THE MOST
TRUSTED NAME
IN TRAVEL

P9-DNY-594

NEW ENGLAND

16th Edition

By Kim Knox Beckius, Leslie Brokaw,
Brian Kevin, Herbert Bailey Livesey,
Laura Reckford, Barbara Rogers, Stillman
Rogers, William Scheller, and Erin Trahan

FrommerMedia LLC

PREVIOUS PAGE: Harborfront skyscrapers shine at night in Boston, New England's biggest city. THIS PAGE: On the western bluffs of Newport, Rhode Island, Castle Hill Lighthouse guards the entrance to Narragansett Bay.

FROMMER'S STAR RATINGS SYSTEM

Every hotel, restaurant, and attraction listed in this guide has been ranked for quality and value. Here's what the stars mean:

★ Recommended
★★ Highly Recommended
★★★ A must! Don't miss!

AN IMPORTANT NOTE

The world is a dynamic place. Hotels change ownership, restaurants hike their prices, museums alter their opening hours, and buses and trains change their routings. And all of this can occur in the several months after our authors have visited, inspected, and written about, these hotels, restaurants, museums, and transportation services. Though we have made valiant efforts to keep all our information fresh and up-to-date, some few changes can inevitably occur in the periods before a revised edition of this guidebook is published. So please bear with us if a tiny number of the details in this book have changed. Please also note that we have no responsibility or liability for any inaccuracy or errors or omissions, or for inconvenience, loss, damage, or expenses suffered by anyone as a result of assertions in this guide.

CONTENTS

Ready for an Atlantic sunrise over Tenants Harbor, Maine.

A LOOK AT NEW ENGLAND

A romantic weekend in a quaint country inn. A bracing day of powder skiing. Antique hunting on winding country roads. Hiking and camping in mountain wilderness, or lake fishing in morning mist. Sun-dazzled days at a dune-edged beach, with lobster dinners every night. Whether you're looking for a crash course in American art, a history lesson brought to life, or a craft-beer pub crawl, you'll find it in the six neighboring northeastern states commonly referred to as New England—Connecticut, Maine, Massachusetts, New Hampshire, Rhode Island, Vermont. Their cities buzz with museums, shopping, and trendy restaurants, yet they're only a short drive from bucolic country landscapes. It's a four-season destination, too, winter snowdrifts melting into brief apple-blossom springs, followed by sparkling summer and the incredible blaze of autumn foliage. Its pleasures are simply inexhaustible.

Harvest time in the bucolic, hilly farmlands of rural Connecticut.

Right on Boston Harbor, the New England Aquarium (p. 74) has lots of hands-on activities, making it a perennial favorite with kids.

Designed to evoke an Italian villa, complete with a serene interior courtyard, the Isabella Stewart Gardner Museum (p. 72) displays one of the country's finest private art collections.

The townhouses of Newbury Street, in Boston's Back Bay, are packed with boutiques and cafes, ideal for a shop-til-you-drop spree. See p. 121.

Based on the children's book *Make Way for Ducklings*, this sculpture is a beloved landmark for children in the elegant Boston Public Garden (p. 85).

Across the river from Boston, in Cambridge, the Harvard University campus has a cluster of intriguing museums. This rare collection of 19th-century glass flowers can be found in the Harvard Museum of Natural History (p. 84).

After a night out at Fenway Park—the oldest professional baseball stadium in America, home to the Boston Red Sox (p. 127)—you'll definitely know how passionate Bostonians are about their sports teams.

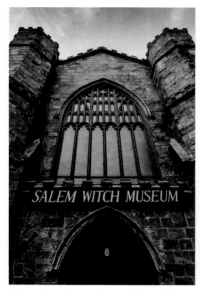

19th-century clipper ships brought wealth to Salem, Massachusetts (p. 155), but today it's better known for its 17th-century history, at sites like the Salem Witch Museum.

The Gloucester Fisherman is an iconic statue in Gloucester, an atmospheric fishing town north of Boston on Cape Ann. See p. 163.

Though there's little left anymore of Plymouth Rock, site of the Pilgrims' landing in 1620, costumed interpreters at the nearby living-history park Plimouth Plantation (p. 176) bring to life the Pilgrims' struggle to survive in their new homeland.

CAPE COD & THE ISLANDS

The long, narrow, curving Cape Cod peninsula is lined with beaches on both sides. Here, a woman totes fishing gear onto Race Point Beach, an Atlantic Ocean beach at the far end of the Cape Cod National Seashore. See p. 247.

A late summer sunset flashes off moored yachts at Allen Harbor, halfway up the Cape in Harwich. See p. 234.

Provincetown, at the Cape's northeast tip, is known for its vibrant LGBTQ community. Among its many flamboyant festivals is the annual Carnival of Gods and Goddesses Parade. See p. 252.

Though its logo merchandise has become a cliché, the dockside Black Dog Tavern (p. 290) is still one of Martha's Vineyard's coziest spots for a bowl of chowder or a lobster dinner.

The quaint fishing village of Menemsha (p. 277) is one of the few towns on the hilly, rural western half of Martha's Vineyard, known as "up-Island."

Gingerbread-trimmed cottages cluster in the Victorian-era "campground" in the Vineyard town of Oak Bluffs. See p. 273.

At the Vineyard's southwest tip, the rugged Aquinnah Cliffs change colors throughout the day, depending on the slant of light. See p. 278.

The 19th-century whaling trade, which made Nantucket Island rich and famous, is explored in fascinating detail at the Nantucket Whaling Museum (p. 299). Dangling from its ceiling, a 46-ft. (14m) skeleton of a sperm whale puts things into perspective.

As the summer season descends on Nantucket Island, hydrangea bushes everywhere burst into colorful bloom. A bike is your best way to explore this small, relatively flat island, which is laced with excellent bike paths.

ELSEWHERE IN NEW ENGLAND

In Shelburne Falls, Massachusetts, the Bridge of Flowers (p. 335)—an abandoned trolley bridge transformed into a show garden—has been delighting pedestrians since 1929.

At Old Sturbridge Village (p. 321), costumed actors and craftspeople—like this skilled potter—recreate the details of life in an 1830s Massachusetts farm village.

Every summer, the Tanglewood Festival (p. 351) brings world-class musical concerts to a beautiful estate in western Massachusetts's Berkshire Mountains.

Autumn foliage brings a blaze of color to the many small lakes that dot the valleys of Connecticut's picturesque Litchfield Hills (p. 384).

The open-air Mystic Seaport Museum (p. 415), on Connecticut's southeast coast, invites visitors to climb aboard vintage boats, explore historic buildings, and learn about maritime crafts such as coopering.

Occupying a landmark 1928 movie palace, the Providence Performing Arts Center (p. 437) is just one element of the Rhode Island capital's downtown renaissance.

Perhaps the most gilded of the Gilded Age mansions in Newport, Rhode Island, Cornelius Vanderbilt II's "cottage," The Breakers (p. 448), dazzles modern visitors.

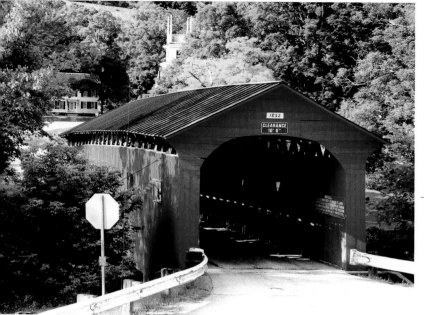

All across New England, quaint covered bridges—like this one near Arlington, Vermont—were built by resourceful countryfolk in the 1800s as protection against the ever-changing New England weather.

One of Vermont's first ski resorts, Stowe (p. 536) remains a popular destination for Eastern U.S. skiers, but it has plenty of competition these days.

In Vermont, a dairy state with a strong strain of hippie counterculture, Ben & Jerry's groovy ice cream factory lures visitors old and young (p. 530).

Open since 1991, the Portsmouth Brewery brewpub (p. 571) is a perennial favorite in the buzzy dining scene of Portsmouth, New Hampshire.

For 150 years, the Mount Washington Cog Railway (p. 590) has been hauling sightseers to the peak of New England's tallest mountain.

New Hampshire's White Mountains offer some of the best hiking in New England, with an abundance of well-laid-out trails and breathtaking mountain views. See p. 583.

The historic Old Port of Portland, Maine, bustles day and night, with several fine restaurants and one of the densest concentrations of bars on the eastern seaboard.

In Kennebunkport, Maine (p. 615), summers are almost synonymous with fresh-caught lobsters.

The Portland Museum of Art (p. 631), housed in a stunning modern building downtown, exhibits a wide range of artwork, often by artists with Maine connections.

The tony 19th-century resort town of Bar Harbor provides lodging and restaurants to the outdoorsy types who visit Acadia National Park, which occupies the rest of Mount Desert Island. See p. 667.

The granite monolith of Mount Katahdin rises above the sparkling lakes and boreal forests of Maine's North Woods, a vast wilderness that beckons hikers, campers, hunters, and paddlers. See p. 695

THE BEST OF NEW ENGLAND

One of the greatest challenges of traveling in New England is choosing from an abundance of superb restaurants, accommodations, and attractions. Where to start? Here's an entirely biased list of our favorite destinations and experiences. Over years of traveling through the region, we've discovered that these are places worth more than just a quick stop—they're all worth a major detour.

THE best OF SMALL-TOWN NEW ENGLAND

- **Essex** (CT): A walk past white-clapboard houses to the active waterfront on this narrow, unspoiled stretch of the Connecticut River rings all the right bells. You won't encounter an artificial note or a cookie-cutter franchise to muddy its near-perfect image. Be sure to take a ride on a vintage steam train or Mississippi-style riverboat. See p. 406.
- **Hanover** (NH): It's the perfect college town: the handsome brick buildings of Dartmouth College, a tidy green, a small but select shopping district, and a scattering of fine restaurants. Come in the fall, and you'll be tempted to join in a touch football game on the green. See p. 578.
- **The Kennebunks** (ME): Chic yet relaxed, this pair of historic shipbuilding towns have long lured summertime visitors with enchanting architecture, first-rate beaches, and the vibrant Dock Square waterfront shopping and dining district. It's still a bit of a best-kept secret, though, that "The Bunks" stay lively in the off-season, when you may get an even better sense of the community spirit that imbues the town with individuality. See p. 615.
- **Marblehead** (MA): This enclave of the yacht set has major picture-postcard potential, especially in summer, when the harbor fills with boats of all sizes. From downtown, stroll toward the water down the narrow, flower-dotted streets. The first glimpse of blue sea and sky is breathtaking. See p. 150.
- **Oak Bluffs** (Martha's Vineyard, MA): Stroll down Circuit Avenue in Oak Bluffs with a Mad Martha's ice-cream cone, and then ride the vintage Flying Horses Carousel. This island harbor town is full of fun for kids and parents. Don't miss the colorful

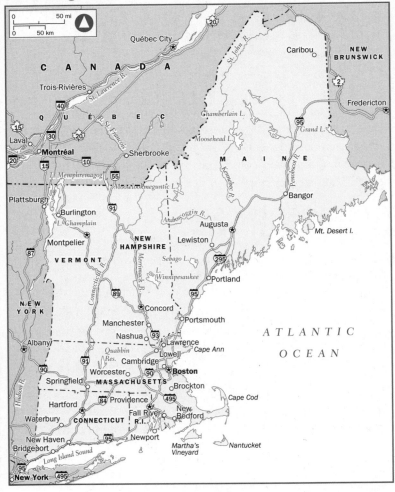

"gingerbread" cottages behind Circuit Avenue. Oak Bluffs also has great beaches, bike paths, and the Vineyard's best nightlife. See p. 273.

- **Northampton** (MA): "Noho" is the cultural center of the Pioneer Valley, the north-south corridor in central Massachusetts that runs along the Connecticut River. Home to Smith College, handsome Northampton beats out neighboring college towns **Amherst** (p. 331) and **South Hadley** (p. 328) by virtue of its diverse restaurants, funky shopping, and top music venues. See p. 329.

- **Stockbridge** (MA): Norman Rockwell famously painted Main Street in this, his adopted hometown in the southern Berkshires. Then, as now, the

Red Lion Inn and the other late-19th-century buildings make up the commercial district, with residential areas a beguiling mix of unassuming saltboxes and Gilded Age mansions. The Norman Rockwell Museum gives an excellent overview of the artist, the town where he worked, and the social issues he addressed in his mid-20th-century art. See p. 346.

o **Woodstock** (VT): Woodstock has a stunning village green, a whole range of 19th-century homes, woodland walks leading just out of town, and a settled, old-money air. This is a good place to explore on foot or by bike, or to just sit and watch summer unfold. See p. 501.

THE best PLACES TO SEE FALL FOLIAGE

o **Camden** (ME): The dazzling trees that blanket rolling hills are reflected in Penobscot Bay on the east side, and in the lakes to the west. Ascend the peaks for views of color-splashed islands in the bay. Autumn usually arrives a week or so later on the coast, so you can stretch out your viewing pleasure. See p. 649.

o **Crawford Notch** (NH): Route 302 passes through this scenic valley, where you can see the brilliant red maples and yellow birches high on the hillsides. In fall, Mount Washington, in the background, is likely to be dusted with an early snow. See p. 590.

o **Kancamagus Highway** (NH): A highway? Don't scoff. NH Route 112 is a relatively new road by New England standards, but it's no interstate. You'll be overwhelmed with gorgeous terrain along this soaring pass cut through the White Mountain National Forest, which was paved for the first time in 1964. See p. 584.

o **The Litchfield Hills** (CT): Route 7, running south to north through the rugged northwest corner of Connecticut, roughly along the course of the Housatonic River, explodes with color in the weeks before and after Columbus Day. Leaves drift down to the water and whirl away with the foaming river. See p. 384.

o **The Mohawk Trail** (western MA): The stretch of Route 2 that runs from the Massachusetts–New York border to the Connecticut River winds wildly and bends in a famous hairpin turn: It was built in 1914 for automobiles that only traveled at leaf-peeping speed. So, take it easy as you travel this 63-mile mountain artery, and pull over when the kaleidoscopic colors splashed across the Berkshire Hills and Hoosac Valley pull your gaze away from the road. See chapter 8.

o **Mount Auburn Cemetery** (Cambridge, MA): More than 5,000 trees spread across Mount Auburn's 175 acres. Each deciduous specimen changes color on its own schedule, and, at the peak of foliage season, each seems to be a different shade of red, orange, or gold. See p. 85.

o **Nashoba Valley** (Harvard and Bolton, MA): An easy day trip from Boston (no need to pay those fall foliage rates at country inns!), this gently rolling area of woodlands and farmland offers an extra autumn treat: loads of orchards where you can pick your own peck of crisp fall apples. See p. 148.

o **Vermont Route 100** (VT): Route 100 wriggles the length of Vermont from Readsboro to Newport, plying the Mad River Valley for a stretch. It's the major north-south route through the Green Mountains, and it's surprisingly undeveloped. You won't have it to yourself on autumn weekends, but as you head farther north, you'll leave the crowds behind. See chapter 11.

o **Walden Pond State Reservation** (Concord, MA): Walden Pond sits surrounded by the woods where Henry David Thoreau built a small cabin and lived from 1845 to 1847. When the leaves are turning and the water reflects the colorful trees, it's hard to imagine why he left. See p. 145.

THE best WAYS TO VIEW COASTAL SCENERY

o **Strolling Around Gloucester** (MA): While nearby Rockport (see p. 166) is often swamped with tourists, the fishing town of Gloucester really delivers the flavor of maritime New England. Walk around the harbor, take a boat tour, and then plunk yourself down at a seafood restaurant with great water views. See p. 163.

o **Getting Back to Nature on Plum Island** (MA): The Parker River National Wildlife Refuge offers two varieties of coastal scenery: picturesque salt marshes packed with birds and other animals, and pristine ocean beaches that bear witness to the power of the Atlantic. See p. 172.

o **Biking or Driving the Outer Cape** (MA): From Eastham through Wellfleet and Truro, all the way to Provincetown, Cape Cod's outermost towns offer dazzling ocean vistas and a number of exceptional bike paths, including the Province Lands trail, just outside Provincetown, bordered by spectacular swooping dunes. See p. 245.

o **Heading "Up-Island" on Martha's Vineyard** (MA): Many visitors never venture beyond the ferry port towns of Vineyard Haven, Oak Bluffs, and Edgartown. Too bad, because the scenery gets more spectacular "up-island." At the western tip of the Vineyard, admire the quaint fishing port of Menemsha, then get that lands-end thrill at the multi-colored sea cliffs of Aquinnah. See p. 277.

o **Cruising Newport's Ocean Drive** (RI): After touring some of the fabulously opulent mansions along Bellevue Avenue, continue by car or bike on shoreline Ocean Avenue. You're in for views of the dancing Atlantic that truly wow, as you drive or pedal past beaches, members-only yacht clubs, historic estates, and oceanside state parks. See p. 453.

o **Walking the Marginal Way** (ME): Don't be surprised to spy students and instructors from the Ogunquit Summer School of Art painting *en plein air* as you follow this just-over-a-mile-long, clifftop path overlooking Atlantic Ocean fireworks. From downtown Ogunquit's Shore Road to Perkins Cove, you'll not only marvel at dramatic scenes, you'll be enchanted by the rhythmic sea symphony. See p. 613.

o **Driving the Park Loop Road at Acadia National Park** (Mount Desert Island, ME): This is the region's premier ocean drive. You'll start high along a ridge with views of Frenchman Bay and the Porcupine Islands, then dip down along the rocky shores to watch the surf crash against the dark rocks. Plan to do this 27-mile loop at least twice to get the most out of it. See p. 670.

THE best PLACES TO EXPLORE THE COLONIAL PAST

o **Plymouth** (Plymouth, MA): Okay, Plymouth Rock is a fraction of its original size and looks like something you might find in your garden. Nevertheless, it makes a perfect starting point for appreciating just how dangerous the Pilgrims' voyage was. Then plan to spend at least a few hours at the living history museum **Plimoth Plantation** to learn how the Pilgrims made a go of it in their new home. See p. 173.

o **Historic Deerfield** (Deerfield, MA): Arguably the best-preserved Colonial village in New England, this town's historic section has more than 80 houses dating back to the 17th and 18th centuries, with none of the clutter of modernity. Ten museum houses on the main avenue can be visited through tours conducted by the organization known as Historic Deerfield. See p. 333.

o **Boston Tea Party Ships & Museum** (Boston, MA): It's the night of December 16, 1773 every day at this interactive attraction, where costumed actors will get your blood boiling over taxation without representation. Sure, it's a little hokey, but it's easy to get caught up in such lively historic fun. See p. 92.

o **Paul Revere House** (Boston, MA): We often study the American Revolution as a political conflict. At this little home in the North End, you'll learn the very human side of the story. The self-guided tour is particularly thought-provoking. Revere fathered 16 children with two wives, supported them with his thriving silversmith's trade—and put the whole operation in jeopardy with his role in the events that led to the Revolution. See p. 77.

o **North Bridge** (Concord, MA): In the opening salvos of the American Revolution, British troops headed to Concord after putting down an uprising in Lexington—and suffered their first defeat in the war. The Old North Bridge (a replica) stands as a testament to the Minutemen and their adversaries who fought that bloody day long ago. Daniel Chester French's iconic "The Minuteman" monument stands near the bridge, a great photo op. See p. 143.

o **Portsmouth** (NH): Portsmouth is a salty coastal city that just happens to boast some of the most impressive historic homes in New England. Start at Strawbery Banke, a historic compound of 42 buildings dating from 1695 to

1820. Then visit the many other grand homes in nearby neighborhoods, such as the house John Paul Jones occupied while building his warship during the Revolution. A self-guided tour of the 27-site Black Heritage Trail tells a long-forgotten side of the city's story. See p. 564.

o **College Hill** (Providence, RI): Here, on the east side of Providence, Rhode Island College was founded in 1764 (you may know it by its current name, Brown University). College Hill is now a National Historic District and has a "Mile of History" in its collection of 18th- and 19th-century houses, Colonial to Victorian, along Benefit Street. See p. 429.

THE best PLACES TO STEP INTO THE 19TH CENTURY

o **Hancock Shaker Village** (Pittsfield, MA): By the time "Mother" Ann Lee died in 1784, the austere Protestant sect she founded, known as the Shakers, had fanned out across the country to form communal settlements from Maine to Indiana. Hancock, edging the Massachusetts–New York border, was one of the most important. The village presents restored buildings, farm animals, and a selection of Shaker crafts, including furniture and home accessories, plus a Shaker-inspired farm-to-table restaurant. See p. 353.

o **Old Sturbridge Village** (Sturbridge, MA): With authentic buildings and costumed staff, this is a re-created rural settlement of the 1830s. Visitors stroll through the village, which is spread across more than 200 acres, to see working versions of a sawmill, a blacksmith shop, a school, and a cooperage. Lazy boat rides are popular, as are historical craft classes. In summertime, a horse-drawn stagecoach traverses the dirt lanes, and, when there's snow, guests can take horse-drawn sleigh rides. See p. 321.

o **Salem** (Boston, MA): Everyone knows about Salem's 17th-century witches, but the city really came into its own as a 19th-century whaling port. That history is very much on view today, from ship captains' houses to a replica merchant vessel to a museum full of curiosities sailors brought home. See p. 150.

o **Nantucket Town** (Nantucket, MA): It looks as though the whalers just left, leaving behind their grand Greek Revival houses, cobbled streets, and a gamut of enticing shops. The Whaling Museum here is one of the best places in New England to learn the story of this now-defunct industry, which brought such riches to the Northeastern coast. See p. 297.

o **Mystic Seaport Museum** (Mystic, CT): It's the only place in America to climb aboard a still-seaworthy wooden whaling ship and to take a short ride on the oldest coal-fired wooden steamboat, and there's much more in store at this living history maritime museum. See p. 415.

o **Mark Twain House & Harriet Beecher Stowe House** (Hartford, CT): Huck Finn and Uncle Tom as neighbors? Yes, it really happened that way, and these two adjacent sites bring to life the late 19th century, when these two famous authors lived next door to each other in an artist's community in the Connecticut capital. See p. 402.

o **Newport** (RI): Newport retains abundant recollections of its storied maritime past, with Colonial-era homes and a thriving harbor clogged with tour boats, ferries, yachts, and majestic sloops. Its chief tourist draw, however, is the ostentatious mansions of America's post–Civil War industrial and financial tycoons, lined up along Bellevue Avenue awaiting visitors. See p. 443.

o **Shelburne Museum** (Shelburne, VT): Think of this sprawling museum as New England's attic. Located on the shores of Lake Champlain, the Shelburne Museum features not only exhibits of quilts and early glass, but also whole buildings preserved like specimens in formaldehyde. Look for the lighthouse, the jail, and the stagecoach inn. This is one of northern New England's "don't miss" destinations. See p. 548.

THE best FAMILY ACTIVITIES

o **Experimenting in the Museum of Science** (Boston, MA): Built around demonstrations and interactive displays that never feel like homework, this museum is wildly popular with kids—and adults. Explore the exhibits, then take in a planetarium show or an IMAX movie on a five-stories-tall screen. Before you know it, everyone will have learned something, painlessly. See p. 74.

o **Grabbing the Brass Ring at the Flying Horses Carousel** (Oak Bluffs, Martha's Vineyard, MA): Some say this is the oldest carousel in the country, but your kids might not notice the genuine horsehair, sculptural details, or glass eyes. They'll be too busy trying to grab the brass ring to win a free ride. After dismounting, stroll around Oak Bluffs. Children will be enchanted with the "gingerbread" houses, a carryover from the 19th-century revivalist movement. See p. 274.

o **Ice skating on Outdoor Rinks:** New Englanders don't take to the outdoors in winter with quite the enthusiasm as, say, the Québécois, but they give it a good shot with outdoor skating. Family-friendly rinks pop up on Boston Common and in downtown Providence and Newport, RI. See pp. 94, 429, and 454.

o **Making Memories at Story Land** (Glen, NH): More manageable and far more affordable than Disney World, but with the same wide-eyed appeal for the preschool set, this enduring White Mountains attraction has been many a kid's first amusement park since it opened in 1954. See p. 588.

o **Riding the Mount Washington Cog Railway** (Bretton Woods, NH): It's exhilarating! It's startling! It's a glimpse of history. Kids love this ratchety climb to the top of New England's highest peak aboard trains that were specially designed to scale the mountain in 1869. As a technological marvel, the railroad attracted tourists by the thousands 150 years ago. They still come to marvel at the sheer audacity of it all. See p. 590.

- **Setting Up along Providence's Rivers for WaterFire** (Providence, RI): On at least 10 nights from spring through fall, thousands of people descend on the riverfront to experience a free nighttime art and music installation featuring more than 80 bonfires right in the water. See p. 431.

- **Taking in a Baseball Game** (Pawtucket, RI): Until at least 2020, McCoy Stadium is home to the Pawtucket Red Sox, a minor league baseball team for the Boston Red Sox (the team will be moving to Worcester, MA, as soon as their new ballfield is built). Games here are not only affordable and fun, they're rife with traditions like fishing for autographs. See p. 430.

- **Taste-testing at the Ben & Jerry Ice Cream Factory** (Waterbury, VT): Kids and ice cream are a natural combination, and the half-hour tours won't tax anybody's patience. Explore the comical Flavor Graveyard, enjoy the playground and hands-on activities, and make sure to save room for a free sample. See p. 530.

- **Visiting Mystic Aquarium** (Mystic, CT): Even tiny tots are mesmerized by Mystic Aquarium's flitting fish, undulating jellies, touchable rays, and performing sea lions. For grown-ups, special encounter programs like Paint with a Whale are, in a word, unforgettable. See p. 415.

- **Walking the Freedom Trail** (Boston, MA): History class is never this much connect-the-dots fun. Just follow the red stripe in the pavement past 16 sights connected with Boston's Revolutionary War history. (For another chapter of history that's often not taught in school, walk the even-more-insightful the Black Heritage Trail—see p. 74.) Pick up a pamphlet for a self-guided adventure; stop for ice cream whenever their legs get tired. See p. 75.

- **Whale-Watching Cruises** (Coastal MA): Boats cruises out to the Stellwagen Bank National Marine Sanctuary, a rich feeding ground for several types of whales. Nothing can prepare you for the thrill of spotting these magnificent creatures feeding, breaching, and even flipper-slapping. Expeditions set sail from **Boston** (p. 89), **Gloucester** on Cape Ann (p. 166), and **Provincetown** (p. 256) and **Barnstable** (p. 211) on Cape Cod.

THE best COUNTRY INNS

- **Captain's House Inn** (Chatham, Cape Cod, MA): An elegant country inn dripping with good taste, this is among the best small inns on the Cape. Sumptuous yet cozy rooms all have fireplaces, antique furnishings, and distinctive touches. Afternoon teas are a cherished tradition, particularly during the holiday season. This could be the ultimate spot to enjoy Chatham's Christmas Stroll festivities. See p. 238.

- **Charlotte Inn** (Edgartown, Martha's Vineyard, MA): Edgartown tends to be the most formal enclave on Martha's Vineyard, and this compound of exquisite buildings is by far the fanciest address in town. The rooms are distinctively decorated: One boasts a baby grand piano, some have fireplaces. The restaurant, **The Terrace,** is also top-notch. See p. 280.

- **Grace Mayflower Inn & Spa** (Washington, CT): Not a tough call at all: Immaculate in taste and execution, the Mayflower is as close to perfection as any such enterprise is likely to be, particularly if you are a spa addict. See p. 389.

- **Grace White Barn Inn & Spa** (Kennebunk, ME): Guests are treated with a graciousness that's hard to match anywhere else in New England. The setting is lovely, too. Rooms, suites, and cottages here are soothing and refined, and the multi-course meals (served in the barn) are among the best in the Northeast. See p. 617.

- **Griswold Inn** (Essex, CT): "The Gris" has been accommodating sailors and travelers as long as any inn in the country, give or take a decade. In all that time, it has been a part of life and commerce in the lower Connecticut River Valley, always ready with a mug of suds, a haunch of beef, and a roaring fire. Tap Room walls are layered with nautical paintings and memorabilia, and they've even added a wine bar to the mix. See p. 410.

- **Hawthorne Inn** (Concord, MA): Everything here—the 1860s building, the garden setting a stone's throw from historic attractions, the vibrant decor, the homemade granola, the accommodating innkeepers—is top of the line. See p. 147.

- **The Inn at Thorn Hill** (Jackson, NH): Spacious and gracious, this White Mountains inn has it all—fireplaces, scenic nooks, and a wide wrap-around porch for enjoying those mountain views. Add to that a full-service spa and top-notch restaurant and you've got a winning formula for a romantic getaway. See p. 601.

- **Land's End Inn** (Provincetown, Cape Cod, MA): Arguably one of the most unique properties in the region, this house high up on Gull Hill in the far west end of town has a panoramic view of the Cape's tip, as the Atlantic Ocean carves away at the peninsula's furthest shores. The rooms, including three tower rooms, are decorated with elegance and a sense of humor. See p. 259.

- **The Pitcher Inn** (Warren, VT): Even though this place was rebuilt in 1997, it's possessed of the graciousness of a longtime, well-worn inn. It combines traditional New England form and scale with modern and luxe touches, plus a good dollop of whimsy. See p. 527.

- **The Porches** (North Adams, MA): The Porches may not be a "country inn" exactly, but it is too much fun to ignore. Constructed from six 19th-century workmen's houses, it sits across from MASS MoCA (the Massachusetts Museum of Contemporary Art). The designers' wit is evident in kitschy art and accessories, while Apple TVs, a hot tub, and free Wi-Fi ensure no 21st-century deprivation. See p. 363.

- **Windham Hill Inn** (West Townshend, VT): This 1823 farmstead sits at the end of a remote dirt road in a high upland valley, and guests are welcome to explore 160 private acres on a network of walking trails. Farm-to-table menus feature ingredients from local growers and the inn's own garden. See p. 498.

THE best MODERATELY PRICED ACCOMMODATIONS

- **The Dean Hotel** (Providence, RI): Sleekly styled, with plenty of artsy touches, this newcomer to the Providence downtown speaks to the city's increasingly hip profile, with a farm-to-table restaurant and a karaoke lounge. See p. 432.

- **Hopkins Inn** (Warren, CT): This yellow farmhouse bestows the top view of Lake Waramaug, and on soft summer days, not much beats savoring robust Alpine dishes at a table on the terrace. Rooms exude country quaintness. The Hopkins Vineyard is adjacent. See p. 389.

- **Lincolnville Motel** (Camden, ME): In the 1950s, this was just another motor-court motel along Route 1 on the shores of Penobscot Bay. A new owner in 2015 transformed it with a hip, stripped-down decor full of witty (sometimes kitschy) touches, and now it's a travelers' fave—but still at motel prices. See p. 654.

- **Nauset House Inn** (East Orleans, Cape Cod, MA): This romantic 1810 farmhouse is like a sepia-toned vision of old Cape Cod. Recline on a wicker divan surrounded by fragrant flowers while the wind whistles outside. Better yet, stroll to Nauset Beach and watch the sun set. Your genial hosts also prepare one of the finest breakfasts around. See p. 240.

- **Newbury Guest House** (Boston, MA): This lovely property would be a good deal even if it weren't ideally located on Newbury Street, Boston's version of Rodeo Drive. Rates even include breakfast. See p. 100.

- **Mad River Barn Inn** (Waitsfield, VT): Families love the woodsy touches at this clean, comfy, sociable inn. Most of the action takes place in the bar and restaurant, where skiers relax and chat after a day on the slopes, and order up comfort food. See p. 526.

THE best RESTAURANTS

- **Al Forno** (Providence, RI): The wood-fired ovens at Al Forno have been turning out delectable Italian-influenced meals from farm-fresh ingredients ever since 1980. This was the restaurant that first put Providence on the gourmet map, and it hasn't missed a beat since. See p. 434.

- **Black Trumpet Bistro** (Portsmouth, NH): Come to this intimate harborside bistro for surprisingly exotic food, borrowing from a range of world cuisines. It's this sort of creative cookery that has made Portsmouth one of New England's liveliest dining scenes. See p. 570.

- **Chantecleer** (East Dorset, VT): Swiss chef Michel Baumann has been turning out dazzling dinners here since 1981, and the kitchen hasn't gotten stale in the least. The dining room in an old barn is magical, the staff helpful and friendly. It's the perfect spot for those who demand top-notch Continental fare but don't like the fuss of a fancy restaurant. See p. 490.

- **Chanticleer** (Nantucket, MA): In this rose-covered cottage in the picturesque village of 'Sconset, this romantic French restaurant has long been the place to celebrate special occasions. The dreamy ambiance is, remarkably, outdone by the cuisine, superbly crafted by Jeff Worster, one of the island's most creative chefs. See p. 315.

o **Centre Street Bistro** (Nantucket, MA): Two of the best chefs on island, Ruth and Tim Pitts, combine their talents at this hole-in-the-wall BYOB restaurant. The best part is that this place features wonderful, creative cuisine at fairly reasonable prices, compared to other island fine-dining restaurants. See p. 313.

o **Fore Street** (Portland, ME): Fore Street is one of northern New England's most celebrated restaurants. The chef's secret? Simplicity and a passion for sustainability. Some of the most memorable meals are prepared over the open, applewood-fired grill. See p. 636.

o **Hen of the Wood** (Waterbury, VT): Waterbury—population: 5,000—seems an unlikely place for a serious culinary adventure, yet Hen of the Wood exceeds the loftiest expectations. Each day, a new menu reflects seasonality and originality. A second outpost inside Burlington's Hotel Vermont makes inspired local fare accessible to city visitors, but dining at the original, beside a waterfall in an old grist mill, is oh-so Vermont. See p. 533.

o **L'étoile** (Edgartown, Martha's Vineyard, MA): Prepare to be wowed at this exquisite venue, a historic sea captain's house, where the island's most famous chef, Michael Brisson, turns out a seasonally driven menu inspired by Vineyard farms and the day's catch from surrounding waters. See p. 285.

o **Mamma Maria** (Boston, MA): The best choice in the restaurant-choked North End is a far cry from the spaghetti-and-meatballs workhorses that crowd this Italian-American neighborhood. The Northern Italian cuisine at this elegant town house is something to write home about. See p. 115.

o **Union League Café** (New Haven, CT): The crème de la crème of New Haven restaurants impresses before you even open the menu. Expect French classics, plus expertly prepared dishes inspired by New England's seasons. See p. 397.

o **T.J. Buckley's** (Brattleboro, VT): This tiny dining car on a dark side street serves up outsize tastes prepared by a talented chef. Forget about stewed-too-long diner fare; get in your mind big tastes blossoming from the freshest of ingredients prepared just right. See p. 500.

o **White Barn Restaurant** (Kennebunk, ME): The setting in a light-splashed, rustic barn is magical. The food? To die for. Your best bet is the Chef's Indulgence Menu: a tasting odyssey starring Maine's bounty, prepared in a way you will never experience again. See p. 623.

THE best LOCAL DINING EXPERIENCES

o **Black Eyed Susan's** (Nantucket, MA): This is extremely exciting food in a funky bistro atmosphere. The place is small, popular with locals, and packed. Sitting at the counter and watching the chef in action is a show in itself. No credit cards, no reservations, and no liquor license—but if you can get past those inconveniences, you're in for a top-notch dining experience. See p. 313.

o **Blue Benn Diner** (Bennington, VT): This 1945 Silk City diner has a barrel ceiling, old-school counter stools, and a vast menu. Don't overlook specials scrawled on paper and taped all over the walls. And leave room for a slice of delicious pie, such as blackberry, pumpkin, or chocolate cream. See p. 489.

o **Captain Frosty's** (Dennis, MA): For generations, Cape Cod summer folks have been stopping in at Captain Frosty's for fried seafood, eaten outdoors at picnic tables, preferably in swimsuits still sandy and damp from a day at the beach. See p. 222.

o **Dot's** (Wilmington, VT): Long a town favorite but a casualty of 2011's floods, Dot's was reborn in its own timeless image. With a menu ranging from hearty diner breakfasts to fiery chili, meatloaf to milkshakes, here's a place to rub shoulders with locals, travelers, and ski bums. See p. 500.

o **Duckfat** (Portland, ME). In a town with no shortage of dining options, Belgian fries and crème anglaise milkshakes keep Portlanders coming back to this laid-back lunch and dinner spot, filling bar stools and patio tables on a brick sidewalk in the historic East End. See p. 637.

o **Durgin-Park** (Boston, MA): Your favorite thing here might be the famous cornbread, the equally famous baked beans, the super-fresh seafood, the gigantic prime rib, the luscious strawberry shortcake, the historic setting, or even the smart-mouthed service. In any case, Durgin-Park has been a magnet for Bostonians and visitors since 1827. See p. 112.

o **Judie's** (Amherst, MA): Don't leave the Pioneer Valley without trying the upbeat, bustling Judie's. The house specialty is stuffed popovers—there are five varieties, from gumbo to shrimp scampi. See p. 337.

o **Louis' Lunch** (New Haven, CT): Not a lot of serious history has happened in New Haven, but boosters claim it was here at Louis' Lunch that hamburgers were invented in 1900. True or not, this little luncheonette lives on, moved from its original site in order to save it. The patties are freshly ground daily, thrust into vertical grills, and served on white toast. Garnishes are tomato, onion, and cheese. No ketchup and no fries, so don't even ask. See p. 399.

o **Lou's** (Hanover, NH): Huge crowds flock to Lou's, just down the block from the Dartmouth campus, for breakfast on weekends. Fortunately, breakfast is served all day here, and the sandwiches on fresh-baked bread are huge and delicious. See p. 583.

o **Pizza** (New Haven, CT): New Haven's claim to America's first pizza is a whole lot shakier than its claim to the first burgers (see above), but the city excels in the ultrathin, charred variety of what they still call "apizza" in these parts, pronounced "ah-beetz." Old-timer **Frank Pepe's,** 157 Wooster St., is usually ceded top rank among the local parlors, but it is joined by such contenders as **Sally's,** 237 Wooster St., and **Modern Apizza,** 874 State St. See p. 398.

o **Woodman's of Essex** (Essex, MA): This busy North Shore institution is still owned and run by descendants of Chubby Woodman: inventor of the fried clam. From chowder to fried seafood of every sort—even lobster—the food is fresh and delicious, and a look at the organized pandemonium behind the counter is worth the (reasonable) price. See p. 169.

THE best OF THE PERFORMING ARTS (WINTER)

o **Iron Horse Music Hall** (Northampton, MA): The premiere honky-tonk music venue of central Massachusetts has folk, bluegrass, and rock music nearly every night, from touring artists to local musicians. There's decent dining, too. See p. 340.

o **Long Wharf Theatre** (New Haven, CT): This prestigious company is known for its success in producing new plays that often make the jump to Off-Broadway and even Broadway itself. See p. 399.

o **The Nutcracker** (Boston, MA): New England's premier family-oriented holiday event is Boston Ballet's extravaganza. When the Christmas tree grows through the floor, even fidgety preadolescents forget that they think they're too cool to be here. See p. 124.

o **Portland Stage Company** (Portland, ME): One of the outstanding regional theaters in the Northeast, their eclectic August-to-May schedule includes both classic and modern shows, such as *The Last Five Years* and *A Christmas Carol;* they have a good track record of developing and producing new American work. See p. 630.

o **Portland Symphony Orchestra** (Portland, ME): They'll knock your socks off from September through May in their series of pops and classical concerts at the Merrill Auditorium. See p. 630.

o **Symphony Hall** (Boston, MA): The Boston Symphony Orchestra's acoustically perfect home also plays host to the Boston Pops and other local and visiting performers worth scheduling a trip around. See p. 123.

o **Trinity Repertory Company** (Providence, RI): In a historic theater building right downtown, this estimable theater company's resident troupe performs a stimulating mix of new plays and dramatic reinterpretations of classics, from October through mid-June. See p. 437.

o **The Wilbur** (Boston, MA): Even in the Athens of America, it's not all high culture. Comedy's biggest national names and some regional up-and-comers take the stage at this historic theater, which occasionally books musical acts and storytelling slams. See p. 129.

THE best OF THE PERFORMING ARTS (SUMMER)

o **Berkshire Theatre Festival** (Stockbridge, MA): An 1887 "casino" and converted barn are homes to stages where both new and classic plays are mounted from June to late October, here in one of the prettiest towns in the Berkshires. See p. 346.

o **The Cape Playhouse** (Dennis, MA) is the oldest continuously active professional summer theater in the country, and still one of the best. A parade of stars from Humphrey Bogart to Judy Kuhn has trod the boards in the decades since the 1920s. Performances are staged from mid-June to early September. See p. 228.

o **Hatch Shell** (Boston, MA): This amphitheater on the Charles River Esplanade plays host to free music and films almost all summer. On the 4th of July, the Boston Pops provides the entertainment. Bring a blanket to sit on. See p. 124.

o **Jacob's Pillow Dance Festival** (Becket, MA): This mountaintop farm turned summertime dance center hosts the world's best and most diverse troupes, often including Pilobolus, the Royal Danish Ballet, and Limón Dance Company. The campus includes a store, pub, tent restaurant, and outdoor stage, where free performances take place most evenings. See p. 348.

o **Marlboro Music Festival** (Marlboro, VT): On the campus of Marlboro College, this mid-July-through-mid-August concert series brings together some of the biggest names in classical music with gifted students—the stars of tomorrow. See p. 495.

o **Newport Folk Festival and Newport Jazz Festival** (Newport, RI): The only thing better than hearing live folk or jazz music in Fort Adams State Park on a summer weekend is anchoring your boat near enough to listen free. These two enduring festivals bring top acts to the City by the Sea. See p. 450.

o **Ogunquit Playhouse** (Ogunquit, ME): This is summer stock. The 750-seat theater has been showcasing lively plays since 1933; famous actors like Bette Davis, Tallulah Bankhead, and Sally Struthers (though not all at the same time!) have taken the spotlight each summer in beloved and brand new musicals. Performances usually run from mid-May through late October. See p. 615.

o **Shakespeare & Company** (Lenox, MA): Sprawled across a bucolic 33-acre property, this theater company presents diverse works indoors and outdoors in the new Roman Garden Theatre. A night here is one of the many civilized ways to enjoy an evening in the Berkshires during the summer and beyond. See p. 350.

o **Tanglewood** (Lenox, MA): By far the most dominating presence on New England's summer cultural front, this magnificent Berkshires estate is the summer playground for the Boston Symphony Orchestra, plus it also makes room for popular artists such as James Taylor and Harry Connick, Jr. See p. 351.

o **Williamstown Theatre Festival** (Williamstown, MA): Classic, new, and avant-garde plays are all presented during the late-June-through-August season at this venerable festival. There are two stages including an intimate venue for less mainstream or experimental plays, typically making their world premiere. See p. 356.

THE best DESTINATIONS FOR ANTIQUES HOUNDS

o **Brimfield Antiques Shows** (Brimfield, MA): The otherwise sleepy town west of Sturbridge erupts with three monster antiques shows every summer, in mid-May, mid-July, and early September. More than 5,000 dealers set up tented and tabletop shops in fields around town. See p. 321.

o **Charles Street** (Boston, MA): Beacon Hill is one of Boston's oldest neighborhoods, and at the foot of the hill is a thoroughfare where hundreds of years' worth of furniture, collectibles, and accessories jam shops along 5 blocks. River Street, which parallels Charles (follow Chestnut Street 1 block), is worth a look, too. See p. 122.

o **Essex, Main Street** (MA): The treasures on display in this North Shore town run the gamut, from one step above yard sale to rare and impressive. Follow Route 133 through downtown and north almost all the way to the Ipswich border. See p. 168.

o **Kittery to Scarborough/Route 1** (ME): Antiques scavengers delight in this stretch of less-than-scenic Route 1, scattered with antiques mini-malls, high-end galleries, and antiquarian bookstores. See p. 610.

o **The Old King's Highway/Route 6A** (Cape Cod, MA): Antiques buffs, as well as architecture and country-road connoisseurs, will have a field day along scenic Route 6A. Designated a Regional Historic District, this former stagecoach route winds through a half-dozen charming villages and is lined with scores of antiques shops. The largest concentration is in Brewster, but you'll find good pickings all along this meandering road, from Sandwich to Orleans. See p. 213.

o **Portsmouth** (NH): Picturesque downtown Portsmouth is home to a half-dozen or so antiques stores and some fine used-book shops. For more browsing, head about 25 miles northwest to Northwood, where more good-size shops flank the highway. See p. 564.

o **Woodbury** (CT): More than 35 high-end dealers along Main Street offer a diversity of precious treasures, near-antiques, and simply funky old stuff. American and European furniture and other pieces are most evident, but there are forays into crafts and assorted whimsies. See p. 384.

NEW ENGLAND IN CONTEXT

2

By Kim Knox Beckius

Most of this book is intended to lead you toward the best or most interesting historical attractions, museums, eating and drinking places, shops, and lodgings in the six New England states. These pages, however, explore the elusive character of New England and its famously resourceful residents. Learn how the region was formed geologically; how it was populated by people and animals; what foods are most crave-worthy and distinctive here; and which books, music, and films written in or about these states best capture its essence. There's also advice here to help you answer the crucial "when to visit?" question, along with a calendar of events that might sway your decision. Ready? Buckle up: Here comes your crash course.

NEW ENGLAND TODAY

Traditionally, people in New England lived off the land. They might have fished for cod, harvested timber, managed gravel pits, or worked in general stores. Or they labored in New England's mills. But hardscrabble work is no longer the primary economic engine in the region.

Today, a New Englander might be a software developer who bounces between freelance gigs; a biotech researcher; a PR consultant who handles business online from home. You'll also find *many* folks whose livelihood depends on tourism—the ski instructor, the family selling maple syrup by the side of a Vermont byway, the math teacher moonlighting as a motel owner, the high school kid working summers in a T-shirt shop, the entrepreneurial chef who sees possibility in a post-industrial downtown.

New England's economy has shifted, from one that was chiefly "blue collar" to something that's much more diverse. This is no longer the province of dairy farms and woolen mills, though those places still exist in pockets. It's a place of light industry, technology, healthcare innovation, arts and entertainment, world-class cuisine—still all informed by a self-sufficiency, flexibility, and creativity rarely seen elsewhere. People tend to double up on jobs around here. And they *all* manage to deal with the fickle weather.

Once a region of distinctive villages, green commons, and prim courthouse squares, New England's landscape has begun to resemble suburbs anywhere else—strip malls dotted with fast-food chains, big-box discount stores, and home-improvement emporia. While undeniably convenient to locals, it's a mixed blessing, because this region has always taken pride in the independent spirit of local merchants.

In many smaller communities, town meetings are still the preferred form of government. Residents gather in public spaces to speak out—sometimes rather forcefully—on the issues of the day: funding for local schools, road repairs, fire trucks, and declarations that their towns are no place for landfills or police shooting ranges. "Use it up, wear it out, make do, or do without" still drives some frugal Yankees, but it's the polar opposite of the artisanal-every-thing ethos favored by a new generation. And therein lies the rub: This region is trying to have it both ways, Norman Rockwell *and* Relais & Châteaux.

Development is a related issue. Many old-timers (and some blow-ins) believe development shouldn't be ushered in regardless of the cultural cost. Others feel the natural landscape isn't sacred, though, and the region has seen a surge of new townhouses of late, covering ski slopes and hillsides through-out these six states. *Nobody's* happy about the rising property taxes and real estate values here—except those already landed in prime locations.

No, development hasn't exploded here. Not yet. But if it ever *does,* many of the characteristics that make New England so unique—and attract those tourist dollars—could disappear. The brick mills and churches, cow pastures, big old maple trees, and whitewashed homes might slowly be replaced by a grayish blanket of condos, Banana Republics, outlet malls, and chain hotels. Would the Green Mountains and the Maine coast still draw tourists if they began to look like any other place in America? Yes, of course, but maybe not as many. It's a tricky balance to maintain.

Then there's the influence of new arrivals, including part-time New Eng-landers. The information age is drawing telecommuters and entrepreneurs to pristine villages: They can run entire businesses and move equities around the world from anywhere in a flash. These folks bring big-city sophistication (and gourmet dining appetites) with them. So how will affluent newcomers adapt to the ticky-tacky lawn ornaments on their neighbors' property, to clear-cut-ting and moose hunting in the countryside nearby, and to increasing numbers of tour buses cruising past village greens? Here's a best case: When Manolo Blahnik honchos George Malkemus and Tony Yurgaitis didn't like the looks of the farm across the street from their Litchfield, CT, weekend home, they bought it . . . and transformed it into the state's prettiest, most headline-grab-bing dairying operation: Arethusa Farm.

Change has seldom come quickly in New England, and this one, too, will take time to play itself out. Most newcomers have a healthy respect for long-time institutions, and some are even investing in preserving the way of life that drew them to New England in the first place.

But you're just visiting, right? So here's what to expect when you get here: decades-old celebrations and towns that cling to their individuality; hardworking people who think fast, move faster, and still find time to lend a hand; antique buildings repurposed rather than demolished—there might be artists' studios or microbreweries in that old factory or shoe mill. Be sure to visit these places and support the cool people who are revitalizing the region. But also set aside time to spend an afternoon rocking and reading on the broad porch of a country inn or old-time general store, or to wander around with no particular destination in mind on roads that follow paths blazed centuries ago.

Because if you crave luscious homemade pie, views of vibrant fall foliage unmatched in the world, exhilarating outdoor experiences, and deep slumber when you return to a 19th-century bed-and-breakfast inn, this is *the* place for you to visit. Yes, it's thoroughly modern; you can sleep in luxury hotels, enjoy indigenous spa treatments, check email from a ski slope, and dine on gourmet fare— food that's the equal of anything in Manhattan or San Francisco. The mix of new and old is *working,* so far, and that's why visitors return season after season.

Finally, Mother Nature has the last word: This remains a sparsely populated place, enduringly quiet and lovely no matter whether it's sparkling with white powdery snow, painted brilliant with autumn leaves, or shimmering with blue sky reflections on lake surfaces on a midsummer's day. It's the perfect backdrop for resetting your biorhythm and your priorities: for declaring independence from anything that limits your wellbeing.

MASSACHUSETTS   The Bay State has always been the place in New England with the most drama and audacity. (Remember the Boston Tea Party and Paul Revere's Ride?) And it still is. The place that brought you the Kennedys was the first U.S. state to issue same-sex marriage licenses. In 2018, it beat all other New England states to the punch in establishing a legal recreational marijuana market, with the aim of filling tax coffers and fueling tourism.

Boston's technology economy is booming, and the ripple effect extends well beyond this city known for education and innovation. The fishing and farming economies, once the state's mainstay, are something less than robust, though. **Cape Cod** and the **Berkshires**—the two glorious landscapes that bookend this state and do a good deal of its touristic trade—are creatively expanding visitor offerings in an effort to become year-round destinations.

Sports teams—the New England Patriots and the Boston Red Sox, Revolution, Bruins, and Celtics—are the single most unifying force in the six New England states. Two recent Super Bowl victories (in 2015 and 2017) for the first team in NFL history to reach 10 championship games brought unspeakable joy to the entire region. The Red Sox have three 21st-century World Series titles to their name after vanquishing the 86-years-long "Curse of the Bambino." Don a jersey or ball cap, and you'll fit right in.

CONNECTICUT   For many years, the state of Connecticut was, quite frankly, basically one big plot of farmland with a strip of shipbuilders on its fringe of a coast. You can still find the odd tobacco barn, boatyard, naval base, or orchard, but otherwise those days are long gone. Today, the state has some interesting niches. The city of **Hartford** has long been the nation's insurance powerhouse, for instance, while its suburb of **Bristol** has found a surprising second life as the world headquarters for ESPN, the planet's largest sports broadcasting network.

Meanwhile, on the southwestern coast, such towns as **Greenwich** and **Fairfield** are now among the most expensive places in the entire country to purchase a home, thanks to their location within commuting distance of New York City. Hedge funds are particularly fond of setting up shop in these parts. Yale University continues to breathe erudite life into **New Haven; Groton** and **New London** are on the upswing thanks to submarine maker General Dynamics Electric Boat's expansion plans; and the many quiet byways stretching into forested hills and still-agrarian realms continue to attract leaf-peepers, second-home buyers, and vacationers.

RHODE ISLAND   Pretty little Rhode Island just goes about its business, staying out of the news and seemingly immune to all the barbs about its size. Quick, what's the top industry in America's smallest state? Tourism? No. Manufacturing? Not. Try "health services" (chain pharmacy CVS is based here, among other companies). There's also a smattering of light industry and business and insurance services, plus tourism as visitors come to gawk at the lovely mansions of **Newport** or enjoy the capital city of **Providence** (home to Brown University). The state *did* hit the news briefly for all the wrong reasons when footage shot in Iceland appeared in a state-funded tourism promotion video. But otherwise, this state only shows up on Hollywood big screens when local sons make movies and TV shows about it (see "New England in Film & TV," p. 29).

VERMONT   Change is afoot in the Green Mountains. Of course, this has always been a place of gorgeous hiking and ski trails, Robert Frostian walks, scenic back-road drives, and wonderful inns. It's the maple syrup capital of the Western world and has more breweries and cheesemakers per capita than any other U.S. state. Yet something else is up: Hotshot chefs are pouring into these parts at what seems like a breakneck pace. Even quite small towns— **Manchester, Essex, Waterbury, Quechee,** and **Vergennes,** to name just a few—have road-trip-worthy restaurants. It's somehow all appropriate for the U.S. state with the smallest capital (**Montpelier,** population 7,500) and the most-loved U.S. senator (Bernie Sanders). The Ben & Jerry's ice-cream factory in **Waterbury** is a must-visit for the kids.

Meanwhile, **Lake Champlain** beckons with its lovely sunsets; and **Burlington** is slowly changing from a hippie town (though tie-dyed shirts are still ubiquitous) into a sophisticated, tech-forward community that supports independent businesses, restaurants, and thinkers. The state's largest city regularly wins quality-of-life awards for its combination of fresh air, lake views, bike trails, a compact walkable downtown, and generous proportions of bookstores, bars, restaurants, and university students. In 2015, it became the first city in America to run entirely on renewable energy.

But life in Vermont's **Northeast Kingdom** *isn't* changing. The region isn't exactly a "kingdom" (or, if it is, black flies and cows are its subjects); instead, it is Vermont at its most primeval. You'll find few fancy inns and restaurants up here; the place is rugged and unpolished as a stone, yet a treasure for mountain bikers, snowmobilers, and skiers.

NEW HAMPSHIRE Like Vermont, fiercely independent New Hampshire is also marching to a new beat—though it still stubbornly resists a state sales tax, which is a boon to visitors. Southern New Hampshire, in particular, is experiencing a sharp demographic shift as leftward-leaning Bostonians filter into the state and use it as a bedroom community. You see this most strongly in places such as **Exeter** and **Portsmouth,** but also in cities such as Nashua and Manchester, where tech and business enterprises are sprouting up.

Some things remain unchanged, thankfully: Portsmouth is still an odd amalgam of pierced baristas, costumed shop clerks, artists, folk musicians, and brazen chefs. **Hanover** still revolves around the tiniest Ivy-League school: Dartmouth College. Lake Winnipesaukee remains a huge, region-defining, active body of water ringed with attractive towns. Finally, the **White Mountains** will *never* change. New England's best backcountry hiking and camping are still found here, and always will be.

MAINE In Maine, the air is clean and pine-tinged, and loons rule the night with their haunting calls. You will want to eat lobsters and fresh-caught fish, and photograph some of the world's most famous lighthouses. The economy isn't going great guns; attracting new, young residents is a struggle. **Portland** remains one of New England's best places to visit and live, with recreation and restaurants that rival anywhere else, while the **Kennebunks** and the **Yorks** offer choice beaches for summer lazing and strolls, plus plenty of distinctive shops. Maine's rocky coast is the stuff of legend, art, and poetry—a list of quaint towns and oceanside drives would fill an entire book and then some.

As you get upcountry, you can feel a difference between affluence (huge summer mansions on Mount Desert Island or around Penobscot Bay) and the hardworking locals who fish, lobster, or wait tables in summer, then tow cars or shovel and plow snow the rest of the year to get by. Land values have shot up in these picturesque regions that are home to tourist towns such as **Freeport, Camden,** and **Rockport.** So many people visit stunning **Acadia National Park** each summer, you may soon have to reserve a time if you want to drive the Park Loop Road past its natural wonders. Finally, Maine's North Woods are a battleground for national park proponents and commercial interests, with millions of pristine acres at the center of the debate. Meanwhile, **Mount Katahdin** and **Baxter State Park** will *always* belong to everyone.

LOOKING BACK AT NEW ENGLAND

Viewed from a distance, New England's history mirrors that of its namesake, England. The region rose from nowhere to gain tremendous historical prominence, captured a good deal of overseas trade, and became an industrial powerhouse and center for creative thought. And then the party ended relatively abruptly, as commerce and culture sought more fertile grounds to the west and south.

To this day, New England remains entwined with its past. Walking through Boston, layers of history are evident at every turn, from the church steeples of Colonial times (dwarfed by glass-sided skyscrapers) to verdant parklands that bespeak the refined sensibility of the late Victorian era.

History is even more inescapable in off-the-beaten-track New England. Travelers in Downeast Maine, northern New Hampshire, Connecticut's Litchfield Hills, the Berkshires, and much of Vermont will find clues to what Henry Wadsworth Longfellow called "the irrevocable past" everywhere they turn, from stone walls running through woods to Federal-style homes.

Here's a brief overview of some historical episodes and trends that shaped New England.

Indigenous Culture

Native Americans have inhabited New England since about 7000 B.C.E. While New York's Iroquois Confederacy had a presence in Vermont, New England was inhabited chiefly by Algonkians. Connecticut was home to some 16 Algonkian tribes, who dubbed the region Quinnetukut.

After the arrival of Europeans, French Catholic missionaries succeeded in converting many Native Americans, and most tribes sided with the French in the French and Indian Wars of the 17th and 18th centuries. Afterward, the Indians fared poorly at the hands of the British and were quickly pushed to the margins. Today, they live in greatest concentrations at several reservations in Maine. The Pequot and Mohegan have established a thriving gaming industry in Connecticut. Several museums in the region, including Connecticut's world-class **Mashantucket Pequot Museum** (see p. 421) preserve the history and culture of New England's First Peoples.

The Colonists

Viking explorers may or may not have sailed southward from Newfoundland into New England—stories abound—but what's certain is the European colonists arrived in the very early 17th century and eventually displaced entirely the Native American culture that existed in the region.

It began in 1604, when some 80 French colonists spent a winter on a small island on what today is the Maine–New Brunswick border. They did not care for the harsh weather of their new home and left in spring to resettle in present-day Nova Scotia. In 1607, 3 months after the celebrated Jamestown, Virginia, colony was founded, another group of 120 settlers (this time from England) established a community at Popham Beach in present-day Phippsburg, Maine. News from home spurred these would-be colonists to abandon their new digs, and they returned to England after only one year.

The colonization of the region began in earnest with the arrival of the Pilgrims at Plymouth Rock in 1620. The Pilgrims—Puritan separatists at odds with the Church of England—established the first permanent colony, although it came at a hefty price: Nearly half the group perished during the first winter. But the colony began to thrive over the years, in part thanks to helpful Native Americans.

The success of the Pilgrims lured other settlers from England, who established a constellation of small towns outside of Boston that became the Massachusetts Bay Colony. Roger Williams was expelled from the colony for his religious beliefs; he founded the city of Providence, Rhode Island. Other restless colonists expanded their horizons in search of lands for settlement. Throughout the 17th century, colonists from Massachusetts pushed northward into what are now New Hampshire and Maine, and southward into Connecticut. The first areas to be settled were lands near protected harbors along the coast and on navigable waterways.

The more remote settlements came under attack in the 17th and early 18th centuries in a series of raids by native peoples, conducted both independently and in concert with the French. These proved temporary setbacks; colonization continued throughout New England into the 18th century.

The American Revolution

Starting around 1765, Great Britain launched a series of ham-fisted economic policies to reign in the increasingly feisty colonies. These included a direct tax— the Stamp Act—to pay for a standing army. The oppressive move provoked strong resistance. Under the banner of "No taxation without representation," disgruntled colonists engaged in a series of riots, resulting in the Boston Massacre of 1770, when British soldiers fired upon a mob of protesters, killing five.

In 1773, the most infamous protest took place in Boston. The British had imposed the Tea Act (giving the East India Company an advantage in the colonial market), which prompted a group of colonists disguised as Mohawk tribesmen to board three British ships and dump 342 chests of tea into the harbor. This incident was dubbed the Boston Tea Party.

Hostilities heightened in 1775, when the British sought to quell unrest in Massachusetts. A contingent of British soldiers was sent to **Lexington** to seize military supplies and arrest high-profile rebels John Hancock and Samuel Adams. The militia formed by the colonists exchanged gunfire with the British at **Concord,** thereby igniting the Revolution ("the shot heard round the world"—see p. 144).

Notable battles in New England included the Battle of **Bunker Hill** outside Boston (see p. 79), which the British won but at tremendous cost; and the Battle of **Bennington** in Vermont (see p. 478), in which the colonists prevailed. Hostilities ended following the British surrender at Yorktown, Virginia, in 1781, and in 1783, Britain recognized the United States as a sovereign nation.

Farming & Trade

As the new republic matured, economic growth in New England followed two tracks. Residents of inland communities farmed and traded furs. Vermont in particular has always been an agrarian state and remains a prominent dairy producer to this day.

On the coast, boatyards sprang up from Connecticut to Maine, and ship captains made fortunes trading lumber for sugar and rum in the Caribbean. Trade was dealt a severe blow by the Embargo Act of 1807, but commerce eventually recovered, and New England ships could be encountered around the globe.

The growth of the railroad in the mid–19th century was another boon. The train opened up much of the interior. The rail lines allowed local resources—such as fine marbles and granites from Vermont—to be shipped to markets to the south.

An Industrial Revolution Arrives

New England's Industrial Revolution found seed around the time of the embargo of 1807. Barred from importing English fabrics, Americans built their own textile mills. Other common household products were also manufactured domestically, especially shoes. Towns such as **Lowell,** Massachusetts (see p. 149); Lewiston, Maine; and Manchester, New Hampshire became centers of textile and shoe production. In Connecticut, the manufacture of arms and clocks emerged as major industries. Industry no longer plays the prominent role it once did—manufacturing first moved to the South, then overseas.

Tourism Boom, Economic Bust

In the mid- and late 19th century, New Englanders discovered a new cash cow: the tourist. All along the Eastern Seaboard, it became fashionable for the affluent and eventually the working class to set out for excursions to the mountains and the shore. Regions such as the **Berkshires** (p. 340), the **White Mountains** (p. 583), and **Block Island** (p. 465) were lifted by the tide of summer visitors. The tourism wave crested in the 1890s in **Newport,** Rhode Island (p. 443), and **Bar Harbor,** Maine (p. 673), both of which attracted society's biggest names. Several grand resort hotels from tourism's golden era still host travelers in the region.

But this economic rebirth would not last long. While railways allowed New England to thrive in the mid–19th century, the trains also eventually played a pivotal role in undermining the region's prosperity. The driving of the Golden Spike in 1869 in Utah, linking America's Atlantic and Pacific coasts by rail, was heard loud and clear in New England, and it had a discordant ring. Transcontinental rail meant farmers and manufacturers could ship goods from the fertile Great Plains and California to faraway markets, making it harder for New Englanders to compete. Likewise, the coastal shipping trade was dealt a fatal blow by this new transportation network. And the tourists set their sights on the Rockies and other stirring destinations in the West.

Beginning in the late 19th century, New England lapsed into an extended economic slumber. Families walked away from their farmhouses (there was no resale market) and set off for regions with more opportunities. The abandoned, decaying farmhouse almost became an icon for New England, and vast tracts of farmland were reclaimed by forest. With the rise of the automobile, many grand resorts closed their doors as inexpensive motels siphoned off their business.

Tourism & Tech: A Second Wind

During the last 2 decades of the 20th century, much of New England rode an unexpected wave of prosperity. A real-estate boom shook the region in the 1980s, driving land prices sky-high as prosperous buyers from New York and Boston acquired vacation homes or retired to the most alluring areas. In the 1990s, the sudden rise of high-tech companies in the Boston area, riding the Internet wave, sent ripples out into suburbs as far-flung as New Hampshire. New York City's rebound as a world-class place to visit and do business brought fresh jobs, money, and homeowners pouring into Connecticut. Tourism experienced a resurgence, as tethered-to-work urbanites of the Eastern Seaboard opted for shorter, more frequent vacations closer to home, particularly during economic dips.

As the 400th anniversary of the Virginia-bound Pilgrims' fateful landing approaches in 2020, New England continues to embrace those seeking to chart a new course. Yankee ingenuity—in the form of 21st-century "inventions" like Harvard-born Facebook—are making our world smaller, more connected, and easier to discover. Yet, there's more joy than ever in ignoring your GPS's instructions and heeding Robert Frost's instead. Take "the road less traveled by" whenever you can.

ART & ARCHITECTURE

Visual Arts

New England is justly famous for the **art** it has inspired, particularly the landscapes painted by **Hudson River School** artists such as Thomas Cole and his student Frederic Church, and the monuments carved by Augustus Saint-Gaudens and Daniel Chester French. Some of the artists who have memorably painted New England landscapes and seascapes include **Winslow Homer** (1836–1910), **Fairfield Porter** (1907–1975), **John Marin** (1870–1953), **Neil Welliver** (1929–2005), and **Andrew Wyeth** (1917–2009), he of the iconic *Christina's World,* painted in a coastal Maine field. Illustrators **Norman Rockwell** (1894–1978) and **Maxfield Parrish** (1870–1966) famously captured the region's faces and places. Art colonies that sprang up around the turn of the 20th century in **Ogunquit,** Maine (p. 613), **Cornish,** New Hampshire (p. 580), and **Old Lyme,** Connecticut (p. 409), remain active arts hubs, thanks to a new, dynamic generation of creators.

There are a surprising number of excellent art museums and galleries throughout New England, even in some rather unlikely places as **St. Johnsbury,** Vermont (p. 558); **Rockland,** Maine (p. 648); and **North Adams,** Massachusetts (p. 357), home to North America's largest contemporary art museum. Consult individual chapters for more details on art offerings.

Architecture

You can often trace the evolution of a town by its architecture, as styles evolve from basic structures to elaborate Victorian mansions. The primer below should aid with basic identification.

○ **First Period** (1600–1700): The New England house of the 17th century was a simple, boxy affair, often covered in shingles or rough clapboards. Don't look for ornamentation; these homes were designed for basic shelter from the elements, and are often marked by prominent stone chimneys. You can see examples at **Plimoth Plantation** (p. 176) and in **Salem** (p. 150), near Boston.

○ **Georgian** (1700–1780): Ornamentation comes into play in the Georgian style, which draws heavily on classical symmetry. Modelled on the building style in vogue in England at the time, Georgian houses were embraced by affluent colonists. Look for Palladian windows, formal pilasters, and elaborate projecting pediments. **Deerfield** (see p. 333) in Massachusetts' Pioneer Valley, is a prime destination for seeing early Georgian homes; **Providence**, Rhode Island (p. 426) and **Portsmouth,** New Hampshire (p. 564) have abundant examples of later Georgian styles.

○ **Greek Revival** (1825–1860): The most easy-to-identify Greek Revival homes feature a projecting portico with massive columns, like a part of the Parthenon grafted onto an existing home. Less dramatic homes may simply be oriented so the gable faces the street, accenting the triangular pediment. Greek Revival didn't catch on in New England the way it did in the South, but some fine examples exist, notably on the island of **Nantucket,** Massachusetts (p. 292).

○ **Carpenter Gothic** and **Gothic Revival** (1840–1880): The second half of the 19th century brought a wave of Gothic Revival homes, which borrowed their aesthetic from the English country home. Aficionados of this style (and its later progeny featuring gingerbread trim) owe themselves a trip to **Oak Bluffs** on Martha's Vineyard in Massachusetts (p. 273), where more than 300 pastel-painted cottages are festooned with scrollwork and exuberant architectural flourishes.

○ **Victorian** (1860–1900): This is a catchall term for the jumble of mid- to late-19th-century styles that emphasized complexity and opulence. Perhaps the best-known Victorian style—almost a caricature—is the tall and narrow Addams Family–style house, with mansard roof and prickly roof cresting. You'll find these scattered throughout the region. The Victorian style also includes squarish **Italianate** homes with wide eaves and unusual flourishes, such as the outstanding Victoria Mansion in **Portland,** Maine (p. 626). Stretching the definition of Victorian a bit is the **Richardsonian Romanesque** style, which was popular for railroad stations and public buildings. The classic Richardsonian building, designed by H. H. Richardson himself in 1872, is **Trinity Church,** in Boston (p. 80).

○ **Shingle** (1880–1900): This uniquely New England style became preferred for vacation homes on **Cape Cod** (chapter 6) and the **Maine** coast (chapter

13). Look for a profusion of gables, roofs, and porches on gray-weathered structures typically covered with shingles from roofline to foundation.

o **Modern** (1900–present): Outside of Boston, New England has produced little in the way of notable modern architecture. In the 1930s, Boston became a center for the stark **International Style** with the appointment of Bauhaus School founder Walter Gropius to the faculty at Harvard. Some intriguing experiments in this style are found on the **M.I.T.** and **Harvard campuses** (p. 82), including Gropius's Harvard Graduate Center and Eero Saarinen's Kresge Auditorium.

THE LAY OF THE LAND

The human history of New England begins thousands of years ago, when Native American tribes fished Atlantic shores and hunted these hills. And even they were here for only a sliver of the long period of time required to cleave mountains and gouge lakes; situations like this call for the word *eons*. The rocks upon which you climb, sun yourself, and picnic are old—staggeringly old.

Before arriving, then, it's a wise idea to acquaint yourself with the natural history of the place. Armed with a little respect and appreciation for the landscape before you, you just might treat it more reverently while you're here—and help ensure that it remains for future generations to behold.

Rocky Road: Geology Sets the Table

The beginnings of New England are perhaps a half-billion years old. That's right: *billion,* with a B.

Liquid magma was moving upward through the earth's mantle, exploding in underground volcanoes, then hardening into granite-like rocks underground. Much later, natural forces, such as wind and water, wore away and exposed the upper layers of these rocks. Their punishment was only beginning, however; soon enough (geologically speaking), what is now eastern North America and most of Europe began to shove up against each other, slowly but inexorably.

This "collision" (which was more like an *extremely* slow-motion car wreck) heated, squeezed, transformed, and thrust up the rocks that now form the backbone of the coastline. Ice ages came and went, but the rocks remained; successive waves of glaciation and retreat scratched up the rocks like old vinyl records, and the thick tongues of pressing ice cut deep notches out of them. The ice swept up huge boulders and deposited them in odd places.

When the glaciers finally retreated for the last time, tens of thousands of years ago, the water melting from the huge ice sheet covering North America swelled lakes and rivers, and left unveiled such distinctively carved places as **Acadia National Park** in Maine (p. 667) and New Hampshire's **Crawford Notch** (p. 590) and **Franconia Notch** (p. 591). The melting ice sheets also laid down tons of silt and sand in their wake, birthing the sandy barrens and gentle hills of central and western Massachusetts.

Life Sets in: Plants & Animals

Once the bones of this landscape were established, next came the plants and animals. After each ice age, conifers such as spruce and fir trees began to take root—alongside countless grasses and weeds. It was tough work: Much of New England has rocky, acidic soil, inhospitable to vegetation. Yet a few plants persevered (as plants tend to do), and evergreens soon formed an impenetrable thicket covering much of the bedrock. When those conifers died of old age, were struck by lightning and caught on fire, or were cut down by settlers (or beavers), different kinds of trees—beeches, birches, brilliant sugar maples—rushed in to replace them.

As trees, flowers, and fruits became reestablished, animals wandered back, too—some are now extinct, but most still thrive in the fields, hills, and woods of the region: Songbirds, deer, and moose attract avid wildlife watchers.

New England's unique position, near the warm Gulf Stream without quite touching it, has also bequeathed the region with an amazing variety of marine life. The warm offshore Gulf current passes over a high, undersea plateau known as the Georges Bank, then collides with the much colder waters of the North Atlantic. This collision creates upwelling currents from the sea floor, bringing loads of microscopic food particles toward the surface—food that sustains a complex variety of microorganisms, the bottom rungs in a ladder of marine life that climbs all the way up to migrating whales, which make for a wonderful spectacle off the New England coast. (Whale-watching cruises set off from **Boston,** p. 89; **Gloucester**, Massachusetts, p. 166; and **Barnstable,** p. 211, and **Provincetown,** p. 256 on Cape Cod.) Seabirds make similar passages, lighting upon the beaches, marshes, and lakes here in spring and fall. The Atlantic also teems (though not as much as it once did) with codfish, lobsters, crabs, and other sea creatures.

The region's coastal tide pools are also worth exploring. This precarious zone, where land and rock meet ocean, is an ever-changing world of seaweed, snails, barnacles, darting water bugs, clams, shellfish, mud-burrowing worms, and other creatures. Interestingly, creatures live in distinct, well-marked "bands" as you get closer to the water. Rocks that are always submerged contain one mixture of seaweed, shellfish, and marine organisms, while rocks that are exposed and then resubmerged each day by the tides have a different mix.

And that's just a sampling of what's out there. Whether you explore New England on foot, by bicycle, by kayak, by horse-drawn carriage, or by charter boat, you're certain to see something you've never seen before. Be attentive, and you'll come away with a deeper respect for all things natural—not only here, but everywhere.

NEW ENGLAND IN LITERATURE

New Englanders have generated entire libraries, from the earliest days of hellfire-and-brimstone Puritan sermons to Stephen King's horror novels set in fictional Maine villages.

Among the more enduring writings from New England's earliest days are the poems of Massachusetts Bay Colony resident **Anne Bradstreet** (ca. 1612–1672) and the sermons and essays of **Increase Mather** (1639–1723) and his son, **Cotton Mather** (1663–1728).

After the American Revolution, Hartford dictionary writer **Noah Webster** (1758–1843) issued a call to American writers: "America must be as independent in literature as she is in politics, as famous for arts as for arms." His decisions, such as removing the "u" common in British spellings like "labour" and "honour," helped mold America's distinct identity. The tales of **Nathaniel Hawthorne** (1804–1864) captivated a public eager for a native literature. His most famous novel, *The Scarlet Letter,* is a narrative about morality set in 17th-century Boston, and he wrote numerous other books and stories (such as the *House of the Seven Gables,* the model for which you can tour in Salem, Massachusetts—see p. 155) that wrestled with themes of sin and guilt, often set in the emerging republic.

Henry Wadsworth Longfellow (1807–1882), the Portland poet who settled in Cambridge, caught the attention of the public with evocative narrative poems focusing on distinctly American subjects. His popular works included "The Courtship of Miles Standish," "Paul Revere's Ride," and "The Song of Hiawatha." Poetry in the mid–19th century was the equivalent of Hollywood movies today—Longfellow could be considered his generation's Steven Spielberg (apologies to literary scholars). It's possible to visit both his boyhood home, the **Wadsworth-Longfellow House** in Portland (p. 632) and his adult home in Cambridge, Massachusetts, **Longfellow House** (p. 84).

The zenith of New England literature occurred in the mid- and late 19th century with the Transcendentalist movement. These writers and thinkers included **Ralph Waldo Emerson** (1803–1882), **Bronson Alcott** (1799–1888), and **Henry David Thoreau** (1817–1862). They fashioned a way of viewing nature and society that was uniquely American. They rejected the rigid doctrines of the Puritans, and found sustenance in self-examination, the glories of nature, and a celebration of individualism. Perhaps the best-known work to emerge from this period was Thoreau's *Walden.* You can visit many sites associated with them in **Concord,** Massachusetts (p. 136), where they lived and worked.

Although she was reclusive, another writer who left a lasting mark on American literature was **Emily Dickinson** (1830–1886), a native of Amherst, Massachusetts, whose precise and enigmatic poems placed her in the front rank of American poets. (Her home is open to visitors—see p. 331.) **James Russell Lowell** (1819–1891), of Cambridge, was an influential poet, critic, and editor, as was **William Cullen Bryant** (1794–1878), who hailed from rural Cummington, Massachusetts. Later poets were imagist **Amy Lowell** (1874–1925), from Brookline, Massachusetts, and **Edna St. Vincent Millay** (1892–1950), from Camden, Maine.

The bestselling *Uncle Tom's Cabin,* the book Abraham Lincoln half-jokingly accused of starting the Civil War, was written by **Harriet Beecher Stowe** (1811–1896) in Brunswick, Maine. She lived much of her life as a neighbor of **Mark Twain** (an adopted New Englander) in Hartford, Connecticut. (To visit their neighboring houses, see p. 402.) Many of his most beloved novels, including *The Prince and the Pauper* and *Adventures of Huckleberry Finn,* were penned there. Another bestseller was the children's book *Little Women,* written by **Louisa May Alcott** (1832–1888), whose father, Bronson, was instrumental in the Transcendentalist movement. (See p. 145 for details on visiting the Alcott home, Orchard House, in Concord, Massachusetts.) **Edith Wharton** (1862–1937) wrote *The House of Mirth* and other blockbusters at The Mount, her home in Lenox, Massachusetts (see p. 349).

New England's later role in the literary tradition may best be symbolized by the poet **Robert Frost** (1874–1963). Though born in California, he lived his life in Massachusetts, New Hampshire, and Vermont. In the New England landscape and community, he found a lasting grace and rich metaphors for life. (Among his most famous lines: "The woods are lovely, dark, and deep/ But I have promises to keep/And miles to go before I sleep/And miles to go before I sleep.") You can visit his former home, **Frost Place,** in Franconia, New Hampshire (p. 594); see his **grave** in Bennington, Vermont (p. 479); or walk the **Robert Frost Memorial Trail** in Middlebury, Vermont (p. 520).

> **Impressions**
>
> *There is a sumptuous variety about the New England weather that compels the stranger's admiration—and regret.*
> —Mark Twain, speech delivered to the New England Society, 1876

New England continues to attract writers drawn to the noted educational institutions and the privacy of rural life. Prominent contemporary writers and poets who live in the region at least part of the year include **Nicholson Baker, Christopher Buckley, Stephen King, P. J. O'Rourke, John Irving, Elizabeth Strout, Wally Lamb, Nathaniel Philbrick, David McCullough,** and **Alice Hoffman.**

NEW ENGLAND IN FILM & TV

New England is frequently captured through the lens of Hollywood, thanks in equal parts to its natural beauty; its slightly spooky history; and the unusual number of star actors, actresses, and directors who were raised here and continue to push forward projects incorporating local storylines or landscapes.

Lillian Gish's 1920 silent film *Way Down East* was perhaps the first movie to bring cinematic attention to the region. Films now regularly depict Boston's grimy underbelly, in films such as *The Departed* (2006) and *Mystic River* (2003); local Red Sox–mania (*Fever Pitch,* 2005); working-class struggle and identity crises (*Good Will Hunting,* 1997, and *Manchester by the Sea,* 2016); and a host of horror films based on books by Maine's Stephen King—from *Carrie* (1976), *The Shining* (1980), and *It* (2017), down through to a welter of TV miniseries—that make it sometimes seem like supernatural forces are at work in all small New England towns. However, King also penned the story upon which *The Shawshank Redemption* (1994), also set in Maine, was based.

The delightful 2012 coming-of-age film *Moonrise Kingdom* seems to be set in Maine but was actually filmed in Rhode Island.

Several television series have been based in New England through the years, such as this wildly popular trifecta: *Cheers* (1982–1993), set in a chummy Boston bar (which is still there beside Boston Common—see p. 133); *Newhart* (1982–1990), in which actor Bob Newhart comically attempted to run a Vermont bed-and-breakfast inn (filmed at the Waybury Inn in East Middlebury, p. 522); and *Murder, She Wrote* (1984–1996), which saw crime novelist Angela Lansbury stumbling across and solving real-life crimes, with seeming ease, from her perch in fictional Cabot Cove, Maine. *Wings* (1990–1997), set at a small airstrip on Massachusetts's Nantucket Island, propelled several actors (Tony Shalhoub, Tim Daly, Thomas Haden Church) on to further fame.

More recently, *Ally McBeal, Boston Public, The Practice,* and *Boston Legal* explored facets of public schools and legal practice in that city. *Gilmore Girls* earned fans who still make pilgrimages to Stars Hollow–like towns in Connecticut. *North Woods Law* has turned Maine and New Hampshire game wardens into celebrities; *Wicked Tuna* has done the same for Gloucester fishermen.

NEW ENGLAND IN POP MUSIC

Talented New Englanders have contributed mightily to the American music scene. Keep these local treasures in mind as you're building a playlist for road trips in the region.

Folk-pop singer **James Taylor** was born in Boston, long ensconced on Martha's Vineyard, and now resides in his beloved Berkshires. The Rock and Roll Hall of Fame band **Aerosmith** also has roots in Boston. The wildly popular '70s rock group **Boston** was fronted by residents of that city. The proto-punk-garage-folk musician **Jonathan Richman,** whose 1975 song "Roadrunner" immortalizes late-night driving around Boston, was born in Natick, MA.

Pop stars **Michael Bolton** and **John Mayer** were both born in Connecticut, while jam-band **Phish** was formed in Burlington, Vermont, by college friends. **Jeffrey Osborne** of the band L.T.D. hails from Providence. The hip-hop group **Bell Biv DeVoe** are from Boston. Nashville singer-songwriter **Patty Griffin** was born and raised in Maine. **Taylor Swift** is famously known for having a seaside house in Westerly, Rhode Island.

With its sizeable student population, Boston has long been an incubator for alternative rock, nurturing such bands such as **The Pixies, J. Geils Band, The Cars,** and **The Lemonheads.** Native sons the **Dropkick Murphys,** a Celtic

---

Moments

Now the first of December was covered with snow
and so was the turnpike from Stockbridge to Boston
Lord, the Berkshires seemed dream-like, on account of that frosting . . .
—James Taylor, "Sweet Baby James"

punk band, sell out shows around St. Patrick's Day. The ska punk band **Mighty Mighty Bosstones** host the annual Hometown Throwdown music festival in Boston between Christmas and New Year's Day.

NEW ENGLAND FOOD & DRINK

New England got a late start in the food game—for a while, it was basically fish, vegetables, simple soup, and whatever was dragged home from a hunt—but it has caught up, in spades. Today, you can dine exquisitely in this region, thanks to some unusually crafty producers and chefs, who use local ingredients to create such things as Maine honey-roasted pumpkin soup, seared Stonington scallops, roasted black sea bass with foraged mushrooms, and wood-grilled, prosciutto-wrapped Vermont rabbit.

Seafood is still king here. All along the coastline, live lobsters can be bought literally off the boat on docks or at **lobster pounds.** You can buy fried fish and clams at **lobster and clam shacks** almost anywhere on the coast, too. More upscale eateries in seaside towns serve the local catch of the day grilled or sautéed with an array of sauces.

Inland, sample local farm products such as the sweet maple syrup, sold throughout the region; it's the best in the world. Look also for Vermont's famous cheeses and cider; Maine's tiny, tasty wild blueberries; and heirloom apples in western Massachusetts.

Every summer, small farmers across the region set up stands at the ends of driveways selling fresh produce straight from the garden. You can find berries, stone fruits, veggies, and sometimes home-baked items here. These stands are rarely tended; just leave what you owe, and maybe a bit of a tip, in the coffee can. Also watch for the appearance of **"pick-your-own" farms** in summertime. For a fee that's typically less than what you pay in a store for the fruit, you fill up containers of strawberries or blueberries and take 'em home. Kids love this.

Restaurateurs haven't overlooked New England's bounty, either. Big-city chefs flock here every year to hang up new shingles and test themselves with the local ingredients; some restaurants maintain their own herb and vegetable gardens. Some of these places stretch the budget a bit, but plenty of others fall squarely into the "road food" category.

Here's an abbreviated field guide to New England's distinctively local tastes.

- **Apples:** Maine, Vermont, Massachusetts, and Connecticut are all well-known for their fall apple harvests. Look for orchards in central and western Maine, the Champlain Valley, the Berkshire Hills, and the lower Connecticut River Valley. Cold Hollow Cider Mill in **Waterbury** (near **Stowe,** VT) is probably the most famous cider purveyor in the U.S.; you can watch the press (and the cider donut robot) in operation daily in the fall.

- **Baked beans:** Boston will be forever linked with baked beans (hence the nickname "Beantown"), but the dish remains extremely popular in parts of Maine, too. Saturday-night church dinners (also known as "bean hole" suppers) usually consist of baked beans and brown bread, plus pasta salads and the like. There's a famous, century-and-a-half-old **B&M Baked Beans** plant in **Portland,** where beans are still slow-baked in 900-pound pots

- o **Blueberries:** One sometimes gets the feeling that Downeast Maine's economy would collapse without the humble blueberry. To taste it, look for roadside stands and diners from the Midcoast north, selling pies made with wild berries from mid- until late summer. These tiny blueberries (which grow on low shrubs on wind-swept rocks or hilltops) are much tangier than the bigger, commercial variety. You can even pick your own pail of berries, for free, high on the slopes of certain hills such as **Blue Hill Mountain** and **Pleasant Mountain.** Look for the bush's egg-shaped, glossy, tealike leaves.

- o **Cheese:** Cheese is a Vermont specialty: Cheddar is the most common variety (you can buy a huge "wheel" of cheddar at any country store worth its salt), but goat cheeses are starting to make a serious run, too. The Northeast Kingdom and Connecticut River Valley are especially rich in cheese. Take a cheese-factory tour in **Grafton** (see p. 502) or **Shelburne Farms** (p. 550) to see what goes into your cheddar, or scour a natural-foods store (often called a "co-op" in Vermont) for cow and goat cheeses produced by nearby farms.

- o **Clam chowder:** The obligatory soup of choice, New England clam chowder consists simply of chopped clams, potatoes, milk or cream, and some butter, flour, and/or salt pork to thicken the mixture. Rhode Islanders eat a clear-broth version, which makes it easier to spot the tender bits of just-dug quahog clams.

- o **Fish chowder:** This coastal dish is the simplest one. In its purest form, fish chowder consists of the day's catch of chopped-up white fish (cod, haddock), enough milk to satisfy a small animal, peeled potatoes, and a nice big chunk of butter. No thickener, cornstarch, or flour—*please.* This dish is best enjoyed with an ocean view, a square of blueberry cake, and a cup of bad coffee. And in the fishing villages of coastal Maine, that's exactly how it's still served to legions of tired and hungry local fisherman as they trundle in after long, cold days out on the water hauling nets or traps.

- o **Johnnycakes:** A Colonial recipe largely lost to time, the Johnnycake still survives in the odd Rhode Island wayside diner: heavy pancakes made from cornmeal and molasses rather than the usual wheat flour and sugar. Rhode Island, tiny as it is, has several idiosyncratic food specialties; see p. 436.

- o **Lobster:** You can buy freshly steamed lobsters at pounds in most Maine fishing towns, usually from a shack right near the main fishing pier. The setting is often as casual it gets—maybe a couple of picnic tables on a patch of lawn. Eating lobster "in the rough," as they say, is still not the most authentic way to go. That would be a traditional lobster bake, in which the crustaceans and other fixings are nestled in seaweed atop fiery-hot rocks in a pit at the beach. **Lobster rolls** consist of lobster meat plucked from the shell, mixed with just enough mayonnaise or melted butter, then served on a buttered hot-dog roll. You'll find them everywhere along the coast.

- o **Maple syrup:** Nothing says New England like maple syrup. You can buy the stuff in any of the New England states, but the best is made in New

made IN NEW ENGLAND

Early in the 20th century, the Maine soda known as **Moxie** actually outsold Coca-Cola. Part of its allure was the fanciful story behind its 1885 creation: A traveler named Lieutenant Moxie was said to have observed South American Indians consuming the sap of a native plant, which gave them extraordinary strength. This "secret ingredient" was key to the drink patented by Maine native Dr. Augustin Thompson, which was initially marketed as Moxie Nerve Food. The backstory is a bunch of malarkey. But the bitter beverage is still quite popular in Maine, and you won't know if you like it until you try it. A tip: Sip it slowly, ice cold.

The New England Confectionery Company (hence the name) in Revere, Massachusetts, has been making powdery **NECCO wafers** since 1847. Rescued from bankruptcy in 2018, the company also produces Mary Janes, Candy Buttons, Clark Bars, and that annual Valentine's Day must: Sweethearts conversation hearts.

Granted, Moxie and NECCO Wafers may be somewhat acquired tastes. But who doesn't love ice cream? New Englanders in particular can't seem to get enough of the stuff—and some of the best is made up in Waterbury, Vermont, at the **Ben & Jerry's Ice Cream Factory** (see box p. 530). Those trademark black-and-white cows on the label make even more sense as you drive through Vermont on your way to take a tour of the operations (and get a free sample at the end!).

Hampshire and Vermont. Visit in late spring (the last week of March is recommended) to get a close look at the process at local sugar houses. Sugarmakers boil up sap and ladle sweet syrup onto pancakes, ice cream, or snow to let you sample before you buy. And you *will* buy.

- **Shellfish:** Mussels, oysters, clams, and scallops can all be bought at fish markets up and down the coast—raw (if you're renting a cottage), steamed, or fried. Look for them on restaurant menus, too. Be sure to know how to choose fresh bivalves at the market if you're cooking for yourself; a single bad one can make a person mighty sick.

- **Smoked fish:** Fish-smoking isn't a huge industry in New England, but it does exist, especially in Downeast Maine. That's not really surprising, given the huge supply of smokeable fish living just offshore.

The Craft Beer Revolution

No survey of food and drink in New England would be complete without serious mention of **beer.** New England has nearly 350 microbreweries, including some of the most acclaimed operations in the nation.

The beers of Vermont, especially, are legion—and they're often in the places you'd least expect to find them: northern Vermont towns such as remote **Greensboro** (Hill Farmstead Brewery, p. 560), the college town of **Middlebury** (p. 518), and **Waterbury** (p. 529), which has the most breweries per capita of any town in the United States. Massachusetts has over 140 microbreweries, including standouts in **Worcester** (CraftRoots Brewery, p. 318) and **Great Barrington** (Barrington Brewery, p. 369). You can even find a microbrewery in the woods of **Damariscotta,** Maine (Oxbow Brewery, p. 642).

Once you get to the cities, the situation gets even better. The concentration of mini-breweries in both **Burlington,** Vermont (p. 543) and **Portland,** Maine (see box p. 634) actually staggers the mind. **Boston** standouts include Samuel Adams and Harpoon (not micro anymore) and nimble newcomer Trillium Brewing Company, which has been stealing their thunder. Resurrected brand Narragansett has transformed a derelict mill in **Pawtucket,** Rhode Island, into one of New England's largest brewing operations.

There are literally *hundreds* more. Go to any package store—or even a local gas station—and check the refrigerator section for local finds.

WHEN TO GO
New England's Seasons

New England has no monopoly on seasonal shifts and splendors. Yet the region dons new outerwear every 3 months or so with unparalleled style and finesse. The ever-changing seasons here are precisely what make New England so distinctive, and there are reasons to embrace all four. Even the unofficial "sprinter," that muddy, sloppy season that marks winter's end and spring's arrival, has fans among the outdoorsy and budget-conscious.

SUMMER   The peak summer season in New England runs from the 4th of July through Labor Day weekend. That's a pretty slim sandwich, only about 8½ weeks. But, wow, does the population of each of these states ever swell between the starting line and summer's checkered flag. Vast crowds surge into New England, particularly on weekends and when temperatures soar.

It's no wonder. Summers here are exquisite, particularly because the daylight lasts so long—until 9 or 9:30pm in late June and early July. In the mountains, cooler temperatures prevail, and this natural air conditioning reinvigorates urbanites. Along the seashore, reliable breezes keep temperatures down even when it's triple-digit steaming in the big cities. In general, expect moderation: In Portland, Maine, the thermometer tops 90°F (32°C) for only 4 or 5 days each year, typically.

Weather in this region is largely determined by winds. Summer's southwesterly winds bring haze, heat, and humidity (to everywhere except the seashore); northwesterly winds bring cool, bright weather and knife-sharp views. These systems tend to alternate during the summer, the heat and humidity building slowly and stealthily for days—then swiftly getting kicked out on their ears by stiff, cool winds pressing down from Canada. Rain is unpredictable in summer—afternoon thunderstorms pop up out of nowhere and roll through at a mighty pace. On average, about 1 day in 3 here will bring some rain.

For most of this region, midsummer is prime time. Expect to pay premium prices at hotels and restaurants. (The exception is around the ski resorts, where you can often find bargains.) Also be aware that early summer brings out scads of biting black flies and mosquitoes as you move inland from the coast in the northern states, a state of affairs that has spoiled many north-country camping trips. Come prepared for these guys.

What to do? Play some golf. Go hiking or kayaking. Body surf in the ocean. Catch a minor-league baseball game. Or indulge in one of our favorite activities: rocking in a chair on a screened porch, reading a book, playing guitar, or just listening intently to the sounds of loons or crickets and watching the night sky for stars you never knew existed.

AUTUMN Don't be surprised to smell the tang of fall approaching as early as mid-August, when you'll begin to notice a few leaves turning blaze-orange on maples at the edges of wetlands or highways. Fall comes early to New England, puts its feet up, and stays for some time. The foliage season begins in earnest in the northern part of the region by September's third week; in the southern portions, it peaks around mid-October.

Fall in New England is one of the great natural spectacles in the world. When the region's rolling hills light up in brilliant reds and stunning oranges, awed motorists pull to the sides of roads to snap photos. The best part? This spectacle is nearly as regular as clockwork, with only a few years truly "bad" for foliage (due to odd storms or invasive, leaf-eating pests).

Keep in mind, however, that autumn is the most popular time of year to travel to the New England states—bus tours flock here like migrating geese in early October. As a result, hotels in renowned leaf towns are invariably booked solid at that time. Reservations are essential. Don't be surprised if rates are $50 or more per night higher than they were just weeks ago at your inn or hotel. Deal with it; you can't buy scenery like this.

Some states maintain seasonal **foliage hotlines and/or websites** to let you know when the leaves are at their peak: **Vermont** (www.vermontvacation. com/fall; ✆ **800/VERMONT** [837-6668]), **Maine** (www.mainefoliage.com; ✆ **888/624-6345**), and **New Hampshire** (www.visitnh.gov/foliage-tracker).

WINTER New England winters are like wine—some years are exceptional, some are lousy. During a good season, mounds of light, fluffy snow fill the deep woods and blanket ski slopes and snowmobile trails. A "classic" New England winter offers profound peace and tranquility, as the fresh snow muffles all noise and brings such a thunderous silence to the entire region that the hiss and pop of a wood fire at a country inn can seem startlingly loud. During these sorts of winters, exploring the forest on snowshoes or cross-country skis is an experience bordering on the magical.

During the *other* winters, the weather fairies instead bring a nasty mélange of rain, freezing rain, and sleet. The woods become filled with crusty snow, the cold is damp and bone-numbing, and it's bleak, as gunpowder-gray clouds lower and linger for weeks. There are ways to beat this, however: The higher in elevation you go into the mountains of northern New England, or the farther north you head (to such places as Jay, VT), the better your odds of finding snow.

The coast in winter is a crapshoot at best, more likely to yield rain (or sticky, heavy "snowball" snow) than powdery snow. Yes, winter vacations on the ocean can be spectacular—think Winslow Homerian waves crashing savagely onto an empty beach—but after a day or two of trying to navigate your car around big, gray, slushy snow banks, you too will soon be heading for Stowe unless hunkering down by a fire is all your soul craves.

Ski areas get crowded. Some *very* crowded. Expect maximum pricing, so-so food, and a herd mentality; this is the price you must pay for enjoying great skiing. The resorts get especially packed during school vacations, which is just when many resorts choose to hike up rates at hotels *and* on the slopes.

By the way, if you visit a small town in this region during winter, there is another pleasure to enjoy during the deepest freeze: public ice skating and ice hockey. You'll find locals skating on town green and public park rinks, lakes, and ponds. How do you find these spots? Look for a clump of cars beside an iconic little warming hut with a wood-burning stove inside, sending up smoke puffs like a signal to the masses. Cities like Boston, Newport, Providence, Portsmouth, and Hartford are also destinations for romantics who want to lace up skates.

SPRING   After the long winter, spring in New England is a tease. She promises a lot and comes dressed in impressive finery (see: delicate purple lilacs, which blossom for just two weeks). There are years when spring lasts only a few weeks, "occurring" around mid-May but up north as late as June. New Englanders often call this time of year "mud season." Warming earth's a gooey mess; rushing waterfalls are worth mucking up your boots.

One morning the ground is muddy, the trees are barren, and gritty snow is still collected in shady hollows and mall parking lots. The next day, it's in the 80s and sunny, maple trees are erupting with little red cloverlike buds; kids are swimming in the lakes where the docks have just been put in; and somewhere in New Hampshire, a blue cover is being ripped off an aboveground pool.

Travelers need to be awfully crafty to experience spring in New England—and, once they get here, they often have trouble finding a room. That's because a good number of innkeepers and restaurateurs close up for a few weeks for repairs or to venture someplace warm. The upside? Rates are never cheaper than in early spring . . . right up until college graduation season. It's jaw-dropping how little you can pay in March for the same room that would cost 3 to 10 times *more* in mid-summer or October.

Boston Average Temperatures & Rainfall

	JAN	FEB	MAR	APR	MAY	JUNE	JULY	AUG	SEPT	OCT	NOV	DEC
Temp. (°F)	35	37	34	52	56	69	73	72	67	61	44	31
Temp. (°C)	2	3	1	11	13	21	23	22	19	13	7	−1
Rainfall (in.)	4.2	3.2	4.2	5.7	3.5	4.9	4.0	1.6	3.7	4.1	1.8	2.5

Burlington, Vermont Average Temperatures & Rainfall

	JAN	FEB	MAR	APR	MAY	JUNE	JULY	AUG	SEPT	OCT	NOV	DEC
Temp. (°F)	18	19	30	43	56	65	70	68	60	49	37	24
Temp. (°C)	−8	−7	−1	6	13	18	21	20	16	9	3	−4
Rainfall (in.)	1.9	1.7	2.2	2.6	3.2	3.7	3.7	3.5	3.4	3.1	2.7	2.2

New England Calendar of Events

For more New England events, check https://www.frommers.com/destinations/new-england/planning-a-trip/calendar-of-events, where you'll find an up-to-the-minute roster of what's happening in the region.

FEBRUARY

Dartmouth Winter Carnival, Hanover, NH. Huge ice sculptures grace the village green during this festive celebration of winter, which includes numerous sporting events. Call ✆ **603/646-3399.** Early February.

APRIL

Patriots Day, Boston area, MA. The events of April 18 and 19, 1775, which started the Revolutionary War, are commemorated with battle reenactments in Lexington and Concord. Call the **Lexington Chamber of Commerce** (www.lexingtonchamber.org; ✆ **781/862-2480**), **Concord Chamber of Commerce.** org; ✆ **978/369-3120**), or **Minute Man National Historical Park** (www.nps.gov/mima; ✆ **978/318-7825**). Claiming to be the "world's oldest" annual marathon, the **Boston Marathon** (www.baa.org) is a cherished feature of Patriots Day. Third Monday in April; a state holiday in Massachusetts and Maine.

Daffodil Festival, Nantucket, MA. Spring's arrival is trumpeted with masses of yellow blooms adorning everything in sight, including a cavalcade of antique cars. Call ✆ **508/228-3643.** Late April.

MAY

Cape Cod Maritime Days, Cape Cod, MA. A multitude of cultural organizations mount special events—such as lighthouse tours—highlighting the region's nautical history. Call ✆ **508/362-3225.** All month.

JUNE

Old Port Festival, Portland, ME. A block party in the heart of Portland's historic waterfront with live music, food vendors, and activities for kids. Call ✆ **207/772-6828.** Early June.

Boston Pride Parade, Copley Square to City Hall Plaza, Boston. New England's largest pride parade caps a weeklong celebration of diversity. Call ✆ **617/262-9405** or go to www.bostonpride.org. Early June.

Market Square Day, Portsmouth, NH. This lively street fair attracts more than 150 vendors and revelers into downtown Portsmouth to dance, listen to music, sample food, and enjoy summer's arrival. Call ✆ **603/433-4398.** Early June.

Annual Windjammer Days, Boothbay Harbor, ME. For nearly 6 decades, antique ships have gathered in Boothbay Harbor to kick off the summer sailing season. Expect fireworks, food, and parades on land and sea. Call ✆ **207/633-2353.** Late June.

Jacob's Pillow Dance Festival, Becket, MA. The oldest dance festival in America features everything from ballet to modern dance and hip-hop. For a schedule of summer's ticketed and free outdoor performances, call ✆ **413/243-0745,** or go to www.jacobspillow.org. Late June through August.

Tanglewood Music Festival, Lenox, MA. The Boston Symphony Orchestra makes its summer home at this fine estate. But that's just the beginning. Tanglewood also hosts a popular artists series, film nights, jazz concerts, touring ensembles, and memorable events. Call the orchestra's home base in Boston at ✆ **617/266-1492,** or go to www.tanglewood.org. Late June through Early September.

Williamstown Theatre Festival, Williamstown, MA. This nationally known festival presents everything from revivals of classics to world premiere comedies and musicals, as well as readings and talks. Contact ✆ **413/458-3253** or www.wtfestival.org. Late June through mid-August.

JULY

Boston Harborfest, downtown Boston, along Boston Harbor, and the Boston Harbor Islands, MA. The city puts on its celebratory best for the 4th of July, a gigantic weeklong celebration of Boston's colonial and maritime history. Events include tours, cruises, reenactments, and the Boston Chowderfest. Contact **Boston Harborfest** (www.bostonharborfest.com; ✆ **617/439-7700**). Early July.

Boston Pops Fireworks Spectacular, Hatch Memorial Shell on the Esplanade, Boston. The patriotic day culminates in the Boston Pops' famous 4th of July concert. People wait from dawn until dark for the music and fireworks to start. Visit www.bostonpopsjuly 4th.org. July 4.

Wickford Art Festival, Wickford, RI. More than 200 juried artists gather in this quaint village for one of the East Coast's oldest art festivals. Call ℂ **401/294-6840,** or go to www.wickfordart.org. Early July.

Maine Lobster Festival, Rockland, ME. Fill up on fresh-cooked lobsters and smoked shrimp at this entertaining 5-day event that toasts Maine's favorite crustacean. Call ℂ **800/576-7512** or go to www.mainelobster festival.com. Late July to early August.

Newport Folk Festival, Newport, RI. Thousands of music lovers congregate at Fort Adams State Park for a heavy dose of performances on a July weekend. It's one of the nation's premier festivals. Go to www.newport folk.org. Late July.

AUGUST

Craftsmen's Fair, Newbury, NH. Quality crafts from several hundred New Hampshire artisans are displayed and sold at this 9-day festival at Mount Sunapee, held for more than 85 years starting the first Saturday of August. Call ℂ **603/224-3375.** Early August.

Newport Jazz Festival, Newport, RI. This 3-day jazz fest brings together some of the best in the music industry to play for a sizzling weekend at waterside Fort Adams State Park. Go to www.newportjazz.org. Early August.

SEPTEMBER

Windjammer Festival, Camden, ME. Come watch Maine's impressive fleet of old-time sailing ships as they parade into Camden's scenic harbor for a weekend of music, nautical fun, and fireworks. Call ℂ **207/236-4404.** Labor Day weekend.

Acadia Night Sky Festival, Bar Harbor, ME. Mount Desert Island, which preserves the darkest night skies on the East Coast, hosts 5 days of workshops and star parties. Mingle with astronomy buffs and see just how bright

the constellations can be. Call ℂ **207/801-2566,** or go to www.acadianightskyfestival. com. Early September.

Norwalk Oyster Festival, Norwalk, CT. This waterfront festival celebrates Long Island Sound's seafaring past. Highlights include oyster slurping contests, harbor cruises, concerts, and rides. Call ℂ **203/838-9444,** or purchase tickets at www.seaport.org. Weekend after Labor Day.

The Big E, West Springfield, MA. "The Big E" is New England's largest agricultural fair, with buildings showcasing the best of all six states, top-name concert acts, artery-clogging fair food, farm animals, rides galore, daily parades, and a rare chance to watch butter sculptors at work. Call ℂ **413/737-2443,** or go to www.thebige.com. Mid- to late September.

OCTOBER

Head of the Charles Regatta, Boston and Cambridge, MA. High school, college, and post-collegiate rowing teams and individuals—some 11,000 athletes in all—race along the Charles River as hordes of fans crowd the banks and bridges. Call ℂ **617/868-6200,** or visit www.hocr.org. Late October.

Salem Haunted Happenings, Salem, MA. Séances, masquerades, fortune-telling, cruises, and spooky tours lead up to an all-day Halloween celebration unlike anything you've experienced. Contact Destination Salem (ℂ **877/SALEM-MA** [725-3662]), or check www.hauntedhappenings.org. All month.

NOVEMBER

Thanksgiving Celebration, Plymouth, MA. The town observes the holiday that put it on the map with America's Hometown Thanksgiving Celebration and Parade the weekend before Thanksgiving. At Plimoth Plantation, dining with the Pilgrims is a Thanksgiving Day treat (reservations accepted starting June 1 for this annual sell-out). Call Destination Plymouth (www.seeplymouth. com; ℂ **508/747-7533**) or Plimoth Plantation (www.plimoth.org; ℂ **508/746-1622**). Mid-November.

Christmas Prelude, Kennebunkport, ME. Join in the merriment of tree lightings, caroling, Santa's lobster boat, a hat parade, fireworks, and the adults-only Fire + Ice with bonfires and hand-carved ice bars. Call ✆ **207/967-0857.** Late November to early December.

DECEMBER

Christmas Stroll, Nantucket, MA. The island stirs from its winter slumber for a weekend of shopping and feasting, attended by costumed carolers and Santa, who arrives by Coast Guard patrol boat. Festivities also include the Nantucket Historical Association's month-long Festival of Trees. Call ✆ **508/228-3643.** Early December.

Candlelight Stroll, Portsmouth, NH. Historic Strawbery Banke revives Christmas and Hanukkah past with old-time decorations and candle lanterns lighting the grounds.

Call ✆ **603/433-1100.** First 3 weekends in December.

Boston Tea Party Reenactment, Boston, MA. A spirited recreation of the events of December 16, 1773. Call ✆ **866/955-0667,** or visit www.bostonteapartyship.com. December 16.

First Night First Day, Boston, MA. The original arts-oriented, no-alcohol New Year's Eve celebration features ice sculptures, arts and crafts, musical performances, kids' shows, and other entertainment. Fireworks light up the sky above Boston Common at 7pm and over Boston Harbor at midnight. For details, contact First Night (www.first nightboston.org; ✆ **617/542-1399**). December 31.

SUGGESTED NEW ENGLAND ITINERARIES

3

Trust your instincts as much as your GPS while you're on the road in New England. Your most memorable experience might await at a lobster shack you hear about from locals, at the end of a hiking trail that overlooks a peaceful lake, or along a tree-lined back road that is the prettiest—not the fastest—route from here to there.

Racing around with a checklist and a beat-the-clock attitude is a recipe for missing out. The happiest visitors to New England are those who stay awhile in one spot, getting to know a manageable area through a mix of well-crafted day trips and serendipitous exploration. Read on for strategies that can help you organize your time.

THE REGIONS IN BRIEF

On a map, New England might look like one compact, highway-veined region you can see in a couple of days. Yet there is so much diversity here that even Connecticut—the third smallest state in the union—can be viewed as having nine distinct areas to explore. These six states have carved out unique identities, shaped by history, geology, water, economics, ethnic heritage, cuisine, dialect—you name it.

BOSTON   Oliver Wendell Holmes dubbed the State House in Boston the "hub of the solar system," and 160 years later, the region's largest city is still known as "the Hub." This alluring metropolis of historic and modern buildings, world-class museums, and top-notch restaurants is a key stop for travelers on any New England trip. **Cambridge,** Harvard's home across the Charles River, is equally engaging.

CAPE COD & THE ISLANDS   The ocean is writ large on **Cape Cod,** an elbowed peninsula with miles of sandy beaches and grassy dunes that whisper in the wind. The carnival-like atmosphere of Provincetown is a draw, as are the genteel charms of **Martha's Vineyard** and **Nantucket** islands.

WESTERN MASSACHUSETTS   In the heart of Massachusetts, Springfield is the gateway to the **Pioneer Valley,** which runs along the Connecticut River—named for 17th-century settlers—has many picturesque towns and colleges. West of the Pioneer Valley, the rolling hills of the **Berkshires** are home to old estates, graceful villages, lots of antiques stores, and an abundance of festivals and cultural attractions.

RHODE ISLAND   The smallest state in the U.S., Rhode Island is mostly coast, deeply indented by Narragansett Bay. The mansions and yachts of **Newport,** that elegant resort town, preside over the mouth of the bay, while Rhode Island's lively, increasingly artsy capital, **Providence,** sits at the top of bay, only a half-hour's drive from Boston.

CONNECTICUT   The **Southeastern Coast,** around the port city of New London, has a maritime flavor, from the submarine base at Groton to the must-see village of Mystic. Heading west, the quaint towns of Essex and Old Lyme sit at the wide mouth of the **Connecticut River Valley.** The main city on the coast is **New Haven,** home to Yale University and several great pizzerias. West of New Haven lie a string of affluent New York City suburbs, dubbed the **Gold Coast.** Connecticut's capital, **Hartford,** sits at the state's very middle. Home to several insurance companies, the city has been struggling but does offer some fine cultural attractions. North and west of Hartford lie the **Litchfield Hills,** a scenic rolling landscape of farms, lakes, and handsome small towns with colonial pasts.

VERMONT   Extending the length of Vermont from Massachusetts to Canada, the **Green Mountains** are a mostly gentle chain of forested hills that beckon those interested in hiking, scenic back-road drives, fantastic inns, and superb bicycling. Vermont's northwest forms half the lakeshore of majestic **Lake Champlain,** with New York's rugged Adirondack Mountains on the far shore. Vermont's largest city, Burlington, faces onto Lake Champlain. Vermont's northeastern counties, called the **Northeast Kingdom,** are rugged, hilly, and unpolished, but with some delightful surprises—not to mention being a source of tasty artisanal cheeses and superb craft beers.

NEW HAMPSHIRE   The **Connecticut River Valley** dividing Vermont and New Hampshire is a world unto itself, full of villages, verdant countryside, covered bridges, cheese farms, and small-town bakeries. It's got smarts, too: Dartmouth College is here. Central New Hampshire is dominated by the towering **White Mountains,** with their stark, windswept peaks, forests dotted with glacial boulders, and clear, rushing streams. South of there, Lake Winnipesaukee is the crown jewel of New Hampshire's **Lakes Region,** but more than 250 other lakes and ponds augment this area's allure. New Hampshire only has 18 miles of Atlantic coastline, but it's packed with beaches and the scrappy, well-preserved city of **Portsmouth:** a smaller (possibly even better) version of Boston.

MAINE   Maine's rocky Atlantic coast is the stuff of legend, art, and poetry. The **southern coast** has the best beaches; to the north, the **Down East** region offers spectacular headlands and **Acadia National Park's** dramatic landscapes. The mostly uninhabited **North Woods** of Maine are still largely owned by timber companies, yet there are some spectacular destinations tucked within them, including big, wild Baxter State Park, home to the state's highest peak, Mount Katahdin. The oft-overlooked region of **Western**

Maine—centered on Bethel but taking in a wide swath of territory north and south of that mountain village—is home to steep slopes, wide rivers, picturesque lakes, stunning foliage, and endless opportunities for quiet hiking and skiing. You might even see a moose.

BOSTON & VICINITY IN 1 WEEK

Basing yourself in Boston or Cambridge allows you to take a hub-and-spoke approach to seeing Massachusetts highlights without packing up luggage each night. On this itinerary, you'll savor a taste of Boston and Cambridge, then set out on day trips to history-rich surrounding towns. You'll venture in roughly chronological order: Start in Plymouth with the Pilgrims; move on to Lexington and Concord to learn about the rebellious colonists; and finally, visit the North Shore, which flourished after the Revolution. If you're renting a car, note that you don't need it for the full week—pick it up on (and don't start paying for it until) Day 4.

Days 1 & 2: Boston ★★★

Begin exploring downtown Boston by walking at least part of the 2.5-mile **Freedom Trail** (p. 75). The whole shebang can be an all-day affair, but if time is short, concentrate on the first two-thirds of the trail, from **Boston Common** through **Faneuil Hall.** Break for lunch at **Faneuil Hall Marketplace** (p. 68), then head into the North End for a stroll on the main drag, **Hanover Street,** and a visit to the **Paul Revere House** (p. 77), the oldest surviving home in downtown Boston. From there, it's an easy walk to Long Wharf or Rowes Wharf, where you can take a **sightseeing cruise** (p. 88) or, if you want to save time and money, a **water taxi ride** (p. 60) to the Charlestown Navy Yard and back. Have dinner at **Legal Sea Foods** (p. 110) on Long Wharf, or return to the North End for Italian food.

On **Day 2,** prearrange tickets for a **Boston Duck Tour** (p. 88), ideally one that leaves from the Prudential Center in the early afternoon. Be at the **Museum of Fine Arts, Boston** (p. 73) when it opens; consider taking a tour to give you an overview before you explore on your own. (The smaller **Isabella Stewart Gardner Museum** (p. 72), a block away, is another excellent option and highly recommended.) Head to the Back Bay for lunch and your Duck Tour, then make a beeline for the retail delights of **Newbury Street.** Newbury dead-ends at the **Public Garden** (p. 85), where you can unwind and perhaps go for a spin on a **Swan Boat** (p. 86). For dinner, check out Boston's take on French cuisine at **Aquitaine Bar á Vin Bistrot,** or **L'Espalier** if you want to pull out the stops (p. 117 and 107, respectively).

Day 3: Cambridge ★★

Start in **Harvard Square** (p. 81) with a student-led or self-guided tour of the main Harvard campus. Up next are the **Harvard Art Museums,** a trio

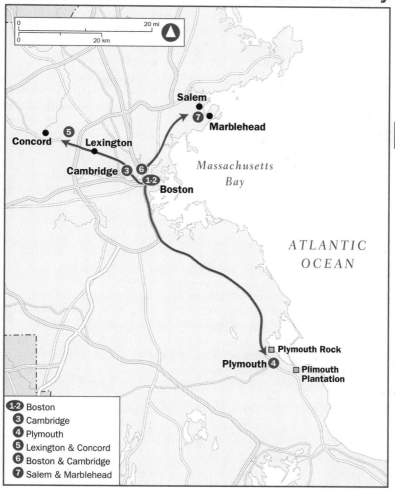

Boston & Vicinity

- **1-2** Boston
- **3** Cambridge
- **4** Plymouth
- **5** Lexington & Concord
- **6** Boston & Cambridge
- **7** Salem & Marblehead

of repositories for masterworks of human creation (p. 83); you may prefer the **Museum of Natural History,** especially if children are along. Then head to lovely Brattle Street and the **Longfellow House–Washington's Headquarters** (p. 84). Rent a Blue Bike from any of the racks around the Square and head to the Charles River, for a meander along the well-maintained bike paths on either side of the water. For a casual evening, have dinner at **Mr. Bartley's Burger Cottage** (p. 121), then hit a bookstore or two; for something more fancy, go to **Craigie on Main** (p. 120).

Day 4: Plymouth ★★

Spend a day with the Pilgrims and their Native American neighbors. Start with a 17th-century reality check at **Plimoth Plantation** (p. 176), where you can mingle with the English "settlers," who stay in character as they chat with visitors, and also interact with descendants of the Wampanoag and other Native Nations, who share their proud history and traditions. In downtown Plymouth, have lunch at the **Lobster Hut** (p. 178), where the deck overlooks the harbor, then explore a bit, starting at **Plymouth Rock** (p. 176). Take in some historic attractions—the 1667 **Jabez Howland House** (p. 177) and the 1640 **Sparrow House** are both nearby—before returning to Boston or Cambridge for dinner.

Day 5: Lexington ★ & Concord ★★★

Spend the morning in Lexington taking a walking tour of the historic sites (p. 138) and acquainting yourself with the earliest events of the Revolutionary War. Have lunch in Concord and explore the beautiful town, perhaps also visiting the **Concord Museum** (p. 142), touring the **North Bridge** within **Minute Man National Historical Park** (p. 143), and stopping at **Walden Pond** (p. 145) to dip your toes. Back in Boston, head to **Top of the Hub** (p. 130) for sunset drinks or dinner.

Day 6: Boston & Cambridge

After 2 days on the road, stick close to "home." Head to the **John F. Kennedy Library and Museum** (p. 72), which is accessible by public transit and offers free parking (you're paying for that rental car, so you might as well get some use out of it). Spend the afternoon at the **Museum of Science** or the **New England Aquarium** (both p. 74), allowing enough time for an IMAX film, if that appeals to you.

Day 7: Marblehead ★★★ & Salem ★★

Begin your day on the picturesque streets of Old Town **Marblehead** (p. 150), a top destination for both sightseeing and shopping. If your hotel room rate doesn't include breakfast, pick up coffee and a delectable breakfast pastry at **Crosby's Marketplace** (p. 159). The **Jeremiah Lee Mansion** (p. 153) is a must if you enjoy house tours. Spend the afternoon in **Salem** (p. 155), where the can't-miss destination is the **Peabody Essex Museum** (p. 155); if time allows, also visit the **Salem Witch Museum** (p. 156) and the **House of Seven Gables** (p. 155). This itinerary leaves you in a handy location for returning to Boston or for heading out to explore the wonders of northern New England.

NEW ENGLAND FOR HISTORY BUFFS

The New England region is rich in history—and luckily, a lot of that history has been beautifully preserved. This 6-day tour, which begins and ends in Boston, visits a handful of sites where the past really seems to come alive.

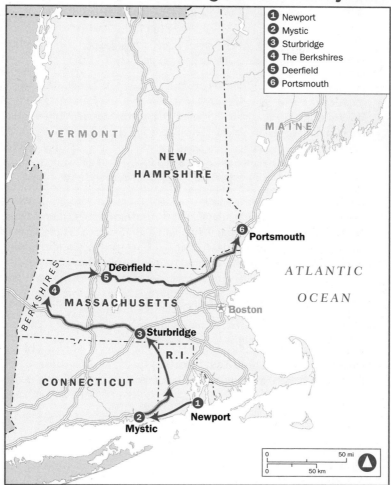

Day 1: Gilded Age Newport ★★★

If you don't hit traffic, you can cover the 75 or so miles between Boston and Newport in about 90 minutes. The city's top attractions are the "cottages"—Newport-speak for "mansions"—that line Bellevue Avenue along the magnificent shore. Don't attempt to tour more than two **cottages** (p. 446) in a day because you'll want to leave time for exploring the picturesque waterfront area. Between the glorious scenery and the serendipitous shopping, Newport is a perfect place to while away an afternoon. Linger into the evening for a drink or dinner near the water.

Day 2: Maritime Mystic ★★★

It'll take about an hour to drive along the coast to Mystic, Connecticut, where your destination is **Mystic Seaport Museum** (p. 415), which recreates an early 19th-century waterfront full of tall-masted sailing ships, and whaling captains. After several hours at the Seaport, head north to Sturbridge, Massachusetts, about an hour and a half's drive.

Day 3: An 1830s Time Machine: Old Sturbridge Village ★★★

What was life like in a New England farming village in 1830? You'll find out in detail by spending a day at this living history museum (see p. 321), full of authentic buildings, costumed interpreters, and craft demonstrations. The get back on the Mass Pike and follow it to the western end of Massachusetts to visit the Berkshires, your base for the next 2 nights.

Day 4: The Berkshires ★★

Begin in the morning in Pittsfield at the **Hancock Shaker Village** (p. 353), which will give you a fascinating glimpse into the practices of this radical Protestant sect. Have lunch in Great Barrington, then, swing by the **Norman Rockwell Museum** (p. 347) in Stockbridge to how the iconic 20th-century artist captured an American way of life that was vanishing even then. Try to schedule this trip to coincide with an evening concert by the **Boston Symphony Orchestra** at **Tanglewood** (p. 351), in Lenox. Spread out a blanket, picnic on the lawn, and enjoy the scene, one of the hallmarks of summer in New England.

Day 5: Colonial Deerfield ★★★

Find a backroads route through the Berkshires to reach **Old Deerfield** ★★★ (p. 333), a perfectly preserved town of historic houses, some from as long ago as the 1600s. A walking tour of the town takes you into a handful of the houses, furnished in period detail. From here, you've got a 2-hour drive to Portsmouth; take Route 2 for more lovely scenery (unfortunately, the end of the drive is on heavily trafficked I-495).

Day 6: Portsmouth ★★

Portsmouth, New Hampshire, is a gem of historic architecture, maritime sights and sounds, and funky shops and cafes. It's worth a trip just for **Strawbery Banke** ★★★ (p. 567), where the historic buildings *are* the displays. More than 40 restored buildings are set around 10 acres, Take a little time afterward to explore Portsmouth's cobblestone downtown before driving back to Boston (the trip should take about an hour unless there's traffic—but there's always traffic).

10 DAYS BY THE SEA FOR FAMILIES

Multiple generations can easily spend a pleasant week or so sharing seaside adventures. You'll start off in coastal Maine, then work your way south to visit

10 Days by the Sea for Families

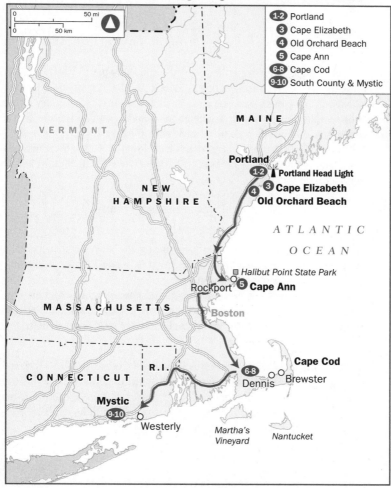

the somewhat warmer waters off Massachusetts and Rhode Island. If you don't have time for this full itinerary, break it in half, doing the Maine-Cape Ann half on one trip and the Cape Cod-to-Mystic trip another time.

Days 1 & 2: Portland ★★★

Portland, Maine, your base for the first 4 days, is a joy for families. The **Children's Museum and Theatre of Maine** (p. 630) is almost exactly in the center of the city, making it a good jumping-off point for a walking tour. The excellent **Portland Museum of Art** (p. 631), right next door, provides teens with something different to do.

In the historic **Old Port** (p. 629), Exchange Street is the key shopping address. Kids will enjoy the ice-cream shops, boats, and quirky gift stores.

The **Maine Narrow Gauge Railroad Co. & Museum** (p. 630) combines a short train ride to the foot of the cliffs framing Portland's east end with a museum.

If the kids need to stretch their legs, the mile-long paved **Eastern Prom Pathway** (p. 629) offers sweeping views of the harbor and offshore islands. (At its eastern end, you can hop on a Casco Bay Lines ferry to sail out to some of those islands.) Stretching inland, rambling Eastern Promenade park is ideal for a picnic or a casual ball game.

For baseball fans, an outing to Hadlock Field to watch the **Portland Sea Dogs** (p. 632) can't be beat; it's one of New Englanders' favorite minor-league parks.

Finally, young and old alike enjoy the sunsets, picnics, sailboat views, and swing sets of the park along the **Eastern Promenade** (p. 629).

Day 3: Cape Elizabeth ★★

Plan to spend at least one afternoon hitting the string of beaches and lighthouses off Route 77 in the quiet town of **Cape Elizabeth** and surrounds, just 15 minutes from Portland.

Don't miss **Portland Head Light** (p. 631) and neighboring Fort Williams Park with its fortress ruins and children's garden. Then, romp around in the sand and surf at **Crescent, Scarborough,** or **Willard Beach.**

Day 4: Old Orchard Beach ★

Drive 30 minutes south of Portland, and you come to **Old Orchard Beach.** This place may strike you as corny at first, but it rarely fails to entertain with its amusement park and miles of sandy beach. On the photogenic pier out over the water, you can find restaurants, bars, bad-for-you eats (mmm… fried dough), and souvenirs.

Day 5: Cape Ann ★★

Leave early for your long drive south. Detour east in Massachusetts to stop off in downtown **Rockport** (p. 166) for souvenirs and fudge, then push on to **Halibut Point State Park** (p. 167), at the tip of Cape Ann, which boasts spectacular views and plenty of room to run around. On your way back to the highway, take Route 133 so you can lunch on fried clams at the legendary **Woodman's of Essex** (p. 169). Skirting Boston, continue on to Cape Cod, where you'll be staying for the next 3 nights. Base yourself in either **Brewster** (p. 236) or **Dennis** (p. 217). Either way, grab a quick and easy seafood dinner at **Captain Frosty's** in Dennis (p. 222).

Days 6, 7 & 8: Cape Cod ★★★

On your Day 6, hang out at the child-friendly beaches that front Cape Cod Bay. On Day 7, get up early enough to be at the **Heritage Museums and Gardens** in Sandwich (p. 183) by 9am, and don't expect to get away without a carousel ride. Book in advance if you want to try the rope course at the adjacent Adventure Park. Then, in the afternoon, head south to Falmouth to visit the **Woods Hole Aquarium.** Cap off the day with some mini-golf or, if it's July or August, an evening watching game in the **Cape Cod Baseball League** (p. 204). Finish off your Cape Cod adventure on Day 8 by visiting the **Cape Cod Museum of Natural History** ★★★ in Brewster (p. 230) and taking a bike ride on the **Cape Cod Rail Trail** (p. 215).

Days 9 & 10: South County & Mystic ★

Work your way west from Cape Cod along the Rhode Island coast, making sure to stop off in **Westerly** (p. 463) for a little beach time or a ride on the vintage carousel. You'll reach Connecticut in time to explore the **Mystic Aquarium** ★★ (p. 415). Stay overnight in the Mystic area and be up bright and early the next morning to spend a full day at the living history park **Mystic Seaport Museum** ★★★ (p. 415).

THE IDEAL 1-WEEK FALL FOLIAGE DRIVE

Set out from Boston on a glorious autumn tour that will renew your gratitude for nature's gifts. Try to start your trip between the last week of September and mid-October, and be sure to make lodging reservations in advance—6 months ahead is not too soon.

Days 1, 2 & 3: Lakes & Mountains ★★

It's a 3-hour straight shot from Boston to **North Conway,** NH, your base for the next 3 days. Give yourself time en route to meander through picture-perfect towns like Wolfeboro, Moultonborough, and Sandwich on **Lake Winnipesaukee**'s eastern shore (p. 582). Stop into the **Old Country Store** in Moultonborough, which modestly claims to be the oldest retail establishment in the nation . . . perhaps to try Moxie (p. 33) and stock up on cheese and penny candy for your road trip.

On **Days 2** and **3,** choose from myriad adventures. Soar above the treetops on the **Cannon Mountain Aerial Tramway** (p. 592) or the canopy tour at **Bretton Woods Mount Washington Resort** (p. 600). Drive scenic Route 302 to **Franconia Notch State Park** and **Flume Gorge** (p. 591). Enjoy a nostalgic **Conway Scenic Railroad** (p. 590) trip or experience the wonder of climbing to New England's highest point aboard the **Mount Washington Cog Railway** (p. 590).

Days 4 & 5: Forests & Farmland ★★★

Drive the high-climbing **Kancamagus Highway** (p. 584) through the White Mountain National Forest on Day 4 to Woodstock, VT, your base for the next 2 nights. Stopping often for photo ops, follow Route 112 to Route 118 South, then turn west on Route 4 in Canaan, NH. Stop en route

1-Week Fall Foliage Drive

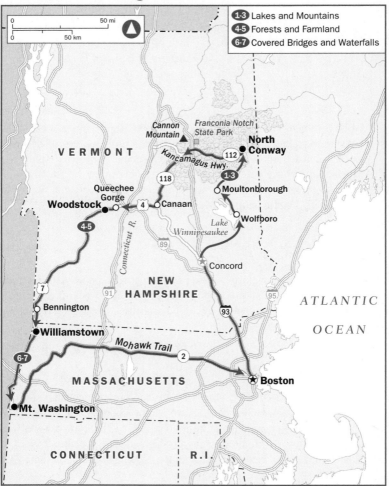

at stunning **Quechee Gorge,** near the town of Quechee (p. 503), to add to your image bank. Also visit the **Simon Pearce** flagship store (p. 509) in Quechee to watch glassblowers at work and to savor a memorable meal overlooking a covered bridge and waterfall.

With its town green edged with antique homes and **Middle Covered Bridge** in the center of the village, Woodstock enchants photographers in the fall. Spend **Day 5** stretching your legs and lungs at the still-working **Billings Farm and Museum** (p. 504) and the neighboring **Marsh-Billings-Rockefeller National Historical Park** (p. 504). South of Woodstock in Reading, you'll bump into fellow shutterbugs at Jenne Farm, reputed to be the most photographed farm in New England.

Days 6 & 7: Covered Bridges & Waterfalls

Leave Woodstock for **Williamstown,** MA, on Day 6 by driving west on Route 4, then south in Route 7. Along the way, in **Bennington,** VT, pause to make a scavenger hunt of finding five covered bridges. You'll also want to take the elevator to the top of the **Bennington Battle Monument** (p. 479) for panoramic foliage views. On Day 7, be among the early birds at **Bash-Bish Falls** (p. 344) in **Mt. Washington,** MA, where a short hike's rewarded with the dramatic scene of Massachusetts' highest waterfall spilling into a shimmering pool. Then, follow the **Mohawk Trail** (Route 2), America's first scenic byway, back east to Boston, stopping to see sights like the famed **Bridge of Flowers** (p. 335) in **Shelburne Falls.**

4 DAYS IN THE WHITE MOUNTAINS

In New Hampshire's White Mountains, four days is barely enough to scratch the dramatic surface, with its mountain crags and crystalline streams. No New England region offers more one-of-a-kind scenes and attractions.

Day 1: "The Kanc" ★★★

Start in Lincoln, at exit 32 off I-93, and drive to North Conway via the incomparably scenic **Kancamagus Highway** (p. 584), stopping for short hikes or a picnic. Indulge in a few shopping forays in town, and savor the views of the Mount Washington Valley. Head to the village of **Jackson** (p. 587) for the night: It's an ideal home base for these four, adventure-filled days.

Relax before dinner at **Jackson Falls,** or take a bike ride along carriage roads at the **Great Glen Trails Outdoor Center** in Gorham.

Day 2: Pinkham Notch ★★

Spend the day embarking on one of five short hikes in **Pinkham Notch** (p. 590) or, if you're feeling ambitious, climb all or part of the **Tuckerman Ravine Trail.** Stop at **Glen Ellis Falls** (p. 590) en route to the base of Mount Washington.

Return to your car and continue north to **Wildcat Ski Area** (p. 596). Take the gondola to the summit for spectacular views of Mount Washington, the Presidential Range, and the Carter Range.

Day 3: Mount Washington ★★★

Drive south on Rte. 16 and west on Rte. 302 through **Crawford Notch** (p. 590). If time allows, stop at the **AMC Highland Center** to see what free programs are scheduled, or have lunch at the grand **Omni Mount Washington Resort.**

Continue driving a loop north through **Carroll** to the **Mount Washington Cog Railway** (p. 590), and take the train ride to the summit of **Mount Washington** (dress warmly).

4 Days in the White Mountains

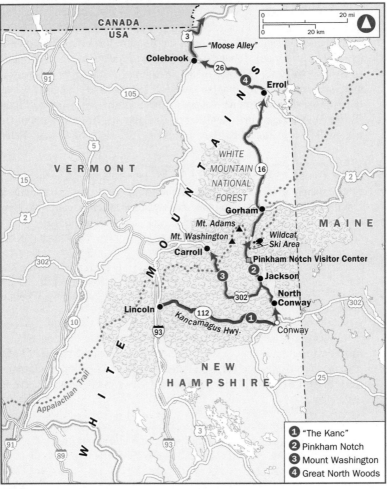

Day 4: Great North Woods ★★

Is your heart set on seeing a moose? Then, drive north on Route 16 to Errol, west on Route 26 through Dixville Notch to Colebrook, and proceed north on Route 3, a.k.a. "Moose Alley," toward the Canadian border. Stay alert and—even though there are no guarantees—keep your camera ready.

EXPLORING THE MAINE COAST

The inlets and peninsulas of the Maine coast make it impossible to plot a straight course. This trip takes you a little more than halfway up (really, across) the coast, allowing time for serendipitous detours. Tack on some extra time at the end to really explore Acadia National Park.

Day 1: York ★★

Drive into Maine from the south on I-95, and head for **York Village** at exit 7 (p. 611). Spend time snooping around historic buildings preserved by the **Old York Historical Society** (p. 612), and stretch your legs on a walk through town.

Drive north through **York Beach** (p. 611), see Nubble Light, stock up on saltwater taffy at the **Goldenrod** (p. 626), and spend the night near the beach.

Days 2 & 3: Portland ★★★

Using the right route, getting to Portland can be as fun as being there. You can hit the antiques shops along stretches of Rte. 1 as you drive north. If you're in a hurry or traveling in summer, avoid the crowds on Rte. 1 by taking I-95.

In **Portland** (p. 626) by afternoon, take a trolley, duck boat, or fire engine tour of the city to get oriented. Plan to stay in the city; to shop for jewelry, souvenirs, or even kites in the Old Port; to taste-test chowder and microbrewed beer; and to soak up the salty air and atmosphere. Don't forget a walk along the **Eastern Promenade** (p. 629) or a **day cruise** (p. 628) on a local ferry.

Day 4: Freeport ★★★, Brunswick ★ & Bath ★★

Head north early to beat the shopping crowds at the outlet haven of Freeport. You can't leave too early for **L.L.Bean** (p. 641)—it never closes!

From Freeport, get off busy Route 1 to meander through charming towns like Bath or **Wiscasset,** the so-called "Prettiest Village in Maine." Spend a relaxing night at a picturesque B&B in the **Boothbay** region (p. 639).

Days 5 & 6: Camden ★★★ & Penobscot Bay

Heading north from the Boothbay area, detour down to **Pemaquid Point** (p. 643) for a late picnic as you watch the surf roll in. Then head back to Rte. 1 and set your sights on the heart of Penobscot Bay.

Rockland (p. 648), which you'll reach first, is the arts-centric part of the equation. The musts here are the excellent museums, galleries, and restaurants. Nearby **Rockport** (p. 649) is a tiny town with harbor views and main street charms.

Finally, head a few miles north to wander around downtown **Camden** (p. 649), poking into gift shops and boutiques. Hike up to one of the summits within **Camden Hills State Park** (p. 652), hop a **ferry** to an island (North Haven and Islesboro are both great for biking), or sign up for a sightseeing sail on a **windjammer.** Getting ice cream and hot dogs down by the harbor is also sheer bliss.

Exploring the Maine Coast

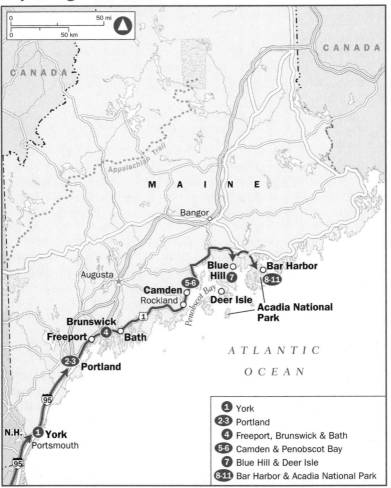

York
Portland
Freeport, Brunswick & Bath
Camden & Penobscot Bay
Blue Hill & Deer Isle
Bar Harbor & Acadia National Park

Day 7: Blue Hill ★★★ & Deer Isle

From Camden, drive up and around the head of Penobscot Bay and then down the bay's eastern shore. The roads here are great for aimless drives, but head for **Stonington** (p. 662), down at the tip of **Deer Isle** (p. 662).

Next, head to scenic **Blue Hill** (p. 662 and 664) for dinner and lodging. You'll love the views from here, and the combination of a Maine fishing town and new-blood book and wine shops and restaurants is quite appealing. Also take a spin around the peninsula to smaller towns such as **Blue Hill Falls** and **Brooklin,** where you'll see boatyards, old-fashioned general stores, and scenes that have long inspired artists. *This* is the real Maine.

Days 8, 9, 10 & 11: Bar Harbor ★★ & Acadia National Park ★★★

Bar Harbor is the perfect base for exploring **Mount Desert Island,** which is well worth 4 (or more) days on a Maine itinerary. Stay at least 2 nights, especially if you have kids along. Bar Harbor offers comforts and services such as a movie theater, bike and kayak rentals, free shuttle buses, and numerous restaurants. Yes, it's more developed than the rest of the island, but think of it as a supply depot.

Hike, bike, boat: There are so many ways to explore the island and **Acadia National Park** (p. 667), one of America's finest. Investigate at your own pace: Take a beginner's **kayak trip** down the eastern shore, a **hike** out to **Bar Island,** or a **horse-drawn wagon trip** along the **carriage roads** built by the Rockefeller family. Only bicycles and horses are allowed on these roads, making them a tranquil respite from the island's roadways, which—almost unbelievably—do get crowded in summer.

The scenic **Park Loop Road** is a great introduction to all Acadia offers (crashing waves, big mountains, drop-dead gorgeous views). Take your time: Your vehicle admission pass is valid for 7 days.

While exploring the rest of the island, be sure to hit some of the non-park towns, too. **Northeast Harbor** and **Southwest Harbor** are fishing towns that tourism has partly transformed into tiny centers of art, music, and shopping. However, they still have small stores where fishermen shop for slickers and Wonder bread.

What about those things you wanted to do but didn't have time for? Do them on your last day in Acadia: Watch a sunrise from the top of **Cadillac Mountain** (p. 673); savor tea and popovers at **Jordan Pond House** (p. 685); take a quick last hike up **The Bubbles** (p. 685); or spread out a blanket on **Sand Beach** (p. 672) at night and stargaze.

NEW ENGLAND FOR ART LOVERS

Why is New England so rich in art museums? As a cultural center from America's earliest days, it has long been home to wealthy patrons and art collectors—but it's also a region where many artists chose to live and work. The combination of the two gives this six-state region an incredible number of top art museums. The challenge is to fit them all into one trip. In this itinerary, we focus on museums with outstanding collections of American art, a particular strength in this region.

If you're starting out from Boston, we'll just assume you've already visited its two great art museums, the **Museum of Fine Arts** (p. 73) and the **Isabella Stewart Gardner Museum** (p. 72). If not, head back to Boston at the end of this itinerary to take them in: Both are world-class repositories of art.

Day 1: Portland, ME ★★

Arriving in Portland, make a beeline for the **Portland Museum of Art ★★★** (p. 631), a stunning modern space right downtown. The museum's permanent collection is broad, but one of its strengths is Maine landscapes by such American masters as Winslow Homer and Andrew Wyeth. If you're on a summer Monday or Friday, be sure to make a reservation to visit **Winslow Homer's studio,** out on nearby Cape Elizabeth—you'll understand better than ever this master's connection to the rocky surf-battered coast of New England.

Day 2: Ogunquit, ME ★★

Driving south from Portland, if you're here between May and October, an essential stop is this small beach town, 45 minutes south of Portland, which just happens to have one of the best small museums in New England. Thanks to Ogunquit's role as an artists' colony since the 1890s, the **Ogunquit Museum of American Art ★★** (see p. 614) has rich holdings in early Modernist works by such Ogunquit painters as Charles Woodbury, Hamilton Easter Field, and Robert Laurent, as well as the Modernist "painter of Maine" Marsden Hartley. Be sure to wander around the sculpture garden overlooking Perkins Cove. Spend your morning here, grab lunch, and then drive on to tonight's base, Worcester, MA (take I-95 to I-395 and you should be there in 2 hours). Worcester has increasingly been developing a foodie scene. Hopefully you've planned ahead and made reservations at the popular gastropub **Armsby Abbey** (p. 320); otherwise, head for the Shrewsbury Street restaurant strip, where you should do well at any number of restaurants.

Day 3: Worcester, MA & Hartford, CT

As this formerly gritty mid-Massachusetts city is rapidly upgrading its image, a major factor has been the well-regarded **Worcester Museum of Art ★★** (see p. 319). Head straight for its American wing to drink in masterpieces by Mary Cassatt, John Singer Sargent, and James Whistler, who in the late 1800s won respect for American painters in European salons. Leave after lunch, taking the Mass Pike to I-84; in about an hour you'll be in Hartford, Connecticut. In the heart of downtown, the venerable **Wadsworth Atheneum ★★★** (p. 403), opened in 1844, is the U.S.'s oldest art museum. It's easy to get distracted by all the marvels in this rambling complex, but head straight for level 3 to focus on its American art, including an amazing stash of Hudson River School landscapes. Back on level 1, the contemporary art collection brings you up to date with works by everyone from De Kooning and Pollock to Sol LeWitt and Cindy Sherman.

If you leave by 5pm, getting onto I-91, you should be in New Haven, CT, by dinnertime—it's only a 40-minute drive. New Haven will be your base for the next two nights. Grab a pizza at any of New Haven's storied pizza joints (see p. 398).

New England for Art Lovers

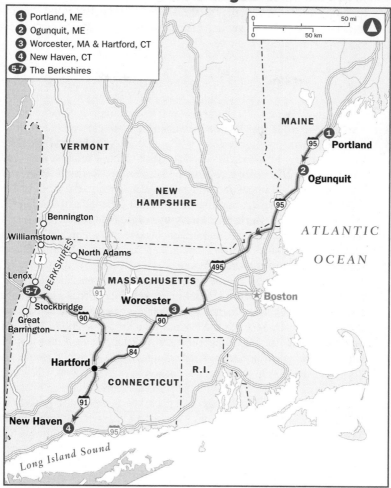

Day 4: New Haven, CT ★★

You could spend a full day in New Haven, strolling around the Yale University campus. With art as your focus, however, you'll probably want to do most of that strolling inside the university's two excellent art collections. The **Yale University Art Gallery** ★★★ (p. 395) has one of the best collections of American art of any museum in the country. Start on the second floor to see treasures of early American art (Trumbull and Copley portraits et cetera), then come down to the first floor to find numerous paintings by American realists of the late 19th and early 20th centuries. And then—well, it's not American art, but while you're here

57

you'll probably also enjoy visiting the **Yale Center for British Art** ★★ (p. 395), the richest repository of British art outside of the U.K. If you haven't scored a reservation at the **Union League Café** (p. 397) for tonight, try your best to get into **Heirloom** (p. 398) or **Zinc** (p. 397).

Days 5, 6 & 7: The Berkshires ★★

On **Day 5,** set out right after breakfast to make the 2-hour drive (Route 8 north to the Mass Pike) to the Berkshire Hills, at the western end of Massachusetts. Base yourself in either Lenox or Williamstown for the next three nights. Your main problem here will be deciding which museums to see first. We recommend pairing museums that are closer to each other. For example, on one day combine a stop at Lenox's **Frelinghuysen Morris House** (p. 349), where abstract artists Suzy Frelinghuysen and George L.K. Morris lived, with a visit to the **Norman Rockwell Museum** (p. 347) in nearby Stockbridge, dedicated to the work of the great 20th-century magazine illustrator. About 20 minutes from Lenox, you'll also find the **Berkshire Museum in Pittsfield** (p. 353), a mix of natural history, history, and art museum; head for the second floor to find 19th-century landscapes by such masters as George Inness, Edwin Church, and Albert Bierstadt.

Farther north, Williamstown has not one but two outstanding museums: the **Williams College Museum of Art** ★ (p. 356), where you'll find works by Whistler, Warhol, and Hopper, as well as a cache of modernist paintings by Maurice and Charles Prendergast; and the **Clark Art Institute** ★★★ (p. 355), which focuses on 19th century European art, but also has works by John Singer Sargent and Winslow Homer. A 20-minute drive north up Route 7 will take you to Bennington, VT, where the **Bennington Museum** ★★ (p. 480) has the world's largest collection of paintings by Grandma Moses. And it's only a few minutes' drive from Williamstown to North Adams, where the superb **Massachusetts Museum of Contemporary Art** (**MASS MoCA,** p. 357), always has something interesting going on. MASS MoCA also features lots of eclectic performing arts—check in advance what's on, to coordinate your visit with a performance you'd enjoy.

While you're in the Berkshires, make time for shopping in Great Barrington, antiquing in Sheffield and Lenox, and some outdoor walks in any of the region's beautiful parks. If you plan ahead, you may also be able to score tickets to one of the area's great summer arts festivals: **Tanglewood** (p. 351) or **Marlboro** (p. 495) for music, **Jacob's Pillow** (p. 348) for dance, and the **Williamstown Theater Festival** (p. 356) for theater. The **Barrington Stage Company** (p. 353) in Pittsfield, The **Berkshire Theatre Festival** (p. 346) in Stockbridge, and **Shakespeare & Company** (p. 350) in Lenox also ramp up their performance schedule in the summer season. There's no shortage of things to do here!

BOSTON & CAMBRIDGE

By Leslie Brokaw & Erin Trahan

Boston wears its history on its sleeve: Just look at its brownstone architecture or take a stroll down its craggy, cobblestone streets. Less visible is its role as a global leader in the high-tech and medical industries. Waves of students pour in each September to attend its colleges and universities, and many stay to work in the region's world-renowned corporate and health institutions. The result is a cosmopolitan city in a state of continual rejuvenation.

In the downtown and waterfront, old meets new. Many visitors walk the 2½-mile Freedom Trail to tread in the footsteps of the country's Founding Fathers—and then head to the newly thriving Seaport District to eat and play. The posh neighborhoods of Beacon Hill and Back Bay recall the city's colonial past and are charged with the full pulse of city life. Cambridge, across the Charles River, offers both academic intensity and a laid-back casualness.

Rich cultural and artistic experiences beckon, of course. Boston's major institution is its Museum of Fine Arts; just a block away is the Isabella Stewart Gardner Museum, a spectacular Venetian-styled palazzo. And you may have heard that Boston has a thing for sports, with often-exemplary pro teams in baseball (Red Sox), basketball (Celtics), hockey (Bruins), and football (New England Patriots). Every April, as well, it hosts elite runners who gather for the Boston Marathon, an inspiring city-wide event. So look around for a place to join in—you're sure to find something to cheer.

ESSENTIALS

Arriving
BY PLANE

Boston's **Logan International Airport** is in East Boston, 3 miles (4.8km) from downtown and across the Boston harbor. Logan is served by all the major U.S. airlines and several international carriers as well (see p. 699 in chapter 14 for details). For information, including real-time flight arrivals and departures, go to **www.massport.com/logan-airport**. Free Wi-Fi is available throughout the airport.

Between the Airport & City Center

Massachusetts Port Authority, or **MassPort** (www.massport.com/logan-airport; ✆ **800/235-6426**), coordinates airport transportation. Public Service information booths are located near baggage claim on the first-floor arrivals level of every terminal.

There are two options for taking **public transport** from Logan into Boston. The **Silver Line SL1 bus** stops at each airport terminal and runs to downtown Boston's South Station, which has connections to the Red Line subway and the commuter rail to the southern suburbs. The 20-minute ride is free and includes a transfer to the Red Line. The other public transport option is to take the **free airport shuttle bus** (either Route 22, 33, 55, or 66) to the stop "MBTA Blue Line" to pick up the subway on the Blue Line. The Blue Line runs daily from approximately 6am to 12:20am. Subway fare is $2.75 with a paper CharlieTicket from a vending machine. See p. 64 for details about the subway system and its fare collection system.

Taxis are available at each terminal. Between airport fees and the initial drop the starting price is about $10; the total fare to downtown runs $25 to $45. There are designated areas at Logan for pick up by **Lyft** (www.lyft.com) and **Uber** (www.uber.com) drivers. Travelers using one of these "Transportation Network Companies" should look for the designated pickup areas on the lower level (Arrivals) and the sign "App Ride/TNC." The fare will include a $3.25 airport fee.

The Logan Airport website lists **private van services** that pick up at the airport and serve local hotels. One-way prices start at $15 per person and can include extra fees.

Because Logan is located just across the Boston harbor from the city, travelers have the option of taking a **ferry or water taxi** from the airport to downtown. The **Harbor Express** ferry trip from Logan to Long Wharf on the downtown waterfront takes about 7 minutes and costs $18.50 one-way. The free no. 66 shuttle bus connects airport terminals to the Logan ferry dock. **Boston Harbor Cruises Water Taxi** (www.bostonharborcruises.com/water-taxi; ✆ **617/227-4320**) and **Rowes Wharf Water Transport** (www.roweswharf watertransport.com; ✆ **617/406-8584**) also serve the airport, the downtown waterfront, and other points around the harbor, for a fare of $12 (kids ages 3–11 ride for just $2 on the Boston Harbor Cruises water taxi). Leaving the airport, ask the no. 66 shuttle-bus driver to radio ahead for water-taxi pickup.

BY TRAIN

Boston has three transportation centers. The biggest, **South Station,** at 700 Atlantic Ave., is a nexus of Amtrak trains, MBTA commuter trains, bus lines, and stops on the subway's Red and Silver Lines. The two other centers are **North Station,** at 135 Causeway St. on the first floor of the TD Garden stadium, and **Back Bay Station,** at 145 Dartmouth St. **Amtrak** (www.amtrak.com; ✆ **800/USA-RAIL**) has stops at all three stations, each of which is also an MBTA subway stop.

Massachusetts

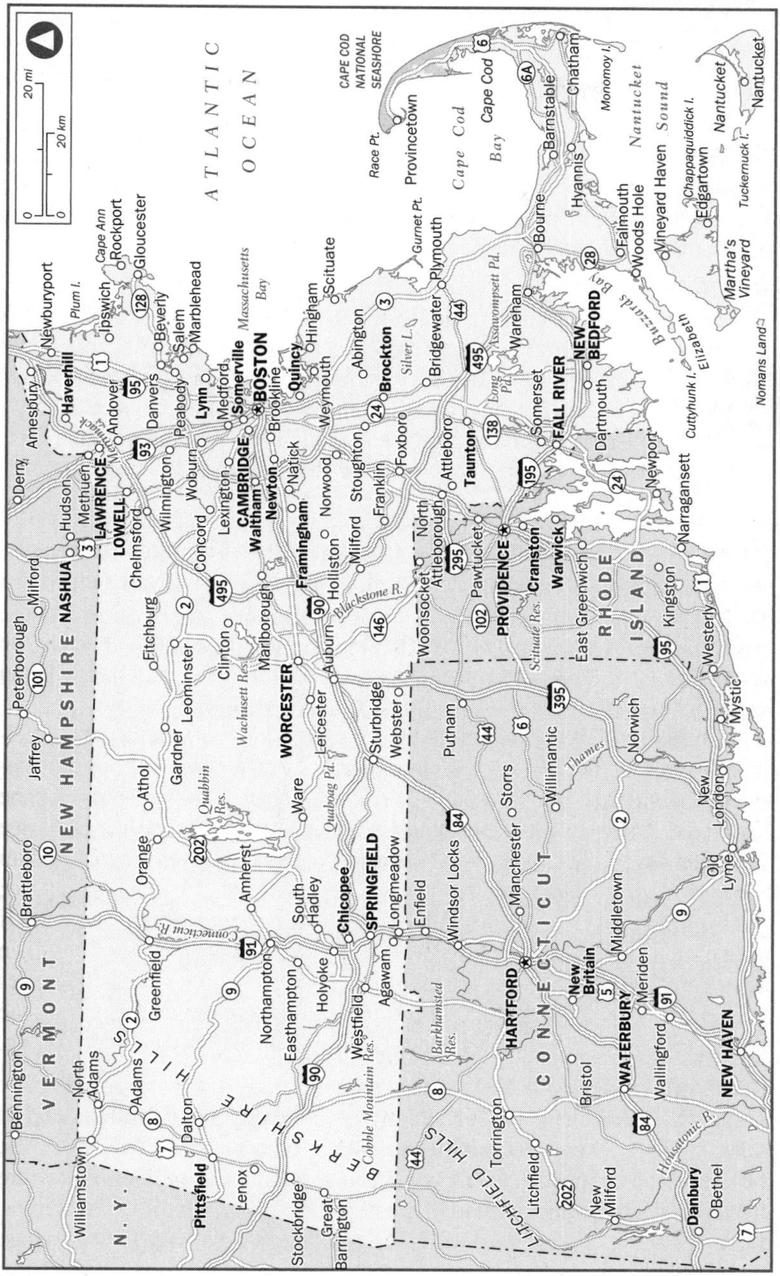

Boston's **commuter rail** operates out of both South Station and North Station (located about a mile apart). South Station serves points south and west of Boston, including Plymouth, MA, and Providence, RI. North Station serves points north and west, including Concord, Ipswich, and Rockport. This rail network is run by the **Massachusetts Bay Transportation Authority,** or MBTA (www.mbta.com; ✆ **800/392-6100** or ✆ **617/222-3200**), which also manages the subway system.

BY BUS

The **South Station Bus Terminal** (www.south-station.net) is at 700 Atlantic Ave., adjoining the train station.

BY CAR

Three major highways converge in Boston. **I-90,** also known as the Massachusetts Turnpike or "Mass Pike," is an east-west toll road. **I-93/U.S. 1** goes north. **I-93/Route 3,** the Southeast Expressway, heads south and toward Cape Cod.

I-95 (Massachusetts Rte. 128) becomes a beltway that circles Boston about 11 miles from downtown, connecting the city to highways in Rhode Island, Connecticut, and New York to the south, and New Hampshire and Maine to the north.

Visitor Information

The **Boston Common Information Center,** 139 Tremont St. (at West Street, inside the park) is open Monday through Friday from 8:30am to 5pm, Saturday and Sunday from 9am to 5pm. The **Copley Place Information Center,** inside the Copley Place mall at 100 Huntington Ave., is open Monday through Friday from 9am to 5pm, Saturday and Sunday from 10am to 6pm. Both are run by the **Greater Boston Convention & Visitors Bureau** (www.bostonusa.com; ✆ **888/SEE-BOSTON** [888/733-267866] or ✆ **617/536-4100**), which also provides maps, multi-language videos, and other resources online. The **Cambridge Office for Tourism** (www.cambridge-usa.org; ✆ **800/862-5678** or 617/441-2884) runs a visitor center at 0 Harvard Square; it's open Monday through Friday from 9am to 5pm, Saturday and Sunday from 9am to 1pm.

USEFUL WEBSITES The City of Boston's website **www.boston.gov/visiting-boston** includes upcoming events and things to do on a budget. **ArtsBoston** (https://calendar.artsboston.org; ✆ **617/262-8632 x229**) is an excellent resource for cultural listings and ticket deals (both day-of and advance sale) and runs the **BosTix discount-ticket** service, with tickets for theater and other performances at 20% to 80% off the original price (see p. 123 for more details). The **Massachusetts Office of Travel and Tourism** (www.massvacation.com; ✆ **800/227-MASS** or ✆ **617/973-8500**) has good regional information on its website. **VSA Arts Massachusetts** (www.vsamass.org; ✆ **617/350-7713;** TTY 617/350-6536), the state's organization on arts and disability, provides details on inclusive and accessible events.

City Layout

Much of Boston still reflects the city's original 17th-century layout, a seemingly haphazard plan that can disorient even longtime residents. You'll see alleys, one-way streets, streets that change names, and streets named after extinct geographical features. Major geographical points of reference include the waterfront, at the city's east end; Boston Common and the adjoining Boston Public Gardens, which separate Beacon Hill from downtown; and the Charles River, which divides Boston from its neighboring town to the north, Cambridge. Storrow Drive runs along the Boston side of the Charles; Memorial Drive runs along the Cambridge side. A handful of bridges span the river, connecting the two cities.

Boston Neighborhoods in Brief

See the map on p. 70 to locate these areas. When Bostonians say **"downtown,"** they usually mean the first six neighborhoods below.

The Waterfront The area along **Atlantic Avenue** and **Commercial Street,** once filled with wharves and warehouses, now boasts luxury condos, tourist-friendly marinas, restaurants, and hotels. Here you'll find the Rose Kennedy Greenway walking path, the New England Aquarium, and docks for harbor cruises and whale watches. Just a block inland from Long Wharf, **Faneuil Hall Marketplace/Quincy Market** is the city's most popular attraction, a cluster of restored market buildings. A block west of Faneuil Hall, **Government Center** is a wide plaza surrounded by state and federal office towers, Boston City Hall, and a central T stop.

The North End Adjacent to the northern end of the waterfront, this is one of the city's oldest neighborhoods and an immigrant stronghold for much of its history. It's still heavily Italian-American, with Italian spoken at many of its restaurants, *caffès*, and shops. **Hanover Street** and **Salem Street** are the main streets. Bars and restaurants cluster on and near **Causeway Street** in the **North Station** area, across from the **TD Garden** sports and performance stadium.

Financial District In the city's banking, insurance, and legal center, skyscrapers surround the landmark Custom House Tower. This area is busy during the day and nearly empty at night. **State Street** separates it from Faneuil Hall Marketplace.

Downtown Crossing The Freedom Trail runs through this bustling shopping and business district a few blocks east of Boston Common. The central Downtown Crossing intersection is where Winter Street becomes Summer Street at **Washington Street,** the most "main" street downtown.

Seaport District Across **Fort Point Channel** from downtown, this hot neighborhood is booming with new restaurants, bars, and hotels. The Boston Convention & Exhibition Center is here, along with the Institute of Contemporary Art.

Chinatown Tucked between Downtown Crossing and the Seaport District is one of the largest Chinese communities in the country, abounding with Asian restaurants and other businesses. Its main street is **Beach Street.** At its western end, Boston's **Theater District** extends about 2 blocks in each direction from the intersection of Tremont and Stuart streets. What's left of Boston's red-light district is also here; be careful in this area at night.

Beacon Hill Narrow, tree-lined streets and architectural showpieces make up this largely residential area near the State House and Boston Common. **Charles Street** is the neighborhood's commercial street.

Back Bay Created out of landfill in the mid-19th century, fashionable Back Bay extends from **Arlington Street,** near the Boston Public Garden, to the student-dominated sections near Massachusetts Avenue, or **Mass Ave.** Main streets include the retail meccas **Boylston** and **Newbury streets** and the largely residential Commonwealth Avenue, or **Comm Ave,** and **Beacon Street.** Unlike downtown, Back Bay is laid out in a grid; its cross streets go in alphabetical order.

South End South of Back Bay, this landmark district, packed with Victorian row houses, has a large gay community and some of the city's best restaurants. Main thoroughfares include **Tremont** and **Washington streets** and **Harrison** and **Columbus avenues.** Tucked within it is the **SoWa Art + Design District** (SoWa is short for "south of Washington street"), with art galleries, boutiques, and design showrooms. **Note:** The South End is not South Boston—"Southie" lies east of highway I-93, near the Seaport District.

Charlestown Across Boston Harbor from the North End is one of the oldest areas of Boston. The Bunker Hill Monument is here, along with the celebrated tall ship the USS *Constitution* ("Old Ironsides"). To get here from the North End, follow **North Washington Street.**

Kenmore Square A landmark white-and-red Citgo sign marks the intersection of

Comm Ave, Beacon Street, and **Brookline Avenue** at Kenmore Square. Boston University students throng its shops, bars, restaurants, and clubs. Fenway Park, home of the Red Sox, is 3 short blocks away.

The Fenway South and west of Kenmore Square, The Fenway surrounds the parklands of the Back Bay Fens. Here you'll find the Museum of Fine Arts, the Isabella Stewart Gardner Museum, and Symphony Hall, as well as several colleges and world-class medical facilities.

Cambridge Across the Charles River from Boston, Cambridge is home to Harvard University and the Massachusetts Institute of Technology. Its backbone, **Mass Ave,** runs from Boston across the Mass Ave Bridge river over the Charles River into Cambridge and beyond.

Getting Around

Boston is nearly flat, and even the tallest hills aren't too steep. Walking is the way to go if you can manage it. Public transportation is readily available, as are taxi, Lyft, and Uber rides. If you drive, check in advance about parking options at your destination or build in some extra time to find on-street parking.

BY PUBLIC TRANSPORTATION

The **Massachusetts Bay Transportation Authority,** or MBTA (www.mbta.com; ✆ **800/392-6100** or ✆ **617/222-3200**), runs subways, trolleys, buses, and ferries in Boston and many suburbs, as well as the commuter rail, which extends as far south as Providence, Rhode Island. The **MBTA trip planner** (www.mbta.com/trip-planner) provides route options.

The **subway system is called "the T"** and consists of the Red, Green, Blue, and Orange lines. Its logo is the letter "T" in a circle. Subway trains and trolleys travel both below ground and above ground. The center of the network is **Park Street station,** located on the northeast corner of the Boston Common. Train tracks are labeled as either "inbound" (toward Park Street and city center) or "outbound" (away from Park Street). Trains start running about 5am (6am on Sundays) and close down at 1 or 1:30am.

The **commuter rail** to the suburbs is shown in purple on T maps, and therefore is often called the Purple Line.

Buses travel through the city and to many suburbs. The **Silver Line,** a bus that travels both above ground and underground, is part of both the subway system and the bus system, with two sections: Riders on the Washington Street branches (SL4 and SL5) pay bus fares; riders on the Waterfront branches (SL1 and SL2), pay subway fares. (Yes, it's confusing even to locals.)

Boston Transit & Parking

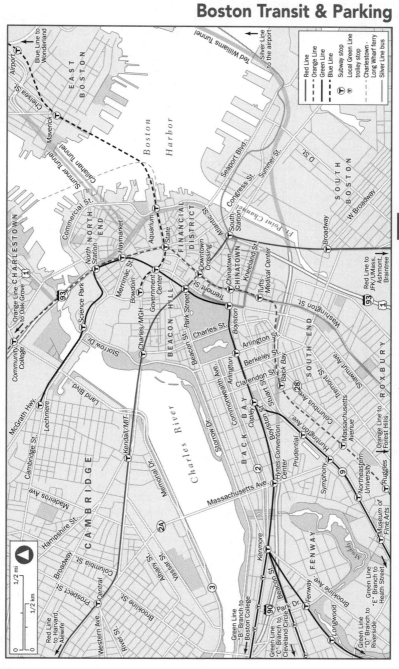

The **Boston Harbor water shuttle** (© 617/227-4321) connects Long Wharf, near the New England Aquarium, with the Charlestown Navy Yard. The ride takes 10 minutes. The one-way fare is $3.50.

ACCESSIBILITY   Newer stations on the Red, Blue, and Orange lines are **wheelchair and stroller accessible**, with elevators. Some (but not all) of the trolley stops on the Green Line are accessible. All MBTA buses have lifts or ramps to accommodate wheelchair passengers. Details are at www.mbta.com/accessibility/subway-guide.

BY BIKE

Boston's bike-sharing program (www.bluebikes.com) started in 2011 as "Hubway" and in 2018 was rebranded Blue Bikes after Blue Cross Blue Shield became a major sponsor. In 2018 the system had 1,800 bikes at 185 stations across Boston and in neighboring Cambridge, Brookline, and Somerville, with plans to expand to 3,000 bikes by 2020. Helmets are not included, so bring your own. A single trip is $2.50, and a 24-hour pass, with unlimited 2-hour trips, is $10. It's a year-round service, with most stations open in the winter months.

BY TAXI/LYFT/UBER

Taxis can be tough to hail on the street. Your best bet is to head to a hotel, since many have cabstands. Both **Lyft** (www.lyft.com) and **Uber** (www.uber.com) are active and popular in the city.

BY CAR

If you drive, keep in mind that road patterns are often confusing—few sections of the city use a grid system, and many streets are one-way. Using GPS or an app such as **Waze** (www.waze.com) on a smartphone will help considerably with navigation.

The T's Fare-Collection System

Most MBTA passengers pay fares with stored-value tickets. The system is complex (and will be changing in 2020 to an all-electronic payment system). For now, travelers have the option of using either paper CharlieTickets or plastic Charlie-Cards; cash is only accepted on buses and above-ground Green Line subway stops. **CharlieTickets** are easiest to find—they're available from kiosks at every station and every airport terminal—and with them the subway fare is $2.75, the bus fare $2. With a plastic **CharlieCard**—available at most downtown subway stations—riders pay less: $2.25 for the subway, $1.70 for the bus, with transfers that are either free or less expensive than with a CharlieTicket. Users can load and reload both the CharlieTicket and the CharlieCard, adding either enough money for one fare or, say, $20 to cover several rides. Tickets can be shared. Children ages 11 and younger ride free (up to 2 children per adult). Cards can also be loaded with **1-Day, 7-Day, or monthly passes**: A 1-Day pass is $12, a 7-Day pass is $21.25, and a monthly pass (calendar month) is $84.50. To use the paper CharlieTicket, insert the ticket into the slot on the turnstile or at the front of the bus and then remove the ticket to keep. To use the plastic CharlieCard, tap the target at a subway turnstile or on the bus. Commuter-rail tickets are available at stations and on the trains, with a surcharge for on-board purchases.

Finding street parking is a matter of good luck in most parts of Boston. If you're driving to a restaurant or performance venue, check in advance if it has discount parking at a lot or valet service. Most parking spaces in Boston are metered until at least 6pm (and sometimes 8pm) Monday through Saturday. **Meters** cost $1.25 to $4 an hour, depending on the neighborhood; as of 2018 the city was testing using "surge rates" for the most popular times in Back Bay and the Seaport District. Older meters only take quarters, while newer meters will take quarters or credit or debit cards. If you don't see a meter, look for a **pay-and-display kiosk** on the block. They accept both cash and cards and print out a receipt that you affix to the inside of your car window facing the sidewalk. In neighborhoods where there is resident-only parking, a few guest spots are reserved for nonresidents, usually for a maximum of 2 hours, between 8am and 6pm.

A full day in a **parking garage** costs between $24 and $45. The bright, well-maintained city-run garage under **Boston Common** (✆ **617/954-2098**) costs $28 for up to 10 hours, with cheaper rates nights and weekends. The entrance is at Zero Charles Street, between Boylston and Beacon streets heading north. For other options, listed by neighborhood, go to **www.boston-discovery-guide.com/parking-in-boston.html**. A good option for finding hourly or overnight parking is **SpotHero** (www.spothero.com/boston/parking)—you prepay for a reservation online, often at a discount, and simply show up at the designated time and flash the barcode that's sent via email.

For most day trips listed in this book you'll want a car. The major **car-rental** companies have offices at Logan Airport and in the city, and most have other area branches. **Zipcar** car sharing is active in Boston.

[FastFACTS] BOSTON & CAMBRIDGE

Area Codes Boston proper, **617** and **857**; immediate suburbs, **781** and **339**; northern and western suburbs, **978** and **351**; southern suburbs, **508** and **774**. *Note:* To complete a local call, you must dial all 10 digits, even if you are in the same area code.

Drinking Laws The legal drinking age is 21. In many bars, particularly near college campuses, and at sporting events, you will probably be asked for ID. Last call typically is 30 minutes before closing time (1am in bars, 2am in clubs).

Emergencies Call ✆ **911** for fire, ambulance, or police.

Hospitals In downtown Boston, the major hospitals are **Massachusetts General Hospital,** 55 Fruit St. (www.massgeneral.org; ✆ **617/726-2000**) and **Tufts Medical Center,** 800 Washington St. (www.tuftsmedicalcenter.org; ✆ **617/636-5000**). In Cambridge, the major hospital is **Mount Auburn Hospital,** 330 Mt. Auburn St.

(www.mountauburnhospital.org; ✆ **617/492-3500**).

Newspapers & Magazines The city's daily papers are the *Boston Globe* and *Boston Herald.* Boxes around Boston and Cambridge dispense free publications including *Improper Bostonian.*

Pharmacies CVS (www.cvs.com) is a major drugstore chain in Boston, with 20 locations in and near downtown. A few are open 24/7, although their pharmacies close earlier. Hours are listed at the website. Some emergency rooms can fill your prescription at the hospital's pharmacy.

Police Call ℰ **911** for emergencies. The police's Sexual Assault Unit can be reached at ℰ **617/343-4400.** For the Massachusetts State Police, call ℰ **508/820-2300.**

Restrooms Bathroom facilities are available at visitor centers, most tourist attractions, hotels, shopping centers, cafes and restaurants (for customers), and public buildings. The interactive map at **www.bostonharborwalk. org** shows restrooms along the waterfront. In Cambridge, a free outdoor public toilet is available 24 hours in Harvard Square at the corner of Massachusetts Avenue and Church Street.

Safety Boston and Cambridge are generally safe cities. As in any urban area, avoid walking alone at night in parks. Be especially alert on the east side of Boston Common, between the Common and Washington Street; in the nearby Theater District; and around North Station. Public transportation is busy and safe, but remember that service stops between 12:30 and 1am.

Smoking Massachusetts prohibits smoking in all workplaces, including clubs, bars, and restaurants. The city of Boston bans smoking in all hotels, inns, and B&Bs.

Taxes The Boston sales tax is 6.25%. It is does not apply to food (groceries), prescription drugs, or clothing that costs less than $175. In Boston and Cambridge, the tax on meals and takeout food is 7% and the lodging tax is 14.95%.

EXPLORING BOSTON & CAMBRIDGE

Top Boston Attractions

Faneuil Hall Marketplace ★★ MALL/PUBLIC SPACE   When Boston's "festival market" opened in 1976, it quickly became a prototype for the concept. With shops, restaurants, food stalls, jugglers, and musicians, the indoor-outdoor Faneuil Hall Marketplace and Quincy Market complex is a popular spot for a meal, shopping, and people-watching.

Five buildings and the outdoor area around them make up the marketplace. The Greek Revival–style center building, called **Quincy Market,** has a long interior corridor that's an enormous food court, with vendors such as **Boston Chowda Co., Steve's Greek Cuisine,** and **North End Bakery** (with savory arancini—stuffed rice balls—in addition to sweet treats). On either side of the building, glass canopies cover restaurants, bars, and pushcarts that hold

Discount Passes

CityPass (www.citypass.com/boston; ℰ **888/330-5008**) is a booklet of tickets providing discount admission to New England Aquarium (p. 74), Museum of Science (p. 74), Prudential Skywalk Observatory (p. 81), and Harvard Museum of Natural History (p. 84) or Boston Harbor Cruises (p. 88). If you visit three or four attractions, the price ($59 for individuals 12 and older, $47 for youths 3–11) provides a decent discount on buying tickets individually (which are $28 for the Aquarium and $25 for the MFA, for instance). Passes are good for 9 consecutive days from date of purchase. They're on sale at participating attractions or online. Tickets in hand mean you can skip ticket lines, too.

Fun on City Hall Plaza, at Government Center

Boston City Hall, located a block from Faneuil Hall Marketplace, is fronted by a large concrete-and-brick plaza. For decades it was rarely used—just a vast wasteland alongside the brutalist-style hall of local government. That has changed. In recent years, a concerted effort has put the space to creative use. A summertime series of **patios** (open 7 days a week) includes a **beer garden,** an **ice cream area,** and **miniature golf.** The plaza also is host to 1- to 3-day events such as **Boston Pizza Festival, Caliente! Music Festival, GospelFest,** the **Puerto Rican Festival,** and a **Donna Summer Roller Disco Party.** A $60-million plan to redesign the space calls for a new seasonal fountain and new trees. Find the event schedule at **www.cityhallplazaboston.com.**

everything from crafts created by New England artisans to hokey souvenirs. Throughout the complex you'll find a mix of chain stores and unique shops. One constant since the year after the original market at this location opened in 1826 is **Durgin-Park,** a traditional New England restaurant (p. 112). Public restrooms are on the lower level.

Faneuil Hall ★ itself is a colonial-era building where many of the great orators of America's past inspired their listeners to rebellion. National Park Service rangers staff the first-floor visitor center and give brief talks in the second-floor Great Hall auditorium.

Bordered by State, Congress & North sts. & Atlantic Ave. Faneuil Hall Marketplace: www.faneuilhallmarketplace.com. ℂ **617/523-1300.** Daily 10am–9pm; restaurants may open earlier & close later. Faneuil Hall itself: www.nps.gov/bost. ℂ **617/242-5601.** Free admission. Daily 9am–5pm (visitor center until 6pm). T: Government Center or Haymarket.

Institute of Contemporary Art ★★ ART MUSEUM   Boston's first new art museum in almost a century opened in 2006 (the institution itself dates to 1936). Its horizon-broadening definition of art encompasses everything from painting and sculpture to film. The collection includes 68 major works of 20th- and 21st-century art by women, including Kara Walker, Cindy Sherman, Cornelia Parker, Tara Donovan, and Louise Bourgeois. The performance theater hosts an eclectic array of programs, from jazz piano and spoken prose to dance and world music concerts. There's an excellent **gift shop.** The upper levels of the building jut out toward the harbor, providing breathtaking views.

In 2018, the ICA opened a seasonal (July–Sept) exhibition space: the **ICA Watershed,** in East Boston. Located in a large, formerly condemned space in the Boston Harbor Shipyard and Marina, it is accessible by ferry from the main ICA, with the ferry ride included in the price of a general admission ticket (ferry spots are limited availability and are first-come first-served). One exciting feature about the ferry service is that the main building looks most spectacular from the water.

100 Northern Ave. www.icaboston.org. ℂ **617/478-3100.** $15 adults, $13 seniors, $10 students, free for kids 17 & under; free to all Thurs after 5pm. Ferry tickets can be reserved online a month in advance, or reserved day-of at box office in ICA main

Boston Attractions

Boston Children's Museum **23**
Boston Fire Museum **24**
Boston Public Garden and Boston Common **9**
Boston Public Library **6**
Boston Tea Party Ships & Museum **22**
Charles River Esplanade **8**
Faneuil Hall Marketplace **18**
Fenway Park **3**
Franklin Park Zoo **4**
Freedom Trail (beginning of route) **13**
Institute of Contemporary Art **21**
Isabella Stewart Gardner Museum **1**
John F. Kennedy Presidential Library
  and Museum **25**

Museum of African American History **11**
Museum of Fine Arts **2**
Museum of Science **14**
New England Aquarium **20**
Nichols House Museum **10**
Old North Church **16**
Otis House Museum **12**
Paul Revere House **17**
Rose Fitzgerald Kennedy Greenway **19**
Skywalk Observatory at the Prudential Center **5**
Trinity Church **7**
USS *Constitution* **15**

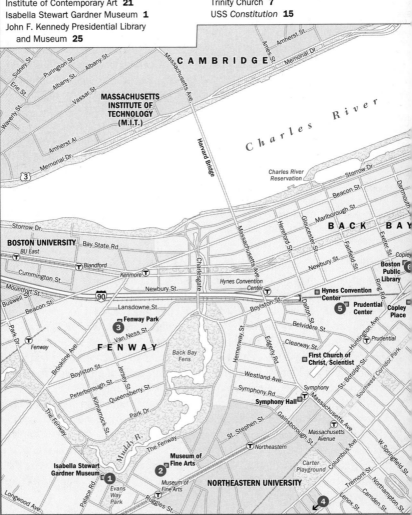

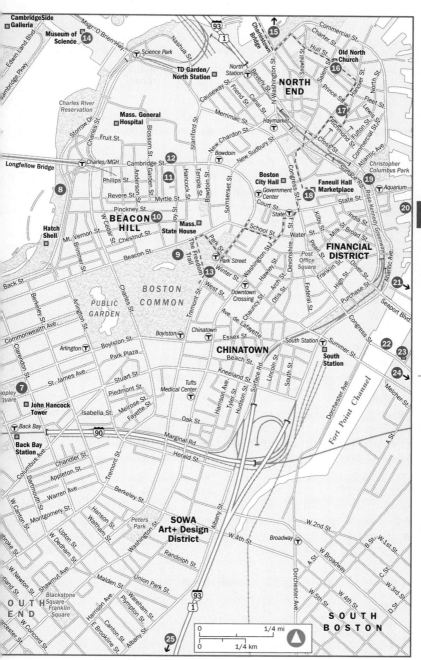

CambridgeSide
Galleria

Museum of
Science 14

Science Park

Edwin Land Blvd

Cambridge Pkwy

Msgr. O'Brien Hwy.

93
1

Charlestown
Bridge 15

Commercial St.
Charter St.
Hull St.
Snow Hill St.
Salem St.
Old North
Church 16
Prince St.
Hanover St.
Fleet St.
Lewis St.
North St.

NORTH
END

Nashua St.

North
Station

TD Garden/
North Station

Beverly St.
Washington St. N.
Causeway St.
Friend St.
Canal St.

17

Richmond St.
Fulton St.
Commercial St.

Charles River
Reservation

Storrow Dr.

Charles St.

Fruit St.

Mass. General
Hospital

Blossom St.

Staniford St.

Merrimac St.

New Chardon St.

Haymarket

Cross St.

Surface Rd.

Atlantic Ave.

Christopher
Columbus Park

Longfellow Bridge

Charles/MGH

Cambridge St.

12

Bowdoin

New Sudbury St.

Boston
City Hall

Congress St.

Faneuil Hall
Marketplace

19

Aquarium

8

Philips St.

Anderson St.

Garden St.

Revere St.

11

Myrtle St.

Hancock St.

Temple St.

Bowdoin St.

Somerset St.

Government
Center
Court St.

18

State St.

Kilby St.

India St.

Broad St.

20

4

Hatch
Shell

BEACON
HILL

W. Cedar St.

Mt. Vernon St.

Chestnut St.

10

Pinckney St.

Mass.
State House

State

School St.

Water St.

Devonshire St.

Pearl St.

Milk St.

FINANCIAL
DISTRICT

Atlantic Ave.

21

Seaport Blvd.

Beacon St.

9

The Freedom Trail

Park St.

Park Street

Winter St.

Hawley St.

Arch St.

Franklin St.

High St.

Oliver St.

Congress St.

Post
Office
Square

Back St.

BOSTON
COMMON

Charles St.

PUBLIC
GARDEN

13

West St.

Downtown
Crossing

Ave. de Lafayette

Summer St.

Purchase St.

Federal St.

22

23

Commonwealth Ave.

Arlington

Boylston St.

Boylston

Chinatown

Essex St.

CHINATOWN

South Station

South
Station

Meicher St.

24

Berkeley St.

Clarendon St.

St. James Ave.

Park Plaza

Stuart St.

Beach St.

Kneeland St.

Lincoln St.

South St.

Dorchester Ave.

Fort Point Channel

7
opley
quare

John Hancock
Tower

Piedmont St.

Melrose St.

Tufts
Medical Center

Harrison Ave.

Tyler St.

Hudson St.

Surface Rd.

Isabella St.

Fayette St.

Oak St.

Back Bay

Marginal Rd.

Back Bay
Station

Columbus Ave.

Dartmouth St.

90

Herald St.

W. Canton St.

Chandler St.

Appleton St.

Warren Ave.

Berkeley St.

Tremont St.

Hanson St.

Waltham St.

Peters
Park

SOWA
Art+ Design
District

Albany St.

W. 2nd St.

W. 1st St.

B St.

Broadway

W. Broadway

A St.

C St.

W. 3rd St.

Upton St.

W. Dedham St.

Washington St.

Randolph St.

W. 4th St.

Dorchester Ave.

OUTH
END

Blackstone
Square
Franklin
Square

Shawmut Ave.

Harrison Ave.

Malden St.

Union Park St.

Plympton St.

Wareham St.

Canton St.

E. Brookline St.

Albany St.

93
1

25

W. 5th St.

SOUTH
BOSTON

W. 4th St.

W. 3rd St.

W. Concord St.

0   1/4 mi
0   1/4 km

building. Main museum: Tues–Sun & some Mon holidays 10am–5pm (until 9pm Thurs–Fri except 1st Fri of month). Watershed: July 4th–early Oct Tues–Sun 10am–5pm. T: Courthouse.

Isabella Stewart Gardner Museum ★★★ ART MUSEUM   An heiress and socialite, Isabella Gardner (1840–1924) was also an avid traveler and patron of the arts. The core of the museum is her private collection of paintings, sculpture, furniture, tapestries, and decorative objects. The largest work of art, though, is the building itself, completed in 1901 and designed to resemble a 15th-century Venetian palace. Three floors of galleries surround a magnificent plant- and flower-filled **inner courtyard,** making the space one of the most unlikely and gorgeous in the city. Galleries feature works by Titian, Botticelli, Raphael, Rembrandt, Matisse, and Sargent—whose monumental *El Jaleo,* a painting of a Gypsy dancer and her musicians, takes up an entire wall in the museum's **Spanish Cloister.** A glass-enclosed wing debuted in 2012 and is a treasure in its own right. (Designer Renzo Piano termed it the "respectful nephew to the great aunt.") It includes the handsome **Café G** (open Wed–Mon) and a concert space, **Calderwood Hall.** The museum has an unfortunate claim to fame: An art heist in 1990 of important works by Rembrandt, Vermeer, and Degas was estimated to be worth more than $500 million, making it the single largest property theft in the world. As of 2018, the case remains unsolved. *Tip:* Gardner was a big Red Sox fan, and the museum offers $2 off adult and senior admission to visitors wearing Red Sox paraphernalia. *One more tip:* All visitors named "Isabella" are admitted free of charge (bring ID as proof).

25 Evans Way. www.gardnermuseum.org. ✆ **617/566-1401.** $15 adults, $12 seniors, $5 students, free for kids 17 & under, military & families. Wed–Mon 11am–5pm (until 9pm Thurs). T: Museum of Fine Arts.

John F. Kennedy Presidential Library and Museum ★★ HISTORY MUSEUM   The Kennedy era springs to life at this dramatic complex overlooking Dorchester Bay, about a half-hour drive south of Boston center (also accessible by T). Photos, memorabilia, and audio and video recordings capture the 35th U.S. president in vibrant style. Visits start with a 17-minute film about his early life, narrated by Kennedy himself, using cleverly edited audio clips. Displays start with the 1960 presidential campaign and include the Cuban Missile Crisis, the president's brother Attorney General Robert F. Kennedy, the civil rights movement, the Peace Corps, the space program, First Lady Jacqueline Bouvier Kennedy, and JFK's 1963 assassination and funeral.

Columbia Point, near UMass Boston. www.jfklibrary.org. ✆ **866/JFK-1960** [535-1930] or 617/514-1600. $14 adults; $12 seniors & college students with ID; $10 youth 13–17; free for 12 & under. Daily 9am–5pm (last intro film at 3:55pm). T: JFK/UMass, then free shuttle bus.

Museum of African American History ★★ HISTORY MUSEUM "Boston's Second Revolution"—the fight against slavery and for the equality of African-Americans—was led in the 1800s by free blacks who made their home in Boston's Beacon Hill and West Side neighborhoods. They were leaders in the Abolition Movement, the Underground Railroad, the U.S. Civil War, and the earliest efforts to bring education and full rights to black Americans. This fascinating museum highlights this history. It occupies the **Abiel Smith School** (1834), the first American public grammar school for African-American children; and the **African Meeting House** (1806), one of the oldest black churches in the country. Changing and permanent exhibits use historic photographs, art, artifacts, documents, and other objects to explore an important era that often takes a back seat in Revolutionary War–obsessed New England. Be sure to visit Holmes Alley, off Smith Court—the narrow passageway is believed to have been a hiding place for fugitive slaves traveling the Underground Railroad. Guided tours of **Boston's Black Heritage Trail** tour (see box p. 74) conclude here.

46 Joy St. www.maah.org. ⓒ **617/725-0022.** $10 adults, $8 seniors & students, free for kids 12 & under. Mon–Sat 10am–4pm. T: Park St. or Charles/MGH.

Museum of Fine Arts ★★★ ART MUSEUM The familiar and the undiscovered meet here, at one of the best art museums in the world. You can take a **mobile guide,** concentrate on a particular period, or head straight to one specific piece. The vast permanent collection soars from classical to contemporary, prints to photography, musical instruments to textiles. The **Impressionism gallery** alone includes Gauguin's masterpiece *Where Do We Come From? What Are We? Where Are We Going?*, the Degas sculpture *Little Fourteen-Year-Old Dancer*, Van Gogh's *Houses at Auvers*, and works by Cézanne, Pissarro, Signac, and Sisley. There's an entire gallery devoted to Monet. Three don't-miss paintings are deeply Boston in subject matter and much beloved: John Singleton Copley's iconic portrait of Paul Revere (1768); John Singer Sargent's *Daughters of Edward Darley Boit* (1882); and Childe Hassam's *At Dusk (Boston Common at Twilight)* (1885–86).

465 Huntington Ave. www.mfa.org. ⓒ **617/267-9300.** Admission (good for 2 visits within 10 days) $25 adults, $23 seniors & students, $10 kids 7–17 on school days before 3pm, otherwise free. Free for kids 6 & under. Voluntary contribution Wed 4–9:45pm. Mobile guide rentals $6 adults, $4 kids 17 & under. Check website for hotel package deals that include museum admission. Sat–Tues 10am–5pm, Wed–Fri 10am–10pm. Closed major holidays (check website). T: Museum of Fine Arts.

The MFA: A Work of Art in Its Own Right

The MFA itself is an architectural landmark. The hub of the original building (1909) is the **rotunda**, accessed from a sweeping staircase. It holds one of the museum's signature elements, John Singer Sargent's Rotunda Murals, which depict mythological figures such as Apollo, Athena, the Muses, and Prometheus. Later additions to the facility were also completed with a splash:

The **Linde Family Wing for Contemporary Art,** designed by I. M. Pei (1981), and the **Art of the Americas wing** (2010), the work of Sir Norman Foster and his firm, Foster + Partners. A central, glass-enclosed 63-foot tall atrium has a 42½-foot-high **lime green glass tower** by Dale Chihuly, which has become a signature icon for the modern MFA.

Museum of Science ★★★ SCIENCE MUSEUM   Considered by many the best indoor family destination in the Boston area, this enormous science museum has sections that focus on the moon, dinosaurs, the human body, and nanotechnology—and that's just to start. Reviewing the website in advance can help you sketch out a game plan for where to visit first. Also check in advance for the schedules for the **butterfly garden, IMAX theater, 4-D films,** and **planetarium,** which all have additional fees. Kids of all ages zip from hands-on activities to interactive displays, and it's fun, educational, and entertaining. The **Discovery Center** is a quieter museum-within-a-museum, designed for the youngest visitors and kept at a limited capacity. Unlike most museums in Boston, this one has its own attached parking lot ($10–$22, depending on length of stay). There's an expansive **gift shop.** Food options include burgers, burritos, pizza, a salad bar, and coffees for exhausted parents and chaperones.

1 Science Park. www.mos.org. ℂ **617/723-2500.** $25 adults, $20 kids 3–11, free for kids 2 & under. Extra fees for butterfly garden, IMAX theater & planetarium; discounted combo tickets available. Daily 9am–5pm (until 9pm Fri); extended hours in summer & school vacations; theater & planetarium close later. T: Science Park.

New England Aquarium ★★★ AQUARIUM   The centerpiece of this well-appointed and popular aquarium is the four-story **Giant Ocean Tank,** which contains sea turtles, sharks, hundreds of colorful reef fishes, and 200,000 gallons of water—a live webcam at www.neaq.org/giant-ocean-tank-web-cam offers a fun sneak peek. A wide ramp travels up and around the tank with exhibits tucked off in every direction. Other sea creatures include seahorses the size of grapes. Seals and sea lions frolic in the open-air marine

Beacon Hill's Black History

Though it's best known for its quaint cobblestones, wrought-iron fences, and patrician air, Beacon Hill has a lesser-known but fascinating other side to its past. In the 1600s, before Brahmin Boston moved in, the north side of "The Hill" was home to free blacks from the West Indies and Africa, and in the 1800s and 1900s, men and women in Boston's free African-American community were leaders in the national fight to end slavery and to achieve equality. During the Civil War, black Bostonians formed the core of the 54th Massachusetts Regiment, fighting alongside white soldiers to preserve the country's union and take down slavery. The **Robert Gould Shaw and 54th Massachusetts Regiment Memorial** (p. 75), at the northeast corner of the Boston Common, commemorates their service. The memorial is also the starting point for **Boston's Black Heritage Trail** (www.maah.org/trail.htm and www.nps.gov/boaf; ℂ **617/742-5415**), a 1.6-mile walking tour of important sites on Beacon Hill, developed by the **Museum of African American History** (p. 72) in partnership with the city of Boston and National Park Service. In summer, 90-minute tours of the Trail, led by National Park Service rangers, begin in Boston Common at the memorial and end at the museum. (Check the NPS website for schedules.) Self-guided tours are also available on the websites, or you can pick up a tour map at the museum's Abiel Smith School or at Faneuil Hall (p. 77).

mammal center, and at the **ray touch tank** visitors can pet the exhibit's leathery-skinned inhabitants. More than 80 penguins greet visitors just inside the front entrance. The facility is big enough to comfortably accommodate the masses of school groups that descend upon it periodically throughout the year. Even if you don't venture inside, you can visit the **Atlantic harbor seals,** whose tank is outside next to the front doors.

1 Central Wharf, ½ block from State St. & Atlantic Ave. www.neaq.org. ✆ **617/973-5200.** $28 adults, $26 seniors, $19 kids 3–11, free for kids under 3. IMAX tickets $10 adults, $8 seniors & kids. Tickets available online in advance. July–Aug Sun–Thurs 9am–6pm, Fri–Sat 9am–7pm; Sept–June Mon–Fri 9am–5pm, Sat–Sun 9am–6pm. T: Aquarium.

The Freedom Trail & its Sights ★★★

A red path—in some stretches brick, in other stretches paint—winds through the streets of old Boston past historic sites of the city's Colonial past. Walking the trail provides a wonderful introduction to the city and its history. It's a 2½-mile self-guided tour that begins at **Boston Common,** although you can certainly join in at any spot. **Freedom Trail tours** with costumed guides ($12 adults, $6.50 kids 6–12) are an option and last 90 minutes; see www.the freedomtrail.org/book-tour/public-tours.shtml.

The Freedom Trail has a website, www.thefreedomtrail.org, and a Twitter feed, @thefreedomtrail. If you follow the full route, plan for 4 hours to allow for walking, reading plaques, spending time inside some of the sights, and taking a serendipitous detour or two.

- **Boston Common.** The Common is the oldest public park in the country (founded in 1634) and a welcome splash of green in redbrick Boston. Over the years, these 45 acres have held pasture, barracks, parade grounds, ball fields, and more. In the wintertime, trees throughout the park are lit with twinkly colored lights. The park **visitor center** (139 Tremont St.) is next to the fountain adjacent to the Park Street subway stop.
- **Robert Gould Shaw and the 54th Massachusetts Regiment Memorial.** At the highest point of the Common, up the hill and near to the State House, is a magnificent bronze sculpture that honors the first American army unit composed of free black soldiers, who fought in the Civil War. The plaque on the back provides rich historical detail. The story of the 54th was told in the 1989 movie *Glory.*
- **Massachusetts State House** (www.sec.state.ma.us/trs/trsgen/genidx.htm; ✆ 617/727-3676). The gracious golden-dome-topped state capitol is a signature work of the great Federal-era architect Charles Bulfinch. Note the symmetry, a hallmark of Federal style, in details as large as doors and as small as moldings. Visitors can take self-guided tours (see www.sec.state. ma.us/trs/trsbok/trstour.htm) or, by prior arrangement, guided tours. Allow time to find the statues and monuments that dot the grounds, including one of President John F. Kennedy captured in midstride.
- **Park Street Church ★,** 1 Park St. (www.parkstreet.org; ✆ 617/523-3383). Most Bostonians know this redbrick church for its 217-foot clock tower and

steeple, which chimes on the quarter-hour. "My Country 'Tis of Thee" was sung on the church's steps for the first time on July 4, 1831. It's open to the public July through August, Tuesday to Saturday, as well as Sundays year-round.

o **Granary Burying Ground ★,** Tremont Street at Bromfield Street. Colonial Boston's residents worked, worshipped, and buried their dead in this area of the city. Established in 1660, this cemetery got its name from the granary, or grain-storage building, that once stood next to it. Wander the walkways to take in the diversity of markers and ornamental carvings, including the "Soul Effigy," a skull or "death's head" with wings on each side. A map near the entrance shows the locations of the graves of Paul Revere, Samuel Adams, Crispus Attucks and the other victims of the Boston Massacre, and John Hancock, whose monument is almost as florid as his signature. Also here: Elizabeth "Mother" Goose, who may or may not be "the" Mother Goose of nursery rhyme fame. It's open daily from 10am to 5pm.

o **King's Chapel and Burying Ground ★,** 58 Tremont St. (www.kings-chapel.org; ✆ **617/523-1749**). Established as an Anglican church in 1686, King's Chapel became Unitarian after the Revolution. The current chapel (1749) is the country's oldest church in continuous use as well as its oldest major stone building. The church hosts **lunchtime concerts on Tuesdays.** The chapel is open year-round Monday to Saturday from 10am, Sunday from 1:30pm, with tours several times a day; check the website for tour schedules and closing times. The burying ground is open daily 9am to 5pm, with shorter hours in winter.

o **Site of the First Public School ★,** 45 School St. A colorful mosaic in the sidewalk marks the original site of the first public school in the United States, Boston Latin, founded in 1634. (The school has moved but is still in operation today, and highly regarded.) Just adjacent is **Old City Hall.** Inside the fence there is an 1856 **statue of Benjamin Franklin**—publisher, statesman, postmaster, scientist—who was born a block away.

o **Old Corner Bookstore Building ★,** 3 School St. The structure here, which today has a restaurant on the ground floor, dates to 1718, making it 300 years old in 2018. In the mid-1800s the building was the center of U.S. publishing and home of publisher Ticknor & Fields, whose authors included Harriet Beecher Stowe, Oliver Wendell Holmes Sr., and Louisa May Alcott.

o **Old South Meeting House ★,** 310 Washington St. (www.osmh.org; ✆ **617/482-6439**). The Boston Tea Party, a pivotal political demonstration of the pre-Revolutionary era, started here in 1773. Displays and exhibits in the former house of worship tell the story in a compelling fashion. It's open daily 9:30am to 5pm, with shorter hours in winter. Admission is $6 for adults, $5 for seniors and students, and $1 for children 5 to 17.

o **Old State House Museum ★,** 206 Washington St. (www.bostonhistory. org; ✆ **617/720-1713**). Like a William Morris flower in a forest of red-woods, this fancy little brick building sits amid towering skyscrapers. On the exterior are vestigial traces of British rule—a lion and a unicorn, both royal symbols that predate the Revolution (when the State House opened in 1713, today's State Street was named King Street). In 1776, the Declaration of Independence was first read to Bostonians from the balcony. Today it houses a history museum (with John Hancock's coat) and a multimedia presentation about the Boston Massacre. Tours are included with admission. The museum is open daily from 9am to 5pm (until 6pm May–early Sept). Admission is $10 adults, $8.50 seniors and students, free for kids 18 and under.

o **Site of the Boston Massacre ★.** A circle of cobblestones underneath the Old State House balcony honors the five men killed by British troops on March 5, 1770. The event fueled the already simmering discontent with British authority; Paul Revere created an engraved image that helped publicize the incident and galvanize rebellion.

o **Faneuil Hall and Faneuil Hall Marketplace ★★,** Dock Square at Congress Street (www.nps.gov/bost; © **617/242-5601**). Faneuil Hall dates to 1742 as a meeting house and site of political activism. The commercial complex behind it—Faneuil Hall Marketplace and Quincy Market—is a popular attraction housed in restored 19th-century buildings. See p. 68.

o **Paul Revere House ★★★,** 19 North Square (www.paulreverehouse.org; © **617/523-2338**). Built about 1680 and now a national historic landmark, this home is one of the few surviving dwellings of its age in the United States. Revere was a talented silversmith who supported a large family—his first wife, Sarah, died after giving birth to their eighth child, and his second wife, Rachel, also bore eight children. When the family moved in in 1770, there were three adults—Revere, Sarah, and Revere's mother Deborah—and the first five children. The home was turned into a museum in 1908. It's open April 15 through October daily from 9:30am to 5:15pm, November through April 14 from 9:30am to 4:15pm (closed Mon Jan–Mar). Admission is $5 for adults, $4.50 for seniors and students, and $1 for children 5 to 17.

o **James Rego Square (Paul Revere Mall) ★,** off Hanover Street, at Clark Street. This narrow, tree-lined, brick-laid plaza is the site of one of the most photographed tableaus of Boston: a statue of Paul Revere atop a horse, with the Old North Church behind him.

o **Old North Church ★★,** 193 Salem St. (www.oldnorth.com; © **617/858-8231**). This beautifully proportioned brick church, officially named Christ Church, overflows with historic associations. It was here that sexton Robert Newman briefly hung two lanterns in the steeple on the night of April 18, 1775, signaling Paul Revere to set out on his "midnight ride" to warn the rebellious colonists that British troops were leaving Boston by water, bound for Lexington and Concord. It contains the oldest American church bells (cast in Gloucester, England) and the Revere family's pew. Somehow, through nearly 300 years of rough New England weather, the original weather vane has survived atop the 191-foot steeple—the tallest in Boston. Tours takes visitors up into the spire and down to the crypt—not for the claustrophobic. It's open daily April through November 15 from 9am to

6pm, and from 10am to 4pm the rest of the year. Talks (5–7 min.) are available. Admission is $8 for adults, $6 for seniors and students, and $4 for kids. Special tours (Behind the Scenes and Bones & Burials) have extra fees: $6 for adults, $5 for students/seniors/military, $4 for children (Bones & Burials tour not suitable for children under 13).

o **Copp's Hill Burying Ground ★,** off Hull Street. The highest point in the North End neighborhood affords a panoramic view across the Inner Harbor to the wishbone-shaped Zakim Bunker Hill Memorial Bridge and the Charlestown Navy Yard, where the three masts of USS *Constitution* (next stop on the tour) poke into view. Boston's first African-American neighborhood was nearby, and an estimated 1,000 of the 10,000 or so people buried in the graveyard at the crest of Copp's Hill were black. The best-known is Prince Hall, who is believed to have fought at Bunker Hill and later founded the first black Masonic lodge. It's open daily from 10am to 5pm. (Fun fact: The 10-foot-wide private home at 44 Hull St., across from the graveyard entrance, is the narrowest house in Boston.)

o **USS Constitution ★★,** Charlestown Navy Yard (www.nps.gov/bost/learn/historyculture/ussconst.htm; ✆ **617/242-7511**). Built in a Boston shipyard and launched in 1797, this magnificent frigate's three masts today loom over the navy yard. The *Constitution* is the oldest commissioned floating warship in the world, and earned its nickname "Old Ironsides" on August 19, 1812, when, during an engagement with HMS *Guerriere* in the War of 1812, cannonballs bounced off its thick oak hull as if it were metal. Old Ironsides never lost a battle, but narrowly escaped destruction several times in its first 2 centuries. Today it is a museum ship and an active-duty posting for the sailors who lead tours (wearing replica post-war 1813 uniforms). Visitors can board the ship, with tours offered every 30 minutes. It's open Wednesday through Sunday from 10am to 4pm year round. Admission to the ship is free. Visitors 18 and older must present a valid federal or state-issued photo ID or passport at the ship's security screening. The adjacent **USS *Constitution* Museum ★** (www.ussconstitutionmuseum.org; ✆ **617/426-1812**) is open daily April through October from 9am to 6pm, and from 10am to 5pm the rest of the year. Suggested donation to the museum is $5–$10 for adults, $3–$5 for kids, or $20–$25 for families. Also at this location is the **Charlestown Navy Yard Visitor Center** (✆ **617/242-5601**), open Tuesday through Sunday from 9am to 5pm year-round. National Park Service rangers are on site for questions.

Take a Ferry Ride

A fun way to return to downtown Boston from Charlestown is on the **Boston Harbor water shuttle** (10 min., $3.50). It connects the Charlestown Naval Shipyard Park, a 30-acre Boston National Historical Park, to Boston's Long Wharf, near the Aquarium.

o **Bunker Hill Monument** ★ (www.nps.gov/bost/planyourvisit/bhm.htm; ✆ **617/242-7275**), Charlestown. The narrow pedestrian streets of Charlestown all seem to lead to this 221-foot granite obelisk at the center of an elegant grassy square. It commemorates the Battle of Bunker Hill on June 17, 1775 (June 17 is now Bunker Hill Day, a holiday in Massachusetts' Suffolk County). The British won that battle, but nearly half of their troops were killed or wounded. Partly as a consequence of the carnage, royal forces abandoned Boston 9 months later. The exhibits in the small but engaging **Battle of Bunker Hill Museum** ★ across the street from the grass lawn (43 Monument Square) tell the story of the fire fight, and the second floor has a 360-degree painting depicting the combat. **Bunker Hill Lodge** adjoins the Monument and houses artwork and a Revolutionary War cannon; this is where you enter if you want to climb up. Think hard before attempting to walk the 294 stairs to the top; it's a tough climb that ends at a small space with tiny windows. National Park Service rangers staff the monument, which is open daily from 9am to 5pm in summer and 1 to 5pm rest of the year. Admission to both the monument and to museum is free.

Other Boston Attractions
HISTORIC HOMES
As a cradle of American history, Boston has several historic homes well worth visiting. The most fascinating is the **Paul Revere House** (p. 77), on the Freedom Trail walking tour, but if that whets your appetite, here are several others.

In the Beacon Hill neighborhood, guided tours are offered of **Otis House** ★, 141 Cambridge St. (www.historicnewengland.org/property/otis-house; ✆ **617/994-5920**), a magnificent 1796 Federal-style mansion designed for Harrison Gray Otis by his friend Charles Bulfinch (who 2 years later completed the Massachusetts State House). The tour illuminates the neighborhood's history as well as the house and its furnishings. Otis was a congressman and mayor of Boston, and Sally Foster Otis appointed their home in grand style. Tours cost $10 for adults, $9 for seniors, $5 for students, and are free for Boston residents (open Apr–Nov Wed–Sun 11am–4:30pm, with tours on the half-hour; closed Dec–Mar).

A few blocks away, **Nichols House Museum** ★, 55 Mount Vernon St. (www.nicholshousemuseum.org; ✆ **617/227-6993**), is also attributed to Charles Bulfinch, but it's really worth visiting as a window on Boston during the lifetime of its most famous occupant, Rose Standish Nichols (1872–1960), a suffragist, feminist, pacifist, and pioneering landscape designer. Nichols traveled the world, returning home with many of the artworks and artifacts that decorate her house—Flemish tapestries, Italian paintings of the 1700s, French table settings. Tours cost $10 adults, $8 seniors, $5 students, free for kids 12 and under (open Apr–Oct Tues–Sat 11am–4pm, Nov–Mar Thurs–Sat 11am–4pm; tours start every hour on the hour).

COPLEY SQUARE & THE PRU ★★
Landmark buildings occupy three sides of Copley Square, the heart of commercial Boston. Named for the celebrated artist John Singleton Copley

With its Federalist townhouses and mansions, gaslights and cast-iron fences, and narrow streets, Beacon Hill is dignified and romantic. **Charles Street** is its main street. Roads with this central a location and tourist flow often capitulate to T-shirt shops and knick-knack stores. Instead, merchants here continue to serve their neighbors as well as visitors, with an appealing collection of bakeries, antiques shops, restaurants, and taverns. Two blocks east of Charles Street, up narrow Mount Vernon Street, is pristine **Louisburg Square.** The fanciest addresses in Boston's fanciest neighborhood surround this small private park. Author Louisa May Alcott lived at #10 after the successful publication of her *Little Women.* One block south of the park is **Acorn Street,** a lane that feels like a surprise. The smaller homes here face the garden walls of larger properties behind them and once housed tradesmen who serviced the neighborhood's wealthier clients. Needless to say, that's no longer the case: The townhouse at #3 Acorn sold in 2016 for $3.7 million. Still, the street continues to be evocative of the past, and is one of the most photographed in the city.

4

(1738–1815), the square is a central locale for summer festivals, a farmers' market, the October **Boston Book Festival** (www.bostonbookfest.org; ✆ **857/259-6999**), and the finish line for April's Boston Marathon (where the city experienced a brutal bombing in 2013). A constant flow of pedestrians enlivens the area and it's a visual treat year-round—it's the hub of The Hub.

The gem of Copley Square is **Trinity Church ★★★**, on the east side of the square at 206 Clarendon St. (www.trinitychurchboston.org; ✆ **617/536-0944**). While the prototypical New England church is simple—white with a towering steeple—Trinity is anything but. The 1877 building is granite and multicolored, trimmed with red sandstone, with a roof of red tiles. The 221-foot tower weighs 90 million pounds all on its own. It is architect H. H. Richardson's masterwork—his style was so distinctive that it now bears his name: Richardsonian Romanesque. Inside, barrel vaults draw the eye up to the 63-foot ceilings, and murals and decorative painting by John La Farge make imaginative use of colored plaster that complements the hues in the stained-glass windows (look for La Farge's window Christ in Majesty, in the west gallery). Among the regular events presented here are **Choral Evensong** on Wednesdays at 5:45pm and an **Organ Recital Series** Fridays at 12:15pm ($10 suggested donation). Admission to the church is free. Guided tours are available (generally one per day, at various times between 11am and 2pm; check website for calendar). The Sunday tour immediately following the worship service is free; otherwise, guided tours are $10 adults, $8 seniors and students, free for children 11 and under. Church hours are Tuesday through Saturday 10am to 4:30pm, Sunday 12:15pm to 4:30pm.

Behind Trinity Church at 200 Clarendon St. is a giant skyscraper with sides of reflecting glass. Long called the John Hancock Tower for its prominent tenant, it was renamed 200 Clarendon in 2015 (though everyone stills calls it

Hancock Tower). It's not open to the public, but its flanks provide wonderful reflections of Trinity Church.

On the south side of Copley Square, the relatively austere facade of the 1912 **Fairmont Copley Plaza ★** (see p. 98) conceals a wildly sumptuous interior that's well worth a look. Its elegant **OAK Long Bar + Kitchen** (p. 135) serves swanky drinks and farm-to-table eats all day long.

On the west side of Copley Square, the main branch of the **Boston Public Library ★★★**, 700 Boylston St. (www.bpl.org; ℭ **617/536-5400**) is a modern public gathering space. A $78-million renovation completed in 2016 created an airy, light-filled front atrium with a welcome center, the vibrant **Newsfeed Café,** loads of cafe-style seating, and an open on-air radio studio for WGBH, one of the city's two public radio powerhouses. A new children's library section doubled the space for kids. The library's calendar lists 5 to 10 events a day, including public lectures, Tinker Tots science activities for the 3-to-5 set, and free tours of the grand building's art and architecture. (Check www.bpl.org/central/tours.htm for tour schedule and downloadable self-guided tours.) Overall, the changes are an architectural marvel and have brought a welcome energy to the public resource, which was built in 1895. On the library's third floor, the **Sargent Gallery** houses a set of religious-themed murals by the celebrated portraitist John Singer Sargent, who worked on them from 1895 through 1916. Many visitors consider this gallery their favorite part of the library. There's also an especially pretty **interior courtyard** designed in the manner of a Renaissance cloister, with a Roman arcade, fountain basin with water jets, and eternally peaceful atmosphere. The library is open Monday to Thursday 9am to 9pm, Friday to Saturday 9am to 5pm, and Sunday 1 to 5pm. *Note:* The Boston Marathon finish line is directly outside the Boylston Street entrance and stays painted on the street year-round.

Finally, for sky-high views, head 2 blocks west of the library to the Prudential Center, and then up to the **Skywalk Observatory,** 800 Boylston St. (www.skywalkboston.com, ℭ **617/859-0648**). When the sky is clear, the 360° panorama from the 50th floor of the Prudential Tower affords views as far as New Hampshire to the north and Cape Cod to the south. Interactive audiovisual displays, including exhibits about immigration, trace Boston's history. Admission is $19 for adults, $15 for seniors and students, and $13 for kids ages 3 to 12. It's generally open daily from 10am to 8pm (until 10pm mid-Mar to early Nov), but call to confirm that it's open, especially on cloudy days.

Exploring Cambridge

Just across the Charles River from Boston, the city of Cambridge is home to **Harvard University, Massachusetts Institute of Technology,** and other schools of higher learning, giving it an academic personality. **Harvard Square ★★** is a people-watching paradise of students, instructors, commuters, shoppers, and sightseers. To be clear, Harvard Square isn't a square or even a plaza—it's only the intersection of Massachusetts Avenue, Brattle Street, and John F. Kennedy Street, with a subway stop and small concrete island at its center. No matter. Restaurants and stores are tightly packed together on the three streets that radiate from the center and the streets that intersect them. Harvard University's undergraduate campus dominates "the Square" proper, with classrooms, dorms, and some of the oldest buildings in the country located just on the other side of a black wrought-iron fence. In the coldest winter months, the streets are busy, and once spring comes, they explode with activity—outdoor cafes, street musicians, and bug-eyed students who are grateful to take a break from staring at computer screens.

To get to Cambridge from Boston, take the Red Line T toward Alewife. Cambridge subway stops are at Kendall/MIT, Central, Harvard, and Porter. The no. 1 bus which runs along Mass Ave also travels from Boston to its end point at Harvard Square.

Traffic and parking in and around Harvard Square are almost as challenging as they are in downtown Boston. If you drive, you'll probably want to park once and walk from there on.

4 HARVARD UNIVERSITY

The oldest college in the country, founded in 1636, Harvard welcomes visitors and offers free guided tours. Even without a guide, the stately main campus— two adjoining quads known as **Harvard Yard ★★**—is interesting to walk through. The school's new **Smith Campus Center,** 1350 Massachusetts Ave. (www.harvard.edu/on-campus/visit-harvard/tours; ℭ **617/495-1000**), was set to open in fall 2018. The center houses a **visitor center** as well as a plaza with cafe seating along Mass Ave at Dunster Street.

From the Harvard T station at Mass Ave, face the black fence that surrounds the campus, and look to your left for an entrance. Once you pass through the gate, you'll be in Harvard Yard, which houses dormitories, libraries, classroom buildings, and churches. The most popular stop is the **John Harvard statue** in front of **University Hall.** The quad they're in is mostly undergraduate dorms, but stroll to the northwestern corner to see **Holden Chapel,** a tiny Georgian building (completed in 1744) which served temporarily as barracks for Revolutionary War troops serving under George Washington. Later it was an anatomy lab; today it's a rehearsal space for undergraduate choral groups.

Walk around University Hall into the second quad and work your way clockwise. **Memorial Church** (ℭ **617/495-5508**), dedicated in 1932, holds nondenominational Protestant services including morning prayer (Mon–Sat at 8:45am during the academic year) and Sunday services at 11am. **Sever Hall** (rhymes with "fever") was designed by H. H. Richardson, the mastermind of Boston's Trinity Church. Architects rave about the brickwork, the chimneys, the roof, and even the window openings. If you stand next to one side of the front door and whisper into the archway, the person next to you won't hear a thing but someone at the other end of the arch can hear you loud and clear. The majestic **Widener Library,** with its dramatic front stairway, is one of the world's most comprehensive research collections in the humanities and social sciences, in more than 100 languages. It's not open to the public.

There are a number of food options nearby, including **Clover Food Lab** (p. 113), **Grendel's Den Restaurant & Bar** (p. 121), **Mr. Bartley's Burger**

Harvard Square & Environs

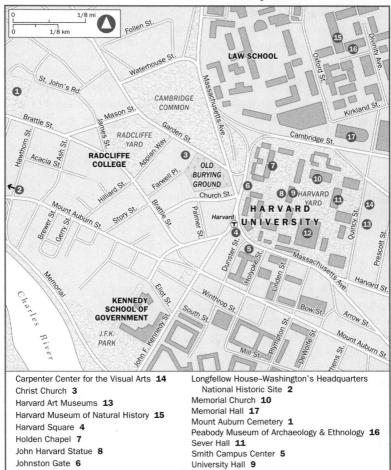

Carpenter Center for the Visual Arts **14**
Christ Church **3**
Harvard Art Museums **13**
Harvard Museum of Natural History **15**
Harvard Square **4**
Holden Chapel **7**
John Harvard Statue **8**
Johnston Gate **6**

Longfellow House–Washington's Headquarters
  National Historic Site **2**
Memorial Church **10**
Memorial Hall **17**
Mount Auburn Cemetery **1**
Peabody Museum of Archaeology & Ethnology **16**
Sever Hall **11**
Smith Campus Center **5**
University Hall **9**
Widener Library **12**

Cottage (p. 121), and four or five food trucks (p. 119) that set up daily on the Harvard Plaza just north of Harvard Yard, near Oxford Street.

Harvard Art Museums ★★ ART MUSEUMS   Three institutions make up the Harvard Art Museums, including the Fogg Museum, focused on Western arts; and the Busch-Reisinger Museums, with art from central and northern Europe. A 6-year, $350-million renovation and expansion, completed in 2014, united the institutions under one roof and added a shop and a cafe (both open to the public without museum admission) as well as a 300-seat lecture hall. The facility is just outside the walls of Harvard Yard on its east side.

32 Quincy St. www.harvardartmuseums.org. © **617/495-9400.** $15 adults, $13 seniors, $10 students, free for kids 17 & under. Daily 10am–5pm. T: Harvard.

Harvard Museum of Natural History ★★ MUSEUM   The most-visited of Harvard's attractions, the museum has dinosaurs—including a Triceratops skull the size of a Smart car and a 42-foot-long prehistoric marine reptile—plus a spectacular Great Mammal Hall with land creatures behind glass at floor level and giant whale skeletons overhead. There's a splashy room of incredible sparkling gemstones, including a 1,600-pound amethyst geode from Brazil. Also here are the world-famous **Blaschka Glass Flowers,** 4,300 vividly realistic models of flowers, leaves, and other plants created by the father-and-son team Leopold and Rudolf Blaschka, from Dresden, Germany. (The gallery that houses many of the glass models was given an extensive renovation in 2016; many of the items nearly glow now.) The museum is just the right size for families with curious children, and a small gift shop has a smart collection of educational items. Note that the galleries are on the building's third floor (up 51 steps) and that the main entrance is not wheelchair-accessible. The North Entrance, on the left side of the building, is fully accessible and has an elevator.

26 Oxford St. www.hmnh.harvard.edu. ✆ **617/495-3045.** $12 adults, $10 seniors & students, $8 kids 3–18, free for kids 2 & under; free for Massachusetts residents year-round. Daily 9am–5pm. T: Harvard.

OTHER CAMBRIDGE ATTRACTIONS

One block from Harvard Yard, **Brattle Street** has been an exclusive address since Colonial times. Its first few blocks are a hodgepodge of interesting commerce, including restaurants, clothing stores, and a movie theater. Buildings then become primarily residential and University-affiliated. This section gained fame—and the nickname "Tory Row"—around the time of the Revolution because of its association with British sympathizers. The loyalists later evacuated, but some of their lovely homes survive.

Starting in the first block of Brattle Street closest to Harvard Square, the 1727 **William Brattle House** (no. 42) is the property of the nonprofit Cambridge Center for Adult Education. The 1969 **Design Research Building** (no. 48) is a splash of modern design, the work of Benjamin Thompson and Associates. The Cambridge Center for Adult Ed also owns the **Hancock-Dexter-Pratt House** (no. 54), constructed in 1811 and immortalized by poet Henry Wadsworth Longfellow, who saw the village blacksmith working here in the late 1830s, in his words, "under a spreading chestnut tree." The 1847 Gothic Revival **Burleigh House** (no. 85), also known as the Norton-Johnson-Burleigh House, adds a note of Victorian spookiness. **Stoughton House** (no. 90), is the work of H. H. Richardson, architect of Boston's Trinity Church, and was completed in 1883.

A few steps further is the star of the street: At No. 105 Brattle, the home of poet Henry Wadsworth Longfellow has been turned into the dual **Longfellow House–Washington's Headquarters National Historic Site** (www.nps.gov/long; ✆ **617/876-4491**). Longfellow lived here from 1843 until his death in 1882. He was first here as a boarder in 1837, but after he married Fanny Appleton, her father made the house a wedding present. The home had an earlier claim to fame, though: Built in 1759, it was George Washington's headquarters in 1775 and 1776, during the siege of Boston. The grounds and gardens are open year-round to visitors, and from May to October free 45-minute guided tours show off the interior (call ahead to confirm hours and tour times). Tours are $3 for adults, free for kids 15 and under.

About a half mile further on, the building at 159 Brattle is the **Hooper-Lee-Nichols House.** The original section of this building was built around 1685, making it the second-oldest house in Cambridge. It now contains the Cambridge Historical Society (www.cambridgehistory.org; ✆ 617/547-4252).

If you continue on Brattle Street about a half mile further, you reach the **Mount Auburn Cemetery ★★**, 580 Mt. Auburn St. (www.mountauburn.org; ✆ **617/547-7105**), dedicated in 1831, a prime example of the "garden cemeteries" that gained popularity as urban centers became too congested for downtown burying grounds. It's a particularly glorious combination of landscaping, statuary, sculpture, architecture, and history (it's on the National Register of Historic Places and a designated National Historic Landmark). Notable people buried here include museum founder Isabella Stewart Gardner, Christian Science founder Mary Baker Eddy, architect Charles Bulfinch, and abolitionist Charles Sumner. Stop by the visitors center in Story Chapel at the front gate, or check the online event calendar for walks, talks, and special events. It's open daily, summer 8am to 8pm and winter 8am to 5pm. Admission & self-guided tours are free, although note that, because Mount Auburn is an active cemetery, pets and picnicking are not allowed. It's a 30-minute walk from Harvard Square and on the 71 and 73 bus lines.

If you've come this far out of Harvard Square, consider going 1 block farther to the popular **Sofra Bakery and Cafe ★★**, 1 Belmont St. (www.sofra bakery.com; ✆ **617/661-3161**). As this compact eatery notes in an equally compact way on its website, "sweet and savory tastes of Turkey, Lebanon, and Greece are served here with a contemporary twist." It's the little sister to the esteemed restaurant **Oleana** (p. 120), on the other side of Cambridge.

Parks & Gardens

Together, the **Boston Public Garden ★★★** and the **Boston Common ★★** are the central green area of the city. Located where the Beacon Hill and Back Bay neighborhoods meet, these public parks are adjacent, but intersected by a busy thoroughfare. They have distinct personalities: Think of the Public Garden as Boston's front yard, carefully maintained and showy, and the Boston Common as the backyard, where the kids run around and play pickup baseball.

Bordered by Arlington, Boylston, Charles, and Beacon streets, the Public Garden is the prettiest park in Boston. Established in 1837, it was inspired by the gardens of Versailles. Today, its 24 acres are crisscrossed with walkways and formally arranged flowers, trees, and shrubs, as well as five fountains. The exquisite flowerbeds change regularly, complementing the perennial plantings. Note that there are no restrooms in here, although there are next door in the Common at its visitors center and Frog Pond.

At the western side of the Public Garden, poised at the Commonwealth Avenue entrance, is a dramatic **equestrian statue of George Washington.** With a backdrop of the city skyline, it creates one of the most picturesque tableaus in the city. The small body of water nearby is called the **lagoon.** It's a triumph of optical illusion—viewed from above, it's tiny, but from anywhere along the curving shore, it looks much more significant. It's home to swans and numerous ducks, who waddle about and swim between the shore and a teeny island in the northern end of the waters. It's crossed by a diminutive footbridge.

In keeping with the Victorian atmosphere of the Public Garden, simple pedal-powered vessels called **Swan Boats ★★** (www.swanboats.com; © **617/522-1966**) provide leisurely 12- to 15-minute rides around the lagoon (employees do the pedaling) from mid-April through early September Tickets are $4 for adults, $2.50 for kids 2 to 15, and free for kids under 2. Boats operate daily 10am to 4pm in spring and 10am to 5pm in summer.

Compared to the Boston Public Garden, the larger, rambling **Boston Common** (www.boston.gov/parks/boston-common) has less charm. Still, it's well used and has lots of foot traffic. At the northeastern end is the appealing **Frog Pond** (www.bostonfrogpond.com), which is a spray pool for children in summer, a popular ice skating rink in winter, and a reflecting pool the rest of the year. Also here is a small carousel and a small playground.

Winding along the eastern edge of the city, roughly following the contours of the waterfront, the **Rose Fitzgerald Kennedy Greenway ★★★** (www.rosekennedygreenway.org) is a new central green space for Boston. A raised highway dominated this part of Boston until 2008, but after the "Big Dig" public works project moved I-93 underground, this much-welcome walkway of connected parks filled in the scar that the highway left behind. The park is 1½ miles long and includes, at its northern end, an enchanting **carousel** (open year-round, subject to weather), fountains (including the family-friendly **Rings Fountain** with jet sprays to play in), the **Trillian Garden beer-garden** (corner of High Street and Atlantic Avenue; closed in winter), and sculptures, murals, and other engaging public artwork. Food trucks dot the cross streets. The Greenway concludes on its southern end near the central transport terminal South Station, at the city's financial district.

Near the northern end of the Greenway, adjacent to Long Wharf at 110 Atlantic Ave., **Christopher Columbus Park ★** (www.cityofboston.gov/parks) is another appealing green spot downtown. It includes a tot lot/jungle gym for smaller children, a fountain spray park, benches and lawn for lounging, a circular performance area that occasionally has musicians, and a dramatic central trellis draped with wisteria vines in warm weather and blue lights in winter.

For many Bostonians, the **Charles River Esplanade ★★** (www.esplanadeassociation.org), along the Boston side of the Charles River, is where we meet friends to go walking (or running, or biking, or skating). Its 64 car-free acres have green spaces for picnicking and paved paths for biking and running (paths on both sides of the river go all the way to Watertown, a suburb 8½ miles northwest of Boston). The **Hatch Shell amphitheater** is here, an Art Deco confection with a grass lawn where concerts are held throughout the summer—including the **July 4th spectacular** with the **Boston Pops** (p. 124). The narrow **Storrow Lagoon** within this park has postcard-pretty footbridges at either end and is surrounded by elaborate plantings and shady trees. The major entrance to the Esplanade is at the Charles/MGH T stop, although the park can be accessed by eight footbridges that cross over Storrow Drive, the highway that divides the city from the park and river.

Midway between the Seaport District and the dense residential streets of South Boston, the delightful **Lawn on D Street ★★**, 420 D St. (www.signature boston.com/lawn-on-d; © 877/393-3393) is an urban playground with a grassy lawn, food concessions, and occasional live music and festivals. Young adults throng here at night to chillax on huge glow-in-the-dark swings. The closest T is World Trade Center, and then it's a 10-minute walk.

Farther afield, in the Jamaica Plain neighborhood, the **Arnold Arboretum of Harvard University ★★**, 125 Arborway (www.arboretum.harvard.edu; © 617/524-1718), is a spectacular living museum of plant species from North America and Asia, and a natural retreat for locals and visitors. Paved and dirt trails weave in and out of towering conifers, hardy rhododendrons, and centenarian trees (100 years and older). In May, acres of lilacs come into bloom, and there's an impeccable bonsai collection on view April through October. After a snowfall the woodsy hills quickly fill with snowshoe and cross-country ski tracks. Because it's operated by Harvard University, there are ample opportunities to learn, including self-guided tours for kids or adults. The

arts, crafts, AND LOTS OF food IN THE SOUTH END

In the South End neighborhood, "SoWa"—which stands for "South of Washington (street)"—vibrates with artistic energy. **The SoWa Art + Design District** is a cluster of warehouses that have been converted to contemporary art galleries, boutiques, design showrooms, and artist studios. The complex at 460 Harrison Ave. (www.sowaboston.com/460-harrison-retail) is home to 40-some spaces running along perpendicular Thayer Street. The neighborhood is a 15-minute walk from the Back Bay T stop.

On Sundays from May through October, the lively outdoor **SoWa Open Market ★★**, 460 Harrison Ave. (www.sowaboston.com/sowa-open-market) brings together a crafts market, a circle of food trucks, and locally made food. Look for **Wild Pops** (www.wildpopsusa.com), whose options include insanely good Dark Belgian Chocolate fudgesicles. A beer garden serves up local beers, ciders, and wines in a converted Trolley Barn at 540 Harrison Ave. There's often live music, and the whole shebang is free and family-friendly (pets are welcome, too). It's open 10am to 4pm.

Throughout the year, **SoWa First Fridays** (www.sowaboston.com/sowa-first-fridays) brings a cocktail-party-like atmosphere to the galleries, shops, and showrooms. It takes place at 450-460 Harrison Ave. on the first Friday of every month from 5 to 9pm.

Hunnewell Building Visitor Center has a giant relief map and is wheelchair accessible, including the restrooms on the ground floor. It's open daily from sunrise to sunset, and admission is free. To get here, take the Orange Line subway to Forest Hills and follow signs to the entrance.

And even further afield, a visit to one or more of the islands that make up the **Boston Harbor Islands National and State Park** ★★ (www.boston harborislands.org) lets you combine a ferry ride, a beach visit, nature walks, and fort-exploring all in one outing. See p. 90 for details.

Organized Tours

TROLLEY TOURS   The fastest way to get the full lay of the land is to take a tour of the city. The orange-and-green **Old Town Trolley Tours** ★★ (www. trolleytours.com; ✆ **855/396-7433**) cover a lot of ground and allow visitors to hop off and then reboard throughout the day. If you buy tickets online they cost $40 (13 and older) and $20 (kids 4–12), and you can just hop on at any of 19 stops in the city. Tickets are also sold at 200 Atlantic Ave. (at the end of the Marriott Long Wharf Hotel, across the street from Faneuil Hall Marketplace), but if you buy tickets in person they cost significantly more—$77 adults, $41 for kids 4 to 12. (Children 3 and under travel free.) This is one case where it really pays to buy in advance.

SIGHTSEEING CRUISES   It's easy and exhilarating to take to the ocean from downtown Boston. The season runs from late March to mid-November.

Harbor cruise options from **Boston Harbor Cruises** ★★, One Long Wharf (www.bostonharborcruises.com; ✆ **617/227-4321**) include a 90-minute Historic Sightseeing Cruise, a 45-minute USS *Constitution* Cruise, a 40-minute Codzilla "high-speed thrill" boat ride, a 90-minute Sunset Cruise, and a 3-hour nighttime Sea the Stars Cruise, produced in conjunction with the Museum of Science (p. 74). Boats leave from the wharf next to the New England Aquarium; check website for times and prices, which vary considerably throughout the season.

Duck Boats: Boston by Land *and* by Sea

Despite safety issues in other cities, tours of Boston in a reconditioned World War II amphibious vehicle remain a popular way to explore the city. "**Duck Boats**" ★★ (www.bostonducktours. com; ✆ **617/267-3825**) trundle around the city streets before slipping into the placid waters of the Charles River basin for a cruise of about 20 minutes. Con-duck-tours (ouch) have licenses to operate the mammoth vehicles on both land and water, and they spin off historical highlights. It's a pricey ticket, but it does provide a unique combination of unusual perspectives and cooling breezes. There are departure points at the New England Aquarium, Museum of Science, or Prudential Center. Tickets are $42 for adults and youth 12 and over, $34 for seniors, $28 for kids 3 to 11, and $11 for kids 2 and under. Discounts are available online. All tickets are for a specific time. Check ahead for schedules. Duck boats operate daily mid-March to late November, from 9am to 1 hour before sunset.

Down in the Seaport District, lunch, dinner and sunset cruises are offered by **Spirit of Boston** (www.spiritcruises.com/boston; ✆ **617/748-1450**). These boats leave from 200 Seaport Blvd., at the Seaport World Trade Center. Prices range from $28 for a 1-hour cruise to $135 for a 3-hour dinner cruise with live music (children 2 and under free).

Lower-key tours of the quieter Charles River are offered by the **Charles Riverboat Company**, 100 CambridgeSide Place, Cambridge (www.charles riverboat.com; ✆ **617/621-3001**). Trips include narrated daytime cruises, narrated architecture cruises, and sunset drinking cruises. Tickets cost $19.50–$28.50 for adults, $12–$24.50 for children 3 to 12, and $3 children 2 and under. Boats leave from the CambridgeSide Galleria mall, a short walk from the Lechmere T station.

WHALE-WATCHING TOURS Straight east from Boston, in the Massachusetts Bay heading toward the Atlantic, there's a large section of ocean designated as the Stellwagen Bank Marine Sanctuary (www.stellwagen.noaa. gov) where whales live—humpback, finback, minke, pilot, and endangered right whales—as well as dolphins. The **New England Aquarium** (p. 74) runs **whale-watch trips** ★★ on customized catamarans (www.neaq.org/exhibits/whale-watch; ✆ **617/227-4321**). Tours run usually 3 hours, sometimes longer depending on where the whales are, and they almost always have a sighting of these magnificent, curious, playful creatures. Naturalists trained by the Aquarium are aboard each trip. Tickets are $53 for adults and youth 12 and older, $45 seniors, $33 kids 3 to 11, and $16 kids under 3. Discounted packages with Aquarium tickets are available. Trips run daily late March to mid-November. Check the website for times and frequency, which vary considerably throughout the season. Note that if you are heading up to Cape Ann (chapter 5) or down to Cape Cod (chapter 6), there will be whale-watch options there as well.

WALKING TOURS In addition to walking the Freedom Trail (p. 75) or the Black Heritage Trail (p. 74), you have many other options for guided walking tours in Boston. Some focus on food, others focus on taverns, and of course many focus on history. From May to October, the nonprofit **Boston by Foot** ★★ (www.bostonbyfoot.org; ✆ **617/367-2345**) conducts excellent historical and architectural tours that focus on neighborhoods or themes. The rigorously trained volunteer guides encourage questions. Tickets are $15 adults, $10 children 6 to 12; online purchases are discounted $2 per ticket. The popular **PhotoWalks** ★★ (www.photowalks.com; ✆ **617/851-2273**) builds tours around the aesthetic beauty of the city, including Beacon Hill, Back Bay, the North End, and the waterfront. Guide Saba Alhadi helps visitors find new angles on old subjects and get the best Instagrammable shots.

BIKE TOURS Urban AdvenTours ★★, 103 Atlantic Ave. (www.urban adventours.com; ✆ **617/670-0637**) offers a half-dozen 2- to 4-hour bike tours including a City View Tour, a Sunset Tour, and Funway to Fenway, which includes a tour of Fenway Park baseball stadium. Some of the tours run primarily on bike paths so are okay for beginning riders and children; others are recommended only for people who are comfortable cycling on city streets.

A DAY TRIP TO THE boston harbor islands

In the waters near South Boston, 34 islands ranging in size from small to miniscule make up the **Boston Harbor Islands National and State Park ★★** (www.bostonharborislands.org). Six are publicly accessible by **ferry** and can be visited for day trips (a couple have campgrounds, too). They offer majestic ocean views, hiking trails, historic sights, rocky beaches, nature walks, and picnic areas.

Visiting the islands is a raw experience: limited concessions, limited toilet facilities, and limited shelter from sun or rain. None are accessible by car. That said, a visit can be an invigorating adventure and one of the most memorable ways to experience Boston and the Atlantic waters.

Georges Island has the historic **Fort Warren** to explore. Built before the U.S. Civil War, it became a prison for Confederate officers; visitors can walk its dark corridors. (Keep an eye out for the Lady in Black ghost.) There are paved and mostly level paths on Georges, and a snack bar that's open daily in summer.

Spectacle Island, the highest point in the harbor, has spectacular views of Boston and the other harbor islands. It has 5 miles of trails, a swimming beach with lifeguards in summer, and a snack bar.

Peddocks Island has **Fort Andrews,** an active coastal fort decommissioned in 1946. Fort Andrew's brick barracks each housed over 100 soldiers; you'll also see elegant officers' quarters and a hospital.

In downtown Boston, the **Boston Harbor Islands Pavilion and Welcome Center** on the Rose Kennedy Greenway at 191 W. Atlantic Ave. (near Faneuil Hall Marketplace) is staffed by National Park Service rangers who can help plan your trip. Ferries (www.bostonharborcruises.com; ✆ **617/227-4321**) serving the islands leave from One Long Wharf behind the New England Aquarium and travel from May through October.

During the summer season, the trip to Georges is 40 minutes, the trip to Spectacle is 20 minutes, and the trip to Peddocks is 1 hour. Check the website for schedules. Round-trip fares are $17 for adults, $12 for seniors & students, $10 for kids.

Most tours are $55 per person; the Fenway Park tour is $119. Tours include bike rentals. Tours run rain or shine unless the company decides the weather conditions are too dangerous.

Especially for Kids

Not only is Boston a great "college town," given the 150,000 or so students who attend its 50-plus colleges and universities each year, but it's also a great city for children. World-class kid-centric museums cater to a range of interests, and there are engaging outdoor options both on land and on sea.

Children 9 and younger will be engaged by the **Boston Children's Museum** (p. 91), **Museum of Science** (p. 74), the **New England Aquarium** (p. 74), the **Harvard Museum of Natural History** (p. 84), and the parks, carousel, and splash fountains along the **Rose Kennedy Greenway** (p. 86). While some will enjoy the land-and-sea **Duck Boat tours** (p. 88), others may be just as happy on the more sedate **Swan Boat** rides (p. 86) in the Public Garden. At the **Museum of Fine Arts** (p. 73), family offerings include 2-hour in-gallery drawing for kids ages 5 to 8 every Saturday morning and a $4 audio/video mobile tour specially designed for ages 6 to 10 (see www.mfa.org/visit/mfa-guide/kids).

Children 10 and older will also like **whale watches** (p. 89), **sightseeing cruises** (p. 88), and a **ferry ride to the Boston Harbor Islands** (p. 90). Kids who love history should beeline to the **John F. Kennedy Library and Museum** (p. 72), the **Paul Revere House** (p. 77), or a walk along the **Freedom Trail** (p. 75). **Boston by Foot** (www.bostonbyfoot.org; ✆ **617/367-2345**) offers a 60-minute guided tour of the Freedom Trail designed especially for kids 6 to 12 years old (called "Boston by Little Feet"); check the website for prices, days, and times.

If you have time for a day trip, kid-centric destinations include the living villages of **Plimoth Plantation** (in Plymouth, a 45-min. drive from Boston; p. 176) **Old Sturbridge Village** (in Sturbridge, a 60-min. drive; p. 321); and the **Amazing World of Dr. Seuss Museum** (in Springfield, a 90-min. drive; p. 325). There's also **swimming at Walden Pond** (in Concord, a 30-min. drive from Boston; p. 145); and, in season, **apple picking** in Nashoba Valley (a 60-min. drive; p. 148).

Boston Children's Museum ★★★ MUSEUM/PLAY SPACE   For kids under 10 or so—the sweet spot is ages 1 to 7—this is one of the best play spaces in the city, with lots of stuff to climb on and crawl through and build on. Kids work in a "construction" area, create giant soap bubbles, shake it on an illuminated dance floor, visit a Japanese house, play grocery store in a bodega in the Boston Black wing, explore the laws of motion by whacking golf balls along room-long ramps, and scramble in and up **a three-story-tall climbing maze**. And that's just for starts. For children 3 and under, the **PlaySpace** room is packed with toys and activities and peers their size. Among several food options nearby, a favorite is **Pastoral** (345 Congress St., p. 114), which is fancy enough to feel special and still accommodating for kids.

308 Congress St. www.bostonchildrensmuseum.org. ✆ **617/426-6500.** $17 adults & children, free for kids under age 1; $1 Fri 5–9pm. Sat–Thurs 10am–5pm, Fri 10am–9pm. Check website for parking garages offering discounts with museum validation. T: Courthouse, or South Station & 10-min. walk.

When Your Child Needs to Run

If you're traveling with young children, you know that sometimes they just need open space to run or a good playground to spend a couple hours. In addition to the **Boston Children's Museum** (above), which is essentially a three-story playground, and the **Rose Kennedy Greenway** (p. 86), which has expanses of nice grass, there's also a small playground at the harbor in **Christopher Columbus Park** (p. 86) and a small playground on the northern end of the **Boston Common** (p. 85). The Common also has **Frog Pond,** which is a spray pool in summer and ice skating rink in winter. If you have a car, the good-sized (and free) **Artesani Playground, Spray Deck & Wading Pool,** 1255 Soldiers Field Rd., along the Charles River in Boston's Allston neighborhood, is a popular option, especially in summer. It's run by the state (www.mass.gov) and has a large, free parking lot.

Boston Fire Museum ★ MUSEUM A block away from the Boston Children's Museum, this small museum housed in a former firehouse displays artifacts from New England firehouses, metal toys, and amazing antique fire trucks. There's a very cool Ephraim Thayer Pumper, a vehicle constructed by Paul Revere in 1793. The volunteers are friendly and give out plastic fire hats to young visitors.

344 Congress St. www.bostonfiremuseum.com. © **617/338-9700.** Free admission. Check website for hours—it's open on a sporadic schedule. T: Courthouse, or South Station.

Boston Tea Party Ships & Museum ★ HISTORY MUSEUM A lot of history about the American Revolution gets crammed into a guided visit here, culminating with visitors participating in a tea party re-enactment by tossing bales of fake tea overboard under the encouragement of costumed patriots. The experience is corny, but many guests love it. The panoramic movie that simulates battlefield action might be intense for young visitors. Tickets are pricey; check online for discounts.

306 Congress St. www.bostonteapartyship.com. © **866/955-0667.** $28 adults, $25 seniors & students, $18 kids 5–12. Apr–Oct daily from 10am (last tour 5pm); Nov–Mar daily from 10am (last tour 4pm). Gift shop & tea room open 1 hr. earlier & stay open 1 hr. later. T: South Station.

Franklin Park Zoo ★ ZOO Boston's zoo is located in Franklin Park, the largest city park, about 6 miles south of city center. The zoo may not be world-class, but it's fine for a family outing. Warthogs and wildebeest live in the area called Serengeti Crossing; the lion and tiger live in Kalahari Kingdom. There's a large, appealing playground. The biggest stink is made about the giant Corpse flowers, which may or may not bloom in a given year. The stench they give off is unbearable but the experience is unforgettable. The closest subway stop is almost 2 miles away on the opposite site of the park, so we recommend driving (there's free parking) or taking a cab. The entrance

BOSTON'S independence day PARTIES

Even though the Declaration of Independence was actually signed in Philadelphia, Boston fervently embraces the July 4th holiday. **Boston Harborfest** (www.boston harborfest.com; © **617/439-7700**), is the city's 6-day party leading up to the Fourth of July concert and fireworks. Events include historical reenactments, boat tours, harborside concerts, and a Chowderfest. July 4th ends with a beloved tradition, the **Boston Pops Fireworks Spectacular** (www.july4th.org). The orchestra plays a free concert at the Hatch Shell amphitheater on the Charles River Esplanade, and spectators (hundreds of thousands, by some counts) spread out along both banks of the river and on the Longfellow and Mass Ave. bridges. Fireworks are set off from river barges.

Revolutionary celebrations of another sort continue later in the month, as a popular **Bastille Day Party** hosted by the French Cultural Center (www.french culturalcenter.org; © **617/912-0400**) takes over Marlborough Street in Back Bay for a nighttime celebration of Francophone cultures. The event sells out, so buy tickets in advance.

Patriots Day is a Massachusetts-only holiday that commemorates the events of April 18 and 19, 1775, when the U.S. Revolutionary War began. Ceremonies take place in Boston's North End at the **Old North Church** (www.oldnorth.com; ✆ **617/523-6676**) and the **Paul Revere House** (www.paulreverehouse.org; ✆ **617/523-2338**). Reenactments take place in suburban **Lexington** (p. 139), where a faux skirmish breaks out on the field now known as the **Battle Green,** and in **Concord** (p. 136), where simulated hostilities rage at the **North Bridge.** Consult the Battle Road Committee (www.battleroad.org) for information. Patriots Day is also **"Marathon Monday,"** the running of the **Boston Marathon** (p. 128).

is on the far eastern side of the park. The entrance is on the far eastern side of the park.

1 Franklin Park Rd. www.zoonewengland.org. ✆ **617/541-5466.** $20 adults and teens, $18 seniors, $14 kids 2–12; 15% discount for online purchases. Apr–Sept Mon–Fri 10am–5pm, Sat–Sun 10am–6pm; Oct–Mar daily 10am–4pm. T: Forest Hills.

Outdoor Activities

BEACHES   There are great beaches for swimming within 45- to 90-minute drives from downtown Boston. All have public parking and some add concessions. **Duxbury Beach** (www.duxburybeachpark.com) on the South Shore and **Plum Island** (p. 170) and **Crane Beach** (p. 162) on the North Shore are serene and beautiful. **Ogunquit Beach** (www.ogunquit.org) is a favorite, and although it's in Maine—see p. 613—it's only 78 miles away. It has a long, sandy beach, seaside parking and concessions, an ocean cliff walk, and a sweet little town with restaurants, a candy shop, and a toy store. It attracts many visitors from Québec, and many of the town's signs are in both English and French. **Walden Pond** (p. 145), in Concord, has a sandy beach and lifeguards in the summer.

BIKING   The **Charles River Bike Path** on both sides of the river goes all the way to Watertown, a suburb 8½ miles northwest of Boston (new bike path extensions even go beyond Watertown). Both sides are busy with bike commuters, runners, and walkers, especially closest to the city. You can enter and exit at many points along the way. Find a good PDF map online: www.mass.gov/eea/docs/dcr/parks/charlesriver/map-chasbasin.pdf.

In Cambridge, a section of **Memorial Drive** nearest to Harvard University is closed to cars on Sundays from 11am to 7pm (from the last Sunday of April to the second Sunday of November) and attracts leisurely and beginning bikers as well as in-line skaters.

In addition to **Blue Bikes** (p. 66), which are designed for short-term rentals (up to 2 hr. at a time) and available at outdoor kiosks all over the city, full-day rentals are available for $40 from **Urban AdvenTours,** 103 Atlantic Ave. (www.urbanadventours.com; ✆ **617/670-0637;** see p. 89 for details on their guided bike tours as well). Massachusetts requires that children 16 and under

Open Studio events (www.boston.gov/departments/arts-and-culture/boston-open-studios-coalition) are opportunities to visit artists in their work spaces and buy art from them directly. In Boston, 11 neighborhoods host open studio weekends, providing a unique way to explore new neighborhoods. Two of the most established are put on by **Jamaica Plain Arts Council** (www.facebook.com/JP OpenStudios) in September and **Fort Point Arts Community** (www.fortpoint arts.org) in May and October.

---

wear helmets. Bicycles can be brought on the MBTA (most subway lines and all buses, on bike racks) during certain hours. See www.mbta.com/bikes for complete details.

CLIMBING   Urban rock climbing space **Brooklyn Boulders Somerville,** 12A Tyler St., Somerville (www.brooklynboulders.com/somerville; ℃ **617/623-6700**) is the go-to spot in the region for indoor climbing. Day passes are $25 to $29 and include full access to the facility. Full gear rentals are $11.

GOLF   *Golf* magazine's "Best Courses You Can Play in Massachusetts" ranking lists **Granite Links Golf Club,** just south of the city in Quincy (www.granitelinksgolfclub.com; ℃ **617/689-1900**), at number 9. It's 6,873 yards and par 72. Greens fees are $75 to $150 depending on the time of day and day of the week and include a required golf cart. There's a strict dress code, detailed on the website.

Also open to the public: **Newton Commonwealth Golf Course,** in suburban Newton (www.sterlinggolf.com/newton; ℃ **617/630-1971**), a challenging 18-hole Donald Ross design. Greens fees are $18 to $40 depending when you play. For a quicker, less challenging outing, 9-hole **Fresh Pond Golf Course,** 691 Huron Ave., Cambridge (www.freshpondgolf.com; ℃ **617/349-6282**) is a 3,161-yard layout adjoining the Fresh Pond Reservoir; it charges $24 (or $35 for two rounds) on weekdays; $27 and $40 on weekends.

GYMS   There are 13 **Boston Sports Clubs** (www.bostonsportsclubs.com) in the city. All have gyms and classes, and a few have **pools,** including the locations at 505 Boylston St., 560 Harrison Ave., and South Station. A day pass costs $15.

ICE SKATING   For outdoor skating, Boston Common's **Frog Pond** becomes a picture-perfect rink in winter, with teeny lights decorating the surrounding trees. (Afterwards, head to nearby **L. A. Burdick Chocolate Shop,** p. 111, to indulge in hot chocolate and a sumptuous pastry.) Admission price is based on the skater's height: everyone 58 inches and over pays $6, everyone else is free. Skate rentals cost $12 for adults and $6 for kids.

For year-round indoor skating, **Warrior Ice Arena,** at 90 Guest St. in Boston's Brighton neighborhood (www.warrioricearena.com; ℃ **617/WARRIOR** [927-7467]), became the new city favorite when it opened in 2016. Built by New Balance (the athletic shoe company has its headquarters next door), it is also used by the Boston Bruins hockey team for training. Admission is $9 for ages 13 and up, $8 for kids 12 and under. Rentals are $5. On Friday nights, **Rock N' Skate** from 8 to 10pm is an all-ages events; admission is $10.

POOLS & SPRAY PARKS   Massachusetts' **Department of Conservation & Recreation** (www.mass.gov/orgs/department-of-conservation-recreation; ✆ **617/626-1250**) oversees dozens of facilities across the state. Its website includes a map of state-managed swimming pools, wading pools, and spray decks. In Boston, there are free spray parks in the Boston Common (p. 85) and on the Rose Kennedy Greenway (p. 86).

RUNNING   Novices and serious runners alike head to the **Charles River Bike Path** (p. 93), which is car-free (except at a handful of intersections) and scenic. The bridges along the river allow for circuits of various lengths. Specialty running shops host group runs that are open to runners of all speeds: check **Marathon Sports,** 671 Boylston St. (www.marathonsports.com; ✆ **617/267-4774**) and **Heartbreak Hill Running Company,** 652 Tremont St. (www.heartbreakhillrunningcompany.com; ✆ **617/391-0897**).

SAILING   In 1966, The Standells immortalized the Charles River with their pop song "Dirty Water"—back when the river was a mess. Today it's cleaner and attracts lots of boaters. Near the entrance to the Esplanade from the Charles/MGH T stop, the **Community Boating** boathouse, 21 David G. Mugar Way (www.community-boating.org; ✆ **617/523-1038**) rents sailboats, kayaks, and stand-up paddleboards to experienced boaters to take into the Charles River basin. Rentals cost $89 to $119 (depending on the vessel) for a sailboat for a day, $45 for a kayak or stand-up paddleboard.

WHERE TO STAY IN BOSTON & CAMBRIDGE

Book ahead if you can if you are traveling to Boston **between April and November,** when conventions, college graduations, and vacations increase demand. The popular **fall foliage season,** in September and October, keeps the city and its hotels busy.

Note that some Boston hotels have begun adding a facility fee of $15 to $30 to each night's room rate, ostensibly to cover access to Wi-Fi and onsite facilities such as fitness centers. Just like all the little fees that show up on a cable TV bill, these facility fees are mandatory for customers and can inflate the quoted room price.

If you're willing to stay outside the city, there are decently priced brand name chain hotels to consider. That can be a good trade-off—limited charm, but at a savings of $100 to $300 a night. Keep in mind that traffic going in and out of the city during rush hour can be stop and go (and truly brutal on the worst days), which cuts into your sightseeing time. Recommended options include **Best Western Plus Waltham Boston** (www.bestwestern. com; ✆ **844/235-7903**), **Hilton Garden Inn Boston Logan Airport**

Boston Hotels

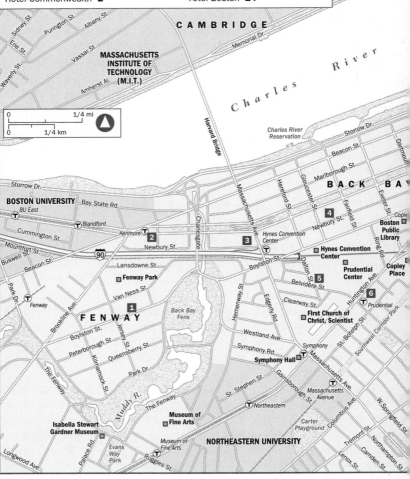

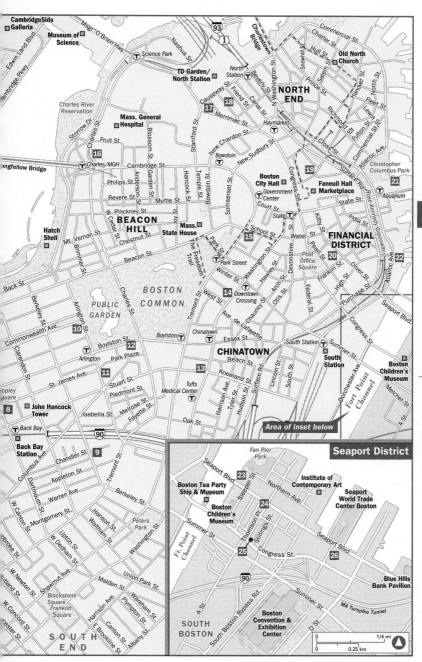

Seaport District

(www.hiltongardeninn3.hilton.com; ✆ **855/618-4697**), and **Sheraton Need-ham Hotel** (www.starwoodhotels.com; ✆ **781/444-1110**).

For an alternative to hotels, bed-and-breakfasts boast homey settings and give visitors an opportunity to connect with locals. They are often less expensive than hotels, too. **The Greater Boston Convention & Visitors Bureau** maintains a small list of B&Bs and inns that it recommends, at www.boston usa.com/hotels/bed-and-breakfast-inns.

Airbnb is active in Boston and the surrounding towns, too. As of late 2018 it lists over 300 rentals of single rooms and whole apartments in Boston alone, at **www.airbnb.com/s/BostonMA**. Keep in mind that proposed Massachusetts regulations for 2019 could add hefty hotel taxes to Airbnb rates (as much as almost 17.5%). The proposed regulations would also require rentals to be in full compliance with fire and other safety codes and be covered by a $1-million liability insurance policy.

4 Back Bay & Beacon Hill

EXPENSIVE

Fairmont Copley Plaza Hotel ★★   Ornate decor and courtly service make this hotel, built in 1912, a Boston classic. Posh furnishings will make you feel at home—if "home" is a mansion. The Copley Square location, across from the Boston Public Library, puts the elegant hotel in the center of the city and just steps from shopping on Newbury Street and in the malls at Copley Place and the Prudential Center. A rooftop health club has panoramic windows overlooking Back Bay, and its **OAK Long Bar + Kitchen** (p. 135) is glamorous. As with other Fairmont properties, pricier Fairmont Gold rooms include a private lounge serving evening hors d'oeuvres and a continental breakfast.

138 St. James Ave. www.fairmont.com/copleyplaza. ✆ **866/540-4417** or 617/267-5300. 383 units. Doubles $289–$729. T: Copley. Parking (valet) $53. **Amenities:** Restaurant; bar; babysitting; concierge; health club (rooftop); Wi-Fi ($11 or $20).

Four Seasons Hotel ★★★   Luxurious, pricey, and one of the loveliest hotels in New England, the Four Seasons offers its pampered guests everything they could ever want—for a price. It looks out onto the sublime **Boston Public Garden** and is close to everything. All rooms were renovated in 2017, heightening the elegance and sophistication of this property. Amenities include an indoor pool with floor-to-ceiling windows and a private Boston Duck Boat tour. The in-house **Bristol Bar** gets consistently good notice for its atmosphere and food.

200 Boylston St. www.fourseasons.com/boston. ✆ **617/338-4400.** 273 units. Doubles from $605. Parking (valet) $57. T: Arlington. **Amenities:** Restaurant; bar; babysitting; concierge; fitness center; indoor pool; spa; Wi-Fi (free).

MODERATE

Boston Park Plaza ★★   If you're looking for a bit of glamour without the price tag of the city's very highest-end options, the updated Park Plaza could be just the ticket. A $100-million overhaul completed in 2016 has spruced up the 1927 building, from the soaring lobby and grand ballroom to guest rooms, which have all been renovated. Keep in mind that the smallest units, called "Run of the House," are just 150 square feet (consider upgrading at least to a Deluxe if you're sharing). With a lot of rooms to fill and a hunger to reestablish itself as a go-to option, its prices are competitive.

50 Park Plaza. www.bostonparkplaza.com. ☏ **617/426-2000.** 1,060 units. Doubles $179–$350. Parking (valet) $51. T: Arlington. **Amenities:** Restaurant; bar; concierge; fitness center; Wi-Fi ($20 mandatory facilities fee).

Colonnade Hotel Boston ★★ Contemporary boutique style, old-fashioned service, and large guest rooms draw business travelers, while families come for all that plus an outdoor rooftop pool (May–Sept). Booking online earns benefits such as a 2pm checkout, a restaurant discount, and an upgrade at check-in.

120 Huntington Ave. www.colonnadehotel.com. ☏ **800/962-3030.** 285 units. Doubles $189–$309. Parking (self-park) $48. T: Prudential. **Amenities:** Restaurant; bar; concierge; fitness center; pool (rooftop; seasonal); Wi-Fi (free).

Eliot Hotel ★★★ A standout, even in a city with lots of options, this exquisite hotel combines the flavor of Yankee Boston with European-style service and amenities—it evokes Brahmin splendor without breaking the bank. Rooms are outfitted with cozy beds, Italian marble bathrooms, and bathrobes for two. On tree-lined Comm Ave, it feels more like a classy apartment building than a hotel, with a romantic atmosphere that belies the top-notch business features. Almost every unit is a spacious suite (others are standard doubles) furnished with antiques, and French doors separate the living rooms and bedrooms. The atmosphere contrasts pleasantly with the bustle of Newbury Street, a block away. Its busy Japanese restaurant, **Uni,** is overseen by celebrity chef Ken Oringer and open for breakfast and dinner—with late-night ramen available Friday and Saturday.

370 Commonwealth Ave. www.eliothotel.com. ☏ **800/443-5468.** 95 units. Doubles $195–$425. Parking (valet) $48. T: Hynes Convention Center. **Amenities:** Restaurant; bar; concierge; Wi-Fi (free).

The Liberty ★★ For some people, this will be a kick: a hotel stay in a former Boston lockup. From 1851 to 1990, the soberly dramatic Charles Street Jail served as the detention facility for Suffolk County. In a first-rate example of historic preservation and urban reuse, renovations turned the facility into an unlikely luxury hotel while keeping distinctly jail-like features: heavy wrought-iron doors, a soaring inner atrium with cat walks lining the perimeter of upper floors, and a former "drunk tank" with barred windows that now houses the hotel bar, **Alibi.** A hidden courtyard once served as the exercise yard for prisoners. The location is a good one, at the base of the handsome Charles Street shopping destination and residential Beacon Hill. The on-site restaurant **Scampo** (Italian for "escape") is helmed by esteemed chef-owner Lydia Shire.

215 Charles St. www.libertyhotel.com. ☏ **617/224-4000.** 298 units. Doubles $149–$515. Parking (valet) $57. T: Charles/MGH. **Amenities:** Restaurant; 2 bars; concierge; fitness center; Wi-Fi ($20 mandatory facilities fee).

Newbury Guest House ★ Housed in a trio of converted 1880s town houses, this sophisticated inn in Back Bay offers comfortable accommodations and New England charm. It's located on fashionable Newbury Street, one of the city's favorite boutique and walking thoroughfares. Full breakfast (eggs, bacon, fruit, croissants) is included.

261 Newbury St. www.newburyguesthouse.com. © **800/437-7668.** 32 units. Doubles $129–$429. Rates include breakfast. Parking (self-park) $20 (limited spots; reservations recommended). T: Hynes Convention Center. **Amenities:** Wi-Fi (free).

Sheraton Boston Hotel ★★ Huge and well-appointed, with tip-top service, this Sheraton has a central location next to the Hynes Convention Center, the Prudential Center shopping mall, and the Copley Place mall. Rooms have large windows (the better to enjoy those city views) and sleek, if generic, furnishings. Convention spouses like it for its fitness center, spa, and salon, while families come for its large indoor/outdoor pool and central locale. It's an easy walk to Fenway Park, Symphony Hall, and the Museum of Fine Arts.

39 Dalton St. www.sheratonbostonhotel.com. © **617/236-2000.** 1,220 units. Doubles $150–$450. Parking (valet) $58. T: Prudential. **Amenities:** Restaurant; concierge; pool (indoor/outdoor saltwater); fitness center; spa; Wi-Fi ($10).

Taj Boston ★★ With a peerless location facing the idyllic **Boston Public Garden,** this property was originally a Ritz-Carlton before the Indian luxury chain took it over. Rooms are stately, spacious for city accommodations, and offer a variety of views. The first-floor bar has floor-to-ceiling windows that face the Garden, while the elegant French Room serves afternoon tea and the rooftop dining room hosts a Sunday brunch from March to November. The hotel was purchased by a group of local real estate firms in 2016, so change may be in its future.

15 Arlington St. www.tajhotels.com/boston. © **617/536-5700.** 273 units. Doubles from $195. Parking (valet) $53. T: Arlington. **Amenities:** Restaurant; bar; babysitting; concierge; fitness center; Wi-Fi ($30 mandatory facilities fee).

The Westin Copley Place Boston ★★★ Travelers who want fresh, recently updated accommodations in the center of Back Bay action will want to stay at this smart hotel connected to the Hynes Convention Center. Even the smallest rooms are a comfortable 400 square feet, and streamlined decor in cool, muted colors make them feel even larger. All guest rooms are located on floors 8 through 36, providing spectacular views of the city. River views are the prettiest, and priciest. There's an in-house spa (with optional in-room treatments) and a 24-hour fitness center.

10 Huntington Ave. www.westin.com/copleyplace. © **617/262-9600.** 803 units. Doubles $151–$489. Parking (valet) $65. T: Copley. **Amenities:** 3 restaurants; bar; concierge; fitness center; Wi-Fi ($16 or $21).

Faneuil Hall Marketplace & Financial District

This area of the city includes the waterfront and harbor, where some of the city's most desirable properties are, and **Downtown Crossing,** just east of the

Boston Common. It also extends north to the newly revitalizing **West End,** which includes **North Station** and the **TD Garden,** where the Boston Celtics basketball team and Boston Bruins hockey team both play.

EXPENSIVE

Boston Harbor Hotel ★★★ Majestic and sweeping, with a 60-foot stone archway at its entrance, this hotel has become a signature structure along Boston's gracefully renovated harbor. It boasts gorgeous rooms to match its exterior, with marble bathrooms, expansive views of either the water or the Boston city skyline, and courtly service. Its **Rowes Wharf Sea Grille** has an appealing outdoor terrace in warm weather in an enclave alongside the harbor walk.

70 Rowes Wharf. www.bhh.com. ℂ **800/752-7077.** 230 units. Doubles $315–$1,045. Parking (valet) $55; self-park $49. T: Aquarium. **Amenities:** 2 restaurants (including outdoor terrace); 2 bars; concierge; health club with pool (indoor); spa; Wi-Fi (free).

Boston Marriott Long Wharf ★★ Across the street from Faneuil Hall Marketplace, next to the New England Aquarium, and jutting directly into the Boston harbor, this hotel is perfectly located for families. Rooms are large, with plenty of natural light, given that the standalone building has no neighbors directly adjacent. Rooms were renovated in 2018, and each unit has a desk, a convenient padded bench, and a comfy chair and ottoman. Bathrooms are sleek with marble tiled showers. A small pool has glassed-in walls and an outside deck to catch some rays.

296 State St. www.marriott.com/boslw. ℂ **617/227-0800.** 415 units. Doubles $265–$600. Parking (valet) $55. T: Aquarium. **Amenities:** Restaurant; concierge; fitness center; pool; Wi-Fi ($13 or $17).

The Godfrey ★★ Do you hear that buzz? The Godfrey opened in early 2016 and was immediately christened one of the coolest new urban hotels in the country by *Travel + Leisure.* Visitors and other press began heaping similar accolades on the facility, terming it "refined simplicity" and raving about **Ruka** (declared one of the city's "sexiest new restaurants" by *Zagat*), its bar (bartender Will Thompson was named best in the city by *Boston Magazine*) and its cafe (run by famed Boston coffee master George Howell). Its Downtown Crossing location is busy during the day with office workers and nearby mid-priced shopping, and quiet at night save for the nearby Boston Opera House, Paramount Center, and other hotels. A neat amenity: The hotel will find guests a "running mate" for a 6:30am run.

505 Washington St. www.godfreyhotelboston.com. ℂ **855/649-4500.** 242 units. Doubles $269–$719. Parking (valet) $55. T: Downtown Crossing. **Amenities:** Restaurant; bar; fitness center; Wi-Fi (free).

MODERATE

The Bostonian ★ Three renovated 19th-century buildings make up this stylish hotel directly across the street from Faneuil Hall Marketplace and on the Freedom Trail, putting visitors in the center of Boston's historic tourist area. Some rooms have balconies, and others have fireplaces.

26 North St. www.millenniumhotels.com/en/boston. ☎ **617/523-3600.** 204 units. Doubles $188–$475. Parking (valet) $51. T: Government Center. **Amenities:** Restaurant; bar; fitness center; Wi-Fi (free).

The Boxer Hotel ★★   Like the **Kimpton Onyx Hotel** (see below) around the block, this boutique hotel, opened in 2013 in a repurposed 1904 building, is in a neighborhood just south of North Station that is in a state of redevelopment. The hotel's slate grey industrial look highlights a fashion-forward urban design, with rooms that are small but sleek. The Boxer is the exclusive hotel partner of **City Winery Boston** (p. 131), a music and dining space a 5-minute walk from the front door.

107 Merrimac St. www.theboxerboston.com. ☎ **617/624-0202.** 80 units. Doubles $220–$485. Parking (valet) $47. T: Haymarket. **Amenities:** Restaurant; bar; fitness center; Wi-Fi (free).

Kimpton Onyx Hotel ★★   Close to Boston's Italian North End neighborhood and just a block from the TD Garden sports and music arena, the Onyx is an obvious option for visitors who are seeing an event at the stadium. The hotel's contemporary boutique decor befits the gentrifying neighborhood. As with many hotels in Boston, pets are welcome here.

155 Portland St. www.onyxhotel.com. ☎ **866/660-6699.** 112 units. Doubles $175–$390. Parking (valet) $47. T: Haymarket. **Amenities:** Restaurant; bar; concierge; fitness center; Wi-Fi ($15 mandatory facilities fee).

The Langham, Boston ★★   Thanks to its location in the heart of Boston's Financial District, the Langham is busy with business visitors during the week—and then does weekend leisure business at discounted prices. The most desirable units in the nine-story building overlook a pleasant park in Post Office Square (buildings surround the other three sides). The fitness center has a small lap pool surrounded by atrium windows. An Afternoon Tea includes sweet and savory nibbles and house tea served on Wedgwood china. Updates are scheduled for 2018.

250 Franklin St. www.boston.langhamhotels.com. ☎ **617/423-2844.** 317 units. Doubles $239–$594. Parking (valet) $49 (Sun–Thurs); $46 (Fri-Sat). T: State. **Amenities:** 2 restaurants; bar; concierge; fitness center; pool; spa; Wi-Fi (free).

Omni Parker House ★   In business since 1855 and claiming the title "America's longest continuously operating hotel," the Parker House offers a range of rooms, with most on the extremely compact end of the scale. The public spaces have a 19th-century old-world grandeur, and the hotel is right on the Freedom Trail. But its real claim to fame is being the acknowledged inventor of both the Boston cream pie and buttery Parker House dinner rolls. Both are available here and generate their own tourist traffic.

60 School St. www.omniparkerhouse.com. ☎ **888/444-6664.** 551 units. Doubles $99–$530. Parking (valet) $51. T: Government Center. **Amenities:** Restaurant; 2 bars; fitness center; Wi-Fi ($10).

Boston has two convention centers, which keep hotels busy on both sides of town. **Hynes Convention Center** is located in the city's sophisticated and established Back Bay, at 900 Boylston St., and is near the Prudential Center and Copley Square. **Boston Convention and** **Exhibition Center** is in the Seaport District, at 415 Summer St., near a burgeoning set of activities and restaurants in that hot neighborhood. **Massachusetts Convention Center Authority** (www. massconvention.com; ✆ **617-954-2000**) has information about both venues.

Seaport District
EXPENSIVE

Envoy Hotel ★★   New in 2015 and named Best Boutique Hotel by *Boston* magazine in 2017, this chic and contemporary property has a nice sizzle: All rooms have floor-to-ceiling windows that look out on either the city skyline or the waterfront, and custom-made furniture includes quirks such as TV stands made from bicycle frames. Beds are pillow-top Serta Perfect Sleepers. The rooftop bar on the sixth floor is at just the right angle to provide a 270-degree view of both the city skyline and the harbor.

70 Sleeper St. www.theenvoyhotel.com. ✆ **617/530-1559.** 136 units. Doubles $340 and up. Rollaway beds are not available. Parking (valet) $49. T: Courthouse. **Amenities:** Restaurant, rooftop bar (May–Oct); concierge; fitness center; Wi-Fi (free).

MODERATE

Residence Inn by Marriott Boston Downtown/Seaport ★★   Name notwithstanding, this hotel is located on the Seaport District side of the Fort Point Channel, in a central location close to excellent restaurants, the Boston Children's Museum, and the Boston Convention and Exhibition Center. In a former life, the historical building was a 1901 warehouse, and rooms boast 12-foot ceilings and exposed beams and brick. All rooms are studios or one-bedroom suites, all with fully equipped kitchens.

370 Congress St. www.marriott.com/bosfp. ✆ **617/478-0840.** 120 units. Doubles $214–$434. Rates include breakfast. Parking (valet) $45; (self-park) $29. T: Courthouse. **Amenities:** Fitness room; kitchenettes; Wi-Fi (free).

Seaport Hotel ★★   A business-traveler favorite—it's across the street from the World Trade Center Boston and boasts a sleek fitness center—this expansive hotel also attracts families for its kid-savvy staff, heated indoor pool, and proximity to the Boston Children's Museum. Guest rooms have a restful, neutral-toned decor, with natural light pouring in through huge windows with either city or harbor views.

1 Seaport Lane. www.seaportboston.com. ✆ **877/732-7678.** 428 units. Doubles $152–$413. Parking (valet) $47; (self-park) $37. T: World Trade Center. **Amenities:** Restaurant; bar; concierge; health club; pool (heated, indoor); Wi-Fi (free).

Yotel Boston ★   New in 2017 and stylish in a bleeding-edge kind of way, this Boston outpost of a small UK-based chain features teeny rooms that it calls "cabins" (inspired, it says, "by the luxury of first-class travel"—the rooms looks like space-age cruise line cabins). They're cleverly designed, but make sure to look at photos before booking to know what you're getting into. There's a lobby-level bar and a beautiful 12th-floor rooftop lounge that is popular on DJ nights. A sister restaurant, **Yo! Sushi**, is down the block at 79 Seaport Blvd. (www.yosushiusa.com; ☎ **857/400-0797**).

65 Seaport Blvd. www.yotel.com/boston. ☎ **617/377-4747**. 326 units. Doubles $115–$529. Parking (valet) $49. T: Courthouse. **Amenities:** Bar (rooftop); fitness center; Wi-Fi (free).

South End
MODERATE
The Alise Boston ★★   Formerly the Chandler Inn, this 56-unit boutique hotel was purchased in 2018 by the Staypineapple hotel chain, which has given it a makeover including all-new beds, bedding, and chill fixtures. It's located in the residential South End, the city's predominant gay neighborhood. It's a good choice to get a taste of Boston that's just off the tourist track. Rooms are small, with no closets and tight bathroom quarters, but its ground floor **Trophy Room** restaurant and bar often stays busy until 2am.

26 Chandler St. www.chandlerinn.com. ☎ **800/842-3450**. 56 units. Doubles $159–$334. No on-site parking. T: Back Bay. **Amenities:** Restaurant; bar; Wi-Fi ($15 mandatory amenity fee).

Chinatown/Theater District
INEXPENSIVE
Hostelling International Boston ★   Well-located in the theater district around the corner from the Wilbur (p. 129) and the Boch Center (p. 125) and a few blocks from the Boston Common, this six-story hostel is popular year-round. Visitors can stay in either shared dorms or private rooms with their own bathrooms. Linens and blankets are provided as well as a free continental breakfast. The hostel is open 24 hours a day. The maximum stay is 14 nights per calendar year and accommodations are only available to guests who live outside a 30-mile radius of the hostel—both to help insure that the clientele are travelers and not locals.

19 Stuart St. www.bostonhostel.org. ☎ **888/464-4872**. 481 beds. Dorm beds $30–$65, private units $100–$230 w/breakfast. No on-site parking. T: Boylston. **Amenities:** Shared guest kitchen; Wi-Fi (free).

Kenmore Square
MODERATE
Hotel Commonwealth ★★   In 2015, the hotel added 96 new rooms in a $50-million expansion that included a new terrace with a view (across the Mass Pike) of **Fenway Park.** As the *Boston Globe* raved: "With mod lighting, cool wall art, a sofa that resembled a Chanel jacket, a sleek bathroom, and a lot of houndstooth upholstery . . . this is exactly what a hotel room should look

and feel like." It was awarded Best of Boston by *Boston* magazine in 2017. The hotel is convenient to Boston University as well as the baseball park.

500 Commonwealth Ave. www.hotelcommonwealth.com. ✆ **866/784-4000.** 245 units. Doubles $179–$529. Parking (valet) $53. T: Kenmore. **Amenities:** 2 restaurants; bar; fitness center; Wi-Fi (free).

Verb ★★ With Verb, Boston finally gets the rock 'n' roll hotel it deserves. Unveiled in 2014 in a renovated 1959 motel, Verb sits in the shadow of the city's historic baseball stadium, Fenway Park, and is rich in the neighborhood's rock history—and managed with care by the former GM of the Four Seasons Hotel Boston. Artwork includes framed covers of the old pop culture magazine *Boston Phoenix* and photos from the beloved (and long gone) Kenmore Square punk venue The Rat. Rooms surround an outdoor pool and some of the windows are candy-colored, lending a cheery pop and sizzle to the retro-chic locale.

1271 Boylston St. www.theverbhotel.com. ✆ **617/566-4500.** 93 units. Doubles $169–$459. Rates include continental breakfast. Parking (valet) $48. T: Kenmore. **Amenities:** Restaurant; bar; pool (outdoor, seasonal); Wi-Fi (free).

Cambridge
EXPENSIVE
The Charles Hotel ★★★ Tucked into the side of Harvard Square next to Harvard University's Kennedy School, Cambridge's finest hotel boasts top-notch accommodations, access to a high-end health club and spa, and a superb in-house jazz club (**Regattabar,** p. 130). The good-size rooms mix and match styles: Unfussy New England Shaker touches contrast with pampering details.

1 Bennett St. Cambridge. www.charleshotel.com. ✆ **800/882-1818.** 295 units. Doubles from $250. Parking (valet) $40. T: Harvard. **Amenities:** 2 restaurants; bar; jazz club; concierge; health club; jazz club; spa; Wi-Fi (free).

MODERATE
Kimpton Marlowe Hotel ★★ This posh business hotel near MIT and the Museum of Science also appeals to families, thanks to its good-sized rooms that are elegantly decorated with funky accents. There's a special "milk and cookies" room service delivery for kids—and, for adults, a complimentary wine and snacks happy hour. The hotel has an appealing courtyard that faces a small canal inlet off the Charles River, and offers free kayaks and bikes for borrowing.

25 Edwin H. Land Blvd. www.hotelmarlowe.com. ✆ **800/825-7140** or 617/868-8000. 236 units. Doubles $146–$330. Parking (valet) $43; (self-park) $30. T: Lechmere. **Amenities:** Restaurant; bar; concierge; fitness center; Wi-Fi ($13; free for IHG Rewards members).

Royal Sonesta Hotel ★★ Like the Kimpton Marlowe Hotel (see above) across the street, this luxurious hotel offers easy access to MIT, the Museum of Science, and Boston itself. Spacious rooms provide river and city views, and there's an atrium-style lap pool with natural light from sliding glass walls and a sun deck in summer. This hotel goes out of its way to call itself a "gay

Cambridge Hotels & Restaurants

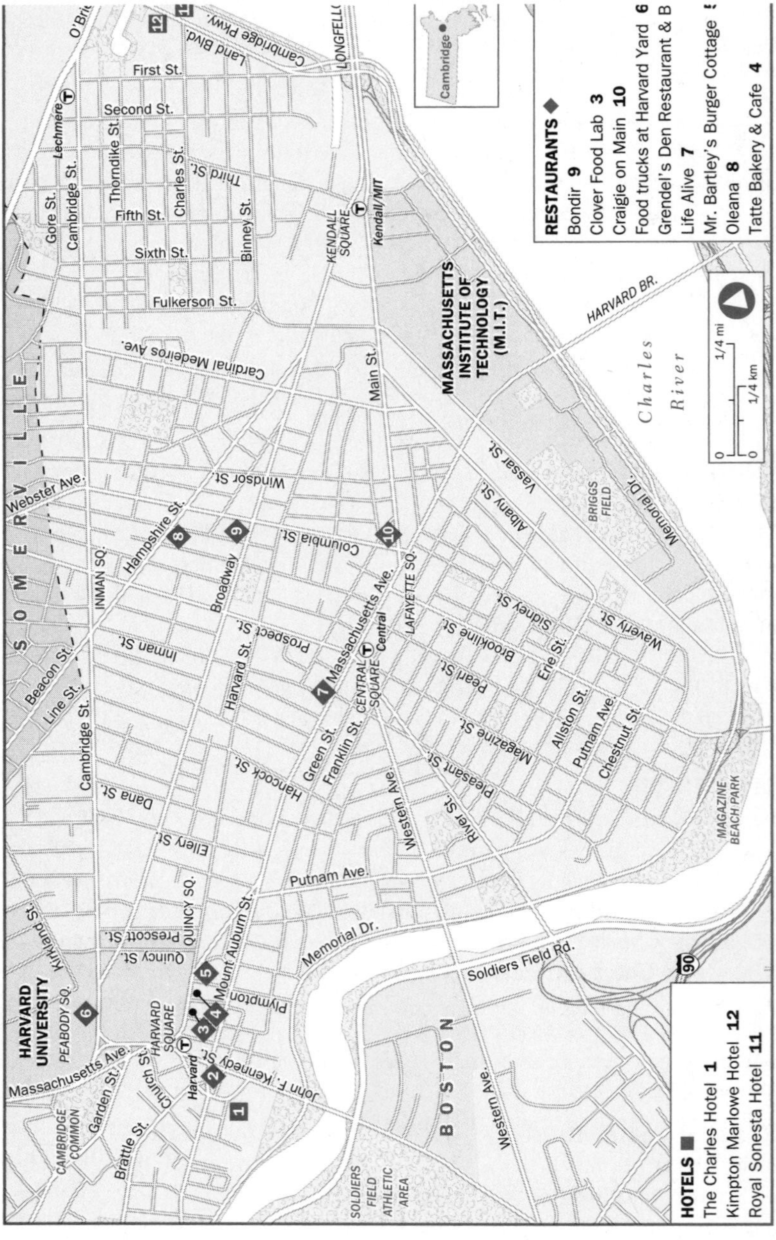

RESTAURANTS ◆

Bondir **9**
Clover Food Lab **3**
Craigie on Main **10**
Food trucks at Harvard Yard **6**
Grendel's Den Restaurant & B
Life Alive **7**
Mr. Bartley's Burger Cottage **!**
Oleana **8**
Tatte Bakery & Cafe **4**

HOTELS ■

The Charles Hotel **1**
Kimpton Marlowe Hotel **12**
Royal Sonesta Hotel **11**

friendly hotel" and state that it "celebrates diversity and supports the LGBT community."

40 Edwin H. Land Blvd. www.sonesta.com/boston. ℭ **617/806-4200.** 400 units. Doubles $159–$529. Parking (valet) $45; (self-park) $42. T: Lechmere. **Amenities:** Restaurant (with riverside patio); bar; concierge; fitness center; indoor pool; Wi-Fi (free).

WHERE TO EAT IN BOSTON & CAMBRIDGE

Many of the country's biggest companies are headquartered in Boston or have major offices here, including General Electric, Liberty Mutual Insurance, the TJX Companies, and Wayfair. Other large employers include the area hospitals, such as Massachusetts General Hospital, and its universities, including Harvard, MIT, and Boston University. Everyone who works in these places needs to eat, and many of them host guests from outside the city. The result is a vibrant and ever-changing food scene, fueled by a thriving economy.

As in other cities, the more expensive restaurants often have less pricey menus at lunchtime. And it's always a good idea to **make reservations** for dinner and lunch at the moderate and high-end venues.

Back Bay & Beacon Hill
EXPENSIVE

Davio's ★★ STEAKS/NORTHERN ITALIAN   Robust cuisine in a business-chic setting makes this excellent restaurant a hit with diners in search of top-notch Northern Italian cuisine, picture-perfect steakhouse offerings, and inventive-comfort-food sides. Steakhouse favorites and creative starters like Philly cheesesteak spring rolls share the menu with Northern Italian classics, including a sumptuous lobster risotto. Somehow, it works beautifully.

75 Arlington St. www.davios.com. ℭ **617/357-4810.** Main courses $20–$59. Mon–Tues 11:30am–10pm; Wed–Fri 11:30am–11pm; Sat 5–11pm; Sun 11am–10pm. T: Arlington.

L'Espalier ★★★ FRENCH   Boston's most esteemed white tablecloth restaurant is elegant, elaborate, and romantic. This is the place to pull out the stops for a special occasion. Tasting menus are featured, although guests can mix and match from anything available that day to create their own menu. Elegant options might include butter-poached lobster with nettles, bok choy, and three-cornered leeks, or foie gras terrine with poached pear, white port Meyer lemon jam, rhubarb, and ginger brioche. As befits a haute cuisine French restaurant, there is a lavish cheese selection. Vintner's tastings are offered that pair with the food tasting menus. After years in an intimate Boston town house, the restaurant is now located inside the Mandarin Oriental hotel.

774 Boylston St. www.lespalier.com. ℭ **617/262-3023.** Lunch main courses $31, tasting menus $68 and $108. Dinner tasting menus only, $98, $118, $280. Tues–Sun 11:30am–2:30pm; daily 5:30–10:30pm; afternoon tea Sat–Sun 1:30–2:30pm. Dress code: "Jacket and tie most comfortable, but not required." T: Copley.

Boston Restaurants

Aquitaine Bar á Vin Bistrot **19**
Artú - Beacon Hill **22**
Artú - North End **36**
The Barking Crab **45**
Barcelona Wine Bar **20**
Boloco **15**
Boston Public Market **25**
Bova's **30**
Clover Food Lab **24**
The Daily Catch **35**
Davio's **13**
Durgin-Park **27**
Faneuil Hall Marketplace food court **28**
Flour Bakery + Café **40**
Galleria Umberto Rosticceria **33**
Hei La Moon **17**
L'Espalier **7**
L. A. Burdick Chocolate Shop **11**
La Famiglia Giorgio **31**
Legal Harborside **44**
Legal Sea Foods - Copley Place **10**
Legal Sea Foods - Park Plaza **14**
Mamma Maria **37**

Mike's City Diner **4**
Mike's Pastry **34**
Modern Pastry **32**
Myers + Chang **21**
Neptune Oyster **38**
Parish Cafe and Bar **12**
Pastoral **41**
Petit Robert Bistro **9**
Pho Pasteur **16**
Piattini Wine Café **6**
Regina Pizzeria **29**
Row 34 **42**
South End Buttery **3**
South End Buttery cafe/market **18**
Sweet Cheeks **1**
Sweetgreen **8**
Tasty Burger **2**
Tatte Bakery & Cafe **23**
Toro **5**
Trade **39**
Union Oyster House **26**
Wagamama **43**

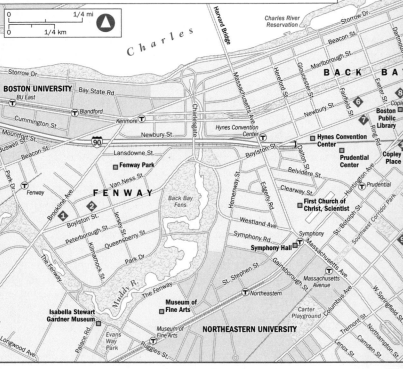

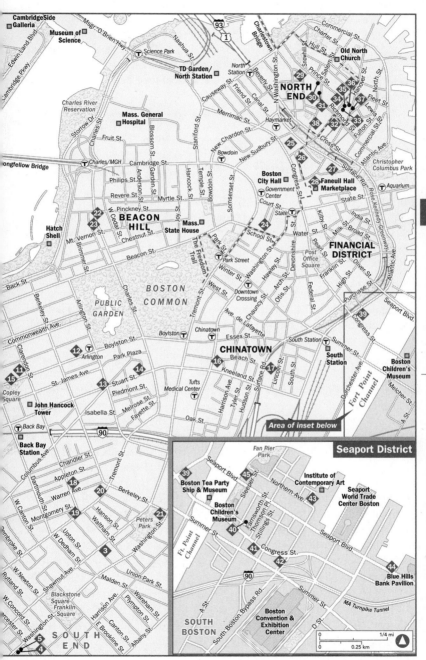

Seaport District

MODERATE

Legal Sea Foods ★★★ SEAFOOD   The city's reigning seafood chain has over a dozen outposts in the area, counting the airport and nearby Cambridge. Its food is uniformly excellent, from starters like oysters and clam chowder and crab cakes to full-on seafood entrees. There's a long dessert menu, but why look farther than Boston cream pie, perhaps paired with a nice tawny port? When in Rome . . . check the website for locations; three prominent ones are listed here.

26 Park Plaza. www.legalseafoods.com. © **617/426-4444.** Main courses $17–$36. Mon–Thurs 11:30am–11pm; Fri–Sat 11:30am–midnight; Sun noon–11pm. T: Arlington. Also in Copley Place mall, 100 Huntington Ave. (© **617/266-7775;** Mon–Thurs 11am–10pm, Fri–Sat 11am–11pm, Sun noon–10pm; T: Back Bay.) Also in the Seaport District, 270 Northern Ave. (© **617/477-2900;** check website for hours at each of 3 restaurants here; T: World Trade Center.

Parish Cafe and Bar ★★ AMERICAN   The conceit here is clever: Ask some of Boston's star chefs for a sandwich recipe, then put them all onto one menu. Parish Cafe has made it work for over 25 years, providing guests sneak peeks into the flavor profiles of restaurants all over the city. The menu has been updated over the years, but it's kept a long-time favorite: the Zuni Roll, by Norma Gillaspie: smoked turkey, bacon, scallions, dill Havarti cheese, and cranberry chipotle sauce in a warm tortilla with a side of sour cream. The restaurant is busy with the office crowd at lunch and after work for drinks, and has an appealing front patio for outdoor dining. The kitchen serves the full menu until 1am, with the bar open until 2am.

361 Boylston St. www.parishcafe.com. © **617/247-4777.** Sandwiches & main courses $10–$20. Mon–Sat 11:30am–1am; Sun noon–1am. T: Arlington.

Petit Robert Bistro ★★ FRENCH   The 2018 closing of downtown's Brasserie Jo sent fans of that classic brasserie looking for new options, and many will be happy to rediscover Petit Robert. The cozy bistro, open since 2005, offers a casual, classic French experience. Starters include escargots and onion soup with a gooey melted cheese crust, and mains include lemon asparagus risotto, steak frites, and the much lauded Coquille Saint Jacques—scallops with braised leeks, saffron sauce, and puff pastry. Weekend brunch offerings run from omelets and quiche to classic moules frites. About 20 wines are offered by the glass. Paris-style, tables are close together; a small front patio buzzes in warm weather. With Symphony Hall a short walk away, it's a good option before or after a Boston Symphony or Pops concert. Petit Robert's sister restaurant, Frenchie Wine Bistro (p. 134), is at 560 Tremont St.

480 Columbus Ave. www.petitrobertbistro.com. © **617/867-0600.** Main courses $22–$32. Mon–Wed 11am–10pm; Thurs–Fri 11am–11pm; Sat 10am–11pm; Sun 10am-10pm. T: Mass. Ave.

Piattini Wine Café ★★ ITALIAN   A great value on the Newbury Street shopping mecca, this café especially shines at lunch, where the pasta, panini, and pizzas are all $8 to $14, with most priced right at $10—including the spinach gnocchi with pesto cream sauce, the homemade fusilli with Bolognese sauce, and the chicken parm panini. There's an outside patio in good weather.

226 Newbury St. www.piattini.com. 📞 **617/536-2020.** Main courses $16–$28. Daily 11am–11pm (lunch begins at 11:30am). T: Copley.

INEXPENSIVE

Boloco ★★ BURRITOS Tasty, consistent, and cheery, this Boston fast-casual chain (there are seven locations in the city—check website for others) is a dependable option for a quick, healthy meal. Burritos and bowls come in flavors such as Bangkok Thai (peanut sauce, Asian slaw, cucumbers, brown rice) and The Summer (mango salsa, melted cheese, black beans, rice), with a full range of protein options including chicken, steak, pork carnitas, and tofu. This branch has an enviable location looking out onto Boston Common.

176 Boylston St. www.boloco.com. 📞 **617/778-6772.** All items $9 or less. Mon–Fri 8am–10pm; Sat–Sun 9am–10pm. T: Boylston.

L. A. Burdick Chocolate Shop ★★ CAFE Cute and cozy, this little cafe—tucked inside a teeny house next to a skyscraper—serves hot and iced chocolate, coffee and tea, and luscious pastries. It's also a retail location for the New Hampshire–based luxury chocolatier (see p. 577 in chapter 12), whose dreamy confections include its signature chocolate mice.

220 Clarendon St. www.burdickchocolate.com. 📞 **617/303-0113.** About $10 for a drink & a pastry. Mon–Thurs 10am–8pm; Fri–Sat 8am–8pm; Sun 10am–8pm. T: Arlington.

Sweetgreen ★★ LIGHT FARE The "salad-as-star" trend is a welcome one, and purveyor Sweetgreen has taken Boston's lunch crowds by storm with its healthy and hearty salads and grain bowls. Dishes are made to order and tossed in a big mixing bowl, making the resulting salad easy to dig right into. Kale Caesar salad and the Harvest Bowl—with kale, apples, sweet potatoes, roasted chicken, goat cheese, and toasted almonds—are popular standbys.

659 Boylston St. www.sweetgreen.com. 📞 **617/936-3464.** Salads and bowls $9–$12. Daily 10:30am–10:30pm. T: Copley. Check website for additional locations.

Tatte Bakery & Café ★★ LIGHT FARE Cozy and bright, Tatte (say "tah-tee") is a perfect place to relax with a pistachio croissant, avocado tartine with peppery arugula, or sweet potato tarte Tatin. Breakfast, lunch, and dinner are served Monday through Thursdays and brunch is offered all day Friday through Sunday at this outpost of the small regional chain, which has eleven locations around Greater Boston. In nice weather, try to snag an outdoor table.

70 Charles St. www.tattebakery.com. 📞 **617/723-5555.** Main courses $9–$14. Mon–Fri 7am–8pm; Sat 8am–8pm; Sun 8am–7pm. T: Charles/MGH. Check website for additional locations.

Faneuil Hall Marketplace & Financial District

The food court in Faneuil Hall Marketplace (www.faneuilhallmarketplace. com/boston-restaurants) has a wide variety of options, including Boston Chowda, Carol Ann Bake Shop, El Paso Enchiladas, Jen Lai Noodle and Rice Co., mmMac n' Cheese, Steve's Greek Cuisine, and Ueno Sushi. There are

Boston's cold winters keeps people indoors for half the year, so when it warms up, folks pour into the outdoors. It used to be difficult to find sidewalk dining outside of **Newbury Street** in Back Bay, but that's changed (although Newbury Street is still a good destination for sidewalk and patio options, such as the Piattini Wine Café, p. 110). On the water, both **The Barking Crab,** 88 Sleeper St. (p. 114) and **Rowes Wharf Sea Grille,** 70 Rowes Wharf at the Boston Harbor Hotel (www.rowes wharfseagrille.com; daily 7am–10pm) have cozy waterside patios. In the Seaport District, **Yotel,** 65 Seaport Blvd. (p. 103) has a rooftop lounge and terrace, and **Legal Harborside,** 270 Northern Ave. (p. 134) has both a patio and a large roof deck, both serving food.

tables indoors, and the Rose Kennedy Greenway and Christopher Columbus Waterfront Park are both a short walk away for picnicking. Food trucks also set up year round on the cross streets of the Greenway.

EXPENSIVE

Trade ★★ MEDITERRANEAN   Chef Jody Adams presents Mediterranean food and cocktails in this upscale, elegant restaurant anchoring a busy corner near the financial district. Select a spread of small plates to share tapas-style—such as Aleppo grilled shrimp, lamb sausage flatbread, and anything with muhammara, a tasty spread made from red pepper, pomegranate molasses, and walnuts—or go for full entrees such as seared Arctic char with cucumbers and mint or lentils with coconut greens and curried mushrooms. Adams' Baked Alaska, featuring mango sorbet, is worth the trip alone.

540 Atlantic Ave. www.trade-boston.com. ✆ **617/451-1234.** Main courses $23–$29. Mon–Thurs 11:30am–10pm; Fri 11:30am–11pm; Sat 5:30–11pm; bar open later every night. T: South Station.

Union Oyster House ★ NEW ENGLAND/SEAFOOD   The country's oldest restaurant (since 1826) is on the Freedom Trail and gets enough tourists to justify a gift shop. The food is pricey—you're paying for *ye olde* atmosphere—but the chowders and oyster options get consistently good marks. There are sit-down tables and counter seats around the oyster shucking bar. President John F. Kennedy apparently was a regular, and the upstairs dining room has a dedicated "Kennedy Booth" at the spot the restaurant says was his favorite.

41 Union St. www.unionoysterhouse.com. ✆ **617/227-2750.** Main courses $22–$39. Sun–Thurs 11am–9:30pm; Fri–Sat 11am–10pm. T: Haymarket.

MODERATE

Durgin-Park ★★ NEW ENGLAND   A true old-timey Boston landmark, with the tagline "Established before you were born," Durgin-Park serves up classic New England fare: Boston baked beans, chicken pot pie, Yankee pot roast, prime rib, boiled scrod, and a full New England Clambake (clam chowder, steamers, lobster, boiled potato, and corn on the cob). Long communal tables with red-and-white-checked tablecloths give the dining rooms a board-inghouse feel, but they're not terribly noisy and the overall ambiance is warm and convivial.

340 Faneuil Hall Marketplace. www.arkrestaurants.com/durgin_park. © **617/227-2038.** Main courses $13–$35. Daily 11:30am–9pm. T: Government Center.

INEXPENSIVE

Boston Public Market ★★ FOOD COURT   New in 2015, this indoor market has given local farmers a permanent downtown home and consumers a year-round market. You can get food to eat here or to take out. Vendors include **Union Square Donuts** (its maple bacon donut is a standout); **Taza Chocolate** (with both iced and hot chocolate drinks), **Boston Smoked Fish Company** (whose haddock is smoked at the Boston Fish Pier); **Beantown Pastrami Company** (for sandwiches), and **Red Apple Farm** (featuring cider from Massachusetts apples).

100 Hanover St. www.bostonpublicmarket.org. © **617/973-4909.** Mon–Sat 8am–8pm, Sun 10am–8pm. T: Haymarket.

Clover Food Lab ★★ VEGETARIAN/VEGAN   A graduate of Boston's food-truck scene, Clover started in 2008 with extremely popular trucks serving vegetarian and vegan fare to MIT students and staff (its founder is an MIT alum), and now has 12 brick-and-mortar locations throughout the Boston, Cambridge, and nearby suburbs. (Check website for other locations.) Standouts include its egg and eggplant sandwich, French fries with rosemary, and mezze platter of vegetables. There's an appealing selection of hot and iced teas, coffees, and fresh juices. Bonus: The restaurant is certified Kosher.

27 School St. www.cloverfoodlab.com. No phone. Most items $10 or less. Mon–Fri 7am–11pm; Sat 8am–11pm; Sun 8am–8pm. T: Park St.

Seaport District

Boston has had seaport activity in this part of the city for over 150 years, but a distinct **"Seaport District"** as a living/working/tourism destination only began to take shape in the early 2000s. Encompassing a long stretch of waterfront and parallel roads, the area has blossomed into a hodgepodge of

---

A Taste of Boston, From Oysters to Boston Cream Pie

What should you eat on a first visit to Boston? Well, Boston is a seafood town, and good plates of **oysters** are ubiquitous. Try them at sit-down restaurants like Legal Sea Foods (p. 110) or Row 34 (p. 114) or modest food stalls inside Faneuil Hall Marketplace (p. 68). Ask for Wellfleet oysters from Cape Cod, which deliver a briny taste of the sea. **Boston baked beans** and **Boston cream pie** are

obvious choices, and both are especially renowned at Durgin-Park (p. 112) and Omni Parker House (p. 102) respectively. **Lobster rolls** are a fun summertime option, with piles of lobster meat served on hot dog buns. Some people like mayo mixed with the lobster, while others prefer warm butter. Both options are sublime. Try them at Neptune Oyster (p. 115) or The Barking Crab (p. 114).

spanking-new luxury housing, retail spaces, and swank hotels, bars, and restaurants. A website by WS Development, www.bostonseaport.xyz, helps keep track of what's new. The neighborhood blends into the **Fort Point** industrial district on the east side of the Fort Point Channel, where warehouses have been reclaimed as office space, artist studios, loft condominiums, and more restaurants.

See p. 134 for the **Legal Sea Foods** at 270 Northern Ave.

MODERATE

The Barking Crab ★ SEAFOOD   New England's coastline is chock-a-block with clam shacks (where the seafood is deep fried) and lobster shacks (with deep pots of water to boil or steam lobsters). At these places, guests often sit elbow to elbow at picnic tables and dig into lobster rolls, whole lobsters with butter, baskets piled high with fried clams, and sides like corn on the cob and potato salad. The Barking Crab offers all that, smack dab in the city. It's located on the Fort Point channel, essentially qualifying it as a seaside restaurant.

88 Sleeper St. www.barkingcrab.com. ✆ **617/426-2722.** Main courses $12–$51. Daily 11:30am–9pm (until 10pm Fri–Sat); bar open 1 hr. later each evening. T: Courthouse.

Pastoral ★★ ITALIAN   With artisan pizza, a roomy main restaurant, and a hopping bar with a wide selection of U.S. and Italian wines and craft beers, Pastoral comfortably accommodates both the nearby work crowd and families who have just come out of the Boston Children's Museum down the block. The fennel sausage pizza is worth the trip alone.

345 Congress St. https://pastoralfortpoint.com. ✆ **617/345-0005.** Main courses $11–$22. Daily 11:30am–3pm and 5–9pm (until 10pm Wed–Sat); bar until 1:30am. T: Courthouse.

Row 34 ★★ SEAFOOD   Plenty of Boston restaurants serve fresh seafood, but Row 34 has emerged as one of the best. The restaurant is at the vanguard of the Seaport District's renaissance, and represents what's both new and classic about this hot neighborhood. It has a short menu—dominated by oysters, crudo, and ceviche, and including a handful of fish dishes and one or two chicken and beef choices—as well as a long list of wine options and an upscale industrial vibe.

383 Congress St. www.row34.com. ✆ **617/553-5900.** Main courses $16–$29. Daily 11:30am–10pm (until 11pm Fri–Sat); Sunday brunch starts 10:30am. T: Courthouse.

Wagamama ★ PAN-ASIAN   The Seaport locale of this London-based chain, opened in 2017, offers seating at long communal tables with an upscale industrial vibe. Some prices are a bit steep—$17 for ramen—but portions tend to be large, and the bowls are packed with fresh veggies and your choice of protein. Stumped by the vast menu? A good go-to is the ginger chicken udon, which has chicken, snow peas, egg, chilies, bean sprouts, pickled ginger, and cilantro atop chewy udon noodles.

100 Northern Ave., behind the ICA. www.wagamama.us. ✆ **617/933-9304.** Main courses $12–$18. Sun–Wed 11am–10pm; Thurs–Sat 11am–11pm. T: Courthouse.

THE sights AND smells OF THE NORTH END

The **Paul Revere House** (p. 77) and the **Old North Church** (p. 77) are the best-known attractions in the **North End ★★★**, Boston's "Little Italy" (although it's *never* called that). Home to Italian immigrants, their assimilated children, and newcomers from around the world, it's dominated by festivals and street fairs on weekends in July and August.

Lively **Hanover Street,** the main artery of this harborside neighborhood, overflows most afternoons and evenings with locals and out-of-towners enjoying its restaurants and cafes. Increasingly sophisticated retail options include quirky boutiques both here and on parallel **Salem Street,** as well as the side streets that connect them.

Popular destinations for a cappuccino and cannoli (tubes of crisp-fried pastry filled with sweetened ricotta cheese) are **Caffè Vittoria** at 290–296 Hanover St. (www.caffevittoria.com; 617/227-7606) and **Mike's Pastry,** 300 Hanover St. (www.mikespastry.com; 617/742-3050). Around the corner, **Salumeria Italiana** at 151 Richmond St. (www.salumeriaitaliana.com; 617/523-8743) is the best Italian grocery store in the neighborhood, with cheeses, meats, fresh bread, sandwiches, pastas, olives, olive oils, and more.

INEXPENSIVE

Flour Bakery + Café ★★ BAKERY   Chef/owner Joanne Chang is a Boston superstar, known for her small chain of high-end bakeries. (She's also the Chang in **Myers + Chang,** p. 118.) Flour's sticky buns, made with caramel and pecan, are justifiably renowned, and its decadent sandwiches, salads, and grain bowls are also first-rate. There are also locations downtown and in Harvard Square. If it's is too crowded here, head to **Sweetgreen** (p. 111) around the corner at 372 Congress St., for a fancy salad to go.

12 Farnsworth St. www.flourbakery.com. 617/338-4333. Baked goods $4–$6, sandwiches $8–$10. Mon–Fri 6:30am–8pm; Sat 8am–6pm; Sun 8am–5pm. T: Courthouse. See website for additional locations.

The North End
EXPENSIVE

Mamma Maria ★★★ NORTHERN ITALIAN   In a town house overlooking North Square and the Paul Revere House, the best restaurant in the North End offers innovative seasonal cuisine in a sophisticated yet comfortable setting. Many come specifically for the fork-tender veal shank *osso bucco* served with saffron risotto Milanese. The restaurant is wildly romantic, with seating in five small dining rooms. Lots of Boston restaurants offer valet parking; here in the crowded North End you may very well want to take advantage of Mamma Maria's offer.

3 North Sq. www.mammamaria.com. 617/523-0077. Main courses $27–$48. Sun–Thurs 5–10pm; Fri–Sat 5–11pm. T: Haymarket.

Neptune Oyster ★★ SEAFOOD   Tiny and crammed, and with a line often extending down the block, Neptune is an open secret: The busy little kitchen produces some of the best seafood in the city. High-end lobster rolls, fried clams, and, of course, oysters all get raves. There are burgers, too—served with fried oysters and garlic mayo.

63 Salem St. www.neptuneoyster.com. (℅ **617/742-3474.** Main courses $21–$39. Sun–Thurs 11:30am–9:30pm; Fri–Sat 11:30am–10:30pm. T: Haymarket.

MODERATE

Artú ★ ITALIAN A neighborhood favorite, known for superb roasted meats and veggies as well as home-style pasta dishes, Artú is a good stop for Freedom Trail walkers. Roast lamb, penne alla puttanesca, and chicken stuffed with ham and cheese are all well-executed. Panini are big in size and flavor—the prosciutto, mozzarella, and tomato is sublime; and chicken parmigiana is tender and filling. Artú isn't great for quiet conversation, especially during dinner in the noisy main room, but it's one of the most reliably satisfying restaurants in the North End. In addition to this location, there's an outpost on Beacon Hill, at 89 Charles St.

6 Prince St. www.artuboston.com. (℅ **617/742-4336.** Main courses $16–$35 (lunch $8–$17). Reservations recommended at dinner. Daily 11:30am–11pm. T: Haymarket.

The Daily Catch ★ SEAFOOD/ITALIAN Follow the aroma of garlic to this tiny storefront (just 20 seats). The lines are long, the specialty is calamari (squid), and everything is delicious. Bring a wad of cash because the restaurant doesn't take credit cards.

323 Hanover St. http://thedailycatch.com. (℅ **617/523-8567.** Main courses $16–$30. Cash only. Daily 11am–10pm T: Haymarket.

La Famiglia Giorgio ★ ITALIAN You want your red sauce? Or maybe an alfredo or Bolognese or puttanesca? You want your bruschetta and garlic bread, your pasta fagioli and fried calamari, your fettuccini, lasagna, and spaghetti and meatballs? You want gigantic portions and reasonable prices? You want old-fashioned family atmosphere, the kind you imagine if you're not Italian? You're looking for Giorgio's.

112 Salem St. www.lafamigliagiorgios.com. (℅ **617/367-6711.** Main courses $10–$23. Sun–Thurs 11am–9pm; Fri–Sat 11am–10pm. T: Haymarket.

INEXPENSIVE

Galleria Umberto Rosticceria ★ ITALIAN Open since the 1960s, the cafeteria-style Galleria Umberto is an excellent eat-and-run spot a few steps off the Freedom Trail. Join the line for tasty pizza, *arancini* (a rice ball filled with ground beef, peas, and cheese), potato croquettes, and calzones. A local fast-casual favorite, it's lunch only and cash only.

289 Hanover St. www.galleriaumbertonorthend.com. (℅ **617/227-5709.** Most items under $5. Mon–Sat 10:45am–2:30pm. Cash only. T: Haymarket.

Regina Pizzeria ★ PIZZA That picture you have in your head of a neighborhood pizza place in an old-time Italian neighborhood? This is it. Regina Pizzeria is a true Boston classic (founded in 1926), on an atmospheric corner of the city's still-traditional Italian neighborhood. There are 14 outlets

"Take the Cannoli"

Cannoli—flaky, deep-fried, filled with sweet ricotta cream—are a specialty of the North End Italian neighborhood. And just as Montréal has a bagel war over which of its great bagel shops is best, there's a minor cannoli battle here between **The Modern** (257 Hanover St.; www.modernpastry.com; ⓒ **617/523-3783**) and **Mike's Pastry,** across the street at 300 Hanover (www.mikespastry.com; ⓒ **617/742-3050**). It's a little too tidy to say "tourists go to Mike's, locals go to the Modern," since both are terrific options for an espresso and cannoli—if you can snag a seat (most people get their pastries to go). On the other hand, if you get your hankering at 2am, there's only one option: **Bova's,** a 4-minute walk away at 134 Salem St. (www.bova bakeryboston.net; ⓒ **617/523-5601**). It's open 24 hours, 7 days a week—and some swear Bova's cannoli are best.

throughout the city and region, but this is the original—an obvious choice if you're walking the Freedom Trail.

11½ Thacher St. www.pizzeriaregina.com. ⓒ **617/227-0765.** Pizza $10–$21. Sun–Thurs 11:30am–11pm; Fri–Sat 11:30am–12:30am. T: Haymarket.

South End

EXPENSIVE

Aquitaine Bar á Vin Bistrot ★★ FRENCH This nook of the South End, radiating out from the corner of Tremont Street and Clarendon Street, is a destination for romantic brunches and dinners. Aquitaine, which has been holding court here since 1998, is part of the reason. The French bistro covers all the essential territory, with a luscious *soupe à l'oignon gratinée,* steak frites, and sole Meunière. It serves up a large menu of brunch items on weekends 9am to 3pm, with an elegant atmosphere to accompany such options as Omelette Alsacienne, shrimp and grits, and malted Belgian waffle. Stroll afterwards to Union Park, a block south—brick row houses surround a small oval park, one of the prettiest settings in the city, with a lawn, trees, flowers, and two bubbling fountains.

569 Tremont St. www.aquitaineboston.com. ⓒ **617/424-8577.** Main courses $25–$38. Mon–Fri 11:30am–3pm; Sat–Sun 9am–3pm; Sun–Wed 5–10pm; Thurs–Sat 5–11pm. T: Back Bay & 10-min. walk.

Toro ★★ SPANISH The draw here is authentic tapas, which guests usually choose as 2 to 3 small plates each to share with the table. With choices so tempting, those small plates can quickly add up. Toro's *maíz asado* (grilled corn on the cob with aioli, lime, Espelette pepper, and aged cheese) is justifiably one of the top dishes in Boston. Other menu favorites include *pimentos del Padron* (spicy fried green peppers), *chorizo Iberico de Fermin* (Spanish pork sausage), and *gambas al ajillo* (garlic shrimp with chilies). Toro is just busy enough at lunch, and noisy, fun, and packed at dinner.

1704 Washington St. www.toro-restaurant.com. ⓒ **617/536-4300.** Tapas $5–$23, with most $10–$16. Lunch weekdays, brunch Sun, dinner daily; check for exact hours, which change seasonally. T: Worcester Square.

MODERATE

Barcelona Wine Bar ★★ SPANISH *The Boston Globe* pegged the trendy Barcelona right when it said that the menu navigates a line "that threads tradition, invention, and ambition." Tapas offerings include both traditional standbys like *pan con tomate* (bread rubbed with tomato, garlic, and olive oil) and *mussels al ajillo* (mussels in garlic sauce) as well as unconventional concoctions such as crispy eggplant with smoked maple and pickled beets with pesto and feta. The atmosphere is festive and the restaurant is usually packed.

525 Tremont St. www.barcelonawinebar.com. © **617/266-2600.** Tapas $5–$11. Daily 4pm–"late"; Sat–Sun 10am–4pm. T: Back Bay & 10-min. walk.

Myers + Chang ★★ ASIAN FUSION Inspired by Southeast Asian street food, this stylish restaurant has small-plate menu items bundled into categories such as "dim sum-y things" and "buns, baos, rolls + a taco." Weekends feature a dim sum brunch. It's a good place to come with a group so you can order a mountain of food to try.

1145 Washington St. www.myersandchang.com. © **617/542-5200.** Main courses $14–$29, small plates $5–$17. Sun–Thurs 11:30am–10pm; Fri–Sat 11:30am–11pm. T: Washington St. @ Herald St.

South End Buttery ★★ CONTEMPORARY AMERICAN Boston's South End is rife with cozy spots for brunch, dinner, and drinks, and few are more appealing than the Buttery. Its small cafe is open from 6am to 6pm, and the attached bar and restaurant are open nightly for dinner and on weekends for brunch. If you are in need of decadent comfort food, the macaroni and cheese here comes with steamed lobster tails and claws. The Buttery also has a cafe/market with a few seats at 37 Clarendon St. (© **617/482-1015**), also in the South End; it's open daily from 6:30am to 6pm.

314 Shawmut Ave. www.southendbuttery.com. © **617/482-1015.** Main courses $18–$25. Restaurant: Sun–Thurs 5–10pm; Fri–Sat 5–11pm; Sat–Sun 9am–3pm; cafe daily 6am–6pm. T: Washington St. @ Union Pk.

INEXPENSIVE

Mikes City Diner ★★ DINER A neighborhood stalwart, Mike's serves huge portions of breakfast classics—eggs, buttermilk pancakes, breakfast burritos—plus hearty Reubens, Philly steak, and fried chicken. It's open for breakfast and lunch daily (no dinner), and is cash only.

1714 Washington St. www.mikescitydiner.com. © **617/267-9393.** Main courses $4–$14. Cash only. Daily 6am–3pm. T: Worcester St.

Chinatown/Theater District

MODERATE

Hei La Moon ★ DIM SUM/CHINESE A gigantic banquet hall with a sea of red and gold tables brings in crowds, especially on the weekend. The best way to sample Chinese food is by trying **dim sum,** the traditional midday meal featuring a variety of dumpling dishes and other small plates. It's especially popular on weekends, when the variety of offerings is greatest, although it's also served on weekdays. If you're uncertain where to start, try the Shrimp

Har Gao (shrimp dumplings) and Char Siu Bao (steamed barbeque pork buns). The restaurant is on the section of Beach Street closest to South Station, and there's a parking lot *above* the restaurant.

88 Beach St. www.facebook.com/pages/Hei-La-Moon. ℂ **617/338-8813.** Items $8–$13. Daily 8am–10pm. T: South Station.

INEXPENSIVE

Pho Pasteur ★★ VIETNAMESE   Boston's Chinatown offers a mélange of Asian cuisine, including Vietnamese. Pho Pasteur has been holding court at this location since 1991 and has a well-earned reputation for inexpensive and tasty food: It's a friendly, bright place for a quick meal. A healthy option is the *bun*—vermicelli noodles, shredded lettuce, fresh mint, and your choice of hot protein, all mixed together. You'll also see lots of patrons with big bowls of *pho,* Vietnamese noodle soup. A giant menu offers over 100 food choices, with another 29 juice and tea options, plus beer and wine.

682 Washington St. www.phopasteurboston.net. ℂ **617/482-7467.** Main courses $9–$14. Daily 9am–10:45pm. T: Chinatown.

Kenmore Square

MODERATE

Sweet Cheeks ★★ BARBEQUE   Casual, big, loud, and extremely popular, this upscale joint near Fenway Park features chef Tiffani Faison's succulent barbecue and hospitable service. Faison, a graduate of TV's *Top Chef,* brings a fun celebrity charisma to her restaurants. Her Southern buttermilk biscuits are so popular that in fall and winter the restaurant sells them as a breakfast grab-and-go option (call ahead to confirm). Faison also runs the equally well-regarded **Tiger Mama** down the block (1363 Boylston St.; www.tigermama boston.com; ℂ 617/425-6262). Its menu is Southeast Asian–inspired: crab and asparagus fresh rolls, claypot chicken, and spring greens pad thai.

1381 Boylston St. www.sweetcheeksq.com. ℂ **617/266-1300.** Main courses $11–$26. Sun–Thurs 11:30am–10pm; Fri–Sat 11:30am–11pm; Sun 8am–5pm. T: Fenway.

Tasty Burger ★ BURGERS   The accurately named Tasty Burger—first established in this location, in a renovated service station—also serves hot dogs and chicken sandwiches. It's the Official Burger of the Boston Red Sox and it's available here and inside the ballpark. This location is open until 2am every night but Sunday, to accommodate the ballpark and bar crowds.

1301 Boylston St. www.tastyburger.com. ℂ **617/425-4444.** All items $7 or less. Mon–Sat 11am–2am. T: Fenway.

Cambridge

Food trucks set up daily (even in winter) at the Harvard Plaza just north of Harvard Yard, near Oxford Street. There are generally four or five options, with the schedule posted at www.commonspaces.harvard.edu/food-truck-schedule. Trucks include **Bon Me,** for Vietnamese sandwiches, salads, and grain bowls; **Roxy's Grilled Cheese,** featuring the Green Muenster with bacon and guacamole; and **Zinnekan's,** for Belgium waffles with toppings such as Nutella, strawberries, and whipped cream. Seating is available at outdoor tables and benches.

There's a branch of **Clover Food Lab** (see p. 113) at 1326 Massachusetts Ave., which provides a selection of local beer. There's also a large outpost of **Tatte Bakery & Café** (see p. 111) a few doors down, at 1288 Massachusetts Ave.

EXPENSIVE

Bondir ★★★ NEW AMERICAN   Settling in for a dining experience at chef Jason Bond's luxuriously inventive restaurant is like visiting the dining room of a friend who happens to be an artisan gourmand: There are barely a dozen tables, rock music sets a casual mood, and a single $68 five-course menu (no a la carte options) means that you give yourself over to whatever the chef has planned for that evening. Menu descriptions might include "Mangalitsa pork shoulder, parsley root, hedgehog mushrooms, and walnuts," or "seared mackerel with foie gras, squash, crosnes, and Perigord truffle vinaigrette."

279A Broadway. www.bondircambridge.com. ✆ **617/661-0009.** 5-course dinner $68. Wed–Sun 5–10pm. T: Central.

Craigie on Main ★★★ NEW AMERICAN   Both polished and rustic, Craigie is one of the city's top restaurants for special meals. A la carte choices are available, but the five- and seven-course tasting menus ($85 and $108) provide a chance to sit back and try plate after innovative plate of seasonal fare. Chef Tony Maws also hosts special events, including Chef's Whim Sundays, burger and beer lunches with Somerville brewery Aeronaut, and a comfy Passover meal with matzoh ball soup. In a partial nod to the many vegetarians in the neighborhood, the restaurant offers a veggie burger—but in the bar room only, and on Tuesdays only. Sirloin, pork shoulder, and a full pig's head (spectacular, if you're game) are more typical of the menu.

853 Main St. www.craigieonmain.com. ✆ **617/497-5511.** Tasting menus $85 and $108; 3-course prix fixe $65; main courses $35. Tues–Sun 5:30–10pm (bar until midnight); Sun 10:30am–2pm. T: Central.

Oleana ★★ MEDITERRANEAN   Emphatic Middle Eastern flavors, seasonal ingredients, and a cozy atmosphere give longtime Oleana its deserved status as a top Cambridge go-to. In cold weather its moussaka—made with smoky eggplant puree, crispy cauliflower, and mint—is a shot of summer, as is its lemon chicken with za'atar spice. Don't miss executive pastry chef Maura Kilpatrick's baked Alaska with coconut ice cream and passion fruit caramel. In good weather, there's a delightful patio. Star chef Ana Sortun has opened similar Turkish-tinged venues in recent years, including the always-packed **Sofra Bakery and Café** (p. 85), west of Harvard Square at 1 Belmont St.

134 Hampshire St. www.oleanarestaurant.com. ✆ **617/661-0505.** Main courses $25–$29. Sun–Thurs 5:30–10pm; Fri–Sat 5:30–11pm. T: Central, 10-min. walk.

INEXPENSIVE

Grendel's Den Restaurant & Bar ★★ AMERICAN   With a faux fireplace and elbow-to-elbow tables, Grendel's, which has been around forever, is a friendly, popular college pub. The food is good—spinach pie, quinoa stew, Portobello Reuben, burgers, and the like—and there's always a daily lunch special for $6. Plus, every day from 5 to 7:30pm, all food is half price with the purchase of a $4 drink (consider the Paulaner Weissbier). In warm weather, a few tables are available on a small, appealing terrace. Open daily until 1am.

89 Winthrop St. www.grendelsden.com. © **617/491-1160.** Main courses $8–$16. Daily 11:30am–1am. T: Harvard.

Life Alive ★★ VEGAN/VEGETARIAN   Cambridge's Central Square neighborhood is the artistic center of the city, with music clubs, a dance complex, yoga studios, and tons of cafes and restaurants from around the world. The fast-casual Life Alive is a good complement to the spectacle, with organic bowls of food and a large selection of fresh juices and smoothies. The Emperor grain bowl is emblematic: tofu, brown rice, corn, shredded carrots, sundried tomatoes, kale, cheddar cheese, sun sprouts, and miso sauce. Portions are generous—you won't leave hungry. Guests order at the counter (at lunch time the line is often to the door) and get food either to go or delivered to a table—there are about a dozen at street level, and about twice as many one floor down, in a cozy, cave-like space.

765 Massachusetts Ave. www.lifealive.com. © **617/354-5433.** All items $10 or less. Mon–Sat 8am–11pm; Sun 10am–10pm. T: Central.

Mr. Bartley's Burger Cottage ★★★ AMERICAN   Elaborate burgers are the thing here, along with phenomenal onion rings, sweet potato fries, and frappes (the regional name for milkshakes). This family business is a high-ceilinged, crowded room plastered with memorabilia. Tables are elbow to elbow and there's often a line to get in. Anything you can think of to put on ground beef is available, from Swiss cheese to grilled pineapple to pickled onions. Good dishes that don't involve meat include veggie burgers, veggie chili, and creamy, garlicky hummus. Closed Sunday and Monday. Cash only.

1246 Massachusetts Ave. www.mrbartley.com. © **617/354-6559.** Burgers $12–$19; main courses, salads, and sandwiches $8–$13. No credit cards. Tues–Sat 11am–9pm. Closed Dec 24–Jan 1. T: Harvard.

BOSTON & CAMBRIDGE SHOPPING

No surprise here: Boston shopping is the full mix of classic and contemporary, chic and practical, high end and hipster. Here, we provide some direction about what you'll find in different neighborhoods.

BACK BAY & BEACON HILL   New England's premier shopping district offers dozens of upscale galleries, shops, and boutiques. **Newbury Street ★★** is a world-famous destination, starting at the Boston Public Garden and running west for 1 mile. At its easternmost end the real estate and merchandise are elegant and pricey (**Burberry** at no. 2, **Tiffany** at no. 5, **Chanel** at no. 6), but shops get quirkier with each passing block (**Johnny Cupcakes** T-shirts at no. 279, **Newbury Comics** music and pop culture tchotchkes at no. 332, the beloved independent **Trident Booksellers & Cafe** at no. 338).

Charles Street, just a few blocks from the eastern end of Newbury, is the charming main street of historic Beacon Hill, with its gaslights, cobblestones, and brick row houses. Commercially dense and picturesque, the ⅓-mile stretch from Cambridge Street (at the Charles/MGH T stop) to Beacon Street (at the entrance to the Boston Public Garden) is chock-a-block with boutiques, antiques stores, and restaurants, plus practical outlets like a pharmacy and a hardware store

COPLEY SQUARE ★ Two high-end indoor **shopping malls** are conveniently located next to each other, with an enclosed pedestrian walkway connecting them: **Copley Place,** 100 Huntington Ave. (www.shopcopleyplace. com; ℂ **617/262-6600**) and **The Shops at Prudential Center,** 800 Boylston St. (www.prudentialcenter.com; ℂ **617/236-3100**). Copley has **Neiman Marcus, Barneys,** and **Stuart Weitzman;** the Prudential Center has **Saks Fifth Avenue, Vineyard Vines**, and **Microsoft Store.** Also in "the Pru" is **Eataly,** a three-story emporium of Italian food and dining.

DOWNTOWN **Faneuil Hall Marketplace** (p. 68) is a visitor-centric indoor-outdoor complex featuring dozens of kiosks with tourist knickknacks and Boston memorabilia, chain stores including **Yankee Candle Company** and **Uniqlo,** and a standalone **Sephora** megastore.

Just a few blocks from Faneuil Hall, the more modest **Boston Public Market** (p. 113) is a year-round farmers market that offers an opportunity to pick up travel-ready local fare, including beer, honey, smoked fish, and yarn.

A gift THAT SAYS "BOSTON"

Need a good Boston souvenir? The **Gurgling Cod Pitcher** from luxury goods store Shreve, Crump & Low (39 Newbury St.; www.shrevecrumpandlow.com; ℂ **617/267-9100**) has a unique fish shape, which causes its contents to give up a *glug-glug* when poured. It's a touch of extravagance from a business founded in 1796. **Red Sox caps** from the shops on Jersey Street next to Fenway Park are good for baseball fans, and **"Harvard" T-shirts** from vendors on the Boston Common or Faneuil Hall Marketplace are a popular option. Merchandise from the **USS *Constitution*** museum (p. 78) is a classy nautical choice, and **bean pots,** available from Old Sturbridge Village (http://shop.osv.org; p. 321), definitely say Boston. The Omni Parker House (p. 102) invented the **Boston cream pie** in 1856 and will ship a modern version anywhere in the U.S. (it's actually not a pie but a cake filled with pastry cream and topped with chocolate). Feeling committed? Get a **"B" tattoo** in the font of the Boston Red Sox logo or a green three-leaf clover in the style of the Celtics. In a last-minute pinch, there's always a pink-and-orange **Dunkin' Donuts mug**—the franchise was founded in 1950, just 30 minutes away in Quincy, and its mugs are available at any of the bajillion locations in the city.

CAMBRIDGE The bookstores, boutiques, and T-shirt shops of **Harvard Square** lie 20 minutes from downtown Boston by subway. Despite the neighborhood association's efforts, chain stores have swept across the Square, and you'll find a mix of familiar national and regional outlets, including quirky gift shop **Black Ink,** 5 Brattle St. (www.blackinkboston.com; © **617/497-1221**); bookstore **The Coop,** 1400 Massachusetts Ave. (www.thecoop.com; © **617/499-2000**), for Harvard merchandise; **The Curious George Store,** 1 John F. Kennedy St. (www.thecuriousgeorgestore.com; © **617/547-4500**), for children's books and toys; tiny poetry powerhouse **Grolier Poetry Book Shop,** 6 Plympton St. (www.grolierpoetrybookshop.org; © **617/547-4648**); and **Mint Julep,** 6 Church St. (www.shopmintjulep.com; © **617/576-6468**), purveyor of candy-colored dresses and sparkly jewelry.

Cambridge's indoor mall, the **CambridgeSide,** 100 CambridgeSide Place (www.cambridgeside.com), is in East Cambridge near the Charles River, with indoor parking; it's a short walk from the Lechmere stop, or a 15-minute walk from the Kendall/MIT stop. **EZRide** (www.crtma.squarespace.com/ezride-shuttle) provides a shuttle bus to the mall from the Kendall/MIT stop ($2 adults, $1 seniors and kids 12–17, free for kids 11 and under).

BOSTON & CAMBRIDGE ENTERTAINMENT & NIGHTLIFE

For information on current arts events, check the websites for **WBUR Artery** (www.wbur.org/artery), *Boston* magazine (www.bostonmagazine.com), and **Scout Cambridge** (www.scoutcambridge.com). Also look for the free magazines *Improper Bostonian* and *DigBoston* in sidewalk boxes.

GETTING TICKET DEALS ArtsBoston (www.calendar.artsboston.org; © **617/262-8632 ext. 229**) is an excellent resource for cultural listings and ticket deals. It runs the **BosTix discount-ticket service** that includes programming from over 100 area performing-arts organizations. Tickets are available online, by phone, or at BosTix booths at Faneuil Hall Marketplace (T: Government Center) and in Copley Square, at the corner of Boylston Street and Dartmouth Street (T: Copley). Tickets are 20% to 80% off the original ticket price: most are 50% off. There is a service fee of up to $8.50 per ticket, even for in-person purchases. The Faneuil Hall booth is open Thursday to Sunday 10am to 4pm; the Copley Square booth is open Tuesday to Friday 11am to 5pm, Saturday to Sunday 10am to 4pm.

The Performing Arts

The city's premier classical performance venue is the acoustically perfect **Symphony Hall ★★★**, 301 Massachusetts Ave. (www.bso.org; © **888/266-1200**). It's primarily host to the resident Boston Symphony Orchestra and Boston Pops, but it books other musical artists and speakers as well.

While Symphony Hall has more high-profile performers, nearby **Jordan Hall ★★**, 30 Gainsborough St. (www.necmusic.edu/jordan-hall;

Several city churches regularly host classical concerts during the work week. On Tuesdays, **King's Chapel** presents a 40-minute recital at 12:15pm, with performances that range from Elizabethan song to Baltic folk music to classical guitar (58 Tremont St.; www.kings-chapel. org; ℂ **617/227-2155**; $5 donation requested). On Thursdays, **Emmanuel Music** puts on free noontime concerts (reserve a spot by phone or online) in the Lindsay Chapel at Emmanuel Church (15 Newbury St.; www.emmanuelmusic. org; ℂ **617/536-3356**). The **Fridays at Trinity Organ Recital Series** presents 30-minute organ concerts at 12:15pm at Trinity Church, the architectural treasure at the heart of Copley Square (206 Clarendon St.; www.trinitychurchboston.org; ℂ **617/536-0944**; $10 donation requested).

ℂ **617/585-1260**) on the campus of New England Conservatory, is also a beautiful venue with wonderful acoustics. The schedule is primarily classical, but the hall also books special events like Cuban jazz and lots of student recitals. Most of the programs are free.

The open-air **Hatch Shell** amphitheater on the Esplanade (www.mass.gov/locations/charles-river-reservation; ℂ **617/727-4708**) is best known as the home of the Pops' Fourth of July concert, but it schedules other events on many summer nights. Family-friendly Free Friday Flicks begin at sunset.

Berklee Performance Center, 136 Massachusetts Ave. (www.berklee.edu/BPC; ℂ **617/747-2261**), presents students and staff members from Berklee College's noted jazz programs, along with touring artists and speakers.

THE MAJOR COMPANIES

Boston Ballet ★★★　One of the top dance companies in the country, the troupe is best known for its annual wintertime performances of *The Nutcracker,* but it presents a full season of classical works as well as playful pieces (such as dances by choreographers Jerome Robbins and William Forsythe) from September through June. Boston Opera House, 539 Washington St. www.bostonballet.org. ℂ **617/695-6955.** Tickets $35–$154. T: Park Street.

Boston Lyric Opera ★★　With four productions a year—in the 2017–2018 season they included *Tosca* and *The Threepenny Opera*—the BLO works hard to make opera accessible, offering two-show subscriptions and a few $25 tickets at each performance, and even reassuring guests that it's OK to wear jeans. Productions are held at the Cutler Majestic Theatre (p. 125), Huntington Theatre (p. 127), and Cyclorama at the BCA (p. 126). www.blo.org. ℂ **617/542-6772.** Tickets $32–$262.

Boston Pops ★★★　The playful sibling of the Boston Symphony Orchestra, the Pops was founded in 1930 by Arthur Fiedler, who in his 50-year tenure as conductor organized the first Fourth of July concert and ushered the Pops into its status as the most recorded orchestra in history. Fiedler was succeeded by composer and Hollywood royalty John Williams; today the Pops are helmed by Keith Lockhart. In addition to performances at **Symphony Hall** (p. 123), the Pops plays the Fourth of July extravaganza at the **Hatch Shell** (p. 124), holiday programs in December, and summer shows at Tanglewood in western Massachusetts (p. 351). Symphony Hall, 301 Massachusetts Ave. www. bostonpops.org. © **888/266-1200** or 617/266-1200 (SymphonyCharge). Tickets $22–$125. T: Symphony.

Boston Symphony Orchestra ★★★   One of the city's cultural jewels, the BSO is among the finest orchestras in the world. The most celebrated programs are classical music, often with a renowned guest artist or conductor. The season runs September through May and performances take place in the ornate, airy **Symphony Hall.** Symphony Hall, 301 Massachusetts Ave. www.bso.org. © **888/266-1200** (SymphonyCharge). Tickets $30–$145; limited availability of $20 tickets for people under 40 and $10 rush tickets. T: Symphony.

THEATER & PERFORMANCE ART

Boston's Theater District is a vibrant one. Two historic venues make up the nonprofit **Boch Center:** the grand **Wang Theatre,** at 270 Tremont St. (www. bochcenter.org; © **800/982-2787**), which seats 3,500; and the smaller **Shubert Theatre** at 265 Tremont St. (© **866/348-9738**), which hosts musicals, opera, and dance productions. The box office for both is at the Wang.

Up the street, **Cutler Majestic Theatre,** at 219 Tremont St. (www.cutler majestic.org; © **617/824-8000**) is an exquisite 1903 Beaux Arts facility that books international theater, dance, and opera, as well as one-time events like The Moth StorySLAM. It's owned by Emerson College. Around the corner, the celebrated **Emerson Colonial Theatre,** 106 Boylston St. (www.emerson colonialtheatre.com; © **888/616-0272**), also owned by Emerson, reopened in 2018 with a 40-year partnership with London's Ambassador Theatre Group, which will develop the programming. The theater was built in 1900 and premiered seminal musicals such as *Anything Goes, Oklahoma!, La Cage aux Folles,* and, in 1935, *Porgy and Bess.*

Wintertime Musical Festivities in Boston

Starting in late November, Boston becomes a wonderland of tiny twinkling lights and decorated Christmas trees, with special holiday programing to match. Annual events include *The Nutcracker* by **Boston Ballet** (p. 124); the **Christmas Revels** multicultural solstice celebration (www.revels.org; © **617/972-8300**); Boston Pops **Holiday Pops** concerts (www.bso.org); **Black Nativity,** the National Center of Afro-American Artists' annual presentation of Langston Hughes' song-play, on track for its 50th anniversary in 2020 (www.blacknativity. org); and **A Christmas Celtic Sojourn** of Celtic, Pagan, and Christian music of the season, hosted by WGBH radio host Brian O'Donovan (www.wgbh.org/music/celtic). To close out the year, **First Night First Day** is an arts-oriented, family-friendly New Year's celebration, and includes music performances, ice sculptures, a parade, and New Year's Eve fireworks (www.firstnightboston.org).

A few blocks away, **Boston Opera House,** 539 Washington St. (www.boston operahouse.com; ✆ **617/259-3400;** tickets from Ticketmaster ✆ **800/982-2787**) hosts touring Broadway musicals as well as the Boston Ballet and its annual production of *The Nutcracker.* Built as an ornate vaudeville house in the 1920s, the Opera House had a gorgeous $54-million restoration in 2004.

About a half mile from the Theater District, in the South End, the **Boston Center for the Arts** complex, 539 Tremont St. (www.bcaonline.org; ✆ **617/ 426-5000**), is home to artists' studios and rehearsal spaces, the Mills art gallery, a couple of good bars, and six theaters, including the **Wimberly Theatre in the Calderwood Pavilion,** the **BCA Plaza Black Box Theatre,** and the **Cyclorama.**

American Repertory Theater (A.R.T.) ★★★ Internationally celebrated artistic director Diane Paulus has brought pizazz to the programming at the renowned Harvard-associated A.R.T. (say each letter), from which many productions move on to Broadway. Performances are at two venues at either side of Harvard Square: the main **Loeb Drama Center** to the north and **club Oberon** to the south, at 0 Arrow Street. 64 Brattle St., Cambridge. www. amrep.org. ✆ **617/547-8300.** Tickets $25 and up. T: Harvard.

ArtsEmerson ★★ Sponsored by Emerson College, ArtsEmerson has swiftly established itself as one of the city's most exciting presenting and producing organizations. It says this of its mission: "Founded in 2010, the year the US Census confirmed there was no single cultural majority in Boston, we committed to building a cultural institution that reflects the diversity of our city." Theater, dance, and film are central, with events that include "Citizen Read," a public dialogue on race and identity in America. Its **Emerson Paramount Center,** a few doors down from Boston Opera House, has three theaters. The organization also presents work at Emerson's **Cutler Majestic Theatre** (p. 125). 559 Washington St. www.artsemerson.org and www.emerson paramount.org. ✆ **617/824-8400.** Ticket prices vary. T: Boylston.

Blue Man Group ★★ The long-running percussive phenom features a trio of cobalt-colored performers backed by a rock band. They enlist audience members, so be ready if you're sitting in the first few rows. Charles Playhouse, 74 Warrenton St. www.blueman.com. ✆ **800/BLUEMAN** (258-3626). Tickets $66–$170. T: Boylston.

Commonwealth Shakespeare Company ★★ A highlight of Boston's summer is the company's "Shakespeare on the Common," a free outdoor production on Boston Common at the Parkman Bandstand. Performances take place Tuesday through Sunday at 8pm, usually mid-July through early August. Bring a blanket to sit on the lawn or rent a lawn chair for $5. Boston Common. www.commshakes.org. ✆ **617/426-0863.** Free admission. T: Park Street.

The Donkey Show ★ Get your Bacchanalian on at this gyrating disco version of Shakespeare's *A Midsummer Night's Dream.* The performance unfolds every Saturday at 10:30pm in club Oberon, among patrons who drink and dance alongside the slinky performers. The club stays open for dancing after the show. 2 Arrow St., Cambridge. www.amrep.org. ✆ **617/547-8300.** Tickets $25–$45. T: Harvard.

Huntington Theatre Company ★★ The well-regarded Huntington presents both contemporary works and revivals. Some productions take place at the Boston Center for the Arts (p. 126). 264 Huntington Ave. www.huntington theatre.org. ✆ **617/266-0800.** Ticket prices vary. T: Symphony.

Jacques ★ Boston's one drag club has performances 7 nights a week, with 2 shows on Saturday and participatory events like the Zumba Fitness Dance Party. Lots of evenings it's packed with bachelorette parties. It has been operating in its Bay Village location (between Back Bay and the Theater District) since the 1950s and looks it—it's basically a dive bar, where drinks are served in clear plastic cups. Cash only. 79 Broadway. www.jacques-cabaret.com. ✆ **617/ 426-8902.** Cover $7–$10. T: Arlington.

Shear Madness ★★ Since 1980, audiences have been helping solve a murder in this madcap show set in a hair salon. It's great fun and never the same twice. Charles Playhouse Stage II, 74 Warrenton St. www.shearmadness.com. ✆ **617/426-5225.** Tickets $56. T: Boylston.

Spectator Sports

Oh, we do love our sports in Boston, from the Red Sox (baseball) and Celtics (basketball) to the Bruins (hockey) and Patriots (football). Tickets to stadium events can be purchased at team websites or at **StubHub** (www.stubhub.com), a ticket-trading site owned by eBay and sanctioned by the teams.

BASEBALL Whether it's your first baseball game of the season or the first game of your life at Boston's famed baseball stadium—built in 1912, it's the oldest ballpark in major league baseball—emerging from the concrete hallways into **Fenway Park** ★★★ and seeing the expansive sky and emerald green field could make your heart grow two sizes. The city's beloved **Red Sox** play here from April to early October (later if they make the playoffs). Tickets are mostly expensive ($20–$197), although prices vary depending on the popularity of the visiting team. Streets adjacent to the stadium become a sort of carnival midway for ticket holders before games, with concession stands and live music.

    Tickets to Red Sox games can be purchased online or in person. The ticket office (www.redsox.com; ✆ **877/REDSOX-9** [733-7699]) is at 4 Jersey St., off Brookline Avenue and just up the hill from the Kenmore T stop. In-season it's open from 10am until 1 hour after the game starts; on non-game days its open 10am to 5pm. A limited number of game day tickets are sold at Gate E on Lansdowne Street, beginning 90 minutes prior to each home game. Fans can start lining up 5 hours prior to game time. Each guest can buy just one ticket and needs to enter the ballpark immediately after purchasing the ticket.

    Security guidelines are tight here, as at other major stadiums. For a list of prohibited items visit www.mlb.com/redsox/ballpark/information/security.

A large variety of **tours of Fenway Park** (www.redsox.com/tours; ✆ **617/ 226-6660**) run year-round. Most include a trip to the stands, the press box, and the luxury seats. Some tours allow visitors to walk the warning track and lay hands on the famed "Green Monster," the left-field wall, nicknamed for both its color and its 37.2 feet (11.3 m) height, which turns a lot of would-be home runs into doubles. Tour tickets can be purchased online up to 30 days in advance; a limited number of same-day tickets are available on a first-come, first-served basis only at Fenway's Gate D. The cost is $14 to $50, and tours take place daily 9am to 5pm or 3 hours before game time on game days. The main tour is one hour and costs $20 for adults and $14 for kids 12 and under.

Loads of Red Sox merchandise is for sale at the **Red Sox Team Store,** 19 Jersey St. (www.mlbshop.com/boston-red-sox; ✆ **800/FENWAY-9**) open 9am to 5pm 7 days a week year round, with extended hours on game nights.

BASKETBALL The **Boston Celtics'** season runs from early October to April or May. Games take place at the **TD Garden ★,** 100 Legends Way, at the North Station transit hub. Tickets (www.nba.com/celtics; ✆ **866/4CELTIX** [423-5849]) include family packs and are available at the team's site, although games often sell out. Resale tickets are sold via Ticketmaster from a link at the Celtics' online ticket page.

FOOTBALL The **New England Patriots ★** (www.patriots.com; ✆ **800/ 543-1776**) are pretty much the most hated sports team in the country, but in Boston they are minor gods. The Pats play from August to December or January at Gillette Stadium in Foxboro, about 45 minutes south of the city. Tickets sell out well in advance, although the website lists availability by game ($95 and way up for "standard" and "verified resale" tickets).

HOCKEY The **Boston Bruins ★** (www.nhl.com/bruins; ✆ **617/634- BEAR**) season runs from early October to April or May. Games take place at the **TD Garden,** 100 Legends Way, at the North Station transit hub. Bruins tickets often sell out (the team has been particularly popular since winning the

---

Rockin' The Boston Marathon

For sports fans, Patriots Day—a Massachusetts-only holiday (see p. 93) that commemorates the events of April 18 and 19, 1775, when the Revolutionary War began—is equally known as "Marathon Monday," for the running of the **Boston Marathon ★★★**. One of the oldest and most famous 26.2-mile races in the world, it begins in Hopkinton, Massachusetts, and ends at Boston's Copley Square. Elite women start at 9:30am and elite men at 10am, which means that runners begin arriving on city streets around 11:30am. Often one of the first really nice days of spring, it's a terrifically festive day. The city experienced a brutal bombing at the finish line in 2013, which killed three spectators and injured another 264 people. Security in the years afterward has been heavy but not disturbing. As all serious runners know, it's competitive even to qualify for an official race number. Contact the **Boston Athletic Association** (www.baa.org; ✆ **617/236-1652**) for details.

Stanley Cup in 2011). You can sign up for email or text alerts to get notified if tickets (day of or next day) become available.

ROWING   On the third weekend of October, the **Head of the Charles Regatta** ★ (www.hocr.org; ✆ **617/868-6200**) draws some 10,000 athletes from around the world to the Charles River in Cambridge for the 2-day rowing competition. It's the country's largest crew event, drawing tens of thousands of fans who line the shore and the bridges to socialize and occasionally even watch the action.

SOCCER   The **New England Revolution** ★ (www.revolutionsoccer.net) play in the Eastern Conference of the U.S. and Canada's Major League Soccer. Like the New England Patriots football team, the Revolution play at Gillette Stadium in Foxboro, about 45 minutes south of the city. The season runs from March to October. Tickets are nearly always available through **Ticketmaster**.

The Club & Music Scene

Clubs in Boston are open until 2am (bars until 1am).

COMEDY

Improv Asylum ★★   With shows 7 days a week—and four on Saturday—Improv Asylum is always hopping. A resident cast presents sketch material and improvisation, taking audience suggestions and ad-libbing vignettes on the spot. Given its appealing location close to Faneuil Hall Marketplace and on the main drag of the tourist-heavy North End, most shows sell out, so get tickets in advance. The company celebrated 20 years in 2018. 216 Hanover St. www.improvasylum.com. ✆ **617/263-6887.** Tickets $7–$33. T: Haymarket.

Laugh Boston ★   Midsized (about 300 seats) and dedicated to stand up, Laugh Boston is just down the block from the Seaport District's Boston Convention and Exhibition Center, and an easy walk to the neighborhood's exploding number of restaurants and activities. There are performances 4 or 5 nights a week, and special events such as Dirty Disney and the storytelling program The Moth. It's located inside the Westin Hotel. 425 Summer St. www.laughboston.com. ✆ **617/725-2844.** Tickets $20–$35. T: World Trade Center.

Wilbur Theatre ★   Built in 1914 and lavishly renovated in 2008, this historic theater in the middle of Boston's compact theater district is Boston's highest-profile comedy venue, bringing in big-names such as Trevor Noah, Maria Bamford, and Jim Jefferies. The space also books musical acts (Wyclef Jean; Blood, Sweat & Tears) when national and local comics aren't in the spotlight. 246 Tremont St. www.thewilburtheatre.com. ✆ **617/248-9700.** Tickets $25–$200. T: Boylston.

DANCE CLUBS

Club Café ★★   With a tagline "Dine Drink Dance," Club Café is the city's top LGBTQ nightlife destination. In addition to a dance club, there's a cabaret room that hosts evenings of jazz standards, sing-a-longs, and comedy (Wed–Sun). 209 Columbus Ave. www.clubcafe.com. ✆ **617/536-0966.** No cover Sun–Thurs & until 11pm Fri–Sat. T: Back Bay.

In 2003, the Massachusetts Supreme Judicial Court became the first state supreme court in the U.S. to rule that same-sex couples have the legal right to marry. A year later, Massachusetts became the first state to issue marriage licenses to same-sex couples. **Boston Pride Week** (www.bostonpride.org; 📞 **617/262-9405**) takes place at the beginning of June and includes a festival, a concert, block parties, and the largest gay-pride parade in New England. Festivities often continue throughout the month, and restaurants, bars, and other venues are likely to fly the rainbow flag during these weeks. *Note:* Additional Pride events are held in February (Black Pride), April (Latinx Pride), and May (Youth Pride).

The Grand ★ New in 2017, this dance club on the third floor of the Seaport District's Scorpion Bar is flashy, although as is often typical in these places, the women look fabulous and the men have to be reminded not to wear ripped jeans. Still, lines can be long to get in. 58 Seaport Blvd. www.thegrandboston.com. 📞 **617/322-0200.** $30 & way up. T: Courthouse.

Royale ★ A former hotel ballroom in the theater district with a stage and a balcony, Royale books concerts, burlesque shows, and DJs. The club's Instagram features a lot of barely dressed women, which sums up the general tenor of this place. 279 Tremont St. www.royaleboston.com. 📞 **617/338-7699.** Most dance nights & concerts free; some events up to $28. T: Boylston.

JAZZ & BLUES

Regattabar ★★ In Harvard Square's posh **Charles Hotel** (p. 105), the 220-seat Regattabar is an appealing locale for music and drinks. Booked by NYC's Blue Note Jazz Club, the schedule can be sporadic—sometimes just a half dozen shows in a month—so check the calendar. In summer, the club hosts free jazz shows by students of the Berklee College of Music in the adjacent outdoor courtyard. In the Charles Hotel, 1 Bennett St. www.regattabarjazz.com. 📞 **617/395-7757.** Tickets $18–$35. T: Harvard.

Top of the Hub Jazz Lounge ★★ The ritzy 52nd-floor lounge atop Boston's soaring Prudential Tower is a gorgeous setting for romance, especially if you arrive late in the afternoon and watch the sunset. Evenings after 7:30, the lounge features jazz ensembles—just the atmosphere for a fancy cocktail, if that's your style. Food options include charcuterie, calamari, burgers, and seafood platters. Dress is business casual (in the adjacent formal dining room, jackets and dress pants are recommended for men). Prudential Tower, 800 Boylston St. www.topofthehub.net. 📞 **617/536-1775.** No cover; no minimum for seats directly at the bar; $24 minimum per person after 8pm at tables. T: Prudential.

Wally's Cafe ★ In the 1940s and '50s, Boston's South End was flush with jazz clubs—the High Hat, Savoy Ballroom, Chicken Lane. Wally's was founded in 1947 by Joseph L. Walcott, said to be the first African American to own a nightclub in New England. Today, this teeny venue serves up jazz (but no food) 365 days a year. There's a jam session from 6 to 9pm every evening, often featuring students from neighboring Berklee College of Music, and then jazz, funk, blues, or Latin salsa from 9:30pm to 2am. 427 Massachusetts Ave. www.wallyscafe.com. ✆ **617/424-1408.** No cover. T: Massachusetts Ave.

ROCK & FOLK

Blue Hills Bank Pavilion ★★ Seating 5,000, this outdoor amphitheater in the Seaport District is open May through September and brings in big-name, old-school acts such as Jackson Browne, Jethro Tull, and Foreigner. It's next door to the giant **Liberty Wharf** (www.libertywharf.co) restaurant space—which includes not just Legal Harborside (p. 134) but Del Frisco's Double Eagle Steak House, Temazcal Tequila Cantina, Tony C's Sports Bar & Grill, and 75 bistro, as well—making it a fun spot for an evening out. 290 Northern Blvd. www.bostonpavilion.net. ✆ **617/728-1600.** Tickets $65 & way up. T: Northern Ave @ Harbor St.

City Winery Boston ★★ Part of a national chain created by the founder of New York's Knitting Factory, City Winery lets guests sit, eat, and drink during most shows. Its calendar is eclectic, from Steve Earle to Altan to Sandra Bernhard. The location is to the south of the TD Garden sports venue and to the west of the North End neighborhood. 80 Beverly St. www.citywinery.com/boston. ✆ **617/933-8047.** Tickets $15–$60. T: Haymarket.

Club Passim ★★ Seating about 100, this Harvard Square folk-music landmark has hosted Joan Baez and Bob Dylan (in the early 1960s), Patty Larkin, Josh Ritter, and Suzanne Vega. Today its calendar features local and national acts 7 nights a week; it offers dinner and a long list of wines and local beers. 47 Palmer St., Cambridge. www.clubpassim.org. ✆ **617/492-7679.** Tickets $10–$50, most shows around $20. T: Harvard.

House of Blues ★ Across the street from Fenway Park baseball stadium, this huge club hops year-round with rock, pop, and blues artists. The restaurant serves the chain's familiar Southern menu. 15 Lansdowne St. www.houseofblues.com/boston. ✆ **888/693-2583.** Tickets $23–$55. T: Kenmore.

Museums, Reimagined at Night

Once a month the **Isabella Stewart Gardner Museum** (p. 72) hosts its **Third Thursdays** evening event. You can stroll the galleries and perch next to the lavish courtyard garden with wine and music—for a few hours, this Venetian-style palazzo is your own play area. The Gardner's programming also includes jazz concerts and special events such as The Red Party, which "brings together fashion, music, and technology." **The**

Museum of Fine Arts (p. 73) has a similar program called **First Fridays,** when it stays open until 9:30pm with music, cocktails, and tapas. And check the calendar of the **Institute of Contemporary Art** (p. 69)—it hosts dance parties on Friday nights in summer on its large harborside patio, and has an annual "White Hot" event in August where most guests dress top to bottom in white.

The Middle East ★★   With three small restaurants and five performance spaces (including a large downstairs room—formerly a bowling alley—a corner bakery, and **Sonia,** in a room formerly occupied by the beloved music club TT the Bears), "The Middle" is an ever-innovative mecca for rock and eclectic alternative music. 472 Massachusetts Ave. www.mideastclub.com. © **617/864-3278.** Most shows $5–$20. T: Central.

The Sinclair ★★★   A welcome and overdue addition to Harvard Square, the Sinclair brings a swank gastropub and the area's first major live music venue to the neighborhood. It's comfortable and smartly booked. 52 Church St. www.sinclaircambridge.com. © **617/547-5200.** Tickets $13–$25. T: Harvard.

TD Garden ★   The city's premier arena is home to the Celtics (National Basketball Association) and Bruins (National Hockey League), but when they're not playing "The Garden" also brings in ice shows and touring rock and pop artists such as Bon Jovi and Maroon 5. 100 Legends Way. www.tdgarden.com. © **617/624-1331.** Ticket prices vary. T: North Station.

Bars, Lounges & Pubs

The Black Rose ★   A location just around the corner from Faneuil Hall Marketplace ensures that there's always a full house in this Irish pub for food, drink, and the Irish musicians who settle in at 9:30pm, 7 nights a week (and at 4pm on Saturday and Sunday). Locals and tourists join in the singing for convivial, blurry nights. Those who can't get enough can come back for breakfast (Saturday and Sunday). 160 State St. www.blackroseboston.com. © **617/742-2286.** Cover $3–$10. T: Aquarium.

Bleacher Bar ★★   Under—*under!*—the Fenway Park bleachers, this standard-issue ground-floor bar has a spectacularly unique feature: a floor-to-ceiling picture window that looks out directly onto centerfield (the bar used to be the visiting team's batting cage). It's accessible from Lansdowne Street, meaning you don't have to be in the stadium to get in. Prime tables enjoy a

Tour the Samuel Adams Boston Brewery

In the Jamaica Plain neighborhood of Boston, an area known as the Brewery Complex is home to the **Samuel Adams Boston Brewery ★★,** 30 Germania St. (www.samueladams.com; © **617/368-5080**). Though it's the smallest of Sam Adams' three beer-making locations, it's the only one that hosts tours. The company's suds started flowing in 1984—not in the revolutionary era as some suppose—but founder Jim Koch tapped into the patriotic fervor that Boston historically had for beer. Before Prohibition this stretch of Jamaica Plain and neighboring Roxbury boasted the most breweries per capita in the U.S. The free tours last about an hour and the visit can be extended to the taproom or beer garden. There's a gift shop on site. Tours take place Monday through Thursday and Saturday 10am to 3pm, and Friday 10am to 5:30pm. Tickets are first-come, first-served. Take the T to Stony Brook, and then it's a 10-minute walk—head for the tower that says "Haffenreffer Brewery."

Boston & Cambridge Entertainment & Nightlife

BOSTON & CAMBRIDGE

fielder's-eye view through one-way glass. On evenings when Fenway Park hosts musical events, a seat here gives you a peek at the backstage and the full show for the cost of a burger. 82A Lansdowne St. www.bleacherbarboston.com. ✆ **617/262-2424.** T: Kenmore.

Bristol Bar ★★   The posh bar in the Four Seasons Hotel is a magnet for a well-heeled older crowd and the perfect place for a martini or glass of wine. A menu of 18 kinds of "bar bites" is available (until 11:30pm Sun–Thurs and 12:30am Fri–Sat). In the Four Seasons Hotel, 200 Boylston St. www.fourseasons.com/boston. ✆ **617/338-4400.** T: Arlington.

The Burren ★★   Further afield of other pubs listed here—it's in Somerville, at the Davis stop on the T's Red Line, two stops after Harvard—the Burren is a top spot in Boston area for Irish music. The front bar has music every evening as well as weekend afternoons, and a larger back room is busy every evening as well, hosting either larger music events or, on quiet nights, programs like trivia and comedy. It's family-friendly and always a good scene. 247 Elm St., Somerville. www.burren.com. ✆ **617/776-6896.** T: Davis.

Cask 'n Flagon ★   Along with its across-the-street competitor **Game On!** (82 Lansdowne St.; www.gameonboston.com; ✆ **617/351-7001**), "The Cask" is busiest when the Red Sox are in town—the team plays at the adjacent Fenway Park—but lively year-round. Gigantic high-def TV screens at every turn and an outdoor urban patio make this a fun option if you don't want to spring for pricey baseball tickets—you can hear the roar of the stadium crowd just fine. Come early for a seat on game days. 62 Brookline Ave. www.casknflagon.com. ✆ **617/536-4840.** T: Kenmore.

Cheers ★   The popular TV show *Cheers,* which ran from 1982 to 1993, featured this Beacon Hill bar's exterior in the opening credits. The outside looks the same—and many visitors pose for a photo right here—although the interior is nothing like the show. "This is a tourist trap for sure," wrote one fan on Yelp, adding: "Lucky for them I love getting trapped. Touristy stuff is a must do for me when traveling." Legions of other visitors agree. Also check out the "replica" *Cheers* in Faneuil Hall Marketplace (✆ **617/227-0150;** T: Government Center.) which looks a lot more like the set, and also has outdoor seating. 84 Beacon St. (Beacon Hill). www.cheersboston.com. ✆ **617/227-9605.** T: Arlington.

Delux Cafe ★   With a kitschy decor (a shrine to Elvis, a sparkly sculpture of Schlitz cans, a painting that does homage to the TV show *The Golden Girls*), good burgers and fish, and local microbrews, the Delux is a friendly hipster bar. Year-round Christmas lights give it a festive glow. The bar attracts a cross-section of the South End, including lots of off-duty chefs. 100 Chandler St. ✆ **617/338-5258.** T: Back Bay.

Drink ★★★   Great martinis are served at this upscale spot in Fort Point, on the western edge of the Seaport District. Here, bartenders put together new variations on familiar themes. Located in the downstairs of an industrial warehouse with street-level windows, the space feels both old fashioned and extremely modern. A small menu of food options is available from 4 to 11:30pm. The bar is part of the family of restaurants by local star Barbara Lynch, and if you're still hungry two of them are steps away: The relaxed **Sportello** is just upstairs, and fancy **Menton** is next door at 352 Congress. 348 Congress St. www.drinkfortpoint.com. ✆ **617/695-1806.** T: Courthouse.

The Four's ★   Especially for hockey and basketball fans, the Four's, across the street from the TD Garden where the Bruins and Celtics play, has been a favorite since 1976. It boasts tons of TVs, abundant memorabilia, and decent pub grub. 166 Canal St. www.thefours.com. ✆ **617/720-4455.** T: North Station.

Frenchie Wine Bistro ★   New to the South End in 2017, the Parisian-styled Frenchie has a few sidewalk tables and an appealing greenhouse. Many guests come for the "frosé," a rosé slushy. 560 Tremont St. www.frenchieboston. com. ✆ **857/233-5941.** T: Back Bay.

The Landing ★   If drinking a neon-colored concoction out of a fish bowl is your thing, then the Landing is your place. It's a large outdoor patio bar on Long Wharf, directly next to the Boston harbor (open seasonally, 10am–11pm daily in good weather). It's managed by the Boston Harbor Cruise company, so lots of patrons are either going to or coming off boat trips. 1 Long Wharf. www.bostonharborcruises.com/the-landing. ✆ **617/227-4321.** T: Aquarium.

Legal Harborside ★★   What a view! The enormous rooftop bar of a 3-floor complex of the **Legal Sea Foods** (p. 110) chain looks out directly over Boston Harbor. It attracts waves of folks bar-hopping through the Seaport District, especially on warm summer nights. Retractable glass walls and ceiling allow the bar to be enclosed in cold months and fully exposed in summer. More than two dozen wines are available by the glass, along with a respectable sushi menu. If you need a bigger food menu, the second floor has a fancy restaurant and the first floor offers casual patio dining. 270 Northern Ave., on Liberty Wharf. www.legalseafoods.com/restaurants/boston-legal-harborside-floor-3-40. ✆ **617/477-2900.** T: World Trade Center.

Boston's Summertime Beer Gardens

Boston's cold weather keeps people indoors for half the year, so when it warms up, folks pour outside. Recent additions to the outdoor drinking scene are **two beer gardens** on the Rose Kennedy Greenway: **Trillium Garden on the Greenway,** at High Street, across from Rowes Wharf (www.trilliumbrewing.com/greenway-garden; Wed–Fri 2–10pm; Sat 11am–10pm; Sun 11am–6pm; check Twitter @trilliumgarden for weather closures and on-tap updates) and **Downeast Back Porch** (in Dewey Square by South Station; www.downeast cider.com/pages/back-porch; Mon, Wed, Fri 4–9pm; Sat noon–9pm; Sun noon–7pm). Neither serve food, but both are near food trucks and both venues invite guests pick up food and bring it in.

After years of contentious debate, Massachusetts now allows casino gambling. **Encore Boston Harbor** (www.encore bostonharbor.com), a major casino development by Wynn Resorts, is scheduled to open summer of 2019 in Everett, a city just north of Boston across the Mystic River from Charlestown. The plan includes over 600 hotel rooms, waterfront dining, and new boat connections to downtown Boston. Check the website for up-to-date details.

Lookout Rooftop and Bar ★★　From a Seaport District perch atop the Envoy Hotel, this sixth floor bar manages to overlook both the Boston harbor *and* the city skyline. (It's located next to **The Barking Crab** restaurant, p. 114.) Dress code is elegant/casual—no baseball caps or tank tops. No food here, just cocktails, wine, and a good selection of local brews. 70 Sleeper St. www.theenvoyhotel.com. ✆ **617/530-1559.** T: Courthouse.

Meadhall ★★　The southeastern corner of Cambridge is home to MIT and tech companies launched by its grads, and both Google and Amazon also have offices here. Geeks that work hard play hard, and many do so at this cavernous, upscale gastropub offering more types of beers than anyone should try in a month. 90 Broadway/4 Cambridge Center, Cambridge. www.themeadhall.com. ✆ **617/714-4372.** T: Kendall/MIT.

Mr. Dooley's Boston Tavern ★★　Far enough off the tourist track to be a favorite with Financial District office workers and homesick expats, Dooley's is an authentically decorated Irish pub. There's live music nightly and a menu that includes shepherd's pie, hot corned beef, and fish and chips. Sometimes an expertly poured Guinness is all you need. 77 Broad St. www.mrdooleys.com. ✆ **617/338-5656.** T: Aquarium.

Oak Long Bar + Kitchen ★★　Voted Best Hotel Bar in 2017 by *Boston* magazine readers, the bar within Fairmont Copley Plaza is an elegant establishment that serves food and drink from early morning to late evening. Dress code is casual but you'll want to be at least neat if you can't muster full-on dapper. In the Fairmont Copley Plaza Hotel, 138 St. James Ave. www.oaklongbarkitchen.com. ✆ **617/585-7222.** T: Copley.

Tiki Rock ★　This cocktail bar comes with a solid pedigree, with menus designed by chefs from top restaurants including **South End Buttery** (p. 118). The drinks menu highlights old-timey favorites such as the Mai Tai and Painkiller—a rum, pineapple, coconut, and orange concoction that comes in a bowl and serves four. 2 Broad St. www.tikirock.com. ✆ **617/670-2222.** T: Aquarium.

Trade ★★　Come for the bar scene, stay for the delectable, shareable flatbreads, small plates, and Mediterranean vegetable sides (pumpkin falafel, beets with muhammara, tabbouleh with pomegranate molasses). Business travelers and foodies are equally happy here. 540 Atlantic Ave. www.trade-boston.com. ✆ **617/451-1234.** T: South Station.

SIDE TRIPS FROM BOSTON

By Leslie Brokaw & Erin Trahan

So many historical movements swirl around Boston—it's a marvel how many trends intersect here. Within an hours' drive from the city, you'll find numerous destinations of historical significance, as well as spots of great beauty that feed the soul. Exploring can take as little as half a day or as long as a week or more.

History buffs won't want to miss a trip west to **Lexington** and **Concord,** rich in American political and literary history. It was here that the U.S. Revolutionary War started, in the days after Paul Revere and William Dawes rode horses from Boston on April 18, 1775, to warn the colonists that British troops were on the march. Also in this region are the wilderness retreat of **Walden Pond State Reservation,** with the legacy of Henry David Thoreau, and Concord's home of *Little Women* author Louisa May Alcott. Farther inland, the mill town of **Lowell** offers tours of its rich textile heritage. North of Boston, **Marblehead, Salem, Newburyport,** and **Cape Ann** embrace their colonial coastal heritage. South of Boston, **Plymouth** is where the American experiment started.

LEXINGTON ★ & CONCORD ★★★

Lexington: 9 miles NW of downtown Boston. Concord: 18 miles NW of Boston.

Lexington and Concord (say "conquered") are often thought of as a joint destination, given their role in early U.S. history. The towns are 9 miles apart and a visit can easily fill a half- or full day. The battles of the U.S. Revolutionary War in 1775 started in Lexington, and the village wears this history proudly. Politically significant sites carry into Concord, which also has sites related to early U.S. literary and artistic movements.

History buffs will probably want to fit in visits to both towns. Those with less interest in the Revolutionary era can probably get

Eastern Massachusetts

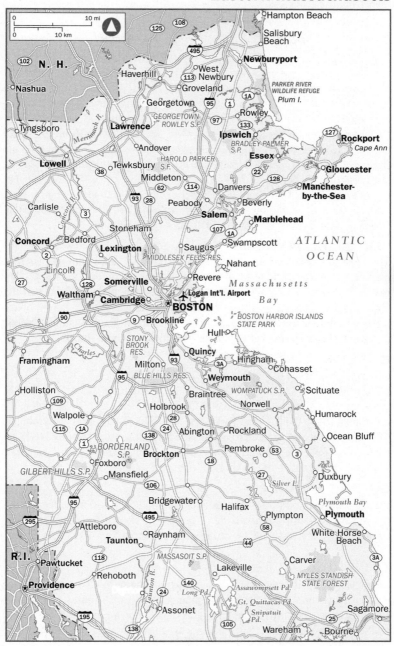

If you don't have the time or inclination to make your own arrangements, consider an escorted tour. One reliable company is **Gray Line Boston** (www.gray lineboston.com; ☎ **781/986-6100**), which offers both half- and full-day excursions.

their fill in a visit to Concord alone, while having other interesting options close by.

Essentials

ARRIVING

From Boston, take Storrow Drive or Memorial Drive to Route 2 to exit 54B, toward downtown Lexington.

Massachusetts Avenue (the same "Mass Ave" you saw in Boston and Cambridge) runs through the center of town. For Concord, stay on Route 2 and exit at 2A, there's metered parking on the street and in several municipal lots, and free parking at the National Heritage Museum and the National Historical Park.

By public transportation, **MBTA** (www.mbta.com; ☎ **617/222-3200**) bus routes no. 62 (Bedford) and 76 (Hanscom) both travel to Lexington from Alewife station, the last stop on the Red Line. Concord is a stop on the Fitchburg Commuter Line, leaving from Boston's North Station.

VISITOR INFORMATION

The **Lexington Visitor Center,** 1875 Massachusetts Ave. (www.tourlexington.us/visitors-center; ☎ **781/862-1450**) distributes maps and information. **Concord's Visitor Center,** 58 Main St. (www.concordma.gov; ☎ **978/318-3100**), is open daily 10am to 4pm mid-April through October. Bikes can be rented from here. The **Greater Merrimack Valley Convention & Visitors Bureau** (www.merrimackvalley.org; ☎ **978/459-6150**) covers both towns.

GUIDED TOURS

Liberty Ride (www.libertyride.us; ☎ **781/862-1450**) offers a 90-minute narrated trolley tour—conducted by guides in period dress—that connects the attractions in Lexington and Concord. Operated by the town of Lexington, it's recommended by the National Park Service. It offers four tours daily from late May through October and on weekends the rest of the year. The fare is $28 for adults, $12 for children 5 to 15, free for children 4 and under. Tickets are available online and at the Lexington Visitor's Center.

GETTING AROUND

Downtown Lexington is easily negotiable on foot, and most of the attractions listed here are within easy walking distance. The sites of Concord are spread out throughout the town, necessitating a car, a bus tour, or a bike to get around.

Exploring Lexington ★★

Lexington's rich Revolutionary War history is shared with visitors through outdoor common spaces, statues and memorials, historic houses and taverns, and museums. Here, we list the highlights of downtown Lexington in a logical **walking tour.** You'll first travel in a clockwise circle (more or less), and then head south on Mass Ave about a mile. These sights can be covered in 1 to 3 hours, depending on how much time you linger and whether you stop by all. (If time is short, head straight to the Buckman Tavern.)

- **Lexington Visitor Center,** 1875 Massachusetts Ave. (www.tourlexington.us/visitors-center; ℂ **781/862-1450**). Start your visit to downtown Lexington in this classic white-with-black-shutters New England Cape that houses the town's tourist center. A diorama and accompanying narrative illustrate the Battle of Lexington. There are public restrooms here. It's open daily from 9am to 5pm (10am–4pm Dec–Mar).

- **Buckman Tavern** ★★, 1 Bedford St. (www.lexingtonhistory.org/visit; ℂ **781/862-5598**). Next door to the visitor center is this appealing sight. If time is short and you have to pick just one house to visit, make it this one. The interior of the tavern (1710) has been restored to approximate its appearance on the day of the battle. The colonists gathered here to await word of British troop movements, and they brought their wounded here after the conflict. Self-paced audio tours are available (so, too, are audio tours of Battle Green and the Old Burying Ground, next on your walking tour), and there's a museum shop. It's open daily April to late November from 9:30am to 4pm. Closed December to March. See **Lexington Historical Society,** below, for ticket information.

GUNSHOTS IN lexington: THE REVOLUTIONARY WAR BEGINS

The battle phase of the U.S. Revolutionary War started in Lexington, with a skirmish on the town common, now called the Battle Green. It began when British troops clashed with local militia members, who were known as "Minutemen" for their ability to assemble on short notice.

British soldiers marched from Boston to Lexington late on April 18, 1775. Tipped off, Paul Revere and William Dawes rode ahead to sound the warning. The Lexington Minutemen, under the command of Capt. John Parker, got the word shortly after midnight, when the British redcoats were still several hours away. The colonists repaired to their homes and Lexington's Buckman Tavern.

Five hours later, some 700 British troops under Major Pitcairn arrived. A tense standoff ensued. Three times Pitcairn ordered the rebel forces to disperse, but the men—fewer than 100, and some accounts say 77—refused. Parker called: "Stand your ground. Don't

fire unless fired upon, but if they mean to have a war, let it begin here!" Finally the captain, perhaps realizing as the sky grew light how badly outnumbered his men were, gave the order to fall back.

As the Minutemen began to scatter, a shot rang out. One British company charged into the fray, and the colonists attempted to regroup as Pitcairn tried unsuccessfully to call off his troops. When it was over, 8 militia members lay dead, and 10 were wounded. A few hours later, the battle moved to Concord, at the North Bridge. The American Revolutionary War had now begun.

Patriot's Day, a Massachusetts state holiday observed on the third Monday in April, commemorates the start of the Revolution. Remembrances include **reenactments of the battles** including a major mock firefight on Lexington's Battle Green at 5:30am—followed by a pancake breakfast hosted by the Boy Scouts. Visit **www.battleroad.org** for information.

Lexington

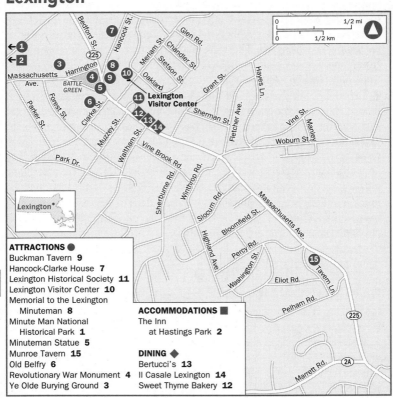

ATTRACTIONS ●
Buckman Tavern **9**
Hancock-Clarke House **7**
Lexington Historical Society **11**
Lexington Visitor Center **10**
Memorial to the Lexington
    Minuteman **8**
Minute Man National
    Historical Park **1**
Minuteman Statue **5**
Munroe Tavern **15**
Old Belfry **6**
Revolutionary War Monument **4**
Ye Olde Burying Ground **3**

ACCOMMODATIONS ■
The Inn
    at Hastings Park **2**

DINING ◆
Bertucci's **13**
Il Casale Lexington **14**
Sweet Thyme Bakery **12**

○ **Battle Green.** Across the street from the visitor center and tavern is a classic town green, which Lexington calls "Battle Green." It's here that the
Battle of Lexington took place. Anchoring this corner of the green (at the
intersection of Mass Ave and Bedford Street) is the famous **Minuteman
statue** (1900), which depicts Capt. John Parker, commander of Lexington's
anti-British militia in 1775. Several other memorials to the period are in the
park, including the **Revolutionary War Monument** (1799), a granite obelisk that marks the grave of seven of the eight colonists who died in the
conflict. The **Old Belfry,** a bell tower, used to be located on Battle Green.
It was this bell that sounded the alarm on the day of the battle, calling the
militia to the field. That Belfry was destroyed in a wind storm in 1909 but
was rebuilt by the Lexington Historical Society in 1910 and now stands half
a block away, at 16 Clarke St.

○ **Ye Olde Burying Ground.** Cross to the western side of the green and walk
across the small Harrington Road. A small sign points to a cemetery whose
gravestones, dating from 1690, are the oldest in Lexington. Those buried
here include Revolutionary soldiers (including Capt. Parker) and many

Civil war soldiers and veterans. Exit back to Harrington Road and head north east. In a few minutes the road dead ends at Hancock Street. Turn left.

o **Hancock-Clarke House,** 36 Hancock St. (www.lexingtonhistory.org/visit; ✆ **781/861-0928**). This 1737 house is where Samuel Adams and John Hancock were staying when Paul Revere arrived to tell them the British were coming (they fled to nearby Woburn). The mustard-colored house contains some original furnishings as well as artifacts of the Battle of Lexington and an orientation film about the town. It's open from 10am to 4pm and has guided tours on the hour. See **Lexington Historical Society,** below, for ticket information. From here, retrace your steps back to Battle Green.

o **Memorial to the Lexington Minutemen.** Back where Hancock Street meets Bedford Street is a small (about 4-ft.-high) sculpture that depicts the battle of Lexington in relief. It was made by artist Bashka Paeff. It's located across the street from Battle Green and is surrounded by a short black iron fence.

o **Lexington Historical Society,** 1846 Lexington Depot (www.lexingtonhistory. org; ✆ **781/8623763**). The historical society oversees the town's non-governmental historic records and three of the sights on this tour: Buckman Tavern, Hancock-Clarke House, and the Munroe Tavern. Admission to all three houses is $12 for adults, $6 for kids 6 to 16. Admission for a single house is $8 for adults, $5 for kids 6 to 16. Tickets (single or for all three properties) are sold at each of the houses and online. There is parking here for $2 a day. Restrooms are also available here as well as at all three houses.

o **Downtown Lexington.** The town's main street, Massachusetts Avenue, has a central downtown section about a quarter mile long that's chock-a-block with quick food options and shopping. Cafes and restaurants include **Sweet Thyme Bakery** (1837 Mass Ave; www.sweetthymebakery.com; ✆ **781/ 860-8818**) for Asian pastries and bubble tea; **Bertucci's** (1777 Mass Ave; www.bertuccis.com; ✆ **781/860-9000**) for pizza, salads, and hearty pasta, chicken, and seafood entrees; and **Il Casale Lexington** (1727 Mass Ave; www.ilcasalelexington.com; ✆ **781/538-5846**) for more upscale sit-down dining. The next stop is about a 15-minute walk down Mass Ave.

o **Munroe Tavern ★,** 1332 Massachusetts Avenue (about 1 mile from the Green; www.lexingtonhistory.org/visit; ✆ **781/862-0295**). The British took over this 1690 tavern to use as their headquarters and, after the battle, field hospital. At this location you'll hear the British side of the battle story, and see furniture carefully preserved by the Munroe family, including the table and chair President George Washington used when he dined here in 1789. The building complex houses a new archives center. See **Lexington Historical Society,** above, for ticket information. The tavern is on bus routes nos. 62 and 76 along Mass Ave.

MINUTE MAN NATIONAL HISTORICAL PARK

If you look at a map of Lexington and Concord, you'll see a 4-mile wide green swath starting west of downtown Lexington. This is **Minute Man National Historical Park** (www.nps.gov/mima; ✆ **978/369-6993**), which sprawls out across Lexington, Concord, and the adjacent town of Lincoln, covering 970 acres. Winding through the park, **Battle Road Trail** traces the route the defeated British troops took as they left Concord. Today, the 5-mile interpretive path is used by runners, walkers, and bikers as much as history buffs. Panels and granite markers along the trail explain the military, social, and natural history of the area.

The park has its own tourist information area, the **Minute Man Visitor Center** ★ on Route 2A., a little more than 2 miles west of downtown Lexington. Its free multimedia program, "The Road To Revolution," plays every 30 minutes. Park rangers provide a battle site exploration called "Parker's Revenge" which details a battle between Capt. John Parker and the Lexington militia and the British (daily mid-June to mid-Aug, 11:30am and 2:30pm). The center is open daily April through October from 9am to 5pm.

Inside Minute Man park are **Whittemore House,** which was inhabited in 1775 during the battle, just a few minutes' walk from the visitor center (open mid-June to early Aug, Mon and Tues 9:30am–5:30pm), and **Hartwell Tavern,** about a mile farther west, also authentic to the period. From mid-June through October, Wednesday through Sunday 9:30am to 5:30pm, costumed park rangers lead programs at the tavern about the Massachusetts militia and minute men, and demonstrate a flintlock musket firing (not recommended for people with hearing impairments or hearing aids).

Exploring Concord ★

By the mid-19th century, this lovely town was the center of the Transcendentalist movement, a philosophical movement that extolled self-reliance and the beauty of nature. Homes of transcendentalism's core practitioners (and literary lions) **Ralph Waldo Emerson, Henry David Thoreau, Nathaniel Hawthorne,** and **Louisa May Alcott** are here and open to visitors, as is their final resting place, **Sleepy Hollow Cemetery.** The nearby body of water made famous by Thoreau, **Walden Pond,** is a popular spot for swimming and hiking. Today Concord is a prosperous pastoral suburb of about 18,000.

The earliest real battle of the Revolutionary War took place at the **North Bridge,** now part of Minute Man National Historical Park (p. 143). For an excellent overview of town history, start your visit at the **Concord Museum.**

Concord Museum ★★ MUSEUM   Informative exhibits tell the story of Concord, incorporating artifacts, murals, films, and maps. Originally a Native American settlement, whose tribes lived along the languid Concord River and shared the Algonquian dialect, Concord later became a U.S. Revolutionary War battleground. Still later, it was a literary and intellectual center with a thriving clock-making industry. Many museum displays focus on the big names: You'll see one of the lanterns Longfellow immortalized in "Paul Revere's Ride" ("one if by land, and two if by sea"), the contents of Emerson's study, and a large collection of Thoreau's belongings. The period furniture and embroidery samplers offer a look at people's daily lives.

53 Cambridge Turnpike. www.concordmuseum.org. ☎ **978/369-9609** (recorded info) or ☎ 978/369-9763. $10 adults, $8 seniors & students, $5 kids 6–18, free for kids under

Concord

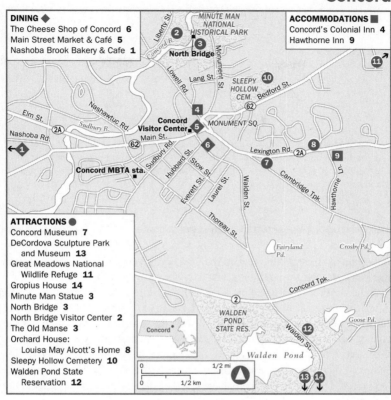

DINING ◆
The Cheese Shop of Concord **6**
Main Street Market & Café **5**
Nashoba Brook Bakery & Cafe **1**

ACCOMMODATIONS ■
Concord's Colonial Inn **4**
Hawthorne Inn **9**

MINUTE MAN
NATIONAL
HISTORICAL PARK

Liberty St.
Concord R.
North Bridge
Lowell Rd.
Lang St.
Monument St.
SLEEPY
HOLLOW
CEM. Bedford St.
Elm St.
Nashawtuc Rd.
Sudbury R.
**Concord
Visitor Center**
MONUMENT SQ.
Nashoba Rd.
2A
62
Main St.
Sudbury Rd.
Hubbard St.
Stow St.
Lexington Rd. 2A
Concord MBTA sta.
Everett St.
Laurel St.
Walden St.
Cambridge Tpk.
Hawthorne Ln.
Thoreau St.
Fairyland
Pd.
Crosby Pd.
Concord Tpk.
WALDEN
POND
STATE RES.
Concord
Goose Pd.
Walden St.
Walden Pond
1/2 mi
1/2 km

ATTRACTIONS ●
Concord Museum **7**
DeCordova Sculpture Park
   and Museum **13**
Great Meadows National
   Wildlife Refuge **11**
Gropius House **14**
Minute Man Statue **3**
North Bridge **3**
North Bridge Visitor Center **2**
The Old Manse **3**
Orchard House:
   Louisa May Alcott's Home **8**
Sleepy Hollow Cemetery **10**
Walden Pond State
   Reservation **12**

6. June–Aug daily 9am–5pm; Apr–May & Sept–Dec Mon–Sat 9am–5pm, Sun noon–5pm; Jan–Mar Mon–Sat 11am–4pm, Sun 1–4pm.

Great Meadows National Wildlife Refuge ★ NATURE PRESERVE
An especially popular destination for birders, the Concord portion of this 3,800-acre refuge includes 2.7 miles of walking trails along the sleepy Concord River and across a flat dike between man-made ponds that attract abundant wildlife. At a board at the entrance, visitors jot down the birds and other creatures they have seen. More than 220 species of native and migratory birds have been recorded, including red-winged blackbirds, great blue herons, and bald eagles. Dogs are not allowed. Parking is limited.

Monson Rd. (off Rte. 62/Bedford St. 1⅓ mi E of Concord center). www.fws.gov/refuge/great_meadows. ℂ **978/443-4661.** $4 Refuge Entrance Pass covers up to 4 adults; children free (look for self-pay station in parking lot). Open daily sunrise–sunset.

North Bridge ★★★ BATTLEFIELD   This site, part of **Minute Man National Historical Park** (p. 141), blends history with great natural beauty. About 0.7 miles from Concord Center, a short walk on an unpaved path from Monument Street (and a large parking lot) leads to this scenic and historically

BATTLE IN CONCORD: A shot HEARD 'ROUND THE WORLD

After the skirmish at Lexington (p. 139) on April 19, 1775, the British continued to Concord in search of stockpiled arms. Warned of the advance, the colonists crossed Concord's North Bridge, evading the "regulars" standing guard. They awaited reinforcements. Soon some 2,000 colonists, known as "Minute Men" for their ability to gather quickly, had arrived at North Bridge, with nearly the same number of militia members pouring in throughout the next hours. The British searched nearby homes and burned any guns they found; the colonists, seeing the smoke, mistakenly thought the soldiers were burning the town. Shots rang out, and soon the British were on the run, leaving behind weapons and equipment as they retreated back toward Boston and their naval ships docked in Charlestown. About 250 British troops and 90 colonists died that day along the 18-mile route from Concord to Charlestown. The news traveled speedily back to England, making this first gunfire of the Revolutionary War "the shot heard 'round the world."

important spot. Sometimes called the Old North Bridge, it's a reproduction of the wooden structure that spanned the narrow Concord River in 1775, a bucolic location surrounded by stone walls, pastures, and rolling countryside. After the skirmish at Lexington, a full battle took place at this bridge (see "Battle in Concord: A Shot Heard 'Round the World"). If you tune out the chatter of visitors you can almost imagine that firefight, which was commemorated in Ralph Waldo Emerson's poem "Concord Hymn." The first stanza of that poem is engraved on the base of the **Minute Man statue** near the bridge. Daniel Chester French, sculptor of the seated Abraham Lincoln at the president's memorial in Washington, D.C., created this iconic image of a militia man with a musket in one hand and a plow handle in the other. A plaque on the other side of the bridge honors the British soldiers who died in the battle.

Up a small hill from the bridge, a **National Park Service visitor center** has a diorama and video program illustrating the battle; rangers are on duty to answer questions. Visitors with mobility issues can park here instead of making the 10-minute walk from the Monument Street parking lot.

Also at this site, next to the bridge, is **The Old Manse** ★, 269 Monument St. (www.oldmanse.org; ⓒ **978/369-3909**), which figures in Concord's rich literary history as well as its political history. Rev. William Emerson built this home in 1770 and watched the terrifying battle from its windows. His grandson Ralph Waldo Emerson later worked on the essay "Nature" in the study. Newlywed Nathaniel Hawthorne (*The Scarlet Letter, The House of the Seven Gables*) moved here in 1842 with Sophia Peabody. On the guided tour you'll see poems that the newlyweds scratched on windows with her diamond ring. Tours are $10 for adults, $9 seniors and students, $5 kids 6 to 12, free for kids 5 and under, $25 families. The house is open for tours mid-April to October

Tuesday to Sunday noon to 5pm, and November to mid-April Saturday to Sunday noon to 4pm.

Two parking lots: Monument St. lot, ½-mile from Concord center; visitor center lot, 174 Liberty St., off Monument St. www.nps.gov/mima/north-bridge-questions. ⓒ **978/369-6993.** Free admission. Grounds daily dawn to dusk. Visitor center daily 9am–5pm Apr–Oct; check ahead for winter hours.

Orchard House: Louisa May Alcott's Home ★★ HISTORIC HOME
The beloved author wrote and set her novel *Little Women* (1868) here. Alcott and her sisters—the models for *Little Women*'s March family—called Orchard House home from 1858 to 1877. The guided tour, the only way to see the house, highlights numerous heirlooms, like Alcott's little desk and the miniature pieces of furniture that appear to be from a dollhouse (they're actually salesman's samples). Check ahead for the extensive schedule of special events.

99 Lexington Rd. www.louisamayalcott.org. ⓒ **978/369-4118.** $10 adults, $8 seniors & students, $5 kids 6–17, free for kids under 6, $25 families. Apr–Oct Mon–Sat 10am–5pm, Sun 1–5pm; Nov–Mar Mon–Fri 11am–3pm, Sat 10am–4:30pm, Sun 1–4:30pm.

Sleepy Hollow Cemetery ★ GRAVEYARD Follow the signs for AUTHOR'S RIDGE in the cemetery's northeast side and climb the hill to the graves of some of the town's literary lights, including the Alcotts, Emerson, Hawthorne, and Thoreau. Many visitors leave pens and pencils on the writers' gravestones. Emerson's bears no religious symbols, just an uncarved quartz boulder. Thoreau is buried nearby.

24 Court Lane, 1 block E of Monument Square. www.nps.gov/nr/travel/massachusetts_conservation/sleepy_hollow.html. Free admission. Daily 7am to dusk.

Walden Pond State Reservation ★★★ PARK/HISTORIC SITE One of the most famous places in New England is also an attractive, surprisingly unspoiled state park property that allows swimming, fishing, hiking, and picnicking. Walden Pond was home to author Henry David Thoreau for a few years in the mid-1840s—he wrote about his time there and his reflections on life in *Walden,* perhaps the most famous American book about living simply—and that legacy helped establish the site as a National Historic Landmark. The wooded park has 462 acres of protected open space, and visitors can pop into a replica of Thoreau's cabin along on the path between the parking lot and the pond. (The real cabin was actually located at the far side of the pond—that site is marked with squat stone pillars surrounding the cabin's original hearth stone.) On the shore, there are condoned-off **swimming areas** in summer with a sandy beach and lifeguards. There are also bathrooms and changing rooms at this end of the pond. You'll often see hearty swimmers slowly traverse the 1.7-mile circumference, which is 102-foot deep in spots and was created by a melted glacier (and if you come at sunrise you're likely to see swimmers who meet to cross the pond together). A striking **visitor center** opened in 2016 and is located in the parking lot; it includes a small store with books, T-shirts, and other Thoreau memorabilia. There are no food concessions here.

Keep in mind that the pond gets half a million visitors a year and on busy days, when it reaches capacity, rangers turn people away. It's an appreciated practice—if you're already inside. To avoid the disappointment of driving up only to see the sign WALDEN POND CLOSED / NO DROP OFFS NO WALK INS / REOPEN TIME 2:30, check the lot's status on Twitter @waldenpondstate or by calling the main number. Plan to arrive by 9:30am on a summer weekend or very hot weekdays.

915 Walden St. (Rte. 126), off Route 2. www.mass.gov/dcr. (C) **978/369-3254.** Free admission to pond; parking $8 Mass. residents, $15 non-residents. No pets or bikes. Weekdays 5am–7:30pm, weekends 7am–7:30pm during summer peak season; confirm hours other times of the year.

NEARBY ART & ARCHITECTURE SIGHTS

DeCordova Sculpture Park and Museum ★★ MUSEUM Four miles south from Concord center, this special museum's main building sits on a rural hilltop, overlooking a pond and an expansive sculpture park. Outdoors and in, contemporary artists are on display, with an emphasis on living New England residents. Much of the outdoor sculpture is both majestic and playful. Picnicking is allowed in the sculpture park; bring your lunch or buy it at the cafe (Mon–Fri 9am–3pm, Sat–Sun 11am–4pm). A handful of tours of the main galleries and the outdoor sculpture park are scheduled each week—check the website for exact days and times. Tours are free with museum admission.

51 Sandy Pond Rd., Lincoln. www.decordova.org. (C) **781/259-8355.** Museum and park: $14 adults; $12 seniors and AAA members; $10 students; free for kids 12 and under; free to anyone who rides a bike to the museum. Late May–early Oct daily 10am–5pm; rest of year Wed–Fri 10am–4pm, Sat–Sun 10am–5pm.

Gropius House ★ HISTORIC HOME/ARCHITECTURE Architect Walter Gropius (1883–1969), founder of the Bauhaus school of design, built this hilltop home for his family in 1938 using traditional materials such as clapboard, brick, and fieldstone, along with components then seldom seen in domestic architecture, including glass blocks and chrome. Its influence was powerful, and the building is now a designated National Historic Landmark. Modernist Marcel Breuer designed many of the furnishings. Decorated in the last decade of Gropius's life, the house affords a revealing look at his career and philosophy.

68 Baker Bridge Rd., Lincoln. www.historicnewengland.org/property/gropius-house. (C) **781/259-8098.** $15 adults, $12 students & seniors. Tours on the hour May–Oct Wed–Sun 11am–4pm; Nov–Apr Sat–Sun 11am–4pm.

Where to Stay in Lexington & Concord

CONCORD

Concord's Colonial Inn ★ The main building of the Colonial Inn has overlooked Concord's pleasant Monument Square since 1716. Like many historic inns, it's not luxurious and is even tired in some spots, but it is comfortable and centrally located. Additions since it became a hotel in 1889 have left the inn large enough to offer modern conveniences and small enough to feel friendly. It's especially popular during the October-November foliage season, and the 15 original guest rooms, decorated in Colonial style, are in great demand. Rooms in the 1970 Prescott House have country-style decor, and four freestanding buildings hold one-, two-, and three-bedroom suites. (Note that there are no elevators.) The **Liberty,** the inn's main restaurant, serves traditional American fare (chicken pot pie, beer battered fish and chips, Yankee pot roast) along with salads and sandwiches. Afternoon tea is served on weekends 3 to 4pm; reservations are required. Food is also served in the **Merchant's Row** restaurant, with drinks in the **Tap Room** and the **Village Forge Tavern.** In warm months, there's a seasonal patio.

48 Monument Sq. www.concordscolonialinn.com. © **800/370-9200** or 978/369-9200. 56 units. $119–$239 double. **Amenities:** 2 restaurants; bar; Wi-Fi (free).

Hawthorne Inn ★★ This quintessential country bed and breakfast is maintained in a careful, thorough manner. Built around 1870, it sits on a tree-shaded property across the street from author Nathaniel Hawthorne's 19th-century home, the Wayside, and down the street from Orchard House, Louisa May Alcott's home. Antiques and handmade quilts enhance the 7 rooms, which aren't huge but are meticulously maintained. Outside, there's a small pond in the peaceful garden. Personable innkeepers acquaint interested guests with the philosophical, military, and literary aspects of Concord's history. The website has a feature that allows you to easily book your exact preferred room. The inn notes that "Children, traveling with well-behaved adults, are always welcome."

462 Lexington Rd. www.hawthorneinnconcord.com. © **978/369-5610.** 7 units. $179–$304 double. Rates include breakfast. 2-night minimum some dates. **Amenities:** Wi-Fi (free).

LEXINGTON

The Inn at Hastings Park ★★ Only a handful of properties in New England are members of the prestigious Relais & Châteaux luxury network. This Lexington inn is one. Located on a stately section of Mass Ave just a short walk from Battle Green, it is made up of three restored buildings and offers 22 rooms that are each uniquely shaped and decorated. Amenities for kids—"Pint Sized Patriots"—include child-sized robes and slippers, room-service-delivered milk and cookies, and children's books about the Revolutionary War. The inn's restaurant, **Artistry on the Green,** receives good notice, featuring clever New England twists: lobster cobb salad, lamb bacon BLT, parsnip cake. Main courses run $24 to $46. The dining room is open for breakfast and lunch 7 days a week (with a Sunday brunch) and dinner Tuesday through Saturday.

2027 Massachusetts Ave. www.innathastingspark.com. © **781/301-6660.** 22 units. From $252 double. Rates include breakfast. **Amenities:** Restaurant; concierge; Wi-Fi (free).

Where to Eat in Lexington & Concord

Besides the restaurant listed below, consider the restaurants at Lexington's **The Inn at Hastings Park** (above) and Concord's **Colonial Inn** (p. 146). In Concord, the **Cheese Shop of Concord,** 29 Walden St. (www.concordcheeseshop. com; © **978/369-5778**) sells sandwiches, soups, and chocolates. **Nashoba**

Brook Bakery & Café, at 152 Commonwealth Ave. in West Concord (www. slowrise.com; ✆ **978/318-1999**) makes its own bread, pastries, soups, salads, and sandwiches.

CONCORD

Main Streets Market & Cafe ★ AMERICAN   Cozy and appealing, serving up breakfast, lunch, dinner, and then music every night starting around 8pm, the family-owned Main Streets has long been a part of Concord's culture—it's been operating here for over 100 years, and it's still a favorite for locals. A big menu includes sandwiches, burgers, grain bowls, and flatbread pizza.

42 Main St. www.mainstreetsmarketandcafe.com. ✆ **866/413-3981.** Main courses $5–$21. Daily 6am–5pm.

NASHOBA VALLEY ★★

Bolton: 40 miles W of downtown Boston and 17 miles from Concord

A little farther west of Concord, the vistas open up into farmland. This is an area of Massachusetts rich in apple orchards (along with pear trees and other fruit). Many people keep horses out here. A drive to Bolton or Harvard for **apple picking** is an annual activity for many Bostonians. There's also skiing here, and extraordinary views of rolling hills as far as the eye can see.

From Boston and Cambridge, take Storrow Drive or Memorial Drive to Route 2 to its end in West Concord, and then pick up Route 111, which goes directly to Harvard, Mass. Bolton is 5 miles south of Harvard Center via Bolton Road (which becomes Harvard Road). Stow is 17 miles south of Harvard on Route 117. Alternately, take I-90, the Mass Pike, from Boston west to I-495 North; there are exits from I-495 for both Bolton and Harvard.

Exploring the Nashoba Valley

Nashoba Valley Ski Area, 79 Powers Rd., Westford (www.skinashoba.com; ✆ **978/692-3033**) has 17 ski trails and a snowtubing park. It stays in business in summertime, too, with 5k races, a volleyball league, paint nights for adults, an outdoor pool, and a tiki bar (www.sunset-tiki.com).

Fruitlands Museum ★ MUSEUM/PARK   It's a quirky destination, but oh, what a view. Set on 210 rural acres, mostly meadows and woods, with five hiking trails, it offers an incredible vista of miles of rolling hills (take a look at Instagram @fruitlandsmuseum). The organization is dedicated to sharing information about the lives of the Transcendentalists, the Shakers, Native Americans, and the artists of the Hudson River School of landscape painting—all folks who had a deep connection to nature—and each group has its own museum. There's also a separate visitor center. A covered-patio café is open for lunch features salads, sandwiches, and—again—that view.

102 Prospect Hill Rd., Harvard. http://fruitlands.thetrustees.org. ✆ **978/456-3924.** $15 adults, $12 students & seniors, $6 kids 5–13, free 4 and under (mid-Nov–mid-Apr $5 for all). Mid Apr–early Nov Mon & Wed–Fri 10am–4pm; Sat–Sun 10am–5pm; rest of year Sat–Sun noon–5pm, some museum buildings closed.

milling around: A TRIP TO LOWELL

A 19th-century textile center that later fell into disrepair, Lowell is a 21st-century success story. A city built around restored mills and industrial canals will never be a glamorous vacation spot, but thousands of visitors a year find Lowell a fascinating and rewarding destination, with sights concentrating on the history of the Industrial Revolution and the textile industry. They include boardinghouses where the "mill girls" lived; the workers, some as young as 10, averaged 14-hour days weaving cloth on power looms.

Start at the **Lowell National Histori- cal Park Visitor Center,** 246 Market St. (www.nps.gov/lowe; **☏ 978/970-5000**), open daily from 9am to 5pm (until 4:30pm in winter). Rangers lead free tours on foot and by trolley. **Boat tours** of the canals ($12 adults, $10 seniors, $8 kids 6-16, free for 5 and under) have limited space; reservations are recommended. Ask for a map of the area, and use it to find your way around downtown.

The **New England Quilt Museum ★**, 18 Shattuck St. (https://www.nequiltmusuem. org; **☏ 978/452-4207**) is within walking distance. Unfortunately, the Smithsonian-affiliated American Textile History Museum closed in 2016.

Both the visitor center and the Quilt Museum are located in the vibrant **Canalway Cultural District** (www.like lowell.com/canalways-cultural-district), which is also home to 10 other art galleries and museums, and over 10 parks and plazas. The **Lowell Summer Music Series** (www.lowellsummermusic.org) takes place at **Boarding House Park,** within the district and near to the small **Jack Kerouac Park** (the writer was a native son).

To drive to Lowell, take Route 3 or I-495 to the Lowell Connector and follow signs north to exit 5B and the historic district. The **MBTA commuter rail** (www. mbta.com; **☏ 800/392-6100** or 617/222-3200) from Boston's North Station takes about 45 minutes.

Honey Pot Hill Orchards ★★ FARM   Apple picking starts in this region in late August, and by mid-September pears are usually ready, too. There are orchards throughout Nashoba Valley, including in Harvard, Bolton, and here in Stow. Honey Pot Hill is a mid-sized operation, accommodating busloads of schoolchildren along with individual guests, and it still feels old-timey. It also has blueberry bushes, which come into season in July for picking. Pick-your-own is cash only. Late August through mid-November, the orchard maintains a Big Green Monster Maze made up of 3,000 hedges—it has six bridges and a lookout gazebo and takes an hour to get through. A smaller Mini Monster Maze is a replica of the maze at England's Hampton Court, a Tunnel Maze serves smaller kids, and there are hayrides. A courtyard next to the farm store has sheep, goats, and bunnies for viewing.

138 Sudbury Rd., Stow. www.honeypothill.com. **☏ 978/562-5666.** Free admission. Pick-your-own apples: one peck bag $18, half-bushel bag $28, cash only. July–Nov daily 9:30am–5pm; closed Dec–June.

Nashoba Valley Winery ★★★ VINEYARD   Atop 52 acres of gently rolling hills, this friendly, mid-sized operation has an orchard, a tasting room, a restaurant, and a brewery. Weddings are held here, but day trippers are welcome, too. Guests are invited to bring blankets and picnics (or pre-order a picnic meal) and spread out on the lawn or at any of the hillside picnic tables

For convenience and flexibility, drive to destinations north of Boston if you can. Renting a car may be cheaper than the commuter rail, if your group is large enough; even if it isn't, flexibility and access are priceless. Most North Shore destinations are about an hour's drive from Boston. Traveling between the destinations listed here can also take as long as an hour. Consider choosing one as home base for a few nights. Each town is rich in history, wonderfully distinct, and worth a close look. The **North of Boston Convention & Visitors Bureau** (www.northofboston.org; ☎ **978/465-6555**) publishes a visitor guide that covers many destinations in this chapter. The website of the **Essex National Heritage Area** (www.essex heritage.org; ☎ **978/740-0444**) is another good resource.

for an afternoon. Tastings are $10 and include a tasting glass and 5 pours. The vineyard produces chardonnay, cabernet, merlot (even a blueberry merlot), and fun options like strawberry rhubarb. Guided tours take place weekends from 11am to 4pm, with six tastings during the tour (tours cost $15; reservations recommended). You can pick your own peaches (usually late July–Aug) and apples (Aug–Oct). Expect crowds on weekends September through October, and quieter visits on weekdays and the rest of the year.

100 Wattaquadock Hill Rd., Bolton. www.nashobawinery.com. ☎ **978/779-5521.** Admission to grounds free; tastings $10; tours $15 adults, $8 children and people not drinking. Tasting room Mon–Fri 11am–5pm, Sat–Sun 10am–5pm. Tours on the hour Sat–Sun 11am–4pm.

MARBLEHEAD ★★★ & SALEM ★★

Marblehead: 15 miles NE of Boston. Salem: 16 miles NE of Boston; 4 miles NW of Marblehead

One of the prettiest of Boston's "North Shore" communities, Marblehead has scenery, history, architecture, and shopping—making it one of the area's most popular day trips for both locals and visitors. The narrow streets of historic Old Town are rich with homes and buildings from the 17th and 18th centuries. Those same streets lead down to the magnificent harbor that helps make Marblehead the self-proclaimed "Yachting Capital of America." Plaques on many homes give the dates of construction as well as the names of the builders and original occupants—a history lesson without any studying.

Marblehead's neighbor, Salem, is a family-friendly destination that's worth at least a half-day visit, perhaps after a stop in Marblehead; it can easily fill a day. If you know Salem only because of its association with witches, you're in for a delightful surprise. Settled in 1626, four years before Boston, for centuries Salem enjoyed international renown as a center of merchant shipping. Its merchant vessels circled the globe in the 17th and 18th centuries, returning laden with treasures. One reminder of that era, a replica of the 1797 East Indiaman tall ship *Friendship,* is typically anchored near the Salem

Maritime National Historic Site (it has been undergoing restoration with a return planned sometime in 2018). Salem also has literary heritage, thanks to novelist Nathaniel Hawthorne, and one of the finest cultural institutions in New England, the Peabody Essex Museum.

Essentials

ARRIVING

BY CAR From Boston, take Route 1A north through Lynn and Swampscott; in Swampscott, take Lynn Shore Drive to Route 129, and follow it into Marblehead. Except at rush hour, allow at least 45 minutes. Parking is tough, especially in Old Town—grab the first spot you see. From Marblehead, take Route 114 west into downtown Salem.

To reach Salem directly from Boston, take I-93 north to I-95 north and then Route 128 north. Exit at Route 114 east and follow Route 114 into downtown Salem. This is also about a 45-minute drive, outside of rush hour. Salem has plenty of metered street parking and a reasonably priced garage opposite the visitor center.

BY BUS MBTA (www.mbta.com; ℭ **800/392-6100** or ℭ 617/222-3200) bus no. 441/442 runs from Haymarket (Orange or Green Line) in Boston to downtown Marblehead on weekdays; on weekends service is from Wonderland station at the end of the Blue Line. During weekday rush hours, bus no. 448/449 connects Marblehead to Boston's Downtown Crossing. The trip takes about an hour. Buses nos. 450/450W to Salem also depart from Haymarket; the trip takes 55 minutes. For either destination, the one-way fare is $4 with a CharlieCard, $5 with a CharlieTicket or cash.

BY TRAIN MBTA commuter trains run to Salem from Boston's North Station. It's a 30- to 35-minute trip; the round-trip fare is $15. The station is about 5 blocks from the downtown area.

BY FERRY From late May through October, the 50-minute **Salem Ferry** (www.salemferry.com; ℭ **877/733-9425** or ℭ 617/227-4321) leaves from Long Wharf in Boston (next to the New England Aquarium and MBTA Blue Line), arriving at Salem's Blaney Street Wharf, off Derby Street, a 15-minute walk from downtown. (It's also on the Salem Trolley route—see p. 152.) Adult fare is $25 one-way, $45 round-trip, with discounts for seniors and children; you can purchase in advance (recommended) online. There are only four or five ferries a day, so always be sure you know the schedule for your return trip.

VISITOR INFORMATION

The **Marblehead Chamber of Commerce,** 62 Pleasant St. (www.marble headchamber.org; ℭ **781/631-2868**), is open Monday, Wednesday, and Friday 9am to 5pm, and Tuesday and Thursday 10am to 6pm. The **information booth** on Pleasant Street near Spring Street is generally open mid-May through October, weekdays noon to 5pm, weekends 10am to 6pm. The **National Park Service Salem Visitor Center,** 2 New Liberty St. (www.nps. gov/sama; ℭ **978/740-1650**), is open daily 9am–5pm from May through October (the rest of the year, it's open Wed–Sun only, 10am–4pm), with historical exhibits, a free film, and brochures and pamphlets, including a walking tour pamphlet. The **Salem Chamber of Commerce,** 265 Essex St., Suite 101 (www.salem-chamber.org; ✆ **978/744-0004**), open weekdays 9am to 5pm, also has brochures and pamphlets.

Information about Salem is also available online at **Destination Salem** (www.salem.org; ✆ **877/SALEM-MA** [725-3662] or ✆ 978/744-3663), the city website **www.salem.com**, and an excellent community website **www. salemweb.com**.

GETTING AROUND

Marblehead's downtown area is fairly compact and moderately hilly, but its narrow streets make driving difficult—your best option is to park the car and hoof it. In congested downtown Salem, walking is also the way to go, but you may opt for riding the **Salem Trolley** ★ (www.salemtrolley.com; ✆ **508/744-5469**), which offers a 1-hour narrated tour and unlimited reboarding at any of its 14 stops. The tour starts at the Essex Street side of the visitor center. It operates daily April through October from 10am to 5pm (last tour at 4pm); check ahead for off-season hours. Tickets ($18 adults, $17 seniors, $8 children 6–14) are good all day.

Exploring Marblehead

Many of the houses in Marblehead's **Old Town** ★★★ have stood since before the Revolutionary War, when this was a center of merchant shipping. Two of these historic homes are open to visitors. Allow at least a full morning to visit Marblehead, but be flexible, because you may want to hang around. A stroll through these winding streets invariably leads to shopping, snacking, or gazing at something picturesque, be it the harbor or a beautiful home. Be sure to spend some time in **Crocker Park** ★★, on the water off Front Street. Especially in warm weather, when boats jam the harbor, the view is breathtaking. The park has benches and allows picnicking. The view from **Fort Sewall,** at the other end of Front Street, is just as mesmerizing. The ruins of the fort, built in the 17th century and rebuilt late in the 18th, are another excellent picnic spot.

Just inland, the **Lafayette House** is a private home at the corner of Hooper and Union streets. Legend has it that one corner of the first floor was chopped off in 1824 to allow Lafayette's carriage to negotiate the turn. In Market Square, on Washington Street near State Street, the **Old Town House** has been a public meeting-and-gathering place since 1727.

By car or on ambitious feet, follow Ocean Avenue across the causeway to look at the swanky residential community of **Marblehead Neck** ★. Veer right at Harbor Avenue to stay on Ocean Avenue. A counterclockwise loop of about 3 miles will lead you past the Massachusetts Audubon Society's **Marblehead Neck Wildlife Sanctuary** (www.massaudubon.org; ✆ 800/AUDUBON [283-8266] or 978/887-9264); look for the tiny sign at the corner of Risley Avenue. Admission is free. You can make another stop at **Castle Rock** for rocky coastline views or continue to the end of "the Neck," at Harbor and Ocean avenues, where **Chandler Hovey Park** has a (closed) lighthouse and a panoramic view.

Marblehead

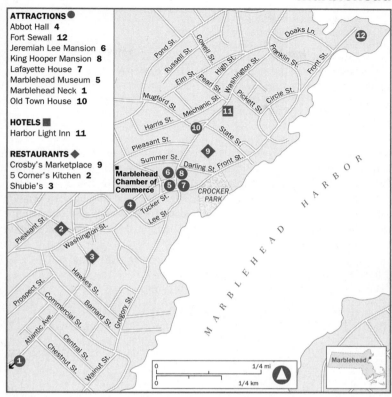

ATTRACTIONS ●
Abbot Hall **4**
Fort Sewall **12**
Jeremiah Lee Mansion **6**
King Hooper Mansion **8**
Lafayette House **7**
Marblehead Museum **5**
Marblehead Neck **1**
Old Town House **10**

HOTELS ■
Harbor Light Inn **11**

RESTAURANTS ◆
Crosby's Marketplace **9**
5 Corner's Kitchen **2**
Shubie's **3**

Abbot Hall ★ TOWN HALL   The town offices and historical commission share Abbot Hall with Archibald M. Willard's iconic painting *The Spirit of '76* ★, on display in the Selectmen's Meeting Room. The thrill of recognizing the ubiquitous drummer, drummer boy, and fife player is the main reason to stop here. Display cases in the halls contain artifacts from the Historical Society's collections.

Washington Sq. www.marblehead.org. ✆ **781/631-0000.** Free admission. Year-round Mon–Tues & Thurs 8am–5pm, Wed 8am–6pm, Fri 8am–12:30pm; June to mid-Oct also open Fri 1–5pm, Sat 10am–5pm, Sun (and Monday holidays) 11am–5pm.

Jeremiah Lee Mansion/Marblehead Museum ★★ HISTORIC HOME Built in 1768 for a wealthy merchant, the Lee mansion is an extraordinary example of pre–Revolutionary Georgian architecture. Rococo woodcarving and other details complement historically accurate room arrangements; the most exciting feature for aficionados is the original hand-painted wallpaper. Ongoing restoration and interpretation by the Marblehead Museum place the 18th- and 19th-century furnishings and artifacts in context. The friendly guides

153

welcome questions and are well versed in the history of the home. The gardens are open to the public. Across the street at 170 Washington St., the **J.O.J. Frost Gallery and Carolyn Lynch Education Center** (free admission, donations welcome) features paintings, wooden models, and carvings by the noted folk artist J.O.J. Frost, a Marblehead native. The Museum also operates the **Civil War & G.A.R Museum,** located within the Old Town House, open to the public on a limited schedule.

161 Washington St. www.marbleheadmuseum.org. ✆ **781/631-1768.** Guided tours $10. June–Oct Tues–Sat 10am–4pm. Closed Nov–May. J.O.J Frost Gallery open Tues–Sat 10am–4pm (closed Sat Nov–May).

King Hooper Mansion/Marblehead Arts Association & Gallery ★

HISTORIC HOME/GALLERY   Shipping tycoon Robert Hooper got his nickname "King" because he treated his sailors so well, but it's easy to think it was because he lived like royalty. Around the corner from the home of Jeremiah Lee (whose sister-in-law was the second of Hooper's four wives), the 1728 mansion gained a Georgian addition sometime after 1745. The **Marblehead Arts Association** stages exhibits in four galleries, schedules special events, and sells members' work in the gift shop. The mansion has a lovely garden; enter through the gate at the right of the house.

8 Hooper St. www.marbleheadarts.org. ✆ **781/631-2608.** Free admission. Sun and Tues–Fri noon–5pm, Sat 10am–5pm.

SHOPPING ★★

Marblehead has charming and upscale shops, boutiques, and galleries grouped in two separate locations, within walking distance of each other. In Old Town, **O'Ramas,** 148 Washington St. (✆ **781/631-0894**), carries fine linens, colorful jewelry and posh pajamas. **Lizzy Loo and Friends,** 108 Washington St. (www.facebook.com/lizzylooandfriends; ✆ **781/639-0746**) batiks its colorful t-shirts and onesies on site. Across the street is **Mud Puddle Toys,** 1 Pleasant St. (www.mudpuddletoys.com; ✆ **781/631-0814**). **F.L. Woods Nautical Merchants,** 76 Washington St. (www.flwoods.com; ✆ **781/631-0221**), has been outfitting local mariners from the same spot since 1938. The other shopping area is on Atlantic Avenue, which locals call Downtown. There's artsy jewelry at **Jambu,** 38 Atlantic Ave. (www.jambujewelry.com; ✆ **781/639-9600**); stylish yet comfy shoes at **Shoe Galley**, 46 Atlantic Ave. (✆ **781/990-1345**); and all things pooch at **Pawsitively Marblehead,** 52B Atlantic Ave. (www. ccpaws.com; ✆ **781/990-0081**). Just a few streets over, you can find books by locals and about local subjects at **The Spirit of '76** bookstore, 107 Pleasant St. (www.hugobookstores.com; ✆ **781/631-7199**).

Exploring Salem

Salem's **historic district** extends well inland from the waterfront (the visitor center can provide a walking-tour pamphlet). Many 18th-century houses, some with original furnishings, still stand. Ship captains lived near the water at the east end of downtown, in relatively small houses crowded close together by today's standards. The captains' employers, the shipping-company owners, built their homes away from the water (and the accompanying aromas). Many lived on the grand thoroughfare of **Chestnut Street ★★**, part of the National Registry of Historic Places.

The House of the Seven Gables ★★ HISTORIC HOME   Nathaniel Hawthorne wrote the 1851 novel that inspired the name of this attraction (and if you haven't read the book since high school or haven't read it at all, keep in mind that it's scary). Visits to the rambling 1668 house are by guided tour. Hawthorne visited his cousin at this home as a young man and tours show off some of the details he included in the book—there's a secret staircase!—and stories of what life in the 1700s was like. The modest home where Hawthorne was born has been moved to the grounds, and visitors are invited to poke around the period gardens that overlook the harbor. The house celebrated its 350th birthday in 2018.

115 Derby St. www.7gables.org. ✆ **978/744-0991.** $15 adults, $14 seniors, $13 kids 13–18, $10 kids 5–12, free for kids 4 & under. Daily 10am–7pm (Nov–June closes 5pm). Closed first 2 weeks Jan; open Fri–Tues only mid-Jan to mid-Feb.

Peabody Essex Museum ★★★ MUSEUM   One of New England's premier art museums, the Peabody Essex originated as a maritime museum (The Peabody) and the county's natural and historical society (the Essex Institute). The two merged in 1992 and have since developed a national reputation for extensive collections of Asian art and photography, American art and architecture, and maritime art. Its curatorial philosophy emphasizes placing objects in context, demonstrating the interplay of influences across time and cultures. The best-known item in the museum's collections is an 18th-century Qing Dynasty house, **Yin Yu Tang,** which was shipped to Salem from rural China; it's the only example of Chinese domestic architecture outside China. Take the audio guide to enjoy an intriguing look at 2 centuries of life in China while exploring the house (you might also need to build your visit around a timed ticket to Yin Yu Tang). Also allow time to check out some of the museum's exceptional traveling shows and lower-profile objects, including regionally made furniture and one of the world's largest shoe collections.

East India Sq., 161 Essex St. www.pem.org. ✆ **866/745-1876** or ✆ 978/745-9500. $20 adults, $18 seniors, $12 students, free for kids 16 & under. Yin Yu Tang additional $6. Tues–Sun & Mon holidays 10am–5pm.

Salem

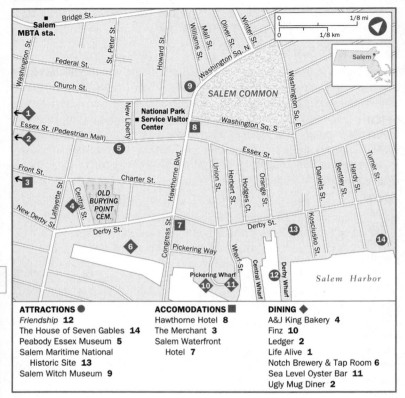

ATTRACTIONS ●
Friendship **12**
The House of Seven Gables **14**
Peabody Essex Museum **5**
Salem Maritime National
   Historic Site **13**
Salem Witch Museum **9**

ACCOMODATIONS ■
Hawthorne Hotel **8**
The Merchant **3**
Salem Waterfront
   Hotel **7**

DINING ◆
A&J King Bakery **4**
Finz **10**
Ledger **2**
Life Alive **1**
Notch Brewery & Tap Room **6**
Sea Level Oyster Bar **11**
Ugly Mug Diner **2**

Salem Maritime National Historic Site ★ OUTDOOR MUSEUM
Docked in the National Park Service's waterfront center is a uniquely memorable exhibit: a full-size (171-ft.) replica of a 1797 East Indiaman merchant vessel. The *Friendship* is open to visitors by guided tour and you can also study it from the shore if you don't want to climb aboard. Note that the ship has been under renovation and was expected to return to Derby Wharf in 2018. Tours include buildings that touch on Salem's trade and literary history—author Nathaniel Hawthorne, for instance, worked in the Custom House. If this location is closed, visit the Park Service's regional center at 2 New Liberty St., a 5-minute walk away.

193 Derby St. www.nps.gov/sama. © **978/740-1650.** Free admission & tours. Summer daily 9am–5pm; winter weekdays 1–5pm, weekends 9am–5pm.

Salem Witch Museum ★ MUSEUM   There are a slew of witch-trial-related sights and walking tours to choose from in Salem and no single option hits every note. Many are seasonal and play up horror over history. This year-round museum, in a building that used to be a church, provides an informative overview of the 1692 hysteria with a slightly dated presentation: A series of dioramas are populated with life-size human figures that light up in sequence as recorded narration, taken from historic documents, describes the pertinent events. The story is grim—most of those accused of "witchcraft" were executed by hanging, and one was pressed to death by stones piled on a board on his chest—but its anti-prejudice message is both clear and timeless.

19½ Washington Sq., at Rte. 1A. www.salemwitchmuseum.com. © **978-744-1692.** $12 adults, $10.50 seniors, $9 kids 6–14, free for kids 5 & under. Daily July–Aug 10am–7pm; Sept–June 10am–5pm; check ahead for extended Oct hours.

SHOPPING ★★

Pickering Wharf, centrally located at the corner of Derby and Congress streets, is a waterfront complex of shops, restaurants, and condos that popular for strolling, snacking, and shopping. Along the retail-rich Essex Street pedestrian mall, there are housewares at **Pamplemousse,** 185 Essex St. (www.pmousse.com; © **978/745-2900**) and, right next door, playful vintage and new clothes at **Modern Millie ★,** 3 Central St. (www.modernmillieshop.com; © **978/745-0231**). Front Street (btw. Central St. and Washington St.) is another nice stretch for shopping; here you'll find clever cards and gifts at **Roost & Company ★,** 40 Front St. (www.roostandcompany.com; © **978/744-4663**).

Several shops specialize in witchcraft accessories and psychic readings. Bear in mind that Salem is home to many practicing witches who take their beliefs very seriously. A team of psychics at **Crow Haven Corner,** 125 Essex St. (www.crowhavencorner.com; © **978/745-8763**), offer readings by appointment; the shop also carries herbs, potions, and spell kits. For a modern twist on the "sacred feminine," **HausWitch Home + Healing,** 144 Washington St. (www.hauswitchstore.com; © **978/594-8950**) has sleek home goods, vegan cleaning products, and community events.

Shops throughout New England sell the chocolate confections of Salem's **Harbor Sweets ★,** Palmer Cove, 85 Leavitt St., off Lafayette Street (www.harborsweets.com; © **800/234-4860** or **978/745-7648**). Its retail store overlooks the floor of the factory; tours begin Tuesday and Thursday at 11am (call ahead to reserve). The deliriously good sweets are expensive, but candy bars and small assortments are available. It's closed Sunday.

Salem Celebrations

In August, the 2-day **Salem Maritime Festival** fills the area around the Salem Maritime National Historic Site (see p. 156) with live music, food, and demonstrations of nautical crafts. The festival kicks off **Heritage Days,** a weeklong event celebrating Salem's multicultural history with musical and theatrical performances and a street fair. (For a schedule of events, go to www.salem. org). Salem's biggest event, however, is its month-long Halloween celebration, **Haunted Happenings ★★** (www.hauntedhappenings.org), which includes ghost tours, costume balls, haunted houses, a street fair, a parade, and family film nights on Salem Common. If you plan to visit then, plan extra time for traffic and make advance reservations where possible.

THE salem witch HYSTERIA & EXECUTIONS

The Salem witch trials that took place in 1692 were a product of old-world superstition, religious control of government, and mass hysteria. The crisis began in Salem Village (now the town of Danvers), in the household of Rev. Samuel Parris. A West Indian slave named Tituba told stories to the girls of the house during the long, harsh winter. The girls—9 and 11—began to act out the tales of sorcery and fortunetelling, claiming to be under a spell, rolling on the ground, and wailing that they were being pricked with pins.

The settlers took the behavior seriously, aware that thousands of people in Europe had been executed as witches in the previous centuries. Tituba and two other women were accused of casting spells. But the infighting typical of the Puritan theocracy surfaced soon enough, and an accusation of "witchcraft" became a handy way to settle a score.

Anyone different was a potential target, from the deaf to the poor.

A special court convened in Salem proper, and although the girls recanted, trials began. Defendants had no counsel, and pleading not guilty or objecting to the proceedings was considered equivalent to confessing. From March 1 to September 22, the court convicted 27 of the more than 150 people accused. In the end, 20 people were executed—14 of them women, by hanging.

The episode's lessons about tolerance have echoed through the years. Arthur Miller's 1953 play The Crucible was a retelling of the Salem trials as well as an allegory about the prosecution and blacklisting of U.S. citizens accused of being communists in the 1940s and '50s. Margaret Atwood based her 1985 dystopian novel The Handmaid's Tale in nearby Cambridge because of the region's history of Puritanism.

Where to Stay in Marblehead & Salem

Nearby **Danvers,** on or near Route 1 north of I-95, has many of the major motel chains. They're all about 30 minutes or less from downtown Salem, 40 minutes from Marblehead.

MARBLEHEAD

Harbor Light Inn ★★   Two Federal-era mansions make up this gracious inn, a stone's throw from the Old Town House. From the wood floors to the 1820s beams to the secluded heated pool, it's both historic and relaxing. Rooms are comfortably furnished in period style, with some attractive antiques; many have canopy or four-poster beds. Eleven have working fireplaces, and five have double Jacuzzis. The best rooms, on the top floor at the back of the building (away from the street), have distant harbor views. The undeniably romantic inn also attracts business travelers. Families with children under age 12 need to make prior arrangements. For longer stays, the Inn also has five apartments.

58 Washington St. www.harborlightinn.com. © **781/631-2186.** 20 units. Summer $249–$299 double; $299–$409 suite. Winter $159–$239 double $249–$309 suite. Rates include breakfast and afternoon refreshments. 2- to 3-night minimum Fri–Sat and holidays. **Amenities:** Tavern; concierge; access to nearby health club ($15); heated outdoor pool; Wi-Fi (free).

SALEM

Salem's busiest and most expensive time of year is Halloween week; reserve well in advance if you plan to travel anytime in October. The **Salem Waterfront Hotel,** 225 Derby St., at Pickering Wharf (www.salemwaterfronthotel. com; © **888/337-2536** or 978/740-8788), is a large, modern establishment with an indoor pool. Double rates in high season start at $209, which includes Wi-Fi.

Hawthorne Hotel ★   This historic hotel, built in 1925, is both convenient and comfortable. The six-story building is centrally located and well maintained, with a traditional atmosphere. Attractively furnished guest rooms vary in size from snug to spacious; some bathrooms are small, and about half of them have only a shower instead of a bathtub. The best units, on the Salem Common (north) side of the building, have better views than rooms that face the street. Ask to be as high up as possible, because the neighborhood is busy.

18 Washington Sq. W. (at Salem Common). www.hawthornehotel.com. © **800/729-7829** or 978/744-4080. 93 units. $200–$300 double; $309–$449 suite. 2-night minimum June–Oct weekends. Limited free self-parking. **Amenities:** Restaurant; tavern; concierge; exercise room; Wi-Fi (free).

The Merchant ★   This chic boutique hotel is within walking distance to most sights. Design enthusiasts will appreciate much about staying here, including the original 1784 interior woodwork and "floating" staircase by prolific local architect Samuel McIntire. Rooms are spacious yet cozy—each has a gas fireplace and heated bathroom floor. Guests can meet up for a daily BYO happy hour in the attractive common area. Rates start at $209 to sleep where George Washington slept, and like him in 1789, you'll have to take the stairs (no elevator). The same hotel group opened the larger, equally chic **The Hotel Salem** in late 2017 (www.thehotelsalem.com; © **978/451-4950**).

148 Washington St. www.themerchantsalem.com. © **978/745-8100.** 11 units. July–Oct $289–$629; Nov–June $149–$349. Rates include breakfast. 2- and 3-night minimum stays in high season. Free off-site self-parking; limited on-site parking $25 per night, reservation required. **Amenities:** Concierge; iPad for duration of stay; Wi-Fi (free).

Where to Eat in Marblehead & Salem

MARBLEHEAD

In Marblehead, the tavern at the **Harbor Light Inn** (see p. 158) offers a limited bar menu in a cozy 18th-century setting. If weather cooperates, find picnic fare at **Crosby's Marketplace,** 115 Washington St. (www.crosbysmarkets. com; © **781/631-1741**) and walk to scenic Crocker Park, just behind the store's parking lot. Or pick up gourmet sandwiches, wine and cheese, from **Shubie's ★★★,** 16 Atlantic Ave. (www.shubies.com; © **781/631-0149**).

5 Corners Kitchen ★★★ BISTRO   One of the North Shore's finest going-out options takes its name from the five street intersection it overlooks. The elegant bar fills early for the ambience, impeccable food, and admittedly, the $1 oysters from 5pm to 6pm. For dinner entrees, try the local skate wing or line caught cod. The sticky toffee pudding is sublime. For brunch (Sundays

Pickering Wharf has several restaurants with outdoor seating or views overlooking the marina. **Sea Level Oyster Bar ★**, 94 Wharf St. (www.sealeveloysterbar.com; ✆ **978/741-0555**) has a good raw bar, local beers on tap, and an open air porch. Main courses start at $15. **Finz,** 76 Wharf St. (www.hipfinz.com; ✆ **978/744-8485**) is a good choice rain or shine, lunch or dinner, with entrees starting at $18. The black and white sesame tuna is a favorite. Note that, in general, seafood entrée pricing fluctuates with the market and some dishes can exceed $30.

from 10am–2pm), Five Corners is in a league of its own: The brioche beignets are must-haves. Count on friendly service and a cosmopolitan vibe.

2 School St. www.5cornerskitchen.com. ✆ **781/631-5550.** Main courses dinner $16–$27; brunch $12–$22. Mon–Sat 5–10pm; Sun brunch 10am–2pm and dinner 5–9pm. Reservations recommended.

SALEM

Near the Salem pedestrian mall, **Life Alive**, 281 Essex St. (www.lifealive.com; ✆ **978/594-4644**) has an organic, vegetarian-friendly menu along with fresh juices and smoothies. Bowls $6.95 to $9.50. **Ugly Mug Diner,** 122 Washington St. (www.uglymugdiner.com; ✆ **978/745-6844**), serves hearty breakfasts, and a few sandwiches, daily 7am to 3pm. Mains $5 to $19.

A. & J. King Artisan Bakers ★★★ BAKERY   Not far from the **Peabody Essex Museum** (p. 155), A. & J. King is a cozy cafe that serves great coffee and outstanding baked goods. Their sandwiches are served on house-made bread and are available after 11am. Consider grabbing something—anything!—to go.

48 Central St. www.ajkingbakery.com. ✆ **978/744-4881.** Baked goods $1–$7. Sandwiches $4–$8. Mon–Fri 7am–6pm; Sat–Sun 7am–4pm.

Ledger ★ NEW ENGLAND   For a rich ambience that captures Salem then—and utterly now—you can't top Ledger. In a renovated Salem Savings Bank building, the ceilings soar and the bar beckons. Warm up with a classic cocktail, then move on to a dinner menu that is both innovative—pan-roasted Romanesco, for example—and nostalgic, with items such as warm popovers and American Chop Suey. If you brought one nice traveling outfit, wear it here. Note that nearby street parking is limited. Several well-marked public parking options are a short walk away.

125 Washington St. www.ledgersalem.com. ✆ **978/594-1908.** Dinner reservations recommended. Main courses $12–$18 lunch, $17–$36 dinner. Tues 5–10pm; Wed–Thurs 11am–2pm and 5–10pm; Fri–Sat 11am–2pm and 5–10:30pm; Sun 10am–2pm and 5–9pm.

Notch Brewing ★★ PUB   Kick back with a house brew and a German pretzel while trying your hand at Skee-Ball at this year-round Tap Room.

Don't count on a meal—the appetizer-sized food is for snacking. Here, beer is the main course. Kids and dogs are welcome with chaperones.

283R Derby St. www.notchbrewing.com. ⓒ **978/238-9060.** Half-liters start $6.50. Mon–Thurs 4pm–11pm, Fri–Sat noon–11pm, Sun noon–8pm.

CAPE ANN

Gloucester: 33 miles NE of Boston, 16 miles NE of Salem. Rockport: 40 miles NE of Boston, 7 miles N of Gloucester.

Four seaside communities make up Cape Ann: **Manchester-by-the-Sea, Gloucester, Rockport,** and **Essex.** Although all four towns have large year-round populations, for tourists they are primarily a summer and fall destination. Many establishments close in fall or early winter through April or May. Some do open on weekends in December.

Jutting out like a nub from the coast, the rocky peninsula of Cape Ann is enchantingly beautiful—and like Cape Cod to the south (see chapter 6) it also has shopping, seafood, and traffic. Its proximity to Boston and manageable scale make it a wonderful day trip and a good choice for a longer stay.

Along with historical attractions, beaches, and glorious scenery, visitors will find quality galleries and crafts shops. With the decline of the fishing industry that brought great prosperity to the area in the 19th century, Cape Ann has played up its long-standing reputation as a haven for artists.

Essentials
ARRIVING
From Boston, the quickest route is I-93 (or Route 1, if it's not rush hour) to Route 128, which ends at Gloucester. From Salem, a slower but prettier approach is Route 1A across the bridge at Beverly to Route 127, which runs through Manchester to Gloucester. Rockport is north of Gloucester along Route 127 or 127A—127 is shorter but more commercial. To take 127A, continue on 128 to the sign for East Gloucester and turn left.

The **commuter rail** (www.mbta.com; ⓒ **800/392-6100** or 617/222-3200) runs from Boston's North Station. The trip takes about 1 hour to Gloucester, 60 to 70 minutes to Rockport. The round-trip fare is $21 to Gloucester, $23 to Rockport.

VISITOR INFORMATION
Gloucester's **Visitors Welcoming Center** (www.gloucesterma.com; ⓒ **800/649-6839** or 978/281-8865) is at Stage Fort Park, off Route 127 at Route 133. It's open in summer daily from 9am to 5pm. The **Cape Ann Chamber of Commerce,** in Gloucester at 33 Commercial St. (www.capeannvacations.com; ⓒ **800/321-0133** or 978/283-1601), is open year-round (summer Mon–Fri 9am–5pm, Sat 10am–5pm, Sun 11am–4pm; winter Mon–Fri 9am–5pm). The **Rockport Chamber of Commerce,** 170 Main St. (www.rockportusa.com; ⓒ **978/546-9372**) operates an information booth on Upper Main Street (Route 127) daily from July 1 through Labor Day and on weekends from mid-May to June and early September through mid-October. It's about a mile from the

town line and a mile from downtown—look for the WELCOME TO ROCKPORT sign.

The **North of Boston Convention & Visitors Bureau** (www.northofboston.org; © **978/465-6555**) also provides abundant visitor information on Cape Ann.

GETTING AROUND

The **Cape Ann Transportation Authority** (www.canntran.com; © **978/283-7916**) runs buses from town to town on Cape Ann and operates special summer routes (except Sunday).

Manchester-by-the-Sea

The scenic route to Cape Ann from points south is Route 127, which runs through Manchester-by-the-Sea, an enchanting village incorporated in 1645. Now a prosperous suburb, it was the setting for the 2016 film *Manchester By The Sea*. It's known for **Singing Beach** (see "Early Birds Get . . . A Spot at the Beach"). Commuter trains from Boston ($10 one-way) stop in the center of the compact downtown area, where there are shops and restaurants. Nearby **Masconomo Park** overlooks the harbor.

early birds GET . . . A SPOT AT THE BEACH

Cape Ann is almost as well known for its sandy swimming beaches as it is for its rocky coastline. Keep in mind that the water is *cold* and that parking can be scarce, especially on weekends. If you can't set out before breakfast, wait until midafternoon and hope that the early birds have begun to clear out. During the summer, lifeguards are on duty from 9am to 5pm at larger public beaches. Keep the tide schedules in mind since high tide can seriously shrink available towel space. Many beaches post tide schedules, parking updates, and insect info on Twitter. The beaches listed here all have bathhouses and snack bars. Parking can cost up to $30.

The best-known North Shore beach is **Singing Beach ★** (www.manchester.ma.us; © **978/526-7276**), in Manchester-by-the-Sea, off Masconomo Street. Because it's so accessible by commuter rail, it attracts a diverse array of beach bunnies up from Boston. From the train station, walk half a mile on Beach Street to find squeaky sand (which gives the beach its name) and lively surf. It costs $7 per person to walk on, cash only.

Nearly as popular is **Crane Beach ★★** (www.thetrustees.org; © **978/356-4354**), in Ipswich, off Argilla Road. It's part of a 1,200-acre barrier beach reservation, with fragile dunes and a white-sand beach leading down to Ipswich Bay. The chilly surf is calmer than that at less sheltered Singing Beach. Also on Ipswich Bay is Gloucester's **Wingaersheek Beach ★** (www.gloucester-ma.gov; © **978/325-5600**), on Atlantic Street off Route 133. (Take exit 13 off Route 128). Wingaersheek has beautiful white sand and a glorious view.

Most other good beaches in Gloucester have almost no nonresident parking. Two exceptions are Half Moon Beach and Cressy's Beach, at Stage Fort Park, off Route 127 near Route 133 and downtown. The sandy beaches and the park snack bar are popular local hangouts.

Whether you're swimming or not, watch out for greenhead flies in July and August. They take little bites of flesh and are miserable company. Bring insect repellent.

The home of the Manchester Historical Museum is the **Trask House,** 10 Union St. (www.manchesterhistoricalmuseum.org; ℂ **978/526-7230**), where Abigail Trask ran a general store and millinery in the early 1800s. Tours ($5 suggested donation) show off the period furnishings and artifacts from the town's maritime history. The museum also operates the **Seaside No. 1 Fire House Museum,** which holds two antique engines and memorabilia of the town fire and police departments. Both buildings are open Saturdays in July and August from 10am to 1pm (with additional winter hours for the Trask House), and by appointment. The museum also has information on three self-guided walking tours around town.

Exploring Gloucester ★★

The ocean has been Gloucester's lifeblood since long before the first European settlement in 1623. The most urban of Cape Ann's communities, Gloucester (which rhymes with "foster") is a working city, not a cutesy tourist town. It's home to one of the last commercial fishing fleets in New England, an internationally celebrated artists' colony, and a large Italian-American community. (At the end of June, the 4-day **St. Peter's Fiesta** celebrates those Italian-American roots with parades, carnival rides, music, food, the "greasy pole" contest, and the blessing of the fleet.)

Miles of gorgeous coastline surround the densely populated downtown area. Allow at least half a day, perhaps combined with a visit to the more touristy Rockport; a full day would be better, especially if you plan a whale watch. The city is exceptionally welcoming—many residents seem genuinely happy to see out-of-towners and to offer directions and insider info.

Start at the water, as visitors have done for centuries. The French explorer Samuel de Champlain called the harbor "Le Beauport" in 1604—some 600 years after the Vikings first visited—and its configuration and proximity to good fishing gave it the reputation it enjoys to this day. On Stacy Boulevard (west of downtown) stands a reminder of the sea's danger: Leonard Craske's bronze statue of the **Gloucester Fisherman,** known as "The Man at the Wheel," with its ominous inscription "They That Go Down to the Sea in Ships 1623–1923." To the west is a memorial to the women and children who waited at home. As you take in the glorious view, consider this: More than 10,000 fishermen lost their lives during the city's first 300 years.

Many travelers know Gloucester from Sebastian Junger's best-selling book, *The Perfect Storm*, and the movie it inspired. **The Crow's Nest,** 334 Main St. (www.crowsnestgloucester.com; ℂ **978/281-2965**), plays a major role in the book, although it technically didn't appear in the movie—its ceilings weren't high enough for it to be a movie set, so the film crew built an exact replica nearby. Still, gawkers like to take a peek into what is otherwise a bar filled with regular folks.

Stage Fort Park, off Route 127 near the intersection with Route 133, offers an excellent view of the harbor and has a busy seasonal snack bar, the

Gloucester

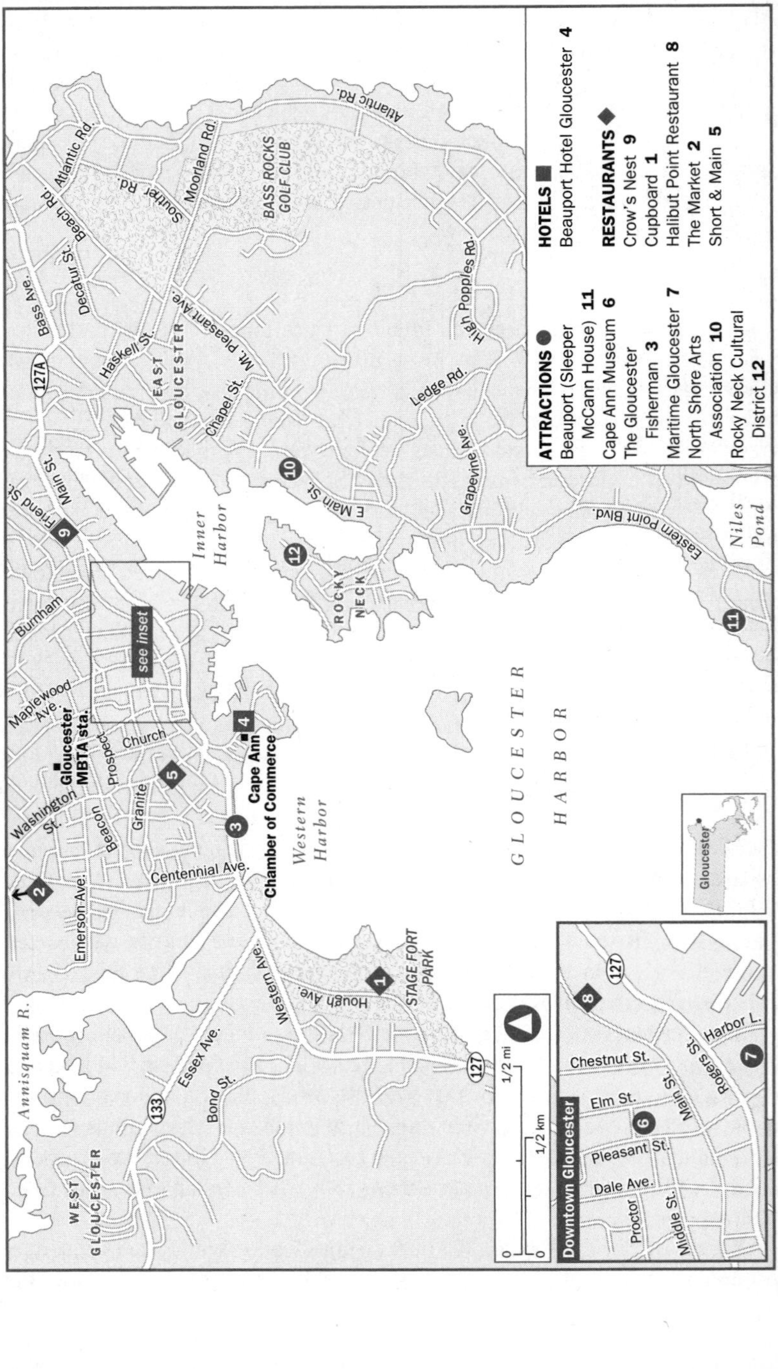

SIDE TRIPS FROM BOSTON | Cape Ann

5

HOTELS ■
Beauport Hotel Gloucester **4**

RESTAURANTS ◆
Crow's Nest **9**
Cupboard **1**
Halibut Point Restaurant **8**
The Market **2**
Short & Main **5**

ATTRACTIONS ●
Beauport (Sleeper
McCann House) **11**
Cape Ann Museum **6**
The Gloucester
Fisherman **3**
Maritime Gloucester **7**
North Shore Arts
Association **10**
Rocky Neck Cultural
District **12**

Downtown Gloucester

Cupboard (© 978/281-1908). The park is a good spot for picnicking, swimming, or playing on the cannons in the Revolutionary War fort.

To reach **East Gloucester,** follow signs as you leave downtown (from Route 128, take exit 9). On East Main Street, you'll see signs for the **Rocky Neck Cultural District** ★ and **Gallery 53,** at 53 Rocky Neck Ave. (www.rockyneckartcolony.org; © 978/282-0917). The oldest continuously operating art colony in the country is based here, and Rocky Neck Avenue abounds with studios and galleries. In summer, most galleries are open daily, hours vary. To explore the area on foot, park your car in the lot on the tiny causeway. The prestigious **North Shore Arts Association,** 11 Pirates Land, off East Main Street (www.nsarts.org; © 978/283-1857), founded in 1922, is open from May through October, Monday through Saturday 10am to 5pm, Sunday noon to 5pm. Admission is free.

Beauport (Sleeper-McCann House) ★★★ HISTORIC HOME Aficionados of house tours will want to build their schedules around a visit to this magnificent property, a National Landmark. It's the product of a uniquely creative mind. Interior designer and antiquarian Henry Davis Sleeper accumulated vast collections of American and European decorative arts and antiques in his summer home. From 1907 to 1934, he decorated the 40-plus rooms to illustrate literary and historical themes. You'll see magnificent arrangements of colored glassware, the "Octagon Room" (with the number 8 as a recurring theme), and the kitchen and servants' quarters. To get there, take East Main Street south from East Gloucester; it becomes Eastern Point Road. Eastern Point Boulevard, a private road, branches off it to the right; Beauport is half a mile down the road.

75 Eastern Point Blvd. www.historicnewengland.org. © **978/283-0800.** Guided tour $15 adults, $12 seniors, $8 students and children 6–12. Tours on the hour. June to mid-Oct Tues–Sat 10am–4pm. Closed mid-Oct to late May.

Cape Ann Museum ★ MUSEUM This meticulously curated museum makes an excellent introduction to Cape Ann's history and artists. It devotes an entire gallery to the extraordinary work of **Fitz Henry Lane** ★★★, the Luminist painter whose light-flooded canvases show off his native Gloucester. The nation's single largest collection of his paintings and drawings is here. Other galleries feature works by 20th-century and contemporary artists, and granite-quarrying tools and equipment. There's also an outdoor sculpture court. The maritime and fisheries galleries display entire vessels, exhibits on the fishing industry, ship models, historic photographs, and a first order Fresnel lens. Check ahead for information about touring the historic houses: The adjacent **Capt. Elias Davis House** (1804), decorated and furnished in Federal style, and the newly restored 1710 **White-Ellery House,** a rare example of First Period architecture about a mile away at 244 Washington St.

27 Pleasant St. www.capeannmuseum.org. © **978/283-0455.** $12 adults, $10 seniors & students, free for kids 11 and under. Tues–Sat 10am–5pm, Sun 1–4pm. Closed Mon and some holidays.

HAVING A whale OF A TIME

The waters off the Massachusetts coast are prime **whale-watching ★★** territory, and Gloucester is a center of cruises. Stellwagen Bank, which runs from Gloucester to Provincetown about 27 miles east of Boston, is a rich feeding ground for the magnificent mammals. The whales often perform by jumping out of the water, and dolphins occasionally join the show. Naturalists on board narrate the trip for the companies listed here, pointing out the whales and describing birds and fish that cross the boat's path.

The season runs from April or May to October. Bundle up—it's much cooler at sea than on land—and wear a hat and rubber-soled shoes. Pack sunglasses, sunscreen, and a camera. If you're prone to motion sickness, take precautions, because you'll be at sea for 3½ to 5 hours.

They'd deny it, but the companies are essentially indistinguishable. Most guarantee sightings and offer morning and afternoon cruises. Check ahead for sailing times, prices (at least $48 for adults, slightly less for seniors and children), and reservations, which are strongly recommended. In downtown Gloucester, there's **Cape Ann Whale Watch** (www.seethewhales.com; ℭ 800/877-5110 or 978/283-5110); **Capt. Bill & Sons Whale Watch** (www.captbillandsons.com; ℭ 800/339-4253 or 978/283-6995), and **Seven Seas Whale Watch** (www.7seas-whalewatch.com; ℭ 978/283-1776).

If your schedule allows, plan to visit **Maritime Gloucester,** 23 Harbor Loop (www.maritimegloucester.org; ℭ **978/281-0470**), before or after your trip. Admission ($10 adults, $7 seniors and children) includes access to its Sea Pocket Aquarium. Open daily 10am to 5pm.

SHOPPING IN GLOUCESTER

Rocky Neck (see p. 165) offers great browsing and craft options. Downtown, Main Street between Pleasant and Washington streets offers some diverting options, such as **Mystery Train Records,** 21 Main St. (www.mysterytrainrecords.com; ℭ **978/281-8911**), which carries vinyl, 8-tracks, and CDs; **Bananas,** 78 Main St. (ℭ **978/283-8806**), which sells vintage women's clothes; and the eclectic **Dogtown Book Shop,** 132 Main St. (www.dogtownbooks.com; ℭ **978/281-5599**).

Exploring Rockport

This handsome little town at the tip of Cape Ann was settled in 1690, and over the years it has been a fishing port, a center of granite excavation, and a thriving summer community whose specialty seems to be selling fudge and refrigerator magnets to visitors. But there's more to Rockport than just gift shops. It's home to a pretty state park and it's popular with photographers, sculptors, jewelry designers, and painters. Winslow Homer, Fitz Henry Lane, and Childe Hassam are among the artists who have captured the local color.

On summer weekends, Rockport can be packed; in winter, from January to mid-April, it's somewhat desolate, but the year-round population is large enough that some businesses stay open with reduced hours. Metered parking spots are available throughout downtown and there's a free parking lot on

Upper Main Street (Route 127). The CATA "park-and-ride" shuttle bus to downtown costs $1, exact change only.

The most famous sight in Rockport has something of an "Emperor's New Clothes" aura—it's a wooden fish warehouse on the town wharf, or T-Wharf, in the harbor. The barn-red shack known as **Motif No. 1** is the most frequently painted and photographed object in a town filled with attractive buildings and surrounded by rocky coastline. The color certainly catches the eye in the neutrals of the surrounding seascape, but you may find yourself wondering what the big deal is. Originally constructed in 1884 and destroyed during the blizzard of 1978, Motif No. 1 was rebuilt using donations from residents and visitors. It stands again on the same pier, duplicated in every detail, reinforced to withstand storms.

On Main Street, behind what looks like a Victorian facade, the **Shalin Liu Performance Center** (37 Main St.; www.rockportmusic.org; ✆ **978/546-7391**) is a stunning modern concert hall with ocean views behind its stage. It was built in 2008–2010 as a home for the acclaimed **Rockport Chamber Music Festival,** held every June. In summers the lobby is usually open to the public 10am to 2pm on Tuesday, Thursday, Friday, and Saturday, with docents giving tours between 11am and 12:30pm, if there's no performance going on.

Throughout town, more than two dozen art galleries display the work of local and nationally known artists. The **Rockport Art Association & Museum,** 12 Main St. (www.rockportartassn.org; ✆ **978/546-6604**), sponsors exhibitions and special shows. It's open daily in the summer, Tuesday through Sunday in the winter.

The 1922 **Paper House,** 52 Pigeon Hill St., Pigeon Cove (www.paper houserockport.com; ✆ **978/546-2629**), is an unusual experience. Everything in it, including the furniture, was built entirely out of 100,000 newspapers. Every item is made from papers of a different period. It's open daily from 10am to 5pm from spring to fall. Admission is $2 adults, $1 children (cash only). Follow Route 127 north from downtown about 1½ miles until you see signs at Curtis Street pointing to the left.

Beyond Pigeon Cove, continue north on Route 127 to the very tip of Cape Ann, surf-battered **Halibut Point State Park** ★★ (www.mass.gov/dcr; ✆ **978/546-2997**). (The point got its name not from the fish, but because sailing ships heading for Rockport and Gloucester must "haul about" when they reach the jutting promontory.) This is a great place to wander and admire the scenery. On a clear day, you can see Maine. About 10 minutes from the parking area, you'll come to a huge water-filled **quarry** (swimming is absolutely forbidden) and a **visitor center,** where staffers dispense information, brochures, and bird lists. There are walking trails, tidal pools, a World War II observation tower, and a rocky beach where you can climb on giant boulders. The park is open daily from Memorial Day to Labor Day, 8am to 8pm; otherwise daily dawn to dusk. Parking costs $10 (for non-MA-residents) from Memorial Day to Columbus Day.

ROCKPORT SHOPPING

Bearskin Neck holds what may be the highest concentration of gift shops in New England. The narrow peninsula has one main street (South Road) and several alleys crammed with shops, galleries, snack bars, and ancient houses. Dozens of little shops here carry clothes, gifts, toys, jewelry, souvenirs, inexpensive novelties, and expensive handmade crafts and paintings. The peninsula ends in a plaza with a magnificent water view.

Along **Main** and **Mount Pleasant streets,** the shopping has more of a retro flavor. Family-owned since 1929, **Tuck's Candy & Gifts** (www.tuckscandy. com; ✆ 978/546-6352) still operates at its original location, 15 Main St. And you can watch taffy being made at **Tuck's Candy Factory,** 7 Dock Square (✆ **978/546-2840**). Near the train station, **Crackerjacks,** 27 Whistlestop Mall, off Railroad Avenue (✆ **978/546-1616**), is an old-fashioned variety store with a great crafts department.

Exploring Essex

West of Gloucester on Route 133 lies a beautiful little town known for Essex clams, salt marshes, a long tradition of shipbuilding, a plethora of antiques shops, and one celebrated restaurant, **Woodman's of Essex** (see p. 169).

Water views here are of the Essex River, a saltwater estuary. The offerings of **Essex River Cruises** ★, Essex Marina, 35 Dodge St. (www.essexcruises. com; ✆ **978/768-6981**) include narrated 90-minute tours of the salt marshes that put you in prime birding territory. They run daily mid-May through mid-October. The pontoon boat, which allows for excellent sightseeing, is screened and has restrooms. Tickets cost $26 adults, $24 seniors, $14 children 4 to 12; reservations are suggested.

Where to Stay Around Cape Ann
GLOUCESTER

Gloucester abounds with B&Bs; for guidance, check with the Cape Ann Chamber of Commerce (www.capeannvacations.com; ✆ **800/321-0133** or 978/283-1601).

Beauport Hotel Gloucester ★ Built where a Birdseye frozen-food plant once stood, the Beauport offers upscale beach-house accommodations in a unique setting, overlooking Gloucester's working waterfront. That means the views are both natural and semi-industrial. Rooms have a classy, nautical feel with crisp linens and marble-topped vanities. Summer is the ideal time to make use of the guest-only rooftop pool or Pavilion Beach, where attendants will set up your beach chair. No matter the season, Beauport's the closest to a full-service resort you'll get on the North Shore. Because it's in a flood zone (one reason some community members opposed its development), the spacious and airy rooms are on upper levels. Since the hotel opened in 2016, it's been in high demand as a destination for weddings.

55 Commercial St. www.beauporthotel.com. ✆ **844/282-0008** or 978/282-0008. 94 units. $200–$275 double; $305–$580 suite. Minimum stay may be required. **Amenities:** Restaurant, seasonal restaurant; beach; concierge; fitness center; pool (rooftop outdoor); spa services; valet parking (free); Wi-Fi (free).

ROCKPORT

When Rockport is busy, it's very busy, and when it's not, it's practically empty. The town's dozens of B&Bs fill in good weather and empty or even close in the winter. There are plenty of **Airbnb** options, from single rooms to entire homes. They can be the most economical option. If you haven't made summer reservations well in advance, cross your fingers and call the Chamber of Commerce to ask about cancellations. Most innkeepers will pick guests up at the train station; if you're not driving, be sure to ask when you reserve.

Bearskin Neck Motor Lodge ★   This recently renovated seasonal motor lodge is all about location. Nestled mid-way out Bearskin Neck (yes, cars can drive on the pedestrian-heavy road), all eight rooms have harbor views and waves can be heard lapping as you drift off to sleep. By day, the hubbub of the nearby shops is right outside the door but evenings are quieter and more serene.

64 Bearskin Neck. www.bearskinneckmotorlodge.com. 𝄢 **978/575-5036.** 8 units. $145–$229 double. Closed mid-Dec to Apr. **Amenities:** Wi-Fi (free).

The Emerson Inn ★   This historic seasonal inn, once a rooming house and later a grand hotel with a "fireproof" garage, maintains the feel of an old-fashioned resort. There's a heated outdoor pool overlooking the Atlantic, and guests can gather for yard games or chat in a lovely parlor. Rooms were updated in 2015 in a clean, uncluttered style with lots of light colors and an eclectic mix of furnishings. Many rooms have ocean views; the best are had from "Balcony" rooms. A nearby walking trail follows the craggy coastline, and Halibut Point State Park (see p. 167) is less than one mile away. Guests who book direct on the Inn's website receive complimentary breakfast. Note that the Inn is closed from November to April.

1 Cathedral Ave. www.emersoninnbythesea.com. 𝄢 **978/546-6321.** 35 units. Doubles $179–$259 low season, $269–$449 high season. Additional person in room charged $25 per night for children under 12, $75 per night for adults. Free self-parking. **Amenities:** Restaurant and bar; concierge; outdoor pool; Wi-Fi (free).

Where to Eat Around Cape Ann

ESSEX

Woodman's of Essex ★★★ SEAFOOD   Legend has it that Woodman's was the birthplace of the fried clam in 1916. Today the thriving family business is *the* spot to join legions of locals and visitors from around the world for lobster "in the rough" (meaning either cooked whole in the shell, or eaten in a casual setting, depending on who you ask), as well as chowder, steamers, corn on the cob, onion rings, and superb fried clams. The line to order is usually long, but it moves quickly and offers a view of the regimented commotion in the food-prep area. You can eat in a booth, upstairs on the deck, or out back at a picnic table.

121 Main St. www.woodmans.com. 𝄢 **800/649-1773** or 978/768-6057. Reservations not accepted. Seafood market price. Sandwiches $3–$24. Fried seafood plates $15–$31. Daily 11am–10pm (until 8pm or 9pm some nights fall through spring; confirm at website).

GLOUCESTER

Halibut Point Restaurant ★ SEAFOOD/AMERICAN   Halibut Point is a friendly tavern that serves good food. Some people come to Gloucester just for its spicy Italian fish chowder, and the "Halibut Point Special"—a cup of chowder, a burger, and a beer—hits the high points. Be sure to check the specials board—in this fishing port, the fresh fish options are bountiful.

289 Main St. www.halibutpointrestaurant.com. © **978/281-1900.** Main courses $6–$21 lunch, $14–$23 dinner. Daily 11:30am–10pm (until 10:30pm Fri–Sat).

Short & Main ★★ PIZZA   Don't let the simple idea of oysters and wood-fired pizza fool you. Short & Main's relaxed sophistication has drawn Boston's foodiest foodies north since it opened in 2013. If you like from scratch, locally sourced cooking, here you go. The cocktails are lovely as well and on most weekends, a bar upstairs serves old school tiki drinks. Its sister restaurant **The Market** ★★★ (33 River Rd.; www.themarketrestaurant.com; © **978/282-0700**) is an equally satisfying dining experience, although it's only open in warmer months and reservations are nearly impossible.

36 Main St. www.shortandmain.com. © **978/281-0044.** Pizzas $12–$23; brunch mains $12–$22. Reservations recommended. Sun 10am–2pm; Sun–Thurs 5–10pm; Fri–Sat 5–11pm.

ROCKPORT

The Rockport dining scene isn't nearly as varied or sophisticated as Gloucester's. A centrally located option, **Roy Moore Lobster Company,** 39 Bearskin Neck (© **978/546-7808**), serves ultra-fresh whole lobsters. Here, the hard part isn't cracking the shell, it's finding a seat.

Feather & Wedge ★ AMERICAN   This intimate restaurant's name is inspired by the tool and process used for harvesting granite, once a vital part of Rockport's economy. Step inside for a clean, modern take on New England cuisine (and, from some tables, harbor views). The menu changes daily but tuna with house-fried rice makes frequent appearances. There's also always an inventive vegetarian option, such as seared eggplant with quinoa and pickled onions. Seasonal bread pudding is a worthy ender. Overall, it's a much-needed addition to a limited restaurant scene. Definitely reserve in advance if possible.

5 Main Street. www.featherandwedge.com. © **978/999-5917.** Mains $15–$30; brunch mains $9–$14. Reservations recommended. Wed–Sun 5–9pm; Sun brunch 10:30am–2:30pm.

IPSWICH, NEWBURYPORT & PLUM ISLAND

Ipswich: 30 miles NE of Boston, 13 miles NW of Gloucester. Newburyport: 38 miles NE of Boston.

Still north of Cape Ann, at the uppermost part of Massachusetts near the New Hampshire border, the coast is magnificent, with outdoor sights and sounds that can only be described as natural wonders. The towns of Ipswich and

Newburyport are charming to visit, but their greatest assets lie outside of town: Ipswich's popular **Crane Beach,** part of a wildlife refuge, and on Newburyport's Atlantic coast, **Plum Island,** one of the country's top nature preserves.

Essentials

ARRIVING

From Boston, take I-93 (or Route 1 if it's not rush hour) to I-95 and follow it to exit 50 for Ipswich (you'll continue on Route 1 to Topsfield Road), exit 57 for Newburyport. Either drive should take around 45 minutes). The two towns are 12 miles apart on Route 1A. From Gloucester, Ipswich is about 13 miles northwest via Route 133.

The **commuter rail** (www.mbta.com; ☎ **800/392-6100** or 617/222-3200) from North Station takes about an hour to Ipswich ($20 round trip) and 70 minutes to Newburyport (round trip $23). On weekends and holidays in the summer, the **Ipswich Essex Explorer** bus (www.ipswichessexexplorer.com; ☎ **978/283-7916**) connects Ipswich station to the attractions, including Crane Beach. A one-way fare is $1.50; the round trip beach pass costs $5 and includes the beach walk-on fee.

VISITOR INFORMATION

The **Ipswich Visitor Information Center,** in the Hall Haskell House, 36 S. Main St., Route 1A (www.ipswichvisitorcenter.org; ☎ **978/356-8540**), is open weekends in May and daily 9am to 5pm from late May through October. For information on Newburyport, check out the **Greater Newburyport Chamber of Commerce and Industry**'s website at www.newburyportchamber.org.

Exploring Ipswich ★

Founded in 1633, Ipswich is dotted with **17th-century or "First Period" houses ★**—reputedly the largest concentration in the United States. The visitor center has a map (and a PDF at its website) of a tour that passes three dozen of them; it also offers an audio tour ($5). Many are private homes, but the **Ipswich Museum,** 54 South Main St. (www.ipswichmuseum.org; ☎ **978/356-2811**) is based in the 1800 **Heard House** and offers tours of the 1677 **John Whipple House,** 1 South Village Green, and other historic properties. Guided tours ($10 each, or $15 for three houses) run Thursday through Saturday from May through October; check ahead for schedules.

If you're traveling with children, consider a stop at **Russell Orchards Store and Winery ★**, 143 Argilla Rd. (www.russellorchards.com; ☎ **978/356-5366**). It's open daily May through Thanksgiving. It has a picnic area, farm animals, and an excellent country store. A hayride is often an option. Be sure to try some cider and doughnuts, too. It's just before Crane Estate, below.

Crane Estate ★★★ HISTORIC HOME/NATURE PRESERVE The 2,100-acre Crane Estate encompasses a National Landmark home, a gorgeous sandy beach, a wildlife refuge, and an exquisite Inn. The home, or "Great House" of **Castle Hill on the Crane Estate,** 290 Argilla Rd. (www.thetrustees.org; ☎ **978/356-4351**), is a Stuart-style mansion built by Richard Teller Crane,

Jr., who made his fortune in plumbing and bathroom fixtures early in the 20th century. Guided indoor tours run April to December. Or you can just roam the grounds; take in the Grand Allée lawn that rolls a half mile down to the Atlantic. The estate is also home to **Crane Beach** (see "Early Birds Get . . . a Spot at the Beach" on p. 162), the **Crane Wildlife Refuge ★★**, a network of hiking trails, and **The Inn at Castle Hill ★★★** (see p. 173).

290 Argilla Rd. www.thetrustees.org. ℰ **978/356-4351.** 1-hr. house tours ($15–$20 for adults, $5 for kids 8–18) Tues–Sun 10am–3pm, late May–Oct; Fri–Sat 10am–1pm Apr–late May and Nov–Dec. Entrance to grounds $15 per car, $5 per motorcycle, $2 per bike in summer). Beach parking $5 motorcycle; $5–$30 cars; $2 bike/foot.

Newburyport ★★ & Plum Island ★★

Newburyport is a singular example of a picturesque waterfront city, with its bustling downtown on the Merrimack River. A substantial year-round population helps make Newburyport less touristy than it appears to be. **Market Square ★**, at the foot of State Street near the waterfront, is the center of a neighborhood packed with boutiques, gift shops, plain and fancy restaurants, and antique stores. It's a great place to eat ice cream and people watch. You can also wander to the water, take a stroll on the boardwalk, and enjoy the action on the river. Architecture buffs may want to climb the hill to High Street, where the **Charles Bulfinch**–designed Superior Court building (1805) is one of several Federal-era treasures.

From downtown, take Water Street southeast until it becomes Plum Island Turnpike. The **Parker River Refuge visitor center,** at 6 Plum Island Turnpike), houses interactive displays and other exhibits about the island's history and ecology. It's open daily 9am to 4pm. Continue on Plum Island Turnpike and take your first right at Sunset Drive, which ends at the refuge's entrance.

Parker River National Wildlife Refuge ★★★ NATURE PRESERVE More than 800 species of plants and animals (including more than 300 bird species) visit or make their home on this narrow finger of land between Broad Sound and the Atlantic Ocean. The 4,700-acre refuge is a complex of barrier beaches, dunes, and salt marshes, one of the few remaining in the Northeast. Wooden boardwalks with observation towers and platforms wind through marshes and along the shore (before bringing children, know that most of the boardwalks lack handrails). The landscape is flat-out breathtaking, whether you're exploring the marshes or the seashore, and it's especially known for **birding ★★★**. Birders come from around the world hoping to see native and migratory species such as owls, hawks, martins, geese, warblers, ducks, snowy egrets, swallows, and Canada geese. Other visitors and residents include

Piping Plovers: Do Not Disturb

All but a small portion of Plum Island's ocean beach closes April 1 to allow piping plovers, listed by the federal government as a threatened species, to nest. The areas not being used for nesting reopen July 1; the rest open in August, when the birds are through. Check with the visitor center for updates.

monarch butterflies, foxes, beavers, and harbor seals. Swimming is allowed but not encouraged: Currents are strong and can be dangerous, and there are no lifeguards. Surf fishing is popular, though, and striped bass and bluefish are found in the area. A permit is required for night fishing and vehicle access to the beach. The seven parking lots fill quickly on weekends when the weather is good, so plan to arrive early.

Refuge Rd., Newbury. www.fws.gov/refuge/parker_river. © **978/465-5753.** Entrance fee $5 per car, $2 per bike, $2 pedestrians (cash only). Open dawn–dusk year-round.

Where to Stay in Ipswich

The Inn at Castle Hill ★★★   Need to deeply exhale? Take a few nights at this serene, impeccably kept bed and breakfast just up the hill from gorgeous Crane Beach. Once a beach cottage for the Crane family, the Inn has been open to the public and operated by a nonprofit nature conservancy since 2000. Rooms are comfy and quiet—you won't find TVs or other distracting gadgetry. At sun-up you can head to the beach (chairs, towels, beach bag, and admission all included). After dark you can stargaze from the formidable stone front porch. The Inn is closed January through March and open weekends only in November and December. Note that the Inn only hosts children ages 13 and up, and only two rooms are able to accommodate a third person.

280 Argilla Rd. www.thetrustees.org. © **978/412-2555.** 10 units. $195–$515 doubles. $40 per additional person. Two-night minimum stay weekends; 3-night minimum holidays. Rates include full breakfast and beach admission. Free self-parking. **Amenities:** Breakfast; hybrid bicycles; iPad for duration of stay; spa services by reservation; Wi-Fi (free).

Where to Eat in Ipswich

IPSWICH

The Clam Box ★ SEAFOOD   This photogenic restaurant, built in 1938, is shaped like a takeout clam box. It's a great place to try fried Ipswich clams, and not easy to sneak past if you have children in the car—or anyone in the car looking for an Instagram-ready image.

246 High St., Rte. 1A/133. www.clamboxipswich.com. © **978/356-9707.** Mid-Feb to mid-Nov Sun–Thurs 11am–7pm; Fri–Sat 11am–8pm. Closed mid-Nov to mid-Feb. Seafood market price. Sandwiches $3–$20. Fried seafood plates $15–$32. Credit cards $10 minimum.

PLYMOUTH ★★

45 miles SE of Boston

Most everyone educated in the United States learns at least a little of the story of Plymouth—about how the Pilgrims, fleeing religious persecution, left Europe on the *Mayflower* and landed at Plymouth Rock in 1620. Many also know that the Pilgrims endured disease and privation, and that just 53 people from the original group of 102 celebrated what we now call "the first Thanksgiving" in 1621 with Squanto, a Pawtuxet Indian associated with the Wampanoag people, and his cohorts.

What many won't grasp until actually visiting is how *small* everything was. The *Mayflower* (a reproduction) seems like a perilously tiny ship, and when you contemplate how dangerous life was at the time, it's hard not to marvel at the settlers' accomplishments. The *Mayflower* passengers weren't even aiming for Plymouth. They originally set out for what they called "Northern Virginia," near the mouth of the Hudson River. On November 11, 1620, rough weather and high seas forced them to make for Cape Cod Bay and anchor at Provincetown. The captain then announced that they had found a safe harbor and refused to continue to their original destination. On December 16, Provincetown having proven an unsatisfactory location, the weary travelers landed at Plymouth.

Plymouth today is a model destination for visitors. The 17th century coexists with the 21st, and most historic attractions are both educational and fun. Visitors jam the downtown area and waterfront in summer, but the year-round population is large enough that Plymouth feels more like the working community it is than just a seaside village trapped in the past. It's a particularly enjoyable excursion from Boston if you're traveling with children; it also makes a good stop between Boston and Cape Cod. The weekend before Thanksgiving, Plymouth hosts **America's Hometown Thanksgiving** (www. usathanksgiving.com; ✆ **508/746-1818**), a 3-day event that includes a large parade on Saturday. Things will be especially festive in **2020, Plymouth's 400th anniversary** (www.plymouth400inc.org).

Essentials

ARRIVING

BY CAR   Take I-93 south and merge onto Route 3 south. To go straight to Pilgrim Memorial State Park and Plymouth Rock, take Exit 6A (Route 44

Tours with a Twist

The Pilgrims arrived Plymouth by sea, and you can too, on narrated ocean cruises run by **Capt. John Boats** (www. captjohn.com; ✆ **508/927-5587**). Departing from State Pier or Town Wharf, these 60-minute cruises hit the water aboard the **Pilgrim Belle paddleboat** ($20 adults and kids 13 and over, $17 seniors, $13 kids 4–12; a few dollars more for the 7pm sunset ride). Cruises run from April or May through October or November. Capt. John's also has **whale watches** ($53 adults and kids 13 and over, $42 seniors, $30 kids 4–12) and **deep-sea fishing excursions** (from 4 hours to 12 hours; check website for prices).

For kids who are into pirates, **Plymouth Cruises Aboard Lobster Tales** (www.plymouthcruises.com; ✆ **508/746-5342**) offers pirate cruises ($19 per person), designed for kids ages 4 to 10. They don hats and face paint and "defend" the boat against marauding buccaneers. The company also offers **lobster excursions** ($18 adults and kids 12 and older, $17 seniors, $15 children 11 and younger), during which passengers help haul up traps and observe marine life (lobsters are catch-and-release).

For a full list of available guided tours, go www.seeplymouth.com/things-to-do/tours.

Plymouth

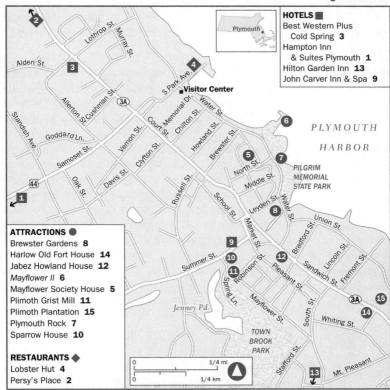

HOTELS ■
Best Western Plus
 Cold Spring **3**
Hampton Inn
 & Suites Plymouth **1**
Hilton Garden Inn **13**
John Carver Inn & Spa **9**

PLYMOUTH

HARBOR

PILGRIM
MEMORIAL
STATE PARK

ATTRACTIONS ●
Brewster Gardens **8**
Harlow Old Fort House **14**
Jabez Howland House **12**
Mayflower II **6**
Mayflower Society House **5**
Plimoth Grist Mill **11**
Plimoth Plantation **15**
Plymouth Rock **7**
Sparrow House **10**

RESTAURANTS ◆
Lobster Hut **4**
Persy's Place **2**

TOWN
BROOK
PARK

0   1/4 mi
0   1/4 km

east). To go directly to Plimoth Plantation, take Exit 4. If it isn't rush hour, the trip from Boston takes about an hour.

BY TRAIN MBTA commuter rail (www.mbta.com; ✆ **800/392-6100** or ✆ 617/222-3200) from Boston's South Station serves Cordage Park, north of downtown Plymouth. The local bus (www.gatra.org; ✆ **800/483-2500**) finishes up the trip, although it doesn't run on Sunday.

VISITOR INFORMATION
There's a **seasonal visitor center** at 130 Water St. (✆ **800/872-1620** or ✆ 508/747-7525), across from Town Pier. Information is available year-round from **Destination Plymouth** (www.seeplymouth.com; ✆ **800/USA-1620** or ✆ 508/747-7533).

GETTING AROUND
America's Hometown Shuttle (www.p-b.com/ahs.html; ✆ **508/746-0378**) runs throughout the town in a loop from late June through late August, daily 10am to 5pm. The fare ($15 adults, $7.50 children 6–11) includes a narrated tour and unlimited reboarding. Its route includes **Plimoth Plantation** (p. 176).

Exploring Plymouth

The logical place to begin is where the Pilgrims first set foot—at **Plymouth Rock ★★**. It's located on the waterfront in the petite **Pilgrim Memorial State Park**, 79 Water St. (www.mass.gov/dcr; ✆ **508/747-5360**), the smallest state park in Massachusetts.

Mayflower II ★ SHIP   A full-scale reproduction of the vessel that brought the Pilgrims to America in 1620, this boat is just 106½ feet long—yet the original transported 102 passengers and some 30 crew members on the perilous voyage from England. Visitors can board the ship, normally berthed in Plymouth harbor at the small Pilgrim Memorial State Park, next to Plymouth Rock. Until 2020, however, it's in at Mystic Seaport in Connecticut (see p. 415), undergoing renovations, which can be followed online at www.plimoth.org/mayflowerII-blog. Until it returns, a waterfront exhibit called *Should I Stay Or Should I Go?* stands in its place, asking visitors to consider what it would it be like to leave everything behind for an unknown world. This is a good place to introduce children to the idea that history is about real people—for instance, ask them to imagine choosing only enough belongings to fit into one minuscule sack.

Pilgrim Memorial State Park, State Pier, 79 Water St. www.plimoth.org. ✆ **508/746-1622.** Should I Stay Or Should I Go? exhibit: $8 adults and kids over 12, $7seniors, $5 kids 5–12, free for 4 and under; combo tickets available with Plimoth Plantation admission.

Plimoth Plantation ★★ LIVING HISTORY MUSEUM   Allow at least half a day to explore this re-creation of the 1627 village. Enter by the hilltop fort and walk down to the farm area. The village approximates the conditions in the early days of the little community, which was settled in 1620 (plans are underway to commemorate 400 years in 2020). Visitors wander the village, stepping into homes and gardens constructed with careful attention to historic detail. Re-enactors and educators assume the personalities of original community members, and they take their roles seriously—they will give mystified reactions to questions about bathrooms or queries from women about cooking techniques (asking a male beside her, "doesn't your wife know how to cook?"). Re-enactors spend their days framing houses, shearing sheep, preserving foodstuffs, and cooking over open hearths, all as it was done in the 1600s. Visitors are invited to join some activities—planting, witnessing a trial, visiting a wedding party. A **Wampanoag Homesite** depicts how 17th-century Native People would have lived. Staff in this section of the village are not actors: They are all either Wampanoag or from other Native Nations, and they talk to visitors as contemporaries, explaining Native history and culture. The visitor center's restaurant, the **Plentiful Cafe,** includes both modern foods and Colonial and Native American-influenced items such as stuffed quahogs, succotash, and something called "17th-century cheesecake."

137 Warren Ave. (Rte. 3). www.plimoth.org. ✆ **508/746-1622.** Admission (good for 2 consecutive days) $28 adults and kids over 12, $26 seniors, $16 kids 5–12, free for 4 and under. Late Mar–Nov daily 9am–5pm. Closed Dec to mid-Mar.

Plymouth Rock ★★ LANDMARK Tradition tells us that the original Plymouth Rock was the landing place of the Mayflower passengers in 1620. From a hunk that was once 15 feet long and 3 feet wide, the boulder has shrunk to about half its original size due to several relocations and chipping away by souvenir hunters. In 1867, the rock wound up here, perched at tide level on the peaceful shore. It's a model attraction: easy to understand, quick to visit, unexpectedly affecting.

A 5-minute walk away is the entrance to **Brewster Gardens,** site of the garden of an original settler, Elser William Brewster. Settle in to enjoy the greenery, or follow Town Brook, a narrow 1½ mile stream, up the hill to Jenney Pond. There, a waterwheel powers the **Plimoth Grist Mill,** a reproduction of a 1636 corn grinder. It's managed by Plimoth Plantation and includes a gift shop, resident ducks and geese, and plenty of room to run around.

79 Water St., within Pilgrim Memorial State Park. www.mass.gov/locations/pilgrim-memorial-state-park. ℂ **508/747-5360.** Free admission. Daily 24 hr. Brewster Gardens: 30 Water St. Plimoth Grist Mill: 6 Spring Ln. www.plimoth.org/what-see-do/plimoth-grist-mill. ℂ **508-746-1622** ext. 8242. $7 adults and kids over 12, $6 seniors, $5 kids 5–12, free for 4 and under; combo tickets available with Plimoth Plantation admission.

Where to Stay in Plymouth

There are over 3 dozen options for hotels, inns, and bed & breakfasts in Plymouth. Big brands are here, including **Hampton Inn & Suites Plymouth,** 10 Plaza Way (www.hamptoninn3.hilton.com; ℂ **800/HAMPTON** [426-7866] or 508/747-5000), less than 10 minutes from the downtown attractions; though it's on a commercial strip near a shopping mall and fast food stores, it does have an indoor pool. High-season double rates start at $185 and include breakfast and Wi-Fi. **Hilton Garden Inn,** 4 Home Depot Dr. (www.hiltongardeninn.com;

Plymouth's Historic Houses

The See Plymouth website (www.seeplymouth.com) lists more than a dozen historic houses in Plymouth and neighboring towns such as Scituate and Duxbury, many of them with costumed guides explaining the homemaking and crafts of earlier generations. For those curious about the original settlers, the 1667 **Jabez Howland House,** 33 Sandwich St. (www.pilgrimjohnhowland society.org; ℂ **508/746-9590;** $6 adults and kids over 12, $5 seniors and students, $2 children), is the only existing house where pilgrims actually lived. The **Sparrow House,** 42 Summer St. (ℂ **508/747-1240**), which has one room open for viewing and a gift/craft shop,

was built in 1640 and is the oldest home in Plymouth.

Other houses open for visits include the 1677 **Harlow Old Fort House,** 119 Sandwich St (www.plymouthantiquarian society.org, free) and the 1754 **Mayflower Society House,** 4 Winslow St. (www.the mayflowersociety.com; ℂ **508/746-3188;** $7 adults, $5 seniors, teens, and AAA members). For a full list, go to www.seeplymouth.com/things-to-do/historic-sites-houses. Most houses are open late May through mid-October, during Thanksgiving celebrations in November, and around Christmas in December. *Tip:* check online for schedules and pay close attention to open days, which are limited.

© **877/782-9444** or 508/830-0200), is also about 10 minutes from downtown and also has an indoor pool. Doubles in high season start at $224 and include Wi-Fi.

Best Western Plus Cold Spring ★★   Convenient to downtown and the historic sites (about a 15-min. walk), this fastidiously maintained chain hotel and its adjacent cottages surround nicely landscaped lawns. Rooms are pleasantly decorated and big enough for a family to spread out; if you want privacy, book a two-bedroom cottage. Registration and breakfast are in a separate building from the room buildings. The tolerable distance from the water makes this place a good deal: The two-story complex is 1 long block inland, set back from the street in a quiet part of town.

180 Court St. (Rte. 3A). www.bestwestern.com. © **800/780-7234** or 508/746-2222. 57 units, includes 2 cottages. $150–$220 double. Rates include full breakfast. Closed Dec–mid Mar. **Amenities:** Fitness center; pool (outdoor heated, open seasonally); Wi-Fi (free).

John Carver Inn & Spa ★   A three-story Colonial-style building with a landmark portico, this hotel offers comfortable, modern accommodations and plenty of amenities. It's within walking distance of the main attractions on the edge of the downtown business district. The indoor "theme pool," a big hit with families, has a water slide and a *Mayflower* replica. The good-size guest rooms are decorated in Colonial style. The best units are the lavish suites with private Jacuzzis; "four-poster" rooms contain king-size beds.

25 Summer St. www.johncarverinn.com. © **888/906-6181.** 78 units. $139–$269 double. **Amenities:** Restaurant; bar; concierge; fitness center; Jacuzzi; pool (indoor, with water slide); spa; Wi-Fi (free).

Where to Eat in Plymouth

Plimoth Plantation (p. 176) has a cafeteria with indoor and outdoor seating.

Lobster Hut ★ SEAFOOD   The deck of Lobster Hut overlooking Plymouth Harbor is the place to be. The seafood restaurant is popular with out-of-towners and locals alike. Order and pick up at the counter, then head to an indoor table or out onto the deck overlooking the bay. Clam chowder, lobster bisque, seafood rolls, fried clams, burgers, and of course lobster are all options.

25 Town Wharf (off Water St.). www.lobsterhutplymouth.com. © **508/746-2270**. Main courses $6–$20; scallops and clams market price. Sun–Thurs 11am–9pm, Fri–Sat 11am–9pm; confirm offseason.

Persy's Place ★ AMERICAN   This small regional chain is known for its extensive breakfast and lunch menus. Breakfast options, which fill six large pages, include both traditional fare and New England variations, such as fish cakes and eggs, Portuguese chourico Benedict, and cranberry-nut pancakes. The diner-style restaurant is a good choice for lunch, too. It's often packed on weekends. This location is in Kingston, 3 miles north of Plymouth.

117 Main St. (Rte. 3A), Kingston. www.persysplace.com. © **781/585-5464.** Breakfast items $3–$15; lunch items $4–$12. Daily 7am–3pm.

CAPE COD

A t only 75 miles long, Cape Cod is a curving peninsula that encompasses miles of beaches, hundreds of freshwater ponds, more than a dozen richly historic New England villages, scores of classic clam shacks and ice cream shops—and it's just about everyone's idea of the perfect summer vacation spot.

More than 13 million visitors flock to the Cape to enjoy summertime's nonstop carnival. In full swing, the Cape is, if anything, perhaps a bit too popular for some tastes. Connoisseurs are discovering the subtler appeal of the off-season, when prices plummet along with the population. For some travelers, the prospect of sunbathing en masse on sizzling sand can't hold a candle to a long, solitary stroll on a windswept beach with only the gulls as company. For that experience, you'll have to come in the springtime, or even better, the fall.

ESSENTIALS

Arriving

BY CAR

There are two routes to Cape Cod: from Boston and the South Shore via **Route 3;** and from everywhere else via I-495 or coastal I-195, which both feed into **Route 25** for the last few miles. Route 3 crosses into Cape Cod via the **Sagamore Bridge;** Route 25 enters over the **Bourne Bridge.** Traffic at both bridges slows to a hellish crawl (if that fast) at the start and end of every summer weekend. You've been warned.

The limited-access **Mid-Cape Highway** (Route 6) runs down the spine of the Cape, from the Sagamore Bridge to Eastham, where it continues as a conventional road on to Provincetown, 63 miles from Sagamore. It's the fastest way to cover long distances, but until Eastham, it has no beachy charm. For that you'll have to go to Route 6A, which traces the north coast (on Cape Cod Bay) or Route 28, which follows the south coast (on Nantucket Sound). And yes, those too get choked with traffic at times in the height of summer.

BY BUS

From Boston, **Peter Pan Bus Lines** (www.peterpanbus.com) stops in Bourne, Falmouth, Woods Hole, and Hyannis. It's about a 1½-hour trip from Boston's South Station to Falmouth (one-way adult fare $31). Frequent **Plymouth & Brockton** buses (www.p-b.com) from Boston stop at Sagamore, Barnstable, and Hyannis; changes

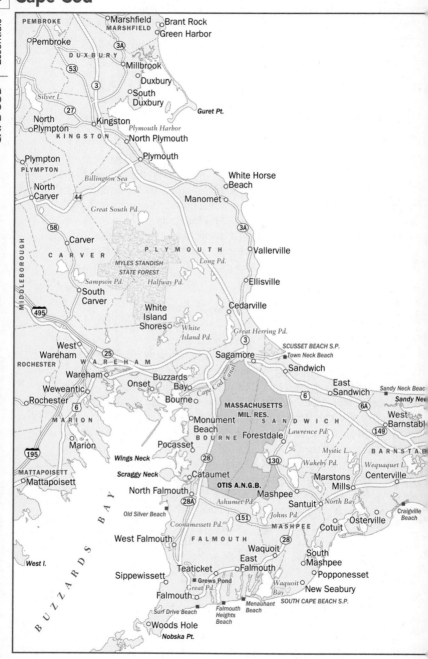

buses at Hyannis to get to several Lower Cape towns en route to Provincetown. It takes 1¾ hours from South Station to Hyannis (one-way adult fare $21).

Greyhound buses (www.greyhound.com) from New York City to Hyannis cost $34 to $61 and take anywhere from 6¾ hours to 9 hours; service continues on to Provincetown, which takes over 9 hours but costs as little as $25.

BY PLANE

Cape Cod's main airport, **Barnstable Municipal Airport,** is in the Mid-Cape town of Hyannis. Flights from New York City via **Jet Blue** (www.jetblue. com) take about an hour; from Boston's Logan Airport it's even quicker, half an hour. **Cape Air** (www.capeair.com) flies from Boston, while **Nantucket Airlines** (www.nantucketairlines.com) flies back and forth to Nantucket Island (see chapter 7). Jet Blue and Cape Air also fly from Boston to **Provincetown Municipal Airport,** at the tip of the Cape; the trip takes about 30 minutes and costs $358 to $405 for a round-trip.

BY FERRY

From mid-May to Labor Day, **Bay State Cruises** (www.provincetownfast ferry.com) runs high-speed (90 min.) and conventional (3 hr.) ferries from Boston to Provincetown; a one-way adult fare is $60 to $63 for the fast ferry, $30 for the regular ferry. **Boston Harbor Cruises** (www.bostonharborcruises. com) also operates a 90-minute fast ferry service from Boston to Provincetown; the one-way adult fare is $61, round-trip $93. Reservations are a must on this popular boat.

BY TRAIN

Launched in 2013, the **Cape Flyer** (www.capeflyer.com; © **508/775-8504**) train runs summer weekend service to Hyannis from Boston; the trip from South Station to Hyannis takes 2 hours and 20 minutes, and costs $22 one-way, $40 round-trip; kids 11 and under ride free, seniors pay half-price. The sleek trains have free Wi-Fi and a cafe car, and passengers can bring bikes and pets on board for free.

Visitor Information

The **Cape Cod Chamber of Commerce** (www.capecodchamber.org; © **888/ 332-2732**) operates two welcome centers: A booth on the road to the Cape, just off Route 3 in Plymouth (© **508/759-3814**), and the main office, just off exit 6 of the Mid-Cape Highway in Centerville (© **508/362-3225**). Both are open daily 9am to 5pm from mid-April to mid-November, with reduced hours the rest of the year.

UPPER CAPE: SANDWICH ★ & FALMOUTH ★★★

Sandwich: 3 miles E of Sagamore; 16 miles NW of Hyannis. Falmouth: 18 miles S of Sagamore; 20 miles SW of Hyannis.

Just over the Cape Cod Canal, the towns of the Upper Cape are the closest to Boston (just over an hour's drive), and they've become bedroom as well as summer communities. They're a bit more staid, more New England-y, than the beach towns farther east, but they're also spared some of the fly-by-night qualities that come with a transient population. Shops and restaurants here tend to stay open year-round.

VISITOR INFORMATION   Just off exit 2 of the Mid-Cape Highway, the **Sandwich Chamber of Commerce,** 520 Route 130 (www.sandwichchamber. com; ✆ **508/681-0918**) has a spiffy visitor center with restrooms. The **Cape Cod Canal Region Chamber of Commerce,** 70 Main St., Buzzards Bay (www.capecodcanalchamber.org; ✆ **508/759-6000**), open year-round Monday to Friday 9am to 5pm, has all the info on Bourne and activities around the Cape Cod Canal. The **Falmouth Chamber of Commerce,** 20 Academy Lane, Falmouth (www.falmouthchamber.com; ✆ **800/526-8532** or 508/548-8500), is open year-round Monday to Friday 9am to 5pm, Saturday 10am to 4pm, and Sunday 11am to 3pm.

Exploring Sandwich ★

Sandwich is the oldest town on the Cape and the quaintest. Towering oak trees, 19th-century churches, and historic houses line its winding Main Street. A 1640 gristmill still grinds corn beside bucolic Shawme Pond. The town had its heyday in the 19th century, however, as a glass manufacturing center—for that slice of history, visit the **Sandwich Glass Museum,** p. 184.

Green Briar Jam Kitchen ★★★ NATURE CENTER/CRAFT DEMON-STRATION   This sweet (in more ways than one) little spot is what is called a "living museum" where visitors can watch and learn how to make home-made jam using old school recipes in a turn-of-the-century kitchen. But that's not all. The kitchen is attached to the Green Briar Nature Center, which offers natural history programs for children and adults year-round. Guided Wild-flower Garden Tours are offered Tuesdays at 10am June, July, and August. The property is a sanctuary located on the shores of Smiling Pool.

6 Discovery Hill Rd., East Sandwich. ✆ **508/888-6870.** Admission by donation. Mon–Sat 10am–4pm, Sun noon–4pm (Jan to mid-Apr, closed on Sun and Mon).

Heritage Museums and Gardens & Adventure Park ★★★ GAR-DENS/MUSEUM   One of the Cape's top attractions, Heritage Museums and Gardens, which sprawls across an exquisitely landscaped 76-acre property, is a particularly good find for families with young children, gardening buffs, and collectors. In recent years, the Adventure Park's elaborate rope course in the trees, on property adjacent to Heritage, has become a major destination for families with pre-teens and teens. On the Heritage property, the Hidden Hollow is a children's play area housed in a 2-acre dry kettle hole that teaches about the outdoors while encouraging creative play. The showpiece of this property will always be the grounds, rolling acres perfect for a stroll, particularly in the spring when the rhododendrons are in bloom, a riot of blooms in all possible shades. (The Rhododendron festival is in May.) Most visitors begin their visit with the collection of cars, from Model T's to a sleek

DeLorean, all housed in a round Shaker barn. Walk along paths through the grounds to reach the Special Exhibition Building along with the American Art and Carousel Gallery on the far end of the property to explore the museum's permanent collections of toy soldiers, Native American artifacts, and American Folk art. An indoor antique carousel offers unlimited rides, and a labyrinth on the grounds is perfect to sap the energy of boisterous children. A free trolley cruises the grounds in the summer for those who would prefer not to walk.

67 Grove St. (about ½ miles SW of Sandwich town center). www.heritagemuseumsand gardens.org. © **508/888-3300.** $18 adults, $8 ages 3–11, free for kids 2 and under. Late May–Aug daily 10am–6pm; mid-Apr to late May and Sept–Oct daily 10am–5pm. No tickets sold 1 hr. before closing. Closed Nov to mid-Apr. **Adventure Park:** www. heritageadventurepark.org. © **508-866-0199.** $49 ages 12 and over, $43 ages 10–11, $38 ages 7–9. July–Aug daily 9am–8pm, mid-Apr to late May and Sept–Oct weekends 9am–7pm (hours are weather dependent and sometimes vary). Combo tickets for Heritage & Adventure Park $59 adults and teens, $48 kids 10–11, $43 ages 7–9.

Hoxie House ★ HISTORIC HOME   One of the Cape's best-preserved historic homes, Hoxie House, circa 1675, is the oldest house on Cape Cod that is open for visitors to tour. It was the home of the town's second minister, Rev. John Smith, who lived here with his wife, Susanna, and their 13(!) children. It is named for Abraham Hoxie, a Sandwich whaling captain, who purchased it in the 1850s. The house was lived in by families up until the 1950s without electricity, central heating, or plumbing, so its authenticity was never "ruined" by those modern conveniences. It is decorated with a few choice pieces appropriate to the period so visitors can see more precisely how its early occupants lived. Nearby is the **Dexter Grist Mill,** one of the earliest water mill sites in the country, worth a look to see how they did it in the olden days. You can take away a bag of freshly ground cornmeal for $5.

18 Water St. (on Shawme Pond, about ¼ mile S of Sandwich town center). © **508/888-1173.** $4 adults, $3 kids 5–15, free for ages 4 and under; combination ticket for Hoxie House and Dexter Grist Mill $5 adults, $3 children. June–Sept Mon–Sat 11am–4:30pm, Sun 1–4:30pm. Closed Oct–May.

Sandwich Glass Museum ★★ MUSEUM   The highlight of this museum is seeing the sunshine from outside glance off the dozens of brightly colored glass displays, refracting multicolored lights. That alone is worth the price of admission. But there is so much more, including glass-blowing demonstrations, which last 20 minutes and take place every hour on the hour.

Sandwich used to be known as Glasstown and to see why, you'll have to visit this museum, which gives a history not only of the glass industry on the Cape but also of the town itself. Sandwich was primarily a farming community until 1825 when Deming Jarves, a Boston businessman, came to town and changed everything. Because of its proximity to a shallow harbor, Jarves chose Sandwich as the base for his Boston and Sandwich Glass Company. The surrounding forest was cut and used to fuel the furnaces and the marsh hay on the coast was used to pack the fragile wares. He brought master glassblowers to the Cape and recruited workers from England and Ireland for his glass factory. The company mass-produced glass products and was very

---

Make Way for Mini-Golf: Upper Cape Edition

The 18-hole **Sandwich Mini Golf**, 159 Route 6A, at the corner of Main Street ((©) **508/833-1905**), is a grassy 1950s classic that encapsulates Cape Cod history. Built on a former cranberry bog, it has an unusual floating green. Hours are Monday to Saturday from 10am to 9pm and Sunday from noon to 9pm. Admission is $8 for adults, $6 for children 12 and under. Add $4 and play two rounds, or 36 holes.

---

successful. Jarves eventually left the company and started a rival firm called Cape Cod Glass Works, also in Sandwich. The glass industry died down after the Civil War when cheaper glass could be made using coal furnaces down south and in the Midwest. In the 1880s, a union strike led to the closing of Sandwich's glass companies. Today, the town is embracing its glass history in the form of a newly formed Glasstown Cultural District (you can take a self-guided walking tour starting at the museum). There are also several art glassblowers in town whose studios are open to the public. Their works are sold in the museum's gift shop.

129 Main St. www.sandwichglassmuseum.org. (©) **508/888-0251.** $10 adults, $2 kids 6–14, free for ages 5 and under. Apr–Dec daily 9:30am–5pm; Feb–Mar Wed–Sun 9:30am–4pm. Closed Jan, Thanksgiving, and Christmas.

SANDWICH BEACHES

Nonresident parking stickers—$90 for the length of your stay—are available at **Sandwich Town Hall Annex,** 145 Main St. (© **508/833-8012**).

o **Sandy Neck Beach ★★★**, off Sandy Neck Road, in East Sandwich (www. town.barnstable.ma.us/sandyneckpark/default.aspx): This 6-mile stretch of silken barrier beach with low, rounded dunes is one of the Cape's prettiest and most unspoiled. It is somewhat isolated, with no commercial businesses or accommodations on the beach. Because it is a Cape Cod Bay beach, the water tends to be warmer than the open ocean, and the waves are never too high. That makes it popular with families. The fact that the beach stretches out for miles makes it a magnet for endangered piping plovers—and their nemeses, off-road vehicles (ORV). That means that the ORV trails are closed for much of the summer while the piping plover chicks hatch. Parking for the beach in the upper parking lot costs $20 per day in season. Up to 4 days of camping in self-contained vehicles is permitted at $20 per night, plus an ORV permit ($85 for Barnstable residents, $170 for non-residents).

o **Town Neck Beach,** off Town Neck Road, in Sandwich: A bit rocky but ruggedly pretty, this narrow beach offers a busy view of passing ships, plus restrooms and a snack bar. Parking costs $15 per day, or you could hike from town (about 1½ miles) via the community-built boardwalk spanning the salt marsh.

o **Wakeby Pond,** Ryder Conservation Area, John Ewer Road (off South Sandwich Rd., on the Mashpee border): The beach, on the Cape's largest freshwater pond, has lifeguards, restrooms, and parking ($15 per day).

GOLF IN SANDWICH

The **Sandwich Hollows Golf Club,** 1 Round Hill Road, in East Sandwich (www.sandwichhollows.com; ✆ **508/888-3384**), is a 6,200-yard, par-71 town-owned course. In season a round costs $30 to $62, depending on the day and time. The 18-hole, par-3 **Holly Ridge Golf Course,** at 121 Country Club Road, in South Sandwich (www.hollyridgegolf.com; ✆ **508/428-5577**), is, at 2,900 yards, shorter and easier. A round costs $34 in season, with afternoon discounts.

SANDWICH SHOPPING

Most shops are concentrated in the town center, and several of the museums in town also have worthwhile gift shops.

ANTIQUES & COLLECTIBLES The **Sandwich Antiques Center,** 131 Route 6A, at Jarves Street (✆ **508/833-3600**), showcases wares from over 100 dealers in 6,000 square feet of rooms. It's headed by a congenial auctioneer and offers virtual one-stop shopping for the likes of Sandwich glass, primitives, country furnishings, and other items. The center is open daily year-round.

BOOKS **Titcomb's Bookshop ★,** 432 Route 6A, East Sandwich, about 4 miles east of the town center (www.titcombsbookshop.com; ✆ **508/888-2331**), has a terrific selection of new and used books relating to Cape Cod and much more. Look for the life-size statue of English Renaissance dramatist Ben Jonson out front.

FOOD & WINE **Crow Farm ★,** 192 Route 6A, ¼ mile east of the town center (www.crowfarmcapecod.com; ✆ **508/888-0690**), is a picture-perfect farm stand purveying sweet corn, tomatoes, peaches, apples, and other produce, as well as flowers. It's closed Sunday in summer but open daily in spring and fall (closed late Dec–Apr). **The Brown Jug,** 155 Main St., in Sandwich (www.thebrownjug.com; ✆ **508/888-4669**), is stocked with delicacies from around the corner and around the world, from fine cheeses and olive oils to rich baked goods and hearty homemade breads.

GIFTS/HOME DECOR The **Weather Store ★,** 146 Main St., Sandwich (www.theweatherstore.com; ✆ **800/646-1203**), has a fascinating collection of meteorological paraphernalia old and new, ranging from antique instruments to coffee-table books. Although technically open year-round, from January through April it's open by chance or appointment.

GLASS For the finest in art glass and a souvenir of your trip to Sandwich, visit **The Glass Studio ★★,** 470 Route 6A, East Sandwich (www.capecodglass.net; ✆ **508/888-6681**), where master glassblower Michael Magyar crafts such one-of-a-kind pieces as his "sea bubbles" series and Venetian-style goblets. Watch glassblowing Thursday through Sunday from 10am to 1pm and 2 to 5pm. At **McDermott Glass Studio & Gallery ★★,** 272 Cotuit Rd., Sandwich (www.mcdermottglass.com; ✆ **508/477-0705**), Dave McDermott creates exquisite handblown art glass, from vases to stemware. Glassblowing takes place Thursday to Saturday from 10am to 5pm.

Exploring Bourne

Most visitors to the Cape know Bourne only as the home of the famous (or infamous, if you're stuck in traffic on a summer weekend) Bourne Bridge and Sagamore Bridge, which span the Cape Cod Canal that divides the Cape from mainland Massachusetts. Two of its villages, Buzzards Bay and Sagamore Beach, are actually on the other side of the canal.

Aptucxet Trading Post Museum ★ MUSEUM/HISTORIC SITE Aptucxet is where to go to learn about shopping, Pilgrim-style. The Algonquin name means "little trap in the river," and the site is where the Manomet and Scusset rivers met, making it a convenient trading place for Native Americans. Historical records indicate that in 1627, the Pilgrims began using the site for early trade with the Wampanoag tribe and the Dutch. The building used for the small museum here is a replica of the Pilgrim trading post and is erected on the original foundation. Excavated in the 1920s, the foundation is considered the earliest remains of a Pilgrim building. Also on the museum grounds you can see a replica **salt works** built by students at the nearby Upper Cape Regional Technical School. Salt-making was a big early industry on the Cape. The first salt-making was done by evaporating seawater placed in large boilers over fire, but after the Revolutionary War, the process was refined and saltworks were built using large wooden vats and solar evaporation. Saltworks used to line the shores of Cape Cod, the most extensive saltworks being on Mashnee Island (those were destroyed by hurricane in 1835). Also on the grounds of the museum is the tiny Victorian-style **Gray Gables Train Depot,** which was built as the personal station for President Grover Cleveland during his second term in the White House (1893–1896). Cleveland had a summer home at Gray Gables in Bourne, chosen for its proximity to rich fishing grounds; the train depot was outfitted with a direct telegraph line to Washington, D.C. The depot was moved to the trading post grounds in 1976.

The Aptucxet Museum is also a good starting spot to explore the Cape Cod Canal bike path (see box p. 188).

24 Aptucxet Rd., off Perry Ave. (about ½ mile west of the town center), Bourne Village. www.bournehistoricalsociety.org. © **508/759-9487.** $6 adults, $5 seniors, $4 kids 6–18, free for ages 5 and under; families $12. July–Aug Tues–Sat 10am–4pm, Sun noon–3pm; Memorial Day–June and Sept–Columbus Day Tues–Sun 11am–3pm. Closed mid-Oct to late May.

OUTDOOR ACTIVITIES

FISHING So plentiful are herring, as they make their spring migration up the **Bournedale Herring Run ★★** (© **508/759-5991;** Route 6 in Bournedale, about 1 mile southwest of the Sagamore Bridge rotary), you can net them once they've reached their destination, Great Herring Pond. You can obtain a shellfish permit from **Bourne Town Hall,** at 24 Perry Ave., Buzzards Bay (© **508/759-0600**). Also plentiful here are pickerel, white perch, walleye, and bass. For freshwater fishing at Flax Pond and Red Brook Pond in Pocasset, you'll need a license from the Bourne Town Hall. You can also obtain a freshwater fishing license at **Red Top Sporting Goods,** at 265 Main St., in

CRUISING THE cape cod canal

You have three ways to get a gander at the wonder that is the Cape Cod Canal: Take a quick look around for the 10 seconds you are driving over the Bourne or Sagamore Bridge; bike along the Cape Cod Canal; or take a **canal cruise ★★**. Most visitors only take Option #1, but Options #2 and #3 are highly recommended.

The gateway to Cape Cod, the 17.5-mile Cape Cod Canal has a fascinating history. The conversation about constructing a canal to serve as a shortcut between Boston and New York is said to have begun as soon as the Pilgrims landed in 1620. (The first known Cape Cod Canal feasibility study, if you will, was commissioned by none other than George Washington.) The project was finally undertaken in the early 20th century by a wealthy industrialist, August Belmont II, who paid for it himself through his Boston, Cape Cod and New York Canal Company, and opened it in 1914 as a private toll waterway. In 1927, he sold the Cape Cod Canal to the US government for what was at the time a whopping price, $11.5 million. To improve navigation, the canal was later widened to 480 feet and deepened to 32 feet.

From the Onset Bay Town Pier (on the northern side of the canal, about 2 miles west of the Bourne Bridge), 2- or 3-hour narrated cruises are operated by Hy-Line (www.hy-linecruises.com;

✆ 508/295-3883), the same company that runs ferries to and from Martha's Vineyard and Nantucket. Tickets cost $15 to $20 adults, half-price or free for children 12 and under. From mid-June to September, there are three or four cruises a day (only two on Sundays); there are no cruises from mid-October through April. (Call for off-season schedules.)

If you want to learn more, the Army Corps of Engineers operates the free **Cape Cod Canal Visitors Center** (www.capecodcanal.us; ✆ 978/318-8816) May through October from 10am to 5pm at the Sandwich Marina, on 60 Moffitt Dr. in Sandwich. It displays exhibits about the canal, and rangers lead walks in the area. **Note:** No swimming is allowed within the Cape Cod Canal because the currents are much too swift and dangerous.

The Corps also maintains a flat, 14-mile loop along the **Cape Cod Canal ★★★**, equally suited to bicyclists, skaters, runners, and strollers. The most convenient place to park (free) is at the Bourne Recreation Area, north of the Bourne Bridge, on the Cape side. You can also park at the Sandcatcher Recreation Area at the end of Freezer Road in Sandwich. As you ride, look for the Railroad Bridge, an unusual vertical lift structure that is used summer weekends for the Cape Flyer train between Hyannis and Boston, as well as a daily train between 5 and 6pm carrying garbage to a landfill off-Cape.

Buzzards Bay (www.redtoptackle.com; ✆ **508/759-3371**). The Cape Cod Canal is a great place to try surf-casting, though the state now requires a $10-per-year permit (free for those over 60). To get one online, go to www.mass.gov/marinefisheries or call ✆ **866/703-1925.**

Exploring Falmouth

Falmouth is a classic New England town, complete with church steeples encircling the town green and a walkable and bustling Main Street. Check out **Falmouth Heights ★★★**, a cluster of shingled Victorian summer houses along Grand Avenue on a bluff east of Falmouth's harbor. At the tip of the peninsula, **Wood's Hole ★★★**, one of Falmouth's eight villages, is home to

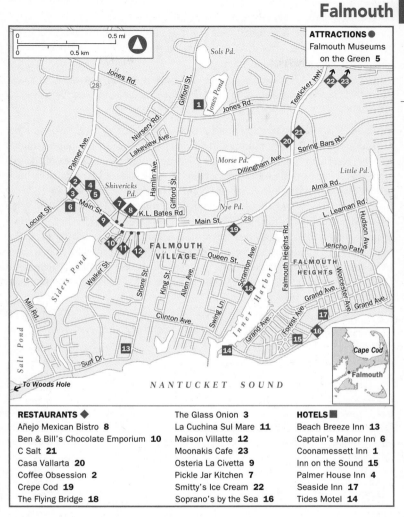

ATTRACTIONS ●
Falmouth Museums
on the Green **5**

RESTAURANTS ◆

Añejo Mexican Bistro **8**
Ben & Bill's Chocolate Emporium **10**
C Salt **21**
Casa Vallarta **20**
Coffee Obsession **2**
Crepe Cod **19**
The Flying Bridge **18**

The Glass Onion **3**
La Cuchina Sul Mare **11**
Maison Villatte **12**
Moonakis Cafe **23**
Osteria La Civetta **9**
Pickle Jar Kitchen **7**
Smitty's Ice Cream **22**
Soprano's by the Sea **16**

HOTELS ■

Beach Breeze Inn **13**
Captain's Manor Inn **6**
Coonamessett Inn **1**
Inn on the Sound **15**
Palmer House Inn **4**
Seaside Inn **17**
Tides Motel **14**

a group of world-renowned oceanic research institutions; it's also where travelers catch the car ferry to Martha's Vineyard, so expect traffic tie-ups at times.

Falmouth Museums on the Green ★★ MUSEUMS   Across the street from the Village Green, where Colonial militia used to train, stand these historically focused museums. The two main museum buildings, inside 18th-century houses, display period furniture, fine art, textiles, and temporary exhibits. The 1790 Dr. Francis Wicks House is set up to show what a doctor's office was like 200 years ago. The Conant House, built about 1730, has revolving exhibits covering topics such as Victorian Life in Falmouth. The museum's visitors' center is inside the reconstructed Hallett Barn, first built in the 18th century. Walking tours of Falmouth depart from the barn at 10am on Tuesday, Wednesday and Thursday mornings in season. Behind the barn is the Cultural Center where many of the museum's activities take place. The gardens—a Colonial-style flower garden, an herb garden, and a Memorial Park—are particularly exquisite.

55 and 65 Palmer Ave. www.museumsonthegreen.org. ✆ **508/548-4857.** $5 adults, free for kids 12 and under. Late June–early Oct Mon–Fri 10am–3pm, Sat 10am–1pm; by appointment early Oct–late June.

Woods Hole Historical Museum ★★ MUSEUM The Woods Hole Museum is a small lively museum that celebrates this fishing village's unique history. The main building, the Bradley House, contains a diorama of the village; revolving exhibits focus on local history, such as old Woods Hole businesses or the Woods Hole Science School. The Swift Barn, built in 1877 by E. E. Swift for $80.71, houses a small boat museum. Displays include an 1890s Woods Hole Spritsail, a Herreshoff 12½ sailboat, and other maritime artifacts and models. In summer there's a boat-building class for families. The Yale Workshop houses a re-creation of the workshop of a local pediatrician, Dr. Leroy Milton Yale Jr., who was an accomplished artist and fly fisherman who made his own rods and flies. The museum hosts walking tours on Tuesdays at 3:30pm in July and August.

579 Woods Hole Rd., Woods Hole. www.woodsholemuseum.org. ✆ **508/548-7270.** Free admission; donations welcome. Mid-June to mid-Sept Tues–Sat 10am–4pm; by appointment during off-season.

Woods Hole Oceanographic Institution Ocean Science Exhibit Center ★ MUSEUM The high point at this small visitor's center is a climb aboard a life-size replica of the DSV *Alvin*, the deep-submergence vehicle that discovered the *Titanic*. But there are a range of other interactive exhibits here that will intrigue children and their parents, including a computer program about whale and dolphin sounds, a hydrothermal vent exhibit, and a presentation about toxic algae. The Woods Hole Oceanographic Institution (called WHOI—rhymes with phooey) is a world-class research organization and a $100-million operation mostly funded by the federal government. It, along with the Marine Biological Laboratory and the National Oceanic & Atmospheric Administration (NOAA), helped make this little fishing village into a world-renowned science community.

15 School St. (off Water St.), Woods Hole. www.whoi.edu. ✆ **508/289-2663.** $2 donation requested. Mid-Apr to Oct Mon–Fri 11am–4pm; Nov–Dec Tues–Fri 11am–4pm. Closed Jan to mid-Apr.

Woods Hole Science Aquarium ★ AQUARIUM The country's oldest marine aquarium, having been established in 1885, makes for a nice little 45-minute visit. Young children will particularly appreciate its charms. Time your visit to coincide with feeding time for the two seals in a special pool out in front of the museum. Their injuries—one is blind—make them unable to be released, so the aquarium is their permanent home. Feeding time is 11am and

4pm most days. The best parts of the aquarium are the touch tanks with lobsters, quahogs, horseshoe crabs, spider crabs, starfish, and hermit crabs. The tanks contain 140 marine animals, mainly fish of the Northeast and Middle Atlantic waters. There are also displays about marine environments, endangered species, and marine science.

166 Water St., at Albatross St. (off the western end of Water St.), Woods Hole. http://aquarium.nefsc.noaa.gov. ℰ **508/495-2001.** Free admission; donations accepted. Mid-June to early Sept daily 11am–4pm; rest of year Mon–Fri 10am–4pm. Adults need picture ID to enter.

NATURE & WILDLIFE AREAS

Falmouth is particularly blessed with some lovely nature preserves. Prime among them is the **Ashumet Holly and Wildlife Sanctuary ★★**, operated by the Massachusetts Audubon Society, at 186 Ashumet Rd., off Route 151 in East Falmouth (www.massaudubon.org; ℰ **508/362-1426**), an intriguing 49-acre collection of more than 1,000 holly trees, representing 65 species culled from around the world. Preserved by the state's first commissioner of agriculture, who was concerned that commercial harvesting might wipe out native species, they flourish here, along with more than 130 species of birds and a carpet of Oriental lotus blossoms, which covers a kettle pond come summer. The trail fee is $4 for adults and $2 for seniors and children 15 and under.

Named for its round shape, **The Knob ★★** (13 acres of trails at Quissett Harbor, at the end of Quissett Road) provides a perfect short walk and lovely views of Buzzards Bay. There's very limited parking at this small, secluded harbor, so try it early or late in the day. The Knob, owned by the nonprofit group Salt Pond Areas Bird Sanctuaries, is free and open to the public.

Families will find a lot to do at the 2,250-acre **Waquoit Bay National Estuarine Research Reserve (WBNERR),** at 149 Waquoit Highway, in Waquoit (www.waquoitbayreserve.org; ℰ **508/457-0495**). The reserve has a 1-mile, self-guided nature trail and a visitor center, open Monday to Saturday from 10am to 4pm, with several interesting exhibits especially for children. The reserve also offers a number of walks and interpretive programs, including the popular "Evenings on the Bluff," on Tuesday nights at 6:30pm, which are geared toward families. On Saturday in season, WBNERR hosts a free 20-minute cruise over to **Washburn Island ★★**, where visitors can explore wooded trails or relax on pristine beaches. The 12-passenger motorboat leaves at 9am and returns by 12:30pm. The reserve also manages 11 primitive campsites on Washburn Island; permits cost $10 a night. These book up 6 months in advance for summer weekends; you'll have better luck with a late-spring or early fall booking. Advance reservations for the cruise and camping are required; call ℰ **877/422-6762.**

FALMOUTH BEACHES

Although Old Silver Beach, Surf Drive Beach, and Menauhant Beach sell 1-day passes, most other Falmouth public beaches require a parking sticker instead. Day passes to Old Silver are $20, to Surf Drive $15, and to Menauhant $10. Renters can obtain temporary beach parking stickers, for $70 per week or $210 for 2 weeks, at **Falmouth Town Hall,** 59 Town Hall Square (☎ **508/548-7611**), or at the **Surf Drive Beach bathhouse** in season (☎ **508/548-8623**), which is open 9am to 4pm daily. The town beaches that charge a parking fee all have lifeguards, restrooms, and concession stands. Some of Falmouth's more notable public shores are as follows:

- **Falmouth Heights Beach** ★★★, off Grand Avenue, in Falmouth Heights: At this family-oriented beach, the parking is sticker-only; some local inns will provide stickers to guests. This neighborhood supported the Cape's first summer colony; the grand Victorian mansions still overlook the beach. The beach has lifeguards and bathroom facilities.

- **Grews Pond** ★★, in Goodwill Park, off Gifford Street, in Falmouth: This freshwater pond in a large town forest stays fairly uncrowded, even in the middle of summer. While everyone else is experiencing beach rage, trying to find parking at Falmouth's popular beaches, here you park for free and can wander shady paths around the pond. You'll find picnic tables, an extra special playground, barbecue grills, a lifeguard, and restrooms.

- **Menauhant Beach** ★★, off Central Avenue, in East Falmouth: A bit off the beaten track, Menauhant is a little less mobbed than Falmouth Heights Beach and better protected from the winds. There are lifeguards, bathroom facilities, and a bathhouse. Day passes are $10.

- **Old Silver Beach** ★★★, off Route 28A, in North Falmouth: Western-facing (great for sunsets) and relatively calm, this warm Buzzards Bay beach is a popular, often crowded, choice. This is the spot for the college crowd and other rowdy young folk. Mothers and their charges cluster on the opposite

Cycle by the Sea

The **Shining Sea Bikeway** ★★★ (☎ **508/548-7611**) is a 12-mile beauty that runs along an old railroad right-of-way from North Falmouth past cranberry bogs, farmland, and the Great Sippewissett Marsh, and then skirts Vineyard Sound from Falmouth center to Woods Hole. This is one of the Cape's most scenic bike paths and one of the few that travels alongside a beach; its name is a nod to Falmouth's own Katharine Lee Bates (1859–1929), who wrote the lyrics to "America the Beautiful," with its verse, "And crown thy good with brotherhood, from sea to shining sea!" The Falmouth Chamber of Commerce offers a map and brochure about the bike path. There is free parking on Locust Street; on Depot Avenue; in West Falmouth, on Old Dock Road;

and at the trailhead on County Road, in North Falmouth.

The closest bike shop—convenient to the main cluster of B&Bs, some of which offer loaners—is **Corner Cycle,** at 115 Palmer Ave., at North Main Street (www.cornercycle.com; ☎ **508/540-4195**). A half-day bike rental is $17 ($12 for children), a 24-hour rental $25 ($18 children). For a broad selection of vehicles—from six-speed cruisers to six-passenger "surreys"—and good advice on routes, visit **Holiday Cycles,** at 465 Grand Ave. in Falmouth Heights (☎ **508/540-3549**), where a half-day (4-hour) bike rental is $20, a 1-day rental $25, and a week rental $75. Surreys rent for $20 to $30 an hour. Holiday Cycles does not accept credit cards.

side of the street, where a shallow pool formed by a sandbar is perfect for toddlers. The beach provides several amenities, including a bathhouse with showers and bathrooms, food concessions, and lifeguards. Sailboards are available to rent in season. Day passes are $20.

o **Surf Drive Beach** ★★★, off Shore Street in Falmouth: About a half-mile from downtown, this beach is easily accessible (it's a 10-minute walk from Main Street) but with limited parking. It's an appealing beach for families: The shallow, calm area between the jetties is called "the kiddie pool." You'll find an outdoor shower, bathrooms, a food concession, and lifeguards. Day passes are $15.

OUTDOOR ACTIVITIES

BOATING **Cape Cod Kayak** (www.capecodkayak.com; ✆ **508/563-9377**) rents kayaks (free delivery in North Falmouth or West Falmouth) by the day or week and offers lessons and ecotours on local waterways. Kayak rentals are $35 to $60 for 8 hours ($5 more for tandems). Lessons are $52 to $65 per hour. Four-hour trips are $49 to $75.

FISHING To go after bigger prey, head out with a group on one of the **Patriot Party Boats,** based in Falmouth's Inner Harbor (www.patriotparty boats.com; ✆ **800/734-0088** or 508/548-2626). Boats leave twice daily, at 8am and 1pm, in season. The *Patriot Too,* with an enclosed deck, is ideal for family-style "bottom fishing" (4-hour trips $45 adults, $30 kids 12 and under; full-day trips $65 adults, $45 kids); equipment and instruction are provided.

GOLF Falmouth has four public golf courses. The most notable is the challenging 18-hole championship course at **The Cape Club,** 125 Falmouth Woods Rd. (www.capeclubresort.com; ✆ **508/540-4005**). Greens fees are $75 (Mon–Thurs) and $80 (Fri–Sun) and include carts; there are reduced afternoon rates.

WATER SPORTS Sailboarders prize Falmouth for its unflagging southwesterly winds. Although Old Silver Beach in North Falmouth is the most popular spot for windsurfing, it's only allowed there before 9am and after 5pm. You can rent gear from **Cape Cod Windsurfing** (www.capecodwind surfing.com; ✆ **508/801-3329**), which can deliver gear to a local beach. There are windsurfers ($70 for a half-day; 2-hr. lessons $75); kayaks ($50 for a half-day), sailboats (a Sunfish costs $150 for a half-day; lessons are $75 an hour); and stand-up paddleboards ($50 for a half-day). There are also jet skis and bikes for rent. The Trunk River area on the west end of Falmouth's Surf Drive Beach and a portion of Chapoquoit Beach are the only public beaches where windsurfers are allowed during the day.

FALMOUTH SHOPPING

Falmouth's spiffy Main Street has a number of stores selling good clothing, home goods, and gifts.

BOOKS **Eight Cousins Books,** 189 Main St., Falmouth (www.eightcousins. com; ✆ **508/548-5548**), specializes in books for children and young adults but also sells books for adults, as well as games, and toys for kids.

FASHION   Don't be too intimidated to browse in **Maxwell & Co.,** 200 Main St. (www.maxwellandco.com; ℂ **508/540-8752**), which may be the highest-end clothier on the Cape. Comfortable Italian fashions for men and women are displayed here in an elegant setting. Its end-of-summer sale in mid-August offers up to 70% off the prices of these exquisite goods. The clothing at **Caline for Kids,** 149 Main St. (www.calineforkids.com; ℂ **508/548-2533**), ranges from practical to elegant, and sometimes manages to be both. Sizes from newborn to 14 are available.

FOOD & WINE   "Pick your own" is the watchword at the long-established **Tony Andrews Farm and Produce Stand ★★**, 394 Old Meeting House Rd. (about 1½ miles north of Route 28), East Falmouth (ℂ **508/548-4717**), where its strawberries early in the summer and tomatoes, sweet corn, squash, sunflowers, and more as the season progresses. Of course, you can just buy them here without picking, though the Puritans wouldn't have approved. It's open daily 10am to 6pm. Also in East Falmouth, **Coonamessett Farm ★★** (www.coonamessettfarm.com; ℂ **508/563-2560**), at 277 Hatchville Rd. (about 1 mile east of Sandwich Rd.), runs a full farm stand of vegetables grown in the fields out back. You can pick your own vegetables, look at the farm animals (including two cute llamas), or rent a canoe for a quick paddle in the on-site pond.

Where to Stay on the Upper Cape

FALMOUTH

For a basic motel with a great location, try the **Tides Motel** (www.tidesmotelcapecod.com; ℂ **508/548-3126**), on Clinton Avenue, at the far west end of Grand Avenue in Falmouth Heights. The 1950s-style no-frills motel (no air-conditioning, no phone) sits on the beach at the head of Falmouth Harbor facing Vineyard Sound. Rates in season for the 29 rooms are $165 to $175 double, $220 suite. It's closed late October to mid-May. Another great value nearby is the **Seaside Inn,** at 263 Grand Ave., Falmouth Heights (www.seasideinnfalmouth.com; ℂ **800/827-1976**), across the street from Falmouth Heights Beach. The 23 rooms, with air-conditioning, TVs, phones with free calls, and some with kitchenettes and decks, are priced at $155 to $199 for a double, $234 to $249 for a deluxe room. Open year-round.

Beach Breeze Inn ★   The big plus of the Beach Breeze is that you are within walking distance—a very pleasant quarter-mile walk at that—of Falmouth's lively Main Street, and yet you're just steps from the placid waters of Surf Drive beach (see p. 193). The rooms, which are in a converted mid-19th-century house, vary in size; they're humble but homey. A few have kitchenettes. There's nothing fancy here, giving you more of an old-fashioned Cape Cod experience.

321 Shore St. www.beachbreezeinn.com. ℂ **800/828-3255** or 508/548-1765. 21 units. Summer $259–$339 double; $1,500–$1,700 weekly efficiencies. **Amenities:** Unheated pool; Wi-Fi (free).

Captain's Manor Inn ★★   One of the town's most historic inns, the Captain's Manor was built in 1849 by a sea captain for his southern bride, which is why the exterior has a plantation style wrap-around veranda. The rooms, decorated with antiques and many with four-poster and canopy beds, are elegantly stylish. New owners have freshened up all the furnishings and fixtures. A full breakfast is an added treat. The location on the historic Village Green puts guests within walking distance of all that Main Street has to offer, with restaurants and activities just steps away.

27 W. Main St. www.captainsmanorinn.com. ✆ **508/388-7336.** 7 units. Summer $150–$399 double. Rates include full breakfast. **Amenities:** Wi-Fi (free).

Coonamessett Inn ★★   Set on 7 acres overlooking Jones Pond, the Coonamessett has been a reliable lodging choice since the 1950s; with new management in recent years, it has undergone significant renovations and a freshening up. Guest are no doubt drawn to the folksy charm of the place, the historic red clapboard farmhouse exterior and gardens resplendent with flowers, and, inside, the large function rooms. Most of the rooms are suites that include a sitting room, which comes in handy if you (or your partner) are an early riser. The location is perfect as a base to explore Falmouth. The tavern is open for guests only for lunch and dinner and an elaborate Sunday brunch. It serves traditional New England fare, like seafood stew and roasted chicken.

311 Gifford St. www.thecoonamessett.com. ✆ **508/548-2300.** 27 units, 1 cottage. Summer $239–$450 double; $350 2-bedroom suite; $200–$350 cottage. Rates include continental breakfast. **Amenities:** Restaurant; Wi-Fi (free)

Inn on the Sound ★★   If a charming waterfront B&B is what you are looking for, look no further. Inn on the Sound sits on a bluff in Falmouth Heights—on a clear day, you can see to Martha's Vineyard. The inn is in a neighborhood made up of Victorian shingle-style homes, many of them beautifully restored. The beach, just a short walk from the inn, is one of Falmouth's best. The 10-room inn itself is small enough to provide a lot of privacy as well as a personal touch. Rooms are decorated in an elegant and crisp style that avoids anything too frilly.

313 Grand Ave., Falmouth Heights. www.innonthesound.com. ✆ **800/564-9668** or 508/457-9666. 10 units, 8 with tub/shower, 2 with shower only. Summer $289–$459 double. Rates include full breakfast. No children 11 and under. **Amenities:** Wi-Fi (free).

Palmer House Inn ★   The Palmer House has a terrific location steps from Falmouth's Village Green and a short walk to Main Street. Of the many B&Bs in the area, this one also rises above the rest by virtue of its warm and welcoming hosts and the amenities, which include sumptuous linens and a top-notch hot breakfast. Rooms are beautifully decorated with an old-world appeal appropriate to this 1879 home. There is one room accessible for those with disabilities and one room that allows pets.

81 Palmer Ave. www.palmerhouseinn.com. ✆ **800/472-2632** or 508/548-1230. 17 units. Summer $259–$389 double. Rates include full breakfast. **Amenities:** Wi-Fi (free).

SANDWICH

In addition to the lodging places listed below, Sandwich has a number of motels along Route 6A. The one with the best location is **Sandy Neck Motel,** at 669 Route 6A, in East Sandwich (www.sandyneck.com; ℂ **800/564-3992** or 508/362-3992), which sits at the entrance to the road leading to Sandy Neck, the best beach in these parts. Rates for the 12 units are $129 to $139 double, and $199 to $299 for one- and two-room efficiencies. It's closed November to mid-April.

The Belfry Inn ★★   What do a converted church, a pink "painted lady" Victorian rectory, and a 19th-century Greek revival house have in common? They all make up the lodging accommodations of the unique Belfry Inn in Sandwich center. The converted church, called the Abbey, makes full winking use of its dramatic space, using an elaborate stained glass window as a headboard, for example, and intricate gothic woodwork as room accents; its six rooms, which have vaulted ceilings and two-person whirlpool bathtubs, are decorated in a dark and bolder palette than the rooms in the other two buildings. (The church also is home to the acclaimed **Belfry Bistro** ★★, see p. 201.) The 11 rooms in the Victorian are more feminine, relying on pastels and a crisper look. The third inn building, called the Village House, offers more casual accommodations and, for the most part, smaller and less expensive rooms. It has a long porch extending across the front of the building with rocking chairs positioned perfectly for guests to watch the world going by.

8 Jarves St. www.belfryinn.com. ℂ **800/844-4542** or 508/888-8550. 23 units. Summer $145–$165 double. Rates include full breakfast. **Amenities:** 2 restaurants, bar; Wi-Fi (free).

The Dan'l Webster Inn and Spa ★★   Centrally located on Main Street in the Cape's oldest town, the Dan'l Webster Inn is named for the prominent 19th-century attorney and U.S. senator, who used to frequent a tavern on the site. The main building contains most of the rooms, as well as the **restaurant** ★★ (see p. 202) and tavern and the full-service Beach Plum Spa; an adjacent fully renovated historic home contains additional upscale rooms. A heated outdoor pool and whirlpool tub are in the courtyard. The rooms range from somewhat plain to luxuriously appointed suites, complete with canopy beds, reproduction antiques, and working fireplaces, a style fit for honeymooners. Besides the convenience of staying at a full-service inn, the Dan'l Webster is also within walking distance or a short drive to almost all the Sandwich attractions. Because it can accommodate groups, this hotel is popular with tour buses.

149 Main St. www.danlwebsterinn.com. ℂ **800/444-3566** or 508/888-3622. 48 units. Summer $244–$304 double; $394–$444 suite. Rate includes $15 breakfast voucher. **Amenities:** Restaurant; tavern/bar; access to health club (2 miles away); outdoor pool; room service; spa; Wi-Fi (free).

WOODS HOLE

Sands of Time Motor Inn & Harbor House ★★   Sure, the rooms may be a tad dated here, but the location can't be beat, right across the street from where ferries leave in the summer for Martha's Vineyard. It is also a short walk to the terrific restaurants and shops of Woods Hole village. There are two very different choices for rooms: a no-frills 1950s vintage motel and a 19th-century shingled house, which definitely feels more like a B&B. Both have rooms with wonderful views of Little Harbor. Lying between the two buildings is a small heated pool.

549 Woods Hole Rd. www.sandsoftime.com. ✆ **800/841-0114** or 508/548-6300. 35 units, 2 w/shared bath. Summer $179–$269 double. Rates include continental breakfast. Closed Nov–Mar. **Amenities:** Outdoor pool; Wi-Fi (free).

Treehouse Lodge ★★   The owner of boutique Woods Hole Inn a few blocks away (see below) has updated this old motel into a freshened-up bargain for families. Many rooms have mini-fridges and some have microwaves. Besides the new decor in all the rooms, the courtyard has been reimagined as a family-friendly outdoor space with "fire ball," which is a large, artistically designed fire pit, and yard games. The motel is walking distance from the ferry to Martha's Vineyard and the village of Woods Hole, which has restaurants and a wide variety of land- and water-based activities.

527 Woods Hole Rd. www.mytreehouselodge.com. ✆ **508/388-4905** or 508-548-1986. 35 units. Summer $148–$299 double. Closed Nov–Mar. **Amenities:** Outdoor heated pool; Wi-Fi (free).

Woods Hole Inn ★★   In a historic inn building in the center of Woods Hole Village, this is the village's boutique-style inn option, with beautiful modern decor, luxury linens and toiletries, and—last but certainly not least—several rooms with balconies and many with views of Great Harbor and Martha's Vineyard in the distance. Bathrooms are up to date, including several with "rain" showers and, for authentic charm, antique clawfoot soaking tubs. The inn is walking distance to restaurants—both fine-dining and casual, including two owned by your innkeeper—as well as historic sites, family activities, world-renowned science institutions, and water-related activities. The inn is across the street from Great Harbor, a stone's throw from the Woods Hole ferry terminal and steps from Eel Pond.

28 Water St. www.woodsholeinn.com. ✆ **508/495-0248.** 13 units. Summer $245–$449 double. Rates include continental breakfast. **Amenities:** Wi-Fi (free).

Where to Eat on the Upper Cape
BOURNE & CATAUMET
The Chart Room ★★ SEAFOOD   Great sunset views over Red Brook Harbor and fresh fish are reason enough to visit this dockside restaurant, housed in a former railroad barge at a busy marina. A piano bar lends a bit of elegance, as does the well-heeled clientele. The only downside is the noise level, due to this restaurant's ongoing popularity. The younger crowd likes to gather at the bar for the mudslides, said to be the best in the region.

1 Shipyard Ln. (in Kingman Yacht Ctr., off Shore Rd.), Cataumet. www.chartroomcataumet. com. ✆ **508/563-5350.** Main courses $10–$27. Dinner reservations strongly recommended. Mid-June to early Sept daily 11:30am–3pm and 5:30–10pm; mid-May to mid-June and early Sept to mid-Oct Thurs–Sun 11:30am–3pm and 5–10pm. Closed mid-Oct to mid-May.

A great place to check your emails and enjoy some coffee or a sandwich is the **Daily Brew Coffee Bar and Café ★**, Cataumet Square, 1370 Rte. 28A, Cataumet (www.thedailybrewcoffeehouse. com; © **508/564-4755**), where you can get delicious espressos, cappuccinos, and baked goods, as well as soups, salads, and sandwiches. Several computers are available for public use upstairs. There is outside seating on a covered patio in back. The cafe is open year-round Monday to Friday 6am to 3pm Saturday and Sunday 7am to 2pm.

Lobster Trap Fish Market & Restaurant ★ CLAM SHACK Since it's just a few miles from the Bourne Bridge, many people make their stop at the Lobster Trap either on the way on Cape or off Cape. After all, why not have one final plate of fried clams instead of sitting in all that traffic? This seafood shack has the benefit of being in a very scenic setting, overlooking the Back River in Monument Beach. All your standard fried fish plates are on the menu, plus some healthier grilled options and more unusual choices like spicy crab sliders or beef Thai sticks. There's live music Thursday evenings and Sunday afternoons in season. Go early or late to avoid crowds.

290 Shore Rd. (take 1st exit from Bourne Bridge Rotary, then left on Shore Rd.), Bourne. www.lobstertrap.net. © **508/759-7600.** Main courses $12–$25. No reservations. May–Oct daily 11am–9pm.

FALMOUTH

You'll see slackers, suits, and surfers all lined up for the best coffee in town at **Coffee Obsession,** 110 Palmer Ave., in the Queen's Buyway Shops (www. coffeeobsession.com; © **508/540-2233**), open 6am to 7pm Monday to Saturday and 7am to 6:30pm on Sunday. The line sometimes extends out the door of **Maison Villatte,** an authentic French bakery on 267 Main St. (© **774/255-1855**). Chef Boris Villatte turns out a dozen kinds of bread in addition to wonderful patisseries, all lined up in a long glass bakery case.

Expensive

C Salt Wine Bar & Grille ★★ NEW AMERICAN This smart beachy-chic restaurant, inside a cozy house on a busy commercial stretch of Route 28, is a respite from all the commotion outside. The menu, American cuisine with French and Asian influences, includes two standouts: Thai pork coconut cashew stir-fry, served over jasmine rice; and the braised short rib, which comes with crispy bacon and Brussels sprouts. The service here is professional and attentive.

75 Davis Straits (Rte. 28). www.csaltfalmouth.com. © **774/763-2954.** Main courses $22–$32. Wed–Thurs 5–9pm, Fri–Sat 5–10pm, Sun 11am–2:30pm and 5–9pm.

The Glass Onion ★★★ NEW AMERICAN Regularly cited as Falmouth's top upscale restaurant, the Glass Onion is a labor of love, and it shows. It's very popular: Try it on an off night if you don't want a long wait for a table. The formal touches here manage to make it feel friendly, if not exactly casual. Have no fear when choosing from this menu; there are no losers. But among the favorites are the poached lobster, shrimp and mussels with a spinach risotto, or the grilled pork chop with creamy polenta. The menu relies heavily on local ingredients, such as Barnstable oysters and Coonamessett Farm greens. There is also homemade gnocchi and fresh pasta.

37 N. Main St. (in the Queen's Buyway). www.theglassoniondining.com. ✆ **508/540-3730.** Main courses $19–$36. Tues–Sat 5–9pm. Open year-round.

Osteria La Civetta ★★★ NORTHERN ITALIAN "The Little Owl" is unique on the Cape for serving food the way they do in Italy, not an Americanized version of it—you could almost imagine you have wandered into this place from a side street in Rome. The dining room, which has a small bar, feels cozy but sophisticated. On the first-course *(primi)* menu, there are the homemade pastas, such as the wild boar pappardelle and tortellini filled with butternut squash and nutmeg. As for the *secondi,* you may have a hard time choosing between the pork tenderloin with fontina pasta and the polenta-encrusted chicken with oven-roasted potatoes. For dessert, a *salame di cioccolato* ("chocolate salami"), a rich chocolate log of goodness, awaits.

133 Main St. www.osterialacivetta.com. ✆ **508/540-1616.** Main courses $16–$28. Reservations recommended. Wed–Sat noon–2:30pm and 5:30–10pm, Sun–Tues 5:30–10pm. Closed Mon off-season.

Soprano's Casino by the Sea ★ ITALIAN The Casino is the place to go for those looking for a meal with views out across Vineyard Sound to Martha's Vineyard. Dining is on two levels, but the best bet is to get a table out on one of the decks overlooking the beach. The menu offers a high-end twist to traditional Italian favorites such dishes as zuppa de clams, with sautéed little necks in a garlic broth; carbonara with applewood bacon; and beef Braciole, simmered in a special aromatic "Sunday gravy."

286 Grand Ave., Falmouth Heights. www.sopranos-ristorante.com. ✆ **508/548-7800.** Main courses $23–$40. Daily 11:30am–10pm; call for off-season hours.

Moderate

Añejo Mexican Bistro & Tequila Bar ★ MEXICAN People love the hip vibe and affordable prices at this popular Mexican restaurant on Falmouth's Main Street. Although the menu features house specials like *pescado encornflecado* (cornflake-crusted cod) and carne asada (Mexican-style grilled skirt steak), the best part of the menu is inspired by Mexican taquerias: enchiladas, burritos, tacos, and tostadas served with Mexican rice and refried beans for great prices ($12–$16). Añejo's popularity (and lack of reservations) means you will often see people standing outside waiting for a table: The wait can be over an hour. Best to try it either early or on the late side.

188 Main St. www.anejomexicanbistro.com. ✆ **508/388-7631.** Main courses $12–$28. Mon–Sat 11:30am–3pm and 4–10pm; Sun 10:30am–3pm and 4–10pm.

The Flying Bridge ★ AMERICAN/CONTINENTAL This dockside cafe is the place to go for traditional Cape cod cuisine with a water view. It's also a great place for boaters who want to step right off the docks of Falmouth

Harbor and onto the restaurant's ample decking. You'll want to go on a sunny day and sit outside under the blue and white awnings, but with two floors and a capacity of 600, there is no shortage of seating. The large menu is focused on traditional club sandwiches and lobster rolls, but you'll also find the occasional unusual offering, like shrimp tacos.

220 Scranton Ave., on Falmouth Inner Harbor. www.flyingbridgerestaurant.com. © **508/548-2700.** Main courses $8–$20. Mid-Apr to mid-Oct daily 11:30am–9pm. Closed mid-Oct to mid-Apr.

La Cucina Sul Mare Italian Ristorante ★★ ITALIAN   It's no wonder this friendly, popular restaurant in the center of town had to double in size a few years back. It all resembles a European bistro, with ceilings elaborately decorated in tin, and 19th-century-style light fixtures. The chef-owner Mark Cilfone will often wander out of the kitchen to chat with customers and find out what they ordered. The classically inclined dishes include lasagna, braised lamb shanks, osso bucco, and lobster fra diavolo over linguine. You'll often see diners waiting outside to get in, so call ahead to put your name on the list.

237 Main St. www.lacucinasulmare.com. © **508/548-5600.** Main courses $18–$35. Daily 11:30am–2pm and 5–10pm; call for off-season hours.

Inexpensive

Casa Vallarta ★ MEXICAN   Large portions of Mexican favorites like tacos, burritos, and enchiladas—piled high with cheese, beans, and guacamole—are standard fare at this bargain-priced option just east of the center of town. Every table starts off with a complimentary basket of warm chips with a salty bean dip and a spicy salsa dip, to get you thirsty for their large menu of margaritas and other specialty cocktails. The interior is brightly decorated with Mexican tiles, and there's outside seating on a patio overlooking the parking lot. Birthdays celebrated here get a fun bonus when all the waitstaff strolls to the table singing a Mexican ballad. A live mariachi band plays Tuesdays from 6 to 9pm in season.

70 Davis Straits (Rte. 28). www.casavallarta.us. © **508/299-8177.** Main courses $14–$20. Daily 11am–10pm.

Crepe Cod ★★ CREPES   Authentic Brittany-style crepes with some North African influences come from this stylish cafe on the east end of Main Street. Those who have traveled to France will recognize the flavors of savory crepes made with mushrooms and an aromatic rich tomato sauce. The sweet crepes—a lovely banana and chocolate version is not to be missed—are also a pleasure.

649 Main St. http://crepecod.business.site. © **774/763-2570.** Most items under $15. Tues–Sat 9am–7pm, Sun 9am–3pm. Closed Mon.

Moonakis Cafe ★★ DINER/BREAKFAST   On summer mornings, people line up to get into this friendly, folksy diner in Waquoit village, east of East Falmouth. Don't bother if you are running late; the line will have already formed. They come for the creative and delicious omelets, like the one with lobster, asparagus, and Swiss cheese. The specials also include special pancakes

Stop by Sandwich's appropriately named **Ice Cream Sandwich ★**, at 66 Route 6A, across from the Stop & Shop (www.icecreamsandwich.net; ℂ **508/888-7237**), for a couple of scoops of the best local ice cream made on premises. Try the Cape Cod chocolate chunk. It's closed November through March. Sandwich's most classic ice cream shop is **Twin Acres Ice Cream Shoppe ★**, 21 Route 6A, Sandwich (www.twinacresicecreamshoppe.com; ℂ **508/888-0566**), which has a wide variety of flavors in hard and soft serve. With its red, white, and blue bunting, this place is right out of a Norman Rockwell illustration.

Falmouth residents are the beneficiaries of a struggle for ice cream bragging rights: **Ben & Bill's Chocolate Emporium ★**, at 209 Main St., in the center of town (www.benandbills.com; ℂ **508/548-7878**), draws crowds even in winter, late into the evening (it's open 9am to 11pm). They come for the homemade ice cream, not to mention the hand-dipped candies showcased in a wraparound display. It's the only place on Cape Cod where you can get surprisingly yummy lobster ice cream; customers can watch the ice cream being made. The competition is **Smitty's Homemade Ice Cream ★**, at 326 E. Falmouth Highway, East Falmouth (ℂ **508/457-1060**), whose proprietor, the cheerful, blond Smitty, is an ice cream man straight out of central casting.

(lemon–poppy seed, cranberry-pecan, and chocolate chip among them) as well as lots of French toast options.

460 Waquoit Hwy./Rte. 28, Waquoit. www.moonakiscafe.com. ℂ **508/457-9630.** All items under $10. No reservations. Mon–Sat 7am–1:30pm; Sunday 7am–noon.

The Pickle Jar Kitchen ★★★ CAFE   This charming cafe is that rare place where after a big meal you feel like you had something healthy, not a belly bomb—for example, a "marathon scrambler," egg whites sautéed with garden fresh veggies and kale, served with homemade toasted bread and home fries. The lunch menu also has unusual offerings, like the open-faced BBQ boneless pork sandwich. The namesake house pickles, including the Mexi-Cali with carrot and jalapeno, are available to purchase by the pound.

170 Main St. www.picklejarkitchen.com. ℂ **508/540-6760.** Breakfast items mostly under $10, lunch items $9–$14. Wed–Mon 7am–3pm.

SANDWICH
Expensive

The Belfry Bistro ★★ NEW AMERICAN   The premier fine-dining spot in Sandwich, located in the **Belfry Inn ★★** (see p. 196), the Belfry Bistro also gets an A for atmosphere. The setting is a converted church: You enter through a majestic arched doorway, and once inside you see the raised floor where the altar used to be and plenty of pretty stained glass windows. This is a roomy space, so couples will find it a good spot; no chance of a neighboring table eavesdropping. The chef takes his cues from the season, revising ingredients to feature the freshest local and regional ingredients. Start the meal with a lovely slow-roasted beet salad or chilled Wellfleet oysters. Main courses include a small but quality selection in the areas of fish, poultry, and meat, be it spring lamb loin with sheep's milk yogurt or day-boat sea scallops with Madras curry.

8 Jarves St. www.belfryinn.com. © **508/888-8550.** Main courses $14–$33. Feb–Dec Wed–Sun 4:30–9pm. Closed Jan.

The Dan'l Webster Inn ★★ AMERICAN   Serving three meals a day in four restaurants plus the tavern, the dining operations of the **Dan'l Webster Inn** ★★ (see p. 196) are busy day and night. But despite the volume, the chef does a top-notch job delivering from a wide-ranging menu that has items to please all manner of eaters. The menu mixes old New England favorites like prime rib with more delicate offerings. An on-site pastry chef means dessert is also freshly made. The "green" menu includes vegetarian selections and uses organic ingredients, including free-range chicken. The tavern menu has soups, sandwiches, pizzas, and burgers. There is fireside dining in the Music or Webster rooms, garden-side dining in the sky-lit Conservatory, and more casual dining in the tavern; you can also dine outside in season.

149 Main St. www.danlwebsterinn.com. © **508/888-3622.** Main courses $18–$39; tavern menu $10–$18. June–Aug daily 7:30–11am, 11:30am–3pm, and 4:30–8:30pm.

Moderate

Pilot House ★★ SEAFOOD   Every town on the Cape has the requisite fish house overlooking the water, and this is Sandwich's version. Almost every seat here has a view of the Cape Cod Canal, the Sandwich marina, or both. (The only minus is the less-than-scenic view of the coal-fired Sandwich power plant.) Best bets are the fish tacos, or dig right in to a boiled lobster dinner. There are also fried seafood, sandwiches, and burger and sandwich options, which are among many reasonably priced options on this large menu. The Summer Sunset Concert Series outside on the lawn daily from 5 to 8pm is a real treat.

14 Gallo Rd. (next to Sandwich Marina). www.pilothousecapecod.com. © **508/888-8889.** Main courses $11–$35. Daily 11:30am–9pm.

Inexpensive

Café Chew ★ SANDWICH SHOP   When in Sandwich, why not have a sandwich? For that, consider Café Chew, which specializes in organic and natural ingredients for its menu items. Choose a classic, like a roast beef sandwich, or something a little more adventurous, like the Bavarian, ham, and brie cheese with sliced Granny Smith apples. Great coffee and breakfast sandwiches here too.

4 Merchant's Rd. www.cafechew.com. © **508/888-7717.** All items under $11. Daily 8am–3pm.

The Dunbar Tea Shop ★★ BRITISH   In this authentic tea room in a historic house overlooking Shawme Pond, you're likely to feel very coddled and leave with a full belly after trying any of the hearty lunches or the afternoon tea. On Fridays and Saturdays, there is a tapas and dinner menu, with pâtés and salads or entree options like chicken pie or quiche. You'd better come early if you want to get a table, though. Besides the cozy indoor seating, there is also an outdoor patio.

1 Water St. (Rte. 130). www.dunbarrestaurant.com. © **508/833-2485.** Main courses $13–$17. May–Oct daily 11am–4:30pm, Fri and Sat 5–9pm; Nov–April Wed–Mon 11am–4:30pm.

Marshland Restaurant ★ DINER   A proven formula of friendly service and comfort food and reasonable prices keeps this joint jumping all year long. Belly up to the counter on one of the old-fashioned diner stools and rub elbows with the locals as you dig into homemade meatloaf, Yankee pot roast, or a steaming plate of fried fish.

109 Rte. 6A. (at Tupper Rd.). www.marshlandrestaurant.com. © **508/888-9824.** Main courses $9–$20. Daily 6am–8pm.

WOODS HOLE

For the best sticky buns anywhere, arrive before 9am at **Pie in the Sky Dessert Café and Bake Shop ★★**, 10 Water St. (© **508/540-5475**), conveniently near the ferry terminal for Martha's Vineyard-bound travelers. Also on Water Street you'll find a branch of Falmouth's popular **Coffee Obsession** (see p. 198), at 38 Water St. (© **508/540-8130**), open daily 6:30am to 9pm.

Landfall ★★ AMERICAN   Falmouth's longest-standing restaurant still run by the same family, Landfall brings to mind old Cape Cod. Buoys, lobster pots, oars, and other flotsam and jetsam hang from the rafters; the huge Gothic window came out of a library, and the stained glass window came from a mansion on nearby Penzance Point. This place is right on the water—boaters can pull up to the dock and have drinks on the small pier, watching ferries come and go while feet dangle just above the waters of Great Harbor. It's no surprise that fish is the focus, with lobsters, swordfish, clams, scallops, and seasonal finfish. The seafood can be ordered fried, broiled, or grilled.

9 Luscombe Ave. www.woodshole.com/landfall. © **508/548-1758.** Main courses $9–$38. Reservations recommended. Mid-May to Sept daily 11:30am–9:30pm; call for off-season hours. Closed late Nov–early Apr.

Quicks Hole Taqueria ★★ MEXICAN   An affordable option in Woods Hole is this authentic take on California-style Mexican street food. Set in a casual atmosphere with most tables on an outside deck where live music is played on summer afternoons, the taqueria is the place to get fish tacos with homemade slaw and sweet Baja shrimp washed down with a refreshing homemade sangria.

6 Luscombe Ave. www.quicksholewickedfresh.com. © **508/495-0792.** Main courses $6–$27. Daily 11am–8pm; call for off-season hours.

Quicks Hole Tavern ★★★ NEW AMERICAN   Close to the ferry terminal, the Quicks Hole Tavern serves upscale tavern food: The burgers come with truffle fries, and the lobster roll is served on a croissant, with basil and lemon. There is a wide array of sandwiches and salads for those looking for a quick bite before catching the ferry, but there are also house specialties for those who want to linger over something like a quinoa succotash soba noodle cake, or chocolate-braised short ribs with wild mushrooms. Climb up to the second floor for a 180-degree view of Vineyard Sound.

29 Railroad Ave. www.quicksholewickedfresh.com. ⓒ **508/495-0048.** Main courses $24–$43. Daily 11am–10pm.

Water Street Kitchen ★★ NEW AMERICAN   Located beside the Eel Pond Drawbridge at the entrance to the pond, this is one of Woods Hole's newer upscale restaurants. In a casual atmosphere of old wooden wide-plank floors and two walls of windows with water views, the common denominators here are home-cooked, made-from-scratch, and fresh. Menu favorites include smoked bluefish pâté, spicy kimchi pancake, and cioppino with lobster, squid, and other delicacies of the sea.

56 Water St. www.waterstreetkitchen.com. ⓒ **508/540-5656.** Main courses $20–$34. Daily 5–10pm.

Upper Cape Entertainment & Nightlife

From late June through August, top talent from college drama departments across the country performs with the **College Light Opera Company** ★ (www. collegelightopera.com; ⓒ **508/548-0668**), which puts on a fast-paced summer repertory at the Highfield Theatre, east of the Falmouth village green at 56 Highfield Ave. The venue, a former horse barn, has been a terrific summer-stock theater for the past half-century. Shows often sell out, so call well ahead or keep your fingers crossed for a scattering of single tickets. Tickets cost about $30 per person. The rest of the year, **Falmouth Theatre Guild** (www. falmouththeatreguild.org) performs on the Highfield Theater stage, offering family-friendly musicals and comedies. Tickets cost about $20 per person.

   The Woods Hole Folk Music Society ★ (www.arts-cape.com/whfolkmusic; ⓒ **508/540-0320**) mounts concerts October through May, on the first and third Sunday of each month, attracting a grassroots crowd to Community Hall on Water Street, by the Eel Pond drawbridge. General admission is $8; discounts are available for members, seniors, and children.

Take Yourself Out to a Ballgame

Sports fans of all ages will enjoy taking in nine innings of the Grand Old Game. The **Cape Cod Baseball League** (www. capecodbaseball.org; ⓒ **508/432-6909**) plays all up and down the Cape, in July and August; games are free and no tickets are required. Players are generally college athletes hoping to be recruited for professional teams; over the years such future MLB stars as Aaron Judge, Jackie Bradley Jr., Dallas Keuchel, and Evan Longoria got their start here. Who knows what stars of the future you'll see? The three Upper Cape teams in the 10-team league are the **Falmouth Commodores** (Guv Fuller Field, 790 Main St. in Falmouth); the **Bourne Braves** (Doran Park, Upper Cape Technical School, Sandwich Road, Bourne); and the **Wareham Gatemen** (Clem Spillane Field, across the Cape Cod Canal at 54 Marion Rd., off Route 6E in Wareham). See p. 210 for Mid-Cape teams; see p. 244 for Lower Cape teams.

Falmouth gets most of the nightlife action on the Upper Cape. One exception is near Otis Air Force Base in Cataumet, near Bourne: On weekends, local bands and DJs draw a crowd of young adults to the **Courtyard Restaurant and Pub,** 1337 County Rd. (www.courtyardcapecod.com; ✆ **508/563-1818**).

In downtown Falmouth, everyone heads to **Liam Maguire's Irish Pub ★**, at 273 Main St. (www.liammaguire.com; ✆ **508/548-0285**), for a taste of the Emerald Isle. Live music is performed on weekends year-round, often by Liam himself; there's no cover charge. **Grumpy's Pub,** at 29 Locust St. (www.grumpyspub.blogspot.com; ✆ **508/540-3930**), is a good old bar/shack with live music (rock, blues, and jazz) Thursday to Saturday nights. Cover is typically $5. Look for free passes on the counter at Coffee Obsession (110 Palmer Ave.) nearby.

Out by Falmouth Heights Beach, grab a stool at the **British Beer Company ★**, 263 Grand Ave. (www.britishbeer.com/local/falmouth; ✆ **508/540-9600**), and choose from a revolving selection of more than 18 drafts from the British Isles as you ponder views of the beach across the street. In Woods Hole, who knows whom you'll meet in the **Captain Kidd Bar ★**, 77 Water St. (www.thecaptainkidd.com; ✆ **508/548-9206**): maybe a lobsterwoman, maybe a Nobel Prize winner. Good grub, too.

THE MID-CAPE: HYANNIS, BARNSTABLE, YARMOUTH & DENNIS

Hyannis: 15 miles E of Sagamore, 44 miles S of Provincetown. Yarmouth: 19 miles E of Sandwich, 38 miles S of Provincetown. Dennis: 20 miles E of Sandwich; 36 miles S of Provincetown.

Visitors who want to be centrally located on Cape Cod choose the Mid-Cape, a good base from which to explore both ends of this endlessly varied peninsula. It's convenient to transportation (the Hyannis airport, ferries to Martha's Vineyard and Nantucket) with plenty of stores and services, yet outside of bustling, commercial Hyannis, you can still find towns with local flavor and good beach access. The real beauty of the Mid-Cape lies in its smaller places: old-money hideaways such as **Osterville ★** to the west, and charming villages such as **Barnstable Village ★**, **West Barnstable ★★**, and **Yarmouth Port ★★**, which can be found along the Old King's Highway (Route 6A) on the northern bay side of the Cape. A drive along this winding two-lane road reveals the early architectural history of the region, from humble Colonial saltboxes to ostentatious sea captains' mansions.

VISITOR INFORMATION   Local sources of tourist info include the **Hyannis Area Chamber of Commerce,** 367 Main St., Hyannis (www.hyannis.com; ✆ **508/775-2201**), the **Yarmouth Area Chamber of Commerce,** 424 Rte. 28, West Yarmouth (www.yarmouthcapecod.com; ✆ **800/732-1008** or 508/778-1008), and the **Dennis Chamber of Commerce** at 238 Swan River Rd. in West Dennis (www.dennischamber.com; ✆ **508/398-3568**). The **Cape**

Cod Chamber of Commerce visitor center is just off the Mid-Cape Highway's exit 6 eastbound ramp in Centerville (www.capecodchamber.org; ℭ **888/332-2732** or 508/362-3225); it's open daily 9am to 5pm from mid-April to mid-November, with somewhat shorter hours the rest of the year.

Exploring Hyannis ★

Hectic Hyannis is the commercial center of the cape, its roads lined with chain stores and mired with maddening traffic. Along routes 132 and 28, you could be visiting Anywhere, USA. And yet this overrun town still has plenty of pockets of charm, especially the waterfront area and Main Street, with a diverse selection of restaurants, shops, and entertainment of all stripes.

For a fun and informative introduction to the harbor, take a leisurely narrated tour aboard one of Hy-Line Cruises' 1911 steamer replicas, **MV _Patience_** or **MV _Prudence._** There are five 1-hour family cruises a day in season, but for a real treat, take the Sunday 3pm "Ice Cream Float," which includes a design-your-own Ben & Jerry's ice-cream sundae. Hy-Line Cruises depart from the

---

CAMELOT ON CAPE COD: THE KENNEDYS IN
hyannis port

It's been more than half a century since those days of Camelot, when JFK was in the White House and America seemed rejuvenated by the Kennedy style, but the Kennedy sites on Cape Cod still attract record numbers of visitors every summer.

The Kennedys always knew how to have fun, and they had it in Hyannis Port. And ever since Hyannis Port became JFK's summer White House, Cape Cod has been inextricably linked to the Kennedy clan. Although the current Kennedys spend time elsewhere—working in Washington or wintering in Palm Beach—when they go home, they go to the Kennedy compound in Hyannis Port, with its large, gabled Dutch Colonial houses still commanding the end of Scudder Avenue.

To bask in the Kennedys' Cape Cod experience, visit the **John F. Kennedy Hyannis Museum ★**, 397 Main St., Hyannis (www.jfkhyannismuseum.org; ℭ **508/790-3077**). Admission is $12 for adults, $6 for children 8 to 17, and $10 for seniors. From June through October

it's open Monday to Saturday 9am to 5pm, Sunday noon to 5pm; in November and mid-April through May, hours are Monday to Saturday 10am to 4pm, Sunday noon to 4pm. The museum shows a documentary on Kennedy, narrated by Walter Cronkite, and contains several rooms featuring photos of the Kennedys on Cape Cod. (In the basement of the museum is the Cape Cod Baseball Hall of Fame & Museum, which is free with admission to JFK Museum.)

Busloads of tourists visit the **Kennedy Memorial** just above Veterans Beach on Ocean Avenue; it's a moving tribute, beautifully maintained by the town, but crowds in season can be distracting. Finally, you may want to drive by the simple white clapboard church, **St. Francis Xavier,** on South Street; JFK's mother, Rose, attended Mass there daily, and Caroline Kennedy and several other cousins got married here.

As Rose once told a reporter, "Our family would rather be in Hyannis Port in the summer than anyplace else in the world." And yours?

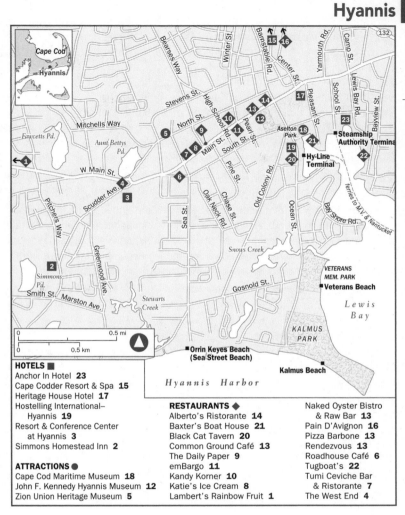

HOTELS ■

Anchor In Hotel **23**
Cape Codder Resort & Spa **15**
Heritage House Hotel **17**
Hostelling International–
  Hyannis **19**
Resort & Conference Center
  at Hyannis **3**
Simmons Homestead Inn **2**

ATTRACTIONS ●

Cape Cod Maritime Museum **18**
John F. Kennedy Hyannis Museum **12**
Zion Union Heritage Museum **5**

RESTAURANTS ◆

Alberto's Ristorante **14**
Baxter's Boat House **21**
Black Cat Tavern **20**
Common Ground Café **13**
The Daily Paper **9**
emBargo **11**
Kandy Korner **10**
Katie's Ice Cream **8**
Lambert's Rainbow Fruit **1**

Naked Oyster Bistro
  & Raw Bar **13**
Pain D'Avignon **16**
Pizza Barbone **13**
Rendezvous **13**
Roadhouse Café **6**
Tugboat's **22**
Tumi Ceviche Bar
  & Ristorante **7**
The West End **4**

Ocean Street Dock (www.hy-linecruises.com; ☎ **508/790-0696**); call for a reservation and schedule. Tickets are $17 for adults and free to $8 for children 12 and under. (The ice-cream cruises are $1 more.) There are 16 departures daily from late June to September; it's closed November to mid-April. Parking is $5 per car.

Two local favorite products offer fun factory tours in Hyannis. Kids in particular will love the free 15-minute factory tours at **Cape Cod Potato Chips,** 100 Breed's Hill Rd. (at Independence Way, off Route 132) (www.capecod chips.com; ☎ **508/775-7253**), which really are the world's best—they're chunkier than the norm. Tours run Monday to Friday from 9am to 5pm in July and August. Call for off-season hours. Adults will appreciate the free brewery tours at **Cape Cod Beer,** 1336 Phinney's Lane (www.capecodbeer.com; © **508/ 790-4200**), Monday through Saturday at 11am.

Cape Cod Maritime Museum ★ MUSEUM   Right down by the harbor, on the east side of Aselton Park, this small but interesting museum displays maritime art, nautical crafts, wooden model boats, a recreated Cape Cod boat builder's shop, and much more. Boat building classes for all ages take place year-round; interactive activities include learning how to tie a proper rope knot. It's a handy place to visit before or after a harbor cruise.

135 South St. www.capecodmaritimemuseum.org. © **508/775-1723.** $6 adults, $5 students and seniors, free for ages 6 and under. Mid-March to mid-Dec Tues–Sat 10am–4pm, Sun noon–4pm. Closed Jan to mid-Mar.

Zion Union Heritage Museum ★ MUSEUM   People of color were very important to the whaling and cranberry industries on Cape Cod, as you'll learn at this fascinating little museum in the former Zion Union Church, a historic African-American church. Displays include artwork and memorabilia reflecting the region's African-American and Cape Verdean heritage, as well as a range of historic documents about well-known community leaders. There are revolving art shows and other exhibits about the African-American community.

276 North St. www.zionunionheritagemuseum.org. © **508/790-9466.** $5 adults, $4 seniors, $3 ages 10–17. May–Oct Tues–Sat 11am–5pm; Nov–Dec Thurs–Sat 10am– 4pm; and Feb–Apr Thurs–Sat 11am–5pm.

HYANNIS BEACHES

In Hyannis itself, you have two choices. Little **Orrin Keyes Beach** ★★ (also known as Sea Street Beach), at the end of residential Sea Street, which is popular with families. **Veterans Beach,** off Ocean Street, is a small stretch of harborside sand adjoining the John F. Kennedy Memorial; it's not tops for swimming, unless you're very young. Parking is usually easy to find, though, and it's walkable from town. The snack bar, restrooms, and playground will see to a family's needs.

Over in Hyannis Port, there's **Kalmus Beach** ★★, off Gosnold Street, an 800-foot spit of sand stretching toward the mouth of the harbor. The surf is tame, the slope shallow, and the conditions ideal for little kids. There are

---

Folk Art in Cotuit

Some 9 miles west of Hyannis in the town of Cotuit, the **Cahoon Museum of American Art** ★ at 4676 Falmouth Rd./ Rte. 28 (just east of the intersection of Rte. 28 and Rte. 130), Cotuit (www. cahoonmuseum.org; © **508/428-7581**), has long been a popular site for art lovers. Located in an 18th-century red clapboard house, the museum is in the former home of Ralph and Martha Cahoon, whose whimsical folk-art paintings featuring mermaids remain popular years after the death of the artists (Ralph in 1982 and Martha in 1999). The museum sponsors frequent gallery talks and other special events. It is open Tuesday through Saturday 10am to 4pm and Sunday 1 to 4pm. Admission is $10 for adults, $8 for seniors and students.

Make Way for Mini-Golf: Mid-Cape Edition

The **Lightning Falls** mini-golf course, 455 W. Main St. in Hyannis (℗ **508/771-3194**), is a nice diversion for young children or for the young at heart. A round costs $8 for adults, $7 for children. Open in season 10am to 11pm. Call for off-season hours.

lifeguards, a snack bar, and restrooms. It makes an ideal launching site for windsurfers, who sometimes seem to play chicken with the steady parade of ferries.

Your best beach bet, however, is west of Hyannis in Centerville: **Craigville Beach ★★★**, a broad expanse of sand off Craigville Beach Road that has lifeguards and restrooms. Once a magnet for Methodist camp meetings (conference centers still line the shore), Craigville these days is also known as "Muscle Beach," a destination for the bronzed and buffed.

OUTDOOR ACTIVITIES

FISHING **Hy-Line Cruises** offers seasonal sonar-aided "bottom" or blues fishing from its Ocean Street dock in Hyannis (www.hylinecruises.com; ℗ **508/790-0696**). The cost for a half-day bottom-fishing trip is $42 per adult, $32 for kids ages 5 to 12 (children 4 and under are prohibited). **Helen H Deep-Sea Fishing,** at 137 Pleasant St. (www.helen-h.com; ℗ **508/790-0660**), offers daily expeditions aboard a 100-foot boat with a heated cabin and full galley. Choose whether you want to fish for porgies and black sea bass or fluke and bluefish. Adults pay $73, children $55 for a half day.

GOLF The **Hyannis Golf Club,** 1840 Route 132 (℗ **508/362-2606**), offers a 46-station driving range, as well as an 18-hole championship course. High-season greens fees are $61. At the scenic 9-hole **Cotuit High Ground Country Club,** at 31 Crockers Neck Rd. in the town of Cotuit, west of Hyannis (www.cotuithighground.com; ℗ **508/428-9863**), an 18-hole round costs $20; it's $15 for juniors and seniors, and for everyone after 4pm.

ESPECIALLY FOR KIDS

The top-of-the-line **Hyannis Youth & Community Center** at 141 Bassett Lane (www.town.barnstable.ma.us/hycc; ℗ **508/790-6345**) has an elevated walking track, an elaborate teen center, two skating rinks, and basketball courts. Day passes cost $5. The center is open 7am to 9pm daily (Fri and Sat until 10pm). Check the website for public skating times and special events.

HYANNIS SHOPPING

Hyannis is undoubtedly the commercial center of the Cape, and you'll find a number of unique shops on Main Street. Sometimes, however, you just need a big indoor shopping mall, and Hyannis has got that, too: The **Cape Cod Mall** at 769 Iyannough Road/Route 28 (www.simon.com/mall/cape-cod-mall; ℗ **508/771-0201**), full of chain stores, chain restaurants, and a multi-screen movieplex, open daily 10am to 9pm (Sun 11am–6pm).

On weekends from late May to mid-June, and daily from mid-June through September, art enthusiasts may want to visit **Harbor Your Arts Artist**

Shanties ★, Ocean Street, along Hyannis Harbor (www.hyartsdistrict.com/visual-arts/art-shanties). In its seven artists' shacks, you can watch the artists at work and buy directly from them. Nearby on **Pearl Street,** a small arts district includes several art galleries and studios clustered together, including the Hyannis Harbor Arts Center at **Guyer Art Barn** (250 South St.; open noon–4pm weekends), giving a chance for the public to see artists at work. The first Thursday of the month in the summer is an **Arts Stroll** in Hyannis, in which galleries offer open houses and musicians serenade strollers on Main Street.

Booklovers will want to drive west of town 9 miles to Cotuit to visit **Isaiah Thomas Books & Prints,** 4632 Falmouth Rd./Route 28 (www.isaiahthomasbooks.com; ℂ 508/428-2752), which has a 60,000-volume collection housed in an 1850 home. Named for the Revolutionary printer who helped foment the War of Independence, the shop is full of treasures, clustered by topic. The owner, James S. Visbeck, is happy to show off his first editions, rare miniatures, and maps; you get the sense that sales are secondary to sheer bibliophilic pleasure.

Exploring Barnstable & Barnstable Village ★★

Just a couple of miles from Hyannis, the bucolic village of Barnstable houses the county courthouse, a line-up of well-kept Colonial houses, and some of the Cape's most charming B&Bs. Barnstable's beaches face onto Nantucket Sound, which means that they are fairly protected and thus not big in terms of surf.

One lovely way to explore the Sound-side coast is to visit the **Long Pasture Wildlife Sanctuary** ★★ at 345 Bone Hill Rd. in Barnstable Village (www.massaudubon.org; ℂ 508/362-7475). On this 110-acre Audubon sanctuary, easy-to-walk trails lead out to a meadow with a view of Barnstable Harbor. Wildlife spottings are likely to include numerous butterflies, dragonflies, and red-tailed hawks. Admission is $4 for adults, $3 for children.

Barnstable's maritime history is celebrated at the **Coast Guard Heritage Museum** ★, set in a former U.S. Customs House in the north side of Barnstable Village (3353 Main St.; www.coastguardheritagemuseum.org; ℂ 508/362-8521). This engaging little museum houses displays of pre–Coast Guard groups, such as the lighthouse service, the lightship service, and the lifesaving service. The village blacksmith shop gives demonstrations daily. Also on the

---

Take Yourself Out to a Ballgame

There's no better way for young sports fans to spend a summer night on the Cape than watching a free baseball game with the **Cape Cod Baseball League** (www.capecodbaseball.org; ℂ 508/432-6909), which gives top college players a chance to be seen by MLB scouts. The three Mid-Cape teams are the **Cotuit Kettleers** (Lowell Park, 10 Lowell Rd., Cotuit), the **Hyannis Harbor Hawks** (McKeon Field, 120 High School Rd., Hyannis), and the **Yarmouth-Dennis Red Sox** (Red Wilson Field, D-Y Regional High School, 210 Station Ave., South Yarmouth). See p. 204 for Upper Cape teams; see p. 244 for Lower Cape teams.

property is the oldest wooden jail in the country, built in the 1600s. Admission is $5; the museum is open from May through October, Tuesdays through Saturdays from 10am to 3pm.

Although Provincetown is closer to the whales' preferred feeding grounds, if you don't have time to drive all the way out there, from Barnstable Harbor you hop aboard **Hyannis Whale Watcher Cruises** (www.whales.net; © **800/287-0374** or 508/362-6088), for a 4-hour voyage on a 100-foot high-speed cruiser. Naturalists provide the narration, and if you fail to spot a whale, your next trek is free. Tickets cost $53 for adults, $45 for seniors (62 and older), and $33 for children 4 to 12 from April through mid-October.

BARNSTABLE'S BEACHES

Barnstable's primary bay beach is **Sandy Neck Beach,** accessed through East Sandwich (p. 185). Beach parking costs $20 a day ($10 at Hathaway's Pond), usually payable at the lot; for a weeklong parking sticker ($70), visit the Recreation Department at 141 Bassett Lane, at the Hyannis Youth & Community Center (© **508/790-6345**), open daily (Mon–Sat 7am–10pm, Sun noon–9pm). *Note:* There is a smoking ban on beaches in the town of Barnstable during the summer.

FISHING

Among the charter boats berthed in **Barnstable Harbor** is Capt. Justin Zacek's *Drifter* (www.driftersportfishing.com; © **774/836-7292**), a 36-foot boat available for half- and full-day trips costing $550 to $775, depending on the length of the trip and the number of people. The township of Barnstable has 11 ponds for freshwater fishing; for information and permits, visit **Town Hall,** at 367 Main St., Hyannis (© **508/862-4044**); or **Sports Port,** 149 W. Main St., Hyannis (© **508/775-3096**). Surf-casting, which now requires a $10 license, is permitted on Sandy Neck (p. 188).

BARNSTABLE SHOPPING

At **West Barnstable Tables** ★, 2454 Meetinghouse Way (off Route 149), West Barnstable (www.westbarnstabletables.com; © **508/362-2676**), you'll see the work of furniture artisans Richard Kiusalas and Steven Whittlesey, who salvage antique lumber and turn it into cupboards, tables, and chairs, among other things (old windows are turned into mirrors). Most of their stock looks freshly made, albeit with wood of unusually high quality. Pieces are priced accordingly: A dining-room set—a pine trestle table with six bow-back chairs—runs more than $4,000. When the wood still bears interesting traces of its former life, it's turned into folk-art furniture.

Exploring Yarmouth ★

Yarmouth represents the Cape at its best—and its worst. **Yarmouth Port ★★,** on Cape Cod Bay, is an enchanting village, whereas the sound-side villages of West and South Yarmouth are a lesson in unbridled development, a nightmarish gauntlet of most tacky accommodations and attractions strung along

Route 28. The attractions listed below are a healthy mix of the two sides of Yarmouth, from tacky to culturally worthy.

Cape Cod Inflatable Park ★★ ATTRACTION   A complete kids' playland, this attraction combines three parks—the Inflatable Park, with all manner of items to jump and bounce on; the Challenge Zone, an obstacle course that includes ziplines and harder climbing attractions; and the H2O, a water park. Onsite is also an arcade and shop. The attraction is next to the Cape Cod Family Resort motel, which offers discounts to the park.

518 Main St./Rte. 28, West Yarmouth. www.capecodinflatablepark.com. *©* **508/771-6060.** Inflatable Park $25 ($20 toddlers); Challenge Zone (must be 48" tall) $25; H2O $25 ($20 toddlers, $15 seniors); 2-park pass $40 ($30 toddlers); 3-park pass $50. Parents who do not go on rides enter free. June–Aug 10am–10pm; mid-Apr to May & Sept to mid-Oct Sat–Sun 10am–5pm. Closed mid-Oct to mid-Apr.

Cultural Center of Cape Cod ★ GALLERY/PERFORMANCE VENUE   In 2000, a group of Yarmouth residents set out to turn the decaying and abandoned Bass River Savings Bank in South Yarmouth into an arts and cultural center. They've transformed it into a happening year-round venue, with a succession of art exhibits in the center's galleries, including the "vault," which has the original bank vault door. In the evenings, even more fun can be had, as the center books local musicians as well as off-Cape musicians to perform.

307 Old Main St. (take exit 8 off Rte. 6 and go south), South Yarmouth. www.cultural-center.org. *©* **508/394-7100.** Admission free. Gallery hours Mon–Fri 9am–5pm; Sat 11am–5pm; Sun noon–5pm (and many evening events).

The Edward Gorey House ★★ HISTORIC HOME   A museum that celebrates such a unique talent as the author/illustrator/playwright Edward Gorey should offer surprises, and this one, inside Gorey's 200-year-old sea captain's home, does just that. The house celebrates the author's passion for collectibles—potato mashers and sea glass were favorites—and animals (he usually had half a dozen cats). The annual exhibits focus on his rich body of work, the quirky and macabre illustrations that were also the basis of his plays, set designs, costume designs, and even stuffed animal–making. This is a fun museum and a must for literary-minded travelers, who will also want to stop in the nearby Parnassus Bookstore (see p. 214), which was one of Gorey's favorite places.

8 Strawberry Lane (off Route 6A, on the Common), Yarmouth Port. www.edwardgorey house.org. *©* **508/362-3909.** $8 adults, $5 students & seniors, $2 kids 6–12, ages 5 and under free. July to mid-Oct Wed–Sat 11am–4pm, Sun noon–4pm. Call for off-season hours. Closed Jan–Mar.

Whydah Pirate Museum ★★ MUSEUM   Billed as the world's only pirate treasure available for viewing, these are the findings of local treasure hunter Barry Clifford. Back in the 1980s, Clifford found evidence of the 1717 wreck of the slave ship *Whydah,* off the beach in Wellfleet. (Research showed it had been captured by "Black Sam" Bellamy, who was said to have plundered 50 ships.) The museum explores legend and lore associated with the find, displaying weapons, jewelry, and clothing; you can also watch a National Geographic special made at the time of Clifford's find. An on-site Sea Lab & Learning Center is devoted to the continuing excavation work of freeing the bounty from the encrustations of the sea.

674 Main St. (Rte. 28), West Yarmouth (just W of Swan Pond River Bridge). www.discover pirates.com. © **508/534-95711.** $19 adults, $17 seniors, $15 kids 5–17, ages 4 and under free. Daily 10am–5pm (last entry 4pm).

YARMOUTH BEACHES

Yarmouth has 11 saltwater and 2 pond beaches open to the public. The body-per-square-yard ratio can be pretty intense along the sound, but so is the social scene, so no one seems to mind. Beachside parking lots charge $15 a day and sell weeklong stickers ($70).

The beaches along the south shore (Nantucket Sound) tend to be clean and sandy, with comfortable water temps (kids will want to stay in all day), but they can also be crowded during peak times. Bring bug spray in July, when Greenhead flies (a kind of horsefly) get hungry. Going from east to west, they include **Bass River Beach** ★ (off South Shore Drive, South Yarmouth), located at the mouth of the largest tidal river on the eastern seaboard; **Parker's River Beach,** also off South Shore Drive, which has a gazebo for the sun-shy; and **Seagull Beach** ★ (off South Sea Avenue, West Yarmouth), which has rolling dunes and a boardwalk. All three have snack bars and restrooms; Bass River also has a wheelchair-accessible fishing pier.

On the north coast, facing onto the tamer waters of Cape Cod Bay, a top option is **Gray's Beach,** off Center Street in Yarmouth Port. It's only a tiny spit of dark sand, but it's good for young children; parking is free, and there's a picnic area with grills. Best of all, it adjoins the Callery-Darling Conservation Area, where the **Bass Hole boardwalk** ★★ over the marshlands offers one of the mid-Cape's most scenic walks.

GOLF

Yarmouth township maintains two 18-hole courses: the seasonal **Bayberry Hills,** off West Yarmouth Road, in West Yarmouth (© **508/394-5597**), and the year-round **Bass River Golf Course,** off High Bank Road in South Yarmouth (© **508/398-9079**). The Bass River course, one of the Cape's most famous, was founded in 1900 and redesigned by Donald Ross. A round at Bayberry costs $85; at Bass River, it costs $45 to $58 to walk and an additional $19 with a cart. Prices are reduced in the afternoon. Another 18-holer open to the public is the par-54 **Blue Rock Golf Course,** off High Bank Road in South Yarmouth (© **508/398-9295**); it's open year-round, and a round costs $30 to $50.

YARMOUTH SHOPPING

Driving Route 6A, the Old King's Highway, in Yarmouth Port, you'll pass a number of antiques stores and fine shops selling household items. Unless you have children in tow, you may want to bypass Route 28 entirely and stay on the pretty north side of Yarmouth.

The most colorful bookshop on the Cape is **Parnassus Books ★**, 220 Route 6A in Yarmouth Port (www.parnassusbooks.com; *©* **508/362-6420**). This jam-packed repository—housed in an 1858 Swedenborgian church—is the creation of Ben Muse, who has been collecting and selling vintage tomes since the 1960s. Relevant new stock, including the Cape-related reissues published by Parnassus Imprints, is sold alongside the older treasures. Don't expect much handholding on the part of the gruff proprietor. You'll earn his respect by knowing what you're looking for or, better yet, being willing to browse until it finds you. The outdoor racks, maintained on an honor system, are open 24 hours a day, for those who suffer from *abibliophobia*—fear of a lack of reading material.

Exploring Dennis ★

In Dennis, as in Yarmouth, virtually all the good stuff—pretty drives, inviting shops, and restaurants with real personality—is in the north, along Route 6A. Route 28, on the other hand, is chockablock with generic motels and strip malls. The main cultural target here is the Cape Cod Center for the Arts campus (below), a nexus for all sorts of arts events.

Cape Cod Museum of Art ★★ MUSEUM   This museum was founded in the 19890s to highlight outstanding artists of Cape Cod and the Islands. The founders felt that unless they began a repository for the Cape's art, it would migrate to museums all over the country, leaving little for locals to enjoy. The museum's several galleries regularly feature multiple exhibits of current and past Cape artists. There is also a fine outdoor sculpture garden with pieces from the museum's permanent collection. The museum is on the grounds of the **Cape Cod Center for the Arts,** which also includes the Cape Playhouse (p. 228) and the Cape Cinema (p. 229).

60 Hope Lane (just north of Route 6A), Dennis Village. www.cmfa.org. *©* **508/385-4477.** $9 adults, $7 seniors, $5 kids 13–18, free for ages 12 and under. Tues–Sat 10am–5pm; Sun noon–5pm.

DENNIS BEACHES

Dennis has more than a dozen saltwater and two freshwater beaches open to nonresidents. The lots charge $15 to $20 per day; for a weeklong permit ($60), visit **Town Hall** at 485 Main St. in South Dennis (*©* **508/394-8300**).

The bay beaches are charming and a big hit with families, who prize the easygoing surf, so soft it won't bring toddlers to their knees. These include, going from west to east, **Chapin Beach ★★**, a nice long bay beach pocked with occasional boulders and surrounded by dunes; 1,200-foot-long **Mayflower Beach ★★**, which has an wheelchair-accessible boardwalk and tide pools kids love to dabble in; and **Corporation Beach ★★**, which has a wheelchair-accessible boardwalk and a children's play area. (Before it filled in with sand, this was once a packet landing for a shipbuilding corporation owned by area residents.) All three have restrooms; Mayflower and Corporation have lifeguards (Chapin doesn't); Corporation also has a snack bar.

The 25-mile-long **Cape Cod Rail Trail** ★★★ (℘ 508/896-3491) starts—or, depending on your perspective, ends—here in South Dennis, on Route 134, a half-mile south of Route 6's exit 9. Once a Penn Central track, this 8-foot-wide paved bikeway extends all the way to Wellfleet (with a few on-road lapses), passing through woods, marshes, and dunes. Sustenance is never too far off-trail, and plenty of bike shops dot the course. At the trail head is **Barb's Bike Shop,** 430 Route 134, South Dennis (www.barbsbikeshop.com; ℘ 508/760-4723), which rents bikes and does repairs. Rates are $16 for 2 hours, and up to $24 for the full day.

The beaches on Nantucket sound tend to attract wall-to-wall families, but the parking lots are usually not too crowded, as so many beachgoers stay within walking distance. A favorite is half-mile-long **West Dennis Beach** ★★, which has lifeguards, a playground, a snack bar, restrooms, and a special kite-flying area (note that the eastern end is reserved for residents).

Inland, you'll find **Scargo Lake,** a large kettle-hole pond (formed by a melting fragment of a glacier) with two pleasant beaches: Scargo Beach, accessible right off Route 6A, and Princess Beach, off Scargo Hill Road, where there are restrooms and a picnic area.

GOLF
The public is welcome to use two 18-hole championship courses: the hilly, par-71 **Dennis Highlands,** on Old Bass River Road in Dennis, and the even more challenging par-72 **Dennis Pines,** on Golf Course Road in East Dennis. For information on either course, call ℘ 508/385-8347 or visit www.dennisgolf.com. Both charge $64 for a round in the morning, $25 to $39 in the afternoon.

DENNIS SHOPPING
You can pretty much ignore Route 28. There's a growing cluster of antiques shops in Dennisport, but the stock is flea-market level and requires more patience than most mere browsers—as opposed to avid collectors—may be able to muster. Save your time and money for the better shops along Route 6A, where you'll also find fine contemporary crafts.

ANTIQUES/COLLECTIBLES The Cape's most prestigious auction house is **Eldred's,** 1483 Route 6A (about ¼ mile west of Dennis Village center), in East Dennis (www.eldreds.com; ℘ 508/385-3116). The gavel has been wielded here for more than 40 years; specialties include Asian art, American and European paintings, marine art, and Americana.

ARTS & CRAFTS Mostly fashioned of lustrous 22-karat gold, the dramatic creations of **Ross Coppelman Goldsmith,** 1439 Route 6A in East Dennis (www.rosscoppelman.com; ℘ 508/385-7900) seem to draw on the aesthetics of some grand, lost civilization. **Scargo Pottery** (www.scargopottery.com; ℘ 508/385-3894), 30 Dr. Lord's Road South in Dennis, is a magical place. Harry Holl set up his glass-ceilinged studio here in 1952; today his work, and

Eighty years after Frederick E. Hebert began a family tradition of making fine candy, his grandson, Ray Hebert, with his wife, Donna, continue the tradition in Dennisport at **Stage Stop Candy ★** (411 Main St.; www.stagestopcandy. com; ✆ **508/394-1791**). Cranberry Cordial has long been the signature candy here, but the white, dark, and milk chocolates are all superlative. The be-all, end-all has to be the Gold Coast truffles, made with special cocoas from around the world. It's open daily in summer from 9am to 5pm (Sun 10:30am–6pm); call for off-season hours.

the output of his four daughters, fills a glade overlooking Scargo Lake. Much of it, such as the signature birdhouses shaped like fanciful castles, is meant to reside outside. The other wares deserve a place of honor on the dining room table or perhaps over a mantel. The hand-painted tiles by Sarah Holl are particularly enchanting.

Where to Stay Mid-Cape

BARNSTABLE

To check on the availability at 17 bed-and-breakfasts along Route 6A from Sandwich to Brewster, head to **www.historiccapecodbay.com**. Being on Route 6A means most of these inns are walking distance to a bayside beach and the shops and restaurants in Barnstable Village.

Ashley Manor Inn ★ This historic B&B is a step up from some of the others along Route 6A, by virtue of the size of the rooms and the amenities. With fancy linens and antique furnishings, it also feels more luxurious, and it's within walking distance of Barnstable Harbor, Millway Beach, and Barnstable Village. The inn was built in 1699, making it one of the oldest B&B buildings on the Cape. Its rich heritage can be seen in the wide-board floors, huge hearth fireplaces, and a secret passageway connecting the upstairs to the downstairs (legend has it that Tories hid here during the Revolutionary War). The patio is a particularly nice place to enjoy the ample hot breakfasts, served here on sunny mornings.

3660 Rte. 6A (just east of Hyannis Rd.). www.ashleymanor.net. ✆ **888/535-2246** or 508/362-8044. 6 units. Summer $259 double; $319 suite. Rates include full breakfast. No children 13 and under. **Amenities:** Bikes; Har-Tru tennis court; Wi-Fi (free).

Lamb and Lion Inn ★ The Lamb and Lion has a lot to recommend it., but most of its laurels stem from the fact that its owners Tom Dott and Ali Pitcher understand hospitality. They also understand fun (Dott is an Elvis impersonator), and they will ensure that you have it. The rooms, which are all different, include some with wood-burning fireplaces or with kitchenettes. From the outside, this is a classic antique Cape house with a beautiful lawn and gardens, with lots of colorful flowerboxes and flower beds. Inside, you'll be surprised to see the guest rooms surround a courtyard with a saltwater pool and large hot tub. There is also a converted 1700s horse stable the size of a small cottage. Also on site is a spa where you can have a massage, facial, or other treatment. The owners are fans of small dogs, and they have several.

2504 Main St./Rte. 6A. www.lambandlion.com. ℂ **800/909-6923** or 508/362-6823. 10 units. Summer $299–$369 double, $419 suite. Rates include continental breakfast. Well-behaved dogs allowed (30-lb. limit). **Amenities:** Hot tub; pool; Wi-Fi (free).

CENTERVILLE

Long Dell Inn ★★　Built in 1849 as a home for Captain Reuben Jones, who made his wealth in the Gold Rush, this pretty Greek Revival is now one of the few B&Bs in this quiet corner of the Mid-Cape—it's welcomed lodgers for over 80 years. The terrific Centerville location means you'll be close to the village's cute general store and a very good ice-cream shop (see box p. 223). From the inn it's just a short walk or drive to Craigville Beach (p. 209), one of the best in the area.

436 S. Main St. www.longdellinn.com. ℂ **508/775-2750.** 7 units. Summer $179–$239. Rates include full breakfast. **Amenities:** Wi-Fi (free).

DENNIS

Isaiah Hall B&B Inn ★★　"Homey" is the word that comes to mind with this B&B, which has been welcoming guests since around 1948. The inn's namesake was a cooper (barrel-maker) whose grandfather Henry Hall is credited with cultivating the first cranberry bog in 1807. The bog, behind the inn, can be visited by guests. The building is an 1857 farmhouse in a quiet residential neighborhood off Route 6A, just steps from the Cape Playhouse (p. 228), Cape Cinema (p. 229), and Cape Cod Museum of Art (p. 214), making it an ideal base for arts lovers. Breakfast is served communally on an antique 12-foot table.

152 Whig St., Dennis. www.isaiahhallinn.com. ℂ **800/736-0160** or 508/385-9928. 12 units. Summer $120–$195 double, $250 suite. Rates include full breakfast. No children 7 and under. **Amenities:** Wi-Fi (free).

Lighthouse Inn ★★　The third generation is now running the Stone family's inn, a slice of old Cape Cod if ever there was one. The inn sits on a placid stretch of Nantucket Sound, its private beach guarded by the decommissioned lighthouse that Everett Stone had the foresight to purchase in 1938. Everett built an inn and cottage colony on the property, and families have been coming back for generations to enjoy this special spot. Lodging choices include the rather spartan rooms in the inn itself (great for singles!) as well as the more expensive cottages, which range from studios to three bedrooms. One of the best parts about this 9-acre compound is there is really no need to leave if you don't want to. The inn's restaurant serves three meals a day. There is a heated outdoor pool, tennis court, volleyball, mini-golf, and shuffleboard also. A beach bar at the entrance has live entertainment on weekends in season.

1 Lighthouse Inn Rd. (off Lower County Rd., ½ miles S of Rte. 28), West Dennis. www. lighthouseinn.com. ℂ **508/398-2244.** 44 units, 24 cottages. Summer $245–$320 double; $305–$335 1-bedroom cottage; $265–$340 2-bedroom cottage; $543–$624 3-bedroom cottage. Rates include full breakfast. Closed mid-Oct to late May. **Amenities:** 2 restaurants; bar w/entertainment; kids' program (ages 3–11) July–Aug; mini-golf; outdoor pool; shuffleboard; tennis court; volleyball; Wi-Fi (free).

HYANNIS & HYANNIS PORT

There are a variety of large, generic, but convenient hotels and motels in Hyannis. **Anchor In,** 1 South St. (www.anchorin.com; © **508/775-0357**), has a great location on Hyannis Inner Harbor and is a short walk to the center of town. It has numerous decks and a heated pool, all with harbor views. During high season, the 42 rooms are priced at $239 to $309, including continental breakfast. Within walking distance of Main Street restaurants, shops, and the ferries to Nantucket and Martha's Vineyard, the **Heritage House Hotel,** 259 Main St. (www.heritagehousehotel.com; © **508/775-7000**) has an indoor and an outdoor pool, a hot tub and saunas, and a restaurant/lounge with entertainment. During high season, its 143 rooms are $132 on weekdays and $188 on weekends.

If you prefer more amenities, the **Resort and Conference Center at Hyannis,** at 35 Scudder Ave., at the West End Circle just off Main Street (www.capecodresortandconference.com; © **866/828-8259**) has an 18-hole par-3 golf course, two restaurants, a fitness center, and indoor-outdoor pools. Summer rates are $190 to $220 double.

Hostelling International–Hyannis ★   This former historic house on the harbor is now a youth hostel with a stellar location, overlooking Aselton Park on Hyannis Harbor and a short walk to Main Street's stores and restaurants, as well as the docks for ferries to the islands. Use of a fully equipped kitchen as well as breakfast are included in the rate.

111 Ocean St. www.capecod.hiusa.org. © **877/683-7990** or 508/775-7990. 37 beds. Summer $39 bed; $115–$135 private room. Rates include continental breakfast. Closed mid-Nov to late May. **Amenities:** Wi-Fi (free).

Simmons Homestead Inn ★★   If you prize uniqueness and informality over routine, this former captain's house may be your B&B of choice. Fun is the buzzword here. Your host, Bill Putnam, has amassed an unusual collection of red sports cars, 55 at last count. As for the B&B itself, it feels like old Cape Cod, except with modern niceties. The rooms are decorated with whimsy in mind, with animal themes reflected in the bedding, artwork, and knickknacks. The interior also reflects the historic nature of the property, with antique reproductions and four-poster beds, for example. There is a billiard room and a backyard with some well-placed hammocks. The inn allows dogs; Putnam has a large number of cats.

288 Scudder Ave. (about ¼ mile W of West End rotary), Hyannis Port. www.simmons homesteadinn.com. © **800/637-1649** or 508/778-4999. 14 units. Summer $170–$210 double; $300 2-bedroom suite. Rates include full breakfast. Dogs welcome. **Amenities:** Bikes; Wi-Fi (free).

YARMOUTH

So many hotels and motels line Route 28 and the shore in West and South Yarmouth that it may be hard to make sense of the choices. The following are some that offer clean rooms and cater to families looking for a reasonably priced beach vacation. For those staying on Route 28, the town runs frequent beach shuttles in season.

The **Cape Codder Resort & Spa ★**, 1225 Iyannough Rd./Route 132 (www. capecodderresort.com; ℂ **888/297-2200** or 508/771-3000) was designed with families in mind. Kids love the top-of-the line Water Park that includes a three-story lighthouse slide for the older kids, a "stormy river" ride, and a pirate cove kiddie pool. Its Hearth 'n Kettle restaurant is a family-friendly choice; adults will appreciate that it also has the Grand Cru Wine Bar and a spa. Summer rates for the 260 rooms are $319 to $369 for a double, $479 to $699 for a suite.

In West Yarmouth, the 100-room **Tidewater Inn,** 135 Main St./Route 28 (www.tidewatercapecod.com/tidewater; ℂ **800/338-6322** or 508/775-6322), is one of the more attractive motels along this strip, a white clapboard double-decker with green shutters and doors. It has indoor and outdoor pools and a restaurant that's open for breakfast, plus it's only a half-mile from a small beach on Lewis Bay. Summer rates are $134 to $176 for double occupancy.

Captain Farris House ★★   This 1849 house, listed on the prestigious National Register of Historic Places, has been done up to the nines. It's located in the very scenic Bass River area, steps from the wide river that divides Yarmouth and Dennis and in the middle of a historic district of other 19th-century homes. The rooms are notable for being extra roomy compared to most B&Bs in the region; some have been remodeled to accommodate Jacuzzi tubs. Luxurious linens and fluffy towels, afternoon tea and cookies, and evening cordials are all among the niceties awaiting guests here.

308 Old Main St. (west of the Bass River Bridge), Bass River. www.captainfarris.com. ℂ **800/350-9477** or 508/760-2818. 9 units. Summer $331–$363 double; $380 suite. Rates include full breakfast. Closed Dec to mid-Feb. **Amenities:** Wi-Fi (free).

The Inn at Cape Cod ★   Though it resembles a southern plantation house with its towering Ionic columns, this B&B was built in 1820 for the Sears family. It is well situated in the village of Yarmouth Port, a pleasant walk to shops, museums, restaurants, and nature trails; and with the bayside beaches not far away. Inside, a grand curving staircase leads up to five of the nine guestrooms. The others are on the ground floor. All are decorated with fine reproductions and outfitted for comfort, from the mattresses to the seating.

4 Summer St., Yarmouth Port. www.innatcapecod.com. ℂ **800/850-7301** or 508/375-0590. 9 units. Summer $320–$395 double; $324–$419 suite. Rates include full breakfast. Closed Dec–Feb. No children 8 and under. **Amenities:** Wi-Fi (free).

Red Jacket Beach Resort ★★   This resort has two really exceptional qualities: the location, between the Parker River and Nantucket Sound, and the activities, which include a free kids' program and numerous family and adult and activities. The same company owns four other nearby resorts (**Blue Rock Golf,** which has a championship golf course; **Green Harbor, Blue Water,** and **Riviera**) and guests get to take advantage of the activities, beaches, and golf at any of the five. The private beach (in addition to indoor and outdoor pools) is a nice plus, also. Particularly for families with young children, this resort is a good choice. The focus for the staff is ensuring guests have a great time and want to come back. And that works well for everyone.

1 S. Shore Dr., South Yarmouth. www.redjacketresorts.com. ℂ **800/672-0500** or 508/398-6941. 170 units, 14 cottages. Summer $409–$479 double; $780–$905 cottages, plus $15 per day resort fee. Closed Nov to mid-Apr. **Amenities:** Restaurant; bar/lounge; concierge; day spa, exercise room; ice cream shop; indoor and outdoor pools; putting green; sauna; tennis court; whirlpool; Wi-Fi (free).

Where to Eat Mid-Cape

The greatest range of dining options in this part of the Cape are in **Dennis** (see below), largely due to the cultural action around the Cape Playhouse, and in **Hyannis** (see p. 223), just because, well, it's Hyannis.

BARNSTABLE

Some say the best coffee on Cape Cod is served at **Nirvana Coffee Company** ★ (ℂ **508/744-6983**), at 3206 Main St. in Barnstable Village, centrally located across from the courthouse.

The Barnstable Restaurant and Tavern ★★ NEW AMERICAN/ITALIAN/PUB   You can almost hear the echoes of horse-drawn carriages at this former stagecoach stop, its wide-board floors and antiques left over from colonial days. A tavern has been on this property for at least 200 years. These days, the popular chef-owned restaurant is notable not just for its New American cuisine but also for very reasonable prices. A grilled tavern burger, thin-crust pizzas, deli sandwiches, and fried seafood are always available, as are Italian specialties like the mushroom ravioli and more upscale offerings like the grilled tuna steak with wasabi or the Mediterranean seafood stew with a garlic-aioli crouton. There is a kids' menu and gluten-free offerings, too.

3176 Main St./Rte. 6A, Barnstable Village. www.barnstablerestaurant.com. ℂ **508/362-2355.** Main courses $10–$20. Daily 11:30am–9pm.

Mattakeese Wharf ★ SEAFOOD   This is the ultimate mid-Cape restaurant to go to for a sunset view, sitting as it does in Barnstable Harbor, with lovely views out to Cape Cod Bay and Sandy Neck. Seafood—have it on the half shell or fried, broiled, or baked—makes up most of the menu. Many people indulge in the lobster dinner with all the trimmings. Prices are high here, since you're paying for that spectacular view. There is entertainment on summer weekends beginning at sunset.

273 Millway, Barnstable Village. www.mattakeese.com. ℂ **508/362-4511.** Main courses $16–$37. May to mid-Oct daily 11:30am–9pm; call for off-season hours.

DENNIS

With a large selection of bakery items plus sandwiches, soups, salads and wraps for lunch, **Buckies Bakery Cafe** ★ (681 Main St.; www.buckies biscotti.com; ℂ **508/398-9700**) is a great place to stock up on picnic foods before a day at the beach. A sister bakery is at 554 Route 28 in Harwichport.

Expensive

Encore Bistro & Bar ★★ NEW AMERICAN   This is where you go after a play at the Cape Playhouse (p. 228) or a movie at Cape Cinema (p. 229). It is right on the cultural campus that includes the theater, cinema and museum; and it uses the same parking lot—very convenient. Fortunately, the food is good too. Appropriate for a place where you might have a snack before a show, there is a pizza menu and a large menu of fancy appetizers, like truffle fries and the lobster mango tower, a sort of vertical lobster salad. For the main course, you can have something light like fish tacos or a big meal, like a shore dinner with lobster and all the fixings. Friday and Saturday, there is a late night menu served from 10 to 11pm, for after-theater hunger pangs.

36 Hope Lane, Dennis Village. www.encoredingcapecod.com. ℂ **508/385-8500.** Main courses $16–$36. June–late Aug Mon–Thurs 11:30–9pm, Sat–Sun 11am–3pm and 4–9pm. Call for off-season hours.

Fin ★★ NEW AMERICAN   Using the best local ingredients, including local fish, is the focus of Fin, an upscale restaurant in a historic house in the Theater Marketplace, a short walk from the Cape Cinema (p. 229), Cape Playhouse (p. 228), and Cape Museum of Art (p. 214). Food is on the rich side and very good. You'll want to have an appetite to eat the likes of foie gras crème brûlée. Among the main courses, there are surprises: The seared peppered yellow-fin tuna comes with a soy-peanut dressing and cucumber-cilantro relish; the poached salmon comes with black-truffle butter.

800 Main St./Rte. 6A, Dennis Village. www.fincapecod.com. ℂ **508/385-2096.** Main courses $27–$34. June–late Aug Tues–Sat 5–9:30pm. Call for off-season hours.

The Ocean House New American Bistro and Bar ★★★ NEW AMERICAN   A regular contender for the Cape's top restaurant, the Ocean House seems to have it all: attentive service, great food, and sensational views of the Sound. The restaurant sits on the beach, with windows giving diners a 180-degree beachfront view. The thoughtful menu means that light bites, a couple of appetizers (spring rolls and calamari), and perhaps a gourmet pizza (artichoke and wild mushroom, or lobster and asparagus), can take the place of a more expansive meal. But if you are steering toward the large plates, consider the lobster ravioli with champagne cream (you can order a half portion) or the Korean BBQ short ribs. Keep in mind that this place is very popular in the summer, so make a reservation unless you don't mind a very long wait.

3 Chase Ave. (at Depot St.), Dennisport. www.oceanhouserestaurant.com. ℂ **508/394-0700.** Main courses $18–$38. June–Sept Tues–Sun 5–10pm (late-night menu to 11pm); call for off-season hours.

The Pheasant ★★★ NEW AMERICAN   Restaurant patrons have been heading to this 200-year-old red barn on the Old King's Highway since 1977, but new owners have updated the decor and reworked the menu to include some surprises. For instance, the selection of charcoal grilled skewers is a choice between local squid, duck hearts, or shiitake mushrooms. As a main course, there is a pork schnitzel as well as the more traditional (for Cape Cod) seared scallops. Desserts are a specialty.

905 Main St., Dennis Village. www.pheasantcapecod.com. © **508/385-2133.** Main courses $19–$33. Wed–Mon 5–9:30pm (late-night menu until 11pm).

Moderate
Gina's by the Sea ★★ SOUTHERN ITALIAN   Just steps from Chapin Beach (see p. 214), Gina's has been pleasing beachgoers for more than 60 years. The restaurant consists of a back room, which is dark and romantic if a little crowded, and the porch-like front room, which is more light and airy. This is old-fashioned Italian food like your mother might have made if she grew up in the old country. The menu is small but full of winners, such as the chicken parmigiana or the fettuccine alfredo. Daily specials are on the blackboard, which might include one of the house specialties, clams casino. This place is very busy in the summer. Come early or late.

134 Taunton Ave., Dennis. www.ginasbythesea.com. © **508/385-3213.** Main courses $10–$27. Apr–Nov Thurs–Sun 5–9pm. Closed Dec–Mar.

Scargo Cafe ★ AMERICAN   When you emerge from the Cape Playhouse (p. 228) late at night and need a place to eat, this is a great choice. Right across the street in a beautifully restored captain's house, the Scargo Café has been satisfying hungry theatergoers for decades. The beauty of this place is the variety of the menu. You can have a burger (try the one on a pretzel roll) or a sandwich (like the caprese chicken) or a full on surf-and-turf meal, with steak and lobster. There's also a menu of gluten-free items.

799 Main St./Rte. 6A, Dennis. www.scargocafe.com. © **508/385-8200.** Main courses $11–$27. Mid-June to mid-Sept daily 11am–11pm; rest of year daily 11am–10pm.

Inexpensive
Captain Frosty's ★ SEAFOOD   This is the ultimate seafood shack, and it's an institution in these parts. Somehow the fried food is not greasy, the breading is flavorful, and the fish is cooked perfectly. Most people sit outside on the picnic tables, but you can also sit inside or get the food to go and take it to nearby Corporation Beach (see p. 214) for a sunset picnic.

219 Rte. 6A, Dennis. www.captainfrosty.com. © **508/385-8548.** Most items under $18. No credit cards. June–Aug daily 11am–9pm; call for off-season hours. Closed late Sept–Mar.

Sesuit Harbor Cafe ★ SEAFOOD   You'll feel like a local if you can find this place, located harborside at Northside Marina just north of Dennis Village. Preferred seating is on picnic tables out on the deck under colorful umbrellas. This is a great place to come to partake of the raw bar, which besides shellfish also has chowder, crab cakes and sashimi. The dinner menu, served from 3:30 to sunset, is heavy on fried seafood, half and full plates of fried clams, scallops, oysters, or shrimp. The lobster roll is a favorite and comes with homemade slaw, as is the tuna shrimp skewer.

357 Sesuit Neck Rd., Dennis. www.sesuit-harbor-cafe.com. © **508/386-5473** (summer) or 508/385-6134 (winter). Main courses $9–$30. Late May–Sept daily 7am–8:30pm; call for off-season hours. Closed mid-Oct to late Apr.

THE ICE-CREAM scoop: MID-CAPE

Since 1934 several generations of summer-goers—including enthusiastic Kennedys—have fed their ice cream cravings at **Four Seas Ice Cream ★★★**, 360 S. Main St. in the center of Centerville (www.fourseasicecream.com; ℭ **508/775-1394**). This place had exotic flavors long before they became the norm: Specialties include rum-butter toffee, cantaloupe, and—at the height of the season—Cape Cod beach plum. Open late May to early September.

Look for the big stuffed bear sitting on a bench to find **Kandy Korner ★★**, 474 Main St., Hyannis (www.kandykorner.com; ℭ **508/771-5313**), an old-fashioned candy store and ice cream shop that's been pleasing strollers on Hyannis's Main Street for decades. The ice cream, chocolates, fudge, and saltwater taffy are all made in-house. Open 10am to 6pm daily.

Another excellent ice cream shop is **Katie's Homemade Ice Cream,** a little farther west at 568 Main St. (www.katiesicecreamcapecod.com; ℭ **508/771-6889**) in the big pink house. All the ice cream (hard and soft serve plus frozen yogurt) is made

here in small batches. There is a deli and lots of outside seating attached. Open late May to Sept daily 10:30am to 11pm.

In South Yarmouth, the **Cape Cod Creamery** company (www.capecod creamery.com; ℭ **508/398-8400**)—which supplies 40 Cape-inspired ice cream flavors wholesale all over the region—also runs a retail shop on the premises. Monomoy mud pie and Patti Page peppermint are favorites. Open year-round, it's at 1199 Route 28, South Yarmouth. Hours are noon to 6pm Monday to Thursday, noon to 9:30pm Friday through Sunday.

A little south of route 28 in Dennisport, **Sundae School ★** (www.sundaeschool.com; ℭ **508/394-9122**) is an old-fashioned ice-cream parlor in a shingled barn with a bright red door. It's full of fun ice-cream memorabilia, and the homemade flavors are sensational, from the Amaretto Nut all the way down to the Turtle (chocolate and butterscotch ice cream with pecans). It's at 381 Lower County Rd. (at Sea Street), open daily 11am to 11pm summer; Saturday and Sunday only in spring and fall; it closes down from mid-September to mid-April.

Wee Packet ★ CLAM SHACK/IRISH   In the days when packet ships plied the local waters, transporting goods from Boston to New York, a "wee packet" was the colloquial name for a small ship. Cape Cod byways used to be lined with little family fish shacks like this. What's fun here is the traditional full Irish breakfast, complete with grilled tomato and baked beans. Lunch is perhaps the most popular meal of the day, featuring traditional fried-fish plates and lobster rolls. For dinner, try a full-on clambake. A new patio offers outdoor seating, though I prefer the cute Formica tables inside. On Thursday nights in season, there is a raw bar with oysters from East Dennis Oyster Farm.

79 Depot St., Dennisport. www.weepacketrestaurant.com. ℭ **508/394-6595.** Main courses $8–$20. July 4–Labor Day daily 7:30am–9pm; call for off-season hours. Closed mid-Oct to May.

HYANNIS
Expensive
Alberto's Ristorante ★★★ NORTHERN ITALIAN   When Alberto's opened in 1984, it was said to be the first Northern Italian in the region. Many

other local restaurants have come and gone since then, but Alberto's, run by the suave Felisberto Barreiro, has remained a consistent choice. It is an elegant venue, with crisp white tablecloths and chandeliers providing romantic lighting, but there's also a lively bar scene, particularly in the summer. The best deal is the three-course prix-fixe dinner, served daily from 4 to 6pm for $22. Favorites include cannelloni and other house-made pastas. There's also a sublime roasted duck, and the signature "Alberto," a delicate veal cutlet with peppers, artichoke hearts, pesto, and a fresh tomato sauce. There's also a good children's menu.

360 Main St. www.albertos.net. ℭ **508/778-1770.** Main courses $16–$27. Daily 11:30am–9:30pm.

Black Cat Tavern ★ NEW AMERICAN Tourists love this traditional restaurant across the street from Hyannis Harbor. The interior is very "mid-century yacht club," with polished brass, sailboat models, and framed nautical flags. The menu hits all the basics, with burgers, steaks and seafood. Four nights a week, the restaurant doubles as a piano lounge with live music. The patio out front is ideal on warm nights, and the **Shack Out Back** is an outdoor patio and raw bar. For a quick bite, the **Black Cat Harbor Shack** next door can handle to-go orders.

165 Ocean St. www.blackcattavern.com. ℭ **508/778-1233.** Main courses $20–$43. Apr–Oct daily 11:30am–10pm; call for off-season hours. Closed Jan.

The Naked Oyster Bistro & Raw Bar ★★★ FRENCH BISTRO Chef Florence Lowell, from Bordeaux, France, runs the show at the Naked Oyster, one of the Cape's top restaurants. Lowell has her own oyster beds in nearby Barnstable Harbor, so the sweet, salty shellfish come straight from the sea to the table, served, ideally, with the mignonette (sauce) of the day. In addition to oysters, served dressed or naked, you might want to start with the French onion soup or the oyster stew, then move on to seared diver scallops served over a roasted-shitake-mushroom risotto. Another winner is the duck confit with thyme gnocchi. A number of items on the menu are gluten-free. Desserts are extra-special here, and the wine list is unrivaled in the region. This bistro is pleasantly cozy and romantically lit, with vibrant paintings shown off the brick walls.

410 Main St. www.nakedoyster.com. ℭ **508/778-6500.** Main courses $24–$35. May–Oct daily 11:30am–9:30pm; Nov–Apr Mon–Sat 11:30am–9:30pm.

Pain D'Avignon ★★★ FRENCH CAFE You'd be hard-pressed to accidentally find this place, located as it is on a side street off Route 132, just north of the airport rotary. It's well worth the hunt, however. Despite the industrial surroundings, stepping into Pain D'Avignon is really like entering a European cafe. It's very stylish, all blacks and whites, including the photos on the walls. Pain D'Avignon began as a wholesale bread business, and breakfast and lunch both feature their exquisite bread, be it a croissant, bagel, brioche, or baguette. The more extensive dinner menu includes as starters Dennis Bay View Oysters, grilled Spanish octopus, and foie gras with a buttered brioche. As a main course, you might try the dish of the day, perhaps the coq au vin or the steak frites, with house-made fries and watercress salad. Desserts are made in-house.

15 Hinckley Rd. www.paindavignon.com. ℂ **508/778-8588.** Main courses $16–$34. Mon–Tues 7am–6pm; Wed–Sun 7am–10pm.

Roadhouse Café ★★ AMERICAN/NORTHERN ITALIAN   In business for more than 30 years, this stalwart wins accolades for its clubby atmosphere and a menu that combines the best of Northern Italian cuisine with New American flair. The best room in the place has a glorious mahogany bar, high-backed booths, and a fireplace that warms the room all winter. The front dining rooms are more formal; the Back Door Bistro, which has a special pizza menu, is where entertainers play 5 nights a week in season (the Monday Night Jazz Ensemble plays from 7 to 10pm year-round). Special dishes include the cioppino, which is a lovely seafood stew, and the lobster ravioli.

488 South St. (near the West End rotary). www.roadhousecafe.com. ℂ **508/775-2386.** Main courses $17–$35. Daily 4–10pm.

The West End ★★ NEW AMERICAN   This restaurant, new in 2018, is the place to dine if you are attending a show at the Melody Tent next door (see p. 228). The menu blends new ideas with the traditional—yes, there are crab-cakes and stuffed quahogs, but also honey-roasted Brussels sprouts and truffle tots, a fancy spin on tater tots. Main courses include fried chicken with mac 'n' cheese, and grilled swordfish with fruit salsa. There is also a raw bar and some less expensive burger options. Sunday morning features a jazz brunch with local musicians.

20 Scudder Ave. (at the West End rotary), Hyannis. www.westendhyannis.com. ℂ **508/ 775-7677.** Main courses $16–$40. Mon–Sat 5–10pm; Sun 11am–2pm and 5–10pm.

Moderate

Baxter's Boat House ★ SEAFOOD   For waterfront dining in Hyannis, you can't do much better than Baxter's, set on a pier on Hyannis Harbor. It's fun to sit out on the deck and watch the ferries, sailboats, fishing boats, and even a pirate cruise come and go from the harbor. The fare here is standard clam-shack cuisine, including fried fish with all the fixings. But you can't argue with success; they've been doing their thing here since 1957, when the Baxter family ran a fish market out of the building. There is a lively bar scene here on summer nights; live entertainment starts at 9:30pm.

177 Pleasant St. www.baxterscapecod.com. ℂ **508/775-4490.** Main courses $11–$25. Late May to early Sept daily 11am–9:30pm; call for off-season hours. Closed mid-Oct to early Apr.

emBargo ★★ NEW AMERICAN   The bar is where most of the action is here, but it also happens to have yummy and sophisticated food—delectables like pan-seared scallops over truffle Parmesan basmati, or baby-back ribs with a mango salsa. Come between 4:30 and 6pm, when there are half-price oysters and tapas. There's a lots of other nibble food on the menu, such as pizza, sushi, sliders, spring rolls, and tacos, prepared with style and pizzazz.

453 Main St. www.embargorestaurant.com. © **508/771-9700.** $13–$30. Mon–Thurs 4:30–9pm, Fri–Sun 11:30am–9pm.

Tumi Ceviche Bar & Ristorante ★★ PERUVIAN   The Cape's only Peruvian restaurant, Tumi features a unique cuisine influenced by Spanish, Japanese, Chinese, and Italian flavors. Specialties include are ceviche (raw fish marinated with lemon and spices and served cold); housemade pastas; and wood-burning grill steaks. Patrons can see the flames in the open kitchen. Many enjoy starting their meal here with a Pisco, a Peruvian alcoholic beverage that is an acquired taste.

592 Main St. (east of the West End rotary). www.tumiceviche.com. © **508/534-9289.** Main courses $11–$20. Daily 11:30am–9pm.

Inexpensive

Common Ground Cafe ★ AMERICAN   This deli, run by members of a Northern Vermont commune, serves wholesome soups, salads, and baked goods in what looks like a mysterious tree fort, with booths made out of carved-out trunks and seemingly tucked into the walls. The menu changes with the seasons, but favorites include tomato soup, tuna melt, and the turkey burrito. Smoothies are a specialty; a retail shop in the back sells natural soaps and similar products.

420 Main St. www.hyanniscommonground.com. © **508/778-8390.** Most items under $10. Mon–Thurs 10am–9pm; Fri 10am–3pm; Sun noon–9pm.

The Daily Paper ★ DINER   Sit at the counter on a swivel stool and chat with your neighbor or grab a booth or a table at this chef-owned and -operated diner. Serving good honest comfort food has been a winning formula (there's now a second Daily Paper just about a mile east at 546 Main St.). The menu has all the diner classics, plus some special offerings, such as lobster Benedict for breakfast and a warm ham-and-brie sandwich for lunch.

644 W. Main St. www.dailypapercapecod.com. © **508/790-8800.** Most items under $10. Mon–Sat 6am–2pm; Sun 7am–1pm.

Pizza Barbone ★★ PIZZA   The competition is over: The best pizza on the Cape is at this small shop on Main Street Hyannis. The Neapolitan wood-fired pizza oven, a 6,000-pound beauty made by third generation oven-makers, was imported from Italy complete with hand-painted glass tiles. The pizza it makes is sublime, a delicate thin crust topped with fresh, unusual ingredients like crushed potato with garlic cream and bacon; pistachio pesto; or the more traditional sweet sausage. The pasta, dressings, sauces, and gelato are all made in-house, and the restaurant even has a roof garden for the organic vegetables used in salads and on the pizzas. As for the flour, it's imported from Italy. The business started as a mobile pizza shop that turned up at parties, and thus the name, which means "vagabond" in Italian.

390 Main St. www.pizzabarbone.com. © **508/957-2377.** Pizzas $9–$14. Daily 11am–9pm.

In Osterville, 6 miles west of Hyannis center, there are two great take-out options. **Earthly Delights ★★** (ⓒ **508/420-2206**), at 15 W. Bay Rd., specializes in natural foods to go. There are different specials prepared every day, but expect to find delicious pizzas and quiches that use organic ingredients.

The family-owned market **Fancy's ★** (ⓒ **508/428-6954**), at 699 Main St., has a deli that's another great place to pick up a picnic lunch. Treat yourself to a panini. In nearby Centerville, **Lambert's Rainbow Fruit ★** (ⓒ **508/790-5954**), at 1000 W. Main St., has the best produce selection in the area, bar none.

Rendezvous Cafe & Creperie ★★★ CREPERIE   Rendezvous's signature dish, whether sweet or savory, is a buttery delight. You haven't lived until you've had a Portobello crepe with blue cheese and baby spinach. Live on the wild side and finish your meal with a wonderfully sweet bananas-Foster crepe. The menu also features hot and cold panini. Coffee is a specialty here, and all manner of cappuccinos made with fair-trade coffee are available. There are open-mic nights and other entertainments scheduled some evenings.

394 Main St. www.rendezvouscafehyannis.com. ⓒ **508/827-4449.** Most crepes and sandwiches $8–$10. Daily 8am–5pm.

YARMOUTH

Inaho ★ JAPANESE   For those who love Japanese food, this restaurant is usually a favorite. The quality of the fish is top-notch and the sushi chef is known as one of the Cape's best. This has been a staple on the local dining scene for years with a word-of-mouth following based on the high quality of the food and service. The atmosphere, with blond wood booths and Japanese screens, is serene and comfortable.

157 Rte. 6A, Yarmouth Port. ⓒ **508/362-5522.** Reservations recommended. Main courses $14–$28. June–Oct daily 5–9pm. Call for off-season hours.

Old Yarmouth Inn ★ NEW ENGLAND   This is the real deal, a stage-coach stop dating from 1686. Today ye olde atmosphere remains, and there's also good food. Burgers and pizzas and similar items are on the tavern menu. The regular dinner menu is more upscale (and more costly), with dishes like roasted panko-and-Parmesan-crusted haddock. Or roasted duck with vanilla bean, strawberry, and rhubarb compote. It's a good place to come off-season, when there's a fire crackling in the hearth.

223 Rte. 6A, Yarmouth Port. www.oldyarmouthinn.com. ⓒ **508/362-9962.** Reservations recommended. Main courses $11–$34. June–Oct Mon 4:30–9pm, Tues–Sat 11:30am–2:30pm and 4:30–9pm, Sun 10am–1pm and 4:30–9pm. Call for off-season hours.

Optimist Cafe ★ AMERICAN   Optimism can take many forms, but this bright-pink gingerbread house on the Old King's Highway can certainly make a claim to one of them. Captain Frederick Howes built this beauty in 1849; as one of the finest examples of Gothic Revival architecture in Yarmouth, it is listed on the National Historic Register. Yet it's a reasonably priced option, with breakfast served all day, an excellent range of lunch choices, and an elegant high tea. Though the menu has room for standards like omelets and sandwiches, what elevates it are dishes like curries and fish tacos.

134 Main St./Rte. 6A, Yarmouth Port. www.optimistcafe.com. ℂ **508/362-1024.** All items under $15. Daily 7:30am–3pm; call for off-season hours. From Rte. 6, take exit 7 (Willow St.) toward Rte. 6A and take a right on 6A.

Tugboats at Hyannis Marina ★ SEAFOOD   Those looking for a lunch overlooking Hyannis Harbor (though technically across the water in Yarmouth) will find this former sail loft an easy choice, informal enough for large parties and children. Large harborside decks provide great views of the comings and goings of boats and ferries. The menu is heavy on burgers, salads, and fried seafood—it's a good place to come if you are craving lobster with all the fixings. There is a kids' menu, too.

21 Arlington St., Yarmouth. www.tugboatscapecod.com. ℂ **508/775-6433.** Main courses $12–$29. Late May–early Sept daily 11:30am–9pm. Closed rest of year.

Mid-Cape Entertainment & Nightlife
PERFORMANCES, PLAYS, & CONCERTS
Cape Cod Melody Tent ★   Built as a summer theater in 1950, this billowy, blue big-top proved even better for variety shows. A nonprofit venture since 1990 (proceeds fund other cultural initiatives Cape-wide), the Melody Tent has hosted the major performers of the past half-century, from jazz greats to comedians, crooners to rockers. Every seat is a winner in this grand oval, only 20 banked aisles deep. Curtains open 8pm nightly from July to early September. 21 W. Main St. (West End rotary), Hyannis. www.melodytent.org. ℂ **508/775-5630.** Tickets $33–$111.

Cape Playhouse ★★   From the first performance at this summer theater ("The Guardsman," starring Basil Rathbone, 1927) to the years when soon-to-be Hollywood stars like Henry Fonda and Bette Davis plied the boards in summer stock, the Cape Playhouse has brought the quintessential summer theater experience to the area. The brainchild of Raymond Moore, a close friend of stage star Gertrude Lawrence, who moved an abandoned 1838 meetinghouse to the present spot off Route 6A, it's considered America's oldest professional summer theater. These days Broadway-caliber Equity actors perform in high-quality traveling shows, usually comedies and musicals. Shows run for about 2 weeks; there are usually six per summer. So many people order a season pass that most of the performances sell out, so plan ahead. 820 Rte. 6A, Dennis Village. www.capeplayhouse.com. ℂ **877/385-3911** or 508/385-3911. Tickets $20–$80; children's theater $12.

Cotuit Center for the Arts   Offering a rich variety of plays, musical performances, art exhibits, and cultural happenings, the Cotuit Center for the Arts, with consistently professional and sophisticated programming, has become a go-to place for those passionate about the arts. 4404 Rte. 28 (½ mile E of jct. rtes. 28 and 130), Cotuit. www.cotuitcenterforthearts.org. ℂ **508/428-0669.** Tickets $30–$35 adults, $2 off for seniors. Gallery Tues–Fri 10am–4pm; Sat 10am–2pm.

Children's Theater

On Wednesday mornings in summer, the **Cape Cod Melody Tent** (see above) offers children's theater productions. Tickets are $12.50 and can be ordered from the Melody Tent online at www.melodytent.org or by calling ✆ **508/775-5630**). On Friday mornings in season, the **Cape Playhouse**, at 820 Route 6A, in Dennis Village (www.capeplayhouse.com; ✆ **508/385-3911**), hosts various visiting companies that mount children's theater geared toward kids 4 and older; tickets ($12) go fast.

Arthouse Cinema

Cape Cinema ★★   The Cape's only year-round art-house theater is a treasure, and it doesn't hurt that it's inside a 1930s Art Deco building complete with a colorful ceiling mural by the artist and book illustrator Rockwell Kent. There is just one large screen, and seating is on black leather armchairs. The cinema was built by Raymond Moore, the same man who started the nearby Cape Playhouse (p. 228). 35 Hope Lane, Dennis Village. www.capecinema. com. ✆ **508/385-2503** or 508/385-5644. Tickets $8.50, seniors $6.50.

LIVE MUSIC

Harvest Gallery Wine Bar ★★   Harvest has become a major destination for the 30- to 60-year-old crowd looking for rootsy music on a Saturday night. The walls also serve as gallery space, brightening up the restaurant and bar areas. Music starts at 7:30pm. Good food too. 776 Main St./Rte. 28, Dennis Village (behind the post office). www.harvestgallerywinebar.com. ✆ **508/385-2444.** No cover.

O'Shea's Olde Inne ★★   At one of the Cape's best Irish venues, Celtic musicians can join the "seisiuns" on Sunday night, when musicians offering jigs, reels, and sing-alongs. On other nights, there's jazz, blues, folk, and even rockabilly. 348 Main St./Rte. 28, West Dennis. www.osheasoldeinne.com. ✆ **508/398-8887.** Cover varies.

Roadhouse Café ★   Duck into this dark-paneled bar, decorated like an English gentlemen's club in burgundy leather, if you're looking for sophisticated entertainment. The bistro area next to the bar has live jazz piano. Insiders know to show up Monday nights to hear local jazz great Lou Colombo. 488 South St., Hyannis. www.roadhousecafe.com. ✆ **508/775-2386.** No cover.

Sand Dollar Bar and Grill ★   Entertainment is 7 nights a week from April through October at this fun and lively venue for the younger crowds. Weekends feature a raw bar, and bands start playing at 4pm. 244 Lower County Rd., Dennisport. www.sanddollarbg.com. ✆ **508/398-4823.** Cover varies.

Sundancers ★   Dancing on the decks overlooking the Bass River is de rigueur at this club, which has been going strong for more than 30 years. Entertainment, from karaoke to '80s night to reggae, is on weekends until Memorial Day nightly during the summer season. 116 Main St./Rte. 28, West Dennis. www.sundancerscapecod.com. ✆ **508/394-1600.** Cover varies.

BARS

Trader Ed's This summer-only hangout at the Hyannis Marina attracts sailors, yachting types, fishermen, and other sea lovers. Besides the location on the harbor, there's also a large pool. On weekends a DJ spins tunes for dancing under the stars. 21 Arlington St., Hyannis. www.traderedsrestaurant.com. *☎* **508/790-8686.** No cover.

THE LOWER CAPE: BREWSTER, CHATHAM & ORLEANS

Brewster: 25 miles E of Sandwich; 32 miles SW of Provincetown. Chatham: 31 miles SE of Sandwich; 35 miles S of Provincetown. Orleans: 31 miles E of Sandwich; 26 miles SE of Provincetown.

With fewer year-rounders, this part of Cape Cod is more summer-oriented. It swings from upscale Brewster to even-more-chi-chi Chatham, a sort of Hamptons North. Orleans serves as a gateway to the Outer Cape (see p. 245).

VISITOR INFORMATION Local sources of tourist information include the **Brewster Chamber of Commerce Visitor Center** (2198 Main St./Route 6A, Brewster; www.brewster-capecod.com; *☎* **508/896-3500**), the **Chatham Chamber of Commerce,** 2377 Main St., South Chatham (www.chathaminfo. com; *☎* **800/715-5567** or 508/945-5199), with its booth at 533 Main St., at the intersection of routes 137 and 28; and the **Orleans Chamber of Commerce,** 44 Main St. (www.capecod-orleans.com; *☎* **508/255-1386**).

Exploring Brewster ★★

Miles of placid Cape Cod Bay beaches and acres of state park land make Brewster an attractive place for families. **Nickerson State Park ★★,** Route 6A and Crosby Lane (www.mass.gov/locations/nickerson-state-park; *☎* **508/896-3491**), is the legacy of a vast self-sustaining private estate that once generated its own electricity (with a horse-powered plant) and had its own golf course and game preserve; notable guests included President Grover Cleveland. Today it's a 1,955-acre nature preserve encompassing eight kettle ponds (stocked year-round with trout), 8 miles of bicycle paths, and 420 campsites (reservations pour in a year in advance to **Reserve America** at *☎* **877/422-6762,** which charges $35 for Massachusetts residents, $55 for out-of-staters).

Cape Cod Museum of Natural History ★★★ NATURE CENTER

One of the top attractions on the Cape, this museum and nature education center is an ideal place to bring the kids, rain or shine. Extensive trails on this 80-acre property make learning about the natural world as easy as taking a walk. Varied habitats include a salt marsh, a stretch of Bay beach between Quivett and Paine's creeks, and Wing's Island. The museum's collection, which covers two floors, includes exhibits about whales and birds and live marine exhibits. In aquariums are fish, eels, turtles, shellfish, and mollusks.

Other topics include archaeology, honeybees, sharks, and erosion. There are educational programs for adults and children as well as nature tours on- and off-site.

869 Rte. 6A. www.ccmnh.org. ℗ **508/896-3867.** $15 adults, $10 seniors, $6 kids 3–12. June–Aug daily 9:30am–4pm; Sept daily 11am–3pm; Apr–May and Oct–Dec Wed–Sun 11am–3pm. Closed Jan–Mar (open for special programs only) and major holidays.

Stony Brook Grist Mill and Museum ★ HISTORIC SITE There is perhaps no sight so welcome during a Cape Cod spring as that of the herring making their way up rivers to spawn in freshwater ponds. Watching the fish flip-flopping their way against the tide is nothing if not an analogy for the gumption needed to overcome life's trials. Most herring runs are deep in the woods, and if you don't know where they are, you won't find them. But Stony Brook, one of the Cape's most productive runs, is right off a main road and set up for visitors. Beginning around 1660, this site has over the years bustled with industry—a mill for grinding corn, a fulling mill, a woolen mill, a tannery, a cotton weaving mill, a carding mill, a paper mill—and nowadays inside the grist mill, a volunteer miller grinds corn into cornmeal that can be bought for $2. Upstairs in the mill, there are artifacts of Cape Cod in the 1800s, including an antique loom.

830 Stony Brook Rd. (at Satucket Rd.), West Brewster. www.brewster-ma.gov/stony-brook-grist-mill-museum. ℗ **508/896-9521.** Free admission. July–Aug Sat 10am–2pm. Closed Sept–June.

BREWSTER BEACHES

Brewster's lovely bay beaches have minimal facilities. When the tide is out, the "beach" enlarges to as much as 2 miles, leaving behind tide pools to splash in and explore, and vast stretches of rippled, reddish "garnet" sand. On a clear day, you can see the whole curve of the Cape, from Sandwich to Provincetown. You can purchase a beach parking sticker ($15 per day, $50 per week) at the **Brewster Visitor Center,** behind Brewster Town Hall, at 2198 Main St./Route 6A, a half-mile east of the General Store (℗ **508/896-3701**).

o **Breakwater Beach** ★★, off Breakwater Road: A brief walk from the center of town, this calm, shallow beach (the only one with restrooms) is ideal for young children. This was once a packet landing, where packet boats would unload tourists and load up produce—a system that became obsolete when the railroads came along.

o **Flax Pond** ★★, in Nickerson State Park (see p. 230): This large freshwater pond, surrounded by pines, has a bathhouse and watersports rentals.

o **Linnells Landing Beach** ★, Linnell Road, in East Brewster: This is a half-mile, wheelchair-accessible bay beach.

o **Paines Creek Beach** ★, off Paines Creek Road, West Brewster: With 1½ miles on which to stretch out, this bay beach has something to offer sun lovers and nature lovers alike. Your kids will love it if you arrive when the tide's coming in—the current will give an air mattress a nice little ride.

GOLF

One of the most challenging courses in the area is **Captain's Golf Course** at 1000 Freemans Way (www.captainsgolfcourse.com; © **508/896-1716**). In season a round at Captain's is $69 to $76, with discounted rates in the afternoon.

BREWSTER SHOPPING

Brewster's stretch of Route 6A has the best antiquing on the entire Cape. Diehards would do well to stop at every intriguing shop; you never know what you might find.

Clayton Calderwood's **Clayworks,** 3820 Main St./Route 6A, East Brewster (© **508/255-4937**), is always worth a stop, if only to marvel at the famous mammoth urns. There's also a world of functional bowls, pots, and lamps, in porcelain, stoneware, and terra cotta.

Collectors from around the world converge at **Sydenstricker Glass,** 490 Main St., Brewster (www.sydenstricker.com; © **508/385-3272**), in which a 1960s-era kiln-fired process uses concepts from the art of enameling to yield unique glassware, especially dishes and stemware.

Though quite a bit spiffier than a "real" general store, the **Brewster Store,** 1935 Main St./Route 6A (www.brewsterstore.com; © **508/896-3744**), an 1866 survivor that was fashioned from an 1852 Universalist church, is a fun place in the center of town to shop for sundries and catch up on local gossip. The wares are mostly tourist-oriented these days, but include some handy kitchen gear (cobalt glassware, for example) and beach paraphernalia. Give the kids a couple of dimes to feed the Nickelodeon piano machine, and relax on a sunny church pew out front as you pore over the local paper.

Exploring Chatham ★★★

Chatham (pronounced "Chatt-um") looks like small-town America the way Norman Rockwell imagined it. Roses climb white picket fences in front of shingled Cape cottages, all within a stone's throw of the ocean, and there's a winding Main Street filled with pleasing shops. Pretty as it is, Chatham is one of the Cape's fanciest towns—and priciest.

If Cape Cod looks like a flexed arm, then Chatham is its elbow, sticking out in the sea. Samuel de Champlain landed here in 1606; in 1656, William Nickerson of Yarmouth built the first house here, next to the wigwam of the local tribal leader. (You'll still see the name Nickerson all over town.) This is where Nantucket Sound turns into the Atlantic Ocean, and the fishing industry is still active. At the tip of the elbow stands a lighthouse.

Dangling south off the elbow lies Chatham's natural bonanza: The uninhabited **Monomoy Islands ★★**, 2,750 acres of brush-covered sand favored by some 285 species of birds migrating along the Atlantic Flyway. Harbor and gray seals are catching on, too: Hundreds now carpet the coastline from late November through May. If you go out during that time, you won't have any trouble seeing them—they're practically unavoidable. From Memorial Day to Columbus Day, **Outermost Adventures** (www.outermostharbor.com; © **508/ 945-5858**) runs boat shuttle service—basically water taxis—to North

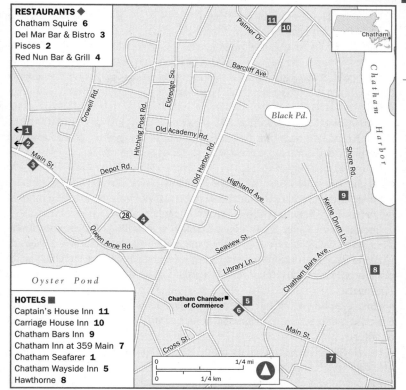

RESTAURANTS ◆
Chatham Squire **6**
Del Mar Bar & Bistro **3**
Pisces **2**
Red Nun Bar & Grill **4**

HOTELS ■
Captain's House Inn **11**
Carriage House Inn **10**
Chatham Bars Inn **9**
Chatham Inn at 359 Main **7**
Chatham Seafarer **1**
Chatham Wayside Inn **5**
Hawthorne **8**

Monomoy. The ride takes 10 minutes; once on the beach, passengers can walk for 2 minutes to the far side of the spit to see seals gathered along the coast. The shuttle runs every 20 minutes from 8am to 4:30pm; its costs $30 for adults, $25 for kids 12 and under. The boats leave from Outermost Harbor, just south of the lighthouse. Follow signs to Morris Island.

The *Beachcomber* ★★ (www.sealwatch.com; ✆ **508/945-5265**) runs **seal-watching cruises** out of Chatham Harbor from mid-May to late September daily in season, weekends in the shoulder seasons. Parking is on Crowell Road, at Chatham Boat Company, near the bakery. There are typically four cruises a day—at 10am, noon, 2pm, and 4pm—depending on the weather. The 90-minute cruises cost $34 for adults, $32 for seniors, and $28 for kids 3 to 15, and are free for children 2 and under. Where there are seals, there may also be their main predator, great white sharks. The large number of seals has attracted sharks in recent years, and passengers should stay alert for sightings.

CHATHAM BEACHES

Chatham has an unusual array of beach styles, from the peaceful shores of the Nantucket Sound to the treacherous, shifting shoals along the Atlantic. For information on beach stickers ($20 per day, $75 per week), call the **Permit Department,** at 283 George Ryder Rd. in West Chatham (📞 **508/945-5180**).

o **Chatham Lighthouse Beach ★★:** Directly below the lighthouse parking lot (where cars can only park for 30 min.), this narrow stretch of sand is easy to get to: Just walk down the stairs. Currents here can be tricky and swift, so swimming is discouraged. The beach has been closed occasionally over the past few years because of shark sightings in the harbor. Great white sharks are attracted to the area's large number of seals, their main source of food.

o **South Beach ★★:** A former island jutting out slightly to the south of the Chatham Light, this glorified sand bar can be dangerous, so heed posted warnings and content yourself with strolling or, at most, wading. A sticker is not required to park here.

o **Oyster Pond Beach ★,** off Route 28: Only a block from Chatham's Main Street, this sheltered saltwater pond (with restrooms) swarms with children. It's free to park here, and there is a lifeguard.

o **Cockle Cove Beach ★, Ridgevale Beach ★, Hardings Beach ★★:** Lined up along Nantucket Sound, each at the end of its namesake road, south of Route 28, these family-pleasing beaches offer gentle surf suitable for all ages, as well as full facilities, including lifeguards. Parking stickers are required.

o **Forest Beach ★:** With limited parking and no lifeguard, this Nantucket Sound landing near the Harwich border is still popular, especially among surfers.

o **North Beach ★★:** Extending all the way south from Orleans, this 5-mile barrier beach is accessible from Chatham only by boat; if you don't have your own, you can take the **Beachcomber,** a water taxi, which leaves from Chatham Fish Pier on Shore Road. Call 📞 **508/945-5265** (www.sealwatch.com) to schedule your trip, though reservations are not necessary. Round-trip costs $25 for adults, $12 for children 3 to 15. The water taxi makes the trip from 10am to 5pm daily in season on sunny days. Inquire about other possible drop-off points if you'd like to beach around.

CHATHAM SHOPPING

Chatham's tree-shaded Main Street, lined with specialty stores, offers a terrific opportunity to shop and stroll. The goods tend to be on the conservative side, but every so often, you'll happen upon a hedonistic delight.

BOOKS **Yellow Umbrella Books,** 501 Main St. (www.yellowumbrella books.net; 📞 **508/945-0144**), sells both new and used books, from rare volumes to paperbacks perfect for a beach read. This full-service, all-ages bookstore invites protracted browsing.

FASHION Catering to fashionable parents and their kids, ages newborn well into the teens, the **Children's Shop,** 515 Main St. (📞 **508/945-0234**), is the best children's clothing store in a 100-mile radius. While according a nod to doting grannies with such classics as hand-smocked party dresses, Ginny Nickerson also stays up-to-speed on what kids themselves prefer.

The flagship store of **Puritan Clothing Company** is at 573 Main St. (www.puritancapecod.com; ✆ **508/945-0326**). This venerable institution, with stores all over the Cape, carries a wide range of quality men's and women's wear, including Polo, Nautica, Eileen Fisher, and Teva, at good prices.

Exploring Orleans ★★

Orleans is where "the Narrow Land" (the early Algonquin name for the Cape) starts to get very narrow indeed. From here on up (or "down," as locals say) to Provincetown, the Cape is never more than a few miles wide from coast to coast. Unfortunately, that also means that Routes 6, 6A, and 28 converge here, continuing north as a single road called Route 6, which often creates a frustrating amount of traffic.

ORLEANS BEACHES

On the eastern side, you're dealing with the wild and whimsical Atlantic, which can be kittenish one day and tigerish the next. While storms may whip up surf you can actually ride, less confident swimmers should wait a few days until the turmoil and riptides subside. In any case, current conditions are clearly posted at the entrance, along with information regarding great white sharks, an increasing hazard in recent years. Weeklong parking permits ($75 for renters) may be obtained from **Town Hall,** at 19 School Rd., Orleans (✆ **508/240-3700**). Day-trippers who arrive early enough—before 10am on weekends in July and August—can pay at the gate (✆ **508/240-3780**).

○ **Nauset Beach ★★★,** in East Orleans (✆ **508/240-3780**): Stretching southward all the way past Chatham, this 10-mile-long barrier beach, which is part of the Cape Cod National Seashore but is managed by the town, has long been one of the Cape's gonzo beach scenes—good surf, big crowds, lots of young people. Full facilities, including a snack bar serving terrific fried fish, can be found within the 1,000-car parking lot; the in-season fee is $20 per car, which is also good for same-day parking at Skaket Beach (see below). Substantial waves make for good surfing in the special section reserved for that purpose, and boogie boards are ubiquitous.

○ **Crystal Lake ★,** off Monument Road, about ¾ mile south of Main Street: Parking—if you can find a space—is free, but there are no facilities.

○ **Pilgrim Lake ★,** off Monument Road, about 1 mile south of Main Street: A beach parking sticker is necessary for this small freshwater beach, which has lifeguards.

○ **Skaket Beach ★,** off Skaket Beach Road to the west of town: This peaceful bay beach is a better choice for families with young children. When the tide recedes (as much as 1 mile), little kids will enjoy splashing about in the tide pools left behind. Parking costs $20, and you'd better turn up early.

OUTDOOR ACTIVITIES

BOATING The **Goose Hummock Outdoor Center,** at 15 Route 6A, south of the rotary (www.goose.com; ⓒ **508/255-2620**), rents out canoes, kayaks, and more, and the northern half of Pleasant Bay is the place to use them; inquire about guided excursions. Canoe and kayak rentals are $35 to $45 per half day.

FISHING Fishing is allowed in Baker Pond, Pilgrim Lake, and Crystal Lake; the latter is a likely spot to reel in trout and perch. For details and a license, visit **Town Hall,** at 19 School Rd. (Post Office Square), in the center of Orleans (ⓒ **508/240-3700**, ext. 305), or **Goose Hummock** (see "Boating," above). Surf-casting—no license needed—is permitted on Nauset Beach South, off Beach Road. **Rock Harbor ★★**, a former packet landing on the bay (about 1¼ miles northwest of the town center), shelters New England's largest sportfishing fleet: some 18 boats at last count. One call (ⓒ **508/255-9757**) will get you information on them all. Or go look them over. Rock Harbor charter prices range from $600 for 4 hours to $800 for 8 hours. Individual prices are also available ($160 per person for 4 hours; $170 per person for 8 hours).

WATERSPORTS The **Pump House Surf Shop,** at 9 Cranberry Highway/Route 6A (www.pumphousesurf.com; ⓒ **508/240-2226**), rents and sells wet suits, body boards, and surfboards, while providing up-to-date reports on where to find the best waves. Surfboards rent for $20 to $30 a day. **Nauset Surf Shop,** at Jeremiah Square, Route 6A, at the rotary (www.nausetsports.com; ⓒ **508/255-4742**), also rents surfboards, boogie boards, skim boards, kayaks, and wet suits.

ORLEANS SHOPPING

Though shops are somewhat scattered, Orleans is full of great finds for browsers and grazers.

BOOKS In the Skaket Corners shopping center, on Route 6A, is a branch of the large retailer **Booksmith/Musicsmith** (ⓒ **508/255-4590**).

GIFTS Birders will go batty over **Bird Watcher's General Store,** 36 Route 6A, south of the rotary (www.birdwatchersgeneralstore.com; ⓒ **800/562-1512**). The brainchild of local aficionado Mike O'Connor, who'd like everyone to share his passion, it stocks virtually every bird-watching accessory under the sun, from basic binoculars to costly telescopes, modest birdhouses to bird-baths fit for a tiny Roman emperor; there's also a good selection of CDs and field guides.

Where to Stay on the Lower Cape
BREWSTER

Candleberry Inn ★ What a showpiece: This grand 1790 Georgian-style structure with its square-rigger design (two chimneys) is among the most regal sea captains' homes in town; it was once owned by the 19th-century author Horatio Alger. There are six rooms in the main house, all graciously decorated with antiques and heirlooms, and Oriental rugs over wide-pine floors. The two rooms in the Carriage House are more modern in style and afford a little extra privacy. Four rooms have working fireplaces. Another big plus for this property are its innkeepers, Stu and Charlotte Fyfe, real Cape Codders who can fill you in on what's where while providing some historical context.

1882 Main St./Rte. 6A. www.candleberryinn.com. ☎ **800/573-4769** or 508/896-3300. 8 units. Summer $159–$279 double; $235–$379 suite. Rates include full breakfast and afternoon tea. Children 10 and over welcome. **Amenities:** Wi-Fi (free).

Captain Freeman Inn ★★ Next to the beloved Brewster General Store, a short walk to two terrific restaurants, and down the street from Breakwater beach, the Captain Freeman Inn occupies an enviable spot in Brewster. Walking up to the inn, you might first notice the magnificent and welcoming wrap-around front porch. The large size of this B&B makes it feel more like a small inn. There are three levels of rooms, the highest having romantic touches like a fireplace and Jacuzzi tub. Breakfast is served on the screened-in porch overlooking the pool. The owners, Byron and Donna Cain, are consummate hosts who know their way around.

15 Breakwater Rd. (at the intersection of Main St./Rte. 6A). www.captainfreemaninn. com. ☎ **508/896-7481.** 10 units. Summer $235–$285 double. Rates include full breakfast and afternoon tea. **Amenities:** Wi-Fi (free).

Ocean Edge Resort & Club ★★ Ocean Edge is for those who like a full-service vacation: The 429-acre property has a private Cape Cod Bay beach, tennis, and an 18-hole golf course designed by Jack Nicklaus. At the resort's center is a 1912 mansion that now houses guest rooms and a restaurant and more casual pub. In the guestrooms, particular attention has been paid to their design, bedding, and bathrooms. The results are modern and fresh, with soothing shades of seafoam, coral, and wheat.

2907 Main St./Rte. 6A. www.oceanedge.com. ☎ **508/896-9000.** 335 units. Summer $255–$559 double; $600–$1,050/night or $2,400–$7,500/week 2- to 3-bedroom villa. $20–$40 resort fee per room per night. **Amenities:** 3 restaurants; fitness center; 18-hole golf course; 6 pools (2 indoor, 4 outdoor); private beach, babysitting; bike trail and bike rentals; children's program (ages 4–12); concierge; room service; 11 tennis courts; Wi-Fi (free).

Old Sea Pines Inn ★★ This inn still has charm and personality, perhaps left over from when it was the Sea Pines School of Charm and Personality for Young Women. A lot has changed since then, but the inn offers an old-fashioned Cape vacation. Guest rooms are spread among three buildings on the 3½-acre property. Bickford Hall, the main building, holds the smallest of the rooms on its second and third floor; they don't have TVs, perhaps because of their proximity. The two cottages have rooms that are more modern, with TVs. The cottages also have the family suites, where children under 8 are welcome. The inn is the site of a dinner theater in season.

2553 Main St./Rte. 6A. www.oldseapinesinn.com. ☎ **508/896-6114.** 24 units, 5 w/shared bath. Summer $89 double w/shared bath; $160–$175 double w/private bath; $210 suite. Rates include full breakfast and afternoon tea. Closed Nov–May. **Amenities:** Wi-Fi (free).

CHATHAM

Chatham's lodging choices are more expensive than those of neighboring towns because it's considered a chichi place to vacation. But for those allergic to fussy, fancy B&Bs and inns, Chatham has several good motel options. Practically across the street from the Chatham Bars Inn (see below), the 26-room **Hawthorne ★**, 196 Shore Rd. (www.thehawthorne.com; © **508/945-0372**), is a no-frills motel with one of the best locations in town: right on the water, with striking views of Chatham Harbor, Pleasant Bay, and the Atlantic Ocean. Rates are $360 for a double, more for an efficiency with kitchenette. It's closed mid-October to mid-May. The **Chatham Seafarer,** 2079 Main St. (www.chathamseafarer.com; © **800/786-2772** or 508/432-1739), is a lovely, personable, well-run motel with an outdoor pool, only about a half-mile from Ridgevale Beach. Rates are $219 to $229 double.

Captain's House Inn ★★★ The highest standards of hospitality have long set the 1839 Captain's House apart from the many other B&Bs in Chatham. The 2-acre property includes not just the grand captain's home but also the converted barn and stables now called the "Carriage House," with 5 units; the "Captain's Cottage," with 3 units; and the luxurious "Stables" building, also with 3 units. All the Stables rooms have fireplaces, and many have whirlpools.

369–377 Old Harbor Rd. www.captainshouseinn.com. © **800/315-0728** or 508/945-0127. 16 units. Summer $305–$390 double, $305–$450 suite. Rates include full breakfast and afternoon tea. Children 9 and under not allowed. **Amenities:** Exercise room; outdoor heated pool; room service; Wi-Fi (free).

Carriage House Inn ★★ Carriage House is a small but well-run newly renovated B&B in an 1890 house and converted horse stables. All the rooms—three in the main house, three in the carriage house—are cozy and decorated in a cheerful Cape Cod style. Room 6 is particularly nice, with a private entrance and outdoor sitting area. The inn is about a mile from downtown. Breakfast includes a hot entrée, such as upside-down apple French toast.

407 Old Harbor Rd. www.thecarriagehouseinn.com. © **800/355-8868** or 508/945-4688. 6 units. Summer $309–$369 double. Rates include full breakfast Children 9 and under not allowed. **Amenities:** Wi-Fi (free).

Chatham Bars Inn Resort & Spa ★★★ Generations of families return year after year here, because there is nothing else this grand on Cape Cod. The location couldn't be better: 25 acres overlooking a private beach and (just beyond a barrier beach) the Atlantic Ocean. Checking in is a treat, as you traverse the veranda and enter the grand lobby to the front desk, the same one used in 1913. Rooms are in the main building or spread in cottages throughout the grounds, many with water views. To save some money, consider a less expensive room with a garden view. There is so much to do here, you won't be spending much time in your room anyway. The list of amenities on site is daunting: restaurants, spa, pools, tennis, and even a 9-hole golf course next door. The inn is a short walk to charming Chatham center.

297 Shore Rd. (off Seaview St.). www.chathambarsinn.com. © **800/527-4884** or 508/945-0096. 205 units. Summer $735–$1,018 double; $1,000–$1,500 1-bedroom suite; $790–$2,625 2-bedroom suite. **Amenities:** 4 restaurants; babysitting; children's program (ages 4 and over); concierge; putting green, 9-hole public golf course; 2 pools; room service; fitness center; gym; 3 tennis courts; Wi-Fi (free).

Chatham Inn at 359 Main ★★ What's extra-nice about this newly renovated small inn is there is a wide choice of size of room, and the small fine-dining restaurant on site means you don't have to compete with the summer crowds in the center of town. It is down on the quiet end of Main Street, a short walk to both Lighthouse Beach and the center of Main Street. Many of the rooms have fireplaces and private balconies. The country breakfast is served in the dining room.

359 Main St. www.359main.com. © **800/332-4667** or 508/945-9232. 18 units. Summer $459–$649 double. Rates include full breakfast. **Amenities:** Restaurant; wine bar; Wi-Fi (free).

Chatham Wayside Inn ★★ Centrally located, this large hotel is popular with groups because of its size as well as its location. A former stagecoach stop, the inn has a completely modern interior. The rooms are comfortable and decorated in a somewhat generic style, though some have four-poster beds and fireplaces. The Wild Goose Tavern has a moderately priced menu with burgers, salads, pizza, and sandwiches.

512 Main St. www.waysideinn.com. © **800/242-8426** or 508/945-5550. 56 units. Summer $425–$495 double; $495–$595 suite. **Amenities:** Restaurant/bar; outdoor heated pool; Wi-Fi (free).

HARWICH

Wequassett Resort and Golf Club ★★★ A secluded, full-service resort, Wequassett has long been in the running for the title of top lodging on Cape Cod. Improvements in recent years have brought the number of restaurants to four, improved the kids' play area, added a lap pool, and increased the size of the beach on Pleasant Bay. The resort's guest rooms and suites, spread out in six buildings, are exceptionally comfortable and stylish—and at these prices, they should be. Rooms without bay views are cheaper but quite a bit less inviting. What guests are really paying for here are all the amenities. Besides the beach, the pools and the restaurants, there are four tennis courts and playing privileges at an exclusive nearby golf club (for $190 a round). The entire 27-acre property sits on a rise above the bay with eastward views beyond to the Atlantic Ocean. The inn's skiff is available to take guests out to North Beach (see p. 234) for a fee. Among the most special amenities here are the fine dining restaurant, **28 Atlantic,** and the **Outer Bar & Grill,** by the pool. Both are exceptional.

2173 Rte. 28 (about 5 mil NE of Chatham ctr., on Pleasant Bay). www.wequassett.com. © **800/225-7125** or 508/432-5400. 120 units. Summer $975 double. $15 per day resort charge. Closed Dec–Mar. **Amenities:** 4 restaurants; babysitting; bike rentals; children's program; concierge; fitness room; 2 heated outdoor pools; room service; 4 tennis courts, pro shop; watersports equipment/rentals; yoga and Pilates classes; Wi-Fi (free).

ORLEANS

The Cove ★   It's just a motel with nothing-fancy rooms, but the Cove has a great location. There is a heated pool and lots of places to sit to look out on adjacent Town Cove—picnic tables, a gazebo, a private dock, a firepit, not to mention decks off some rooms. Hardwood floors and beadboard paneling add a beach-cottage feel to the bland but soothing decor. Some rooms are suites and have kitchenettes.

13 S. Orleans Rd./Rte. 28. www.thecoveorleans.com. ☎ **800/343-2233** or 508/255-1203. 47 units. Summer $165–$195 double; $245 suite or efficiency. **Amenities:** Outdoor pool; grilling area; Wi-Fi (free).

A Little Inn on Pleasant Bay ★★   Part of the fun here are your hosts, two British sisters and the German husband of one of them. They have extensively renovated this 1798 house and two adjacent buildings into a very modern and comfortable B&B. The property is beautifully landscaped, with flowers everywhere, and it sits high up on a knoll with exquisite views of Pleasant Bay—very peaceful. The nine rooms are named after the kinds of boats you might see sailing by, such as Beetle Cat and Knockabout.

654 S. Orleans Rd. www.alittleinnonpleasantbay.com. ☎ **888/332-3351** or 508/255-0780. 9 units. $295–$380 double. Extra person $30/night. Rates include continental breakfast and evening sherry. No children under 10. Closed Oct–late May. **Amenities:** Wi-Fi (free).

Nauset House Inn ★★   This inn is a slice of old Cape Cod, a simple 1810 farmhouse that has been family-owned and -operated since 1982. The folksy rooms have hand-painted furniture, floral stencils, and trompe l'oeil walls. This is one of the few inns on the Cape that has some rooms with shared bathrooms; these are significantly less expensive in-season than anything else around. The main house has nine guest rooms, including six with shared baths. An outbuilding, the Carriage House, has larger rooms, and the standalone Outermost House, set in the apple orchard, is even more private. The inn is a short walk from Nauset Beach.

143 Beach Rd., East Orleans. www.nausethouseinn.com. ☎ **800/771-5508** or 508/255-2195. 14 units, 6 w/shared bath. Summer $99–$125 double w/shared bath; $145–$220 double w/private bath. Rates include full breakfast. Closed Nov–Mar. No children 12 and under. **Amenities:** Wi-Fi (free).

The Orleans Inn ★   This eye-catching Victorian mansion on Town Cove has quite a rich history. Captain Aaron Snow built it in 1875; it soon became known as "Aaron's Folly" because of its large size. Today's owners, the Maas family, have brought the inn back to its glory as a big part of the community. It is a popular function and wedding site. The restaurant and bar on the first floor are convenient for guests. A short walk across a parking lot brings guests to Goose Hummock (see p. 236), which rents kayaks for exploring the Cove. Rooms are simple but adequate, and half have Cove views.

3 Old Country Rd./Rte. 6A. www.orleansinn.com. ☎ **800/863-3039** or 508/255-2222. 11 units. Summer $250–$275 double; $375–$450 suite. Rates include full breakfast. Closed Jan to mid-Feb. Dogs allowed. **Amenities:** Restaurant/bar; Wi-Fi (free).

Where to Eat on the Lower Cape

BREWSTER

In a sweet little country gift shop, the **Hopkins House Bakery,** at 2727 Main St. in Brewster (📞 **508/896-3450**) sells standout hermit cookies (molasses, raisins, and nuts), as well as excellent breads and muffins. Its hours are limited, however: in July and August it's open only Thursdays through Sundays, 8am to 4pm, and in June and September it's weekends only.

The Brewster Fish House ★★ NEW AMERICAN If a restaurant's quality can be judged by how hard it is to get in, this one wins hands down. Patrons are so loyal to this lovely little restaurant in a cottage that they fill it night after night. The menu is very inventive—just when you think you have it figured out, you try something like Spanish octopus with pesto or scallop sashimi with watermelon. As you'd expect, this is an excellent place to order fish. Desserts are particularly good here, but there is no escaping the chocolate bread pudding.

2208 Main St./Rte. 6A, Brewster. www.brewsterfishhouse.com. 📞 **508/896-7867.** Main courses $23–$38. Reservations not accepted. May–Aug daily 11:30am–3pm and 5–9pm; call for off-season hours. Closed Dec–Apr.

Brewster Inn & Chowder House ★ SEAFOOD/AMERICAN Every town has its tavern, and this is Brewster's. It's friendly and homey, serving reasonably priced chowder, burgers, and fish several ways (baked, broiled, and, of course, fried). Next door is the **Woodshed,** a busy bar with bands most nights in season.

1993 Rte. 6A. www.brewsterchowderhouse.com. 📞 **508/896-7771.** Main courses $10–$25. Late May to mid-Oct daily 11:30am–3pm and 5–10pm; call for off-season hours.

Chillingsworth ★★★ FRENCH Two separate kitchens, two separate auras at this restaurant that's been a mainstay since 1976. One kitchen serves the fancy and formal main dining rooms, where guests can order a la carte or choose the five-course prix-fixe option. The other kitchen serves the more relaxed bistro area, where you can get away with a couple of appetizers and call it a night. In the dining rooms, dishes like the Creole lobster bisque starter and the main course of pesto rack of lamb with a goat cheese, fig, and herb brûlée are favorites. As for the bistro, there are lots of good choices, but the gnocchi with a mushroom-butter fondue and the pan-seared sea scallops both

Where Your Local Barista Knows Your Name

Snowy Owl Coffee Roasters, 2624 Main St. in Brewster (www.socoffee.co; 📞 **774/323-0605**), is an artsy gathering place in a repurposed barn. This friendly coffee house hosts open mic nights and a Sunday morning local music series from 11am to 1pm. Hours are Mondays to Fridays 6:30am to 5pm; Saturdays and Sundays 7:30am to 4pm. They also have a second location at 483 Main St. in Chatham.

stand out. House-made desserts are a specialty here, and you are wise to save room, however hard that may be. Three country-style rooms upstairs rent for $135 to $185 a night.

2449 Main St./Rte. 6A. www.chillingsworth.com. ℰ **508/896-3640.** 5-course fixed menu $68–$73; bistro main courses $21–$38. Mid-June to Aug Tues–Sat 6–9:30pm (Bistro opens 5pm). Call for off-season hours. Closed Dec to mid-May.

Cobie's ★ AMERICAN This roadside clam shack, in business since 1948, is a stone's throw from the Cape Cod Rail Trail (see p. 215). Pack a picnic or just grab a table and settle in with a steaming plate of fried clams and French fries or onion rings, Cape Cod style.

3260 Rte. 6A. www.cobies.com. ℰ **508/896-7021.** Main courses $5–$23. Late May–early Sept daily 11am–9pm. Closed early Sept–late May.

CHATHAM

Chatham Squire ★★ AMERICAN At some point, everyone in town ends up around the Squire's big bar. But don't be fooled into thinking a place this popular can't possibly serve good food. Besides the prize-winning chowder, the menu has dishes from much farther afield, including France (the sole), Asia (shrimp and chicken stir-fry), and Italy (cioppino—a fish stew).

487 Main St. www.thesquire.com. ℰ **508/945-0945.** Main courses $11–$32. May–Oct Mon–Sat 11:30am–10pm, Sun noon–10:30pm.

Del Mar Bar & Bistro ★★ BISTRO This cool nightspot specializes in modern bistro cuisine, such as wood-fired thin-crust pizzas and substantial steaks, like the 14-ounce rib-eye with mashed sweet potatoes and bourbon-soaked black cherries. Don't forget to check out the nightly blackboard specials, where you might find BLT pizza or the native fluke baked in parchment, with couscous flavored with dry apricots. There's a lively bar scene, with a young crowd sipping cocktails.

907 Main St. www.delmarbistro.com. ℰ **508/945-9988.** Main courses $15–$32. Daily 5–10pm.

Pisces ★★ NEW AMERICAN This small chef-owned spot has an unpretentious homey feel, even though there is sophisticated cooking going on in the kitchen. The meal begins with homemade rosemary focaccia for dipping in garlicky white bean spread. With a name like Pisces, you might as well stick to the fish. Start with calamari from Point Judith, Rhode Island, which is sautéed with garlic and Kalamata olives. For a substantial but special meal, try the Mediterranean fisherman's stew, which has cod and all manner of shellfish in a spicy lobster broth.

2653 Main St./Rte.28, South Chatham. www.piscesofchatham.com. ℰ **508/432-4600.** Reservations recommended. Main courses $18–$38. Tues–Sun 5–10pm.

Red Nun Bar & Grill DINER This is a real fisherman's bar. The small menu has a few choice items, mainly fried fish, soup, and salads: The fish tacos are great. The line forms around dinnertime here, so plan to arrive early if you want a bite before catching a Cape Cod Baseball League game at the field next door.

746 Main St. www.rednun.com. ☎ **508/348-0469.** Main courses $12–$20. May–Sept daily 11:30am–10pm; call for off-season hours. Closed Jan 15–Mar.

HARWICH

28 Atlantic ★★★ NEW AMERICAN The wow factor starts when you enter the dining room at 28 Atlantic to see a 180-degree view of Pleasant Bay through a wall of 8-foot-tall windows. Chandeliers, snow-white tablecloths, and fine china hint of the elegant experience to come. The menu is rich with delicacies, such as foie gras, that are served in a non-traditional way—with grilled watermelon and smoked maple syrup, for instance. A playful twist on tradition continues with the main courses, which might include butter-braised lobster with cashew curry, or duck breast with pistachio praline. With top-notch service to boot, it all adds up to a meal fit for a very special occasion. The dress code urges "smart casual" and prohibits jeans, T-shirts, or shorts. For casual dining, the **Outer Bar & Grill,** a hip bar overlooking the pool and the bay, is the perfect venue.

> ### A Life of Pie
>
> It all started in 1947, with Marion making chicken pot pies in her home. She built a bakery next door and was soon making fruit pies. Though Marion is no longer at the stove, **Marion's Pie Shop ★**, at 2022 Route 28 in Chatham (www.marionspieshopofchatham.com; ☎ **508/432-9439**) still churns out sublime sweet and savory pies using her special pastry crust recipe. It's open daily 8am to 6pm (closes at 4pm on Sundays).

2173 Rte. 28 (at the Wequassett Resort, see p. 239). www.wequassett.com. ☎ **508/430-3000.** Main courses $21–$44. May–Nov daily 7–11am, 5:30–10pm; call for off-season hours. Closed Dec to mid-Apr.

ORLEANS

The Hot Chocolate Sparrow ★★ Opened in 1994, this cafe provides specialty coffee drinks, desserts, and hand-dipped chocolates to a community that embraces every single espresso, smoothie, and caramel turtle. There are also free-range-egg sandwiches for breakfast and grilled sandwiches on focaccia for lunch. With the best community bulletin board in town, this is also a place to meet locals and find out what's going on.

5 Old Colony Way. www.hotchocolatesparrow.com. ☎ **508/240-2230.** Apr–Oct daily 6:30am–11pm; Nov–Mar Sun–Thurs 6:30am–9pm, Fri–Sat 6:30am–11pm.

Land Ho! ★★ AMERICAN John Murphy opened this pub, known as the Ho, in 1969, and it's been the social center of Orleans pretty much ever since. At this hangout, everyone feels welcome. It is always very busy, but the late-night service (serving food sometimes until 10pm) can be a godsend. Orleans business signs hang on every available space. Fried seafood, burgers, and salads are among the mainstays.

38 Rte. 6A (at Cove Rd.). www.land-ho.com/orleans. ☎ **508/255-5165.** Main courses $10–$25. Mon–Sat 11:30am–10pm; Sun noon–10pm.

Hoping to see the next Aaron Judge or Jackie Bradley, Jr. competing to win an MLB spot? The 10-team **Cape Cod Baseball League** (www.capecodbaseball.org; ⓒ 508/432-6909) is one of the country's top collegiate showcases. Running from July through August, games are free and fun to attend. The four Upper Cape teams are the **Brewster** **Whitecaps** (Stony Brook School, 384 Underpass Rd., Brewster), the **Harwich Mariners** (Whitehouse Field, 75 Oak St., Harwich), the **Chatham Anglers** (Veteran's Field, 702 Main St., Chatham), and the **Orleans Firebirds** (Eldredge Park, 78 Eldredge Park Way, Orleans). See p. 204 for Upper Cape teams; see p. 210 for Mid-Cape teams.

The Lobster Claw Restaurant ★ SEAFOOD   Your basic family fish shack, this big red barn of a restaurant has been at it for almost 50 years. You can get your seafood baked, broiled, or steamed, but most people get it fried. This is also a good place to get a full-fledged lobster clambake. No problem if the kids get too loud here; everyone else's are, too. So pick a picnic table and settle in. We're all family.

42 Rte. 6A. www.lobsterclaw.com. ⓒ **508/255-1800.** Main courses $12–$30. Apr–Oct daily 11:30am–9pm. Closed Nov–Mar.

The Yardarm ★ PUB GRUB   John Sully has been running this popular tavern since 1972. You can rub elbows with all manner of locals here: fishermen, lawyers from the Orleans courthouse, local politicians, and working people. The menu features the award-winning chowder, in addition to knockwurst, homemade fish cakes, and other tavern favorites.

48 Rte. www.the-yardarm.com. ⓒ **508/255-4840.** Main courses $9–$21. Daily 11:30am–3pm and 5:30–10pm.

Lower Cape Entertainment & Nightlife

Although most towns host some comparable event, Chatham's free **band concerts**—40 players strong—are arguably the best on the Cape and attract crowds in the thousands. This is small-town America at its most nostalgic, as the band, made up mostly of local folks, plays those standards of yesteryear that never go out of style. Held in **Kate Gould Park** (off Chatham Bars Ave., in the center of town) from July to early September, it kicks off at 8pm every Friday. Better come early to claim your square of lawn (it's already a checkerboard of blankets by late afternoon), and be prepared to sing—or dance—along. Call ⓒ **508/945-5199** for information.

THEATER

Summer theater is alive and well on the Lower Cape, with well-respected theater troupes in each of the three main towns. About 2½ miles east of Brewster center, the **Cape Cod Repertory Theatre** ★ (3299 Rte. 6A; www.caperep.org or www.theatermania.com; ⓒ **866/811-4111** or 508/896-1888), mounts performances Tuesday to Saturday nights at 7 or 8pm, as well as a

Sunday 2pm matinee, from early July to early September. Tickets are around $35. This shoestring troupe tackles the Bard, as well as serious contemporary fare, at an indoor theater as well as an outdoor theater on the old Crosby estate (now state-owned and undergoing restoration). On Tuesday and Thursday mornings at 10am they also offer plays for kids.

Chatham's entry is the **Monomoy Theatre** ★ (776 Route 28; www.monomoy theatre.org; ✆ **508/945-1589**), a small historic theater where a company combining college students and professional actors steals the show with eight productions a summer, mid-June to August. The schedule usually offers a well-balanced mix of comedies, classics, musicals, and a Shakespeare play or two. Not only do they perform Tuesday through Saturday at 8pm, they also have a 2pm matinee on Thursday. Tickets are $25 to $30.

Over in Orleans, **The Academy Playhouse,** 120 Main St. (www.apacape. org; ✆ **508/255-1963**), makes a fine platform for local talent in the form of musicals and drama, recitals, and poetry readings. The 162-seat arena-style stage is housed in the town's old town hall (built in 1873). Tickets are $24 to $28. July through August, there are generally shows Tuesday to Sunday at 8pm, as well as a children's theater series ($10 per ticket) on Friday and Saturday mornings. The Academy Playhouse hosts performances year-round; check the website for a schedule.

BARS & LIVE MUSIC

Hot local bands take the tiny stage seasonally at the **Woodshed,** at the Brewster Inn & Chowder House, 1993 Route 6A (✆ **508/896-7771**), a far cry from the glitzy discos on the southern shore. If your tastes run more to Raitt and Buffett than techno, you'll feel right at home in this dark, friendly dive. Cover charge $5.

In Orleans, **BNI** (✆ **508/255-0212**) is a big old barn of a bar that might as well be town hall: It's where you'll find all the locals exchanging juicy gossip and jokes. Live music ranges from jazz to rock to blues. There's never a cover. There's also often live music at **Land Ho!** (see p. 243), the best pub in Orleans. Performers are on the bill on Monday and Tuesday nights in season, and Thursday and Saturday off-season. There's usually no cover.

THE OUTER CAPE: WELLFLEET & PROVINCETOWN ★★★

Wellfleet: 42 miles NE of Sandwich; 14 miles S of Provincetown. Provincetown: 56 miles NE of Sandwich; 42 miles NE of Hyannis.

It's only on the Outer Cape that the landscape and even the air feel really beachy. You can smell the seashore just over the horizon—in fact, everywhere you go, because you're never more than a mile or two from sand and surf.

VISITOR INFORMATION The **Wellfleet Chamber of Commerce** (www. wellfleetchamber.com; ✆ **508/349-2510**) operates an information center off Route 6, open 9am to 6pm daily in summer; call for off-season hours. The

Provincetown Chamber of Commerce, 307 Commercial St. (www.ptown chamber.com; © **508/487-3424**), is open daily from 9am to 5pm in summer; call for off-season hours. The gay-oriented **Provincetown Business Guild** at 3 Freeman St. (www.ptown.org; © **508/487-2313**) is open Monday to Friday from 10am to 2pm.

Exploring Wellfleet ★★

With the well-tended look of a classic New England village, and surrounded by beaches, Wellfleet is the chosen destination for artists, writers, off-duty psychiatrists, and other contemplative types who hope to find more in the landscape than mere quaintness or rusticity. To this day, Wellfleet remains remarkably unspoiled. Once you leave Route 6 commercialism is kept to a minimum; the town boats plenty of appealing shops, distinguished galleries, and a couple of very good New American restaurants.

And where else could you find a thriving drive-in movie theater right next door to an outstanding nature preserve? The vintage **Wellfleet Drive-In** (51 State Highway/Route 6; www.wellfleetcinemas.com; © **508/349-7176**), built in 1957, shows double features of current first-run pictures nightly throughout the summer; there's a flea market, snack bar, mini-golf, and even indoor movie house on the same grounds. Adjoining it is the 937-acre **Wellfleet Bay Wildlife Sanctuary** (291 State Highway/Route 6; www.massaudubon.org; © **508/349-2615**), which has walking trails through saltmarshes and pine woods, teeming with fiddler crabs, green herons, and all sorts of other wildlife. It's open daily 8am to dusk; admission is $8 adults, $5 seniors, $3 kids ages 2 to 12.

WELLFLEET BEACHES

Dominating the beach scene in Wellfleet is the magnificent **Cape Cod National Seashore** (see box below). The town has several beaches, both within and outside of the Seashore—ocean beaches, bay beaches, and freshwater pond beaches. There's just one problem: Very few of them have parking for nonresidents. To visit them you'll have to walk or bike in, or see if you qualify for a sticker ($55 for 3 consecutive days, $90 per week). Bring proof of residency to the seasonal Beach Sticker Booth, on the Town Pier, or call the **Wellfleet Beach Sticker Office** (© **508/349-9818**). Parking is free at all beaches and ponds after 4pm.

- **Marconi Beach ★★**, off Marconi Beach Road, in South Wellfleet: A National Seashore property, this cliff-lined beach (with restrooms) charges an entry fee of $20 per day ($10 for motorcyclists; $3 for pedestrians/bicyclists), or $60 for the season. *Note:* The bluffs are so high that the beach lies in shadow by late afternoon.

- **Mayo Beach,** Kendrick Avenue (near the Town Pier): Right by the harbor, facing south, this warm, shallow bay beach (with restrooms) is very central; it will please young waders and splashers. This is one of the few beaches on the Cape with free parking. Make sure you go at high tide; at low tide,

CAPE COD NATIONAL seashore

No trip to Cape Cod would be complete without a visit to the **Cape Cod National Seashore,** on the Outer Cape, and a barefoot stroll along "The Great Beach," where you see exactly why the Cape has attracted so many artists and poets. On August 7, 1961, President John F. Kennedy signed a bill designating 27,000 acres in the 40 miles from Chatham to Provincetown as the Cape Cod National Seashore, a new national park. Perhaps surprisingly, the Seashore includes 500 private residences, the owners of which lease their land from the park service. Convincing residents that a National Seashore would be a good thing for Cape Cod was an arduous task back then, and Provincetown still grapples with Seashore officials over town land issues.

The Seashore's claim to fame is its spectacular beaches—in reality, one long beach—with dunes 50 to 150 feet high. This is the Atlantic Ocean, so the surf is rough (and cold), but a number of the beaches have lifeguards. Seashore beaches include **Marconi Beach,** in Wellfleet; **Head of the Meadow Beach,** in Truro; and Provincetown's **Race Point** and **Herring Cove beaches.** A $60 pass will get you into all of them for the season, or you can pay a daily rate of $20.

The Seashore also has a number of walking trails—all free, all picturesque, and all worth a trip. In Eastham, **Fort Hill** (off Route 6) has one of the best scenic views on Cape Cod and a popular boardwalk trail through a red-maple swamp. The **Nauset Marsh Trail** is accessed from the Salt Pond Visitor Center, on Route 6, in Eastham. **Great Island,** on the bay side in Wellfleet, is surely one of the finest places to have a picnic; you could spend the day hiking the trails. On **Pamet Trail,** off North Pamet Road, in Truro, hikers pass a decrepit old cranberry-bog building (restoration is in the works) on the way to a trail through the dunes. Don't try the old boardwalk trail over the bogs here; it has flooded and is no longer in use. The **Atlantic White Cedar Swamp Trail** is located at the Marconi Station site; **Small Swamp** and **Pilgrim Spring trails** are found at Pilgrim Heights Beach; and **Beech Forest Trail** is at Race Point, in Provincetown.

The best bike path on Cape Cod is the **Province Lands Trail,** 5 swooping and invigorating miles, at Race Point Beach. Race Point is also a popular spot for surf-casting, which is allowed from the ocean beaches.

Pick up a map at the Cape Cod National Seashore's **Salt Pond Visitor Center,** in Eastham (www.nps.gov/caco; ✆ **508/255-3421**). Another visitor center is at **Race Point.** Both centers have ranger activities, maps, gift shops, and restrooms. Seashore beaches are all off Route 6 and are clearly marked. Additional beaches along this stretch are run by individual towns, and you must have a sticker or pay a fee.

oyster farmers take over. You could grab a bite (and a paperback) at the Bookstore Restaurant across the street, which serves three meals a day and sells used books.

○ **White Crest & Cahoon Hollow beaches ★★★**, off Ocean View Drive, in Wellfleet: The town runs White Crest—big with surfers—which is open to all ($20 per day to park). As with all the oceanside beaches on the Outer Cape, large sand dunes border the beach, which is a wide-open and beautiful expanse. It has a snack bar and restrooms. Massive erosion in recent years has damaged Cahoon Hollow Beach's parking lot and now the parking is leased by the onsite restaurant/nightclub, **The Beachcomber** (see p. 252), which is located in the beach parking lot. Parking is free for those with a Wellfleet town sticker or a season pass to the Beachcomber. Others pay $20 to park, but that includes a $20 voucher for the restaurant. Grab lunch at the Beachcomber, spend time on the beach, and segue to an evening of live music and dancing.

OUTDOOR ACTIVITIES

BOATING **Jack's Boat Rental,** 2616 Route 6 (www.jacksboatrental.com; ✆ **508/349-9808**), rents out canoes, kayaks, surfboards, and Sunfish. Renting a kayak or canoe for the day costs $50. Sunfish sailboats are $230 for 3 days. Rentals come with a roof rack. Delivery within 20 miles is $20 each way. There are many wonderful places to canoe in Wellfleet—for example, a trip across the harbor from Wellfleet's Town Pier to Great Island.

WATERSPORTS Surfing is restricted to White Crest Beach, and sailboarding to Burton Baker Beach, at Indian Neck, during certain tide conditions; ask for a copy of the regulations at the Beach Sticker Booth on the Town Pier. **Eric Gustafson** (www.funseekers.org; ✆ **508/349-1429**) offers windsurfing instruction ($140 for 2 hours); surfing ($70 for 1 hour); and, for the most adventurous, kite-boarding lessons ($250 for 3 hours). He also teaches stand-up paddleboarding ($70 per hour) in the ocean and estuaries of Wellfleet.

WELLFLEET SHOPPING

ANTIQUES/COLLECTIBLES Wheeler-dealers should head for the **Wellfleet Flea Market,** part of the Wellfleet Drive-In campus at 51 Route 6, north of the Eastham-Wellfleet border (www.wellfleetcinemas.com/flea-market; ✆ **508/349-0541**). A few days a week in summer and during the shoulder seasons, the parking lot of the Wellfleet Drive-In Theater "daylights" as an outdoor bazaar with as many as 300 booths. Though a great many vendors stock discount surplus, there are usually enough collectibles dealers on hand to warrant a browse through. Summer hours are Wednesday, Thursday, Saturday, and Sunday from 8am to 3pm. Lookers are charged $2 to $3 per carload.

ARTS & CRAFTS One of the more distinguished galleries in town, the smallish **Cove Gallery,** at 15 Commercial St. (www.covegallery.com; ✆ **508/ 349-2530**)—located by Duck Creek, with a waterside sculpture garden—carries the paintings and prints of many well-known artists, including the late John

---

Make Way for Mini-Golf: Outer Cape Edition

No conceivable nocturnal treat beats an outing to the **Wellfleet Drive-In Theater**—unless it's by a game at the adjacent **Wellfleet Mini-Golf** while you're waiting for the sky to darken. A round costs just $5 for adults and $3.50 for kids; it's open daily 10am to 9pm. The restaurant on-site is the **Dairy Bar and Grill,** which specializes in fried seafood and is open from 11:30am to 10pm daily in season.

One of the last working farms in the Outer Cape, **Truro Vineyards of Cape Cod,** 11 Shore Rd./Route 6A, North Truro (www.trurovineyardsofcapecod. com; ✆ 508/487-6200) uncorked its first homegrown chardonnay and cabernet franc in the fall of 1996, and Muscadet and merlot soon followed. Inside the main house on this pastoral property, the living room, with its exposed beams, is decorated with interesting wine-related artifacts. From late May through October, wine tastings are every half hour at $10 per person. Free winery tours are offered at 1pm and 3pm. On the premises you'll also find the **South Hollow Spirits** distillery, offering 20 Boat Rum and Dry Line Gin. Distillery tours are at noon and 2pm. Events take place all summer with live music and high-end food truck vendors; check website for details. Open Monday to Saturday from 11am to 6pm, Sunday noon to 7pm.

Grillo, whose work delights with boldly painted tango-themed paintings, watercolors, and prints. It's closed mid-October through April.

Also by Duck Creek, the **Left Bank Gallery,** 25 Commercial St. (www. leftbankgallery.com; ✆ **508/349-9451**) is set inside a 1933 American Legion Hall that makes an optimal display space. Crafts make a stronger stand than art here; although the paintings occupying the former auditorium sometimes verge on hackneyed, the "Potter's Room" overlooking the cove is packed with sturdy, handsome, useful vessels, along with compatible textiles.

FASHION **Karol Richardson,** 11 W. Main St. (www.karolrichardson.com; ✆ **508/349-6378**), is owned and operated by its namesake, an alumna of the London College of Fashion and a refugee from the New York rag trade. She has a feel for sensual fabrics and a knack for lovely clothes that, in her own words, are "wonderfully comfortable but sophisticated at the same time and very flattering to the less-than-perfect body." It's closed mid-October through April.

GIFTS North of Wellfleet in the town of Truro, **Jules Besch Stationers,** 3 Great Hollow Rd. (www.julesbesch.com; ✆ **508/487-0395**), specializes in papers, ribbon, gift cards, handmade journals and albums, desktop pen sets, guest books, and unusual gift items. It's closed January through March.

Where to Stay in Wellfleet & Truro
TRURO
Hostelling International–Truro ★   By far the most scenic of the youth hostels on the Cape, this Hopperesque house on a lonely bluff a short stroll from Ballston Beach was once a Coast Guard station; these days it's used as an environmental-studies center in the winter. During the summer, it's a magnet for hikers, cyclists, and surfers.

111 N. Pamet Rd. www.capecod.hiusa.org. ✆ **508/349-3889.** 42 beds. $46 bed in dorm room; $139 private room. Closed early Sept–late June.

WELLFLEET

Even'tide ★★   This motel in a pine forest off Route 6 ranks as one of the best on the Cape by virtue of its location—on the Cape Rail Trail bike path and a short walk to Marconi Beach—and also its amenities, which include a large pool and loads of kid-friendly stuff on site. There is a basketball court, five-hole mini-golf, horseshoe pit, badminton, shuffleboard, and table tennis. All the motel rooms have mini-fridges and coffeemakers and HBO on the TV, so you are all set if the weather is rainy. In addition to the motel rooms, there are eight cottages and a four-bedroom house for rent on the property. Ask for a cottage with an outdoor shower; those are a real treat.

650 Rte. 6, South Wellfleet. www.eventidemotel.com. ℂ **800/368-0007** or 508/349-3410. 40 units. Summer $171–$242 double; $250–$388 efficiency. Closed Nov–early May. **Amenities:** Playground; heated indoor pool; Wi-Fi (free).

Surf Side Cottages ★★   For fans of mid-century Cape Cod style, these cottages have it in spades, simple, boxlike clapboard-sided units with big windows and roof decks. Even better is the location, just steps from the dunes near LeCount's Hollow beach in South Wellfleet. With kitchens, barbecues, and outdoor showers, these make the perfect base for a family vacation. Although it began as a cottage colony, the units are now individually owned condos, but they are still rented in much the same way and are, for the most part, only available by the week in season. The managers of the property also rent out about a dozen additional houses in the area.

Ocean View Dr. (at LeCount Hollow Rd.), South Wellfleet. www.surfsidecottages.com. ℂ **508/349-3959.** 18 cottages. Summer $1,300–$2,800 weekly; off-season $125–$250 per day. No credit cards. Closed Nov–Mar. Pets allowed in some cottages off-season. **Amenities:** Wi-Fi (some cottages).

Where to Eat in Wellfleet

EXPENSIVE

Mac's Shack ★ SEAFOOD   Run by two brothers, Mac and Alex Hay, this upscale restaurant in a mammoth 19th-century house serves updated classics, like their grandmother's cracker-crusted bluefish, or more experimental dishes, such as grilled oysters with absinthe and halibut in a saffron lobster broth. A sushi chef is on hand, and there's also a raw bar that's open 2 hours before the restaurant. This is a very popular place in the summer, and if you don't have reservations, you'll need to find a strategic off night to get in.

91 Commercial St. www.macsseafood.com. ℂ **508/349-6333.** Main courses $12–$39. Mid-June–early Sept daily 11:30am–10pm (raw bar 3–9:30pm); call for off-season hours. Closed mid-Oct to mid-May.

Pearl ★★ SEAFOOD   Pearl is a glorious harborfront restaurant serving fish, fried as well as grilled, baked, and sautéed. Ample multi-level outdoor decks allow unobstructed views of boats going in and out of Wellfleet Harbor. Another deck faces the marsh in the back of the building, and that is where live music is performed from 3 to 5pm daily in summer. Fresh fish cooked to order in the open kitchen is the thing here. The oysters on the half-shell, set up at the raw bar made from an old fishing boat, come from a shellfish area you can see from the upper deck of the restaurant. Lobster, steaks, chicken, and BBQ ribs are all popular menu items.

250 Commercial St. www.wellfleetpearl.com. © **508/349-2999.** Main courses $19–$34. Mid-May to mid-Oct daily 11:30am–9pm. Closed mid-Oct to mid-May.

The Wicked Oyster ★★ NEW AMERICAN   Housed in a big red weathered building from 1750, this sophisticated bistro is a dependable choice for breakfast, lunch, or dinner. The best seats are on the enclosed porch, where summer breezes come free. No surprise that the small but creative menu has a focus on seafood. There are those Wellfleet oysters, a seafood stew, and pan-fried sole. On the less expensive side, there are fish-and-chips and fried oysters, as well as burgers, including a veggie burger that is among the best around.

50 Main St. www.thewickedo.com. © **508/349-3455.** Main courses $11–$30. June–Aug daily 8am–2pm and 5–9:30pm; call for off-season hours. Closed Dec to mid-Jan.

Winslow's Tavern ★★ NEW AMERICAN   Winslow's is a fancier option in the center of town, located in an 1805 captain's house and former governor's mansion. Tables set out on the sloping lawn are the ideal places to sit on a pleasant summer day or night. The perfect appetizer would have to be Wellfleet oysters; they have them six ways. The beet salad is heaven. As for main courses, fish is a specialty, but there's also a very sophisticated crisp lamb belly dish with beluga lentils and pickled mustard.

316 Main St. www.winslowstavern.com. © **508/349-6450.** Main courses $16–$27. Late May–Aug daily noon–3pm and 5:30–10pm; call for off-season hours. Closed late Oct to mid-May.

MODERATE

The Lighthouse ★ AMERICAN   This is where to rub elbows with locals at the bar. Breakfast is your best bet here (the blueberry pancakes are keepers) but come early if you want a table. Thursday is Mexican Night, when the usual New England fare gets a spicy shake-up. The place rocks with live music on some summer evenings.

317 Main St. © **508/349-3681.** Main courses $10–$25. May–Oct daily 8am–9pm; call for off-season hours. Closed mid-Feb to mid-April.

INEXPENSIVE

Mac's on the Pier ★   This was the first restaurant for Wellfleet's Hay brothers, who have four fish markets and three restaurants (see Mac's Shack, p. 250). It is a no-fuss take-out clam shack, perfectly located on the Wellfleet pier. You order from the window and find a picnic table on the sand, steps from the lapping waters of the harbor. It is dining alfresco, Cape Cod style. The usual fried fish dinners are here, but there's also grilled tuna with summer vegetables, fish tacos, and even jambalaya. Ice cream, both soft-serve and hard, gets its own window.

265 Commercial St. www.macsseafood.com. © **508/349-9611.** Most items under $15. Mid-May to Sept daily 11am–7pm. Closed Oct to mid-May.

Moby Dick's Restaurant ★ SEAFOOD   The first codfish sandwich was made here in 1983, and it's been hopping ever since at this popular and family-friendly fish shack. Lines go out the door around dinnertime in the summer, so try to visit before 5pm or after 8pm. And if you see a full parking lot, keep on driving. The restaurant is set up for counter service. The way it works is you stand in line to place your order, then you find a seat among the picnic tables and a waitress brings your order when it is ready. Good grub. The restaurant is BYOB.

3225 Rte. 6. www.mobydicksrestaurant.com. ✆ **508/349-9795.** Main courses $8–$20. May to mid-Oct daily 11:30am–9:30pm.

Wellfleet Entertainment & Nightlife

THEATER

The principals behind the **Wellfleet Harbor Actors' Theatre (WHAT),** 2357 Route 6 (next to the post office; www.what.org; ✆ **508/349-9428**), aim to provoke—and usually succeed, even amid this very sophisticated, seen-it-all summer colony. The company goes to great lengths to secure original work, some local and some by playwrights of considerable renown, with the result that the repertory rarely suffers a dull moment. The sublime theater experience offered by **Harbor Stage Company**, 15 Kendrick Ave. (www.harborstage.org; ✆ **508/514-1763**) comes in part from its intimate home in a harborfront building. This professional troupe performs three shows a summer—expect excellent thought-provoking theater.

NIGHTLIFE

On Cahoon's Hollow Beach, **The Beachcomber** ★★ (1120 Old Cahoon Hollow Rd.; www.thebeachcomber.com; ✆ **508/349-6055**) is the only nightclub on Cape Cod with an Atlantic Ocean view. Built as a lifesaving station in 1897, since 1978 this been THE dance club for those in the know on the Cape. The club also serves lunch and dinner, and the food is surprisingly good, with fish tacos a standby; frozen drinks and a great selection of draft beer complete the picture. As for the music, the acts have been mostly the same for years; cover charges range from $10 to $25. The Beachcomber now controls the Cahoon's Hollow Beach parking lot; parking costs $20, but includes a $20 voucher for a meal at the restaurant. (After 5pm parking is free.) It's open daily from late June to early September, noon to 1am. The Beachcomber also runs the **free Funk Bus,** to shuttle restaurant patrons and beachgoers from the nearby White Crest Beach parking lot to and from Cahoon's Beach daily in the summer from 11am to 6pm.

Exploring Provincetown

You've made it all the way to the end of Cape, to one of the most interesting spots on the eastern seaboard. Explorer Bartholomew Gosnold must have felt much the same thrill in 1602, when he and his crew happened upon a "great stoare of codfysshes" here. The Pilgrims, of course, were overjoyed when they slogged into the harbor 18 years later. And Charles Hawthorne, the painter who "discovered" this near-derelict fishing town in the late 1890s and introduced it to the Greenwich Village intelligentsia, was besotted by this "jumble of color in the intense sunlight accentuated by the brilliant blue of the harbor."

While at times it can feel like a commercial circus, the whole town is dedicated to creative expression, both visual and verbal, and a prevailing atmosphere of open-mindedness. That may account for Provincetown's ascendancy as a gay and lesbian resort. In peak season, the streets are a celebration of the individual's freedom to be as "out" as imagination allows. But the street life also includes families, art lovers, and gourmands. In short, Provincetown has something for just about everyone.

If you plan to spend your entire vacation in Provincetown, you don't need a car, because everything is within walking or biking distance. And because parking is a hassle in this tiny town, consider leaving your car at home and taking a boat from Boston (see p. 182).

Once you're settled, you can enjoy the vintage fleet of the **Mercedes Cab Company** (www.mercedescab.com; © **508/487-3333**). They charge only $8 per person to take passengers from MacMillan Pier to just about anywhere in town. Provincetown is such a funky place that it seems perfectly ordinary to use **Ptown Pedicabs** (www.ptownpedicabs.com; © **508/487-0660**), "chariots for hire," for your transportation needs. These cheerful bikers will ferry you up and down Commercial Street for whatever you want to pay. That's right: You pay what you think the ride was worth. If you need to get from a gallery opening in the East End to dinner in the West End, this is the best way to do it.

Pilgrim Monument & Provincetown Museum ★★ LANDMARK/MUSEUM

The tallest all-granite structure in the country, the 252-foot Pilgrim Monument is the town's way of reminding everyone that the Pilgrims arrived here first. (Take that, Plymouth.) A climb to the top is a must—from that height, you can appreciate the curl of the Cape's arm and how the Cape's tip is essentially a sandbar, between Cape Cod Bay and the Atlantic Ocean. The museum at the foot of the monument contains a variety of colorful exhibits. Is that a polar bear over there? Yes, because Admiral Donald Macmillan, the first to the North Pole, was raised in Provincetown. There are playbills from the Provincetown Players, a group that had Eugene O'Neill as a member, and even a replica dune shack, of the type lived in by Harry Kemp, who was called "the poet of the dunes."

High Pole Hill Rd. (off Winslow St., north of Bradford St.). www.pilgrim-monument.org. © **508/487-1310.** $12 adults, $10 seniors, $4 kids 4–14. July to mid-Sept daily 9am–7pm; off-season daily 9am–5pm. Last admission 45 min. before closing. Closed Dec–Mar.

Provincetown Art Association & Museum ★★★ MUSEUM

In 1914, a group of Provincetown artists and businesspeople who supported the arts came together to build a collection of works by Outer Cape artists. Now, a century after that first group gathered, PAAM has collected 3,000 works and morphed into a pillar of the community, with exhibitions, lectures, workshops and cultural events. The contemporary wing, built onto an old captain's house

The Outer Cape: Wellfleet & Provincetown

CAPE COD

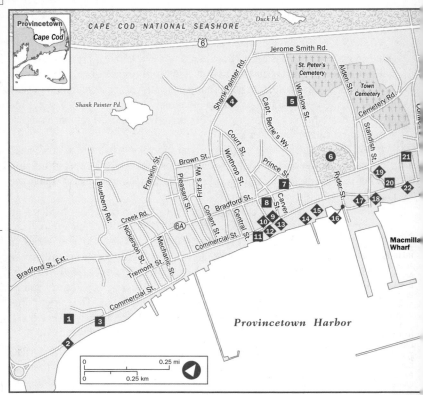

in 2006, has given the museum more space for exhibits and classes, not to mention an air of contemporary sophistication.

460 Commercial St. (in the East End). www.paam.org. © **508/487-1750.** $10; free for kids 12 and under. July–Aug Mon–Thurs 11am–8pm, Fri 11am–10pm (free 5–10pm), Sat–Sun 11am–5pm; call for off-season hours.

ORGANIZED TOURS

Art's Dune Tours ★★   In 1946, Art Costa started driving sightseers out to ogle the decrepit "dune shacks," where such transient luminaries as Eugene O'Neill, Jack Kerouac, and Jackson Pollock found their respective muses; in one such hovel, Tennessee Williams cooked up *A Streetcar Named Desire.* The park service wanted to raze these eyesores, but luckily, saner heads prevailed: They're now National Historic Landmarks. The tours conducted by Art's son and others, via Chevy Suburban, typically take about 1 to 1½ hours and are filled with wonderful stories of local literati and other characters.

Meet at the corner of Commercial and Standish sts. www.artsdunetours.com. © **800/894-1951** or 508/487-1950. 1-hr. tour costs $32 adults, $20 children 6–11; sunset tours (2 hr.) $49 adults, $27 children. Call for schedule and reservations.

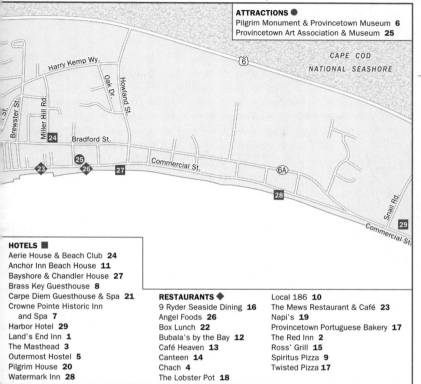

ATTRACTIONS ●
Pilgrim Monument & Provincetown Museum **6**
Provincetown Art Association & Museum **25**

Harry Kemp Wy.

Oak Dr.

Howland St.

Brewster St.

Miller Hill Rd.

24 Bradford St.

25
26 **27**

Commercial St.

23

CAPE COD
NATIONAL SEASHORE

6

6A

28

29

Snail Rd.

Commercial St.

HOTELS ■
Aerie House & Beach Club **24**
Anchor Inn Beach House **11**
Bayshore & Chandler House **27**
Brass Key Guesthouse **8**
Carpe Diem Guesthouse & Spa **21**
Crowne Pointe Historic Inn
  and Spa **7**
Harbor Hotel **29**
Land's End Inn **1**
The Masthead **3**
Outermost Hostel **5**
Pilgrim House **20**
Watermark Inn **28**

RESTAURANTS ◆
9 Ryder Seaside Dining **16**
Angel Foods **26**
Box Lunch **22**
Bubala's by the Bay **12**
Café Heaven **13**
Canteen **14**
Chach **4**
The Lobster Pot **18**

Local 186 **10**
The Mews Restaurant & Café **23**
Napi's **19**
Provincetown Portuguese Bakery **17**
The Red Inn **2**
Ross' Grill **15**
Spiritus Pizza **9**
Twisted Pizza **17**

Bay Lady II ★★ In sightseeing aboard this 73-foot reproduction gaff-rigged Grand Banks schooner, you'll actually add to the scenery for onlookers on shore. The sunset trip is especially spectacular.

Leaves from MacMillan Wharf. www.sailcapecod.com. ✆ **508/487-9308.** 2-hr. sail costs $34–$38 adults, $20 kids 12 and under. Mid-May to mid-Oct daily at 10am, 12:30pm, 3:30pm, and 7pm; call for reservations. Closed mid-Oct to mid-May.

PROVINCETOWN BEACHES

Provincetown has miles of beaches. The 3-mile bay beach that lines the harbor, though certainly swimmable, is not all that inviting compared to the magnificent ocean beaches overseen by the National Seashore. The two official access areas (see below) tend to be crowded; however, you can always find a less densely populated stretch if you're willing to hike.

Note: Local beachgoer activists have been lobbying for "clothing-optional" beaches for years, but the rangers, fearful of voyeurs trampling the dune grass, are firmly opposed and routinely issue tickets, so stand forewarned (and clothed).

whale-watching: A PRIME P-TOWN PASTIME

In 1975, 4 years after the U.S. government—fearing the species' extinction—called an official halt to whaling, fisherman Al Avellar noticed that they seemed to be making a comeback in the Stellwagen Bank feeding area, 8 miles off Provincetown. Together with marine biologist Charles "Stormy" Mayo of the Center for Coastal Studies, he came up with the notion of a new kind of hunt, spearheaded by tourists bearing cameras. An immediate success, the **Dolphin Fleet/Portuguese Princess ★★**, (www.whalewatch.com; *©* **800/826-9300** or 508/240-3636), was widely copied up and down the coast. Prices for whale-watching trips are $52 for adults, $31 for children 5 to 12, and free for children 4 and under. Discounts of $3 off are available for AAA members; coupons are also available at the chamber of commerce. Boats depart from MacMillan Wharf. See p. 211 for information on whale-watching trips out of Barnstable harbor.

On most cruises, running commentary is provided by naturalists with various qualifications. (The naturalists aboard the *Portuguese Princess* are Center for

Coastal Studies scientists who do research crucial to the whales' survival, and some of the proceeds go to the center's efforts.) Because these waters are still the whales' prime feeding grounds, all the whale-watching fleets can confidently "guarantee" sightings—they offer a rain check should the cetaceans fail to surface. Serious whale aficionados can take a daylong trip to the Great South Channel, where humpbacks and finbacks are likely to be found by the dozen.

Some tips for first-timers: Dress very warmly, in layers (it's cold out on the water), and definitely take along a windbreaker, waterproof if possible. The weather is capricious, and if you stand in the bow of the boat, the best viewing point, you can count on getting drenched. Veteran whale-watchers know to bring a spare set of dry clothes, as well as binoculars—although if the whales seem to be feeling friendly and frisky, as they often are, they'll play practically within reach of the boat. And last but not least, if you're prone to seasickness, bring along some motion-sickness pills: It can get pretty rough out there.

- **Herring Cove ★★★ & Race Point ★★★:** Both National Seashore beaches are spectacular, with long stretches of pristine sand, and they are very popular. Herring Cove, facing west, is known for its spectacular sunsets; observers often applaud. Race Point, on the ocean side, is rougher, and you might actually spot whales en route to Stellwagen Bank. Calmer Herring Cove is a haven for same-sex couples. Parking costs $20 per day, $60 per season.

- **Long Point ★:** Trek out over the breakwater and beyond by catching a water shuttle to visit this very last spit of land, capped by an 1827 lighthouse. Locals call it "the end of the earth." Shuttles run hourly from 9am to 5pm in July and August—$10 one-way, $15 round-trip; hourly in season, or by demand off-season—from Flyer's Boat Rental (see "Boating," below), located at slip 2 on MacMillan Wharf (*©* **508/487-0898**).

OUTDOOR ACTIVITIES

BICYCLING   North of town, nestled amid the Cape Cod National Seashore preserve, is one of the more spectacular bike paths in New England, the 7-mile

Province Lands Trail ★★, a heady swirl of steep dunes (watch out for sand drifts on the path) anchored by wind-stunted scrub pines. With its free parking, the **Province Lands Visitor Center** ★ (www.nps.gov/caco; ☎ **508/487-1256**) is a good place to start: You can survey the landscape from the observation tower to try to get your bearings before setting off amid the dizzying maze. Signs point to spur paths leading to Race Point or Herring Cove beaches.

The most centrally located bike rental store is **Arnold's Where You Rent The Bikes** (☎ **508/487-0844**), at 329 Commercial St., near MacMillan Wharf. Bike rentals are also offered May through October at **Gale Force Bikes,** at 144 Bradford St. (www.galeforcebikes.com; ☎ **508/487-4849**), in the West End. The Province Lands Trail begins nearby. (The Beach Market, on-site at Gale Force Bikes, offers delicious sandwiches and wraps and other picnic fare for your ride.) There's also **Ptown Bikes,** at 42 Bradford St. (www.ptown bikes.com; ☎ **508/487-8735**), where you should reserve several days in advance during high season. Bike rentals cost $22 to $25 for 24 hours.

BOATING   In addition to operating a Long Point shuttle from its own dock (see "Beaches," p. 256), **Flyer's Boat Rental,** at 131A Commercial St. in the West End (www.flyersboats.com; ☎ **508/487-0898**)—established in 1945—offers all sorts of crafts, from kayaks ($30–$50 half-day for singles and tandems) to various sailboats ($60–$90 for a half-day).

PROVINCETOWN SHOPPING

ART GALLERIES   Berta Walker is a force to be reckoned with, having nurtured many top artists through her association with the Fine Arts Work Center before opening her own gallery in 1990. At **Berta Walker Gallery,** 208 Bradford St., in the East End (www.bertawalker.com; ☎ **508/487-6411**), the historic holdings span Charles Hawthorne, Milton Avery, and Robert Motherwell. Closed late October to late May.

The **Fine Arts Works Center** displays weekly shows that are always worth checking out in its Hudson D. Walker Gallery at 24 Pearl St., in the center of town (www.fawc.org; ☎ **508/487-9960**). The center is the heart of creativity in town, supporting a crew of creative artists and writers on fellowships in residence every year.

Julie Heller started collecting early P-town paintings as a child—and as a tourist at that. She chose so incredibly well that her roster at **Julie Heller Gallery** ★★, 2 Gosnold St., on the beach in the center of town (☎ **508/487-2166**), and at 465 Commercial St. (www.juliehellergallery.com; ☎ **508/487-2169**), reads like a who's who of local art. Hawthorne, Avery, Hofmann, Lazzell, Hensche—all the big names from Provincetown's past are here, as well as some contemporary artists. Closed weekdays January to April. Open winter weekends by chance or appointment.

At the far east end of town, a former church building houses one of the town's top galleries, **Schoolhouse Gallery** ★, 494 Commercial St. at Howland Street (www.schoolhouseprovincetown.com; ☎ **508/487-4800**), which specializes in modern and contemporary painting, photography, and printmaking.

BOOKS   **Provincetown Bookshop,** 246 Commercial St. (© **508/487-0964**), has the most complete selection in town. You'll find all the bestsellers, as well as books about the region and local lore.

DISCOUNT SHOPPING   **Marine Specialties** ★, 235 Commercial St., in the center of town (www.marspec.net; © **508/487-1730**), is packed with useful stuff, from discounted Doc Martens to Swiss Army knives and all sorts of odd nautical surplus whose uses will suggest themselves to you eventually. Be sure to look up: Hanging from the ceiling are some real antiques, including several carillons' worth of ships' bells.

Where to Stay in Provincetown

For last-minute availability, check out www.ptown.org to see a list of all available rooms in town.

EXPENSIVE

Anchor Inn Beach House ★★

This inn is in a historic waterfront house that's closer to the west end of town, not right in the middle of things but a 2-minute walk to the center. Decor in the rooms varies, from cottage-style, with wicker, to handmade furniture from the West Indies and classic English chintz. The suites have 2-person whirlpool tubs and balconies overlooking the harbor. The waterview rooms are more expensive and worth the price.

175 Commercial St. www.anchorinnbeachhouse.com. © **800/858-2657** or 508/487-0432. 23 units. Summer $275–$415 double. Rates include continental breakfast. **Amenities:** Wi-Fi (free).

Brass Key Guesthouse ★★★

This was the first hotel to bring luxury lodging to Provincetown, and it remains one of the top inns in town. The property consists of a number of historic homes, including the 1790s main inn building, that have been converted into hotel rooms. Rooms are spread out in 10 buildings, including three small cottages that have just one unit apiece. Just as the buildings in the compound are of different architectural styles, the rooms are all different, but the common denominator is comfort. From the beds to the seating areas to the amenities, every need has been anticipated. There are two dog-friendly rooms ($40 per day).

67 Bradford St. www.brasskey.com. © **800/842-9858** or 508/487-9005. 43 units. Summer $419–$579 double, $499–$729 suites. Rates include continental breakfast and afternoon wine-and-cheese hour. Closed Jan–Mar. No children 18 and under. **Amenities:** Bar; hot tub; outdoor heated pool; Wi-Fi (free).

Carpe Diem Guesthouse & Spa ★★★

The owners of this first-class inn in the heart of Provincetown are continually upgrading and improving. The 2006 addition of a second house to the property allowed the creation of a Zen garden between the two buildings. In 2007, the Namaste Spa, offering massage, aromatherapy, and wraps, opened. In 2013, the inn expanded again with a large yoga and meditation room. In the morning, the inn serves a

German-style breakfast (the home country of the owners), complete with eggs cooked to order, Belgian waffles, and quiche.

12–14 Johnson St. www.carpediemguesthouse.com. © **800/487-0132** or 508/487-4242. 19 units. Summer $299–$499 double; $449–$459 suites; $529 cottage. Rates include full breakfast and wine-and-cheese hour. **Amenities:** Spa; 6-person hot tub; Wi-Fi (free).

Crowne Pointe Historic Inn and Spa ★★

Located on Bradford Street, a block from the Commercial Street hub, this historic sea captain's house, restored and expanded, has been turned into a luxury hotel with a fine restaurant and a spa. Six buildings make up the compound; although all the rooms differ in size, and some have fireplaces and whirlpool tubs, they all have very comfortable beds with high-end linens. The decor is modern, with muted colors. There's one dog-friendly room.

82 Bradford St. www.crownepointe.com. © **877/CROWNE1** (276-9631) or 508/487-6767. 35 units. Summer $369–$439 double, $579–$739 suites. Rates include full breakfast, afternoon tea and cookies, and wine-and-cheese hour. No children under 16. **Amenities:** Restaurant (dinner only); bar; 2 outdoor Jacuzzis; heated outdoor pool; spa; Wi-Fi (free).

Land's End Inn ★★★

Probably the most unique property in a town of unique properties, this house was originally built as a bungalow in 1904, high up on Gull Hill, which is on the far west end of Commercial Street. Subsequent owners turned it into a guest house and later an over-the-top valentine to Victoriana that straddled the line, and sometimes crossed over, into kitsch. The decor style has been upgraded and toned down, but some Victoriana remains. The tower rooms (there are three), which have 360-degree views of the Cape's tip, are perhaps the most exceptional rooms on the Cape. It is a long walk into town from here. Consider renting a bike if you plan to make the trek often. Dogs are allowed in seven rooms.

22 Commercial St. (in the West End). www.landsendinn.com. © **800/276-7088** or 508/487-0706. 18 units. Summer $360–$590 double; $460–$570 tower rooms. Rates include continental breakfast and wine-and-cheese hour. **Amenities:** Wi-Fi (free).

Watermark Inn ★★

It is often hard to get a reservation at the Watermark in season, because those who discover it go back year after year. It is a find. The inn sits directly on the sand, the water sometimes lapping up to the stairs from your unit down to the beach. The interiors are light, breezy, and modern. Each unit is a suite with a kitchenette and a private deck. A couple of the suites do not face the water—you want one that does.

603 Commercial St. (in the East End). www.watermark-inn.com. © **508/487-0165.** 10 units. Summer $240–$560 suite; weekly $1,530–$3,580. **Amenities:** Wi-Fi (free).

MODERATE

Aerie House & Beach Club ★★

There is a lot of variety in the rooms here, which are decorated in a beachy contemporary style. Those in the house on Bradford Street are less expensive and include rooms with shared baths. The four deluxe rooms at the Beach Club property at 425 Commercial St. are steps from the beach and have waterfront decks. There are also suites and efficiencies for those who prefer to have a kitchenette. In season, the inn provides a fleet of bicycles for guests.

184 Bradford St. (in the East End). www.aeriehouse.com. ℂ **800/487-1197** or 508/487-1197. 11 units, 3 with shared bathroom. Summer $190 double w/shared bath; $190–$395 double. Well-behaved dogs allowed with prior permission. **Amenities:** Bikes; Jacuzzi; Wi-Fi (free).

Bayshore and Chandler House ★★
Twenty-five individually decorated apartments can be found at Bayshore (16 units) and Chandler House (6 units) on the east end of town, and 77 Commercial St. (1 unit) on the far west end of town, perhaps the ideal place to stay if you want extra privacy and a water view. All the buildings are on the beach side of Commercial Street. The units, which are weekly rentals in summer, all have separate entrances and complete kitchenettes. The Bayshore property is perhaps the prettiest with a courtyard full of flowers in season.

Bayshore: 493 Commercial St. Chandler House: 480 Commercial St. www.bayshorechandler.com. ℂ **508/487-9133.** 23 units. Summer $1,450–$3,800 weekly; shoulder season daily $110–$295. Dogs allowed w/advance notice. **Amenities:** Wi-Fi (free).

Harbor Hotel ★★
This is one jazzy motel. It is way off the main drag, though, so guests have to bike or take a free town shuttle bus, taxi, or pedicab to get to the center of town, where parking is almost impossible in season. The contemporary and primarily white rooms are enlivened with vibrant colors on the walls and bedding. The Whaler's Lounge serves three meals daily, and there's also a poolside bar.

698 Commercial St. (at Rte. 6A, in the East End). www.harborhotelptown.com. ℂ **800/422-4224** or 508/487-1711. 129 units. Summer $189–$252 double. Rates include continental breakfast. Open year-round. Dogs allowed. **Amenities:** Restaurant; outdoor pool; Wi-Fi (free).

The Masthead ★★
The harborfront compound offers a wide range of lodging options, from singles with shared bathrooms to three-bedroom suites with water views. The property was popular with celebrities in decades past, which is why some rooms have names like the Isabella Rossellini Cottage, Mrs. Bob Hope room, Billy Joel efficiency, and Helena Rubinstein cottage. Hang out on the sun deck along the 450-foot private beach and you never know who you might meet.

31–41 Commercial St. (in the West End). www.themasthead.com. ℂ **800/395-5095** or 508/487-0523. 21 units (2 w/shared bath), 4 cottages. Summer $125–$130 double w/ shared bath; $289–$379 double; $289–$455 efficiency and 1-bedroom; $422–$739 2-bedroom apt; $2,954–$4,844 cottage weekly. **Amenities:** Wi-Fi (free).

Pilgrim House ★★
In a historic house set back from the street, this sleek, modern, and hip hotel is in the heart of P-town's Commercial Street. Recently renovated, the rooms are decorated boutique-style with textured wallpaper and streamlined deco furnishings. An onsite restaurant, The Landing Bistro &

Bar, offers a fine-dining alternative without having to venture into the Commercial Street bustle a few steps away.

336 Commercial St. www.pilgrimhouseptown.com. © **508/487-6424.** 19 units. Summer $269–$309 double. **Amenities:** Restaurant; Wi-Fi (free).

INEXPENSIVE

Outermost Hostel ★   If you feel like roughing it, head over to this tiny compound of tiny houses, P-town's version of a hostel. Rates are the best in town. The hostel consists of five units filled with bunk beds, so you share those with other guests, as in a typical hostel. The bunks fill up fast.

28 Winslow St. (near the Pilgrim Monument). www.outermosthostel.com. © **508/487-4378.** 40 beds. Summer $25 per bunk.

Where to Eat in Provincetown
EXPENSIVE

9 Ryder Seaside Dining ★★★ ITALIAN   This is a real find, a harbor shack converted into an intimate little restaurant. Candles twinkle and historic photos of old Provincetown line the walls. Servers are a bit more professional than usual on the Cape, the better to explain the menu items and make educated recommendations. That's how I ended up eating the divine native littleneck clams in white wine sauce. Menu items are recognizable as traditional old-fashioned Italian cuisine—scampi and chicken parmigiana, for instance—but made with very high-quality ingredients that make them seem new. Gluten-free pasta is available on request.

9 Ryder St. (on the pier at Fisherman's Wharf). www.9ryder.com. © **508/487-9990.** Main courses $18–$34. Open mid-May to mid-Oct.

The Mews Restaurant & Cafe ★★ INTERNATIONAL/AMERICAN FUSION   This granddaddy of the Provincetown restaurant scene can be counted on for great food and service. Downstairs is more formal, where the sandy beach is right out the window and the menu has the likes of filet mignon with Béarnaise sauce. Upstairs is an upscale lounge, and the menu includes lower-priced bistro fare. This is where to find roasted chicken with lingonberry cream sauce and top-notch burgers.

429 Commercial St. www.mews.com. © **508/487-1500.** Main courses $21–$37. Mid-June to early Sept daily 6–10pm, Sun brunch 11am–2:30pm; early Dec to mid-Feb daily 6–10pm; call for off-season hours.

Napi's ★★ INTERNATIONAL   Checking out Napi's art collection is one of the main reasons to come to this big barn of a restaurant. Antique stained glass, carousel horses, and even a gorgeous chimney are worth the trip. The menu is massive and hits almost every country worth its culinary salt, including Chinese, Greek, and Japanese, and that's just in the appetizer section. Fish served a variety of ways is a specialty. There is a large portion of the menu that's vegetarian.

7 Freeman St. (at Bradford St.). www.napis-restaurant.com. © **800/571-6274.** Main courses $13–$36. May to mid-Sept daily 5–9:30pm; Oct–Apr daily 11:30am–4pm and 5–9pm.

The Red Inn ★★ NEW AMERICAN   It's a lovely expedition to go to the far west end of Commercial Street to this bright red restaurant, which is set on the harbor, covered with flowers, and looks like something out of a fairy tale. Dinner here is best done for very special occasions, when price is no object and its formality will be appreciated. The best part is the view; there are no bad seats. Be prepared for a substantial meal. The lobster and artichoke fondue, is very hard to resist, so don't even try. Sitting this close to the water, it's hard to pass up fish. The local scallops are served with orzo and a buttery citrus sauce. The warm bread pudding comes with a white-chocolate and Frangelico sauce.

15 Commercial St. www.theredinn.com. © **508/487-7334.** Main courses $28–$46. Mid-May to early Oct daily 5:30–10:30pm, call for off-season hours.

Ross' Grill ★★★ NEW AMERICAN BISTRO   This is the most unabashedly urban restaurant in P-town, one that wouldn't be out of place in Boston or even New York. The restaurant is on the second floor of Whaler's Wharf, with terrific views out to the harbor. But in such a clubby atmosphere, you almost feel like turning your back to the view and focusing on the matters at hand, the fine food and the expert service. This is one for the meat-lovers, with filet mignon and oven-roasted rack of lamb. The wine list is one of the most extensive in town. Tapas are served at happy hour, when a raw bar is also on hand.

237 Commercial St. (in Whaler's Wharf). www.rossgrillptown.com. © **508/487-8878.** Main courses $20–$42. May to mid-Sept Mon and Wed–Sat noon–2:30pm and 5:30–9:30pm, Sun noon–3pm and 5:30–9pm; call for off-season hours.

MODERATE

Bubala's by the Bay ★ INTERNATIONAL   People-watching is the name of the game here. There is really no better place to do it than the immense patio in the front of the restaurant. Inside, there is a large colorful wall mural that speaks to the lightheartedness of the whole enterprise. The international flavor is apparent on the menu where there are quesadillas next to Thai spring rolls. This isn't fine dining and if anything, it is a little overpriced for what it is, but it's good for lunch or a light snack.

185 Commercial St. (in the West End). www.bubalas.com. © **508/487-0773.** Main courses $11–$32. Mid-Apr to late Oct daily 11am–11pm. Closed late Oct to mid-Apr.

Cafe Heaven ★★ AMERICAN   Cafe Heaven, a double storefront cafe in the west end of town with a sophisticated urban feel, wins the prize for best breakfast in Provincetown. Colorful paintings adorn the walls and the large windows and bar area look out on bustling Commercial Street. Freshly baked breads, omelets overstuffed with veggies, and stacks of pancakes with fruit toppings are all on the menu. In high season, get here early before all the tables fill up. Lunch features European-influenced sandwiches and salads, such as the avocado and goat cheese on a baguette. Dinner, featuring burgers and pasta, is also a winner.

199 Commercial St. (in the West End). www.cafeheavenptown.com. © **508/487-9639.** Main courses $15–$28. Late June–Aug daily 8am–2pm, 6–10pm; call for off-season hours. Closed Nov–May.

The Lobster Pot ★ SEAFOOD   Yes, it is an institution. And you could do a lot worse than making your way to the upper level of the Lobster Pot and ordering a steaming bowl of Tim's clam chowder while you watch the boats come and go from the harbor. Or make a meal of it and order one of the signature bouillabaisses and stews, including cioppino.

321 Commercial St. www.ptownlobsterpot.com. ℂ **508/487-0842.** Main courses $12–$34. Mid-June to mid-Sept daily 11:30am–10:30pm; call for off-season hours. No reservations. Closed Dec–Mar.

Local 186 ★★ BURGERS   Hands-down the best burgers in town, and the house-made condiments, including the bacon jam, are wonderful, as are the fries. They also have great veggie burgers. On the lower level, the Grotto Bar has wild local acts and DJ dance parties late at night on weekends. A guest house upstairs has four rooms available.

186 Commercial St. (in the West End). www.local186.com. ℂ **508/487-7555.** No reservations. Main courses $15–$22. July–Aug daily 11am–10pm; call for off-season hours. Closed Feb–May.

INEXPENSIVE

The Canteen ★★★ INTERNATIONAL   The owners of this restaurant were inspired by summer dinner parties to create a twist on summer shack favorites like lobster rolls and fish-and-chips. This is a good place to try something you've never had, like kale and quinoa salad or the very unusual but delicious cod *bánh mì* (a sandwich with marinated cod, pickled daikon radishes, and carrots, cucumber, cilantro, mint, aioli and Sriracha sauce). There are also more typical items like fish and chips, which for some reason taste much better here.

225 Commercial St. www.thecanteenptown.com. ℂ **508/487-3800.** Main courses $7–$16. June–Aug daily 8am–11pm. Call for off-season hours. Closed Nov–Apr.

Chach ★ DINER   This take on the classic diner is chef-owned (by Chach, natch)—everything is homemade. Breakfast options, like the French toast with blackberry crumble or the breakfast quesadilla, really are worth waking up for. For lunch, try the beer-battered crispy cod sandwich with homemade coleslaw, or the Reuben, piled high with corned beef. Chach is off the beaten path a bit, but those in the know fill the place up early in season.

73 Shank Painter Rd. (off Bradford St.). www.chachprovincetown.com. ℂ **508/487-1530.** Most items under $15. July–Aug Fri–Tues 8am–2pm. Call for off-season hours. Closed Mar.

Spiritus Pizza ★ PIZZA/ICE CREAM   At one o'clock in the morning, this is the unofficial center of town, as bar habitués head here for a late-night snack and the front patio becomes an after-hours meet-and-greet (a polite way of saying a hook-up joint). The pizza here has a thin, chewy crust; it's a little greasy and pretty satisfying when you're hungry. Pizza is served until 1am and beyond, depending on demand. Emack and Bolio's ice cream finishes the meal.

190 Commercial St. www.spirituspizza.com. ℂ **508/487-2808.** Slices $2.75–$3.75. Full pizzas $23–$28. No credit cards. Apr–Oct daily 11:30am–2am. Closed Nov–Mar.

The Outer Cape: Wellfleet & Provincetown

CAPE COD

One thing you absolutely have to do while in town is to sample the *pasties* (meat pies) and pastries at **Provincetown Portuguese Bakery,** 299 Commercial St. (✆ 508/487-1803). Point to a few and take your surprise package out on the pier for delectation. It's open daily 7am to 11pm, and shuts down from November to early April. Also near Macmillan Wharf, some tasty pizza slices can be found at **Twisted Pizza ★,** at 293 Commercial St. (www.twistedpizza ptown.com; ✆ 508/487-6973); their creative toppings include breaded eggplant. It's open from 10am to 2am. Just up the street at 353 Commercial St., many of the offerings at **Box Lunch** (www.boxlunch.com; ✆ 508/487-6026) are ideal for a strolling lunch, especially the "rollwiches"—pita bread packed with a wide range of fillings. It's open 8:30am to 8pm. In the East End, **Angel Foods,** 467 Commercial St. (www. angelfoods.com; ✆ 508/487-6666), is an upscale takeout shop with Italian specialties and other scrumptious prepared foods to go; it's open 7am to 5pm.

Provincetown Entertainment & Nightlife
PERFORMANCE
Art House ★★   Art house films are just the beginning of the programming at this centrally located modern movie palace on Commercial Street. The summer season is packed with a parade of well-known performers, be they drag legends, like Varla Jean Merman, nationally known comedians, like Andrea Martin, or musicians, like Well Strung, a hunky classical quartet. Performances are given mid-May to mid-September from 7 to 10pm. Films are shown in the off-season. 214 Commercial St. www.ptownarthouse.com. ✆ **508/487-9222.** Tickets $25–$30.

The Provincetown Theater ★★   Provincetown is considered the birthplace of modern American theater. Both Eugene O'Neill and Tennessee Williams spent time here. O'Neill even lived in the old coast guard station and staged his first plays in a shack on a P-town wharf. New plays and revivals are staged here in the summer; many are exciting works that may be bound for Boston or even New York. Other events take place here year-round including readings, movies, lectures and more. 238 Bradford St. www.provincetowntheater. org. ✆ **800/791-7487** or 508/487-9793 (box office), 508/487-7487, or 866/811-4111 (Theatre Mania). Ticket prices vary.

THE CLUB SCENE
The Atlantic House ★   The "A-House" is the only year-round dance club in P-town. The three sections of the club are the Little Bar, which has a jukebox; the Macho Bar, a leather bar, and the Big Room, for dancing. The building is actually one of the oldest in town (1798) and some of the club's history can be seen from the photos on the walls, including a famous one of Tennessee Williams walking along in the buff along a Provincetown beach. Though the clientele is predominantly gay, everyone is welcome. 6 Masonic Pl. (off Commercial St.). www.ahouse.com. ✆ **508/487-3821.** Cover $5–$10 for the Big Room.

Crown & Anchor ★ The Crown & Anchor is the biggest and most varied entertainment venue in town—it even has hotel rooms and a restaurant, including an outdoor bar/patio area. The massive complex in the center of town has six separate gay bars including the largest nightclub (The Paramount); a video bar (Wave); a cabaret venue; a poolside bar; a piano bar; and a leather bar (The Vault). Closed November to April. 247 Commercial St. www. onlyatthecrown.com. ℂ **508/487-1430.** Cover $20–$30 for shows.

Post Office Café and Cabaret ★ No nightclub listing is complete without the Post Office, a small club that tends to have the top acts in town, particularly in the realm of drag and comedy. Closed November to April. 303 Commercial St. www.postofficecabaret.com. ℂ **508/487-0006.** Cover $22.

BARS

1620 Brewhouse ★ One of the town's newer hangouts, this bar/restaurant smartly occupies a central spot in time for the town's 400th anniversary in 2020. A specially brewed beer made off-Cape for this establishment may be traded for a brewery in town sometime in the future. But for now, this is just a great open-air place to meet friends for drinks in the center of town. 214 Commercial St. www.1620brewhouse.com. ℂ **774/593-5180.**

Governor Bradford ★ A good old bar with pool tables, drag karaoke (summer nights at 9:30pm), and disco. 312 Commercial St. ℂ **508/487-2781.**

Harbor Lounge ★★ Walk through a long courtyard and pass some stores to find this modern, minimalist bar overlooking the beach. It only serves drinks, no food. But what a terrific place to have a cocktail: You are essentially in a three-sided glass box (sliders that can open and let the breeze through) overlooking the beach. Seating is on leather sofas. A little pier sticks out the back. The bar is open noon to 10pm. 359 Commercial St. www.theharbor lounge.com. ℂ **508/413-9527.**

Nor'East Beer Garden ★ This open-air bar also features good food. There are 16 craft beers on draft, like Founders Curmudgeon out of Grand Rapids, and 26 more in bottles. 206 Commercial St. www.thenoreastbeergarden. com. ℂ **508/487-BEER (2337).** Closed mid-Oct to mid-May.

Patio ★ A large outdoor seating area on Commercial Street makes this a terrific place to sip summer cocktails and people-watch. Tasty appetizers, desserts, light fare, and even whole dinners are served until 11pm. The interior holds a sleek, attractive bar. 328 Commercial St. www.ptownpatio.com. ℂ **508/ 487-4003.**

The Squealing Pig ★★ No, it's not a gay bar, but there are usually gay people here. It's not a sports bar either, but there is often sports on the TVs. It might be a pickup bar, but everyone seems to know everyone else. In a town of great bars, this is one of the best. Good food, too. 335 Commercial St. ℂ **508/487-5804.**

MARTHA'S VINEYARD & NANTUCKET

Although they are often lumped together, the two major islands off the coast of Cape Cod—Martha's Vineyard and Nantucket—are surprisingly different from each other. Martha's Vineyard, by far the larger of the two, has six distinct towns with striking variety. In parts of the Vineyard, you might feel like you are in Vermont, it is so rural, whereas the down island port towns feel more akin to other New England harbor communities. Nantucket, on the other hand, is small enough that the entire island is a historic district, composed of one main town—also called Nantucket—and a couple of beachy outlying villages. The cobblestone streets and most of the buildings downtown look just as they did 150 years ago—quaintness intact.

Martha's Vineyard is much closer to the Cape Cod mainland—just 3 nautical miles, a 45-minute ferry ride from Woods Hole in Falmouth—and no matter which town you arrive in (boats land in Vineyard Haven, Oak Bluffs, and Edgartown), it's worthwhile to explore other parts of the island, whether by car, bus, or bike. Nantucket is 30 miles off the coast of Cape Cod, though a fast ferry gets you there in an hour, and mainly everything a visitor could want to see is in walking distance of the ferry terminals.

Both islands have excellent beaches, shopping, and loads of things to do. Whichever you pick—or visit them both!—you won't be disappointed.

MARTHA'S VINEYARD

New England sea captains' houses framed with white picket fences. Flying horses alongside ice cream shops. Colorful gingerbread cottages on one end of the island and an authentic fishing village on the other. Lighthouses pierce the fog with their signals. A Native American community preserves its identity amid miles of pristine beaches and rolling farmland. Martha's Vineyard is a picturesque island indeed.

If you can imagine Martha's Vineyard as the shape of a humpbacked whale, up on the "hump" you'll find two of the island's main towns, bustling **Vineyard Haven** and resort-y **Oak Bluffs.** The coast slopes from there down to the "head," **Edgartown,** with its more dignified (some would say snooty) New England charm. The "underbelly" is a long stretch of ocean beach, deeply indented with ponds and inlets, leading to the glorious Aquinnah cliffs, the western "tail" of the island. The Vineyard's western half—**"up island"** as the locals say—is hilly and rural, with a few tiny but delightful hamlets.

Essentials

ARRIVING BY FERRY

Most visitors arrive via ferry service; if you're traveling via car or bus, you will most likely catch the ferry from Woods Hole, in the town of Falmouth, on Cape Cod. Passenger-only boats also run from Falmouth Inner Harbor, Hyannis, New Bedford, Rhode Island, New York, and New Jersey.

Tip: If you're interested in visiting both Martha's Vineyard and Nantucket in one day trip (admittedly, that's a very full day where you'll only scratch the surface of either island), check out Hy-Line Cruises' **Around the Sound** excursions from Hyannis (see p. 295).

CAR FERRIES The state-run **Steamship Authority** (www.steamship authority.com) runs the show in Woods Hole (✆ 508/477-8600 early Apr to early Sept, daily 8am–5pm, or 508/693-9130 daily 8am–5pm), with about 20 crossings a day in season. It maintains the only year-round ferries to Martha's Vineyard and the only ferries that accommodate cars in addition to passengers. The large ferries make the 45-minute trip to Vineyard Haven year-round; some boats go to Oak Bluffs from late May to late October (call for seasonal schedules). If you're bringing your car over to the island, plan to get to the Woods Hole terminal at least 30 minutes before your scheduled departure.

Many people prefer to leave their cars on the mainland, take the ferry (often with their bikes), and then rent a car, Jeep, or bicycle on the island. You can park your car at the Woods Hole lot (always full in the summer) or at one of many lots in Falmouth and Bourne that absorb the overflow of cars during the summer months; parking is $10 to $15 per day, depending on the time of year. Plan to arrive at the parking lots in Falmouth at least an hour before sailing time.

Free shuttle buses (some equipped for bikes) run regularly from the outlying lots to the Woods Hole ferry terminal.

The cost of a round-trip car passage from April through October is $137 to $157 (depending on the size of your car); in the off season, it drops to $87 to $107. On top of that, each passenger needs to pay a round-trip fare of $17 adults and $9

Plan Ahead

During the summer, you'll **most definitely** need a reservation to bring your car on the ferry to Martha's Vineyard. Word to the wise: You must reserve *months in advance* to secure a spot. Contact the Steamship Authority at www.steamshipauthority.com, or by calling ✆ 508/693-9130.

children 5 to 12. (Kids 4 and under ride free.) Bikes add an extra $8 round-trip. You do not need a reservation on the ferry if you're traveling without a car.

PASSENGER FERRIES   Passengers without cars can ride the car ferry from Woods Hole (see above for prices). **From Falmouth,** the passenger-only *Island Queen* at Falmouth Inner Harbor (www.islandqueen.com; ✆ 508/548-4800) makes a 35-minute crossing to Oak Bluffs, late May to mid-October. The round-trip fare is $22 for adults, $12 for kids 12 and under, and an extra $8 for bikes. No reservations are needed. Parking will run you $15 per calendar day. Credit cards are not accepted. *Tip:* It pays to buy a round-trip ticket on the *Island Queen;* it's cheaper than two one-way tickets. The **Falmouth–Edgartown Ferry Service,** 278 Scranton Ave. (www.falmouthedgartownferry.com; ✆ 508/548-9400), operates a 1-hour passenger ferry, called the *Pied Piper,* from Falmouth Inner Harbor to Edgartown. The boat runs from late May to mid-October, and reservations are required. Round-trip fares are $60 for adults and $40 for kids 6 to 12. Bicycles are $10 round-trip. There are several options for parking. Parking is $20 for the day; $25 for overnight.

From Hyannis, the traditional **Hy-Line** ferry runs daily from Ocean Street Dock (www.hy-linecruises.com; ✆ 800/492-8082), to Oak Bluffs, late May through mid-October. Trip time is about 1 hour and 40 minutes; round-trip costs $59 for adults; $39 for kids 5 to 12 ($14 round-trip for bikes). Parking at the Hy-Line lot is $25 per calendar day in season (spring and fall $20, $8–$12 off-season).

From New Bedford, Massachusetts, a fast 1-hour ferry travels to Martha's Vineyard six times a day in season (late May–Oct). The fare is $70 round-trip for adults; $40 round-trip for kids 12 and under. Contact **Seastreak Martha's Vineyard** for details (www.seastreak.com; ✆ 866/683-3779).

From **North Kingstown, Rhode Island,** to Oak Bluffs, **Vineyard Fast Ferry** (www.vineyardfastferry.com; ✆ 401/295-4040) runs its high-speed catamaran *Millennium* daily from mid-June through October. The trip takes 90 minutes. Round-trip rates are $89 to $104 for adults, $66 to $81 kids 4 to 12, $16 bikes. Parking next to the ferry port is $10 per calendar day.

From **New York City and New Jersey** to Oak Bluffs, **Seastreak Martha's Vineyard** (www.neferry.com, ✆ 866/683-3779) runs a high-speed catamaran from late May to mid-October. Round-trip fares are $240 to $310 adults, $135 to $310 children, $30 bikes. The catamaran leaves Thursdays and Fridays from New York and takes 6½ hours from New York to Oak Bluffs. The ferry makes the return trip Sundays, Mondays, and Tuesdays.

ARRIVING BY AIR

You can fly into **Martha's Vineyard Airport,** also known as Dukes County Airport (www.mvyairport.com; ✆ 508/693-7022), in West Tisbury, about 5 miles outside Edgartown. **Cape Air/Nantucket Airlines** (www.flycapeair.com; ✆ 800/352-0714) connects the island year-round with Boston (trip time 34 min., about $187 one-way); Hyannis (trip time 20 min.; $49 one-way); Nantucket (15 min.; $49 one-way); Providence RI (trip time 25 min.; $124 one-way); and New Bedford MA (trip time 20 min.; $49 one-way). **US**

Airways (www.usairways.com; © **800/428-4322**) flies from Boston for about $304 round-trip and also has seasonal weekend service from LaGuardia Airport, in New York City (trip time 1¼ hour), which costs approximately $400 round-trip.

ARRIVING BY BUS

Peter Pan Bus Lines (www.peterpanbus.com; © **888/751-8800** or 508/548-7588) connects the Woods Hole ferry port with South Station and Logan Airport in Boston, as well as with New York City and Providence, Rhode Island. (To get to Falmouth Inner Harbor instead, passengers disembark at the Falmouth Bus Station and take a taxi to the harbor or, in summer, a free shuttle bus that gets you a short walk away.) The trip from South Station takes about 1 hour and 35 minutes and costs about $40 one-way; from Logan Airport, the cost is $30 one-way; from Providence, the 2½-hour trip to Woods Hole costs $30 one-way; from New York, the bus trip takes about 6 hours and costs approximately $74 one-way. The trip from South Station to Woods Hole takes about 1 hour and 35 minutes and costs about $40 one-way; from Logan Airport, the cost is $30 one-way; from Providence, the 2½-hour trip to Woods Hole costs $30 one-way; from New York, the bus trip takes about 6 hours and costs approximately $74 one-way. After arriving in Woods Hole, bus passengers then need to buy tickets for the Steamship Authority ferry (see "Car Ferries," p. 267).

Both Peter Pan and **Plymouth-Brockton** (www.p-b.com) bus lines go from South Station and Logan to Hyannis. See p. 292 for details.

ARRIVING BY LIMO

Falmouth Taxi (www.falmouthtaxi.com; © **508/548-3100**) also runs limo service from Boston and the airport. It charges $165 plus a gratuity.

VISITOR INFORMATION

The **Martha's Vineyard Chamber of Commerce,** at 24 Beach St., Vineyard Haven (www.mvy.com; © **800/505-4815** or 508/693-0085), just 2 blocks up from the ferry terminal, is open Monday to Friday 9am to 5pm year-round, plus weekends in season. There are also information booths at the ferry terminal in Vineyard Haven; across from the Flying Horses Carousel in Oak Bluffs; and on Church Street in Edgartown.

GETTING AROUND

The down-island towns of Vineyard Haven, Oak Bluffs, and Edgartown are fairly compact, and if your inn is located in the heart of one of these small towns, you will be within walking distance of shopping, beaches, and attractions in town. Frequent shuttle buses can whisk you to the other down-island towns and beaches in 5 to 15 minutes. In season you can also take the shuttle bus up-island. Otherwise you will have to drive, bike, or take a cab.

BY CAR   If you're coming to the Vineyard for a few days and you're going to stick to the down-island towns, it's best to leave your car at home—traffic and parking can be brutal in summer. If you're staying longer or want to explore up-island, bring your car or rent one on the island (my favorite way to tour the Vineyard is by Jeep). Keep in mind that car rental rates soar during peak season and gas is expensive. All the national car rental chains have desks at the airport and offices in Vineyard Haven and Oak Bluffs. Local agencies also operate out of all three port towns; in Vineyard Haven, you'll find **Adventure Rentals,** Beach Road (www.islandadventuremv.com; © **508/693-1959**), where a regular car costs about $140 per day; a Jeep will run you about $199 to $249 per day in season. In Edgartown, try **AAA Island Rentals,** 31 Circuit Ave. (www.mvautorental.com; © **508/627-6800**); they're also at Five Corners in Vineyard Haven (© **508/696-5300**).

BY SHUTTLE BUS & TROLLEY The **Martha's Vineyard Regional Transit Authority** (www.vineyardtransit.com; © **508/693-9440**) operates shuttle buses year-round on about a dozen routes around the island. The buses, which are white with purple logos, cost about $2 to $5 depending on distance. The formula is $1 per town. For example, Vineyard Haven to Oak Bluffs is $2, but Vineyard Haven to Edgartown (passing through Oak Bluffs) is $3. A 1-day pass is $7, and a 3-day pass is $15. The main down-island stops are **Vineyard Haven** (near the ferry terminal), **Oak Bluffs** (near the Civil War statue, in Ocean Park), and **Edgartown** (Church Street, near the Old Whaling Church). From late June to early September, they run frequently—from 6am to midnight, every 15 minutes or half-hour. Hours are reduced in spring and fall.

In Edgartown, there's a Downtown Shuttle that circles throughout town, and South Beach buses circle that head out to South Beach every 20 minutes in season. Both stop at the free parking lots just north of the town center, which means you won't waste your time circling downtown Edgartown vainly searching for a parking spot. Buses also go out to Aquinnah year-round (via the airport, West Tisbury, and Chilmark), leaving every couple of hours from down-island towns and looping about every hour through up-island towns. The trip from one of the down island towns to Aquinnah is $5 to $6.25, depending on which town.

BY BICYCLE See box below.

BY MOPED The number of accidents involving mopeds seems to rise every year, and many islanders are opposed to these vehicles. If you rent one, be aware they are considered quite dangerous on the island's busy, narrow, winding, sandy roads. Moped renting is banned in Edgartown, and there is a movement to ban mopeds on the island entirely. To rent a moped, try **Adventure Rentals,** Beach Road (www.islandadventuremv.com; © **508/693-1959**). In Oak Bluffs, there's **Sun 'n' Fun,** 26 Lake Ave. (www.sunnfunrentals.com; © **508/693-5457**).

BY TAXI Upon arrival, you'll find taxis at all ferry terminals and at the airport, and there are permanent taxi stands in Oak Bluffs (at the Flying Horses Carousel) and Edgartown (next to the Town Wharf). Most taxi outfits operate cars as well as vans for larger groups and travelers with bikes. Cab companies on the island include **AdamCab** (www.adamcabmv.com; © **800/360-8629** or 508/627-4462), **Martha's Vineyard Taxi** (www.mvtaxi.com; © **508/693-8660**), and **Atlantic Taxi** (www.atlanticcabmv.com; © **508/693-7110**). Rates

cycling THE VINEYARD

You shouldn't leave without exploring the Vineyard on two wheels, even if only for a couple of hours. There's a little of everything for cyclists, from paved paths to hilly country roads, and you don't have to be an expert rider to enjoy yourself. Plus, biking is a relatively hassle-free way to get around the island.

What's unique about biking on Martha's Vineyard is that you'll find not only the smooth, well-maintained paths indigenous to the Cape, but also long stretches of road with virtually no traffic that, while rough in spots, pass through breathtaking country landscapes with sweeping ocean views. It is only a few miles but a very scenic ride between Vineyard Haven and Oak Bluffs. A few more miles gets you to Edgartown along a nice flat bike path.

Bike rental operations are ubiquitous near the ferry landings in Vineyard Haven and Oak Bluffs, and there are also a few outfits in Edgartown. Bike rentals cost about $28 to $38 a day. In Vineyard Haven, try **Martha's Bike Rentals,** Lagoon Pond Road (© **800/559-0312** or 508/693-6593). In Oak Bluffs, there's **Anderson's,** Circuit Avenue Extension (© **508/693-9346**), which rents bikes only; and **Sun 'n' Fun,** 26 Lake Ave. (www.sunnfunrentals.com © **508/693-5457**). In Edgartown you'll find bikes at **R. W. Cutler Edgartown Bike Rentals,** 1 Main St. (www.edgartownbikerentals.com; © **800/627-2763**); and **Wheel Happy,** with two locations, at 204 Upper Main St. and 8 S. Water St., both in Edgartown (www.wheelhappybicycles.com; © **508/627-5928**).

The chamber of commerce has a great bike map available at its office on Beach Road, in Vineyard Haven (see p. 269).

from town to town in summer are generally flat fees based on where you're headed and the number of passengers on board. A trip from Vineyard Haven to Edgartown would probably cost around $23 for two people. Late-night revelers should keep in mind that rates double after midnight until 7am.

ORGANIZED TOURS

For a 2½-hour bus tour of the island, call **Martha's Vineyard Sightseeing Bus Tours** (www.mvtour.com; © **508/627-8687**). The buses are stationed at the ferry terminals in Vineyard Haven and Oak Bluffs from late May to the end of September. Tours are $33 per person.

Exploring Vineyard Haven

Vineyard Haven, where the big car ferries pull in, has the salty flavor of a New England fishing town (like Gloucester, say, or New London). It can get crowded when a ferry has just arrived, but it also has some very good seafood restaurants and lots of stores (this is where island residents, particularly up-islanders, come to do their everyday shopping).

In downtown Vineyard Haven, **Owen Park Beach** is a tiny strip of harborside sand just off Main Street. Adjoining a town green with swings and a bandstand, it will suffice for young children. There's a lifeguard but no restrooms here, although it's a quick walk from most Vineyard Haven inns. A more popular spot is **Lake Tashmoo Town Beach** ★, off Herring Creek Road. It's also a tiny strip of sand, but it's the only spot on the island where

Martha's Vineyard

Nantucket Sound

Vineyard Sound

ATLANTIC OCEAN

Ferry to Hyannis (Year-round)
Ferry to Nantucket (Seasonal)
Ferry to Falmouth (Seasonal)
Ferry to Rhode Island (Seasonal)
Ferry to Falmouth (Seasonal)
Ferry to Woods Hole (Year-round)
Ferry to New Bedford (Year-round)

Cape Pogue Bay
Dyke Bridge
East Beach (Wasque)
Wasque Point
Pocha Pond
Chappaquiddick Island
Litchfield Rd.
Katama Bay
Norton Point
Chappaquiddick Rd.
Edgartown Harbor
Lighthouse Beach
Edgartown
Katama Rd.
Herring Creek Rd.
South Beach (Katama Beach)
Edgartown Great Pond
Edgartown Pond
Joseph A. Sylvia State Beach
Oak Bluffs Town Beach
Seaview Ave.
East Chop
Oak Bluffs
Lagoon Pond
Owen Park Beach
Barnes Rd.
Beach Rd.
County Rd.
Edgartown–Vineyard Haven Rd.
Edgartown–W. Tisbury Rd.
Meeting House Rd.
Main St.
West Chop
Vineyard Haven
Main St.
Tashmoo Lake
Lambert's Cove Rd.
Lake Tashmoo Town Beach
Lamberts Cove
Airport Rd.
Martha's Vineyard Airport
MANUEL F. CORRELLUS STATE FOREST
Old County Rd.
Oyster Pond
Tisbury Great Pond
North Tisbury
State Rd.
West Tisbury
South Rd.
Chilmark Pond
Middle Rd.
Menemsha Beach
North Rd.
Menemsha
Chilmark
Menemsha Pond
Lobsterville Beach
Menemsha Harbor
South Rd.
Lucy Vincent Beach (restricted to residents)
Squibnocket Beach (restricted to residents)
Squibnocket Pond
State Rd.
Aquinnah
Moshup Trail
Aquinnah Beach

Beach
Ferry
Lighthouse
Popular Bike Trail

0   2 mi
0   2 km

ATTRACTIONS●
Alley's General Store 8
Aquinnah Cliffs 1
Cape Poge Wildlife Refuge 16
Cedar Tree Neck Sanctuary 11
Cottage Museum 14
Felix Neck Wildlife Sanctuary 15
Flying Horses Carousel 13
Long Point Wildlife Refuge 6
Martha's Vineyard Museum 12
Polly Hill Arboretum 9
Wasque Reservation 17

UP-ISLAND HOTELS ■
Beach Plum Inn 2
The Captain R. Flanders House 5
Hosteling International
Martha's Vineyard 7
Menemsha Inn and Cottages 3

UP-ISLAND RESTAURANTS ◆
Beach Plum Inn Restaurant 2
Home Port 4
State Road Restaurant 10

lake meets ocean, giving beachgoers a choice between the Vineyard Sound beach with mild surf or a placid lake beach. Parking is limited and the water is often brackish. It's an easy bike ride from downtown Vineyard Haven.

Off Franklin Street you'll find the **West Chop Woods,** an 85-acre preserve with marked walking trails.

Martha's Vineyard Museum ★★ MUSEUM   In summer 2019, this museum should be opening in its new home, in the historic 1895 Vineyard Haven Marine Hospital, overlooking the harbor and Lagoon Pond. This museum tells the story of this multi-faceted island with rotating themed exhibits, while preserving significant artifacts of its history, from arrowheads to whaling-ship logs to vintage tourism souvenirs. Oral history projects feature portrait photos of old time Vineyarders and quotes from them about how life used to be, and a special exhibit displays the 1,000-prism **Fresnel lens** of the Gay Head Lighthouse (Aquinnah's former name), which aided mariners from 1854 to 1951. The public will also have access to the island's archive of source material from the 17th to the 21st century. The museum will continue to have exhibits at the Cooke House in Edgartown (see p. 275) as well.

151 Lagoon Pond Rd. (near Five Corners). www.mvmuseum.org. ✆ **508/627-4441.** $7 adults, $6 seniors, $4 children 6–15. Mid-May to mid-Oct Mon–Sat 10am–5pm, Sun noon–5pm; mid-Oct to mid-May Mon–Sat 10am–4pm.

VINEYARD HAVEN SHOPPING

Bunch of Grapes Bookstore, 23 Main St., Vineyard Haven (www.bunchof grapes.com; ✆ **508/693-2291**), is a popular bookstore a short walk from the Steamship Authority terminal. Stop by **C. B. Stark Jewelers,** 53A Main St. (www.cbstark.com; ✆ **508/693-2284**), where proprietor Cheryl Stark started fashioning island-motif charms back in 1966. Feel like whipping up your own lobster feast? For the freshest and biggest crustaceans on the island, head to the **Net Result,** 79 Beach Rd. (www.mvseafood.com; ✆ **508/693-6071**). Run by the Larsen family, here you'll also find everything shrimp, scallops, swordfish, bluefish, and tuna, as well as prepared foods, including sushi.

Exploring Oak Bluffs

A popular resort town since the 19th century, Oak Bluffs is a place of Victorian gingerbread houses, a vast seaside town green, and a touch of beach-town honkytonk around the vintage Flying Horses carousel.

Stretching along Seaview Avenue from both sides of the ferry wharf, **Oak Bluffs Town Beach** is a convenient place to linger while you wait for the next boat, and within easy walking distance for visitors staying in Oak Bluffs. The surf is consistently calm and the sand smooth, so it's also ideal for families with small children. Public restrooms are available at the ferry dock, but there are no lifeguards.

From the harborfront, turn south on Central Avenue to enter the **Martha's Vineyard Camp Meeting** grounds, a neighborhood of tiny Victorian cottages grouped around a central green. First started as a Methodist Revival colony in the 1800s, this area hosted multi-week religious meetings in the summers.

Back then, instead of cottages, there were tents where families would stay during the course of the meetings; some families began to decorate their tents and expand them and eventually the tents became homes. There would be three prayer services daily in the nearby 1878 Trinity Methodist Church; or the 1879 open-sided **Trinity Park Tabernacle** ★★, which today is used for Sunday morning services, but also concerts and sing-alongs. The tabernacle is the largest wrought-iron structure in the country.

Mile-long **Joseph A. Sylvia State Beach** ★★★, one of the Vineyard's most popular, sits midway between Oak Bluffs and Edgartown, along the Beach Road causeway. Flanked by a paved bike path, this placid beach has views of Cape Cod and Nantucket Sound and is prized for its gentle and (relatively) warm waves. The wooden drawbridge is a local landmark—visitors and islanders alike have been jumping off it for years. The shuttle bus stops here, and roadside parking is also available—but it fills up fast, so stake your claim early. There are no restrooms, and only the Edgartown end of the beach, known as Bend-in-the-Road Beach, has lifeguards.

Cottage Museum ★ HISTORIC HOME   As you walk around the 34-acre Camp Meeting Grounds in Oak Bluffs and admire the more than 300 tiny colorful cottages in the compound, you may find yourself wanting to take a look inside. This museum is your ticket. Decorated with period furnishings, it offers a glimpse into what the Campground was like in its late Victorian heyday.

1 Trinity Park (within the Camp Meeting Grounds). www.mvcma.org. ℂ **508/693-7784.** $2 donation requested. Mid-June–Sept Mon–Sat 10am–4pm. Closed Oct–mid-June.

Flying Horses Carousel ★★ CAROUSEL   The oldest operating platform carousel in the country, the Flying Horses has been designated as a National Historic Landmark. But for generations of islanders, the carousel is just simply a lot of fun. Kids and their parents reach to grab the rings, hoping for a brass one, which gives the bearer a free ride. The horses are majestic steeds, intricately carved, with real horsehair and glass eyes. Charles Dare, a renowned maker of carousel, constructed this one in 1876 for Coney Island.

33 Circuit Ave. (at Lake Ave.). www.mvpreservation.org. ℂ **508/693-9481.** $3 per ride. Late May–early Sept daily 10am–10pm; call for off-season hours. Closed mid-Oct to mid-Apr.

OAK BLUFFS SHOPPING

Oak Bluff's main shopping street, **Circuit Avenue,** begins at the Flying Horses and runs along the southeastern edge of the Camp Meeting Grounds. My favorite place for gifts in Oak Bluffs is **Craftworks,** 149 Circuit Ave. (www.craftworksgallery.com; ℂ **508/693-7463**), which is filled to the rafters with whimsical, colorful contemporary American crafts, some by local artisans.

A little art gallery cluster called "The Arts District" in Oak Bluffs, just beyond the gingerbread cottage colony, is worth a visit. A short walk away, on Dukes County Avenue, there are interesting shops, including **Alison Shaw Gallery** (88 Dukes County Ave.; www.alisonshaw.com; ℂ **508/696-7429**), featuring the exquisite photographs by this artist.

Exploring Edgartown

There's more of a Colonial air to Edgartown, with its stately sea captains' mansions, white-steepled churches, brick sidewalks, mature shade trees, and a Main Street lined with striped awnings. Divided from Edgartown by a narrow inlet, **Chappaquiddick Island** (see box p. 276) is a world unto itself.

A stroll around Edgartown reveals how the 19th-century whaling trade enriched this part of the world. Begin at 99 Main St. with the **Dr. Daniel Fisher House,** built in 1840 in Greek Revival style. Fisher, a successful whaling merchant, founded the Martha's Vineyard National Bank. Behind the Fisher House, off Main Street between Planting Field Way and Church Street, you'll find the oldest surviving dwelling on the island, **Vincent House,** a modest gray shingled Cape-style house built in 1672. Next to the Fisher House, at Main Street and Church Street, the Greek Revival **Old Whaling Church** (1843) was designed by local architect Frederick Baylies, Jr. It's still a Methodist church, though its major role these days is as a performance venue (see p. 291).

Continue down Main Street 2 blocks and turn left on North Water Street to admire the many grand sea captain's homes. At 56 North Water Street, what is now the **Edgartown Inn** was originally built in 1798 as the home of whaling captain Thomas Worth. Converted into an inn a few years later, it is considered the longest-operating lodging on the island; in the 1830s a young Nathaniel Hawthorne lived here on and off for nearly a year while writing the short stories that would be later collected as *Twice-Told Tales*. At 59 North Water St., the **Daggett House** was built in 1750 as a conversion of a 1660 tavern.

Edgartown is blessed with beaches—northwest of town is popular **State Beach** (see p. 274), and the 3-mile-long sweep of **South Beach ★★★** (Katama Beach) lies about 4 miles south of Edgartown, on Katama Road. If you have time for only one beach day while on Martha's Vineyard, go with this popular barrier strand. It boasts heavy wave action (check with lifeguards for swimming conditions), sweeping dunes, and, most important, relatively ample parking space. It's also accessible by bike path or shuttle. Lifeguards patrol some sections of the beach, and there are sparsely scattered toilet facilities. The rough surf here is popular with surfers. *Tip:* Families tend to head to the left, college kids to the right.

Felix Neck Wildlife Sanctuary, along the Edgartown–Vineyard Haven Road (www.massaudubon.org; ✆ **508/627-4850**), is an easy 2-mile bike ride from Edgartown. A Massachusetts Audubon Property, it has a complete visitor center staffed by naturalists who lead bird-watching walks, among other activities. You'll see osprey nests on your right on the way to the center. Pick up a trail map at the center before heading out. Several of the trails pass Sengekontacket Pond, and the orange trail leads to Waterfowl Pond, which has an observation deck with bird-sighting information.

Martha's Vineyard Museum ★★ HISTORIC HOME   Although much of this history museum will have moved to its new home in Vineyard Haven (see p. 273) in summer 2019, the previous Edgartown site, the **Thomas Cooke House,** will remain open as a historic house. This shipwright-built

Colonial, dating to between 1720 and 1740, was home to the U.S. Customs collector, Thomas Cooke.

59 School St. (corner of Cooke St.). www.mvmuseum.org. ℰ **508/627-4441.** $7 adults, $6 seniors, $4 children 6–15. Mid-May to mid-Oct Mon–Sat 10am–5pm, Sun noon-5pm; mid-Oct to mid-May Mon–Sat 10am–4pm.

EDGARTOWN SHOPPING

Edgartown Books, at 44 Main St. (www.edgartownbooks.com; ℰ **508/627-8463**), has a lively presentation of timely titles highlighting local endeavors; inquire about readings and signings. Closed January to March. **The Great Put On,** 1 Dock St. (www.thegreatputonmv.com; ℰ **508/627-5495**), dates back to 1969 but always keeps up with the latest styles, including lines by Vivienne Tam, Moschino, and BCBG. **Katydid** is another high-fashion option, at 38 Main St. (ℰ **508/627-1232**).

Exploring Up Island

The western half of Martha's Vineyard feels completely different from the eastern half—hilly, rural, and rugged. The town centers of West Tisbury and

---

THE beachy charm OF CHAPPAQUIDDICK ISLAND

Accessible by ferry from Edgartown (see below), quiet Chappaquiddick is home to two sizable preserves run by the Trustees of Reservations. The **Cape Poge Wildlife Refuge ★★★** and **Wasque Reservation ★★★** (www.thetrustees.org), covering much of the island's eastern barrier beach, have 709 acres that draw flocks of nesting or resting shorebirds, including egrets, herons, terns, and piping plovers. Also on the island, 3 miles east on Dyke Road, is another Trustees of Reservations property, the distinctly poetic and alluring **Mytoi,** a 14-acre Japanese garden that is an oasis of textures and flora and fauna.

Within Wasque (pronounced Way-squee) Reservation are two fine beaches. Half-mile-long **Wasque Beach ★★**, is the easier to get to and has all the amenities—lifeguards, parking, restrooms—without the crowds. If you are not a Trustees member you must pay at the gatehouse; it's $5 to park your car here and go to the beach. **East Beach ★★**, is one of the Vineyard's best-kept secrets, and rarely crowded, since few

people make the effort to hike or bike this far. Most people park their car near the Dyke Bridge and walk the couple hundred yards out to the beach. Admission is $5 per person. Because of its exposure on the east shore of the island, the surf here is rough. Pack a picnic and make this an afternoon adventure. Sorry, no facilities.

Biking on Chappaquiddick is one of the great Vineyard experiences, but the roads can be sandy and are best suited for a mountain bike. You may have to dismount during the 5-mile ride to Wasque.

The **On-Time ferry** (www.chappyferry.net; ℰ **508/627-9427**) runs the 5-minute trip from Memorial Wharf, on Dock Street in Edgartown, to Chappaquiddick Island (a distance of about 500 ft.) from June to mid-October daily, every 5 minutes from 6:45am to midnight. Passengers, bikes, mopeds, dogs, and cars (three at a time) are all welcome. A round-trip is $4 per person, $12 for one car/one driver, $6 for one bike/one person.

Chilmark are little more than a cluster of modest buildings; the fishing hamlet of Menemsha, a 5-minute drive northwest of Chilmark, has an end-of-the-road quality. North of West Tisbury, State Road splits into three equally lovely country roads, somewhat prosaically named North Road, Middle Road, and South Road; with very little car traffic, they are wonderful for cycling. The three roads reconvene at the Chilmark crossing, beyond which State Road winds past Menemsha and Squibnocket Ponds to wind up at the spectacular Aquinnah cliffs (formerly known as Gay Head, before adopting the name of the native peoples). It's a lot of scenery packed into just a few square miles.

Most of the up-island shoreline is privately owned or restricted to residents and thus off limits to transient visitors. Renters in up-island communities, however, can obtain a beach sticker (around $35–$50 for a season sticker) for those private beaches by applying with a lease at the relevant **town hall:** West Tisbury, ✆ **508/696-0147;** Chilmark, ✆ **508/645-2100;** or Aquinnah, ✆ **508/645-2300.** Also, many up-island inns offer the perk of temporary passes to residents-only beaches such as Lucy Vincent Beach.

Menemsha Beach ★★, next to Dutchers Dock in Menemsha Harbor, is a small but well-trafficked strand, with lifeguards and restrooms. Popular with families, in season it's virtually wall-to-wall colorful umbrellas and beach toys. The nearby food vendors in Menemsha are a plus (get a lobster dinner to go at the famous **Home Port** restaurant, see p. 291) and it's an ideal place to watch a sunset.

Down by Aquinnah, you have two beach options. The 2-mile beauty **Lobsterville Beach ★★**, at the end of Lobsterville Road on Menemsha Pond, has calm, shallow waters that are ideal for children. It's also a prime spot for birding—just past the dunes are nesting areas for terns and gulls. Parking, however, is for residents only—it's a great beach for bikers to hit on their way back from Aquinnah. Just east of the colorful cliffs, **Aquinnah Beach ★★★** (Moshup Beach), off Moshup Trail, is a peaceful half-mile beach. Parking costs $15 a day (note that the lot is small and a bit of a hike from the beach); in season, shuttle buses from down-island stop at the parking lot at the Aquinnah cliffs, from which you can walk to the beach. Although it is against the law, nudists tend to gravitate here. Remember that climbing the cliffs or stealing clay for a souvenir here is against the law, for environmental reasons: The cliffs are suffering from rapid erosion. Restrooms are near the parking lot.

In this woodsy area, it's not surprising that there are some wonderful nature preserves. The 300-acre **Cedar Tree Neck Sanctuary ★★★** (www.sheriffs meadow.org; ✆ **508/693-5207**) on State Road in Tisbury, has several trails leading through ponds, fields, woods, and bog to a picturesque bluff overlooking Vineyard Sound and the Elizabeth Islands. To get there, take State Road to Indian Hill Road to Obed Daggett Road and follow signs. The 633-acre **Long Point Wildlife Refuge ★★★**, off Waldron's Bottom Road in West Tisbury (www. thetrustees.org; ✆ **508/693-7392**), offers heath and dunes, freshwater ponds, a popular family-oriented beach, and interpretive nature walks for children. In season there's a $10 parking fee, plus $5 per person ages 16 and older. The **Menemsha Hills Reservation,** off North Road in Chilmark (www.thetrustees.org;

West Tisbury Farmers' Market

This seasonal outdoor market (www.wtf market.org; ℃ **508/693-9561**), open Wednesdays and Saturdays 9am to noon, is among the biggest and best in New England, and certainly the most rarefied, with local celebrities loading up on prize produce and snacking on pesto bread and other international goodies. The fun starts in June and runs for 18 Saturdays and 10 Wednesdays. It's located at the Old Agricultural Hall, West Tisbury, just up the road from Alley's General Store (facing).

℃ **508/693-7662**), encompasses 210 acres of rocks and bluffs, with steep paths, lovely views, and even a public beach.

Alley's General Store ★ HISTORIC SITE   In business since 1858—it's the oldest operating retail business on Martha's Vineyard—this prime example of that endangered species, the true New England general store, nearly foundered in the 1980s. Luckily, the Martha's Vineyard Preservation Trust interceded to give it a new lease on life, along with a much-needed structural overhaul. The stock is still the same, though: basically, everything you could possibly need, from scrub brushes to fresh-made salsa. The no-longer-sagging front porch still supports a popular bank of benches, along with a blizzard of bulletin-board notices. For local activities and events, check here first.

State Rd., West Tisbury. ℃ **508/693-0088.** Summer Mon–Sat 7am–7pm, Sun 7am–6pm; closes 1 hr. earlier in winter.

Gay Head Lighthouse & Aquinnah Cliffs ★★ SCENIC LOOKOUT
It is a bit of a journey to go all the way up island to see the famous red cliffs of Aquinnah and the iconic red brick Gay Head Lighthouse, but it's well worth the trip. From the large parking lot, a steep slope leads up to a small compound with several shops with tourist trinkets and Native American crafts, as well as a couple of casual though pricey eateries. But it is free to walk to the viewing platform to look out at the magnificent panoramic view of the cliffs and the ocean. The lighthouse nearby, which was recently moved away from the rapidly eroding cliff, is open daily in season.

65 State Rd., Aquinnah. www.gayheadlight.org. ℃ **508/645-2300.** $6 lighthouse admission, free for kids under 12. June–Aug daily 10am–4pm. Additional sunset tours 6-8pm Thurs and Fri. Call for off-season hours.

Polly Hill Arboretum ★ GARDENS   This is a magical place, particularly mid-June to July when the Dogwood Allee is in bloom. Horticulturist Polly Hill developed this 20-acre property over the past 40 years and allows the public to wander the grounds. Wanderers will pass old stone walls on the way to the Tunnel of Love, an arbor of bleached hornbeam. There are also witch hazels, camellias, magnolias, and rhododendrons. To get there from Vineyard Haven, go south on State Road, bearing left at the junction of North Road. The arboretum entrance is about a half-mile down on the right.

809 State Rd., West Tisbury. www.pollyhillarboretum.org. ℃ **508/693-9426.** $5 admission. Guided tours at 2pm. Visitor center and plant sale open 9:30am–4:30pm. Grounds open daily sunrise–sunset.

UP ISLAND SHOPPING

Chilmark Pottery, 145 Field View Lane, off State Road in West Tisbury (℅ **508/693-6476**), features tableware fashioned to suit its setting. Geoffrey Borr takes his palette from the sea and sky and produces serviceable stoneware with clean lines and a long life span. Two miles down the road, at **Martha's Vineyard Glass Works,** 683 State Rd. (www.mvglassworks.com; ℅ **508/693-6026**) world-renowned master glassblowers sometimes lend a hand just for the fun of it, at this handsome rural studio/shop. Another 2 miles down State Road is **The Field Gallery** (1050 State Rd.; www.fieldgallery.com; ℅ **508/693-5595**), where Tom Maley's playful figures set in a rural pasture have enchanted locals and passersby for decades. You'll also find paintings by Albert Alcalay and drawings and cartoons by Jules Feiffer. Their Sunday evening openings are high points of the summer social season. Closed mid-October to mid-May. The **Granary Gallery at the Red Barn** (www.granary gallery.com; ℅ **800/472-6279**), at 636 Old County Rd. (off Edgartown–West Tisbury Road, about ¼-mile north of the intersection), displays astounding prints by the late longtime summerer Alfred Eisenstaedt, dazzling color photos by local luminary Alison Shaw, and a changing roster of fine artists—some just emerging, some long since "discovered." A fine selection of country and provincial antiques is also sold here. Open April to December, and by appointment only January through March.

Outdoor Activities on Martha's Vineyard

FISHING Deep-sea excursions can be arranged aboard **North Shore Charters** (www.bassnblue.com; ℅ **508/645-2993**), out of Menemsha, locus of the island's commercial fishing fleet (you may recognize this weathered port from the movie *Jaws*). Charter costs are about $700 for a half-day.

Cooper Gilkes III, proprietor of **Coop's Bait & Tackle,** at 147 W. Tisbury Rd. in Edgartown (www.coopsbaitandtackle.com; ℅ **508/627-3909**), offers rentals as well as supplies. He's available as an instructor or charter guide and is even amenable to sharing hard-won pointers on local hot spots. For shellfishing you'll need to get information and a permit from the appropriate town hall. Popular spots for surf-casting (requires a $10 license available at town halls) include **Wasque Point** (Wasque Reservation), on Chappaquiddick (see p. 276).

GOLF The 9-hole **Mink Meadows Golf Course,** at 320 Golf Club Rd., off Franklin Street, in Vineyard Haven (www.minkmeadowsgc.com; ℅ **508/693-0600**), despite occupying a top-dollar chunk of real estate, is open to the general public. There is also the semiprivate, championship-level 18-hole **Farm Neck Golf Club,** off Farm Neck Way, in Oak Bluffs (www.farmneck.net; ℅ **508/693-3057**). The Cafe at Farm Neck serves a wonderful lunch overlooking the manicured greens. In season, greens fees at Mink Meadows are $70 for 9 holes and $100 for 18 holes; at Farm Neck, it's $175 (including cart) for 18 holes.

MOUNTAIN BIKING The adventurous **mountain biker** will want to head to the 8 miles of trails in the **Manuel F. Correllus State Forest** (www.mass.gov/locations/manuel-f-correllus-state-forest; ℅ **508/693-2540**), a vast spread of scrub oak and pine smack-dab in the middle of the island that also boasts paved paths and hiking and horseback-riding trails. For those seeking an escape from the multitudes, the trails are so extensive that even during peak summer season, it is possible to not see another soul for hours. On most of the conservation land on the Vineyard, mountain biking is prohibited, for environmental reasons.

WATERSPORTS **Wind's Up,** 199 Beach Rd., Vineyard Haven (www.winds upmv.com; © **508/693-4252**), rents out canoes, kayaks, and various sailing craft, including sailboards, and offers instruction on-site, on a placid pond; it also rents surfboards and boogie boards. Canoes and kayaks rent for $20 per hour and $50 for a full day.

Where to Stay on Martha's Vineyard

In the summer season, overnight lodging is expensive on Martha's Vineyard. Prices start to come down to earth in the fall with great deals to be had in the winter and spring. But if you are set on visiting in summer, consider renting a cottage for a week, where you can take advantage of a kitchen for meals.

EDGARTOWN

Charlotte Inn ★★   The hotel version of a Ralph Lauren advertisement, this stately inn in the center of town has a hushed quality about it. The rooms are full of intriguing antiques and knickknacks, elaborate boudoir sets and statuary. The rooms are all completely distinct. Take room 14: You enter through mahogany doors to an elegant accommodation with a fireplace and a baby grand. It's time travel, Vineyard-style. The inn's fine-dining restaurant, The Terrace at the Charlotte Inn, is set in the conservatory dining room and out on the adjacent terrace. Local fare from the island's farms and fishermen is enlivened with French and Italian preparations.

27 S. Summer St. www.thecharlotteinn.com. © **508/627-4151.** 19 units. Summer $425–$750 double; $895–$1,000 suite. No children 13 and under. **Amenities:** Restaurant; Wi-Fi (free).

The Christopher ★★   This handsome old whaling captain's house, a block from Edgartown Harbor, is now part of the Lark Hotel Group, which are boutique hotels with a playful sense of style. This is a very well-run property, spotlessly clean and well maintained. Rooms are freshly remodeled with colorful contemporary decor in a style they call "coastal chic." The breakfast is so plentiful that you might be able to skip lunch.

24 S. Water St. www.thechristophermv.com. © **508/627-4784.** 15 units. Summer $259–$639 double. Rates include full breakfast. Closed Dec–Mar. **Amenities:** Wi-Fi (free).

Edgartown Inn ★   Built as the 1798 residence of the whaling captain Thomas Worth (see p. 275), this is perhaps the island's oldest continuously operating lodging house. As other inns have become more and more pricey, this one has stayed fairly reasonable—making it one of the best lodging bargains on the island. Furnishings are charmingly old-fashioned, with lots of floral wallpapers, ruffled gauze curtains, and wicker and rattan furniture; several are named after famous people who've stayed here, from Daniel

Edgartown

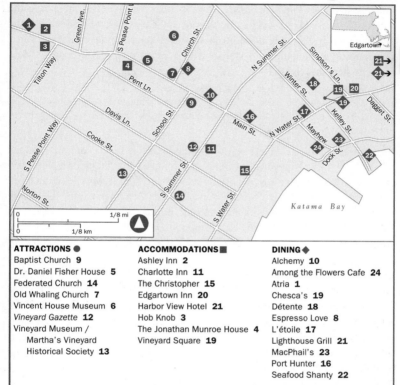

ATTRACTIONS ●
Baptist Church **9**
Dr. Daniel Fisher House **5**
Federated Church **14**
Old Whaling Church **7**
Vincent House Museum **6**
Vineyard Gazette **12**
Vineyard Museum /
   Martha's Vineyard
   Historical Society **13**

ACCOMMODATIONS ■
Ashley Inn **2**
Charlotte Inn **11**
The Christopher **15**
Edgartown Inn **20**
Harbor View Hotel **21**
Hob Knob **3**
The Jonathan Munroe House **4**
Vineyard Square **19**

DINING ◆
Alchemy **10**
Among the Flowers Cafe **24**
Atria **1**
Chesca's **19**
Détente **18**
Espresso Love **8**
L'étoile **17**
Lighthouse Grill **21**
MacPhail's **23**
Port Hunter **16**
Seafood Shanty **22**

Webster and Nathaniel Hawthorne to John F. Kennedy. The inn has long been known for its country breakfasts, which are open to the public.

56 N. Water St., Edgartown. www.edgartowninn.com. ℂ **508/627-4794.** 14 units. Summer $175–$375 double. Rates include continental breakfast. Free parking. Closed Nov–Mar. No children 12 and under. **Amenities:** Wi-Fi (free).

Harbor View Hotel & Resort ★★   Still a grand old hotel, the Harborview occupies a commanding spot. Relaxing in a rocking chair on the huge verandah overlooking the harbor is something guests here have been doing for more than 100 years. The 114 rooms here are in three areas: the main building, the Governor Mayhew building, and in cottages on the grounds. Rooms have in common a high-toned elegance, on the fancy side of beachy. The two main restaurants, **Lighthouse Grill** and **Henry's** (see p. 285), serve, between them, three meals a day; casual poolside food is also served at **North 41.**

131 N. Water St. www.harbor-view.com. ℂ **800/225-6005** or 508/627-7000. 114 units. Summer $499–$650 double; $1,200 1-bedroom suite; $1,500 2-bedroom suite; $1,800–$2,100 3-bedroom suite. **Amenities:** 3 restaurants; heated outdoor pool; babysitting; concierge; fitness center; room service; spa; Wi-Fi (free).

The Hob Knob ★★★ This very stylish B&B was inspired by the owner's grandparents, bon vivants who gallivanted around the Ohio countryside, overflowing silver tumblers in hand. Now an eco-friendly boutique hotel, the building has served as a lodging house since at least 1947, when a windblown Senator John F. Kennedy is said to have stayed here during a sailing regatta. The interior is exceptionally stylish with a sense of humor—a cow theme crops up here and there.

128 Main St. www.hobknob.com. ℰ **800/696-2723** or 508/627-9510. 17 units, 3-bedroom and 4-bedroom cottage. Summer $599–$720 double. Rates include full breakfast and afternoon tea. No children 6 and under. **Amenities:** Rental bikes ($20 per day); exercise room; room service; spa; Wi-Fi (free).

Vineyard Square Hotel ★★ A large boutique hotel, centrally located in Edgartown, the Vineyard Square is in a complex that includes a salon and day spa, fitness center, art gallery, and boutique. The rooms have all been redone in recent years in what you might call "beach modern." The more expensive ones have views of Edgartown Harbor. There's quite a variety in size, with the smallest called "cozy" rooms. Continental breakfast is a large buffet spread for guests in season. The inn's roof deck, with wonderful harbor views, is outstanding.

38 N. Water St. www.vineyardsquarehotel.com. ℰ **800/627-4701** or 508/627-4711. 28 units. Summer $395–$525 double; $590–$1,095 suite or efficiency. Rates include continental breakfast. Closed Dec–Mar. Pets allowed in designated rooms. **Amenities:** Restaurant; fitness room; spa; Wi-Fi (free).

Winnetu Oceanside Resort ★★★ This resort, set near one of the Vineyard's best full-surf beaches, has more amenities than any other island resort—and prices to match. The rooms are all suites with one to four bedrooms. Winnetu is very much set up with families in mind. There is a children's day program, a parent/toddler program, tennis club, heated swimming pools, a fitness facility, free fitness classes and yoga on the lawn, and, perhaps most important, shuttle transportation by land or water taxi to Edgartown's Main Street. A nearby sister compound has home rentals and vacation condos.

31 Dunes Rd. (at South Beach). www.winnetu.com. ℰ **866/335-1133** or 508/310-1733. 54 units. Summer $550–$835 1-bedroom suite; $920–$1,595 2- to 4-bedroom suite; $1,485–$1,975 2-bedroom cottages. Closed Nov–Mar. **Amenities:** Restaurant; children's program (early June–early Sept); free in-season hourly shuttle to Edgartown; concierge; fitness room; general store; outdoor heated pool; putting green; tennis courts w/pro; Wi-Fi (free).

OAK BLUFFS

The Dockside Inn ★★ The family-friendly Dockside is located just steps from Oak Bluffs Harbor. Its rooms are comfortable, though decor is upscale motel-like; they open onto a double-decker wrap-around balcony, and several rooms have views of the harbor. There are several clubs nearby, which may or not be a good thing—streets are definitely hopping around here until

1am. There are two-person rooms, four-person rooms, and five-person suites which also have kitchenettes.

9 Circuit Ave. Ext. www.vineyardinns.com. © **800/245-5979** or 508/693-2966. 21 units. Summer $319–$369 double; $389–$429 suite. Rates include continental breakfast. Closed late Oct–early Apr. Pets allowed. **Amenities:** 6-seat hot tub; Wi-Fi (free).

Isabelle's Beach House ★ At what's the best in a line-up of B&Bs across from the ocean in Oak Bluffs, you could while away the afternoon in a rocker on the front porch. As is typical with a converted Victorian house, some of the rooms are a tad small. There are plenty of old-fashioned touches, like wicker beds and pedestal sinks in the bedrooms. Since the inn is oceanfront, when a storm blows in, the windows of the old place have quite a rattle.

83 Seaview Ave. www.isabellesbeachhouse.com. © **800/674-3129** or 508/693-3955. 11 units. Summer $375–$395 double; $450–$575 suite. Rates include continental breakfast. Closed late Oct–early May. **Amenities:** Wi-Fi (free).

The Oak Bluffs Inn ★ After seeing all the fancifully decorated gingerbread cottages in Oak Bluffs, you may want to stay in one yourself. Here it is, a big pink confection with elaborate trim and turrets. This is a terrific location for an easy walk to restaurants, shops, clubs, and the harbor. Rooms are simply and tastefully decorated in soothing muted colors.

64 Circuit Ave. (at Pequot Ave.). www.oakbluffsinn.com. © **800/955-6235** or 508/693-7171. 9 units. Summer $280–$380 double; $600 2-bedroom suite. Rates include continental breakfast. Closed Nov–Apr. **Amenities:** Wi-Fi (free).

Summercamp ★ This Victorian hotel, in continuous operation since 1879 (formerly known as The Wesley), has had a top-to-bottom upgrade and name change under new management, the Lark Hotel chain of boutique hotels. One of the larger hotels on the island, it overlooks Oak Bluffs Harbor, so many rooms offer terrific harbor views. Rooms are outfitted with colorful modern decor in a distinctly playful style. *Note:* The bathrooms have showers only, no tubs.

70 Lake Ave. www.summercamphotel.com. © **800/638-9027** or 508/693-6611. 95 units. Summer $350–$495 double; $355–$525 suite. Closed late Oct–Apr. **Amenities:** Wi-Fi (free).

VINEYARD HAVEN

Mansion House on Martha's Vineyard ★ A rambling shingled hotel right on Vineyard Haven's Main Street and steps from the ferry, this is a nice location for people who like to be in the thick of it. This is one of the few Vineyard lodging choices with a pool, and it's a beauty, a 75-foot pool in the basement. Some rooms have a view of the harbor from private balconies; all are decorated in a modern minimalist style, fresh and clean. Beds are particularly comfortable. The **Copper Wok** restaurant (see p. 289) is downstairs.

9 Main St. www.mvmansionhouse.com. © **800/332-4112** or 508/693-2200. 32 units. $309–$409 double; $349–$619 suite. Rates include full buffet breakfast. Pets accepted in some rooms (call ahead). **Amenities:** Restaurant; indoor pool, health club; room service; Wi-Fi (free).

Beach Plum Inn ★★   Under the same ownership as the Menemsha Inn next door (see below), this upscale hotel has one of the island's top restaurants, the **Beach Plum Restaurant** (see p. 290), on site. The main inn building and cottages are set in a 7-acre garden property with colorful flowers throughout. The rooms, some in cottages and some in the main house, vary widely in size, but all are decorated in a pleasing French country style. Many of the rooms in the main house have balconies, screened-in porches, or patios, the better to enjoy harbor breezes.

50 Beach Plum Lane (off North Rd.), Menemsha. www.beachpluminn.com. ✆ **508/645-9454.** 11 units. Summer $380–$770 double or cottage. Rates include full breakfast in season, continental off-season. Closed Jan–Apr. **Amenities:** Restaurant; babysitting by arrangement; croquet court; tennis court; Wi-Fi (free).

The Captain R. Flanders House ★   This 1700s country farmhouse is on the west end of the island, on 60 rolling acres of farmland, with horses and sheep grazing and the aptly named Bliss Pond. The house, simply decorated with period antiques, has four rooms, with two that share a bathroom and two with private bathrooms. There are also two small stand-alone cottages, each with a bedroom, sitting area, and kitchenette.

440 North Rd., Chilmark. www.captainflandersinn.com. ✆ **508/645-3123.** 4 units, 2 w/ shared bath; 2 cottages. Summer $190 double w/shared bath; $225 double w/private bath; $300 cottage. Rates include continental breakfast. Closed Nov–early May. **Amenities:** Private beach pass; shuttle bus to beach, bikes to borrow; Wi-Fi (free).

Hostelling International–Martha's Vineyard ★   Set in a large forest in the geographic center of the island, this hostel isn't the most conveniently located. Bikes are an option for getting around, but a shuttle bus also stops here. The facility is run with efficiency, and staff members are known for their friendliness, which, for a traveler, may be the most important quality of all. The rooms are set up with bunk beds, 4 to 10 beds per room.

525 Edgartown–West Tisbury Rd., West Tisbury. www.capecod.hiusa.org. ✆ **888/901-2087** or 508/693-2665. 67 beds, 1 family room. Beds $29 for HIUSA members; $42 for nonmembers; $150–$200 private room. Closed mid-Oct to mid-May. **Amenities:** Wi-Fi (free).

Menemsha Inn & Cottages ★★★   This is a casual down-to-earth place, a far cry from the touristy part of the Vineyard. It's a brisk quarter-mile walk from this 25-acre estate to the center of the fishing village of Menemsha. But mostly a stay here is about getting away from it all. The Carriage House and the Tea House have 15 rustic rooms; the large stone fireplace in the Carriage House is a gathering spots for guests to plan their day. The mainstay suite is by itself, above the reception area in the inn's main building. In addition, there are 12 Sea View Cottages of one or two bedrooms, with kitchens, wood-burning fireplaces, and great views of Menemsha Harbor.

12 Menemsha Rd., Menemsha. www.menemshainn.com. ✆ **508/645-2521.** 15 units, 12 cottages. Summer $370 double; $550–$735 suite; $1,995–$3,300 1-bedroom cottage, $3,995 per week 2-bedroom cottage. Rates include continental breakfast (not in

cottages). Closed Dec to mid-Apr. Dogs allowed in certain rooms. **Amenities:** Fitness room; tennis court; Wi-Fi (free).

Where to Eat on Martha's Vineyard

Note that outside Oak Bluffs, Edgartown, and Vineyard Haven (also known as Tisbury), all of Martha's Vineyard is "dry," but you can bring your own wine or other alcoholic beverage; some restaurants charge a small fee for uncorking. **Jim's Package Store,** at 27 Lake Ave. in Oak Bluffs (www.jimspackage store.com; ℂ **508/693-0236**) is the place to pick up supplies.

EDGARTOWN
Expensive

Atria/Brick Cellar Bar ★★★ NEW AMERICAN Many of the Vineyard's fanciest restaurants, including Atria, also have a more casual dining area (and less expensive menu). The Brick Cellar Bar here, with live music, bumper pool, and fish tanks, has perhaps the Vineyard's best burger menu, from the PETA (vegetarian, with a marinated Portobello) to the Atria classic, with cheddar, sautéed onions, mushrooms, apple-smoked bacon and béarnaise sauce. The pleasures of the bar cannot be overstated, but upstairs, the main dining room offers the more lauded experience. Traditional surf-and-turf is turned on its head with Georges Bank scallops and red wine–braised short ribs. A 2-pound lobster is wok-fired and served with whipped potatoes. It's all delicious.

137 Main St. www.atriamv.com. ℂ **508/627-5850.** Atria main courses $34–$60, Brick Cellar Bar $16–$26. June–Aug daily 5:30–10pm; call for off-season hours. Closed Dec to mid-Mar.

Chesca's ★ ITALIAN What distinguishes this classic Italian restaurant may be a boisterous bar scene where you can catch a game on TV while dining. The casual and lively restaurant also includes an enclosed porch for a quieter dining experience. This is the place to bring a large group and enjoy a big bowl of pasta—perhaps lobster ravioli and seared scallops or pappardelle Bolognese?—for a fun night out.

At the Colonial Inn, 38 N. Water St. www.chescasmv.com. ℂ **508/627-1234.** Main courses $30–$40. Mid-June to mid-Oct daily 5:30–9:30pm; call for off-season hours. Closed Nov to mid-Apr.

L'étoile ★★★ CONTEMPORARY FRENCH Long known for being the fanciest restaurant in a town of fancy restaurants, L'étoile now has a bar menu if you want the experience of eating the exquisite cuisine of Chef Michael Brisson without the intimidating prices. Locally caught and sourced fish, meat, and vegetables are the mainstay here. What it all has in common is care in combinations, flavors, colors, and presentation.

22 N. Water St. (off Main St.). www.letoile.net. ℂ **508/627-5187.** Main courses $31–$55; chef's tasting menu $99. Mid-June to mid-Sept 6–10pm; call for off-season hours. Closed Dec–Apr.

Lighthouse Grill/Henry's Pub ★★ NEW AMERICAN Whether you prefer the fancy atmosphere of the Lighthouse Grill, a special occasion summer-only restaurant with big windows offering views out to Edgartown Lighthouse and Edgartown Harbor, or the clubby gastropub atmosphere of Henry's Pub, you are assured of good food. Both restaurants have a selection of small dishes suitable for sharing in addition to the traditional menu. Bistro fare at Henry's includes local chicken with a sweet-potato puree and pig cheek Bolognese with fresh rigatoni. At Lighthouse Grill, you might find unabashedly fancy choices on the menu, like duck with rhubarb coulis, or Faroe Island salmon with snap peas and a wasabi potato spring roll. Desserts are not to be missed here, in particular the pear bombe, which is a pear mousse with a Chinese five-spice cake.

At the Harbor View Hotel, 131 N. Water St. www.harbor-view.com/dining. ☏ **508/627-3761.** Lighthouse Grill main courses $30–$50; Henry's small plates $12–$26. June–Aug both restaurants open 6–10pm; Henry's also open daily 7–10:30am and 11am–5pm; Lighthouse also open Sunday brunch 10am–2pm. Call for off-season hours. Lighthouse Grill closed mid-Sept to late May.

Restaurant Détente ★★ NEW AMERICAN   Both this hidden gem and its menu are small but expertly executed and innovative. People book days in advance for dishes like local monkfish with Spanish octopus, mint, grapefruit, and hazelnut ravioli. As a main course, choose between Vineyard fluke with buttermilk risotto or perhaps squid ink fettuccine with Menemsha lobster. It all gets pricey, but it's worth it for a special occasion.

15 Winter St. (in Nevin Sq., behind the Colonial Inn). www.detentemv.com. ☏ **508/627-8810.** Main courses $32–$44. 6-course tasting menu $75. June–Aug daily 5:30–10pm; call for off-season hours. Closed Jan–mid-Apr.

Moderate

The Port Hunter ★ AMERICAN   This casual flatbread pizza and burgers place is also the best live (and loud) music venue in Edgartown. The menu always has creative specials like tempura shrimp with a ginger dipping sauce; catch of the day like grilled scup (porgy) with mixed greens; and vegetarian choices including pastas. There is also a raw bar with local shellfish. The music—local bands and others—is typically 10pm to midnight.

55 Main St. www.theporthunter.com. ☏ **508/627-7747.** Main courses $16–$32. Mid-May to Nov daily 5:30–10pm; call for off-season hours.

The Seafood Shanty ★ SEAFOOD   What distinguishes this seafood shack from others along the waterfront is the two levels of indoor and outdoor dining. The roof deck overlooking Edgartown Harbor is really the ultimate place to enjoy a meal in this quaint seaside town. The menu includes sushi and sashimi, with special rolls and platters served all day and evening. The owners strive to serve only sustainable and locally caught seafood and shellfish, prepared in a healthful manner.

31 Dock St. www.theseafoodshanty.com. ☏ **508/627-8622.** Lunch $13–$22; dinner $13–$34. June–Aug daily 11am–9pm; call for off-season hours. Closed Nov to mid-May.

Inexpensive

Among the Flowers Cafe ★★ AMERICAN   A charming little cafe, Among the Flowers is where to go for a moderately priced lunch or dinner that feels like visiting a friend. Outdoor seating on the patio is particularly pleasant. For breakfast, best bets are apple cinnamon French toast and omelets loaded with veggies. Lunch, though, is really the standout here, with lobster rolls, turkey wraps, and even scallop kebobs.

17 Mayhew Lane. www.mvol.com/menu/amongtheflowers. ✆ **508/627-3233.** Main courses $10–$18. Late June–early Sept daily 8am–9:30pm; late Apr–June and Sept to mid-Oct daily 8am–4pm. Closed late Oct to mid-Apr.

Espresso Love ★★ AMERICAN   The place is a little difficult to find, tucked back behind a parking lot off Main Street in Edgartown. But once you find it, you'll be glad you did. The MV Blue Beast Sandwich (roast beef, caramelized onion, blue cheese, and mayo) may be reason enough to visit this deli/gourmet restaurant. It's a go-to place for breakfast and lunch, with burgers, salads, and soups the mainstays. In season, they also serve dinner.

17 Church St. (off Main St., behind the courthouse). www.espressolove.com. ✆ **508/627-9211.** Main courses $12–$18. July–Aug daily 6:30am–8pm; off-season Mon–Sat 6:30am–6pm, Sun 6:30am–4pm.

MacPhail's Corner Café ★ DINER   Six oranges go into each glass of fresh-squeezed juice and muffins are baked daily at this top-notch diner steps from the harbor. Breakfast is all day and the bacon, egg, and cheese sandwich is a winner. For lunch, there is clam chowder, lobster rolls, and huge cookies.

18 Dock St. ✆ **508/939-3090.** All items under $15. July–Aug daily 8am–6pm.

The Newes from America ★★ PUB GRUB   If you're looking for a pub with atmosphere, this one has it. Set in the basement of a 1742 building, the Newes has beams, brick walls, and a hearth. The pub food includes bangers and mash; curry fries; and of course fish and chips. The beer menu's extensive, too.

At The Kelley House, 23 Kelley St. www.kelley-house.com. ✆ **508/627-4397.** Main courses $11–$17. Daily 11:30am–11pm.

OAK BLUFFS
Expensive
Martha's Vineyard Chowder Company ★★ NEW AMERICAN Located across from the Flying Horses carousel, this restaurant has sort of a dark, clublike atmosphere when you enter. As you might hope, the signature soup is indeed special—made from scratch with a thin cream base, bacon, and lots of clams ($9 for a cup; $12 for a bowl). Other highlights on the menu are fresh seared scallops with a corn and herb risotto, and the prosciutto-wrapped fresh cod with potato gnocchi.

9 Oak Bluffs Ave. www.mvchowder.com. ✆ **508/696-3000.** Main courses $27–$29. May–Nov daily 11am–10pm; call for off-season hours.

The Red Cat Kitchen at Ken 'N' Beck ★★★ NEW AMERICAN Chef Ben DeForest has created a winner here, in this quirky little hole-in-the-wall on a side street in Oak Bluffs. DeForest's signature dish is Island Fresca, a soup of corn broth, tomatoes, corn, and butter, topped with Parmesan and basil oil. Fresh from the Vineyard, it tastes like a summer day. The rest changes with the season. You won't be disappointed.

14 Kennebec Ave. www.redcatkitchen.com. ℰ **508/696-6040.** Main courses $25–$48. May–Nov daily 6–10pm; call for off-season hours.

Sweet Life Cafe ★★ FRENCH/AMERICAN

Set in a restored Victorian house, this high-end choice has a large outdoor patio, with tables lit by candles and under Japanese umbrellas. It is lovely on a summer evening. Inside is casual elegance. If it's on the menu when you visit, try the striped-bass ceviche in season as an appetizer. Among the main courses, king salmon with broccoli-rabe risotto, sun-dried tomatoes, and white anchovies is a pleasing—and filling—combination. Grass-fed sirloin comes with greens from the Vineyard's Morning Glory Farm and, at the other end of the dining spectrum, there's a house-made fettuccine with roasted broccoli pesto on ginger carrot puree.

63 Circuit Ave. www.sweetlifemv.com. ℰ **508/696-0200.** Main courses $32–$40. Mid-May to Aug daily 5:30–9pm. Closed late Sept to mid-May.

Moderate

Coop de Ville ★ SEAFOOD

The beauty of this place is the outdoor raw bar where you can sit facing Oak Bluffs harbor and watch the boats come and go. There is no indoor seating, but there is an awning over the seating. Fried fish, hamburgers, chicken wings, and lobster dinners are the staples here, washed down with a cold brew ($10 on draft, $12 in bottles).

Dockside Market Place. www.coopdevillemv.com. ℰ **508/693-3420.** Main courses $6–$25. June–Aug daily 11am–10pm; call for off-season hours. Closed late Sept–Apr.

Linda Jean's ★ DINER

A summer staple in Oak Bluffs since 1976, this diner with a long counter and cozy booths and tables is a particularly good choice for breakfast, although by mid-morning in season, the line waiting for a table goes out the door.

25 Circuit Ave. ℰ **508/693-4093.** Main courses $6–$24. June–Aug daily 8am–7pm; call for off-season hours.

Sharky's Cantina ★ MEXICAN

With many menu items under $15, this high-octane Mexican restaurant is a great place for budget travelers. On the menu are the usual burritos and chimichangas, but also an entire wings menu with fun flavors like tango mango teriyaki. Beverages are a specialty here, with carefully made margaritas and frozen drinks. Note that Sharky's gets fairly loud on weekend evenings in summer.

31 Circuit Ave. www.sharkyscantina.com. ℰ **508/693-7501.** Main courses $10–$29. June–Aug daily 11am–12:30am; call for off-season hours.

Slice of Life ★ DELI

This cafe serves upscale deli food at breakfast, lunch, and dinner at reasonable prices. A lunch favorite is the meatloaf sandwich on a ciabatta roll. At dinner, you could have pan-seared salmon with sweet-potato hash or even fish and chips.

50 Circuit Ave. www.sliceoflifemv.com. ℰ **508/693-3838.** Main courses $11–$29. June–Aug daily 8am–8pm; call for off-season hours.

New Englanders do like their ice cream, and the Vineyard's go-to ice cream outfit is **Mad Martha's ★**. Founded in 1971, it now has shops in Oak Bluffs (117 Circuit Ave.), Edgartown (7 N. Water St.), and Vineyard Haven (48 Main St.). They offer just over a dozen homemade flavors, and they're so good, you'll wish there were even more. The scoops are huge (one is plenty). It's cash only here, and the ice-cream counter is open daily 11am to midnight, May through September only.

Wherever you find a Mad Martha's, you can bet there'll be a **Murdick's Fudge ★** shop (www.murdicks.com) down the street—they're at 5 Circuit Ave. in Oak Bluffs, 21 N. Water St. in Edgartown, and 79 Main St. in Vineyard Haven. This velvety sugar-laden concoction is the top fudge on the island, made from the same recipe since 1887; kids enjoy watching it being made right there in the storefront. Shops are open in summer daily 10am to 11pm; call for off-season hours.

Inexpensive

Martha's Vineyard Gourmet Cafe & Bakery ★ BAKERY   You can't imagine the heavenly smell and then taste of a chocolate donut pulled fresh out of the oven at midnight on Martha's Vineyard. That is when people line up at Back Door Donuts (the alleyway in the back of this coffee shop) for extraordinary baked goods—donuts and apple fritters—fresh out of the oven.

5 Post Office Sq. www.backdoordonuts.com. © **508/693-3688.** Mid-Apr to Oct daily 6am–10pm. Back Door Donuts 7:30pm–1am. Call for off-season hours. Closed mid-Oct to mid-Apr.

VINEYARD HAVEN
Expensive

Garde East ★★ NEW AMERICAN   You may go for the view, a calming expanse of Vineyard Haven Harbor, but you'll remember the cuisine: French-inspired of-the-moment (okay, trendy) preparations of all the bounty the island has to offer. Diners might start with cauliflower tartar with Okinawan sweet potato chips and harissa yogurt; move on to lobster cavatelli with black trumpet mushrooms; and follow that with a pan-seared sea bass with chorizo emulsion. Homemade desserts include a hazelnut mousse with Vineyard smoked sea salt caramel ice cream.

52 Beach Rd. (at the Vineyard Haven Marina). www.gardeeast.com. © **508/687-9926.** Main courses $28–$38. June–Sept daily 5–9:30pm; call for off-season hours.

Moderate

Copper Wok ★ PAN ASIAN   Pan-Asian is how the cuisine is described at this sleek restaurant in the Mansion House hotel (see p. 283), steps from the ferry in Vineyard Haven. Besides Chinese food, there are dishes from India and Thailand, as well as a full 20-seat sushi bar. The Chinese items on the menu are a bargain for the Vineyard; the sushi is on the pricey side, with rolls starting at $7 and going up to $23.

9 Main St. (at the Mansion House). www.copperwokmv.com. © **508/693-3416.** Main courses $12–$19. June–Sept daily 11:30am–9:30pm; call for off-season hours.

THE LEGEND OF THE black dog

Back in 1969—or so the story goes—Captain Robert Douglas, a local sailor, spent a late cold night in Vineyard Haven and wanted a good meal. There were no restaurants open, and the only food he could find was a packaged stale donut from a convenience store. From that experience, he got the idea of building a good year-round tavern on the harbor in Vineyard Haven. The rest is (marketing) history, as the tavern logo—a silhouetted Black Lab—has been plastered on t-shirts, sweatshirts, coffee mugs, and just about everything else possible. You'll find the gear sold all over the island (and on Cape Cod as well); go to www.theblackdog.com for locations. Or buy the stuff on the website and just say you went to Martha's Vineyard to get it.

Nevertheless, the **Black Dog Tavern** (Beach St. Ext.; www.theblackdog.com; ✆ **508/693-9223**) remains on the Vineyard Haven harborfront, open all winter long for breakfast, lunch, and dinner (summer hours are 7am–9pm; call for off-season hours.) You can still get a steaming cup of quahog chowder on a winter day here, as well as fish and chips and chicken potpie. Old-time favorites are clams casino, grilled swordfish and, for meat-lovers: bacon-wrapped meatloaf. Friday is lobster night: On sunny days, try to get a seat on the porch next to the harbor. Main courses range from $20 to $45. Reservations are a very good idea.

Just as popular is the **Black Dog Bakery** ★ (11 Water St.; ✆ **508/693-4786**), which is the first place you pass as you get off the ferry in Vineyard Haven; this is where travelers in the know get their coffee and snack for the ferry ride. Muffins are a specialty, as are—naturally—dog biscuits.

Inexpensive

Art Cliff Diner ★★ DINER   Every town should have a really good diner with a sense of fun. At Art Cliff, even the menu is playful. Green eggs and ham? That's an omelet with Swiss cheese, spinach, and ham. There are frittatas, crepes and wonderful Drunken Sailor Pancakes (pecan pancakes with real rum sauce). Go early or late or you'll never make it in the door. If the wait's too long, there's always the food truck parked out front, with burgers, hotdogs, and pulled-pork sandwiches, and Parmesan fries.

39 Beach Rd. www.artcliffdiner.com. ✆ **508/693-1224.** No reservations. Main courses all under $15. No credit cards. July–Aug Thurs–Tues 7am–2pm; call for off-season hours. Closed Nov to mid-Apr.

CHILMARK, MENEMSHA & WEST TISBURY

The Beach Plum Inn Restaurant ★★★ NEW AMERICAN   This secluded restaurant in the Beach Plum Inn (see p. 284) is one of the best on the island. A big long table is the focus point, though there are also individual tables. The focus here is on local food, be it a salad of North Tabor Farm greens or Menemsha mussels. In a restaurant with views of the harbor, you can't go wrong with fish, either. This is Chilmark and that means BYOB.

At the Beach Plum Inn, 50 Beach Plum Lane (off North Rd.), Menemsha. www.beachpluminn.com. ✆ **508/645-9454.** Prix fixe $80. Mid-June to early Sept Thurs–Mon 6–8:30pm; call for off-season hours. Closed Dec to mid-May.

Home Port Restaurant ★★ SEAFOOD   At some point after 1930, when the Home Port opened on the slope overlooking Menemsha Harbor, it became not just a casual clam shack but an institution, a place that defined summer for Vineyard visitors. It's still a place for lobster dinners and sunsets, but now it's also about sustainable fisheries and using fish caught by local fishermen. Best bets are the fish taco or the varied fried fish platters. The sunset's thrown in for free. BYOB.

512 North Rd., Menemsha. www.homeportmv.com. © **508/645-2679.** Main courses $14–$54. July–Aug daily 5–9pm; call for off-season hours. To-go window 11:30am–9pm. Closed Labor Day to mid-May.

State Road Restaurant ★★ NEW AMERICAN   The restaurant, located way off the tourist track in North Tisbury, bills itself as a "contemporary American tavern," and though it is open year-round, it is certainly more upscale than the usual tavern. The restaurant's stone fireplace, rough-hewn beamed ceiling, shingle-sided porch, and paintings by the rural master Alan Whiting make it resemble a farmhouse. The menu focuses on Island products, from the Vineyard greens salad to the Briar Patch farm rabbit with Parmesan polenta. The drinks list features ciders, craft beers, and carefully selected wines by the glass and bottle.

688 State Rd., West Tisbury. www.stateroadrestaurant.com. © **508/693-8582.** Main courses $24–$52. July–Aug daily 5:30–10pm; Sunday 8am–2pm. Call for off-season hours.

Martha's Vineyard Entertainment & Nightlife

THEATER & DANCE

Old Whaling Church ★★   This magnificent 1843 Greek Revival church functions primarily as a 500-seat performing-arts center offering lectures and symposiums, films, plays, and concerts. It's also the Edgartown United Methodist Church, with a 9am service on Sundays. 89 Main St., Edgartown. www.mvpreservation.org. © **508/627-4440.** Ticket prices vary.

Vineyard Playhouse ★   In an intimate (112-seat) black-box theater, carved out of an 1833 church-turned-Masonic lodge, Equity professionals put on a rich season of favorites and challenging new work, followed, on summer weekends, by musical or comedic cabaret in the gallery/lounge. Children's theater selections are performed on Saturdays at 10am. Townspeople often get involved in the outdoor Shakespeare production, a 3-week run starting in mid-July, at the Tashmoo Overlook Amphitheatre, about 1 mile west of town. Tickets for the 5pm performances Tuesday to Sunday run only $15 to $25. Open June to September Tuesday to Saturday at 8pm, Sunday at 7pm; call for off-season hours. 24 Church St., Vineyard Haven. www.vineyardplayhouse.org. © **508/696-6300.** Tickets $40–$60.

PUBS, BARS, DANCE CLUBS & LIVE MUSIC

The Lampost/The Dive Bar ★   Young and loud are the watchwords at this pair of clubs in Oak Bluffs; the larger features live bands or DJs and a dance floor, the smaller (down in the basement), acoustic acts. This is where

Want to travel between Martha's Vineyard and Nantucket? **Hy-Line Cruises** (www.hy-linecruises.com; ☎ **800/492-8082** or 508/228-3949) runs passenger-only high-speed inter-island ferry service from Oak Bluffs, on Martha's Vineyard, to Nantucket and back, from late May to early September (there is no car-ferry service between the islands). Each crossing takes 1 hour and 10 minutes; service runs three times a day. The one-way fare is $36 for adults, $24 for kids 5 to 12, and $7 extra for bikes; round-trip is $65 adults, $45 kids, $14 bikes.

the young folk go, and the performers could be playing blues, reggae, R&B, or '80s music. Call for a schedule. Closed November to March. 6 Circuit Ave., Oak Bluffs. www.divebarmv.com. ☎ **508/696-9352.** Cover $1–$5.

Offshore Ale Company   In 1602, the first barley in the New World was grown on Martha's Vineyard. The Vineyard's only brewpub features eight locally made beers on tap ($4–$7). It's an attractively rustic place, with high ceilings, oak booths lining the walls, and peanut shells strewn on the floor. Local acoustic performers entertain 6 nights a week in season. Open June to September daily, noon to midnight; call for off-season hours. 30 Kennebec Ave., Oak Bluffs. www.offshoreale.com. ☎ **508/693-2626.** Cover $2–$3.

The Ritz Café ★   Locals and visitors alike flock to this down-and-dirty hole-in-the-wall that features live music every night in season and on weekends year-round. The crowd—a boozing, brawling lot—enjoy the pool tables in the back. Call for a schedule. 4 Circuit Ave., Oak Bluffs. www.theritzmv.com. ☎ **508/693-1454.** Cover $3.

The Sand Bar & Grille   This cool-cat bar is the place to hang out in Oak Bluffs near the harbor to listen to the latest local bands. 6 Circuit Ave., Oak Bluffs. www.mvsandbar.com. ☎ **508/693-7111.** No cover.

NANTUCKET

Herman Melville wrote in *Moby-Dick,* "Nantucket! Take out your map and look at it. See what a real corner of the world it occupies; how it stands there, away off shore . . ." More than 100 years later, this tiny island 30 miles off the coast of Cape Cod still defines itself, in part, by its isolation. At only 3½ by 14 miles in size, Nantucket is smaller and more insular than Martha's Vineyard, with only one town of any size (also called Nantucket). But charm-wise, Nantucket stands alone—all the creature comforts of the 21st century wrapped in an elegant 19th-century package.

Essentials

ARRIVING

BY FERRY   Two companies compete for ferry passengers from Hyannis to Nantucket: the **Steamship Authority** and **Hy-Line Cruises,** with terminals on opposite sides of Hyannis Harbor. Tickets on the Steamship Authority are

less expensive than tickets on the Hy-Line, by about $10. Parking in the Steamship Authority lots is also a couple dollars less expensive.

From the South Street Dock in Hyannis, the **Steamship Authority** (www. steamshipauthority.com; ✆ **508/477-8600** or 508/228-3274 on Nantucket) operates year-round ferry service, for cars, passengers, and bicycles, to Steamboat Wharf in Nantucket. The Steamship Authority's **fast ferry** to Nantucket, **MV *Iyanough*** (✆ **508/495-3278**), is for passengers only (no cars). It takes 1 hour and runs four to five times a day. Tickets in season cost $36.50 one-way ($69 round-trip) for adults, $18.75 one-way ($35 round-trip) for kids 5 to 12, free for ages 4 and under. Bikes cost $14 round-trip. Reservations are highly recommended. The Steamship Authority's **conventional ferries** carry cars as well as passengers and bikes. A one-way ticket on the conventional ferry is $18.50 ($37 round-trip) for adults, $9.50 ($19 round-trip) for children 5 to 12, and $14 round-trip for bikes. Car rates are significantly more—$400 to $450 in season (see box p. 294); drivers and passengers must also buy individual ferry tickets on top of that. No advance reservations are required for passengers traveling without cars, but car reservations must be made months

Bringing a Car to Nantucket

Given Nantucket's size and the excellence of its public transportation options, there really is no need to bring a car with you to Nantucket. From April through October, a round-trip fare on the Steamship Authority car ferry costs a whopping $400 to $450 (depending on the length of the car—you must specify make and model when you make your reservation); even during the off season, from November through March, it's $280 to $320. (Do you get the impression they don't want you to bring a car?)

If you must bring a car to the island, you need to reserve *months in advance* to secure a spot on the conventional ferry. Only five boats make the trip daily in season (three boats daily off-season). Before you call, have alternative departure dates.

Arrive **at least** 1 hour before departure to avoid your space being released to standbys. If you arrive without a reservation and plan to wait in the standby line, there is no guarantee you will get to the island that day. There is a $10 processing fee for cancelling reservations 14 days or more in advance of the trip; no refunds are issued if you cancel less than 14 days before the trip.

in advance. Steamship Authority parking costs $15 per day in season ($12 off-season). Also, no need for parking reservations for the Steamship Authority. The Authority operates four lots, two close to the docks, and two farther away that are served by a free shuttle.

Operating from Hyannis' Ocean Street Dock, **Hy-Line Cruises** (www.hy-linecruises.com; © **800/492-8082** or 508/228-3949) sail to Straight Wharf on Nantucket. Hy-Line's **high-speed passenger catamaran**, the *Grey Lady,* makes five to six hourly trips per day year-round. A one-way fare costs $41 for adults ($77 round-trip), $29 for kids 5 to 12 ($51 round-trip), and $7 for bicycles ($14 round-trip). Pets are allowed on the *Grey Lady.* The *Grey Lady IV* also has a first-class section, with tickets costing $89 round-trip ($48 one-way), for all ages. No pets are allowed in the first-class section.

Parking for Hy-Line ferries costs $25 per day in summer (only $8–$12 in winter and $20 in spring and fall). Hy-Line passengers can reserve a parking space in advance, but it's not essential: Hy-Line has several lots (a free shuttle serves its off-site lot), and while they can fill up in the summer but other companies offer parking nearby for similar rates.

From Harwich Port, Cape Cod: You can avoid the summer crowds in Hyannis and board a passenger-only ferry to Nantucket run by **Freedom Cruise Line** (www.nantucketislandferry.com; © **508/432-8999**). From mid-May to early October, boats leave from Saquatucket Harbor in Harwich Port (702 Route 28, across from Brax Landing). They make two or three trips a day in season and one trip per day in the shoulder season. The trip takes 1 hour and 15 minutes. A round-trip ticket is $76 for adults, $51 for kids 2 to 11, $6 for ages 1 and under, and $14 for bikes. Parking is free for day-trippers; it's $22 overnight. Advance reservations are highly recommended.

Tip: All of the above ferries are equipped with Wi-Fi.

BY AIR You can also fly into **Nantucket Memorial Airport** (www. nantucket-ma.gov; © **508/325-5300**), which is about 3 miles south of Nantucket Road, on Old South Road. The flight to Nantucket takes about 30 to 40 minutes from Boston, 20 minutes from Hyannis, and a little more than an hour from New York City airports. There is frequent shuttle bus service from Nantucket Airport terminal to town for $2. **Cape Air/Nantucket Airlines** (www. flycapeair.com; © **866/227-3247** or 508/771-6944) flies year-round from Hyannis (about $80–$185 round-trip, $39–$95 one-way), Boston (about $240–$350 round-trip, $175 one-way), Martha's Vineyard ($89 each way), and New Bedford ($99–$169 each way). **US Airways Express** (www.us airways.com; © **800/428-4322**) flies to Nantucket year-round from Boston ($223 and up round-trip) and LaGuardia Airport in New York City ($1,033 and up round-trip). **Delta Airlines, United Airlines,** and **JetBlue Airways** run flights from JFK Airport in New York City to Nantucket. Delta and United charge about $500 round-trip for a 1-hour-and-20-minute flight. Jet Blue charges $140 round-trip for a 1-hour-and-10-minute flight.

VISITOR INFORMATION

For information, contact the **Nantucket Island Chamber of Commerce,** at 48 Main Street (www.nantucketchamber.org; © **508/228-1700**). The **Nantucket Visitor Services and Information Bureau** at 25 Federal St. (© **508/228-0925**) is open 9am to 5pm daily from June to September; it closes on Sundays from October to May. Visitor Services have the most up-to-date listings on accommodation availability; they can help with 1-night stays and a list of current events.

   Nantucket Accommodations (www.nantucketaccommodation.com; © **866/743-3440** or 508/228-9559), a fee-based private service, can arrange advance reservations for 95% of the island's lodgings. Last-minute travelers can use the **Nantucket Visitors Service and Information Bureau** (© **508/228-0925**), a daily referral service, rather than a booking service. It always has the most updated list of available accommodations.

GETTING AROUND

Nantucket is easily navigated on bike, moped, or foot, and also by shuttle bus or taxi. If you're staying outside of Nantucket Town, however, or if you simply prefer to explore by car, you might want to bring your own car or rent one when you arrive. Adventure-minded travelers may even want to rent a Jeep or

---

See It All in One Day

From mid-June to mid-September Hy-Line also operates a 1-day round-trip **Around the Sound** cruise from Hyannis, with stops in Nantucket and Oak Bluffs, Martha's Vineyard. It's a full-day expedition, departing at 9:30am and returning at 7:30pm, allowing 4 hours for exploring at each of the islands. The price is $79 for adults, $44 for kids 5 to 12, and $21 for bikes. For details, contact Hy-Line (www.hy-linecruises.com; © **800/492-8082** or 508/228-3949).

other four-wheel-drive vehicle, which you can take out on the sand—a unique island experience—on certain sections of the coast (a permit is required—see p. 297, below). Be advised, however, that in-town traffic can reach gridlock in the peak season, and parking can be a nightmare.

BY BIKE & MOPED   When I head to Nantucket for a few days, biking is my preferred mode of transportation. The island itself is relatively flat, and paved bike paths abound—they'll get you from Nantucket Town to Siasconset, Surfside, and Madaket. There are also many unpaved back roads to explore, which make mountain bikes a wise choice when pedaling around Nantucket.

A word of warning to bikers: One-way street signs and all other traffic rules apply to you, too! This law is enforced in Nantucket Town, and don't be surprised if a tanned but stern island policeman requests that you get off your bike and walk. Helmets are required for children 15 and under. Bikers should also remember not to ride on the sidewalks in town, which are busy with pedestrians strolling and exiting shops.

Mopeds and scooters are also prevalent, but watch out for sand on the roads. Be aware that local rules and regulations are strictly enforced. Mopeds are not allowed on sidewalks or bike paths—stay on roads. You'll need a driver's license to rent a moped or a scooter, and state law requires that you wear a helmet.

The following shops rent bikes and scooters (all are within walking distance of the ferries): **Cook's Cycle Shop, Inc.,** 6 S. Beach St. (www.cookscycles nantucket.com; © **508/228-0800**), which rents bikes and mopeds; **Nantucket Bike Shop,** at Steamboat and Straight wharves (www.nantucketbikeshop. com; © **508/228-1999**), which rents bikes and scooters; and **Young's Bicycle Shop,** 6 Broad St. at Steamboat Wharf (www.youngsbicycleshop.com; © **508/ 228-1151**), which rents bikes and also does repairs. Bike rentals average $30 for a full day. Most places renting scooters or mopeds require the operator to be 18 or older. Rentals cost about $70 for a one-seater or $90 for a two-seater for 24 hours.

BY SHUTTLE BUS   Inexpensive shuttle buses, with bike racks and accessibility for those with disabilities, make frequent loops through Nantucket Town and beaches, and to outlying spots. For routes and stops, contact the **Nantucket Regional Transit Authority** (www.nrtawave.com; © **508/228-7025**), or pick up a map and schedule at the visitor center on Federal Street or the chamber of commerce office on Main Street (see p. 295). The shuttle permits you to bring your clean, dry dog along, too. There's room for two bikes on a first-come, first-served basis. The cost is $2 to $3, exact change required. A 1-day pass can be purchased at the visitor center for $8 and a 3-day pass for $18.

Shuttle routes and fares are pretty simple. Downtown shuttle stops are located on the corner of Salem and Washington streets (for South, Miacomet, and Airport loops); on Broad Street, in front of the Foulger Museum (for

Madaket Loop and Beach Express); and on Washington Street, at the corner of Main Street (for 'Sconset loops). Most shuttles run approximately every 30 minutes for most of the season; from July until Labor Day, the Mid-Island Loop runs every 15 minutes, and the Miacomet Loop every 20 minutes.

BY CAR & JEEP   I recommend a car if you'll be here for more than a week or if you're staying outside Nantucket Town. However, there are no in-town parking lots; parking, although free, is limited to Nantucket's handful of narrow streets, which can be a problem in the busy summer months. Also, gas is much more expensive on Nantucket than it is on the mainland.

Four-wheel-drive vehicles are your best bet, as many beaches and nature areas are off sandy paths; be sure to reserve at least a month in advance, if you're coming in summer. If you plan on doing any four-wheeling in the sand, you need to get an Over-Sand Permit ($140) from the **Nantucket Police Department** (✆ 508/228-1212). To drive in the Coskata-Coatue nature area, you need a separate permit from the **Trustees of Reservations,** at the gatehouse (✆ 508/228-0006). A season pass is about $160; if you have a dayrental four-wheel-drive that comes with the Over-Sand Permit, the gate fee is $75. Dogs are not allowed, even in a car.

The following on-island rental agencies offer cars, Jeeps, and other four-wheel-drive vehicles: **Hertz,** at the airport (www.hertz.com; ✆ 800/654-3131 or 508/228-9421); **Nantucket Windmill Auto Rental,** at the airport (www. nantucketautorental.com; ✆ 800/228-1227 or 508/228-1227); and **Young's 4×4 & Car Rental,** 6 Broad St. at Steamboat Wharf (www.youngsbicycle-shop.com; ✆ 508/228-1151). A standard car costs about $129 to $139 per day in season; a four-wheel-drive rental is about $199 to $229 per day (including an Over-Sand Permit).

BY TAXI   You'll find taxis (many are vans that can accommodate large groups or those traveling with bikes) waiting at the airport and at all ferry ports. During the busy summer months, I recommend reserving a taxi in advance to avoid a long wait upon arrival. Rates are flat fees set in advance for various destinations, based on one person riding before 1am, with surcharges for additional passengers, bikes, and dogs. The most centrally located taxi stand is at the bottom of Main Street, in front of the Club Car restaurant. A taxi from the airport to Nantucket Town will cost about $15, plus $1 for each additional person. Reliable cab companies on the island include **All Point Taxi & Tours** (✆ 508/228-5799); **Canty's Cab** (✆ 508/228-2888); **Chief's Cab** (✆ 508/284-8497), which is run by the island's former fire chief; and **Val's Cab Service** (✆ 508/228-9410).

Exploring Nantucket Town

Sophisticated Nantucket Town features bountiful stores, quaint inns, cobblestone streets, interesting historic sites, and pristine beaches. In the days when Nantucket was the whaling capital of the world, Nantucket Town was a place to be reckoned with. Impressively, it has managed to preserve the beauty of that era without feeling stuck in the past.

You don't even need to leave town to go to the beach. In a protected cove just west of busy Steamship Wharf, small **Children's Beach** ★ has a park, a playground, restrooms, lifeguards, a snack bar (the beloved Downy Flake, famous for its homemade doughnuts), and even a bandstand for free weekend concerts. A half-mile west of Children's Beach, on North Beach Street, **Jetties Beach** ★★★ is another family favorite for its mild waves, lifeguards, bathhouse, and restrooms. Facilities include the town tennis courts, volleyball nets, a skate park, and a playground; watersports equipment and chairs are also available to rent. There is also **The Jetties,** an upscale concession stand, complete with bar, serving lunch and dinner. The Fourth of July fireworks are held here, and every August, Jetties hosts an intense sand-castle competition. There's a large parking lot, but it fills up early on summer weekends.

To visit Nantucket's numerous historic sites, you may want to buy a Nantucket Historical Association **All Access Pass,** good for 10 sites around town. It costs $20 for adults, $18 for seniors and students, and $5 for kids 6 to 17. Even better, take one of the historical association's walking tours—a downtown tour runs daily at 10:30am in summer, and there's also a historic house and gardens tours at 1:30pm. Tickets ($10 adults, $8 seniors and students, $4 kids 6–17) can be purchased at the historical association's front desk at 15 Broad Street. For more information, go to **www.nha.org**.

Hadwen House ★★   In the mid–19th century when Nantucket was a wealthy boomtown, successful whaling ship captains and merchants built luxe houses like this Greek Revival beauty on Upper Main Street. Docents give a good feeling for the time period as they give tours around this 1845 mansion, a twin to the house next door. Whaling merchant William Hadwen hired a builder who specialized in intricate carving to construct the house's five-bayed facade, colossal pilasters, and pedimented ionic portico. Inside is period furniture, while outside are gardens maintained in period style.

96 Main St. (at Pleasant St.). www.nha.org. © **508/228-1894.** $6 adults, $3 children; also included in NHA's All Access Pass (see above). Apr–Dec daily 10am–5pm; call for off-season hours. Closed Dec–Mar.

Jethro Coffin House ("The Oldest House") ★★   If you're only going to see one historical site, it should be the Whaling Museum (see p. 299), but if you have time for two sites, this should be your second choice. On an island of historic buildings, this is officially the oldest, built in 1686 as a wedding gift for Jethro Coffin, a blacksmith, and his wife Mary Gardner; it is the sole surviving structure from the island's original 17th-century English settlement. The interior gives an example of the spare existence of the early settlers. A kitchen garden and an apple orchard also help put the house into historic perspective.

16 Sunset Hill Lane (off W. Chester Rd.). www.nha.org. © **508/228-1894.** $6 adults, $3 children; also included in NHA's All Access Pass (see above). Late May to mid-Oct daily 11am–4pm. Closed mid-Oct to late May.

Maria Mitchell Association ★ SCIENCE CENTER/HISTORIC HOME Maria Mitchell (1818–89), considered America's first professional astronomer, grew up on Nantucket, looking at the stars. She used to scan the sky from the roof of the Pacific National Bank, where her father was a cashier. While in her 20s, she was scanning the skies one day with a telescope when she found an object not in her charts. She had discovered a comet. She later became a professor of astronomy at Vassar College and traveled the world giving talks on her discovery. The Maria Mitchell Association on Nantucket has developed a campus of five buildings, including two observatories, dedicated to scientific inquiry and education. Perhaps most of interest for any member of the family is the **Loines Observatory** at 59 Milk St. Extension (© **508/228-9273**), which is open for viewing the stars on Monday, Wednesday and Friday from 9 to 10:30pm in July and August; September to June, it's open 2 nights per month near to the first quarter of the moon. The **Hinchman House Natural Science Museum** (© **508/228-0898**) at 7 Milk St. (at Vestal Street) houses a visitor center with science exhibits. Programming for adults and children include bird-watching, nature walks, and discovery classes. A small **aquarium** at 28 Washington St. is open Monday to Saturday 10am to 4pm.

4 Vestal St. (at Milk St.). www.mmo.org. © **508/228-9198.** Single-site admission $6 adults, $5 children; museum pass (for birthplace, aquarium, science museum, and Vestal St. Observatory) $10 adults, $8 children ages 6–12. Early June–late Aug Mon–Sat 10am–4pm; call for off-season hours.

Whaling Museum ★★★ MUSEUM   One of New England's top museums, this is a must-see on Nantucket. The museum building is a former candle factory, built by the Mitchell family immediately following Nantucket's Great Fire of 1846; it was operated as a candleworks until the end of whaling in 1860. One of the museum's most arresting exhibits is a 46-foot-long skeleton of a sperm whale. Besides a comprehensive history of the island of Nantucket and also of whaling, the museum has fine collections of the island arts of Nantucket baskets, scrimshaw and sailor's valentines.

13 Broad St. www.nha.org. © **508/228-1894.** All Access Pass ($20 adults, $18 students and seniors, $5 children 6–17) includes Whaling Museum and historic sites. Late May–Nov daily 10am–5pm. Closed Dec–late May.

NANTUCKET SHOPPING

ANTIQUES   **Rafael Osona Auctions** is the island's top antiques vendor, where the high prices reflect the high value of the items on view. Specialties include highly sought-after examples of Nantucket crafts like lightship baskets, scrimshaw, and sailors' valentines. It is located at the American Legion Hall at 21 Washington St. (www.nantucketauctions.com; © **508/228-3942**). Auctions take place May to December; see website for dates and viewing times.

ART & CRAFTS   The **Artists' Association of Nantucket** has the widest selection of work by locals, and the gallery at 19 Washington St. (www.nantucketarts.org; © **508/228-0294**) is impressive. Classes and workshops are at the Visual Arts Center at 24 Amelia Dr. (© **508/228-0722**). In February and March, it's open by appointment only.

Exquisite art-glass pieces, as well as ceramics, jewelry, and basketry, can be found at **Dane Gallery,** 28 Centre St. (www.danegallery.com; ☎ **508/228-7779**), where owners Robert and Jayne Dane show top-quality work. You'll be amazed at the colors and shapes of the glassware.

BARGAINS   Nantucket Cottage Hospital Thrift Shop, 17 India St. (www.nantuckethospital.org; ☎ **508/228-1125**), is where you go to find a Dior gown—or just an elegant summer dress—at bargain-basement prices.

BOOKS   Mitchell's Book Corner, 54 Main St. (www.mitchellsbookcorner.com; ☎ **508/228-1080**), features an astute sampling of general-interest books and an entire room dedicated to regional and maritime titles. **Nantucket Bookworks,** 25 Broad St. (www.nantucketbookworks.com; ☎ **508/228-4000**), is a charming bookstore, strong on customer service.

FASHION   Blue Beetle, 12 Main St. (www.bluebeetlenantucket.com; ☎ **508/228-3227**), is the place to find summer cocktail dresses, cashmere throws, and the bling to pull it all together.

Eco-fashionista **Cheryl Fudge,** 24 Easy St. (www.cherylfudge.com; ☎ **508/228-9155**), sells what she calls up-cycled clothing, turning scarves into halter tops, for instance. Her funky dresses and vintage jewelry and ACK Green line of organic clothing have a passionate following. **Current Vintage,** 4 Easy St. (www.currentvintage.com; ☎ **508/228-5073**), is one of the most original shops to open in recent years, with gorgeous vintage gowns and accessories, such as antique bags and jewelry, as well as special wines from small wineries.

Haul Over, 7 Salem St. (☎ **508/228-9010**), is where you go for basic, wear-it-all-summer-long sportswear, perfect for a day on the sailboat or an evening singing oldies at the piano bar at the Club Car. **Hepburn,** 3 Salem St. (☎ **508/228-1458**), sells ultrafashionable women's clothing and accessories, a cut above the usual fare.

Satisfying Nantucket's Sweet Tooth

Ambrosia Chocolate & Spices, 29 Centre St. (www.ambrosianantucket.com; ☎ **508/292-3289**), is an exquisite little organic chocolate and spice shop. Its specialty of the house is the otherworldly hazelnut "noisette," a delicate treat for coco connoisseurs. **Petticoat Row Bakery,** at 35 Centre St. (www.petticoatrowbakery.com; ☎ **508/228-3700**), has beautiful cupcakes, cookies, and muffins. **Sweet Inspirations,** Zero India St. (www.nantucketchocolate.com; ☎ **508/228-5814**) purveys artisan chocolate, carefully crafted on-site, often with beautiful Nantucket-themed packaging, which makes this a great place to come for gifts. The Rainbow Fleet tin containing chocolate scallop shells, clipper-ship medallions, and Nantucket mints, among other chocolates, is a delight.

At 12 Broad St., **The Juice Bar** ★★ (☎ **508/228-5799**) is the ice cream shop on the island, with homemade ice cream and frozen yogurt. It is crowded most of the day, as well as after the bars let out, when people gather for one last treat before bedtime. (In summer it's open until 11:30pm on Fridays and Saturdays, 9pm the rest of the week.) Closed mid-October to mid-April.

THE LEGEND OF nantucket reds

Martha's Vineyard may have spawned "Black Dog" fever (see box p. 290), but this island boasts the inimitable "Nantucket reds"—cotton clothing that starts out tomato red and washes out to salmon pink. The fashion originated at **Murray's Toggery Shop,** 62 Main St. (www.nantucketreds.com; © **800/368-2134** or 508/228-0437). Legend has it that the original duds were colored with an inferior dye that washed out almost immediately. However, customers so liked the thick cottons and instant aged look that the proprietor was forced to search high and low for more of the same fabric. Roland Hussey Macy, founder of Macy's, got his start here in the 1830s. Today's management also keeps up with current trends.

Lilly Pulitzer's In The Pink has sensational vibrant summer minidresses at 5 South Water St. (© **508/228-0569**). **Zero Main,** at 34 Centre St. (© **508/228-4401**), has a limited but fine selection of elegant yet casual women's clothes, shoes, and accessories.

GIFTS/HOME DECOR **Nantucket Looms,** at 51 Main St. (www.nantucketlooms.com; © **508/228-1908**), is the place to ogle exquisite brushed-mohair chaise throws and other handmade woven items. The weaving studio is upstairs, where they also make blankets and sweaters of cotton and cashmere. **Erica Wilson Needle Works,** 25 Main St. (www.ericawilson.com; © **508/228-9881**), features the designs of its namesake, an islander since 1958 and author of more than two dozen books on needlepoint. The shop offers hands-on guidance for hundreds of grateful adepts, as well as kits and handiwork of other noteworthy designers.

NEWSSTAND **The Hub,** 31 Main St. (© **508/325-0200**), offers a selection of newspapers, magazines, and books, as well as greeting cards by local artists. On an island without convenience stores, this is *the* go-to place for a cold drink, newspaper, or quick gift.

TOYS **The Toy Boat,** 41 Straight Wharf (www.thetoyboat.com; © **508/228-4552**), is keen on creative toys that are also educational. In addition to the top commercial lines, owner Loren Brock stocks lots of locally crafted, hand-carved playthings, such as "rainbow fleet" sailboats, part of the Harbor Series that includes docks, lighthouses, boats, and everything your child needs to create his or her own Nantucket Harbor. There are also stackable lighthouse puzzles replicating Nantucket's beams.

Exploring the Rest of Nantucket Island

The rest of the island is mainly residential, but for a couple of notable villages. **Siasconset** (nicknamed 'Sconset), on the east side of the island, is a tranquil community with picturesque, rose-covered cottages and a handful of businesses, including a pricey French restaurant, the Chanticleer (see p. 315). Sunset aficionados head to **Madaket,** on the west coast of the island, for the evening spectacular.

Fresh from the Farm

In the 1800s, Nantucket had 100 family farms, and one was run by the Bartlett family on a large parcel near Hummock Pond. Today, **Bartlett's Farm ★★** (www.bartlettsfarm.com; ✆ **508/228-9403**) is Nantucket's oldest and largest (125 acres) farm; the seventh generation is running the operation. A Bartlett's truck with its wonderful fresh produce is parked in town in the summer from 9am to 1pm Monday through Saturday. It's well worth the trip to head out to the farm itself to stock up on goodies, including prepared foods. Take Main Street to the Civil War monument; go left on Milk Street to Hummock Pond Road, and follow that to Bartlett Farm Road. The farm, at 33 Bartlett Farm Rd., is open to visitors April to December daily 8am to 7pm.

The lay of the land on Nantucket is rolling moors, cranberry bogs, and miles of exquisite public beaches. The vistas are honeymoon-romantic: an operating windmill, three lighthouses, and a skyline dotted with church steeples. About one-third of Nantucket's 42 square miles are protected from development. Contact the **Nantucket Conservation Foundation,** at 118 Cliff Rd. (www.nantucketconservation.org; ✆ **508/228-2884**), for a $4 map of its holdings, which include the 205-acre **Windswept Cranberry Bog** (off Polpis Road), where bogs are interspersed amid hardwood forests; and a portion of the 1,100-acre **Coskata-Coatue Wildlife Refuge,** comprising the barrier beaches beyond Wauwinet.

Nantucket Shipwreck and Lifesaving Museum ★ MUSEUM   The Lifesaving Museum preserves the memory of those islanders who risked their lives to save shipwrecked mariners. The building is a replica of Nantucket's Life-saving station. Inside is an interesting display of objects on the topic including historic photos and actual surfboats from the Massachusetts Humane Society, the predecessor of the Coast Guard. The collection includes film footage of the sinking of the *Andrea Doria,* which took place off the coast of Nantucket in 1956. Kids will like the exhibit on Coast Guard sea dogs. The museum is about 3 miles from town and is a nice stop by bike for those riding the path to Surfside Beach; the shuttle bus stops here as well.

158 Polpis Rd. www.nantucketshipwreck.org. ✆ **508/228-1885.** $10 adults, $7 seniors and students, $5 kids 6–18; free ages 5 and under. Late May to mid-Oct Mon–Sat 10am–5pm, Sunday noon–5pm.

BEACHES AROUND THE ISLAND

In distinct contrast to Martha's Vineyard, virtually all of Nantucket's 110-mile coastline is free and open to the public. Though the pressure to keep people out is sometimes intense (especially when four-wheel-drivers insist on their right to go anywhere, anytime), islanders are proud that they've managed to keep the shoreline in the public domain.

○ **Cisco Beach ★★**: About 4 miles from town, in the southwestern quadrant of the island (from Main Street, turn onto Milk Street, which becomes

Hummock Pond Road), Cisco enjoys vigorous waves—great for the surfers who flock here, not so great for the waterfront homeowners. Restrooms are available, and lifeguards are on duty.

o **Coatue ★**: This fishhook-shaped barrier beach, on the northeastern side of the island, at Wauwinet, is Nantucket's outback, accessible only by four-wheel-drive vehicles, watercraft, or the very strong-legged. Swimming is strongly discouraged because of fierce tides.

o **Dionis Beach ★★★**: About 3 miles out of town (take the Madaket bike path to Eel Point Road) Dionis enjoys the gentle sound surf and steep, picturesque bluffs. It's a great spot for swimming, picnicking, and shelling, and you'll find fewer children than at Jetties or Children's beaches. Stick to the established paths to prevent further erosion. Lifeguards patrol here, and restrooms are available.

o **Madaket Beach ★★★**: Accessible by Madaket Road, the 6-mile bike path that runs parallel to it, and by shuttle bus, this westerly beach is narrow and subject to pounding surf and sometimes serious crosscurrents. Unless it's a fairly tame day, you might content yourself with wading. It's the best spot on the island for admiring the sunset. Facilities include restrooms, lifeguards, and mobile food service.

o **Siasconset ('Sconset) Beach ★★**: The eastern coast of 'Sconset is as pretty as the town itself and rarely, if ever, crowded, perhaps because of the water's strong sideways tow. You can reach it by car, by shuttle bus, or by a less scenic and somewhat hilly (at least for Nantucket) 7-mile bike path. Lifeguards are usually on duty, but the closest facilities (restrooms, grocery store, and cafe) are back in the center of the village.

o **Surfside Beach ★★★**: Three miles south of town via a popular bike/skate path, broad Surfside—equipped with lifeguards, restrooms, and a surprisingly accomplished little snack bar—is appropriately named and commensurately popular. It draws thousands of visitors a day in high season, from college students to families, but the free parking lot can fit only about 60 cars. You do the math—or better yet, ride your bike or take the shuttle bus.

CYCLING nantucket

Several lovely, paved bike paths radiate from the center of town to outlying beaches. The **bike paths** run about 6¼ miles west to Madaket, 3½ miles south to Surfside, and 8¼ miles east to Siasconset. To avoid backtracking from Siasconset, continue north through the charming village and return on the Polpis Road bike path. Strong riders could do a whole circuit of the island in a day. Picnic benches and water fountains stand at strategic points along all the paths.

For a free map of the island's bike paths (it also lists Nantucket's bicycle rules), stop by **Young's Bicycle Shop,** at Steamboat Wharf (www.youngsbicycle shop.com; ℭ **508/228-1151**). It's definitely the best place for bike rentals, from basic three-speeds to high-tech suspension models. In operation since 1931—check out the vintage vehicles on display—they also deliver to your door. See p. 296 for more bike rental shops.

Outdoor Activities

FISHING ★   For shellfishing, you'll need a permit from the **marine coastal resources office** at 34 Washington St. (© **508/228-7261**), which costs $25 for nonresidents for the season. You'll see surf-casters all over the island ($10 permit required). Deep-sea charters heading out of Straight Wharf include Capt. Bob DeCosta's *The Albacore* (www.albacorecharters.com; © **508/228-5074**); Capt. Josh Eldridge's *Monomoy* (www.monomoychartersnantucket.com; © **508/228-6867**); and Capt. David Martin's *Absolute* (www.absolute sportfishing.com; © **508/325-4000**). For a typical fare, expect a 5-hour bass-fishing trip for up to six people to cost $1,350 plus $125 per person; for 2½ hours, it might be $675 plus $105 per person.

GOLF   Two pretty courses are open to the public: the 18-hole **Miacomet Golf Course,** 12 W. Miacomet Rd. (www.miacometgolf.com; © **508/325-0333**), and the 9-hole **Siasconset Golf Club,** off Milestone Road (© **508/257-6596**). You'll pay $125 for 18 holes at Miacomet. At Siasconset, playing 9 holes costs $35.

WATERSPORTS   **Jetties Sailing Center** manages the concession at **Jetties Beach** (www.nantucketcommunitysailing.org; © **508/228-5358**), which offers lessons and rents out kayaks, sailboards, sailboats, and more. Rental rates for single kayaks are $45 per hour; windsurfers $40 per hour; and Sunfish $50 per hour. **Sea Nantucket Paddle Sports Rentals,** on tiny Francis Street Beach, off Washington Street (www.seanantucketkayak.com; © **508/228-7499**), also rents stand-up paddleboards and kayaks; it's a quick sprint across the harbor to beautiful Coatue. Single kayaks rent for $45, and tandems for $75, for 4½ hours. **Nantucket Island Community Sailing** (www.nantucketcommunity sailing.org; © **508/228-6600**) gives relatively low-cost private and group lessons from the Jetties pier for adults (16 and up) and children; a seasonal adult membership covering open-sail privileges costs $250 for 4 weeks. One 2-hour private lesson costs $125.

Where to Stay on Nantucket

Perhaps it goes without saying, but it's worth a reminder: Nantucket is a very expensive place to stay overnight. From the cost per night of hotel rooms—averaging about $700 in the summer—to the cost of dinner at a "moderate" restaurant, where you should expect to pay about $100 per person, this is a hard place for bargain hunters. Many summer visitors rent houses by the week or month, which brings the cost per night way down; others may have to content themselves with a day trip. Consider visiting in the shoulder seasons in the fall or spring or even in the winter, when Nantucket's beauty is still on full display and there are far fewer people around to spoil the views.

It's also worthwhile checking **Airbnb.com** and **Vrbo.com**—they may significantly beat hotel prices, or even have more last-minute availability than the island's limited stock of hotel rooms.

Nantucket Town

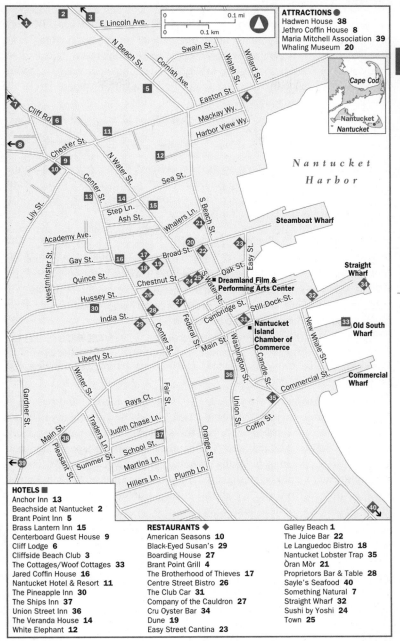

ATTRACTIONS ●
Hadwen House **38**
Jethro Coffin House **8**
Maria Mitchell Association **39**
Whaling Museum **20**

Cape Cod

Nantucket
Nantucket

Nantucket Harbor

Steamboat Wharf

Straight Wharf

Old South Wharf

Commercial Wharf

Dreamland Film & Performing Arts Center

Nantucket Island Chamber of Commerce

HOTELS ■
Anchor Inn **13**
Beachside at Nantucket **2**
Brant Point Inn **5**
Brass Lantern Inn **15**
Centerboard Guest House **9**
Cliff Lodge **6**
Cliffside Beach Club **3**
The Cottages/Woof Cottages **33**
Jared Coffin House **16**
Nantucket Hotel & Resort **11**
The Pineapple Inn **30**
The Ships Inn **37**
Union Street Inn **36**
The Veranda House **14**
White Elephant **12**

RESTAURANTS ◆
American Seasons **10**
Black-Eyed Susan's **29**
Boarding House **27**
Brant Point Grill **4**
The Brotherhood of Thieves **17**
Centre Street Bistro **26**
The Club Car **31**
Company of the Cauldron **27**
Cru Oyster Bar **34**
Dune **19**
Easy Street Cantina **23**

Galley Beach **1**
The Juice Bar **22**
Le Languedoc Bistro **18**
Nantucket Lobster Trap **35**
Òran Mòr **21**
Proprietors Bar & Table **28**
Sayle's Seafood **40**
Something Natural **7**
Straight Wharf **32**
Sushi by Yoshi **24**
Town **25**

NANTUCKET TOWN
Expensive

Beachside at Nantucket ★   Simple and clean and a little nondescript, the Beachside is the equivalent of a Hampton's Inn on the island. But then again, you will not be spending much time in your room anyway, right? It's a 10-minute walk to Steamboat Wharf and the heart of downtown in one direction, and about the same distance to Jetties Beach the other way. The rooms are more spacious than what you might find in a historic house B&B; the 'poolside' rooms are more private.

30 N. Beach St. www.thebeachside.com. (℃ **800/322-4433** or 508/228-2241. 90 units. Summer $452–$561 double; $661–$1,030 suite. Rates include continental breakfast. Closed late Oct–late Apr. Dogs allowed. **Amenities:** Outdoor pool; Wi-Fi (free).

The Cottages/Woof Cottages at the Boat Basin ★★★   In a prime location on a wharf overlooking Nantucket Harbor, the Wharf Cottages comprise 24 units with one-, two-, and three-bedroom options. Your neighbors are the private yachts that line the harbor. These are sweet units, with up-to-date kitchens and comfortable seating areas, beautifully maintained and decorated in a crisp nautical modern style. Though it's not a typical hotel, there's a concierge available and daily housekeeping services are provided. All the complimentary extras have been thought of—beach chairs and umbrellas, bicycles, fishing rods for kids, even a welcome treat for your pet upon arrival. Spa services are available from a sister property nearby (the White Elephant, see below), and there's a free shuttle bus to the beach.

24 Old South Wharf. www.thecottagesnantucket.com. (℃ **866/838-9253** or 508/325-1499. 33 units. Summer $790–$1,226 studio and 1-bedroom; $750–$1,196 2-bedroom; $1,246–$1,546 3-bedroom. Closed mid-Oct–May. Pets accepted. **Amenities:** Spa; shuttle bus; concierge; Wi-Fi (free).

Nantucket Hotel & Resort ★★   Thoroughly modern and renovated, but with generous nods to the island's rich history, this grand lady of island hospitality caters to those who prefer a full-service experience. It is especially geared to families with children. The hotel can handle groups of anywhere from 2 to 17 people in its tastefully designed and comfortable rooms. There is a complimentary children's program during the day; it's also offered 3 nights a week with a fee. You can hop aboard either the antique fire truck or antique bus to be shuttled to Surfside or Jetties Beach.

77 Easton St. www.thenantuckethotel.com. (℃ **508/228-4747.** 12 units, Summer $450–$1,095 double; $990–$1,350 2-bedroom. **Amenities:** Restaurant, 2 outdoor pools (1 adults only), fitness facility and spa, fitness classes, kids' program, shuttle; Wi-Fi (free).

White Elephant ★★★   The White Elephant has long been one of the island's top luxury accommodations. A 2-minute walk from Steamboat Wharf, many of the finely appointed rooms and suites have harbor views and private decks—others have garden views—several with their own fireplace. Garden-view cottages have one, two, or three bedrooms and a there is a three-bedroom loft. The **Brant Point Grill** provides a decent breakfast but is best known as one of the island's top steak joints, with an afternoon raw bar.

50 Easton St. www.whiteelephanthotel.com. © **800/445-6574** or 508/228-2500. 52 units, 11 cottages. Summer $960–$1,375 double; $1,060–$1,860 suite & 1-bedroom cottage; $2,465 2-bedroom cottage; $2,465 3-bedroom cottage. Rates include full breakfast. Closed Nov–Mar except for 1 week during Christmas Stroll, in early December. **Amenities:** Restaurant; concierge; exercise room; room service; spa; Wi-Fi (free).

Moderate

Anchor Inn ★   In 1806 Captain Archelaus Hammond, considered the first man from Nantucket to kill a sperm whale in the Pacific Ocean, built the building that now houses the Anchor Inn, and it still has the old floorboards and antique paneling from days gone by. The rooms, each named after a whaling ship, are simple, and some are smallish, but for authentic Nantucket feel and hospitality, this inn can't be beat.

66 Centre St. www.anchor-inn.net. © **508/228-0072.** 11 units. Summer $375–$425 double. Rates include continental breakfast. Closed Jan–Feb. **Amenities:** Wi-Fi (free).

Brant Point Inn ★   Located about halfway between downtown and Jetties Beach, the Brant Point Inn and its almost-identical twin across the driveway, the Atlantic Mainstay, have fairly spacious rooms with queen or twin beds decorated in a homey country style, with wooden post-and-beam construction throughout. A common living room is for reading and relaxation.

6 N. Beach St. www.brantpointinn.com. © **508/228-5442.** 8 units. Summer $285–$325 double; $375–$450 suite. Rates include continental breakfast. Closed Nov–Apr. **Amenities:** Wi-Fi (free).

Brass Lantern Inn ★★   In a shingled 1847 Greek Revival house, this long-established B&B is a very good moderately priced option: first by virtue of its location—far enough from the thick of things to be very quiet but close enough for a quick walk—and second, by its amenities, which are a step up from some similar properties. Yes, it has the expected antiques and hardwood floors, but, you can also expect luxurious bedding and top-notch toiletries, and several rooms (and bathrooms!) are much more spacious than the vintage buildings of most Nantucket B&Bs usually afford.

11 N. Water St. www.brasslanternnantucket.com. © **800/377-6609** or 508/228-4064. 16 units. Summer $345–$625 double; $625–$725 2-bedroom suite. Rates include continental breakfast. Dogs allowed. **Amenities:** Wi-Fi (free).

Centerboard Guest House ★★   Located in the center of town, this whaling captain's home has always been one of the better area B&Bs. It is the only one in the Victorian style, lending it a certain elegance that comes with the 12-foot ceilings and spacious rooms. The rooms are luxurious, and the bedding is particularly plush here.

8 Chester St. www.centerboardguesthouse.com © **877/228-2811** or 508/228-9696. 7 units. Summer $399–$450 double; $599 suite. Rates include continental breakfast. Closed Nov–Apr. **Amenities:** Wi-Fi (free).

Jared Coffin House ★   This inn, with its majestic brick facade, has a terrific location, just steps from all restaurants and stores in the downtown center. The rooms have been freshened up, but still retain a feeling of yester-year, particularly in the old wallpaper and furnishings. An upscale steakhouse is the onsite restaurant.

29 Broad St. (at Centre St.). www.jaredcoffinhouse.com. ✆ **800/248-2405** or 508/228-2400. 60 units. Summer $402–$692 double. **Amenities:** Restaurant; Wi-Fi (free).

The Ships Inn ★   The abolitionist Lucretia Mott was born in this 1831 house, and today it is one of the island's best moderately priced inns. Rooms are fresh and cheerful, not overly frilly. None are alike, and unfortunately some are small or awkwardly configured. A very good restaurant is in the basement.

13 Fair St. www.shipsinnnantucket.com. ✆ **888/872-4052** or 508/228-0040. 12 units, 2 w/shared bath. Summer $195 single w/shared bath; $385–$405 double. Rates include continental breakfast. Closed late Oct to mid-May. No children 8 or under. **Amenities:** Restaurant; Wi-Fi (free).

Union Street Inn ★★   The Union Street Inn is a B&B that acts like a hotel, with refinements that bring it several notches above the usual "mom and pop" operation. The entire inn is decorated in a combination of bright and rich colors, with luxurious wallpapers and wood paneling. This is the only Nantucket B&B to serve a full breakfast (it's a zoning thing), and there are fresh cookies in the afternoon.

7 Union St. www.unioninn.com. ✆ **888/517-0707** or 508/228-9222. 12 units. Summer $379–$619 double; $619 suite. Rates include full breakfast. Closed Nov–Mar. **Amenities:** Wi-Fi (free).

The Veranda House ★★   Calling itself a retro-chic boutique hotel, the Veranda House, originally built in 1684, is one of the island's most stylish B&Bs. Inside, it looks like nothing else on island: There's rattan mixed with club chairs mixed with zebra striped benches in the common areas. The rooms have colorful artwork and accents. The smallest ones—very tiny, in the third-floor attic space—are well priced for budget travelers, particularly off-season.

3 Step Lane. www.theverandahouse.com. ✆ **877/228-0695** or 508/228-0695. 18 units. Summer $359–$679 double; $679 suite. Rates include continental breakfast. Closed mid-Oct to late May. **Amenities:** Wi-Fi (free).

Inexpensive

Cliff Lodge ★   This 1771 captain's home is along the initial ascent of Nantucket's Cliff Road, where some of the island's oldest and most sough-after homes are located. A climb to the widow's walk gives a panorama of downtown Nantucket and the harbor. The bright and cheery rooms range from a tiny single tucked into an alcove to a spacious room on the first floor with a king-sized bed. The apartment is a good fit for a small family. Wine and cheese is served in the afternoon.

9 Cliff Rd. www.clifflodgenantucket.com. ✆ **508/228-9480.** 12 units. Summer $235–$425 double; $442–$465 apt. Rates include continental breakfast. No children 10 and under. **Amenities:** Wi-Fi (free)

The Pineapple Inn ★★　This B&B is one of the Summer House group of small inns and B&Bs, so if one is booked up, they can refer you to another. A stay here also means that you can take advantage of the pool, private beach, and other amenities at the Summer House Inn and Cottages in 'Sconset. As for the Pineapple, it is a lovely property, with rooms decorated with 19th-century antiques and reproductions, like handsome four-poster beds and oriental rugs. Rooms are, for the most part, spacious, and it has a good location, steps from downtown shops and restaurants.

10 Hussey St. www.pineappleinn.com. ℘ **508/257-4577.** 12 units. Summer $255–$455 double. Rates include continental breakfast. Closed early Dec to mid-Apr. No children 8 or under. **Amenities:** Wi-Fi (free).

ELSEWHERE ON THE ISLAND

Cliffside Beach Club ★★★　If you can swing the hefty nightly room rate and the 4-night minimum stay, this beachfront property is the ultimate place to stay on Nantucket. The name "beach club" is apt, because when you walk into the unpretentious lobby, you feel like you are entering an old-money private club, one where the fresh-faced staff acts genuinely glad to see you. The on-site restaurant, **Galley Beach** (see p. 315), is one of the island's best, and all the amenities, from the health club to the in-room extras are top-notch. But the biggest selling point is the beach. Get one of the Beach Club rooms, with private decks right on the sand. They cost a little more but are worth it. Better yet, reserve slightly off-season, in May or October, to get a much better rate for the same room. Then just cross your fingers on the weather.

46 Jefferson Ave. (about 1 mile NW of town ctr.). www.cliffsidebeach.com. ℘ **800/932-9645** or 508/228-0618. 25 units, 1 cottage. Summer $445–$1,120 double; $1,350 suite; $3,500 2-bedroom apt; $1,235–$2,600 cottage. 5.3% service charge added. Rates include continental breakfast. Closed mid-Oct–mid-May. **Amenities:** Restaurant; babysitting; concierge; exercise room; pool; steam saunas; indoor hydrotherapy spa; Wi-Fi (free).

Robert B. Johnson Memorial Hostel ★　The price is under $40 a night and the location is priceless. Yards away from a private walk to the popular Surfside Beach, this hostel was once a life-saving station where men headed out in treacherous conditions to rescue sailors from shipwrecks along the island's south shore. Now it is a lifesaver of another sort, saving cash-strapped visitors from being priced off the island.

31 Western Ave. (on Surfside Beach, about 3 miles S of town ctr.). www.hiusa.org. ℘ **888/901-2084** or 508/228-0433. 49 beds. $32–$35 for HIUSA members; $38 for non-members; $200 private room. Closed mid-Oct to mid-May.

The Wauwinet ★★　If refuge is what you want, refuge is what you'll get at this luxury property at the head of the harbor, a 20-minute car ride northeast from town. It's also at the edge of some 1,400 acres of Nantucket's most cherished, protected land. The property has 32 guestrooms and 6 cottages that are richly appointed with equestrian oil paintings and fine linens and have views of the bay or the garden (planted with opulent hydrangeas). The manicured lawn leads to a private beach on the harbor side, and there's a path to a private beach on the Atlantic side. Complimentary Sunfish sailboats and bicycles are available during the day, and a shuttle runs back and forth to town hourly. Other perks include a bay cruise, excursions to Great Point Lighthouse, lawn games, and tennis (two clay courts). The restaurant, Topper's, is excellent.

120 Wauwinet Rd. (about 8 miles E of town ctr.). www.wauwinet.com. © **800/426-8718** or 508/228-0145. 25 units, 10 cottages. Summer $525–$995 double; $1,020–$1,450 1- and 2-bedroom cottages. Rates include full breakfast and afternoon wine and cheese. Closed mid-Oct–mid-May. Children 12 and older only. **Amenities:** Restaurant; spa; concierge; mountain bikes; croquet lawn; tennis courts; rowboats, sailboats, sea kayaks; room service; Wi-Fi (free).

Where to Eat on Nantucket

Keep in mind that Nantucket restaurateurs need to make most of their year's income during the short summer season—and need to pay their staff a living wage on an island where living is not cheap. So yes, dining out can be expensive here. If you're lucky enough to be staying somewhere with a kitchen, use it for most meals, the better to treat yourself when you do dine out.

Broad Street, just steps from Steamboat Wharf, is the place to go for cheap takeout eats any time. Good choices are **Island Coffee,** 4 Broad St. (© **508/228-2224**), where you can treat yourself to rich coffee and chocolate croissants with Nutella; **Stubby's,** 8 Broad St. (© **508/228-0028**), for burgers; and **Walter's Deli,** 10 Broad St. (© **508/228-0010**), for sandwiches. Walter's and Stubby's are open until 2am.

During the two Nantucket Restaurant Weeks (early Jun and late Sept), you can get three-course menus for the same price as an entree costs on a typical night. Think of it as two or three meals for the price of one.

NANTUCKET TOWN
Expensive

American Seasons ★★ AMERICAN   A leader among Nantucket's restaurants for 25 years, American Seasons attracts an older crowd in an upscale subdued, even formal, atmosphere. Fancy offerings like foie gras and rabbit terrine for a starter, and braised veal cannelloni with chanterelles, change with the seasons. The candlelit dining room is decorated with old-fashioned Americana and pleasing agrarian-themed murals. Seating in the summer is outside on a trellis-covered patio.

80 Centre St. www.americanseasons.com. © **508/228-7111.** Main courses $32–$48. Apr to mid-Dec daily 5:30–9:30pm. Closed mid-Dec to Mar.

The Club Car ★★ CONTINENTAL   No list of restaurants on Nantucket would be complete without the Club Car, a classic since it was founded in 1977. The restaurant got a recent remodel and has updated the decades-old French-themed menu in favor of New American cuisine, with a range of unique tapas choices like grilled lamb skewers and special toasts with sweet pea or roasted mushroom. For dinner, you can go big with a whole black bass with chickpeas. After dinner, diners can wander into the club car section—an actual train car from when a train used to run from downtown Nantucket out to 'Sconset. This piano bar is loads of fun in the summer.

1 Main St. www.theclubcar.com. ✆ **508/228-1101.** Main courses $34–$45. July–Aug daily 11am–4pm and 6–9:30pm; call for off-season hours. Closed late Oct–Apr.

Company of the Cauldron ★★★ NEW AMERICAN   A longtime contender for the honor of most romantic restaurant on Nantucket, this place maintains its special qualities year after year. You enter its little red building from the tree-shaded sidewalk while candles flicker and a harpist performs classical music. There's just one three-course, fixed-price menu every night, so that everyone is served the same dishes and it feels a bit like a private dinner party. You check the menus in advance to be sure they are serving something you want. For example, it might be salad Niçoise; beef Wellington; or for dessert, pineapple upside-down cake. Monday's single seating always includes lobster three ways (for instance, bisque, grilled, and with mac and cheese).

5 India St. (btw. Federal and Centre sts.). www.companyofthecauldron.com. ✆ **508/228-4016.** 3-course prix fixe $65–$115. Early July–early Sept Tues–Sat, seatings 6 and 8:30pm, Sun 11am–2pm, and one dinner seating at 7pm; Mon seating 7pm only. Call for off-season hours. Closed mid-Oct to mid-Apr, except Thanksgiving weekend and 1st 2 weeks Dec.

Cru Oyster Bar ★ SEAFOOD   Formerly the Ropewalk, this upscale raw bar with an enviable location has long been the place where the yachting crowd goes to toast the day. And why not? They can hop off their boats and be at the bar in a few steps. There are a dozen kinds of oysters on the menu ($3.75–$5.75 apiece), a revolving selection from around the region. The bistro-style menu has classics like steak frites and seared sea scallops with lobster broth. Keep in mind, the million-dollar view and up-close look at the rich and famous is reflected in your check. Wine is $17 a glass and appetizers hover around $20 apiece.

1 Straight Wharf. www.crunantucket.com. ✆ **508/228-9278.** Main courses $29–$49. Late May–Aug daily 11am–10pm. Call for off-season hours. Closed mid-Oct to Apr.

Dune ★★ NEW AMERICAN   Sleek and modern, Dune may seem at first a little out of place on Nantucket, but the restaurant's creator, Chef Michael Getter, a longtime resident, knows what he's doing. Lovely colorful choices with an Asian inspiration change with the seasons, but you will certainly see items on the menu you have never seen anywhere else. A spring offering might be a pea bisque with smoked mushrooms and ham with lavender yogurt. A grilled steak comes with bok choy and green garlic potato puree. The outdoor patio is the place to be in summer but you must request it when you reserve.

20 Broad St. www.dunenantucket.com. ✆ **508/228-5550.** Main courses $28–$38. July–Sept daily noon–3pm and 5:30–9:30pm; call for off-season hours.

Le Languedoc Bistro ★★ NEW AMERICAN/FRENCH   Run since 1978 by the same owners, this bistro remains a place where locals feel comfortable coming in for a warm lunch—a cheeseburger with garlic fries perhaps, or a bowl of lobster bisque on a crisp fall day. The beauty of the dinner menu is that you can order half-portions for a more affordable meal that still lets you appreciate the riches of this food. Among the appetizers are the roasted fresh quail and veal sweetbreads saltimbocca. Main courses include the foie-gras-infused chicken or pan-roasted lobster with creamy polenta. Downstairs has a casual bistro atmosphere; upstairs is white tablecloth fancy.

24 Broad St. www.lelanguedoc.com. ⓒ **508/228-2552.** Main courses $19–$49 (half-portions $15–$16). June–Sept Tues–Sun 11:30am–2pm and 5:30–9:30pm; call for off-season hours. Closed mid-Dec to mid-May.

Òran Mór Bistro ★★★ INTERNATIONAL   Climbing the copper steps in this historic building to enter Òran Mór, you can tell you are in for a special evening. The vibe is surprisingly down to earth. No white tablecloths or crystal here, and the small handsome bar and attentive service put you at ease. The first course might be marinated grilled baby octopus, or perhaps a Nantucket lobster po'boy atop grilled focaccia. As for the main course, you might find beer-braised pork short ribs with a parsnip puree, or a miso-marinated cod with sweet-potato lasagna. Desserts are a sublime specialty: Save room for vanilla cream-filled brioche doughnuts with brown butter and roasted pear puree.

2 S. Beach St. www.oranmorbistro.com. ⓒ **508/228-8655.** Main courses $30–$44. June to mid-Oct daily 6–9:30pm; mid-Oct to mid-Dec and mid-Apr to May Thurs–Tues 5:30–9pm. Closed mid-Dec to mid-Apr.

Straight Wharf ★★★ NEW AMERICAN   Perhaps the most lauded chefs on an island of lavishly praised chefs, Amanda Lydon and Gabriel Frasca run the elegant Straight Wharf beside Nantucket Harbor as a sort of chef's restaurant, a place where foodies flock for the best of the best in creative cuisine. The menus change nightly, adjusting to what's fresh at the market. In contrast to some other Nantucket restaurants, this food is neither heavy nor overly rich. You might begin with a butter pear and celery salad, and continue with the seared Nantucket fluke with island vegetables and garden herbs, adding on pan-roasted broccoli rabe and heirloom grits. Finish the meal off with a chilled melon soup with a cantaloupe sorbet. See what I mean? Ethereal.

6 Harbor Sq. (on Straight Wharf). www.straightwharfrestaurant.com. ⓒ **508/228-4499.** Main courses $26–$39. July–Aug Tues–Fri 11:30am–2pm and 5:30–9:45pm, Sat–Sun 11am–2pm and 5:30–10pm; call for off-season hours. Closed late Sept–mid-May.

Town ★★ INTERNATIONAL   The peaceful aesthetic when you enter Town is not an illusion. This restaurant featuring global cuisine is all about balancing the yin and the yang. The decor inside and on the outdoor patio is features muted colors and soft textures, black and ivory, wicker and rattan, cozy booths and cushioned couches. Besides sushi, you might find red Thai curried chicken and orecchiette with grilled eggplant. At the outdoor Tree Bar, which is under a shady tree, you can order appetizers from the menu like salt cod fritters with tomato confit, and sweet corn bisque.

4 E. Chestnut St. www.townnantucket.com. ⓒ **508/325-TOWN** [8696]. Main courses $24–$32. July–Aug Mon–Fri 5:30–9pm, Sat–Sun 11am–2:30pm and 5:30–9pm.

Moderate

Note that "moderate" on Nantucket would mean "pricey" anywhere else. To keep your food budget down, consider having your big meal at lunch and visiting the to-go places on Broad Street, or any of our Inexpensive listings (beginning on the next page) for your evening meal. Take your meals over to the harbor or a picnic table at Children's Beach for a sunset picnic.

Black-Eyed Susan's ★★ ASIAN/AMERICAN   Foodie friends have said they would like to have every meal at this funky diner. Some seating is right at the counter: The food is cooked right behind it, for all to see—and even better, to smell. Breakfasts of huevos rancheros or Pennsylvania Dutch buttermilk pancakes with Jarlsberg cheese will leave you so full that you might want to skip lunch. At dinner, you might have your choice of tandoori salmon with mango coulis; beef tenderloin in red wine sauce with rigatoni; or paprika-dusted diver scallops with a lemon-Madeira demi-glace and kale risotto. Note that the diner's cash only; there's an ATM not far away on Centre Street. It's also BYOB: A liquor store is a few blocks away, on Main Street. Finally, they don't take reservations, so that the line out the door. A typical wait in season is an hour.

10 India St. www.black-eyedsusans.com. © **508/325-0308.** Main courses $24–$29. Apr–Oct daily 7am–1pm; Mon–Sat 6–10pm. Closed Nov–Mar.

Centre Street Bistro ★★★ NEW AMERICAN   At this little cafe, two of the island's top chefs, Ruth and Tim Pitts, create wonderfully creative meals in an intimate atmosphere. It's a very unpretentious place to have what is sure to be a memorable meal—the menu changes nightly. Main courses on a given night might include tofu pad Thai, sesame-crusted shrimp with red curry rice, and pan-seared duck breast with fruit chutney and homemade ricotta gnocchi. The restaurant is BYOB; the nearest liquor store is a few blocks away on Main Street.

29 Centre St. www.nantucketbistro.com. © **508/228-8470.** Main courses $19–$25. June–Sept Mon and Wed–Fri 11:30am–2pm and 5:30–9:30pm; Sat–Sun 8am–1pm and 6–9pm; call for off-season hours.

Nantucket Lobster Trap ★ SEAFOOD   This is Nantucket's version of your typical clam shack, though keep in mind, it is far more expensive than the Cape Cod version. Seating is at picnic tables, and there's an extensive raw bar and an outdoor patio area. Standard fried fish dinners are on the menu as well as lobster dinners. There are also some pasta entrees that take advantage of the seafood, such as linguini with clam sauce and lobster scampi.

23 Washington St. www.nantucketlobstertrap.com. © **508/228-4200.** Main courses $24–$30. June–Sept daily 5–10pm; call for off-season hours. Closed late Oct–early May.

The Proprietors Bar & Table ★★ NEW AMERICAN   Although much of the food here has global inspirations, the focus is on sourcing ingredients from small Nantucket and New England farms. The menu has a selection of unique small plates of light bites, like pig ear fries with cilantro. Sharing is the thing to do here but hungry people will need three or four to satisfy them, so you might want to just come for a drink and an appetizer if you're on a budget. There are also traditional main courses on the menu, like the seared Nantucket fluke with olive oil, lemon, and tomato juice. The flavors are a revelation. The dining room is very beautiful, a sort of hip ode to the island's history. It's fun to sit at the bar and soak in the atmosphere.

9 India St. www.proprietorsnantucket.com. © **508/228-7477.** Main courses $21–$36. Half portions $12–$18. July and August 5–10pm, Sunday 10am–1:30pm and 5–10pm; call for off-season hours. Closed Dec to mid-May.

Inexpensive

The Brotherhood of Thieves ★ PUB   The unusual name of this 1840s

bar comes from an 1844 anti-slavery pamphlet written on Nantucket. It's best for classic pub fare like burgers or even a fish burrito, washed down with craft beer (they have a couple dozen unusual ones available on tap and in bottles.) After a major fire damaged the restaurant, the basement was retained as the old whaling tavern and upstairs rooms were redone in a more upscale mode. There is also an outside patio seating area, which is a great option in the summer months.

23 Broad St. www.brotherhoodofthieves.com. © **508/228-2551.** Main courses $16–$38. Mar–Jan Mon–Sat 11:30am–midnight; Sun noon–10pm. Closed Feb.

Easy Street Cantina ★   Among the many fast food places along Broad

Street, this is your best bet for a good meal to go, mainly by virtue of the size of the menu and the choices you have. But this isn't typical fast-food fare. The fish tacos are nicely spiced and come with homemade slaw, and the breakfast sandwiches are sublime.

2 Broad St. © **508/228-5418.** All under $15. July–Aug Mon–Sat 7:15am–2am, Sun 8:30-2am. Call for off-season hours.

Sayle's Seafood ★★   A great bargain option is to pick up fried seafood

platters or fish sandwiches at Sayle's, which is a short walk from the harbor, and eat it by the water. This is water-view dining on the cheap, and the fish here is among the best you can get on the island.

99 Washington St. Ext. www.saylesseafood.com. © **508/228-4599.** $7–$25. No credit cards. May–Nov daily 8am–9pm.

Brewing Up a Fun Afternoon

It used to be that the typical Nantucket visitor would not get to **Cisco Brewery ★★** (www.ciscobrewers.com; © **508/325-5929**) because it is too far to drive from the downtown area. But now a free shuttle bus, leaving from the Nantucket Visitor Services Center at 12:30pm, will take you there (5 Bartlett Farm Rd., just down the road from Bartlett's Farm, see box p. 302). Many afternoons there's live music on the property, and food service provided by different island restaurants: Buy a drink at the brewery and enjoy a concert of local music. There are tours of the brewery, winery, and the Triple Eight Distillery on site, lasting about an hour and costing $20 per person, which includes tasting of two beers, two wines and two liquors. It's open April through December, Monday through Saturday 11am to 7pm, Sunday noon to 6pm.

Something Natural ★★   This is the place to stop on your bike while heading out for a day at Jetties Beach. Big overstuffed sandwiches (they sell halfs too) and homemade cookies are the specialties.

50 Cliff Rd. www.somethingnatural.com. ⓒ **508/228-0504.** All items under $15. Apr to mid-Oct daily 8am–6pm. Closed mid-Oct to Mar.

Sushi by Yoshi ★★   On an island 30 miles out to sea, it makes sense that you would be able to find terrific sushi. Here is your supplier. The small store-front lends itself to takeout, and what could be better than a sushi feast while sitting by the harbor watching the sunset? Be ready for a long wait here on summer nights.

2 E. Chestnut St. www.sushibyyoshi.com. ⓒ **508/228-1801.** Rolls from $11 and up. No reservations. May to mid-Oct Daily 11:30am–2:30pm, 4:30–9:30pm; mid-Oct to Apr Thurs–Sat 11:30am–9pm, Sun–Wed 5–9pm.

ELSEWHERE ON THE ISLAND

The Chanticleer ★★★ FRENCH   This famous restaurant in a rose-covered cottage continues to exceed expectations. The chef-owner Jeff Worster, who is known for his creativity, has reinvented the strictly French menu to reflect modern ways of dining. That means, just taking a sampling from the appetizers menu, that the ahi tuna tartare comes with ancho chili and a scallion pancake, and corn-crusted Alabama catfish comes with andouille sausage and okra risotto. Still, this remains one of the island's most formal dining experiences—a place for special occasions, especially in the romantic garden dining alfresco.

9 New St., Siasconset. www.chanticleernantucket.com. ⓒ **508/257-4499.** Jackets preferred for men. Main courses $24–$46. June–Aug Tues–Sun 11:30am–2pm and 6–8:30pm; call for off-season hours. Closed mid-Oct to late May.

Galley Beach ★★★ NEW AMERICAN   This is really more of an experience than a restaurant. An intake of breath is the typical response as you walk into the dining room, set right on a beautiful wide beach with views across the sand to the ocean. Salt breezes accompany your meal. You might expect a place this fabulous to have so-so food because people will come no matter what. But not so here. The menu is wonderfully summery. On the starter list, you might have cured salmon tartare with crème fraîche and caviar, or crab tortellini with fennel cream and ginger vinaigrette. As a main course, there is the luxurious warm lobster tail or the pork belly with roast parsnips and pickled pear. This restaurant boldly prices most of its entrees in the 40-dollar-range; that delicious lobster tail is $59.

At Cliffside Beach Club, 54 Jefferson Ave. www.galleybeach.net. ⓒ **508/228-9641.** Main courses $32–$59. Summer Mon–Fri 11:30am–2:30pm and 5:30–10pm, Sat–Sun 10am–2:30pm and 5:30–10pm; call for off-season hours. Closed late Sept–late May.

Nantucket Entertainment & Nightlife

Nantucket's newest entertainment venue is **Dreamland Theater,** 17 South Water St. (www.nantucketdreamland.org; ⓒ **508/228-1784**), an impressive complex housing a cinema and performing arts space.

Theatre buffs will want to spend an evening at the **Theatre Workshop of Nantucket,** 2 Centre St. (at the Methodist Church; www.theatreworkshop. com; ⓒ **508/228-4305**). This shoebox-size theater assays thought-provoking plays as readily as summery farces. The season runs 8 months, well into the fall. Tickets are $64 for adults, $57 for seniors and $42 for children age 5 to 12.

Nantucket usually has an attractive crowd of bar-hoppers making the scene around town. You'll find good singles scenes at the **Boarding House** at 12 Federal St. (www.boardinghousenantucket.com; ⓒ **508/228-9622**), **The Club Car,** at 1 Main St. (see p. 310), or **Slip 14 on South Wharf** at 14 Old South Wharf (www.slip14.com; ⓒ **508/228-2033**).

Live music comes in many guises on Nantucket, and there are a number of good itinerant performers who play at different venues. Meanwhile, it may be Reggae Night at **The Chicken Box,** 16 Daves St. (www.thechickenbox.com; ⓒ **508/228-9717**), when the median age of this rocking venue rises by a decade or two. For a fun, laid-back bar outside of town, try the **Muse,** 44 Surfside Rd. (www.themusenantucket.com; ⓒ **508/228-6873**). Cover about $5.

CENTRAL & WESTERN MASSACHUSETTS

By Herbert Bailey Livesey & Leslie Brokaw

While Boston and its maritime appendage Cape Cod face the sea and embrace it, inland Massachusetts turns in upon itself. Countless ponds and lakes shimmer in its folds and hollows, often hidden by deep forests and granite outcroppings. Farms and vestiges of industrial buildings speckle the north-south valleys of the Connecticut and Housatonic rivers.

The heartland Pioneer Valley, enclosing the Connecticut River, earned its name in the early 18th century, when European trappers and farmers first began to push west from the colonies clinging to the edges of Massachusetts Bay. They were followed by ambitious capitalists who erected redbrick mills along the river for the manufacture of textiles and paper. Most of those enterprises failed or faded in the post–World War II movement to the milder climate and cheaper labor of the South, leaving a miasma of economic hardship that has yet to be completely resolved. But those industrialists also helped fund many of the distinguished colleges for which the valley is now known, and the educated populations that come out of these schools provide the region with youthful energy and a rich cultural life.

Roughly the same pattern applied in the Berkshires, the twin ranges of rumpled hills that define the western band of the state. The development of this region in the 19th century was prompted mainly by the construction of the railroad from New York and Boston. Artistic and literary folk made a favored summer retreat of it, followed by wealthy urbanites attracted by the region's reputation for creativity and bohemianism. Many of their extravagant mansions, dubbed "Berkshire Cottages," still survive, and the region continues to attract the town-and-country crowd, who support a vibrant summer schedule of the arts and then steal away as the crimson leaves fall and the Berkshires grow quiet beneath 6 months of snow.

WORCESTER

44 miles W of Boston; 52 miles NE of Springfield

Massachusetts's second-largest city, Worcester (pronounced *Wuss*-ter, or, locally, *Woos*-tah) has a number of good museums and eating venues. There are enough attractions here to fill an overnight. The student population draws from over a dozen schools, including Clark University, Worcester Polytechnic Institute, and College of the Holy Cross.

Worcester was the site of the first National Women's Rights Convention, in 1850, 2 years after the 1848 Seneca Falls Woman's Rights Convention.

Essentials

ARRIVING

Worcester is 2 miles north of the east-west Massachusetts Turnpike (I-90) via I-290, which bisects the city. Driving can be tricky in Worcester, with the convergence of highways and its one-way streets, so get detailed directions to your destination. **Amtrak** (www.amtrak.com; © **800/USA-RAIL** [872-7245]) stops here daily each way on its route between Boston and Chicago.

VISITOR INFORMATION

The tourism organization **Discover Central Massachusetts** (www.discover centralma.org; © **508/753-1550**) has an active website of events going on in the city and area.

Exploring Worcester

CraftRoots Brewery ★ BREWERY   Small-batch breweries are all the rage, and New England is right in the scrum of the trend. There are over 140 artisanal breweries in Massachusetts alone. CraftRoots is a standout: Not only is it the first fully woman-owned brick-and-mortar brewery in the history of Massachusetts, but in 2018 it was named the fastest-growing small and independent craft brewery in the U.S. by the Brewers Association. All of the grain and hops used to make its beer is grown in nearby states. It's located about 25 miles southeast of Worcester, and guests are invited to bring their own food (and kids) to the taproom—decorated in bright lime-green and earth-tone colors—to try out the beer and see how the process works.

4 Industrial Rd., Milford. www.craftrootsbrewing.com. © **508/381-1920.** Wed–Thurs 5–9pm, Fri 3–10pm, Sat noon–10pm, Sun noon–6pm.

Crompton Collective ★★ SHOPPING MALL   Located in an 1860 Worcester mill building listed on National Register of Historic Places, the funky Crompton Collective describes itself as "a curated boutique marketplace" with items by independent artisans. The dozens of vendors who rent space here include both antique dealers and makers of original arts and crafts—housewares, jewelry, gifts—many using cleverly repurposed materials. Founder Amy Lynn Chase helped put **Worcester's Canal District**, where the Collective is located, on the map. Stop by **BirchTree Bread**

(www.birchtreebreadcompany.com; © **774/243-6944**), located inside the same building, for breads, pastries, coffee, and music.

138 Green St. www.cromptoncollective.com. © **508/753-7303.** Free admission. Tues–Sun 11am–5pm (to 6pm Wed, Fri, and Sat, and to 8pm Thurs).

EcoTarium ★ NATURE CENTER   This indoor-outdoor discovery center is set on a woodsy campus crossed by meandering nature trails. Primarily directed at young children, the complex includes a **planetarium** and a museum with interactive displays as well as live and taxidermied animals. Outside, there are bald eagles, otters, and owls, and the **Explorer Express Train,** a one-third-scale model of an 1860s steam engine that takes a 12-minute loop through the grounds.

222 Harrington Way. www.ecotarium.org. © **508/929-2700.** $18 adults, $14 seniors, students, and ages 2–18. Planetarium $5, Explorer Express Train $3. Tues–Sat 10am–5pm; Sun noon–5pm.

Worcester Art Museum ★★ MUSEUM   WAM boasts an impressive collection of artworks, from 2nd-century Buddhist pieces to 20th-century American photos. Special exhibits of contemporary work give some fizz and pop to the hushed classical setting, which features a beautiful interior court-yard. Particular strengths are the American wing, with canvases by Cassatt, Sargent, and Whistler; some memorable works by anonymous Colonial art-ists; and silver by Paul Revere. The Europeans on the second floor include Gauguin, Monet, Dürer, and Gainsborough. There's a 12th-century **Gothic chapter house,** once used by Benedictine monks, transported from France and said to be the first medieval room to come to the U.S. After the nearby Higgins Armory Museum closed, WAM took over the extensive **collection of knightly armor and swords.** A cafe offers soups and sandwiches from 11:30am to 2pm (Wed–Sat), with an outdoor courtyard in warm months.

55 Salisbury St. www.worcesterart.org. © **508/799-4406.** $16 adults, $14 seniors, $6 ages 4–17; free 3 and under; free for all 1st Sat of month. Wed–Sun 10am–4pm (until 8pm 3rd Thurs of month).

Outdoor Activities

Ten miles south of Worcester center, **Purgatory Chasm State Park,** Purgatory Road, Sutton (www.mass.gov/locations/purgatory-chasm-state-reservation; © **508/234-3733**), is a distinctive spot for a family hike for folks of moderate-to-good condition. It can include traveling through a quarter-mile-long gap between massive granite walls (if you're slender, you'll be able to explore the narrowest nooks and crannies). The main trail runs down the middle of the gap with several return options; the shortest is a ½-mile loop. Restrooms are avail-able at a visitor center. Parking is $5 for Massachusetts residents and $10 for all others.

Where to Stay in Worcester

Most of the accommodations in and around the city are chain motels. **Stur-bridge**, 21 miles away, has atmospheric options in its **Publick House** (p. 322) and **Old Sturbridge Inn** (p. 322).

Beechwood Hotel ★★   A 10-minute drive from downtown, the Beechwood is located across the street from the University of Massachusetts Medical School and Medical Center complex—a location that's both safe and quiet. Guestrooms have a modern-country-cozy feel and include bathrobes, Keurig coffeemakers, and pillowtop beds. Sunday brunches ($35 adults, $17 children) and dinners in the **Sonoma Restaurant** receive local notice. (Beer fans will want to check out the options from the local **Wormtown Brewery**, on tap here.) The hotel is well kept and boasts its status as the only AAA Four Diamond Hotel in Central Massachusetts.

363 Plantation St. (at Rte. 9). www.beechwoodhotel.com. 📞 **800/344-2589** or 508/754-5789. 73 units. $189–$286 double. Rates include continental breakfast. Free parking. **Amenities:** Restaurant; bar; exercise room; room service; Wi-Fi (free).

Where to Eat in Worcester

Just a few blocks east of the downtown train station, a strip of restaurants and cafes line Shrewsbury Street. Among them are **VIA Italian Table,** 89 Shrewsbury St. (www.viaitaliantable.com; 📞 **508/754-4842**), and a handsome steakhouse, **111 Chop House,** 111 Shrewsbury St. (www.111chophouse.com; 📞 **508/799-4111**), both run by the same group behind Sole Proprietor (see below). A few blocks away is **Bocado Tapas Bar,** 82 Winter St. (www.bocadotapasbar.com; 📞 **508/797-1011**).

Armsby Abbey ★★★ PUB FARE   This popular gastropub opened in 2008 and went on to win 66 awards in its first 9 years in Worcester Magazine's Best of Worcester polls. We're big fans, too. The Armsby's coziness is infectious, and its menu and beer selection make it a must-visit. An enticing cheese plate continues to be a highlight, with some dozen New England cheeses to choose from each day. Burgers and flatbreads are also available. A large chalkboard details the more than 20 beers on tap, and there are creative cocktails. Even its website is best of breed, with its draft beer menu updated daily.

144 N. Main St. www.armsbyabbey.com. 📞 **508/795-1012.** Main courses $12–$23. Reservations recommended. Mon–Fri 11:30am–midnight; Sat–Sun 10am–midnight (kitchen until 10pm Sun–Thurs and until 11pm Fri–Sat).

Sole Proprietor ★★ SEAFOOD   A well-run property, from the congenial staff to the long wine card (over 30 available by the glass), this is a standout restaurant. Fish options range from the simple (broiled, grilled, or blackened, Cajun style) to the fanciful (rainbow trout served over pumpkin and sage ravioli). It's been named the city's best seafood restaurant annually for more than 30 years in *Worcester Magazine*'s Best of Worcester polls, and it's been the recipient of *Wine Spectator*'s "Award of Excellence" every year since 2001. Most lunch mains are $12 to $16, and generously portioned. There are two dining options here, depending on your needs: An elegant dining area on one side, and a clubby bar on the other.

118 Highland St. (Rte. 9). www.thesole.com. 📞 **508/798-3474.** Main courses $17–$40; Sun–Mon 11:30am–9pm, Tues–Thurs 11:30am–10pm, Fri—Sat 11:30am–11pm; bar open 1 hr. later.

STURBRIDGE & OLD STURBRIDGE VILLAGE ★★★

59 miles W of Boston; 22 miles SW of Worcester; 35 miles E of Springfield

Sturbridge is a quiet New England town of 9,268 residents that offers two reasons to visit. The first is **Old Sturbridge Village,** a living outdoor/indoor museum on 200 acres with costumed "residents" who demonstrate the pursuits of the period (see below). It's one of the top tourist destinations in central Massachusetts and deservedly popular. The other reason is an **antiques show** that sets up three times a year in the adjacent town of Brimfield (see below).

Essentials

ARRIVING

Sturbridge is at the intersection of the Massachusetts Turnpike (I-90) and I-84. Rtes. 20 and 131 are the main roads in town. Note that some "Main Street" addresses are on Route 20 and others are on Route 131.

VISITOR INFORMATION

The **Sturbridge Area Tourist Association Visitor Center** is at 46 Hall Rd. (www.sturbridgetownships.com; © **800/628-8379** or 508/347-2761). The town's website, www.visitsturbridge.org, offers a PDF of its annual visitor guide.

Exploring Sturbridge

Old Sturbridge Village ★★★ LIVING HISTORY MUSEUM   Spread across 200 acres, Old Sturbridge Village uses authentic 19th-century buildings to re-create a rural settlement of the 1830s. Among the sights on the large property are a saw mill, a country store, a blacksmith shop, a school, a cooperage, a printing office, and a parson's home. At the edges of the village are a working farm and an herb garden. Lazy boat rides are popular, as is the horse-drawn stagecoach which traverses the dirt lanes. When there's snow guests can take horse-drawn sleigh rides.

Visitors stroll through the village, where costumed docents demonstrate musketry, barrel-making, and plowing with oxen (guests are sometimes invited to help). The operators have gotten inventive in recent years, adding a craft beer and roots music festival in July, a cider festival in October, and

---

Antiques Road Trip #1: Brimfield

Brimfield is a normally quiet village just to the west of Sturbridge, but in mid-May, mid-July, and early September tens of thousands of dealers and shoppers gather along a 1-mile stretch of Route 20, the main drag through town, for the **Brimfield Antiques and Collectible Shows** ★ (www.brimfield.com and www.brimfieldexchange.com). Each event is actually a collection of almost two dozen individual shows running side by side that have their own opening times, contact information, and admissions (most are free to attend). Each overall show runs for 6 days (Tues–Sun).

live-action theater that works its way through the village (including, in 2018, a production of *Charlotte's Web* that featured real animals). Popular, too, is the participatory Dinner in a Country Village—where guests stay after-hours to pitch in and make a typical meal of the times on a massive hearth by candlelight and then gather around a single table to enjoy the fruits of their labor—and Christmas in a Country Village, which takes place on select evenings in December and includes song, storytelling, and a nightly tree lighting.

1 Old Sturbridge Village Rd. www.osv.org. © **800/733-1830.** $28 adults, $26 seniors, $14 children 4–17 and college students, free for children 3 and under. Memorial Day–Labor Day Wed–Sun 9:30am–5pm and some Mon holidays. Reduced days and hours rest of year; confirm before visiting.

Where to Stay in Sturbridge

Old Sturbridge Village operates two lodgings a short walk away from the Village: the **Old Sturbridge Inn** (the 10-room Oliver Wight House, built in 1789) and 29-room **Reeder Family Lodges** (each unit a cross between a classic New England Cape and an updated motel) at 369 Main St. For information go to www.osv.org/stay-dine-shop/inn or call © **508/347-5056.**

Familiar chains include the **Comfort Inn & Suites,** 83 Hall Rd. (www.sturbridgecomfortinn.com; © **508/347-3306**) and **Hampton Inn of Sturbridge,** 328 Main St. (Route 131; www.hamptoninn3.hilton.com; © **508/347-6466**). **Airbnb** (www.airbnb.com) lists over 250 rentals in Sturbridge and 150 in Brimfield.

Publick House ★ This has long been the high-profile historic lodging in the Sturbridge area, although the **Old Sturbridge Inn,** above, has presented some formidable competition in recent years. The most desirable rooms are the 17 in the main **Historic Inn.** Built in 1771, it's heavy on atmosphere, with Colonial reproduction pieces, quilts on some beds, and floors and ceilings that long ago settled into not-quite-right angles. A downstairs **tavern** with fireplace, used mainly by guests, is a jovial venue. Suites in the adjacent **Chamberlain House** are larger and somewhat more contemporary and also recommended. The **Country Lodge,** on the back side of the property, is a motor inn with an outdoor pool. Meals are available in the tavern and the more refined **Tap Room**, which serves American cuisine. A small "bake shoppe" does brisk business throughout the day.

277 Main St. (Rte. 131). www.publickhouse.com. © **800/782-5425** or 508/347-3313. 108 units. $103–$199 double in Historic Inn; $103–$199 in Chamberlain House; $69–$145 in Lodge. Pets accepted in some rooms of Country Lodge. **Amenities:** 2 restaurants; bar; A/C; outdoor pool; Wi-Fi (free).

Where to Eat in Sturbridge

B.T.'s Smokehouse ★★ BARBECUE B.T.'s offers Texas roadhouse-style barbeque that's slow-cooked—pulled pork, beef brisket, smoked chicken, and pork ribs—and has become a regional best of breed. The $4 mini-sandwiches, the size of an apple, have ¼ pound of meat and are a perfect snack, but you can load up on sandwiches or platters of BBQ along with catfish po'boys, bison burgers, brisket chili, black-eyed peas, hush puppies, and onion rings. In warm weather, patrons flock to the outdoor tables.

392 Main St. (Rte. 20). www.btsmokehouse.com. ✆ **508/347-3188.** Main courses $7–$21. Tues–Sat 11am–9pm; Sun noon–8pm.

SPRINGFIELD

90 miles W of Boston; 26 miles N of Hartford

This once-prosperous manufacturing city on the east bank of the Connecticut River shows signs of redevelopment throughout downtown, with recycled loft and factory buildings standing beside modern glass towers. As of 2018 it has something new to boast about: a Las Vegas–style MGM Resorts casino.

Essentials

ARRIVING

BY CAR   Springfield is located at the juncture of the east-west Massachusetts Turnpike (I-90) and north-south I-91.

BY PLANE   The primary airport serving Springfield is **Bradley International Airport** (www.bradleyairport.com; ✆ **860/292-2000**), in Windsor Locks, Connecticut, about 20 miles to the south (see p. 400). The major **car rental** companies all have counters here.

BY TRAIN   **Amtrak** (www.amtrak.com; ✆ **800/USA-RAIL** [872-7245]) trains running both east-west and north-south stop in Springfield. From Boston, it's a 2½-hour trip, with fares starting at $23; the trip time from New York City is 3½ hours, and fares start at $50.

BY BUS   **Peter Pan Bus Lines** (www.peterpanbus.com; ✆ **800/343-9999**), which serves much of New England, is based right in Springfield. Founded in 1933, it was named after the founder's favorite bedtime story. Buses from Boston take 2 hours to get to Springfield, and fares start at $10. Buses from New York City take 3½ to 4 hours, with fares starting at $14.

VISITOR INFORMATION

The **Greater Springfield Convention and Visitors Bureau** (www.explore westernmass.com; ✆ **413/787-1548**) has regularly updated information at its website along with a PDF of its Springfield Downtown Cultural and Walking Tour Map. There's a **visitor center** inside the Naismith Memorial Basketball Hall of Fame (see p. 324).

Exploring Springfield

MGM Springfield Casino ★ CASINO   After years of contentious debate, the Massachusetts electorate voted to allow casino gambling in the state. MGM Springfield was set to open in August 2018. The $960-million hotel and casino complex will have slots, table games, and poker rooms, along with 250 on-site hotel rooms, a steakhouse, an Italian restaurant, a sports bar, and a spa and fitness center. The casino will be a new city anchor on the

During the last 2 weeks in September, the Big E—the Eastern States Exposition (www.thebige.com; ℂ **413/737-2443**)—is held in West Springfield, at 1305 Memorial Avenue. It's a huge old-fashioned agricultural fair with 4-H presentations, equestrian shows (in a 5,900-seat Coliseum), a wine and cheese barn, a midway, and entertainment from the likes of B.B. King's Blues Band and The Marshall Tucker Band. Admission to the fair is $15 for adults and kids 13 and older, $10 for kids 6 to 12, free for kids 5 and under.

Included on the expo grounds is **Storrowton Village** (www.storrowtonvillage.com; ℂ **413/205-5051**), a re-creation of a 19th-century village. During the Big E event, admission to Storrowton is included in the Big E entrance fee. Storrowton is also open on its own mid-June to mid-August as well as the first weekend of December and the following week for Yuletide celebrations. It's free to enter and stroll the grounds during these periods, while tours of the houses cost $7 per person (children under 6 free). Call to confirm opening hours.

eastern end of Main Street and along Interstate 91, and the hope is that it will bring new zest to that part of the city.

One MGM Way. www.mgmspringfield.com. ℂ **413/273-5000.** Check website for opening hours and details.

Naismith Memorial Basketball Hall of Fame ★★ SPORTS MUSEUM
A feast for fans, the Basketball Hall of Fame celebrates its 60th anniversary in 2019. The complex has an Honors Ring with biographies of the more than 300 athletes who have been inducted—women, too, who finally began making the list in 1985—and there are interactive displays with vast quantities of memorabilia of the sport, which was invented by Dr. James Naismith in Springfield in 1891 (early teams included the Philadelphia Hebrews and the Chicago Studebakers). On the ground floor is a basketball court where clinics and shootings contests are held. A large gift shop sells T-shirts, jerseys, and the like. Six chain restaurants occupy the complex and there's an adjacent Hilton Garden Inn hotel.

1000 Hall of Fame Ave., just off I-91. www.hoophall.com. ℂ **877/446-6752.** $24 adults 16 and older, $18 seniors, $16 kids 5–15, free for ages 4 and under. Daily 10am–4pm (sometimes until 5pm depending on day and season; check website).

Springfield Museums at the Quadrangle ★★ MUSEUM   A library
and five museums surrounding a small grassy quadrangle constitute this worthwhile destination for all ages. It's a peaceful respite, with marble benches throughout the small park. The newest venue, opened in 2017, is the **Amazing World of Dr. Seuss Museum ★★** (see box p. 325), which includes interactive exhibits that look like the amazing machines depicted in Seuss's children's books. Exhibit information is presented in both English and Spanish. Due to its popularity, the museum uses timed ticketing to control visitor flow. For advance reservations, contact **www.springfieldmuseums.org/tickets**. On the quad's library end, the **Dr. Seuss National Memorial Sculpture Garden**

features sculptures of the author himself (who was born in Springfield), the Cat in the Hat, the Grinch, Thing One and Thing Two, and other creations of his fertile mind. The sculptures are free to visit.

Elsewhere in the complex, the **Michele and Donald D'Amour Museum of Fine Arts** ★★ has over a dozen galleries. A permanent **Currier & Ives gallery** ★ features exhibits by the printmakers. Other galleries have Colonial paintings from Gilbert Stuart and John Copley of the Revolutionary period all the way up to 20th-century abstract expressionists such as Frank Stella and Helen Frankenthaler. On the end of the quad, the **George Walter Vincent Smith Art Museum,** housed in an 1896 Italian Renaissance–style mansion, displays Japanese samurai weaponry surrounding a carved 1805 Shinto shrine, with pastoral scenes by George Inness, Thomas Cole, and Albert Bierstadt upstairs. An Art Discover Center here has costumes and armor for kids to play dress-up. The **Springfield Science Museum** features a planetarium, dioramas of African animals, and a small Dinosaur Hall. The **Lyman and Merrie Wood Museum of Springfield History** details the city's manufacturing roots and the products made here, from motorcycles to firearms to Milton Bradley board games.

21 Edwards St. www.springfieldmuseums.org. ⓒ **413/263-6800.** One admission for all museums: $25 adults, $16.50 seniors & college students, $13 kids 3–17. Advance purchase recommended for Dr. Seuss museum. Mon–Sat 10am–5pm, Sun 11am–5pm.

Where to Stay in Springfield

The August 2018 opening of the MGM Springfield Casino and its 250 hotel rooms in downtown Springfield is going to change the game for hotels in the city: Other hotel operators will need to spruce themselves up (and offer discounts online) to compete with the attention and splash that will be paid to the

dr. seuss's NEIGHBORHOOD

Author and illustrator Theodor Seuss Geisel, better known as Dr. Seuss, grew up in Springfield and is a much beloved native son. In 1937, he named the first of his books, *And to Think That I Saw It on Mulberry Street,* after the Springfield avenue where his grandparents lived. (The book was rejected by 27 publishers before finding a home at Vanguard Press.)

Classics such as *The Cat in the Hat* and *How the Grinch Stole Christmas* followed. Hundreds of millions of copies of his dozens of books have been sold, and they've been translated into 15 languages.

Geisel spent most of his adult life in California, but much of his inspiration

can be traced to Springfield. Bartholomew Cubbins's castle bears a strong resemblance to the Howard Street Armory, and some of his landscapes look as if they were recalled from his playtime in Forest Park, near his boyhood home at 74 Fairfield St.

Mulberry Street is about a half-mile from the **Amazing World of Dr. Seuss Museum** and **Dr. Seuss National Memorial Sculpture Garden** (p. 324) and still has glimpses of its heyday charm, with Victorian manses and undistinguished apartment buildings along its length. The website **www.seussin springfield.org** has more information about the author.

very big new kid in town. The Greater Springfield Convention and Visitors Bureau lists **hotel packages** at www.explorewesternmass.com/lodging.

The most central downtown chain options are **Tower Square Hotel Springfield**, 2 Boland Way (www.thetowersquarehotel.com; ✆ **413/781-7111**), which was a Marriott until its rebranding in 2017, and the atrium-style **Sheraton Springfield Monarch Place,** One Monarch Place (www.sheraton-springfield.com; ✆ **800/325-3535**), directly across the street.

See also "Where to Stay in the Pioneer Valley" (p. 335) for hotels within easy driving distance of Springfield.

Where to Eat in Springfield

Springfield in 2018 began offering permits to restaurants for outdoor seating on public sidewalks. Look for new outdoor options on your visit.

Red Rose Pizzeria Restaurant ★ ITALIAN   Gigantic portions, consistently high quality, and seating for 400 are hallmarks of this long-time family business, which has held court on this modest block in Springfield for decades. A long menu features traditional renditions of Italian classics: baked manicotti, tortellini alfredo, chicken piccata, and shrimp scampi, along with pizza. The iconic business is on the cusp of a new challenge and opportunity: The one-story restaurant sits in the literal shadow of the colossal new MGM Springfield Casino, which was built next door.

1060 Main St. www.redrosepizzeria.com. ✆ **413/739-8510.** Main courses $10–$23. Tues–Thurs 11am–10pm; Fri–Sat 11am–11pm; Sun noon–10pm.

Student Prince (The Fort) ★ GERMAN/AMERICAN   In 1935, German immigrants opened this venue to serve schnitzels and sauerbraten. That year might not have seemed the precise historical moment to ensure the success of such an enterprise, but somehow the restaurant thrived and became a city icon, especially during the Christmas season. It almost shut down in 2014, but was saved by a new team of owners, led by the CEO of the local Peter Pan Bus company. Wiener schnitzel, bratwurst, and sauerbraten are obvious choices, and they're supplemented by big steaks, stuffed shrimp, and Boston scrod. Over 20 beers are on tap. An enormous stein collection fills shelves all the way to the ceiling.

8 Fort St. www.studentprince.com. ✆ **413/734-7475.** Main courses $13–$31. Mon–Wed 11am–9pm; Thurs–Sat 11am–11pm; Sun 11am–8pm.

Springfield Entertainment & Nightlife

Symphony Hall, 34 Court St. (www.symphonyhall.com; ✆ **413/788-7033**), is a venue for children's shows, country music singers, juggling troupes, and the **Springfield Symphony Orchestra** (www.springfieldsymphony.org; ✆ **413/733-2291**). The orchestra's main season runs October through May. The box office is around the corner at 1441 Main St., suite 121.

Downtown in past years has been eerily quiet at night. The new casino (p. 323) will, presumably, bring more foot traffic to its section of the city.

THE PIONEER VALLEY ★★

South Hadley: 5 miles N of I-90; Northampton: 17 miles N of I-90; Amherst: 24 miles N of I-90; Deerfield: 34 miles N of I-90; Turners Falls: 43 miles N of I-90 and 91 miles NW of Boston (via Rte. 2).

Low hills and quilted fields channel the Connecticut River as it runs south toward Long Island Sound, forming the Pioneer Valley. The earliest European settlers came here in the mid-1600s for what proved to be uncommonly fertile soil, and they were followed in the 19th century by men who harnessed the power of the river and became wealthy textile and paper manufacturers.

These industrialists took the lead in funding the prestigious institutions of higher learning that are now the pride of the region: **Smith, Mount Holyoke, Amherst,** and **Hampshire colleges.** The town of Amherst also is home to the sprawling **University of Massachusetts,** with nearly 22,000 undergrads. All five schools contribute mightily to the cultural life of the valley and the towns of South Hadley, Northampton, and Amherst. In the north, closer to Vermont, the old section of the village of Deerfield preserves the architecture and atmosphere of Colonial New England, while Turners Falls is a town-that-time-forgot being remade by an infusion of new artists.

Essentials

ARRIVING

BY CAR   While there are local buses, you really need a car to explore this area.I-91 and the smaller Route 5 traverse the valley from south to north, more or less parallel to each other. On the interstate, the region takes less than an hour to drive from bottom to top. From Boston and upstate New York, take the Massachusetts Turnpike (I-90) to Springfield, then I-91 or Route 5 north. From New York City, take I-95 north to New Haven, CT, where you can pick up I-95 north.

BY PLANE   The nearest major airport is **Bradley International** (www. bradleyairport.com; ✆ **860/292-2000**), in Windsor Locks, Connecticut. **Valley Transporter** (www.valleytransporter.com; ✆ **800/872-8752**) offers van shuttles between the airport and the towns and schools of the Pioneer Valley. Reservations are recommended.

BY TRAIN   The north-south **Amtrak** (www.amtrak.com; ✆ **800/USA-RAIL** [872-7245]) *Vermonter* stops in Amherst. It runs from St. Albans, Vermont, in the north to Washington, D.C., in the south, traveling through New York City, Philadelphia, and Baltimore. There is no train service from Boston.

BY BUS   **Peter Pan Bus Lines** (www.peterpanbus.com; ✆ **800/343-9999**) has regular bus service connecting the towns of the Valley to New York City and Boston.

VISITOR INFORMATION

Downloadable maps of the Pioneer Valley overall, Northampton, and Amherst are at **www.explorewesternmass.com/travel-tools**. You can also request, through the website, a hard copy of the Western Mass Visitors & Recreation Guide.

The Pioneer Valley

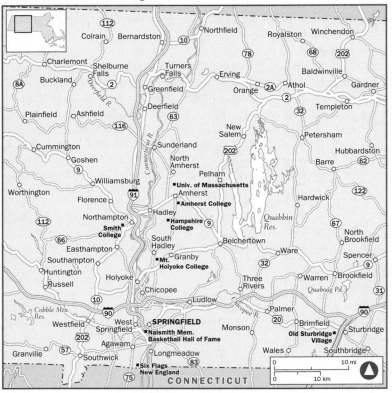

Exploring South Hadley ★

90 miles W of Boston; 12 miles N of Springfield

This stately town pops up on Route 116 alongside farming and working-class communities because of **Mount Holyoke College.** Pioneer educator Mary Lyon founded the school, then a seminary, in 1837, making the college the oldest continuously operating women's college in the nation. The campus, which was landscaped by Frederick Law Olmsted, designer of New York City's Central Park, is well worth a stroll. The college also has an excellent **Art Museum ★** (www.mtholyoke.edu/artmuseum; ✆ **413/538-2245**), which focuses on works from Asia, Egypt, and contemporary America, with emphasis on female artists. Hours are Tuesday through Friday from 11am to 5pm, Saturday and Sunday from 1 to 5pm. Admission is free.

J. A. Skinner State Park (www.mass.gov; ✆ **413/586-0350**) straddles the border between South Hadley and Hadley. On its 400 acres are picnic grounds and 40 miles of trails. At the top is the historic **Summit House,** a former hotel, with panoramic views of the valley (closed for repairs at this writing, so call ahead). The 1½-mile road to the summit is open to cars from mid-April to the end of October and to walkers year-round. Possible activities include cross-country skiing, horseback riding, mountain biking, and snowshoeing. The park entrance is on Mountain Road, off Route 47, in Hadley. Parking is $5 for Massachusetts residents, $10 for others.

Exploring Northampton ★★

11 miles NW of South Hadley; 20 miles N of Springfield.

Known locally as "Noho," Northampton is the cultural center of the valley, liveliest in the warmer times toward the starts and ends of the school year. Then the streets fill with students, parents, vendors, latter day hippies, returning alumnae, panhandlers, and occasional musicians. Try to allow at least an overnight or a long day in the area. The diversity and number of restaurants is far greater than most cities its size can boast (for a college town), and its many stores are as kicky as any devout shopper could hope. Events range from chamber music to art exhibitions to an autumn **film festival** (www.northampton filmfestival.com). The city also has a large LGBTQ population, with an elaborate **Pride Event** is held every May (**www.nohopride.org**).

Smith College, one of the largest colleges for women in the United States, is Northampton's dominating physical and spiritual presence. Its campus sprawls along Main Street just west of the commercial center.

Historic Northampton Museum & Education Center ★ MUSEUM
This small center hosts a smattering of readings, film screenings, and special exhibits, and houses items from the 1700s, memorabilia from former U.S. President Calvin Coolidge, and silk dresses from the 19th century. It has a rich collection of online resources, including the history of the Goody Parsons witchcraft case and photocopies of the *Hampshire Gazette* from the 1700s.

46 Bridge St. (Rte. 9). www.historicnorthampton.org. ℂ **413/584-6011.** Admission $3. Wed–Sat 10am–4pm; Sun noon–5pm.

Calvin Coolidge: Keeping a Low Profile in Northampton

U.S. President Calvin Coolidge practiced law in Northampton both before and after his occupancy of the Oval Office (1923–29). The White House website notes this vignette about Coolidge: "Both his dry Yankee wit and his frugality with words became legendary. His wife, Grace Goodhue Coolidge, recounted that a young woman sitting next to Coolidge at a dinner party confided to him she had bet she could get at least three words of conversation from him. Without looking at her he quietly retorted, 'You lose.'" Coolidge lived in houses at 21 Massasoit St. and on Hampton Terrace, but these are not open to the public. The **Forbes Library,** 20 West St. (www.forbeslibrary.org; ℂ **413/587-1011**), maintains the **Calvin Coolidge Presidential Library & Museum,** the only presidential collection hosted by a public library in the United States. It's open just to researchers, although a number of Coolidge photos and links to Coolidge information are posted at the library website. More items connected to Coolidge are displayed at the **Historic Northampton Museum** (above).

Smith College ★ COLLEGE CAMPUS   Equal parts tranquil and heady, the Smith campus is a bucolic mélange of rolling hills, broad lawns, and architecture in the Gothic, Greco-Roman, Renaissance, and medieval traditions. Landscape architect Frederick Law Olmsted laid out much of the original design, and the campus contains wooded walks and **botanic gardens** (www.smith.edu/garden; daily 8:30am–4pm; suggested donation $2). Smith is one of the largest women's colleges in the U.S., with just women undergraduates and both women and men admitted to its graduate programs.

Elm St. www.smith.edu. ✆ **413/584-2700.**

Smith College Museum of Art ★★ MUSEUM   Part of this museum's mission is collecting works by both white and black female artists, to join its impressive permanent collection of paintings by Degas, Monet, Cezanne, Picasso, Sargent, and Winslow Homer. With programming that includes free Second Fridays, Community Days, and lectures, this facility is on equal footing with New England's finest college art museums. A 5-year plan that began in 2017 aims to make the museum even more experiential, diverse, and accessible to the public. There's no museum parking lot, so look for a metered street spot.

20 Elm St. www.smith.edu/artmuseum. ✆ **413/585-2760.** $5 adults, $4 seniors, free for students and youth. Tues–Sat 10am–4pm (until 8pm Thurs); Sun noon–4pm; 2nd Fri of month until 8pm, with free admission 4–8pm.

OUTDOOR ACTIVITIES

Just northwest of Northampton on Route 9, families gravitate to the 150-acre **Look Memorial Park,** 300 N. Main St., Florence (www.lookpark.org; ✆ 413/584-5457), which has woods, a lake, pedal boats, miniature golf, a small steamer train, tennis courts, and picnic grounds. The park hosts frequent special events for children and families and has an outdoor amphitheater for concerts. Parking is $4 April to October, $2 November to March, with fees for activities.

Three miles southwest of Northampton on Route 10, the **Arcadia Wildlife Sanctuary,** 127 Combs Rd., Easthampton (www.massaudubon.org; ✆ 413/584-3009), is a preserve operated by the Massachusetts Audubon Society. Bordering the Connecticut River, the sanctuary contains marshes, woods, trails, and a nature center. Visitors often spot beavers, turtles, hawks, hummingbirds, and great blue herons. Admission is $4 for adults, $3 for seniors and children ages 2 to 12.

NORTHAMPTON SHOPPING

Northampton enjoys the most diverse shopping in the valley. Its half-mile-long Main Street, from Bridge Street at the eastern end to the Smith College campus on the western end, is rich with diverse restaurants, art galleries, acupuncture clinics, buskers, and jewelry and clothing boutiques. Downtown is equal parts funky and chic, and it's as easy to find vegan chocolate and organic egg omelets as it is UGG boots and expensive glass artworks.

Thorne's Marketplace, 150 Main St. (www.thornesmarketplace.com), is a former department store reconfigured into two dozen boutiques and casual eating places. **Booklink,** on the main floor, is an admirable bookseller and carries an excellent card selection, with bargain books and an espresso bar on the upper floor. Down the hall is **Refinery,** whose "distinctive accessories" include bags, scarves, clogs, and sandals, many of them hand-made.

Burnishing the city's reputation as a small town with an unusually vigorous arts community is the prestigious **R. Michelson Gallery,** 132 Main St. (www. rmichelson.com; ℂ **413/586-3964**), which occupies a Greek Revival former bank (the vault serves as an exhibition space) and puts on shows that range from Leonard Baskin prints to largely figurative paintings and sculptures. One gallery is devoted to children's book illustrations by such luminaries as Jules Feiffer, William Steig, and Dr. Seuss. **Essentials,** 88 Main St. (℃ **413/584-2327**), sells hip housewares, including kitschy "Japanistic" items, French ware (Tintin, the Little Prince, and the like), and shoulder bags of all sizes.

A half-dozen independent bookstores continue to persevere in downtown. They are listed at **www.ravenusedbooks.com**, the website of **Raven Used Books,** 4 Old South St. (℃ **413/584-9868**).

Exploring Amherst ★

8 miles NE of Northampton; 23 miles N of Springfield

Another Pioneer Valley town defined by its educational institutions, this one has an even larger student population than most, with distinguished **Amherst College** occupying much of its center, **Hampshire College** off South Pleasant Street, and the vast **University of Massachusetts** campus to its immediate northwest. The name of the town is properly pronounced without the "H." It was the first permanent English settlement in the area, in 1727.

The best strolling is within a few blocks any direction of the town green. At the northeast corner of the green is the **Town Hall,** a fortress-like Romanesque Revival creation of Boston's noted architect, H. H. Richardson.

Amherst College ★ COLLEGE CAMPUS   Amherst's campus cuts through the heart of the town and makes for a pretty stroll. Its **Mead Art Museum ★**, routes 116 and 9 (℃ **413/542-2335**), specializes in American art, including Hudson River School landscapes and modern works by Louise Bourgeois, Frank Stella, Cindy Sherman, and Ai Weiwei.

S. Pleasant and College sts. www.amherst.edu. ℂ **413/542-2000.** Museum admission free. Daily except Mon.

Emily Dickinson Museum: The Homestead and The Evergreens ★ HISTORIC HOME   Designated a National Historic Monument, the Homestead is where poet Emily Dickinson was born in 1830, lived until she was 10, and then moved back to when she was 25. The Evergreens was the next-door home of her brother Austin, his wife Susan, and their three children. Dickinson stayed here at this home until her death 31 years later. The "Belle of Amherst" (see box p. 332) was the granddaughter and daughter of local movers and shakers, the source of her support while she produced her groundbreaking poetry, even as she withdrew into near-total seclusion. The two

THE BELLE OF AMHERST: emily dickinson

Born in 1830 into a well-known Amherst family—her lawyer father, Edward Dickinson, served as treasurer of Amherst College for nearly 40 years—Emily Dickinson lived most of her life in the family homestead on Main Street. Her parents saw to it that she and her sister received a rigorous education, unusual for girls of that era. Yet she rarely left the town of Amherst, except for a few months in Boston when she was 14, 10 months attending nearby Mount Holyoke College in South Hadley (p. 328), and a month-long family trip in 1855. (Though she did not complete her Mount Holyoke education, that hasn't stopped the college from claiming her as one of its most illustrious alumnae.) Over the years Dickinson became increasingly reclusive and odd, devoting herself to household tasks and gardening, known for dressing almost exclusively in white. Even when her father died, she did not attend the funeral, only sitting in an adjacent room with the door cracked open so she could listen to the service.

Yet at the same time Dickinson carried on lively correspondence with various friends, many of whom knew her passion for writing poetry. A good half of her poetry was written in a creative blaze in the years 1860 to 1864. A handful of her poems were published in her lifetime, including several in the Springfield Republican, but upon her death (probably from Bright's Disease) in 1886, her sister Lavinia discovered a locked chest with around 1,800 poems, many of them neatly copied out as if ready for publication. Four years later, a volume of her poetry was published by some of her literary friends, and became a surprise best-seller. In the 1920s, as modernism took hold, Dickinson's poetry grew in critical stature. While the early volumes heavily edited Dickinson's idiosyncratic spellings, syntax, and punctuation, when they were republished in 1955 as originally written down, Dickinson's startling originality finally blossomed in the public eye. The feminist movement of the 1960s embraced her work even more, and today she is regarded as one of America's boldest and most inventive poets.

buildings now make up Emily Dickinson Museum, with a free Tour Center, bookshop, and exhibit space in the Homestead, and guided tours (for a fee) of both homes.

280 Main St. www.emilydickinsonmuseum.org. ✆ **413/542-8161.** Admission free to center and bookshop. Entrance to Homestead and Evergreens by guided tour only: $15 adults, $13 seniors, $10 students, under 18 free. Tour Center Mar–Dec Wed–Sun 11am–4pm (until 5pm June–Aug), guided tours 1–3:30pm. Closed rest of year. Reservations recommended.

National Yiddish Book Center ★ MUSEUM   This airy complex on the Hampshire College campus is devoted to rescuing the language of Ashkenazi Jews from central and eastern Europe. That means collecting and distributing Yiddish-language books and celebrating Yiddish culture through films, lectures, and other public events—including **Yidstock**, an annual music festival held every July. It's the world's first museum of its kind and is located in an apple orchard that has gardens and picnic tables.

1021 West St. (on Hampshire College campus). www.yiddishbookcenter.org. ✆ **413/256-4900.** Free admission. Sun–Fri 10am–4pm.

University of Massachusetts Fine Arts Center ★ PERFORMANCE VENUE/GALLERY   On the expansive 1,450-acre UMass campus north of the town center, UMass Amherst's FAC books a variety of dance, jazz, global arts, and contemporary ensembles.

151 Presidents Dr., on UMass campus (follow signs to CONCERT HALL). https://fac.umass. edu/online. ☏ **413/545-2511.** Free admission to Gallery. Tues–Fri 11am–4:30pm; Sat–Sun 2–5pm.

OUTDOOR ACTIVITIES
The **Norwottuck Rail Trail ★** (www.mass.gov/locations/norwottuck-rail-trail; ☏ **413/586-8706,** ext. 12) is a mostly level, paved bike path that connects Hadley, Northampton, and Amherst. Built on the former Boston and Maine rail bed, it travels for 11 miles more or less parallel to Route 9. In the midsection, it passes through open farmland.

AMHERST SHOPPING
Amherst Books, 8 Main St. (☏ **413/256-1547**) has an exceptionally well-chosen selection, from a full complement of bestsellers to titles far more esoteric. **Clay's,** 32 Main St. (☏ **413/256-4200**), has funky, flowing women's clothes in natural fibers. It's one of a chain of New England locations that feature brands manufactured in the region. **Amherst Typewriter & Computer,** 41 N. Pleasant St. (☏ **413/253-7122**), has a fascinating collection of antique and just old typewriters on display.

Exploring Old Deerfield ★★★
16 miles N of Northampton; 35 miles N of Springfield.

Meadows cleared and plowed nearly 350 years ago still surround this historic town between the Connecticut and Deerfield rivers. An invaluable fragment of American history, Deerfield has been designated a National Historic Landmark village. Massacres of Deerfield's English settlers by the French and Indian enemies of the British nearly wiped out the town in 1675 and again in 1704. In the latter raid, 47 people were killed and another 112 were taken prisoner and marched north to French Quebec.

Follow the signs to "Old Deerfield" or "Historic Deerfield," a turn-off of Route 5. The main thoroughfare of Old Deerfield, simply called **The Street,** is only about a mile long, but this small neighborhood has more than 80 homes built in the 17th, 18th, and 19th centuries. (The museum houses are located a few blocks either direction of the visitor center.) Most are private, but 10 can be visited mid-April through December by either self-guided tours or by guided tours conducted by **Historic Deerfield,** a local tourism organization (see below). Also on the main street is the prep school **Deerfield Academy,** which was founded in 1797.

Historic Deerfield Neighborhood Walking Tour ★★★ WALKING
TOUR   To stroll the main street and visit the 10 properties open for viewing, start at the **Visitor Center at Hall Tavern.** While there are no charges for walking the neighborhood, the only way to get inside most of the houses

during the mid-April to December tour season is to buy a ticket for a **guided tour.** If you want to stroll on your own, the visitor center sells walking tour booklets—or just download a village map from the website. The houses on the tour were constructed between 1730 and 1850. Inside them you'll see period furnishings, textiles, ceramics, silver, and pewter, as well as implements used from the mid–17th century to 1850, including many items made in the Connecticut River Valley during its prominence as an industrial center.

Visitors can also stop in at the **Flynt Center of Early American Life** ★, which has exhibitions of textiles, paintings, and decorative arts relevant to the local history. Unlike the historic homes, it's open year-round.

Nearby you'll also find the **Channing Blake Meadow Walk,** a marked trail that begins beside the Rev. John Farwell Moors House, a Historic Deerfield holding on the west side of The Street. Its route winds through a working farm, past the playing fields of Deerfield Academy, and through pastures beside the Deerfield River. Along the trail, sheep and cattle are seen up close; for that reason, dogs aren't allowed. There is no charge to walk the trail.

A **museum store** sells a judicious selection of evocative items such as cookbooks, jigsaw puzzles, and reproductions of household items found in the village houses.

84B Old Main St. www.historic-deerfield.org. Ⓒ **413/775-7214.** Tour admission (includes all properties open to public, plus Flynt Center) $18 adults, $5 kids 6–21, free for 5 and under. Mid-Apr to Dec daily 9:30am–4:30pm; no tours Jan to mid-Apr. Flynt Center also open Jan to mid-Apr Sat–Sun 9:30am–4:30pm; off-season admission to Flynt Center only, $7 adults, $5 kids 6–17.

Yankee Candle Village ★ STORE   Lots of people love Yankee Candles, and for them especially, this place will be a kick. The emporium is the company's flagship store (the "scenter of the universe"), and it befits a kingdom built on Americans' insatiable need for candles that are scented like cider donuts and "tranquil mist." In addition to miles of aisles of candles, this huge complex features a toy store, a flavored popcorn stand, and a year-round **Bavarian Christmas Village** with and indoor snow showers every 4 minutes. It's packed on weekends in autumn and near Christmas.

25 Greenfield Rd. (Rte. 5), South Deerfield. www.yankeecandle.com/south-deerfield-village. Ⓒ **877/636-7707.** Free admission. Daily 10am–6pm.

Exploring Turners Falls

5 miles NE of Old Deerfield; 22 miles N of Northampton; 40 miles N of Springfield.

Built in the 1860s as a mill town along the Connecticut River, the village of Turners Falls became home to immigrants from Germany, French Canada, Lithuania, and Ireland, all coming to chase their dreams. As with other riverside communities in the region, the village began a long economic slide when the mills started closing in the 1940s. But the community's profile has risen in recent years, thanks to an active partnership among cultural and commercial groups.

The **Turners Falls Cultural District,** designated by Massachusetts in 2017, is the central part of the village. Here historic buildings have been restored, some turned into affordable housing and others preserved to the standards of the national historic register. **Turners Falls River Culture** (www.turnersfallsriverculture.org), a partnership of leaders from the business and arts communities, has helped usher in the ongoing creative and artistic development. Its website provides extensive information about the town and its cultural attractions.

Start your visit at the **Great Falls Discovery Center,** 2 Avenue A (www.greatfallsdiscoverycenter.org; © **413/863-3221**), where you can see dioramas of the shoreline and birding culture along the Connecticut River. It's open daily mid-May through mid-October, Wednesday through Sunday the rest of the year. Admission is free.

Bicyclists can park here and take a ride along the paved 3.6-mile-long (6km) **Canalside Rail Trail** (www.mass.gov/locations/canalside-rail-trail). It begins at the canal and heads off to the left, toward Deerfield, traveling along a scenic stretch of the Connecticut River.

The **Shea Theater Arts Center,** 71 Avenue A (www.sheatheater.org; © **413/648-7432**), is the district's center of entertainment. Built in 1927 and renovated in 2016, it has 330 seats and hosts touring regional, national, and international artists as well as community artists and musicians.

Turners Falls lays claim to being the home of the first pinball-only arcade in Western Mass: **Mystic Pinball,** just down the block from The Shea at 104 Avenue A (www.mysticpinball.com; © **413/863-5760**), opened in 2017 and has more than 20 pinball machines from over 6 decades. It hosts a weekly tournament on Tuesday nights.

Bridge of Flowers ★ BRIDGE/GARDEN From April through October, consider a drive 14 miles west of Turners Falls to Shelburne Falls for a stroll across this **1908 trolley bridge** over the Deerfield River. It was converted in 1929 into an eye-popping garden pathway (foot traffic only) that has been maintained ever since by the Shelburne Falls Area Women's Club. Gladiolus, peonies, roses, clematis, daisies, snapdragons, wisteria, and more weave together to form an ever-changing quilt of color. If you continue 27 miles on Route 2 from Shelburne Falls, you'll reach **North Adams** (p. 357), the northern end of the Berkshires.

Bridge St. www.bridgeofflowersmass.org. Shelburne Falls. Free admission. Daily Apr–Oct.

Where to Stay in the Pioneer Valley

The website of the **Massachusetts Office of Travel & Tourism** (www.go-massachusetts.com; © **800/227-6277** or 617/973-8500) has an easy-to-use search function for lodgings. Room rates rise considerably at graduation time (mid-May) and when parents come through to drop off students (late Aug and early Sept).

If lodging gets tight, remember that Springfield hotels (see p. 325) are close enough to be an overnight option as well.

AMHERST

Though technically not in Amherst but in Hadley, the **Courtyard by Marriott Hadley Amherst ★**, 423 Russell St. (Route 9), Hadley (www.marriott.com/hadley; ✆ **413/256-5454**), has a handy location just west of the Amherst College campus, near the intersection of routes 9 and 116. It's a chain property, but with a sleek decor and the abundant amenities of a more expensive property.

The Lord Jeffery Inn ★★   After a massive renovation and expansion completed in 2012, the "Lord Jeff" once again established itself as the most desirable lodging in the area. First impressions are made by the two large rooms inside the entrance, with a fireplace, very comfortable seating, and the tone of a spiffed-up yesteryear. The changes undertaken become more obvious with the bedrooms (some with gas fireplaces), cosmetically enhanced, and with sparkling new baths. Drinks and light food can be taken on a large rooftop deck and around the firepit of the gaslit front patio. The in-house restaurant **30Boltwood** (www.30boltwood.com; ✆ **413/835-2011**) presents a short but thoughtfully crafted menu. Complimentary coffee and newspapers are set out in the lobby each morning.

30 Boltwood Ave. www.lordefferyinn.com. ✆ **844/860-4258** or 413/835-2001. 49 units. $205–$265 double. Street parking. **Amenities:** Restaurant; bar; fitness center; same-day dry cleaning; Wi-Fi (free).

DEERFIELD

Deerfield Inn ★★   Built in 1884, this inn in the middle of Old Deerfield is one of the best-known stopping places in the valley. The innkeepers have restlessly scoured the establishment, replacing bathroom fixtures, refinishing the older furniture, and installing new carpeting and flatscreen TVs. Antiques and reproductions are carefully mixed throughout, and all rooms have private baths. With blazes in the several fireplaces and an atmospheric tavern in which to linger, this is as pleasant a setting as you'll find in the area. **Champney's Restaurant and Tavern** is open daily for breakfast, lunch, and dinner.

81 Old Main St., Deerfield. www.deerfieldinn.com. ✆ **413/774-5587**. 24 units. $175–$270 double. Rates include full breakfast. **Amenities:** Restaurant; bar; Wi-Fi (free).

NORTHAMPTON

As central as Northampton is to the Pioneer Valley, there aren't many options for accommodations in town. Route 9, which runs between Noho and Amherst, has some chain options including **Holiday Inn Express Amherst-Hadley,** 400 Russell St./Route 9 (www.ihg.com; ✆ **413/582-0002**); the **Hampton Inn Hadley Amherst,** 24 Bay Rd./Route 47 (www.hamptoninn3.hilton.com; ✆ **413/586-4851**); and **Courtyard by Marriott Hadley Amherst** (above). Closer to the center of town is **Fairfield Inn & Suites**, 115A Conz St. (www.reservationcounter.com/hotels; ✆ **844/423-1845**). Anticipate higher rates and limited vacancies during graduation and homecoming periods as well as the usual holiday weekends.

Hotel Northampton ★   Built in 1927, the main brick building of this hotel is a grand focal point at the center of town and close to restaurants and evening activities. Rooms vary considerably (ask about options when booking and ask to see several, if possible, when checking in) and contain Colonial reproductions, feather duvets, and assorted Victoriana. A newer building behind the driveway, called Gothic Garden, offers the most updated rooms. The hotel's **Wiggins Tavern** is an atmospheric watering hole with dark beams and three stone fireplaces; the **Coolidge Park Cafe** has an outdoor terrace in warm weather and a good-looking bar.

36 King St. (Rte. 5 at Rte. 9). www.hotelnorthampton.com. © **800/547-3529** or 413/584-3100. 106 units. $251–$301 double. Limited free parking (first-come, first-served). **Amenities:** 2 restaurants; bar; exercise room; 24-hour business center; room service; Wi-Fi (free).

Where to Eat in the Pioneer Valley

Keep in mind that all of the historic inns listed above also have restaurants that are considered some of the area's top dining options.

AMHERST

For a morning cappuccino and sticky bun or an evening cocktail, check out **Amherst Coffee,** 28 Armory St. (www.amherstcoffee.com; © **413/256-8987**) This is a spacious, stretched-out coffeehouse, perfect for conversation or powering through a laptop, but you'll have to take meals elsewhere. Open daily. Additional options include the venues listed in the nightlife section on p. 340.

Johnny's Tavern ★ AMERICAN   Three dining areas and a central bar are kept dim (at lunch) and dimmer (dinner). Hanging Edison lamps illuminate the menu, with a plurality of Italian-inspired dishes—braised beef pappardelle and squid-ink spaghetti, among them—but plenty of room for the likes of upscale pork porterhouse adorned with bourbon bacon jam and an apple demi-glace, or pan-roasted duck breast with an almond honey crust, cherry compote, parsnip puree, fingerling potato, and greens. In other words, you might choose to skip the appetizers. The kitchen endeavors to utilize only sustainable seafood (example: barramundi, a Pacific sea bass) and organic produce. Ample parking in front. Note that the address is Bolton *Walk,* not nearby Bolton *Avenue.*

30 Bolton Walk. www.johnnystavernamherst.com. © **413/230-3818.** Main courses $9–$26. Sun–Thurs 11:30am–10pm; Fri–Sat 11:30am–11pm.

Judie's ★★ AMERICAN   Don't leave Amherst without eating at upbeat, bustling Judie's. The place has an infectious good cheer. Throughout the day, folks drop by for a cup of seafood bisque or one of the trademark savory popovers (basil pesto chicken, for example). Dinner entrees don't stint, including lobster ravioli *with* grilled chicken, and a prodigious seafood gumbo with that includes shrimp, sausage, scallops, salmon, *and* lobster. This being a college town, portions are prodigious, the better to assuage raging young metabolisms. (For the record, there are also "small meals," too—scallop and tomato tartine, for one.)

51 N. Pleasant St. www.judiesrestaurant.com. © **413/253-3491.** Main courses $9–$20. Daily 11:30am–10pm (Fri–Sat until 11pm).

NORTHAMPTON

For a sweet treat, keep in mind **Herrell's,** 8 Old South St. (www.herrells.com; ✆ **413/586-9700**), a celebrated New England super-premium ice-cream emporium. It scoops a huge variety of flavors, including malted vanilla, burnt sugar and butter, and black raspberry.

Bombay Royale ★ INDIAN   With its low prices and vast selection of tempting choices, this spot is hugely popular with all ages, locals, and visitors, so expect a crowded room. The menu features the usual—lamb vindaloo, samosas, kebabs, masalas—abetted by less ordinary items, such as *meen molee* (mahi-mahi poached in turmeric coconut stew) and *chettinadu* (vegetables in spicy black pepper and roasted coconut sauce). Order riata to cool the heat. The buffet lunch is only $9.95.

1 Roundhouse Plaza. www.bombayroyale.com. ✆ **413/341-3537.** Main courses $14–$25. Tues–Fri noon–2:30pm and 5–9:30pm (Fri until 10pm), Sat–Sun noon–3pm and 5–9:30pm.

Eastside Grill ★★ AMERICAN   This white-clapboard building with a vaguely nautical look is particularly appealing to the over-40 set looking for refuge from the prevailing collegiate tone of Northampton. Beef, such as the tenderloin with gorgonzola butter, is prominent on the card, but seafood choices are impressive, too. Half-portions of several popular items constitute the bar menu.

19 Strong Ave. www.eastsidegrill.com. ✆ **413/586-3347.** Main courses $12–$28. Mon–Fri 5–10pm; Sat 4–10:30pm; Sun 4–9pm.

Fitzwilly's ★ AMERICAN   Occupying an 1898 building, this ingratiating pub makes the most of its atmospheric stamped-tin ceilings and cavernous two-story space. As many as fourteen beers are on tap, pulled the night we were there by the burly bartender who engages patrons in discussions about literature (his college major). Patrons dive into such pub faves as pulled pork and Reuben sliders, racks of ribs, nachos, Buffalo chicken, and seven burger fabrications, including a veggie version. Food is available until midnight every day.

23 Main St. www.fitzwillys.com. ✆ **413/584-8666.** Main courses $7–$20. Daily 11:30am–midnight; bar until 1am.

Jake's ★ CAFE   This folksy joint takes breakfast seriously—all the way past lunch—then it closes in mid-afternoon. After one of these heaped platters, you probably won't need dinner. Aggressively farm-to-table and locally sourced when possible, the dishes are hyper-seasonal, as with the eggs Benedict, which during a springtime visit came with asparagus and fiddleheads. Eggs pairings include shrimp and grits, "Hash of the Day," and scrambled with Jack cheese and spinach. There are also tacos and a pork belly BLT. Efficient servers bring all this to copper-topped tables in two rooms with a bar in the middle.

17 King St. www.jakesnorthampton.com. ✆ **413/584-9613.** Main courses $7.50–$14. Daily 7am–3pm.

Osaka ★ JAPANESE   One reviewer called Osaka's menu "Japanese-French," and it self-describes itself as "Japanese Fusion." A glance through the ten-page dinner menu certainly raises questions about authenticity. Never mind. Osaka makes a case for sushi and filet mignon in company, and the blend regularly wins the readers' favorite awards. The menu lists dozens of sushi rolls, many with such off-the-wall names as Foxy Lady, Yellow Submarine, and Hot Lover, as well as dozens of a la carte *nigirizushi* and sashimi. Then it takes a deep breath before adding soups, chef's specials, teriyaki, bento boxes, and hibachi dinners.

7 Old South St. www.osakanorthampton.com. ✆ **413/587-9548.** Rolls $6–$16; sushi a la carte $3–$15; main courses $12–$30. Mon–Sat 11:30am–11pm (Fri–Sat until midnight); Sun noon–11pm.

Paul & Elizabeth's ★ SEAFOOD/VEGETARIAN   The combination of honest food in ample portions and low to moderate prices assures a steady flow of diners young and old. The venue is a light-filled space in **Thorne's Marketplace** (see p. 330) with gleaming wood floors beneath an original pressed-tin ceiling. Allegiance to its healthy food mission doesn't bring about the blandness carnivores might fear. On the contrary, consider the Guatemalan shrimp sauté in Thai basil pesto, or the day-boat sea scallops teriyaki-style. Monster salads incorporate hummus and super-fresh produce. By all means, start with a cup or bowl of the fish chowder, dense with chunks of the catch of the day. With all those hard surfaces, expect loud.

150 Main St. www.paulandelizabeths.com. ✆ **413/584-4832.** Main courses $10–$21. Sun–Thurs 11:30am–9pm, Fri–Sat 11:30–9:45pm, Sun brunch 11am–2pm.

TURNERS FALLS

For sweet snacks and light lunch, **2nd Street Baking Co.,** 104 4th St. (www. facebook.com/2ndstreetbakingco; ✆ **413/863-4455**), makes its own rustic breads, vegan cookies, and soups. It's open daily from 6:30am to 4pm.

Five Eyed Fox ★ CAFE   The two women who own and run this new restaurant list upwards of 20 farms on their website that they source from, embracing seasonality and locality. The short menu might include sweetbreads with caramelized leeks and pea shoots, sesame Pollock with cauliflower, or squash and shrimp with chicken of the woods mushrooms. The food is beautifully conceived and prepared—and Instagram-ready, too.

37 3rd St. www.fiveeyedfox.com. ✆ **413/863-5654.** Main courses $9–$16. Wed–Thurs 11:30am–10pm, Fri 11:30am–midnight, Sat 10am–midnight, Sun 10am–10pm.

The Lady Killigrew Café & Pub ★ CAFE   One jewel of the area is about 5 miles from Turner's Falls, in the small town of Montague. The Lady Killigrew Café is cozy oasis perched nearly on top of the small Sawmill River and has peaceful, woodsy views. Menu items include healthy snacks (brown rice salad, peanut-ginger udon noodles) and a choice of wines (no espresso drinks, however). The restaurant is one of a half-dozen small businesses inside a repurposed gristmill from 1834. The other prominent tenant is the rambling **Montague Book Mill** (www.montaguebookmill.com; ✆ **413/367-9206**), whose tagline is "Books you don't need in a place you can't find." It's not too difficult to find, actually: From Turners Falls, head south on Third Street about a mile and take the right fork; that road turns into Route 47 (Turners Fall Road). The mill comes up on your right after 4½ miles.

442 Greenfield Rd., Montague. www.theladykilligrew.com. ℂ **413/367-9666.** All items under $11. Daily 8am–11pm.

Pioneer Valley Entertainment & Nightlife

Northampton is the nightlife magnet of the valley. For a rundown of what's on the calendar, check out the *Valley Advocate* (www.valleyadvocate.com).

An old favorite, the **Iron Horse Music Hall ★★**, 20 Center St. (www.iheg. com; ℂ **413/586-8686**), is a New England honky-tonk that hosts a wide variety of artists most nights, from cabaret performers to jazz combos to folksingers. Latin dance nights have free admission, but cover charges otherwise are typically between $10 and $25. There's also decent food here. A sister venue, the larger **Calvin Theatre and Performing Arts Center,** 19 King St. (www. iheg.com; ℂ **401/586-8686**), offers a similarly broad palette, including comedians along the lines of Randy Rainbow and touring old-timers such as The Cowsills or Gary Puckett and the Union Gap.

Academy of Music, 274 Main St. (www.academyofmusictheatre.com; ℂ **413/584-9032**), is the granddaddy of the region. Open since 1891, it shows art-house and foreign films and provides a venue for symphony concerts, jazz and blues concerts, ballet, story slams, children's shows, theatricals, and even rock bands like the Red Hot Chili Peppers. Smith's **Sweeney Concert Hall,** 50 College Lane (www.smith.edu/smitharts/calendar.html; ℂ **413/586-8686**) hosts classical and chamber music.

Students and other young adults tend to gravitate toward the livelier music scene in Northampton, but Amherst does offer some nighttime entertainment. **The Black Sheep,** 79 Main St. (www.blacksheepdeli.com; ℂ **413/253-3442**), has a scattering of music performances throughout the week and at lunch time on weekends to go along with its sandwiches and appealing desserts. **Amherst Brewing Company,** 24 N. Pleasant St. (www.amherstbrewing.com; ℂ **413/253-4400**), features craft beers and appropriate eats on two floors; it also hosts live music some nights.

Amherst College's **Buckley Recital Hall** (ℂ **413/542-2195**) hosts chamber music performances that include classical quartets and solo pianists. Also check the schedule of the **University of Massachusetts Fine Arts Center** (p. 333).

THE BERKSHIRES ★★★

More than hills but less than mountains, the Taconic and Hoosac ranges that define this region at the western end of Massachusetts go by the collective name "The Berkshires." The hamlets, villages, and one small city have long drawn sustenance from the region's kindly Housatonic River and its tranquil tributaries, and are as New England as can be.

The Berkshires

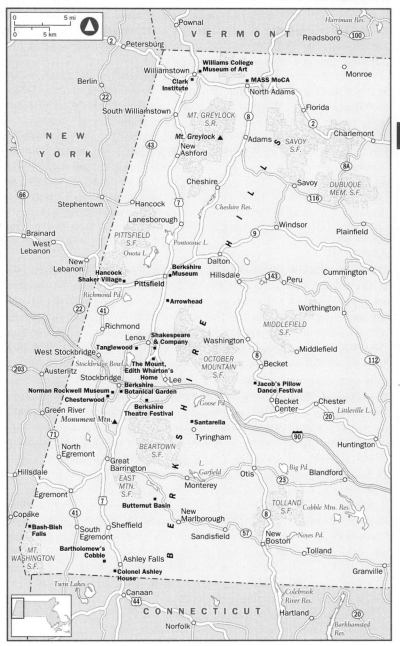

Mohawk and Mohegan lived and hunted here, and while white missionaries established settlements at Stockbridge and elsewhere in an attempt to Christianize the native tribes, the Indians eventually moved west. Farmers, drawn to the narrow but fertile flood plains of the Housatonic, were increasingly supplanted in the 19th century by manufacturers, who erected the brick mills that drew their power from the river.

At the same time, artists and writers were attracted by the mild summers and seclusion that these hills and lakes offered. Nathaniel Hawthorne, Herman Melville, and Edith Wharton were among those who put down temporary roots. By the late 19th century and the arrival of the railroad, wealthy New Yorkers and Bostonians had discovered the region and begun to erect extravagant summer "cottages." With their support, culture and the performing arts found a hospitable reception. By the 1930s, theater, dance, and music performances had established themselves as regular summer fixtures. Tanglewood, Jacob's Pillow, and the Berkshire and Williamstown Theatre festivals draw tens of thousands of visitors every summer (see box p. 343).

Essentials

ARRIVING

The **Massachusetts Turnpike** (I-90) runs east-west from Boston to the Berkshires, with an exit near Lee and Stockbridge. From New York City, the scenic **Taconic State Parkway** connects with I-90 not far from Pittsfield. To reach the southern end of the county, exit the Taconic at Route 20 heading toward Hillsdale, New York, and Great Barrington, Massachusetts.

Amtrak (www.amtrak.com; ✆ **800/USA-RAIL** [872-7245]) has stops daily in Pittsfield from trains operating out of Boston and New York's Penn Station.

VISITOR INFORMATION

The **Southern Berkshire Chamber of Commerce** maintains an information booth near the Great Barrington town hall at 362 Main St. (www.southern berkshires.com; ✆ **413/528-1510**), open Tuesday through Sunday from 10am to 5pm. May through October, the **Stockbridge Chamber of Commerce** (www.stockbridgechamber.org; ✆ **413/298-5200**) offers information opposite the row of stores depicted by native son Norman Rockwell.

Spring through early fall, the **Lee Chamber of Commerce** (www.lee chamber.org; ✆ **413/243-1705**) operates an information center on the town common, Route 20 (✆ **413/243-0852;** closed Sunday) that offers help with finding lodging, often in local guesthouses and B&Bs—something to remember when every other place near Tanglewood is either booked or quoting prices of $300 a night. The **Lenox Visitors Center,** at 4 Housatonic St. (www.lenox.org; ✆ **413/637-3646**), advises on area recreational and cultural possibilities and can make lodging arrangements.

The **Berkshire Visitors Bureau,** 66 Allen St., Pittsfield (www.berkshires.org; ✆ **413/743-4500**), can also assist with questions and lodging reservations.

In the summer months, the Berkshires turn into a performing art magnet, thanks to the influence of the **Jacob's Pillow Dance Festival** ★★★ in Becket (see p. 348) and the **Tanglewood Festival** ★★★ in Lenox (see p. 351). Following in their wake, the **Williamstown Theater Festival** ★★★ in Williamstown (p. 356), the **Berkshire Theatre Festival** ★★ in Stockbridge (p. 346), **Shakespeare and Company** ★★ in Lenox (see p. 350), and the **Barrington Stage Company** ★ in Pittsfield (p. 353) make it possible to line up a string of great performances in just a few days in the Berkshires. And don't forget to check out what's on tap at the **Massachusetts Museum of Modern Art (MASS MoCA)** ★★★ in North Adams (p. 357).

Exploring Great Barrington ★

135 miles W of Boston, 130 miles NE of New York City, 52 miles NW of Springfield

Even with a population barely over 7,000, this pleasant retail center is the largest town in the southern part of Berkshire County. Rapids in the Housatonic provided power for a number of mills in centuries past, most of which are now gone. In 1886, this was one of the first communities in the world to have electricity on its streets and in its homes. Nowadays a bearded post-Woodstock hippie subculture persists with many of its residents.

While Great Barrington itself has few sights of particular significance, you'll want to browse its many antiques galleries and specialty shops. In recent years, a Main Street makeover brought new street furniture, bicycle lanes, sidewalk extensions, and lamps, giving the town a more upmarket tone.

Great Barrington makes a convenient touring base for excursions to such outdoorsy nearby attractions as **Monument Mountain** (below), **Bash-Bish Falls** (p. 344), and **Butternut Basin** (p. 359). Another perennial draw is **Tanglewood concerts** (p. 351). Great Barrington has also become a dining destination, with an alleged 71 eating places. A **farmers market** is held at 18 Church St. on Saturdays from 9am to 1pm mid-May to late October.

OUTDOOR ACTIVITIES

Open to the public, the **Egremont Country Club,** at 685 South Egremont Rd. (Route 23) (www.egremontcountryclub.com; ✆ **413/528-4222**), has a scenic 18-hole golf course and a restaurant and bar. Required tee times can be arranged up to a week in advance. Greens fees are $45 on weekends and $30 on weekdays for visitors.

Four miles north of town, west of Route 7, **Monument Mountain** has two hiking trails to the summit. The easier route, the Indian Monument Trail, is about an hour's hike to the top; the more difficult one, the Hickey Trail, isn't much longer but takes the steep way up. The summit, called Squaw Peak, offers splendid views.

See also local skiing options on p. 359.

GREAT BARRINGTON SHOPPING

Downtown, central Railroad Street and the nearby blocks on Main Street offer the town's best shopping. Start on the corner with Main Street, at **T. P. Saddle Blanket & Trading Co.** (www.tashapolizzi.com; ✆ 413/528-9400). An unlikely emporium that looks as if it was lifted whole from the Rockies, it's packed with stylish boho-western clothing, boots, hats, Indian jewelry, and blankets. **Church Street Trading Company,** 4 Railroad St. (✆ **413/528-6120**), defies easy categorization, with walking sticks, dog collars, and home furnishings all on display. Primary wares are sturdily stylish North Country sweaters, and pricey-but-worth-it casualwear for both men and women.

The Chef's Shop, 31 Railroad St. (www.thechefsshop.net; ✆ **413/528-0135**), features a bounty of gadgets and cookbooks, as well as cooking classes. A couple of blocks south of Railroad is **One Mercantile,** 8 Castle St. (www.one-mercantile.myshopify.com; ✆ **413/528-1718**), a housewares shop that purveys clocks, candles, coasters, cushions, cords, ceramics, cookbooks, canvas bags, and such necessities as tortilla warmers.

Stay on Route 7, going north of the center, and you'll pass a large mall with an anchoring Kmart. In that unlikely location is one of the best bookstores in the area: **The Bookloft,** Barrington Plaza (www.thebookloft.com; ✆ **413/528-1521**).

Exploring South Egremont

4 miles SW of Great Barrington

If you're coming to the Berkshires from the Taconic Parkway in New York, you can't help but drive through the town of Egremont. Its larger, busier half South Egremont, once a stop on the stagecoach route between Hartford and Albany, retains many structures from that era, including mills that utilized the stream that still rushes by.

OUTDOOR ACTIVITIES

Scenic **Bash-Bish Falls State Park ★★**, on the south side of Egremont on Falls Road on Mt. Washington (www.mass.gov; ✆ **413/528-0330**), makes a rewarding outing for a day of hiking, birding, and fishing. To get here, drive west on Route 23 from town, turning south on Route 41, and immediately right on Mount Washington Road. Watch for signs directing the way to Mount Washington State Forest and Bash-Bish Falls. After 8 miles, a sign indicates a right turn toward the falls; look for it opposite a church with an unusual steeple. The road begins to follow the course of a mountain stream, going downhill. In about 3 miles is a large parking place next to a craggy promontory.

The sign also points off to a trail down to the falls, which should be negotiated only by reasonably fit adults. First, mount the promontory for a splendid view across the plains of the Hudson Valley to the pale-blue ridgeline of the Catskill Mountains. You'll be able to hear, but not yet see, the falls, which are down to the left. If this trail seems too steep, continue driving down the road to another parking area, on the left. From here, a gentler trail, a little over a mile long, leads to the falls. The falls themselves are quite impressive, crashing down from more than 80 feet. The park is open from dawn to 30 minutes after sunset. Apart from accessible restrooms, there are no services inside the park. Picnicking is permitted, but alcoholic beverages are not. No dogs allowed, and no swimming.

Exploring Sheffield ★

7 miles S of Great Barrington

Located on a flood plain beside the Housatonic River, with the Berkshires rising to the west, Sheffield has long been defined by agriculture. There's a **farmer's market** outside the Old Parish Church, 125 Main St., Saturdays from late May to early October. A lot of other residents, although not as many as 20 years ago, sell antiques (see box below), as you'll see driving along Route 7, also known as Main Street or Sheffield Plain. The meticulously maintained houses cultivate an impression of prosperous tranquility.

Ashley House ★ HISTORIC HOME   Built by Colonel John Ashley in 1735, this modified saltbox is believed to be the oldest house in Berkshire County and is part of the **Berkshire 18th Century Trail** (www.berkshire18th centurytrail.org). Ashley was a person of considerable repute in Colonial western Massachusetts: a pioneer settler, an officer during one of the French and Indian Wars, and later a lawyer and a judge. He achieved great material success and over 3,000 acres of land—in part due to his ownership of five slaves. One of them, **Mum Bett**, sued the colonel for her freedom and won in 1781. It was the beginning of the end of slavery in Massachusetts.

117 Cooper Hill Rd. www.thetrustees.org. *C* **413/298-3239.** Admission to grounds free; house tours $5 adults, $3 kids 6–12. Grounds open year-round, house open (guided tours only) July–Aug Sun noon and 1pm.

Antiques Road Trip #2: Sheffield

Sheffield has long laid claim to the title of "Antiques Capital of the Berkshires"—no small feat, given what seems to be an effort by half the population of the Berkshires to sell collectibles, oddities, and true antiques to the other half. These are canny, knowledgeable dealers who know exactly what they have, so expect high quality and few bargains.

Painted Porch Country Antiques, 102 S. Main St. (www.paintedporch.com; *C* **413/229-2700**), specializes in furniture and accessories from provincial France, England, and Canada. Housed in an 1815 house, it is open all year. Farther north along Route 7, **Dovetail Antiques & Restorations,** 440 Sheffield Plain (*C* **413/ 229-2628**), sells and restores furniture

from the 19th and early 20th centuries, notably Georgian, Victorian, and Edwardian. Continuing along Route 7, on the left at the edge of town is **Susan Silver**, 755 N. Main St. (www.susansilver antiques.com; *C* **413/229-8169**), with meticulously restored 18th- and 19th-century English library furniture (desks, reading stands) and French accessories.

There are about a dozen other dealers along this route. Most of them stock the **free directory** of the Berkshire County Antiques Dealers Association (www.bcaada.com), which lists member dealers from Sheffield to Cheshire and across the border in Connecticut and New York. The association will mail out its free map and guide of the region.

OUTDOOR ACTIVITIES

Beside an oxbow bend in the Housatonic River lies the 278-acre nature reservation called **Bartholomew's Cobble** ★, 105 Weatogue Rd./Route 7A (www.thetrustees.org; ✆ 413/229-8600). A "cobble," by local definition, is a "scenic, rocky eminence rising from the valley floor." Five miles of trail cross pastures, penetrate forests, and provide vistas of the river valley from the area's high point, 1,000-foot Hurlburt's Hill. Picnicking is permitted, as are canoeing, kayaking, skiing, and snowboarding. Birders will want their binoculars. No dogs allowed. Trails are open from sunrise to sunset. Admission is $5 for cars of nonmembers, plus $5 for nonmember adults, $1 for kids 6 to 12.

Exploring Stockbridge ★★

8 miles N of Great Barrington, 48 miles NE of Springfield.

Readily accessible from Boston and New York (about 2½ hr. from each), in the Gilded Age Stockbridge was transformed from colonial frontier settlement into a summer retreat for the rich. One of the Berkshires' hottest destinations, Stockbridge is jammed on warm weekends and during foliage season. Along and near Main Street are a number of historic homes and other attractions, enough to fill up a long weekend, even without a Tanglewood concert.

The town has long been popular with artists and writers. World-renowned illustrator Norman Rockwell, who lived here for 25 years, portrayed the Main Street of his adopted town and many of its inhabitants in his paintings. A prominent event occurs on the first weekend in December, when antique cars are parked along Main Street to re-create a Christmas scene painted by Rockwell decades ago (www.stockbridgechamber.org/christmas.html).

Berkshire Botanical Garden ★ GARDEN Fifteen acres of flower beds, ponds, and vegetable and herb gardens are an inviting destination for strollers and picnickers. The first weekend in October features a popular harvest festival.

5 West Stockbridge Rd. www.berkshirebotanical.org. ✆ **413/298-3926.** $15 adults, $14 seniors, $12 students, free for kids 11 and under. May–Columbus Day daily 9am–5pm. Tours offered Sat–Sun June–Aug.

The Berkshire Theatre Festival ★★ From June to August, and on a smaller scale throughout the rest of the year, the Berkshire Theatre Festival

---

A Charming Woodland Village

Twelve miles southeast of Great Barrington, the rural town of New Marlborough, settled in 1738 and officially incorporated in 1775, covers about 48 heavily wooded square miles with several streams and small rivers running through. The first Europeans were drawn here by the agricultural opportunities and, later, by the growth of mills. A current issue is the prospect of local commercial marijuana production. A significant draw here is the charming **Old Inn on the Green** (see p. 362).

puts up classic and new plays, comedy shows, and music events. Its Fitzpatrick Main Stage is in a "casino" built in 1887 to plans by the celebrated Gilded Age architect Stanford White. Ticket charges vary widely according to season and production, from as little as $10 to $70 or more.

6 East St. www.berkshiretheatre.org. ⓒ **413/999-4444.** Tickets $10–$70.

Chesterwood ★ HISTORIC HOME   Sculptor Daniel Chester French, best known for the Lincoln Memorial in Washington, D.C., used this estate as his summer home for more than 30 years. His Minute Man statue at the Old North Bridge in Concord (p. 144), completed in 1875 when the artist was 25 years old, launched his highly successful career. The 122-acre grounds are used for an annual show of contemporary sculpture. Visitors can take self-guided tours of the studio, residence, and property. Guided tours are offered, but times and dates should be confirmed and reserved, so call ahead. If you like, bring a lunch for picnicking.

4 Williamsville Rd. www.chesterwood.org. ⓒ **413/298-3579.** $18 adults, $17 seniors, $9 military and teenagers, children free. May–Oct daily 11am–4pm.

Naumkeag ★ HISTORIC HOME   The Gilded Age is on full display here: In 1886, Stanford White designed this summer estate for Joseph Hodge Choate, who served as U.S. ambassador to the Court of St. James. The client dubbed it Naumkeag, a Native American name. His mansion of many gables and chimneys is largely of the New England shingle style, but with many delightful quirks, and surrounded by impressive gardens with fabulous views to the west. Admission is by guided tour only; it's worth it to explore the rich 44-room interior. Tucked away in a dark corner upstairs are several original Goya etchings. There's a cafe for sandwiches and snacks.

5 Prospect Hill Rd. www.thetrustees.org. ⓒ **413/298-3239.** $15 adults, kids 6–12 free. Mid-Apr to late May Sat–Sun 11am–4pm, late May to mid-Oct daily 10am–5pm, closed rest of year.

Norman Rockwell Museum ★★ MUSEUM   This striking museum opened in 1993, at a cost of $4.4 million, to house the works of Stockbridge's favorite son. The illustrator used both his neighbors and the town where he lived to tell stories about small-town America, working from 1916 until his death in 1978. Most of Rockwell's paintings adorned covers of the *Saturday Evening Post:* warm and often humorous depictions of homecomings, first proms, and visits to the doctor. He addressed serious concerns, too, notably with his poignant portrait of a little African-American girl being escorted by U.S. marshals into a previously segregated school. Critics long derided his paintings as sentimental, but a reconsideration in recent years has led to widespread appreciation for his storytelling prowess and deft brushwork. The 36-acre grounds also contain Rockwell's last studio (open May–Oct). The museum and rest of the grounds are open year-round.

9 Glendale Rd. (Rte. 183). www.nrm.org. ⓒ **413/298-4100.** $20 adults, $18 seniors, $17 veterans, $10 college students, free for kids 18 and under. May–Oct daily 10am–5pm; Nov–Apr Mon–Fri 10am–4pm, Sat–Sun 10am–5pm.

Exploring Lee & Becket

Lee: 6 miles NE of Stockbridge. Becket: 11 miles E of Lee

While Stockbridge and Lenox were developing into luxurious recreational centers for the upper crusts of Boston and New York, Lee was a thriving paper-mill town. That meant that it was shunned by the wealthy summer people and thus remained essentially a blue-collar town of workers and merchants. It has a somewhat raffish—though not unappealing—aspect, with its center bunched with shops and offices and few of the stately homes that characterize neighboring communities. A farmers market is held on the town green at 25 Park Place Saturdays from late May to early October.

Jacob's Pillow Dance Festival ★★★ ARTS FESTIVAL   In 1933, modern dance pioneers Ted Shawn and Ruth St. Denis decided to put on a show in the barn—dubbed "Denishawn"—and so was Jacob's Pillow born. After decades of advance and retreat and evolution, Jacob's Pillow is now to dance what Tanglewood is to classical music in the Berkshires: A must-see experience of the summer. Once a regular summer venue for famed dancer and choreographer Martha Graham, one of Shawn and St. Denis' early disciples, the theater has long welcomed troupes of international reputation, including the Paul Taylor Dance Troupe, the Royal Danish Ballet, Les Grands Ballets Canadiens, and Twyla Tharp. In 2018, the Pillow's 85th anniversary, there was an ambitious centennial tribute to Jerome Robbins. The season runs from mid-June to late August, and tickets go on sale April 1; the schedule is usually available by March 1. Prominent companies are seen in the main **Ted Shawn Theatre**, while other troupes are assigned to the **Doris Duke Studio Theatre**. Admission is free to the **Inside/Out**, an outdoor stage. The growing campus includes a store/cafe, a coffee bar, and exhibition space. Picnic lunches can be preordered 24 hours in advance.

358 George Carter Rd., Becket. www.jacobspillow.org. ✆ **413/243-0745.** Tickets $10–$78.

Santarella ★ HISTORIC HOME   With no obligatory historic homes or museums to see in Lee, visitors often make the short excursion 8 miles south to a fairy-tale structure called Santarella, known by most as the "Tyringham Gingerbread House." Conical turrets top towers and the shingled roof rolls like waves on the ocean. It served as a studio for sculptor Henry Hudson Kitson from 1930 to 1947 and now is used for weddings and other special events. The garden, which includes a lily pond and stream, is open to visitors.

75 Main Rd., Tyringham. www.santarella.us. ✆ **413/243-2819.**

OUTDOOR ACTIVITES

October Mountain State Forest (www.mass.gov; ✆ **413/243-1778**), 7 miles north of Lee center, has 47 campsites (with showers) and more than 16,000 acres for hiking, canoeing, mountain biking, cross-country skiing, and snowmobiling. Camping season is from mid-May to mid-October; reservations are suggested.

Exploring Lenox ★★ & Tanglewood ★★★

7 miles NE of Stockbridge, 7 miles S of Pittsfield

Stately homes and fabulous mansions mushroomed in this former agricultural settlement from the 1890s until 1913, when the 16th Amendment, authorizing income taxes, put a severe crimp in that impulse. But Lenox remains a repository of extravagant domestic architecture surpassed only in such fabled resorts of the wealthy as Newport, Rhode Island, and Palm Beach, Florida. And because many of the cottages have been converted into inns and hotels, it is possible to get inside some of these beautiful buildings, if only for a cocktail or a meal. The reason for so many lodgings in a town with a population of barely 5,000? **Tanglewood,** a nearby estate where a wildly popular series of concerts by the Boston Symphony Orchestra is held every summer.

If you're here on a Friday afternoon between June and mid-September, stop by the farmers market outside St. Ann Church, 134 Main St.

Berkshire Scenic Railway Museum ★ VINTAGE TRAIN This museum rolls: It's a long train of vintage engines, passenger coaches, and even a caboose that makes 90-minute trips between Adams and North Adams. The restored 1903 Lenox station is open to visitors on the days the nostalgic excursions take place. Uniformed conductors narrate the trips, mostly along the pretty Housatonic River. At this writing, there are Saturday train trips from late May to early September and Christmastime excursions (complete with Santa) on several days in December, but scheduling is elastic with this volunteer-run enterprise, so it is wise to call ahead to confirm details.

10 Willow Creek Rd. (Housatonic St.). www.berkshirescenicrailroad.org. © **413/637-2210.** $20 adults, $16 children ages 4–14. Sat only, Memorial Day–Sept, plus several days in Dec.

Frelinghuysen Morris House & Studio ★ HISTORIC HOME Built on 46 acres next to the Tanglewood property in the early 1940s, this Bauhaus-influenced house was the home of abstract artists Suzy Frelinghuysen and George L.K. Morris. Their chosen style was Cubism, which they pursued long after it had been abandoned by better-known practitioners. Lesser works by some of those artists—Braque, Léger, Gris, Matisse, and Picasso—can be viewed alongside the canvases of the owners. Visits are by hourly tours only.

92 Hawthorne St. www.frelinghuysen.org. © **413/637-0166.** $15 adults, $14 seniors, $7.50 students, free for kids 11 and under. Late June to early Oct Thurs–Sun 10am–3pm.

The Mount, Edith Wharton's Home ★ HISTORIC HOME Wharton, who won a Pulitzer for her 1920 novel *The Age of Innocence*, was singularly equipped to write that deftly detailed examination of the upper classes of the Gilded Age and the first decades of the 20th century. Born into that stratum of society in 1862, she traveled in the circles that made the Berkshires a regular stop on their restless movements between New York, Florida, Newport, and the Continent. Wharton had her villa built on this 130-acre lakeside property in 1902 and lived here 10 years before leaving for France, never to

Lenox

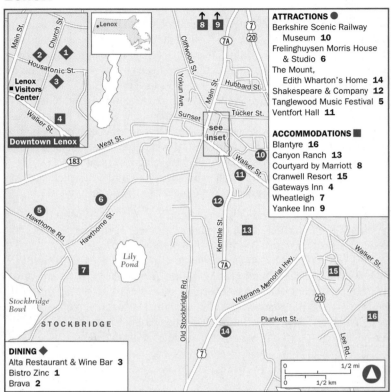

ATTRACTIONS ●
Berkshire Scenic Railway Museum **10**
Frelinghuysen Morris House & Studio **6**
The Mount, Edith Wharton's Home **14**
Shakespeare & Company **12**
Tanglewood Music Festival **5**
Ventfort Hall **11**

ACCOMMODATIONS ■
Blantyre **16**
Canyon Ranch **13**
Courtyard by Marriott **8**
Cranwell Resort **15**
Gateways Inn **4**
Wheatleigh **7**
Yankee Inn **9**

DINING ◆
Alta Restaurant & Wine Bar **3**
Bistro Zinc **1**
Brava **2**

return. She took an active hand in the creation of The Mount, which makes the mansion a notable rarity—it's one of the few designated National Historic Landmarks designed by a woman. Guided tours focus on the house and the gardens (there's also a spooky 90-min. ghost tour that is not recommended for children). The Mount also serves as a cultural center, hosting readings, films, and lectures. The Terrace Cafe serves light fare.

2 Plunkett St. (jct. rtes. 7 and 7A). www.edithwharton.org. © **413/551-5111.** $18 adults, $17 seniors, $13 students, free for kids 18 and under. May–Dec 10am–4pm, Jan–Apr Sat–Sun 11am–4pm.

Shakespeare & Company ★★ PERFORMANCE VENUE/PARK Spread out on a campus that includes four theaters and three studio spaces, the Company is devoted to the dramatic arts, including a Center for Actor Training. There are walking trails on the grounds, and a cafe in the theater lobby serves drinks and light fare. Picnickers are welcome. Free outdoor performances are staged before evening curtain times. There are shows and staged readings on certain weekends through the winter, with longer, more elaborate productions in the warmer months. Some outdoor productions are staged at

The Mount nearby (p. 349). Combination FLEXpasses carry substantial discounts for packages of three or six shows, $129 to $269.

70 Kemble St. www.shakespeare.org. ✆ **413/637-3353**. Tickets $15–$60.

Tanglewood Music Festival ★★★ ARTS FESTIVAL   Lenox has been filled with music every summer since 1937, and the undisputed headliner is the **Boston Symphony Orchestra (BSO)** (p. 125) directed most recently by Andris Nelsons. Concerts are given at the famous Tanglewood estate, usually beginning in July and ending the weekend before Labor Day. While the BSO is Tanglewood's 800-lb. cultural gorilla, the season features a menagerie of other performers and musical idioms, running the gamut from popular artists (James Taylor, Sting, Judy Collins, Boz Scaggs) to jazz musicians (Diana Krall, Wynton Marsalis) to classical soloists (Itzhak Perlman, Yo-Yo Ma) to appearances by the Boston Pops.

The **Koussevitzky Music Shed** is an open auditorium that seats 5,700, surrounded by a lawn where an outdoor audience lounges on folding chairs and blankets. Chamber groups and soloists appear in the smaller **Seiji Ozawa Hall.** Major performances are on Friday and Saturday nights and Sunday afternoon. During the Leonard Bernstein Centennial celebration in 2018, there were fully staged performances of his musicals *On the Town* and *Fancy Free.*

Tickets usually go on sale in late January and can sell out quickly (you can buy them online). To go at the last minute, take a blanket or lawn chair and get tickets for lawn seating, which is almost always available. You can also attend open rehearsals during the week, as well as the rehearsal for the Sunday concert on Saturday morning (fee charged).

The estate itself (✆ **413/637-5165;** June–Aug), with more than 500 acres of lawns and gardens, much of it overlooking the lake called Stockbridge Bowl, was put together starting in 1849. Admission to the grounds is free when concerts aren't scheduled. Picnicking is allowed, and baskets and bento boxes can be ordered in advance (call Boston Gourmet at ✆ **413/637-5152**). There are four casual eating places, as well as more substantial buffet dinners and Sunday brunch at **Highwood Manor House** (reserve at ✆ **413/637-4486**). Summer Sundays from noon to 2pm bring rosters of family activities which include face painting, games, yoga, and food tastings.

297 West St. www.tanglewood.org. ✆ **617/266-1492**. Tickets $20–$125 Shed and Ozawa Hall, $19–$25 lawn (free for kids 11 and under). Limited $20 tickets for patrons under age 40 available after May 1. Kids 4 and under not allowed in the Shed or Ozawa Hall. Higher prices for opening nights and some special appearances.

Ventfort Hall ★ HISTORIC HOME   The painstaking renovation of this Gilded Age mansion (which even managed to snag the web address "www.gildedage.org") has been an ongoing project. The Elizabethan Revival manse, termed a "cottage," was originally constructed at the behest of a sister of J. P. Morgan in 1893. One of its most striking features is the collection of 29-inch porcelain dolls modeling elaborate women's fashions of the period 1855 to 1914; creator John Burbidge used to design wedding dresses for such prominent brides as the daughters of Presidents Johnson and Nixon. A "Tea &

Talks" lecture series is offered June-early Sept, $26 to $32. The exterior was used in the film *The Cider House Rules*.

104 Walker St. www.gildedage.org. ✆ **413/637-3206.** $18 adults, $17 students & seniors, $7 kids 5–17, free 4 and under. Guided tours daily on the hour, usually 10am–3pm.

OUTDOOR ACTIVITIES

Pleasant Valley Wildlife Sanctuary, 472 West Mountain Rd. (www.mass audubon.org; ✆ **413/637-0320**), has a small museum and 7 miles of hiking and snowshoeing trails crossing its more than 1,100 acres. Beaver lodges and dams can be glimpsed from a distance, and waterfowl and other birds are found in abundance—bring binoculars. The nature center is open Tuesday through Sunday from 10am to 4pm; admission is $5 adults, $3 seniors and children 2 to 12.

More extensive trails can be found at **October Mountain State Forest** (see p. 348) near Lee, or at **Beartown State Forest,** 69 Blue Hill Rd., in nearby Monterey (www.mass.gov; ✆ **413/528-0904**). The **Appalachian Trail,** which runs from Maine to Georgia, connects here with a 1.5-mile loop trail around 35-acre Benedict Pond, where there is swimming. Fishing, cross-country skiing, and snowmobiling are possibilities in their seasons. True to its name, black bears and other wild animals are a presence.

LENOX SHOPPING

The Bookstore, 11 Housatonic St. (www.bookstoreinlenox.com; ✆ **413/637-3390**), with author signings and poetry readings, helps fill a yawning gap in the Berkshires, a region curiously short on comprehensive bookstores. A sign at the entrance reads "This store welcomes all immigrants and refugees." Inside the marvelously quirky emporium, find an eclectic selection of books chosen by the amiable owner, who operates a wine bar off in a side space that he calls *Get Lit*.

For fashion-forward clothing for men and women, much of it Italian-made, check in at **Casablanca,** 21 Housatonic St. (✆ **413/637-2680**). L.L.Bean, it isn't. Out on Route 7, heading toward Pittsfield, serious cooks should watch for **Different Drummer's Kitchen,** 374 Pittsfield Rd. (www.differentdrummers kitchen.com; ✆ **413/637-0606**).

Antiques Road Trip #3: Lenox

Those in pursuit of art and antiques cannot easily exhaust Lenox's possibilities. Top among them are **Charles Flint Fine Art & Museum-Quality Antiques** (5 Housatonic St.; www.flint.cc; ✆ **413/637-1634**), **Coffman's Antiques Market** (69 Church St.; ✆ **413/637-1884**), where some 20 dealers show their wares; and, down Route 20 on the way to Lee, the fun **Retro Pop Shop** (395 Laurel St., ✆ **413/243-0025**) for vintage 1950s and 1960s memorabilia. Stroll down the 2 blocks of Church Street in the Lenox town center and you'll also pass over a half-dozen art galleries.

Exploring Pittsfield

15 miles NE of Great Barrington, 52 miles SW of Springfield, 137 miles W of Boston, 7 miles N of Lenox

Berkshire County's largest city (pop. 42,825) gets little attention in most tourist literature. A commercial and industrial center, Pittsfield doesn't have the charm that marks Stockbridge and Lenox. But this blue-collar city has made inroads in reinventing itself, with a smattering of worthwhile attractions, restaurants, and nightlife. Emblematic of this shift was the 2006 reopening of the **1903 Colonial Theatre,** once again home to dance, comedy, and music from classical to country (www.thecolonialtheatre.org). Fun fact: A document discovered in 2004 that banned the playing of baseball within 80 yards of the main church in 1791 suddenly gave Pittsfield claim to the invention of the game, 48 years before Cooperstown, New York.

A Saturday-morning farmers market is held at The Common Park on 1st Street, mid-May to mid-October.

Barrington Stage Company ★ THEATER At intervals throughout the year, but with concentrations from late June to October, this nonprofit theater group mounts musicals, comedies, and dramas at the **Mainstage** on Union Street and two smaller venues. Past productions have included Stephen Sondheim's *Company,* the thriller *Gaslight,* and the musical *Bye Bye Birdie.* They also mount a cabaret series in summer.

30 Union St. www.barringtonstageco.org. ℰ **413/236-8888.** Tickets $15–$35 adults (discounts for seniors), $10 students.

Berkshire Museum ★ MUSEUM Holdings bounce from Babylonian cuneiform tablets to tanks of live fish to archaeological artifacts such as a delicate necklace from Thebes, dating to at least 1500 B.C. Included in the permanent collections are works by such 19th-century portraitists and landscapists as George Inness, Edwin Church, and Albert Bierstadt. Temporary exhibitions are frequent and professionally mounted. An auditorium seating 300 serves as the "Little Cinema," which shows art and foreign films during the warmer months. A controversial plan to sell off forty of its paintings and sculptures, including two major Norman Rockwell illustrations, was challenged by the state attorney general, but eventually permitted by a judge. One of those paintings, Rockwell's "Shuffleton's Barbershop," is temporarily on display at the **Norman Rockwell Museum** (p. 347) before moving to the new Lucas Museum of Narrative Art, in Los Angeles.

39 South St. (Rte. 7). www.berkshiremuseum.org. ℰ **413/443-7171.** $13 adults, $6 ages 4–17. Mon–Sat 10am–5pm; Sun noon–5pm.

Hancock Shaker Village ★★★ LIVING HISTORY MUSEUM The serenity of the setting, among low hills and meadows, and the carefully considered placement of the buildings and their relationships with each other, are the essence of Shaker philosophy, "Order is Heaven's law." Twenty restored buildings make up the village, which explores the religious practices and

shaker society & ITS HISTORY OF CRAFTSMANSHIP

The former Ann Lee, once imprisoned in England for her excess of religious zeal, arrived in New York with eight disciples in 1774, just as the disgruntled American colonies were about to burst into open rebellion. She had anointed herself leader of the United Society of Believers in Christ's Second Coming and was known as Mother Ann. The austere Protestant sect was dedicated to simplicity, equality, and celibacy. They were popularly known as "the Shakers" for their spastic movements when in the throes of religious ecstasy.

By the time Mother Ann died in 1784, the Shakers had many converts, who then fanned out across the country to form communal settlements from Maine to Indiana. One of the most important Shaker communities, **Hancock,** edged the Massachusetts–New York border, near Pittsfield.

Shaker society produced dedicated, highly disciplined farmers and craftspeople whose products were much in demand in the outside world. They sold seeds, invented early agricultural machinery and hand tools, and erected large buildings of several stories and exquisite simplicity. Their spare, clean-lined furniture and accessories anticipated the so-called Danish Modern style by a century and in recent years have drawn astonishingly high prices at auction.

All of these accomplishments required a verve owed at least in part to sublimation of sexual energy, for a fundamental Shaker tenet was total celibacy for its adherents. The society grew through converts and adoption of orphans (who were free to leave, if they wished). But, by the 1970s, the movement had a bare handful of believers. The string of Shaker settlements and museums that remain testify to their dictum, "Hands to work, hearts to God."

lifestyle habits of the austere Protestant sect. Its signature structure is the **1826 round stone barn:** The Shaker preoccupation with functionalism joined with purity of line and respect for materials has never been clearer than it is in the design of this building. Its round shape expedited the chores of feeding and milking livestock by arranging cows in a circle, and the precise joinery of the roof beams and support pillars is a joy to observe. The other must-see is the brick dwelling that contained the village's communal dining room, kitchens, and sleeping quarters. Sexes were separated at meals, work, and religious services, and there are staircases leading to male and female "retiring rooms."

While artisans and docents demonstrate Shaker crafts and techniques, only some dress in period clothing to portray Shaker inhabitants. All are knowledgeable about their subject and dispense nuggets about the Shaker discipline such as the requirement to dress the right side first and to step with the right foot first. The museum shop is excellent, and the **Seeds Market Cafe** serves lunches in summer and fall, as well as occasional dinners, with some dishes based on Shaker recipes. (Note that if you're only here to eat at the Cafe, you don't have to pay Village admission.) New management has initiated programs such as farm-to-table dinners, music series, lectures, art exhibits, and even goat yoga classes.

Many parts of the complex are wheelchair accessible, but not most of the original buildings.

1843 West Housatonic St. (Rtes. 20 and 41). www.hancockshakervillage.org. © **413/443-0188.** $20 adults, $8 ages 13–17, free 12 and under. 90-minute farm tours $30. Mid-Apr to June daily 10am–4pm; July to mid-Nov 10am–5pm, late Nov to mid-Dec Sat–Sun only 10am–4pm.

OUTDOOR ACTIVITIES

Plaine's Bike, Ski & Snowboard, 55 W. Housatonic St. (www.plaines.com; © 413/499-0294), rents bikes and ski and snowboard equipment. It's on Route 20, west of downtown.

Pittsfield State Forest, at 1041 Cascade St. (www.mass.gov; © **413/442-8992**), a little over 3 miles west of the center of town, includes 65 acres of wild azalea fields that explode in pink blossoms in June. There's also camping, boating, fishing, hiking, biking, and cross-country skiing here. Open daily from sunrise to sunset. Admission is $5 per car for state residents from early May to mid-Oct, $10 for out-of-state residents.

Onota Boat Livery, 463 Pecks Rd. (© **413/442-1724**), rents canoes and motorboats on Onota Lake, conveniently located at the western edge of the city. It's open Monday through Saturday from 7am to 5:30pm.

Exploring Williamstown ★★

21 miles N of Pittsfield; 67 miles NW of Springfield; 202 miles N of New York City; 131 miles NW of Boston.

This community and its prestigious liberal-arts college were both named for Col. Ephraim Williams, who was killed in 1755 in one of the French and Indian Wars. He bequeathed the land for creation of a school and a town. Williams College grew, spreading east from the central common along both sides of Main Street (Route 2). Over Williamstown's long history, buildings have been erected in styles of the times, making Main Street a virtual museum of institutional architecture, with representatives of the Georgian, Federal, Gothic Revival, Romanesque, and Victorian styles (and a few yet to be labeled). Inserted into this diverting display is the '62 Center for Theatre and Dance, a thoroughly contemporary structure that serves as home of the **Williamstown Theatre Festival** (p. 356). It stands at dignified distances from the older buildings, so that what might have been a tumultuous visual hodgepodge is instead a stately lesson in historical design.

It's a great destination for art lovers, given the one-two punch of the **Sterling and Francine Clark Art Institute** and the **Williams College Art Museum**. The Clarks were more disciplined in their acquisitions than most wealthy collectors, and their museum qualifies as one of the great cultural resources of New England.

A farmers market is held at the base of Spring Street Saturday mornings from late-May to mid-October.

Clark Art Institute ★★★ MUSEUM   Within these walls are canvases by Renoir (34 of them), Degas, Gauguin, Toulouse-Lautrec, Pissarro, and Corot.

Look for J.M.W. Turner's splendid seascape, *Rockets and Blue Lights.* Also on display is a version of the famed Degas sculpture *Little Dancer,* his only three-dimensional piece and a signature work of the Institute. In addition to these standouts are works by 15th- and 16th-century Dutch portraitists, European genre and landscape painters, and Americans Sargent and Homer, as well as fine porcelain, silver, and antiques. The Clark Center wing houses a gallery for special exhibits, a store, and a cafe. In warmer months, the terrace has tables and chairs that overlook a reflecting pool and the surrounding hills.

Tip: Discount ticket packages are available for admission to the Clark and **MASS MoCA** in North Adams (p. 357) or the **Norman Rockwell Museum** in Lenox (p. 347).

225 South St. www.clarkart.edu. (*C*) **413/458-2303.** $20 adults, free for kids 17 and under. July–Aug daily 10am–5pm; rest of year Tues–Sun 10am–5pm.

Williams College Museum of Art ★ MUSEUM

The second leg of Williamstown's two prominent art repositories exists in large part thanks to Williams College's collection of almost 400 paintings by the American modernists Maurice and Charles Prendergast. The museum also has works by Gris, Léger, Whistler, Picasso, Warhol, and Hopper. Increasingly important among its holdings is its African collection, containing ceremonial vessels, dolls, masks, and agricultural implements, most of them from East Africa. The museum hosts frequent special exhibitions and lecture series.

15 Lawrence Hall Dr. http://wcma.williams.edu. (*C*) **413/597-2429.** Free admission. Tues–Sat (and some Mon holidays) 10am–5pm (until 8pm Thurs); Sun 1–5pm.

The Williamstown Theater Festival ★★★ ARTS FESTIVAL

Stargazing doesn't always involve the night sky in the Berkshires. Some head, instead, to the Williamstown Theatre Festival where Matthew Broderick, Mary-Louise Parker, Bradley Cooper, Gwyneth Paltrow, and other well-known actors regularly take the stage. They come here not just because there are few lovelier places to spend a summer than Williamstown, but because this theater has gained a reputation as an incubator for new works, both plays and musicals. Along with the '62 Center for Theatre and Dance mainstage (right on the Williams College campus), there's a smaller venue for more experimental works and a cabaret. The theater also puts on free outdoor shows for kids. The season runs from late June to mid-August, and tickets go on sale online June 1st.

1000 Main St., on the campus of Williams College. www.wtfestival.org. (*C*) **413/458-3253.** Tickets usually $25–$60.

OUTDOOR ACTIVITIES

Mount Greylock State Reservation ★ contains the highest peak (3,491 ft./1,064m) in Massachusetts, as well as a section of the Appalachian Trail. A long, narrow, bumpy road allows cars almost to the summit, where the War Memorial Tower affords vistas of the Taconic and Hoosac ranges, far into Vermont and New York (parking $2). The ride down is popular with mountain bikers. Trails radiate from the parking lot near the reservation's **Bascom Lodge** (www.bascomlodge.net; (*C*) **917/680-0079**), a grandly rustic creation of the Civilian Conservation Corps in the New Deal 1930s. See p. 365 for details on staying at the lodge.

WILLIAMSTOWN SHOPPING

In the small downtown shopping district, **Library Antiques,** 70 Spring St. (www.libraryantiques.com; ⓒ **413/458-3436**), was once filled with English chess sets and Polish stoneware, but the inventory now seems to be shifting to clothing. South of town on Route 7, **Collectors Warehouse,** 723 Cold Spring Rd. (ⓒ **413/458-9686**), has a little bit of everything—jewelry, books, dolls, furniture, and glassware.

Exploring North Adams

58 miles NW of Springfield, 6 miles E of Williamstown

In the mid-1990s, it seemed impossible that this then-comatose mill town could recover. Its unemployment rate was the highest in the state, and over two-thirds of its storefronts were empty. A land developer once even suggested that the town be flooded to create lakefront property.

But then North Adams experienced a whiplash turnaround, and today many of those once-abandoned storefronts are taken up with restaurants, galleries, and high-tech start-ups. The unlikely reason, to almost everyone's agreement, is an art museum that opened in 1999. An abandoned industrial complex has been converted, despite early hoots of derision, into a thriving center for the visual and performing arts. It is called the **Massachusetts Museum of Contemporary Art,** nicknamed MASS MoCA, and it has strikingly altered the socioeconomic dynamic of North Adams (see more below).

Saturday mornings from mid-June to late October, a farmers market is held at the parking lot on St. Anthony Drive near Marshall Street. The first Sunday of October is **Fall Foliage Day** (www.fallfoliageparade.com), with a parade of fire engines, marching bands, and Clydesdales. Balloons, hot dogs, and cotton candy are on sale at sidewalk stands.

About 27 miles east of North Adams on Route 2, the **Bridge of Flowers** (p. 335) in Shelburne Falls has stunning displays of blooming shrubs and gardens from April through late autumn.

Massachusetts Museum of Contemporary Art (MASS MoCA) ★★★ MUSEUM

A lot of excitement and anticipation surrounded this ambitious project, the conversion of a 27-building mill complex into a center for the arts. Even before its official opening in 1999, it had a nickname—MASS MoCA—and immediately started hosting performances by the likes of David Byrne, Patti Smith, and the Merce Cunningham Dance Company. Works on display often cross traditional aesthetic boundaries to marry elements of both performing and visual arts. The center's chief virtue—from the standpoint of those contemporary artists who choose to work on a grand scale—is the vastness of the spaces available. That capaciousness was more than augmented by the 2017 opening of another enormous, formerly empty building that doubled the museum's gallery space. Today, to walk the perimeter of every gallery, a visitor would travel 4 miles. Popular performing arts programs and music festivals are held here as well, such as **Bang on a Can** and **Solid Sound**, curated by the band Wilco. The museum has also presented a variety of experimental films, comedy festivals, and dance parties, and is attracting small tenant companies working the vineyards of technology, including software, video, and e-commerce. The **Kidspace** area includes the hands-on ArtBar, where visitors are invited to make art that is thematically connected to current exhibitions. The snacky **Lickety Split** (✆ **413/346-4560**) on the ground floor of the museum serves breakfast until 11am and light fare the rest of the day (closed Tuesday). In addition, there is now a craft brewery and taproom.

1040 Mass MoCA Way. www.massmoca.org. ✆ **413/662-2111.** $20 adults, $18 seniors & veterans, $12 students, $8 kids 6–16, free ages 5 and under. Summer Sun–Wed 10am–6pm, Thurs–Sat 10am–7pm; rest of year Wed–Mon 11am–5pm.

Where to Stay in the Berkshires

Note that many inns in this in-demand area routinely stipulate minimum 2- or 3-night stays in summer and over holiday weekends, and often require advance deposits.

GREAT BARRINGTON

Great Barrington has a number of unremarkable but entirely adequate motels north of the center along or near Route 7. The most desirable is **Holiday Inn Express,** 415 Stockbridge Rd. (www.ihg.com; ✆ **413/528-1810**), which has an indoor pool, Jacuzzi, small fitness room, and rooms with Jacuzzi tubs and/ or fireplaces; rates include breakfast. Motels in the area tend to fill up more slowly on weekends than the better-known inns. The **Chamber of Commerce** operates a lodging hotline at ✆ **800/269-4825** or 413/528-4006.

Wainwright Inn ★ Evidences of the 1776 tavern that once stood here are still visible in lower ceilings and wide-plank floors in parts of the present building. Walking past the front parlor, with its large bare center space and chairs pushed against the walls, may prove a disappointing first impression, but the inn grows on you. Near the doorway are carafes of sherry and port for pouring after dinner. There's a dining room past that, where three-course cooked-to-order hot breakfasts are served. Up the steep stairs are nine rooms on the second and third floors. Most are uncommonly spacious, with private baths, most of which have been recently updated. Two have king beds. A carriage house at the end of the back parking lot has two bedrooms, a living room, and a kitchen—just the thing for families.

518 South Main St. www.wainwrightinn.com. ✆ **413/528-2062.** 11 units. $129–$169 in low season, $189–$229 in high season. Rates include full breakfast. **Amenities:** A/C; Wi-Fi (free).

HANCOCK

The Country Inn at Jiminy Peak ★ This is one of the better lodging deals in the Berkshires, if your idea of luxury is space. All units are suites with full kitchens, one to three bedrooms, and sofa beds—perfect for families. Downhill skiing and snowboarding is directly on site, and in summer there's downhill mountain-biking along with bobsled rides on an alpine slide, a

BERKSHIRES skiing

Butternut Basin, on Route 23, 2 miles east of Great Barrington (www.ski butternut.com; ℂ **413/528-2000**), is known for its strong family ski programs, including programs for children of varying levels of experience and Learn to Ski and Learn to Ride programs for first-timers. An eight-lane tubing park provides another downhill option. On weekends, full-day lift tickets cost $60 for adults, $50 for seniors and ages 7 to 13, and $25 for kids 6 and under.

Twenty-four miles east of Williamstown, **Berkshire East Mountain Resort,** 22 East Mountain Rd., Charlemont (www. berkshireeast.com; ℂ **413/339-6617**) maintains 43 trails for skiing, tubing, and snowboarding. The Base Area Tour, near the main lodge, is for families and beginners ($30 adults, $20 seniors and youth). Ski lifts take more venturesome clients up to the Mountain Top Tour, with seven tower-to-tower lines, and the Valley Jump Tour, which sails at ever greater lengths and speeds over the forest canopy. Advance reservations are required. There are lodgings and a cafe on the grounds. Over the summer, whitewater rafting is also offered, and the resort' activates its three ziplines, which it claims are the longest in New England.

At the western edge of South Egremont, touching the New York border, the **Catamount Ski Area,** on Route 23 (www.catamountski.com; ℂ **413/528-1262**), is understandably popular with

New Yorkers, being only about 2 hours from Manhattan. It has 36 trails, including the daunting double-diamond Catapult (the steepest run in the Berkshires), and seven chairlifts, as well as a 400-foot half-pipe for snowboarders. Night skiing and rentals are available. On weekends, full-day lift tickets cost $68 for adults, $57 for seniors and ages 7 to 13, and $30 for kids 6 and under.

South of Pittsfield's city center, the **Bousquet Ski Area** (pronounced Boskay) on Dan Fox Drive (www.bousquets. com; ℂ **413/442-8316**). Bousquet has 23 trails, with a vertical drop of 750 feet, three double lifts, and two carpet lifts. Night skiing is available Monday through Saturday. Rentals and lessons are offered. Lift tickets cost $20 to $47; snow tubing costs $20.

Jiminy Peak ★, 14 miles northwest of Pittsfield in Hancock (www.jiminypeak. com; ℂ **413/738-5500**), has skiing and snowboarding on 45 trails (18 open at night) with nine lifts. Winter activities are supplemented the rest of the year with horseback riding, trapshooting, fishing in a stocked pond, a rock-climbing wall, tennis, mountain biking, pools, and golf at the nearby Waubeeka Springs course. There's lodging at the resort (see p. 358), with lift tickets included in the room rates. For day-trippers, all-day tickets cost $65 for adults and $43 for juniors on the weekend, $39 for adults and $29 for juniors during the week.

bungee-trampoline, a climbing wall, a giant swing, trout fishing, and minigolf. A convenience store on the property has groceries, wine, and beer.

37 Corey Rd., Hancock. www.jiminypeak.com. ℂ **413/738-5500.** 105 units. $129–$909 1–3 bedroom suite. Winter rates include lift tickets. Children 17 and under stay free in parent's room. **Amenities:** 2 restaurants; 2 bars; babysitting; exercise room; outdoor and indoor pools; tennis courts; Wi-Fi (free).

LEE

Applegate ★ This B&B utilizes a gracious 1920s Georgian Colonial-style manse to full advantage. The nicest unit has a canopy bed, Queen Anne reproductions, sunlight filtering through gauzy curtains, a steam shower, and a fireplace (with real wood). All rooms have stoves or fireplaces, and most have wet bars, TVs, and mini-fridges. Chocolates and brandy await guests at bedside, and there are robes in the closet. The full breakfast is by candlelight, and the innkeepers set out wine and cheese in the afternoon. There are eight rooms in the main building, and four each in two separate cottages, with Jacuzzis in the barn cottage and a full kitchen in the other. The country club across the street has golf and tennis and is open to the public.

279 W. Park St., Lee. www.applegateinn.com. © **800/691-9012** or 413/243-4451. 11 rooms and suites. June–Oct $210–$410 double; Nov–May $170–$305 double. Rates include breakfast. **Amenities:** Fitness room; pool (heated outdoor); tennis court; Wi-Fi (free).

Black Swan Inn ★   From the road, the Black Swan looks like a conventional motel, and stepping inside doesn't dispel that impression. But ah! Book a room in back and find yourself gazing directly upon a lovely, unspoiled lake. Half the 52 rooms enjoy that vista, so by all means ask for one (although the rooms facing the road are usually larger). Vanities are separate from the rooms housing the toilet and tub. Picnic areas encourage guests to get out in the sun on the lawn, and kayaks and boats are available for rent. There's an Indian restaurant, **Mint**, inside the inn and facing the lake (www.mintlee.us).

435 Laurel St. www.blackswaninnberkshires.com. © **413/243-2700.** 52 units. $98–$155 winter, $139–$179 summer**. Amenities:** Restaurant; exercise room; Wi-Fi (free).

Chambéry Inn ★   This was originally the Berkshires' first parochial school (1885), named for the French hometown of the nuns who ran it. That accounts for the extra-large bedrooms, about 500 square feet each—they were formerly classrooms. Six of them, with 13-foot ceilings and the original woodwork and blackboards, are equipped with whirlpool tubs and gas fireplaces. A breakfast basket is delivered to guests' doors each morning. Terry robes are provided.

199 Main St., Lee. www.chamberyinn.com. © **800/537-4321** or 413/243-2221. 10 units. $135–$170 double. Rates include breakfast. No children 15 and under. **Amenities:** A/C; Wi-Fi (free).

Federal House Inn ★★   When new owners pulled up the wall-to-wall carpeting installed in every room here, they discovered floors dating from 1834 in pristine condition. Inspired, they set about bringing their property to highest Berkshires standard. All the bedding is new and there are two easy chairs in every room. All have private baths, gas or electric fireplaces, robes, and extra pillows. All but one room have queen beds (#7 has a king). Breakfast in the common areas of the ground floor starts with coffee and tea from 6am on. The meal itself starts later with a buffet of fruit, granola, yogurt, and hard-boiled eggs, followed by a freshly cooked sweet or savory main course. A guest pantry has coffee and soft drinks for the taking and there are complimentary wine and snacks afternoons in front of the fire. Although technically located in the town of Lee, it's closer to downtown Stockbridge.

1560 Pleasant St. (Rte. 102). www.federalhouseinn.com. © **800/243-1824** or 413/243-1824. 9 units. $125–$195 in low season, $185–$295 high. Rates include breakfast. **Amenities:** A/C; Wi-Fi (free).

LENOX

Most inns in Lenox proper can accommodate only small numbers of guests. Because the Tanglewood concert season is a powerful draw, prices are highest in summer, as well as during the brief foliage season in mid-October. Minimum 2- or 3-night stays are usually required during Tanglewood, foliage season, weekends, and holidays. *Note:* If you're planning to come during the Tanglewood season, reserve far in advance—February isn't too soon.

Some inns here are so rule-ridden and facility-free that they come off as crabby—no kids, no pets, no phones, no breakfast before 9am, shared bathrooms—while costing twice as much as nearby motels that have all those conveniences. Routes 7 and 20 north and south of town harbor a number of properties you may want to consider instead, including a **Days Inn** (www.wyndhamhotels.com; ✆ **413/637-3560**), the **Hampton Inn & Suites Berkshires-Lenox** (www.hamptoninn3.hilton.com; ✆ **413/499-1111**), and the **Lenox Inn** (www.thelenoxinn.com; ✆ **413/499-0324**).

Expensive

Cranwell Resort ★★★ The main building of this all-season resort looks like a castle in the Scottish Highlands, but no 17th-century laird lived this well. That's where the most expensive rooms are; the rest are in four smaller outlying buildings. Furnishings and general decor hop along a spectrum from English country manor to Adirondack cottage, and all surround guests in immediate comfort. In addition to the very attractive, expansive grounds (serving as cross-country ski trails in winter), there is an 18-hole golf course (greens fees $39–$79, depending on season). Three dining rooms range from formal to pubby, and live music is often featured. The resort is the summer home (July–Aug) of the Capitol Steps political satire group. An enormous 35,000-square-foot spa offers many beauty treatments, an indoor pool, lounges with fireplaces, and 17 spa treatment rooms.

55 Lee Rd. (Rte. 20). www.cranwell.com. ✆ **800/272-6935** or 413/637-1364. 107 units. Summer $299–$449 double, winter $179–$279 double. **Amenities:** 4 restaurants; bar; babysitting; bikes; golf course; health club & spa; pools (outdoor and indoor); room service; tennis courts; Wi-Fi (free).

Gateways Inn ★★ Built in 1912, this grand home's most impressive feature is the staircase that winds down into the lobby. Designed by McKim, Mead, and White, it's a stunner, just the thing for a grand entrance—which is why so many weddings are staged here. The eleven bedrooms and suites are named for female Shakespearean characters; six have gas fireplaces. The piano bar features 200 whiskies, a menu of light dishes, and music nightly in summer, weekly in winter. In addition to the formal dining room, there is a terrace available for light meals and desserts after dinner until midnight.

51 Walker St. www.gatewaysinn.com. ✆ **888/492-9466** or 413/637-2532. 11 units. June–Oct $380–$700 double; Nov–May $180–$450 double. Rates include breakfast. **Amenities:** Restaurant; lounge; Wi-Fi (free).

Moderate

Courtyard by Marriott ★★★ This new entry on the Lenox lodging scene sets an exemplary vision of what the chain can be: near-luxury at an

PAMPERING & POSH DIGS FOR THE one percent

It's hardly surprising that an area that attracted the super-rich of the 19th-century Gilded Age would retain some vestiges of that time. That it does, with several grand estates, undeniably posh, but with breathtaking tariffs for rooms that rent nightly for $1,000—and up. The sumptuous 1902 Tudor-Norman mansion called **Blantyre** (www.blantyre.com; © **413/637-3556**) was modeled after the founder's ancestral home in the town of Blantyre in Lanarkshire, Scotland. The property also includes a 14-room carriage house. New owners took over in 2017 and have said they'll invest additional capital into the property. **Wheatleigh** (www.wheatleigh.com, © **413/637-0610**), a persuasive 1893 replica of a 16th-century Tuscan palazzo, has always been very expensive, currently topping out at $1,600 a night. (Note that some of its so-called "superior" rooms measure only 10×14 ft.) **Canyon Ranch** (www.canyonranch.com; © **800/742-9000**) is essentially a high-toned fat farm for the well-to-do, featuring spa services, relentless exercise, Botox sessions, and spartan meals sans alcohol. By comparison, the estimable **Cranwell Resort** (p. 361) is a luxurious bargain.

upper-middle price point. Here, instead of the self-serve snack alcove characteristic of its brothers, is "The Bistro," where breakfast is served—morning eggs are cooked to order—and, later in the day, cocktails are poured by live attendants. Other menu options include quesadillas, prosciutto flatbreads, and substantial sandwiches and pasta. Rooms are spacious and crisply furnished, with sitting areas, walk-in showers, microwave ovens, and unstocked fridges. TVs allow guests to stream Netflix, Amazon, and other services. The decently equipped fitness center is open 24/7 and the adjacent indoor pool 8am to 10pm.

70 Pittsfield Rd. www.marriott.com. © **413/551-7700.** 89 units. $154–$184 double. **Amenities:** Lobby cafe/lounge; fitness center; pool (indoor, with whirlpool); Wi-Fi (free).

Yankee Inn ★ Of the several motels strung along Route 20 east of Lenox center, this is a place to remember when the area's actual inns are filled. It is congenial for families: children are welcome, as they are not in many B&Bs. Housekeeping is of a reasonably high standard, and furnishings, while routine in design, are as fresh-looking as might be expected in a city hotel. Some rooms have gas fireplaces and unstocked fridges. Long, empty corridors don't enhance the experience, but the indoor/outdoor pool, convenient location, and moderate prices (for the Berkshires) compensate. It's a sister hotel to the local Courtyard by Marriott (p. 361).

461 Pittsfield Rd. (Rte. 20). www.berkshireinns.com. © **800/835-2364** or 413/499-3700. 96 units. $139–$275 double in summer, $94–$125 double in winter. Rates include breakfast. **Amenities:** Lounge; exercise room; pools (heated indoor and outdoor); Wi-Fi (free).

NEW MARLBOROUGH

The Old Inn on the Green ★★ The inn, a former stagecoach stop from 1760, and the adjacent 18th-century Thayer House are under the ownership of the chef and his wife. The five rooms in the main inn are authentically restored and evocative of their original years, with wide floorboards and period latches;

several include access to a second-story veranda. Rooms in Thayer House are larger, with combinations of fireplaces and whirlpool tubs. The intimate dining rooms in the pre-Revolutionary tavern have fireplaces, and the only other illumination at dinner is from candles. Menus are nothing startling, but carefully rendered, often featuring lamb shanks, brook trout, and diver scallops, and closing with a large selection of regional cheeses. Selections are a la carte every night but Saturday, when the four-course prix fixe is $75 per person plus wine. The always-available chef's tasting menu is $95. Reservations are strongly advised, especially on summer weekends and off-season, when hours and days are shorter. There is outdoor dining in warmer weather. Pets are allowed, and dinner and room packages are good deals.

134 Hartsville-New Marlborough Rd. (Rte. 57). www.oldinn.com. ℘ **413/229-7924.** 11 units. $260–$395 double. 10% discount when reserving by phone or website. Rates include breakfast. **Amenities:** Restaurant; taproom; courtyard pool; Wi-Fi (free).

NORTH ADAMS

True to its erstwhile company slogan, there are certainly no surprises at the **Holiday Inn Berkshires** (40 Main St.; www.ihg.com; ℘ **413/663-6500**), but its downtown location is a plus, and its tariffs, from a summer high of $168 double to a winter low of $97, are attractive to budget-watchers.

By the time you read this, **Tourists,** a new 48-room boutique hotel at 915 State Rd. (www.touristswelcome.com; ℘ **413/346-4933**) should be open. It features a farm-to-table restaurant called **Loom,** helmed by an honored California chef. Other big plans for downtown North Adams include another hotel with 110 rooms, along with a clutch of museums meant for exhibitions of motorcycles, clocks, virtual reality devices, and model railroads.

The Porches ★★ "Retro-rural chic" might describe this row of six detached 19th-century workingmen's houses stitched together by an uninterrupted streetside veranda, the spaces in between roofed over and fitted with indoor catwalks and patios. Rooms are witty tributes to the past, with kitschy/ironic lamps and paint-by-numbers pictures on the walls. Down duvets, bathrobes, and cushy sofas make things even cozier. Ask for one of the second-floor king rooms with balcony. Coffee, croissant, and a newspaper in a rocking chair on the porch on a warm morning is a singular pleasure. Evening cocktails are available, too.

231 River St. www.porches.com. ℘ **413/664-0400.** 47 units. Mid-May to early Nov $180–$335 double; mid-Nov to early May $130–$195 double. Rates include breakfast. 2-night minimum stay Fri–Sat May–Nov and holidays. **Amenities:** Exercise room; Jacuzzi; year-round outdoor pool; sauna; Wi-Fi (free).

PITTSFIELD

Crowne Plaza ★ The tallest building in town at 14 stories, this has the unsurprising bells and whistles expected of the familiar chain, but it's more family-friendly than many smaller lodgings in the region. Kids are readily occupied with the heated indoor pool and PlayStations in every room (and they won't mind the dated seen-it-before furnishings). The Elle Day Spa provides a variety of massage therapies, facials, and body treatments. With 179 rooms, there's also a good chance of copping a bed here on hectic Tanglewood weekends.

1 West St. www.berkshirecrowne.com. © **877/227-6963** or 413/499-2000. 179 units. $88- $235 double. Free self-parking in garage. **Amenities:** Restaurant; bar; babysitting; exercise room w/Jacuzzi; heated indoor pool; Wi-Fi (free).

Hotel on North ★ Echoing wide spaces mitigate against any suggestion of coziness in this refurbished late 19th-century Victorian edifice, but otherwise it provides the conveniences and gadgets 21st-century travelers expect: minibars, safes, bathrobes, and streaming HDTVs. Some rooms have gas fireplaces and antique chests, and a few even have washer-dryers or kitchenettes. Much of the furniture was commissioned by local artisans. Large common rooms on the top two floors (of four) are fitted out with comfortable chairs and couches, and shelves of books and board games.

297 North St. www.hotelonnorth.com. © **413/358-4741.** 45 units. $143–$197 winter, $349–$409 summer. **Amenities:** Restaurant; bar; Wi-Fi (free).

SOUTH EGREMONT

The Egremont Village Inn ★ This 1786 farmhouse was renovated in Greek Revival style in 1835. Many guest rooms have four-poster beds with quilts, three are kings, and a few have fireplaces. Some travelers may be put off by the fact that there are no television sets in the bedrooms (others will love it), but two common spaces have TVs. Dogs are allowed in some rooms. The separate carriage house has two more bedrooms. A big draw is **The Barn ★**, at the back of the same property, which offers live music Wednesday through Sunday most of the year and features a wagon wheel chandelier, a bar, and a stage large enough for bands of four or more musicians; dancing often ensues. Eats include burgers, quesadillas, and wings (organic, of course). A public golf course is next door to the inn.

17 Main St. (Rte. 23). www.theegremontvillageinn.com. © **800/528-9580** or 413/528-9580. 12 units. $125–$275 double; $350–$400 suite. Rates include breakfast and afternoon tea. **Amenities:** A/C; pool (outdoor); Wi-Fi (free).

STOCKBRIDGE

Inn at Stockbridge ★ A little over a mile north of Stockbridge center, the main 1906 building has a grandly columned porch set well back from the road on 12 acres. Several bedrooms have fireplaces and whirlpool tubs, and there are eight suites in a remodeled barn and separate cottage. Coffee and snacks are available in the dining room, as is a computer for guest use. *Note:* The inn's sign out on Route 7 is small and easy to miss.

30 East St. (Rte. 7). www.stockbridgeinn.com. © **888/819-2373** or 413/298-3337. 16 units. June–Oct $200–$420 double; Nov–May $99–$275 double. Rates include full breakfast and afternoon refreshments. No children 11 and under. **Amenities:** A/C; exercise room; heated outdoor pool; Wi-Fi (free).

Kripalu Center for Yoga & Health ★ This is, in fact, a resort hotel of a sort, with bedrooms, lounges, restaurants, and sweeping vistas of lake and hills. But its focus, obvious from its name, is on the healing arts, including yoga, meditation, aromatherapy, acupressure, tai chi, and massage—not to mention classes in crafts and non-stressful cooking. Room styles run from dormitories with bunk beds to twin or queen bedrooms with shared half baths, some of which are private. Decor is strictly utilitarian, or, if you prefer, minimalist. Rates include the accommodation, three meals daily, use of the fitness room and sauna, workshops, and yoga and meditation classes. Scheduled classes and other events start at 6:30am and end mid-evening. There's access to the beach of Lake Mahkeenac, down the hill from the Center. Note that there is *no* air conditioning, and (by design) Wi-Fi is available only in the cafe and the Annex.

57 Interlaken Rd. www.kripalu.org. *©* **866/200-5203.** 650 beds. $292–$351 w/private bath, $205–$247 w/shared bath. Rates include 3 meals per day. **Amenities:** Dining room; cafe; beachfront; exercise room; hiking trails; Wi-Fi (annex & cafe only, free).

The Red Lion Inn ★★   So well known that it serves as a symbol of the Berkshires, this busy inn had its origins as a stagecoach tavern in 1773. The rocking chairs on the porch are the place to while away an hour reading or people-watching. An ancient birdcage elevator carries guests up to halls and rooms filled with antiques ranging in styles that span 2 centuries. Floors creak and tilt, as might be expected, but modern comforts are provided. Six satellite buildings are within 3 miles of the inn. Dining choices include the pricey traditional dining room, the casual and atmospheric Widow Bingham Tavern, the Lion's Den pub, and, in good weather, the courtyard out back. The pub has nightly live entertainment, often of the folk-rock variety. Book your room far in advance.

30 Main St. www.redlioninn.com. *©* **413/298-5545.** 108 units (14 w/shared baths). Jan to late May $145–$295 double, $295–$455 suite; late May–late Oct $165–$455 double, $389–$590 suite; late Oct–Dec $114–$219 double, $215–$485 suite. 2-night minimum stay Memorial Day–Oct, Dec, and holidays. Pets accepted ($40 per pet per night). **Amenities:** 3 restaurants; 2 bars; babysitting; exercise room; Jacuzzi; year-round heated outdoor pool; tennis and golf privileges nearby; Wi-Fi (free).

WILLIAMSTOWN

This is a college town, so in addition to the usual peak periods of July, August, and the October foliage season, accommodations fill up during graduation and on football weekends. The largest lodging in town is the **Williams Inn,** 1090 Main St. (www.williamsinn.com; *©* **800/828-0133** or 413/458-9371), which despite the name is a standard motel, with a dining room, tavern, and indoor pool.

In Mount Greylock State Reservation (see p. 356), **Bascom Lodge** (www.bascomlodge.net; *©* **917/680-0079**) offers simple dormitory beds ($40 per bunk) and private family rooms ($125–$150) accommodating a total of 34 guests from mid-May to October. Family-style meals are available (reservations required for breakfast and dinner; no reservations needed for lunch). The lodge has stone fireplaces for lounging after a hike and an enclosed porch with expansive views of the mountain range. Wi-Fi is available and free. *Note:* Bascom Lodge's website says that GPS is not always accurate for getting to the building. Detailed directions, depending on which direction you are coming from, are provided online.

Field Farm Guesthouse ★   After an extended vacation of B&B-hopping, there may come a time when one more tilted floor or wobbly Windsor chair will send even a devout inn-lover over the edge. Here's an antidote. This pristine example of postwar modern architecture rose in 1948 on a spectacular 296-acre estate with 4 miles of trails. Most guest rooms look over meadows to Mount Greylock. The Scandinavian Modern furniture was made to order for the house, and three guest rooms have decks while two have fireplaces. Don't expect TV or phones, but there is Wi-Fi. Breakfasts are hearty meals of waffles and five-cheese omelets making use of herbs and vegetables grown on the property. No children under 12.

554 Sloan Rd. www.thetrustees.org/field-farm. ✆ **413/458-3135.** 5 units. $200–$325 double. Rates include breakfast. **Amenities:** Heated outdoor pool; tennis court; Wi-Fi (free).

The Orchards ★   An upscale country-club atmosphere pervades: the Orchards is the sort of place where afternoon tea is an event. Public and private rooms enjoy a mix of antique and reproduction English-style furniture. Even standard units are sizeable, all with separate dressing cubicles, and those with working fireplaces have chaise lounges and deeply padded chairs. There is live piano in the lounge on weekends.

222 Adams Rd. www.orchardshotel.com. ✆ **800/225-1517** or 413/458-9611. 49 units. $239–$319 (summer); $119–$219 double (winter). **Amenities:** Restaurant; bar; exercise room w/sauna and Jacuzzi; heated outdoor pool; Wi-Fi (free).

Where to Eat in the Berkshires

Also consider the restaurants in the region's various historic inns, notably the **Old Inn on the Green** ★★ in New Marlborough (p. 362) and the **Red Lion Inn** ★★ in Stockbridge (p. 365).

GREAT BARRINGTON
Expensive

Aegean Breeze ★ GREEK   Almost hidden on the heavily commercial street leading north from Great Barrington to Stockbridge, this commendable taverna occupies a building with an enclosed porch, an open terrace, and three dining rooms. The menu is laid out in the traditional manner, with sections for *mezedes, salates,* seafood, poultry, and lamb. Execution counts here, elevating such standards as *moussaka* (potatoes, eggplant, and ground beef with béchamel) and lamb *plaki* (with mushrooms, Vidalia onions, and feta baked in a clay pot). Especially appealing are the fish and shellfish—16 varieties of them—utterly fresh and simply prepared. Thursdays are lobster specials, and if you absolutely must, there are five kinds of burgers.

   A similar menu, with Lebanese accents, diversions, and spellings, is offered a block away at **Naki's,** 401B Stockbridge Rd., ✆ **413/528-5540.** The big difference is in the lower prices, with dinner entrees from $14 to $20.

327 Stockbridge Rd. www.aegeanbreezeonline.com. ✆ **413/528-4001.** Main courses $15–$32. Daily 11am–10pm.

Allium ★ ECLECTIC The menu changes often depending on seasonal availability and chef's whim, but in the recent past it has included *khaso soi* (braised chicken, wheat noodles, and coconut curry broth), steamed pork belly buns (with radish, scallions, hoisin, and Sriracha) and cod fritters—which, with crisp outer shells enclosing a creamy brandade with a drizzle of aioli, were as good as the dish can be. Small and shared plates are popular, especially in the lively bar, with options such as carnitas and fish tacos, fluke crudo, and manila clams with bacon and celery.

42/44 Railroad St. www.mezzeinc.com. ℭ **413/528-2118.** Main courses $20–$34. Sun–Thurs 5–9:30pm; Fri–Sat 5–10pm (bar open until 2am).

Cafe Adam ★★ NEW AMERICAN *The* place in the landlocked town for seafood, Cafe Adam serves oysters on the half shell all year (usually for $3.75, but a bargain on Thursday nights at $2 each). Perfectly shucked and presented, they might precede a dish of five pan-fried scallops with bits of pink grapefruit, slips of radish, and creamy whipped parsnips, or the full-on "Downeast" bouillabaisse—the Mediterranean stew crammed with clams, mussels, squid, scallops, fennel, and chunks of fish of the moment. Those adverse to edible creatures from the deep are not forgotten: The confit duck farro, perhaps? Or the "Almost Vegan" tumble of cauliflower, sweet potato, pickled red onions, black lentils, pomegranate, almonds, and beet sour cream? Beef tenderloin and smoked salmon carbonara are additional possibilities. The rooms are woody, the tables unadorned, the lighting low. Servers and bussers, dressed in black, are efficient and as friendly as the frequent crush of visitors allow.

420 Stockbridge Rd., in the Jenifer House Commons complex. www.cafeadam.org. ℭ **413/528-7786.** Main courses $24–$34.Wed–Sat 5–9pm, Sun 5–8pm.

Prairie Whale ★ NEW AMERICAN Much of what you need to know about this place is that they tear up yesterday's menu every morning and use the pieces for scrap paper, reinventing their offerings depending upon what's available from markets and local farmers. The owner is restaurateur Mark Firth, who made his bones in the white-hot dining scene of Williamsburg, Brooklyn, with his celebrated Marlow & Sons eatery. Here, he and his chefs let their fancies wander. For a very general idea, think quinoa with flatbread, feta, roasted beets, Swiss chard, and yogurt. There's a cheeseburger at $14 and, usually, a rib-eye with foie gras at $38; most mains are under $25. Imaginative cocktails use the wares of local distilleries. There are five dining areas with several communal tables and a sheet-metal-topped bar, all housed in a 19th-century Colonial.

178 Main St. ℭ **413/528-5050.** Main courses $14–$38. Mon, Thurs–Fri 5–10pm, Sat–Sun 11am–3pm and 5–10pm.

Moderate

Aroma ★ INDIAN Aroma touts itself in ads as the "best Indian restaurant in the Berkshires," and so it is. Never mind that there's not all that much competition: The restaurant's owners act like they have something to prove, which means dinner has over 64 main course possibilities plus seven breads, all baked on the premises. It's hard to go wrong with a couple of vegetable or meat samosas (crispy turnovers), chicken or fish tikka (marinated chunks grilled on skewers), sides of basmati rice and mango chutney, and spinach naan (flatbread stuffed with fresh spinach). Lunch specials are $10 to $12. Note that when the menu or waitress says "spicy," believe it. They'll tone down the heat on request.

485 Main St. www.aromabarandgrill.com. © **413/528-3116.** Main courses $10–$18. Sun–Thurs 11:30–3pm and 4:30–10:30pm, Fri–Sat 11:30–3 and 4:30–11pm (closed Mon lunch).

Fuel ★ BISTRO/COFFEE SHOP   Having moved from smaller digs across the street, Fuel tries to be all things to all comers—both a hipster coffee bar and a place for substantial breakfast, sandwiches, and more. It offers dinner from Thursday to Saturday, Sunday brunch, and adult beverages from Thursday to Sunday, with a menu that ranges wildly from fish and chips to pad thai to butternut risotto. Story slams, musical performances, and "drag queen bingo" are among the periodic entertainment offerings. The setting is supremely casual, with an exposed brick wall, a collection of empty picture frames, and a row of vivid photos of surrealist bent. There are sidewalk tables in decent weather. The only certainty? Change.

239 Main St. www.fuelgreatbarrington.com. © **413/528-5505.** Main courses $13–$15. Mon–Sat 7am–midnight, Sun 8am–11pm.

Inexpensive

Rubiner's ★ DELI/CAFE   A former neoclassical bank building has been transformed into a true gourmet shop. The imposing inner space displays dozens of cheeses of both American and European origin, along with freshly baked breads, charcuterie, pickles, condiments, and platters of prepared foods. Around back, at the edge of a parking lot, the attached cafe **Rubi's** (same address) serves espresso drinks, wine, and a selection of creative sandwiches and main courses, with prices ranging from $5.50 to $15.

264 Main St. www.rubiners.com. © **413/528-0488.** Daily 10am–6pm (until 4pm Sun). Rubi's cafe: Mon–Fri 7am–6pm, Sat 8am–6pm, Sun 8am–5pm. Store:

LEE

Chez Nous ★★ FRENCH BISTRO   A warren of tightly packed dining rooms, a full bar, and a terrace compose this ode to the Gallic canon (with the addition of classic North African dishes). Although the menu changes with the seasons, odds are good that you'll encounter rack of lamb, chicken tagine, and a crispy cod brandade. Distinctions are typically found in the accompaniments, as with items like local ramps, which have a short growing season. A most welcome innovation is the policy of offering both half and full portions of all entrees (except the foie gras burger)—an economic and ethical savings for diners with smaller appetites who hate leaving food on the plate. Notable starters are the house-made pâté and artisanal cheese selections. Hours and open days vary by season, swinging from 6 nights a week in July and August to only 4 in deepest winter and a month off mid-March to mid-April; confirm online or by calling ahead. The restaurant is always dinner-only.

QUICK BITES: EAT this. THEN EAT that.

For a town that is not that large, Great Barrington has a remarkable number of eating places. Many focus on specialty products, or close or open at unpredictable times, or emphasize artisanal procedures. In addition to the restaurants listed above, here are some of our other favorites:

o **Baba Louie's** ★ (285 Main St.; www.babalouiespizza.com; ℂ **413/528-8100**) sells sandwiches and soups too, but the reason to go is their maddeningly tasty sourdough pizzas. That they avoid cliché is evident in the ingredients of just one (of over ten choices), the Dolce Vita: spinach, mozzarella, figs, gorgonzola, prosciutto, Parmesan, tomato sauce, and rosemary oil. Gluten-free and vegan choices are available, and it's open daily, all year, for lunch and dinner.

o **The Barrington Brewery** (420 Stockbridge Rd.; www.barringtonbrewery. net; ℂ **413/528-8282**) started years before the recent craft beer blowup. All their beers are handcrafted on the premises; signature ales are always on tap, supplemented by seasonal brews. Flights of five samples are a good way to sample the wares. Chili and eight burgers are available. Open daily for lunch and dinner.

o **Berkshire Co-op Market Café** (42 Bridge St.; www.berkshire.coop; ℂ **413/528-9697**) is attached to a back-to-the-earth, locally sourced, artisanal, vegetarian-friendly, and very earnest supermarket that stocks few products with familiar national names. The café is attached to one side, with tables inside and on the large terrace. Sandwiches are inspired by the store's zeitgeist: The "Bridge Street BLT," with hickory-smoked bacon, lettuce, tomato, and sprouts with chipotle mayo on whole grain bread is typical. Open daily 8am to 8pm.

o **The Bistro Box** (937 S. Main St.; www.thebistrobox.rocks; ℂ **413/717-5958**), run by two graduates of the Culinary Institute of America, follows the Shake Shack formula of elevating fast foods' quality. Its sandwiches, burgers, dogs, soups, and salads may sound ordinary, but their execution is superb. (Observe the stacked fries coated with Parmesan cheese and truffle oil! One of five types!) They're open 11am to 4pm Sunday to Tuesday, closed on Wednesdays, and open 11am to 7pm Thursday to Saturday. Almost all items are well under $10, passed from the window of a roadside shack, to be gobbled up at the picnic tables or taken away.

o **Great Barrington Bagel** (777 Main St.; www.gbbagel.com; ℂ **413/528-9055**) does bagels right—the 16 varieties are boiled, then baked at pizza-level temperature. There are 30 filling options, from nova & egg to whitefish salad. Open daily.

o **SoCo Creamery** (5 Railroad St.; www.sococreamery.com; ℂ **413/717-4035**) makes its ice creams, sorbets, and gelatos from scratch in flavors from the expected to the unimagined: Banana Brownie, Ginger, and Mexicali Chocolate among them. Open daily from noon.

o **Patisserie Lenox** ★★ (313 Main St.; www.patisserielenox.com; ℂ **413/591-8747**) is a small chain that started in Lenox, thus the name. A Francophile's dream of a bakery-cafe, its long glass case offers dazzling fresh-that-morning brioche, eclairs, cream puffs, flourless chocolate cakes, colorful fruit tarts, and, of course, varieties of sublimely flaky Parisian-style croissants. You won't find better this side of the Atlantic. Open daily for breakfast and lunch, which includes a classic croque monsieur and salmon tartine.

LENOX

Two of the three restaurants recommended below serve lunch, in a region where many don't open until evening. Note that in winter Berkshire restaurants are apt to close for weeks or months, so always call ahead.

Chocoholics will want to check out the **Chocolate Springs Café,** 55 Pittsfield Lenox Rd./Route 7 (www.chocolatesprings.com; ✆ 413/637-9820). The entire spectrum of the dark confection is explored, from bonbons to truffles to pastries. They serve afternoon tea at one end of the space, with live music on weekends between 3pm and 5pm.

For a fascinating dining experience, consider **Table Six** (www.tablesix lenox.com; ✆ 413/637-4113) in the **Kemble Inn** (2 Kemble St.). Featured offerings often include prix-fixe or wine dinners and three-course meals with musical entertainment, as well as lunch and weekend brunch. As is characteristic of the Berkshires, hours and days fluctuate during the year, so check ahead.

Alta Restaurant & Wine Bar ★★ MEDITERRANEAN

The scene is as fizzy as prosecco at this wine-centric resto, especially in the summer months when diners bask in the breeze on the big covered porch and eye the parade of tourists and music-lovers. The lunch menu ranges from paninis served on excellent, locally baked focaccia to wraps, omelets of the day, burgers, and cobb salad. Dinner dishes include pan-seared trout, beef au poivre, and wild mushroom penne. There's even grilled organic tofu, if that's your desire. Wine is featured, and the ample three-glass flight is a way to test the cellar. There is also an excellent selection of locally brewed, artisanal beers and ales. Lunch items are significantly less costly than dinner. Don't even *think* of coming here without a reservation during the Tanglewood season.

34 Church St. www.altawinebar.com. ✆ **413/637-0003.** Main courses $22–$33. Daily 11:30am–2:30pm and 5–9pm (until 10pm Sat).

Bistro Zinc ★★ FRENCH

Zinc occupies the upper echelon of Berkshires eateries. For one thing, it is the best-looking restaurant in town, with its eponymous zinc bar, stamped-tin ceiling, flowers, and butcher paper over white tablecloths. The cuisine and wine list adhere with some rigor to the French-bistro repertoire. Past menus have listed such toothsome entrees as pork schnitzel with braised spinach, Faroe island salmon with quinoa and chimichurri sauce, and roasted cod and clams with chorizo with lemon spaetzle. Otherwise, standards boeuf bourguignon, coq au vin, and steak frites are done well. A remarkable 24 wines are available by the glass, and there's a five-cheese tasting option. The owner has the admirable philosophy of staying open year-round—you can always find a meal here, and the bar is open until 1am. Reservations recommended.

56 Church St. www.bistrozinc.com. ✆ **413/637-8800.** Main courses $18–$34. Daily 11:30am–3pm and 5:30–9pm (bar until 1am).

Brava ★ TAPAS

They don't take reservations, so arrive early or expect to wait. The inner space is snug, low-ceilinged, filled with crowds of happy adults of all ages. Spanish tapas—crispy calamari, garlic shrimp, *patatas bravas*—dominate the menu, with occasional Italianate diversions. They are served on plates the Spanish call *raciones,* much larger than the daintier few-nibbles tapas size. Most diners are likely to find one or two adequate. Take on more and the bill can also run up very quickly.

28 Housatonic St. ℂ **413/637-9171.** Tapas $5–$17. Daily 5pm–1am.

NEW MARLBOROUGH

Colonial-style dining at the **Old Inn on the Green ★★** (p. 362) is your top option in New Marlborough.

Cantina 229 ★ ECLECTIC   The name misleads. Although they throw big Tacos Tuesdays, this isn't a predominantly Mexican stopover. Instead, the card dances among the chef-owner's changing whims: Chicken flautas, yes, but also Sichuan dumplings, Rueben eggrolls, a Maui poke, cold sesame noodles, and *pa jun* (a Korean pancake). And that's just the appetizers. Mains include pulled pork curry, bibimbap (Korean rice bowl), seared cape scallops, and the wonderment of "New Marlborough Cavatelli"—house-made pasta tossed with garlic cream, confit chicken, peas, bok choy, pecorino, toasted crumbs, and chili flakes. The owners raise chickens and pigs on the property and buy much of what else they need from local farmers. The restaurant is in a rustic shed with a concrete floor, and a glass wall takes in a wide lawn that fades into a distant treeline.

229 Hartsville-New Marlborough Rd. www.cantina229.com. ℂ **413/229-3276.** Main courses $16–$28. Fri–Tues 5–9pm.

NORTH ADAMS

Gramercy Bistro ★ BISTRO   This quiet retreat has ruled the North Adams culinary roost for years, although it has more competition now. On the menu, organic and "locally sourced" meet creative and global: coq au vin, veal schnitzel, and spicy Thai mussels. A whopper of a paella is adorned with chicken, shrimp, chorizo, squid, mussels, clams, *and* peas. There are a few venturesome outreaches—sweetbreads *au beurre noir* with preserved lemon and artichokes—while ravioli and crabcakes counter with tradition.

87 Marshall St. www.gramercybistro.com. ℂ **413/663-5300.** Main courses $20–$28. Wed–Mon 5–9pm; Sun brunch 11am–2pm.

Jack's Hot Dog Stand ★ DINER   What a hoot is Jack's! There's its history—on this site, a narrow street in downtown North Adams, since 1917, and still operated by the grandson of the founder. There is the crush—12 stools at the counter with room for a single file of eager eaters leaning against the wall, sitters and standees politely making room for families and old people. And there is the frenzy—counter people making jokes and shouting orders: "Got two here! What's waitin'? Three cheese!" The menu and its prices seem to be preserved in amber: Two dogs, two burgers, two fries, and two Cokes cost $9.80 total. Take that, Golden Arches.

12 Eagle St. www.jackshotdogstand.com. ℂ **413/664-9006.** All items under $3. No credit cards. Mon–Sat 10am–7pm.

Public Food + Drink ★★★ NEW AMERICAN   Public is a feel-good restaurant, with a clean uncluttered look, an attractive young waitstaff, and 12 taps at the bar for a rotation of artisanal beers. The farm-to-table menu follows the lead of its sister place in Pittsfield, the **District Kitchen & Bar** (below), categorizing its dishes as "Smalls" or "Bigs," supplemented by burgers and flatbreads. Appetites both raging and dainty are thus served. For the hungry, there are the grilled 10-oz. strip steak or the chicken leg and thigh braised in red wine with mushrooms, Portobellos, and carrots. For the peckish but not famished, there are fun jerk chicken tacos as well as shrimp and grits with an orange and chorizo cream sauce. In between, burgers come with a choice of toppings, including fried eggs and pulled pork.

34 Holden St. www.publiceatanddrink.com. ✆ **413/664-4444.** Most mains $19–$24. Thurs–Sun 11:30am–2pm and 4pm–late, Mon–Wed 4pm–late.

PITTSFIELD

An unusual number of downtown eateries serve only breakfast and lunch, supplemented by a few Mexican and Asian places. One alternative is **Eat on North** ★, the in-house restaurant of the **Hotel on North** (p. 364). It serves all three meals and has a raw bar and pub-grub menu that includes pizza.

District Kitchen & Bar ★ GASTROPUB   What a refreshing antidote to the largely forlorn Pittsfield dining landscape this is! Edison bulbs in glass pots hang over the central bar, the walls are lined with atmospheric scenes from Old New York, and copper pipes and small spotlights on the ceiling fill out the industrial look. Food is laid out as "Smalls" (soups and salads), "Mids" (sandwiches and tacos), and "Bigs" (duck, fish, steak, pasta). The District Burger, either ground beef or vegetable, can be heaped with as many as twelve toppings, from brie to a fried egg.

40 West St. www.district.kitchen. ✆ **413/442-0303.** Main courses $17–$28. Daily from 4pm.

SOUTH EGREMONT

The Old Mill ★   The first item on the menu is "Soup of Yesterday"— pointing to the fact that soups often deepen in flavor a day after they are made. This is not to suggest that there's anything plodding about this kitchen. Skip on down the card and you'll find items such as skillet shrimp in dry sherry with white beans, and grilled focaccia and panko-crusted sweet-potato-quinoa cake. Rainbow trout, calves liver, and strip steak experience similar flourishes. The venue is an 1832 flour mill with wide-plank floors, dark beams overhead, and iron sconces on the walls. Service is warm, and there's a full bar.

53 Main St. (Rte.2–3). www.oldmillberkshires.com. ✆ **413/528-1421.** Main courses $26–$41. Dinner Tues–Sun 5–9pm; occasional Sunday brunch (call ahead).

STOCKBRIDGE

The famed **Red Lion Inn** ★★ (p. 365) offers three dining options, ranging from the formal dining room to a casual tavern and pub.

Once Upon A Table ★ NEW AMERICAN   Find this cozy place down an alley off Main Street, east of the Red Lion Inn. Depending on the time of day, options might include Prince Edward Island mussels steamed in white wine, grilled salmon burger, and mac and cheese—which is actually penne with panko and bacon. More venturesome tastes might prefer the carrot coconut soup or escargot pot pie. For dessert, perhaps a strawberry shortcake with a Rhode Island–style Johnny Cake on the bottom? In high season, expect a wait.

36 Main St. www.onceuponatablebistro.com. ℂ **413/298-3870.** Reservations recommended in high season. Main courses $15–$29. Mon–Sat 11:35am–3pm and 5–9pm; Sun 11am–6pm (shorter hours in winter).

WILLIAMSTOWN

Food is on the uptick in Williamstown, compared to past years.

Mezze Bistro & Bar ★ BISTRO   The enthusiasm for small plates is addressed in the name and on the menu, with tapas-type starters like Sriracha-fried chickpeas, or roasted mussels with Marcona almonds, chimichurri, and pomegranate seeds. Among the more ambitious main dishes are skate with parsnip puree and duck breast with beluga lentils, bacon, and beets. Tuesday through Thursday the "staff menu" offers twists on bar faves such as duck wings and octopus tacos.

16 Water St. www.mezzerestaurant.com. ℂ **413/458-0123.** Main courses $18–$32. Daily 5–9pm (until 9:30pm Fri–Sat), bar open later as business requires.

Spice Root ★ INDIAN   Catch an irresistible whiff of this Indian eatery and thoughts of anything else vanish. Students like it for the student-only $13 dinner special, and everyone finds the $11 weekday lunch buffet agreeable. The a la carte menu is rewarding, too, with 13 starters, 20 vegetarian or vegan dishes, and 6 tandoor specialties.

23 Spring St. www.spiceroot.com. ℂ **413/458-5200.** Main courses $16–$26. Tues–Sun 11:30am–2:30pm; daily 5–10pm.

The Berkshires Entertainment & Nightlife

Beyond the many summer arts festivals (see box p. 343), Great Barrington is the hub of most nightlife activity in the Berkshires. Its grand old vaudeville theater, opened in 1905, is now the **Mahaiwe Performing Arts Center,** 14 Castle St. (www.mahaiwe.org; ℂ **413/528-0100**). After restoration to some of its century-old glory, it now stages a surprising variety of music, dance, and drama. The **Aston Magna Festival** (www.astonmagna.org; ℂ **800/875-7156** or 413/528-3595) features classical music performed on period instruments. Concerts are held at irregular intervals throughout the year at St. James Church, Main Street and Taconic Avenue. The **Triplex Cinema,** 70 Railroad St. (www.thetriplex.com; ℂ **413/528-8886**), programs independent and foreign films as well as major studio releases.

In Williamstown, the Williams College Department of Music sponsors concerts and recitals. Call its **Concertline** (ℂ **413/597-3146**) for information on upcoming events. In addition, the **Clark Art Institute** (p. 355) hosts frequent classical-music events.

CONNECTICUT

By Kim Knox Beckius

Coast. Cities. Countryside. Casinos. Connecticut's gifts begin with this superfecta of backdrops. Add classic and cutting-edge attractions, and it's easy to build a playlist of adventures, or . . . just hit "shuffle" and explore. So compact, you could drive from corner to corner in about two hours, New England's threshold will introduce you to all of the region's best-loved experiences.

Established in 1636 by disgruntled English settlers who didn't like the way things were going in the Massachusetts Bay Colony, Connecticut occupies the fulcrum position between New York City and Boston. Linger here on your way to more far-flung parts of New England, and you will discover that the state's dualities are a plus, not a minus.

Connecticut's personality derives from the presence of water. In addition to having Long Island Sound along its southern coast, its hills and coastal plain are sliced through by significant rivers and their tributaries: the Housatonic, Naugatuck, Quinnipiac, Connecticut, and Thames. These waterways provided power for 19th-century mills and the towns that grew around them.

While many once-prosperous industrial localities have had to reinvent themselves, Connecticut has preserved scores of classic villages, from the Litchfield Hills to Mystic to the wildly scenic Connecticut River Valley towns in between. These areas are as placid and timeless as they were in the 1700s—while, at the same time, as polished and sophisticated as transplanted urbanites can make them. A salty maritime heritage is palpable in the old boat-building and fishing villages at the mouths of rivers.

Connecticut is New England's front porch. Pull up a chair and stay awhile.

THE GOLD COAST: FAIRFIELD COUNTY

Stamford: 40 miles NE of New York City; Norwalk: 48 miles NE of New York City; Westport: 53 miles NE of New York City; Ridgefield: 57 miles NE of New York City

Mansions, marinas, and luxury apartment blocks nudge up against each other along the deeply indented Long Island Sound shoreline

Connecticut

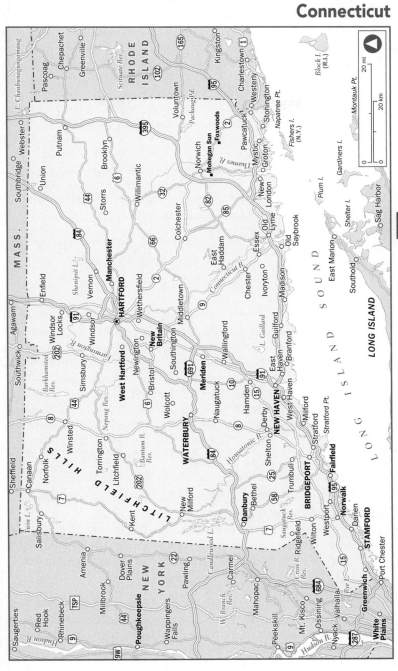

in the southwestern corner of the state. This is one of the most heavily developed and wealthiest stretches of the coast. Fairfield County has long been known as "the Gold Coast," especially to real estate agents. As the land rises slowly inland from the water's edge, woods thicken, roads narrow, and pockets of New England unfold. Yacht country becomes horse country.

The first suburbs formed in the mid-19th century, when train rails started radiating north and east from New York's Grand Central Terminal. This part of the state was made accessible for summertime refugees from the big city, and eventually weekend houses became permanent dwellings. Corporate executives liked life outside the concrete jungle, so after World War II, they moved their companies closer to their new homes. Stamford became a city; Greenwich, New Canaan, Darien, and Westport were the bedroom communities of choice—pricey, exclusive, and redolent of the good life. (Of course, Fairfield County also contains Bridgeport, the state's largest city, which struggles with unemployment and crime.)

For visitors, the fashionable "exurbs" (beyond suburban) and their beaches, paddling outfitters, playhouses, restaurants, and upscale shops are the draw, along with the villages farther north, especially Ridgefield, that hint of Vermont, all within 1½ hours of Times Square.

Essentials

ARRIVING

From New York and points south, take I-95 or, preferably, the more scenic Hutchinson River and Merritt Parkways. From eastern Massachusetts and northern Connecticut, take I-84 west to Danbury, then Route 8 or Route 7 south into Fairfield County.

Metro-North (www.mta.info/mnr; ✆ **877/690-5114**) has many trains daily from New York's Grand Central Terminal, with stops at Greenwich, Stamford, Darien, Norwalk, Westport, and additional stations all the way to New Haven. Express trains make the trip to Greenwich in as little as 40 minutes.

VISITOR INFORMATION

The **Western Connecticut Visitors Bureau** (www.visitfairfieldcountyct.com; ✆ **800/663-1273**) provides information for Fairfield County's destinations.

FESTIVALS & SPECIAL EVENTS

The ticketed **Norwalk Oyster Festival** (www.seaport.org; ✆ **203/838-9444**), held in early September, attracts over 90,000 visitors for its slurping competitions, big-act concerts, boat tours, crafts show, amusement rides, and food.

Exploring Stamford

A trickle of corporations started moving their headquarters from New York, 40 miles northeast, to Stamford in the 1960s. That flow became a stream by the 1980s, and today more than a half-dozen Fortune 1000 companies direct their operations from here. They have erected shiny midrise towers that give the city of 131,000 residents an appearance more like the new urban centers of the Sun Belt than those of the Snow Belt.

One result is a lively downtown that other, less prosperous, Connecticut cities surely envy. It has three movie theaters, tree-lined streets with many shops and a large mall, and a number of stylish restaurants, sidewalk cafes, and clubs patronized by the city's large cohort of young single professionals. For more details on this ever-changing scene, check **www.stamford-downtown.com**.

Stamford Museum & Nature Center ★ NATURE CENTER/MUSEUM This fine, family-oriented resource has a maple sugaring house, a pond that is home to frolicking river otters, an exotic wild animal exhibit (Heckscher WILD!), and a 10-acre working farm with heritage breeds of goats, cattle, pigs, and chickens. May and June mark the arrival of newborn chicks, kids, calves, and piglets. On the grounds are a gift shop, nature trails, a small observatory, and an oddball Tudor-Gothic house, the Bendel Mansion, with galleries of art, natural history, and American culture.

39 Scofieldtown Rd. (at High Ridge Rd, 1 mile N of Merritt Pkwy., exit 35.). www.stamford museum.org. ✆ **203/322-1646.** $10 adults, $8 seniors, $6 students, $5 children 4–17. Bendel Mansion Mon–Sat 9am–5pm, Sun 11am–5pm; Heckscher Farm and Nature's Playground daily 9am–5pm (until 4pm Nov–Mar); Heckscher WILD! Tues–Fri noon–4pm, Sat–Sun plus summer and school vacations 10am–4pm.

STAMFORD SHOPPING

United House Wrecking ★ ANTIQUES/HOME DECOR   The name may not sound promising, but this sprawling emporium of oddities got its start selling architectural remnants salvaged from building demolitions. Still home to vintage decor pieces harvested from old homes, it also showcases imported antiques and new furniture in over 43,000 square feet of space. 535 Hope St. www.unitedhousewrecking.com. ✆ **203/348-5371.** Tues–Sat 10:30am–6:30pm, Sun 10:30am–5pm.

STAMFORD ENTERTAINMENT & NIGHTLIFE

The **Palace Theatre,** 61 Atlantic St. (www.palacestamford.org; ✆ **203/325-4466**), presents a busy line-up of popular music concerts, comedy performances, and children's stage shows; it is also home to the Stamford Symphony.

Exploring Norwalk

In this city known for oystering, the rehabilitation of several blocks of 19th-century row houses transformed the waterfront South Norwalk neighborhood into a trendy precinct that has come to be called "SoNo." Concentrated around Washington, Water, and North and South Main Streets, SoNo is readily accessible from the South Norwalk railroad station. Clustered with shops and more than 30 bars and restaurants—their tables spilling out onto sidewalks when the weather is nice—this feels like a chunk of New York City picked up and moved to a place where the air is fresh and the rents aren't sky high.

Lockwood-Mathews Mansion Museum ★ HISTORIC HOME   Completed in 1868, this granite mansion in the Second Empire style is topped with peaked and mansard slate roofs and has 62 rooms arranged around a stunning,

Excursions by 49-passenger ferry to **Sheffield Island** and its historic 1868 lighthouse are offered by the **Norwalk Seaport Association,** 4 North Water St. dock (www.seaport.org; ☏ **203/838-9444**), departing from near the Maritime Aquarium. Weather permitting, the boat sets out one to three times daily in July and August and on Saturday and Sunday in May, June, and September. Tales of pirates, rum runners, and local history make the 40-minute trip fly by, and passengers debark for about 90 minutes on the island. Fares are $25 for adults, $15 for ages 4 to 12, and $5 for ages 3 and under. Thursday evenings from 6 to 9:30pm in season bring clambakes to the island. Other outings include sunset and acoustic cruises and occasional haunted lighthouse adventures. Purchase tickets online in advance.

sky-lit, octagonal rotunda. Marble, gilt, marquetry, and frescoes were commissioned and incorporated with abandon. Visits are by guided tour.

295 West Ave. www.lockwoodmathewsmansion.com. ☏ **203/838-9799.** $10–$20 adults, $8–$18 seniors, $6–$16 ages 8–18, free for children 7 and under. Wed and Sun, check online for available 45- and 90-min. tour times. From I-95 southbound, take exit 15; from I-95 northbound, take exit 14.

The Maritime Aquarium at Norwalk ★★ AQUARIUM   This facility remains the centerpiece of revitalized SoNo, and cruises aboard its *R/V Spirit of the Sound,* a stealthily quiet catamaran that is the first hybrid-electric-powered research vessel in North America, are its most dynamic offering. The main attractions, though, are the marine and land creatures on view. Crowds gather to watch daily training sessions with six harbor seals that wriggle up on the rocks and even rest their heads in their handler's lap. Additional exhibits include a duo of river otters, an open petting pool swirling with sharks and rays, and tanks alive with jellies and other creatures, including sea turtles and sharks. Although the exhibits mostly focus on the waters of Long Island Sound, some cover Africa and the tropics. A six-story IMAX screen shows nature films.

10 N. Water St. www.maritimeaquarium.org. ☏ **203/852-0700.** $25 adults, $23 seniors, $18 children ages 3–12 (admission includes one IMAX movie). July–Labor Day daily 10am–6pm; Sept–June daily 10am–5pm.

NORWALK SHOPPING

Serious shoppers have several choices, primarily among the boutiques and galleries along Washington and Main streets. **A Taste of Holland,** 83 Washington St. (www.kaasnco.com; ☏ **203/838-6161**), run by Dutch expatriates, features all manner of goods from their homeland, including Delftware, herring, cheese, wooden shoes, candies, and Dutch girl dolls. **Knotted Bone Leatherworks,** 68A Washington St. (www.knottedboneleatherworks.com; ☏ **203/939-9871**), showcases handcrafted medieval-inspired leather and chain-mail accessories. **Beadworks,** 139 Washington St. (www.beadworksnorwalk.com; ☏ **203/852-9194**), sparkles with jewelry-making supplies and offers beginner-friendly classes.

Exploring Westport

After World War II, the housing crunch had young couples scouring the metropolitan area for affordable housing along the three main routes of what is now known as the Metro-North transit system. Some wound up in this pretty village where the Saugatuck River empties into Long Island Sound. Most of the new commuter class found Westport to be too far from Manhattan (it's still more than 1 hr. each way on the train), and it was deemed the archetype of the far-out bedroom communities that were dubbed the exurbs.

Notable for its contingent of people in creative fields, the town also appeals to CEOs and executives, many of whom solved their commuting problem by moving their offices to nearby Stamford. (The food company Newman's Own, founded by the late actor and Westport resident Paul Newman, is based here, too.) The result is a bustling community with surviving elements of its rural New England past wrapped in a sheen of Big Apple panache. Outdoor recreation—from paddle sports and saltwater fishing to languid beach days and nighttime concerts—entice visitors, who are often surprised these pleasures await so close to the nation's largest metropolitan area.

West of the town center, the 74-acre nature center **Earthplace** (10 Woodside Lane; www.earthplace.org; ✆ **203/557-4400**) offers walking trails, a wildlife rehab center, and a hands-on nature museum. The center is open Monday through Saturday from 9am to 5pm, Sunday from 1 to 4pm; the grounds are open daily from dawn to dusk. Admission is $7 adults, $5 for children 2 and up.

Rent a sailboat, kayak, canoe, or SUP or arrange a lesson at **Longshore Sailing School,** 260 Compo Rd. South (www.longshoresailingschool.com; ✆ **203/226-4646**). Rentals are $20 to $52 per hour; small boat private lessons are $90 per hour.

BEACHES

Connecticut's first state park, **Sherwood Island State Park,** Sherwood Island Connector (www.ct.gov/deep/sherwoodisland; ✆ **203/226-6983**) has two long swimming beaches separated by a picnic grove. Surf fishing is a possibility from designated areas, and the park has concession stands, restrooms, and a nature center. The park is open daily year-round from 8am to sunset. Leashed pets are allowed October through mid-April. Admission for out-of-state cars from Memorial Day to September is $15 Monday through Friday; $22 Saturday, Sunday, and holidays; $7 after 4pm any day. **Compo Beach,** 60 Compo Beach Rd., is a long municipal strand not far from downtown; the in-season parking fee here is a whopping $40 weekdays, $65 weekends, so you may consider parking elsewhere and using a taxi or ride-hailing service to get to the beach.

Exploring Ridgefield

No town in Connecticut has a grander, more imposing Main Street. Ridgefield's, laid out in 1721 at 132 feet wide, is lined with ancient elms, maples, and oaks, and bordered by massive 19th-century houses, most of them in Classical Revival and late Victorian styles. Impressive at any time of the year,

One of the oldest theaters on the straw-hat circuit, the **Westport Country Playhouse,** 25 Powers Court (www.westportplayhouse.org; ☎ **203/227-4177**), had its first performance in 1931. The centuries-old red barn and its theatrical goings-on got a 21st-century shot in the arm when actress Joanne Woodward took the helm as Artistic Director. Now under the direction of acclaimed stage director Mark Lamos, the theater produces a full schedule of comedies, dramas, and musicals from late May through late December. Tickets are priced from about $24 bm to $50.

the thoroughfare is in its glory during the brief blaze of the October foliage season and twinkling with white lights during holiday shopping evenings. Only a little over an hour from New York City (57 miles northeast), the town (pop. 25,000) is nonetheless a true evocation of the New England character. The bustling shopping district has few franchise outlets.

Aldrich Contemporary Art Museum ★★★ MUSEUM   Larry Aldrich was a fashion designer who used his superb collection of late-20th-century paintings and sculptures to establish this museum. The original 18th-century clapboard structure in which he housed his increasingly contemporary collection soon doubled in size. But before Aldrich died in 2001, the museum turned in another direction. The collection was sold off, and the museum was closed while a new building was fashioned—an angular, natural-light-flooded new structure, opened in 2004. Its spacious galleries on two floors and 2-acre Sculpture Garden are devoted to revolving exhibitions of work by emerging and mid-career contemporary artists.

258 Main St. www.aldrichart.org. ☎ **203/438-4519.** $10 adults, $5 seniors and students 13 and up, free for K–12 teachers and children 12 and under; 3rd Sat of month free to all. Sun–Mon and Wed–Fri noon–5pm; Sat 10am–5pm.

Keeler Tavern ★ HISTORIC SITE   This circa 1713 stagecoach inn was providing sustenance to travelers between Boston and New York long before the Revolutionary War, but that conflict left a lasting mark. A British cannonball has been embedded in one of its walls since the Battle of Ridgefield in 1777. The tavern is now a museum of Colonial life, with period furnishings and costumed guides. And it has another claim to fame: It was long the summer home of architect Cass Gilbert (1859–1934), who designed the Supreme Court Building in Washington, D.C., and the support towers for the George Washington Bridge in New York. Visits are by guided tour.

132 Main St. www.keelertavernmuseum.org. ☎ **203/438-5485.** $8 adults, $5 seniors, students, and children under 18. Wed and Sat–Sun 1–4pm. Closed Jan.

Where to Stay in Fairfield County

The Gold Coast has a reputation for being pricey, but stick close to the I-95 corridor, and there are ample chain hotels offering rooms in the $100 to $150 per night range.

NORWALK

EVEN Hotel Norwalk ★★   The prototype EVEN Hotel is, by design, healthy for you, your budget, and the environment. Overnight rates here typically trounce local competitors, and *you* can stay strong and well for whatever vacay days throw your way by using in-room workout gear including resistance bands and a stability ball. Bed linens are all-natural eucalyptus fiber, toiletries are botanical, and cocktails are mixed with organic spirits. Plus, this is the rare hotel where the walls talk. Don't worry: Affirmations like "Dream Big" are meant to soothe and encourage, not give away secrets.

426 Main Ave./Rte. 7. www.ihg.com/evenhotels. © **203/846-9355.** 129 units. $105–$232 double. Free parking. Pets accepted. **Amenities:** Fitness center; local shuttle; Wi-Fi (free).

RIDGEFIELD

West Lane Inn ★★   An inn that fits most images of a romantic country getaway, this one also works for businesspeople, offering some rooms with kitchenettes that are ideal for longer stays. Some rooms have fireplaces; most have four-poster beds. The 1849 house stands on a property blessed with giant shade trees. Take breakfast on the porch in good weather; the continental version is included, but hot a la carte dishes are extra. The inn is smoke-free.

22 West Lane (off Rte. 35). www.westlaneinn.com. © **203/438-7323.** 18 units. $210–$255 double. Rates include breakfast. Free parking. **Amenities:** In-room refrigerators; Wi-Fi (free).

WESTPORT

The Westport Inn ★   This 1960-motel-turned-boutique hotel feels fresh and refined. Property highlights include an indoor pool and a lobby warmed by a fire when days turn brisk. **Bistro | B** (© **203/557-8145**), the in-house restaurant, presents local-harvest-inspired, French-American fare. It's open for breakfast daily and for dinner Monday through Saturday and brunch on Sunday. The inn is 3 miles east of Main Street and the Saugatuck River, on Route 1.

1595 Post Rd. E. (Rte. 1). www.westportinn.com. © **203/557-8124.** 117 units. $94–$359 double. **Amenities:** Restaurant; bar; exercise room; heated indoor pool; Wi-Fi (free).

Where to Eat in Fairfield County

NORWALK

Barcelona Waypointe ★ MEDITERRANEAN   Tapas are the attraction here, one of five such outposts in western Connecticut. The kitchen looks all over the Mediterranean and down to South America for inspiration. Two or three tapas per person make a meal, and sharing is inevitable. Start with *charcutería,* either an assortment of Spanish cheeses or of cured meats and sausages. The day's additional delectables might be *chorizo* with sweet and sour figs, garlic shrimp, or sea-salted *shishito* peppers. Paella and *parrillada* (mixed grill) "for the table" are main course options. An enclosed patio is open year-round.

515 West Ave. www.barcelonawinebar.com. © **203/854-5600.** Tapas $4.50–$15; main courses $15–$27. Daily 4pm–1am (Fri–Sat until 2am), Sat–Sun brunch 11:30am–4pm.

Kazu ★ JAPANESE   Each sushi plate is more artful than the last at this endur-ing destination for truly fresh fish and rolls both traditional and inventive. In the latter category are jalapeño and spicy tuna with Sriracha sauce and a lobster tail tempura roll. Bountiful bento boxes are a favorite. Build yours with a choice of two entrees, such as spicy beef and grilled salmon, and the chef will accessorize with two appetizers in addition to the included soup, salad, and California roll.

64 North Main St. (near West Ave.). www.kazusono.com. ✆ **203/866-7492.** Main courses $17–$25. Mon–Fri 11:30am–2:30pm and 5–10pm (Fri until 11pm); Sat 5–11pm; Sun 4:30–9:30pm.

Match ★★ NEW AMERICAN   SoNo's original hot spot still strikes all the right notes. Don't expect elegance: Walls are bare brick, the ceiling is exposed wood joists, and industrial lamps provide lighting. There is the expected craft cocktail menu, which morphs with the seasons. Five different kinds of designer pizza emerge from the wood-fired oven. As much eating as drinking goes on at the steel-topped main bar, with happy diners making the most of such *mmm*-inducing edibles as truffled fried local oysters, and "8-hour" veal osso bucco.

98 Washington St. (btw. Broad and Main sts.). www.matchsono.com. ✆ **203/852-1088.** Main courses $10–$38. Daily 5pm–11am (Fri–Sat until 2am).

RIDGEFIELD

Fans of classy low-brow eats will want to make a stop at **Chez Lenard ★** (www.chezlenard.com; ✆ **203/431-1313**), on the sidewalk toward the north end of the shopping district, opposite Ballard Park. It's an open-air hot-dog cart with foot-longs that come with such trappings as peppers and onions ("Le Hot Dog Excelsior") and cheese fondue ("Le Hot Dog Garniture Suisse"). The boss gallantly stays open right through winter.

Bernard's ★★ FRENCH   A piano in the dining parlor is played Friday and Saturday nights and for the festive Sunday brunch, and there's live music upstairs in Sarah's Wine Bar Wednesday through Saturday, but it's the kitchen that really hits a high note. Main courses, which transform with the seasons, are about 50/50 land- and ocean-based proteins, and a creative vegetarian option, such as pumpkin, leek, and wild mushroom ravioli, muddies the decision-making for carnivores. Then again, house-cured bacon selections and a weekly wild game special aren't everyday temptations. Equally alluring lunch entrees run nearly half the price, but the romantic music and lighting are reserved for evenings. Men might want to wear a jacket.

20 West Lane (near jct. of Rte. 7). www.bernardsridgefield.com. ✆ **203/438-8282.** Main courses $26–$45. Wed–Sat noon–2:30pm and 5–9pm (Fri–Sat until 10pm); Sun noon–2:30pm and 5–8pm.

STAMFORD

Coromandel ★ INDIAN   This restaurant is part of a chainlet of Indian winners striving to make diners aware that Indian eateries don't have to be feebly decorated dives with sullen waiters. Here are white tablecloths, lustrous woods, and bold art as setting for food that tantalizes all the senses before a

CONNECTICUT   The Gold Coast: Fairfield County

fork even touches it. Standouts are *dahi dhani jhinga* (jumbo shrimp cooked with yogurt and coriander) and *mamsam koora* (lamb in a chili-fired gravy), and just about anything from the tandoor oven. Brunch/lunch buffets are a good deal ($12.71 weekdays, $18.03 weekends).

68 Broad St. (at Summer St.). www.coromandelcuisine.com. © **203/964-1010.** Main courses $15–$26. Mon–Fri noon–2:30pm and 5–10pm (until 10:30pm Fri); Sat noon–3pm and 5–10:30pm; Sun noon–3pm and 5–10pm.

Layla's Falafel ★ MIDDLE EASTERN   This looks like just another strip-mall-ethnic joint, and the handful of tables and bad paintings of Arabian street scenes do little to alter the original impression. But the welcome is cordial, especially for the regulars who pile in after work for takeout. Choose from an enticing menu of bountiful one-plate meals such as the Arabic lamb *shawarma,* the central ingredient rolled in flatbread and briefly grilled, then joined with a tossed green salad and a thick puddle of perfect hummus.

936 High Ridge Rd. (Rte. 137). www.laylasfalafel.com. © **203/461-8004.** Most items under $10. Daily 11am–9pm.

WESTPORT

Black Duck Café ★ BAR FOOD   A floating barge on the Saugatuck River is Westport's quirkiest place to grab a beer and a bite. You can't beat the view, especially when sunset paints the water hot pink. Named for owner and champion powerboat racer Peter Aitkin's speedboat, this Duck is a place to slow down and savor a cheese-stuffed burger, lobster Reuben, or whole belly clam po'boy.

605 Riverside Ave. www.blackduckwestport.com. © **203/227-7978.** Main courses $12–$32. Daily 11:30am–1am (Fri–Sat until 2am, Sun until 11pm)

Tavern on Main ★ BISTRO   Hobnob with Westporters at this multi-experience landmark in the town's Historic District. Local merchants, women who lunch, and busy executives all crowd the clubby bar, the outdoor patio, and the more formal dining room. The main room has fragments of the building's earliest 19th-century years—hand-hewn beams and three brick fireplaces. While menu items are neither over-the-top nor overly daring, the kitchen does toy with convention. For example, the trademark lobster roll consists of hot (not chilled) chunks of the crustacean bathed in white wine, butter, and garlic. Similar twists are taken with Cape Cod mussels in a distinctive sherry broth seasoned up with herbs, garlic, and smoky paprika and with seared branzino with butternut squash green pea risotto.

150 Main St. www.tavernonmain.com. © **203/221-7222.** Main courses $16–$30. Daily 11:30am–9pm (Fri–Sat until 10pm).

Terrain Garden Café ★★ NEW AMERICAN   A gourmet dining experience inside a garden shop? Granted, Terrain is more Eden than your typical outdoor retailer, but it's still surprising to find a conservatory-like indoor-outdoor restaurant hidden inside. Every dish here is crafted with locally grown, raised, caught, and produced ingredients, from heirloom carrots to Mystic oysters; every dish is as colorfully fresh as the lush surroundings.

From the moment a warm loaf of bread baked in a clay flower pot is planted on your table, you're in for a sensory feast.

561 Post Rd. E. www.shopterrain.com/westport-restaurant. © **203/226-2732.** Main courses $22–$32. Brunch daily 10am–3pm; dinner Wed–Sun 5–9:30pm.

THE LITCHFIELD HILLS ★★

Woodbury: 89 miles NE of New York City, 142 miles SW of Boston. Litchfield: 106 miles NE of New York City, 135 miles SW of Boston.

When the Hamptons got too pricey, too visible, and too chichi back in the 1980s, financiers, CEOs, and celebs discovered the Litchfield Hills, arguably the most fetchingly rustic yet uber-sophisticated part of Connecticut.

The topography and, to an extent, the microculture of the region are defined by the river that runs through it, the Housatonic. Broad but not deep enough for vessels larger than canoes, it waters farms and forests along its course, provides opportunities for recreational angling and paddling trips, and, over the millennia, helped to shape these foothills, which merge in the north with the Massachusetts Berkshires.

Firehouses hold pancake-breakfast fundraisers; neighbors rally to each other's aid; Appalachian Trail hikers wander through. That's one side of these bucolic hills, less than 2 hours from Manhattan. Increasingly, the other side is fashioned by refugees from Brooklyn. These seekers of tranquility and relatively affordable real estate are buying up pre-Revolutionary saltboxes and Georgian Colonials on Litchfield County's warren of back roads and bringing urban expectations with them. Agriculture thrives in new forms: This is a land of gourmet dairies, farmstead breweries, estate wineries, and the state's best farm-to-table restaurants. Online businesses hum along in antique homes, barns, even a caboose. And, yes, it's increasingly easy to find fancy coffee.

Consider the Litchfield Hills the best of two worlds: a place—in every season—to stretch your legs and still exercise your mind.

Essentials

ARRIVING

From New York City, follow the Hutchinson River Parkway to I-684 north to I-84 east, taking exit 7 onto Route 7 north. Continue on Route 7 for New Milford, Kent, West Cornwall, and Canaan. For Washington Depot, New Preston, and Litchfield, branch off at New Milford onto Route 202.

From Boston, take the Massachusetts Turnpike west to I-84. From I-84, just past Hartford, branch off onto Route 4 (for Litchfield) or Route 6 (for Woodbury).

VISITOR INFORMATION

The useful 112-page *Unwind* getaway planner and map is produced by the **Western Connecticut Visitors Bureau** (www.litchfieldhills.com; © **860/567-4506**).

Exploring Woodbury ★

The chief distinction of this attractive town west of Waterbury is its over 35 high-end antiques stores. On sunny weekends, Route 6 is clogged with cars

full of antiquers trolling for treasures. Yet Woodbury has other charms to recommend it: Significant Colonial history, a pair of pleasant town greens, and—surprising in this neck of the woods—paved walking trails along the main drag, Route 6, which offer locals and visitors an opportunity to stretch their legs while taking in white-steepled churches and other New England-y vistas.

Flanders Nature Center ★   At this 1,400-acre nature center, yearly events include maple syrup and wreath-making, and each spring, a Botany Trail planted with 100 species of wildflowers and plants bursts into bloom. Maps of hiking trails are available online.

Church Hill and Flanders Rd. www.flandersnaturecenter.org. ⓒ **203/263-3711.** Free admission. Welcome Center Mon–Fri 9am–5pm; trails daily dawn to sundown.

Glebe House Museum & Gertrude Jekyll Garden ★   This circa 1740 house, on a street of fine 18th-century houses, has the distinction of being the Episcopal Church's birthplace in America. Inside are furnishings

ON THE WOODBURY antiques TRAIL

Pick up the **Woodbury Antiques Dealers Association** directory (www.antiques woodbury.com) at one of the member stores. Start off at **Monique Shay Antiques**, 920 Main St. South (www. moniqueshay.com; ✆ **203/263-3186**), and explore six rustic barns full of vintage French Canadian furnishings. **Abrash Galleries Rugs and Antiquities**, 40 Main St. North (✆ **203/263-7847**) is Connecticut's finest destination for Persian, Indian, Chinese, and Turkish carpets—antique and new. At **Martell & Suffin Antiques** (www.martellandsuffinan tiques.1stdibs.com; ✆ **203/263-1913**), the owners favor 18th- and

early-19th-century European furniture as well as Asian works of art. Of similar high order is the stock of **Country Loft Antiques,** 557 Main St. South (www. countryloftwoodbury.com, ✆ **203/266-4500**), largely 19th-century French furnishings and *objets* displayed in a fine old barn. New is a five-room B&B decorated with these same French country heirlooms.

The **Woodbury Antiques & Flea Market,** 44 Sherman Hill Rd. (www.woodbury flea.net; ✆ **203/263-6217**), brings extra treasure-hunting traffic to town on Saturdays and Sundays from 7:30am to 2:30pm, March through early December.

true to the period; outside is the only surviving U.S. example of a Gertrude Jekyll–designed garden.

49 Hollow Rd. www.glebehousemuseum.org. ✆ **203/263-2855.** Admission $7 adults, $2 children ages 6–12, $2 garden only. May–Oct Wed–Sun 1–4pm.

Exploring Washington ★★

Settled in 1734 and renamed in 1779 to honor the first American president, Washington occupies the crown of a hill beside Route 47. Its village green, with the impressive 1802 Congregational Meeting House surrounded by white buildings and sheltered by shade trees, is an example of a municipal arrangement found all over New England—but rarely to such perfection.

Adjacent Washington Depot, down the hill beside the Shepaug River, serves as the commercial center, with banks and a cluster of shops. Stop in at the **Hickory Stick Bookshop,** 2 Greenhill Rd. (www.hickorystickbookshop.com; ✆ **860/868-0525**), fiercely independent for more than 60 years, and you might stumble upon an author signing books.

Nearby **Steep Rock Preserve** (www.steeprockassoc.org; ✆ **860/868-9131**) is a wildlife and nature reservation of 998 acres, a lovely spot for hiking, fly-fishing, or cross-country skiing. (Dogs are welcome but must be leashed.)

A few minutes' drive from the green, in a part of Washington known as New Preston, beautiful Lake Waramaug is mostly monopolized by private homes. But **Lake Waramaug State Park ★**, 30 Lake Waramaug Rd. (www. ct.gov/deep/lakewaramaug; ✆ **860/868-2592**), at the northwest tip of the chair-shaped lake, gives the public access to Waramaug's charms. In warmer months, canoes and kayaks are for rent, and there's a swimming beach as well as picnic tables, plus 76 camping sites and rustic cabins.

Institute for American Indian Studies ★   This rather hidden museum owns more than 300,000 Native American artifacts: one of the largest collections in New England. Tour a recreated, 17-century, pre-contact-with-Europeans Algonkian village, stroll through the healing plants garden, and see if you could survive in 1518 by participating in an escape room–style challenge.

38 Curtis Rd. (off Rte. 199). www.iaismuseum.org. ℂ **860/868-0518.** $10 adults, $8 seniors, $6 children ages 3–12. Wed–Sat 10am–5pm; Sun noon–5pm.

Exploring Litchfield ★★

Possessed of a stately treed green reconfigured around the turn of the 20th century by the Frederick Law Olmsted landscaping firm (Olmsted designed New York's Central Park), Litchfield reflects the taste and affluence of Yankee entrepreneurs who built it up in the late 18th and early 19th centuries from a Colonial farm community to an industrial center. Factories and mills were dismantled around the 19th century's end, and those who'd profited settled back to enjoy their uncommonly large homes.

The town is now the domain of fashionable New Yorkers, who find it less frenetic than the Hamptons. Their influence is seen in the quality of store merchandise and restaurant fare, as well as in the lofty prices houses command.

Litchfield's houses and tree-lined streets reward leisurely strollers. From the stores and restaurants along West Street, walk east, and then turn right on South Street. On the opposite corner is the **Litchfield History Museum,** at South and East streets (www.litchfieldhistoricalsociety.org; ℂ **860/567-4501**), containing an eclectic array of local artifacts, including the world's largest collection of works by 18th-century portraitist Ralph Earl. It's open free from mid-April through November, Tuesday through Saturday from 11am to 5pm and Sunday from 1 to 5pm.

Walking down South Street, on the right, is the **Tapping Reeve House and Law School** (www.litchfieldhistoricalsociety.org; ℂ **860/567-4501**). The house was built in 1773, while the adjacent 1784 building was the first law school in America. It counted among its students Aaron Burr and Noah Webster. Hours are the same as the Litchfield History Museum (see above), and admission is also free. An introductory video and opportunities to don period garb and roleplay breathe life into this institution that shaped early America's decision-makers.

When you begin to see more modern houses, walk back to the green and cross over to the north side. You can't miss the magisterial **First Congregational Church,** built in 1828: It's one of New England's most photographed churches. A voluminous used bookstore in the basement, open weekends, raises money for charity.

The **White Memorial Conservation Center,** 80 Whitehall Rd. (Route 202; www.whitememorialcc.org; ℂ **860/567-0857**), a 4,000-acre environmental education center and recreational facility, has 40 miles of trails for hiking, cross-country skiing, and horseback riding. On the grounds is a museum of natural history, open year-round, Monday through Saturday from 9am to 5pm

It opened in 1927, with a Wurlitzer organ to accompany silent films; since the 1960s, it's been focused on foreign and independent films (on two screens since 1997). **Bantam Cinema ★★**, off Route 202 just southwest of Litchfield center, has found its niche, screening thought-provoking films for a discriminating audience. It's sort of a chicken-and-the-egg question: Does Bantam Cinema thrive because NYC/Boston escapees and local artists want to see intriguing mainstream and indie films, or does the presence of Bantam Cinema educate a home-grown film audience? Either way, this is a unique movie-going experience in a savvy setting where everyone pays attention and everyone gets the jokes. Go to www.bantamcinema.com to find out what's playing this week.

and Sunday from noon to 5pm. Admission is $6 for adults, $3 for children 6 to 12.

Haight-Brown Vineyard ★ WINERY This winery, established in the 1970s, has grown and prospered, and presently offers 10 drinkable bottlings including summery Strawberry Bliss. Its tasting room is open year-round—sample portfolio wines for $12, or add on reserve wines for $15. Haight-Brown is part of the 26-vineyard **Connecticut Wine Trail**. A map is online at **www.ctwine.com**.

29 Chestnut Hill Rd. (at the corner of Rte. 118). www.haightvineyards.com. ℂ **860/567-4045.** Fri and Sun noon–6pm; Sat noon–6:30pm.

OUTDOOR ACTIVITIES

This is horse country, so consider a canter across the meadows and along the wooded trails of **Topsmead State Forest,** Buell Road (www.ct.gov/deep/topsmead; ℂ **860/567-5694**). The park's Tudor-style mansion can be toured the second and fourth weekends from June through October. The grounds are open from 8am to sunset. Horses can be hired nearby at **Lee's Riding Stable,** 57 East Litchfield Rd., off Route 118 (www.windfieldmorganfarm.com/lees.html; ℂ **860/567-0785**). Group trail rides cost $50 per hour; private half-hour lessons are available for $50.

Where to Stay in the Litchfield Hills

LITCHFIELD

The Litchfield Inn ★ Yes, it's white clapboard with black shutters like everything else in Litchfield, but this is not a historic inn. If you like your floorboards even and your bathrooms up-to-date, however, it's a good option, only a 2-minute drive west of Litchfield town center, set back among woods at the head of a manicured lawn. Standard rooms are pleasantly decorated in a generic blue-and-tan color scheme, with two queen beds and a bit more room than you'd get in a chain hotel (king-bed rooms also have a pullout couch and can sleep four). The hotel also has 12 king-bed theme rooms, each with its own striking look; these have gas fireplaces, and some have Jacuzzis.

While the themed decor is bold, they're not corny or kitschy, and the rooms are spacious enough to carry it off, with plenty of fun details. (Check photos on the website, though they don't do the rooms justice). The in-house restaurant, **Tavern Off the Green**, is open for dinner Wednesdays through Sundays, serving upscale New American food.

432 Bantam Rd., Litchfield. www.litchfieldinnct.com. ℭ **860/567-4503.** 32 units. $159–$179 double. Rates include breakfast. **Amenities:** Restaurant; fitness room; mini-fridges; microwaves; Wi-Fi (free).

WARREN

Hopkins Inn ★   A family named Hopkins started farming this land in 1787, long before summer visitors began to plant handsome second homes around the shores of the adjacent lake. In 1847, they opened this white Italianate Victorian as a hilltop country inn with sweeping views of Lake Waramaug. (Other Hopkins descendants turned the neighboring farm into a vineyard and winery in 1979—see www.hopkinsvineyard.com.) Guest rooms are light and airy, though on the small side, decorated in country antiques and flowered wallpapers; two rooms share bathrooms. The restaurant serves an old-school menu of dishes from the Swiss and Austrian Alps, such as wiener schnitzel and veal piccata (main courses $23–$31). Warren is a 15-minute drive north from Washington Depot or a 20-minute drive west from Litchfield.

22 Hopkins Rd., Warren. www.thehopkinsinn.com. ℭ **860/868-7295.** 14 units, some with shared bath. $125–$160 double, $160–$250 apartments. Rates include breakfast (except Mon). 2-night minimum weekend May–Nov. No smoking. Restaurant closed Jan–Mar. **Amenities:** Restaurant, bar; lake beach; Wi-Fi (free).

WASHINGTON

Grace Mayflower Inn & Spa ★★★   Galaxies of stars have been scattered over this, one of the state's courtliest manor inns, but be warned: The prices are also out of this world. The spa—open only to overnight guests—is as posh, professional, and progressive as you'll find in Connecticut, with body therapies matched to your composition and outdoorsy experiences like forest bathing. The main building's porches look out across manicured lawns and gardens to 58 acres of deep woods. Most rooms have fireplaces, the bathrooms are done with brass fittings and mahogany wainscoting—all is as close to perfection as such an enterprise is likely to be. The accomplished restaurant features top-drawer ingredients drawn from local farms and Atlantic fisheries.

118 Woodbury Rd. (Rte. 47), Washington. www.gracehotels.com/mayflower. ℭ **860/868-9466.** 30 units. $740–$1,790 double. Take Rte. 202 north 2 miles past New Preston, turn south on Rte. 47 through Washington Depot and up the hill past Washington Common. Entrance is on the left. **Amenities:** Restaurant; tap room; concierge; extensive spa and health club; heated outdoor pool; room service; tennis court; putting green; Wi-Fi (free).

WOODBURY

Curtis House Inn ★   An inn since 1754, this white clapboard landmark claims to be Connecticut's oldest lodging property. Never mind that it made an appearance on Gordon Ramsay's *Hotel Hell* and is rumored to host a ghost.

Any building with colonial bones exudes charm, and the clean, simple rooms are priced at a steal. The on-site restaurant and pub is a plus: Specials like $18 three-course pasta dinners on Thursdays are popular with locals.

506 Main Street South (Rte. 6), Woodbury. www.curtishouseinn.com. © **203/263-2101.** 17 units. $70–$135 double. **Amenities:** Restaurant; bar; Wi-Fi (free).

Where to Eat in the Litchfield Hills

BETHLEHEM

Oliva on Main ★ MEDITERRANEAN In a simple yellow farmhouse across from the town green in the low-key farming town of Bethlehem, chef Riad Aamar turns out deeply flavorful Mediterranean food, from rustic wood-fired pizzas to roasted lamb shank with mushrooms, prunes, and chickpeas or sautéed cod with leeks, capers, cilantro, and tomatoes. His previous New Preston location built a fan base of savvy weekenders; they've followed him here, so make reservations in advance.

15 Main St. S (Route 61), Bethlehem. www.olivacafe.com. © **203/266-5558.** Main courses $16–$30. Wed–Sun 5:30pm–closing.

LITCHFIELD

@the Corner ★★ BISTRO/AMERICAN Striking a perfect balance between casual and sophisticated, this friendly brick-walled spot across from Litchfield's town green ticks all the boxes: "handhelds" (hearty sandwiches, tacos, and burgers), "greens" (salads), and "bowls" (rice or noodle, loaded with veggies), with a few more hearty entrees added at dinnertime. Local and seasonal ingredients come to the fore in dishes like the artisanal beet salad with farro, mesclun greens, sliced apples, and crumbled goat cheese; or the ancient grains bowl with grilled asparagus, roasted eggplant, and squash. Soups are so soothing, you'll wish you'd gone for the bowl instead of just a cup. There's a cozy sidebar cafe with espressos and lattes; the bar serves an impressive list of regional craft beers and stylish cocktails.

3 West St., Litchfield. www.athecorner.com. © **860/567-8882.** Main courses $12–$27. Daily 8am–midnight.

Patty's ★ BREAKFAST/LUNCH Breakfast lovers, Patty's has your back. It's *the* local place for apple and sausage omelets, walnut pancakes, and shaved steak wraps. It's the kind of country cafe seen in scores of other towns—a counter with stools, tables with chairs of a sort first seen sometime around Truman's election. Posh, it isn't, but don't let that stop you. Here's food with flavors and earthy panache rarely encountered in such settings, served up with a sense of humor. Expect to share the room with farmers, merchants, work-men, and weekenders, but few outsiders. Breakfast and lunch only.

499 Bantam Rd. (Rte. 202). www.pattyslitchfield.com. © **860/567-3335.** Most items under $10. No credit cards. Mon–Sat 6am–2pm; Sun 7am–noon.

West Street Grill ★ NEW AMERICAN When this contemporary bistro opened more than 25 years ago, local and big-city reviewers were enthralled. Known as an incubator for some of Connecticut's best chefs, several of whom went off to open their own places, it hasn't always merited the raves. But despite frequent changes and tinkering, the restaurant's fortunes have more often waxed than waned. Recently, entrees have run the European gamut, and you can never go wrong with the lunch favorite fish and chips made with Atlantic-caught cod.

43 West Street (on the Green). www.weststreetgrill.com. ② **860/567-3885.** Reservations recommended for dinner, essential on Fri–Sat. Main courses $24–$36. Wed–Sun 11:30am–2:30pm and 5:30–9pm (lunch until 3pm and dinner until 10pm Sat–Sun).

WASHINGTON DEPOT

For a casual meal, assemble a picnic from the delectable array of soups, quiches, sandwiches, and salads at **The Pantry,** 5 Titus Rd., Washington Depot (② **860/868-0258**). Or, eat there at one of the dozen tables.

G.W. Tavern ★ CONTEMPORARY AMERICAN   The tavern's atmospheric bar has booths and a fireplace, while the simulated attached barn is airier, with a deck that looks down on the Shepaug River. The kitchen concerns itself with interpretations of such robust Americana as crab cakes, meatloaf, chicken potpie, and Buffalo wings. Daily specials nearly outnumber the items on the regular menu (lighter fare is served 2:30–5:30pm).

20 Bee Brook Rd. (Rte. 47). www.gwtavern.com. ② **860/868-6633.** Main courses $13–$36. Mon–Tues and Thurs–Fri 11:30am–9pm; Sat 11:30am–2:30pm and 5:30–10pm; Sun 11:30am–3pm and 5–9pm.

WOODBURY

Charcoal Chef ★ DINER   In pre-Interstate 1956, when Route 6 was still the main highway through this part of Connecticut, Charcoal Chef opened as a roadside stop for truckers and travelers, offering charcoal-grilled burgers, steaks, and seafood. Blessedly, very little has changed since then. Still owned by the same family (the Sandersons), Charcoal Chef offers all the aforesaid comfort food classics, plus grilled cheese sandwiches, fried chicken, franks 'n' beans, and pie a la mode. The dining room is a perfect time capsule of 1960s "Early American" decor. Service is friendly and quick; local folks are regulars here. Portions aren't huge, but they don't have to be at these prices (where else are you going to find a $6 BLT?). One last 1950s grace note: They make one mean martini.

670 Main St. N (Rte. 6), Woodbury. www.thecharcoalchef.com. ② **203/263-2538.** Main courses $6–$24. Mon–Sat 8am–closing, Sun noon–8pm.

Good News Restaurant & Bar ★★ NEW AMERICAN   This enduring Connecticut favorite has cheery staff and rooms doused in ripe primary colors. The food? Europe meets Asia, touching down in parts of the Americas. The results are spirited, but never bizarre. Examples: antelope burger with melty Manchego cheese and horseradish mayo; or pasta and asparagus with capers, sage, gorgonzola, spiced pecans, and balsamic drizzle. Ingredients, whenever possible, are purchased from local farms. Desserts tend to be gooey and caloric—pair your choice with a boozy milkshake composed of Litchfield

Along gloriously scenic Route 7, heading up through western Connecticut to the Berkshires (see p. 340), you'll find no end of red barns, covered bridges, tree-tufted hills, and other New England-y vistas. The Berkshire foothills town of **Kent ★★** is an essential stop-off, half an hour's drive west of Litchfield or just 8 miles from the Tenmile River train station across the New York border in Amenia. Though it's only a few blocks long, Kent's eminently strollable Main Street offers an unexpected mix of antiques stores, art galleries, and restaurants to woo parents of three nearby private schools, plus coin-operated showers for Appalachian Trail hikers.

You can eat high-end or casual at **Ore Hill & Swyft** (3 Maple St.; www.orehill andswyft.com), grab diner fare at the **Villager** (28 N. Main St.; www.villagerkent. com), or go old-school at the venerable **Fife 'n Drum** (53 N. Main St.; www.fifen drum.com). In October, the Gilmore Girls Fan Fest embraces Kent as Connecticut's closest incarnation of the TV show's fictional town of Stars Hollow.

Not up to tackling the entire Appalachian Trail? A 5-mile **River Walk** segment of the Trail along the Housatonic River from Kent to Cornwall, CT, is a worthy day trek (see www.berkshirehiking.com for details), or you can head to the 263-acre, trail-laced **East Kent Hamlet Nature Preserve**, an abandoned Girl Scout camp (39 Kent Hollow Rd.; www. kentlandtrust.org). Five miles north of town on Route 7, **Kent Falls State Park** (non-resident parking fee $15 on weekends and holidays Memorial Day weekend through October) is an ideal picnic spot with a 250-foot waterfall providing the background music.

Distillery bourbon and ice cream from Litchfield's Arethusa Farm. There's outdoor dining in summer.

694 Main Street South (Rte. 6). www.goodnewsrestaurantandbar.com. © **203/266-4663.** Main courses $18–$32. Mon and Wed–Sat 11:30am–10pm; Sun noon–10pm.

NEW HAVEN

80 miles NE of New York City

With an impressive line-up of free cultural attractions and more than 120 restaurants within walking distance of its 16-acre green, this Sound-side city is as Manhattan-y as Connecticut gets. This is not to paper over the reality that more than a quarter of its citizens live at or below the poverty line, with the attendant urban afflictions that suggests. But this hub of education and innovation has much to offer leisure travelers: music venues, theaters, outstanding museums, college football rivalries that date back over 140 years, and a growing number of destination restaurants.

Much of what is worthwhile about New Haven can be credited to the presence of one of the world's most prestigious schools. Yale University both enriches its community and exacerbates the usual town-gown conflicts—a paradox with which the institution and civic authorities have struggled since the Colonial period.

Relatively little serious history has happened here, but there are a number of "firsts" that boosters love to trumpet. Noah Webster compiled his first

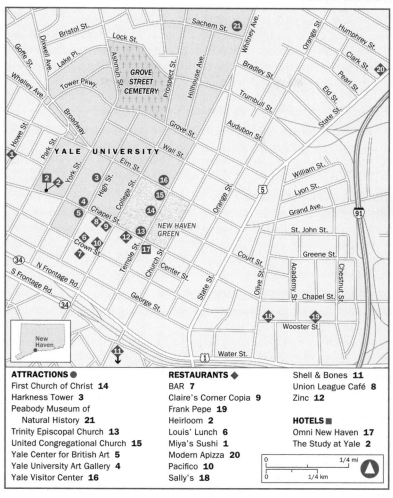

ATTRACTIONS ●

First Church of Christ **14**
Harkness Tower **3**
Peabody Museum of
   Natural History **21**
Trinity Episcopal Church **13**
United Congregational Church **15**
Yale Center for British Art **5**
Yale University Art Gallery **4**
Yale Visitor Center **16**

RESTAURANTS ◆

BAR **7**
Claire's Corner Copia **9**
Frank Pepe **19**
Heirloom **2**
Louis' Lunch **6**
Miya's Sushi **1**
Modern Apizza **20**
Pacifico **10**
Sally's **18**

Shell & Bones **11**
Union League Café **8**
Zinc **12**

HOTELS ■

Omni New Haven **17**
The Study at Yale **2**

dictionary here, Eli Whitney perfected his cotton gin, and a local man named Colt invented an automatic revolver in 1836. The first telephone switchboard was made here, and so were the first lollipops. And, the first hamburger was allegedly cooked and sold here, as was—even less certainly—the first pizza.

Essentials

ARRIVING

BY CAR   I-95 between New York and Boston skirts the shoreline of New Haven; I-91 from Springfield, Massachusetts, and Hartford, Connecticut, ends here. Connections can also be made from the south along the Merritt and Wilbur Cross Parkways. Downtown is congested at the usual rush hours; there are ample parking lots and garages near the New Haven Green and Yale University.

BY TRAIN   Amtrak (www.amtrak.com; 🕾 **800/USA-RAIL** [872-7245]) runs several trains, including the Acela Express, daily between Boston and New York that make stops in New Haven. To or from New York takes about an hour and 40 minutes; to or from Boston, a bit over 2 hours. **Metro-North** (www.mta.info/mnr; 🕾 **877/690-5114**) commuter trains make many daily trips between New Haven and New York. Metro-North tickets are much cheaper than Amtrak's, but its trains take a smidge longer.

BY PLANE   Tweed–New Haven Airport (www.flytweed.com; 🕾 **203/466-8833**) primarily handles private and charter traffic, but scheduled commercial passenger flights are offered by **American Airlines** (www.aa.com) to its hub in Philadelphia. The airport is located southeast of the city.

VISITOR INFORMATION

Visit New Haven (www.visitnewhaven.com; 🕾 **203/777-8550**) maintains an office at 5 Science Park. **INFO New Haven,** at 1000 Chapel St. (www.infonew haven.com; 🕾 **203/773-9494**), is open daily year-round (Mon–Sat 10am–9pm; Sun noon–5pm). In addition to stocks of useful brochures, attendants are on-hand to offer suggestions.

FESTIVALS & SPECIAL EVENTS

Important events are the **International Festival of Arts & Ideas** (www.artidea. org), held at sites around the city for 15 days in June, and summer's free **Music on the Green** (www.infonewhaven.com/activities/music-on-the-green).

Exploring Yale University & New Haven

Most major attractions are Yale-affiliated and, except for the Peabody Museum, are within walking distance of the **New Haven Green,** which is bounded by Elm, Church, Chapel, and College Streets and divided by north-south Temple Street, with government buildings, including the Gothic Revival City Hall, bordering it on its east. There's a retail district on the south and older sections of the vast Yale campus to the north and west

Facing Temple Street are three churches, all dating from the early 19th century: **Trinity Episcopal Church,** a brownstone Gothic Revival structure; the post-Georgian **First Church of Christ/Center Church;** and the Federal-style **United Congregational.** Center Church is of greatest interest, built atop a crypt with tombstones inscribed as early as 1687. Crypt tours are conducted Saturdays between 11am and 1pm April through October.

The oldest house in New Haven is now the **Yale Visitor Center,** facing the north side of the Green at 149 Elm St. (🕾 **203/432-2300**). While its primary mission is to familiarize prospective students with Yale, the public is invited along on 1-hour **guided walking tours.** The center also has an introductory video and maps for self-guided tours. It's open Monday through Friday 9am to 4:30pm; Saturday and Sunday 11am to 4pm. Free tours are available weekdays at 10:30am and 2pm, Saturday and Sunday at 1:30pm.

It is impossible to imagine New Haven without Yale, so pervasive is its physical and cultural presence. After all, it helped educate four of the last eight U.S. presidents, as well as 27th president William Howard Taft, Noah Webster, Nathan Hale, and Eli Whitney. Established in 1702 in the shoreline town now known as Clinton, the young college was moved here in 1718 and named for Elihu Yale, who made a major financial contribution.

The most evocative quadrangle of the sprawling institution is the **Old Campus,** which can be entered from College, High, or Chapel Streets. Its mottled green is enclosed by Federal and Victorian Gothic buildings and dominated by **Harkness Tower,** a 1921 Gothic Revival campanile that looks far older. It houses the 54-bell Yale Memorial Carillon, which is played at least once daily.

Peabody Museum of Natural History ★ MUSEUM   Head to the third floor and work your way down. At the top are dioramas with taxidermied animals in various environments: bighorn sheep, Alaskan brown bears, bison, and musk oxen. On the same floor is a small collection of ancient Egyptian artifacts. The first floor's Great Hall of Dinosaurs is the museum's claim to fame, although exhibits devoted to human and mammalian evolution also captivate. Guided tours are offered hourly on Saturday and Sunday 12:30 to 3:30pm, as well as Thursday at 2:30 and 3:30pm.

170 Whitney Ave. (at Sachem St.). http://peabody.yale.edu. © **203/432-8987.** $13 adults, $9 seniors, $6 children 3–18; free to all Thurs 2–5pm (donations encouraged). Tues–Sat 10am–5pm; Sun noon–5pm.

Yale Center for British Art ★★ MUSEUM   What looks like a parking garage from outside is a great deal more impressive inside. Underwritten by Paul Mellon and designed by Louis I. Kahn, this museum is said to be the most important repository of British art outside the United Kingdom, with holdings of more than 2,250 paintings and sculptures. Most are from the 16th through early 19th centuries. It's a dazzling array, with canvases by such luminaries as Hogarth, Gainsborough, Hockney, and the glorious J.M.W. Turner.

1080 Chapel St. (at High St.). http://britishart.yale.edu. © **203/432-2800.** Free admission. Tues–Sat 10am–5pm; Sun noon–5pm.

Yale University Art Gallery ★★★ MUSEUM   While this museum displays art of many epochs and regions, it's most noted for works by French Impressionists and American realists of the late 19th and early 20th centuries. Architect Louis I. Kahn, also responsible for the nearby Center for British Art (above), designed the largest of three buildings, and an interior renovation markedly increased exhibition space. The top floor is primarily for special exhibitions; third-floor galleries are devoted to contemporary art and the museum's newest collection of nearly 2,000 Indo-Pacific carvings, textiles, and ceremonial items. The second floor is commanded by compelling Asian artworks and treasures of early American art, as well as notable works by European masters. The first floor's galleries showcase African, ancient, and American decorative arts.

1111 Chapel St. (at York St.). http://artgallery.yale.edu. © **203/432-0600.** Free admission. Tues–Fri 10am–5pm (Thurs until 8pm Sept–June); Sat–Sun 11am–5pm.

NEW HAVEN SHOPPING

Atticus Bookstore Café, 1082 Chapel St. (www.atticusbookstorecafe.com; ℂ **203/776-4040**), could be listed under "Where to Eat," because half of this store consists of a bakery/lunch counter locally famous for its scones. The rest is devoted to the best bookstore in town. Much the same description might be applied to **The Book Trader Cafe,** 1140 Chapel St. (www.booktradercafe. net; ℂ **203/787-6147**), which serves healthy and tasty soups, sandwiches, and salads and stocks used books in good condition.

A retail time machine, **Group W Bench,** 1171 Chapel St. (ℂ **203/624-0683**), was started in 1968 and is still packed with beads, antique toys, peace emblems, rubber chickens, and far-out attire. You can get a nostalgia contact high just walking in the door. **Ten Thousand Villages,** 1054 Chapel St. (www. tenthousandvillages.com/newhaven; ℂ **203/776-0854**) displays fascinating handicrafts from Third World artisans, both utilitarian and decorative. The shop endeavors to observe fair income practices, and prices are reasonable, too.

Where to Stay in New Haven

New Haven lodgings are both limited and, with one notable exception, largely devoid of either charm or distinctiveness. Still, motels and hotels fill up far in advance for Yale football weekends, reunions, and graduation, so reserve ahead during those periods.

Omni New Haven Hotel at Yale ★★   Its location next to the Green couldn't be improved—the Omni is within easy walking distance of theaters, the Yale campus, and two of the Yale museums. This is a conventional member of the reliable brand, and its 19th-floor restaurant, **John Davenport's at the Top of the Park ★,** offers fine views of the Green and surrounding cityscape.

155 Temple St. (south of Chapel St.). www.omnihotels.com. ℂ **888/444-6664** or 203/ 772-6664. 306 units. $220–$509 double. **Amenities:** Restaurant; bar; concierge; exercise room; room service; Wi-Fi (free).

The Study at Yale ★★★   This boutique hotel is a standout in a city otherwise served primarily by midlevel national hotel chains. The cuisine and vibe at in-house dining room **Heirloom** (p. 398), surpass what you'd expect to find within hotel walls. Rooms are furnished in sublimely contemporary taste, every unit equipped with stylish lamps and leather chairs. In the eight "Study" suites, guests get an alcove with two chairs with footstools and views over the peaked slate roofs of the Yale campus.

1157 Chapel St. (btw. York and Park Sts.). www.thestudyatyale.com. ℂ **203/503-3900.** 124 units. $209–$399 double. **Amenities:** Restaurant; bar; virtual concierge; exercise room; room service; Wi-Fi (free).

Where to Eat in New Haven

Few college towns are without at least one low-cost vegetarian restaurant, and **Claire's Corner Copia,** 1000 Chapel St. at College Street (www.claires cornercopia.com; ℂ **203/562-3888**), has ruled in New Haven since 1975.

Options include soy bacon BLT, veggie burgers, quesadillas, and many vegan options. Open daily.

EXPENSIVE

Pacifico ★ NUEVO LATINO   The restaurant's name refers to the cuisines of the western coast of Latin America, but while the kitchen draws inspiration from that region, it takes liberties with traditional dishes. This means lighter, less robustly seasoned food than found in Mexico, Colombia, Peru, and Ecuador. Downstairs in Barcito, couples canoodle over exotic-flavored mojitos and tapas like bacon-wrapped dates, steak and bleu cheese flatbread, and Chihuahua cheese fondue. Upstairs, crispy whole Mediterranean sea bass is the dish most likely to turn heads when it splashes out of the kitchen. Presentations are pretty but unfussy. A particularly good deal is the two-course *prix fixe* Sunday brunch at $20.

220 College St. (at Crown St.). www.pacificonewhaven.com. ℂ **203/772-4002.** Main courses $14–$28. Daily noon–midnight (until 12:30am Thurs and 1:30am, Fri–Sat).

Shell & Bones Oyster Bar and Grill ★★ SEAFOOD   To dine closer to the water, you'd need a boat. Whether on the deck by a fire pit or inside the floor-to-ceiling-windowed dining room, New Haven Harbor's undulations will whet your appetite for sea delicacies. The name Shell & Bones isn't just a playful twist on Yale's famous Skull and Bones secret society: It's an homage to the surf *and* turf origins of locally grown, caught, and raised ingredients. The eponymous signature dish pairs Thai-braised short ribs with barbecued shrimp.

10 S. Water St. (at Howard Ave.). www.shellandbones.com. ℂ **203/787-3466.** Main courses $24–$48. Mon–Tues 4–10pm; Wed–Thurs and Sun 11am–10pm; Fri–Sat 11am–11pm.

Union League Cafe ★★★ FRENCH   A grand salon that retains an air of the site's and the building's rich past, this gentlemen's club turned French brasserie is the city's crème de la crème of special occasion spots. Chef/owner Jean Pierre Vuillermet has cooked for U.S. and foreign presidents, and the executive orders his team follows ensure a polished, exceptional experience. Classics like duck confit are always on the menu, but as fiddleheads and ramps sprout and shad swim up the Connecticut River, these regional delicacies find their way into precisely prepared dishes. Wines are almost exclusively French; save room for cheeses and dessert.

1032 Chapel St. (btw. High and College sts.). www.unionleaguecafe.com. ℂ **203/562-4299.** Main courses $23–$41. Mon–Thurs 11:30am–2:30pm and 5–9:30pm; Fri 11:30am–2:30pm and 5–10pm; Sat 5–10pm.

Zinc ★★ NEW AMERICAN   On site for 20 years, this contemporary bistro can be fairly credited with igniting the city's restaurant renaissance, presaging all but the Union League Cafe (above) as a pinpoint of light in the once-dreary New Haven night. The interior is of mahogany and zinc, Manhattan-esque, but with elbow room. Chef/co-owner Denise Appel is adventurous without being daunting. Hot sauces of many origins are frequently incorporated into dishes, as with the Thai tomato broth that enlivens mussels and cod. Try the smoked duck nachos and slow-roasted pork belly, too. Zinc pays particular attention to its cheese menu and offers more than a dozen wines by the glass. Look for **Kitchen Zinc,** an artisan pizza bar around back, at 966 Chapel St. (www. kitchenzinc.com; ✆ **203/772-3002**).

964 Chapel St. www.zincfood.com. ✆ **203/624-0507.** Main courses $25–$35. Mon 5–9pm; Tues–Fri noon–2:30pm and 5–9pm (Fri until 10pm); Sat 5–10pm.

MODERATE

Heirloom ★★ NEW AMERICAN   The Study at Yale (p. 396) embellishes its high-quality image even more with this buzzing bar and restaurant. A seasonally changing, heritage produce–focused menu ratchets up familiar fare in taste and visual appeal. Bouillabaisse, for example, nudges that Provençal standard in a New England direction with lobster bisque as its base. You may know sea scallops, but not with the tangy-sweet accoutrement of capers, citrus, sultanas, and a bed of caramelized spaghetti squash. At lunch, grass-fed Connecticut beef burgers topped with Vermont cheddar, horseradish jam, and homemade pickles beckon.

1157 Chapel St. (btw. Park & York sts.). www.heirloomnewhaven.com. ✆ **203/503-3919.** Main courses $23–$36. Daily 7–10am, 11am–2pm, and 5:30–11:30pm.

Miya's Sushi ★★ JAPANESE   If you care for fish at all, you owe yourself a visit to the planet's first sustainable sushi restaurant, where hand-plucked shellfish, wild-foraged plants, and invasive species populate the encyclopedic menu. Activist chef Bun Lai, whose mother established this conscientious restaurant more than 35 years ago, crafts futuristic cuisine with the health of diners and their world in mind. Don't expect tuna rolls: Most species of tuna are overfished. This is your chance to gobble up sustainable rolls like Californikacion, made with blue crab, Icelandic smelt roe, artichoke hearts, and organic cream cheese (Lai harvests the wild seaweed just offshore). Or to help clean up Long Island Sound by nibbling Asian shore crabs, an invasive predator. Wash your adventurous meal down with Firecracker sake.

68 Howe St. (at Chapel St.). www.miyassushi.com. ✆ **203/777-9760.** Main courses $6–$22. Tues–Sun 4pm–midnight (Fri–Sat until 1am).

THE NEW HAVEN pizza WARS

On the scene for most of the last century, **Frank Pepe** ★, 157 Wooster St. (www.pepespizzeria.com; ✆ **203/865-5762**), has long laid claim to the local pizza crown in the face of substantial competition. In exchange for almost unimaginably thin-crusted pies, pilgrims put up with long lines, nothing decor, and an often sullen staff the management prefers to think of as "seasoned." A big fave is the white clam pie.

You can do every bit as well at **Sally's** ★, 237 Wooster St. (www.sallys apizza.com; ✆ **203/624-5271**), just down the street (new owners have vowed to sustain this 1938 institution). **BAR**, 254 Crown St. (www.barnightclub. com; ✆ **203/495-8924**), also makes a mean thin-crust pie. But many knowledgeable pizza lovers believe that **Modern Apizza** ★, 874 State St. (www. modernapizza.com; ✆ **203/776-5306**), holds the edge over other contenders.

INEXPENSIVE

Louis' Lunch ★ DINER   The claim, unprovable but gaining strength as the decades roll on, is that America's first hamburger was sold in 1900 at this little luncheonette founded by Louis Lassen and still owned by his descendants. Although the low brick building was relocated to escape demolition, not much else has changed. The wooden counter and tables are carved with the initials of a century of patrons. The beef is freshly ground each day, thrust onto cast-iron grills, and then served on white toast. The only allowable garnishes are tomato, onion, and cheese—don't even ask for ketchup or mustard. There are no fries, either, just chips or potato salad and homemade pies. Soup is served seasonally, and, during late hours from Thursday through Saturday, franks and steak sandwiches, too . . . sometimes.

261 Crown St. (btw. High and College sts.). www.louislunch.com. ✆ **203/562-5507.** All items under $7. Cash only. Tues–Wed 11am–3:45pm; Thurs–Sat noon–2am. Closed Aug.

New Haven Entertainment & Nightlife

The presence of a highly educated faction ensures cultural life in New Haven equals that of many larger cities.

THE PERFORMING ARTS

The **Shubert Performing Arts Center,** 247 College St. (www.shubert.com; ✆ **800/745-3000** or 203/562-5666), presents musicals, plays, concerts, and such touring troupes as the Mark Morris Dance Group. The well-regarded **Yale Repertory Theatre** (www.yalerep.org; ✆ **203/432-1234**) mounts a late September through mid-May season of modern productions at two venues: University Theatre, 222 York St., and Yale Repertory Theatre, 1120 Chapel St.

Away from downtown, but worth the cab fare, the prestigious **Long Wharf Theatre,** 222 Sargent Dr. (www.longwharf.org; ✆ **203/787-4282**) is known for producing new plays that often make the jump to Off-Broadway and even Broadway itself. The season runs from October through May.

Yale campus venues, including **Sprague Memorial Hall,** 470 College St.; **Sudler Hall,** 100 Wall St.; and **Woolsey Hall,** 500 College St., host performances by resident organizations, including the New Haven Symphony Orchestra, Civic Orchestra of New Haven, Yale Concert Band, Yale Glee Club, Yale Philharmonia, and Yale Symphony Orchestra. To find out what's being performed when, visit **http://music.yale.edu**.

THE CLUB SCENE

The biggest and best venue for live rock, hip-hop, and pop is **Toad's Place,** 300 York St. (www.toadsplace.com; ✆ **203/624-TOAD** [8623]), which welcomes the likes of The Voidz and Arch Enemy, with a smattering of tribute bands and regional groups on the schedule.

For something less frenetic, the popular **BAR,** 254 Crown St. (www.bar nightclub.com; ✆ **203/495-8924**), has a brewpub and pool table in front—open to the street on warm nights—and a dance floor in back. On Thursday, Friday, and Saturday nights, there's a cover charge to join the 21-and-over party starting at 9:30pm. It's open 365 nights a year and Wednesday through Sunday for lunch. Rich beers are produced on site, and the kitchen's leading entry in the eternal New Haven pizza wars (see box p. 398) is a mashed potato pie.

The gentrifying Ninth Square neighborhood has a cool bar and jazz concert space, **Firehouse 12,** 45 Crown St. (www.firehouse12.com; ✆ **203/785-0468**). It's open Tuesday through Sunday nights, featuring local beers, throwback cocktails, and light bites. Jazz performances are typically Friday nights in the spring and fall.

HARTFORD

114 miles NE of New York City; 100 miles SW of Boston

Connecticut's capital, Hartford was born out of a political squabble, as a group of dissidents fled the Massachusetts Bay Colony and settled here in 1636. Three years later, they drafted the "Fundamental Orders," essentially the world's first written constitution—hence the state's nickname, "the Constitution State."

Today, Hartford is home to several major insurance company headquarters. More than one-third of the population is of Puerto Rican heritage, making it the most Puerto Rican city on the U.S. mainland. A Puerto Rican Day Parade and Festival del Coquí (www. hartfordprparade.com) is held in the city each June.

Downtown is a mixed bag. Dominated by Dunkin' Donuts Park, the Connecticut Science Center, the august Wadsworth Atheneum, and the gold-domed capitol building, it also has recently been on the brink of bankruptcy. However, the city has a strong arts and entertainment scene, a thriving riverfront, and some cosmopolitan restaurants, and there are museums worth the trip. Most of a day-long or overnight visit can be contained within a few blocks radiating around the Old State House. The Twain and Stowe houses (both p. 402) are 1½ miles east of the city center.

Essentials

ARRIVING

BY CAR Interstates 84 and 91 intersect in Hartford. The city is almost exactly halfway between New York and Boston, just over a 2-hour drive from either city.

BY PLANE **Bradley International Airport** (www.bradleyairport.com; ✆ **860/292-2000**), in Windsor Locks, about 15 miles north of the city, is served by major U.S. airlines, including American (www.aa.com), Delta (www.delta.com), JetBlue (www.jetblue.com), Southwest (www.southwest.com), and United (www.united.com).

BY TRAIN Amtrak (www.amtrak.com; ✆ **800/USA-RAIL** [872-7245]) has several trains that stop daily in Hartford, on a branch line that heads north from New Haven and goes through Springfield, MA, on up into Vermont.

VISITOR INFORMATION

The Hartford Visitor Information Center is located in the **Old State House,** 800 Main St. (✆ **860/522-6766**). It's open Monday to Saturday 10am to 5pm,

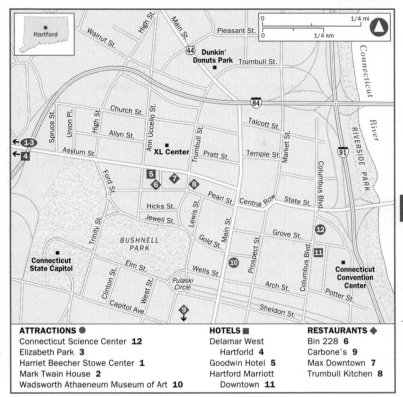

ATTRACTIONS ●
Connecticut Science Center **12**
Elizabeth Park **3**
Harriet Beecher Stowe Center **1**
Mark Twain House **2**
Wadsworth Athaeneum Museum of Art **10**

HOTELS ■
Delamar West
    Hartford **4**
Goodwin Hotel **5**
Hartford Marriott
    Downtown **11**

RESTAURANTS ◆
Bin 228 **6**
Carbone's **9**
Max Downtown **7**
Trumbull Kitchen **8**

Sunday noon to 5pm. Also check out the on-line listings at the Hartford Business Improvement District's website www.hartford.com.

GETTING AROUND

In addition to regular city buses, a free "dash Shuttle" run by CT Transit (www.cttransit.com; ✆ **860/525-9181**) makes a loop past all the venues mentioned in this section, except for the Twain and Stowe houses, on weekdays from 7am to 7pm and on weekends during special events. You can print out a map of the route from the service's website.

FESTIVALS

For 3 days in mid-July, the **Greater Hartford Festival of Jazz** (www.hartford jazz.com) offers free performances at the pavilion in Bushnell Park.

Exploring Hartford

In nice weather, use Constitution Plaza as a launching point for a riverside stroll. You'll find 16 sculptures related to U.S. President Abraham Lincoln positioned in parks on the west and east banks of the Connecticut River (www.riverfront.org/parks/art-in-parks).

Connecticut Science Center ★ MUSEUM

Adjacent to the revitalized waterfront along the Connecticut River, this science museum holds more than 165 interactive exhibits and a 3D theater. From character appearances to coffee club learning opportunities for adults, the schedule of events is enthralling.

250 Columbus Blvd. www.ctsciencecenter.org. © **860/724-3623.** $24 adults, $22 seniors, $17 children 3–17, free ages 2 and under. Additional fee for 3-D movies, stage shows, and butterfly encounter, with combo tickets available. Tues–Sun and some Mon holidays 10am–5pm. July–Aug also Mon 10am–5pm.

Elizabeth Park ★★ PARK

In the city's West End, this 100-acre park is an inviting place to stop and smell the roses: There are some 15,000 bushes including many heirloom specimens within the oldest municipal rose garden in America. At its peak in June, when you'll bump into brides and grooms beneath archways laden with fragrant blossoms, the photogenic rose garden is surrounded by walking paths, additional gardens, and lawns perfect for picnicking. Summer's free events include concerts, movie nights, and yoga sessions. The waterside **Pond House Café** offers indoor-outdoor dining within the park, featuring dishes constructed from locally grown, organic ingredients: Vegetarian options abound.

1561 Asylum Ave. www.elizabethparkct.org. © **860/231-9443.** Admission free. Daily sunrise to sunset.

Harriet Beecher Stowe Center ★★ HISTORIC HOME

Though rarely read nowadays, Stowe's landmark 1852 book *Uncle Tom's Cabin* was a massive bestseller in the U.S., England, Europe, and Asia, opening the world's eyes to the abuse endured by enslaved people in the United States. The author and her professor husband moved into this modest house in 1873, joining what was then a tight-knit artist community known as Nook Farm; the following year, Mark Twain would move in next door (see below—you'll save money if you visit both houses the same day). At the time Stowe was in her 60s and already world-famous, while Twain was not yet 40 and still had much of his greatest work ahead of him. Renovated in 2017, Stowe's home is the backdrop for interactive, conversational tours that explore the issues of her day and their still-relevant place in American discourse.

77 Forest St. www.harrietbeecherstowecenter.org. © **860/522-9258.** $16 adults, $14 seniors and students, $10 children 5–16, free for children 4 and under. Mon–Sat 9:30am–5pm; Sun noon–5pm. Visits by guided tour only.

Mark Twain House & Museum ★★ HISTORIC HOME

Samuel Clemens, whose pseudonym, Mark Twain, was a term used by Mississippi riverboat pilots to indicate a water depth of 2 fathoms, lived here from 1874 to 1891, a period when he wrote some of his most beloved tales including *The Adventures of Huckleberry Finn* and *A Connecticut Yankee in King Arthur's Court*. The 25-room house is a fascinating example of the late-19th-century style known as "Picturesque Gothic," with steeply peaked gables and brick walls with varying patterns highlighted by black or orange paint. The High Victorian interior was the work of distinguished designers including Louis Comfort Tiffany, who provided both advice and stained glass. Twain's enthusiasm for newfangled gadgets—his *Life on the Mississippi* is said to be the first novel written on a typewriter—led to the installation of an exasperatingly primitive telephone in the entrance hall. More than a house museum, this vibrant institution is devoted to exploring Twain's many passions via lectures, events, writing workshops, and experiences such as Get A Clue Murder Mystery Tours, featuring Twain-inspired "suspects" portrayed by members of Hartford's own Sea Tea Improv troupe.

351 Farmington Ave. www.marktwainhouse.org. © **860/247-0998.** $20 adults, $18 seniors, $12 children 6–16, free for children 5 and under. Daily 9:30am–5:30pm. Closed Tues Jan–Feb.

Wadsworth Atheneum Museum of Art ★★★ MUSEUM   Opened in 1842, the first public art museum in the United States remains a repository with few equals in New England. The strength of the collection lies primarily in its American paintings, especially its 65-plus landscapes of the Hudson River School of the 19th century. Also represented are Andrew Wyeth, Milton Avery, and Norman Rockwell; kinetic works by Alexander Calder; and canvases by abstract expressionists and pop and op artists of the 1950s and 1960s, including Willem de Kooning and Robert Rauschenberg. Other holdings include ancient Greek and Roman antiquities, European and Colonial decorative arts, African-American art, and the Samuel Colt firearms collection. As if reflecting the art within, the original castle-like Gothic Revival building has been much expanded over the years, each addition expressing the architectural tastes of its time.

600 Main St. www.thewadsworth.org. © **860/278-2670.** $15 adults, $12 seniors, $5 students, free for children 17 and under; free admission Wed–Sat 4–5pm and second Sat of month 10am–1pm. Wed–Fri 11am–5pm; Sat–Sun 10am–5pm.

Where to Stay in Hartford & West Hartford

Delamar West Hartford ★★   Don't need to stay right downtown? Go west 4 miles to Greater Hartford's newest major property. This Delamar—the third incarnation in an upscale, Connecticut-only chain (the others are in Greenwich and Southport)—is an instant classic, with stylish rooms, a full-service spa, and art on loan from the nearby New Britain Museum of American Art. West Hartford's thriving Blue Back Square shopping, dining, and entertainment development is right outside, but you'll be hard-pressed to find a better meal than the one you can enjoy at the hotel's own farm-to-table **Artisan** restaurant. Alfresco dining in the garden is the capital region's best-hidden treat.

1 Memorial Rd., West Hartford. www.delamar.com © **860/937-2500.** 114 units. $239–$399 double. Rates include welcome champagne and breakfast buffet. Free valet parking. Dogs welcome. **Amenities:** Restaurant; bar/lounge; spa; fitness center; courtesy vehicle within 5 miles; Wi-Fi (free).

The Goodwin Hotel ★★   The capital city's grande dame was resuscitated in 2017, 9 years after its sudden closure. The terracotta-and-redbrick exterior still speaks of Victorian splendor, and enough interior details have been preserved to honor the landmark's past, even though its contemporary styling and amenities are a quantum leap forward. The hotel's gourmet donut shop morphs at night into the city's most inventive cocktail spot, **Piña;** the attached restaurant **Porrón** serves an enticing tapas menu.

1 Haynes St., Hartford. www.goodwinhartford.com. ✆ **860/246-1881.** 124 units. $179–$649 double. Rates include breakfast buffet. Valet parking $25. **Amenities:** Restaurant; bar/lounge; fitness center; yoga studio; local shuttle; Wi-Fi (free).

Hartford Marriott Downtown ★★ Guest rooms here come complete with cushy mattresses as well as refrigerators and flatscreen TVs. The main restaurant, **Vivo,** goes in for imaginative interpretations of the Mediterranean oeuvre. The **L Bar** is mod and experiential, with a strong line-up of Connecticut-brewed beers and a pub-food-made-posh menu.

200 Columbus Blvd., Hartford. www.hartfordmarriott.com. ✆ **860/249-8000.** 409 units. $259–$390 double. Valet parking $23; self-parking $19. **Amenities:** Restaurant; bar/lounge; concierge; concierge-level rooms; fitness center; whirlpool; indoor pool; room service; spa; Wi-Fi (free).

Where to Eat in Hartford

In addition to these restaurants (and the hotel restaurants mentioned above), the venues listed in "Hartford Entertainment & Nightlife" (below) all serve food.

Bin 228 ★ WINE BAR This petite, intimate, friendly bistro has a wine list that will wow you, with more than 50 selections available by the glass. The menu concentrates on light fare: salads, small plates, bruschette, and panini sandwiches. The prosciutto, fig, caramelized onion, and asiago cheese panini packs a flavor punch. (The recipe is at Epicurious.com.) This is a romantic spot with Euro casualness, although solo eaters settle in quite comfortably alongside business folks in jeans and cashmere.

228 Pearl St. www.thebin228.com. ✆ **860/244-9463.** Main courses $10–$16. Mon–Thurs 11:30am–10pm; Fri 11:30am–midnight; Sat 4pm–midnight; Sun call ahead.

Carbone's Ristorante ★★ ITALIAN The Caesar is tossed and desserts are flamed before your eyes, but tableside theatrics are not what's kept diners returning to this family-owned South End stalwart for more than 80 years. Sashay back to a time when service was polished and Chianti-fueled conversation was ample entertainment. Whether you're celebrating an anniversary or were just lured in by a craving for rigatoni Bolognese like Grandma used to make, expect to feel like it's a once-in-a-lifetime occasion.

588 Franklin Ave. www.carbonesct.com. ✆ **860/296-9646.** Main courses $23–$49. Mon–Thurs 11:30am–9pm; Fri 11:30am–10pm; Sat 4:30–10pm.

Max Downtown ★★ NEW AMERICAN Hartford's prime-time power lunch venue is nearly always packed with business folks at midday and a be-seen crowd at night. A 2017 renovation reenergized this long-time go-to, swapping stuffy white tablecloths for warm woods and vibrant paint, art, and upholstery. Diners are indulged with hefty chophouse favorites—"Tomahawk

Ribeye" steak with bacon marmalade, perhaps?—and lighter efforts, such as simply prepared Hawaiian ahi tuna. Over two dozen wines are available by the glass. A sister restaurant, **Trumbull Kitchen,** just around the corner at 150 Trumbull St., also caters to lawyers, techies, and execs but offers up a long menu of creative global grazing noshes. It's cheaper, with main courses from $13 to $31 at dinner and $8 to $18 at lunch, and several notches more casual.

185 Asylum St. www.maxdowntown.com. © **860/522-2530.** Main courses $20–$50. Mon–Thurs 11:30am–2:30pm and 5–10pm; Fri 11:30am–2:30pm and 5–11pm; Sat 5–11pm (bar opens at 4pm); Sun 4:30–9:30pm.

Hartford Entertainment & Nightlife

PERFORMING ARTS   The Bushnell, 166 Capitol Ave. (www.bushnell. org; © **860/987-5900**), hosts diverse events in its two theaters, from Broadway shows to Hartford Symphony concerts to Connecticut Forum panel discussions. **Hartford Stage,** 50 Church St. (www.hartfordstage.org; © **860/527-5151**), mounts a variety of heart-warming and thought-provoking plays including an annual holiday-season production of *A Christmas Carol.*

Big name touring rock and pop acts appear in summer at the **XFINITY Theatre,** 61 Savitt Way (www.livenation.com; © **860/548-7370**), a huge outdoor amphitheater near Riverside Park, north of downtown. Smaller acts take advantage of the excellent acoustics at 500-seat **Infinity Hall,** 32 Front St. (www.infinityhall.com; © **860/560-7757**).

SPECTATOR SPORTS   The XL Center, One Civic Center Plaza (www. xlcenter.com; © **860/249-6333**), is the city's sports and concerts arena. The UConn men's and women's basketball and men's ice hockey teams play here, and so does the Hartford Wolf Pack American Hockey League team.

BARS & CLUBS   City Steam Brewery, 942 Main St. (www.citysteam.biz; © **860/525-1600**), is housed in a gorgeous 1877 building that once held the state's largest department store. On tap are over a dozen beers brewed on-site to accompany a menu of pub grub. It hosts the **Brew Ha Ha Comedy Club** Friday and Saturday nights.

Black-Eyed Sally's, 350 Asylum St. (www.blackeyedsallys.com; © **860/278-7427**), known for its BBQ ribs and other Southern-style treats, presents live blues bands and jams almost every night. The **Arch Street Tavern,** 85 Arch St. (www.archstreettavern.com; © **860/246-7610**), around the corner from the convention center, is a pub/restaurant with DJ and live music.

THE CONNECTICUT RIVER VALLEY ★★

Essex: 114 miles NE of New York City, 125 miles SW of Boston. East Haddam: 124 miles NE of New York City, 132 miles SW of Boston. Old Lyme: 112 miles NE of New York City, 120 miles SW of Boston.

The Connecticut River, New England's longest, originates near the Canadian border, some 410 miles from where it ends at Long Island Sound. It separates

Vermont from New Hampshire, splits Massachusetts in half, then flows into Connecticut, takes a 45-degree turn, and makes its final run to the sea.

Native Americans called the river *Quinnetukut,* which, to the tin ears of English settlers, sounded like "Connecticut." Because the river was navigable by relatively large ships as far as Hartford, its lower part became important for boat-building and industries associated with the international clipper trade. The valley retains a nautical flavor and has miraculously avoided the development and decay that afflict most of the region's rivers. Nearly 600 acres of salt marsh at the mouth of the Connecticut River are preserved within the Roger Tory Peterson Wildlife Area, named for the Connecticut artist renowned for his bird illustrations.

Given the unspoiled, upper-class, scenic atmosphere here, the valley is a popular spot for weekend getaways year-round. River cruises are obvious attractions, supplemented by a selection of worthy inns and shops, rides on a steam-powered train, a venerable musical theater, and a quirky castle on a hilltop.

Essentials

ARRIVING

Route 9 runs parallel to the Connecticut River, along the west side of the valley. It connects I-91 south of Hartford to I-95 near Old Saybrook, making the valley readily accessible from all points in New England. **Amtrak** train service between Boston and New York City stops in Old Saybrook.

VISITOR INFORMATION

Check out the **Experience Essex** website (www.essexct.com) for an events calendar and listings of local shops, restaurants, and hotels. It covers not only Essex but also the neighboring towns of Ivoryton and Centerbrook.

Exploring Essex ★★ & Ivoryton

It is difficult to imagine what improvements might be made to bring Essex, a dream of a New England waterside town, nearer to perfection. Tree-bordered streets are lined with shops and homes that retain an early-18th-century flavor, but without the frozen-in-amber quality that can afflict towns as postcard-pretty as this. Essex is ideal to stroll through: Park on Main Street, head to the river, and then wander off on side streets.

About 6,500 people live and work here, and bustle along Main Street, which runs down to the Essex Town Dock and the Connecticut River Museum. Many houses have plaques noting their heritage, such as "Gamaliel Conklin c. 1803" (#20 Main Street) and "Uriah Hayden 1847" (#24). Streets have such names as Novelty Lane and Methodist Hill. In the Tap Room at the Griswold Inn (p. 410), you might hear The Jovial Crew singing sea shanties: Live music fills this antique pub every single night of the year.

Ivoryton is one of three villages in Essex. It was once a center for the ivory trade, with factories fabricating piano keys and toothpicks. The village long ago subsided into residential quietude, but it perks up a bit in summer, when the **Ivoryton Playhouse,** 103 Main St. (www.ivorytonplayhouse.com; ⓒ **860/**

767-7318), conducts much of its mid-March through mid-November theatrical season. It's also home to the estimable **Copper Beech Inn** (see p. 410). Look for large-scale modern sculpture pieces on Main Street lawns near the inn.

Connecticut River Museum ★ MUSEUM   All you ever wanted to know about the Connecticut River is explained here, with model ships, paintings, and artifacts that relate the story of shipbuilding in the valley, which began in 1733 and made this a center of world trade far into the 19th century. Be sure to see the replica of America's first submarine (1776), a wooden, grenade-shaped, one-man contraption called the *American Turtle*. While you're here, go outside onto the museum's dock—steamboat service was fully operational here in 1823, and the existing dock dates from 1879—and gaze at the river's wide mouth, as gulls circle overhead and ducks hang around hoping for a discarded tidbit. In winter, when bald eagles come to these lower reaches of the river, the museum sponsors boat trips for viewing (Fri–Sun, early Feb to late Mar); trips costs $40 per person.

67 Main St. www.ctrivermuseum.org. ℂ **860/767-8269.** $10 adults, $8 seniors, $7 students, $6 ages 6–12, free children 5 and under. Daily 10am–5pm Memorial Day to Columbus Day; Tues–Sun 10am–5pm rest of the year.

Essex Steam Train ★ VINTAGE TRAIN RIDE   Chug along the river to the hamlet of Deep River on a 1920s steam locomotive. The excursion takes about an hour. The same operation offers cruises on a beautiful Mississippi-style riverboat named *Becky Thatcher.* Combo train and riverboat trips are available, as are themed excursions and dinner trains with a four-course meal for $83. Santa Special and North Pole Express trains are an annual holiday-season sellout.

1 Railroad Ave. (at Rte. 154 and Rte. 9). www.essexsteamtrain.com. ℂ **800/377-3987** or 860/767-0103. Train ride $20 adults, $18 seniors, $10 children 2–11; train plus boat $30 adults, $27 seniors, $20 children 2–11. Daily mid-June to late Aug and late Sept–late Oct; less frequently mid-May to mid-June and early Sept; themed trains Nov–Apr.

Exploring Chester ★, East Haddam & Hadlyme

Seven miles north of Essex, the well-turned-out riverside hamlet of **Chester** is teeny but alluring. Its old-fashioned Main Street and adjacent country lanes offer up enough gift shops, art galleries, and somewhat precious boutiques to fill an hour of browsing. Stop in at **R. J. Vickers Herbery**, 26 Waters St. (www.rjvickers herbery.com; ℂ **860/526-4061**), for a stroll through the garden and to browse the array of take-home plants and handcrafts.

While Chester sits on the west side of the Connecticut River, **East Haddam** and **Hadlyme** are directly on the east. To get from one to the

---

A Ferry Tale

From April through November, take the **Chester-Hadlyme Ferry** (ℂ **860/662-0701**), at the end of Route 148, 2 miles from Chester center. It's a designated state historical landmark: a ferry has operated here since 1769. The current one carries about eight cars and walkons ($5–$6 for vehicles, $2 for pedestrians and bicyclists). The pretty ride takes only minutes. Be sure to ask if eagles are active; they often are here.

other, take the **Chester-Hadlyme Ferry** (see box p. 407), or drive 4 miles upriver to Route 82 and the East Haddam Bridge.

East Haddam might never have attracted much attention if a wealthy thespian, William Gillette, hadn't decided to build an oddball hilltop castle here (see Gillette Castle, below). Hikers, birders, and anglers will also want to head for **Devil's Hopyard State Park,** 366 Hopyard Rd. (Route 434) in East Haddam (www.ct.gov/deep/devilshopyard; © **860/526-2336**), which has extensive woodland trails and streams teeming with brook trout. Its main feature is Chapman Falls, with its distinctive round potholes beneath the shimmering cascade. Early settlers posited they had been struck into the stone by the hooves of the devil.

Gillette Castle State Park ★ HISTORIC HOME   Hartford-born William Gillette (1853–1937) was an actor and playwright, most famous in his time for portraying Sherlock Holmes on stage. He took his money and built a 24-room mansion. It's difficult to believe he thought the result resembled the medieval fortresses that inspired him. The stone exterior has the dripping look of a sandcastle built by wet globs that fell through children's fingers. Inside, Gillette designed oddities such as a dining-room table that slides into the wall. But it's dramatic, and no one can argue with the location. The mansion sits atop the east bank of the Connecticut River and has superlative vistas upriver and down. The expansive grounds, which are owned and managed by the state, have picnic areas and nature trails. The park and the castle's terrace can be entered for free, making it a grand destination even to just take in the **river views** ★★.

67 River Rd. www.ct.gov/deep/gillettecastle. © **860/526-2336.** Grounds free; castle admission $6, ages 6–12 $2, free for children 5 and under. Grounds daily 8am–sunset; castle daily 10am–5pm Memorial Day weekend through Labor Day.

Goodspeed Musicals ★★ THEATER   The dominant building in teeny East Haddam is a restored 1876 Victorian opera house of splendid proportions and white-frosting curlicues. Located directly on the Connecticut River, it has been home to Goodspeed Musicals since its beginning. Today, Goodspeed stages shows on the order of *Oliver!* and *The Will Rogers Follies.* It also helps develop new works and hosts a festival of new musicals every January.

6 Main St. www.goodspeed.org. © **860/873-8668.** Tickets $29–$79.

RiverQuest ★ NATURE CRUISE   These 90-minute river tours specialize in providing information on the birds of the Connecticut River, which include eagles, hawks, ospreys, tree swallows, and ducks. The boat operates most months, including February and March for Winter Wildlife Eagle Cruises, when the birds are particularly populous.

Eagle Landing State Park, 14 Little Meadow Rd., Haddam (west bank of the river). www.ctriverquest.com. © **860/662-0577.** $20 adults, $18 seniors (Mon, Wed, Thurs mornings only), $15 ages 2–12; higher prices for longer specialty excursions. July–Labor Day trips daily except Tues, less frequently rest of year.

Exploring Old Lyme

Back at the wide mouth of the Connecticut River, across the bridge from Essex, Old Lyme is as quiet and undeveloped a town as the coast can claim. It was the favored residence of generations of seafarers, and many of their 18th- and 19th-century homes have survived, some as inns and museums. These preserved houses are best seen on **Lyme Street,** also home to the Florence Griswold Museum (below) and Bee and Thistle Inn (p. 411). Preservationists and community activists proudly point out this is the only main street in the region bisected by interstate highway 95 that continues to thrive.

Florence Griswold Museum ★ MUSEUM   After the shipbuilding and merchant trade had all but flickered out at the end of the 19th century, the "American Impressionists" took a fancy to this area. These artists received encouragement, food, and shelter from "Miss Florence" (1850–1937), the daughter of a sea captain. She opened her Georgian–Federal 1817 mansion to boarders and made it a country retreat for artists. Some notables painted directly on the dining room walls. Among her guests was Childe Hassam, the grand master of the American Impressionists.

Now, the "Flo Gris" and its modern Krieble Gallery, which opened in 2002, showcase masterworks from the permanent collection as well as changing exhibitions. Visitors can stroll the 13-acre landscape to take in its old-fashioned gardens, picnic on the banks of the Lieutenant River, or even do some painting.

96 Lyme Street (Rte. 1). www.florencegriswoldmuseum.org. © **860/434-5542.** Admission $10 adults, $9 seniors, $8 students, free for 12 and under. Tues–Sat 10am–5pm; Sun 1–5pm.

BEACHES

Set right on Long Island Sound, **Rocky Neck State Park** (www.ct.gov/deep/rockyneck; © **860/739-5471**) is at 244 W. Main St. (Route 156), in East Lyme, about 5 miles east of Old Lyme. Its crescent-shaped beach is popular with families; there are bathrooms and a food stand here. The park also has 160 camping sites. It's open daily from 8am to sunset; out-of-state residents must pay a per-vehicle entry fee of $22 weekends, $15 weekdays.

Where to Stay & Eat in the Connecticut River Valley

CHESTER

River Tavern ★ NEW AMERICAN   Offering some urban panache in a bucolic setting, the high-design River Tavern is equal parts swanky, funky, and Northern California. Undulating felt ceiling panels muffle the noise of the tall room, which is brightly decorated with orange bands of paint and abstract prints. A short menu (two fish, three meat, and one vegetarian entree on a typical night) is sourced almost entirely locally, with a list of farms, orchards, cheesemakers, and other providers thanked on the restaurant's website.

Proceeds from $10 children's meals on Sundays support healthy school lunches in local schools.

23 Main St. www.rivertavernrestaurant.com. ℂ **860/526-9417.** Main courses $26–$34. Mon–Sat 11:30am–2:30pm and 5–9pm (Fri–Sat until 10pm); Sun 11am–2:30pm and 4:30–9pm.

ESSEX

For a more modest meal than what's offered in the dining rooms of the area's historic inns, check out the gourmet take-out at **Olive Oyl's,** 6 Main St. (www.oliveoylscarryout.com; ℂ **860/767-4909**).

Griswold Inn ★★ Art-filled, folksy, and forever besieged by drop-in yachties, anglers, locals, and tourists, the main building at "the Gris" dates to 1776. The mahogany-heavy taproom started life as a schoolhouse and was moved here in 1800. There's live entertainment every night, from four guys singing sea shanties to a '60s rock band. The Sunday Hunt Breakfast buffet is popular, and food in the evenings, while hearty (think roasted cod with crab and butter crumb crust), has taken a turn toward the innovative. A newish **wine bar** has a smattering of small plates, artisanal cheeses, and 50 wines by the glass. Bedrooms are bright, comfortable, and individual; some have fireplaces, none have TVs.

36 Main St. www.griswoldinn.com. ℂ **860/767-1776.** 33 units. $160–$335 double. Rates include breakfast. **Amenities:** Restaurant; 2 bars; Wi-Fi (free).

HADDAM

Gelston House ★ AMERICAN Right on the banks of the Connecticut River and next door to the Goodspeed Opera House, the Gelston House has soothing views and a dining room with some old-fashioned grandeur. It offers a special *prix fixe* menu ideal for theatergoers and a pub menu if you're looking for a lighter bite post-show. There are four overnight rooms here, although they are underwhelming and pricey ($150–$225).

8 Main St. www.gelstonhouse.com. ℂ **860/873-1411.** Main courses $21–$36. Tues–Thurs 11:30am–9pm; Fri–Sat 11:30am–11pm; Sun 11:30am–9pm.

IVORYTON

Copper Beech Inn ★★ The centuries-old tree that gave this enduring inn its name succumbed to disease in 2017, but the stately Copper Beech still oozes elegance and luxury. It offers four rooms replete with antiques in the 19th-century main building and 18 more contemporary rooms in the Carriage House, converted barn, and Comstock House. You need not spend a night to partake of a meal at the **Oak Room,** where the fireplaced bar attracts casual diners, or in the fancier dining room (dinner entrees $19–$38). Breakfast is served daily, lunch Friday and Saturday. Sunday brunch is the best of both worlds, with a playful menu of rich dishes like lobster eggs Benedict.

46 Main St. (take exit 3 from Rte. 9). www.copperbeechinn.com. ℂ **860/767-0330.** 22 units. $179–$499 double. Rates include breakfast. No children 15 and under in hotel. **Amenities:** Restaurant; bar; Wi-Fi (free).

OLD LYME

Bee and Thistle Inn and Spa ★   On bucolic acreage beside the Lieutenant River (and next door to the Florence Griswold Museum, see p. 409), the main draws of the Bee and Thistle are the 1756 core structure and the romantic "English countryside" grounds and gardens. Public areas are a jumble of antiques, while most rooms boast four-poster beds and river views. Dinner is served in the **Chestnut Grille** Wednesday through Sunday, 5 to 9pm (main courses $26–$39).

100 Lyme St. (Rte. 1). www.beeandthistleinn.com. © **860/434-1667.** 10 units. $229–$289 double. **Amenities:** Restaurant, lounge; Wi-Fi (free).

MYSTIC ★★★ & THE SOUTHEASTERN COAST

New London & Groton: 127 miles NE of New York City, 106 miles SW of Boston. Mystic: 135 miles NE of New York City, 99 miles SW of Boston.

From New London east to Rhode Island, the shoreline is studded with towns that bear the stamp of their maritime pasts. Mystic and its major attractions, Mystic Aquarium and Mystic Seaport, are the prime reasons for a stay—the Seaport alone can easily occupy most of a day. Mystic village itself sustains a nautical vibe, with eclectic shops and restaurants to suit most tastes. The tranquil neighboring borough of Stonington is home to a small commercial fishing fleet, the last in the state, and is making a name for itself with the quality of its scallop and deep-water red shrimp harvest. You'll recognize its antique streets lined with cute shops and well-kept historic homes if you've seen the Meryl Streep and Tommy Lee Jones film *Hope Springs*.

If you're visiting in July, August, or on weekends from May to Columbus Day, pack some patience. That's when attractions are most crowded and lines for lobsters longest. Hotel rooms are often booked months in advance at peak season rates.

Essentials

ARRIVING

Take I-95 to exit 84 (New London), exit 85 (Groton), exit 90 (Mystic), or exit 91 (Stonington). Driving from New York City, you can avoid the heavy truck and commercial traffic of the western segment of I-95 by taking the Hutchinson River Parkway, which becomes the Merritt Parkway (Route 15) and merges with the Wilbur Cross Parkway. At exit 54, pick up I-95 for the rest of the trip. From Boston, take I-95 straight down.

BY TRAIN   **Amtrak** train service (www.amtrak.com; © **800/USA-RAIL** [872-7245]) between New York, Providence, and Boston stops at New London and Mystic.

BY BUS   The regional bus company **Southeast Area Transit,** or **SEAT** (www.seatbus.com; © **860/886-2631**), connects many of the towns along the coast.

BY FERRY **Cross Sound Ferry** (www.longislandferry.com; ☎ **860/443-5281**) provides year-round service for cars between New London and Orient Point on Long Island, in New York. A one-way voyage takes about 80 minutes. One-way reserved fares are $55 for a car and driver, $15.75 for additional adults, $6 for children. Reservations are recommended. Seasonal, passenger-only, high-speed Sea Jet trips take only 40 minutes, but the cost is a bit higher.

There's also passenger-only service to Block Island, RI (see p. 465) from New London, via **Block Island Express** (www.goblockisland.com; ☎ **860/444-4624** or 401/466-2212), from late May to September. Round-trip day fares are $47.50 adults, $23.50 children.

VISITOR INFORMATION

A good source of information is the **Greater Mystic Chamber of Commerce Welcome Center**, located across the street from Mystic Seaport (62 Greenmanville Ave.; Mystic; www.mysticchamber.org; ☎ **860/572-9578**). The **Mystic & Shoreline Visitor Information Center** (www.mysticinfocenter.com; ☎ **860/536-1641**) is located at the **Olde Mistick Village shopping center,** adjacent to the Mystic Aquarium.

Exploring New London

New London's protected deep-draft harbor at the mouth of the Thames River was responsible for its long and influential history as a whaling port. With an architecturally interesting downtown and vibrant waterfront, the city is of note to travelers particularly because it's a hub for ferry lines connecting the mainland with Rhode Island (Block Island) and New York (Long Island). New London is home to the **U.S. Coast Guard Academy** (www.cga.edu).

Lyman Allyn Museum of Art ★ MUSEUM   Standing on a hill looking toward the U.S. Coast Guard Academy, this neoclassical granite building has a collection built upon the enthusiasms of private collectors. Its strongest areas are Colonial American paintings as well as landscapes by Hudson River School artists Frederic Edwin Church and John F. Kensett; it also has a fine collection of Victorian toys. Special exhibitions bring fresh work into the venue.

625 Williams St. www.lymanallyn.org. ☎ **860/443-2545.** $10 adults, $7 seniors and students over 18, $5 students 12–18, free for children 11 and under. Tues–Sat 10am–5pm; Sun 1–5pm.

BEACHES

Not far from downtown is the throwback **Ocean Beach Park** (www.oceanbeach-park.com; ☎ **860/447-3031**), with a broad sand beach, a boardwalk, an Olympic-size pool, a kiddie spraypark, a carousel and amusement rides, an arcade, miniature golf, bathhouse with lockers and showers, and a café and concession stands. Parking is $17 weekdays, $23 weekends, $7 after 6pm, which includes park admission for everyone in the car.

Mystic

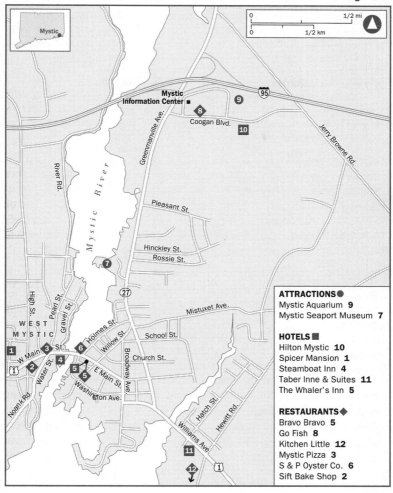

Mystic
Information Center ■

Mystic
Coogan Blvd.

95

Jerry Browne Rd.

River Rd.

Mystic River

Greenmanville Ave.

Pleasant St.

Hinckley St.
Rossie St.

27

Mistuxet Ave.

High St.
Pearl St.
Gravel St.

WEST
MYSTIC

W Main St.
Water St.
Holmes St.
Willow St.
School St.

Broadway Ave.
Church St.

E Main St.
Washington Ave.

Noank Rd.

Hatch St.
Hewitt Rd.

Williams Ave.

ATTRACTIONS●
Mystic Aquarium **9**
Mystic Seaport Museum **7**

HOTELS■
Hilton Mystic **10**
Spicer Mansion **1**
Steamboat Inn **4**
Taber Inne & Suites **11**
The Whaler's Inn **5**

RESTAURANTS◆
Bravo Bravo **5**
Go Fish **8**
Kitchen Little **12**
Mystic Pizza **3**
S & P Oyster Co. **6**
Sift Bake Shop **2**

Exploring Groton

Just across the Thames River from New London, Groton is a major naval-industrial town. The U.S. Navy has a submarine base here, and General Dynamics Electric Boat designs, constructs, and maintains subs at its Groton shipyard.

History buffs will enjoy **Fort Griswold Battlefield State Park,** Park Avenue (www.ct.gov/deep/fortgriswold; © **860/449-6877**). It was here, in 1781, that Benedict Arnold, who fought for American independence before trading allegiances, led a British force against American defenders and ruthlessly

Mystic Whaler Cruises, at City Pier, 35 Water Street, New London (www.mystic whalercruises.com; ℂ **800/697-8420**), offers various tall ship outings, ranging from $60 sunset cruises to a $95 lobster dinner cruises that includes a classic New England meal. Also departing from New London, at 2 Ferry St., **Block Island Express** (www.goblockisland. com; ℂ **860/444-4624** or 401/466-2212), the same company that runs the ferries to Block Island (see p. 412), also runs 2-hour narrated cruises daily from late May through September and on October weekends and Wednesdays ($30 adults, $15 children 2–11). Two itineraries showcase lighthouses and other coastal sights. From downtown Mystic, **Argia Mystic Cruises,** 12 Steamboat Wharf (www.argiamystic.com; ℂ **860/ 536-0416**) offers trips on a replica of a 19th-century schooner that docks just south of the Mystic River drawbridge. Two-hour sailing trips and sunset cruises are $52 for adults, $49 for seniors, and $42 for children under 18. Cruises operate from May through mid-October.

ordered the massacre of 88 prisoners after they had surrendered. Entrance is free, as is a cell phone tour you can access by dialing ℂ **860/424-4005**.

Submarine Force Library and Museum ★ MUSEUM   The centerpiece of this museum at the edge of the U.S. Naval Submarine Base is the USS *Nautilus,* a 319-foot-long sub that was commissioned in 1954 and in operation until 1980. It's moored and ready for boarding, welcoming visitors to take a walk through the control rooms, attack center, galley, and sleeping quarters of the world's first nuclear-powered ship. It is difficult to imagine how the sub could possibly contain a crew of 116 men, especially on its fabled 1958 cruise between Pearl Harbor and the North Pole. The museum also displays artifacts and replicas from its 33,000-item collection of early submarines, torpedoes, deck guns, and periscopes.

1 Crystal Lake Rd. (Naval Submarine Base). www.ussnautilus.org. ℂ **800/343-0079** or 860/694-3174. Free admission. Wed–Mon 9am–5pm (Nov–Apr closes at 4pm). Closes 1–2 weeks in spring for upkeep.

Exploring Mystic ★★★

New England's maritime spirit is captured in many ports along its indented coast, but nowhere more precisely than beside the Mystic River estuary and its harbor. This was a dynamic whaling and shipbuilding center during the Colonial period and into the 20th century. Even though whaling is dead and shipbuilding on the decline, Mystic doesn't appear to be suffering—no derelict barges or rotting piers degrade views or waterways. The town is home to one of New England's most singular attractions, the **Mystic Seaport Museum** (p. 415), a re-created seaport of the mid-1800s, fully evoking that romantic era of clipper ships and the China trade.

Mystic and West Mystic are stitched together by a **drawbridge**, the hourly raising of which causes regular traffic stoppages but rarely shortens tempers.

There are complaints by some that the town has been commercialized, but the more touristy shops and chain hotels have been restricted to the periphery, especially up near exit 90 off I-95. A good collection of New England history books is available in downtown Mystic at the "locally owned, fiercely independent" **Bank Square Books,** 53 W. Main St. (www.banksquarebooks.com; *©* **860/536-3795**).

Mystic Aquarium ★★ AQUARIUM Enter this indoor/outdoor complex, and you're met by sweet-faced beluga whales that swim right up to the glass in a specially chilled tank. Mystic is the only New England aquarium to host the Arctic white whales. Watch them squeal and twirl for their trainers at feeding times or even touch and view them up close during a "Beluga Encounter" ($179; reservations required), one of several unforgettable interactive experiences offered. Children love to pet stingrays in the touch pool (the rays arc up like cats to skim along children's hands), and little "Nemo" fans flock to the tank of orange-and-white-striped clownfish. There also are sea lion shows, penguins, and 4-D movies.

55 Coogan Blvd. www.mysticaquarium.org. *©* **860/572-5955.** $37 adults, $32 seniors, $32 youth 13–17, $27 ages 3–12, free for children 2 and under. Tickets good for 2 consecutive days (must be validated before exit). Apr–Labor Day daily 9am–5:50pm; slightly shorter hours daily rest of year.

Mystic Seaport Museum ★★★ LIVING HISTORY MUSEUM Dubbed "the museum of America and the sea," Mystic Seaport Museum is a re-created 19th-century waterfront settlement. Historic buildings were transported here from across New England, and there are historic vessels like the *Charles W. Morgan,* the world's only surviving wooden whaling ship, to scramble over, too. Set aside 2 or 3 hours—if not an entire day—for exploring. The village center has about 30 rescued **shops and artifacts** including a cooperage, a printing office, a general store, and a hand-pumped fire engine from the 1850s. In the warm months, a boathouse offers rentals of sailboats or rowboats ($15 an hour) and pedal-powered boats ($15 per half-hour).

Out on the Water: Fishing Expeditions

Charter and public **fishing trips** are available between early May and mid-November from the Sunbeam Fleet, based at **Captain John's Sport Fishing Center,** 15 First St., Waterford (www.sunbeamfleet.com; *©* **860/443-7259**). Waterford is immediately west of New London, and the dock is next to the Niantic River Bridge (Route 156). Public trips last from 5½ to 8 hours, and include half-day blues and bass fishing trips, departing at 6am and 1pm on weekends, as well as 8am some weekdays. The cost is $63 adults, $58 seniors, $33 children 12 and under, plus $7 rod rental; bait is included. Check for exact days and times and reservation policies. Based in Groton, the 114-foot *Hel-Cat II,* 181 Thames St. (www.helcat.com; *©* **860/535-2066** or 860/535-3200) runs trips lasting either 4 hours ($55 adults, $30 ages 12 and under, as well as non-fishing adults) and 7 hours ($70 adults, $35 ages 12 and under and non-fishing adults). Tackle can be rented.

On one end of the village is a **working shipyard** where carpenters demonstrate historically accurate methods. The *Mayflower II,* a full-scale replica of the Pilgrims' famous ship, is undergoing restoration here in preparation for 2020's 400th anniversary of these religious dissidents' transatlantic voyage. The village's other end has many activities for smaller children. There's a creepy display of wide-eyed wooden **figureheads** that might incite strange dreams, as well as a planetarium, where presentations explain how critical celestial navigation was to early mariners.

In high season, visitors can expect all exhibits to be open and the village to have an energetic buzz. Docents are friendly and highly competent at crafts they demonstrate, always ready to impart as much information as visitors care to absorb. It can be a bit of a ghost town in the colder months: From early January through early February, the village and shipyard are closed.

75 Greenmanville Ave. (Rte. 27). www.mysticseaport.org. © **860/572-0711.** $29 adults, $27 seniors, $19 children 4–14, free for children 3 and under. Tickets good for 2 consecutive days (must be validated before exit). Late Mar–late Oct daily 9am–5pm; Nov daily 10am–4pm; Dec–Mar Thurs–Sun 10am–4pm.

Exploring Stonington ★ & North Stonington

These slumbering villages are only lightly brushed by the 21st century despite the glitz of heavily touristed Mystic nearby. Incorporated in 1801, coastal Stonington Borough's two lengthwise streets are lined with well-preserved Federal-style and Greek Revival homes. North Stonington, 7 miles inland, is as peaceful a New England town as you'll find, with hardly any commercialization. Its village historic district is listed on the National Register of Historic Places.

Drive south in Stonington along its main **Water Street,** which is thick with boutiques and restaurants. At the end is **Stonington Point,** where there's a petite **public beach.** The misty blue headland across the sound is Montauk Point, the eastern extremity of New York's Long Island. At Stonington Point, the **Old Lighthouse Museum,** 7 Water St. (www.stoningtonhistory.org; © **860/535-1440**), was America's first lighthouse museum. Built of stone recycled from a predecessor beacon in 1840, the lighthouse was active until 1889. Exhibits of scrimshaw and export porcelain inside relate to the maritime past of the area. Admission ($10 adults, $8 seniors, $6 ages 6–12) includes the chance to climb tower stairs for views of three states. It's open May through October, daily except Wednesday, from 10am to 5pm.

Stonington Vineyards, 523 Taugwonk Rd., Stonington (www.stonington vineyards.com; © **860/535-1222**), has a sunlight-drenched tasting room. Sample six wines, with an aged-in-oak Chardonnay leading the pack. Visitors are welcome to bring a picnic, buy a bottle, and settle in at a table overlooking the vines. The winery is open daily year-round from at least 11am to 5pm (until 7pm on summer and early fall Saturdays), with a free vineyard tour at 2pm.

Where to Stay on the Southeastern Coast

Plenty of notable historic properties and ho-hum but adequate hotels are available to soak up the tourist traffic at all but peak periods, meaning weekends from late spring to early fall plus weekdays in July and August

MYSTIC

Hilton Mystic ★   Unlike most Mystic properties, the Hilton is full-service, with all the amenities found in its big-city cousins: indoor pool, courtyard lounge with fire pits, room service, complimentary shuttle. It's located across the street from Mystic Aquarium. Renovations have upped the comfort factor and given the property, particularly its nautical gastropub **The Irons,** local flair.

20 Coogan Blvd. www.hiltonmystic.com. ℰ **860/572-0731.** 182 units. $115–$390 double. **Amenities:** Restaurant; lounge; exercise room; indoor pool; room service; Wi-Fi (free).

Spicer Mansion ★★★   This boutique inn's local owners saw potential in a tattered, forlorn sea captain's home that had stood on a hilltop overlooking downtown Mystic since 1853. Two years of meticulous restoration—plus over-the-top amenities like Duxiana beds, curated fine art, picnic basket lunches, behind-the-scenes experiences, and a basement speakeasy accessed through a hidden door—have transformed the dilapidated mansion into the village's most upscale and unusual place to dream.

15 Elm St. www.spicermansion.com. ℰ **860/245-4621.** 8 units. $395–$850 double. **Amenities:** Restaurant; bar/lounge; pass to local gym; complimentary bicycles; Wi-Fi (free).

Steamboat Inn ★★   Mystic's most romantic lodging is easily overlooked from land but readily apparent from the water, as it's perched directly on the bank of the Mystic River. The windowed structure has large, handsome rooms with wood-burning fireplaces (upstairs bedrooms) or kitchenettes (downstairs bedrooms). Each is decorated differently—Laura Ashley was a likely muse—and all but one have a view of the water and the sailboats that make up the traffic.

73 Steamboat Wharf (or 9 Water St. for GPS directions). www.steamboatinnmystic.com. ℰ **860/536-8300.** 11 units. $170–$300 double. Rates include breakfast. Parking available. **Amenities:** Boat dockage; Wi-Fi (free).

Taber Inne & Suites ★   Not quite an inn but more than a motel, this ever-popular complex has something to suit most tastes and budgets. It's made up of 12 buildings with basic units, hedonistic suites with fireplaces and decks, and two-bedroom town houses. The Carriage House has a fireplace, two bedrooms, a sitting room, and a two-person Jacuzzi. Standard rooms are clean, neat, and bland. It's located a little less than a mile from town center.

66 Williams Ave. (Rte. 1). www.taberinne.com. ℰ **866/822-3746** or 860/536-4904. 32 units. $110–$185 double; suites $165 and up. Rates include breakfast. 2-night minimum stay on weekends May–Oct and holiday weekends. **Amenities:** Heated indoor pool; Wi-Fi (free).

The Whaler's Inn ★   Smack in the middle of all the action, Whaler's is a stone's throw from shops and restaurants. There are five buildings including the main inn, the motel-like Stonington House, and the Hoxie House, which has the most elegant (and expensive) digs. There, adults-only rooms have gas fireplaces, whirlpool baths, and luxurious linens. More modest rooms are clean and no-frills. Stonington House has long porches, although the view is of the parking lot. The restaurant **Bravo Bravo** (see below) is on the first floor of the main inn building.

20 E. Main St. www.whalersinnmystic.com. © **860/536-1506.** 48 units. $189–$289 double. Rates include breakfast. **Amenities:** Gym access; complimentary bicycles; Wi-Fi (free).

STONINGTON

The Inn at Stonington ★★   Combining the intimacy of a small inn with the comforts of a luxury hotel, the elegant Inn at Stonington exceeds expectations. Most rooms have gas fireplaces, and many have decks for taking in Stonington Harbor and Fishers Island Sound. The design is a contemporary interpretation of country decor, and no two rooms are alike. It's so quiet here you might think you are alone—but head to the bar in the early evening to meet other guests for complimentary wine and cheese.

60 Water St. www.innatstonington.com. © **860/535-2000.** 18 units. $195–$490 double. Rates include breakfast and evening wine and cheese. 2-night minimum weekends. No children 13 and under. **Amenities:** Wi-Fi (free).

Where to Eat on the Southeastern Coast

GROTON

Olio ★ INTERNATIONAL   Look past the unassuming location at the intersection of two highways. Inside, Olio is a contemporary, lounge-y space with a creative menu. Pastas dominate the offerings, from red beet linguini and scallops to spinach ricotta-filled gnocchi with chicken and Marsala goat cheese sauce. Tasty appetizers, such as Cajun swordfish tacos, fill out the menu. With bare tables and hard surfaces everywhere, it can be loud, and take the reading glasses, because there are only guttering candles and a few dim pin lights to illuminate the menu.

33 Kings Hwy. (south of I-95 at Rte. 1). www.olioct.com. © **860/445-6546.** Main courses $19–$35. Mon–Thurs 11:30am–4pm and 4:30pm–9pm; Fri–Sat 11:30am–10pm; Sun 4:30–9pm.

MYSTIC

Bravo Bravo ★ CONTEMPORARY ITALIAN   Reserve or plan to wait, because this enduring favorite is reliably packed. Bravo Bravo can get as noisy as a disco, but it's a fun place for an animated night out, and it's right in the center of town. Half the entrees involve pasta—lobster ravioli, champagne risotto, seafood with tomato fettuccine in a lobster cream sauce—with alternatives like stuffed veal with a shiitake mushroom sauce.

20 E. Main St. www.bravobravoct.com. © **860/536-3228.** Main courses $24–$35. Tues–Thurs 11:30am–9pm; Fri 11:30am–10pm; Sat 8am–10pm; Sun 8am–9pm.

Go Fish ★ SEAFOOD   Brash and boisterous, Go Fish is dominated by a sprawling granite bar at its center, often surrounded by younger drinkers and grazers. At the far end is an enclosed sushi bar, while near the front entrance is a room usually populated by older folks and families. Local or regional seafood is employed as much as possible, including Stonington sea scallops and Mystic oysters. Daily specials rely on fresh catches. Portions are abundant, so you might want to skip appetizers, enticing though they are (the creamy lobster bisque, for one). During weekday happy hour, from 4:30 to 6pm, the bar food menu is half-price.

Olde Mistick Village, 27 Coogan Blvd. at Rte. 27. www.gofishct.com. *©* **860/536-2662.** Main courses $19–$34. Sun–Thurs 11:30am–9pm; Fri–Sat 11:30am–9:30pm.

Kitchen Little ★ DINER   This cheery breakfast and lunch joint at Mystic River Marina promises "A.M. Eggstasy." Don't miss dozens of distinct brunchy choices (try the Portuguese fisherman plate or Eggs Benedict topped with fresh-caught lobster or filet mignon). Expect a wait and tight quarters inside. Try to snare a table on the shaded deck for views of boats coming and going. To get to Mason's Island, take Mason's Island Road south from Route 1, just east of the Mystic drawbridge.

36 Quarry Rd., Mason's Island. www.kitchenlittle.org. *©* **860/536-2122.** Main dishes $2.59–$20. Mon–Fri 7:30am–2pm; Sat–Sun 6:30am–1pm.

Mystic Pizza ★ PIZZA   In a state known for pizza, this downtown parlor's pies aren't Oscar-worthy, but fans of the eponymous Julia Roberts movie still head here for nostalgia and a "slice of heaven."

56 W. Main St. www.mysticpizza.com. *©* **860/536-3700.** Pizzas and dinners $9–$18. Daily 10am–11pm.

S&P Oyster Co ★★ SEAFOOD   In the center of town (across from Bravo Bravo, p. 418), S&P is Mystic's big fish restaurant. Its location assures that it will be busy, but the food delivers. Seafood white bean chili is a spicy blend of crawfish, scallops, and shrimp, served with homemade corn chips. The seafood pasta is piled so high with mussels, shrimp, scallops, and calamari, you'll have to mount an expedition to uncover the tagliatelle. The dining rooms are elegant without being too formal and look out over the Mystic River. There's reasonable value here: Nothing's inexpensive, but the portions are generous. You'll leave satisfied.

1 Holmes St. www.sp-oyster.com. *©* **860/536-2674.** Main dishes $25–$38, with most under $30. Daily 11:30am–9pm (until 10pm Fri–Sat).

Sift Bake Shop ★★ BAKERY   Chef, perfectionist, performance artist, and Food Network "Best Baker in America" winner Adam Young and his team are hard at work in the wee hours to ensure cases are filled with artisanal loaves, flaky croissants, exotic pastries, and too-pretty-to-eat macarons. An open kitchen allows salivating fans to spy on their efforts. Long hours and caffeinated beverages make this the perfect pick-me-up stop morning, noon, or eve.

5 Water St. www.siftbakeshopmystic.com. *©* **860/245-0541.** All items under $10; most under $4. Daily 7am–7pm.

NOANK

Abbott's Lobster in the Rough ★★ SEAFOOD   Located in pictur-esque Noank, about 3 miles south of downtown Mystic, Abbott's is a nitty-gritty lobster shack with picnic tables and not a frill to be found—it's as if a wedge of the Maine coast has been punched into the Connecticut shore. While options include hot dogs and chicken, the classic shore dinner rules: clam chowder, cocktail shrimp, steamed mussels and clams, and a tasty lobster, with coleslaw, chips, and drawn butter. Abbott's doesn't have a liquor license, but you can bring your own beer or wine.

117 Pearl St. www.abbottslobster.com. ✆ **860/536-7719.** Main courses $4–$40. Daily late May–Labor Day 11:30am–9pm; weekends only early May and Sept–early Oct.

STONINGTON

Water Street Cafe ★ NEW AMERICAN   With a pressed-tin ceiling, rustic walls and banquettes, and a huge French mahogany bar, this cheery, casual restaurant on Stonington's main shopping drag is pleasantly unpreten-tious. Local oysters from the raw bar are consistently good, as are lobster spring rolls, fluke tempura, skillet-roasted chicken, and the pulled pork sandwich.

143 Water St. www.waterstcafe.com. ✆ **860/535-2122.** Main courses $9–$30. Mon–Thurs 5–9:30pm, Fri–Sat 5–10:30pm, Sun 10am–3pm and 5–9pm.

THE CASINOS: FOXWOODS RESORT & MOHEGAN SUN

Foxwoods and Mohegan Sun: 134 miles NE of New York City, 106 miles SW of Boston

There was little but forest here when the Mashantucket Pequot (pronounced *Pee*-kwat) tribe received clearance to open a casino on ancestral lands. Nearly overnight, the tribal bingo parlor was expanded into the **Foxwoods Resort Casino.** That was in 1992. Expansion ensued—more hotels, more gaming areas, a golf course, a museum devoted to Native American culture, an indoor outlet shopping mall, and an on-site brewery.

All this wasn't lost on the Mohegan tribe, which in 1996 opened a compet-ing casino, **Mohegan Sun.** The complexes are about 10 miles apart by car, with Mohegan Sun on the west in Uncasville nearer to New London, and Foxwoods on the east side of the Thames River in the Mashantucket area of the town of Ledyard.

Foxwoods was once the world's largest casino (and it's still the second-biggest in the U.S.), and it does look dramatic, rising like Oz above the rolling green hills. Recent years, though, have taken some of the bloom off the rose. With brand new competition just across the state line in Massachusetts, Fox-woods and Mohegan Sun are collaborating in a way that is unprecedented in the 400-year history of these once-warring tribes. Their $300-million casino joint venture is projected to open in East Windsor in 2020.

Essentials

ARRIVING

Foxwoods and Mohegan Sun are about 10 miles apart on Route 2/2A. For Foxwoods, take I-95 to exit 92 and head directly north on Route 2. For Mohegan Sun, take I-395 north from I-95 to exit 9 and follow Route 2A east to Mohegan Sun Boulevard.

A bewildering number of companies operate **buses** to Foxwoods and Mohegan Sun, from major players like Greyhound (www.greyhound.com), Academy (www.academybus.com), and MBT (www.mbtworldwide.com) to several smaller regional companies. Tickets range from $18 to $37 for Foxwoods and $35 to $40 for Mohegan Sun, and often include a $10 or $15 coupon to spend at the casinos. For specific options from your location, go to the casinos' websites or call ✆ **888/BUS-2-FOX** [888/287-2369] for Foxwoods or ✆ **888/770-0140** for Mohegan Sun.

VISITOR INFORMATION

Just about any question you could have about the casinos is answered at their websites: **www.foxwoods.com** and **www.mohegansun.com**.

Exploring the Casinos

Foxwoods Resort Casino ★ CASINO/SHOPPING/ENTERTAINMENT
One of the largest casino complexes in the world at 9 million square feet, Foxwoods boasts more than 250 tables including $1 Blackjack, a 3,600-seat bingo hall, and 4,800 slot machines. In addition to gaming, the resort is home to high-end boutiques, a Tanger Outlets mall, 4 hotels, and the **Grand Theater.** The theater is one of the busiest venues in the region, with such acts as comedian Jerry Seinfeld and singer Toby Keith. Foxwoods has also become Connecticut's adrenaline zone with the addition of the 60-mph High Flyer Zipline, the Thrill Tower free fall, XD Dark Ride, and an indoor karting center. Restaurant options range from unremarkable to high end; see "Where to Eat," p. 423. Larger-than-life sculptures depicting indigenous people are prominent throughout the buildings.

350 Trolley Line Blvd., Mashantucket. www.foxwoods.com. ✆ **800/369-9663.** Free admission. 24/7. Gaming areas restricted to ages 21 and older; bingo area 18 and older.

Mashantucket Pequot Museum & Research Center ★ MUSEUM
$193 million from the flood of cash washing over Connecticut's resurgent Indian Nation was diverted to develop this world-class museum, located a mile or so south of Foxwoods Resort Casino. From a chilly simulation of an Ice Age crevasse to a recreated Pequot village from pre-Contact days (before European settlers arrived in North America) and a recreated 18th-century farmstead, the museum explores the history of the Pequot nations and their relationship to their native environment. Films, murals, dioramas, and interactive displays engage museum visitors (life-size replicas of mastodons and giant beavers!); the on-site cafe serves Native American dishes; even the

architecture reinforces the message, with its glass-and-steel wigwam-like Gathering Place, an observation tower, and several underground floors nestling gently into the landscape.

110 Pequot Trail, Mashantucket. www.pequotmuseum.org. ℂ **800/411-9671.** $20 adults, $15 seniors, $12 ages 6–17, ages 5 and under free. Wed–Sat 10am–5pm, late Mar–early Dec.

Mohegan Sun ★ CASINO/SHOPPING/ENTERTAINMENT   Foxwoods' big competitor has three distinct casinos, the Earth and Sky hotel towers (see below), and a mall of pricey shops. There also are three venues for entertainment: a 10,000-seat **Arena** that hosts performers such as singer Justin Timberlake as well as the WNBA's Connecticut Sun, a professional women's basketball team; the **Comix Comedy Club;** and the free **Wolf Den,** located smack dab in the center of the circular "Earth" casino, with acts ranging from Herman's Hermits to The Wallflowers. Gamblers try their luck at Texas Hold 'em, blackjack, live-feed horse track betting, and more than 5,000 slot machines. Look up, and you'll see a tree canopy, an animated water wall, or a planetarium dome; the spaces are aesthetically pleasing, although few of the avid players seem to notice. One time-warp feature stands out strongly: Unlike almost all public areas in Connecticut including Mohegan Sun's restaurants and venues, smoking is allowed in most gaming rooms. High-tech ventilation systems keep the haze down.

1 Mohegan Sun Blvd., Uncasville. www.mohegansun.com. ℂ **888/226-7711.** Admission free. Daily 24 hours. Gaming areas restricted to ages 21 and older. Licensed child care available for ages 6 weeks to 12 years at Kids QueStreet.

Where to Stay by the Casinos

Foxwoods has four hotels on-property; Mohegan Sun has two. There are also familiar chain hotels and quiet B&Bs in the area. Many visitors to the casinos stay in the Mystic area (see p. 417 for Mystic area hotels).

Fox Tower at Foxwoods ★★   Attached to the original casino by an indoor walkway, the Fox Tower opened in 2008, and although a branding deal with MGM expired, the hotel and its pool still feel trendy and plush. Many rooms in the 30-story hotel have views of the surrounding evergreen woods, and decor is minimalist with dark earth tones. Fox Tower has its own G Spa, bars, restaurants, and Vegas-style **Shrine** night club. Smoke-free rooms are not guaranteed, although some suites are non-smoking.

39 Norwich-Westerly Rd., Ledyard. www.foxwoods.com/fox-tower-hotel. ℂ **800/369-9663.** 825 units. $139–$268 double. Free valet parking. **Amenities:** Fitness center; outdoor pool (warm months only); room service; spa w/waterfall whirlpool; Wi-Fi (included in resort fee).

Mohegan Sun Sky Tower ★★   The asymmetrical grouping of soaring, silver-skinned wedges that make up Mohegan Sun's first and largest hotel provokes the intended "Wow!" response. The slanting columns are arrayed around a reflecting pool in abstract homage to woodland ponds, and the nearly

1,200 rooms in the 34-story building are a minimum of 450 square feet each. A newly reimagined spa and an attractive indoor/outdoor pool are appealing features. Lobby escalators carry guests down to the restaurants, shops, and gaming areas of the casino complex. In 2016, Mohegan Sun added 400 additional rooms with high-tech amenities: The **Earth Tower,** a short walk from the hubbub of the casino, has its own pool, spa, and outdoor patio.

1 Mohegan Sun Blvd., Uncasville. www.mohegansun.com. ⓒ **888/777-7922.** 1,563 units. $159–$1,309 double. Free valet parking. **Amenities:** Many restaurants; many bars; concierge; fitness centers; indoor/outdoor pools; room service; spas; Wi-Fi (free).

Where to Eat Near the Casinos

Foxwoods has more than 35 restaurants and fast-food operations situated throughout the hotel-casino complex. Unlike in Atlantic City or Vegas, there are few bargains to be found. The popular **Festival Buffet** offers an extensive all-you-can-eat spread. Casual, wow-factor eateries like **Sugar Factory** and **Guy Fieri's Kitchen + Bar** are moderately priced. The high-end options are **VUE 24,** with a seafood- and steak-heavy menu; **Alta Strada,** which features crisp pizzas and homemade pastas; and **Cedars,** a steakhouse that grills a $140, 42-ounce, bone-in ribeye for two. These three venues expect business casual attire for guests. Reservations for any of the Foxwoods restaurants can be made online at www.foxwoods.com or through the main number, ⓒ **800/369-9663.**

Mohegan Sun has more than 40 dining spots. Among the top venues are **Jasper White's Summer Shack** (www.summershackrestaurant.com; ⓒ **860/862-9500**), for seafood; fellow celeb **Todd English's Tuscany** (ⓒ **860/862-3236**), for contemporary Italian; and an outpost of **Michael Jordan's Steak House** (mjshconnecticut.com; ⓒ **860/862-8600**).

RHODE ISLAND

By Barbara Radcliffe Rogers & Stillman Rogers

Water defines "Little Rhody" as much as mountain peaks characterize Colorado. The Atlantic Ocean borders its southeastern side, not in one smooth coastline but in a delightfully ragged, sea-fringed edge of islands, inlets, and the large basin that is Narragansett Bay. Indeed, while this tiny state measures only 37 miles east to west—you can easily drive from end to end in under an hour—within those 37 miles Rhode Island tucks in some 400 miles of seacoast. No wonder its official nickname is the Ocean State!

At the northern point of Narragansett Bay, 30 miles from the open ocean, lies Providence, the state capital, founded in 1636 by theologian Roger Williams. A couple of years later, another group of Puritan exiles established a settlement on an island in the Narragansett Bay known to the Narragansett tribe as Aquidneck. Settlers thought their new home resembled the Isle of Rhodes in the Aegean, so the region's name became "Rhode Island and Providence Plantations"—a title that eventually came to be used for the entire state.

Rhode Island's most important coastal town, Newport, is the best reason for an extended visit here. Newport's first era of prosperity was during the Colonial period, when its ships plied new mercantile routes to China. The city also was central to the reprehensible "Triangle Trade" of rum from New England, molasses from the West Indies, and enslaved peoples from Africa. Smuggling and evading taxes brought the ship owners into conflict with their British rulers and the occupying British army all but destroyed Newport during the American Revolution. About a hundred years later, after the U.S. Civil War, the town began its transformation to luxury resort. Millionaires arrived and built astonishingly extravagant mansions, dubbed their summer "cottages." (Their lives spawned what authors Mark Twain and Charles Dudley Warner sneeringly described as the "Gilded Age" in their 1873 novel *The Gilded Age: A Tale of Today*.) Those mansions remain intact, and many are open to visitors. Newport also became a yachting destination: Sailing's most famous trophy, the America's Cup, was moved to the city in 1930 and Newport continues to be a recreational sailing center with a

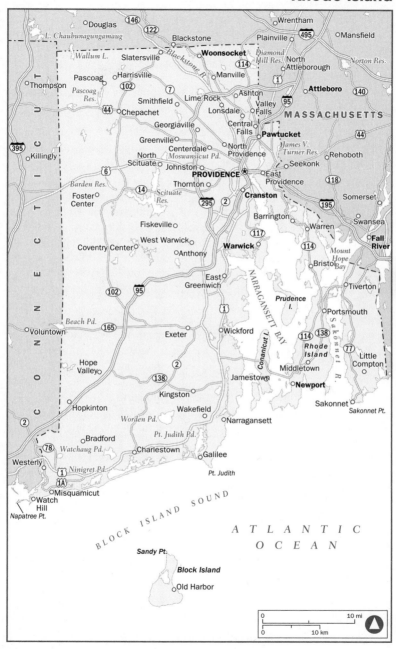

packed summer cultural calendar. The result is a city with a little of everything: Visitors who want nothing more than to listen to the surf can happily coexist with history buffs.

Finally, there is Block Island. Beloved by both year-round residents and vacationers, it's a 1-hour ferry ride from the southern coast of the state. It's a quieter and less chic summer destination than Martha's Vineyard (p. 266), the Massachusetts island about 50 miles to its east. "The Block" has few mandatory sights, leaving visitors free simply to explore its lighthouses, hike its cliffside trails, and hit the beach.

PROVIDENCE ★★

50 miles S of Boston, MA; 57 miles NE of New London, CT

From a neglected, run-down industrial has-been in the 1970s, Providence has re-created itself into a thriving, lively arts and creative center, alive with an energy that sets it apart from other small and midsize New England cities. Rivers have been uncovered to form canals and waterside walkways (and host a popular summer event called **WaterFire**); distressed buildings from the 1800s have been reclaimed and made into residences and office spaces; and construction has wrought new hotels and large public/private partnerships such as **Providence Place**, a mega-mall opened in 1999 that brought national department stores here for the first time.

Prosperity is evident in the resurgent Downcity business center and emerging adjacent neighborhoods, the Arts & Entertainment District to its west and Jewelry District to its south. Also on the rise is the West Side, a former industrial enclave adjoining Federal Hill, the city's traditional "Little Italy." All this new energy has attracted creative young people and restaurants, shops, bars, and entertainments they crave. A current key initiative, City Walk, is part of an Urban Trail plan that will strengthen the connections between neighborhoods, celebrating their diversity and culture through public art, signage and attractive public spaces.

The key historic figure of the region is **Roger Williams** (1603–83), a theologian who established a colony in Providence in 1636 after being banned from the Massachusetts Bay Colony for his views on religious freedom. Williams had good instincts for town building. He planted the seeds of his settlement on a steep rise overlooking a swift-flowing river at the point where it widened into a large protected harbor. That part of the city, called the East Side and dominated by the ridge now known as College Hill, is one of the most attractive city districts in New England, second only to Boston in the breadth of its cultural life and rich architectural heritage.

Essentials

ARRIVING

BY CAR I-95, which connects Boston and New York, runs right through the city. Going to or from Cape Cod, pick up I-195 West.

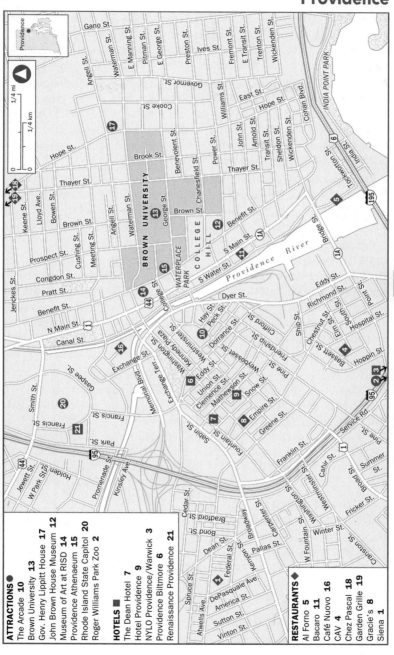

Providence

ATTRACTIONS ●
The Arcade **10**
Brown University **13**
Gov. Henry Lippitt House **17**
John Brown House Museum **12**
Museum of Art at RISD **14**
Providence Athenaeum **15**
Rhode Island State Capitol **20**
Roger Williams Park Zoo **2**

HOTELS ■
The Dean Hotel **9**
Hotel Providence **9**
NYLO Providence/Warwick **3**
Providence Biltmore **6**
Renaissance Providence **21**

RESTAURANTS ◆
Al Forno **5**
Bacaro **11**
Café Nuovo **16**
CAV **4**
Chez Pascal **18**
Garden Grille **19**
Gracie's **8**
Siena **1**

10

RHODE ISLAND | Providence

427

BY TRAIN Amtrak (www.amtrak.com; ✆ **800/USA-RAIL** [872-7245]) runs several trains daily between Boston and New York that stop at the attractive station at 100 Gaspee St., near the State House. The train journey from Boston takes anywhere from 35 minutes to 1 hour, depending on how many stops the train makes; tickets cost $12 and up. The trip from New York takes 3 or 3½ hours, with fares $50 and up.

BY PLANE **T. F. Green/Providence Airport** (www.pvdairport.com; ✆ **401/737-8222** or 401/691-2000) in Warwick, south of Providence (I-95, exit 13), handles domestic and international flights into the state. Most major U.S. airlines fly here, along with **Air Canada** (www.aircanada.com), and the European carriers **Azores Airlines** (www.azoresairlines.pt), and low-cost **Norwegian Airlines** (www.norwegian.com).

Between the Airport & the City Center

The **Rhode Island Public Transit Authority,** or **RIPTA** (www.ripta.com; ✆ **800/244-0444** or 401/781-9400), provides transportation between the airport and the city center. Taxis are also available, about $30 to $35 for the 20-minute trip; shared shuttle van rides cost $11.

VISITOR INFORMATION

The **Providence Warwick Convention & Visitors Bureau** runs an information center in the Rhode Island Convention Center, 1 Sabin St. (www.goprovidence. com; ✆ **800/233-1636** or 401/751-1177). Their website is full of good information, too, and you can request a visitors' guide booklet to be mailed to you in advance. The center is open Monday through Saturday from 9am to 5pm.

CITY LAYOUT

Downcity is the center for business, government, and entertainment, with City Hall, the convention center, the best large hotels, and venues for music, dance, and theatrical productions. Most points of general interest are found in the **East Side** and **College Hill,** which lie—as their names imply—east and uphill from downtown. To downtown's north, across the Woonasquatucket River, is the imposing State House, as well as the Amtrak station. To its west, on the other side of I-95, is **Federal Hill,** a residential area bearing a primarily Italian ethnic identity, although increasingly permeated by more recent immigrant groups.

GETTING AROUND

Traffic on local streets isn't bad, even at rush hour. But hailing a taxi is not easy; few can be found outside even the largest hotels, and when called from restaurants they can take up to an hour. The **RIPTA bus** Green and Gold Lines, which look like old-time trolleys, have routes that reach most major hotels and tourist destinations. Each ride costs $1.75; you can buy tickets at RIPTA ticket vending machines, the Kennedy Plaza ticket window, or onboard.

Exploring Providence

City boosters are understandably proud of downtown Providence's **Waterplace Park & Riverwalk** ★★, which encircles a tidal basin and borders the Woonasquatucket River down past where it joins the Moshassuck to become the Providence River. It incorporates an amphitheater, boat landings, landscaped walkways, and vaguely Venetian bridges. Summer concerts and other events are held here, including the popular **WaterFire** ★★ (see p. 431).

At the park's eastern end is a singular attraction, **La Gondola** (www.gondolari.com; ☏ **401/421-8877**). A faithful replica of the Venetian original, it carries up to six passengers along the Woonasquatucket and Providence rivers May through October. Especially popular for rides during the WaterFire events, its rates run from $179 (2 persons) to $279 (6 persons) for WaterFire nights, or $89–$169 (2–6 persons) for a 40-minute Viaggio Dei Sogni experience—about what it would cost in the Italian city itself, minus the airfare.

South of the river and west of Exchange Street, expansive **Kennedy Plaza** lies in the heart of downtown. In winter, a huge **outdoor ice skating rink** (www.theprovidencerink.com; ☏ **401/331-5544**) is set up here; it's fully utilized almost every evening in cold weather, with skate rentals, lockers, and a snack bar are on site. In summer the Plaza is home to special events.

Brown University ★★   The nation's seventh-oldest college was founded in 1764 and has a reputation as the most experimental institution among its Ivy League brethren. The evidence of its pre-Revolutionary origins is seen in

Stroll the Historic Neighborhoods

To get a sense of Providence's evolution from a colony of dissidents to a contemporary center of commerce and government, take a leisurely walk from downtown (or "Downcity," as it's called here) across the river toward Brown University; you'll pass most of the prominent Providence attractions.

Start at **Providence City Hall** (built in 1878), at Kennedy Plaza and Dorrance Street. Walk 1 block south, turn left onto Westminster, then right in 1 block at the Arcade (see p. 432), then left onto Weybosset. Follow Weybosset until it joins Westminster, and continue along Westminster across the Providence River. Turn right, along the river on South Water Street as far as James Street, just before the I-195 overpass. Turn left onto James, cross South Main, and then turn left on Benefit Street.

Here on Benefit Street is the start of the so-called **Mile of History** ★★. Lined with 18th- and 19th-century houses, it is enhanced by gas streetlamps and sections of brick herringbone sidewalks. Along the way are opportunities to visit, in sequence, the 1786 **John Brown House,** the **Providence Athenaeum** (p. 431), and the **Museum of Art at the Rhode Island School of Design** (p. 430). The grand **Gov. Henry Lippitt House Museum** (p. 430) is a half-mile from the RISD museum and worth a stop if you're touring on a Friday.

The area from Benefit up to the right (east) is **College Hill** ★, site of the former Rhode Island College (founded in 1764), which was later renamed Brown University. Now a National Historic District, College Hill has several square miles of 18th- and 19th-century Colonial and Victorian houses lining its streets. In the middle of the Brown campus, parallel to Benefit, is **Thayer Street,** a funky shopping district.

The **Rhode Island Historical Society** (www.rihs.org; ☏ **401/331-8575**) offers guided walking tours of the city's neighborhoods starting from the John Brown House Museum (52 Power St.).

University Hall, built in 1771. Free tours of the campus are intended primarily for prospective students, but anyone can join. Reservations are not necessary, but call ahead to check the schedule, which changes frequently. Tours begin at Stephen Robert '62 Campus Center located at 75 Waterman St.

Office of Admissions, 45 Prospect St. (at Angell St.). www.brown.edu. ✆ **401/863-1000.**

Gov. Henry Lippitt House Museum ★ HISTORIC HOME   This 1865 mansion is as magnificently true to its grandiose Victorian era as any residence on the Continent. Expanses of stained glass, meticulously detailed stenciling, and inlaid floors make this one of the treasures of College Hill. Visits are by guided tour only.

199 Hope St. (at Angell St.). www.preserveri.org. ✆ **401/453-0688.** Guided tour $10. Tours May–Oct Fri and 3rd Sat of month: 11am–3pm on the hour (last tour at 2pm); Nov–Apr by appointment only.

Museum of Art at the Rhode Island School of Design ★★ MUSEUM   Prestigious RISD (pronounced *Riz*-dee) supports this center of fine and decorative arts. Of New England's many excellent college and university museums, this ranks near the top for the breadth of its collection. Holdings include textile arts and French Impressionist paintings, with works by such masters as Monet, Cézanne, Rodin, Picasso, and Matisse. Allow extra time for the American wing, which contains paintings by John Singleton Copley and John Singer Sargent, and the contemporary collection, which includes sculpture by Louise Bourgeois and videos by Bruce Nauman. The Gorham silver collection, including work by Colonial silversmith Paul Revere, is itself worth the price of admission.

224 Benefit St. (at Waterman St.) or 20 N. Main St. www.risdmuseum.org. ✆ **401/454-6500.** $15 adults, $12 seniors, $3 college students, free under age 18. Free to all 3rd Thurs of month 5–9pm, Sun 10am–1pm, and last Sat of month. Tues–Sun 10am–5pm (3rd Thurs of month until 9pm).

Pawtucket Red Sox Baseball at McCoy Stadium ★ SPECTATOR SPORTS   Just 6 miles north of Providence is Pawtucket, a working-class city with a great attraction: the minor league ballpark for the Pawtucket Red Sox, a Triple A baseball team. As the step just before the big leagues with the Boston Red Sox, Pawtucket is the place to catch both up-and-coming stars and big name players recovering from injuries. Baseball at McCoy Stadium is old-timey American: The crowds are friendly, the prices are modest, the baseball is good, and the music is low-key. You can even get your photo taken with the mascots (Paws and Sox) for free. Fun fact: McCoy was witness to the longest game in baseball history—33 innings, played over 2 days in 1981 (the Paw Sox won). *Note:* In 2018 it was announced that the PawSox will be moving to a new stadium in Worcester, Massachusetts in 2021. Goodbye PawSox, hello WooSox!

1 Columbus Ave., Pawtucket. (Take I-95 to exit 27, 28, or 29 and follow signs.) www.pawsox.com. ✆ **401/724-7300.** Box seats $14; general admission $9 adults, $6 senior, military and children 12 and under. Limited free parking; paid parking nearby. Season runs Apr–Sept.

Providence Athenaeum ★ LIBRARY   The Providence Athenaeum commissioned this 1838 Greek Revival building to house its lending library, the fourth-oldest in the United States. Edgar Allan Poe courted Sarah Whitman, his "Annabel Lee," among the stacks here. Glances through the old card catalog reveal handwritten cards dating well back into the 1800s; bibliophiles will lose themselves in this evocative place. Rotating exhibits of rare books and works by local artists are additional attractions.

251 Benefit St. (at College St.). www.providenceathenaeum.org. ✆ **401/421-6970.** Free admission. Mon–Thurs 9am–7pm; Fri 9am–5pm; Sat 1–5pm. Also Sun 1–5pm Sept–May. Closed 1st 2 weeks Aug.

Rhode Island State House ★ ARCHITECTURE   Constructed of white Georgian marble that blazes in the sun, Rhode Island's capitol building dominates the city center. This near-flawless example of neoclassical governmental architecture (by McKim, Mead & White; 1885–1904) is crowned by one of the world's largest self-supported domes. The gilded figure on top represents "Independent Man," the state symbol. Inside the State Room is a portrait of George Washington, one of several painted by Gilbert Stuart (1755–1828), a Rhode Island native.

82 Smith St. (at State St.). sos.ri.gov/divisions/Civics-And-Education/State-House-Tour. ✆ **401/277-2357.** Free admission. Guided tours by appointment.

Roger Williams Park Zoo ★ ZOO   One of the country's oldest zoos (founded in 1872), its mission is to engage visitors' interest in animals and to promote their conservation in the wild. The 40-acre zoo is divided into six habitats: Tropical America, North America, the Plains of Africa, Madagascar, Australia, and the Marco Polo Trail. Featured animals include giraffes, elephants, harbor seals, and snow leopards. Halloween brings special programs including a huge display of jack-o-lanterns and "spooky zoo" parties.

1000 Elmwood Ave. (exit 16 or 17 from I-95). www.rwpzoo.org. ✆ **401/785-3510.** $18 adults, $16 seniors, $13 ages 2–12, free for children 1 and under; 50% discount for retired and active military. Admission half-price Jan–Feb. Free parking. Daily 9am–4pm.

WaterFire Providence ★★ OUTDOOR EVENT   The signature event of the Providence summer and early fall are the WaterFire nights. Along the three rivers that run through the city, an installation of 100 floating bonfires creates a haunting glow, with world music adding to the scene. Thousands of people descend to the shores to witness the event, held a dozen times from late

Stroll Federal Hill

Federal Hill, on the west side of the city, has long been a tourist destination. It's a traditionally Italian neighborhood—the television show *Brotherhood* was filmed in the area, as was the 1994 movie *Federal Hill*—complete with traditional Italian eateries, but since about 1990 it has seen a rise in non-Italian restaurants and new boutiques and galleries (see "Shopping," p. 432). Atwells Avenue is the neighborhood's main artery.

spring to early fall. It takes place along Memorial Boulevard and the Providence and Woonasquatucket Rivers, running for just over a half-mile from Providence Place to the Crawford Street Bridge.

Basin of Waterplace Park and along the river, downtown Providence. www.waterfire. org. ℂ **401/273-1155.** Free admission, donations accepted at site. Late May–Oct, from 20 min. after sunset until midnight. Check website for schedule.

Shopping

On the East Side of the city, **Thayer Street,** the main commercial district for Brown University, is good for browsing. The official **Brown Bookstore** is here, at no. 244 (corner of Olive St.). **Wickenden Street,** which crosses Thayer at its southern end, also has interesting shops and art galleries.

Downtown, **Providence Place,** a 170-store mall at One Providence Place (www.providenceplace.com; ℂ **401/270-1000**), is home to Nordstrom, Tiffany & Co., Coach, Apple Store, J. Jill, and Build-A-Bear Workshop, among others. There's also a National Amusements IMAX movie theater. The mall's parking garage rates are reasonable for a midsize city (2 hours free, 2–5 hours $2, 5–8 hours $15 and up).

The Arcade ★, 66 Weybosset St. (ℂ **401/454-4568**) is the granddaddy of all U.S. shopping malls, having opened in 1828. While its upper floors have now been made into "small lofts", the first floor continues the shopping history with nine shops. **Carmen and Ginger** specializes in items including jewelry, clothing, and bric-a-brac—you might say light antiques. **Chamonix Antiques** sells furniture and art (both old and contemporary). The Arcade also has **Lovecraft Arts and Sciences**, a book and gift store devoted to Providence native son H. P. Lovecraft, the early 20th-century master of horror and spooky fiction; it also serves as headquarters for occasional literary events and the biannual Necronomicon convention.

Foodies will want to stroll Federal Hill, Providence's "Little Italy," west of I-95 (see box p. 431). Head to Atwells Avenue, the main drag. Keep an eye out for **Costantino's Venda Ravioli ★,** 275 Atwells Ave. (www.vendaravioli. com; ℂ **401/421-9105**), a pasta store that has expanded into a small empire of prepared foods, packaged Italian specialties, and large cheese and meat sections. There's an espresso bar, as well as cafe tables for noshing either inside or on a terrace.

Where to Stay in Providence

The Renaissance Providence, listed below, is across the street from the State House. Three others recommended are downtown—"Downcity," as it's called here—and one is just south of the city near TF Green Airport. Tip: Hotel demand goes through the roof for Brown University commencement weekend; even if you are lucky enough to snag a free room, expect rates to soar well above usual.

The Dean Hotel ★★   As cheeky and hip as the city itself, The Dean is a newcomer to Downcity but rooted firmly in its idiosyncratic traditions. Take the karaoke lounge for example, or the stylish furniture that combines the work of local craftspeople with "previously owned" finds. There's a sociable vibe going on here, in the welcoming public areas and in the no-phone-no-reservations-no-menu restaurant, **North ★**, where ingredients are sourced from local growers and producers. Stylish rooms are decorated with original art and works of RISD photographers, and range from cozy double-bunk dens to Guardian Suites with king-size beds and seating for six.

122 Fountain St. (btw. Snow and Mathewson sts.). www.thedeanhotel.com. © **401/455-3316.** 52 units. $109–$209 double. Valet parking $28. **Amenities:** Restaurant; coffee bar; cocktail lounge; karaoke lounge; rain showers; complimentary bikes; Wi-Fi (free).

Hotel Providence ★★
A dazzling contribution to the emerging downtown arts and entertainment district, this boutique hotel, combining two buildings, gained instant membership in the selective Small Luxury Hotels of the World marketing group. The owners filled the public areas with fine 18th- and 19th-century European antiques and artworks, and commissioned custom reproductions for the bedrooms to carry the image through. Pillow-top beds are cozy and enveloping. Guests are serenaded at 15-minute intervals by the pealing of the 16 tower bells of Grace Church, across the street, so light sleepers will want a room away from that side of the hotel.

139 Mathewson St. www.hotelprovidence.com. © **855/861-8990** or 401/861-8000. 80 units. $199–$239 double. Valet parking $25. Small pets accepted ($75 fee). **Amenities:** Restaurant; bar; concierge; small exercise room; room service; Wi-Fi (free).

NYLO Providence/Warwick ★
Outside the center on the airport (south) side of the city, the NYLO's minimalist loft rooms overlook the Pawtuxet River or have views of Downcity. Rooms are 300 square feet, suites double that, all with king-size beds and industrial-chic decor of brick walls and cement floors. The Skyline Suite adds a 300-square-foot private terrace. Some rooms have heating/air conditioning units behind the bed, which can be noisy at night. An outdoor patio lounge overlooks the river, and the in-house restaurant serves Italian/New England dishes. Shoppers like the NYLO's location opposite the Warwick Mall, a complex of 80 stores, restaurants and a movie theater. Special airport packages include free parking and shuttle to TF Green Airport.

400 Knight St. (off Greenwich Ave.), Warwick. www.nylohotels.com/warwick. © **401/734-4460.** 163 rooms. $107–289 double. Free parking. Pets accepted ($50 per pet for up to 3 nights). **Amenities:** Restaurant; bar; allergy-free rooms available; Wi-Fi (free).

Providence Biltmore ★★
A grand staircase beneath the stunning Deco bronze ceiling dates the centrally located building to the 1920s, and a plaque in the lobby shows the nearly 7-foot-high water level reached during the villainous 1938 hurricane. From the lobby, the dramatic glass elevator shoots skyward, exiting outdoors to scoot up the side of the building. Most guest rooms are large (over half are suites averaging 600 sq. ft.), and California king beds are standard in all rooms. The in-house restaurant, **McCormick & Schmick's**, specializes in seafood and steaks, with an Oyster Night every Thursday.

11 Dorrance St. www.providencebiltmore.com. © **800/294-7709** or 401/421-0700. 292 units. $169–$234 double. Valet parking $24. Pets accepted ($35/night). **Amenities:** Restaurant; bar; fitness center; room service; Wi-Fi (free).

Renaissance Providence ★★★ Here's a story: In the late 1920s, the Masons were building a neoclassical temple a couple of blocks west of the State House. When they ran out of money, construction suddenly ended, leaving the building an empty shell. There it stood for 78 years, unoccupied, a magnet for graffiti vandals and thieves. A $100-million renovation by the Marriott company transformed it into this ambitious luxury hotel, which opened in 2007. Immediately, the Renaissance Providence rivaled the best the city has to offer. A grand lobby with a fireplace welcomes guests, and **Temple,** the flashy in-house restaurant-bar, was an instant hit with locals as well as out-of-towners. Two executive-level floors have a private club/lounge with honor bar. The hotel is a 5-minute walk from the Amtrak station and across from the State House.

5 Ave. of the Arts (formerly Brownell St.). www.renaissancehotels.com. © **866/238-4218** or 800-468-3571. 272 units. $209–$299 double. Valet parking $30. **Amenities:** Restaurant; bar; babysitting; concierge; executive-level rooms; fitness center; room service; Wi-Fi ($13/day).

Where to Eat in Providence

Providence has a sturdy Italian heritage, hence its profusion of tomato-sauce and pizza joints, especially on **Federal Hill**. That identity is changing, but a stroll along the Hill's main drag, Atwells Avenue, can set off furious hunger alarms. Another fruitful strip to explore for lower-cost and ethnic dining options is that part of **Thayer Street** bordering the Brown University campus.

An interesting phenomenon in Providence, and indeed throughout the state, is its customer loyalty: Outstanding restaurants stay popular as long as they stay good.

Al Forno ★★★ CREATIVE ITALIAN In the 1980s if you'd asked almost anyone in Providence the best place to eat, they'd most likely have said "Al Forno" without a second thought. When chef-owners Johanne Killeen & George Germon opened this Italian-influenced restaurant in 1980, farm-to-table was a new idea that didn't even have a name yet, wood-fired ovens were rare, and Providence was just beginning to make a name as a dining mecca. That nearly four decades later Al Forno is still one of the city's top dining spots is testament to its continuing excellence. Ingredients from New England farms and waters are transformed over hardwood charcoal and in blistering hot ovens, creating memorable dishes such as roasted stuffed rabbit, duck confit and roasted duck with grapes, or an entrée of wood-grilled and roasted vegetables. The signature dessert, Grand Cookie Finale, is so abundant that it comes with a bag for the leftovers.

577 South Water St. www.alforno.com. © **401/273-9760.** Reservations recommended. Main courses $24–$34. Tues–Fri 5–10pm; Sat 4–11pm. RIPTA bus 60.

Bacaro ★ ITALIAN A standout for what might be called Italian tapas—small dishes that allow for an evening of grazing and tasting—Bacaro's menu seems made for sharing with friends. Diners choose from 30 such *cicchetti* options here, from fried smelts with lemony aioli to wild boar sausage on crispy polenta crostini served with blueberry chutney. You can also order from an expansive *salumeria* menu of cured meats and robust cheeses—ask for advice and start there. Bacaro's location on South Water Street offers views of the Providence River and is a logical destination after touring the historic east side of the city.

262 S. Water St. (near Williams St.). www.bacarorestaurant.net. © **401/751-3700.** Reservations recommended. Main courses $25–$35; cicchetti $5–$12. Tues–Sat 5–10pm (Sat from 4pm). RIPTA bus 35 or 78.

Cafe Nuovo ★★★ INTERNATIONAL   This spacious room of glass, marble, and burnished wood, on the ground floor of a downtown office tower, overlooks the confluence of the Moshassuck and Woonasquatucket rivers. (It makes an ideal overlook for the WaterFire events, p. 431.) Unlike some of its competitors, Cafe Nuovo takes reservations, is open for lunch *and* dinner, and impresses with every course, from dazzling appetizers to stunning pastries. The fare skips lightly among inspirations—Greek, Portuguese, and Japanese among them.

1 Citizens Plaza (access from Steeple St. bridge). www.cafenuovo.com. © **401/421-2525.** Reservations recommended. Main courses $31–$50. Mon–Fri 11:30am–3pm; Mon–Thurs 5–10:30pm; Fri–Sat 5–11pm. RIPTA bus 1 or 23 (5-min. walk from Kennedy Plaza).

CAV ★★ INTERNATIONAL   No corporate design drudge had a hand in *this* warehouse interior, a Jewelry District pioneer. CAV is an acronym for "Cocktails/Antiques/Victuals," and patrons are surrounded by tribal rugs, African carvings, and assorted antiques (most for sale). Turkish *kilims* under glass cover the tables. The resulting bohemian air is not unlike Greenwich Village in the 1960s. Select from such strenuous menu swings as pistachio-crusted crab cake with Sriracha aioli and taro root chips to such modern comfort foods as braised lamb with poppy seed port wine demi-glace, butternut squash custard, and Israeli couscous. Consult a map or the directions at the restaurant's website before heading out.

14 Imperial Place (at Basset St.). www.cavrestaurant.com. © **401/751-9164.** Reservations recommended. Main courses $22–$32. Mon–Thurs 11:30am–10pm; Fri 11:30am–1am; Sat 10am–10pm; Sun 10:30am–10pm. RIPTA bus 3, 22, or 92.

Chez Pascal ★★ FRENCH   Located about 2 miles north on Hope Street from the Brown University campus, this warm little bistro is worth the trip. The kitchen works in the French tradition but isn't dogmatic about it. The variety of house-made pâtés and charcuterie is unusually large, from a root vegetable terrine to the pork and fennel sausage. Pascal always offers a "local pork of the day" dish, but it also caters to non-meat-eaters with a vegetarian tasting menu that often features lentil ragout with roasted sugar pumpkin. Winning desserts have included pear upside-down cake with Great Hill blue cheese and walnuts, caramel sauce, and crème fraiche. Reserve well ahead.

960 Hope St. (at 9th St.). www.chez-pascal.com. © **401/421-4422.** Main courses $25–$31. Mon–Thurs 5:30–9:30pm, Fri–Sat 5:30–10pm. RIPTA bus line 1.

Garden Grille ★ VEGETARIAN   Animal-free meals are not so easy to find as you might expect in this college town, but a long-time favorite is this

big TASTES HIDE IN little RHODY

You'd think that, in an age of instant communication, no flavorful food tidbit would stay unknown for long. Regional specialties often become national staples—think Buffalo wings, Carolina blooming onions, Texas burritos. But Rhode Island's food specialties remain mysteriously secret. Even residents of neighboring states are in the dark about a lot of them. So while you're visiting, be sure to check out some of the following:

o **Stuffies:** These come in as many versions as there are cooks. At Flo's Clam Shack (p. 431), in Newport, big quahog clams are chopped up with hot and sweet peppers and bread crumbs, packed inside the two shell halves, and shut, the whole held together by a rubber band and baked.

o **Rhode Island clam chowder:** This is a potato, onion, and clam (often quahog) soup of clear broth. It's neither cream-based (such as the well-known New England chowder) nor tomato-based (such as Manhattan chowder).

o **Coffee milk and cabinets:** Obligatory Rhody beverages. Coffee milk is made with milk and sweet coffee syrup (available in any Rhode Island grocery store). Cabinets are what most of the rest of America calls a milkshake (and some parts of New England call a frappe): milk, ice cream, and flavorings such as chocolate syrup.

o **Johnnycakes:** Also spelled *jonny-cakes*, these are breakfast fodder. Sometimes they're as thin as crepes, sometimes as thick as griddlecakes. Their primary ingredient is corn-meal. Honey is a common topping.

o **New York System Wieners:** These have only a passing acquaintance with Big Apple franks. In Rhode Island, the wieners are served on soft steamed buns and topped (usually) with a chili-type meat sauce, minced sweet onion, and mustard. Try them from **Olneyville New York System,** 2014 recipient of the James Beard Foundation America's Classics Award (two Providence locations; see www.olneyvillenewyorksystem.com).

small restaurant a few steps across the town line into Pawtucket. Go for the food, not the atmosphere, which is non-existent and somewhat cramped. But the menu has something for almost every food preference: gluten-free, vegan, vegetarian, Kosher—and when possible, the vegetables come from local farms. Along with the expected quesadillas, stir-fry bowls, and veggie burgers, you'll see seitan mushroom burgers, tofu BLTs with avocado or egg, pastrami seitan Reubens, and vegan mac 'n' cheese. Meat-lovers will never miss the meat in Garden Grille's tamales, stuffed full of mushrooms and sweet potatoes, with walnuts, quinoa polenta, wilted greens, and cumin-scented tomatoes.

727 East Ave. (at Lafayette St.), Pawtucket. www.gardengrilleri.com. © **401/726-2826.** No reservations. Main courses $9–15. Mon–Sat 11am–10pm, Sun 11am–9pm. RIPTA bus line 1.

Gracie's ★ NEW AMERICAN   Pin lights in the ceiling hint at the night sky, and white tablecloths and well-spaced tables carry out the romantic theme. The menu changes seasonally, but the first course might be house-made potato gnocchi or crispy veal sweetbreads with wild leeks. Carnivores will be more than sated by the lamb duo with bok choy, green garlic panisse, and beech mushrooms. *Prix-fixe* menus of three, five, seven, and nine courses are available with appropriate wine pairings.

194 Washington St. (1 block from Empire St.). www.graciesprov.com. ⓒ **401/272-7811.** Reservations advised. Main courses $26–$39; 3-course prix fixe $50. Tues–Sat 5–10pm.

Siena ★ ITALIAN   Federal Hill's days as a tomato gravy and pizza destination are fading, replaced by upbeat, contemporary chefs and owners who value quality and are alert to trends. Promising "Tuscan Soul Food," Siena draws all ages (including an occasional shrieking child). Waitstaff is patient and more knowledgeable and attentive than average. Antipasti and thin, wood-grilled, upscale pizzas may distract your attention from the rest of the card, but give full consideration to the *pollo al diavolo,* chicken breasts with an herb and hot red pepper rub; and the *aragosta cioppino,* a San Francisco fish stew of lobster, shrimp, clams, mussels, swordfish, and calamari in a spicy broth.

238 Atwells Ave. www.siena.com. ⓒ **401/521-3311.** Reservations advised. Main courses $15–$29. Mon–Thurs 5–10pm; Fri 5–11pm; Sat 4:30–11pm; Sun 3–9pm. RIPTA bus 92.

Providence Entertainment & Nightlife

This being a college town, there is no end of music options. A good source of information is www.goprovidence.com, which publishes a calendar of events and nightlife.

THE PERFORMING ARTS

Big-ticket touring musicals on the order of *Hamilton* are showcased at the **Providence Performing Arts Center,** 220 Weybosset St. (www.ppacri.org; ⓒ **401/421-ARTS** [2787]). At the **Trinity Repertory Company,** 201 Washington St. (www.trinityrep.com; ⓒ **401/351-4242**), works by Shakespeare, and adaptations such as Marcus Gardley's *Black Odyssey,* share the stage with the revival of classics like *Little Shop of Horrors.*

The **Dunkin' Donuts Center,** 1 La Salle Square (www.dunkindonuts center.com; ⓒ **401/331-6700**), hosts big-name performers, monster truck events, and NCAA basketball games.

Opera Providence (www.operaprovidence.org; ⓒ **401/524-1638**) stages productions at a variety of locations, including Blithewold (p. 440) in Bristol and Hopkins Square Park in Providence. The **Rhode Island Philharmonic,** 67 Waterman Ave., East Providence (www.ri-philharmonic.org; ⓒ **401/248-7000**) puts on one or two concerts a month from September through May, often at the Veterans Memorial Auditorium (1 Avenue of the Arts in Providence).

For art-house films and midnight cult movies, check the **Avon Cinema,** 260 Thayer St., at Meeting Street (www.avoncinema.com; ⓒ **401/421-AVON** [2866]).

THE CLUB & MUSIC SCENE

Live concert venues include **Alchemy** on the second floor at 71 Richmond St. (www.alchemyri.com, ⓒ **401/383-6336**) and **Fête Music Hall,** 103 Dike St.

Providence claims the invention of the diner, starting with a horse-drawn wagon transporting food down Westminster Street in 1872. The tradition is carried forward by the likes of the **Seaplane Diner,** 307 Allens Ave. (www.facebook.com/seaplanediner; ℂ **401/941-9547**), a silver-sided classic with tableside jukeboxes.

While shopping in the Arcade, stop into **Livi's Pockets** (www.livispockets.com) for locally sourced Middle Eastern street foods; **Rogue Island Local Kitchen and Bar** (www.rogueisland-group.com), a burger joint/bar that sources local ingredients (ask for a rum drink, for example, and you'll have a choice of New England brands); or **New Harvest** (www.newharvestcoffee.com), which serves locally roasted coffee, along with beer and whiskey.

Speaking of locally roasted coffee, if you're shopping the boutiques along

Wickenden Street, **Coffee Exchange** (207 Wickenden; www.thecoffee exchange.com) is a local favorite. Wickenden also has an adorable crepe/cupcake cafe, **The Duck and Bunny** (312 Wickenden; www.theduck andbunny.com), which bills itself as a "snuggery."

Another local culinary institution arrives in Kennedy Plaza on wheels every afternoon around 4:30pm. The grungy aluminum-sided **Haven Bros.** (ℂ **401/861-7777**) is a food tractor-trailer with a counter and six stools inside; it's a good deal for decent burgers and even better fries, sold from its parking space next to City Hall. No new frontiers here, except that it hangs around until way past midnight to dampen the hunger pangs of clubgoers, lawyers, night people, and workaholic pols.

(www.fetemusic.com; ℂ **401/383-1112**). **The Columbus Theatre** is an old-fashioned theater, where you can see live bands, plays, and films in opulent surroundings of murals and stained glass, at 270 Broadway (www.columbus theatre.com; ℂ **401/621-9660**). **AS220,** at 115 Empire St. (www.as220.org; ℂ **401/831-9327**), is a community arts space for mostly local visual, musical, and performance artists, with events every day.

At the **Trinity Brewhouse,** 186 Fountain St. (www.trinitybrewhouse.com; ℂ **401/453-2337**), home-brewed, award-winning beers are the main event. As the website puts it, "We sell heaven by the pint." There's often live music in the evenings.

Providence has plenty of bar choices, from after-work stops and quiet neighborhood retreats to raucous bar scenes. Downcity, there's **The Eddy,** a small cocktail bar at 95 Eddy St. (www.eddybar.com; ℂ **401/831-3339**), and **Boombox,** a karaoke lounge at the Dean Hotel (122 Fountain St.; www.thedeanhotel.com; ℂ **401/455-3316**).

On the east side, **The Wild Colonial Tavern,** near Brown and RISDI at 250 South Water St. (www.wildcolonial.com; ℂ **401/621-5644**) is an old brick bar with darts, pool tables, and occasional trivia nights. In good weather, **The Hot Club** at 25 Bridge St. in Fox Point (www.hotclubprov.com; ℂ **401/861-9007**) has nice riverside tables.

On the west side of town, **Lili Marlene's** (422 Atwells Ave.; ☏ **401/751-4996**) is a darkened lounge on Federal Hill. If you've a taste for retro and kitsch, **Ogie's Trailer Park** at 1155 Westminster St. (www.ogiestrailerpark.com; ☏ **401/383-8200**) is a fun tiki bar on the West Side. **The Avery**, on Luongo Square (www.averyprovidence.com; ☏ **401/751-5920**) is a classy little Art Deco bar hidden away in a residential neighborhood on the West Side. **Justine's** (☏ **401/454-4440**) is a speakeasy-style cocktail lounge hidden behind a store on Olneyville Square.

BRISTOL

16 miles SE of Providence; 15 miles N of Newport

About halfway between Providence and Newport, Bristol is perhaps the best-kept secret in Rhode Island. First settled in 1680, this beautiful waterfront town sits on a peninsula straddling the Narragansett and Mount Hope Bays. It makes for a soothing excursion from the urbanity of Providence and the concentration of sights and activity that is Newport.

Bristol is best known as home to the nation's oldest 4th of July parade, which has run annually here since 1785. The parade, which now draws up to 200,000 spectators, is the highlight of the year for what some residents call "America's Most Patriotic Town." The main boulevard, Hope Street, replaces the double yellow line in favor of a red, white, and blue band marking the 1.8-mile parade route.

Bristol's past also includes the notoriety of being the former home to the DeWolfs, the largest slave trading family in U.S. history. During much of the 1700s and the first decade of the 1800s, Rhode Island was the business epicenter of the "Triangle Trade," the trade of rum from New England, molasses from the West Indies, and enslaved peoples from Africa.

Today, though, Bristol is known for its historic homes and quaint downtown. In the past 15 years, it has undergone a gentrification from industrial town to tourist haven, with shops, a few fine dining spots, and cafes comprising a landscape of what used to be abandoned mills and fading industry.

Note that in the off season, November through April, most museums and small inns close.

Essentials

ARRIVING
From Providence, it's fastest to take I-195 to Route 136, but the more scenic route is to take I-195 to exit 7 and follow Route 114S toward Barrington. Follow Route 114 all the way into Bristol; on the way, you'll pass marinas and historic buildings and traverse scenic bridges.

VISITOR INFORMATION
Tourism information (www.explorebristolri.com; ☏ **401/253-7000**) is available in the Town Hall at 10 Court St. (Mon–Fri 8:30am–4pm), and in the Burnside Building at 400 Hope St. (Sat–Sun 10am–5pm).

Exploring Bristol

The city's quiet charm is in its well-preserved historic district, which runs along Hope Street and down side roads to Thames Street (pronounced "TH-aymz"), which borders the Bristol Harbor. Start here and stroll past homes dating back to the 1700s and 1800s. Former industrial sites at the harbor have been gentrified into high-end condos in converted mill buildings. There is 1- and 2-hour parking available along most streets, and a municipal parking lot on Thames.

Bristol was named one of the Distinctive Destinations in the U.S. by the National Trust for Historic Preservation, which called it a "quintessential New England waterfront town" with an "unwavering commitment" to preservation. Also cited by the Trust are town attractions Blithewold Mansion, Coggeswell Farm Museum, Herreshoff Marine Museum and America's Cup Hall of Fame, and Colt State Park, all listed below.

Blithewold Mansion, Gardens, and Arboretum ★★ HISTORIC HOME
This 45-room waterfront estate was built in 1907 as a summer home to Augustus Van Wickle. Featuring beautiful gardens and landscaping, it's now a museum that feels like a rural English manor. Open for tours, the estate is preserved much as it was in the early 1900s. The gardens bordering the water are a particular treat, and in mid- to late April, thousands of blooming daffodils provide a magnificent scene.

101 Ferry Rd. (Rte. 114). www.blithewold.org. ✆ **401/253-2707.** $15 adults, $14 seniors, $11 military and full-time students, $6 children 6–17, children 5 and under free. House open mid-Apr to mid-Oct only, Tues–Sun 10am–4pm. Gardens open daily 10am–4pm year-round.

Coggeshall Farm Museum ★ LIVING HISTORY MUSEUM
Set on 50 acres abutting Colt State Park (see p. 441), this museum is worth a visit even if just to walk around and enjoy the atmosphere of centuries-old farmland. In its 1790s farmhouse and several small antique farm buildings, costumed staff answer questions and demonstrate farm life of the 18th century.

Off Poppasquash Rd. (turn off Rte./Hope St. and follow signs). www.coggeshallfarm. org. ✆ **401/253-9062.** Weekdays $5 adults, $3 seniors and children; weekends $7 adults, $5 seniors and children. Tues–Sun 10am–4pm; closed some holidays.

Herreshoff Marine Museum and America's Cup Hall of Fame ★ MUSEUM
This maritime museum highlights the history of the Herreshoff Manufacturing Company, a boat builder of everything from U.S. Navy torpedo boats to championship America's Cup yachts; it was once the centerpiece of industry in Bristol. The facility houses the America's Cup Hall of Fame and features a collection of 35 boats, including the famous "*America³*," winner of the 1992 America's Cup race.

1 Burnside St. (off Hope St./Rte. 114). www.herreshoff.org. ✆ **401/253-5000.** Admission $3. Mon–Sat 10am–5pm; Sun noon–5pm.

Outdoor Activities

Once the estate of Samuel Colt, of the same family as the famous firearms manufacturer, **Colt State Park** (www.riparks.com; ✆ **401/253-7482**) encompasses 464 acres of land bordering Narragansett Bay. Open year-round sunrise to sunset, it offers stunning views over the water, especially at sunset. There are trails for biking, walking, jogging, or cycling, and bridle paths for horseback riding. In warmer months, families come for the day to barbecue, play volleyball, and otherwise enjoy the bucolic atmosphere. You'll also find anglers casting lines and kayakers paddling on the bay. Entry and parking are free, but there is a $2 charge for picnic tables and grills.

The **East Bay Bike Path** (www.dot.ri.gov/community/bikeri/eastbay.php) is a 14.5-mile paved trail running between Bristol and Providence, built atop a converted train track. After passing through Colt State Park, it spends much of the trip skimming Narragansett Bay. The trail is used by runners, skaters, and walkers as well as bikers. Access to the path is free.

Shopping in Bristol

The most interesting shopping in Bristol is in the historic downtown area. The highest concentration of shops is along Hope Street (Route 114), with more on Thames Street and the short side streets between them. **Jesse/James Antiques,** 44 State St. (www.jessejamesantiques.wordpress.com; ✆ **401/253-2240**), open since 1992, has notable pieces of china, glassware, and period furniture. **Harbor Bath & Body,** 251 Thames St. (✆ **401/396-9170**), offers a variety of natural and organic bath products, many of which are made in New England. **Epilogues,** 274 Hope St. (✆ **401/254-8958**), mixes antiques and vintage finds with handcrafted works.

Where to Stay in Bristol

There are a handful of inns and bed-and-breakfasts in Bristol, but no large hotels, so plan to pay slightly more for a room here than you would at a major hotel chain. Summer months are busy, so book a room well in advance at the end of May—when Roger Williams University holds commencement ceremonies—and around the July 4th holiday.

Bristol Harbor Inn ★   Situated at the newly renovated Thames Street Landing complex along the waterfront, the Bristol Harbor Inn has a range of options, from standard rooms to waterfront rooms to plush suites with gas fireplaces. The least expensive units are no-frills but perfectly agreeable, while the pricier suites are more finely adorned. This is not a destination hotel but rather a good, basic, affordable alternative to higher-priced B&Bs nearby. 259 Thames St. www.bristolharborinn.com. ✆ **866/254-1444** or 401/254-1444. 40 units. Apr–Oct $135–$249 double; Nov–Mar $95–$135 double. Rates include continental breakfast. 2-night minimum weekends Apr–Oct. Free parking. **Amenities:** Restaurant; pub; spa; Internet (free).

William's Grant Inn ★   In the center of town, five impeccably furnished guest rooms welcome guests to an historic Federal-style clapboard home built in 1808 by William Bradford III, the third generation of one of the original settler families. Three rooms have gas fireplaces and all have private baths; rooms are bright and airy, decorated in a cozy country style with bed quilts and antiques but also up-to-date features like air-conditioning.

154 High St. www.williamsgrantinn.com. © 800/596-4222 or 401/253-4222. 5 rooms. June–Sept $214–$327, Oct–May $180–$282. Rates include full breakfast. Free parking. 2- or 3-night minimum stay some holiday weekends. **Amenities:** Guest barbeque area; Wi-Fi (free).

Where to Eat in Bristol

Once strictly home to family restaurants, sub shops, and pizza joints, Bristol has seen a number of upscale restaurants pop up in recent years. For coffee and pastry or a custom-built lunch sandwich, there's **Angelina's** (301 Hope St.; © **401/396-5592**) and **The Beehive Café,** overlooking the harbor at 10 Franklin St. (© **401/396-9994**).

DeWolf Tavern ★ NEW AMERICAN Located in a renovated 1818 warehouse, this interesting tavern's decor consists of the building's original stone and mortar walls and exposed wooden beams. The menu is contemporary American with a tilt toward Bristol's seafaring heritage and a dash of the East: steamed mussels in coconut milk with curry leaf and chili; tandoori marinated swordfish. Don't miss roasted Brussels sprouts and cornbread hash from the selection of side dishes.

259 Thames St. www.dewolftavern.com. © **401/254-2005.** Main courses $14–$42. Mon–Fri 11:30am–10:30pm, Sat–Sun 8am–2pm and 2:30–10:30pm.

Le Central Bistro ★★ FRENCH Typical French bistro dishes served in this lively local gathering spot include traditional steak frites, salade Niçoise, charcuterie plates, country style *pâtés*, Moroccan chicken, and rack of lamb. Lunch specialties include a bistro burger with fries or lobster BLT. Try the warm lemon-ricotta crepes with seasonal fruits for dessert.

483 Hope St. www.lecentralbristol.net. © **401/396-9965.** Main courses $16–$24. Mon–Sat 11am–2pm, Sun 10am–2pm; dinner daily 5pm "til closing."

The Lobster Pot ★★★ SEAFOOD A consistent winner of *Rhode Island Monthly's* Best of RI Award for seafood, this traditional waterfront restaurant has sat overlooking the Bristol harbor since 1929. For all its fame, the atmosphere is friendly and unpretentious. Sleek it isn't; it's a traditional shore-hall, but with white tablecloths—the image of places all along the New

England shore. Build your own seafood platter of littlenecks, cherrystones, oysters, lobster, and jumbo shrimp, or order from a menu of traditional seafood dishes created from impeccably fresh fish and shellfish.

119 Hope St. www.lobsterpotri.com. ✆ **401/253-9100.** Main courses $17–$40. May–Oct Mon–Fri noon–9pm, Sat–Sun noon–10pm; Nov–Apr Tues–Sun noon–9pm.

NEWPORT ★★★

71 miles S of Boston; 178 miles NE of New York City

Look out today across the marina filled with pleasure craft and it's hard to imagine how vital Newport was during the Colonial and Federal periods, rivaling Boston and even New York as a center of New World trade and prosperity. In the following century, wealthy industrialists, railroad tycoons, coal magnates, financiers, and robber barons were drawn to the area, especially between the Civil War and World War I. They bought up property at the ocean's rim to build what they called summer "cottages"—which were, in fact, mansions of immoderate design and proportions, patterned after European palaces.

Today's Newport reflects all these eras. Immediately east and north of the business district are blocks of Colonial, Federal, and Victorian houses, many of them designated National Historic Sites. Happily, they are not frozen in amber but very much in use as residences, restaurants, offices, and shops. Taken together, they are as visually appealing as the 40-room cottages of the super-rich, the Gilded Age sites that draw so many visitors to Newport.

Newport has been spared the coarser intrusions that afflict so many coastal resorts. T-shirt emporia have been kept within reasonable limits—a remarkable feat, considering that some 4 million visitors come through its narrow streets every year.

Despite Newport's prevailing image as a collection of ornate mansions and regattas for the rich and famous, the city is largely middle class and not too excessively priced. Scores of inns and B&Bs ensure lodging even during festival weeks, at rates from budget to ultra-luxury level. In almost every respect, this is the "First Resort" of the New England coast.

Essentials

ARRIVING

BY CAR Newport occupies the southern tip of Aquidneck Island in Narragansett Bay and is connected to the mainland by bridges and a ferry. From New York City, take I-95 to exit 3, picking up Route 138 east and crossing the Newport toll bridge, which takes you slightly north of the downtown district; the drive should take around 3½ hours. From Boston and the north, it's a 1½-hour drive; take Route 24 through Fall River, picking up Route 114 into town.

BY BUS The **Rhode Island Public Transit Authority,** or **RIPTA** (www. ripta.com; ✆ **800/244-0444** or 401/781-9400), has buses that run between Providence's Kennedy Plaza and the Newport Visitor Information Center. The trip is 75 minutes and the one-way fare is $1.75. **Peter Pan Bus Lines** (www. peterpanbus.com) also provides service from Providence, but it takes twice as

Newport

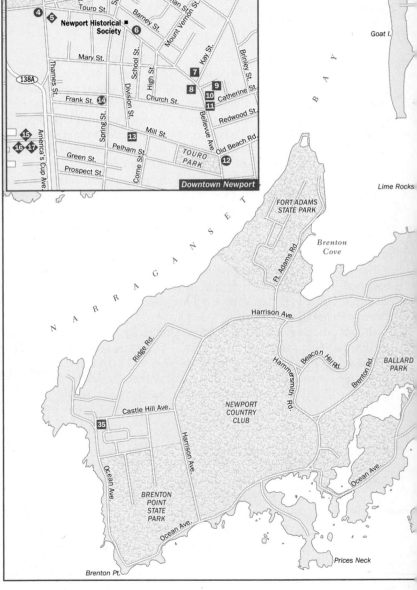

Downtown Newport

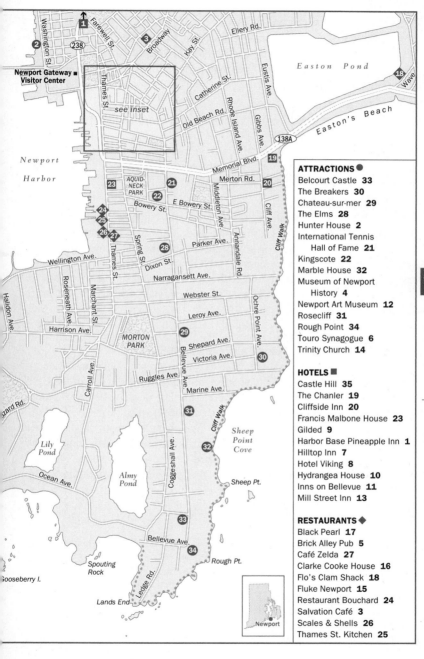

ATTRACTIONS ●
Belcourt Castle **33**
The Breakers **30**
Chateau-sur-mer **29**
The Elms **28**
Hunter House **2**
International Tennis
  Hall of Fame **21**
Kingscote **22**
Marble House **32**
Museum of Newport
  History **4**
Newport Art Museum **12**
Rosecliff **31**
Rough Point **34**
Touro Synagogue **6**
Trinity Church **14**

HOTELS ■
Castle Hill **35**
The Chanler **19**
Cliffside Inn **20**
Francis Malbone House **23**
Gilded **9**
Harbor Base Pineapple Inn **1**
Hilltop Inn **7**
Hotel Viking **8**
Hydrangea House **10**
Inns on Bellevue **11**
Mill Street Inn **13**

RESTAURANTS ◆
Black Pearl **17**
Brick Alley Pub **5**
Café Zelda **27**
Clarke Cooke House **16**
Flo's Clam Shack **18**
Fluke Newport **15**
Restaurant Bouchard **24**
Salvation Café **3**
Scales & Shells **26**
Thames St. Kitchen **25**

long, requires a transfer, and costs $21. There's no reason to use them when RIPTA is so much faster and cheaper.

VISITOR INFORMATION

The Newport Gateway Transportation and Visitor Center, 23 America's Cup Ave. (www.gonewport.com; ✆ **800/976-5122** or 401/845-9123), adjacent to the bus station, is open daily from 9am to 5pm. It has attendants on duty to help with lodging and local events.

GETTING AROUND

Except for the mansions, most of Newport's attractions can be reached easily on foot. **RIPTA** runs a trolley in Newport (Route 67, also called the Yellow Line) that travels to the mansions daily year-round. In summer, the line is extended to Rough Point. Service originates at the Gateway Transportation and Visitor Center. A 24-hour pass is $6.

CITY LAYOUT

Newport's perimeter resembles a heeled boot, its toe pointing west, not unlike Italy. About where the laces of the boot would be is the downtown business and residential district. Several wharves push into the bay, providing support and mooring for flotillas of pleasure craft. Much of the strolling, shopping, eating and quaffing happens along this waterfront and its parallel streets: America's Cup Avenue and Thames Street (Americanized to "Thaymz" after the Revolution).

Exploring Newport

"THE COTTAGES": NEWPORT'S MANSIONS

"The Cottages" is what wealthy people called the almost unimaginably sumptuous mansions they built in Newport in the era between the end of the Civil War and the beginning of World War I—the last decades before the 16th Amendment to the Constitution permitted an income tax.

Say this for the wealthy of the Gilded Age, many of whom obtained their fortunes by less than honorable means: They knew a good place to put down roots when they saw it. These are the same people who developed Florida's Palm Beach for the winter months, New York's Hudson Valley for the spring,

---

The Lowdown on Newport Parking

There's a huge parking lot and garage next to the Newport Gateway Visitor Center (above)—take advantage of it. In-town parking lots aren't cheap, and while there is metered parking along Thames Street, it's closely monitored by police, and fines are steep (note that Nov–Apr, meter parking is free for up to 3 hr.). Newport Visitor's Bureau can provide you with a list of parking lots with hours and rates, but leaving your car at the Gateway center is still your best bet, unless you're staying at a hotel or inn in town that offers parking. The lot is open May through October, 8am to midnight. Parking costs $2 for the first half-hour, $1.50 each additional half-hour, up to a maximum of $24.50. You can walk or taxi to the center of town, or catch a RIPTA bus (see above).

and the Berkshires of Massachusetts (p. 340) for the autumn. Newport was for summering, and the mansion owners and their friends swept from house to luxurious house with the insouciance of a bejeweled matron dragging her sable down a grand staircase.

Ticket & Other Visitor Information

Walking the length of Bellevue Avenue to see the mansions is a serious trek for most people (from Kingscote, at #253, to Rough Point, at #680, is about 2 miles, and that's before touring any of the homes or grounds). Plan to bike or drive to the cottage district, but keep in mind that parking is limited. Narrated bus tours are also available; see p. 454.

Many of the residences are still privately owned (and yes, some do regularly come up for sale). The grounds and interiors of about a dozen houses, however, are open to the public, by guided tour only. Six of those listed here (The Breakers, Kingscote, The Elms, Chateau-sur-Mer, Rosecliff, and Marble House) are maintained by the **Preservation Society of Newport County** (www.newportmansions.org; © **401/847-1000**). Belcourt Castle and Rough Point are run independently; ticket and other information is listed with their descriptions below.

Tickets for the mansions run by the Preservation Society are available in a range of combinations, listed at **http://tix.newportmansions.org** (text "Newport" to 82672 for updates and offers). A wide variety of tours are offered, such as Beneath the Breakers, Tuesday at Chateau, Servant Life, garden tours, and even a Cliff Walk tour. Sample prices: One house might cost $20 adults, $10 youth; five houses might be $35 adults, $12 youth; Servant Life costs $15 adults, $7.50 youth; a Saturday Garden Tour costs $20. Special events, such as festive Thanksgiving and Christmas celebrations, cost extra. Children age 5 and under are admitted free, but strollers are not allowed inside. Parking is free at all the Society properties.

Tip: Because their sheer opulence can become numbing after a while, you might want to visit only one or two per day. Budget about 45 minutes to an hour for each mansion's guided tour, plus extra time for exploring the grounds.

Tickets can be purchased online or at any of the mansions; you need to specify times when ordering online. The Preservation Society has a **visitors' center** at its base in the middle of the district at 424 Bellevue Ave.

The Breakers and Rosecliff are fully **wheelchair accessible**. Marble House and the Elms are partially wheelchair accessible.

During the **winter**, three Preservation Society mansions remain open, with limited hours: The Breakers, Marble House, and the Elms. In **summer**, the properties are all open daily. However, because of a highly variable schedule over the course of the year, confirm online or by phone which mansions are open on the day of your travel.

Note: The properties are listed here in the order in which they're encountered when driving south on Bellevue Avenue, starting at Memorial Boulevard.

Kingscote ★ HISTORIC HOME

This mansion is a reminder that well-to-do Southern families often had second homes north of the Mason-Dixon line to avoid the sultry summers of the deep South. Architect Richard Upjohn designed the mansion in the same Gothic Revival style he used for Trinity Church in New York, with romantic towers and medieval arches. Kingscote was built in 1841, nearly 40 years before the Gilded Age, but is considered one of the Newport Cottages because it was acquired in 1864 by a sea merchant who furnished it with porcelains and textiles accumulated in the China trade. The dining room is notable for its Tiffany glass panels.

253 Bellevue Ave. See p. 447 for Preservation Society of Newport County information.

The Elms ★★ HISTORIC HOME   Architect Horace Trumbauer is said to have been inspired by the Château d'Asnières, a mid-18th-century French chateau outside Paris, when designing the Elms. Its opulent exterior and interior details (such as those in the ornate dining room) are indeed suitable for at least a marquis. Marble hallways lead to rooms filled with Louis XIV and XV furniture, and paintings and accessories are true to the late 18th century. Sunken gardens are laid out and maintained in the formal French manner.

367 Bellevue Ave. See p. 447 for Preservation Society of Newport County information.

Chateau-sur-Mer ★ HISTORIC HOME   If you try, you may be able to imagine being one of the more than 2,000 guests who attended a "country picnic" here in 1857. This "Castle by the Sea" is High Victorian in style, which means it drew from many inspirations including Italian Renaissance and French Second Empire. It features a central atrium that reaches up three levels to a stained-glass skylight, with balconies at every level. A park designed in a style true to the period of the cottage features copper beech and weeping willows around its garden pavilion.

474 Bellevue Ave. See p. 447 for Preservation Society of Newport County information.

The Breakers ★★★ HISTORIC HOME   If you're going to see only one of the cottages, make it this one. Architect Richard Morris Hunt was commissioned to create this replica of an Italian Renaissance palazzo, and he was unrestrained by costs: The 50×50-foot great hall has 50-foot-high ceilings and is sheathed in French marble; a room with double mirrors creates an illusion of an endless row of crystal chandeliers; a Flemish tapestry drapes along a wall above a gurgling interior fountain; and French provincial furnishings include chairs that look like red velvet thrones (all furnishings on view, by the way, are original). Bathrooms, far from common at the time, were provided with both fresh and salt running water, hot and cold.

Built over 3 years (1892–95), the house had platoons of artisans—some 2,000—imported from Europe to apply 24-karat gold leaf to the ceilings, carve wood and marble, and provide mural-size baroque paintings. Images of oak leaves and acorns, which stand for long life and strength, are employed throughout the decor. The small family that lived here had 70 rooms in which to roam and was attended by a staff of 40 servants. The children would sled down the grand staircases on silver platters.

Such mind-numbing extravagance shouldn't really be surprising—the home was built for Cornelius Vanderbilt II, grandson of railroad tycoon Commodore Vanderbilt (and great-grandfather of CNN news anchor Anderson Cooper, whose mother is Gloria Vanderbilt). The house was passed on to Cornelius Vanderbilt II's youngest daughter, Gladys, in 1934, and purchased by the Preservation Society in 1972 from her heirs. Not surprisingly, the Breakers is designated a National Historic Landmark. The cottage sits atop a 30-foot cliff, with the Atlantic Ocean "breaking" below—hence the home's name.

Note: The Breakers is one of the few mansions not on Bellevue Avenue. From Bellevue, turn west on Ruggles Avenue after Chateau-sur-Mer, and then left on Ochre Point Avenue. The Breakers is on the right and a parking lot on the left.

44 Ochre Point Ave. See p. 447 for Preservation Society of Newport County information.

Rosecliff ★ HISTORIC HOME   Of all the mansions listed here, Rosecliff may be the prettiest upon first approach, glowing white across an expansive lawn. To get a preview, rent the 1974 film *The Great Gatsby,* starring Robert Redford: This mansion was used as a setting for some of that movie's scenes. Rosecliff is modeled on the garden retreat of Louis XVI at Versailles and was built for the flamboyant Tessie Fair Oelrichs, heiress to the thickest vein of silver mined in Nevada. The home has 40 rooms, a storied heart-shaped grand staircase, and the largest ballroom of all the cottages.

548 Bellevue Ave. See p. 447 for Preservation Society of Newport County information.

Marble House ★★★ HISTORIC HOME   Architect Richard Morris Hunt outdid himself for his clients William and Alva Vanderbilt, William being the younger brother of the Vanderbilts who built the Breakers (p. 448). Some 500,000 cubic feet of marble were used both outside and in, with a lavish hand that rivals the palaces of France's Louis XIV. The mansion reaches its apogee in the ballroom, which is encrusted with three kinds of gold. Money did not buy love, however, and in 1895, 4 years after being given the house as a 39th birthday present, Alva divorced William. Adding insult to injury, she married a neighbor and moved to his Belcourt Castle (below). Alva reopened Marble House after her second husband's death and held a benefit there in 1913 to raise money for the campaign for women's right to vote. Dishes in the scullery reflect this part of her history, bearing the legend "Votes for Women."

596 Bellevue Ave. See p. 447 for Preservation Society of Newport County information.

Belcourt Castle ★★ HISTORIC HOME   After her second marriage, Alva Vanderbilt repaired to this only slightly less grand mansion down the road from Marble House (see above). While the Vanderbilts were avid yachtsmen, Alva's new husband, Oliver Hazard Perry Belmont, was a fanatical horseman. His 60-room house contained extensive stables on the ground floor where his beloved steeds slept under monogrammed blankets. Intended to resemble a European hunting lodge, the castle has a ponderously masculine character, designed as it was for the bachelor before he won over the vivacious Alva. Tours for many years emphasized the dim spookiness of its neo-medieval architecture and decor, while behind its dark walls the building was quietly deteriorating. Then it closed and stood empty, deteriorating further in neglect. Recently bought by the owner of Sakonet Vineyards, Belcourt is being completely restored, using the latest discovery and restoration techniques coupled with green technology. The task is staggering: the 11,000-square-foot Vaulted Room took 40 gallons of primer and 40 of paint to refresh, and one chandelier required cleaning 20,000 individual pieces. You can watch it happening, in fascinating tours during its reconstruction process, which is expected to last at least through 2019.

657 Bellevue Ave. www.belcourtcastle.com. Tours $17 adults, $8 ages 4–17.

Rough Point ★★ HISTORIC HOME The fabled 1887 Gothic-Tudor home of the late tobacco heiress and art collector Doris Duke made its long-awaited opening in 2000, 7 years after Duke's death. (Duke bequeathed Rough Point and its furniture to the Newport Restoration Foundation, which Duke had founded and used to preserve 83 homes in Newport during her lifetime.) Only a portion of the 105 rooms are open for viewing, but tours do cover the entire

NEWPORT HAS A festival FOR EVERYTHING

The first big event of the summer is the June **Great Chowder Cook-Off** (www.riwaterfrontevents.com; ✆ **401/846-1600**), a 1-day event that includes three stages of entertainment. In the 3rd week of July, the **Black Ships Festival** (www.blackshipsfestival.com; ✆ **401/846-2720**) celebrates all aspects of Japanese culture with performances, sumo wrestling, sushi-, sake-, and tea-tasting.

July brings the **Newport Folk Festival** (www.newportfolk.org), which celebrates its 60th anniversary in 2019, and the **Newport Jazz Festival** (www.newportjazz.org), which started in 1954. Both are held at Fort Adams State Park.

In July and early September, 10 lush private gardens are open for a **Secret Garden Tour** (www.secretgardentours.org;

✆ **401/439-7253**) Advance tickets are $20; day-of tickets cost $25.

Bowen's Wharf holds a number of seasonal events. The **Bowen's Wharf Seafood Festival** (www.bowenswharf.com; ✆ **401/849-3478**) in October is among the most popular, as is **Oktoberfest** (www.newportfestivals.com; ✆ **401/846-1600**) on Columbus Day weekend.

Winter is relatively quiet, but even then there's a festival: **Christmas in Newport** (www.christmasinnewport.org; ✆ **401/849-6454**), a city-wide celebration with events each day in December. The city has a special beauty that month, with businesses, city buildings, and homes using clear and white bulbs to simulate candle glow throughout the harbor, the wharves, and the Victorian and Colonial residential streets.

first floor and Duke's bedroom. Look for the ivory inset side tables bearing the marks of Catherine the Great in what is called the Yellow Room. Other highlights are Duke's collections of Ming-dynasty vases, Flemish and French tapestries, and paintings by van Dyck and Gainsborough. Tours are wheelchair accessible and Rough Point is air-conditioned.

680 Bellevue Ave. www.newportrestoration.org. © **401/849-7300.** Admission $25, ages 13–18 $10. Visits at reserved times by 75-min. guided tour only. Garden tour Tues–Fri at 2pm free with admission. Museum tours Tues–Sun 9:30, last tour at 2pm. Parking is available.

OTHER NEWPORT ATTRACTIONS

Historic Hill (also called the Old Quarter) is the large district of Colonial Newport that rises from America's Cup Avenue, along the waterfront, to Bellevue Avenue, the beginning of Victorian Newport. **Spring Street** ★ is the Hill's main drag, and it's a treasure trove of Colonial, Georgian, and Federal structures. Chief among its visual delights is the 1725 **Trinity Church** ★, at the corner of Church Street. The church is not open for tours, but it is a visual icon of the city. Said to have been influenced by the work of the legendary British architect Christopher Wren, it certainly reflects that inspiration in its belfry and distinctive spire, seen from all over downtown Newport and dominating Queen Anne Square, a greensward that runs to the waterfront.

Hunter House ★★ HISTORIC HOME   With Gilded Age mansions getting so much attention, it's easy to overlook Newport's illustrious earlier history and outstanding homes from the Colonial and Federal periods. One of the dozen finest Colonial homes remaining in America, Hunter House served as the Revolutionary War headquarters of the commander of the French fleet after the British were driven out of Newport. Five of the rooms are fully paneled, the most remarkable being a parlor with faux marble and painted cherubs; two others have wooden paneling painted to imitate walnut. Hunter House has some of the finest examples of the work of the famed Newport cabinet makers, Townsend and Goddard.

54 Washington St. www.newportmansions.org. © **401/847-1000.** $30 adults, $8 ages 6–17. Daily 10am–5pm mid-May to early Oct.

International Tennis Hall of Fame & Museum ★ MUSEUM   On Bellevue Avenue, there was in the 1870s an exclusive men's club called the Newport Reading Room. One member was James Gordon Bennett, Jr., the wealthy publisher of the *New York Herald.* The story goes that Bennett persuaded a friend to ride a horse into the club, the outraged members reprimanded Bennett, Bennett had an instant snit that they hadn't enjoyed his little jest, and he went right out and bought a property on the other side of Memorial Boulevard to build his own club. Architects McKim, Mead & White produced a shingle-style edifice of lavish proportions, with turrets and verandas and an interior piazza for lawn games, equestrian shows, and a new game called tennis. In 1881, this "Newport Casino" held the first U.S. National Lawn Tennis Championships and hosted the event until it moved to Forest

Hills, New York, and became known as the U.S. Open. Today, the building still has a grass lawn open for play.

194 Bellevue Ave. (at Memorial Blvd.). www.tennisfame.com. ℭ **800/457-1144** or 401/849-3990. $15 adults, $11 seniors, $12 students & military. Daily 10am–5pm. Jan–Mar closed Tues.

Museum of Newport History ★ MUSEUM   Maintained by the Newport Historical Society, this museum is in the refurbished 1772 Brick Market (not to be confused with the nearby shopping mall Brick Marketplace). It houses a printing press, boat models, antique silverware, and a ship figurehead, and shows videos on Newport history.

127 Thames St. (at Touro St.). www.newporthistory.org. ℭ **401/841-8770.** Suggested donation $4 adults, $2 children 6 and older. Daily 10am–5pm.

Newport Art Museum ★ MUSEUM   Exhibitions here focus on the visual arts of Newport and southeastern New England, with solo shows by contemporary artists. There also are weekly arts programs for young children and lectures on everything from stone walls in Rhode Island to the myths and reality of America's robber barons. The museum is housed in a 1862 building constructed in Victorian stick style and was the first Newport commission of Richard Morris Hunt, who went on to design many of the mansions along Bellevue Avenue.

76 Bellevue Ave. (1 block N of Memorial Blvd.). www.newportartmuseum.org. ℭ **401/848-8200.** $10 adults, $8 seniors, $6 students, free for ages 5 and under. Tues–Sat 10am–5pm, Sun noon–5pm (Nov–Apr closes at 4pm).

Touro Park ★ PARK   Opposite the Newport Art Museum (above), this small park provides a shaded respite. At its center is an Old Stone Mill. Dreamers like to believe that its eight columns were erected by Vikings. Realists say it was built by Benedict Arnold, a governor of the colony long before his great-great-grandson committed his infamous act of treason during the Revolution.

Bellevue Ave. (btw. Pelham and Mill sts.).

Touro Synagogue ★ RELIGIOUS SITE   Dating from 1763, this grand building is the oldest existing synagogue in the United States. A Jewish community, largely refugees from Spain and Portugal, first arrived in Newport in

---

Newport and America's Cup

Competition among extravagant pleasure yachts established Newport's reputation as a sailing center. In 1851, the schooner *America* defeated a British boat in a race around the Isle of Wight. The prize trophy became known as the America's Cup, which remained in the possession of the New York Yacht Club (which moved its America's Cup venue from New York to Newport in 1930). In 1983, *Australia II* shockingly snatched the Cup away from *Liberty* in the last race of a four-out-of-seven series. Since then possession of the cup and locations for the race have moved to different locations around the world, but Newport remains a bastion of world sailing and a destination for long-distance races.

1658. Roger Williams, the dissident who founded Providence after being banished from the Massachusetts Bay Colony for being too fervent about freedom of religion, welcomed the immigrants. The temple's congregation later received assurance from none other than President George Washington, who wrote in a letter in 1790 that the United States "gives to bigotry no sanction, to persecution no assistance." The synagogue has an active membership of 140 families and holds Shabbat services Friday at 6pm and Saturday at 8:45am. It is orthodox, with separate seating for men and for women.

85 Touro St. www.tourosynagogue.org. © **401/847-4794.** $12 adults, $10 seniors, $8 students and military, ages 12 and under free (buy tickets at the Loeb Center). Admission by guided tour only; tours begin every half-hour. May–June Sun–Fri 9:30am–2:30pm, July–Aug Sun–Fri 9:30am–4:30pm, Sept–Oct Sun–Fri 9:30am–2:30pm; Nov–Apr Sun only 10:30am–2:30pm.

Outdoor Activities

Cliff Walk ★★ offers a dramatic way to see some of the biggest highlights of Newport. The walk skirts the water's edge of the southern section of town and travels behind many of the mansions, providing even better views of many than can be seen from Bellevue Avenue. Traversing its length, high above the crashing surf, is more than a stroll but less than an arduous hike. For the full length (3.5 miles from Memorial Boulevard at the north to Lands' End/Ledge Road at the south), start at the access point near the intersection of Memorial Boulevard and Eustis Avenue. For a shorter walk, there's an entrance/exit at the stone staircase known as Forty Steps, at the end of Narragansett Avenue. Be warned that there are some mildly rugged sections to negotiate and no facilities. Keep an eye out for poison ivy. The walk is open from sunrise to sunset. There are no parking lots nearby, so plan to get here by public transportation or cab. For more information, go to www.cliffwalk.com and www.cliffwalkmap.com.

Biking is one of the best ways to get around town, especially out to the mansions and along **Ocean Drive ★★**. Rentals are available from **Newport Bicycle,** 130 Broadway (© **401/846-0773**), open daily, with bicycles for $7 per hour, $35 for a full day and $95 per week.

The best beach for **swimming** is **Easton's Beach ★**, 175 Memorial Boulevard (www.cityofnewport.com; © **401/845-5810**), just east of the Cliff Walk. It's the longest and most popular beach and has lifeguards, a boardwalk, a bathhouse, eating places, picnic areas, a carousel, bumper boat rides, chair and umbrella rentals, and the **Save the Bay Exploration Center and Aquarium** (www.savebay.org/aquarium; © **401/324-6020;** admission $8). The beach is open from Memorial Day to Labor Day. Parking costs $10 weekdays.

A quieter option is **Gooseberry Beach ★**, 130 Ocean Ave. (© **401/847-3958**), on a beautiful stretch of Ocean Avenue just past the Rough Point mansion. Like Easton's, it has silky sand, but it's set in a cove, so the waves are smaller. It's privately owned but open to the public. Parking costs $20.

Fort Adams State Park (www.riparks.com; © **401/847-2400**) is on the thumb of land that partially encloses Newport Harbor. It can be seen from the downtown docks and reached by driving or biking south on Thames Street, west on Wellington Avenue, and then west on Harrison Avenue. The park is the site of the summer jazz and folk music festivals (see box p. 450) and of Civil War reenactments. Ocean swimming, fishing, and sailing are all possible here. The park is open year-round and entrance is free. The sprawling **1820s fort** (www.fortadams.org; © **401/841-0707**) for which the park is named can be viewed by guided tour only. Tours are $10 for adults, $5 for ages 6 to 17, and free for children 5 and under, and run every hour from 10am to 4pm daily Memorial Day through Columbus Day.

If you're driving or biking Ocean Avenue to take in the mansions and the scenery, keep in mind **Brenton Point State Park ★**. There's free parking along its Ocean Avenue edge, where you'll find grand vistas over the water—there's nothing to impede the waves rolling in and collapsing on the rock-strewn beach. You'll often see people parked here to eat lunch or just take a snooze in the late day sun. On windy days it's a prime spot for kite flying.

In the winter, an **outdoor skating rink** is set up at the **Sovereign Bank Family Skating Center** (www.skatenewport.com; © **401/846-3018**), at the Newport Yachting Center, 4 Commercial Wharf, at America's Cup Avenue. The rink is open daily from about mid-November into March, depending upon weather. Admission is $7 for adults and children 12 and older, $5 for seniors and children ages 3 to 11, and free for children 2 and under. Skate rentals are available for $3 to $5.

Organized Tours & Cruises

Bus tours of the mansions are offered by **Viking Tours** (www.viking toursnewport.com; © **401/847-6921**), based at the Visitor Center, 23 America's Cup Ave. Tours run daily in summer and on Saturday from November to April. The 1½-, 3-, or 4-hour tours range in cost from $25 to $54 for adults and $23 for children age 6 to 17.

Walking tours of downtown's historic Colonial neighborhoods are offered by the **Newport Historical Society,** 82 Touro St. (www.newporthistory.org; © **401/846-0813**). Tours are offered year-round, with a wide variety of itineraries, including the "Pirates & Scoundrels Tour" and "Old House ABCs." Tickets are generally $15 adults, $10 military, $5 ages 5 to 17.

Options abound for getting out on the water from spring through fall. **Classic Cruises of Newport ★**, Bannister's Wharf (www.cruisenewport.com; © **800/395-1343** or 401/847-0298), runs narrated 90-minute trips on its 72-foot schooner *Madeleine* and 75-minute trips aboard its classic speedboat *RumRunner II*. Rates for *Madeleine* are $27 for adults, $22 for children, $35 for a cocktail cruise. Rates for *RumRunner II* are $18 for adults, $13 for children, and $25 for the cocktail cruise. Reserve early to ensure space. Daily 90-minute cruises of the bay and harbor are also offered on the 80-foot schooner *Adirondack II ★*, Bowen's Wharf (www.sail-newport.com; © **401/847-0000** or 212/209-3370). Tickets are $33–$43 adults, $28 ages 4 to 11, $30 seniors, $5 ages 3 and under. Reservations must be made in advance.

Newport Helicopter Tours (www.newporthelicoptertours.com; © **401/843-8687**) offers a helicopter sightseeing tour costing $75 to $190.

Newport Shopping

Shopping fans will find plenty to do in Newport: Much of the downtown is given over to shopping, with wharfs that have been converted to small mini-malls and smaller side streets lined with local and chain operations.

Most of the shopping nearest to the waterfront seems designed entirely to sop up tourist dollars. There are chain clothing stores and such places as **Frazzleberries,** 475 Thames St. (www.frazzleberries.com; ✆ **401/841-9899**), which sells Newport-centric souvenirs, including reproductions of local beach signs and nautical charts. More interesting shopping is found in the smaller stores along **Lower Thames Street. Spring** and **Franklin streets** are both noted for their antiques shops.

Newport Mansions Stores, located at The Breakers, Marble House, The Elms, Rosecliff, and on Bannister's Wharf in downtown Newport, are good places to buy quality souvenirs and gifts, while helping to support the historic properties. The shops are filled with reproductions of china and decorative items you've seen in the mansions, such as Votes for Women plates and tea-pots, as well as period jewelry and nautical-themed decor. Each also has a wide selection of books on historical subjects, decorating, and the Gilded Age.

Where to Stay in Newport

Reserve well in advance, especially for summer weekends (2 months ahead is not too soon). The properties listed here generally have wide ranges in rates depending upon seasonal demand. A $300 room on weekends in July might be half that in March. The summer season is Memorial Day to Columbus Day.

Note that the usual gaggle of moderately priced national chain hotels are clustered outside the historic area along Route 114; you can save money and avoid hassle by staying there, driving to the Gateway Visitors Center parking lot (see p. 446), and taking a RIPTA bus into the harborfront action.

EXPENSIVE

Castle Hill Inn & Resort ★★   The setting—40 oceanfront acres on a near-island bordered by the Narragansett Bay and Atlantic Ocean—is the over-whelming attraction of this 1874 Victorian mansion, the highest-profile resort in Newport. There is no more enticing ritual in Newport than taking to one of the Adirondack chairs that dot the slope from the inn down toward the water, cocktail in hand, watching boats returning while the sun turns the water to gold. The best values are the Harbor Houses, which have porches overlooking the bay. Breakfast buffets are expansive, and dinners (inside or on the terrace) are among the most accomplished in Newport.

590 Ocean Dr. www.castlehillinn.com. ✆ **888/466-1355** or 401/849-3800. 35 units. $835–$945 double. Rates include breakfast and afternoon tea. **Amenities:** Restaurant; bar; Wi-Fi (free).

The Chanler at Cliff Walk ★★   Now an elegant boutique hotel with only 20 units, this French Empire structure dates from 1873 and stands above the northern end of the Cliff Walk, overlooking the surf. All rooms have gas fire-places, separate sitting areas, and, except for one suite, double Jacuzzis and rain showers. Each is jaw-droppingly decorated to a different theme—Mediterranean, Renaissance, Tudor—with chairs, sofas, and mattresses that are uniformly plush. The restaurant, **Spiced Pear** ★★ (www.spicedpear.com; ✆ **401/847-2244**), has surged to elite status, offering prix fixe and tasting menus.

117 Memorial Blvd. www.thechanler.com. ✆ **866/793-5664** or 401/847-1300. 20 units. $595–$1,399 double. Rates include breakfast. **Amenities:** Restaurant; bar; concierge; room service; Wi-Fi (free).

Cliffside Inn ★★   One of Newport's grandest inns, once the home of the eccentric artist Beatrice Turner, is in the capable hands of new owners. All units have at least one working fireplace, and most have whirlpool baths. Antiques are generously deployed, including Eastlake and Tiffany originals and Victorian fancies such as plush fainting couches. A favorite is the two-story Garden Suite, with its private garden and waterfall. All guests enjoy the inn's elegant perennial gardens and wrap-around porch. Full breakfasts, served in the grand parlor, include fresh-baked breads and muffins and creative entrees that change daily; there's complimentary wine and hors d'oeuvres for guests each afternoon. The inn is walking distance from the popular Easton's Beach (p. 453).

2 Seaview Ave. (left off of Cliff Ave.). www.cliffsideinn.com. ✆ **800/845-1811** or 401/847-1811. 16 units. $240–$575 double. Rates include breakfast and afternoon wine reception. 2-night minimum weekends. Free parking. **Amenities:** Wi-Fi (free).

Hilltop Inn ★   Owned and renovated by the innkeepers behind the Francis Malbone House (p. 457), this 5-unit Craftsman-style inn has an excellent location at the end of Bellevue Avenue, a short uphill walk from the wharf area. If you need to avoid the climb up the long staircase, reserve the first-floor Stewart Room, which has its own porch and whirlpool tub. All but one of the rooms have king-size beds.

2 Kay St. www.hilltopnewport.com. ✆ **800/846-0392.** 5 units. $275–$450 double. Rates include breakfast and afternoon tea. No children 12 and under. **Amenities:** Exercise room; Wi-Fi (free).

Hotel Viking ★   On the Newport scene since 1926, this neo-Georgian sprawl of a hotel was built to accommodate the summer guests of Newport's wealthiest families. A recent renovation has sparked up many rooms and added 10 luxury suites. The Viking is less expensive than the grander options in town *and* boasts a fitness room and spa, an indoor pool, a good location, and a pleasant staff. The rooftop bar with views of the harbor is an especially outstanding feature. Be sure to ask for an updated room.

1 Bellevue Ave. www.hotelviking.com. ✆ **800/556-7126** or 401/847-3300. 209 units. $319–$429 double. Pets accepted ($75 fee). **Amenities:** Restaurant; bar; health club & spa; indoor pool; room service; Wi-Fi ($7 per day).

Hydrangea House ★   A deep violet exterior catches the eye before you enter this long-established inn. Its opulent breakfast room has one long table, beneath a crystal chandelier, where ample breakfasts are served—perhaps raspberry pancakes or scrambled eggs in puff pastry. Morning coffee can be taken on the veranda in back. Upstairs bedrooms and suites are each distinctively decorated, and all have steam showers and gas fireplaces. The inn is located in the heart of the Historic Hill district and an easy walk to downtown.

16 Bellevue Ave. www.hydrangeahouse.com. ✆ **800/945-4667** or 401/846-4467. 10 units. $295–$475 double. Rates include breakfast. 3-night minimum summer weekends. Free parking. **Amenities:** Wi-Fi (free).

Mill Street Inn ★ Something different from most Newport inns, this is a converted 19th-century sawmill, scooped out and rebuilt from the walls in. This is an all-suite facility, where even its smallest unit has a queen-size bed and a sofa bed. The duplexes have private balconies, but everyone can use the rooftop decks, where breakfast is served on warm days. Where full breakfast and afternoon tea are included at other area properties, breakfast is relatively skimpy here. But the spacious rooms and excellent beds and bedding make up for it. There are three floors but no elevator. The inn is a member of the "Green" Hotels Association and uses resource-efficient technologies.

75 Mill St. (2 blocks E of Thames). www.millstreetinn.com. ✆ **800/392-1316** or 401/849-9500. 23 units. $330–$630. Rates include breakfast. 2-night minimum stay summer weekends. **Amenities:** Wi-Fi (free).

MODERATE

Francis Malbone House ★★ In 1996, nine modern rooms were added in a wing attached to this original 1760 Colonial house. They are very nice, with king-size beds and excellent reproductions of period furniture. Four of them share two sunken gardens, and three have Jacuzzi tubs built for two. Given a choice, though, choose a room in the old section, where antiques outnumber repros and Oriental rugs adorn buffed wide-plank floors. All but two units enjoy gas fireplaces. The adjacent Benjamin Mason House, a Colonial home from 1750, adds a suite and another guest room. An opulent tea service is set out each afternoon. The location is good for walkers, with the most interesting parts of the waterfront right outside the property.

392 Thames St. (east of Memorial Blvd.). www.malbone.com. ✆ **800/846-0392** or 401/846-0392. 20 units. $225–$375 double. Rates include breakfast and afternoon tea. 2-night minimum Fri–Sat, 3-night minimum selected weekends. Free parking. No children 12 and under. **Amenities:** Wi-Fi (free).

Gilded ★★ Distinct Art Deco flair makes the rich colors and smart contemporary style of this hotel especially refreshing in a town so largely given over to Colonial and over-the-top Beaux-Arts decor. On a quiet residential street a block from Bellevue Avenue, Gilded's rooms include thoughtful details like bathrobes, USB charging outlets, and complimentary iPads loaded with local information. Public spaces include a billiards room, guest lounge, and patio. At the included breakfast, along with the usual scones, fruit breads, and chocolate croissants, you'll be offered tapas-style savories that could include open-faced pulled-pork-and-egg sandwiches or caprese baked eggs with basil and tomato.

23 Brinley St. www.gildedhotel.com. ✆ **401/619-7758.** 17 units. $129–$549 double. Rates include breakfast. Free parking (limited spaces). **Amenities:** Concierge; croquet lawn; Wi-Fi (free).

MODERATE/INEXPENSIVE

The Inns on Bellevue ★   Three separate inns, all on the same block of Bellevue Avenue and only 2 blocks from Thames Street shops and restaurants, offer the same level of comfort but in three different styles. Check in for all three at the principal property, an elegantly decorated home built in 1891 at the corner of Bellevue Avenue and Catherine Street, where daily continental breakfast is served to guests. The Inn on Bellevue has adjoining rooms for families, while suites with two or three bedrooms are available in Bellevue Manor. The third, Bellevue House, offers value-priced rooms that are more basic, but have the same level of service as the other locations.

30 Bellevue Ave. www.innsonbellevue.com. ℂ **401/848–6242** or 800/718-1446. 31 rooms and suites. $119–$289 (may be higher midsummer weekends). Rates include continental breakfast. Free on-site parking. **Amenities:** Jacuzzis (some units); kitchenettes (some units); pets accepted in some rooms (extra charge); Wi-Fi (free).

INEXPENSIVE

Harbor Base Pineapple Inn ★   Upgrades carried out by new owners have brought this plain-Jane motel up several notches. Comfortable rooms are decorated in a generic Colonial reproduction style; they're not luxurious, but a good value in a town where even moderate hotel prices are rare. It's a short drive from the waterfront attractions, close to the main routes into Newport. For those traveling without a car, it's a 5-minute walk to the RIPTA stop for buses to Thames Street and the main attractions.

372 Coddington Hwy., off Rte. 114. www.pineapple-inn.com. ℂ **401/847-2600** or 877/847-2601. $99–$213 double. Free parking. **Amenities:** Wi-Fi (free).

Where to Eat in Newport

In addition to the recommendations below, the dining rooms at **Castle Hill** (p. 455) and **The Chanler** (p. 455) are open to anyone unintimidated by the cost. Do make reservations, even in the off-season. Non-summer hours and days of operation vary considerably at Newport's restaurants, and some venues close for months between November and April.

EXPENSIVE

Black Pearl ★ SEAFOOD/AMERICAN   This long building near the end of the wharf contains The Tavern, an atmospheric bar and room with marine charts on the walls, and the pricier Commodore's Room, with linens, candles, and

---

Dine in Gilded Age Style

The Gilded Age moguls who built their mansions in Newport often traveled by private rail car, and so should you. For something different, the **Newport Dinner Train,** 19 America's Cup Ave. (www. trainsri.com; ℂ **800/398-7427** or 401/841-8700), offers meals during a 22-mile train trip along Narragansett Bay. It leaves at 6:30pm for dinner and 11:30am or 2pm for lunch. Reservations are required. Fares range from $30 for lunch excursions to $50 for dinner. The train runs from mid-April to mid-December.

19th-century sailing prints. And in warm months, there's a waterside patio and raw bar. Most of the preparations of fish, duck, lamb, and beef are familiar but of good quality. Don't miss the clam chowder, which has been winning prizes since forever. Other Tavern staples include the Pearlburger and chicken potpie, which arrives with a high golden-brown dome that explodes in steam when punctured. In summer, the restaurant adds a "Hot Dog Clam Chowder Annex."

Bannister's Wharf. www.blackpearlnewport.com. ⓒ **401/846-5264.** Reservations and jackets for men required for dinner in Commodore's Room. Main courses $15–$33 in Tavern, $28–$48 in Commodore's Room. Daily 10:30am–1am in summer; until 10pm in winter. Closed Jan to mid-Mar.

Clarke Cooke House ★★ NEW AMERICAN

For many, this is *the* quintessential Newport restaurant. Most of its several levels are open to the air in summer and glassed-in in winter, and several bars serve to lubricate conversation. Up on the formal third floor, you can start with oysters on the half shell or tuna ceviche, perhaps moving on to a 12-oz classic steak au poivre. Other rooms have more casual personalities: The Bistro wraps around a fireplace and center bar; the main floor, called the Candy Store, serves full meals, snacks, sandwiches, and drinks. All levels have access to the wide choices of a big wine cellar, and all are steeped in nautical decor.

24 Bannister's Wharf. www.clarkecooke.com. ⓒ **401/849-2900.** Weekend reservations recommended in summer. Main courses $23–$55. Daily 11:30am–1am. Limited hours in winter; call to confirm.

Fluke Newport ★★ NEW AMERICAN

The second-floor houses the formal dining room, but climb the steps to the third level to find a happy space with a small slip of a bar and bare tables, views of the harbor and a convivial crowd. Set the mood with a specialty cocktail, the Juniperotivo, perhaps (gin, pomegranate molasses, lemon juice, and fresh mint), or one of nearly a score of wines by the glass—pours are generous. Begin with bacon-wrapped dates filled with Marcona almonds before a main of crispy skin-on striped bass with attention-grabbing cilantro-habanero sauce, or pan-seared skate with pastrami spices, mustard seed, and citrus capers.

41 Bowen's Wharf. www.flukenewport.com. ⓒ **401/849-7778.** Main courses $26–$38. Daily 5–10pm in summer; Thurs–Sun 5–10pm in winter.

Thames Street Kitchen ★★

Newport all but flew the flag at half-staff when this favorite closed in 2015, but they are back, reopening in the spring of 2018 with a fresh new menu. Check it out online, but don't depend on its being the same when you get there, because these chefs are full of surprises, changing with the season's freshest ingredients and the moment's inspiration. So expect the unexpected—oysters served with rhubarb mignonette, escargot with bone marrow, halibut in ramp broth with nasturtium and fiddleheads. The wine list is short but respectable, with all available by the glass. Cocktails are phenomenal—like the jalapeno mezcal drink, a blend of Del Maguey Vida, pineapple honey syrup, jalapeno, lime and bitters.

509 Thames St. www.tsknpt.com. ⓒ **401/846-0400.** Main courses $28–$34. Tues–Sun 5:30am–10pm.

MODERATE

Brick Alley Pub ★ AMERICAN   The Brick is loud, large, and good-natured, and is probably Newport's favorite hangout. Families, tourists, working stiffs, and yachtsmen squeeze through the doors into the thronged dining rooms, the bar, and the terrace. The cab of a 1938 Chevy pickup sits next to the soup-and-salad bar, with the decor also incorporating kid-size vehicles, license plates, vintage photos, and a model train. The voluminous menu is pub grub squared: stuffed clams, Cajun catfish, nachos, burgers, pizzas, steaks, stuffies, meatloaf, and squid-ink spaghetti with cream, scallops, and crabmeat. There's a children's menu for kids 10 and under, and a caution that "unattended children will be given two free puppies and a double espresso." Expect a wait.

140 Thames St. www.brickalley.com. ✆ **401/849-6334.** Main courses $8–$30. Reservations advised. Mon–Fri 11:30am–10pm; Sat 11:30am–10:30pm; Sun 10:30am–10pm.

Cafe Zelda ★ SEAFOOD   The cafe's bar is a local favorite populated by neighborhood regulars, while the two-level dining room, where engravings of sailboats line the walls, is more often occupied by 40-plus tourists. The big deal here is the chicken-fried lobster: Lobster flesh is taken out of the shell, dipped in batter, and flash-fried, producing a dish resembling tempura. Another winner is the bouillabaisse, with fish and shellfish in a leek and tomato saffron broth; and the wood-grilled hanger steak with *frites* is commendable. At lunch, by all means go for the Zelda burger.

528 Thomas St. www.cafezelda.com. ✆ **401/849-4002.** Main courses $10–$35. Reservations recommended for dinner. Fri–Sun 11am–3pm; daily 5–10pm.

Restaurant Bouchard ★★ FRENCH   Invitingly elegant, Bouchard serves French classics using a wider range of fresh ingredients, and with such panache that each dish seem newly invented each night. You might begin with sautéed foie gras with a raspberry reduction sauce or a warm tomato tart with Boursin and goat cheese topped with truffle aioli. Try the Gallic approach to New England's favorite seafood with asparagus and lobster in puff pastry, or stuffed roasted lobster and scallops with truffle, Gruyere cheese, and lobster sauce. Dress for the occasion; this is one place you won't want to arrive from the beach in shorts and a T-shirt.

505 Thames St. www.bouchardnewport.com. ✆ **401/846-0123.** Main courses $18–$38. Complimentary off-street parking available; ask when you reserve. Weds–Mon 5:30pm "til closing."

Salvation Café ★ NEW AMERICAN   About a half-mile away from the waterfront, this friendly, eclectically decorated cafe attracts an artsy, 30s-to-50s crowd. It's as funky-hip as Newport gets, and so popular with locals that the tourists who discover it are barely visible. 1950s record covers occupy the walls and tables are close together, with diners elbow to elbow. Teriyaki salmon with lemon coconut rice and sesame Sriracha aioli is a winner, as is the braised lamb rigatoni. Call for weeknight and before-7 specials.

140 Broadway. www.salvationcafe.com. ✆ **401/847-2620.** Main courses $17–$27. Daily 4:30pm–midnight. Sometimes closed mid-Feb to mid-Mar.

Scales & Shells ★★ SEAFOOD   The graceless name reflects the uncompromising character of this clangorous fish house: It's fish and shellfish *only* here (with one vegetarian pasta option). Diners looking for a little elegance in the summer season should head for the upstairs room, called UpScales (it's closed in winter). On the first floor, which is open year-round, options are listed on a big blackboard next to the open kitchen, with guileless preparations that allow the natural flavors to prevail. Portions are substantial: The "large" appetizer of fried calamari is enough for four. Swordfish grilled over hardwood and topped with roasted peppers is typical. A new feature is a new Oyster Room, ½ Shell, next door, open weekends off-season, full-time summer.

527 Thames St. www.scalesandshells.com. ℭ **401/846-3474.** Main courses $17–$30. Reservations for patio seating. Sun–Thurs 5–9pm, Fri–Sat 5–11pm (Fri–Sat closes 10pm off-season). Closed mid-Dec to mid-Jan.

INEXPENSIVE

Flo's Clam Shack ★ SEAFOOD   Just past Easton's Beach over the Newport/Middletown line, this old-timer is a lopsided shanty, where you step up to the order window and choose from the handwritten menu. This is the place to get clams, on a plate or on a roll. They're cooked swiftly to order, and meltingly tender. This is also the place to sample "chowda" and that Rhode Island specialty, stuffies (see box p. 436). Upstairs are a raw bar and deck even more happily ramshackle than below.

4 Wave Ave., Middletown. www.flosclamshacks.com. ℭ **401/847-8141.** Main courses $5–$25. No credit cards. Daily 11am–9pm Memorial Day–Labor Day; Mar–Memorial Day and Labor Day–Dec Wed–Sun 11am—9pm. Closed Jan–Feb.

Newport Entertainment & Nightlife

Many of the restaurants listed above have chummy bars for a drink and snack. The most likely places to spend a full evening lie along **Thames Street.** One of the most obvious possibilities, **The Red Parrot,** 348 Thames St., near Memorial Boulevard (www.redparrotrestaurant.com; ℭ **401/847-3800**), has handsome windows overlooking the street and the look of an Irish pub.

A full schedule of live music is on the plate at the **Newport Blues Cafe ★**, 286 Thames St., at Green Street (www.newportblues.com; ℭ **401/841-5510**). There's music nightly in summer, weekends in the off season. With its fireplace and dark wood, the cafe has a touch of class. (Dinner is served here 6–10pm nightly, with main courses such as porterhouse steak and chicken parmesan running $16–$26.)

In 2018, the **1908 Public House** replaced the long-time favorite Mudville Pub at 8 W. Marlborough St. (www.1908publichouse.com; ℭ **401/619-0800**). It's across the street from **Cardines Field**, a small baseball stadium near the visitor center, where the **Newport Gulls** (www.newportgulls.com), a collegiate team, play in the summer. Fans and players alike stop in after games, and it can get packed.

THE RHODE ISLAND COAST: NARRAGANSETT TO WATCH HILL

Narragansett: 32 miles SW of Providence; 14 miles W of Newport

Travelers rushing through the state on I-95 between Providence and the Connecticut border miss some of the best beaches and most congenial fishing and resort villages of New England. **South County**—an unofficial designation that refers, loosely, to the coast from Narragansett west to Watch Hill at the Connecticut border—undersells the beguilements of the area. Locals, however, are well aware of its charms; try to avoid weekends in July and August, when the crush of day-trippers can turn the region's two-lane roads into parking lots.

Essentials

ARRIVING

From I-95, take exit 9 to pick up Route 4. This merges with Route 1, arriving in **Narragansett** in about 20 miles. Turn east on Route 1A for a few miles to reach Narragansett Pier. Alternately, from Newport, take Route 138 to Route 1A south, which comes right into Narragansett Pier after 14 miles.

    Westerly is 25 miles west of Narragansett along Route 1; it's also accessible via I-95, exit 91 or 92 (both of which are actually in Connecticut). Westerly also is a stop on **Amtrak**'s (www.amtrak.com) Northeast corridor service, with four or five trains daily. It's 30 to 45 minutes by train from Providence, around 3 hours from New York City, and 1½ to 2 hours from Boston.

VISITOR INFORMATION

The **Narragansett Chamber of Commerce** maintains a **visitor center** inside the Towers, 36 Ocean Rd. (www.narragansettcoc.com; ✆ 401/783-7121). The **South County Tourism Council** (www.southcountyri.com; ✆ 800/548-4662 or 401/789-4422), has a vacation planner, *South County Style,* that you can view online or request a free copy be mailed to you.

Exploring the Narragansett Coast

This is a good section of coastline for a drive or a swim. You'll pass some of the most desirable beaches in New England, with swaths of fine sand, relatively clean waters, and summer water temperatures that average about 70°F (21°C). When there are storms, the water kicks up enough to justify getting out the surfboard; this is the best place in the state to catch the waves.

NARRAGANSETT ★

Traveling from east to west (you'll also be going north to south), start at **Narragansett Pier,** a village that extends inland from the shoreline. Pick up Ocean Road here. You'll pass under the **Towers,** a massive stone structure that spans the road, with cylindrical towers topped by conical roofs on either side. It is all that remains of the Gilded Age Narragansett Casino, lost in a 1900 fire. In the seaward tower is the Narragansett **visitor center** (see above).

About 3 miles after the Towers is the entrance to **Scarborough State Beach ★★** (www.riparks.com; ✆ **401/789-2324**), the most popular beach in the state. Noticeably well kept, with a row of pavilions for picnicking and changing, it has ample parking and surroundings unsullied by brash commercial enterprises. The beach is largely hard-packed sand. While the mild surf makes this a good option for families with young children, sections are often also jammed with teenagers and college students. Weekend parking costs $14 for nonresidents ($12 on weekdays, $7 for nonresident seniors).

About 2½ miles past the beach entrance is the **Point Judith Lighthouse,** 1470 Ocean Rd. (✆ **401/789-0444**). Built in 1857 and restored in 2000, the brownstone tower is a photo op that can be approached but not entered.

In July and August, **whale-watching expeditions** leave from near here, offered by **Frances Fleet,** 33 State St. (www.francesfleet.com; ✆ **800/662-2824** or 401/783-4988). Boats go out on Tuesdays and Thursday through Sunday, leaving at 1pm and returning at 5:30pm. Tickets are $50 adults, $45 seniors, and $40 children 11 and under. Chances are good that a whale will show itself, although, as the company website notes, "whether or not you sight these marvelous creatures is entirely up to the whales." To get to the dock from the lighthouse, double back about 1 mile, turn left onto Point Judith Road, go two-fifths of a mile and turn left onto Galilee Escape Road, go 1 mile and turn right onto Great Island Road, and make the first left onto State Road. This is the **Port of Galilee,** where year-round ferries to **Block Island** (p. 465) also depart.

WATCH HILL ★ & WESTERLY

In the most southwest corner of Rhode Island, peacefully semirural Westerly is home to the pretty land's-end resort village of Watch Hill. Grand summer mansions and Queen Anne gingerbread houses remain from the post–Civil War period, when Watch Hill gained its popularity as a summer retreat.

In Watch Hill, on Bay Street, the small **Carousel Beach** is good for younger children. Its **Flying Horse Carousel,** which dates to 1867, is for kids only. There's shopping nearby for the adults. *Note:* Parking is extremely limited in Watch Hill. Expect to pay $15 or more in a commercial lot.

For quiet hiking and bird-watching (hawks in the fall, especially), head for the white crescent beach on **Napatree Point ★**, a long spit of land jutting into the Atlantic at the tip of Watch Hill. While you can enter the Napatree wildlife preserve for free, there are no facilities; you'll need to park in town and walk in. The 1.5-mile stroll along the shore from the Watch Hill Yacht Club to the end of the point takes about 30 minutes. Stay off the dunes to prevent dune erosion and steer clear of the grass (and wear long pants) to avoid ticks.

For swimming, eating, and nightlife, the half-mile long **Misquamicut State Beach ★** (www.riparks.com; ✆ **401/596-9097**), 257 Atlantic Ave., is parallel to and south of Route 1. Along with fine-grained sand, gentle surf, and gradual drop-offs, the beach has parking, a pavilion, a carousel, minigolf, batting cages, paddle boats, restaurants, beach stores, and music at night. It fills up during summer days, so arrive early. The beach is open May through Labor Day, and parking is $14.

Where to Stay in Watch Hill & Westerly

See also chapter 9 (p. 411), for options in nearby Mystic, Connecticut.

Shelter Harbor Inn ★   Parts of the main building date to 1810, accounting for the creaking floorboards and doors that don't quite close. A genteel tone prevails. Several bedrooms have fireplaces, decks, or both. Furnishings are clean and simple with a touch of Ye Olde Inne, but comfortable enough. A shuttle takes guests to a private beach a mile away (or guests can drive themselves and park); a rooftop hot tub is open all year; and guests are welcome to play paddle tennis, croquet, and bocce during the summer. A creative **restaurant ★** (main courses $11–$29) and honored wine cellar round out the picture. The inn and restaurant are open 365 days a year—unusual for this area of New England.

10 Wagner Rd. (just S of Rte. 1), Westerly. www.shelterharborinn.com. ℂ **800/468-8883** or 401/322-8883. 24 units. $192–$258 double; from $106 off-season. Rates include breakfast. **Amenities:** Restaurant; bar; rooftop Jacuzzi; Wi-Fi (free).

Watch Hill Inn Apartments ★   Savor sunsets over the marina from this century-old clapboard lodge. Modern suites are either in the main lodge or the annex building. Most have kitchenettes and/or decks, and some accommodate up to five people. The location is great: There's access to a beach, and the inn is walking distance to Napatree Point (p. 463), Carousel Beach (p. 463), and Olympia Tea Room (below). It's also just 8 miles from Mystic, Connecticut (p. 411). In summer months, meals also are offered at the in-house **Seaside Cafe,** which has indoor and outdoor seating.

38–44 Bay St., Watch Hill. www.watchhillinn.com. ℂ **855/677-7686.** 22 units. $415 and up for suites. Rates include breakfast. **Amenities:** Restaurant; bar; Wi-Fi (free).

Where to Eat Along the Narragansett Coast
NARRAGANSETT

With your beachside meal, you might want to give the local **Narragansett Beer** (www.narragansettbeer.com) a taste. In 2020 it will celebrate its 130th birthday, having survived even Prohibition from 1920 to 1933. Available in cans or longnecks, it's still brewed in Providence and Pawcatuck, RI.

Coast Guard House ★ SEAFOOD   Adjacent to the Towers (see p. 462), this 1888 former Coast Guard headquarters is now a restaurant that enjoys unobstructed views of the beach and breakers crashing a few feet below its windows—a diversion from the corporate-looking interior. You can enjoy appetizers and raw-bar options on the hugely popular outdoor deck.

40 Ocean Rd. www.thecoastguardhouse.com. ℂ **401/789-0700.** Main courses $17–$33. Mon–Thurs 11:30am–9pm, Fri–Sat 11:30am–10pm, Sunday 10am–9pm.

Crazy Burger Cafe & Juice Bar ★ LIGHT FARE/VEGETARIAN   This funky burger joint serves burgers made from beef, lamb, turkey, and salmon, and vegetarian and vegan options that include the Just Plain Nuts burger of toasted cashews, walnuts, lentils, and zucchini. The sweet potato fries are to die for, and the ketchup is homemade. Drinks include espresso, fresh juices, and chai.

144 Boon St. www.crazyburger.com. ⓒ **401/783-1810.** Burgers and main courses $9–$15. Daily 7am–8:30pm (Fri–Sat until 9:30pm).

Spain of Narragansett ★★ SPANISH   About a mile south of Scarborough Beach, this is deservedly the most popular restaurant on this stretch of shore. Partly it's the congenial staff, partly the terraces overlooking the sea. But the greatest share of credit goes to the creative riffs on the Spanish tapas tradition and such favorites as *paella Valenciana* (mildly seasoned shrimp, sea scallops, clams, mussels, chicken, chorizo, calamari, saffron rice) and the irresistible fried calamari tossed with very un-Spanish hot peppers. Pay special attention to the delectable dishes listed as "Shellfish Combinations."

1144 Ocean Rd. www.spainri.com. ⓒ **401/783-9770.** Main courses $20–$38. Tues–Sat 4–10pm (Fri–Sat until 11pm); Sun 1–9pm.

WATCH HILL & WESTERLY
See also chapter 9 (p. 418), for options in nearby Mystic and Stonington, Connecticut.

Olympia Tea Room ★ NEW AMERICAN   The genteel tone of Watch Hill is undergirded by the Olympia, long a favorite meet-and-eat retreat for wealthy locals. The layout includes a warren of wooden booths, into which the kitchen cranks out imaginative food. If available, jump for the appetizer of plump, lightly fried oysters on wilted spinach and corn salsa. The stuffies and lobster rolls are as good as you're likely to enjoy in coastal New England. Be sure to read the "Watch Hill History" in the front of the menu—it's quite entertaining. There are no highchairs, emphasizing that this is not a venue for young children.

74 Bay St., Watch Hill. www.olympiatearoom.com. ⓒ **401/348-8211.** Main courses $16–$38. Daily 11:30am–10pm in summer, Thurs–Sun 11:30am–8pm spring and fall. (Hours and days vary frequently; call ahead.) Closed Nov–Apr.

Two Little Fish Westerly ★★ CLAM SHACK   Celebrating 21 years as a local gathering spot, Two Little Fish is a clam shack with a cafe vibe. The lobster rolls (served hot or cold) are packed with tender meat, or you can get rolls packed full of sizzling scallops, whole belly clams, fried shrimp, or calamari (Rhode Island–style, with hot cherry peppers). And, of course, fish 'n' chips. Half a dozen of Tim's Clam Fritters ($5.99) or Kevin's Clam Cake Combo (four with chowder for $7.99) make a light lunch or a good pm pick-me-up.

300 Atlantic Ave, Westerly (at Misquamicut Beach). www.twolittlefishseafood.com. ⓒ **401/348-9941.** Main courses $17–$30, seafood sandwiches and rolls $12–$20. Apr–Oct daily 11am–6pm, June–Aug 11am–8pm (hours vary, so call ahead).

BLOCK ISLAND ★★

Viewed from above or on a map, Block Island looks like a pork chop with a big bite taken out of the middle. (That "bite" is **Great Salt Pond,** almost cutting the island in two and creating a fine protected harbor.) Only 7 miles long and 3 miles wide, Block Island is edged with long stretches of beach, lifting at points into dramatic bluffs. The interior, dimpled with undulating hills, only rarely reaches above 150 feet in elevation. Its hollows and clefts cradle more than 350 sweet-water ponds, some no larger than a backyard swimming pool.

The only significant concentration of houses, businesses, hotels, and people is at **Old Harbor,** on the lower eastern shore, where most ferries from the mainland arrive and most of the remaining fishing boats moor.

Named for Adrian Block, a Dutch explorer who briefly stepped ashore in 1641, the island's earliest European settlement was in 1661. For years, it attracted the kinds of people who nurture fierce convictions of independence: farmers, pirates, fishermen, smugglers, scavengers, and entrepreneurs, all willing to deal with the realities of isolation, lonely winters, and occasional killer hurricanes. Today it's home to about 1,000 permanent residents.

After the Civil War, during America's first taste of mass tourism, sun, sand, sea and a sense of other-worldliness transformed Block Island from an off-shore afterthought into an accessible summer retreat for the urban middle class. Unlike other regions, Block Island has preserved many hotels from that Victorian era: They crowd around Old Harbor, providing most of the lodging base. Smaller inns and B&Bs add more tourist rooms, most in converted Victorian-era houses. Only a few establishments even resemble motels. Tasteful Yankee understatement is the baseline.

Away from the sand and surf, this is an island of peaceful pleasures. Police officers wear Bermuda shorts and ride bikes. Children tend lemonade stands in front of picket fences and low hedges. Clumps of hydrangeas tangle with beach roses and honeysuckle, hiding the foundations of farmhouses with shingles scoured gray by sea winds. The island is in the middle of a flyway for migratory birds, and egrets, ducks, goldfinches, and kingfishers are seen in abundance.

No wonder Block Island was included on a list of the "Last Great Places" in the Western Hemisphere by the Nature Conservancy. Conservation groups have created abundant walking trails throughout the island. Deer were introduced only about 30 years ago, to the islanders' regret, bringing Lyme disease and the four-hoofed enthusiasm for turning flowerbeds into salad bars.

Essentials

ARRIVING

BY PLANE   **Westerly State Airport** (http://westerly.stateairportri.com), near the Connecticut border, is the base for over a dozen regular flights to and from Block Island via **New England Airlines** (www.blockislandsairline.com; ℂ **800/ 243-2460,** 401/596-2460 in Westerly, or 401/466-5881 on Block Island). Flights depart hourly in summer, taking 12 to 15 minutes. Fares are $109 round-trip for adults, slightly less for children. Reserve in advance and allow for the possibility that coastal fogs or high winds will delay or even cancel flights.

BY FERRY   The **Interstate Navigation Company** (www.blockislandferry. com; ℂ **866/783-7996** or 401/783-7996) runs year-round passenger-and-vehicle ferries between Newport's Point Judith and Old Harbor on the Block. Boats

Block Island

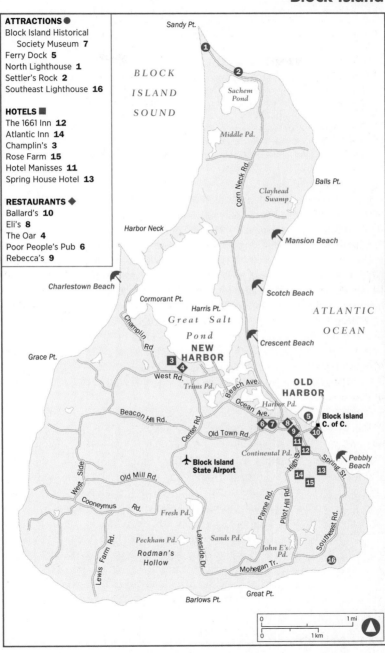

ATTRACTIONS ●
Block Island Historical
  Society Museum **7**
Ferry Dock **5**
North Lighthouse **1**
Settler's Rock **2**
Southeast Lighthouse **16**

HOTELS ■
The 1661 Inn **12**
Atlantic Inn **14**
Champlin's **3**
Rose Farm **15**
Hotel Manisses **11**
Spring House Hotel **13**

RESTAURANTS ◆
Ballard's **10**
Eli's **8**
The Oar **4**
Poor People's Pub **6**
Rebecca's **9**

Sandy Pt.

*BLOCK
ISLAND
SOUND*

Sachem
Pond

Middle Pd.

Corn Neck Rd.

Balls Pt.

Clayhead
Swamp

Harbor Neck

Mansion Beach

Charlestown Beach

Cormorant Pt.

Harris Pt.

*Great Salt
Pond*

NEW
HARBOR

*ATLANTIC
OCEAN*

Scotch Beach

Champlin Rd.

Grace Pt.

West Rd.

Crescent Beach

Trims Pd.

Beach Ave.

OLD
HARBOR

Harbor Pd.

Ocean Ave.

Block Island
C. of C.

Beacon Hill Rd.

Center Rd.

Old Town Rd.

Continental Pd.

High St.

Spring St.

Pebbly
Beach

Block Island
State Airport

West Side

Old Mill Rd.

Payne Rd.

Pilot Hill Rd.

Cooneymus Rd.

Fresh Pd.

Lewis Farm Rd.

Peckham Pd.

*Rodman's
Hollow*

Lakeside Dr.

Sands Pd.

John E's
Pd.

Southeast Rd.

Barlows Pt.

Mohegan Tr.

Great Pt.

| 0 | | 1 mi |
| 0 | | 1 km |

10

RHODE ISLAND | Block Island

Given the cost of taking a car, consider parking in a long-term lot at Point Judith or New London (see p. 412) and going car-less once you're on Block Island. The island is small, rental bicycles and mopeds are readily available, there are cabs for longer distances, and most hotels and inns are within a few blocks of the docks. There are even car-rental agencies on the island. If you intend to take a car anyway, understand that it's important to make ferry reservations well in advance, at ☏ **866/783-7996** Monday through Friday between 5am and 4pm. Two months' advance reservations aren't too early for weekend departures.

If you do decide to bring your car to the island, top off the gas tank before rolling onto the ferry. The only gas station on the island, on Corn Neck Road, is only open Monday to Saturday 8am–3pm, Sunday 11am–3pm.

depart up to nine times daily in high season, once daily in mid-winter; sailing time is 55 minutes. Ferries leave Point Judith (Fort Adams) at 9:15am and return from Block Island at 4:45pm. Sailing time is 2 hours. Reservations aren't required, but get to the dock early; boats tend to fill up quickly (see box above). Round-trip passenger fares are $26 adults, $22 seniors, and $12 for children, but getting a car to Block Island is considerably more expensive: Passenger vehicles cost an additional $95 to $115, with different fees for bicycles, mopeds, and motorcycles. **Car reservations** must be made by phone at ☏ **866/783-7996, ext. 3.** Drivers, be prepared: You are expected to *back* your car into the close quarters of the ferry's main deck.

High-speed passenger-only service operates from Point Judith (and also from Fall River, MA) via **Island Hi-Speed Ferry** (www.blockislandferry.com; ☏ **866/783-7996**), which makes several daily round-trips from late May to early October. Sailing time is 30 minutes; fares to and from Newport are $50 adults ($26 child 5–11).

Block Island Express (www.goblockisland.com; ☏ **860/444-4624** or 401/466-2212) also runs high-speed catamarans to Block Island, with service from both New London, CT (see p. 412) and Orient Point, Long Island, NY. The trip takes 80 or 90 minutes, depending on the boat. (Some Long Island trips take over 2 hours and involve a connection through New London.) Service operates daily mid-June through August and less frequently in May, early June, and September; round-trip fares are $47.50 to $52.50 adults, $23.50 to $26.25 children ages 2 to 11, depending on whether you return the same day or stay overnight on Block Island. The ferry takes passengers, bicycles, and surfboards (for a fee), and crated dogs (free). Reservations are wise.

Tip: Try to avoid the last ferry Sunday nights in summer, when boisterous weekend drunks roll on board from the bars along Water Street.

VISITOR INFORMATION

The **Block Island Chamber of Commerce** has a year-round information office at the ferry landing at Old Harbor (www.blockislandchamber.com; ☏ **800/383-BIRI** [2474] or 401/466-2474). Its attendants can answer questions and help find lodging. In the same building are lockers for day-trippers and one of the island's few ATMs. At Corn Neck Road and Ocean Avenue is the only bank, which also has an ATM.

Most streets on Block Island have no house numbers, and some roads have no names. Leave your dog at home: Hotels and B&Bs won't accept them, they are banned from the beaches, and they are supposed to be leashed at all times.

Daily newspapers from Boston, New York, and Providence are sold at the **B.I.G.** (© **401/466-2949**), the grocery store on Ocean Avenue (near Corn Neck Road). When they become available, however, depends on the ferry from Port Judith to which they are delivered each morning.

GETTING AROUND

Cars are allowed on the island, but roads are narrow, winding, and without shoulders, and drivers must contend with runners and flocks of bicycles and mopeds. Unless your party includes people with mobility problems or small children, we recommend leaving your car on the mainland and joining the two-wheelers.

If you'd like to rent a car after you arrive, **Block Island Bike & Car Rental,** on Ocean Avenue (www.blockislandbikeandcarrental.com; © **401/466-2297**), has offices near Payne's Dock and will pick you up at the ferry or airport; reserve ahead. Convenient sources near Old Harbor for 2-wheeled transportation include **The Moped Man,** 435 Water St. (© **401/466-5444**) on the main business street, renting bikes as well as mopeds; **Old Harbor Bike Shop,** at the ferry dock (© **401/466-2029**); and **Island Moped & Bikes,** Water Street (www.bimopeds.com; © **401/466-2700**). Rates for bikes are $20 per 5 hours, per day $30, 3 days $40, less with widely available discount coupons. Moped rates vary but are usually from $45 an hour to $135 per full day. Bargaining often brings prices down, especially early in the week after the weekenders have left, or if your rental is for 3 or more days. Keep in mind that mopeds aren't allowed on dirt roads, which provide access to many beaches.

Some inns also rent bicycles, so it's possible to take a taxi from the ferry or airport to your inn, drop off luggage, and get around by bike after that. Two such inns are the **Seacrest,** 207 High St. (© **401/466-2882**), and **Rose Farm** (see p. 472) on Roslyn Road (www.beachrosebicycles.com; © **401/466-5925**). Inquire about bike rentals when making room reservations at other places as well.

Exploring Block Island

With no golf course and a lone museum that takes only 15 minutes to see, little on the island distracts from the central missions of sunning, cycling, hiking, lolling, and ingesting copious quantities of lobster, clams, and chowder. A driving tour of every site on the list takes no more than 2 hours.

The **Block Island Historical Society Museum,** 18 Old Town Rd. at Ocean Avenue (www.blockislandhistorical.org; © **401/466-2481**), was an 1871 inn that now contains a miscellany of photos, ship models, and tools. An upstairs room reflects the Victorian period. The museum is open weekends, 11am to

4pm in the summer, with limited hours in the spring and fall. Admission is $6 adults, $4 seniors and students, free for children 15 and under.

Proceed north on Corn Neck Road, skirting Crescent Beach, on the right. Look for the **Clay Head Trail** sign on your right and drive down the dirt road to the trail head: After a half-mile moderate hike, the trail splits, going right to a beautiful sandy beach or left up the bluff for breathtaking views high above the ocean. Watch out for unmarked grassy trails leading away from the bluff. You can while away an entire afternoon on these trails, known as **The Maze.**

Farther along Corn Neck Road, the pavement ends at **Settler's Rock ★★★,** with a plaque naming the English pioneers who landed here in 1661. This is one of the island's loveliest spots, with **Sachem Pond** behind the Rock and a scimitar beach curving out to **North Lighthouse (© 401/466-3200),** erected in 1867. In between is a **national wildlife refuge** of particular interest to birders. The lighthouse, reached by a mile-long walk on a rocky beach, contains an interpretive center of local ecology and history (and the only public restroom for miles); it's open from July 5 to Labor Day daily from 10am to 4pm.

Alternatively, a couple of miles south of Old Harbor, on what starts out as Spring Street is the **Southeast Lighthouse (© 401/466-5009),** an appealing Victorian structure built in 1874. A National Historic Landmark, the lighthouse had to be moved 245 feet back from the eroding precipice in 1993. While a small exhibit on the ground floor can be seen for free, the admission fee to the top is $10. Continuing along the same road—which changes names and makes a sharp right turn inland—watch for the left turn onto West Side Road. In a few hundred yards is the sign for **Rodman's Hollow,** a geological dent dug by a passing glacier. It's deeper than it looks, the bottom a few feet below sea level and laced with walking trails beneath a thick mantle of low trees.

Much of what you see here, and elsewhere on the island, is designated forever wild, for the Nature Conservancy has purchased about a third of the island's surface to protect it from development. There are about 25 miles of trails, only occasionally signed with granite Greenway markers and wooden turnstiles. You can purchase a map of the trail network at the Chamber of Commerce building at the ferry landing or at the **Nature Conservancy** office, 352 High St. (© **401/466-2129**).

Block Island Beaches

Immediately south of the Old Harbor, past the breakwater, is the northern end of **Pebbly Beach,** a section informally known as **Ballard's Beach** for the popular restaurant located there (see p. 473). Crowded with sunbathers and swimmers, it is one of only two on the island with lifeguards. The surf is often rough. Drinks are served at your towel.

North of Old Harbor starts the 3-mile-long **Crescent Beach** (also known as Frederick J. Benson Town Beach, or simply Town Beach). The southern section, with a sandy bottom that stays shallow well out into the gentle surf, is known as **Baby Beach** because of its relative safety for children. Farther along is the main part, a broad strand served by a pavilion with a snack bar, restrooms, and showers. You can rent chairs, umbrellas, and boogie boards. The surf is higher here and rolls straight in; lifeguards are on duty.

Farther north, **Scotch Beach** has a small parking lot reached by a dirt road off Corn Neck Road. Consider this grown-up and R-rated, dominated by young summer workers and residents. Still farther north is **Mansion Beach,** with a dirt road of the same name leading in from Corn Neck Road. Somewhat more secluded, it is usually less crowded than the others.

On the west side of the island, running south from the jetty that marks the entrance to New Harbor, is **Charlestown Beach.** Uncrowded and relatively tranquil during the day, it draws anglers from dusk into the night surf-casting for striped bass.

Outdoor Activities

Parasailing has become popular here; chutes can be seen lifting riders up to heights of 1,200 feet above the ocean. You must reserve in person with **Block Island Parasail** (www.blockislandparasail.com; ✆ **401/864-2474**) at the office near the Old Harbor ferry landing. Rates start at $80 for 500 feet and increase by altitude; observers are charged $20 each. The company also offers banana boat and jet boat rides, as well as dive trips.

A more old-fashioned form of transportation is provided by horseback rides at **Rustic Rides Farm,** on 1173 West Side Rd. (✆ **401/466-5060**). A walking attendant handles the reins and protects children on the trail. Several options are available, priced from $55 for a slow 1-hour ride to $100 for a 2-hour beach ride.

The name to know for fishing, kayaking, and canoeing is **Pond & Beyond** (www.pondandbeyondkayak.com; ✆ **401/578-2773**). Guided tours include family paddles, kids and kayaks, and full moon paddles. Tours last 2½ hours and cost $50 per person. **Block Island Fishworks,** Ocean Avenue (www.sandypointco.com; ✆ **401/466-5392**) sells fishing tackle and arranges charter boat outings for both inshore and deep-water angling. Another source is **Champlin's Resort,** on Great Salt Pond (www.champlinsresort.com; ✆ **401/466-7777**), which rents bumper boats and Zodiacs as well as kayaks.

Where to Stay on Block Island

Most inns are in buildings over 100 years old, so expect wavy floors, narrow hallways, steep staircases, and rooms of odd configuration. Air-conditioning is rare on the island, and such amenities as TV and Wi-Fi cannot be assumed. There's basically a 4-month year for businesses serving tourists, so cost differences between moderate and very expensive room rates are narrow. Two- or 3-night minimum stays are routinely required.

A note on Wi-Fi Service: As service is being expanded on the island, more and more sites are accessible. Things change minute to minute—although be aware that even where service available it is sometimes weak.

The 1661 Inn/Hotel Manisses ★★
Emus, llamas, kangaroos, lemurs, two camels, and a Scottish Highland steer graze in the meadow behind the

Hotel Manisses, the most visible property of an island-wide hospitality empire. The Victorian hotel tends toward older couples. Guest rooms utilize oak antiques and lots of wicker; some have fireplaces. The Manisses parlor serves desserts and flaming coffees in the evening, and stylish dining is featured in the main dining room, with comparable fare in the more casual Gatsby Room. Up the hill at the 1661 Inn, substantial champagne breakfast buffets and afternoon wine and cheese are served to guests of all nine of the properties. The 1661 Inn is now open year-round, although the restaurants are closed in winter.

1 Spring St. www.blockislandresorts.com. © **800/626-4773,** 401/466-2421, or 401/466-2063. 73 units. $210–$440 double. Rates include breakfast. **Amenities:** 2 restaurants; bar; babysitting; concierge; Wi-Fi (in lobby; free).

Atlantic Inn ★★   Perched on 6 rolling acres south of downtown, this 1879 Victorian hotel beguiles with its long veranda and broad views. Bedrooms are furnished mostly with antiques. Drawn by the restaurant's changing menu of appetizers—Ahi tuna carpaccio for example—people start assembling at 4pm each summer day, taking up the Adirondack chairs on the sloping lawn to settle in for spectacular sunsets, lubricated by cocktails and the island's most diverse beer and wine selection. The kitchen is one of the two most accomplished on the Island, and you will need reservations from June to September.

359 High St. www.atlanticinn.com. © **800/224-7422** or 401/466-5883. 21 units. $215–$330 double. Rates include breakfast. Closed Nov–Apr. **Amenities:** Restaurant; bar; 2 tennis courts; Wi-Fi in lobby, some rooms, and cottage.

Champlin's ★★   Families are welcome at this all-inclusive resort, with 225 slips in the marina for visiting yachters. Those who are put off by Victorian fuss and frills will be pleased by the simpler lines and muted fabrics here. All rooms have fridges and microwaves (another plus for families). There's live music in the bars on weekends, picnic grounds with grills, a pizza bar and ice-cream parlor, a laundry facility, and even a theater showing first-run movies. Once you've unpacked, there isn't much to compel you to leave, but the resort provides a shuttle van for trips to other parts of the island. Cars, mopeds, kayaks, and pontoon boats are available for rent.

Great Salt Pond (from Old Harbor, drive west on Ocean Ave. turning left on West Side Rd.). www.champlinsresort.com. © **800/762-4541** or 401/466-7777. 30 units. $325–$415 double. Closed mid-Oct to early May. **Amenities:** Restaurant; 2 bars; bike rentals; outdoor pool; 2 tennis courts; watersports equipment/rentals; Wi-Fi (free).

Rose Farm ★   Spot deer and pheasant on the 20 acres surrounding the 1897 farmhouse that was the original inn. It is complemented by an additional house across the driveway. Four of the rooms feature Jacuzzis and decks. Some have canopied beds, most have ocean views, and their furnishings are often antique. Afternoon refreshments, usually iced tea and pastries, are served. Bicycles are available for rent on the property.

1005 High St. www.rosefarminn.com. © **401/466-2034.** 19 units (2 w/shared bathroom). $229–$369 double. Rates include breakfast. Children 13 and over welcome. Closed Nov–Apr. **Amenities:** Bike rentals; Wi-Fi (free).

Spring House Hotel ★   Marked by its red mansard roof and wraparound porch, the island's oldest hotel (dating from 1852) has hosted Ulysses S. Grant, Mark Twain, and the Kennedy clan. The young staff is congenial, if occasionally a bit scattered. Bedrooms in the two buildings all have queen-size or double beds, some also with pull-out sofas; most are large. Formal meals are served in the all-white dining room, while a bistro menu is available in the parlor and veranda cafe. Friday is Jazz Club Night with live music.

902 Spring St. www.springhouseblockisland.com. ℂ **800/234-9263** or 401/466-5844. 50 units, 4 houses, 6 condos. $275–$450 double. Rates include breakfast. Closed mid-Oct to May. **Amenities:** Restaurant; bar; Wi-Fi (free).

Where to Eat on Block Island

Expect mostly lobsters, fried and grilled fish and chicken, and routine burgers and beef cuts. Chowders are usually surefire, especially the creamy New England version. Clam cakes—deep-fried fritters that are more cake than clams—are a staple. Lobster dishes are usually sold at fluctuating market prices.

Several inns and hotels (see p. 471) have dining rooms worth noting, but even there, neither jackets nor ties are required. Due to the island's seasonal nature, note that its restaurants can change policies, menus, and—most important—chefs, in a twinkling.

Ballard's ★ AMERICAN   Everyone at some point winds up at Ballard's. Behind the long front porch is a warehouse-like hall where a monster whale skeleton hangs, and beyond that a terrace beside a crowded beach. Several bars and frequent live bands fuel drinkers and diners from lunch until midnight. The menu is all over the map, with something for everyone and an emphasis on seafood. Complementing the lobster rolls and fish and chips is a seafood pasta with lobster, clams, scallops, and shrimp. Kids have their own menu, and they can make as much noise and mess as they want. This place gets pricey for families, though, so you might want to go for lunch and order sandwiches.

42 Water St. www.ballardsbi.com. ℂ **401/466-2231** or 844/405-3275. Main courses $12–$38. Daily 11am–midnight. Closed Oct to mid-May.

Eli's ★★ NEW AMERICAN/VEGETARIAN   One of the island's most popular spots, this tiny place can serve only 50 diners at a time, and the no-reservations policy means waits of up to 2 hours. Once inside at table, order tuna nachos, or pan-seared sea scallops in salsa verde with smoked pork and hominy stew. There is an especially good vegetarian menu, with dishes such as spinach fettuccini in smoked walnut basil cream. Huge portions defy anyone to finish.

456 Chapel St. www.elisblockisland.com. ℂ **401/466-5230.** Main courses $19–$36. May–Oct daily 6–9pm (Sat–Sun until 10pm); Nov–Dec Sat–Sun 5:30–10pm. Closed Jan–Apr.

The Oar ★ AMERICAN   This former good-time bar is open for breakfast, lunch, and dinner, and the menu has a full range of choices from mahi mahi, sirloin, and fried chicken to the standard fries, lobster rolls, and calamari.

A deck and a bar with a picture window take in sea views. Inside, the ceiling and walls are hung with scores of oars—all of them painted with cartoons or graffiti.

West Side Rd. (Block Island Marina). ℂ **401/466-8820.** Main courses $13–$25. Daily 8am–midnight (bar until 1am). Closed late Oct–May.

Poor People's Pub ★ Lots of on-tap beers and good burgers and pub fare keep regulars coming back. Faves are the lobster-and-corn chowder packed with lobster chunks, the stuffed clams, and the smoked salmon sandwich with charred cherry tomatoes, arugula, and pesto on a baguette. The menu is varied, with pizzas and multiple mac 'n' cheese variations.

33 Ocean Ave. www.pppbi.com. ℂ **401/466-8533.** Sandwiches and burgers $11–$15. Daily 11:30am–1am.

Rebecca's Seafood Takeout ★ Though it's opposite the ferry dock, and a popular breakfast stop for those taking the morning ferry, Rebecca's is best known for its affordable lobster rolls and batter-fried shrimp. Chicken wraps are popular, too. Eat at picnic tables or at one of the few indoors.

435 Water St. www.rebeccasseafood.com. ℂ **401/466-5411.** Rolls and sandwiches $5.75–$17; main courses $12–$16. Daily 7am–8pm.

10 Block Island Nightlife

Block Island nightlife isn't of the raunchy, rollicking South Florida variety, but the bars don't close at sunset, either. Among the prime candidates for a potential rockin' good time is **Captain Nick's,** at 34 Ocean Ave. (www.captain nicksbi.com; ℂ **401/466-5670**), opposite the Block Island Grocery, which has pool tables, three bars, and a large dance floor inside, as well as dollar beers, cheap burgers, and live music most nights in season out on the terrace. A block away, **McGovern's Yellow Kittens,** 214 Corn Neck Rd. (www.yellow kittens.com; ℂ **401/466-5855**), also presents live bands in summer, inside or

---

Do-It-Yourself Shore Dinners

Should you have housekeeping facilities in your lodging, you might wish to put together an iconic New England shore dinner.

Lobster is the central component, of course, and you can even buy yours straight off the fishing boats—each afternoon from about 4 to 5:30pm, boats put in at both Old Harbor and the Great Salt Pond on Block Island. A more reliable source is **Finn's Fish Market,** at the Old Harbor ferry landing (ℂ **401/466-2102**). Its lobster prices are similar, and it also carries oysters, clams, shrimp, and fish.

For the other fixings, stop at either the **Block Island Grocery** (known as the B.I.G.), on Corn Neck Road (ℂ **401/466-2949**), a conventional supermarket; or **Block Island Depot,** 101 Ocean Ave. (ℂ **401/466-2403**), which carries a line of cheeses and specialty foods. The best-stocked wine and liquor store is the **Red Bird Package Store,** 233 Dodge St. (ℂ **401/466-2441**), around the corner from the north end of Water Street. Toward the other end of Water Street, **Seaside Market** (ℂ **401/466-5876**) has a good wine selection and some groceries.

out on the deck. Darts, pool tables, foosball, and video games help fill the winter nights. Pub food, pool tables, and foosball are also attractions at **Club Soda,** 35 Connecticut Ave. (📞 **401/466-5397**).

Ballard's (p. 473), 42 Water St., has live rock or pop most afternoons out on the terrace and nightly inside. An occasional live-music venue is the lounge of the **National Hotel,** 36 Water St. (www.blockislandhotels.com; 📞 **401/466-2901**). Yachtsmen and other sailors docked or moored at Champlin's Marina settle in on the end of the main dock at **Trader Vic's,** at New Harbor (www.champlinsresort.com; 📞 **401/466-2641**). The bar is downstairs, with a DJ or band out on the deck most afternoons. In addition to the sunset drinks and tapas on the front lawn of the **Atlantic Inn** (p. 472), many visitors settle in on the porch of the equally well-situated (and less expensive) **Narragansett Inn,** on Water Street (www.narragansettinn.net; 📞 **401/466-2626**). On Payne's Dock at the end of Water Street, **Mahogany Shoals** (www.paynesdock.com; 📞 **401/466-5572**), always has a lively bar scene, often with live music.

VERMONT

By William Scheller

Vermont's rolling hills, shaggy peaks, grazing cows, sugar maples, spectacular fall foliage, and quaint towns give it a distinct sense of place. This state is filled with the dairy farms, dirt roads, and small-scale enterprises that bring joy to the hearts of back-road travelers. And the towns are home to an intriguing mix of old-time Vermonters, back-to-the-landers who showed up in VW buses in the 1960s and never left (many got involved with municipal affairs or put down business roots—think Ben & Jerry); and newer, mon-eyed arrivals from New York or Boston who came to ski or stay at B&Bs and ended up buying second homes—more than a few of which ended up becoming first homes.

The place captures a sense of America as it once was—because here it still is. Vermonters share a sense of community, and they still respect the ideals of thrift and parsimony above those of commercialism. (It took years for Walmart to get approval to build its first big-box store in Vermont, and Montpelier is America's only state capital without a McDonald's.) Locals prize their villages, and understand what makes them special. That counts for a lot in an age when so many other small towns have been swallowed up by suburban sprawl or otherwise faded away with changing times.

Vermont remains a superb destination of country drives, mountain rambles, and overnights at country inns. A good map opens the door to back-road adventures, and it's not hard to get a taste of Vermont's way of life. The state's total population is just a shade over 600,000, making it one of only seven states with more senators (two) than representatives (one) in Congress. It does sometimes feel like the cows still outnumber the humans here, although that hasn't been true since the early 1960s.

Southern Vermont has mostly resisted the encroachments of progress (except at ski resorts on winter weekends), and remains a great introduction to the state. You'll find plenty of antiques shops, handsome inns, fast-flowing streams (with fish!), and inviting restaurants.

Northern Vermont is different. On the region's western edge, along the shores of Lake Champlain, Burlington—the state's largest, liveliest city—is ringed by fast-growing suburban communities

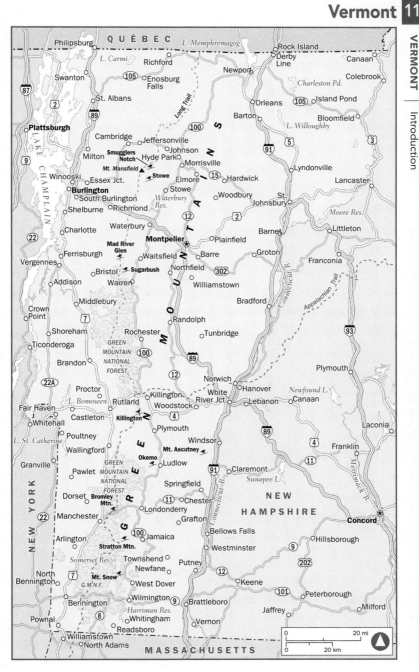

and industrial parks of the non-smokestack variety. But drive an hour east and you're deep in the Northeast Kingdom, the state's least developed, most lost-in-time region.

There are remnants of older industries here—marble quarries in Danby, converging train tracks at White River Junction, a GE plant in Rutland that makes jet engine parts—but mostly it's still rural living: cow pastures high in the hills, clapboard farmhouses under spreading trees, maple-sugaring operations, and the distant sound of timber being cut in woodlots. New and old co-exist here peaceably, and there are few better places to be on a summer or fall afternoon—winter, too, if you love the season's sports. (April mud season? Not so much . . .)

BENNINGTON, MANCHESTER & ENVIRONS

Bennington: 143 miles NW of Boston; 126 miles S of Burlington. Arlington: 15 miles N of Bennington. Manchester: 24 miles N of Bennington.

Bennington (motto: "Where Vermont Begins") owes its significance to a handful of eponymous moments, places, and things. There's the Battle of Bennington, fought in 1777 during the American War of Independence (although the battle actually occurred across the border in New York State); Bennington College, a small, prestigious liberal-arts school just outside town; and Bennington pottery, which traces its ancestry back to the original factory in 1793 and is still prized by collectors for its superb quality.

North of Bennington, a string of closely spaced villages—Arlington, Manchester, and Dorset—presents Vermont at its most Vermont, making the area an ideal destination for a romantic getaway, antiquing trip, or even a serious outlet-shopping trip. This corner of the state is also renowned among anglers because of a winding tributary of the Hudson River called the Battenkill, home of wily populations of brook and brown trout.

Each of the towns has its own unique charm; you can even visit all of them in a single day if you sleep locally and get up early. That would be a pity, though—even a week's travel would reveal only a portion of the superb lodging and dining possibilities in an area that offers sophisticated hospitality along with bucolic beauty.

Essentials

ARRIVING

Bennington is at the intersection of Vermont state routes 9 and 7. If you're coming from the south, the nearest interstate access is via the New York State Thruway at Albany, about 35 miles away. (But you have to drive through the city of Troy first, which takes time; figure 45 min. or more from the Thruway to downtown Bennington.) From the east, I-91 is about 40 miles away at Brattleboro via Route 9 (the Molly Stark Trail). Arlington and Manchester lie north of Bennington on Historic Route 7A, which runs parallel to and west of

Route 7 (it's 15 miles to Arlington, 24 miles to Manchester). Dorset is 7 miles north of Manchester Center on Route 30.

VISITOR INFORMATION

The **Bennington Area Chamber of Commerce,** 100 Veterans Memorial Dr. (www.bennington.com; ✆ **802/447-3311**), maintains a visitor center on Route 7 about 1 mile north of downtown, near the veterans' complex. This office is open weekdays 9am to 5pm year-round, and also on Saturdays until 1pm mid-May through mid-October. There's also a **downtown welcome center** (✆ **802/442-5758**) in a former blacksmith shop at South and Elm streets; look for the big blue flag. Operated by the other BBC—the Better Bennington Corporation, of course—it's open Monday through Friday year-round, and has a big map of the area to orient you.

There's a **Manchester Visitors Center** at 4802 Main St. in Manchester Center; information on the town is also available at **www.manchestervermont. com** or **www.manchesterdesigneroutlets.com**. **Arlington** maintains its own small, self-serve visitor information center at the Stewart's gas station on Route 7A. Just take what you need.

For information on outdoor recreation, the **Green Mountain National Forest** maintains a district ranger office (✆ **802/362-2307**) in Manchester Center at 2538 Depot St. It's open Monday through Friday from 8am to 4:30pm.

Exploring Bennington ★

Today visitors will find a Bennington of two faces. Historic Bennington (more commonly known as **Old Bennington ★★**), with its handsome white clapboard homes and magnificently steepled Old First Church, sits atop a hill west of town off Route 9. **Downtown Bennington,** on the other hand, is a pleasant commercial center where practical shops mix with a brew pub, a craft shop in an old bank, and a diner that harks back to the '50s. The downtown boasts a fair number of architecturally striking buildings. In particular, don't miss the stern marble Federal building (formerly the post office) with six fluted columns at 118 South St., and the massive granite Sacred Heart-St. Francis DeSales church.

Turn off Route 9 in Old Bennington's little traffic circle to visit the **Bennington Battle Monument ★★** (✆ **802/447-0550**). Dedicated in 1891, this 306-foot obelisk of blue limestone resembles a shorter, paunchier Washington Monument. (This is not the battle site—that's about 6 miles northwest of here in New York State—but the monument marks the spot where American munitions were stored.) The monument's viewing platform, which is reached by elevator, is open daily from 9am to 5pm from mid-April through October, and affords wonderful views that extend into New York and Massachusetts. A diorama depicting the battle is on view at ground level. A small fee ($5 adults, $1 kids ages 6–14) is charged. On holidays and during the last 2 weeks of each year, the monument is lit up.

Near the monument, you'll find distinguished old homes lushly overarched with ancient trees. Be sure to spend a minute exploring the **old burying**

"I Had a Lover's Quarrel with the World."

That's the epitaph on the tombstone of Robert Frost, who is buried in the cemetery behind the 1806 First Congregational Church in Old Bennington, down the hill from the Bennington Monument. Signs point the way to the Frost family grave. Travelers often stop here to pay their respects to the man many still consider the true voice of New England. Closer to the church, look for the old tombstones—some decorated with urns and skulls—of other Vermonters who lived much less famous lives.

ground ★ behind the First Congregational Church, where the great poet Robert Frost and several Vermont governors are buried (see "I Had a Lover's Quarrel with the World" box, left). The chamber of commerce provides a walking-tour brochure that helps you make sense of this neighborhood's formerly vibrant past.

Bennington College ★, just northwest of downtown Bennington, was founded in the 1930s as an experimental women's college. It later went co-ed and garnered a national reputation as a liberal-arts school with a special reputation for teaching writing: Pulitzer Prize–winning poet W. H. Auden, novelist Bernard Malamud (*The Natural*), and novelist John Gardner (*Grendel*) all taught here. In the 1980s, Bennington produced a fresh wave of prominent young authors, including Donna Tartt, Bret Easton Ellis, and Jill Eisenstadt. The pleasant campus north of town is worth wandering; to get there, take the North Bennington Road (Route 67A) turnoff north of downtown (near the Bennington Square Shopping Center) and follow it about 2 miles north. There are also three attractive **covered bridges** near the college.

The Bennington Museum ★★ MUSEUM   This eclectic and intriguing collection is one of the best small museums in northern New England. The museum traces its roots back to the 1850s, although it has occupied its current stone-and-column home overlooking the valley since "only" 1928. Expansive galleries feature a range of exhibits on local arts and industry, including early Vermont furniture, glass, paintings, and Bennington pottery. Of special interest are the many colorful primitive landscapes by Grandma Moses (1860–1961), who lived much of her life nearby. (This museum has the largest collection of Moses paintings in the world.) There's also lots of American glass; a globe by Vermonter James Wilson, the nation's first globe maker; the Bennington flag, the oldest surviving stars–and–stripes flag; and a 1925 Martin Wasp luxury car. (Only 16 were ever made, handcrafted in Bennington by Karl Martin between 1920 and 1925.) Surprisingly—given the museum's antiquarian character—substantial space has recently been given to 20th-century artists such as Rockwell Kent and Helen Frankenthaler. Rotating special exhibits bring in serious art that's sometimes unrelated to local history, such as a show of rarely shown works by Renoir, Monet, and Degas or a show of Haitian quilts. This is a great find.

75 W. Main St. (Rte. 9 btw. Old Bennington and downtown). www.benningtonmuseum. org. © **802/447-1571.** $10 adults, $9 seniors and students, free for kids 17 and under, $19 family. June–Oct daily 10am–5pm; Feb–May and Nov–Dec Thurs–Tues 10am–5pm; closed Jan.

Exploring Arlington, Manchester & Dorset ★★★

Driving north from Bennington on Route 7A, you'll come first to the tiny town center of **Arlington ★★**. With its auto-body shop, hub-of-town gas station/convenience store, ice-cream shop, and redemption center (all remnants of a time when the main highway passed right through town), this is a real, functioning Vermont village. It also has a great riverside campground (**Camping on the Battenkill;** www.campingonthebattenkill.com), an unusual number of good farmhouses-converted-into-inns on the surrounding roads, and an enduring connection with Norman Rockwell, who lived in Arlington from 1939 to 1953. There's a Rockwell Exhibition at a maple products shop called the **Sugar Shack** (Route 7A; ✆ **802/375-6747**), with reproductions of paintings and magazine covers for which he used local folks as models; several still live in the area.

Some 8 miles north of Arlington on 7A, Manchester (also sometimes called Manchester Village) and Manchester Center share a blurred town line and proximity, but maintain very different characters. The more southerly **Manchester ★★★** has an old-moneyed elegance and a prim, campus-like main street centered on the resplendently columned Equinox Resort (see p. 488). There's also a neat row of shops, a wonderful golf course, a town library, a former Lincoln home (p. 482), and a fly-fishing museum (below). Just a mile and a half north along Main Street, **Manchester Center** is the major mercantile center for these parts; it almost feels like a small city, with its dozens of outlet stores (see box p. 482), doughnut shop, big-box grocery store, golden-arched fast food, and surprising traffic jams at the main intersection.

Follow Route 30 north out of Manchester Center for about 7 miles to reach **Dorset ★★,** an exquisitely preserved village of white-clapboard architecture and marble sidewalks. While it has no sightseeing attractions, it's definitely worth visiting, with a pair of delightful country inns (see p. 486).

American Museum of Fly Fishing ★★ MUSEUM   If the legendary Battenkill has brought you to Manchester, you'll want to tear yourself away from streamside to visit the world's largest collection of angling art and items under one roof. The complex, which includes a gallery space, library, reading room, store, and historical resources, was specially built for the purpose. You can browse through an impressive collection of antique rods (including some owned by Daniel Webster, Ernest Hemingway, and Winslow Homer), reels, and 200-year-old flies (there are over 22,000 flies in the museum's trove), plus photos, instructional videos, sketchbooks, and historical items. Recent exhibitions have even chronicled the growing popularity of saltwater fly fishing. This is a surprisingly fun place to while away an hour; about the only thing missing is, well, fish. The museum is neatly positioned right between the Equinox Resort (p. 488) and the Orvis fly-fishing store (see box p. 482), where there are fish, in a trout pond where you can try out the famed company's wares.

4070 Main St. (Rte. 7A), Manchester. www.amff.com. ✆ **802/362-3300.** $5 adults, $3 kids 5–14, $10 family. Tues–Sun 10am–4pm. Closed major holidays.

Hildene ★★ HISTORIC HOME   Robert Todd Lincoln, Abraham Lincoln's only child to survive to adulthood, built this 24-room Georgian Revival mansion in 1905, and summered here until his death in 1926. Unlike many showpiece homes of the era, Hildene has an atmosphere of comfort and livability—even with its sweeping central staircase and thousand-pipe 1908 Aeolian organ, played today during house tours. Lincoln chose a gorgeous natural setting for his retreat, and enhanced it with formal gardens designed after the patterns in a stained-glass window. Outstanding views of the flanking mountains make this one of southern Vermont's most popular wedding spots every summer and fall. The home and grounds can be viewed only on group tours that start at an informative visitor center; budget 2 to 3 hours for the tour plus extra time exploring the pretty grounds and diversions, such as a restored 1903 Pullman private railroad car. Cross-country skiing and snowshoeing are allowed with admission to the grounds in winter. A visit during Christmastime is a special treat—the house is decorated as it would have been in the Lincolns' day.

Historic Rte. 7A (just south of Equinox Resort), Manchester. www.hildene.org. © **802/ 362-1788.** Admission to house and grounds $23 adults, $6 ages 6–16, free for kids 5 and under. Guided tour of house or archives, $7.50. Daily 9:30am–4:30pm.

Southern Vermont Arts Center ★★ MUSEUM/PERFORMANCE SPACE   Located in a striking Georgian Revival home surrounded by more than 55 hillside acres, overlooking land that once belonged to fly-fishing magnate Charles Orvis, the center's galleries display works from its permanent

Manchester: Shopping Mecca

Manchester Center has one of the best concentrations of outlet shops in New England, both in terms of the number of shops in a compact area (it's very walkable and parkable, so you won't get tired) and the quality of the merchandise. Among the designers and retailers with outlet shops here are: Brooks Brothers, Coach, Michael Kors, Ann Taylor, Talbot's, Eddie Bauer, BCBG Max Azria, Giorgio Armani, Kate Spade, Polo Ralph Lauren, and Theory. Most of the shops are in little mini-mall clusters in and around the busy little intersection at the heart of town. Hungry from shopping and window-shopping? In season there's an outdoor stand scooping Ben & Jerry's ice cream, and a brand new cafe serves good sandwiches, lunches, and coffee to the shopped-out masses.

If your interests include fishing or outdoorsy fashion of the genteel,

country manor variety, though, head instead for Orvis, the Manchester-based local company that has crafted a worldwide reputation for manufacturing topflight fly-fishing equipment and the associated gear. The massive, woodframed **Orvis Company Store** ★★★ (https://stores.orvis.com/us/vermont/ manchester; © **802/362-3750**) between Manchester and Manchester Center sells housewares, men's and women's clothing—both for daily wear and sturdy outdoor use—plus, of course, more fly-fishing equipment than you'll ever need (budget close to three grand for one of their signature bamboo rods). Two small ponds just outside the shop allow prospective customers to try the gear before buying. A sale room, with even more deeply discounted items, is directly behind the main store.

collection, as well as frequently changing exhibits of contemporary Vermont artists. An appealing modern building across the drive displays additional works, and there is an extensive sculpture garden. Check the center's schedule before you arrive; you may be able to sign up for an art class or workshop, or attend one of the frequent live music performances. Leave time to enjoy a light lunch at the **Garden Cafe** and wander the lovely grounds.

West Rd., Manchester. www.svac.org. ✆ **802/362-1405.** $8 adults, $3 students, free for kids 12 and under; Tues free. Open June–Sept Mon–Sat 10am–5pm; Sun noon–5pm.

Skiing

See also **Mount Snow,** p. 483.

Bromley Mountain Ski Resort ★   Bromley is a great place to learn to ski if you don't already know how. Gentle and forgiving, the mountain features long, looping, intermediate runs that are tremendously popular with families and beginners; *Ski* magazine once named it the second-best ski destination in the entire country for families. The slopes are mostly south-facing, which means they receive the warmth of the sun and protection from the harshest winter winds. There's one ski school for kids, another for adults; the base-lodge scene is mellower than at many other resorts; and the experience is nearly guaranteed to be relaxing. Even snowboarders and telemark skiers are made to feel welcome. This is not a fancy-pants resort, however, and there are no quintuple-diamond, by-the-seat-of-your-pants runs here; if you crave that, bypass Bromley.

3984 Rte. 11, Peru (8 miles NE of Manchester Center). www.bromley.com. ✆ **802/824-5522.** Day lift tickets $80–$84 adults, half-day $65–$69; discounts for youths and seniors, and for spring skiing.

Stratton Mountain Ski Resort ★★   Founded in the 1960s, Stratton labored in its early days under the belief that Vermont ski areas needed to be Tyrolean to be successful—hence the Swiss-chalet feel of the architecture. In recent years, though, Stratton has worked to shed its image as a haven of alpine quaintness. In a bid to attract a younger set, new owners spent more than $25 million in improvements, mostly in snowmaking, which covers 95% of the mountain. Now this mountain is consistently ranked among the nation's best-groomed by skiers, and also picks up big kudos for its lifts, dining choices, and customer service. The slopes here are especially popular with snowboarders; expert skiers should check out Upper Middlebrook, a twisting run off the summit.

5 Village Lodge Rd., Stratton Mountain (16 miles SE of Manchester Center). www.stratton.com. ✆ **800/787-2886** or 802/297-4000. Day lift tickets $115 adults, half-day $85; discounts for seniors, children, and online purchase.

Other Outdoor Activities

HIKING & BIKING   Scenic hiking trails ranging in difficulty from "very challenging" to "easy-as-an-after-dinner-stroll" can be found in the hills a short drive from town. At the Green Mountain District Ranger Station in

Manchester (see "Visitor Information," p. 479), ask for the free brochure listing hiking trails easily reached from the town.

A scenic drive 30 to 40 minutes northwest of Manchester Center takes you to the **Delaware and Hudson Rail-Trail,** approximately 20 miles of which have been built in two sections in Vermont. The southern section of the trail runs about 10 miles from West Pawlet to the state line at West Rupert, over trestles and past vestiges of former industry. Like most rail-trails, this one is perfect for exploring by mountain bike. You'll bike sometimes on the original ballast, other times through grassy growth. To reach the trail head, drive north on Route 30 from Manchester Center to Route 315, then continue north on Route 153. In West Pawlet, park at the trailhead on Egg Street, then set off on the trail southward from the old D&H freight depot across the street.

Vermont's famed **Long Trail** offers a more rugged hiking experience. It crosses Routes 11/30 east of Manchester Center, and continues north to Bromley Mountain and south to Stratton. For information, contact the Green Mountain Club (www.greenmountainclub.org; ☎ **802/244-7037**).

The hills around Manchester are full of other great touring rides, too. Your headquarters should be **Battenkill Sports Bike Shop** (www.battenkillbicycles.com; ☎ **800/340-2734** or 802/362-2734), at 1240 Depot Street, in downtown Manchester Center. It's a wonderful little place, with free local bike maps, great bikes for sale, and a range of rentals from hybrids to touring cycles to mountain bikes ($40–$45 per day; locks and helmets are included).

CANOEING   For a duck's-eye view of the rolling hills, stop by **BattenKill Canoe Ltd.** (www.battenkill.com; ☎ **800/421-5268** or 802/362-2800) at 6328 Route 7A (about halfway between Arlington and the Equinox Resort). This friendly outfit offers daily canoe rentals for exploring the Battenkill River and surrounding areas, as well as guided trips ranging from 2 hours to all day, and the firm specializes in multiple-night, inn-to-inn canoe packages. The shop is open daily in season (which runs from about May–Oct) from 9am to 5:30pm, and Wednesday through Friday only during the rest of the year—but check ahead if you're coming during those months.

FLY-FISHING   Why not learn from the best? Aspiring anglers can sign up for fly-fishing classes taught by skilled instructors affiliated with **Orvis** (☎ **866/531-6213**), the famous fly-fishing supplier and manufacturer based in Manchester (see box p. 482). The shop's ½- to 2-day classes ($140–$489 per person per day, with occasional two-for-one deals) include instruction in knot-tying and casting, plus some catch-and-release fishing on a company pond and the Battenkill River. Classes are held from late April until mid-October. Room rate discounts are sometimes available at the Equinox Resort (see p. 488) for visiting Orvis students.

Where to Stay in the Bennington/ Manchester Area

The choices below mostly fall into the "luxury country inn" category, but there are plenty of other options in this valley, too.

ARLINGTON

West Mountain Inn ★★ Sitting atop a grassy bluff at the end of a dirt road a half-mile from Arlington center, this rambling, mid–19th-century white-clapboard farmhouse with the stone walkway has an immediate visual appeal that practically shouts "Vermont inn." Guest rooms, named for famous Vermonters, are nicely furnished in country antiques (some have canopied beds) and Victorian reproductions; they vary widely in size and shape, but even the smallest has lots of charm and character. (No rooms have phones, the idea being that you're here to get away from it all.) The expansive Rockwell Kent Suite offers a four-poster canopy bed in a very wood-paneled bedroom, plus a wood-burning fireplace in a sitting room with French-style couches. A delightful little wood cottage in back has been divided up into three units (the living room is shared among guests), and three town houses have been carved out of a former millhouse on the grounds. These feature TVs, river views and, in one, a kitchen. A century–old post-and-beam barn is often rented for weddings and reunions, and the 150 acres of meadows invite exploring. In addition to the included breakfast (which you can skip for a discount in the town houses), the dining room also serves hearty regional dinners nightly in a wood-paneled dining room.

River Rd. (at Rte. 313), Arlington. www.westmountaininn.com. ⓒ **802/375-6516.** 20 units. $175–$305 double. Rates include full breakfast (except for town houses). 2-night minimum stay Fri–Sat or Sat–Sun. **Amenities:** Restaurant; kitchenette (some units); Wi-Fi (in inn units; free).

BENNINGTON

The Four Chimneys Inn ★★ This 1912 Colonial Revival catches your eye as you roll into Bennington from the west; it's right at the edge of Old Bennington, and the towering Bennington Monument looms just over its shoulder. Set back from Route 7 on 11 landscaped acres, the three-story mansion features—no surprise—four prominent chimneys. Guest rooms are divided among the main inn, an ice house, and a carriage house; they're serene, airy, and uncluttered, with color-coordinated wallpaper and upholstered furniture. Some units sport wood-burning fireplaces burning real wood, and many have nice Jacuzzis, four-poster beds, and/or mountain views from patios. Room no. 11 has a private glassed–in porch and more windows than most of the other units; the brick carriage house (room no. 9) has a cathedral ceiling. Room no. 8, in the ice house, is a two-level affair with exposed brick walls, a circular wooden staircase, and a gas fireplace. The inn is a popular wedding venue—among couples who married here are the owners, Pete and Lynn Green.

21 West Rd. (Rte. 9, just west of downtown), Bennington. www.fourchimneys.com. ⓒ **802/447-3500.** 11 units. $129–$399 double. Rates include full breakfast. 2-night minimum stay foliage and holiday weekends. Children 12 and over accepted. **Amenities:** Dining room; full bar; Wi-Fi (free).

Paradise Inn ★ Bennington's best motel justifies its upscale name with furnishings and amenities that match its higher-than-most-motels rates. It's clean, well-managed, and within walking distance of town. Tidy, generously sized accommodations are further bolstered by such surprising features as kitchenettes in some suites, a tennis court, and a heated pool. The very central location and neighborhood views aren't bad, either. Try to reserve a spot in the North Building, in spite of its unprepossessing exterior—each unit has an outdoor terrace or balcony. The more up-to-date Office Building is done in Colonial Revival style.

141 W. Main St., Bennington. www.vermontparadiseinn.com. ✆ **800/575-5784** or 802/442-8351. 77 units. $80–$175 double; $125–$240 suite. **Amenities:** Restaurant; exercise room; heated outdoor pool; tennis court; Wi-Fi (free in lobby and some units).

South Shire Inn ★   A locally prominent banking family hired architect William Bull in 1880 to design and build this Victorian home, with leaded glass on its bookshelves and intricate plasterwork in the main dining room. Five guest rooms in the main inn building are furnished with handsomely carved canopy or poster beds and working fireplaces (burning Duraflame logs, not wood); the two best rooms here are probably the former master bedrooms (Otto and Gold), with their king beds and tile-hearth fireplaces. Four newer, more modern guest rooms—with such names as Jim Dandy—are located in an adjacent carriage house. They each sport extra amenities and lovely exposed pine flooring (rooms in the main inn have all been carpeted). All four of these rooms have televisions with DVD players, ceiling fans, and Jacuzzis.

124 Elm St., Bennington. www.southshire.com. ✆ **802/447-3839.** 9 units. $125–$185 double; foliage season $155–$265 double. Rates include breakfast. 2-night minimum stay during foliage season. Not appropriate for children. **Amenities:** Wi-Fi (free).

DORSET

Barrows House ★   Just a short stroll from Dorset village, this compound of eight venerable buildings is set on 12 leafy acres. The 1784 main house has welcomed travelers since 1900; in keeping with its pedigree, rooms have a timeless, quiet elegance, and have been completely renovated—along with public areas—following a recent ownership change. Some units have gas or wood fireplaces, while several cottages (one of which doubles as the pool house) offer additional space and privacy for families. If you're looking for old Vermont charm, this is the place; if not, some of the more luxe quarters in Manchester village might be a better option. The inn's superb **restaurant** and tap room (p. 490) feature menus built largely on locally sourced fare, including Vermont craft beers and cheeses.

3156 Rte. 30, Dorset. www.barrowshouse.com. ✆ **802/867-4455.** 28 units. $185–$295 double; $235–$355 suite and cottage; $355–$465 luxury suite. **Amenities:** Restaurant/bar; bikes; heated outdoor pool; sauna; 2 tennis courts; Wi-Fi in limited areas (free).

Dorset Inn ★★   Set in the center of genteel Dorset, this three-story former stagecoach stop built in 1796 claims to be the oldest continuously operating inn in Vermont. Anyplace with two dozen rooms stretches the definition of "inn," but we'll make an exception for an establishment exuding this much sedate, time-burnished elegance. Prices are surprisingly reasonable given the competition in Manchester, and the Bryant family—who also own Dorset's

Barrows House (see above) and the Mountain Top Resort in Chittenden (p. 515)—have upgraded everything from room decor to the restaurant. Guest rooms, some located in a well-crafted addition next door that dates from the 1940s, are named for famous local people and places (Frost, Saddleback, Marsh, Owls Head). They're furnished in upscale country style, in a mix of reproductions and antiques, including some canopy and sleigh beds. All units are air-conditioned, though a few still lack televisions and most don't have telephones; about one-quarter have Jacuzzi tubs, sitting rooms, and fireplaces. The excellent **restaurant and tavern** (see p. 491) feature local and regional ingredients. A small day spa operates on the premises.

8 Church St. (at Rte. 30), Dorset. www.dorsetinn.com. © **877/367-7389** or 802/867-5500. 25 units. $165–$485 double. Rates include full breakfast. Pets allowed by prior permission at additional cost. Children 6 and over welcome. **Amenities:** Restaurant; bar; spa; Wi-Fi (in all but 2 units; free).

MANCHESTER CENTER

Barnstead Inn ★   Here's a worthwhile alternative to the steep room tariffs charged by most establishments within walking distance of lively Manchester Center. Most of the guest rooms are housed in an 1830s hay barn; appropriately, a rustic aesthetic prevails, right down (up?) to the barn's exposed beams. The departure from country chic comes in the form of vinyl bathroom floors, office-grade carpeting, and a mix of motel-modern and antique furnishings in most rooms. The nicest units include the two above the office (with two double beds, and showing off those beams) and any of the pricier suites—including the Green River Suite, with a lovely fireplace of big, hand-laid stones, Oriental carpets, a kitchenette, and a two-person Jacuzzi. All in all, a good value and one of the closest lodgings to the outlet stores.

349 Bonnet St. (P.O. Box 988), Manchester Center. www.barnsteadinn.com. © **800/331-1619** or 802/362-1619. 15 units. $109–$199 double, $270–$375 suite; foliage-season rates higher. Children 13 and over welcome. **Amenities:** Outdoor pool; Wi-Fi (free).

Palmer House Resort Motel ★   Despite the name, this hostelry doesn't quite qualify as a resort; but it's several rungs above the vast majority of motels. Owned and operated by the same family for about a half-century, its rooms are furnished with antiques and other unexpected niceties; ask for one of the somewhat larger rooms in the newer rear building if you want more space. Ten spacious suites each offer a king bed, sitting room, gas fireplace, two-person Jacuzzi, and private deck overlooking a trout-stocked pond and the mountains beyond—these are much more expensive than regular rooms, and lack the charm of traditional country inn accommodations, but they will do as a romantic retreat when those are booked solid. The buildings are set on 16 well-kept acres, part of which constitute a free par-3 golf course just for guests (clubs are free).

5383 Main St. (Rte. 7A), Manchester Center. www.palmerhouse.com. © **800/917-6245** or 802/362-3600. 50 units. $179–$209 double; $294–$324 suite. 2-night minimum stay some weekends. Children 12 and older welcome. **Amenities:** 9-hole golf course; exercise room; Jacuzzi; 2 pools (1 outdoor, 1 heated indoor lap); sauna; 2 tennis courts; Wi-Fi (free).

MANCHESTER VILLAGE

The Equinox Resort & Spa ★★★ Manchester's grand resort harks back to the days when well-heeled sojourners—including Robert Todd Lincoln, before he built his own nearby summer retreat Hildene (see p. 482)—relaxed in rockers on the broad, pillared veranda. The Equinox's earlier incarnations date to 1769, but what you'll find today is a modern resort complete with a full-service spa, lovely indoor pool, scenic (and challenging) golf course, free business center, and extensive sports facilities. Rooms are moderately sized but have been kept up to date; the big surprise, for travelers partial to grand public spaces, is the lack of one big, welcoming lobby. This is because the hotel predates steel construction—those columns, defining smaller spaces, are there for a reason. The resort also owns the nearby B&B style **1811 House**—a place of cozy rooms, authentically uneven pine floors, and antique furniture—as well as the adjacent **Charles Orvis Inn.** Suites in the Orvis Inn are big and modern, and use of a private billiards room is included. The resort offers plenty of activities on its 1,300-plus acres of grounds, including skeet shooting, falconry, and the Land Rover off-road driving school. Of the resort's three restaurants, the **Chop House** (see p. 492) is best; **The Marsh Tavern** is nearly as good, serving both pubby and formal lunches and dinners, while the **Falcon Bar** is not to be missed—an outdoor brazier has recently been added, making it a convivial place to sip drinks beneath the stars.

3567 Rte. 7A (P.O. Box 46), Manchester Village. www.equinoxresort.com. ✆ **802/362-4700.** 183 units. Main inn and Charles Orvis Inn peak season $341–$899; off season $269–$679. **Amenities:** 3 restaurants; bar; babysitting; bikes; concierge; golf course; exercise room; indoor and outdoor pools; room service; sauna; spa; 3 tennis courts; Wi-Fi (free).

The Inn at Manchester ★★ On the outside, it looks like a prosperous 19th-century Manchester home, but this is a special B&B. An inn since 1978, it's just a half-mile from the outlet stores that draws so many to Manchester, and handy to the village, resort, and golf course; yet it has a true country feel. Guests arrive here from around the U.S., often booking far in advance, drawn by the location, the rooms, and the amazing hospitality that comes with family ownership—owners Frank and Julie Hanes are as helpful as can be. Rooms are in the main inn and an adjacent carriage house dating from the mid-1800s, both decorated with art and sculpture from around the world. The public spaces are whitewashed and lovely, with fireplaces, staircases, and wingback chairs tucked throughout its various corners and angles. Most of the 18 rooms and suites have televisions (no phones, though), and some also have poster beds and/or good direct views of Mount Equinox. All units feel clean and fresh, with distinctive looks—the Sage Suite is popular for its walk-out deck, sitting room, whirlpool tub, and that Equinox view. Four acres of gardens and grounds, a brook, and a lazy front porch complete the peaceful experience.

3967 Main St. (Rte. 7A), Manchester Village. www.innatmanchester.com. ✆ **802/362-1793.** 21 units. Main building, $165–$315; carriage house and celebration barn, $235–$315. Rates include full breakfast. **Amenities:** Outdoor pool; Wi-Fi (free).

The Reluctant Panther ★★★ A quick walk from the Equinox, this property began life as a somewhat funky '60s B&B, but after a 2005 fire destroyed the main house, it was reborn as a true luxury inn. All rooms now sport a fireplace (one in each room, in the deluxe suites), whirlpool tub, thick duvets, fluffy robes, and flatscreen TVs. In the main house, the woodsy Akwanok room is furnished with Orvis nightstand lamps and a birch headboard handcrafted in the Adirondacks, while Lady Slipper sports a claw-foot Jacuzzi and king poster bed. Other rooms are decorated according to themes, too: horses in the John Morgan Suite; flowery murals in the Florist Suite; green hues in the Fallen Spruce Suite. In the outbuildings, standouts are the Garden Suite's living room and see-through fireplace, as well as the expansive Panther Suite's four-poster bed, grandiose bathroom, and regal, columned Jacuzzi. The Pond View Suite, in the carriage house, is bigger than many Vermont cottages. The dining room (see p. 492) is outstanding; a pub menu is also served on a patio (weather permitting) and in the Panther Pub.

17-39 West Rd., Manchester Village. www.reluctantpanther.com. © **800/822-2331** or 802/362-2568. 20 units. $199–$449; higher in foliage season. Rates include full breakfast. Pets allowed on limited basis ($50 per night). **Amenities:** Restaurant; pub; exercise room; Wi-Fi (free).

Where to Eat in the Bennington/ Manchester Area

In addition to the selections below, most of the inns listed above offer good to excellent dinners on site in their dining rooms, often in romantic settings. For informal dining or a beer, locals head for **Mulligan's** (www.mulligans-vt. com; © **802/362-3663**), a pubby family eatery on Route 7A near the Equinox Resort in Manchester. **Mrs. Murphy's Donuts** (© **802/362-1874**), a locals' favorite on the outlet strip in Manchester Center, is a nice alternative to chain fast-food breakfasts.

BENNINGTON

Blue Benn Diner ★ DINER There are maybe a half-dozen true diners in Vermont. The qualification aficionados insist on is that a diner be prefabricated of stainless or enameled steel, and be delivered to its site. The Blue Benn, which rolled down the ways in Paterson, NJ, in 1945, fits the bill—and meets diner mavens' culinary standards as well. Expect the classics: meat loaf, chicken-fried steak, liver and onions . . . and, since this is a college town, offerings include veggie burritos, falafel, and a Cuban pork sandwich. Daily dinner specials include soup or salad, rolls, pudding, and coffee or tea; breakfast, served all day, is a hearty and imaginative panoply of omelets and pancakes. No credit cards.

314 North St. (Rte. 7), Bennington. © **802/442-5140.** Breakfast $3–$7.50; sandwiches and entrees $3.50–$14; dinner specials $13. Mon–Tues 6am–5pm; Wed–Fri 6am–8pm; Sat 6am–4pm; Sun 8am–4pm.

Madison Brewing Co. ★ AMERICAN Bennington's first and only brew pub is a lively downtown spot where Bennington College types mingle with townies and travelers. The lunch and dinner menus—served in upstairs and downstairs, rehabbed 19th-century brick-and-beam dining areas—run to well-executed, tried-and-true comfort dishes such as pot roast, mac and cheese, fish and chips, flatiron steak, and generous sandwiches. Imagination flourishes in the house-brewed beer selections: You'll find the IPAs that are practically written into the Vermont constitution, but also experiments involving maple, coffee, blackberries, and peanut butter. One seasonal stout, the "Nor'beaster Chocolate Imperial," slides down like malted milk but packs a 10% alcohol wallop. Live music Friday and Saturday nights.

428 Main St., Bennington. www.madisonbrewingco.com. © **802/442-7397.** Lunch items $8–$15; main courses $12–$20 at dinner. Mon–Thurs 11am–9pm; Fri–Sat 11:30am–10:30pm; Sun 11:30am–9:30pm.

Pangaea ★★ INTERNATIONAL   This upscale little culinary campus is a bit hard to find (tucked away in workaday North Bennington), but it's worth trying to locate. Chef/owner Bill Scully offers his distinctive cuisine (using local and organic ingredients whenever possible) in a lounge as well as a fine-dining room. At the latter, start with Vermont boar-and-brie Wellington, or ricotta agnolotti with *fines herbes* butter. Entrees could include rack of lamb with mint pistachio pesto, pan-seared sea scallops over creamy adobe polenta, or herb-crusted baked halibut. Next door in the lounge, sip a Vermont beer or craft cocktail while deciding among items such as a Vermont cheese plate, fried oysters, Vietnamese spring rolls, and burgers available in beef, salmon, or black bean versions. The small card of desserts is notable, especially for the chocolate cake.

1-3 Prospect St. (Rte. 67A), North Bennington. www.vermontfinedining.com. © **802/442-7171.** Lounge items $9–$15; main courses $31. Tues–Sat 5–9pm.

DORSET

Barrows House Restaurant and Tap Room ★★ NEW AMERICAN The restaurant at the Barrows House (see p. 486) is a worthy manifestation of the modern gastropub, Vermont style. Start off in the pub with a flight of local beers or a craft cocktail, then settle down to study an uncluttered, satisfying menu built around starters (call them small plates if you aren't heading on to an entrée) such as tandoori chicken tacos, beet carpaccio, and tuna nachos. Your main course might be built around house-made pasta; or go with tried-and-true steak frites or short ribs. There's always a daily special flatbread, and; fish specials and vegetarian choices, too. A dessert standout is the sour cherry flourless chocolate torte.

Rte. 30, Dorset (in Barrows House). www.barrowshouse.com. © **802/867-4455.** Small plates $8–$15; main courses $26–$32. Daily 5:30–9pm.

Chantecleer ★★★ CONTINENTAL   First–rate continental fare finds a home in an atmosphere of rustic elegance at Chantecleer, which consistently serves some of the best food in southern Vermont—inside a century-old dairy barn. Just outside Dorset, the restaurant's tidy exterior doesn't hint at how pleasantly romantic the interior is, even if it feels almost Pennsylvania Dutch.

The owner, Swiss chef Michel Baumann, changes his menu frequently. Appetizers lean toward seafood, especially shellfish (mussels, oysters, octopus, and escargot). For the main course, he might feature whole Dover sole, venison and duck breast medallions, veal sweetbreads, or a classic veal schnitzel with spaetzle. Whatever you eat, you must finish with Baumann's delicious "Matterhorn" sundae—Vermont ice cream shingled with toasted hazelnut nougatine and topped with Toblerone hot fudge.

Rte. 7A (3½ miles N of Manchester Center), East Dorset. www.chantecleerrestaurant. com. ✆ **802/362-1616.** Reservations recommended. Main courses $30–$49. Wed–Sun 5:30–9pm. Closed 1st 3 weeks of Nov, and Apr to mid-May.

Dorset Inn Restaurant ★★ NEW AMERICAN   Menus at the Dorset Inn's (see p. 486) restaurant and tavern strike an admirable balance between sophistication and down-home Vermont culinary values—with an emphasis on seasonal fare and locally sourced meats and produce. Start with house-smoked local duck pâté, PEI mussels, Maine crab cakes, or a plate of locally crafted cheese. The entrée card—changing with the seasons—might include a rosemary-and-garlic grilled pork ribeye, roast duck breast in a cranberry-maple demi-glace, or grilled trout with a Meyer lemon butter. Burgers rule the tavern menu, where the star side is sweet potato fries with cilantro lime sour cream for dipping. Desserts are also stellar, from New York–style cheesecake with fresh berries to maple crème brûlée, and New England bread pudding— also with maple. Brunch is served Saturday and Sunday.

8 Church St. (Rte. 30), Dorset (in the Dorset Inn). www.dorsetinn.com. ✆ **802/867- 5500.** Reservations recommended. Brunch items $12–$16, main courses $22–$34. Mon–Thurs 8–9:30am and 5:30–9pm; Fri–Sun 8am–2pm and 5:30–9pm.

MANCHESTER CENTER

Little Rooster Cafe ★ DINER   Roosters don't nest—they roost—but never mind: The seats here are painted like birds' nests. The farm motif runs to the extreme at this spot near the outlets and the traffic circle, but there are gourmet touches as well. Breakfast choices might include Cajun omelets, corned-beef hash (with béchamel sauce!), or flapjacks with Vermont (what else?) maple syrup. Lunchtime features creative sandwiches—for instance, a good roast beef number with sauerkraut and a horseradish dill sauce. This is the best non-inn spot in town for eggs, pancakes, or a filling lunch, and quite affordable. Cash only.

4645 Main St (Rte. 7A S.), Manchester Center. ✆ **802/362-3496.** Breakfast and lunch items $4.50–$8.50. No credit cards. Daily 7am–2:30pm. Closed Wed in off season.

Mistral's at Toll Gate ★★ FRENCH   This place is a little hard to find (take a left turn off Route 11/30 as you ascend east into the mountains above Manchester Center), but it's worth it. The best tables are along the windows, which overlook a lovely creek spotlighted at night. Inside the tollhouse of a long-since-bypassed byway, the restaurant is a romantic mix of modern and old. The French menu changes seasonally, with dishes that might range from fish to cannelloni stuffed with Atlantic salmon to a Chateaubriand for two, stuffed with shallots, mushrooms, and garlic, served with Béarnaise sauce. This kitchen is run with skill by the owner-chef, Dana Markey, and his wife, Cheryl, who have been doing an admirable job here for 30 years. Plenty of *Wine Spectator* awards testify to the phenomenal quality of the Mistral cellar.

10 Toll Gate Rd. (east of Manchester Ctr. off Rte. 11/30), Manchester Center. www. mistralsattollgate.com. ✆ **802/362-1779.** Reservations recommended. Main courses $28–$40. July–Oct Thurs–Tues 6–9pm; Nov–June Thurs–Mon 6–9pm.

MANCHESTER VILLAGE

The Chop House ★★★ STEAK   Truly great steakhouses aren't that easy to find in Vermont (family-style restaurants, on the other hand, are everywhere). For the past decade, though, this omission has been splendidly corrected at the Equinox Resort (see p. 488) in Manchester Village. Executive chef Daniel Black broils the expected porterhouses, rib-eyes, and filet mignons, and serves up the traditional steakhouse sides (creamed spinach and baked potatoes, of course, but also roasted cauliflower and Brussels sprouts). Prime rib (available Fri and Sat only), double lamb chops, and seafood round out the entrée menu. The appetizers would be right at home on a Manhattan menu: lobster bisque, iceberg wedge/blue cheese salads, tuna tartare, and a terrific shrimp cocktail.

3567 Rte. 7A, Manchester Village (in the Equinox Resort). www.equinoxresort.com. ✆ **800/362-4747** or 802/362-4700. Reservations recommended. Main courses $34–$65. Daily 5–10pm.

The Reluctant Panther ★★★ NEW AMERICAN   This award-winning dining room—part of the inn of the same name (see p. 492), with a lovely dining room looking out onto Mount Equinox—has become one of the best fine-dining options in Manchester. The kitchen reaches for and attains a high level with cuisine that's both New American and Continental. Starters could include such things as lobster and brie fondue, hearty soups, duck confit, or a Vermont cheese and charcuterie board. For the main course, you might choose from braised venison osso bucco, pan-seared pheasant, freshly made fettuccine with leeks and butternut squash, or short ribs braised in Vermont's own Switchback ale. Desserts are stunning and beautifully presented; the wine list is long and well chosen, though predominantly of California vintages. Patio dining in season.

39 West Rd., Manchester Village. www.reluctantpanther.com. ✆ **800/822-2331** or 802/362-2568. Reservations required. Main courses $22–$32. Mon–Sat 5:30–9pm.

BRATTLEBORO ★ & THE SOUTHERN GREEN MOUNTAINS

Brattleboro: 105 miles NW of Boston; 148 miles SE of Burlington. Wilmington: 20 miles E of Brattleboro

The hills and valleys around the bustling town of Brattleboro, in Vermont's southeast corner, have some of the state's best-hidden treasures. Driving along the main valley floors—on roads along the West or Connecticut rivers, or on

Route 100—tends to be only moderately interesting. To really soak up the region's flavor, then, turn off the main roads and wander up and over rolling ridges into the narrow folds of mountains hiding peaceful villages. If it looks as though the landscape hasn't changed all that much in the past 2 centuries, you're right. It really hasn't.

Set in a scenic river valley, Brattleboro is more than just a wide place in the road to fill the gas tank and stock up on provisions (though some parts of town do lend themselves best to that). In fact, this compact, hilly former mill town has a healthy working downtown, where 19th-century brick facades are enlivened by locally owned shops selling books, clothing, cookware, vinyl and CDs, camping supplies, and many other things that elsewhere have migrated to malls. That counterculture edge you may detect dates to Brattleboro's attraction to newcomers of 50 years ago. Keep that in mind when a gent with a gray ponytail walks by.

Essentials

ARRIVING

BY CAR Brattleboro is easily accessible by car via exits 1 and 2 on I-91. From the east or west, Brattleboro is best reached via Route 9, which comes in from Albany and Bennington to the west and Keene, New Hampshire, to the east. From New York City via Hartford, it's about 3 hours without traffic, up to 4 hours with traffic. Wilmington sits at the junction of routes 9 and 100; Route 9 offers the most direct access. The Mount Snow area is north of Wilmington on Route 100.

BY TRAIN Brattleboro is a stop on **Amtrak**'s (www.amtrak.com; ⓒ **800/872-7245**) once-daily Vermonter service from Washington, D.C., and New York to northern Vermont. From New York's Penn Station, the ride takes about 5½ hours and costs $67 one-way; from Washington's Union Station, it's about 9 hours and $97 per person. Brattleboro's Union Station sits by the river in a stone building at 10 Vernon Avenue (Route 142), just downhill from Main Street's concentration of shops.

BY BUS **Greyhound** (www.greyhound.com; ⓒ **800/231-2222**) also stops in Brattleboro, running two buses daily from New York's Port Authority bus terminal. The ride takes 5½ hours and costs $54 one-way, but as little as $36 if nonrefundable and booked online. The bus station is tucked away behind a Citgo gas station in the Route 5/9 traffic circle on the north side of town (about 2½ miles from the train station). A handy, free black-and-white shuttle bus known as the **MOOver** (www.moover.com; ⓒ **802/464-8487**)—it's spotted to look remarkably like a cow—connects the two stations two or three times a day.

VISITOR INFORMATION

The **Brattleboro Chamber of Commerce** office, at 180 Main St. (www.brattleborochamber.org; ⓒ **877/254-4565** or 802/254-4565), dispenses tourist information when it's open for business (Mon–Fri 8:30am–5pm; closed holidays). The **Mount Snow Valley Chamber of Commerce** (www.visitvermont.com; ⓒ **877/887-6884** or 802/464-8092) maintains a visitor center at 21 West

Main St. Open daily year-round from 10am to 5pm, the chamber offers a room-booking service, which is helpful for booking smaller inns and B&Bs. (To investigative or book on-the-mountain accommodations, however, it's best to check directly with **Mount Snow's** lodging bureau at ✆ **800/451-4211.**)

Exploring Brattleboro

Here's a useful two-phase strategy for exploring Brattleboro: Park. Walk. The commercially vibrant downtown is blessedly compact, and strolling it is the best way to appreciate its human scale and handsome commercial architecture. It invites casual browsing without an itinerary.

Brattleboro has a trio of museums devoted to local history, manufactures, and the arts. The **Brattleboro Historical Society's History Center and Museum** ★ (196 Main St.; www.brattleborohistoricalsociety.org; ✆ **802/258-4957**) exhibits artifacts and photos highlighting the history of the city and the Connecticut River Valley, and offers walking tours concentrating on history and architecture; open Thursday 2 to 4pm and Saturday 10am to noon. A donation is requested. The **Brattleboro Museum & Art Center** ★ (10 Vernon St.; www.brattleboromuseum.org; ✆ **802/257-0124**) is housed inside the city's 1916 train station. The focus is on changing exhibits of both classic and contemporary sculpture and art from local and regional artists. The museum is open daily except Tuesday, 11am to 5pm. Admission is $8 for adults, $6 for seniors, $4 for students, and free for kids 5 and under. The **Estey Organ Museum** (108 Bridge St.; www.esteyorganmuseum.org) is devoted to what was once Brattleboro's most famous export. From 1846 to 1860, the town's Estey Organ Company not only built church organs, but also the parlor models that graced many a middle-class home before radio and its electronic descendants took over. The Museum's collections range from reed and pipe organs, to the electronic models produced during the firm's final years. Many are working organs, and visitors are invited to bring their own sheet music and play. Open 2 to 4pm weekends, mid-May through mid-October. A $5 donation is requested.

Wholly Cow!

Parodying the annual Running of the Bulls in Pamplona, Spain, Brattleboro's "Strolling of the Heifers" has become an early June tradition that includes live entertainment, food vendors, a cycling tour, a "Famous Farmers Breakfast," and of course a Main Street parade led by docile young Holstein-Friesian cows who aren't about to run amok (sorry, Hemingway fans). For information, contact Strolling of the Heifers, a local not-for-profit that promotes healthy food and area artists (www.strollingoftheheifers.com; ✆ **802/246-0982**).

Exploring Wilmington/Mount Snow ★

Wilmington, 20 miles east of Brattleboro along Route 9, has a nice selection of antiques shops, boutiques, and pizza joints. Except on busy holiday weekends, when it's inundated by visitors driving oversized SUVs, it feels like a gracious mountain village untroubled by the times. From Wilmington, the ski resort of **Mount Snow** (see below) is easily accessible to the north via busy

The Marlboro Music Festival

The renowned **Marlboro Music Festival** (www.marlboromusic.org; © **215/569-4690**) is a series of summertime classical concerts, performed by accomplished masters as well as by highly talented younger musicians, on weekends from mid-July through mid-August in the agreeable village of Marlboro, east of Wilmington on Route 9. The musical retreat was founded by Rudolf Serkin in 1951 and has hosted countless noted musicians such as Pablo Casals, Van Cliburn, Emanuel Ax, and Joshua Bell. Concerts take place in the 700-seat auditorium at Marlboro College, and advance ticket purchases are strongly recommended. Ticket prices usually range from about $15 to $40 per concert.

Route 100, which is close to impassable on sunny weekends in early October. Heading north, you'll first pass through **West Dover,** an attractive classic New England town with a prominent steeple and acres of white clapboard.

Skiing

Mount Snow ★ Mount Snow is noted for its widely cut runs on the front face of the mountain (disparaged by some skiers as "vertical golf courses"), yet it still remains an excellent destination for intermediates and advanced intermediates. More advanced skiers migrate to the North Face, another world of bumps and open glades. This is also a great spot for snowboarding. Because it's the closest Vermont ski area to Boston and New York (about a 4-hour drive from Manhattan), the mountain can get more crowded than other Vermont hills on weekends. But Mount Snow's village is attractively arrayed along the base of the mountain; the most imposing structure is a balconied hotel overlooking a small pond, but the overall character here is still shaped mostly by unobtrusive smaller lodges and homes. Once famed for a groovy singles scene, the hill's post-skiing activities have mellowed somewhat and embraced the baby-boomer and family markets, though 20-somethings can still find a good selection of après-ski activities.

39 Mount Snow Rd., West Dover. www.mountsnow.com. © **800/245-7669** or 802/464-3333. Day lift tickets $75 adults, half-day $63; discounts for youths and seniors.

Outdoor Activities

The **Vermont Canoe Touring Center** (www.vermontcanoetouringcenter.com; © **802/257-5008**), open seasonally, is at 451 Putney Road, just north of Brattleboro. This is a great spot to rent a canoe or kayak to poke around for a couple of hours, half a day, or a full day. Explore locally, or arrange for a shuttle upriver or down. The owners are helpful about providing information and maps to keep you on track. Among the best spots, especially for birders, are the marshy areas along the lower West River and a detour off the Connecticut River, known locally (and with some slight exaggeration) as "the Everglades." Get a gourmet sandwich to go at the Brattleboro Food Co-op (see p. 499) and make a day of it.

Bike rentals and advice on day-trip destinations are available at the **Brattleboro Bicycle Shop,** 165 Main St. (www.bratbike.com; ⓒ **802/254-8644**). Hybrid bikes, ideal for exploring area back roads, can be rented by the day or week. It's open daily from spring through summer, closed Sundays in fall, and closed Sundays and Mondays in winter.

Where to Stay in the Southern Green Mountains

Budget-priced chain motels flank Route 5 north of Brattleboro, especially around the Route 5/9 traffic circle leading to Keene, New Hampshire. The best choice here is probably the **Hampton Inn Brattleboro,** 1378 Putney Rd. (www.hamptoninn.com; ⓒ **866/238-4218** or 802/254-5700). But it isn't as cheap as most of the other motel options.

Fortunately, inns abound in this part of Vermont, and some are priced quite affordably.

BRATTLEBORO

See also the **Chesterfield Inn ★★** in West Chesterfield, NH (chapter 12, p. 575), about a 10-minute drive east of Brattleboro.

Colonial Motel & Spa ★   Operated by the same family for 3 decades, this sprawling 7-acre compound set back from Route 5 is a far better deal than the highway chains. The rear building's rooms, set farther back from road noise, are also larger and more comfortably furnished, if still somewhat motel-generic. There's a cozy lounge and basic restaurant on-site—but the best feature is a 75-foot indoor saltwater lap pool in the spa building, where there's also a dry sauna, steam room, and a simple fitness center where massages are available. A second pool accommodates kids and casual swimmers.

Putney Rd., Brattleboro. www.colonialmotelspa.com. ⓒ **800/239-0032** or 802/257-7733. 68 units. $63–$90 double; $108–$120 suite; higher in foliage season. Pets welcome. Rates include continental breakfast (Mon–Fri only). **Amenities:** Restaurant; bar; exercise room; Jacuzzi; 2 pools; sauna; Wi-Fi (free).

Latchis Hotel ★   At downtown Brattleboro's main intersection, this hotel fairly leaps out in Victorian-brick Brattleboro. Built at in 1938 in understated Art Deco style (there's only one other true Deco building in Vermont; it's in Rutland, see p. 511), the Latchis was once the cornerstone for a small chain of hotels and theaters. It no longer has its own orchestra or commanding dining room, but the movie theater (showing first-run films) remains, and the place still has an authentic period flair. Some units have been upgraded over the past few years, with newer furnishings and sunny art prints on the walls; other rooms and hallways, however, say "1938" in a way that will captivate some guests, and leave others wishing for more modern surroundings. About two-thirds of the rooms have limited views of the river, though those views include the sounds of cars crawling down Main Street early every morning. If you need quiet, sacrifice the views and ask for a room in back—or ask for a sound-masking machine, available at no charge. You can walk to the museum, food co-op, or shops of Main Street from here without breaking a sweat.

50 Main St., Brattleboro. www.latchis.com. © **800/798-6301** or 802/254-6300. 30 units. $100–$180 double; $190 suite. Rates include continental breakfast. **Amenities:** Wi-Fi (free).

NEAR MT. SNOW

The Mount Snow area has a surfeit of lodging options, ranging from basic motels to luxury inns and slope-side condos; rates in most of them drop quite a bit in summer, when the region slips into a pleasant lethargy. In winter, though, the high prices reflect the relatively easy drive from New York and Boston. The best phone call to make first is to Mount Snow's **central reservations line** (© **800/451-4211** or 800/245-7669) to ask about vacation packages and condo accommodations.

Deerhill Inn ★★   Set on a hillside above Route 100 in West Dover with views of the rolling mountains, Deerhill Inn was built as a ski lodge in 1954, but subsequent innkeepers have given it more of an upscale country character. It's not quite in the luxury category (rooms do not have phones), but makes for a nice alternative to more rustic B&B accommodations. In summer, the property features attractive gardens and a nice stonework pool; in winter, the ski slopes are just a short drive away. Guest rooms vary from the small and cozy to the spacious, some with Jacuzzis and/or flatscreen TVs; several more are located in a motel-like annex (these rooms all have balconies). The Tamarack Room features a king bed, double Jacuzzi, and attractive stone fireplace; Dahlia has a Jacuzzi, small fireplace, and walk-out private deck. The "garden" rooms are cheaper and less luxe, but cheerful and charming. Dining-room fare, available only to inn guests, is a highlight (the wine cellar is impressive), and all guests can use the two upstairs sitting rooms stocked with books.

14 Valley View Rd., West Dover. www.deerhill.com. © **802/464-3100.** 13 units. $145–$295 double; $240–$355 suite. Rates include breakfast. 2-night minimum stay Sat–Sun. Children 8 and over welcome. **Amenities:** Dining room; bikes; outdoor pool; Wi-Fi (free).

Grand Summit Resort Hotel at Mount Snow ★★

Like a house of several dozen gables (you'll probably stop counting), Mount Snow's premier lodging rambles along the base of the big mountain's ski trails—but the attractions here are year-round, and the resort is as handily located for summer and foliage-season pursuits as it is for skiing and snowboarding. You won't find country-inn coziness here (after all, there are nearly 200 rooms and suites), although the common areas are lodge-y enough, with natural surfaces and the de rigueur big stone fireplace. The star factor is the number and variety of guest accommodations: choices range from kitchenette-equipped studios, to hotel rooms, to full-kitchen one-, two-, and three-bedroom suites (including penthouse suites) sleeping up to six. The prime offerings are the suites with loft bedrooms (that explains all those gables), making "send the kids up to bed" a literal option. Many units have decks; some have fireplaces, and a few come with a sauna. Opportunities for pampering and recreation also far exceed the small-inn norm, with chairlift rides, a heated outdoor pool, hot tubs, a fitness center, the holistically oriented **Naturespa,** and the 18-hole, Geoffrey Cornish-designed championship **Mount Snow Golf Club.** Mountain biking, hiking trails, and kids' Outdoor Exploration Camp are all part of the scene.

39 Mount Show Rd., West Dover. www.mountsnow.com. ℰ **800/498-0479.** 196 units. $112–$197 double; $187–$650 suites; higher in winter. **Amenities:** 2 restaurants; spa; health club; pool; golf course; Wi-Fi (free).

Vintage Motel ★ The stereotype of the thrifty Vermonter plays out for real at this perfect pick for travelers planning to be on the go rather than chilling in their rooms. These are basic units that are actually quite nice-looking, if predictably "motelish" with office-standard carpeting, TVs, phones, minifridges (in deluxe rooms), and durable furniture. There's a common room with a microwave. In winter, the place fills up with skiers and with local and visiting snowmobilers: A major trail passes through the motel's backyard.

195 Rte. 9, Wilmington. www.vintagemotel.net. ℰ **800/899-9660** or 802/464-8824. 18 units. $77–$115 double; $125–$225 deluxe rooms. Rates include continental breakfast, weekends and holidays only. 2-night minimum stay Fri–Sat; 3 nights some holidays. Pets allowed in 3 units ($15 per pet). **Amenities:** Kids' play area; Wi-Fi (free).

FARTHER AFIELD

The Old Tavern at Grafton ★★ Carved into the stone doorstep of this beautiful historic property are the words "Montani Semper Liberi"—mountaineers are always free. The inn (which isn't free) is actually a series of accommodations spread throughout the village (see p. 502); only about a dozen rooms are in the handsome, colonnaded 1801 main building, which wears its age gracefully though not without a charming tilt to some of the corridors. The remaining rooms are in the nearby Homestead and Windham buildings across the road. Antiques and Americana are everywhere; all rooms have phones, but none have televisions. Room nos. 6 and 8 feature lovely white-canopied beds, as do many units in the Windham Cottage. Rooms in the Homestead "Cottage"—not a cottage at all, but two historic homes joined together—on the other hand, have more of a modern, hotel-like character. The Cricketers Suite is in yet another building, and has a small refrigerator, coffeemaker, and whirlpool tub where toddlers are welcome. In all, six units have suite-like layouts. Some suites have fireplaces. Four rental homes in the village are also available; call ℰ **802/234-8700** for information.

92 Main St (Rtes. 35 and 121), Grafton. www.old-tavern.com. ℰ **800/843-1801** or 802/843-2231. 30 units. $189–$269 double; $249–$319 suite. Rates include breakfast. 2- to 3-night minimum stay winter weekends, holidays, and foliage season. Closed Mar to mid-Apr. Children 4 and under welcome in Homestead Cottage and Cricketers Suite. **Amenities:** Restaurant; pub; bikes; fitness center; Jacuzzi; swimming pond; tennis court; Wi-Fi (most units; free).

Windham Hill Inn ★★★ This Relais & Châteaux property pretty much defines what luxury Vermont innkeeping is all about. Situated on 160 acres at the end of a dirt road in a high upland valley in West Townshend (about 20 miles/30 min. from Mount Snow), this 1823 farmhouse remained in the same family until the 1950s, when it was converted into an inn. Guest rooms are wonderfully appointed in elegant country style and floral prints; many feature Jacuzzis or soaking tubs; balconies or decks; 15 rooms have gas fireplaces—and *all* have good views. Especially nice are the third-floor Jesse Lawrence Room, with its lovely modern soaking tub, plush chairs, cherry pencil-poster king bed, and gas stove; and Forget-Me-Not, on the second floor, which has a similar setup plus a window nook. An annex (the White Barn) contains eight units, the choicest of which is the great top-floor Meadowlook with lots of windows, fieldstone fireplace, soaking tub beneath a skylight, double shower—and a big, open private deck. The inn's superb **dining room** ★ features creative Continental and New American cooking; outside, the pastoral acreage includes 6 miles of groomed cross-country ski trails.

311 Lawrence Dr., West Townshend (turn uphill at West Townshend country store and continue uphill 1¼ miles to dirt road and turn right). www.windhamhill.com. ⓒ **800/944-4080** or 802/874-4080. 22 units. $299–$329 double; $359–$489 suite. Rates include full breakfast. 2- to 3-night minimum stay Sat–Sun and some holidays. Children 12 and over welcome. **Amenities:** Restaurant; outdoor heated pool; tennis court; Internet (in lobby; free).

Where to Eat in the Southern Green Mountains
BRATTLEBORO

In addition to the choices listed below, the subterranean coffee shop **Mocha Joe's** ★, at 82 Main St. (www.mochajoes.com; ⓒ **802/257-7794**), is connected with a coffee roasting outfit, and draws an eclectic crowd of locals. It sports a friendly, laid-back vibe, brews a good cup of joe or espresso, and pours fresh-squeezed "-ades" in the summer. If you like what you're drinking, you can buy the beans and have them shipped home. Try the maple latte if you're craving something different.

Another upscale choice is the restaurant of the **Chesterfield Inn** (see chapter 12, p. 575) in West Chesterfield, NH, a 10-minute drive on Route 9 from Brattleboro.

Brattleboro Food Co-op ★ DELI   Selling wholesome foods since 1975, this huge store also has a deli counter great for takeout meals. Grab a quick and filling lunch that won't *necessarily* be tofu and sprouts—you can also get a smoked turkey and Swiss-cheese sandwich or a crispy salad. (The "Happy Hippie" sandwich has pesto, roast peppers, and mozzarella, although Vermont doesn't yet have retail outlets for what makes hippies really happy.) Check out the eclectic selection of wines and cheeses as well as the natural bath products (some locally made) and the hand-cut steaks in the butcher section. Sausages are made and stuffed on premises, too, and the place is renowned for "case lot specials": deep discounts on oversized quantities of health food. (Stash a case of organic cheese puffs in the trunk for the road.) The store section stays open until 9pm every night, a boon in early-closing Vermont. The co-op, located in a small strip mall downtown near the New

Hampshire bridge, has lots of parking—though the mini-mall plaza is hard to notice as you whiz downhill and around the town's main bend.

2 Main St. (in Brookside Plaza, on right at bottom of Main St. hill), Brattleboro. www.brattleborofoodcoop.com. © **802/257-0236.** Sandwiches $5–$8, prepared foods usually around $6–$8 per lb. Mon–Sat 8am–9pm; Sun 9am–9pm.

Peter Havens Restaurant ★★ AMERICAN   You're likely to feel at home right away in this locally popular dining spot, which has just 10 tables. Chef Zachary Corbin has taken the menu away from its former seafood tilt—although you'll still find oysters on the half shell, ahi tuna tartare, and grilled salmon and swordfish—and balanced it with worthy interpretations of dishes such as braised lamb shank (pepped up with star anise), pan-roasted duck breast, and house-made potato gnocchi with roast squash in a brown sage butter. Sides, offered steak-house style at a separate tariff, are headlined by a mushroom-saffron risotto and fries cooked in duck fat. The bar is convivial and popular, but make a reservation if you're visiting on a weekend: The place gets packed with a mix of locals and tourists.

32 Elliot St., Brattleboro. www.peterhavens.com. © **802/257-3333.** Reservations recommended. Main courses $23–$35. Wed–Sun 5:30–9pm; June–Oct lunch on the patio Wed–Sat 11:30am–3pm.

T.J. Buckley's ★★ NEW AMERICAN   Brattleboro's best restaurant, little T.J. Buckley's, is housed in a classic old diner on a dim side street. But this is *far* from diner food—so far, in fact, that the full name of the place is "T.J. Buckley's Uptown Dining." Un-dinerlike touches such as slate floors and golden lighting have created an intimate space that seats fewer than 20 when full; any more clients, and there wouldn't be room for the chef, sous-chefs, and server, all of whom miraculously perform their culinary ballet without bumping into each other and you. Iconoclastic chef/owner Michael Fuller's menu is always limited, with just a few entree choices each night, but the food nearly always dazzles in its execution. Expect the usual New American appetizers and entrees: beet carpaccios, wondrous pâtés, crab, seared scallops, steak, duck, and fish-of-the-day dishes—all beautifully prepared and presented, sometimes more adventurously than you might expect. (Whatever Fuller feels like making, he makes—*his* way.) **Note:** The tab for a dinner party of three or more *will* run into the hundreds, so hit a bank first (well, not in the John Dillinger sense) and bring a wad of big bills.

132 Elliot St., Brattleboro. www.tjbuckleysuptowndining.com. © **802/257-4922.** Reservations strongly recommended. Main courses $32–$45. No credit cards. Winter Thurs–Sun 5:30pm "til closing;" open Wed in summer and foliage season.

NEAR MT. SNOW

Dot's ★ DINER   A casualty of catastrophic flooding brought on by 2011's Tropical Storm Irene, but Dot's was rebuilt and revived as a local's favorite. The rule here is good, inexpensive food, served in a classic diner setting—pine paneling, swivel stools at the counter, and checkerboard-patterned linoleum tiles. It's regionally famous for its chili (kicked up with jalapeño peppers), but other good choices include great pancakes, French toast, shakes, daily chicken specials, hot open-faced sandwiches, and the Cajun skillet: a medley of sausage, peppers, onions, and fries sautéed and served with eggs and melted Jack cheese. There's now a second Dot's—known as "Dot's of Dover"—in Dover (𝄞 **802/464-6476**), 7 miles north on Route 100.

3 E. Main St., Wilmington. No website. 𝄞 **802/464-7284.** Breakfast items $3–$9, lunch and dinner items $4–$19. Beer and wine served. Daily 5:30am–8pm (to 9pm Fri–Sat).

Jezebel's Eatery ★ AMERICAN   Ample portions of comfort food stand-bys, with an inventive twist, rule the menu at this downtown Wilmington spot nestled into the handsomely restored 1836 Lyman House. Settle into a big Windsor chair and tuck into a half-pound burger, overstuffed Reuben, or muffaletta sandwich at lunch; come back later (OK, the next day) and choose among entrees ranging from classics such as meatloaf, mac and cheese, and chicken and waffles, to herb-crusted prime rib and the not-so-subtly named "hunk of beef," a big strip steak. Comfort takes on a slightly more sophisticated accent in butternut squash ravioli, a tapenade-stuffed chicken breast, and a vegetable-studded risotto. Equally hearty breakfasts, sad to say, are only served on weekends—look for house-baked muffins, heaps of corned beef hash, and plump omelets known to keep skiers off the slopes 'til noon. They'll be back later—summer sojourners and leaf-peepers too—for Vermont beers and spirits at the cheery bar.

28 West Main St. www.jezebelseatery.com. 𝄞 **802/464-7774.** Lunch items $9–$14; main courses $15–$29. Mon–Fri 11am–9pm; Sat 8am–10pm; Sun 8am–5pm.

FARTHER AFIELD

The Free Range ★ AMERICAN   Eight miles north of Grafton, on the town common in Chester, this showcase for local provender features chef Jason Tostrup's take on standards like chili (made here with white beans and chicken), beef bourguignon (served with truffled mashed potatoes), and that now-ubiquitous vegetarian option, gnocchi, made with by-no-means ubiquitous buckwheat. Wash down brunch—go for the ever-changing hash bowl—with an "Ultimate Bloody Mary," garnished with maple candied bacon and a shrimp. The well-thought-out wine list features 20 wines by the glass.

90 The Common, Chester. www.thefreerangevt.com. 𝄞 **802/875-3346.** Brunch items $10–$16, main courses $17–$27. Tues–Sat 5–9pm; Sun 5–8pm. Lunch Fri noon–3pm; brunch and lunch Sat–Sun 10am–5pm.

WOODSTOCK ★★

Woodstock: 265 NE of New York City; 140 miles NW of Boston; 98 miles SE of Burlington; 16 miles W of White River Junction.

For more than a century, the resort community of Woodstock has been considered one of New England's most exquisite villages, and its attractiveness has benefited from the largesse of some of the country's most affluent citizens. Even the surrounding countryside is mostly unsullied—it's pretty difficult to drive here via any route that isn't pastoral and scenic, and by the time you're here you're already feeling as if you're in another era. Few New England villages can top Woodstock for grace and elegance; the tidy downtown is

One of Vermont's most scenic and well-preserved villages, **Grafton** ★★★ was founded in 1763 and soon grew into a thriving settlement. But as the agriculture and commerce shifted west and to bigger cities, Grafton became a shadow of a town—by the Depression, many of the buildings here were derelict.

Then something remarkable happened. In 1963, Hall and Dean Mathey of New Jersey created the Windham Foundation and began purchasing and restoring the dilapidated center of town, including the old hotel. This foundation eventually came to own some 55 buildings and 2,000 acres around town—even the cheese cooperative was revived. The village sprung back to life, and it's now teeming with history buffs, antiques hounds, and tourists (instead of farmers and merchants). The Windham Foundation has taken great care in preserving this village, even to the point of burying utility lines so as not to mar the village's landscape with wires.

Grafton is best seen at a slow pace, on foot, when the weather is welcoming. Unfortunately, none of the grand (and privately owned) historic homes you see in the village are open for tours; it's a village to be enjoyed with aimless walks outdoors. Start at the **Grafton Village Cheese Co. ★**, 533 Townsend Rd. (www.graftonvillagecheese.com; ✆ **800/472-3866**), a small, modern building where you can buy a snack of the great award-winning cheese and peer through plate-glass windows to observe the cheese-making process. (No tours are allowed for sanitary reasons.) It's open daily, 10am to 5pm. Sometimes they sell big wheels of the cheese at deep discounts, too.

From the cheese shop, follow the trail over a nearby covered bridge, and then bear right on the footpath along a cow pasture to the cute **Kidder Covered Bridge.** Head into town via Water Street, and then turn onto Main Street, where white clapboard homes and shade trees are about as New England as it gets.

On Main Street, stop by the **Grafton Historical Society Museum ★** (www.graftonhistoricalsociety.com; ✆ **802/843-2584**)—open Friday to Monday from Memorial Day to Columbus Day (daily in foliage season)—to peruse photographs, artifacts, and memorabilia of Grafton. The suggested donation is $5 per adult. Afterward, have a look at **The Old Tavern at Grafton ★★** (see p. 498), the impressive town anchor that has served as a social center since 1801. Partake of a beverage at the rustic **Phelps Barn Lounge** or a meal in one of the dining rooms. If you'd like to see Grafton from a different perspective, inquire at the inn about a horse-and-buggy ride.

To reach Grafton, take I-91 to exit 5 or 6, and follow signs to Bellows Falls via Route 5. From here, take Route 121 west for 12 miles to Grafton. Grafton's informal **information center** is located in a gift shop inside the Grafton Inn's Daniels House, right behind the Old Tavern. The town also maintains a comprehensive website at **www.graftonvermont.org**.

compact and neat, populated by a handful of shops, galleries, and boutiques. The lovely village green is surrounded by handsome homes, creating what amounts to a comprehensive review of architectural styles of the 19th and early 20th centuries. You could literally throw a stone (but don't) from the town center and hit a very attractive covered bridge.

The village, on the banks of the gently flowing Ottauquechee River, was first settled in 1765 and rose to prominence as a publishing center at one time: No fewer than five newspapers were being published in this tiny town in 1830.

It soon began to attract wealthy families seeking cool solace from the big-city summers. A Vermont senator, in the late 19th century, said "the good people of Woodstock have less incentive than others to yearn for heaven," and that still (partly) applies today. This town is about as upscale as it gets in this low-key state, but it got there with Yankee good taste—for glitz and glamour, look elsewhere.

The town is also a center for winter outdoor recreation. In fact, the very first ski tow (a rope tow powered by, yes, an old Buick motor) in the U.S. was built in 1933 at the Woodstock Ski Hill near the present-day Suicide Six ski area. There are no huge mountains hereabouts, which is why the center of the Vermont skiing universe moved to Stowe (some would say Killington). Woodstock is a great place in summer, winter, or fall to hike, bike, skate, cross-country ski, snowshoe, or simply window-shop or leaf-peep.

In addition to Woodstock, this region also takes in nearby White River Junction, Quechee, and Norwich, three towns of distinctly different lineages along the Connecticut River on the New Hampshire border. While here you'll also want to cross that river over to Hanover, New Hampshire (p. 577), a lovely town that's also home to Dartmouth College.

Essentials

ARRIVING

Woodstock is located 13 miles west of White River Junction on Route 4 (take exit 1 off I-89). It's about 20 miles due east of Killington and Rutland, also via Route 4.

VISITOR INFORMATION

The **Woodstock Area Chamber of Commerce,** 3 Mechanic St. (www.wood stockvt.com; ✆ **802/457-3555**), staffs a helpful information booth on the green, open daily from June through October. The chamber's website is a great quick reference to all the key local sights, restaurants, and inns, with hyperlinks.

Exploring Woodstock

Much of Woodstock is on the National Register of Historic Places already, and—as if that weren't enough—the Rockefeller family deeded 500 acres surrounding Mount Tom (see p. 504) to the National Park Service just to protect even more of it from developers. Not just the park, but all of downtown Woodstock could probably be renamed "Rockefeller National Park," for all the attention and cash that family has lavished on it. (Yes, Rockefeller money also built the faux-historic Woodstock Inn and paid to bury unsightly utility lines around town to preserve its character.)

The heart of the town is the shady, elliptical **Woodstock Green,** faced by the stately **Woodstock Inn** (p. 507), the handsome **Norman Williams Library,** and some of the town's grandest homes (for a look inside, come to Woodstock during December's Winter Wassail Weekend and take the house tour).

You can get a good background in local history at the **Woodstock History Center** ★ (www.woodstockhistorycenter.org; ✆ **802/457-1822**) at 26 Elm St.

Housed in the 1807 Charles Dana House, this beautiful home has rooms furnished in Federal, Empire, and Victorian styles, and has displays of dolls, costumes, and early silver and glass. The Dana House museum and adjoining buildings with more exhibits are open to the public, but only from late May through mid-October, Wednesday to Saturday 1 to 5pm and Sunday 11am to 4pm.

Billings Farm and Museum ★★★ OUTDOOR HISTORY MUSEUM This remarkable working farm offers a striking glimpse into an era when Vermont still looked like something out of a Grandma Moses painting, yet when forward-thinking agriculturists were already experimenting with scientific farming. The museum encompasses the model farm of Frederick Billings, a native Vermonter who was credited with completing the Northern Pacific Railroad. (Billings, Montana, is named after him.) Billings returned home to create a managed forest along the principles of George Perkins Marsh, who was born in Woodstock and wrote the 1864 groundbreaking ecological study *Man and Nature*. As a 19th-century dairy farm, it was renowned for its scientific breeding of Jersey cows (and also its fine architecture, particularly its gabled 1890 Victorian farm manager's house). A tour includes hands-on demonstrations of farm activities, exhibits of farm life, a look at an heirloom kitchen garden, and a visit to active milking barns. Programs for kids include wagon rides, preschool activities, and sleigh rides; there are also many holiday events. Because they're so close to each other, adults would do well to buy the 2-day combination ticket granting admission to the farm and the national historic park (see below).

River Rd. (approx. ½-mile N of town on Rte. 12), Woodstock. www.billingsfarm.org. © **802/457-2355.** $16 adults, $14 over 62, $8 kids 5–15, $4 kids 3–4, free for ages 2 and under; combination ticket with national historic park $21 adults, $16 over 62. Daily 10am–5pm; to 4pm Nov–Feb.

Marsh-Billings-Rockefeller National Historic Park ★★★ HISTORIC HOME/PARK   Billings Farm and the National Park Service have teamed up to manage this newer park, the first and only national park focused on the history of conservation. It's more or less right across the street from the Billings Farm (see above), and is closely related. Here you'll learn more about the life of George Perkins Marsh, one of the first writers to warn against his era's breakneck exploitation of resources, especially forests. You'll also discover how Woodstock native/rail tycoon Frederick Billings, who read Marsh's *Man and Nature,* eventually returned and purchased Marsh's boyhood farm, putting into practice many of the principles of restorative forestry Marsh espoused. The property was later purchased by Laurance Rockefeller and his wife Mary, Billings' granddaughter, who in 1982 established the nonprofit farm; a decade later, they donated more than 500 acres of forest land and their elaborate Victorian mansion, filled with exceptional 19th-century landscape art, to the Park Service. Visitors can tour the mansion, walk the graceful carriage roads surrounding Mount Tom, and view one of the oldest professionally managed woodlands in the nation. Mansion tours accommodate only 12 people at a

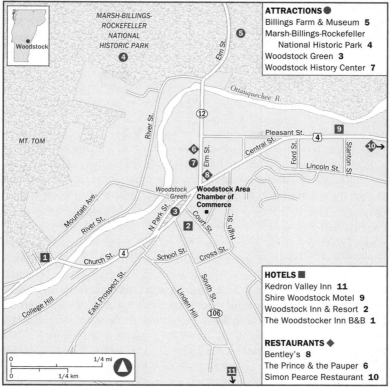

ATTRACTIONS ●
Billings Farm & Museum **5**
Marsh-Billings-Rockefeller
  National Historic Park **4**
Woodstock Green **3**
Woodstock History Center **7**

HOTELS ■
Kedron Valley Inn **11**
Shire Woodstock Motel **9**
Woodstock Inn & Resort **2**
The Woodstocker Inn B&B **1**

RESTAURANTS ◆
Bentley's **8**
The Prince & the Pauper **6**
Simon Pearce Restaurant **10**

time, so advance reservations are highly recommended; check in at the visitor center, located inside a carriage barn, to reserve one (or call ahead).

54 Elm St., Woodstock. www.nps.gov/mabi. ℂ **802/457-3368.** Free admission to grounds; mansion tour $8 adults, $4 over 62, free for kids 15 and under; combination ticket with Billings Farm $21 adults, $16 over 62, $15 kids 16–17. Late May–Oct daily 10am–5pm.

Outdoor Activities

BIKING The rolling, hilly terrain around Woodstock is ideal for exploring by road bike for those in reasonably good shape. **Woodstock Sports,** 30 Central St. (ℂ **802/457-1568**), has road, mountain, hybrid, and fat tire bikes for rent. They'll provide maps for road cyclists, and info on local mountain biking trails.

CROSS-COUNTRY SKIING The area's best cross-country skiing is at the Woodstock Inn & Resort's **Nordic Center ★★** (www.woodstockinn.com; ℂ **802/457-6674**), at the Woodstock Country Club, just south of the village center on Route 106. The center maintains about 38 miles of trails in meadow and woodland trail networks. It's not all flat, either; the high and low points along the trail system vary by some 750 feet in elevation. The ski center has a lounge and restaurant, as well as a large health and fitness center accessible via the ski trail. Lessons and tours are available. Skiing here is free if you're a Woodstock Inn guest; it costs $22 per day for nonguests (discounts for youths and half-day tickets). Skis and snowshoes can be rented on site, and there's a small discount for inn guests on the rental fees.

DOWNHILL SKIING The ski hill **Suicide Six** ★ (http://suicide6.com; ✆ **802/457-6661**) has an intimidating name, but at just 650 vertical feet, it doesn't pose much of a threat. There are, however, 24 trails, not just the original six. Owned and operated by the Woodstock Inn (just like the Nordic Center), this family-oriented ski resort (which opened in 1934 using a gas-powered rope tow) has quad and double chairs, a J-bar for beginners, and a modern base lodge and restaurant. Beginners, intermediates, and families with young children alike will be content here; expert skiers will find only seven trails, none very long. Again, inn guests always ski free—a big boon if you're staying there. For all others, lift tickets cost $35 to $72 for adults, with discounts for seniors and youths. It's located about 2 miles north of the village, on Pomfret Road (take Route 12 north past the Billings Farm and Museum, and bear right).

HIKING **Mount Tom** ★★ is the prominent hill overlooking Woodstock, its low summit providing great views over the village and to the Green Mountains. It's part of the Marsh-Billings-Rockefeller National Historic Park (p. 504), but you can ascend the mountain right from the village: Start at **Faulkner Park** ★★, a town-owned park named after Mrs. Edward Faulkner, who had the oddly zigzagging trail up the mountain built to encourage locals to exercise. To reach the trailhead from the green, cross the Middle Covered Bridge (visible from the green) and continue straight ahead on Mountain Avenue. The road bends left and soon arrives at the grassy park; from here, it's less than an hour to the summit. The trail winds uphill gradually, employing one of the most slowly climbing sets of switchbacks you'll ever see.

HORSEBACK RIDING Aspiring equestrians head to the **Kedron Valley Stables** ★ (www.kedron.com; ✆ **802/457-1480**), about 4½ miles south of Woodstock on Route 106. One-hour beginners' lessons run about $60. The stables offer pony rides for kids; run seasonal **sleigh and carriage rides** ★; and maintain an indoor riding ring for lessons in inclement weather. In spring there's a maple-syrup operation here as well. Kedron Valley is open daily except on Thanksgiving and Christmas—but credit cards aren't accepted.

Where to Stay in Woodstock

Kedron Valley Inn ★★ Here's the television star among Woodstock hostelries: Christmas after Christmas, it appeared as the oh-so-Vermont background in Budweiser commercials (the real stars, of course, were the famous Clydesdales hoofing through the snow). The inn occupies a clutch of Greek

Revival buildings 5 miles south of Woodstock, and its guest rooms are splendidly furnished in antiques (real and reproduction), poster beds, and heirloom quilts; most have wood-burning fireplaces, and a few have Jacuzzis. Rooms in the newer log building by the river are less expensive, but the motel-like exterior is redeemed, inside, by canopied beds, custom oak woodwork, and fireplaces; one (a simple two-level suite) even has a private streamside terrace and kitchenette. Units 12 and 17 in the main house are upstairs suites, and are among the most popular Kedron accommodations. Both have lovely period fireplaces and double Jacuzzis. There are two dining spaces, a formal dining room and a tavern, and alfresco dining on the porch in summer. The inn's own spring-fed pond features a sandy beach, toys for kids, and a lifeguard.

4778 South Rd. (Rte. 106), South Woodstock. www.kedronvalleyinn.com. (✆ **800/836-1193** or 802/457-1473. 25 units. $169–$249 double, $239–$289 suite; higher during foliage season and Christmas week. Rates include breakfast. Closed Apr and briefly prior to Thanksgiving. Pets allowed in some units; $15 per night. **Amenities:** Restaurant; pub; swimming pond; Wi-Fi (in public rooms; free).

The Shire Woodstock Motel ★ If you don't mind a short stroll to the Green—or saving a fair bit of money—the Shire is an attractive option. It's far better appointed than most places with "motel" in their names, featuring bright, nicely decorated rooms, most of which face the Ottauquechee River and have ample windows to take advantage of the view. At the end of the second-floor porch there's a veranda where you can sit on rockers overlooking the river and enjoy a cup of coffee. Luxury-level rooms add amenities like porches, gas fireplaces, Jacuzzis, or more antique furniture. No, it's not a luxury inn—don't look for 400-count sheets or inch-thick towels. But for a motel, this place offers incredible views and is both friendly and decently priced.

46 Pleasant St., Woodstock. www.shirewoodstock.com. (✆ **802/457-2211.** 42 units. $149–$229 double; foliage-season rates higher. **Amenities:** Wi-Fi (free).

Woodstock Inn & Resort ★★★ Central Vermont's best full-scale, in–town resort sets back from the Green, in a rambling brick building that looks like it's been there forever. Except it hasn't: Though an inn has stood on this site since 1793, the current iteration dates only to 1969. Philanthropist and resort mogul Laurance Rockefeller bought the property a year earlier, and determined that the 1891 structure housing the inn was beyond repair. He tore it down and replaced it with the faux-colonial gem you see today. Inside, guests are greeted by a broad stone fireplace, the appealing smell of wood smoke, plenty of exposed woods, and sitting areas tucked throughout the giant open lobby. Guest rooms are tastefully decorated in country pine or a Shaker-inspired style—the best units, in the newer wing (built in 1991), have plush carpeting, refrigerators, and fireplaces. One huge bonus here is that all guests get *free* use of the inn's downhill and cross-country **ski facilities** (p. 506 and 507), all nearby (free shuttle), plus discounts for golf at the Woodstock Country Club. The fitness center has squash courts, racquetball, and steam room. The two restaurants—the more formal red Rooster and the snug Richardson's

Tavern—have gotten on the locavore bandwagon with produce from the inn's own gardens.

14 The Green, Woodstock. www.woodstockinn.com. © **800/448-7900** or 802/457-1100. 141 units. $265–$569 double; $474–$1,479 suite. 2-night minimum stay Sat–Sun. Pets welcome; $125 charge. **Amenities:** 2 restaurants; bar; golf course; putting green; health club; indoor and outdoor pools; room service; 12 tennis courts, babysitting; bikes; concierge; Wi-Fi (free).

The Woodstocker Inn B&B ★★

At the foot of Mount Tom, this 1830-built inn—so yellow it's impossible to miss—has recently been renovated and upgraded to a sumptuous fare-thee-well. The top-of-the-line Morgan Horse suite is spacious enough for you to bring your own—he'd have his own garden entrance—with a 160-square-foot bedroom and a parlor twice that size, plus a private sauna. The Woodstock room has two, count 'em, two clawfoot tubs and a separate shower. The Whispering Wolf and Willard rooms evoke, respectively, a mountain cabin and the craftsmanship of a Vermont covered bridge (there's one just down the road). Six of the rooms have infrared fireplaces; all have flatscreen TVs—though none have in-room phones. In the morning, look for house-baked brioche (a nice departure from those ubiquitous B&B muffins), and selections including organic yogurt and granola made from scratch; smoked trout with blini, and the now-go-climb-Mt. Tom "Vermonter" that packs in a cheddar omelet, local sausage, a pancake, and home fries. Or, have a continental breakfast brought to your room.

61 River St., Woodstock. www.thewoodstockerbnb.com. © **802/457-3896.** 9 units. $209–$289 double; foliage season $289–$399. Rates include full breakfast. Children not allowed. **Amenities:** Wi-Fi (free).

Where to Eat in Woodstock

Bentley's ★ AMERICAN

Standing right at Woodstock's main intersection, Bentley's is just about the only downtown dining choice at lunchtime or after 9 o'clock at night—barring, of course, the pricier options at the Woodstock Inn (p. 507). The two-level dining room, located beyond an English pub-feeling bar (except for the Red Sox on the tube), is eclectically Victorian, with floor and table lamps from Grandma's house. Expect burgers and big sandwiches for lunch, while the dinner menu is more refined, but hardly sophisticated, leaning toward chicken, salmon, steaks, fish and chips, and a big cider-brined pork chop. The sausages are made in house. It's often very crowded here at night both at the bar and in the dining room, when it becomes the closest thing Woodstock has to a "scene." Try to reserve a table if you'll be coming on a weekend night.

3 Elm St., Woodstock. http://bentleysrestaurant.com. © **877/457-3232** or 802/457-3232. Reservations recommended for parties of four or more. Main courses $11–$20 at lunch, $20–$29 at dinner. Mon–Thurs 11:30am–9:30pm; Fri–Sat 11am–10pm; Sun 11am–9pm; 'til 2am for live music and dancing on Fri–Sat.

The Prince and the Pauper ★★ NEW AMERICAN

Tucked down Dana Alley (next to the Woodstock Historical Society's Dana House), this intimate, informal spot offers some of Woodstock's best meals. Start with a drink in the taproom, and then move over to the elegantly simple little dining room. The menu (appetizer, salad, and entrée at a fixed price) changes daily, but might feature wine-braised short ribs, veal scallopini sautéed in Madeira, Grand Marnier–tinged magret of duck, or cedar-planked Arctic char. A la carte dishes may be ordered as well. On the bistro menu, there's an inexpensive choice of gourmet hearth-baked pizzas, as well as steaks, salmon, curry, and more.

24 Elm St., Woodstock. www.princeandpauper.com. © **802/457-1818.** Reservations recommended. Bistro main courses $16–$26 (not available Sat or holidays), prix-fixe dinners $51. Sun–Thurs 5:30–8:30pm; Fri–Sat 5:30–9pm. Lounge opens 5pm.

Simon Pearce Restaurant ★★ NEW AMERICAN   Housed in a restored 19th-century woolen mill with wonderful views of a waterfall, this adjunct to the famed glassworks is a collage of exposed brick, pine floorboards, and handsome wooden tables and chairs. Meals are served on pottery and glassware made right here (downstairs, you can watch glassblowers at work)—if you like your place setting, you can buy it afterward at the sprawling retail shop in the mill. The atmosphere is a good mix of formal and informal. Chef Jeremy Conway's lunch menus include Vermont cheddar soup, sesame chicken, coquilles Saint Jacques, lamb burgers, shepherd's pie, and a daily quiche. At dinner look for entrees like horseradish-crusted blue cod with crisped leeks, pan-seared Arctic char with leek and scallop succotash, pan-roasted sirloin in a cabernet demi-glace, or spiced pork osso bucco. Recent desserts have included roasted-apple tarts, blackberry cobbler, a bittersweet chocolate pudding cake with a cappuccino semifreddo, and a walnut meringue.

1760 Main St. (inside the Mill), Quechee. www.simonpearce.com/ourrestaurant. © **802/295-1470.** Reservations recommended for dinner (not accepted for lunch). Main courses $14–$18 at lunch, $23–$36 at dinner. Daily; lunch 11:30–2:45pm; dinner 5:30–9pm. Bar opens 4pm Sun–Thurs; 11:30am Fri–Sat, and closes . . . when it closes.

KILLINGTON & RUTLAND

Rutland: 240 miles NE of New York City, 170 miles NW of Boston, 55 miles N of Bennington, 65 miles S of Burlington, 25 miles W of Woodstock.

Killington: 12 miles E of Rutland.

In 1937, a travel writer described the village near Killington Peak as "a church and a few undistinguished houses." The rugged, remote area was isolated from Rutland by imposing mountains, and accessible only through the daunting Sherburne Pass.

But that was before Vermont's second-highest mountain was developed into the Northeast's largest ski area, and before a wide, 5-mile-long access road was slashed through the forest right up to the mountain's base. (It was also before Route 4 was widened and upgraded, improving access to Rutland considerably.) Today, Route 4 is one of the most heavily traveled routes through the Green Mountains, and a sea of condos, restaurants, and other tourist-related entities have moved in and taken possession of the pass.

So know this: Killington is plainly not the Vermont pictured on calendars and postcards. The region around the mountain boasts Vermont's most active winter scene, with loads of distractions both on and off the mountain. The area has a frenetic, where-it's-happening feel in winter. (That's not the case in summer, when the vast, empty parking lots trigger a mild, where-did-everybody-go panic, tempered by relief at the sinking prices of lodging.) The people happiest here are (a) skiers who like their skiing BIG; (b) singles in search of aggressive mingling on the mountain; and (c) travelers who want a wide choice of lodgings, eats, and fun stuff to do—and are willing to sacrifice a good portion of Vermont's usual charm in exchange for that.

About a dozen miles to the west, the city of Rutland lacks immediate charm, too. It's a working-class city with compact downtown, a rich history, and a wide array of services for travelers—most of them arrayed along two cluttered edge-city strips that inch close to the city center. Today it's undergoing a slight renaissance, with new residents who enjoy the small-city atmosphere, free summer outdoor concerts, cheap real estate, and quick access to the mountains. But even though it's lost its status as Vermont's second-largest city—South Burlington passed it in the 2000 census—it retains an urban, workaday atmosphere.

If you like the action of Killington but not the prices, sleeping in Rutland and then driving 25 or 30 minutes up to the ski area in the morning—or taking the local shuttle bus there—will work just fine. If you don't mind waking up to zero scenery, that is.

Essentials

ARRIVING

BY CAR   It's easy to get to Rutland. From New York City, it's about a 4½-hour drive via the New York State Thruway; from Boston it's about 3 hours via I-89. The city sits right at the intersection of two old U.S. highways, routes 7 and 4. Killington lies east on Route 4, through the mountains. Killington Road, the main access road to the mountain, extends southward off routes 4 and 100. This turnoff is about 10 or 12 miles (25 minutes) east of Rutland, on your right.

BY TRAIN   Amtrak (www.amtrak.com; ✆ 800/872-7245) offers a daily service from New York City up the Hudson River Valley to Rutland (the Ethan Allen Express). The ride takes a shade under 6 hours and costs $73 one-way. From Rutland there are connecting shuttles to the mountain and various resorts—or you can call a taxi.

BY PLANE   Rutland is served by several daily direct flights from Boston's Logan International Airport on **Cape Air** (www.capeair.com; ✆ **800/227-3247**); the flight takes about an hour. Some local hotels and inns offer shuttles from Rutland airport.

VISITOR INFORMATION

The **Rutland Region Chamber of Commerce,** at 50 Merchants Row in Rutland (www.rutlandvermont.com; ✆ **800/756-8880** or 802/773-2747), staffs an information booth at the corner of routes 7 and 4W from Memorial Day until Columbus Day. The chamber's main office is open year-round, weekdays from 8am to 5pm. The **Killington Pico Area Association** (www.killington pico.org; ℂ **802/422-5722**) staffs an information booth on Route 4 at the base of the access road; it's open weekdays from 9am to 5pm, shorter hours on weekends in winter and spring.

For information on accommodations in the area and travel to Killington, contact the resort's central reservations service (www.killington.com; ℂ **800/621-6867**) directly.

GETTING AROUND

The Marble Valley Regional Transit District (www.thebus.com; ℂ **802/773-3244**) operates the **Diamond Express**—a very handy daily shuttle service between Rutland and Killington. The ride costs just $2 per person, one-way.

Exploring Rutland

Rutland is the regional hub for central Vermont, with a daily newspaper (well, daily in print Tuesday through Saturday; online Sunday and Monday) and a long line of big box stores, fast-food chain restaurants, and businesses stretched out along crowded Route 7 both north and south of the downtown center. At times this "edge city" comes perilously close to looking like one big, outdated strip mall; the concept of zoning got here too late, if it ever got here at all. Still, Rutland has the feel of a real place full of real people eating normal food—a good antidote when you've spent a little too much time in cuckoo-clock shops or the lift lines.

A stroll through Rutland's historic downtown might delight architecture buffs. Look for the detailed marblework on many of the buildings, such as the **Paramount Theater** (30 Center St.) or the handsome commercial buildings lining **Merchants Row.** Note especially the **Service Building** at 128 Merchants Row—at seven stories tall, it was Vermont's first "skyscraper" when it was built in 1930, one of Vermont's two significant Art Deco structures (the other is Brattleboro's Latchis Hotel and Theater, p. 496). Nearby **South Main Street** (Route 7) also has a good selection of handsome homes built in elaborate Queen Anne style.

Another stop worth making, especially as a rainy-day diversion, is the **Chaffee Art Center ★,** at 16 S. Main St. (www.chaffeeartcenter.org; ℂ **802/775-0356**). Housed in a fairy-tale-like 1896 building with a prominent turret and mosaic floors in its archway vestibule—it's on the National Register of

---

Fair Time in Rutland

The **Vermont State Fair ★** (www.vermontstatefair.net; ℂ **802/775-5200**) has attracted fairgoers for more than a century and a half—since 1846, to be precise. Expect a conjunction of clowns, carnival rides, snacks, and country music acts, not to mention Bingo, racing pigs, magic shows, and plenty more. Admission is $1 to $10 per adult, depending on the date, with big discounts for kids. There's also a small charge for parking (free to $3 per day). The fair is held for 5 days in mid-August. Look for the expansive fairgrounds on Route 7, just south of Rutland's city center on the right-hand side as you leave town. Gates open at 8am daily.

Historic Places, the glorious parquet floors now restored to their original luster—the arts center showcases local talent from Rutland and the hills beyond, with changing exhibits of their work, much of it for sale. It's open daily Wednesday to Saturday from 10am to 5pm, and Sunday from noon to 4pm; admission is by donation.

Exploring Killington

Killington lacks a town center, a single place that makes you feel you've arrived, and perhaps it lacks a soul as well; Killington is, basically, "wherever you parked." This town is so tied to the ski hill that it actually renamed itself after the mountain and resort in 1999; before that, it had been called Sherburne.

Since the mountain was first developed for skiing in 1958, dozens of restaurants, hotels, and stores have sprouted up along Killington Road (which shoots off Route 4 at a sudden angle) to accommodate the legions of skiers who descend upon the area during the ski season, which typically runs from October well into May, and sometimes even into June (Killington always makes a big deal about being the first area to open and the last to close). There's little to love about Killington Road—it's strung out, clear-cut, unattractively landscaped—and the culinary offerings along its sides are very average at best. But this is the only access road in; it's a fact of life if you're skiing here. Learn to find the few diamonds in the rough.

The ski area itself (see "Skiing," below) is massive, stretching to encompass seven mountainsides, including Pico Peak; it's considered the biggest resort in the northeastern U.S.

"silent cal" COOLIDGE, SON OF VERMONT

One of two Vermont-born presidents (the other was Chester A. Arthur)—and the only one born on the Fourth of July—Calvin Coolidge has never ranked among the nation's top chief executives, although he has long been credited with the simple virtues and rock-solid integrity that Vermonters prize. The President Calvin Coolidge State Historic Site ★★ (3780 Rte. 100A, Plymouth; http://coolidgefoundation.org; © **802/672-3773**) takes in just about all of the tiny mountain hamlet of Plymouth where he grew up. About a dozen unspoiled buildings are open to the public, and a number of other private residences can be observed from the outside. On August 3, 1923, in his boyhood home—the Coolidge Homestead, open for tours—Vice President Coolidge was awakened and informed that President Warren Harding had died. His own father, a notary public, administered the presidential oath of office by kerosene light.

A welcome addition to the older structures is a modern visitor center, where films, Coolidge association items, and special exhibits illuminate the free-wheeling "Roaring Twenties" over which the taciturn Vermonter presided. Coolidge is buried in the cemetery across the road, where every July 4th a wreath is laid at his simple grave in a quiet ceremony. Admission to the site is $9 adults, $2 kids 6 to 14, $25 family. It's open late May to mid-October, daily 9:30am to 5pm.

For a look at Coolidge's years practicing law in Northampton, MA, see p. 329 in chapter 8.

Skiing

DOWNHILL

Killington ★★ A love-it or hate-it kind of place, New England's largest and most bustling ski area offers more vertical drop—and variety of experiences—than any other New England resort. It's certainly exciting. You'll find a huge choice of slope types across the seven peaks, from long, narrow, old-fashioned runs to killer moguls high on the mountains' flanks or tree-glade skiing. This is the Vermont choice of serious skiers. (It's also a huge operation, run with efficiency and not much personality, where tickets and passes are referred to as "products.") It's easy for kids to get separated from friends and family, and the resort seems to attract boisterous packs of young adults, so families should stick to Ramshed (the family area) or head to another resort such as Sugarbush (p. 525), Stowe (p. 536), or Suicide Six (p. 506). But for a big-mountain experience, with lots of evening activities and plenty of challenging terrain, this is still a great choice—maybe Vermont's best.

4763 Killington Rd., Killington. www.killington.com. © **800/734-9435.** Day lift tickets $115 adults; discounts for children and seniors, for multi-day passes, and for online ticket purchases.

CROSS-COUNTRY

Nearest to the ski resort (just east of Killington Road on Route 100/4) is **Mountain Meadows Cross Country & Snowshoe Area** ★ (www.xcskiing.net; © **800/221-0598**), with more than 35 miles of trails groomed for both skating and classic skiing. The trails are largely divided into three sections, with beginner trails closest to the lodge, an intermediate area a bit farther along, and an advanced 6-mile loop farthest away. Rentals and lessons are available at the lodge. For adults, a 1-day pass is $19, and a half-day (after 1pm) pass is $16. Kids ages 6 to 12 pay $8 per day, $6 per half-day.

The intricate network of trails at the **Mountain Top Nordic Ski & Snowshoe Center** ★★ (www.mountaintopinn.com; © **802/483-6089**), part of the Mountain Top Inn (p. 515), has long had a loyal local following. (It was one of the first commercial cross-country ski facilities in the East.) The 35-mile trail network offers pastoral views through mixed terrain, most of it groomed for classic and skate skiing. Trails here are often deep with snow, owing to the inn's ridge-top position high in the hills. Adults pay $22 for 1-day trail passes, $18 for half-day passes (after noon). This is challenging and picturesque terrain.

Other Outdoor Activities

Vermont is loaded with fine golf courses, public and private, lovely in summer and outstandingly scenic in fall. The acknowledged top course is **Green Mountain National Golf Course** ★★★ (www.gmngc.com; © **802/422-4653**) on Route 100, about 3 miles north of the Route 100/Route 4 junction in Killington. Greens fees run from $68 to $78 per adult, not including the cost of a motorized cart (mandatory Fri–Sun and holidays). Discounts are available if you begin after 3pm, and from opening day until June 21. Rentals, instruction, and a driving range are also available.

Where to Stay in the Killington/Rutland Area

Rutland's one true "inn" closed years ago, and B&Bs are not to be found. On the other hand, the city has an unusually wide selection of roadside motels and chain hotels, mostly clustered on or along Route 7 either right downtown or just south of town, in the lower-to-middle price range for the most part. None of these is much better or different from any of the others. Check with the chamber of commerce (see p. 511) if you need help weeding through these; most can easily be booked online from the comfort of your own home.

Skiers, especially families, headed to Killington for a week or so should also consider the condominium option. Talk to a representative at the **Killington Central Reservations Bureau** (www.killington.com; ✆ **800/621-6867**), and check online for special deals. (Killington will also help you book a stay at area inns and motels that it does not own.)

Blueberry Hill Inn ★★ The simple, homey Blueberry Hill Inn, dating from 1813 and run by the same family since 1971, lies in the heart of the Moosalamoo recreation area amid 180 acres of forest and meadows, about 45 minutes northwest of Killington—it's halfway to Middlebury. It's hard to top this place for access to outdoor activities—there's superb hiking, biking, canoeing, swimming, and cross-country skiing all around. An inn brochure put it like this: "We offer you no radios, no televisions, no bedside phones to disturb your vacation." There are also no Jacuzzis or fancy fireplaces (and quite a few double and twin beds), surprising given the (seasonally) high room rates. Instead, you get a clean room, solid construction, plenty of wood, and lots of Americana-themed quilts. The original inn building houses four units; an attached conservatory contains three loft-style rooms, all reached via stairs, and there are four more in a pond-side 1987 addition plus the Moosalamoo Cottage, with a queen bed downstairs and three twin beds in the loft (the cottage, and one pond-side room, are dog-friendly). Family-style meals are served in a rustic dining room with a great stone fireplace and original wooden beams. The menu is Continental, with fusion touches—things like snapper cakes with guacamole and roasted free-range chicken. And the inn's famous cookie jar is always full. There's also a cross-country ski center on the property; a day pass is about $20.

1245 Goshen-Ripton Rd., Goshen. www.blueberryhillinn.com. ✆ **802/247-6735.** 12 units. $175–$315 double; higher in foliage and holiday seasons. Rates include breakfast. MAP rates $50 additional per person. **Amenities:** Babysitting; bikes; sauna; Wi-Fi (in public areas; free).

Inn at Long Trail ★ The Inn at Long Trail is situated in an architecturally undistinguished building (three stories of beige), poised at a significant crossroads: the intersection of the highway (Route 4) and the Long and Appalachian trails at the Sherburne Pass. It's also only a 10-minute drive from Killington's ski slopes. The rustic character of the place merges with real hospitality; it's popular with young hikers and families alike. The interior here makes up for what the exterior lacks—tree trunks support beams in the lobby, where you'll also find log furniture and banisters carved from birch. The oldest rooms in the inn (built in 1938 as an annex to a long-gone lodge) are furnished simply, in ski-lodge style—but more modern suites with fireplaces, telephones, TVs, and (sometimes) Jacuzzis and fireplaces are housed in a motel-like annex—they're the preferable accommodations. The dining room is fun, with a stone ledge that pokes right through the wall from the mountain behind the inn; it serves straight-ahead family fare plus a kids' menu. There's also a pub.

709 Rte. 4, Killington. www.innatlongtrail.com. © **800/325-2540** or 802/775-7181. 19 units. Summer and fall $90–$145 double; foliage season $120–$170. All rates include breakfast; foliage and holiday rates also include dinner. 2-night minimum stay Fri–Sat and foliage season weekends. Closed late Apr–late May. Pets allowed with prior permission, $10 per night (certain suites only). **Amenities:** Dining room; pub; Wi-Fi (in public areas, free).

Killington Grand Resort Hotel ★★

It's pricey, but you can't do better than this behemoth when it comes to spacious, modern accommodations and the convenience of being right on the mountain. There's a choice of standard queen-bedded rooms; studios; suites with sitting rooms; and two-bedroom, two-bathroom penthouses with full kitchens and gas fireplaces, all decorated in comfortable if predictable country condo style. More than half of the units have kitchen facilities. Some can sleep up to eight people—this resort has really placed an emphasis on catering to families. The staff is more helpful than you've probably come to expect at ski hotels this size, and you can ski right onto the mountain from your room (or walk to the resort's golf course) via a special bridge. A shuttle runs you to Killington Road if you must sample the nightlife. There's a great health club here (two Jacuzzis with views, a big heated pool), plus a newer addition—the **Killington Grand Spa,** offering Swedish massage, Vichy showers, stone massages, nail care, and more.

228 E. Mountain Rd. (near Snowshed base), Killington. www.killington.com. © **802/734-9435.** 200 units. $179–$267 double, suites $202–$574. 5-night minimum stay during Christmas and school holidays; 2-night minimum stay Sat–Sun. **Amenities:** 2 restaurants; 2 bars; food court; children's programs; concierge; health club and spa; Jacuzzi; outdoor pool; room service; sauna; spa; 2 tennis courts; Wi-Fi (free).

The Mountain Top Inn & Resort ★★

They couldn't have come up with a more appropriate name for this property, which sprawls across 1,300 acres on a high ridge of the Green Mountains with one of Vermont's best inn views and an incomparable location flanking pristine Chittenden Reservoir, a half-hour's drive from the Killington ski area. It has the feel of one of those places where people used to while away whole summers, lolling on the front porch in Adirondack chairs, playing croquet, riding horses, paddling canoes, and simply relaxing. The pleasures may be old-fashioned, but the accommodations are not: Even the lowest-priced rooms have been updated in woods, leathers, and tartan. Luxury rooms and suites come outfitted with sofas, double-sided fireplaces, jetted tubs, and kitchenettes. The standard rooms are smaller and simpler but still come with fresh paint, rocking chairs, and views. The inn rents five cabins on the grounds described as "rustic" (but they're quite nice, with TVs and big fireplaces), and can also arrange a stay in local ski chalets. Activities run from trap and skeet shooting to fly-fishing lessons, from tennis to cross-country skiing and dog-sledding . . . and, of course, those horses and canoes. Although the resort no longer has a golf course (Eisenhower once played here), trips to several nearby courses can be arranged. For evening entertainment, there are performances of jazz and orchestral music. The dining room and tavern are pretty good, too.

195 Mountain Top Rd., Chittenden. www.mountaintopinn.com. ✆ **802/483-2311.** 55 units. $275–$445 double; $495–$545 suite; $395–$545 cabin. Resort fee of 15% additional. 2-night minimum stay Fri–Sat; Pets welcome in cabins only ($25 fee). **Amenities:** 2 restaurants; bar; outdoor pool; kitchenette (some units); free Wi-Fi in public areas.

Where to Eat in Killington & Rutland
KILLINGTON
Charity's 1887 Saloon & Restaurant ★ PUB FARE   Bustling and laid-back, Charity's has upgraded its menu in recent years, adding entrees including pot roast, BBQ ribs, and a mixed shellfish over angel hair pasta dish, but maintains its cachet as a lively young crowd's watering hole and burger stop. Who was Charity? She worked an old profession in the bar's original American home. Ask a staffer if you want to know more.

2194 Killington Rd., Killington. www.charitystavern.com. ✆ **802/422-3800.** Reservations not accepted. Main courses $9–$15 at lunch, $11–$25 at dinner. Mon–Thurs 4–9pm; Fri 4–10pm; Sun 12–9pm.

Choices Restaurant and Rotisserie ★ CONTINENTAL   Locals like this unpretentious place on the access road, and indeed it's one of the mountain's better options. Seafood and fresh pastas are a specialty (try the various fettuccine dishes), plus meats from a roaring front-and-center rotisserie. There's no theme, really, other than a Continental touch; you might just as well find curry, snails, or lamb chops on the menu as a smoked-salmon potato pancake, fish salad, nachos, or a cut of filet mignon dolled up with blue cheese. Full dinners come with salad or soup and bread. The atmosphere is nothing to write home about, but quality, variety, and care in preparation make up for prices higher than at the burger joints nearby

2820 Killington Rd. (at Glazebrook Center), Killington. www.choicesrestaurantkillington. com. ✆ **802/422-4030.** Main courses $20–$23; pasta selections available in small portions. Wed–Thurs 5–10pm; Fri–Sat 5–10:30pm; Sun 5–9pm.

The Foundry ★ AMERICAN   Tucked just off the road to the slopes, this deceptively rustic-looking establishment sits right on the shores of Summit Pond. The all-season views are spectacular—especially when it's warm enough to perch on the deck with a drink. Menus lean heavily towards the standards, but with imaginative and flavor-forward variations: rack of lamb roasts in a slathering of mustard and golden raisins; swordfish with a glaze of mango and sweet chilis; scallops crusted in ground hazelnuts—even risotto, that tried-and-true meatless option, stands out with ricotta and Manchego cheeses filling in for the usual Parmigiano. Steak comes in four iterations,

from the humble hanger to a lordly porterhouse, with stops at strip, rib-eye, and filet mignon (in steakhouse style, the sides are a separate buy—go for the cornbread and creamed spinach; as for mac and cheese, to each their own). The star at lunchtime is the Wagyu burger; at brunch, a heroic smoked pork, black bean, and cheddar omelet muscles up against more typical waffles and crepes. Wines can get a little pricey, but there are a few decent bottles that won't break the bank, and the selection circles the globe from Italy to Australia. Live music.

63 Summit Path, Killington. www.foundrykillington.com. © **802/422-5335.** Brunch and lunch items $9–$18; main courses $20–$35. Mon–Thurs 3–10pm; Fri 3–11pm; Sat 11am–11pm; Sun 10am–10pm.

The Garlic ★ ITALIAN   Might as well not beat around the bush . . . or the bulb: This aptly named place is a monument to the pungent little cornerstone of southern Italian cuisine. It turns up in dishes such as pasta puttanesca, linguini in clam sauce, scallops fra diavolo, a garlic-marinated rack of lamb, and of course in a classic Caesar salad. Garlic averse? Options include cedar plank-roasted salmon, the ubiquitous New York strip, and chicken alfredo. The wine list skews Italian, and happily includes plenty of under-$40 bottles; there's also a specialty martini card designed to horrify gin-and-vermouth purists. It's all served up in a cheery atmosphere, heavy on the primary colors.

1724 Killington Rd., Killington. www.thegarlicvermont.net. © **802/422-5055.** Main courses $19–$33. Daily 5–10pm.

RUTLAND

Little Harry's ★ INTERNATIONAL   Located in downtown Rutland, on the first floor and in the basement of a strikingly unattractive building, Harry's has a wonderfully eclectic menu. Main courses could range from a stuffed loin pork chop to jerked scallops, fish and chips to pad Thai (there's *always* something Thai on the menu here). Appetizers are equally eclectic: Marinated olives, curried mussels, and pan-fried crabcakes might make appearances. The food here spans the globe—to paraphrase Thoreau, you can travel extensively in Rutland, via Little Harry's.

121 West St. (at Merchants Row), Rutland. No website. © **802/747-4848.** Reservations recommended. Main courses $18–$27. Daily 5–10pm.

The Palms ★ ITALIAN   Here's an opportunity to celebrate a little-known facet of local history: One fine fall day in 1948, on these very premises, Giuseppe and Giovannina Sabataso served Vermont's first pizza. The Sabatasos had been running their restaurant since 1933, but it had taken those 15 years for the Neapolitan staple to inch its way up from New York. Still in the family, three generations later, The Palms continues to turn out its distinctive square pizza, with dough made fresh daily and ingredients hand-cut. The menu also includes the southern Italian standbys—antipasto with salami and provolone; manicotti; linguini and red or white clam sauce; eggplant, chicken, and veal parmigiana—along with steaks and chops. You don't come here for innovation, or for "northern" dishes that look down on the lordly tomato, but a taste of Italian Rutland, 1933.

36 Strongs Ave., Rutland. www.palmsvermont.com. ✆ **802/747-6100.** Main courses $12–$24; pizzas $13–$18, plus extra toppings. Mon–Thurs 5–9pm; Fri–Sat 5–9:30pm.

Table 24 ★★ AMERICAN   When he opened Table 24, chef Stephen Sawyer energized the once-moribund Rutland dining scene. Look for hearty lunches of soup, salad, mac and cheese, sausage jambalaya, and burgers—you get the idea. These are cooked with a little more flair and care than your mom-and-pop diner would, though, and the restaurant uses Vermont-sourced ingredients wherever possible. Dinner is the real star—diner staples, but also things like baby back ribs, maple-cured pork tenderloin, seafood stew, grilled steaks with compound butter, chicken stuffed with prosciutto and Gouda, and a vegetable plate redolent of wood-fired Portobellos and pumpkin seed pesto. Dessert choices, too, are the pudding-and-pie diner classics, but raised several notches above the ordinary. The high ceiling, exposed rafters, and a long copper-top bar add to the restaurant's convivial feeling.

24 Wales St. (just off Rte. 4), Rutland. www.table24.net. ✆ **802/775-2424.** Reservations recommended. Lunch items $10–$24, dinner main courses $15–$34. Mon–Sat 11:30am–9pm.

MIDDLEBURY ★★

Middlebury: 35 miles S of Burlington, 85 miles N of Bennington, 65 miles NW of White River Junction.

Middlebury is a gracious college town set among rolling hills and pastoral countryside. The town center is idyllic in a New-England-as-envisioned-by-Hollywood way, and for many travelers it's the perfect combination of small-town charm, close access to the outdoors (the Adirondacks and Green Mountains are both pretty close at hand), and a dash of sophistication. (Foodies, rejoice.)

The worldly influence of a college (and its international student body), relocated artisans, and assorted other out-of-staters who've blown in here has led to the establishment of a natural-foods store, ethnic restaurants, a growing microbrewery, and more arts, crafts, and books than you'd expect to find in a place several times its size—especially in Vermont.

Essentials
ARRIVING
Middlebury is on Route 7, almost exactly midway between Rutland and Burlington, about 30 miles (45 min.) from both of Vermont's largest cities. From New York City, it takes 5 or more hours to get here by car.

One popular route is to drive to the village of Fort Ticonderoga, then take a **cable ferry across Lake Champlain** (✆ **802/897-7999**). Some form of ferry boat has crossed the lake here since way back in 1759; this one operates from May through October, about three times per hour from 7am until 6pm (to 7pm July–Labor Day); the cost for autos is $12 one-way, $18 round-trip, but it

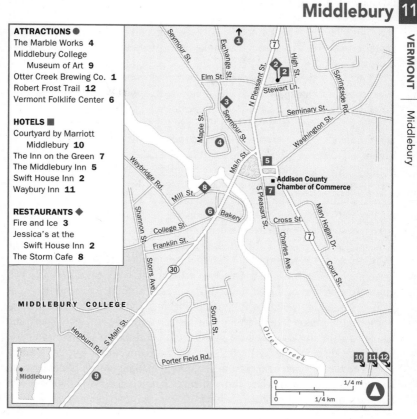

ATTRACTIONS ●
The Marble Works **4**
Middlebury College
    Museum of Art **9**
Otter Creek Brewing Co. **1**
Robert Frost Trail **12**
Vermont Folklife Center **6**

HOTELS ■
Courtyard by Marriott
    Middlebury **10**
The Inn on the Green **7**
The Middlebury Inn **5**
Swift House Inn **2**
Waybury Inn **11**

RESTAURANTS ◆
Fire and Ice **3**
Jessica's at the
    Swift House Inn **2**
The Storm Cafe **8**

takes just 7 minutes. In very severe weather, the ferry doesn't run, but this is Vermont: It almost always does run.

VISITOR INFORMATION

The **Addison County Chamber of Commerce,** 93 Court St. (www.addison county.com; ⟨ **802/388-7951**), is just south of downtown. Brochures and assistance are available Monday through Friday during business hours (9am–5pm), and sometimes on Saturday and Sunday as well (early June through mid-Oct). Ask for a map and guide to downtown Middlebury, which lists local shops and restaurants and is published by the Downtown Middlebury Business Bureau.

Exploring Middlebury

Middlebury's tiny main street has plenty of things to see—used-book shops, cafes, souvenir and stationery shops, and the like. It's a bit cutesy, but you'll find enough shopping interest to occupy an hour or two. The **Vermont Folklife Center ★** (www.vermontfolklifecenter.org; ⟨ **802/388-4964**), at 88 Main St., is a gallery of changing displays of local art from Vermont and beyond—visual art, but also music. You might even listen to recordings of old Vermonters reminiscing telling stories in a vanishing Yankee dialect. The gift shop sells heritage books, foods, baskets, and other traditional crafts. The center is open Tuesday through Saturday from 10am to 5pm. Admission is by donation.

Take the footbridge over the river and find your way to **The Marble Works,** an assortment of wood and rough-marble industrial buildings on the far bank, converted to a handful of interesting shops and restaurants (p. 523).

Atop a low ridge, with beautiful views of the Green Mountains to the east and farmlands rolling toward Lake Champlain in the west, prestigious **Middlebury College ★** (founded in 1800) has a handsome, well-spaced campus of gray limestone and white marble buildings best explored on foot. The architecture of the college is primarily Colonial Revival, giving it a rather stern Calvinist feel. The view from the marble **Mead Memorial Chapel ★,** built in 1917 and overlooking the campus green, is especially nice.

At the edge of campus, the architecturally engaging Mahaney Center for the Arts, at 72 Porter Field Rd., houses the good little **Middlebury College Museum of Art ★★** (http://museum.middlebury.edu; ✆ **802/443-5007**), with a sampling of European and American art both old and new. Classicists will enjoy the displays of Greek painted urns, vases, and bits of stone frieze, as well as Florentine panels, a Rembrandt etching, and other Renaissance and Baroque artworks. Modern-art aficionados can check out the permanent and changing exhibits; also, look for works from the museum's public sculpture collection, displayed at various places around the campus. The museum is open Tuesday through Friday from 10am to 5pm, Saturday and Sunday noon to 5pm. (It's closed mid-Dec through early Jan, when college is out of session.) Admission and parking are free.

Brewhounds should schedule a stop at the **Otter Creek Brewing Co.,** 793 Exchange St. (www.ottercreekbrewing.com; ✆ **802/388-0727**) for a pub lunch (soup, chili, panini, cheese plates) and one of their seasonal ales or year-round IPAs. The pub and gift shop are open daily 11am to 6pm, but, sad to say, brewery tours are no more.

One recommended walk for people of all abilities—and especially those of literary sensibilities—is the **Robert Frost Memorial Trail ★,** dedicated to the memory of New England's poet laureate. Frost lived in a cabin on a farm across the road for 23 summers. (The cabin, a National Historic Landmark, is not open to visitors.) It's on Route 125, about 6 miles east of Middlebury's village center. The trail itself is a relaxing, easy mile-long loop with excerpts of Frost's poems posted on signs all along the way—a wonderful idea. There's also information about the natural history of the trail area. This is a nice taste of the local mountains, with a pleasant poetic tint thrown in. If you have questions about the trail, call the Green Mountain National Forest's Middlebury Ranger District office, south of town on Route 7 (✆ **802/388-4362**), which administrates it.

Where to Stay in Middlebury

If you're looking to save a few dollars, the outskirts of Middlebury, especially Route 7 south of the village green, are home to a clutch of budget motels and inns, some locally owned and some chain-run. These are in various states of upkeep and comfort, but they're uniformly cheap—$120 a night or less, in most cases. But don't expect anything but the bare bones.

By far the best motel choice in these parts, especially for families, is the 89-room **Courtyard by Marriott Middlebury** (www.marriott.com; ✆ **800/ 388-7775** or 802/388-7600) on Route 7 (309 Court St.) a half-mile south of the village green. Yes, it's a chain and nothing out of the ordinary, but it supplies the basics plus an indoor swimming pool. Some big spa suites have gas log fireplaces, Jacuzzi tubs, and fuller amenities; all rooms come with free Wi-Fi. There's also a bistro-style restaurant for breakfast and dinner, and a coin-op laundry.

The Inn on the Green ★★ This handsome, robin's-egg-blue village inn is a case study in changing 19th-century architectural tastes—it was built in 1803, along chaste Federal-era lines, and given its Second Empire mansard tower in the 1860s. It's comfortable, too, and nicely situated within a short walk of the town green. Rooms are furnished in a mix of solid antiques and reproductions (pencil-poster beds, sleigh daybeds, and the like). Exposed wooden floors and boldly colored walls of harvest yellow, peach, and burgundy keep things bright, and everything is smartly maintained. The suites are most spacious, but every unit offers enough elbow room; those in the front of the house are wonderfully flooded with afternoon light. A continental breakfast (delivered to your room) is always included, though there are no Jacuzzis or fireplaces; this is not a luxury property, but rather a cozy Vermont experience. 71 S. Pleasant St., Middlebury. www.innonthegreen.com. ✆ **888/244-7512** or 802/388-7512. 11 units. $159–$209 double; $249–$299 suite. Rates include continental breakfast. 2-night minimum stay Fri–Sat. **Amenities:** Free use of bikes; Wi-Fi (free).

The Middlebury Inn ★★ Oddly enough, one of the rarest finds on the lodging scene—even in tradition-heavy New England—is the small, non-chain hotel, that institution that lies between country inns and full-scale hotels. Perhaps more than any other Vermont hostelry, the Middlebury Inn fits the description. The most upscale lodging experience in town, it occupies a stately 1827 brick building facing the main village square; tucked alongside and in the rear are two more structures that bring the inn's total to 71 rooms and suites. Units are mostly on the big side, outfitted with either a sofa or upholstered chairs; Colonial-reproduction furniture; and vintage bathroom fixtures. Room nos. 116 and 246 are spacious corner units entered via foyers; no. 129, though smaller, has a four-poster bed, view of the green, and Jacuzzi. Rooms in the Porter Mansion next door also have a pleasantly historic feel, but the adjacent Courtyard annex is more motel-like, with double- and twin-bedded units. When you book, specify the main building or the mansion—but be prepared to put up with some traffic noise from Route 7, especially if you have a front room. **Morgan's Tavern,** the inn's restaurant, specializes in locally sourced ingredients and is open for breakfast, lunch, dinner, and afternoon tea.

14 Court Sq., Middlebury. www.middleburyinn.com. © **800/842-4666** or 802/388-4961. 71 units. $135–$229 double; $216–$279 suite. Rates include continental breakfast. Pets accepted in Courtyard annex ($25 fee). **Amenities:** Restaurant; tavern; day spa; Wi-Fi (in main inn, free).

Swift House Inn ★★ This historic complex of three whitewashed houses sits above broad, sloping lawns 2 blocks from downtown Middlebury. Several waves of recent ownership have improved it with such touches as a friendly wine bar, improved pricing of the excellent **house restaurant ★★** (see p. 523), and a "green" designation from the state of Vermont for environmentally sound practices. The five rooms in the roadside Gate House are lowest-priced and have a B&B feel, but with luxuries such as plush carpets, gorgeous wooden floors, and bathrooms. Nine units in the main Federal-style inn, built in 1814, are thoroughly imbued with the history of the place (a Vermont governor lived here at one time); inside, it's decorated in antiques and reproduction furnishings. And the carriage house's six suites are ideal for honeymooners or business travelers. They're the biggest and most luxurious, almost all of them furnished with Jacuzzis and fireplaces.

25 Stewart Lane, Middlebury. www.swifthouseinn.com. © **866/388-9925** or 802/388-9925. 20 units. $149–$275 doubles and suites. Rates include full breakfast. 2-night minimum stay some Fri–Sat. **Amenities:** Restaurant; room service (breakfast only); Wi-Fi (in main inn; free).

Waybury Inn ★ Photos of Bob Newhart and "Larry, his brother Darryl, and his other brother Darryl" grace the wall behind the desk at this 1810 inn, located 5 miles east of Middlebury. That's because the inn was featured in the 1980s TV show *Newhart*—the handsome exterior, anyway, which was painted white for television (it's now green). (The interior was created on a Hollywood sound stage.) The rooms here vary in size and price, as they do in most old inns; the more you pay, the more space you get, though none have in-room phones. Two of the rooms are suites, with sitting rooms, four-poster king beds, Jacuzzis, and claw-foot tubs. Room no. 9, the Robert Frost Suite (the poet, who summered nearby, was a frequent guest), has a secret stash of previous guests' notes, while the New England Room features the work of local artist Warren Kimble. The inn's restaurant, the **Pine Room,** features an inventive continental menu, and the convivial tavern serves lighter meals and libations.

457 E. Main St. (Rte. 125, about 1½ miles past Rte. 7 S. turnoff), East Middlebury. www.wayburyinn.com. © **800/348-1810** or 802/388-4015. 12 units (1 w/bath across hall). $140–$315 double; $260–$335 suite. Rates include breakfast. Pets allowed with restrictions; call first ($50 per stay). **Amenities:** Restaurant; pub; Wi-Fi (free).

Where to Eat in Middlebury

In addition to the eateries listed below, Middlebury possesses an abundance of delis, sandwich shops, and the like—perfect for a quick lunch or a picnic.

Tops among these is **Costello's** (9 Maple St., in the Marble Work complex; www.costellosmarket.com; ⓒ **802/388-3385**), an Italian deli to rival any in New York or New Jersey. Takeout subs, with names like "The Soprano" and "The Don Corleone" (take the "Fredo" fishing, if you dare) bulge with delicious Italian cold cuts and cheeses; prices run from $8.95 to $13.

Fire and Ice ★ AMERICAN   Done up in the Busy Americana look—there's even a speedboat in the lobby—this Middlebury institution ticks off the usual steak, chops, chicken, seafood and pasta boxes, but the best reason to drop by is for the salad bar and prime rib. The former is an unlimited-trip extravaganza featuring shrimp, vegetable "sushi," and a fresh-baked bread bar (don't fill up on it, as Mom warned), while the latter comes in three sizes, culminating in a nearly 2-pound bone-in leviathan. The attached **Big Moose Pub** offers a burger-intensive menu, also available in the restaurant at lunch.

26 Seymour St., Middlebury. www.fireandicerestaurant.com. ⓒ **800/367-7166.** Main courses $22–$35; lunch and pub items $15–$18. Mon–Thurs 5–9pm; Fri–Sat noon–10pm; Sun noon–9pm.

Jessica's at the Swift House Inn ★★ AMERICAN   This restaurant consists of two dining rooms on the ground floor of the main inn (see p. 522). Since coming on board, chef Rob Fenn has brought the menu back to its American roots, after several years of Continental leanings. You might start with panko-crusted crab cakes, or a shaved Brussels sprout salad with bacon and almonds; then move on to slow-braised pork shank with white beans, pan-roasted salmon, or seared duck breast kissed with a cherry gastrique and accompanied by duck confit. Vegetarian offerings are several cuts above the usual, with a five-cheese gluten-free ravioli and Portobello mushroom Wellington. Ice cream (salted caramel!) is made in-house, and the banana bread pudding is ambrosial. Vermont and New Hampshire artisanal cheeses are served mix and match, at $3 the selection. Some tables in the dining room look out onto the inn's grounds—and, by default, sunset over the mountains to the west. Ask for one.

25 Stewart Lane, Middlebury. www.jessicasvermont.com. ⓒ **802/388-9925.** Reservations recommended. Main courses $16–$31. Wed–Sun 5:30–9pm (Thurs–Sun only Jan–May).

The Storm Cafe ★★ NEW AMERICAN   Popular with locals and travelers alike, this tiny, casual chef-owned spot has great river views on the ground floor of a stone mill near the downtown Otter Creek waterfall. The menu is simple, but great care is taken in the selection of ingredients and cooking. Salads are especially good, with the pear and gorgonzola a standout. Interesting lunch selections include "The Berber" (pan-fried salmon in African spices on a baguette, with lemon aioli), and a spicy pile of Prince Edward Island mussels steamed in wine. Dinner brings appetizers and main courses of roasted garlic and potato soup; cod with sundried tomatoes, roasted eggplant, and spinach; and locally raised chicken with pesto, roasted red peppers, and wild mushrooms. There's a tiny wine list, too. And the Storm is now open for break-fast. Ultrafancy this place is not, but locals enjoy it, and for good reason.

3 Mill St., Middlebury. www.thestormcafe.com. © **802/388-1063.** Reservations recommended. Main courses $9–$10 lunch, $20–$31 dinner. Tues–Sat 9am–2:30pm; Sun 9am–2pm. Dinner Fri and Sat 5–8pm.

THE MAD RIVER VALLEY ★★

Warren: 3 miles S of Waitsfield; 205 miles NW of Boston; 43 miles SE of Burlington

Save for a couple of telltale signs, you could drive Route 100 through **Warren** and **Waitsfield** and never realize you're just a couple miles downhill from some of the choicest skiing in the entire state. There's no rampant condo or strip-mall development here—the valley seems to have learned from the sprawl that afflicts such resort areas as Mount Snow and Killington. (Even the Mad River Green, a tidy strip mall on Route 100 just north of Route 17, is disguised as an old barn; it's scarcely noticeable from the main road.) Some Vermont travelers say the valley still looks much like the Stowe of 30 years ago. That's a good thing.

The region's character becomes less pastoral along the access road to the Sugarbush ski resort, however; at least the best inns and restaurants tend to be tucked back into the forest or set along rushing streams. Make sure you get good directions before setting out in search of accommodations or food in this valley, and try not to do so at night unless absolutely necessary—hardly any of the roads in this part of Vermont are lit by streetlights. (That's why you're in Vermont, remember?)

Hidden up a winding valley road, Mad River Glen, the area's older ski area, has a pleasantly dated quality that pointedly sticks a thumb in the eye of rock-stardom (we're looking at you, Sugarbush and Killington). It has an almost crunchy granola sort of charm, cute and unprepossessing, and it's many Vermonters' favorite ski hill for that very reason.

Essentials

ARRIVING

Warren and Waitsfield are close to each other on Route 100, north of Killington and south of Waterbury—figure on almost an hour's drive from either Burlington or Killington. The quickest access from a major interstate is via exit 10 (Waterbury/Stowe) off I-89; then you drive about 20 miles south on Route 100 until you hit Waitsfield. Warren is 5 or 6 more miles down the same road.

VISITOR INFORMATION

The **Mad River Valley Chamber of Commerce** (www.madrivervalley.com; © **802/469-3409**) is at 4601 Main St. (that's Route 100) in Waitsfield, inside the General Wait House, which is next to the elementary school. It's open daily during regular business hours in summer, foliage season, and ski season; during slower times of the year, it sometimes closes weekends, or closes earlier.

Skiing

Mad River Glen ★★ Mad River Glen is at once the radical dude and the Zen master of Vermont's skiing universe—a place whose motto is still "Ski it if you can!" High-speed detachable quad chairs? Forget it; up until 2007, the main lift here was a 1948 single-chair lift that slowly creaked its way a mile up to the summit. Snowmaking? Very little, and not a whole lot of grooming, either. This hill functions according to the whims of Mother Nature. Snowboarding? No, it's forbidden. Gourmet restaurants? A lodge? Toll-free number? Fancy website? No, no, no, and definitely not. Mad River long ago attained cult status among "soul skiers" (for lack of a better term), and its fans seem determined to keep it this way. Owned and operated by a cooperative since 1995, it claims to be the only cooperatively owned ski area in the country—you can even buy a small share of the resort yourself, and get discounts on tickets afterward. But don't mistake this gentler approach for easier skiing; the slopes here are twisting and narrow, hiding some of the steepest drops in New England. (Nearly half of Mad River's runs are classified as "expert.") A ski school, kids' program, and telemarking classes are all offered, and care is taken to both preserve and explain the mountain's ecology. Tickets are pretty affordable, too, especially midweek. A renegade spirit perseveres here, even in the face of the sport's (and Vermont's) inexorable upscaling process. If you're interested in a different skiing experience, or one that's more "ecotouristy," this is it.

PO Box 1089, Waitsfield. www.madriverglen.com. ✆ **802/496-3551.** Day lift tickets $89 adults, half-day $59; discounts for youths and seniors.

Sugarbush ★★ Now more than a half-century old, Sugarbush is a fine intermediate-to-advanced ski resort comprising several mountains linked by a long, high-speed chairlift that crosses several ridges. (A shuttle bus offers a warmer way to traverse the hills, and the resort also recently acquired a "Snow Cat" transporter.) The number of high-speed lifts, plus the excellent snowmaking, makes this a desirable destination for serious skiers—and there have been serious improvements over the past two decades. But this is not Killington. The "Bush" remains a pretty low-key area with great intermediate cruising runs on its north slopes and challenging, old-fashioned expert slopes on Castlerock Peak. Mount Ellen features a terrain pipe and half-pipe, and the resort has made "green" strides by fueling all its equipment and shuttle buses with biodiesel (vegetable oil and/or reused waste oil). This is a good choice if you seek great, exciting skiing but find Killington's sprawl a little overwhelming.

102 Forest Dr., Warren. www.sugarbush.com. ✆ **800/537-8427** or 802/583-6300. Day lift tickets $119–$129 adults, half-day $99–$108; discounts for youths and seniors.

Outdoor Activities

A rewarding 14-mile **bike trip ★★** along paved roads begins at the village of Waitsfield. Park near the covered bridge, then follow East Warren Road past the Inn at Round Barn Farm and up into hilly, farm-filled countryside. (Don't be discouraged by the long hill at the outset.) Near the village center of War-ren, turn right at Brook Road to connect to Route 100. Return north on bus-tling but scenic Route 10 to Waitsfield, minding the traffic carefully.

Clearwater Sports, at 4147 Main St. (Route 100) in Waitsfield, north of the covered bridge (www.clearwatersports.com; ✆ **802/496-2708**), has rented mountain bikes, snowshoes, kayaks, and skis out of a blue-and-white Victo-rian-era house since 1975; these folks are well-liked locally. Staff members are helpful, offering suggestions for routes and tours. The shop is open daily, year-round, and offers shuttle service for canoe and kayak rentals.

Where to Stay in Mad River

In addition to the choices listed below, Sugarbush has condos to rent—call the resort's main switchboard at ✆ **800/537-8427** and ask for lodging services.

Inn at the Mad River Barn ★ This classic 1960s-style ski lodge attracts a clientele that's nearly fanatical in its devotion to the place. One reason might be its charismatic former owner Betsy Pratt, who co-owned the Mad River Glen ski area before she created (and then sold it to) the cooperative that runs the mountain now. She's since sold the inn as well, to Andrew and Heather Lynds, who have maintained its distinctive and eclectic character. Accommo-dations are in a two-story barn behind the white clapboard main house, and in an annex building that trades a bit of character for a more upscale feel. *Don't* come expecting a fancy place—furnishings are simple and rustic—but rather to relax in a ski-lodge/aunt's-home/youth-hostel-like atmosphere. It's all knotty pine and Americana here; the spartan guest rooms (there are no phones in the rooms) and countrified common spaces (a mounted moose head by the stone fireplace, for instance) get visitors feeling at ease right away. The inn restaurant serves a hearty, hungry-after-skiing menu, and there's a chummy little pub.

2849 Mill Brook Rd. (Rte. 17), Waitsfield. www.madriverbarn.com. ✆ **802/496-3310.** 18 units. $130–$155 double; holiday rates higher. Rates include breakfast. 2-night mini-mum stay holidays and Fri–Sat in winter. **Amenities:** Restaurant and pub; exercise room; game room; sauna; fridge (some units); Wi-Fi (most units; free).

Inn at the Round Barn Farm ★★ Appropriately enough, you arrive via a covered bridge. It doesn't get much more Vermont than this—a classic farmhouse and a big round barn, wearing its century-plus age gracefully, all set on 235 pillowy acres with views in all directions. Guest rooms in the house (the barn is a venue for weddings, art shows, even church services) are fur-nished in an elegant, understated country style with wingback chairs, poster beds, love seats, marble gas fireplaces, and luxe trimmings. The less expen-sive units in the older section of the home are comfortable, if comparatively small; the larger luxury units sport soaring ceilings beneath old log beams, and include such extras as Jacuzzis, gas fireplaces, and cable televisions. There's also one suite (the Abbott), with CD and DVD players, a steam shower, Jacuzzi, and pullout sofa bed. There's no restaurant—not even a bar—and some rooms don't have phones, but you'll love the place anyway.

1661 E. Warren Rd., Waitsfield. www.theroundbarn.com. ✆ **802/496-2276.** 12 units. $179–$289 double; $359 suite. Rates include breakfast. 3-night minimum stay during holidays and foliage season. Closed Apr 15–30. Children 15 and over welcome. **Amenities:** Indoor pool; cross-country ski center; Wi-Fi (most units; free).

The Pitcher Inn ★★★

Every ski-and-foliage mecca in New England has one inn that outdoes all its neighbors in luxury, decor, amenities, dining . . . and price. In the Warren-Waitsfield area, it's the Pitcher Inn. Set in the tiny but picturesque village of Warren, the business *and* inn were rebuilt from the ground up after a 1993 fire, which gave local architect David Sellers the opportunity to create a space seamlessly blending modern convenience, whimsy, and classic New England decor. Inside, all 11 "themed" rooms share a gracefulness and a sense of humor—each is like a miniature installation of art and artifacts appropriate to the overall upcountry aesthetic. The carved goose on the ceiling of the Mallard Room (we know, Mallards are ducks), for example, is attached to a weathervane on the roof; it rotates with the vane. The Trout Room feels like a riverside campground with its antique oars, a desk for fly-tying, a porch extending over a rushing steam, and a fireplace of river stones. The Mountain Room has antique snowshoes and a rustic fireplace. Most rooms have wood-burning or gas fireplaces, all have Jacuzzis, and most have steam showers; among the choices are a pair of two-bedroom suites in the barn.

275 Main St., Warren. www.pitcherinn.com. ✆ **802/496-6350.** 11 units. $375–$725 doubles. Rates include breakfast and afternoon tea. 2-night minimum stay Sat–Sun; 3-night minimum holiday weekends; 5-night minimum at Christmas. Children 15 and under accepted in suites only. **Amenities:** Restaurant; spa; Jacuzzi; babysitting; room service; Wi-Fi (free).

West Hill House ★★

Guests consistently rank this small, cozy B&B as one of the best in Vermont. Innkeepers Peter and Susan MacLaren have taken advantage of their quiet country-road location to provide one of the most relaxed inn experiences in the Mad River valley, just a few minutes from the slopes of Sugarbush. Built in the 1850s, the farmhouse boasts three common rooms, including a bright, modern addition with a handsome fireplace, an outdoor patio, and a game room with a pool table. Guest rooms are decorated in an updated country style—updated meaning air-conditioning, memory-foam mattresses on the beds, gas fireplaces or woodstoves, and steam showers or Jacuzzis. The Paris Suite, inspired by the MacLarens' time living near Versailles, is the prettiest. The owners are unfailingly kind, even supplying snowshoes in winter, while in summer they maintain lovely perennial gardens and ponds.

1496 W. Hill Rd., Warren. www.westhillbb.com. ✆ **802/496-7162.** 9 units. $140–$295 double; $210–$260 suite. Rates include breakfast. 3-night minimum stay foliage and holiday weekends; 2-night minimum Fri–Sat. Children 12 and over welcome. **Amenities:** Honor-system bar; Wi-Fi (free).

Where to Eat in Mad River

On Friday and Saturday nights, **American Flatbread ★★**, on Route 100 in Waitsfield (www.americanflatbread.com; ✆ **802/496-8856**), serves terrific-tasting, organic-flour pizzas from 5:30 to 9pm. Founder George Schenk's delicious vision of pizza-as-whole-food has since been expanded to a small, thriving northern New England chain and frozen-pizza operation; this place is where it all started. Get there up to an hour early and put your name on the waiting list; no reservations are taken. The chef also creates inventive weekly salad and non-pizza entree specials.

You can pick up thick, inexpensive sandwiches on fresh bread at most any country store in the area, such as the **Warren Store** (www.warrenstore.com; ✆ **802/496-3864**), on Main Street in Warren. Just up Route 100 in Waitsfield, a good spot for a hearty informal meal is **The Big Picture Café and Theater** (www.bigpicturetheater.info; ✆ **802/496-8994**), where "dinner and a show" means sauntering across the lobby separating the homey restaurant from a movie house showing first-run films. It's open daily for breakfast and lunch, and for dinner Tuesday through Saturday from 5pm to 9pm.

For a fancy meal, the restaurant at the **Pitcher Inn ★★** (see p. 527) is superlative, and many other area inns also open their kitchens to the public.

Chez Henri ★★ FRENCH   Back in the early 1960s, Henri Borel came to Sugarbush from France to manage a ski club. In 1964 he opened Chez Henri on the resort's access road, and the restaurant—and Henri, now in his early nineties—have been going strong ever since. This is the last place in Vermont where you can find the old-time religion of French provincial cuisine, from bouillabaisse to *poulet provençal* (chicken with tomatoes, garlic, and white wine); from escargot in puff pastry to filet of beef au poivre with Béarnaise sauce. The bistro menu is no less traditional, featuring cheese fondue, onion soup, mussels in cream and wine, and a *croque monsieur.* Of course there's crusty French bread, a wine bar, and a big roaring fireplace. Sadly, Henri only keeps his place open during ski season, when he still hits the trails himself.

80 Sugarbush Village Rd. www.chezhenrisugarbush.com. ✆ **802/583-2600.** Main courses $26–$38. Daily in winter 11:30am "til closing."

The Hyde Away ★ AMERICAN   Located on the winding route that leads to Mad River Glen, this inn has a ski-club atmosphere—nine guest rooms attract the Mad River "Ski It If You Can" crowd—as well as a cheery tavern with a big stone fireplace and a slew of Vermont craft beers, and a restaurant several cuts above the access-road standard. Locally produced provender (OK, not in the tuna tartare) takes the fore, in dishes such as a cheese and charcuterie plate, Misty Knoll chicken breast in a maple *beurre blanc,* and steak frites featuring beef from nearby Neill Farm. Wednesday is Italian night, BBQ ribs star on Thursday, and Tuesday tacos are $2.50 a pop. Sandwiches, burgers (beef or elk), and a beef brisket poutine might accompany your microbrew in the tavern. Dining on the patio in season.

1428 Mill Brook Rd. (Rte. 17). www.hydeawayinn.com. ✆ **802/496-2322.** Main courses $18–$27. Daily 5–10pm (tavern from 4pm).

MONTPELIER ★★, BARRE & WATERBURY

Montpelier: 178 miles NW of Boston; 39 miles SE of Burlington. Barre: 9 miles SE of Montpelier. Waterbury: 13 miles NW of Montpelier.

Montpelier might be the most down-home, low-key state capital in the nation (and it's definitely the one with the smallest population). The glistening gold dome of Vermont's capitol building is practically the only showy or pretentious thing in the entire city; behind it, there's no cluster of mirror-sided skyscrapers, but rather a thickly forested hill. Montpelier, it turns out, isn't a self-important center of politics; it's just a small town that happened to become the home of state government.

Restaurants, coffee shops, and cultural offerings have flowed here as a result, and it's an agreeable place to pass an afternoon or stay the night if you want to know how small-town Vermont ticks. The city is centered around two main boulevards: State Street, lined with handsome government buildings; and Main Street, where many of the town's stores and restaurants are found. Everything's compact here. The downtown sports a pair of hardware stores, decent small-town shopping, and one of the best art movie houses in northern New England: the **Savoy Theater** (www.savoytheater.com; ✆ **802/229-0598**), where concession prices are almost criminally low.

Nearby **Barre** (pronounced "Barry") is more commercial and less charming, with a blue-collar, workaday feel. It remains the hub of Vermont's granite quarrying industry—you can still see granite curbstones lining Barre's long Main Street, not to mention signs for many businesses carved from it. Barre attracted talented stone workers from Italy and Scotland (there's a statue of Robert Burns here), who helped give the turn-of-the-20th-century town a lively, cosmopolitan flavor.

About 10 miles west of Montpelier, **Waterbury** ★ is at the junction of Route 100 and I-89, making it a commercial center by default if not by design. Set along the Winooski River, it has sprawled along the valley more than other Vermont towns, largely because it has attracted an impressive number of food companies (Ben & Jerry's ice-cream empire, Keurig Green Mountain Coffee's big-time java business, Cold Hollow Cider Mill's cider operations, and several craft breweries) that have built factories and outlets in what were once dairy pastures. Despite its drive-through quality, Waterbury makes a decent overnight base for further explorations of the Green Mountains, Burlington (just 25 miles west), or nearby Montpelier.

Essentials

ARRIVING

Montpelier is accessible by car via exit 7 off I-89. For Barre, take exit 8; Waterbury is just south of exit 10 (the same exit as Stowe). Burlington's airport, with daily flights from New York, is about 45 miles away by car.

TASTE OF SUCCESS: THE STORY OF ben & jerry

A clutch of doleful cows standing amid a bright green meadow on Ben & Jerry's ice-cream pints have almost become *the* symbol of Vermont, but Ben & Jerry's cows—actually, they're Vermont artist Woody Jackson's cows—also symbolize friendly capitalism (or "hippie capitalism," as some prefer).

The founding of this company is legend in small-business circles. Two friends from Long Island, Ben Cohen and Jerry Greenfield, started the company in Burlington in 1978 with $12,000 and a few mail-order lessons in ice-cream making. The pair experimented with flavor samples obtained free from salesmen, and sold their product out of an old downtown gas station.

Embracing the outlook that work should be fun, they gave away free ice cream at community events, staged outdoor movies in summer, and plowed profits back into their local community. This free-spirited approach, plus the exceptional quality of the product—their machines stir out most of the air bubbles as the ice cream freezes, creating a denser ice cream that's more expensive to manufacture—built a hugely successful corporation.

Since then, they've faced tough competition from a zillion other upstart gourmet ice-cream makers, plus a gradual national shift toward healthier diets. Yet Ben and Jerry are still at it. Though the friends sold their interest to the huge multinational food concern Unilever—a move that raised not a few eyebrows among its grassroots investors—its heart and soul (and manufacturing operations) remain squarely in Vermont.

The **main factory** in Waterbury might be Vermont's most popular tourist attraction. The plant is located about a mile north of I-89 on Route 100, and the grounds have almost a Woodstockian feel to them. During summer, crowds arrive early, milling about and making new friends while waiting for the half-hour **factory tours** to begin. Tours are first-come, first-served, and run at least every 30 minutes from 9am to 9pm from July to mid-August (last tour departs at 8pm). Tour hours are shorter the rest of the year, but they're always running from at least 10am to 5pm. Afternoon tours fill up quickly, so get there early to avoid a long wait.

Once you've got your ticket, browse the small museum (learn the long, strange history of Cherry Garcia), buy a cone of your favorite flavor at the scoop shop, or lounge along a promenade scattered with Adirondack chairs and picnic tables. Tours cost $4 for adults, $3 for kids and seniors, and free for kids 12 and under. There's also a package deal where you get a tour, a half-hour session helping out in the Flavor Lab, a T-shirt, a cone, and a pint of the good stuff for $125. (That was probably the boys' first week's take at the gas station.) Kids can enjoy the "Stairway to Heaven," which leads to a playground, and a "Cow-Viewing Area," which is self-explanatory. The tours are informative and fun, and conclude with a sample of the day's featured product. For more information, go to www.ben jerry.com or call ✆ **802/882-2047.**

Amtrak (www.amtrak.com; ✆ **800/872-7245**) runs one daily train (the Vermonter) from New York City to Montpelier. The trip takes a long 8 hours, and costs $71. The train also stops in Waterbury.

Greyhound (www.greyhound.com; ✆ **800/231-2222**) runs buses to Montpelier as well. From New York City, the ride takes 8 hours (change buses in White River Junction) and costs about $64 to $83 one-way; from Boston, it's a 4-hour ride costing about $23 to $33 each way.

VISITOR INFORMATION

The **Central Vermont Chamber of Commerce** (www.central-vt.com; ℂ **802/229-5711**) is on Stewart Road in Barre, just off exit 7 of I-89. Turn left at the first light; it's a half-mile farther on the left. The chamber is open weekdays from 9am to 5pm.

Exploring Montpelier

Start your exploration of Montpelier with a visit to the gold-domed **State House** ★ at 115 State St. (ℂ **802/828-2228**), guarded out front by a statue of Ethan Allen. Three capitol buildings have risen on this site since 1809; the present building retained the portico designed during the height of Greek Revival style in 1836. Modeled after the temple of Theseus in Athens, it's made of Vermont granite (of course). You can take a self-guided tour anytime the capitol is open, any weekday (except holidays) from 8am to 4pm. Free guided tours are offered every half-hour between late June and mid-October, Monday through Friday from 10am to 3:30pm and Saturday from 11am to 2:30pm. The informative and fun tour is worthwhile if you're in the area, but not worth a major detour.

Next door to the State House is the **Vermont Historical Society Museum** (www.vermonthistory.org; ℂ **802/828-2291**) at 109 State St. The museum is housed in a brick replica of the elegant old Pavilion Building, a once-prominent Victorian hotel, and contains artifacts relating to three centuries of Vermont history. From May through mid-October, it's open Tuesday to Saturday from 10am to 4pm. Admission is $7 for adults, $5 for students or seniors, and $20 for families. There's also a gift shop. The Society also operates the **Vermont History Center** (60 Washington St.; Barre; ℂ **802/479-8500**), with similar hours and admission fees. The Center offers a series of special exhibits—one recent show chronicled the influence of the counterculture on 1970s Vermont.

Where to Stay in the Montpelier Area

MONTPELIER

Capitol Plaza Hotel ★   The favorite hotel of folks here to do business with the state government (those may be lobbyists you see in the lobby), this four-story brick hotel stands right across from the capitol and makes a good base for visitors. The first floor houses a decent restaurant (see p. 532); guest rooms on the three upper floors adopt a light, faux-Colonial tone and have more amenities than you might expect. It has the feel of a place best suited for conventions—clean, comfortable, and convenient, nothing more; the big attraction is location, since you're here to explore Montpelier, not luxuriate in an inn. The more expensive rooms add wingback chairs, Ralph Lauren bedding, and high-speed Internet access, while three still-fancier suites add Jacuzzis, fridges, sofas, and bigger televisions.

100 State St., Montpelier. www.capitolplaza.com. ℂ **800/274-5252** or 802/223-5252. 56 units. $185–$335 double and suite; foliage season higher. **Amenities:** Restaurant; Wi-Fi (free).

WATERBURY

The Old Stagecoach Inn ★ This columned and gabled home, within walking distance of Waterbury's downtown, is full of interesting detailing: painted wood floors, two porches, an old library with a stamped tin ceiling, and a chessboard. Built in 1826, the house was gutted and revamped in 1890 in ostentatious period style by an Ohio millionaire. After years of disuse, it was converted to an inn in the late 1980s by owners who preserved the home's historical touches; there are still Oriental rugs, an organ, a tapestry, and a parrot. Eight guest rooms and three suites are furnished mostly in oak and pine furniture and antiques. This isn't a polished, luxury-inn experience in any way, but the price is right if you're looking to save, and the full breakfasts are good. Two third-floor rooms show off original exposed beams and skylights, while three back rooms share one bathroom and feel a bit more like paying to stay in some family's farmhouse than an actual vacation. (Unlike the Stagecoach, though, that family won't have a bar in their library.)

18 N. Main St., Waterbury. www.oldstagecoach.com. © **802/244-5056.** 12 units (3 w/ shared bath). $100–$120 double with shared bath; $150–$170 double with private bath. Rates include breakfast. 2-night minimum stay and higher rates during foliage season and holidays. **Amenities:** Bar; Wi-Fi (free).

Where to Eat in the Montpelier Area

Unlike good beds, dining options in Montpelier are many and varied. That's largely due to the influence of the wonderful New England Culinary Institute (NECI) campus on the edge of town. **La Brioche Bakery & Café,** 89 Main St. (© **802/229-0443**), which is essentially NECI's pastry laboratory, occupies a key corner at State and Main streets. A deli counter here offers baked goods such as croissants and baguettes. Get them to go, or settle into a table in the afternoon sun outdoors. It's open daily from as early as 6am, usually until 6pm (to 2pm Sundays).

Another spot to while away an hour is the cleverly named **Capitol Grounds** ★, at 27 State St. (www.capitolgrounds.com; © **802/223-7800**), a stone's throw from the gold dome of the state capitol building.

MONTPELIER

J. Morgan's ★ AMERICAN Just when you've come to expect Vermont restaurants to sport that rustic counterculture look, here's a place that would look at home in a big city, even a big state capital. Settle into a plush banquette and select from a true steakhouse menu, featuring classic New York strip (with or without bone), Porterhouse, rib-eye dry-rubbed with Montreal seasoning or dried porcini, filet mignon, and a monster cowboy bone-in rib-eye—pork and veal chops, too. For a side, order the "Millionaire's baked potato," a spud studded with lobster, crab, shrimp, bacon, and four-cheese sauce. Burgers dominate the lunch menu, but don't overlook flatbreads, quesadillas, and the "Crazy BLT" glorified with brie and avocado. The wine list is extensive and quite reasonable. Sunday brunch is the best in town, and, this being a hotel restaurant, there's breakfast each weekday.

100 State St., Montpelier. www.capitolplaza.com. (C) **802/223-5222.** Main courses $22–$42; lunch items $10–$22. Open daily. Lunch 11am–2pm; dinner 4–9pm; Sat breakfast buffet 7am–noon; Sun brunch 8am–2pm. Breakfast Mon–Fri 7–10: 30am.

Neci on Main ★★ NEW AMERICAN   This modern restaurant serves as a classroom and ongoing exam for students of the New England Culinary Institute. It's not unusual to see knots of students, toques at a rakish angle, walking around. You can eat in the first-level dining room, watching street life through the broad windows, or hang out in the homey bar downstairs. The menu changes often, but keeps a "farm-to-table" thread going throughout the year. Dinner might start with a mushroom ragout tartine or an ambrosial bowl of onion soup, followed by a butter-basted chicken breast with polenta, cod in a tempura-like batter of Vermont ale and chickpea flour, or a two-person (or one very hungry person) prime rib-eye prepared sous vide prior to grilling. A vegetable shepherd's pie tops vegetarian offerings, and there's always a pasta selection. On the lighter side, burgers come in beef, turkey, and meatless versions, all of which can be glorified with—among other toppings—Vermont's celebrated Jasper Hill blue cheese.

118 Main St., Montpelier. www.neci.edu. (C) **802/223-3188.** Main courses $16–$25. Tues–Sat 3:30–5:30pm for light fare; 5:30–9pm for dinner.

Sarducci's ★ ITALIAN   The only top-drawer Italian restaurant for miles around may or may not have been named after *Saturday Night Live* character Father Guido Sarducci, but it's a good guess that the worldly Vatican gossip columnist would have appreciated his namesake's hearty menu. Start with a copious antipasto, or maybe polenta with a creamy sauce of sun-dried tomato and mushroom; move along to penne Bolognese; capellini with spinach, artichokes, olives, tomatoes, and goat cheese; or one of several pasta and seafood combinations. The big wood-burning pizza oven doubles as the cooker for baked penne with sausage, peppers, mushrooms, and mozzarella; spinach ravioli in a mushroom cream sauce; and other specialties. Sit in the main dining room, and you can enjoy the glow of the oven; or take a table on the enclosed porch, and watch the Winooski River flow by.

3 Main St., Montpelier. www.sarduccis.com. (C) **802/223-6003.** Main courses $10–$13 at lunch; $11–$23 at dinner. Pizzas $10–$12; gluten free extra. Mon–Thurs 11:30am–9pm; Fri–Sat 11:30am–9:30pm; Sun 4–9pm.

WATERBURY

Hen of the Wood ★★★ NEW AMERICAN   Since 2005, Chef Eric Warnstedt has made this open-kitchen concept restaurant into one of the premier dining destinations in Vermont. The menu, divided between small and large plates, changes daily; while it leans on ideas borrowed from France and Italy, most of the preparations are solidly New American: scallops crudo; a board of local bread, cheese, and prosciutto; fried rabbit with sunchoke and smoked crème fraiche; grass-fed rib-eye steaks with a tarragon-inflected aioli; and short ribs braised in red wine. There are also plenty of artisanal cheeses to sample here—the place is practically a master class in the modern art of Vermont cheesemaking—plus a long wine list. There's a Burlington branch, too, at 55 Cherry Street (© **802/540-0534**).

92 Stowe St., Waterbury. www.henofthewood.com. © **802/244-7300.** Reservations recommended. Main courses $22–$35. Tues–Sat 5–9pm.

Prohibition Pig ★ AMERICAN   In recent years Waterbury has become the capital of Vermont's craft beer scene (the state now has some 60 breweries, the most per capita in the U.S.), and "The Pig" builds its menu around suds from its own brewing operation, located on nearby Elm Street (you can drop by daily; © **802/244-4120**). What goes with the house brews? At lunch, look for pork rinds, chips, quesadillas, burgers, and burritos; come dinnertime, tuck into mac and cheese, poutine made with duck fat fries, and the house specialty, beef brisket dry-rubbed, smoked for 12 hours, and served with bacon BBQ sauce. Also emerging from the smoker are half chickens, and pork shoulder served chopped and vinegary, North Carolina-style. To wash it all down, count on at least a dozen Pig beer offerings—plus selections from other Vermont breweries, including legendary Hill Farmstead.

23 South Main St., Waterbury. www.prohibitionpig.com. © **802/244-4120.** Main courses $8–$12 at lunch; $17–$21 at dinner. Mon–Thurs 4–10pm; Fri–Sun 11:30am–10pm.

STOWE

Stowe: 10 miles N of Waterbury, 35 miles E of Burlington, 75 miles NE of White River Junction

There's no other place in Vermont quite like Stowe. A wonderful destination in summer, fall, or winter—and one of Vermont's original winter-vacation resorts—it's set in beautiful hills beneath bigger mountains. Yet it's also struggling with growing pains, as condo developments and strip-mall-style restaurants have arrived en masse. The village's main street has mostly preserved its New England character and great views of the surrounding mountains and farmlands, but this is one of the few places in the state where you'll find yourself cursing out traffic as a 2-mile line snakes through the center of town on a weekend.

Most attractions are strung out along Mountain Road (Route 108), which runs from the village center all the way to the base of Mount Mansfield and the Stowe ski resort, and a free trolley bus connects the village with the mountain during ski season (mid-December to March). Not a skier? That's okay; you can still play. Mount Mansfield (Vermont's tallest) is a lovely driving or hiking trip, ablaze with foliage in fall to photograph and full of plenty of rewarding views in summer. Smugglers' Notch is one of New England's most fun passes to squeeze your car through. And the concentration of resorts here rivals anywhere else in New England. Period.

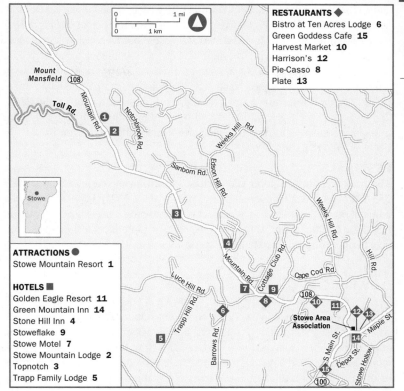

RESTAURANTS ◆
Bistro at Ten Acres Lodge **6**
Green Goddess Cafe **15**
Harvest Market **10**
Harrison's **12**
Pie-Casso **8**
Plate **13**

ATTRACTIONS ●
Stowe Mountain Resort **1**

HOTELS ■
Golden Eagle Resort **11**
Green Mountain Inn **14**
Stone Hill Inn **4**
Stoweflake **9**
Stowe Motel **7**
Stowe Mountain Lodge **2**
Topnotch **3**
Trapp Family Lodge **5**

Essentials

ARRIVING

Stowe is on Route 100, about 10 miles north of Waterbury; simply take I-89 to exit 10 and head north, continuing past all the tourist stuff until you reach the village center. In summer, Stowe can also be reached from Burlington or Montpelier (after some back-roading) via Smugglers' Notch on Route 108. This scenic pass, which squeezes narrowly between rocks, is not recommended for RVs or trailers, but it is one of the state's most scenic drives. The pass is closed in winter, and absolutely packed with parked cars on both shoulders (try squeezing past that) in October.

Stowe has no direct train or bus service, though **Amtrak**'s (www.amtrak. com; ℂ **800/872-7245**) Vermonter service does make one daily run from New York City to Waterbury, 10 miles away. The ride takes nearly 9 hours and costs $71 one-way. Once there, though, you'll probably have to call a local taxi.

VISITOR INFORMATION

The **Stowe Area Association** (www.gostowe.com; ℂ **802/253-7321**) maintains a great, professional **tourist information office** right in the village center at 51 Main St. It's open 9am to 8pm weekdays, plus 10am to 5pm weekends during summer, fall-foliage season, and winter ski season (during other seasons, weekend hours are more limited). The staff here can help you book a room even on short notice, give you enough maps and brochures to keep you reading all week long, and point you to a good restaurant. They also maintain clean bathrooms.

The **Green Mountain Club** (www.greenmountainclub.org; ℂ **802/244-7037**), a statewide association devoted to building and maintaining walking trails in the mountains, has its headquarters and visitor center on Route 100 between Waterbury and Stowe.

FESTIVALS

The weeklong **Stowe Winter Carnival** (www.stowewintercarnival.com; ℂ **802/253-7321**) has been held annually in January since 1921. The fest features a number of wacky events involving skis, snowshoes, and skates, as well as nighttime entertainment. Don't miss the snow-sculpture contest or snow golf, played on a snow-covered course.

Skiing

DOWNHILL

Stowe Mountain Resort ★★★   Stowe was one of the first ski resorts in the U.S. when it opened in the 1930s. Its regional dominance has eroded somewhat over the years since—Killington, Sunday River, and Sugarloaf, among other resorts, have snagged big shares of the New England ski market, and iconic hills like Mad River and Jay Peak have carved out niches, too. But this resort still has loads of charm and plenty of excellent runs, and it's one of the best places to get that full New England ski experience: a combination of beautiful ski trails and pastoral Vermont views. This is a tremendous challenge for advanced skiers, with winding, old-style trails—especially notable are the legendary "Front Four" trails (National, Starr, Lift Line, and Goat), which have humbled more than a handful of folks. The mountain also has several good, long lifts that go all the way from bottom to top—not the usual patchwork of shorter lifts you find at many other ski areas. For après-ski, the resort operates the very tony **Stowe Mountain Lodge** (see p. 540) and maintains a couple of upscale restaurants with bar areas—not to mention the obligatory spa.

5781 Mountain Rd., Stowe. www.stowe.com. ℂ **888/253-4849** or 802/253-3000. Day lift tickets $99 adults; discounts for youths and seniors.

CROSS-COUNTRY

The **Trapp Family Lodge Nordic Ski Center ★★** (www.trappfamily.com; ℂ **800/826-7000** or 802/253-5755) on Luce Hill Road was the nation's first cross-country ski center. It remains one of the most gloriously situated in the Northeast, set atop a ridge with views across the broad valley and into the folds of mountains flanking Mount Mansfield. The center maintains some 30 miles of groomed trails (plus perhaps another 60 miles of natural backcountry trails) on 2,700 acres of rolling forestland; basically, for the cross-country ski nut, this is sheer heaven. Rates are $25 per adult for a full-day trail pass (less for kids and half-days), and $25 per day to rent skis.

There's also good ski touring at the **Stowe Mountain Resort Cross-Country Touring Center** (www.stowe.com; ℂ **888/253-4849** or 802/253-3000), with about 20 miles of groomed trails and 25 miles of backcountry trails at the base of Mount Mansfield. Full-day passes cost $28 for adults, $24 half-day; about half that much for kids ages 6 to 12; private and group lessons are also available here.

Summer Outdoor Activities

Stowe's name is synonymous with winter recreation, but it's also a delightful summer destination. The area's lush, rolling hills are great for hiking and biking—and all of it's towered over by craggy Mount Mansfield, Vermont's highest peak.

Besides going to the top of Mount Mansfield (see box below), a popular local attraction is the **Stowe Recreation Path ★★**, winding for more than 5 miles from behind the Stowe Community Church in the village and up the valley toward the big mountain, ending behind the Topnotch Tennis Center. This appealing pathway is heavily used by local walkers, hikers, and bikers in summer; in winter it becomes an equally popular cross-country ski trail. Get onto the pathway at either end, or at points where it crosses side roads leading to Mountain Road. No motorized vehicles or skateboards are allowed.

THREE WAYS TO THE TOP OF mount mansfield

The **auto toll road ★★** (ℂ **802/253-3500**), part of the Stowe Mountain Resort, traces its lineage back to the 19th century, when it served horse-drawn vehicles bringing passengers to a former hotel near the mountain's crown. (That hotel was demolished in the 1960s.) Drivers now twist their way up the road and park in a lot, after which there's still a 2-hour hike along well-marked trails to get to the summit, which offers unforgettable views of Lake Champlain and the Adirondacks. The toll road is open 9am to 4pm from mid-May until mid-October. The fare is a steep $24 per car and driver, plus $9 for each additional passenger age 5 and over. Trailers, RVs, and RV vans are prohibited. Climbing the mountain on foot is free, but bicycles and motorcycles are not allowed.

Another option is the **Stowe gondola ★** (ℂ **802/253-3500**), which whisks visitors to the summit at the Cliff House Restaurant. Hikers can explore the rugged, open ridgeline, and then descend via gondola before twilight. The gondola runs from mid-June to mid-October. The full round-trip costs $29 for adults and $20 for kids ages 5 to 12. There are family discounts, and you can also pay for a one-way ride. The lift is open 10am to 5pm daily in season.

The budget route up Mount Mansfield—the most rewarding, but of course the most physically demanding—is entirely on **foot ★**, with at least nine options for an ascent. This requires a good map. Ask for the Visitor's Guide Hiking Map at Stowe Mountain's guest-services desk, the local tourism office, your inn, or the Green Mountain Club headquarters on Route 100 (about 4 miles south of Stowe's village center)—it's open weekdays, and the GMC can also offer you advice on other area trails.

According to the tourism office, some 300 bikes are available for rental from shops near the Rec Path.

Where to Stay in Stowe

Stowe is blessed with the highest concentration of luxury resorts in New England: There are five in this little village, plus several smaller inns that vault into the ultraluxe category. There are also plenty of basic motels of varying quality along Mountain Road, serving travelers who don't want or need to stay in the resorts.

Golden Eagle Resort ★   The first thing you learn about Stowe is that there isn't all that much to the village—it's a charming 3-block stretch, but it is a three-block stretch. The next thing you learn is that with one major exception—we'll get to that—the big resorts are scattered along Route 108, the Mountain Road that leads to the ski area and Smugglers Notch. Heading out of the village, the first of these is the family-friendly Golden Eagle. Here's the whole package—a children's play area, three swimming pools, two ponds for fishing, a regulation tennis court, 80 acres of private woods laced with hiking trails, and even a small spa offering kids' massages. For adults, the draws are the romantic cottages and suites with fireplaces and whirlpools behind the main building. Standard units are more basic, but some do have sitting areas or porches. The small spa area includes a popular indoor Jacuzzi, and a cafe serves breakfasts built from local provender. Don't come if you're expecting white-glove service, valet parking, or a fancy restaurant; but the Golden Eagle is a fine casual family resort. The hotel also rents out several apartment units with full kitchens and kitchenettes.

511 Mountain Rd., Stowe. www.goldeneagleresort.com. 𝒞 **866/970-0786** or 802/253-4811. 89 units. $149–$229 double; $249–$339 suites and apartments. **Amenities:** Cafe; 3 pools (2 outdoor, 1 indoor); spa; fitness center; tennis court; fridges; Wi-Fi (some units; free).

Green Mountain Inn ★★★   And here's the resort set right in the village—a stately historic inn that dates to way before Stowe discovered skiing (or vice-versa), and became so closely identified with the local snow sports scene that legendary broadcaster and avid skier Lowell Thomas broadcast from here on his winter trips to the area. Guest rooms are spread out among several buildings; rooms are tastefully decorated in a motif befitting the 1833 vintage of the main building, which houses the most traditional (and smaller and simpler) units. More than a dozen units have Jacuzzis and/or gas fireplaces, and the Mill House has rooms with CD players, sofas, and Jacuzzis that open into the bedrooms from behind folding wooden doors. The deluxe Mansfield House adds double Jacuzzis, marble bathrooms, and 36-inch TVs with DVD players. The inn's well-regarded restaurant, **The Whip ★**, is complemented by a more informal tavern eatery.

18 Main St., Stowe. www.greenmountaininn.com. 𝒞 **800/253-7302** or 802/253-7301. 100 units. $149–$389 double; $209–$419 suite; $229–$899 apartments and townhouses. 2-night minimum stay summer and winter weekends and in foliage season. Pets

allowed in some rooms (call ahead; $20 per night). **Amenities:** 2 restaurants; exercise room; Jacuzzi; heated outdoor pool (year-round); limited room service; sauna; steam room; Wi-Fi (free).

Stone Hill Inn ★★   Smallest of the luxe Stowe accommodations options— it only has nine rooms—Stone Hill is contemporary yet romantic. Located partway between Stowe village and the mountain, it's a very fancy place, with top-drawer amenities and furnishings in every room: four-poster king beds, Egyptian cotton towels, and gas fireplaces that front double Jacuzzis in the oversized bathrooms. Suite layouts are all roughly similar, yet each room has a distinct color scheme with fabric and wall hues of gold, purple, bordeaux, and the like. The high-ceilinged common rooms sport fireplaces and billiards tables, while a guest pantry offers complimentary beverages around the clock. Breakfast is served in a bright dining room, and snacks are set out each evening. An outdoor hot tub is good for a relaxing soak, and the inn has snowshoes and a toboggan for guests. Stone Hill hasn't got the sprawl of the bigger Stowe resorts, or the history of the Trapp Family Lodge or the Green Mountain Inn, but it can't be beat for quiet, luxury, and romance.

89 Houston Farm Rd. (off Mountain Rd.), Stowe. www.stonehillinn.com. ✆ **802/253-6282.** 9 units. $295–$450 double. Rates include breakfast. 2-night minimum stay Sat–Sun and foliage season; 3-night minimum stay holiday weekends; 4-night minimum stay Christmas week. Closed Apr and Nov. Not suitable for children. **Amenities:** Jacuzzi, no phones in rooms; Wi-Fi (free).

Stoweflake ★★   This resort with the cutesy name is on Mountain Road en route to the ski resort, less than 2 miles from the village. In terms of setting, facilities, and amenities, it runs neck-and-neck with its nearby competitor, Topnotch (see p. 540). The resort has several categories of guest rooms in two wings; the "standard" and "classic" rooms in the west wing are a bit cozy, okay for an overnight, but you're better off requesting "deluxe," "luxury," or "premier" rooms if you will be staying a few days, as they offer more space and better views. Many of these units have tubs with jets. The spa and fitness facilities have been upgraded, and now include waterfalls and universal soaking pools, along with 30 plush treatment rooms. There's a decent-size fitness room with Cybex equipment, a squash/racquetball court, co-ed Jacuzzi, spinning studio, and a small indoor pool. Stoweflake also manages a small collection of fine town houses nearby (two are dog-friendly; $40 per day extra). All rooms and town houses are wired for either high-speed Internet or Wi-Fi—free of charge.

1746 Mountain Rd, Stowe. www.stoweflake.com. ✆ **800/253-2232** or 802/253-7355. 95 units. Winter, foliage season, and summer $198–$308 double; $408–$766 suites and townhouses; off–season $188–$288 double; $388–$726 suites and townhouses. 2-night minimum stay most weekends; 4-night minimum stay in peak winter season and during holidays. **Amenities:** 2 restaurants; health club; spa; indoor and outdoor pool; racquetball/squash court; 2 tennis courts; bikes; babysitting; children's center; limited room service; Wi-Fi (free).

Stowe Motel and Snowdrift ★   This is one of the very best choices in Stowe if you're traveling on a budget. Units are spread out among three buildings on 16 acres; rooms are basic, but some have couches and coffee tables, and all have small fridges, televisions, and phones. The slightly more expensive efficiency units add two-burner stoves for in-room cooking; some have fireplaces. The place looks like a roadside stop at first glance, but the grounds are surprisingly extensive and include tennis courts, a pool, hammocks, and an outdoor hot tub—quite a deal at the price, especially since continental breakfast is included. They even lend out snowshoes and mountain bikes to guests. If you need more space, the motel rents out a few local houses and apartments nearby, some with hot tubs and washer/dryers.

2043 Mountain Rd., Stowe. www.stowemotel.com. ✆ **800/829-7629** or 802/253-7629. 60 units. $124–$134 double; $139–$159 efficiencies. Pets allowed (1 per room, $10 per night). **Amenities:** Bikes; Jacuzzi; outdoor heated pool; tennis court; fridges; Wi-Fi (free).

The Stowe Mountain Lodge ★

When it opened a decade ago, this resort marked Stowe's entry into the Aspen-Vail lodging echelon (in fact, Vail recently bought the ski area, though not this hotel). The Lodge stands right across from (and a short gondola ride to) the ski lifts on Mount Mansfield; the Spruce Peak lifts are alongside. The Lodge is handsome in the best posh-ski tradition, its public areas scattered with cushy leather armchairs set before massive stone fireplaces in open areas lit by floor-to-ceiling windows; guestrooms are just as grand. Look for 12-foot ceilings, solid and elegant alpine-esque furnishings in woodsy colors, and marble-clad bathrooms. The gym and spa are first-rate: they're spacious and well-equipped, with an abundance of both free weights and machines. Kids love the place, thanks to the game room and a heated indoor/outdoor four-season pool. So how successful has the Lodge been in copying that Rocky Mountain resort panache and service? After a bumpy start—and decidedly mixed reviews in its early years—management has mostly smoothed out service glitches that included longer-than-acceptable waits for fixing room complaints, and being short-handed in staff during busy periods. One continuing source of irritation has been parking—guests can't self-park, and mandatory valet parking runs $23 per night, in addition to the room tariff. At that price, vehicles should all but magically appear, but instead the wait can be a long one. Dinner at the handsome **Solstice** restaurant is expectedly pricey, as befits a grand slopeside establishment, but the solid, unfussy menu stands up well against other first-class Stowe eateries. At breakfast, however—where you're more of a captive audience—prices are nose-dive-steep, whether you're virtuously sipping an açai smoothie or wolfing a $32 steak-and-egg combo. But you probably didn't come here to economize.

7412 Mountain Rd., Stowe. www.stowe.com. ✆ **888/478-6938** or 802/253-3560. $219–$566 double and studio; $341–$1,286 suite; town houses higher. **Amenities:** Skiing, ski equipment rental; ski-to-door access; ski valet service; 2 restaurants; bar; spa; gym; indoor/outdoor heated pool; game room; playground; room service; dogs accepted ($125 per stay); Wi-Fi (free).

Topnotch ★★★

Once you get past the underwhelming exterior of Topnotch, you'll discover the style and substance of a first-class resort. The main lobby suggests a traditional north country lodge—all stone and wood, with a huge moose head on the wall; guest rooms carry on the rustic motif, mostly in country pine. Some units have wood-burning fireplaces, some have Jacuzzis, and third-floor rooms soar with cathedral ceilings. The main attraction is the huge 35,000-square-foot **spa ★,** free for guests (nonguests pay a $60 fee). This spa has such nice touches as fireplaces in the locker rooms (and in the couples' massage suites), a 60-foot indoor pool, a hot tub with waterfall, and a range of aerobics classes, weight-training programs, and revitalizing treatments for face, skin, and body. Outdoors you can ramble on 120 acres of grounds, doing anything from horseback riding to cross-country skiing.

4000 Mountain Rd., Stowe. www.topnotchresort.com. © **844/258-7212** or 802/253-8585. 92 units. $229–$429 double, $629 suite; holidays $649–$749 double, $849 suite. 6-night minimum stay Christmas week. Pets allowed. **Amenities:** 2 restaurants; concierge; exercise room; Jacuzzi; 3 pools (1 indoor, 2 outdoor); sauna; spa; tennis courts (4 indoor, 10 outdoor), limited room service; Wi-Fi (free).

Trapp Family Lodge ★★ Even people who have never been to Stowe, maybe never even heard of the place, know the story behind this most famous of the region's resorts. With a bit of embellishment here and there, *The Sound of Music* told the tale: The Trapp family fled Nazi Austria under cover of darkness and wound up on this lovely Vermont hillside, farming, singing, and eventually building a lodge with the best views of any Stowe resort. (The original burned in 1980; this is a copy.) Baroness Maria von Trapp's grandchildren now manage the resort and have added a bakery, microbrewery, and a gorgeous fitness center with outdoor hot tub and indoor pool. Even standard rooms are big, many with expansive balconies and views of the Green Mountains (ask about a corner unit). Family suites like no. 421 are positively huge, while a half-dozen luxury suites in the newer Millennium Wing feature touches like wood-burning fireplaces, kitchenettes, wine glasses, or stylish European-style bathrooms with Jacuzzis and open showers. You can even sleep in Maria's own room, which sports a full brick fireplace, full kitchen, four-poster bed, and the best views in the house. Hiking, biking, and skiing trails interlace 2,000-plus acres of grounds (see "Cross-Country Skiing," p. 536), and the lodge rents mountain bikes. Do be aware, though, that the Lodge is a popular bus tour destination during foliage season. All those folks have seen the movie. To get there, drive westward out of Stowe on Route 108; after 2 miles bear left at a fork near a white church, and continue up the hill, following signs for the lodge.

700 Trapp Hill Rd., Stowe. www.trappfamily.com. © **800/826-7000** or 802/253-8511. 120 units. $225–$430 double; $325–$715 suite. Rates include meals during holidays and foliage season. 3-night minimum stay Presidents' Day weekend and foliage season; 5-night minimum stay Christmas week. **Amenities:** 2 restaurants; health club; Jacuzzi; sauna; 3 pools (1 heated indoor, 2 outdoor); 4 tennis courts; bikes; babysitting; limited room service; Wi-Fi (free).

Where to Eat in Stowe

Packing a picnic? The **Harvest Market ★,** at 1031 Mountain Rd. (www. harvestatstowe.com; © **802/253-3800**), is a great place for picking up takeout gourmet. You can browse Vermont products and imports, or snag fresh-baked goods to bring back to the ski lodge or take for a picnic. It's open daily, 7am until 7pm; in off season it closes at 5:30pm on Friday, Saturday, and Sunday.

The Bistro at Ten Acres Lodge ★★★ NEW AMERICAN

It doesn't take much to get off the beaten track in Stowe, the beaten track being the Mountain Road between the village and the ski resort. A 10- or 15-minute drive from either point, however, delivers you to this dining spot that does everything well. The classically New England setting features colorful walls, well-spaced tables, and lots of sound baffles that keep noise to a pleasant hum. The bar is run by one of the owners, a competent mixologist who infuses liquors in-house, hand-squeezes juices, and pours from a creative list of craft beers and wines. The kitchen staff forages their own mushrooms and grow herbs in a small garden out back, and even the mustard is made on site. The Bistro is deservedly known for its roasted pork shank, a caveman-worthy hunk of meat that's falling off the massive bone and given oomph by a terrific BBQ sauce. But don't write off the seafood dishes, which are also excellent—the linguini and clams, made with fresh pasta and sweet manila clams, is a study in a simple dish done right. Save room for dessert, especially the bourbon and dark chocolate pecan pie.

14 Barrows Rd., Stowe. www.tenacreslodge.com. ✆ **802/253-6838.** Main dishes $19–$35. Wed–Sun 5–10pm.

Green Goddess Cafe ★ BREAKFAST/AMERICAN

We're off that beaten path again—this time, to a modest little spot (you order at the counter and carry your own dish to a table) that serves perhaps the finest breakfast in Stowe. Crafted from local ingredients like newly laid eggs, sharp Vermont cheddar, and whatever fruits and vegetables are in season (the restaurant is a proud member of the Vermont Fresh Network, an alliance of farmers and chefs) the food is cooked with care and creativity. One morning you might enjoy a "Mexican standoff scramble," marrying eggs with smoked ham, jalapeno, black beans, and charred red onion; next day, you might head back and tuck into traditional buttermilk pancakes doctored with blueberries, bananas, or chocolate chips. Lunches have an international flair, ranging from a classic Cubano sandwich to gyros to a chicken pesto panini. Alas, the Green Goddess is not open for dinner.

618 S. Main St., Stowe. www.greengoddessvt.com. ✆ **802/253-5255.** Main dishes $9–$13. Mon, Tues, Thurs, Fri 7:30am–3pm, Sat 8am–3:30pm, Sun 8am–3pm.

Harrison's Restaurant and Bar ★★ INTERNATIONAL

Mother-and-son restaurateurs Kathi and Andrew Kneale aren't running a speakeasy here, though that may come to mind as you descend into a basement on Stowe's main drag. What they have been running, since 2003, is one of the ski town's most reliable eateries, offering a menu with a sound American base and just enough ventures into foreign cuisines to make things interesting. Off the grill come rib-eyes, steak tips, and pork tenderloin, along with a wine-marinated flank steak imaginatively served with bacon, grilled onion, and bleu cheese crumbles. But you'll also find tacos filled with Sriracha-glazed shrimp, fried chicken perked up with Korean barbecue sauce, and a chicken piccata that would do honor to an all-Italian menu. Dessert? The word "decadence" is a tired cliché in restaurant-speak, but you'll forgive the Kneales' applying it to a sumptuous chocolate ganache on a graham cracker crust. Andrew mans the bar, pouring the requisite Vermont beers, a decent single-malt selection, and wacky martinis that might terrify a gin-and-vermouth purist. The wine list covers the under-$40 basics, but also reaches amply into the triple digits for skiers celebrating a flawless challenge of Stowe's Front Four.

25 Main St., Stowe. www.harrisonsstowe.com. ℂ **802/253-7773.** Main dishes $16–$34. Sun–Thurs 4:30–9:30pm, Fri–Sat 4:30–10pm.

Pie-casso ★★ PIZZA/AMERICAN   Stowe is rightly known for its abundance of high–end restaurants, but it has its share of decent, humbly priced establishments too. Exhibit A is this wittily named pizzeria where customers are encouraged to create their own "masterpieces," ordering individually sized rounds of dough slathered with barbecue sauce, pesto, classic red sauce, or a white béchamel-style sauce. On top of that, the restaurant offers a wealth of farm-fresh ingredients as toppings, from dots of locally made goat's cheese to wild mushrooms, quality sausages, and every veggie you can name. Despite its name, pizza is just the start of what's on offer at Pie-casso. Its kitchen also sends out tasty and unusual salads, classic sandwiches, a number of other Italian entrees, and guilty-pleasure desserts. The bar hosts weekly events like trivia nights, live music concerts, and even stand-up comedy

1899 Mountain Rd., Stowe. www.piecasso.com. ℂ **802/253-4411.** Large pizzas $13–$22; main dishes $10–$19. Sun–Thurs 11am–11pm.

Plate ★★★ AMERICAN   You don't have to head up the Mountain Road to reach Plate—it's right on Main Street, in a former storefront with big glass windows facing the white-steepled church. The menu balances comfort food with more imaginative dishes, offering burgers and matzoh ball soup for those who just want a hearty, simple meal; and more exotic offerings like gnocchi with kimchi and braised beef cheek, or monkfish with a side of white beans with fennel and tomato. Just count on flavor being paramount; the chefs aren't afraid to pair smoked salmon with horseradish cashew cream, or brighten roast chicken with a mint chimichurri. An expert bar staff crafts well-balanced cocktails, and the wonderfully friendly waitstaff make toddlers and grandmas feel equally at home. Best of all: Plate is significantly less expensive than Stowe's other fine-dining options.

99 Main St., Stowe. www.platestowe.com. ℂ **802/253-2691.** Main courses $16–$35. Wed–Sun 5–10pm.

BURLINGTON

Burlington: 215 miles NW of Boston; 98 miles S of Montreal; 154 miles NE of Albany, NY

Right at the doorstep of Lake Champlain, Burlington is Vermont's biggest city (though it isn't all that big, with a population of just over 40,000). It's a vibrant college town—home to the University of Vermont, known locally as UVM—and Champlain College, with flavors of hippie, yuppie, and vintage Vermont mashed and mixed in like a scoop of Ben & Jerry's super fudge chunk. Speaking of Ben & Jerry, they completely epitomize this place: two city hippies-gone-big-time who found the city to be their ideal testing ground. (Look for the sidewalk plaque at the corner of St. Paul and College streets commemorating their original ice-cream shop.)

It's really no wonder that Burlington has become a magnet for those seeking an alternative to big-city life, and for students who stay on after graduation. The downtown occupies a superb position overlooking the lake and the Adirondack Mountains to the west. To the east, the Green Mountains rise dramatically, with two of their highest peaks (Mount Mansfield and Camel's Hump) stretching above an undulating ridge.

Downtown's Church Street pedestrian mall is enjoyable, and the city's extensive bus system is absurdly cheap.

Essentials
ARRIVING
BY CAR   Burlington is at the junction of I-89, Route 7, and Route 2. From New York City, it's between a 5- and 6-hour drive via either I-91 and I-89 or the New York State Thruway; from Boston, figure on 3 to 3½ hours' driving via I-93 and then I-89.

BY PLANE   Burlington International Airport, about 3 miles east of the city center, is served daily by nonstop flights on **Delta** (www.delta.com) from Atlanta, New York LaGuardia, and Detroit; **American** (www.aa.com) from Charlotte, Philadelphia, Chicago, and Washington Reagan; **United** (www. united.com) from Newark, Washington Dulles, and Chicago O'Hare; **JetBlue** (www.jetblue.com) from New York JFK; and, in ski season only, **Porter** (www. flyporter.com) from Toronto. Car rentals are available from a half-dozen national chains inside the terminal; a bus ride into the city on a CCTA bus (bus no. 1; departs every 30 minutes, every hour on Sunday) costs just $1.25.

BY TRAIN   Amtrak's (www.amtrak.com; ✆ **800/872-7245**) Vermonter service offers one daily departure to Essex Junction (connected by bus to downtown Burlington) from New York, New Haven, Springfield, Massachusetts, and points beyond such as Baltimore and Washington, D.C. It's a cheap ride ($71 one-way) from New York—but it also takes almost 9 hours from New York.

BY BUS   Greyhound (www.greyhound.com; ✆ **800/231-2222**) has a bus depot at the airport, with connections to Albany, Boston, Hartford, and New York. From New York, it's a 10- to 14-hour slog (change in Boston), costing $52 to $79 one-way; from Boston, it takes 4½ to 5 hours and costs $26 to $59 one-way.

VISITOR INFORMATION
The **Lake Champlain Regional Chamber of Commerce,** 60 Main St. (www. vermont.org; ✆ **877/686-5253** or 802/863-3489), maintains an information center in a brick building near the waterfront and a short walk from Church

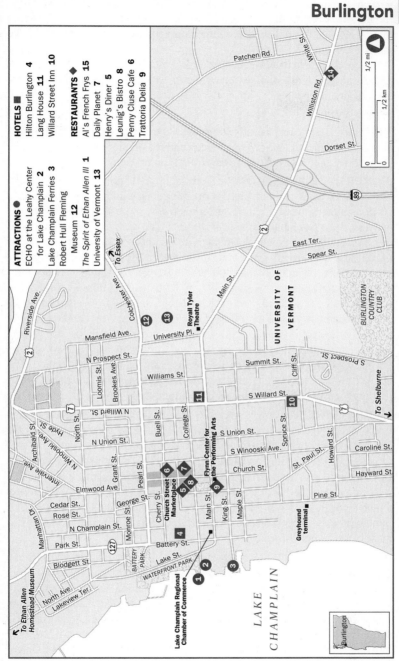

Street Marketplace. It's open weekdays only. (On weekends, helpful maps and brochures are left in the entryway for visitors.) In summer, an information kiosk is also staffed at the Church Street Marketplace, at the corner of Church and Bank streets.

The excellent free local weekly paper, *Seven Days* (www.7dvt.com), carries great local articles and dining reviews plus a very good listing of local events, exhibits, and happenings.

CITY LAYOUT

For visitors, Burlington basically comprises three distinct areas: the UVM campus on top of the hill, a downtown area centered on the active Church Street Marketplace, and a thin strip of waterfront running along Lake Champlain.

UNIVERSITY OF VERMONT Founded in 1791 (funded by a state donation of 29,000 acres of forest land), Vermont's public university has since grown to accommodate nearly 12,000 undergraduates, more than 1,500 graduate students, and a few hundred medical students. The campus is set on 400 acres atop a small hill overlooking downtown Burlington and Lake Champlain to the west; it also has a pretty good view of the Green Mountains to the east. The campus is large, with more than 400 buildings, many of which were designed by noted architectural firms such as H. H. Richardson (Billings Library, now housing special collections) and McKim, Mead, and White (Waterman Building; Ira Allen Chapel). What UVM *doesn't* have is the usual college strip of beery bars, bagel shops, and bookstores adjacent to campus. Downtown serves that function, 5 blocks away; College Street connects the two, as does the free **College Street Shuttle** (it looks like an old-fashioned trolley). The shuttle runs between Burlington's waterfront boathouse and the UVM campus year-round, every 15 to 30 minutes from 11am until 9pm. Use it.

CHURCH STREET Downtown centers around the largely traffic-free Church Street Marketplace, a pedestrian corridor that jumps with activity most of the year—it's most fun in summer, obviously. This is the place to wander without purpose, people-watching and snacking. While the shopping and grazing are excellent here, don't overlook the superb historic commercial architecture that graces much of the area. (Unfortunately, a controversial 14-story mixed-use complex now towers over it all, at the corner of Church and Cherry streets.) A number of side streets radiate out from Church Street, too, with a mix of restaurants, shops, and offices.

THE WATERFRONT Once a shabby, half-derelict relic of Burlington's heyday as a terminal for shipping on Lake Champlain, the city's waterfront now boasts a marina, cruise boat dock, and floating waterside restaurant (Splash), along with a scenic stretch of the Burlington Bike Path, which separates here into lanes for cyclists and pedestrians. It's also the home of **ECHO at the Leahy Center for Lake Champlain** (www.echovermont.org; ✆ **802/ 864-1848**), dedicated to showcasing the natural diversity of the Lake Champlain watershed with aquarium and animal exhibits that kids will find fascinating.

Exploring Burlington

Aside from its spectacular natural setting and the retail, dining, drinking, and people-watching scene along the Church Street Marketplace, Burlington's attractions are largely of the indoor, cultural variety, with a significant exception being the annual June **Discover Jazz Festival** (www.discoverjazz.com), with its myriad outdoor performances. The **Flynn Center for the Performing Arts** (www.flynncenter.org; ✆ **802/863-5966**) a beautifully restored Art Deco movie palace on Main Street opposite City Hall, fills its calendar with world-class acts; while UVM's **Lane Series** (www.uvm.edu/laneseries; ✆ **802/656-4455**) likewise draws top talent.

Ethan Allen Homestead Museum ★ HISTORIC HOME A quiet retreat on one of the most idyllic, least-developed stretches of the Winooski River, this museum just north of the city center is a shrine to Vermont's favorite son; even today, centuries later, he and his Green Mountain Boys remain larger-than-life figures in this state. Though Allen wasn't actually born in Burlington, he settled here later in life on property confiscated from a British sympathizer during the Revolution. Inside this red reconstruction of a farmhouse, an orientation center gives an intriguing multimedia account of Allen's life, plus info about colonial life and regional history. Even if you're not a Vermont history buff, the footpaths along the river (no charge) make for a fine outing.

Rte. 127, Colchester. www.ethanallenhomestead.org. ✆ **802/865-4556.** $10 adults, $6 students 5–17; under 5 free. Daily May–Oct 10am–4pm. From city center, follow Pearl St. (at north end of Church St. Marketplace) to Rte. 127 and continue 2 miles N. From I-89, take exit 17 to North Ave., or exit 15 to Rte. 15.

Lake Champlain Ferries ★★ BOAT RIDE Car ferries chug across the often placid, sometimes wind-whipped waters of Lake Champlain from Burlington to Port Kent, New York, between late May (or later, depending on weather) and early October, and it's a good way to cut out miles of driving if you're heading west toward the Adirondacks. It's also a great way to see the lake, leaves, and mountains on a pleasant, inexpensive 1-hour cruise. Reservations are taken for the Burlington route only, which operates 10 to 20 times per day. It's wise to make reservations at least a day in advance. Two other ferries also cross the lake—much more quickly, in just 12 to 20 minutes—linking Grande Isle, Vermont, with Plattsburgh, New York (daily, year-round); and Charlotte, Vermont, with Essex, New York (spring–fall; opening and closing dates vary). Note that credit cards are not accepted for fares on these two shorter rides. Between June and mid-October, narrated, musically accompanied, or dinner-inclusive lake cruises are also offered by the ferry company; call ✆ **802/864-9669** for details. Note that these three ferries are unaffiliated with the "cable ferry" at Ticonderoga, New York, a fourth Champlain crossing (see p. 518).

King St. Dock, Burlington. www.ferries.com. ✆ **802/864-9804.** Burlington–Port Kent $30 one-way car and driver, $8 additional adults, $6.80 seniors, $3.10 kids 6–12; Charlotte–Essex and Grande Isle–Cumberland Head $10.75 one-way for car and driver, $4.50 additional adults, $4 seniors, $2.25 kids 6–12.

Robert Hull Fleming Museum ★ MUSEUM Housed in a 1931 McKim, Mead, and White building—it's in the great firm's late, largely uninspired Colonial Revival style—the University of Vermont's art museum possesses a globe-girdling collection of more than 25,000 objects. Holdings include art and anthropological artifacts from Europe, the Americas, Africa, ancient Egypt, East Asia, and the Middle East. A tour of the Fleming's galleries can take you from works by artists such as Goya and Corot, to a mummy and sarcophagus dating to the 6th century B.C.E. A selection of paintings by 20th-century Vermont artists is also on permanent display. The museum's website lists frequent talks, generally connected with temporary special exhibits. (*Note:* If you drive to the museum on weekdays, you must feed the museum's parking meters, which cost 75¢ per hour, and you must also obtain a pass from the reception desk; on weekends, there's a free parking lot nearby.)

61 Colchester Ave. (UVM campus), Burlington. www.uvm.edu/~fleming. © **802/656-0750.** $5 adults, $3 seniors and students, $10 family. Labor Day–late May Tues–Fri 10am–4pm (Wed to 7pm), Sat–Sun 12–4pm; May–Labor Day Tues–Fri noon–4pm, Sat–Sun 1–5pm. Closed during school recesses and vacation; check website for schedules.

Shelburne Museum ★★★ OUTDOOR MUSEUM Established in 1947 by sugar and railroad heiress Electra Havemeyer Webb, the Shelburne houses one of the nation's best collections of American folk and decorative art. The museum occupies three dozen buildings spread out across 45 rolling acres, about 7 miles south of Burlington, and no less than the *New York Times* has opined that "there is nothing like Shelburne in the museum universe." The holdings total some 150,000 items in all—the expected quilts, tools, duck decoys, and weather vanes, a wonderful circus collection of posters and miniatures, and entire *buildings* gathered from around New England and New York, which are a highlight. The structures include an 1890 railroad station, an entire lighthouse, a stagecoach inn, an Adirondack lodge, and a Vermont round barn. Even a 220-foot Lake Champlain steamship, the 1906 sidewheeler *Ticonderoga,* stands landlocked and immaculately preserved, from staterooms to engine room, on the museum's grounds. Rotating special exhibits highlight specific aspects of Americana such as Shaker design, African-American quilt work, the art of John James Audubon, and similar topics. With the opening of the Pizzagalli Center for Art and Education, housing galleries and performance spaces, the museum is now a year-round destination. As if this weren't enough, there are annual events ranging from "Lilac Sunday" to a classic automobile festival.

Route 7, Shelburne. www.shelburnemuseum.org. © **802/985-3346.** $25 adults, $23 seniors and AAA members, $15 college students, $14 ages 13–17, $12 ages 5–12, under 5 free, families (2 adults and children) $65 (Nov–Apr prices reduced to $10 adults, $5 ages 5–17, under 5 free). Discounts for Vermont residents; active military free.

The Spirit of Ethan Allen III ★ SIGHTSEEING CRUISE The vistas of Lake Champlain and the Adirondacks haven't changed much since Samuel de Champlain first explored the area in 1609—but travel sure has. This tour ship, holding 500 passengers on three decks, offers a more genteel touring alternative to taking a ferry ride. The enclosed decks are air-conditioned, and food and drink are served from a deli and cash bar. In addition to four-times-daily narrated tours (1½ hours; sunset cruise more expensive than the others), there are many specialty trips involving lunch, brunch, dinner, music, or even a murder (dramatically, for mystery buffs; not a real one). Parking is available at an additional cost.

Burlington Boathouse, Burlington. www.soea.com. © **802/862-8300.** Narrated 90-min. tours $22.15 adults, $8.45 kids 3–11; meal and specialty cruises $34–$53 adults, $16–$33 kids 3–11. Narrated cruises daily mid-May to mid-Oct; specialty cruises mid-May to early Oct. Check website for schedules.

Where to Stay in Burlington

Several excellent resort properties are located within a half-hour's drive of the city. If those are too rich for your blood, a number of chain motels cluster along Route 7 (Shelburne Road) and along Route 2 (Williston Road), each in South Burlington, about a 5- to 10-minute drive from downtown. While they lack even a trace of New England charm, they're mostly clean, modern, and reliable.

Basin Harbor Club ★★   For over 130 years, five generations of the Beach family have operated this classic lakeside resort. Their careful steward-ship has resulted in a vacation environment as timeless, and as relaxing, as any in Vermont. Splendidly integrated into its natural setting on Lake Champlain about 40 minutes south of Burlington, Basin Harbor offers cottage accom-modations as well as units in the main inn building. Many of the cottages, which are situated to feel isolated despite their convenience to dining and activities, have fireplaces, work desks, sofas, and Jacuzzis. You won't find televisions here, so borrow or rent bikes, kayaks, canoes, or a speedboat; hit the little golf course; or grab a tennis racquet (lessons are available) and head to the clay courts. A program of events and activities includes art classes and lectures, although the most appealing activity might just be lounging in an Adirondack chair and gazing out at the lake (and the actual Adirondacks, on the other side). Dining is at three good restaurants of various types—you choose from among B&B, MAP, or full dining plans in spring and fall, while all meals are included in summer rates. (It was only recently that Basin Harbor dropped the requirement that gentlemen over age 12 wear jackets and ties to dinner in the main dining room—but you still won't see the guy at the next table wearing a ball cap.) An excellent kids' program completes the sense of having stepped into an upscale summer camp from another century. Summer-time bonus: Thursday nights bring lobster dinners and live jazz to the beach. To get there from Burlington, follow Route 7 south about 20 miles, turn right onto Route 27A and follow into Vergennes; just after the bridge, turn right onto Panton Road (watch for Basin Harbor signs), then bear right after 1½ miles onto Basin Harbor Road; continue about 5 more miles to resort. (Or just fly in, piloting your own plane and landing on the resort's private strip.)

4800 Basin Harbor Rd., Vergennes. www.basinharbor.com. © **800/622-4000** or 802/475-2311. $197–$445 double, rooms and suites; $312–$818 cottage. B&B, MAP, and full American plan available at extra charge. Rates do not include 18% service fee. 2-night minimum stay some weekends. Closed mid-Oct to mid-May. Well-behaved pets allowed in cottages ($20 per pet per night). **Amenities:** 3 restaurants; babysitting; bikes; children's programs; concierge; golf course; exercise room; outdoor pool; 5 tennis courts; watersports equipment/rentals; Wi-Fi (free).

Hilton Burlington ★   The glass-boxy, nine-story Hilton started out as a Radisson, then did time as a Wyndham, but has retained its late-70s International-style looks throughout the franchise transfers and interior updates. It stands conveniently between the waterfront and Church Street Marketplace, and offers nice lake and Adirondack views from rooms on the west-facing side. Otherwise, don't expect more than standard chain-hotel accommodations. A few "cabana" units by the pool area are convenient for families, while executive-floor rooms are bigger and feature more amenities. The airport shuttle is a plus, and the staff is friendly and competent. Eat elsewhere, though—downtown Burlington's cornucopia of restaurants is only a short walk away.

60 Battery St., Burlington. www.hilton.com. © **866/238-4218** or 802/658-6500. 257 units. $139–$239 double. Parking $15 per night. **Amenities:** Restaurant; babysitting; concierge; exercise room; Jacuzzi; indoor pool; room service; Wi-Fi (free).

The Inn at Essex ★   Just east of Burlington's outer suburbs, this inn bills itself as "Vermont's Culinary Resort"—a claim that dates from the property's former partnership with the New England Culinary Institute but still rings true in light of the cooking classes offered to guests. Set on 20 hillside acres with views of Mt. Mansfield, it's less of a top-tier resort than a plush semi-rural alternative to staying in the city. Some rooms—particularly the suites outfitted for longer stays, built with full kitchens (including Hearthstone gas stoves)— are decked out with fireplaces, CD players, Jacuzzis, four-poster beds, and the like. Other units, though, are fairly ordinary for the high prices. The **spa** is the best full-service facility in the Burlington area, there's an airport shuttle and kids' play area, and The Tavern (see p. 554), the inn's restaurant, is a worthwhile dining destination even if you're not a guest.

70 Essex Way, Essex. www.essexresort.com. © **800/727-4295** or 802/878-1100. 120 units. $169–$319 double, $219–$479 suite. **Amenities:** Restaurant; bikes; exercise room; golf course; heated outdoor pool; room service; spa; Wi-Fi (free).

The Inn at Shelburne Farms ★★   The numbers behind this elaborate mansion on the shore of Lake Champlain tell the story: 60 rooms, 10 chimneys, 1,400 acres, all the one-time domain of railroad magnate William Seward Webb. It's a whimsical house, a tourist attraction in and of itself, as is adjacent **Shelburne Farms,** another Webb legacy that showcases model agricultural practices and includes an award-winning cheesemaking operation open for tours (© **802/985-8498**). Yet from May through October, you can sleep here and pretend it's all yours. Built in 1899, the sprawling Edwardian "farmhouse" is a place to fantasize about the lifestyles of the Gilded Age. Famous architect Frederick Law Olmsted helped design the grounds—the concept was an "agricultural estate" complete with grazing cows on the lawns and a sustainable dairy operation, but also super-plush (for the time) bedrooms and fittings. Restored to its Webb-era grandeur, but still possessing the feel of a country estate, the inn offers French design touches, floral wallpapers, and a sunny elegance. Units here vary considerably in decor and amenities: About a quarter of the rooms share hallway bathrooms with other rooms, for example (the Oak Room is probably best of these)—but you can also rent luxurious digs like Overlook, the original master bedroom of owner Lila Webb, with its frilly draperies, big king bed, and views of the lake, meadows, and grounds. The Louis XVI room was furnished with whitewashed furniture when the home was built in 1899, and that furniture is still here, complemented by a design scheme popular at that time. Whether you're an inn guest or not, try to reserve an outdoor table for summer Sunday brunch.

1611 Harbor Rd., Shelburne. www.shelburnefarms.org. © **802/985-8498.** 26 units (7 w/ shared bath). $160–$230 double with shared bath; $180–$530 double w/private bath; $270–$850 cottage. 2-night minimum stay Sat–Sun. Closed mid-Oct to early May. **Amenities:** Restaurant; babysitting; tennis court; Wi-Fi (free).

Lang House ★   The signature architectural trend of upper-middle-class Burlington during late Victorian times was Queen Anne style (there's no satisfactory explanation for the name; Anne lived 175 years earlier), characterized by turrets, wraparound porches, and quirky asymmetry. This lovely 1881 example, on the steep main drag between downtown and the University of Vermont, luckily avoided conversion into student apartments and wears its age well, right down to the polish on its rich cherry and maple woodwork. Rooms vary in size, though most have smallish bathrooms and quite small TVs, and are a bit on the pricey side; but you're staying right in the middle of Burlington and you're not in a cookie-cutter hotel. Two of the best rooms are corner units: no. 101 on the first floor, and no. 202 on the second floor, with a sitting area tucked into the turret. Breakfast is ample and tasty, and the owners have a liquor license, so they can sell you a bottle of wine or beer. Only cautions? There's no elevator, and you're sleeping practically right on a big university campus with a national reputation for its parties. So you might *hear* some of that partying late at night.

360 Main St., Burlington. www.langhouse.com. © **877/919-9799** or 802/652-2500. 11 units. $199–$299 double. Rates include breakfast. Free parking. **Amenities:** Wi-Fi (free).

Willard Street Inn ★★   Here's another in-town inn, likewise occupying a splendid 1881 Queen Anne mansion. Located farther up the hill than the Lang House, on a less busy cross street a few minutes' walk from the university campus, it has the look of a place built by a family just a wee bit more prosperous. The proprietors have done right by the grand brick pile, having decorated all rooms in genuine and reproduction antiques. Some have down comforters and gas fireplaces, and many have interesting slopes, angles, and eaves; four-poster beds and handsome, not-too-frilly decor are the norm here. Among the best units are the third-floor Tower Room (in the turret), which boasts a small, wicker-furnished sitting area and the best views of the lake; and Champlain Lookout, on the second floor, with its spacious bedroom and bathroom and more great lake views. The Nantucket Room also has a lovely antique tub. Walk (no elevator) down the marble staircase and check out the marble-floored solarium, green lawns, and English gardens. This inn's owners really go the extra mile to ensure guests' satisfaction—breakfasts are truly sumptuous.

349 S. Willard St. (2 blocks south of Main St.), Burlington. www.willardstreetinn.com. © **800/577-8712** or 802/651-8710. 14 units (1 w/bath across hall). $165–285 double. Rates include full breakfast. Free parking. 2-night minimum stay Sat–Sun. Children 12 and older welcome. **Amenities:** Wi-Fi (free).

Where to Eat in Burlington

Al's French Frys ★ FAST FOOD   For over 70 years—since the surrounding strip malls were farmland—this quirkily spelled roadside joint between Burlington and its airport has been beloved by locals and travelers alike. Al's is both fun and efficient, and the fries here (which you can order by the cup, pint, or even quart) draw locals back time and again. Other offerings—hamburgers, dogs, wraps, chicken strips, and grilled cheese sandwiches—are okay, but you're here for the fries—add a side order of cheese, gravy, or chili sauce if you want to get experimental. There's no beer here, but you can order cola, shakes (in five flavors), or—this being Vermont—a cup of plain or chocolate milk.

1251 Williston Rd. (Rte. 2, just east of I-89), South Burlington. www.alsfrenchfrys.com. © **802/862-9203.** Fries $2–$6, sandwiches and burgers $3–$6. No credit cards. Sun–Thurs 10:30am–11pm; Fri–Sat 10:30am–midnight.

The Daily Planet ★ INTERNATIONAL   Named for Superman alter-ego Clark Kent's day-job newspaper, this popular spot often fills with college students and/or downtown folks getting out of work. It's central (on Central Street) and keeps up its youthful appeal, even though it's been here going on 30 years. The mild chaos in the dining room only adds to the experience, which begins with a fun, eclectic menu—better than you might expect given the pubby look to the place and its largely college-age clientele. Look for almond-crusted swordfish steak; spicy Korean barbecue duck; a sirloin graced with caramelized onion, cider demi-glace, and gruyere fondue; or pan-roasted lamb "lollipops" crusted in mustard and herbs—most available as large- or small-plate entrees. On the bar menu, pork carnitas and Vietnamese beef sandwiches make the microbrews go down with a little spice. The vegetarian entrees here are among the very best in town. Desserts are creative and tempting, too—choices might include a lavender crème brûlée, a praline sundae, or a hazelnut-topped cheesecake. There's a decent selection of wines by the glass, and a loony martini menu.

15 Center St., Burlington www.dailyplanetvt.com. © **802/862-9647.** Reservations recommended for parties of 5 or more. Main courses $14–$26. Sun–Thurs 4–9pm, Fri–Sat 4–9:30pm (limited late-night menu until 11pm Sun–Thurs, midnight Fri–Sat. Bar daily 'til 2am.

Henry's Diner ★ AMERICAN   Henry's isn't a diner in the stainless steel, straight-out-of-Jersey mode. If the exterior is in any mode at all, it's stucco-Southwestern-Deco, which makes it even more of an anomaly half a block off the Church Street Marketplace. Unlike a lot of places that call themselves diners, there's nothing self-consciously retro here; if it looks like it's been around since 1925, that's because it has (there is an original Jersey-made prefab hidden under the stucco). All the diner requisites are in place: counter seating, squeezy little booths, milkshakes, and an all-day breakfast that rings the changes on eggs, including hearty combos served in an iron skillet. For lunch (or a very early dinner) the burger array and the classic hot open-faced turkey sandwich are supplemented by gyros, spanakopita, and souvlaki, along with Philly cheese steaks and those true diner throwbacks, liver with bacon and onions, and a gravy-and-onion smothered hamburger steak.

155 Bank St., Burlington. www.henrysdinervt.com. © **802/862-9010.** Breakfast items $6–$14; lunch $7–$12. Daily 6am–4pm.

Leunig's Bistro ★ CONTINENTAL   Is that Edith Piaf you hear? If not, it should be, at this determinedly retro-Parisian bistro, with its marble bar, crystal chandeliers, and oversized posters. The inventive menu uses regional ingredients, prepared with a Continental (usually a French) hand. Lunches run to good, upscale bistro-style sandwiches and soups (you can add truffled fries or duck pâté poutine to any lunch, if that gives you a sense of it). But dinner is where things *really* get cranked up and daring: On the nightly menu, you might find a rack of wild boar ribs, cavatappi carbonara with roast chicken and bacon, or swordfish marinated in fennel and orange. The side dishes, salads, and Vermont-oriented cheese plates here are also outstanding. An upscale brunch is served Saturday and Sunday, with the requisite omelets and eggs Benedict supplemented by unexpected items such as poached eggs on crab cakes, a chicken and biscuit napoleon, and—again topped with poached eggs—tournedos of beef *and* butter-poached lobster.

115 Church St., Burlington. www.leunigsbistro.com. © **802/863-3759.** Reservations recommended. Main courses $15–$21 at lunch, $18–$36 at dinner. Mon–Thurs 11am–10pm; Fri 11am–11pm; Sat 9am–11pm; Sun 9am–10pm.

Penny Cluse Cafe ★ CAFE   First question: Why are all those people waiting in line? Second question: Why are they waiting in line at breakfast time? The answer to both questions is that they're Penny Cluse regulars—or folks who've just heard about the place consistently rated as serving the best breakfast in Burlington. This casual spot, a block off the Church Street Marketplace, is the go-to place when you want to ease into your day with buttermilk or gingerbread pancakes; banana bread with maple cream cheese; breakfast sandwiches; a "tofu scram;" and the Zydeco breakfast of eggs, black beans, andouille sausage, and corn muffins. Lunch plates range to chorizo tacos, chicken and biscuits, a smoked-salmon plate, and good sandwiches—including some terrific veggie options. The breakfast prices are at the high end of the usual Vermont breakfast price scale, but unless you have a gargantuan appetite, you're probably going to save by skipping lunch. Just be prepared to be part of that hungry sidewalk line, especially on weekend mornings.

169 Cherry St., Burlington. www.pennycluse.com. © **802/651-8834.** Breakfast and lunch items $7–$14. Mon–Fri 6:45am–3pm; Sat–Sun 8am–3pm.

Can't decide where to eat? An approximately 1.5-mile walk includes food samplings at five restaurants, along with an entertaining narrative of the rich culinary and architectural history of the Queen City. During your walk, you'll learn the colorful stories of twelve immigrant groups that built Burlington, including the Abenaki, African Americans, Jews, and Italians. Tours run from mid-June to mid-October, Thursday through Saturday from 1 to 4:15pm. Tickets must be purchased at least 24 hours in advance through Seven Days Tickets at www.sevendaystickets.com, or through the tour's website at **www.burlingtonediblehistory.com**.

The Tavern ★ AMERICAN   No longer affiliated with the New England Culinary Institute, the Inn at Essex has gone the informal route with this snug taproom serving simple and satisfying fare—barbecue sliders, poutine, burgers, and heartier items like short-rib pot roast, maple-seared tuna, and mac and (Vermont, of course) cheddar. As befits the state with the nation's largest number of breweries per capita (60 and counting), the bar here sprouts 33 taps dispensing Vermont craft beers and ciders. All in all a good stop if you're heading out Route 15, the back road towards Smugglers Notch and Mt. Mansfield.

70 Essex Way, Essex. www.essexresort.com. ℭ **802/878-1100.** Lunch and dinner items $12–$25. Breakfast Mon–Sat 7–11am, Sun 8–11am; lunch Mon–Sat 11:30am–5pm, Sun 11am–3pm; dinner Mon–Thurs 5–10pm, Fri–Sat 5–11pm, Sun 3:30–10pm.

Trattoria Delia ★★★ ITALIAN   More than 20 years ago, when Lori and Tom Delia opened their intimate, one-flight-down trattoria in what had once been a sugarhouse-themed restaurant (hence the rustic atmosphere and big stone fireplace), Burlington's Italian dining experience had largely been centered around spaghetti and meatballs. The Delias have moved on to other ventures, but new owners have continued to educate local palates in the ways of sophisticated Italian cuisine. You have to start with the Antipastone, a long wooden board bedecked with handmade salumi, Vermont and Italian cheeses, and house-cured vegetables (share if you must). Move on to pasta dishes both familiar and not so—for example, house-made gnocchi with lamb meatballs, in a wine-infused brodo—then tuck into ambrosial, melting short ribs in a red wine sauce or a Calabrian seafood stew. The wine list? It's a splendid map of Italy.

152 Saint Paul St., Burlington. www.trattoriadelia.com. ℭ **802/864-5253.** Reservations recommended. Main courses $20–$40. Daily 5–10pm.

THE NORTHEAST KINGDOM ★

St. Johnsbury is 60 miles N of White River Junction, 75 miles E of Burlington, and 125 miles N of Brattleboro

Vermont's Northeast Kingdom has a wilder, more remote character than the rest of the state. Consisting of Orleans, Essex, and Caledonia counties, the

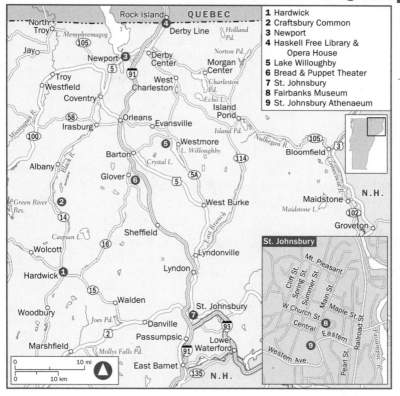

1 Hardwick
2 Craftsbury Common
3 Newport
4 Haskell Free Library & Opera House
5 Lake Willoughby
6 Bread & Puppet Theater
7 St. Johnsbury
8 Fairbanks Museum
9 St. Johnsbury Athenaeum

region was given its memorable nickname in 1949 by Vermont Senator George Aiken. What gives this region its character is its stubborn, old-fashioned insularity. It looks and feels much more like hardscrabble parts of neighboring New Hampshire (which it faces across the Connecticut River) than the farmhouses and outlet malls of Manchester, country stores of the Mad River Valley, sprawling farmland of the Champlain lowlands, or ski trails of Stowe. You won't find any designer fly-fishing shops in these parts.

The landscape here is open and spacious, its dairy pastures ending abruptly at the hard edge of dense boreal forests. The leafy woodlands of the south quickly give way to spiky woods of spruce and fir. Accommodations and services for visitors aren't plentiful or easy to find here, but a growing number of inns are sprouting up in these hills.

Even if your time is limited, stop in St. Johnsbury, which holds two excellent attractions. Also try to cruise through at least a couple of small towns here before heading elsewhere. The fall foliage can be brilliant, although it arrives a bit earlier here (from late September to very early October, usually) than elsewhere in New England.

The entire tour described below, from Hardwick to St. Johnsbury by way of Newport, Derby Line, and Lake Willoughby, is about 90 miles by car. Allow at least a full day for it if you plan to hike, bike, or photograph in the region.

Visitor information is available from the **Northeast Kingdom Chamber of Commerce** (www.nekchamber.com; ✆ **800/639-6379** or 802/748-3678), at Green Mountain Mall, 2000 Memorial Drive, in downtown St. Johnsbury.

DRIVING TOUR: **THE NORTHEAST KINGDOM**

START:	**Hardwick**
FINISH:	**St. Johnsbury**
TIME:	**One full day**

Begin in Hardwick at the intersection of routes 14 and 15, about 23 miles NW of St. Johnsbury and 26 miles NE of Montpelier:

1 Hardwick

A small town with rough edges set on the Lamoille River, Hardwick has a single main street with some intriguing shops, a couple of casual, family-style restaurants, and one of Vermont's best natural-foods stores (the **Buffalo Mountain Food Co-op Café,** 39 S. Main St.). A 2005 fire claimed part of this downtown block, but it has since been rebuilt.

From Hardwick, head north 7 miles on Route 14 to the turnoff to Craftsbury and:

2 Craftsbury Common ★★

An uncommonly graceful village, Craftsbury Common is home to a small academy and a large number of historic homes and buildings spread along a central green and the village's main street. The town occupies a wide upland ridge and offers sweeping views to the east and west; be sure to stop by the old cemetery on the south side of town, too, where you can wander among historic tombstones of pioneers—they date back to the 1700s. Craftsbury is an excellent destination for mountain biking and cross-country skiing.

From Craftsbury, continue north to reconnect to Route 14. Pass through the towns of Albany and Irasburg as you head north. At the village of Coventry, veer north on Route 5 to the lakeside town of:

3 Newport

This small city is struggling with renewal but it has a terrific setting on the southern shores of big Lake Memphremagog, a stunning 32-mile-long lake that's just 2 miles wide at its broadest point (the bulk of it actually lies across the border in Canada). It's worth stopping here for the **Northeast Kingdom Tasting Center** (150 Main St., ✆ **802/334-0599**), where you can sample cheese, cider, maple products, baked goods, and more. From Newport, continue north on Route 5 (crossing under I-91) about 7 miles more to the border town of Derby Line. This outpost has a handful of restaurants and antiques shops; if you've got your passport, you can also park and walk across the bridge to poke around the Quebec town of Stanstead, also known as Rock Island.

Back in Derby Line, look for the:

4 Haskell Free Library & Opera House ★

At the corner of Caswell Avenue and Church Street, this handsome neo-classical building (www.haskellopera.com; ✆ 802/873-3022) contains a public library on the first floor and an elegant opera house, modeled after the old Boston Opera House, on the second. The theater opened in 1904 with advertisements promoting a minstrel show featuring "new songs, new jokes, and beautiful electric effects." It's a beautiful theater, with a scene of Venice painted on the drop curtain and carved cherubim adorning the balcony.

What's coolest about this building, though, is that it lies half in Canada and half in the United States. (The Haskell family donated the building jointly to the towns of Derby Line and Rock Island.) A thick, black line runs right beneath the seats of the opera house, marking the border between nations. Because the stage portion is set entirely in Canada, legends abound of frustrated U.S. marshals sitting in the audience watching fugitives perform on stage, free as birds. (Those stories are almost certainly false.) More recently, the theater has been used for an occasional extradition hearing. Performances still take place here. Tours are also available, from May through October, anytime during regular library hours; a $5 per person donation is suggested. (The library is open Tues–Sat.)

From Derby Line, retrace your path south on Route 5 to Derby Center and the junction of Route 5A. Continue south on Route 5A to the town of Westmore, on the shores of:

5 Lake Willoughby ★★

This underappreciated lake might be one of the most scenic in Vermont—it almost looks like something from Switzerland. Carved out by glaciers and set in an unpopulated area, the lake is best viewed from the north, where its shimmering sheet of water appears to be pinched between the base of two low mountains at its southern end. Route 5A as it runs along the lake's eastern shore is lightly traveled, thus good for biking or walking.

Head southwest on Route 16, which branches off Route 5A just north of the lake. Follow Route 16 through the peaceful villages of Barton and Glover. About 1 mile south of Glover, turn left on Route 122. On your left, look for the farmstead that serves as home to the:

6 Bread & Puppet Theater

For nearly 3 decades, Polish artist and performer Peter Schumann's Bread & Puppet Theater staged an elaborate annual summer pageant at this farm, attracting thousands of attendees who gaped at the theater's brightly painted puppets (crafted of fabric and papier-mâché, they could be an amalgam of Ralph Nader and Hieronymus Bosch). The huge puppets marched around the farm grounds, acting out dramas that typically featured rebellion against tyranny of one sort or another. It was like Woodstock, minus the music.

Alas, the event became too popular—and attracted drifters of questionable character. In 1998, a murder at an adjacent campground prodded Schumann to shut down the circus for a while. His troupe still designs and builds puppets here, however, and periodically takes its unique shows on the road—or offers live performances in Glover. (For the latest schedules, check the troop's website, **www.breadandpuppet.org**.)

Between June and October, you can still visit the venerable, slightly tottering barn, home of the **Bread & Puppet Museum** ★ (© **802/525-3031**), which preserves many of the puppets from past events. This remarkable display shouldn't be missed if you're near the area. Downstairs, in former cow-milking stalls, smaller displays include mournful washerwomen doing laundry and King Lear addressing his daughters. Upstairs, the vast hayloft is filled with soaring, haunting puppets, some up to 20 feet tall. Admission is free, though donations are encouraged. It's open daily 10am to 6pm June through October.

From Glover, continue south through farmlands to Lyndonville, where you pick up Route 5 South to:

7 St. Johnsbury

This is by far the largest community in the Kingdom, and its major center of commerce. First settled in 1786, the town enjoyed a buoyant prosperity in the 19th century, largely stemming from the success of platform scales (which were invented right here in 1830 by Thaddeus Fairbanks, and are still manufactured here). The place hasn't yet been overtaken by sprawl, outlet shops, boutiques, or brewpubs, and the downtown features an abundance of commercial architecture in two distinct neighborhoods connected by steep Eastern Avenue.

The commercial part of town lies along Railroad Street (Route 5) at the base of the hill, while the most visually pleasing section of town runs along Main Street at the top of the hill. There you'll find the local library (with its fine art museum; see below), the St. Johnsbury Academy, and a second museum. This northern end of Main Street is also notable for its grand residential architecture.

In St. Johnsbury, at the corner of Main and Prospect streets, find the:

8 Fairbanks Museum ★★

The collections housed in this imposing Romanesque red-sandstone structure hark back to that Victorian phenomenon known as the "cabinet of curiosities." Built in 1889 to hold the accumulations of obsessive amateur collector Franklin Fairbanks, grandson of the inventor of the platform scale, the museum is a great trove of ethnographic and natural history exhibits from all over the world, with special emphasis on Vermont and the Northern Forest. Here are more than 175,000 objects including mounted birds, mammals and reptiles, as well as old toys, weapons, fossils, general exotica ... and Fairbanks scales. There's also a children's area, with hands-on exhibits and a full schedule of special programs. There's also a **planetarium** ★—it's tiny, but does offer accurate star shows. Also quite accurate—everyone hopes—are the weather reports issued each day from the meteorological center in the basement of the museum and broadcast throughout the state on Vermont Public Radio.

The museum (www.fairbanksmuseum.org; ✆ **802/748-2372**) is open daily from 9am to 5pm, and Sunday from 1 to 5pm; closed 2 weeks in early January. Admission is $9 for adults, $7 for seniors and kids ages 5 to 17, and $25 per family (maximum of two adults). Admission to planetarium shows is separate—$5 for 30 minutes, $7 for 1 hour.

Also on Main Street, just south of the museum at 1171 Main St., find the:

9 St. Johnsbury Athenaeum ★★

Inside a brick building with a blunt mansard tower, St. Johnsbury's public library—one of only 15 libraries in the nation to be declared a national historic landmark—houses an extraordinary little art gallery dating to 1873. It claims to be the oldest unadulterated art gallery in the nation, and has indeed been kept unchanged since its inception. It remains a remarkable record of the artistic tastes of a century and a half ago.

The gallery may be small, but your first view of it is spectacular: you round a corner and find yourself gazing across Yosemite National Park— or, at least, a pretty good facsimile. The luminous 10×15-foot oil painting of the park here, *The Domes of the Yosemite* ★★★, was made by painter Albert Bierstadt in 1867, just 3 years after President Lincoln created the California park. Horace Fairbanks later bought it and built this gallery specifically for the painting.

That's not all there is here. Along with copies of Renaissance works, and paintings by second-tier Victorian artists, are a few originals from Hudson River School painters such as Asher B. Durand, Thomas Moran, and Jasper Cropsey.

The Athenaeum (1171 Main St.; www.stjathenaeum.org; ✆ **802/748-8291**) is open Monday, Wednesday, and Friday 10am to 5:30pm, Tuesday and Thursday noon to 7pm, and Saturday 10am to 3pm. Admission is $5.

Skiing
DOWNHILL

Jay Peak ★★ Just south of the Canada border, Jay Peak has long been famous for its staggering snowfall—an average of about 30 ft. annually, more than anywhere else in New England. That much hasn't changed—but over the past decade, just about everything else here has. Formerly known as a big mountain with a wide variety of terrain and no lodging options other than a small, tacky, fading hotel, Jay now boasts bells and whistles to match its natural setting. There are two hotels, the smaller Tram Haus and the bustling Hotel

Jay—the latter features an indoor water park—as well as a year-round indoor ice rink, a golf course, several restaurants, and a summit-station deli in what used to be a forbidding concrete outpost with a couple of vending machines. The 60-person gondola cables its way up the mountain in winter, summer, and early autumn, offering spectacular views—and, in ski season, a cosmopolitan flavor, as half of the conversations you'll hear are in Quebec French. The skiing? It's as good as ever, with twin peaks, plenty of trails in all categories, and glades for every skill level.

830 Jay Peak Rd, Jay. www.jaypeakresort.com. *C* **802/988-2611.** Adults $84 day lift tickets, $67 half-day; discounts for youths, students, seniors, and VT residents.

CROSS-COUNTRY

The Craftsbury Outdoor Center maintains more than 50 miles of cross-country trails through the gentle hills surrounding the village of Craftsbury. These forgiving, old-fashioned trails, maintained by the center's **Nordic Center ★★** division (535 Lost Nation Rd; www.craftsbury.com; *C* **802/586-7767**), emphasize landscape over speed. They even guarantee skiable snow from January until the second Sunday in March. A trail pass costs $10 per person per day, while a full setup of rental equipment costs just $15 per day more—an outstanding value, given the local scenery.

Another option is the **Highland Lodge Ski Touring Center ★** (www.highlandlodge.com; *C* **802/322-4456**), on Caspian Lake in Greensboro, with more than 30 miles of roller-packed trails (some of which are further groomed) through rolling woodlands and fields. When you stay at the lodge (see below), you ski for free.

Where to Stay & Eat in the Northeast Kingdom

Don't miss the **P&H Truck Stop ★** (*C* **802/429-2141**) in Wells River, right at exit 17 off I-91. It's a must-stop on the way to Jay Peak or St. Johnsbury.

Highland Lodge ★   Built in the mid-19th century, this Northeast Kingdom B&B has been accommodating guests since 1926, with only a short interval during a recent change of ownership. Just across the road from lovely Caspian Lake, long a quiet old-money retreat, it has 10 rooms furnished in a comfortable country style, plus 10 nearby cottages, most equipped with kitchenettes. In summer, you'll feel like you've gone to camp: activities include swimming, boating on the lake, cycling, and playing tennis on a clay court. In winter, the lodge maintains its own cross-country ski area (see "Cross-Country Skiing," above) with miles of packed and groomed trails. Behind the lodge is an attractive 136-acre nature preserve for exploration. Rates here include a hearty country breakfast, and free use of the canoes, kayaks, and most of the other equipment scattered about the property. For off-site diversion, visit nearby **Hill Farmstead** brewery, makers of beers rated among the world's best; and, in Greensboro village, **Willey's Store,** a rambling emporium that exemplifies 21st-century small-town Vermont's shellac-to-Shiraz mercantile style.

1608 Craftsbury Rd., Greensboro. www.highlandlodge.com. © **802/322-4456.** 20 units. $160–$220 double rooms and suites; $220–$260 cabins. Dogs (cabins only) $30 per day. From Hardwick, take Rte. 15 east 2 miles to Rte. 16, and then drive 2 miles north to East Hardwick. Follow signs 6 miles to inn. **Amenities:** Weekend dining; bikes; children's program; tennis court; watersports equipment/rentals; Wi-Fi (entire main inn and some cottages; free).

WilloughVale Inn ★★   The only full-service inn on five-mile-long, fjord-like Lake Willoughby, the WilloughVale offers stunning views across the water to the twin mountains, Pisgah and Hor, bracketing the southern end of the lake. It's ideal for a quiet retreat with some books, a kayak, or a bicycle; Robert Frost stayed here in 1909 and even wrote a poem about it ("A Servant to Servants"). Rooms in the main lodge are tastefully appointed, much of their furniture crafted right here in Vermont. Some have private sections of porch and have been thoroughly updated with Jacuzzis, big-screen satellite televisions, gas fireplaces, and similar touches. Just make sure you snag a room facing the lake—there's no view out back. The cottages—four right on the lake with kitchenettes (including the one Frost stayed in), plus three others nearby with lake views—give off a rustic, Adirondack-lodge feeling, albeit with modern comforts. All these cottages now have wall-unit air-conditioning and televisions, and some have fireplaces or Jacuzzis, yet still feel rustic thanks to their exposed woodwork. Note that this inn's restaurant is seasonal, opening in spring and closing in fall; it serves good food with a superb view of the lake, but in winter you'll have to hunt for other options.

793 Rte. 5A S., Westmore. www.willoughvale.com. © **800/594-9102** or 802/525-4123. 10 rooms and suites; 8 cottages. $99–$259 double; $199–$349 cottage. Weekly rates available (summer only). Rates include continental breakfast. 2-night minimum stay in cottages, and in lodge during July, Aug, and fall-foliage season. Small dogs sometimes accepted ($40 per night; call ahead). **Amenities:** Restaurant; tavern; bikes; watersports equipment/rentals; Wi-Fi (free).

NEW HAMPSHIRE

12

By Barbara Radcliffe Rogers & Stillman Rogers

Geographically, New Hampshire drives a long wedge between two neighboring states that early on carved out their public tourism identities, staking claim to cherished of New England icons. While Vermont became the quintessence of white-spired villages in bucolic green landscapes sweetened by maple syrup, Maine defined itself in piney woods and rockbound shore. New Hampshire was only left with being itself—and it does a smashing good job of it (wicked good job, a New Englander would say).

Sure, the state tourism office hires a NY public relations firm to send out press releases calling attention to Portsmouth's innovative chefs and the beauties of fall foliage in the White Mountains, but they could just as well save their scarce tax revenue (NH famously has neither a sales nor income tax). Once seen and experienced, New Hampshire sells itself.

New Hampshire is where New Englanders themselves vacation—just look at the license plates in the parking lots of its ski areas and attractions. Tourists looking for authentic New England will find it in New Hampshire, from its rugged landscapes (NH's White Mountain summits are rocky and open, not rounded and tree-covered) to the locals' dry self-deprecating humor and genuine hospitality. Yep, what New Hampshire does best is be itself.

That's not to say they don't get a little fun out of it. The state gets its most attention, aided by the national news, every 4 years during the presidential primaries, when NH residents play tongue-in-cheek games with the press, donning plaid shirts and hunting caps and brushing up their "ayuhs" to deliver pithy opinions on the state of the nation. But surely they can be forgiven the play-acting every 4 years. Some of the best of these small-town "rustics" on the porch of the country store are retired professionals from Manchester and Nashua. They never miss a cue: "You lived here all your life?" "Not yet."

New Hampshire is a four-season state for tourism: green in the summer, plenty of snow for skiers in the winter, brilliant foliage in the fall, lilac- and apple blossom-painted landscapes in the spring.

New Hampshire

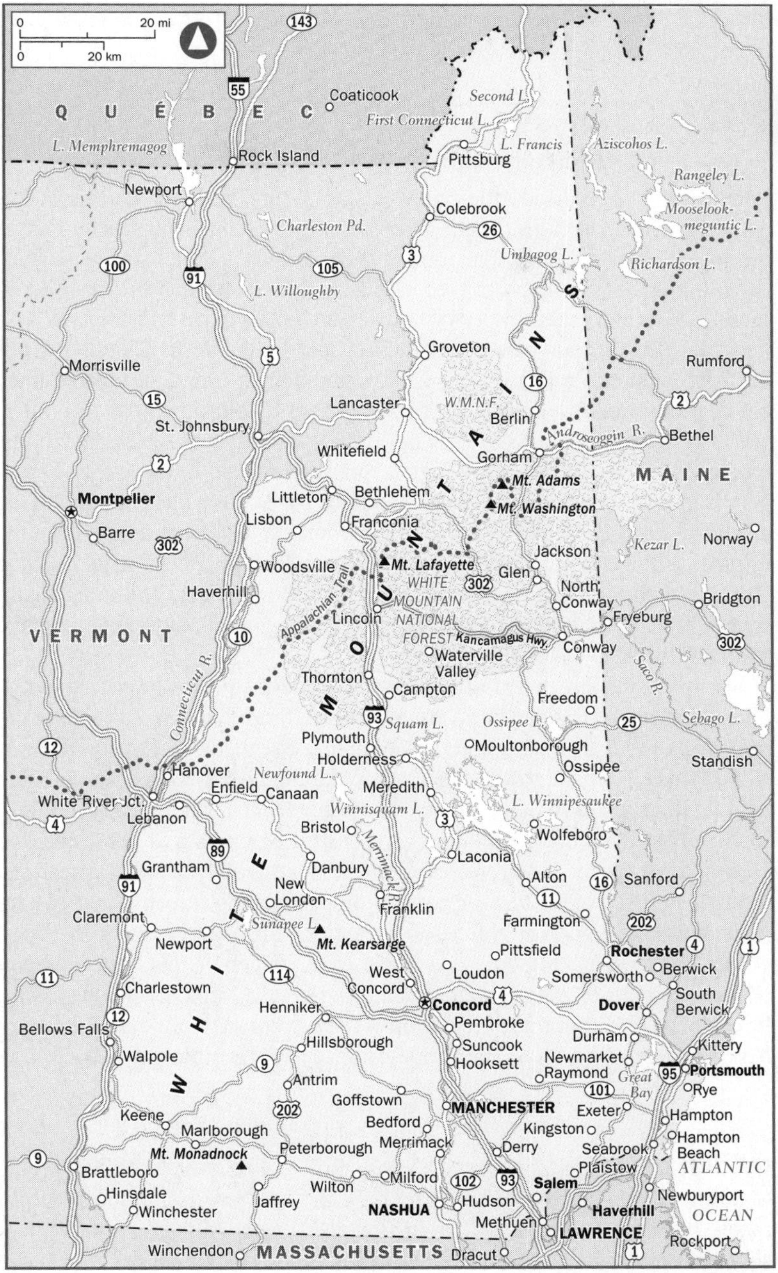

12

NEW HAMPSHIRE | Introduction

November and late March can be a bit drab, but there are indoor pleasures in those quiet months: concerts and theater productions, art galleries and museums, fine dining and inviting country inns. Any time of year, it's a nice place to be.

12 PORTSMOUTH ★★

55 miles N of Boston; 54 miles S of Portland ME.

Portsmouth is a civilized little gem of a seaside city, filled with elegant 18th- and 19th-century architecture that's more intimate than intimidating. Part of the appeal is its variety: Upscale coffee shops and art galleries stand alongside old-fashioned barbershops and second-hand stores. Despite a steady influx of money in recent years, the town still retains an earthiness that serves as a tangy vinegar for more saccharine coastal spots to the north. It invites strolling—through streets lined by Federal-period homes, along its tugboat-lined colonial-era waterfront, or through Prescott Park's colorful gardens.

History runs deep here. For 5 centuries, Portsmouth has been the hub of the coastal Maine/New Hampshire region's maritime trade. In the 1600s, Strawbery Banke (it wasn't called Portsmouth until 1653) was a major center for the export of wood and dried fish to Europe. Portsmouth spread rapidly from the original settlement around the wharf, and that "Puddle Dock" neighborhood changed with the centuries. Today the unique **Strawbery Banke Museum** brings those 4 centuries to life, preserving buildings and interpreting life there from the 1600s to the 1950s.

Just across the Piscataqua River in Maine, the Portsmouth Naval Shipyard— founded in 1800—evolved into a prominent base for the building, outfitting, and repairing of U.S. Navy submarines. Within living memory, Portsmouth was still a "sailor town," a rowdy place of smoke-filled bars and cheap boarding houses. But those days are long gone, replaced by an air of casual gentility.

Visitors to Portsmouth will discover a surprising number of experiences in such a small space—good shopping in the boutiques on Market Street and throughout much of the historic downtown; good eating at many small restaurants and bakeries; great coffee; and plenty of history to explore in period houses, gardens, and museums. As if that weren't enough, this is the only part of New Hampshire that meets the ocean, and beaches are only minutes away. New Hampshire's seacoast may be only 18 miles or so, but it contains one of New England's best-loved summer vacation spots, **Hampton Beach.**

Essentials

ARRIVING

BY CAR   Portsmouth is on exits 3 through 7 on I-95. The most direct route to downtown is via Market Street (exit 7), the last New Hampshire exit just before the bridge into Maine. From Boston's Logan Airport, Portsmouth is about a 1-hour drive via I-95; from Portland Jetport or Manchester airport, the trip is an hour at most.

Portsmouth

ATTRACTIONS ●
Black Heritage Trail **19**
John Paul Jones House **5**
Moffatt-Ladd House **11**
Prescott Park **20**
Rundlet-May House **3**
Strawbery Banke **21**
Warner House **17**
Wentworth-Gardner House **22**

Piscataqua River

STRAWBERY BANKE

PRESCOTT PARK

HOTELS ■
Ale House Inn **18**
Courtyard Portsmouth **1**
Hilton Garden Inn **10**
Hotel Portsmouth **4**
Martin Hill Inn Bed & Breakfast **2**

RESTAURANTS ◆
Black Trumpet Bistro **12**
Breaking New Grounds **15**
Ceres Bakery **16**
Dolphin Striker **13**

Flatbread Company **7**
Friendly Toast **8**
Jumpin' Jay's Fish Cafe **6**
Portsmouth Brewery **14**
Row 34 **9**

BY BUS   **Greyhound** (www.greyhound.com; ✆ **800/231-2222**) and **C&J** (www.ridecj.com; ✆ **800/258-7111** or 603/430-1100) each run about five buses daily from Boston's South Station directly to Portsmouth (trip time: 1¼ hr.); C&J also runs from Boston's Logan Airport. Greyhound is probably the better choice, because it drops you off right in Market Square, while C&J calls at a modern but distant bus station about 5 miles south of the city. (A "trolley" [bus] shuttles between the station and the city about once an hour—though *no* shuttle on Sunday. Otherwise, you'll need to call a taxi or have a rental car outfit pick you up.) A Greyhound ticket from South Station costs $19–$30 each way depending on the level of service. The trip from Logan Airport costs $23 one-way on C&J. From New York City, a one-way Greyhound ticket to Portsmouth costs about $56 to $96 (trip time: 7½ hours); C&J's fare is $79 (trip time: 5 hr.).

BY TRAIN   It's also possible to get here by **train**—sometimes. **Amtrak** (www.amtrak.com; ✆ **800/872-7245**) runs five trains daily from Boston's North Station to downtown Dover, New Hampshire, about 12 miles from Portsmouth; a one-way ticket is $21 to $31 per person, and the trip takes about

90 minutes. You can then take a no. 2 COAST bus (www.coastbus.org; ℂ **603/743-5777**) from Dover station to the center of downtown Portsmouth, a 45-minute trip that costs $1.50. This bus runs frequently on weekdays, eight times a day on Saturday, and does not run on Sunday.

VISITOR INFORMATION

The **Greater Portsmouth Chamber of Commerce,** 500 Market St. (www. portsmouthchamber.org; ℂ **603/610-5510**), has an information center on the road into town at exit 7 from I-95—it's on the right, in a grey shingle building. From Memorial Day to Columbus Day, it's open daily until at least 5pm (later Thurs–Fri); the rest of the year, it's open weekdays only. During summer a staffed information hut opens in Market Square in front of the Breaking New Grounds coffee shop.

Exploring Portsmouth

Black Heritage Trail ★★ WALKING TOUR   It may come as a surprise to learn that Portsmouth was a landing point for slaves, who were sold to locals on Long Wharf, near today's Strawbery Banke. Black culture of the Colonial and Federal periods is documented on 24 signboards and enhanced with personal stories of some of the hundreds of slaves who lived here. The self-guided Black Heritage Trail begins, appropriately, at the Long Wharf site of the auction block.

Long Wharf. www.pbhtrail.org. Admission free.

John Paul Jones House ★ MUSEUM   This 1758 home didn't belong to Revolutionary War hero Jones ("I have not yet begun to fight"), but he's believed to have rented a room here in 1777 while in town to oversee construction of his sloop, the *Ranger* (probably the first ship ever to sail under the U.S. flag; a model is on display). Jones sailed out of Portsmouth the next year and never returned, but that brief connection was enough for the Portsmouth Historical Society to appropriate his name for this museum. Today it's the home of the Portsmouth Historical Society's collections, shown in exhibits illustrating life in Portsmouth from 1623 onward. Especially worth seeing are exceptional examples of local furniture and decorative arts, both high-style and vernacular. Textile collections show three centuries of clothing, along with fine needlework, and there's a fascinating look at the influence of local people on the Portsmouth Peace Treaty of 1905 that ended the Russo-Japanese War.

43 Middle St. (corner of State St.). ℂ **603/436-8420.** $6 adults, free for children & active military. Memorial Day–Oct daily 11am–5pm (last tour at 4:30pm). Closed Nov to mid-May.

Moffatt-Ladd House & Garden ★★ HISTORIC HOME   Built for a family of prosperous merchants and traders, this 1763 home is as notable for its elegant gardens as it is for the home's great hall and elaborate carvings. Now a National Historic Landmark, it belonged to a single family from 1763 until 1913, when it became a museum. As a result, many of the furnishings here have never left the premises; aficionados of Early American furniture and painting, take note.

154 Market St. www.moffattladd.org. © **603/436-8221.** Admission to house and gardens $8 adults, $2.50 kids 11 and under; gardens only $2 per person. Tours mid-June to mid-Oct Mon–Sat 11am–5pm; Sun 1–5pm (last tour at 4:30pm). Closed mid-Oct to mid-June.

Rundlet-May House ★ HISTORIC HOME/GARDENS

Along with the Moffat-Ladd House, garden lovers shouldn't miss the impressive grounds and gardens of the Rundlet-May House, which still retain their original design from the time of the house's building in 1807. The house itself is interesting for its modernity, featuring the most up-to-date home improvements of its time: central heating, an indoor well, and the latest in kitchen equipment, including a Rumford range and a ventilation system.

364 Middle St. www.historicnewengland.org. © **603/436-3205.** $8 adults, $7 seniors, $4 students. June–mid-Oct 1st and 3rd Sat of month 11am–4pm. Closed mid-Oct to mid-June.

Strawbery Banke ★★★ OUTDOOR HISTORY MUSEUM

In 1958, the city of Portsmouth was finalizing plans to raze this neighborhood (which was settled in 1653!) to make way for "urban renewal." A group of local citizens resisted the move, and they prevailed, establishing an outdoor history museum that's become one of the largest and best in New England. Today the attraction consists of 10 downtown acres and more than 40 historic buildings, some restored with period furnishings, others featuring historic exhibits. (The remainder can be viewed only from the outside, but are mostly well restored.) The focus is on the buildings, architecture, and history. Several working crafts shops demonstrate Colonial skills and craftwork. The most intriguing home might be the Drisco House, half of which depicts life in the 1790s and half of which shows life in the 1950s—nicely demonstrating how houses grow and adapt to each era.

Visitor center at 14 Hancock St. (at Marcy St.). www.strawberybanke.org. © **603/433-1100.** $19.50 adults, $9 kids 5–17, free for kids 4 and under, $48 per family (fees lowered in winter). May–Oct daily for self-guided tours 10am–5pm; Nov–Apr 90-min. guided tours on the hour Sat–Sun only 10am–2pm; extra tours in Dec.

Warner House ★ HISTORIC HOME

This house, built in 1716 for a merchant and ship owner, was later the New Hampshire governor's mansion during the mid-18th century (when Portsmouth was the state capital). The brick structure with Georgian architectural elements is a favorite of architectural historians for its wall murals (said to be the oldest such murals still in place in the U.S.), early wall marbleizing, and white-pine paneling. It is a bit hard to find, although it's very close to Market Square—from the square, walk past the post office toward Memorial Bridge; look to your left for a brick house with dormers and a white picket fence.

150 Daniel St. www.warnerhouse.org. © **603/436-5909.** $8 adults, $7 seniors and students, $4 kids 7–12, ages 6 and under free. Mid-June to mid-Oct Tues and Thurs–Sat noon–4pm. Closed mid-Oct to mid-June.

Wentworth-Gardner House ★★ HISTORIC HOME   This 1760 mansion is considered one of the nation's prime examples of Georgian architecture, with many period elements, including pronounced *quoins* (blocks on the building's corners), pedimented window caps, plank sheathing, an elaborate doorway with Corinthian pilasters, a broken scroll, and a paneled door topped with a pineapple (even then, the symbol of hospitality). For all its elegant detail, though a grand home of the Colonial era, it's fairly modest in size. From the Prescott Park rose gardens (across from Strawbery Banke), walk 1 block and make a left toward the bridge. Take right onto Mechanic Street; house is 2 blocks farther on right.

50 Mechanic St. (at Gardner St.). www.wentworthgardnerandlear.org. ✆ **603/436-4406.** $6 adults, $3 students under 18, kids 7 and under free. Mid-June to mid-Oct Thurs–Sun noon–4pm. Closed mid-Oct to mid-June.

Side Trip from Portsmouth: Hampton Beach

Follow the shore south from Portsmouth along Route 1A and you'll pass several sandy beaches before you come to Hampton Beach's 700-foot-long stretch of soft white sand. It measures 150 feet wide at high tide—plenty of room for swimming, sunning, beachcombing, flying a kite, or building sand castles (there's a big competition here in mid-June). Hampton is a classic old-time beach town, with arcades, a boardwalk, soft ice cream, fried clams and the century-old **Hampton Beach Casino Ballroom** (www.casinoballroom. com; ✆ **603/929-4100**), which draws top entertainers. If you like smaller beaches, stop short of Hampton at **Wallis Sands** or **Jenness Beach.** Route 1A is lined with lodging and seafood restaurants that increase in concentration as you travel south.

Where to Stay in Portsmouth

Downtown accommodations are preferable, as everything is within walking distance, but prices tend to be high. The **Courtyard Portsmouth** (www. marriott.com; ✆ **603/436-2121**), at 1000 Market St., is big and modern, with business amenities and comfortable beds. The **Hilton Garden Inn** (www. hiltongardeninn3.hilton.com; ✆ **603/431-1499**), also downtown, has an indoor pool.

Ale House Inn ★★   Locations don't get any better than the urban-chic rooms at this former 1800s brewery warehouse adjacent to the Seacoast Repertory Theatre. Strawbery Banke, historic houses, and downtown restaurants and shops are a few steps away, and guests can use the hotel's Trek cruiser bicycles to roam farther afield. They also enjoy discounts on nearby golf, cruises, and cooking classes, and can search local attractions on the in-room iPads. No breakfast is served, but in-room Keurig coffee makers with organic coffees and teas help start the day, and several cafes are close by (see box p. 570).

121 Bow St. www.alehouseinn.com. ✆ **603/431-7760.** 10 rooms. $129–339 doubles. **Amenities:** Fridges; Wi-Fi (free).

The Hotel Portsmouth ★   In a favored location, quietly residential but close to Market Square and most of the city's attractions, the Hotel Portsmouth is a boutique hotel, in an exquisite Queen Anne–style building. It retains the details that made it a showplace in its heyday as a private residence, furnished in a nice blend of antique and contemporary. Rooms have iPod decks and bathrooms feature soaking or whirlpool tubs. The personal concierge service and a 24-hour front desk are rare among small inns.

40 Court St. (at Middle St.). www.thehotelportsmouth.com. ✆ **603/433-1200.** 32 units. $149–$359 doubles, $179–$469 suites. Rates include continental breakfast. **Amenities:** Wi-Fi (free).

Martin Hill Inn Bed & Breakfast ★   In a residential neighborhood a half-mile west of Market Square, this B&B consists of two attractive buildings: a main house (built around 1815) plus a guesthouse built 35 years later. Rooms have queen-size beds, writing tables, and sofas or sitting areas, and are appointed in handsome wallpapers, antiques, and four-poster or brass beds; some even have private porches. There are no in-room televisions. A stone pathway leads to a small water garden. The full breakfast might include johnnycakes, "goldenrod" eggs, quiche, nutty waffles, or cooked fruit. Check-in is limited to 4–6pm; there's a mandatory $3 charge for housekeepers' tips on your first night; children 11 and under aren't accepted.

404 Islington St. www.martinhillinn.com. ✆ **603/436-2287.** 7 units. May–Nov $145–$260 double; rest of year $145–$180 double. 2-night minimum stay summer and holiday weekends. Rates include full breakfast. Children 12 and over welcome. **Amenities:** Wi-Fi (free).

Wentworth by the Sea ★★★   A photogenic grand hotel, Wentworth by the Sea was built on a commanding spot on New Castle Island in 1874 and was the location of the international conference that ended the Russo-Japanese War in 1905. As befits an old grand hotel, rooms vary in size, but most are spacious, with good views of ocean or harbor. The suites in the three turrets have some of the more interesting views. Some units have gas fireplaces or private balconies. Luxury water-side suites have modern kitchens and marble bathrooms with Jacuzzis—plus access to a private dockside pool. A full-service spa offers a range of treatments, and there's a handsome lounge area as well as a **dining room** in the main building; in summer a seasonal deck grill opens adjacent to the Marina Suites. You can golf at the 18-hole Wentworth golf course (a 5-minute walk down the road). From downtown, take Route 1A (Miller Avenue) to Route 1B and continue 1½ miles to hotel.

588 Wentworth Rd., New Castle. www.wentworth.com. ✆ **866/384/0709.** 161 units. Peak season $259–$459 double, $439–$899 suite; off season $179–$229 double, $259–$599 suite. **Amenities:** 2 restaurants; bar; 2 pools (1 indoor, 1 outdoor); spa; kitchenettes (some units); tennis; golf course; Wi-Fi (free).

Where to Eat in Portsmouth

Beyond the options listed below, you could visit the dining room at the **Wentworth by the Sea** (see p. 569), on Route 1B a few miles south of the city; the resort's **Latitudes** grill has a simpler menu but offers terrace dining.

For casual dining in downtown Portsmouth, look for **Flatbread Company** (www.flatbreadcompany.com; *℃* **603/436-7888**), at 138 Congress St. It's *the* place to eat a terrific organic wheat-crust pizza.

Black Trumpet Bistro ★★★ BISTRO   Popular local chef Evan Mallett is known for his house-made charcuterie (he's a great believer in using nose-to-tail meats). He's also an expert mycologist, which accounts for the restaurant's name and the abundance of foraged mushrooms on the menu. His exotically spiced comfort food is served as small plates, medium plates or full entrees, and is influenced by cuisines of southern France, Spain, Africa, and Latin America. The intimate two-story restaurant is in a former warehouse at the harbor.

29 Ceres St. www.blacktrumpetbistro.com. *℃* **603/431-0887.** Reservations recommended. Small plates $7–$13; main courses $19–$30. Sun–Thurs 5:30–9:30pm; Fri–Sat 5:30–10pm.

Dolphin Striker ★ SEAFOOD/AMERICAN   In an old brick warehouse on one of Portsmouth's most charming streets, the Dolphin serves traditional New England seafood dishes—some of them dressed up in new ways, such as a mushroom-crusted fillet of cod or salmon "lacquered" in tomato-y balsamic vinaigrette and then grilled. But the Maine lobster potpie recipe hasn't changed since, well, probably 1700. Seafood avoiders can find refuge in the beef Wellington, steak au poivre, and other meaty choices. The main dining room has a rustic, public-house atmosphere with wide pine-board floors;

Portsmouth: Coffee Capital

Portsmouth has perhaps the best cafe scene in northern New England. **Breaking New Grounds** (14 Market Sq.; *℃* **603/436-9555**), serves outstanding espresso shakes, with tables out on the square; the cheery **Friendly Toast** (113 Congress St.; www.thefriendlytoast.net; *℃* **603/430-2154**) serves eggs and other breakfast dishes all day long; and **Me and Ollie's** (254 Lafayette St.; www. meandollies.com; *℃* **603/433-6588**) is a local favorite for its good bread, sandwiches, and homemade granola. Several more bakeries and coffee shops are within shouting distance of Market Square. The funky **Ceres Bakery** (51 Penhallow St.; www.ceresbakery.com; *℃* **603/436-6518**), on a side street off the main square, has a handful of tables and a tray of just-made sandwiches for those in a hurry. Nibble on sweet baklava with your coffee or tea at **Caffe Kilim,** a quarter-century-old Turkish coffee shop on Islington Street (www. caffekilim.com; *℃* **603/436-7330**). For a good pot of organic tea, walk a bit farther on Islington Street to no. 601, the cozy **White Heron Tea & Coffee** (www.whiteherontea.com; *℃* **603/294-0270**).

downstairs is a comfortable pub known as the Spring Hill Tavern, with a lighter, tavern-style menu and quite good acoustic acts.

15 Bow St. www.dolphinstriker.com. © **603/431-5222.** Reservations recommended. Main courses $18–$27. Daily 5–11pm.

Jumpin' Jay's Fish Café ★★ SEAFOOD   Attracting a younger, more culinarily attuned clientele than most other spots in town, Jay McSharry's signature restaurant is the place for anyone who wants to eat a fish cooked in something other than a deep-fryer. The sleek, spare dining room features an open kitchen and a polished-steel bar, and the fresh catch of the day is posted on the blackboards. You pick your fish and the way you want it cooked, then pair it with one of the sauces, such as an orange-sesame glaze, a lobster velouté, or simply olive oil with herbs. Starters include escargots, fish stews, crab cakes, and fried oysters; a few pasta dishes are also available. Great fresh fish and the attention to detail make this one of Portsmouth's iconic spots, a place that wouldn't feel right anywhere else.

150 Congress St. www.jumpinjays.com. © **603/766-3474.** Main courses $17–$39. Mon–Thurs 5:30–9pm (summer to 9:30pm), Fri–Sat 5–10pm; Sun 5–9pm.

Portsmouth Brewery ★ PUB FARE   In the heart of the historic district (look for the tipping tankard suspended over the sidewalk), New Hampshire's first brewpub opened here in 1991 and still draws a loyal local clientele with its superb beers and boisterous atmosphere. The airy tin-ceilinged, brick-walled dining room is redolent of hops. Brews are made in 200-gallon batches and include specialties such as Old Brown Dog ale and a delightfully creamy Black Cat Stout—plus some cool offbeat styles like cream ale, and a medieval-style "braggot." Along with the expected pizzas, burgers, and sandwiches, a changing selection of specials trots the globe adventurously—things like Asian rice noodles in a coconut broth or meatloaf spiked with chipotle peppers.

56 Market St. www.portsmouthbrewery.com. © **603/431-1115.** Reservations accepted for parties of 10 or more. Main courses $9–$26. Daily 11:30am–12:30am.

Row 34 ★★★ SEAFOOD   Locals sneak out of work early to get to Row 34 before 5pm for the $1 oysters at the raw bar. The bivalves come from the best Atlantic oyster beds still tasting of the sea, and go down well with any of the 20 or so on-tap brews that line one wall of the industrial-chic interior. In good weather, grab a sidewalk table on tiny Portwalk Place and join smartly dressed young professionals for dinner; go for the daily whole fish or the incomparable house-cured shrimp or salmon.

5 Portwalk Pl. www.row34nh.com. © **603/319-5011.** Main courses $13–$30. Mon–Thurs 11:30am–10pm, Fri–Sat 11:30am–11pm, Sun 10:30am–10pm.

Portsmouth Entertainment & Nightlife
PERFORMING ARTS
The Music Hall ★★   This historic theater near Market Square dates to 1878 and was more recently restored to its former glory. A variety of shows

are staged here, from lots of film to comedy revues, *The Nutcracker,* and concerts by visiting pop artists. Call or check the website for a current calendar. 28 Chestnut St. www.themusichall.org. © **603/436-2400.**

Rudi's Portsmouth ★   There's live jazz on weekends in the classy surroundings of a white-tablecloth restaurant at Rudi's Portsmouth. The lounge and wine bar are popular after-work spots on weeknights, with drink specials and $6 appetizers. 20 High St. www.rudisportsmouth.com. © **603/430-7834.** Main courses $12–$34.

Spring Hill Tavern ★   Quality acoustic noodling, live jazz, classical guitar, and/or low-key rock are on top most nights of the week here in the pub located right downstairs from the popular Dolphin Striker seafood restaurant (see "Where to Dine," above). Expect anything from a seasoned New Orleans–style blues band to a local singer-songwriter's nascent efforts. There are also sometimes fun free-form jam sessions. 15 Bow St. www.dolphinstriker.com. © **603/431-5222.** Cover varies.

THE MONADNOCK REGION ★

Keene: 220 miles NE of New York City, 102 miles W of Portsmouth, 93 miles NW of Boston

The region roughly surrounding Mount Monadnock and stretching west to the Connecticut River is often called New Hampshire's Quiet Corner. Commercial hubs are the small city of Keene and the town of Peterborough. It's a low-key area, marked by pretty villages of white clapboard houses set around green commons and overlooked by white church spires. Covered bridges sit picturesquely astride its streams and the mountain that gives it its name forms a backdrop to rural views. Amid these pastoral settings lurks quite a different layer—a thriving art and music scene, a high concentration of craft studios, fine dining, and luxury country inns that make travel here a delightful surprise. Couple this with the fact that—except in the fall, when its roads are busy with what locals call genially "leaf-peepers"—it is largely bypassed by tourists.

Within a half hour's drive of Keene, you'll find any number of postcard New England towns—look especially for **Walpole** (northwest of Keene on Route 12), **Fitzwilliam** (on Route 12 southeast of Keene), **Jaffrey Center** (on Route 124 southeast of Keene), **Harrisville** (east of Keene, a little ways north of Route 101), and **Hancock** (east of Keene, at the crossing of routes 123 and 137). You'll need a car to truly appreciate why the Monadnock region is one of New Hampshire's best-kept travel secrets.

Essentials

ARRIVING

You can reach Keene from Boston in about 2 hours via Route 3 or I-93 to Nashua and then Route 101. From New York and Hartford, take I-91 north to Brattleboro, Vermont; cross the river on Route 9 to Keene—it typically takes about 5 hours.

Pick up a state map for exploring the region's many little villages and towns, as the winding country roads can be confusing without one.

VISITOR INFORMATION

The **Monadnock Travel Council** website (www.monadnocktravel.com) includes lodging, dining, and attractions listings, although it's not always up to date. The **Greater Peterborough Chamber of Commerce** (www.peterborough chamber.com; © **603/924-7234**) has a year-round information center at 10 Wilton Road (just east of the intersection of routes 101 and 202). The center is open weekdays, 10am to 4pm. Several historic villages in this area maintain their own visitor websites, including **Jaffrey Center** (www.jcvis.org), **Harrisville** (www.historicharrisville.org), and **Fitzwilliam** (www.fitzwilliam.org).

Exploring Keene

Keene is the hub of the Monadnock region, a small city with a comfortable small-town air, but a surprising variety of arts and cultural options. Several of these—the **Thorne-Sagendorph Art Gallery** and frequent concerts and performances—are on the 170-acre campus of **Keene State College**, founded in 1909 (229 Main St.; www.keene.edu).

Adjacent to the college on Main Street is the **Horatio Colony House** (199 Main St.; www.horatiocolonymuseum.org; © **603/352-0460**), which is not your ordinary old house museum. Writer, philanthropist, and collector Horatio Colony was a highly cultured 19th-century gentleman who traveled extensively, collecting what struck his fancy, from fine furniture to folk crafts. Long before the eclectic look, Colony mixed styles and periods, surrounding himself with everything from carved Chinese furniture to bronze sculptures and highly improbable collections of cribbage boards and silver napkin rings. Today Colony's house looks as though he had just stepped out a few minutes ago. From May through mid-October, it's open Wednesday through Sunday, 11am to 4pm (rest of year by appointment). House tours are free of charge.

Keene's downtown shops and restaurants fill well-kept brick mercantile blocks circling the tree-shaded Central Square and lining its famously wide Main Street. Wander from the square along Court or Washington Street to see distinguished Victorian homes.

Outdoor Activities

Mount Monadnock ★★ rises impressively above the gentler hills of southern New Hampshire. Though it's only 3,165 feet (965m) in altitude, its lone position magnifies its height. Reputed to be the most oft-climbed mountain in the world—largely because it's relatively close to so many major population centers—its rocky peak is scaled by more than 100,000 hikers each year. It's clearly not a place for solitude on a beautiful September weekend, but climbers are spread across some 40 miles of trails that network the various slopes of the mountain. About a third of these are open in the winter for cross-country skiers.

The most popular and best-marked trails leave from near the entrance to **Monadnock State Park** ★★ (© **603/532-8862**), about 4 miles northwest of

Covered Bridge Tour

The NH state road map marks covered bridges, so it's easy to follow a circuit from Keene that includes five in a short distance. Leave Keene on Winchester Street (Route 10) and turn left onto Matthews Road to find **Cresson Bridge** at its end. Through the bridge, a left turn at the end of the road leads to Route 32. Go right, then left on Carleton Road to cross the 1790s **Carleton Bridge.**

Return to Route 32 and continue south (left), taking Swanzey Lake Road to the right. When it ends, turn right into West Swanzey, going left on Main Street and through **Thompson Bridge.** At the other side, turn right, then left when the street ends at Route 10. Two covered bridges are just off this road, the first on **Westport Village Road,** which forks to the left. Go through the bridge and continue until the road rejoins Route 10. Turn left and look for the sign to 1837 **Coombs Bridge.** Return to Route 10 and continue south into Winchester. A right on Route 119 leads along the river into the village of Ashuelot, where you'll find the most elaborate and largest of the bridges, **Village Bridge,** built in 1864.

Jaffrey Center off Route 124. (It's about 12 miles east of Keene via routes 101 and 124.) A round-trip hike up and down the most direct, crowded routes (the **White Dot** and **White Cross** trails, which begin at the end of a paved road) should take someone in decent shape 3 to 4 hours. Keep your eyes on the trail and be careful, as some sections are steep and some involve broken-up rock or ledges.

The final ascent is pretty steep; if you're afraid of heights, stop to snap pictures at one of the overlooks on the way up. On a clear day you can just see Boston and bits of other New England states from the top, if you know where to look. The state park is open year-round (a ranger is on duty in summer). Admission costs $5 for adults, $2 for kids 12 and over. No pets are allowed in this park. There's also camping at about two dozen sites in a small camping area, some available by reservation only; the sites cost $25 per night, and there are no water or electrical hookups.

Where to Stay in the Monadnock Region

Benjamin Prescott Inn ★ The three-story farmhouse, built by the sons of a veteran of Battle of Bunker Hill, dates from 1853, a handsome yellow Greek Revival building about 2 miles east of Jaffrey's town center. Throughout the inn, there's a strong sense of history and a connection to the past. Rooms are simply furnished—cranberry-hued Col. Prescott's Room is furnished with two armchairs and a desk, Susannah's Suite has a sitting room with a couch; all rooms have ceiling fans and the two suites are air-conditioned; Guests can wander the farmlands beyond the inn or drive a short way up the road for giant ice cream cones at **Kimball Farm.**

433 Turnpike Rd. (Rte. 124), Jaffrey. www.benjaminprescottinn.com. ✆ **888/950-6637** or 603/532-6637. 10 units. $105–$179 double; $235 suite. Rates include full breakfast. 2-night minimum some holidays and peak-season weekends. Children 12 and over welcome. **Amenities:** Wi-Fi (free).

Birchwood Inn ★ This quiet retreat offers affordable rooms and a thoroughly British experience. Thoreau visited the inn during one of his many rambles through New England and the inn still has the feeling of a 19th-century wayside hostelry. Decorated in an informal country style and operated by a pair of affable guys, it has rooms with a different themes (musical instruments, train memorabilia, country-store) bordering on the kitschy. The tavern downstairs, opens 5 nights a week, serves actual English-style pub food and beer.

340 Rte. 45, Temple (1½ miles S of Rte. 101). www.thebirchwoodinn.com. ℂ **603/878-3285.** 5 units. $99–$159 double. Rates include full breakfast. 2-night minimum stay during foliage season. No credit cards. Children 11 and over welcome. **Amenities:** Pub; Wi-Fi (free).

Chesterfield Inn ★★★ It's hard to say which is the more compelling reason for a stay at this elegant country inn—its spacious rooms with terraces overlooking the Connecticut River valley, or its outstanding dining room. Instead of being retrofitted into the circa 1780s farmhouse, guest rooms occupy a wing renovated especially to accommodate modern travelers who want a little more space, and no stairs to climb with luggage. This also allows the rooms to have large gas fireplaces and individual entrances, as well as panorama windows and thicker walls than most old-house conversions allow. All are eclectically appointed in a mix of modern and antique furniture; each has a fridge, CD player, television, and phone. The two priciest units have two–person Jacuzzis and private decks with mountain and meadow views. The main house is given over to large public spaces: a gracious parlor with wing chairs and a fireplace, and the **dining room** ★★. Here you'll find a small menu of exceptionally well-prepared seasonal dishes. The chef, Robert Nabstedt, has a passion for local ingredients and wild game, so you'll almost always find pheasant, wild boar, or venison on the menu. Main courses ($25–$33) might include items like tea-smoked duck breast served over sesame and peanut-flavored soba noodles; grilled salmon with a guava mango glaze; maple- and bourbon-basted barbecued shrimp over an autumn risotto; or an elk osso bucco with ragout.

While in the area, stop to hike through **Chesterfield Gorge,** on Route 9 east of the inn.

20 Cross Road, West Chesterfield (off Rte. 9 west of Keene). www.chesterfieldinn.com. ℂ **603/256-3211.** 8 rooms in the main building, 6 in adjacent cottages. $149–$345 doubles. Rates include full breakfast. 2-night minimum stay foliage season and holidays. Pets accepted in some units; $25 charge. **Amenities:** Restaurant; electric car charging station; fridges; Wi-Fi (free).

Hancock Inn ★★ The Hancock Inn, built in 1789, claims to be New Hampshire's oldest. You'll find classic Americana inside, from braided oval rugs and original wall murals to guest rooms appointed in understated Colonial decor. The Rufus Porter Room has an original 1820s wall mural by that foremost American primitive artist and the Moses Eaton Room features the designs of that famed stencil artist, who lived in Hancock. The Ballroom (it really was one) has a high, vaulted ceiling and Jacuzzi. This inn has the same historical charm as other historic inns in this area, but with more upscale rooms. The Fox Tavern serves excellent dinners based on local ingredients.

33 Main St. (Rte. 123/137), Hancock. www.hancockinn.com. © **800/525-1789** or 603/525-3318. 14 units. High season $289–$379 double; $409 suite. Low season $177–$262 double; $260–$290 suite. Rates include breakfast. Pets accepted in 1 unit (free). **Amenities:** Restaurant; Wi-Fi (most units; free).

Monadnock Inn ★   In the middle of one of New Hampshire's most idyllic villages, this architecturally eclectic inn was built around 1830 and offers one of the region's best values. Its rooms are updated in traditional New England style—some with four-poster or canopy beds—without losing the eccentricities that give old country inns their special appeal. Some rooms have TVs; all have goose-down comforters. A big front porch overlooks the shaded lawn and village, where several historic sites are within walking distance (see the town website, **www.jcvis.org**, for details). Parson's Pub is a convivial local gathering place and Thorndike's Restaurant serves well-above-average dinners.

379 Main St., Jaffrey Center. https://monadnockinn.com. © **877/510-7019** or 603/532-7800. 11 rooms. $110–$160 double. Rates include continental breakfast. Minimum stays required during foliage and holiday weekends. **Amenities:** Restaurant; pub; Wi-Fi (most units; free).

Where to Eat in the Monadnock Region

Nearly all of the inns listed above maintain restaurants serving dinner to both their own guests and the public. You'll find a number of good restaurants in downtown Keene, two of which overlook Central Square: **The Stage ★★** (www.thestagerestaurant.com; © **603/357-8389**) and **Luca's Mediterranean Café ★★** (www.lucascafe.com; © **603/358-3335**).

Harrisville General Store ★   DELI/BAKERY   Overlooking the 19th-century mill complex (a National Historic Landmark), Harrisville General Store was saved by a community effort to remain the town's gathering point as it has been for nearly 200 years. Order a BLT made with bacon from nearby Mayfair Farm and locally grown tomatoes. Take home some local honey or jams made at a nearby farm while you're there. Knitters and weavers should stop across the street at **Harrisville Designs** (www.harrisville.com; © **603/827-3333**) to revel in the dreamy yarns and woolcraft supplies.

29 Church St., Harrisville. www.harrisvillegeneralstore.com. © **603/827-3138.** Mon–Sat 8am–6pm, Sun 8am–4pm (grill closes 2pm).

Nicola's Trattoria ★★★   ITALIAN   Well-spaced tables, romantic lighting (but so you can still read the menu), and professional service complement the dependably fine Italian cuisine of chef/owner Nicola Bencivenga. Taste the flavors of his native Calabria in an appetizer of polenta with fontina cheese in a delicate mushroom sauce, or his deftly seasoned takes on Italian classics like veal saltimbocca. Seafood is a specialty: fettucine topped by sautéed shrimp and scallops in a blend of Alfredo and marinara sauce, or his signature cioppino brimming with shrimp, clams, calamari, sea scallops, mussels and fish. Reserve the table nearest the open kitchen to watch the well-choreographed ballet as Nicola and his team prepare your dinner.

51 Railroad St., Keene. www.facebook.com/nicolastrattoria. © **603/355-5242**. Main dishes $21–$30. Tues–Thurs 5–9pm, Fri–Sat 5–10pm.

The Restaurant at Burdicks and Burdick's Chocolates ★★★

BISTRO   A few steps from Walpole's pretty town common with its white bandstand (yes, there are band concerts there on summer evenings) is a winning combination of premier chocolate shop/cafe and notable dining spot. The latter serves a traditional French bistro menu—think pot au feu, grilled quail, duck ragout, or steak frites—in a smartly subdued atmosphere with an excellent wine list. Ingredients are locally sourced, many from nearby Connecticut Valley farms. Go at lunch time for the Lyonnaise Salad or the savory quiche. Head straight into the adjoining chocolate shop to inhale the rich aromas and take home a wooden box of Burdick's signature chocolate mice. Burdick's modestly claims to be the "World's Finest Gourmet Handmade Chocolates" and we can't argue with that. The display cases also include mouthwatering tortes and pastries, and there are tables if you have room for dessert.

47 Main St, Walpole (off Rte. 12 N of Keene). www.47mainwalpole.com. © **603/756-9058**. Main courses $17–$31. Tues–Sat 11:30am–9pm, brunch Sun 10am–2pm.

Twelve Pine ★ DELI   This inviting deli and market, in a former railroad building behind Peterborough's main street, is a great spot to nosh and linger. Select a premade meal or made-to-order sandwich heaped with filling and find a table among the locals who lunch here regularly. Between meals, stop for a fresh-from-the-oven scone and gourmet coffee. On your way out, stock up on local and imported cheeses in the market and wine shop.

11 School St. (in Depot Sq.), Peterborough. www.twelvepine.com. © **877/412-7463** or 603/924-6140. Sandwiches around $6, salads priced per lb. Mon–Fri 9am–7pm; Sat 9am–5pm; Sun 9am–4pm.

THE DARTMOUTH-LAKE SUNAPEE REGION ★

North of the Monadnock region, the Dartmouth-Lake Sunapee region hugs the broad, fertile valley of the Connecticut River and encompasses one of the state's loveliest lakes, its shoreline unspoiled by mass tourism. North of Lake Sunapee is Hanover, home of the Ivy League school Dartmouth College, a cultural center for the region. Close to Lake Sunapee, New London is another, smaller college town, another center for the arts, with a well-known summer playhouse. The area's scenic beauty has long provided inspiration for artists—a highlight is visiting the studio/home of sculptor Augustus Saint-Gaudens in Cornish.

Essentials

ARRIVING

BY CAR   To reach Hanover or New London from Boston, Concord NH, or Manchester NH, take I-93 to I-89N. From Brattleboro or St. Johnsbury VT, take I-91 north to Hanover; from Montpelier or Burlington VT, take I-89S to I-91N in White River Junction, head north a few miles, then exit for Norwich and cross the river.

BY BUS   Daily direct bus service connects Hanover and New London to Boston and Hanover to New York. **Dartmouth Coach** (www.dartmouthcoach. com; © **800/637-0123**) travels to and from Boston, stopping in New London, nine times per day, an easy 2½-hour ride costing $52 round-trip. From New York City, there are three Dartmouth Coach trips daily ($159 round-trip, 5 hr.).

BY TRAIN   Amtrak (www.amtrak.com; © **800/872-7245**) also runs one train daily (7 hr.; $56 one-way) from New York City to **White River Junction** VT, about 4½ miles away. From there, you'll need to take a cab on weekends, but on weekdays there is also a free public transit system from White River Junction to Hanover, on Advance Transit; take the Orange Route (www. advancetransit.com/routes/orange).

VISITOR INFORMATION

Hanover Area Chamber of Commerce (www.hanoverchamber.org; © **603/643-3115**) at 53 S. Main St. is open weekdays during normal business hours. Bonus: The chamber's members include businesses across the river in Norwich, Vermont, too.

SPECIAL EVENTS

In early to mid-February, look for the fantastic and intricate ice sculptures marking the return of the annual **Dartmouth Winter Carnival.** Call Dartmouth College's student affairs office at © **603/646-3399** for more information.

Exploring Hanover ★★

Hanover was settled in 1765 by early colonists who'd been granted a charter by King George III to establish a college here. That school, Dartmouth College—one of only nine colleges chartered in the colonies before the American Revolution—has had a profound impact in shaping the town, and its stately buildings ring three sides of the handsome village green. Hanover's compact downtown offers plenty of good restaurants, galleries, shops, and pubs.

Hanover is a great town to explore on foot, by bike, or even by *canoe* (see p. 579). Start by picking up a map of the **Dartmouth campus** at the college's information center on the green (summer and fall only), or across the street at the Hanover Inn (see p. 581). Free guided tours of the campus are also offered during summer, and the expansive, leafy neighborhood is a delight to walk through—especially the fraternity district, which, believe it or not, is full of grand old homes. **Baker-Berry Library,** facing the green, houses a little-known 20th-century art treasure: an entire reading room lined with powerful floor-to-ceiling murals painted by Jose Clemente Orozco.

On the south side of the green, next door to the Hanover Inn, is the modern **Hopkins Center for the Arts ★★** (http://hop.dartmouth.edu; ℂ **603/646-2422**). Locally known as "The Hop," the center attracts national acts to its 900-seat concert hall and stages top-notch dance and theatrical performances in its Moore Theater. Wallace Harrison, who later famously designed Lincoln Center in New York, was the building's architect.

Enfield Shaker Museum ★ OUTDOOR MUSEUM   About a 20-minute drive southeast of Hanover, this cluster of historic buildings on Lake Mascoma—"The Chosen Vale" (as the 350 Shakers who lived here in the mid-1800s called it)—was founded in 1793. Dominating the village is the Great Stone Dwelling, an austere granite five-plus-story structure that was once the tallest building north of Boston. While this is a far more modest museum of Shaker life than the outstanding **Canterbury Shaker Village** (www.shakers.org) farther south near Concord, the self-guided walking tour of the surrounding village is a good introduction to this historic sect.

447 Rte. 4A, Enfield. www.shakermuseum.org. ℂ **603/632-4346.** $12 adults, $8 ages 11–17, $3 ages 6–10, free for ages 5 and under. Mon–Sat 10am–5pm; Sun noon–5pm (last tour 4pm).

Hood Museum of Art ★★ MUSEUM   Often overlooked by visitors to Hanover (maybe because it's not even visible from the street, but rather set back behind other buildings), this modern, open structure beside the Hopkins Center houses one of the oldest college museums in the country. The permanent collection holds some 65,000 items, including a superb selection of 19th-century American landscapes; significant holdings of African, African-American, and Native American art and artifacts; and six stone reliefs dating from 900 B.C.E. Assyria. Reopening in 2019 after a massive renovation, the museum has increased its gallery space by 40%.

Wheelock St. (adjacent to Hopkins Center). http://hoodmuseum.dartmouth.edu. ℂ **603/646-2808.** Free admission. Tues–Sat 10am–5pm (Wed to 9pm); Sun noon–5pm.

Ledyard Canoe Club ★ OUTDOOR ACTIVITY   One idyllic way to spend a lazy afternoon in Hanover is by drifting along the Connecticut River in a canoe or kayak—assuming you know how to paddle one safely, that is. At Dartmouth's historic boating club, just downhill from the campus at the river's bank (turn upstream at the bottom of the hill west of the bridge and follow signs), you can rent a boat (and the required life jackets) for a few hours and explore the tree-lined river. The club also rents stand-up paddle boards.

Off W. Wheelock St. www.ledyardcanoeclub.org. ℂ **603/643-6709.** Canoe and kayak rentals $10/hr., $30/day Mon–Fri, $40/day Sat–Sun. Summer Mon–Fri 11am–7pm, Sat–Sun 10am–7pm; spring and fall Mon–Fri noon–6pm, Sat–Sun 10am–7pm. Open mid-May to mid-Oct. or whenever river temperature is above 50°F (10°C).

Exploring Sunapee & New London ★

Big **Lake Sunapee ★★** (about 30 miles southeast of Hanover via I-89) is said to be one of the purest in the nation, and it's much deeper than it looks.

GARDENS OF stone

There was a seriously thriving artists' colony in the little village of **Cornish,** about 20 miles south of Hanover, in the early 20th century; today, the chief relic of those heady days is the **Saint-Gaudens National Historic Site ★★** (www.nps. gov/saga; ℂ **603/675-2175**), a remarkable little spot off Rte. 12A. The Irish-born sculptor Augustus Saint-Gaudens arrived here in 1885, having received an important commission to create a statue of Abraham Lincoln. His friend Charles Beaman, a Manhattan lawyer who owned several homes in the area, assured him he could find a plenty of "Lincoln-shaped men" in the area. Saint-Gaudens came, found them, and stayed for the rest of his life, creating work that today fills American museums, cemeteries, and parks. (He even designed a U.S. coin, the lovely "double eagle").

Saint-Gaudens' hillside home and studio **Aspet**—named for the village in Ireland where he was raised—are superb places to learn more about the artist. Grounds are open year-round, while the buildings are open to the public daily from late May through October, 9am to 4:30pm. Admission is $10 for adults, free for kids 16 and under during that season. There's no charge to visit the grounds during the off season.

Sunapee is a longtime favorite summer resort of Bostonians, and offers excellent swimming, boating, and fishing. But its shores have never been scoured by bulldozers to make room for big resorts, so they remain largely tree-clad.

The only way to see the often sumptuous summer "cottages" is from the water. Luckily the *MV Mt Sunapee II* obliges with 90-minute narrated cruises filled with tales from the lake's quirky history, and unobstructed views of Mt Sunapee and the lake's eight islands and three lighthouses (www.sunapee cruises.com; ℂ **603/938-6465**; fares $20 adults, $19 seniors and military, $10 ages 6–12). Or sightsee over a roast beef dinner as the sun sets, aboard the replica steamship *MV Kearsarge* (www.sunapeecruises.com; ℂ **603/938-6465;** fares $41 adults, $31 ages 12 and under). Both set sail from **Sunapee Harbor,** a good place to grab an ice cream cone and watch the boats come and go.

The steep Mt Sunapee—which, together with the beach, forms **Mount Sunapee State Park** (ℂ **603/763-5561**)—is a fine place to hike in the summer or ski in the winter. Family-friendly **Mount Sunapee Ski Resort** (www. mountsunapee.com; ℂ **603/763-3500**) is always listed among New England's best for snowmaking and grooming. Although it has only 1,500 feet of vertical drop, the 66 trails pack in a lot of skiing for all skill levels and the state-of-the-art terrain park has 50 features for boarders You might see a famous face with your cone, too; members of the band Aerosmith own homes in the harbor area.

For a glimpse at the early vacationers who chose Lake Sunapee as a summer retreat, stop at **The Fells,** 456 Route 103A in Newbury (www.thefells. org; ℂ **603/763-4789**). This historic home was built in the late 1800s by U.S. Secretary of State John Hay, former personal secretary to President Abraham Lincoln. The gardens are beautiful, varying from flower-bordered terraces and walled garden rooms to a rock garden surrounding a brook that tumbles into a rocky glen. The grounds are open daily 9am to 4pm; from mid-June through Labor Day the house is open Wednesday through Sundays 9am to 4pm (weekends only late spring and early fall, closed Columbus Day–Memorial Day), with a docent-led tour at noon. House admission is $10 adults, $8 seniors and students, $4 ages 6 to 17, $25 families.

On the east side of the lake, pretty **New London ★** is an attractive college town with lots of fine homes, art galleries, a few restaurants, and an outstanding summer musical theater. The **New London Barn Playhouse** (www. nlbarn.org; ℂ **603/526-6710**) produces quality Broadway shows from June through August.

Where to Stay in the Dartmouth-Lake Sunapee Region

There are plenty of midprice chain hotel and motel properties clumped together along a strip just off the interstate in **West Lebanon,** 5 miles south of Hanover. Take exit 20 off I-89 to find them.

HANOVER

The Hanover Inn ★★   The venerable white-and-brick Hanover Inn is one of the oldest lodgings in the state, but kept up-to-date with sophisticated and tailored decor in its spacious rooms. Those in front overlook the pretty green. The professional service has a boutique warmth and there's a clubby sort of Dartmouth flair (the college does own it, after all), but not enough to put off non-Ivy League alums. Walkways connect the inn to the Hood Museum of Art and Hopkins Center for the Arts, a convenience especially appreciated in the winter. The high-end **Pine** farm-to-table restaurant (see p. 583) has a terrace of outdoor tables fronting the green.

Wheelock St., Hanover. www.hanoverinn.com. ℂ **800/443-7024** or 603/643-4300. 108 units. $180–$430 double. Valet parking $23/day. Pets $50 per night. **Amenities:** Restaurant; business center; fitness center; room service; Wi-Fi (free).

Six South Street Hotel ★★   There's an upbeat hospitality that begins with the valet parking and bright open lobby; there's the feel of a boutique hotel despite its 69-room size. The contemporary rooms in Hanover's newest hotel are well-designed with large desks, good lighting, coffee makers, and dramatic (but not jarring) cocoa-and-red color schemes; many have comfortable seating areas. Roomy, smartly decorated public spaces off the lobby are inviting, opening into a bar that has quickly become a local gathering spot. The adjoining restaurant, Bistro at Six, serves breakfast and dinner.

6 South St. (just off Main St.), Hanover. www.sixsouth.com. ℂ **603/643-0600.** 69 rooms. $115–$299 (higher rates on fall football weekends and Dartmouth events). **Amenities:** Restaurant; fitness room; library; valet parking $20; Wi-Fi (free).

NEW LONDON

New London Inn ★   Welcoming travelers since 1870, this historic inn sits in the center of New London, next to Colby-Sawyer College campus and close to the New London Barn Playhouse. Good-sized rooms are simply furnished and uncluttered, with large windows; one has a double Jacuzzi and

New Hampshire's largest lake, Winnipesaukee has 44,000 spring-fed acres of water, studded with more than 250 islands. Around it are several other glacier-carved lakes, giving New England its own beautiful Lakes Region, defining the central region at the foothills of the White Mountains. The lakelands are beloved by families who return summer after summer to lakeside cottages, which up here are called camps, many of them (especially those along the wooded shore of coveted Squam Lake) owned by the same family for generations.

Views from Winnipesaukee take in the Belknap range and stretch north to Mt. Washington on a clear day. The favorite way to take in those views is from a boat. On the east side of Winnipesaukee, in the lively tourist center of **Wolfeboro,** you can board a scenic lake tour on the 65-foot *Winnipesaukee Belle,* a replica 19th-century paddleboat (www.wolfeboroinn.com; ☎ **603/569-3016**). In the summer season the 230-foot *M/S Mount Washington* and two smaller mail boats (www.cruisenh.com; ☎ **603/366-5531**) depart daily on 2½-hour scenic cruises from Weirs Beach, stopping at either Wolfeboro, Alton Lake, or Meredith and Center Harbor. Or if you'd prefer to propel yourself on the lake, you can rent kayaks and aquacycles at **EKAL Activity Center** in Meredith, at the lake's northwest corner (www.ekalactivitycenter.com; ☎ **603/677-8646**).

Not all the region's activities are water-borne. **Gunstock Mountain** (www.gunstock.com, ☎ **603/293-4341**), overlooking Winnipesaukee on its southern shore, is well known as a full-service ski area in the winter, but has an expanding four-season presence as a family recreation park. Among its attractions is New

England's largest aerial obstacle course, the **Aerial Treetop Adventure,** which includes log ladders, bridges, swings, foot bridges, seesaws, and zip lines. There's an Explorer Course just for kids, a 4,100-foot **Mountain Coaster,** bungee jumping, a climbing wall, Segway trail tours, scenic chairlift rides to the summit (especially beautiful in the fall) and a small lake with paddle boats, kayaks, and stand-up paddle boards.

Not on Lake Winnipesaukee, but on neighboring **Squam Lake** (made famous as the film setting for *On Golden Pond*), **Holderness** is home to the **Squam Lakes Natural Science Center** (www.nhnature.org; ☎ **603/968-7194;** $20 adults, $15 kids 3–15), where you can see local wildlife and learn about the lakeside ecosystem. The center also offers naturalist-led boat tours of Squam Lake to spot eagles and loons.

Meredith and Wolfeboro are the two main centers for lodging, dining, and shopping. **Mills Falls Marketplace** (www.millfalls.com) in Meredith houses nine shops ranging from an independent book store to clothing, quality handcrafts, antiques, and fine art. Dine overlooking the lake in Meredith at the summer-camp-themed **Camp** (www.thecman.com; ☎ **603/279-3003**), where you can finish off a dinner of comfort foods with s'mores for dessert, or the equally casual **Town Docks,** known for seafood and its outdoor Tiki Bar (www.thecman.com; ☎ **603/279-3445**). Just up the road at **Hart's Turkey Farm,** a New Hampshire landmark, you'll find traditional turkey dinners and sandwiches (www.hartsturkeyfarm.com; ☎ **603/279-6212**). For more on the attractions around Lake Winnipesaukee, visit **www.lakesregion.org.**

fireplace. Public areas include a cozy common room, a porch with rocking chairs, and spaces for local artists to display their works. The inn's **Coach House Restaurant** serves a somewhat traditional menu, but dishes are nicely prepared and with creative touches. The dining room spills outdoors onto the terrace in good weather.

353 Main St., New London. www.thenewlondoninn.com. © **603/526-2791.** 23 rooms. $154–$259 double. Rates include breakfast. **Amenities:** Restaurant; use of nearby sports complex; passes to Town Beach; Wi-Fi (free)

Where to Eat in Hanover

Note also that all the inns listed above have in-house restaurants that welcome non-guests.

Lou's ★ BAKERY/DINER   Lou's has been a Hanover institution since the 1940s, attracting hordes of students for breakfast on the weekends and a steady local clientele during the week. This is a no-frills diner, just a black-and-white-checkerboard linoleum floor, maple-and-vinyl booths, and a harried but efficient crew of waiters. Breakfast is served all day (real maple syrup on your pancakes costs extra, though), and the sandwiches, served on freshly baked bread, are huge. Locals know to pop in after the diner closes at 3 to buy the day's remaining baked goods (if any are left) until 5pm.

30 S. Main St. www.lousrestaurant.net. © **603/643-3321.** Breakfast items $3–$7; lunch items $5–$8. Mon–Fri 6am–3pm; Sat–Sun 7am–3pm (opens 8am Sun in winter). Bakery daily to 5pm.

Pine Restaurant ★★★ FARM-TO-TABLE   Showcasing locally raised and sustainable ingredients, Pine's menu runs the gamut from the Hanover Burger (with Vermont cheddar, bacon, crispy onions, and chipotle aioli) to Yuzu-glazed duck breast served with spring vegetables and a sweet-sour sauce of cherries and rhubarb. Simple or complicated, it's served in stylish presentations. It's located in the Hanover Inn (p. 581).

Wheelock St. www.pineathanoverinn.com. © **603/646-8000.** Reservations recommended. Main courses $14–$18 lunch, $16–$36 dinner. Daily 6:30am–11pm.

THE WHITE MOUNTAINS ★★★

The first road through the seemingly impenetrable barrier of the White Mountains opened in 1775, but their beauties and recreation potential weren't fully realized until the 1820s, when a tragic landslide brought attention—and chroniclers—to the dramatic landscapes and fresh mountain air. The latter was particularly appealing to wealthy city dwellers, who soon began to decamp here each summer—entire families, maids and all—for a social season at the grand hotels that began to spring up. From then on, the White Mountains became northern New England's outdoors and recreation capital, and the season now extends year-round.

The Appalachian Trail, the Maine-to-Georgia hiking route, crosses the rocky summits of Mount Washington and its neighbors in one of the most scenic stretches of the entire trail. Each of the peaks has its own trail from the base, and climbers who "collect" 4,000-footers have a heyday here. But these mountains aren't just for hikers—outdoor lovers of all stripes scale its cliffs, fish its lakes and streams, cycle its winding roads, ski its well-groomed trails, and seek photographs of the illusive moose.

The **White Mountain National Forest** covers most of this vast landscape, nearly 800,000 acres of rocky, forested terrain, more than 100 waterfalls, dozens of backcountry lakes, and miles of cascading streams. A vast network of hiking trails (more than 1,000 miles' worth) dates back to the 19th century, ranging from easy strolls to almost vertical rock scrambles.

The heart of the White Mountains is 6,288-foot **Mount Washington,** often cloud-capped and white with snow from October through April or May. It's so big, you can see it from the Maine coast, 100 miles away. For all its majesty (not to mention its forbidding weather) it's highly accessible. You can reach its peak by climbing trails ranging from moderate to brutal, ride a historic cog railway or a van, or drive your own car to the top. It's a lofty and panoramic, but not lonely, peak.

Flanking Washington is the **Presidential Range,** wind-blasted granite peaks named for U.S. presidents and offering similarly sweeping views. Two notches (glacially scoured mountain passes)—Crawford and Franconia—cross the range, and together form a driving loop that includes some of New England's best mountain scenery. Another lofty drive is the **Kancamagus Highway** (Route 112), running east-west between Conway and Lincoln, an officially designated Scenic Byway with well-placed pullouts to picnic and snap photos.

North Conway is the lodging capital; on the western side of the mountains, **Lincoln** and **North Woodstock** are smaller centers for lodging and dining. The towns of **Bethlehem, Jackson,** and **Franconia,** plus a handful of little villages, offer even more variety.

Essentials

ARRIVING

BY CAR   North Conway and the Mount Washington Valley sit on routes 16 and 302. Route 16 connects to the Spaulding Turnpike, then to I-95 to Boston and New York; Route 302 zigzags from Maine to Vermont. Traffic can be vexing in this valley on holiday weekends in summer, and it gets *really* bad on foliage weekends in fall, when backups several miles long are common. You can avoid the worst of this by taking North-South Road from Route 302, just before (east of) the Route 16 intersection; it ends a block away from downtown North Conway.

I-93 runs right through **Franconia Notch,** about 2¼ hours by car from Boston via I-93, or about 5½ hours from New York City via I-84 and I-93.

BY BUS   Concord Coach (www.concordcoachlines.com; © **800/639-3317**) runs two daily buses from Boston's South Station and Logan Airport to North Conway, stopping at the Eastern Slope Inn (Route 16/302) and in Conway at the First Stop Market on West Main Street (across from the middle school). Concord Coach also runs two daily buses from Boston to Lincoln (3½ hr., $32 one way) and Franconia (4 hr., $32 one-way).

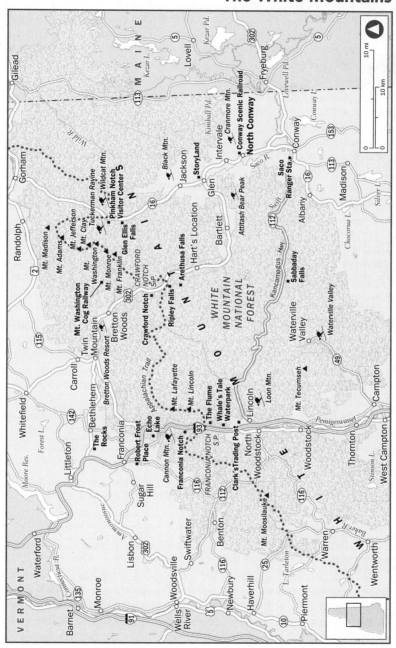

VISITOR INFORMATION

For information on the entire area, contact **White Mountain Attractions** (www.visitwhitemountains.com; ℰ **603/745-8720**), online or at their visitors center at 200 Kancamagus Highway in North Woodstock.

In the eastern part of the region, the very helpful **Mount Washington Valley Chamber of Commerce** (www.mtwashingtonvalley.org; ℰ **877/948-6867** or 603/356-5701) operates an information booth opposite the North Conway village green; it's open daily in summer, weekends only in winter. The **Jackson Area Chamber of Commerce** (www.jacksonnh.com; ℰ **800/866-3334** or 603/383-9356), based in the Jackson Falls Marketplace on Route 16B, has information about lodging and attractions. Farther north, on Route 16 between Jackson and Gorham, the rustic **Pinkham Notch Visitor Center** (ℰ **603/466-2721**), operated by the Appalachian Mountain Club, offers maps, some outdoor supplies, and helpful advice; it has a cafe, travel store, even overnight accommodations and meals (at the adjacent Joe Dodge Lodge; see p. 601). It's open daily, year-round, from 6am to 10pm.

Just north of the White Mountain National Forest, the **Twin Mountain–Bretton Woods Chamber of Commerce** (www.twinmountain.org; ℰ **800/245-8946**) provides general information and lodging advice from a booth near the intersection of routes 302 and 3 (look for the retired Cog Railroad engine). It's open late May through mid-October.

Along the I-93 corridor, the year-round (weekends only in the winter) **White Mountains Visitor Center** ★ (ℰ **603/745-3816**), just off exit 32, includes National Forest staff as well as information on White Mountain attractions and travel. The **Flume Gorge Visitor Center** (ℰ **603/745-8391**), open mid-May to mid-October, is at exit 34A. Farther north, off exit 38, the **Franconia Notch Chamber of Commerce** (www.franconianotch.org; ℰ **603/823-5661** in summer or 603/823-3450 in winter) maintains a helpful visitor information hut at 421 Main St., next to the town hall in Franconia. It's open spring through fall.

Exploring North Conway ★

North Conway: 150 miles N of Boston, 62 miles NW of Portland ME

North Conway is the commercial heart of the White Mountains, with the highest concentration of lodgings and shops. Shoppers are drawn to the outlets that line route 302/16 south of the center. On rainy weekends and during foliage season, that road can resemble a linear parking lot. But look up from the clutter and you'll see the peaks of the Whites and the ski trails of Cranmore Mountain forming a scenic backdrop.

Sprawl notwithstanding, North Conway is beautifully situated along the broad Saco River valley (known here as the Mt. Washington Valley). Gentle, forest-covered mountains, some with sheer cliffs that could be distant cousins of those in Yosemite, border the bottomlands. Northward up the valley, hills rise in a crescendo to Mount Washington. You can get a closer look at the mountain and its infamous weather at the **Mount Washington Observatory Weather Discovery Center** on Main Street (www.mountwashington.org; ℰ **603/356-2137**).

The central village is trim and attractive, with colorful shops, eating places, a splendid Victorian railway station overlooking an open green, and attractive old mercantile buildings along its main street (which is, unfortunately, also the main road and often congested).

Exploring Mount Washington & Environs ★★

A gateway to **Mount Washington ★★★** and its massive surrounding peaks, **Jackson ★★** is a quiet place in a picturesque valley just off Route 16. It's only about a 15-minute drive north of North Conway—yet a world apart. The compact village center, approached via a single-lane covered bridge, has

A Magic Place for the Younger Set

Parents can buy peace of mind (and have fun themselves) at **Story Land ★★**, at the northern junction of routes 16 and 302 (www.storylandnh.com; ✆ **603/383-4186**), just south of Jackson. This old-fashioned fantasy village is filled with 30 acres of magical rides, cuckoo clocks, story-book houses, mini-trains, a pumpkin coach, pirate ship, swan boats, fairy-tale creatures, and plenty of other enchanted beings. It's especially good for very young children, although a newer section will keep older kids entertained, with more age-appropriate thrill rides. It's open weekends 9am–5pm from Memorial Day to mid-June; daily 9am–6pm from mid-June to Labor Day; and again weekends only 9am–5pm through Columbus Day. Admission is $31 per person for ages 3 and over; children 2 and under enter free. *Tip:* Enter the park during the last 3 hours any day (after 3pm July and Aug, 2pm other days), and receive a free pass for the next day, or any other day that season.

retained its old-world elegance—reminders of a time when Jackson was the favored destination of those who could afford to summer at grand hotels.

Today, thanks to its scenic golf course and one of the nation's most elaborate, well-maintained cross-country ski networks, Jackson has found renewed purpose as a resort in summer *and* winter. It's no longer undiscovered, but it does still feels a bit out of the mainstream, especially compared to the busy scene just to the south.

Just north of Jackson, in the heart of the White Mountain National Forest, **Mount Washington** (see box p. 589) is the region's star attraction. It's the highest mountain in the northeast U.S., but it's also the New England mountain with the most options for getting to its summit. Visitors can ascend via a **cog railway** (see p. 588); by car, along a snaky **toll road** to the summit; in an all-terrain vehicle (ATV), using the same road; in a guide-driven van; or **on foot.** Twice a year—during two annual thigh-punishing races to the summit—you can even climb **by bike.** The races are for pros only, as the grade increases steeply to 22% near the top, where even pros have flipped over backwards.

The best place to learn about Mount Washington and its approaches is the **Pinkham Notch Visitor Center** (✆ **603/466-2721**), operated year-round by the Appalachian Mountain Club, on Route 16 between Jackson and Gorham. The **Joe Dodge Lodge** (see p. 601) is here, and a number of hiking trails depart from here, with several loops and side trips.

About a dozen **trails** lead to the mountain's summit, ranging in length from about 4 to 15 miles. (Detailed information is available at the visitor center.) The most direct and dramatic way is via the **Tuckerman Ravine Trail ★★★**, which departs right from Pinkham Notch. It's a true full-day's endeavor. Healthy hikers should allow 4 to 5 hours for the ascent, 2 to 4 hours for the return trip. Be sure to allow enough time to enjoy the dramatic glacial cirque of Tuckerman Ravine, which attracts extreme skiers to its sheer drops as late as June, and often holds patches of snow well into the summer.

The **Mount Washington Auto Road** ★★ (www.mtwashingtonautoroad. com; © **603/466-3988**) opened in 1861 as a carriage road and has since remained a wildly popular attraction. The steep, winding 8-mile road (with an *average* grade of 12%) is partly paved and incredibly dramatic; your breath will be taken away at one curve after another. The ascent will test your iron will; the descent will test your car's brakes. This trip is not worth doing, though, if the summit is in the clouds—wait for a **clear day.** Located on Route 16 just north of Pinkham Notch, the road is open daily from early May until late October, 8am to 5pm (hours may be slightly different early or late in the season). The cost is $31 per vehicle and driver, plus $9 for each additional adult ($7 per child age 5–12); it's $14 for a motorcycle and its operator. This price includes an audiocassette or CD narration pointing out sights along the way and the famous bumper sticker proclaiming "This car climbed Mt. Washington." No trailers, RVs, or mopeds are allowed, and some other vehicle restrictions protect against breakdowns and logjams. (For example, Acuras, Hondas, Saturns, Sterlings, and Jaguars with automatic transmissions must show a "1," "L," or "S" on the shifter to be allowed on the road; only H-3 version Hummers can ascend.)

If you'd prefer to leave the driving to someone else—or it's winter—**van tours** ascend throughout the day in safe weather, allowing you to relax, enjoy the views, and learn about the mountain from informed guides. The cost is $36 for adults, $31 for seniors, and $16 for kids ages 5 to 12, and includes a short stay on the summit. Vans leave from the Great Glen Trails Outdoor Center and reservations are not necessary.

In summer, an enclosed gondola known as the **Wildcat Express** ★ at the Wildcat Mountain ski area, just north of Pinkham Notch on Route 16 (see p. 596), carries passengers up the mountain for views of Tuckerman Ravine and Mount Washington's summit. The lift operates daily July 1 through Labor Day, weekends through Columbus Day. It costs $15 per adult to ride the gondola, with discounts for seniors and kids, but it doesn't run in bad weather. There's now also a "ziprider," a zipline ride down a similar track—it costs $5

Mount Washington 101

The impressive statistics about **Mount Washington** ★★★ don't always succeed at evoking the scenic, windblown peak—or its hellish weather. But here are a few anyway. At 6,288 feet (1,916m), Washington is *the* highest mountain in the Northeast. It also has some of the worst weather in the world. It still holds the world's record for the highest wind speed ever recorded on land—231 mph in 1934. Winds topping 150 mph are routinely recorded here, a result of the mountain's position at the confluence of three major storm tracks. The average temperature atop the mountain is 30°F (–1°C). (The record low was –43°F/–42°C, and the warmest temperature ever recorded atop the mountain, in August, was 72°F/22°C.) Even in August, bring warm clothing in case blustery, cold weather moves in suddenly. Wearing only shorts and a T-shirt, with nothing else as backup, is a bad idea.

Scenic Hiking Around Pinkham Notch

Just south of the Pinkham Notch Visitor Center (see p. 586), look for signs to **Glen Ellis Falls ★★**, an easy 10-minute walk along the Glen Ellis River—until the path suddenly seems to drop off the face of the earth. The stream plummets 65 feet down a cliff here; observation platforms are at the top and near the bottom of the falls, some of this area's most impressive after a heavy rain.

From the same visitor center, it's about 2.5 miles up to **Hermit Lake** and

Tuckerman Ravine ★★★ via the Tuckerman Ravine Trail (see p. 588). Even if you're not planning to continue on to the summit, the ravine—with its sheer sides and lacy cataracts—might be the most dramatic destination in the White Mountains. The trail is wide and only moderately demanding; allow 2 hours if you're in good shape. Bring a picnic and lunch on the massive boulders that litter the ravine's floor.

extra, and you must be between 75 and 275 lb., and between 4'4" and 6'8". There's also **Frisbee golf** on the mountain (15 per person, $10 with your own disc).

Exploring Crawford Notch ★★★ & Bretton Woods

Crawford Notch is a wild, rugged mountain valley that angles right through the heart of the White Mountains. There's a surplus of history here. For nearly all the colonial period, this was an impenetrable wilderness—a barrier to commerce that blocked trade between the upper Connecticut River Valley and the harbors of Portland and Portsmouth. Eventually the notch was discovered, and a primitive road was built in 1775, followed by a railroad, making this into an important route.

A few miles beyond the head of the notch is the village of Bretton Woods; the Notch itself is in the town of Harts Location, one of the state's smallest in population (at last count, 41).

A splendid way to see Crawford Notch is from the lofty vantage point of the original railroad route along its precipitous western side. The **Conway Scenic Railroad ★★** (www.conwayscenic.com; ✆ **603/356-5251**) makes the 5-hour round trip daily from North Conway to the little Victorian station at the head of the notch. During the height of fall colors, mid-September to mid-October, it travels 15 minutes farther to Bretton Woods. Tickets are $59 to $85 adults, $41 to $55 for kids ages 4 to 12, $40 for children under age 4.

Mount Washington Cog Railway ★★★ VINTAGE TRAIN RIDE Mount Washington's Cog Railway was a marvel of engineering when it opened in 1869, and it remains so today. Part moving museum, part slow-motion roller-coaster ride, the Cog Railway climbs to the mountain's summit at a determined, "I think I can" pace of about 4 mph. But you'll still get some adrenaline thrills, especially when the train crosses Jacob's Ladder, a trestle 25 feet high that angles upward at a grade of more than(!) 37%. Passengers enjoy the expanding views on the 3-hour round-trip, which includes important stops to add water to the steam engine and change the track switches to allow other trains to ascend or descend. A 20-minute stop at the summit gives you a little time for photos and a look around the little museum, or you can return on a later train. For it first century or so this ride was more than a little sooty, but in the interests of the environment, state-of-the-art biodiesel engines have replaced the coal-burning originals, just as picturesque and a lot cleaner for passengers—and the mountain air. For traditionalists who don't mind the soot, steam trains make the first run at 9am most mornings.

Base Rd., Bretton Woods (From Rte. 302, turn onto Base Rd. at Fabyan's Station Restaurant, continue 6 miles to station.). www.thecog.com. ℂ **800/922-8825** or 603/278-5404. $79 adults, $68 seniors, $41 ages 4–12, free for ages 3 and under. Memorial Day–late Oct daily (Sat–Sun in May) usually on the hour 9am to 3 or 4pm (check website or call for schedule). Reservations recommended.

Exploring Franconia Notch ★★★

The approach to **Franconia Notch** is dramatic. As travelers drive north on I-93, the Kinsman Range to the west and the Franconia Range to the east begin converging, and the two mountain ranges press inward on either side like a closing book, forming "the Notch." This narrow defile offers little in the way of civilization or services, but a whole lot of natural drama. Plan on a leisurely ride through the notch, allowing extra time to get out of your car and explore the local forests, peaks, and eateries. Too bad the Old Man of the Mountain isn't here anymore (see box below), but even without his watchful stone eye, this drive is high on our "must-do" list for northern New England.

FRANCONIA NOTCH STATE PARK ★★

Franconia Notch State Park's (ℂ **603/745-8391**) 8,000 acres, inside the much bigger White Mountain National Forest, includes a number of attractions easily accessible from I-93 and the Franconia Notch Parkway.

The Flume ★★ is a rugged 800-foot gorge through which the Flume Brook tumbles. A popular attraction as far back as the mid-19th century, it's 90 feet deep and as narrow as 20 feet at the bottom; visitors explore it by a series of boardwalks and bridges on a 2-mile-long walk through the forest that includes a waterfall, some glacial boulders, and a covered bridge. The Flume

---

The Old Man of the Mountain

On the side of Cannon Mountain, overlooking Franconia Notch, the Old Man of the Mountain was a distinctive 40-foot natural stone profile that became the official symbol of New Hampshire. Nathaniel Hawthorne immortalized it in his short story "The Great Stone Face," it was a prime tourist attraction, and its image decorated souvenirs for more than a century. Then sometime the night of May 3, 2003, the five granite ledges that composed the famous face slid off into the rock tumble below it. To many in New Hampshire and beyond, it was like losing an old friend. Eulogies were penned, people left flowers, and a memorial was built at the former viewing point to show what it looked like.

is open daily 9am to 5pm from early May through mid-October, weather permitting—it stays open a half-hour later in July and August. Admission costs $16 for adults, $14 for kids ages 6 to 12, and is free for younger children. There is no charge to walk or snowshoe here in the off season.

Echo Lake ★ sits at the head of the notch, directly beneath the steep slopes of Cannon Mountain and Mount Lafayette. A good swimming beach with lifeguards lines one side of the 39-acre lake, and you can admire the views of the notch and mountains from picnic tables or from the bike path along the shore (it continues for 8 miles through the notch). Inexpensive canoe and kayak rentals are available at the beach. For beautiful views of the lake and notch, make the 1.5-mile climb to **Artists' Bluff,** the rock ledge you can see above the north shore. The beach is open daily from mid-June through early September; admission costs $4 per adult, $2 for ages 6 to 11, and is free for younger kids. Lifeguards are on duty 9am–6pm mid-May through Labor Day.

For a dramatic high-altitude view of Echo Lake, Franconia Notch, the Presidential Range—and into Canada on a clear day—board the **Cannon Mountain Aerial Tramway ★★** (www.cannonmt.com; ✆ **603/823-8800**). This 80-passenger cable car serves the ski hill (see p. 595) in winter; in summer, it takes sightseers to the summit of the 4,180-foot mountain. Once up top, you can walk along the Rim Trail for dramatic views into the notch, directly below. Be prepared for cool, gusty winds, though. The tramway operates from mid-May through mid-October, and costs $18 round-trip for adults, $16 for kids ages 6 to 12. *Tip:* If you're planning to do both the Aerial Tramway and Flume Gorge, you can buy a Discovery Pass at either attraction (adults $30, ages 6–12 $24) that combines the two on one ticket.

Outdoor Activities in the White Mountains
BACKPACKING

The White Mountains have some of the most challenging and scenic backpacking in the eastern U.S. The huge **White Mountain National Forest** encompasses several 5,000-plus-foot peaks and miles of wilderness trails that range from easy rambles to wind-buffeted ridgeline paths. The **Appalachian**

Fun for Kids in Franconia Notch

Two attractions just south of Franconia Notch are of interest to parents with young children. **Clark's Trading Post** (www.clarkstradingpost.com; ✆ **603/745-8913**) is best known for its trained bears, which seem to be having as much fun as the audience as they cavort on swings, ride scooters, play basketball and eat ice cream. Learn about these native animals (all of whom were rescued as orphaned cubs) as they play.

A steam train ride, water games, and a fun house are all one-offs, made especially for this family-owned fun park, and several of the attractions relate to White Mountain history and lore. The more traditional **Whale's Tale Waterpark** (www.whalestale waterpark.net; ✆ **603/745-8810**), 2 miles north on Route 3, is good for a hot summer day, with a wave pool and water-soaked rides.

Trail ★★★ passes through New Hampshire, entering the state at Hanover and running along the highest peaks of the White Mountains before exiting into Maine along the scenic, tough-to-climb Mahoosuc Range northeast of Gorham. The trail is well maintained in these stretches, though it tends to attract crowds along the highest elevations in summer. The **Appalachian Mountain Club** (www.amc-nh.org or www.outdoors.org; ✆ **603/466-2727**) is an excellent source of information about the region's outdoors offerings.

HIKING

The essential guide to hiking in this region is the Appalachian Mountain Club's *White Mountain Guide,* which contains up-to-date and detailed descriptions of every trail in the area. The guide is available at bookstores and outdoor shops.

The Appalachian Mountain Club's **Highland Center at Crawford Notch ★★** (✆ **603/278-4453**), on Route 302 in Bretton Woods, is a multipurpose facility on 26 acres of AMC-owned land. It's a one-stop headquarters for hikes into the surrounding mountains. You can book a tour, hike the path that passes nearby (two AMC huts are each a short hike away), bunk down for the night, eat communal dinners, and use L.L.Bean gear for free (yes, really—hiking boots, jackets, snowshoes and more, all free). It's open year-round.

From June through mid-September, the center is also the hub for two AMC **hiker shuttles** (✆ **603/466-2727**). These vans cruise the mountains daily (and on weekends through mid-Oct), depositing and picking up hikers. They're pricey, but make it possible to hike longer trails without backtracking. Rides cost $24 one-way, regardless of length; AMC members get a $4 discount.

BACKCOUNTRY FEES

The White Mountain National Forest requires anyone using the backcountry—for hiking, mountain biking, picnicking, or any other activity—to pay a recreation fee. Anyone parking at a trailhead must display a permit on the dashboard; those lacking a permit face a fine. Permits are available at ranger stations and many stores in the region. An annual permit costs $20, and a 7-day pass is $5. You can also buy a day pass for $3, but it covers only the site where you bought it. (If you drive anywhere else on the same day and park again, you'll have to pay another $3.) You're much better off with the 7-day or annual pass.

RANGER STATIONS

The Forest Service's new **White Mountain National Forest headquarters** (www.fs.usda.gov/detail/whitemountain; ✆ **603/536-6100**) are located at 71 White Mountain Drive in Campton (take exit 27 from I-93 and follow signs). The facility also houses a handy visitor center that's open daily, year-round, 8am to 4:30pm. There are two more stations in the mountains: the **Saco Ranger Station,** at 33 Kancamagus Highway, 300 feet west of Route 16 in Conway (✆ **603/447-5448**); and the **Androscoggin Ranger Station,** at 300 Glen Road in Gorham (✆ **603/466-2713**).

WHOSE woods THESE ARE, I THINK I KNOW

The great American poet Robert Frost lived in New Hampshire from the time he was 10 until he was 45. Today his former farmhouse, the **Frost Place** (Ridge Rd., Franconia; www.frostplace.org; ℂ 603/823-5510) is a quietly respectful tribute in the form of an arts center and gathering place for local writers. The poet and his family moved to this small-ish, humble farmhouse in 1915; his first two books of poetry were published while he lived here. Walking the grounds, it's not hard to see how his granite-edged poetry evolved here at the fringes of the White Mountains. First editions of Frost's works are on display; a nature trail in the woods nearby is posted with excerpts from some of his poems. In early July every year, there's a **Frost Day** celebration with lectures and readings from resident poets.

Admission is $5 adults, $4 seniors, $3 students 6 to 18 (age 12 and under free) From July to early October, it's open Wednesday to Monday 1 to 5pm; in late May and June it's open weekends from 1 to 5pm; it's closed mid-Oct to mid-May. From Franconia, travel south 1 mile on Route 116 to Ridge Road (a gravel road) and follow signs a short way to the house.

Skiing

For up-to-date information on the state's ski areas, both downhill and cross-country, contact SkiNH (www.skinh.com; ℂ **603/745-9396**).

DOWNHILL

Attitash ★★   One of New England's most scenic ski areas, Attitash is an especially good mountain for skiers at the intermediate-to-advanced level. The resort consists of 68 trails (plus tree skiing and terrain parks) across two peaks: 2,250-ft. high (686m) Attitash and adjacent Bear Peak. Dotted with rugged rock outcroppings and full of sweeping views of Mount Washington and the Presidential Range, this is an eye-popping place—with excellent skiing. Look for great cruising runs and a handful of challenging drops. You can stay right at the mountain's base in a 143-unit hotel. As with many of these New Hampshire ski areas, though, the base area is sleepy at night; if you're looking for a beer or some live music, you'll have to drive 15 minutes to North Conway.

775 Rte. 302, Bartlett. www.attitash.com. ℂ **877/677-7669** or 603/374-2600. Day lift tickets $79 adults mid-week, $85 weekends; discounts for seniors, students, and children.

Black Mountain ★★   Dating back to the 1930s, Black Mountain was one of the White Mountains' pioneering ski areas. It hasn't gone all modern like many of New England's other ski hills, instead remaining a quintessential family mountain—modest in size, nonthreatening, ideal for beginners—though there's also glade skiing for more advanced skiers. Its retro feel adds to the charm; this place isn't even on the radar of the Aspen set. The views from the Presidentials are very good, and a lift ticket is surprisingly inexpensive compared with the other resorts in the area—on a weekday, an adult can ski for less than $45, an unheard-of bargain. Bonus: Most of the 44 trails are pointed due south, so no frigid north winds blast your face. The resort also offers two compact terrain parks for snowboarders, as well as lessons, rentals, day-care for small kids, a ski school, and a base lodge with a cafeteria and pub. Nice place.

373 Black Mountain Rd., Jackson. www.blackmt.com. © **800/475-4669** or 603/698-4490. Day lift ticket $42 adults weekday, $59 weekends/holidays; discounts for students, children, seniors, and military.

Bretton Woods (Mount Washington Resort) ★★

In terms of acreage, Bretton Woods/Mount Washington is New England's biggest ski resort; it's also one of the most family-friendly. The resort does an award-winning job taking care of kids—there are tons of programs for them, and *Ski* magazine annually ranks it among the nation's best family ski areas. The low-key attitude is a big part of that. Accommodations are available both on the mountain and nearby, notably at the grand, red-roofed **Mount Washington Resort** (see p. 600), though nightlife there is pretty sedate. Views are straight across the valley to Mt. Washington, and trails feature plenty of glades and wide cruising runs, perfect for beginners and families, as well as a few more challenging options for advanced skiers (they're not the most radical slopes in the state, though). There's also night skiing; four freestyle terrain parks; and an excellent cross-country ski center.

Rte. 302, Bretton Woods. www.brettonwoods.com. © **800/314-1752** or 603/278-1000. Day lift tickets $66–$74 adults ($10 discount for Mt. Washington Resort guests); $50–$56 half-day; discounts for teens and children, none for seniors.

Cannon Mountain ★★

One of New England's very first ski mountains, Cannon remains famed for its challenging runs and exposed faces, and although the mountain has some runs for beginners and intermediates, it still attracts mainly serious skiers. (The scenery is knockout-gorgeous, too—ranked second-best in the Eastern U.S. by *Ski* magazine.) Many of the old-fashioned New England–style trails here are narrow and steep (but sometimes icy, because they're constantly scoured by the notch's winds), and the enclosed tramway is an elegant way to get to the summit. There's no base lodge scene to speak of, though.

Franconia Notch Pkwy., Franconia. www.cannonmt.com. © **603/823-8800** or 603/823-7771. Day lift tickets $77 adults, $55 half-day; discounts for seniors, teens, and youths. Tues & Thurs special rates.

Cranmore Mountain Resort ★★

Ski pioneer Hannes Schneider brought recreational downhill skiing to America in 1939, at what's now New England's oldest operating ski area. (You can learn more about this at the **New England Ski Museum,** next to Schouler Park.) Cranmore's slopes and trails have something for every level, but are best for beginners and intermediates. It's worth a few runs just for the views of the snow-covered Presidential range. In recent years Cranmore has added a big snow-tubing center, a 2,390-foot-long 728m) Mountain Coaster, an Aerial Adventure Course, disk golf, and more facilities that have turned it into a year-round attraction. It's ideal for families, thanks to the relaxed attitude, range of activities, and not-outrageous ticket prices.

1 Skimobile Rd., North Conway. www.cranmore.com. © **800/786-6754.** Day lift tickets $75 adults; discounts for youths and seniors.

Wildcat ★★ Set high in Pinkham Notch, Wildcat combines a rich heritage as a venerable ski resort with some of the best views of any ski area in the White Mountains. This mountain offers plenty of intermediate trails and challenging expert terrain. It's skiing the way it used to be—no base-area clutter, just a single lodge and no on-slope hotels, condos, or other accommodations (but there are plenty of lodging options within an easy 15-min. drive).

Rte. 16, Pinkham Notch. www.skiwildcat.com. © **888/754-9453** or 603/466-3326. Day lift tickets $79 adults midweek, $85 weekends/holidays; discounts for seniors, teens, and kids 6–12.

CROSS-COUNTRY

The state's premier cross-country destination is **Jackson Ski Touring Association** (www.jacksonxc.org; © **800/927-6697** or 603/383-9355), which maintains more than 50 miles of lovely trails in and around the scenic village of Jackson, near the base of Mount Washington. Jackson is ranked among the top cross-country sites in the U.S., largely thanks to the nonprofit **Jackson Ski Touring Foundation,** which created and maintains the extensive trail network. The terrain is wonderfully varied; many trails are rated "most difficult," which will keep advanced skiers from getting bored. But novice and intermediate skiers also have plenty of good options spread out along the valley floor. Start at the base lodge, near the Wentworth Resort in the center of Jackson, and ski right through the village and into the hills. Gentle trails traverse the valley floor, with more advanced trails winding up the mountains. One-way ski trips with shuttles back to Jackson are available. Given the extensive and well maintained trails, passes are a good value at $21 for adults, $17 for seniors, and $10 for kids ages 10 to 17. Rentals are available at the ski center (ticket/rental packages are available); snowshoes can be rented, too ($10 all ages)—there are specifically groomed trails for snowshoers.

Another good Nordic center is at **Bretton Woods Resort** (www.bretton woods.com; © **800/314-1752** or 603/278-3322; see p. 595 for downhill skiing info). Adults pay $21 per day to ski the trails here; ski rentals are available.

Where to Stay in the White Mountains
NORTH CONWAY

Route 16 in North Conway is lined with basic motels (many family-run), which are affordably priced in the spring or late fall, but often disappointingly expensive during the summer, ski-season weekends, and fall-foliage season. They vary wildly in upkeep from place to place. For a relaxing stay outside of North Conway's constant buzz but close enough to access all its activities, drive a few miles south to the pretty lakeside village of Eaton Center, neighboring Madison, or to Albany, at the beginning of the Kancamagus Highway scenic drive.

camping IN THE WHITE MOUNTAINS

The White Mountain National Forest maintains about two dozen drive-in campgrounds scattered throughout the region. Campsites cost in the $20 range per night. Online reservations are accepted at many of these campsites through the **National Recreation Reservation Service** (www.recreation.gov; ℂ 877/444-6777). Most of the National Forest campsites are rather basic—in fact, some have only pit toilets—but all of them are well maintained. Remember that some sites require reservations at least a week in advance (in other words, no walk-ins), and there are 2- to 3-night minimum stays some weekends during peak season.

Of all these, the biggest (and least personal) is **Dolly Copp Campground** (ℂ 603/466-2713), near the base of Mount Washington. Still, it has a superior location and great views from the open sites. Along the Kancamagus Highway, **Covered Bridge Campground** (ℂ 603/447-2166), about 6 miles west of Conway and adjacent to an 1858 covered bridge, is a short drive to some delightful river swimming at the Rocky Gorge Scenic Area. These campgrounds are open from mid-May until mid-October.

New Hampshire State Parks (www.nhstateparks.org; ℂ 603/271-3628) also offer camping in northern New Hampshire, including four in the White Mountains. Most have more facilities than the National Forest sites (White Lake has a beach, Lafayette Place a camp store, all have showers). You can reserve these state campgrounds online at www.reserveamerica.com.

Backcountry tent camping is free throughout the White Mountains, and no permit is needed. (You *will* need to purchase a parking permit to leave your car at the trail head, however; see p. 593.) Check with a ranger station and the forest-service website about updated camping rules. Three-sided log lean-tos are also scattered throughout the backcountry, providing overnight shelter. Some of these are free; at others, a backcountry manager will collect a small fee. Any of the three ranger stations (see p. 593) can give details and locations.

Briarcliff Motel ★   Of North Conway's dozens of roadside motels, the Briarcliff is one of the best choices. Located about a half-mile south of the village center, this is your basic U-shaped motel with standard-size rooms, but all its units have been redecorated in rich colors, much like B&B rooms. You have to pay extra for a room with a "porch" and mountain view; the porches are actually part of a long enclosed sitting area, separated by partial partitions. Soda, irons, a microwave, and ski lockers are all in the common room. But this is still a bargain, and well kept up.

Rte. 16, North Conway. www.briarcliffmotel.com. ℂ **800/338-4291** or 603/356-5584. 30 units. Summer and fall $99–$179 double; rest of the year $69–$189 double. 2-night minimum stay holidays and foliage season. **Amenities:** Outdoor pool; Wi-Fi (free).

Cranmore Inn ★   The Cranmore Inn has the feel of a 19th-century boardinghouse—which is appropriate, because that's what it is. Open since 1863, this three-story Victorian home is a short walk from North Conway's village center. Its heritage adds charm and quirkiness, but comes with occasional old-house drawbacks such as uneven water pressure and winding hallways. Still, it offers good value, handy location, hospitable innkeepers, and nicely maintained rooms. Some family-friendly units in the main inn consist of two bedrooms, connected in the middle by a bathroom. Three big "kitchen units" are housed in an annex; these suites come with separate dining rooms, living rooms, and even personal computers.

80 Kearsarge St., North Conway. www.cranmoreinn.com. ℂ **800/526-5502** or 603/356-5502. 19 units (some with bath across hall). Peak season $169–$479 double, foliage season $219–$519 double, Jan to mid-Mar & Nov $129–$409 double. Rates include full breakfast (except kitchenette units). 2-night minimum stay weekends, holidays, and in foliage season. **Amenities:** Jacuzzi; outdoor pool; kitchenette (some units); Wi-Fi (free).

Darby Field Inn ★★   Want to feel like you're in the middle of the wilderness? Darby Field Inn is in the tiny corner of Albany that's not inside the vast White Mountain National Forest. Ten miles of hiking and cross-country ski trails converge at the back door, and rooms (we like the Mt. Washington Suite for its double-sided fireplace and big Jacuzzi) have views of Mt. Washington. A large common room with a stone fireplace invites relaxing, or you can stroll in the flower gardens or lie in a hammock and watch the autumn leaves turn orange. Cooked-to-order breakfasts are served in a room hung with the works of local artists. Conway's restaurants are nearby, but in-house **Littlefield's Tavern** is a powerful reason to "stay home" for dinner.

185 Chase Hill Road, Albany. www.darbyfield.com. ℂ **603/447-2181.** 13 rooms and suites. $160–$280 double, foliage and Christmas week $185–$300. Rates include breakfast. **Amenities:** Outdoor pool; snowshoes; Jacuzzis and fireplaces in deluxe rooms; Wi-Fi (free).

Huttopia ★★   A cross between camping and a posh cottage resort, Huttopia, which opened in 2017, adds outdoor fun to a family vacation without the fuss of packing and unloading gear and setting up a campsite. The safari-style tents have wooden floors, real beds, and electricity. Some have running water, equipped mini-kitchens (with real wine glasses), and even en-suite loos. All sites have coolers or refrigerators, propane grills, and fire rings. The big pool and adjoining terrace (where a food trailer serves espresso and French crepes for breakfast) is a gathering spot where evening shows delight the kids. French ownership and management lends an exotic touch.

57 Pine Knoll Road, Albany. https://canada-usa.huttopia.com/en. ℂ **603/447-3131.** High season $90–$200 double; low season $90–$125. **Amenities:** Swimming pool; playground; canteen (w/wine); pétanque court; lake beach w/kayaks and paddle boards; Wi-Fi in lounge area (free).

Kearsarge Inn ★★   Also in a 19th-century house a few steps from North Conway's Main Street shops and restaurants, Kearsarge Inn is more upscale, but also with rooms and suites that are perfect for families. Some rooms have sleep-sofas for children and there are suites and cottages for larger families. It's a long climb with luggage, but the third-floor penthouse suite is a family-friendly lair with two large rooms, each with a gas fireplace. Guest rooms are furnished tastefully in antiques and reproductions, with no frilly curtains or stacks of decorative throw pillows. The entire front of the inn is circled by a wraparound porch, where guests can watch the world go by from wicker easy chairs. Or they can play croquet on the lawn.

42 Seavey St., North Conway. www.kearsarginn.com. © **603/356-8700** or 855/532-7727. 18 rooms and suites. High season $99–$219 double; low season $69–$229 double. **Amenities:** Gas fireplaces (most rooms); Wi-Fi (free).

Purity Spring Resort ★★   Summer or winter, there's plenty to do at this down-home resort that feels like a summer camp—and in fact includes a day camp for the kids. Choose from several options: the century-old inn, cottages, luxury rooms overlooking Purity Lake, and ski-in-ski-out rooms in the base lodge at the resort's King Pine ski area. Here skiers can boot-up in their room, stepping out the door and into skis at the bottom of the slope. Skiing is free with lodging, as are skating, tubing, the pool and summer activities; there's no added resort fee. Some suites have kitchenettes, but the restaurant, **Traditions** ★, is so popular that most families leave cooking to the chef.

1251 Eaton Rd., Madison (Rte. 153, south of Conway). www.purityspring.com. © **603/367-8896** or 800/373-3754. High season $202–$288 double, low season $134–$161 double. Summer rates include all meals; off-season rates include breakfast. **Amenities:** Restaurant; indoor and outdoor pools; fitness center; tennis; spa; skiing (downhill and Nordic); skating; tubing; kids' camp; Wi-Fi (free).

Snowvillage Inn ★★★   High on a hillside, with panoramic views of the Presidential Range, Snowvillage Inn combines the charms of a traditional inn with a sophisticated dining room, **Max's,** that draws as many locals as inn guests, especially on Tuesday for the Local's Night menu or Thursday for the Oyster Orgy. Rooms in the main inn vary from the cozy Queen Room to the bright King Suite with its 180-degree above-the-treetops view of the White Mountains. The adjacent Chimney House has four queen-size rooms with gas fireplaces; knotty-pine-clad Carriage House rooms can sleep up to four. Breakfast is cooked to order, served in the common room where guests gather in the evening in front of the massive stone fireplace.

136 Stewart Rd., Eaton Center. www.snowvillageinn.com. © **603/4472818.** 16 rooms. High season $179–$289 double; low season $139–$249 double. Rates include breakfast. **Amenities:** Snowshoe Center; access to private lake beach; Wi-Fi (free).

Stonehurst Manor ★★★   In the days before air conditioning, wealthy city people packed up trunks of clothes and moved, along with the maids and valets, to summer "cottages" in cooler mountain air. You can relive those days at this 1874 stone estate with spectacular views of Mt. Washington. Most of the 16 opulently decorated rooms in the manor have fireplaces and/or Jacuzzis, and 10 more in the newer Mountain View Wing are also individually decorated. Adjacent modern condos accommodate families and include use of the swimming pool and resort facilities. Cocktails in the lush Library Lounge are an evening tradition, and the Manor's **Wild Rose Restaurant** is known for generous cuts of prime rib, pit-smoked, aged, and slow-roasted. The grilled rack of lamb, crabcakes, and fresh-made pasta are equally good.

3351 White Mountain Hwy, North Conway. www.stonehurstmanor.com. © **800/525-9100** or 603/356-3113. 26 units. $156–$296 double. Rates include full breakfast and dinner. **Amenities:** Restaurant; outdoor pool; tennis court; Wi-Fi (free).

BRETTON WOODS

A number of motels, cottage clusters, and campgrounds line routes 3 and 302 in Twin Mountain, just west of Bretton Woods. It's not the most charming stretch of road, but convenient to attractions in both Crawford and Franconia notches.

Mount Washington Resort ★★ At the foot of New Hampshire's highest peak, this gleaming white five-story resort surrounded on three sides by porches looks like a classic ocean liner sailing across the valley. Built in 1902, it has an illustrious history as the scene of the 1944 International Monetary Conference that established the World Bank and International Monetary Fund. Thomas Edison designed its electrical system and it has hosted presidents and royalty. The 900-foot-long porch, as well as windows in the grand octagonal dining room, look directly up at the massive mountain and down onto the resort's golf course, pool, and tennis court. Guest rooms vary in size and decor, but many have grand views. There are lots of family and kids' programs and activities (such as fly-casting lessons). A change in management—it's now an Omni property—have given it more of an urban business hotel feel, but it still rings of the grand resort hotel era. Also included in the resort are the **Bretton Arms Inn ★★** (next door to the big hotel) and **The Lodge ★**, more modern and motel-like, across the highway.

Rte. 302, Bretton Woods. www.omnihotels.com. © **888/444-6664** or 603/278-1000. 200 units. $169–$579 double. Minimum stay during holidays. **Amenities:** 2 restaurants; babysitting; bikes; children's programs (summer); concierge; 2 golf courses; Jacuzzi; 2 pools (1 indoor, 1 outdoor); room service; sauna; free shuttle to ski area and other facilities; Wi-Fi (free).

Notchland Inn ★★★ In a hand-cut granite house built in the mid-1800s, the Notchland Inn is a standout in many different ways. First, it's a surprise to see such an elegant mansion perched grandly beside the road deep in an otherwise wild stretch of Crawford Notch. Inside, you'll discover from your gregarious hosts that its parlor and fireplace were designed by Gustav Stickley, a founder of the Arts & Crafts movement. Guest rooms are no less memorable, each different and each infinitely appealing and comfortable. Our favorite is the Evans suite, with its three-corner tub and skylight over the bed for stargazing. But we also like the Zealand for its suite of Eastlake furniture and the rosy Victorian feel of the Crawford room. Two new cottages on the hillside are pet-friendly. Don't worry that it's a bit of a drive away from it all—you'll want to have a glass of wine in the solarium and dinner overlooking the birch trees in your own back yard. With luck, one of the menu choices will be the grapevine-skewered lamb kabobs or chicken breast crusted with pistachios. Finish with maple pecan pie (made with NH maple syrup). Non-guests can dine here as well, although they should reserve in advance.

2 Morey Rd. (just off Rte. 302), Hart's Location. www.notchland.com. © **800/866-6131** or 603/374-6131. 8 rooms, 5 suites, 2 cottages. $199–$285 double; $295–$395 cottages and suites. Rates include full breakfast. 2- to 3-night minimum stay weekends, foliage season, and some holidays. Children 12 and over welcome. **Amenities:** Dining room; Jacuzzi; Wi-Fi (free).

PINKHAM NOTCH

The Inn at Thorn Hill ★★★ This elegant inn is a good choice for a romantic getaway, and although there are three cottages, we'd opt for the main inn, whose rooms are spacious and elegant, with fireplaces, whirlpool tubs, steam showers, lush bathrobes, and DVD players. The inn's common areas are exceptionally large and gracious—comfy leather sofas by the fireplace, cozy game tables, a scenic nook under the tower, a convivial bar, and a wide wrap-around porch overlooking the mountains. A beautifully appointed spa with a full menu of services hides downstairs (the inn's a lot bigger than it looks), along with a redwood sauna and a wine cellar that provides the dining room with the state's largest wine list. The **dining room** ★★ is one of the best in the valley, featuring farm-fresh local ingredients in a menu of classic favorites—melt-in-the-mouth braised short ribs, Statler chicken, shallot-marinated hanger steak—and daily specials. Cooked-to-order breakfasts feature four different entrees each day (and never repeat during your stay).

Thorn Hill Rd., Jackson. www.innatthornhill.com. © **603/383-4242.** 16 rooms, 3 cottages. $220–$320 double. Rates include full breakfast, afternoon tea. 2- to 3-night minimum stay Sat–Sun and some holidays. Children 16 and over welcome. **Amenities:** Restaurant; bar; limited room service; outdoor pool; spa; Wi-Fi (free).

Joe Dodge Lodge at Pinkham Notch ★ Guests come to this Appalachian Mountain Club lodge as much for the camaraderie as for the accommodations, knowing they will meet and share experiences with fellow hikers and outdoors enthusiasts. Situated at the base of Mount Washington, far from commercial clutter and with easy access to many hiking trails, the lodge is somewhat like a tightly run youth hostel. Guests share bunkrooms, dormitory-style bathrooms, and meals at family-style tables in the main lodge. (A few private rooms provide double beds and family accommodations, but try to book these well ahead.) Breakfast and dinner are included in the prices, although bunks-only rates are sometimes available. The festive atmosphere is wonderful, as is the can't-be-beat location. You can also buy a trail lunch to-go in the cafeteria.

Rte. 16, Pinkham Notch. www.outdoors.org. © **603/466-2721.** 108 beds, in 2-, 3-, and 4-bed rooms and family rooms (all w/shared bath). $98–$112 per person high season; $79–$90 off-season (discounts for AMC members). Rates include breakfast and dinner. Children 3 and over welcome. **Amenities:** Cafeteria; Wi-Fi (free).

Whitney's Inn at Jackson ★ Welcoming guests since the mid-1800s, Whitney's is one of the oldest hostelries in the White Mountains, and it's a favorite of generations of families. Rustic decor (many rooms have tree-log

The **Appalachian Mountain Club** ★ (www.amc-nh.org) maintains eight sturdy mountain huts ★, small cabins with bunkrooms and great campfire conviviality; hearty breakfasts and dinners are included with your rates, which are about $139 per adult, $116 for members. Other AMC cabins and lodges in the mountains include the 16-bed **Shapleigh Bunkhouse** in Crawford Notch (a bunk plus breakfast costs $60 for non-AMC members) and the **Highland Center** at Crawford Notch.

beds) and the old-time convivial atmosphere add to the away-from-it-all feeling. In the winter you can ski right out the door and onto the lifts at Black Mountain ski area (see p. 594), one of the sweetest family-friendly mountains in the east. Tiny "hiker rooms" are the best bargain, but many rooms accommodate four people, making the inn a good budget choice for families. Two-room suites and two-bedroom cottages have stone fireplaces and mini-kitchens. The adjacent three-story post-and-beam barn is now The **Shovel Handle Pub,** with a menu of old favorites such as chicken pot pie, fish and chips, and some more ambitious specialties like mahogany-roasted duck.

357 Black Mountain Rd. www.whitneysinn.com. ⓒ **603/383-8916.** 17 rooms, 8 suites, 2 cottages. $99–$199 doubles, $169–$229 suites, $219–$299 cottages. **Amenities:** Restaurant; downhill and cross-country skiing; outdoor heated pool; trout pond on property; Wi-Fi (free) in the main inn.

FRANCONIA NOTCH

Adair Country Inn ★★★   Close to Franconia Notch and within easy reach of Mt. Washington, Adair Country Inn gives modern-day travelers a chance to sample the century-ago luxuries of wealthy city families who retired to the mountains annually to escape the summer's heat. The mansion looks much as it did in the 1920s, when it was aglow with summer dinner parties, and still displays the original owner's hat and book collections. Arrive for afternoon tea in the airy parlor and stay for **dinner** ★★ overlooking authentically restored gardens designed by premier landscape architect Frederick Law Olmstead. The chef favors local ingredients, enhancing traditional dishes with some more exotic touches: fried chicken breast is crusted with pecans, topped with maple bourbon sauce, and served on creamy risotto. The breakfast popovers are heavenly.

80 Guider Lane, Bethlehem. www.adairinn.com. ⓒ **603/444-2600.** 11 rooms. High season $209–$309 double, low season $159–$269 double. Rates include breakfast and afternoon tea. **Amenities:** Restaurant; gardens; snowshoe trails; Wi-Fi (free).

Sugar Hill Inn ★★★   This classic New England inn, with wraparound porch and sweeping mountain panoramas, is as welcoming and comfortable a spot as you'll find in the Whites. Some of the stylish, individually decorated rooms have gas Vermont Castings stoves; some suites have double Jacuzzis, as do the spacious new cottages on the hillside above the inn. All rooms have Nespresso coffee makers. The **dining room** ★★, one of the area's best, serves upscale eclectic dinners in a cozy, white-linens setting. The four-course dinner ($69) offers half a dozen entrée choices, which might include "A Tasting of Duck"—sautéed breast, confit, and foie gras ravioli. An outstanding collection of original art decorates the inn's rooms and public spaces.

116 Rte. 117, Sugar Hill. www.sugarhillinn.com. © **800/548-4748** or 603/869-7543. 12 units. $180–$265 double; $284–$410 suite and cottage. Rates include full breakfast. 2- to 3-night minimum stay in foliage season and holiday weekends. **Amenities:** Restaurant; outdoor pool; spa; Tesla charging station; Wi-Fi (free).

Where to Eat in the White Mountains

NORTH CONWAY

North Conway is a hub of family-style restaurants, fast-food chains, pubs, and, increasingly, fine dining. Inns in the smaller surrounding towns (see "Where to Stay," p. 596) often have excellent dining rooms.

For a good breakfast or lunch, look for the peach-colored house on Route 16 in North Conway—it's a popular spot called, appropriately, **Peach's** (www.peachesnorthconway.com; © **603/356-5860**). Expect eggs, Belgian waffles and sandwiches. It's open daily from 7am until 2:30pm. The **Metropolitan Coffee House** (www.metcoffeehouse.com; © **603/356-2332**) has free Wi-Fi and good coffee. It's open daily from 7am until 9pm.

Also on Main Street are our kids' favorites, **Flatbread Company** (www.flatbreadcompany.com; © **603/356-4470**), an organic-pizza place inside the Eastern Slope Inn, just north of the village center, and **Horsefeathers** (www.horsefeathers.com; © **603/356-2687**), a pub and ice-cream shop.

Chef's Bistro ★★★ In a town filled with after-ski watering holes and family-oriented restaurants, the somewhat urban feel of Chef's Bistro comes as a bit of a surprise. But the menu is grounded in local, local, local, conceived by a chef with a passion for using what is grown and produced by area farmers. He preserves seasonal produce in-house to use throughout the seasons, and the sources of each day's vegetables, meats, and cheeses are shown on a blackboard in the dining room. The menu, which draws inspiration from all over the world, includes vegetarian, vegan, and gluten-free options. Step up to the bar for creative cocktails and generous pours.

2724 White Mountain Hwy (Main St.), North Conway. www.chefsbistronh.com. © **603/356-4747**. Sandwiches/burgers $10–$12, main courses $19–$29. Daily 11am–9pm.

Locavore Seal of Approval

For meals using local ingredients prepared fresh daily in a locally owned restaurant, look for the yellow **Valley Originals** flag or check the website (www.thevalleyoriginals.com) for the list of members. They shun the ubiquitous frozen entrees and look-alike menus for a dining experience that's unique to the locale and to each establishment. The 22 members, spread from Albany to Crawford Notch, span fine dining, casual pubs, take-out spots, bakeries, and country inns, but they're all committed to the same high standards. That's not to say that others aren't, but their directory is a good place to start.

Delaney's Hole In the Wall ★★ What would a ski trip be without a friendly pub at the end of the day? Après-ski or hike (or for that matter, a hard day's shopping), locals head just north of town to Delaney's for wings, stuffed quahogs or burly burgers. Ten-to-one they'll stay for a dinner of baby back ribs or the house favorite, Seafood Extravaganza. The bar serves a good selection of local brews amid a prodigious collection of sports memorabilia.

2966 White Mountain Hwy. (Rte. 16/302), North Conway. www.delaneys.com. ☏ **603/356-7776.** Main courses $16–$24. Lunch daily from 11:30am; dinner Sun–Thurs 4–10pm, Fri–Sat 4–11pm.

JACKSON

J-Town Deli and Country Store ★ More than just a convenient spot for breakfast or lunch right across from Jackson Ski Touring, J-Town is a community meeting place. The store is redolent of fresh-baked breads, and the cupcakes are legendary. Choose from a blackboard of custom-built sandwiches or pick a salad from the showcase and find a table overlooking the mountains. If there are none free, a local regular will probably move over for you. Self-catering travelers can get ready-to-heat full dinners here or grill up some of the deli's made-in-house sausage.

174 Main St., Jackson. www.jtowndeli.com. ☏ **603/383-8064.** Daily 7am–6pm. Sandwiches $9, full breakfast $5–$11.

Shannon Door Pub ★ Once you get over the notion of an Irish pub specializing in pizza, order your Guinness, choose from the 21 options for pizza toppings, and settle in to enjoy the authentic Irish music and lively craic. Or pay the extra buck and order the pizza "loaded" for an assortment that the tender thin crust barely supports. The rest of the menu is filled with classic standbys—shepherd's pie, Irish stew, corned beef and cabbage, and a selection of 14 beers on tap. This is a favorite après-ski stop, but it's a lively "local" all year round.

Rte 16. (jct. of rtes. 16 and 16A N), Jackson. www.shannondoor.com. ☏ **603/383-4211.** Main courses $9–$18, pizza $7–$11. Mon–Wed 4–10pm, Fri–Sat 4–11:30pm, Thurs & Sun 4–11:30pm (full dinners served until 9pm daily).

Wildcat Tavern ★ Take your pick of local bands, acoustic guitar, or open mic—every night there's something going on here. The menu is as good as the music, and you won't find better braised beef short ribs, cider-brined pork loin, or chicken saltimbocca in the mountains. Along with a great vibe and live music, the lively Jackson watering hole offers frequent money-saving specials, including Wednesday Dinner for Two and Tuesday night twin lobsters. If the music isn't your scene, you can enjoy a quiet diner in the dining room or al fresco on the front porch in the summer.

94 Main St., Jackson. www.wildcattavern.com. ☏ **603/383-6502** or 603/228-4245. Dinner daily 5–9:30pm, lunch Tues–Sat noon–4pm. Main courses $18–28, burgers and sandwiches $11–$17. Daily 5–9:30pm, lunch Tues–Sat noon–4pm.

FRANCONIA NOTCH

In addition to the dining rooms in the two inns described above (p. 602), you'll find multiple choices in the neighboring towns of **Littleton** and **Bethlehem,** both nearby and reached from I-93.

Polly's Pancake Parlor ★★ This family-style favorite on the road up to the little village of Sugar Hill may look modest, but they can brag about the James Beard Foundation medal they were awarded in 2006! Along with a sweeping mountain view, the restaurant serves a wonderful assortment of pancakes (order a combo of three for a sampling). Of course, all are served with real New Hampshire maple syrup and sugar from the farm on which Polly's sits. Kids love this place, and there's also a good gift shop that doubles as a display for antique farm implements. They also serve sandwiches and salads (which is not why you're here), plus maple-inflected desserts (which is). Breakfast and American-road-food aficionados shouldn't miss it. If you can't live without more, you can mail order their pancake mixes and syrup year-round.

672 Sugar Hill Rd. (Rte. 117), Sugar Hill. www.pollyspancakeparlor.com. ✆ **603/823-5575.** Breakfast and lunch items $4–$10. Daily 7am–3pm.

Sunny Day Diner ★★ DINER This 1958 diner moved around the state a bit before finding its sweet spot next to Clark's Trading Post in Lincoln, where it serves bountiful breakfasts in a cheery chrome and red-and-white-checkered atmosphere. The banana bread French toast is legendary. Real maple syrup drizzles down the stacks of fluffy pancakes and the lemony hollandaise sauce on the eggs Benedict is made fresh in-house. Heartier appetites will rejoice to see pork chops and eggs on the breakfast menu. The staff is as cheerful as the decor, so you'll leave smiling in addition to well-fed.

90 US Rte. 3 (next to Clark's Trading Post), Lincoln. https://sunnydaydiner.business.site. ✆ **603/745-4833.** Breakfast main courses $4.50–$10. Summer and fall daily 7am–2pm, winter and spring Fri–Sun 7am–2pm.

MAINE

By Brian Kevin

" **I** would really rather feel bad in Maine than feel good anywhere else," favorite son E. B. White once famously declared. It's a testament to the kind of loyalty the Pine Tree State commands, from both its modest population of 1.3 million natives and a good chunk of the 35 million-ish tourists and seasonal residents (or "summer people") who drop in on Maine each year.

It's fitting that White made the comment in the context of complaining about the weather, as Maine can be meteorologically taxing. Spring is almost universally referred to as "mud season." November features bitter winds alternating with gray sheets of rain. Winter brings a mix of blizzards and ice storms—and sometimes lasts 6 months.

But summer and fall are the payoff for your year-long patience. You can drink in a huge dose of tranquility during these all-too-brief seasons in Maine, and it's almost like medicine to city-jangled nerves.

Summer in Maine doesn't truly arrive until mid-June, bringing the smell of salt air, osprey diving for fish off wooded points, puffy cumulus clouds and fog banks building over the sea, and the haunting whoop of loons. It brings long, lazy days when the sun rises over the beaches and the Atlantic Ocean very early, well before travelers do—by 8 o'clock in the morning, it already feels like noon. It brings a special, haze-tinted coastal light that can't be described (but has been painted by some wonderful artists down through history). And, of course, summer brings lobsters.

Autumn (read: October) is every bit as nice: brilliant foliage against rippling, blue bay waters; tart apples ripening in the orchards; the wonderful smell of wood smoke.

The trick is finding the *right* spot in which to enjoy Vacationland. The main road along Maine's coast, Route 1, is for long stretches an amalgam of convenience stores, fast-food restaurants, and shops selling slightly tacky souvenirs. And traffic isn't restricted to Route 1, either: Even the most beautiful places along the coast—the loop road, beaches, and most popular mountain peaks in Acadia National Park, for instance—can get pretty crowded in summer. Arriving without a room reservation in high season is just a bad idea.

On the other hand, Maine's remote position and size *can* work to your advantage. This state has an amazing 5,500 miles of coastline,

Maine

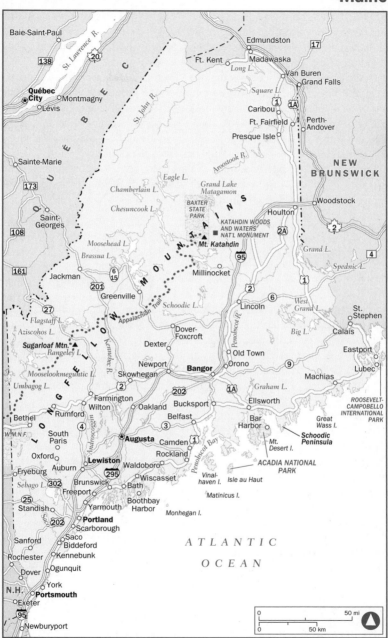

plus 3,000 or so coastal islands. For those who love deep woods, wild mountain trails, and trout-rich lakes and streams, the state's inland reaches are an unspoiled, underappreciated playground. With a little homework, you can find that perfect little cove or lakeside camp, book a room in advance, and enjoy Maine's extremely lovely scenery without battling traffic jams, lines, or rising blood pressures.

Getting to know the locals is fun, too. Their ancestors were mostly fishermen and other seafaring folk (as opposed to the farmers who colonized the rest of New England), and crunchy back-to-the-landers have left their cultural mark on the region since the '70s. Today, Mainers—even transplanted ones—tend to exhibit a wry sense of humor, a gregariousness, and a libertine streak that can seem at odds with New England's stodgier corners.

For even more detailed coverage of the state's gorgeous coastline, pick up *Frommer's Maine Coast* to supplement your travels. It's a great resource for enjoying this region in even more detail.

THE SOUTHERN MAINE COAST ★★

York: 45 miles SW of Portland, 10 miles NE of Portsmouth NH, and 65 miles NE of Boston

Tourist bureau statistics show that Maine's southern coast—stretching from the state line at Kittery to Portland—is the primary destination of most leisure travelers to the state. In season, it takes some doing to find privacy or remoteness here, despite a sense of history in the coastal villages (some of them, anyway). Still, it's not hard to find a relaxing spot, whether you prefer dunes, the lulling sound of breaking waves, or a carnival-like atmosphere in a beach town.

Nearly all of Maine's best sand beaches lie along this stretch of coastline. Waves depend on the weather; during a good Northeast blow, they pound the shores, rise above the roads, and threaten beach houses built decades ago. During balmy midsummer days, though, the ocean can be gentle as a farm pond, its barely audible waves lapping timidly at the shore as the tide creeps in, inch by inch, covering tidal pools full of crabs, barnacles, and sea snails.

One thing all the beaches here share in common: They're washed by the chilled waters of the Gulf of Maine, which makes for, er, invigorating swimming. Though the beach season is generally brief and intense, running only from July 4th to Labor Day, the tourism season increasingly stretches into the stunningly colorful month of October, with most restaurants and hotels these days staying open to accommodate carloads of "leaf peepers."

Essentials

ARRIVING

BY CAR   The main roads along the coast are **I-95** or **Route 1,** with well-marked exits. Note that near the Yorks, I-95 (the Maine Highway) becomes a toll road. Ogunquit is on Route 1, about halfway between York and Wells; it's

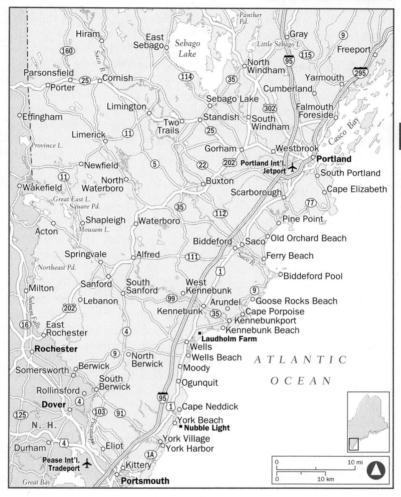

accessible from both exit 7 (the Yorks) and exit 19 (Wells) of the Maine Turnpike. To reach Kennebunkport, take the exit for Kennebunk and continue through town on Port Road (Route 35) for about 3½ miles. At the traffic light, turn left and cross the small bridge.

BY TRAIN   Amtrak (www.amtrak.com; ⓒ **800/872-7245**) operates five trains daily into southern Maine from Boston's North Station (note these trains do *not* connect directly to Amtrak's national rail network, which operates out of Boston's South Station—you'll need to take a subway or taxi between the two stations). A one-way ticket from Boston starts at $15; the trip takes 1¾ hours to reach the station outside Wells, about 10 miles away from the Yorks, and inland. From Wells, you'll need to call a local taxi or arrange for a pickup to get to your final destination on the beach.

BY BUS The two chief bus lines serving this stretch of Maine are **Greyhound** (www.greyhound.com; ✆ **800/231-2222**), which has service to Wells, and **C&J Trailways** (www.ridecj.com; ✆ **800/258-7111**), which runs a seasonal weekend service from New York to Ogunquit, Memorial Day through Columbus Day. Taking a Greyhound from New York City's Port Authority to Wells costs from $50 to $100 one-way and takes 7 to 9 hours; from Boston, figure on paying a fare of $12 to $30 one-way and a ride of 1¾ hours. A New York–to–Ogunquit trip on C&J Trailways runs $80 and takes 6 hours. Note that you can also take a bus or train to Portsmouth, New Hampshire (p. 564), which is very close to Kittery—you can actually walk over a bridge into Maine from Portsmouth.

VISITOR INFORMATION

The **Maine State Visitor Information Center** (✆ **207/439-1319**) operates at a well-marked rest area on I-95. It's full of info and helpful staff; it has a pet exercise area and copious vending machines; and it's open daily from 8am to 6pm in summer, from 9am to 5:30pm the rest of the year. (The vending machines and restrooms are open 24 hours a day)

The **Greater York Region Chamber of Commerce** (www.gatewayto maine.org; ✆ **207/363-4422**) operates another helpful visitor center, one that mirrors the shape of a stone cottage. It's across Route 1 from the Maine Turnpike access road (right beside the Stonewall Kitchen headquarters and cafe) on Stonewall Lane. In peak season, it's open Monday to Saturday from 9am to 5pm and Sunday from 10am to 4pm; from Labor Day through June, it's open Monday to Friday 9am to 4pm, Saturday from 10am to 2pm, and Sunday 9am to 1pm. The **Ogunquit Welcome Center** (www.ogunquit.org; ✆ **207/646-2939**) is easy to miss: It's on the east side of Route 1, just south of the main intersection. The center is open daily from Memorial Day through Columbus Day (until 8pm during summer weekends), and daily except Sunday during the off season. Yes, it has restrooms. The helpful **Kennebunk-Kennebunkport Chamber of Commerce** (www.visitthekennebunks.com; ✆ **207/967-0857**) can answer questions year-round by phone or in person at its offices at 17 Western Avenue (Route 9), beside the H.B. Provisions general store.

Exploring Kittery ★

Driving into Maine from the south, as most travelers do, you'll find that **Kittery ★** is the first town to appear after crossing the big bridge spanning the Piscataqua River from New Hampshire. Once famous for its (still operating) naval yard, Kittery is now better known for its dozens of factory outlets, clustering along both sides of Route 1, about 4 miles south of York.

Since 2012 or so, the historic **Foreside neighborhood** has become Kittery's snug, hip town center. Once a rough-around-the-edges district catering to off-duty shipyard workers, Foreside now hosts a few of the state's most acclaimed bars and restaurants, plus indie-fied enterprises like eclectic arts venue **The**

More than 100 outlet stores flank Route 1 in Kittery, in more than a dozen strip malls—not the prettiest sight in Maine, but if you're looking to score a deal, you just might find it beautiful. Among the various complexes are a Gap outlet, a lululemon shop with a wide selection, a small but elegant Coach store, a Nike factory store, Polo Ralph Lauren, J. Crew (good prices on sweaters), an Orvis sporting goods outlet (I found a fly rod here for a fraction of the retail cost), and a useful Crate & Barrel outlet. On rainy summer days, hordes of disappointed beachgoers head here and swarm the aisles; at those times, parking is especially tight. Information on current outlets is available from the **Kittery Outlet Association.** Call (C) **888/548-8379,** or visit the website at www.thekitteryoutlets.com

Dance Hall (www.thedancehallkittery.org; (C) **207/703-2083**) and rustic-mod accessories boutique **Folk** (www.shop-folk.com; (C) **207/703-2526**). It's a great few blocks where you can crush a craft beer or a cruller while mingling with student scenesters, young families, and Navy folks in their digital blues.

The latter are based at the **Portsmouth Naval Shipyard,** which faces Portsmouth, New Hampshire, across the river. This active shipyard isn't open to the public for security reasons, but you can visit the **Kittery Historical & Naval Museum** (www.kitterymuseum.com; (C) **207/439-3080**) to see ship and sub models, lighthouse lenses, scrimshaw work, diving suits, and the like. From June through October, the museum's open Wednesday through Sunday, from 10am to 4pm; in the off-season, it's only open Wednesdays and Saturdays, with the same hours. Admission is $5 for adults, $3 for children, and $10 for a family. Find it by taking Route 1 to the Kittery traffic circle, then exiting for Route 236 south; that's Rogers Road. Continue to the end and Rogers Road Extension.

From Kittery, an attractive alternative route north to York follows winding Route 103 to the historic, lost-in-time village of **Kittery Point.** It's perfect for driving, though a bit busy and narrow for biking. Kittery Point homes seem to be just inches from the roadway and there are not one but *two* historic forts; both are parks open to the public.

Exploring the Yorks ★★

"The Yorks," just to the north of Kittery, are three towns that share a name but little else. In fact, it's rare to find three such well-defined and diverse New England archetypes within such a compact area. **York Village ★** is full of 17th-century American history and architecture and has a good library. **York Harbor ★★**, the most relaxing and scenic of the three, reached its zenith during America's late Victorian era, when wealthy urbanites constructed cottages at the ocean's edge. Finally, **York Beach ★★** is a fun beach town with amusements, taffy shops, a small zoo, gabled summer homes set in crowded enclaves, a great lighthouse, and two excellent beaches with sun, sand, rocks, surf, surfers, and fried-fish stands.

From mid-June through Labor Day, a trackless **trolley** (a bus painted to look like a trolley) runs back and forth between Short Sands and Long Sands beaches in the Yorks, providing a convenient way to explore without having to be hassled with parking. Hop on the trolley (www.yorktrolley.com; © **207/363-9600**) at one of the well-marked stops; it's $4 each way, $3 to sit on board for the entire loop without debarking.

The best town center for walking around in is **York Village ★★**. First settled in 1624, the village opens several homes to the public.

Museums of Old York ★★★ HISTORIC BUILDINGS   York's local historical society oversees the bulk of the town's collection of historic buildings, some of which date to the early 18th century. Tickets are available to eight Old York-operated properties; one good place to start is at the **Jefferds Tavern ★**, across from the handsome **old burying ground ★**. Changing exhibits document various facets of early life. Next door is the **School House ★**, furnished as it might have been in the 19th century. A 10-minute walk along lightly traveled Lindsay Road brings you to **Hancock Wharf** (see box below), next door to the **George Marshall Store.** Also nearby is the **Elizabeth Perkins House,** with its well-preserved Colonial Revival interiors. Finally, there are two "don't-miss" buildings in the society's collection. The barn-red, hill-topping **Old Gaol ★★**, built in 1719 as a jail to hold criminals, debtors, and other miscreants, is said to be the oldest surviving public building in the United States; you can still see the dungeons. Just down the knoll from the jail, the bright yellow **Emerson-Wilcox House ★**, built in the mid-1700s and periodically added onto through the years, is a virtual catalog of architectural styles and early decorative arts.

207 York St., York. www.oldyork.org. © **207/363-1756.** Admission per building $8 adults, $5 kids 6–15; pass to all buildings $15 adults, $10 kids 6–15. Museums open late May–Labor Day Tues–Sat 10am–5pm, Sun 1–5pm (some properties have shorter hours). Labor Day—mid-Oct open Thurs–Sun only; closed mid-Oct to late May.

Father of Our Country; Flop as a Wharf Owner

John Hancock is justly famous for his oversize signature on the Declaration of Independence, his tenure as governor of Massachusetts, and the insurance company and tall Boston building that were named for him. What's not so well known is his involvement as a proprietor of York's **Hancock Wharf,** a failed 18th-century wharf-and-warehouse enterprise that went bust. Hancock never actually set foot on the wharf, but for years locals believed he used it to stash arms, contraband, and/or goods he didn't want taxed by those tax-happy British. It now appears that wasn't the case, but it still makes for one of the many intriguing sites and stories in the **York Village** section of downtown York. (See Museums of Old York, above, for more details on this neighborhood.)

Surprisingly, the wharf has a happy ending: It's more famous today than it was then, the only 18th-century warehouse still standing on the York River. It has been designated a National Historic Site, and the York Historical Society sometimes uses it to launch or receive the occasional historic boat passing through town.

BEACHES

York Beach actually consists of *two* beaches, **Long Sands Beach** ★★ and **Short Sands Beach** ★, separated by a rocky headland. Both have plenty of room for sunning and Frisbees when the tide is out. (When the tide is in, though, both become narrow and cramped.)

Short Sands fronts the honky-tonk town of **York Beach,** and it offers candlepin bowling, taffy-pulling machines, and video arcades. It's a better pick for families traveling with kids who have short attention spans. Long Sands has views of the lighthouse known as Nubble Light and runs along Route 1A, directly across from a line of motels, summer homes, and convenience stores. Parking at *both* beaches is metered in summer; pay heed, as enforcement is strict and you must feed the meters with quarters until 9pm, all 7 days of the week. (At the end of summer, though, they decapitate the meters—literally— and parking is subsequently free and plentiful until the next Memorial Day.)

SHOPPING IN THE YORKS

Stonewall Kitchen's flagship store (© **207/351-2712**) is in York, on Stonewall Lane (behind the huge tourist information center on Route 1). Sample the company's jams before buying; the store is open daily until 8pm; the cafe, though, closes at 3pm.

Exploring Ogunquit ★★

Ogunquit (oh-GUN-quit) is a bustling little beachside town that has attracted vacationers and artists for more than a century. Although it's certainly notable for its abundant and elegant summer-resort architecture and nightlife, Ogunquit is most famous for its 3½-mile white-sand beach, backed by grassy dunes and served by a beautiful seaside walking path, one of Maine's best. This beach is the town's front porch, and almost everyone ends up here at least once a day if the sun is shining.

Despite its architectural gentility and overall civility, the town can become overrun with tourists and cars during summer weekends. If you despise crowds and the processes of jockeying for parking spots and beach space, visit during the off season or during summer weekdays instead.

Ogunquit's entrance is a horrid three-way intersection that seems intentionally designed to cause massive traffic tie-ups. Turn seaward at the confusing intersection and follow Shore Road—the southernmost of the two spurs—to reach Perkins Cove and the best shops, accommodations, and restaurants. (For the best beach access, take the *other* prong of the intersection to Beach Street) Expect traffic to creep along Route 1 during summer weekends. Parking in and around the village is tight and relatively expensive for small-town Maine ($10–$25 per day in various lots). My advice? The town is best navigated on foot, by bike, or by using the local shuttle bus (see "Trolley Ho!," below).

The village center is good for an hour or two of browsing among the boutiques, or sipping a cappuccino at one of the several coffee emporia. From the village, you can walk to scenic Perkins Cove along **Marginal Way** ★★★, a mile-long oceanside pathway that departs across from the Seacastles Resort

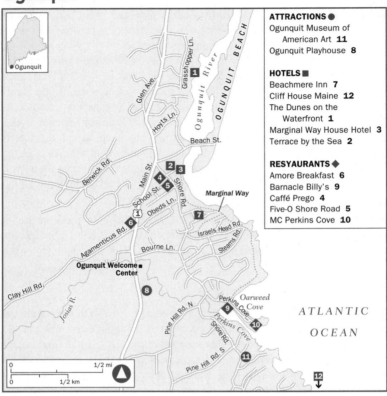

ATTRACTIONS ●
Ogunquit Museum of
American Art **11**
Ogunquit Playhouse **8**

HOTELS ■
Beachmere Inn **7**
Cliff House Maine **12**
The Dunes on the
Waterfront **1**
Marginal Way House Hotel **3**
Terrace by the Sea **2**

RESYAURANTS ◆
Amore Breakfast **6**
Barnacle Billy's **9**
Caffé Prego **4**
Five-O Shore Road **5**
MC Perkins Cove **10**

on Shore Road. It passes tide pools, pocket beaches, and rocky, fissured bluffs, all worth exploring. The seascape can be spectacular, even if Marginal Way can get quite crowded with walkers during fair-weather weekends. Early morning is a good time to avoid crowds.

Perkins Cove ★, accessible either from Marginal Way or by driving south along Shore Road and then veering left at the Y intersection, is a small, well-protected harbor that attracts lots of visitors (sometimes too many). A handful of galleries, restaurants, and T-shirt shops cater to tourists here. Also at the cove, an intriguing pedestrian drawbridge is operated by whomever happens to be handy.

Ogunquit Museum of American Art ★★★ MUSEUM   Not far from Perkins Cove, this is one of the best—and most beautiful—small art museums in the nation (that's not just me talking; the director of New York's Metropolitan Museum of Art said so, too). It's only open in summer and fall, however. Set back from the road in a grassy glen overlooking the rocky shore, the museum's spectacular view initially overwhelms the artwork as visitors walk through the door. But stick around for a few minutes—the changing exhibits in this architecturally engaging modern building of cement block, slate, and glass will get your attention soon enough. Its curators have a track record of staging superb shows and attracting national attention. The permanent collection holds work by seascape master Marsden Hartley and many members of the Ogunquit Colony, including Woodbury, Hamilton Easter Field, and Robert Laurent.

543 Shore Rd. www.ogunquitmuseum.org. ℓ **207/646-4909.** $10 adults, $9 seniors and students; kids under 12 free. May–Oct, daily 10am–5pm

Ogunquit Playhouse ★★ THEATER For evening entertainment, head to this 750-seat summer stock theater right on Route 1 (just south of the main intersection) with an old-style look that has garnered a solid reputation for its careful, serious attention to stagecraft. The theater has entertained Ogunquit since 1933, attracting noted actors such as Bette Davis, Tallulah Bankhead, and Sally Struthers, performing in shows like *A Chorus Line* and *Guys and Dolls.* Performance tickets generally cost in the range of $40 to $80 per person, and the season runs from May through December.

10 Main St. www.ogunquitplayhouse.org. ℓ **207/646-2402.**

Exploring the Kennebunks ★★

"The Kennebunks" consist of the side-by-side villages of **Kennebunk** and **Kennebunkport,** both situated along the shores of small rivers and both claiming a portion of the rocky coast. First colonized in the mid-1600s, the area flourished after the American Revolution when ship captains, boat builders, and prosperous merchants constructed imposing, solid homes. Linked by a photo-op bridge, the Kennebunks are each famed for their striking historical architecture, shopping, dining, fine inns and hotels, ocean views (the Bush family owns a summer home here), and long, sandy beaches. Be sure to take time to explore both towns.

Several higher-end inns in these two towns offer shuttle services to the downtown areas. Otherwise, a local **trolley** (actually a bus that looks like a trolley) makes several convenient stops in and around the Kennebunks, and also serves the best local beaches; it picks up about once per hour from 10am until 4pm (3pm in spring and fall). It's expensive, though: The fare comes in the form of a day pass costing $16 per adult or $6 per child. At least the pass includes unlimited opportunities to jump on and off the trolley during the day you are using it. Call © **207/967-3686** for more details, or check the trolley's schedule online at **www.intowntrolley.com**.

EXPLORING KENNEBUNK

Kennebunk's downtown is inland, just off the turnpike, and is a dignified, compact commercial center of clapboard and brick. If you're a history buff, the **Brick Store Museum ★**, 117 Main St. (www.brickstoremuseum.org; © **207/ 985-4802**), should be your very first stop in town. The museum hosts showings of historical art and artifacts throughout summer, switching to contemporary art exhibits in the off season. And they've got extensive local historic archives, too. The museum is housed in a former brick store plus three adjacent buildings renovated to a polish. Adult admission costs $7, seniors $6, and $3 for kids 6 to 16. Half-hour **walking tours ★** of the downtown cost an additional $5 per person. (They're a must, if you have time and interest.) The museum opens Tuesday to Friday from 10am to 5pm, Saturday from 10am until 4pm, and Sunday from noon until 4pm.

When en route to or from the coast, be sure to note the extraordinary homes that line Port Road (Route 35). This includes the famously elaborate **Wedding Cake House ★**, which you should be able to identify all on your own.

EXPLORING KENNEBUNKPORT

Dock Square has a bustling feel to it, with low buildings of mixed vintages and styles. The boutiques in the area are attractive, and many feature creative artworks and crafts, but sometimes they're a bit crowded. Kennebunkport's real attraction is found in the surrounding blocks, where side streets are lined with one of the nation's richest collections of Early American homes.

Many of the beautiful Federal-style houses here have been converted to B&Bs (see "Where to Stay," p. 617). Also look for the amazing meeting-house-style **South Congregational Church ★★**, with its big clock faces, just off Dock Square at North and Temple streets; it's well worth the short detour.

Ocean Drive (marked by a post in Dock Square) runs out to and beyond the Bush compound at **Walkers Point ★**, and the route is lined with opulent summer homes. Take a quick look at the presidential palace, snap a pic, and move on—there's plenty more to see out here, including outstanding ocean and shore views.

KENNEBUNKS BEACHES

The coastal area around Kennebunkport is home to several of the state's best beaches. Southward across the river (technically, this is Kennebunk, though it's much closer to Kennebunkport) are **Gooch's Beach ★★** and **Kennebunk Beach ★★**. Head eastward from the intersection of routes 9 and 35 along—yes—Beach Street past the White Barn Inn (see p. 617), and, in a few minutes, you'll arrive at the ocean and a handsome row of eclectic, shingled summer homes.

The narrow road continues to twist past sandy strands and rocky headlands for a few miles, and this portion is well worth exploring, too. It can get congested in summer, though; avoid gridlock by parking and wandering on foot or by bike.

(Also take note of local parking regulations: You're only permitted to park along some stretches of these beaches if you're a local or have moseyed down to the police station on Route 1 and bought a temporary parking permit, which few summer visitors know to do. Some local inns and hotels will give you a temporary day pass.) Again, if you can avoid bringing a car to the beach, do.

Where to Stay on the Southern Maine Coast

Airbnb rentals proliferate around Kittery and the Yorks, many of them right on the water. While there aren't many genuine bargains to be had, you're more likely to find last-minute lodging through online rental services than at the hotels, which fill up months in advance for peak season. If you've arrived without a room (not recommended), turn up at the York visitor center (see "Visitor Information," p. 610) and ask about vacancies.

THE KENNEBUNKS

Beach House Inn ★★   This is a good choice if you'd like to be close to the people-watching, dog-walking action on and above Kennebunk Beach. The inn was built in 1891 but has been extensively modernized and expanded. The rooms here aren't necessarily historic, but most have Victorian furnishings and accents, plus nice framed photographs of beach landscapes. Suites have lovely panoramic views of the ocean across the road. But the main draw is the lovely front porch, where you can stare out at the water and watch passing walkers and cyclists. The inn has bikes and canoes for guests to use, and provides beach chairs and towels.

211 Beach Ave., Kennebunk. www.beachhseinn.com. ✆ **207/967-3850.** 34 units. $129–$249 double; $200–$560 cottage and suite. Rates include continental breakfast. 2-night minimum on weekends. Closed Jan–March. **Amenities:** Bikes; canoes; spa; fitness studio; free Wi-Fi in common areas.

Grace White Barn Inn & Spa ★★★   As it has long done, the venerable White Barn goes the extra mile and sets a standard to which other resorts can only hope to aspire. This is arguably the state's best inn-style lodging, with its best inn dining (see p. 623). Upon checking in, guests are shown to a parlor and served a drink, while valets gather luggage and park cars. The atmosphere here is distinctly European, with an emphasis on service. Rooms are individually decorated in an upscale country style that's been recently recast to reflect the color schemes of the nearby sea. Many units have wood-burning fireplaces and Jacuzzis; renovations in 2016 include new double walk-in showers and marble tubs. Suites (in an outbuilding beside the main inn) border on spectacular, each with a distinct color theme and flatscreen television, whirlpool, or similar perks. There are plenty of other amenities such as fresh flowers daily, turndown service, an attractive spa, a lovely outdoor swimming pool, and complimentary afternoon scone service. A handful of cottages, on the Kennebunk River across the road, are cozy and nicely equipped with modern kitchens and bathrooms.

37 Beach Ave., Kennebunk. (¼ mile E of jct. of rtes. 9 and 35). www.whitebarninn.com. ✆ **207/967-2321.** 26 units, 4 cottages. $300–$710 double; $520–$1290 suite; $410–$1,290 cottage. Rates include afternoon tea. 2-night minimum weekends; 3-night

minimum holiday weekends. **Amenities:** Restaurant, bar, free bikes; free canoes; concierge; conference rooms; outdoor heated pool; valet parking; room service; free Wi-Fi.

Hidden Pond ★★★

It's not easy to pull off crunchy carefree rusticity across a resort that costs more per night than many urban monthly rents. And make no mistake, Kennebunkport's Hidden Pond is trying extremely hard. The manicured organic farm in the middle of the wooded cottage campus? The rough-hewn Adirondack chairs surrounding the nightly bonfire? Even the cottages, with their riverstone fireplaces, screen porches, outdoor showers, and (would you believe) clapboard siding? It's an achievement for a place to seem this authentically bucolic and homespun when, in fact, you're surrounded by luxurious details and perks. The spa, the two heated outdoor pools (one is adults-only), and the vast weekly activity schedule (Pilates and yoga sessions, ice cream socials, watercolor clinics, mixology lessons) are among the reminders that this is a chi-chi resort and not some kind of bougie granola commune. The entrees at **Earth,** the on-site farm-to-table restaurant, are exquisite, and it's the nicest barn you'll ever have dinner in.

354 Goose Rocks Rd., Kennebunkport. www.hiddenpondmaine.com. © **207/967-9050.** 44 cottage units. $288–$869 1-bedroom; $508–$1629 2-bedroom. 3-night minimum July–Aug. **Amenities:** Restaurant; bars; free bikes; beach shuttle; golf cart rentals; kids programs; fitness center; spa; two outdoor heated pools; free Wi-Fi.

Lodge at Turbat's Creek ★

This simple, clean motel isn't exactly a "lodge," but it does sit in a quiet residential neighborhood an easy 5-minute drive from Dock Square. It's a good value, if dated, in a town that usually gives you sticker shock. The grounds are attractive and endowed with Adirondack chairs; the inn also supplies free mountain bikes for guests who want to cruise to town, and there's a big, seasonally open heated pool as well. Rooms, on two floors, are standard motel size. They're decorated in rustic pine furniture and painted cheerfully. The continental breakfast can be taken outside, on the lawn, in good weather.

7 Turbat's Creek Rd., Kennebunkport. www.lodgeatturbatscreek.com. © **207/967-8700.** 27 units. $79–$199 double. Rates include continental breakfast. Closed Dec–Apr. Pets allowed; inquire before arriving. **Amenities:** Free use of mountain bikes; heated outdoor pool; free Wi-Fi.

The Yachtsman Lodge & Marina ★★

River views, proximity to Dock Square, and value are the selling points at this airy spot right off the marina. Nice touches abound, such as down comforters, granite-topped vanities, high ceilings, CD players, and French doors that open onto patios just above the river. While rooms are all standard motel size and on one level, their simple, classical styling is far superior to anything you'll find at a chain motel. And the service is seriously kicked up a notch.

59 Ocean Ave., Kennebunkport. www.yachtsmanlodge.com. © **207/967-2511.** 30 units. $119–$339 double. Rates include continental breakfast. 2-night minimum stay weekends and holidays. Closed mid-Dec to mid-Apr. **Amenities:** Free bikes and canoes; free Wi-Fi in common areas.

KITTERY

Water Street Inn ★★ This handsome 1899 home is just across the river from downtown Portsmouth, New Hampshire (p. 564), a pleasant half-mile walk across a drawbridge. New owners took over in summer 2018 and have refreshed the place top-to-bottom, transforming the formerly stuffy-ish B&B into a "modern Victorian" boutique inn with contemporary art, brightly colored furniture, and self-registration. Despite the lack of a front desk (you'll get a door code upon reservation), there's a concierge staff that can point you to local dining, beaches, and events.

6 Water St. www.waterstinn.com. ✆ **207/439-4040.** 6 units. May–Oct $210 double; Nov–Apr $90 double. **Amenities:** Guest bikes; library; free Wi-Fi.

OGUNQUIT

In addition to the selections below, there are loads of family-owned budget- to moderately priced motel operations around town. Private-stay Airbnb rentals can be had, though there aren't many seaside places (and hospitality culture is so woven into the fabric of Ogunquit, it's kind of a shame to miss out on it). Simply cruising Route 1 can yield dividends (don't forget your AAA card, if you're a member).

Beachmere Inn ★★ In a town of motels, simple B&Bs, and condos, the Beachmere excels. Operated by the same family since 1937, this quiet, well-run cliff-top inn sprawls across a scenic lawn where repeat visitors have reclined for decades. Nearly every unit gives you an amazing look up or down the beach, and all have kitchenettes. The original Victorian section dates from the 1890s and is the most fun; it's all turrets, big porches, angles, and bright, beachy interiors. Next door is the modern Beachmere South, with spacious rooms and plenty of private balconies or patios—those on the end have absolutely knockout views. A new wing (Beachmere West) was added in 2008, with a small but nice little hot tub, exercise room, and children's play area; units in this wing have sitting rooms and bigger bathrooms. The adjacent Marginal Way footpath (see "Exploring Ogunquit," p. 613) is terrific for walks and beach access, and groups can inquire about several off-property cottages a short walk away. The inn is now open year-round: You can rent snowshoes in winter to (carefully) stroll the path.

62 Beachmere Pl. www.beachmereinn.com. ✆ **800/336-3983** or 207/646-2021. 53 units. June–Aug $190–$295 double, $360–$395 suite, $560 cottage; May and Sept to mid-Nov $90–$220 double, $200–$314 suite, $295–$424 cottage; mid-Nov to May $70–$125 double, $160–$215 suite, $260 cottage. Rates include continental breakfast. 3-night minimum in summer. **Amenities:** Lounge; beach access; children's play room; Jacuzzi; spa; restaurant; free Wi-Fi.

Cliff House Maine ★★ This complex of modern buildings replaced a grand hotel and completed a monster renovation in 2016. Keeping up with the ever-expanding southern Maine tourism season, it's now a year-round resort, and it offers some of the best hotel-room ocean views in Maine: nearly a 360-degree panorama, in some cases. There are a number of different styles of rooms, but the overall vibe is clean seaside contemporary, with minimalist art on the walls, digital everything, midcentury-looking folding chairs, and crisp Cuddledown linens. A vanishing-edge pool fronting the sea does indeed seem to disappear into the blue yonder, and there's an upscale restaurant with knockout vistas. The spa and fitness facility, brand-new in 2016, dispenses a wide range of soothing treatments and exercise programs.

591 Shore Rd. www.cliffhousemaine.com. © **207/361-1000** or 855/502-5433. 227 units. June–Aug $389–$639 double, $729–$1799 suite; Sept–Nov $279–$439 double, $729–$989 suite; Dec–May $209–$379 double, $579–$729 suite. Holiday rates are higher. Dogs welcome ($100 fee). **Amenities:** Restaurants; art gallery; bar; fitness center; Jacuzzi; indoor pool; outdoor pool; fire pits; room service; spa; free Wi-Fi.

The Dunes on the Waterfront ★★

This classic motor court (built around 1936) has made the transition into the modern luxury age more gracefully than any other vintage motel I've seen. It has one six-unit motel-like building, but most of the rooms are in gabled cottages of white clapboard and green shutters; these have full kitchens and bathrooms. Plenty of old-fashioned charm remains in many of the units, with vintage maple furnishings, oval braided rugs, maple floors, knotty pine paneling, and louvered doors. Most of the cottages also have wood-burning fireplaces. The complex is set on 12 acres, wedged between busy Route 1 and the ocean, but somehow stays quiet and peaceful; Adirondack chairs overlook a lagoon, and guests can borrow a rowboat to get across to the beach.

518 Rte. 1. www.dunesonthewaterfront.com. © **888/623-5882.** 36 units. $115–$390 double; $205–$575 cottage. Mid-June to mid-Sept 3-night minimum stay in guest rooms, 1-week minimum stay in cottages (3-night minimum rest of year); July–Aug 2-week minimum stay in 2-bedroom cottages. Closed Nov–late Apr. **Amenities:** Outdoor pool; watersports equipment rental; free Wi-Fi.

Marginal Way House Hotel ★

This simple, old-fashioned compound centers on a four-story, mid-19th-century guesthouse with summery, basic rooms and white-painted furniture. The whole complex is plunked down on a large, grassy lot on a quiet cul-de-sac, and it's hard to believe you're smack in the middle of busy Ogunquit. But you are: The beach and village are each just a few minutes' walk away. The main building is surrounded by four more contemporary buildings that lack historic charm: the Cottage House has only double beds, but the Wharf House has a cool quietude about it, enhanced by white linens and shady trees. Some units have little decks with views; all rooms have refrigerators and televisions, but none have phones. The property also maintains some one- and two-bedroom efficiency apartments (some have minimum stays); inquire when booking.

22-24 Wharf Lane. www.marginalwayhouse.com. © **207/646-8801.** 30 units (1 w/bathroom down hall). Early June–Labor Day $129–$299 double; mid-Apr to early June and early Sept to mid-Nov $79–$209 double. $15 extra charge for more than 2 people (except kids under 3). Closed mid-Nov to mid-Apr. Pets allowed off season only; advance notice required. **Amenities:** Free Wi-Fi.

Terrace by the Sea ★

Overlooking Ogunquit Beach, this cluster of six modern buildings offers wide-open ocean views from many rooms. A landscaped lawn dotted with deck chairs overlooks the water, while a board-walk leads to the beach, a 5-minute walk away. There's also a nice heated outdoor pool, free Wi-Fi, and excellent customer service. Rooms of varying size and price range are simply furnished with colonial reproductions; eight rooms have kitchenettes, and many have private decks. Children ages 5 and under are welcome in the off season.

23 Wharf Lane. www.terracebythesea.com. ℰ **207/646-3232.** 61 units. Late May–Oct $123–$330 double; late Mar–early May and Nov to mid-Dec $83–$225 double. Closed Jan–Mar. **Amenities:** Outdoor pool; free Wi-Fi.

THE YORKS

Besides the properties listed below, York Beach is stocked with plenty of condo and house rentals and motel rooms right on Long Sands Beach, plus a bunch more on Short Sands. The quality of these places is highly variable, but at least all of them can truthfully boast that you can literally walk across the street to the beach.

Dockside Guest Quarters ★ David and Harriette Lusty established this quiet retreat in 1954; more recent additions and new management (son Eric and wife Carol) haven't changed the friendly, maritime flavor of the place. Situated on an island connected to the mainland by a small bridge, the inn occupies nicely landscaped grounds shady with maples and white pines. A few of the rooms are in the cozy main house, built in 1885, but the bulk of the accommodations are in small, shared, town-house-style cottages added between 1968 and 1998 down by the water. These are simply furnished, but bright and airy; most have private decks overlooking the entrance to York Harbor. Several also have woodstoves, fireplace, and/or kitchenettes (though you do pay quite a bit extra for the kitchenette units and suites). The inn also maintains a simple restaurant (run by Philip Lusty, yet another son, and his wife, Anne), and offers personalized boat tours of the harbor from its own private dock.

22 Harris Island Rd., York Harbor. www.docksidegq.com. ℰ **888/860-7428** or 207/363-2868. 25 units. $162–$263 double; $291–$350 suite. Rates include breakfast. Closed late Oct–Apr. 2-night minimum stay weekends in summer. **Amenities:** Restaurant; badminton; bike rentals; boat tours; croquet; rowboats; free Wi-Fi.

Union Bluff Hotel ★★ With its turrets, dormers, and porches, the Union Bluff looks like a 19th-century beach hotel—but it was actually built in 1989, replacing the previous (ca. 1870) version of the hotel, which had burned down. Inside, the hotel is modern if bland; rooms have oak furniture, wall-to-wall carpeting, and small refrigerators. There are about 20 rooms in an annex next door, but the main inn's rooms and views are better—the best ones are the suites on the top floor, with beach vistas (and some Jacuzzis, fireplaces, and decks). It's amazing how low rates can plummet here midweek and off-season; but weekends, even before and after the summer, are quite expensive. The vibe is often festive, with families letting loose and a constant stream of wedding parties. The hotel's seafood-heavy restaurant is not half bad. Step outside and you're a half-block from Short Sands beach, T-shirt and shell shops, and a bowling alley and throwback arcade. The hotel assigns one parking spot for each room, which is great because parking is supertight in summer in Short Sands; but if you've brought an RV or second car, you'll need to use the big town parking lot adjacent to the hotel—bring quarters. Lots of quarters.

8 Beach St., York Beach. www.unionbluff.com. © **800/833-0721** or 207/363-1333. 71 units. Mid-June–Aug $89–$469 double and suite; rest of year $79–$289 double and suite. **Amenities:** Restaurant; pub; free Wi-Fi.

Where to Eat in Southeastern Maine
THE KENNEBUNKS

The Clam Shack ★ SEAFOOD   A Kennebunks institution, found right on the bridge separating the Lower Village from Dock Square, The Clam Shack's biggest claim to fame may be its lobster roll. Served on a round yeast roll (a break from the traditional split-top hot dog bun), the Clam Shack roll comes with butter, mayo, or both, complementing fresh-off-the-boat, saltwater-boiled lobster. And, crucially, they get the ratio right: plenty of meat without overwhelming the balance with the toasted bun. Light and fresh, the namesake fried clams are worth stopping for too (get 'em by the half-pint, pint, or quart).

2 Western Ave., Kennebunk. www.theclamshack.net. © **207/967-3321.** Sandwiches $5–$21; seafood baskets $17–$32. Daily 11am–8pm.

Hurricane ★ AMERICAN/SEAFOOD   The Kennebunks' fine-dining old guard, Hurricane hasn't missed a step in some three decades. Lunch might start with a cup of lobster chowder, small plates of carpaccio or mussels, a lobster Cobb salad, or oysters Rockefeller; the main course could be a Cubano sandwich or a "Maine Surf & Turf" burger (with lobster meat, natch). Local seafood shines among the dinner entrees, which run to such items as a Mediterranean-inflected, lobster-based cioppino, roasted garlic shrimp, or terrific seared scallops with quinoa. Finish with desserts such as vanilla bean crème brûlée, legit Maine blueberry pie, panna cotta, or s'mores.

29 Dock Sq., Kennebunkport. www.hurricanerestaurant.com. © **207/967-1111.** Reservations recommended. Main courses $22–$50; small plates $10–$17. Daily 11:30am–10:30pm weekends (9:30pm weekdays). Closed Jan–Mar.

Pier 77 Restaurant ★★ REGIONAL   Under the steady hand of owners Peter and Kate Morency—and thanks to Peter's training at the Culinary Institute of America and 20 years in top kitchens in Boston and San Francisco—Pier 77 has become that rare combination of a tourist destination and a locals' favorite in the lovely little village of Cape Porpoise, between Kennebunkport and Biddeford. Lunches skew toward slightly upscale comfort food such as barbecue, spaghetti and meatballs, cheddar burgers, and fried clams. At dinner it's again about traditional favorites (pasta, steak, lobster), but there are also some slightly more adventurous dishes: housemade dolmas or a tomato-y seafood stew, for instance. The restaurant has racked up quite a few awards of excellence from *Wine Spectator.* Worth noting: a casual section of the restaurant known as the Ramp Bar & Grill stays open all day long, even between lunch and dinner service, offering lighter meals.

77 Pier Rd., Cape Porpoise (Kennebunkport). www.pier77restaurant.com. © **207/967-8500.** Reservations recommended. Main courses lunch $15–$26, dinner $16–$35. Daily 11:30am–9pm.

The White Barn Restaurant ★★★ REGIONAL/NEW AMERICAN

The centerpiece of the **Grace White Barn Inn** (see p. 617), this classy dining room—carved out of, yes, a barn—attracts gourmands from far and wide. The space is half the fun, with its soaring interior and an eclectic collection of country antiques displayed in a hayloft; window displays are changed with the seasons. Chef Matthew Padilla took over the kitchen in 2018, and he's continued his predecessors' traditions of changing up the menu frequently and privileging local produce, fish, and game: Recent options on the prix-fixe menu included a pan-roasted duck breast with fennel, fregola, chanterelles, and duck confit. Fresh, terrific intermezzo courses of fruit soups or sorbets are still a standard. The tasting menu is similarly seasonal, if a bit more exotic (think smoked bone marrow with bacon jam and chimichurri) and paired with selections from a first-in-class wine cellar. Service is astonishingly attentive and knowledgeable, capping the experience. A new, more casual bistro next door is meant to appeal to more casual diners (there's no dress code, for instance), but it's hard to beat the original dining room. Still one of Maine's best meals.

37 Beach Ave., Kennebunk. (¼ mile E of jct. of routes 9 and 35). www.whitebarninn. com. © **207/967-2321.** Reservations recommended. Fixed-price dinner $125; tasting menu $165 per person. Mon–Thurs 6–9:30pm; Fri 5:30–9:30pm. Closed 2 weeks in Jan.

KITTERY

Anju Noodle Bar ★★ PAN-ASIAN   Locals start filling this Foreside hotspot at lunch time, and the crowds don't let up until well after dark. The five varieties of kimchi are a draw, as are the sweet-and-spicy Korean and Japanese chicken wings. But really, everybody's coming for the ramen—big, fragrant bowls of wavy-thin noodles, bone broth, slow-roasted pork shoulder, and more, complex and savory and damn near medicinal.

7 Wallingford Sq. www.anjunoodlebar.com. © **207/703-4298.** Small plates $7–$12; noodle bowls $13–$17. Sun–Thurs noon–9:30pm, Fri–Sat noon–10:30pm.

The Black Birch ★★★ GASTROPUB   Assessing this boxy, bland former post office from the outside, you wouldn't imagine that there's regularly a line out the door by 5pm on weekends. But the magic's all inside: a long bar and tables made of reclaimed wood, 24 taps of esoteric regional beers and obscure imports, a turntable spinning classic vinyl, and a kitchen run by chef Jake Smith turning out totally indulgent and inventive comfort foods. Think deep-fried short ribs and the best poutine outside of Quebec, with duck confit on top and melted local cheese curds.

2 Government St. www.theblackbirch.com. © **207/703-2294.** Small plates $9–$12; main courses $11–$17. Reservations not accepted. Tues–Thurs 3:30–10pm; Fri–Sat 3:30–11pm.

Bob's Clam Hut ★ FRIED SEAFOOD Operating since 1956, Bob's manages to retain an old-fashioned flavor—despite now being surrounded on all sides by factory outlet malls, and with prices that have steadily escalated out of the "budget eats" category. Plump and perfectly golden heaps of clams and other seafood are served with tremendous efficiency in baskets alongside French fries and coleslaw. Order at the window and stake out a table inside or on the deck (with its lovely view of, er, Route 1). The food is surprisingly light, cooked in cholesterol-free vegetable oil; the onion rings are especially good. The lobster roll attracts foodie pilgrims from around the country. To ensure that your diet is irrevocably busted, Bob's also dishes up soft-serve ice cream.

315 Rte. 1 (west side). www.bobsclamhut.com. © **207/439-4233.** Sandwiches $4–$23; main courses $10–$35. Mon–Thurs, Sun 11am–7pm; Fri–Sat 11am–8pm.

OGUNQUIT

Amore Breakfast ★★ BREAKFAST Amore is a breakfast-only place—but what a breakfast it is. (This is *not* a place for weight-watchers. But you're on vacation, right?) Look for numerous variations on the eggs Benedict theme (including a popular one with a big hunk of lobster on top), plus good Belgian waffles, a calorific bananas-Foster-style French toast with pecans outside and cream cheese inside, French toast topped with blueberries, and more than a dozen tasty variations on an omelet. Bloodies and mimosas, too. Italian owner Leanne Cusimano is a local fixture; Amore has gone through several incarnations since it opened in 1994, though it's only inhabited its cheery mod-diner space at The Admiral Inn since 2018.

87 Main St. www.amorebreakfast.com. © **207/646-6667.** Breakfast items $7–$18. Summer daily 7:30am–1pm; off season closed Wed–Thurs. Also closed mid-Dec to Apr.

Barnacle Billy's ★★ SEAFOOD An Ogunquit classic right on the harbor, Barnacle Billy's has been the place to get fresh-off-the-boat lobster in town since 1961. It's loud and busy, and the terrific patio sitting is often filled with tourists who've had one too many plastic cups of the house specialty rum punch—but that's all part of the appeal. There's a lovely garden separating the original restaurant from a neighboring annex, which serves a wider menu of fried seafood baskets and swordfish steaks and stuffed shrimp.

50 Perkins Cove Rd. www.barnbilly.com. © **800/866-5575** or 207/646-5575. Market prices for lobster, sandwiches $5–$20, dinner main courses and baskets $17–$20. April–early Nov daily 11:30am–9pm; rest of year closed.

Caffé Prego ★ ITALIAN BISTRO Beloved for its brick oven pizzas and classic pasta dishes like a rich Bolognese and veal saltimbocca, Prego also offers a small plates menu with simple dishes like salted cod and a house ricotta plate, perfect for a midday snack. Hearty breakfasts, too. The outdoor seating area has lovely landscaping and overlooks the heart of town. Word to the wise: Caffé Prego is known for its desserts, from more than 25 flavors of creamy, house-made gelato to airy and rich éclairs and tartufate.

44 Shore Rd. www.cafeprego.com. ℭ **207/646-7734.** Breakfast items $7–$18. Sandwiches $10–$23. Dinner main courses $14–$25. Daily 7:30am–9:00pm. Closed late Oct–early Apr.

Five-O Shore Road ★★ NEW AMERICAN A fine choice if you're looking for a meal you can brag about without spending a whole day's vacation budget. Chef James Walter got a 2016 Chef of the Year nod from the state's restaurant association; his menu is eclectic in a brasserie/supper-clubby kind of way. You might order terrific steak frites or a roasted lamb loin, but also great clam chowder and pasta dishes. Of course, you can get a Maine lobster in season, too, perhaps served with shaved truffles and cream. There's also a cool cocktail lounge with a long list of creative martinis. It's like the Rat Pack wanted a casual coastal place to kick back in.

50 Shore Rd. www.five-oshoreroad.com. ℭ **207/646-5001.** Reservations strongly recommended in summer. Small plates $10–$20, main courses $22–$39. May–Sept Mon–Sat 5–9pm, Sun 10am–2pm and 5–9pm; call for hours outside peak season.

MC Perkins Cove ★★ SEAFOOD/NEW AMERICAN Chef-partners Mark Gaier and Clark Frasier endeared themselves to Ogunquit (and picked up a coveted James Beard Award) with a groundbreaking, white tablecloth, farm-to-table restaurant called Arrows back in the '90s. It closed years ago, but not before "M" and "C" opened this sleek bistro on the best real estate in town. MC Perkins Cove manages to be fun rather than stuffy. Okay, no bathing suits are allowed in the dining room, but still: Expect big food, even on the "small" plates. Lobster rolls, chopped salads, calamari, oysters on half shell, and crab cakes give way to more sophisticated starters such as mussels in curry sauce, smoked trout rillette, and country ham pâté. Entrees might include steamed lobster, sesame-encrusted trout, Kobe burgers, grilled tuna, hanger steak, or a piece of plank-roasted fish, plus one of the so-labeled "evil carbos" (cheesy mashed potatoes, onion rings, and so forth). Desserts are wonderful: brown-butter brownies with vanilla ice cream, burnt orange caramel, and candied orange peel; toffee pudding with bourbon caramel; a bittersweet chocolate cake with chocolate sauce and pistachio crème anglaise; or peppermint stick ice cream with cookies.

111 Perkins Cove Rd. www.mcperkinscove.com. ℭ **207/646-6263.** Reservations recommended. Lunch main courses $13–$30; dinner main courses $24–$37. Late May to mid-Oct daily 11:30am–9pm; rest of year closed Mon and Tues. Closed Jan.

THE YORKS

Fox's Lobster House ★ SEAFOOD Fox's is unabashedly commercial, and charges more than it could, but so what? You're sitting outside, eating pre-cracked lobsters and breathing salt air, on a headland that would be worth zillions in real estate terms—looking straight at Nubble Light. Fox's has been here since 1966, and I can see why: It delivers a pretty intensively "Maine" experience just a few miles across the state line. You can also dine inside, in a wood-and-nautical-themed dining room, where you can get platters including side dishes: a better deal for families, just without that great lighthouse view. There's an ice-cream window for kids as well.

8 Sohier Park Rd., York Beach. www.foxslobster.com. © **207/363-2643.** Lobsters $25 and up. May–June, Sun–Thurs 11:30am–8pm, Fri–Sat 11:30am–9pm; July–Aug, daily 11:30am–9pm; Sept–Oct, daily 11:30am–8pm. Closed Nov–Apr.

The Goldenrod ★ TRADITIONAL AMERICAN   Follow the neon to this beach-town classic—a York summer institution ever since it opened in 1896. It's easy to find: Look for visitors gawking through plate-glass windows at ancient machines hypnotically churning out taffy (millions of pieces a year). The restaurant, across from the candy-making operation, is low on frills but big on atmosphere: Diners sit on stout oak furniture around a stone fireplace or elbow-to-elbow at an antique soda fountain. Breakfast offerings are New England standards, and for lunch you can eat soups, burgers, and overpriced sandwiches. But what saves the place is the candy counter, where throngs line up to buy boxes of wax-wrapped taffy "kisses" (check the striping on each candy for its flavor; I'm a peanut-butter guy, myself), almond-pocked birch bark, and other penny-candy treats. The shakes, malts, and sundaes are on the sweet side.

Railroad Rd. and Ocean Ave., York Beach. www.thegoldenrod.com. © **207/363-2621.** Lunch and dinner main courses $5–$10. Memorial Day–Labor Day daily 8am–10pm (until 9pm in June); Labor Day–Columbus Day Sat–Sun 8am–3pm. Closed Columbus Day–Memorial Day.

Stonewall Kitchen ★★ CAFE   Stonewall Kitchen's York-based gourmet-foods operation packs them in at this quality, inexpensive cafe, smartly located right at its York headquarters next to the local tourist information office. The cafe has a lovely dining patio and serves simple, hearty items such as fish chowder, soups, lobster rolls, lobster BLTs, muffulettas, turkey wraps with cranberry spread, and more; check the board to find out what's being served that day. Finish with a dessert such as lemon squares, brownies, or fresh-baked cookies. The cafe kitchen also prepares gourmet meals to go, and there's an espresso machine, too.

2 Stonewall Lane (set back from Rte. 1), York. www.stonewallkitchen.com. © **207/351-2719.** Sandwiches and salads $8–$14. Mon–Sat 8am–4pm, Sun 9am–4pm.

PORTLAND ★★

Portland: 106 miles N of Boston

Urban amenities, lively street culture, and a dense concentration of the East Coast's most lauded restaurants—all in a town you can bike end-to-end in 20 minutes. That's what draws transplants and travelers alike to Maine's biggest city (still fewer than 70,000 souls), which radiates out from a hammerhead-shaped peninsula extending into glittering Casco Bay. If you came to Maine for bucolic coastal seclusion, you might be tempted drive right past **Portland**

Portland

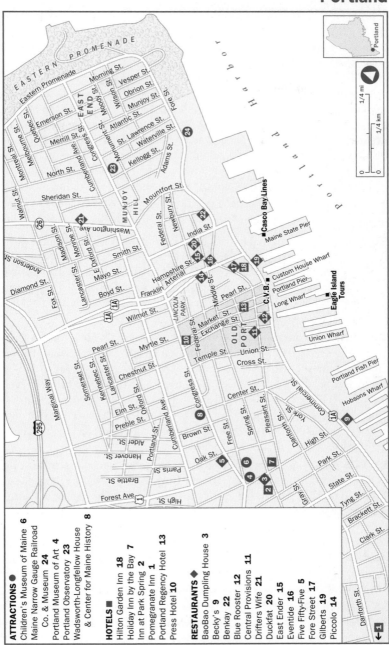

Portland

Casco Bay Lines

Maine State Pier

Custom House Wharf

Portland Pier

C.V.B.

Long Wharf

Eagle Island Tours

Union Wharf

Portland Fish Pier

Hobsons Wharf

ATTRACTIONS ●
Children's Museum of Maine **6**
Maine Narrow Gauge Railroad
  Co. & Museum **24**
Portland Museum of Art **4**
Portland Observatory **23**
Wadsworth-Longfellow House
  & Center for Maine History **8**

HOTELS ■
Hilton Garden Inn **18**
Holiday Inn by the Bay **7**
Inn at Park Spring **2**
Pomegranate Inn **1**
Portland Regency Hotel **13**
Press Hotel **10**

RESTAURANTS ◆
BaoBao Dumpling House **3**
Becky's **9**
Benkay **22**
Blue Rooster **12**
Central Provisions **11**
Drifters Wife **21**
Duckfat **20**
East Ender **15**
Eventide **16**
Five Fifty-Five **5**
Fore Street **17**
Gilberts **19**
Piccolo **14**

on I-295, admiring the skyline at 60 miles an hour. But you'd be missing out on one of the country's most vibrant up-and-coming small metros.

Portland is worth at least an afternoon's detour, and a long weekend isn't too much time to spend here. This historic city has plenty of charm—not only in the Old Port, with its brick sidewalks, but in several lovely residential neighborhoods of striking views and architecture, some of which look out onto Casco Bay.

You can catch a quick ferry to an offshore island, browse boutiques, crack lobsters, walk empty beaches, and pose beside lighthouses—then top off your day with top-shelf food and drink, as Portland is now a recognized culinary destination, blessed with an uncommonly high number of excellent restaurants, craft breweries and distilleries, micro-roasteries, and so on for a city its size. And there's still a salty tang to local culture that you'll occasionally still glimpse in the waterfront bars and chowder houses.

Essentials

ARRIVING

BY CAR   Coming from the south by car, downtown Portland is most easily reached by taking exit 44 off the Maine Turnpike (I-95), and then following I-295 (no toll) into the city. Exit onto Franklin Arterial (exit 7), and continue straight to the city's ferry terminal. Turn right onto Commercial Street, and continue a few blocks to parking meters and the visitor center on the right (see below). Get oriented there.

BY TRAIN   Amtrak (www.amtrak.com; © **800/872-7245**) runs a daily *Downeaster* service from Boston's North Station to Portland (passengers from other cities must change stations from South Station to North Station in Boston by taxi or subway). The train makes five round-trips daily (time: 2½ hr.), for $20 to $30 each way. Downtown is a short bus, cab, or Uber ride or a drab 45-minute walk from the station, which is out on Thompson's Point (although a new recreational development in an old train repair facility has made Thompson's Point a destination itself—see p. 629).

BY BUS   Two big carriers, **Concord Coach** (www.concordcoachlines.com; © **800/639-3317** or 603/228-3300) and **Greyhound** (www.greyhound.com; © **800/231-2222**), provide bus service to Portland. The Greyhound bus terminal is at 950 Congress Street, about a mile south of the downtown core. Greyhound runs buses from both Boston (around 2 hr., $15–$30 one-way) and New York City (8 hr., $33–$64 one-way). Concord Coach runs more than a dozen buses daily between Portland and Boston's Logan Airport (2 hr., $29 one-way; discounts for round-trips), plus two buses a day to NYC (6 hr., $69 one- way). Concord Coach's bus terminal is next to the Amtrak station

BY PLANE   **Portland International Jetport** (www.portlandjetport.org; © **207/874-8877**) is the largest airport in Maine, served by most major airlines. A taxi ride to the city is about $30 with tip; some hotels near the airport and downtown will shuttle you to your digs for free. Ask when booking.

Car rentals are available from a half-dozen chain outfits at the terminal. Also, the no. 1 **Metro city bus** ($1.50) passes nearby about twice per hour (only once per hr. on Sun); limos and vans can be called to pick you up; a taxi into the city center costs about $22, tip included; rideshare services Uber and Lyft cost roughly half as much as a taxi.

VISITOR INFORMATION

The **Convention and Visitors Bureau of Greater Portland** (www.visit portland.com) maintains *four* information centers in and around the city. The **main info center** (© 207/772-5800) is located on the Ocean Gateway Pier, at the far northern end of Commercial Street past the Casco Bay Ferry docks. Most of the time, it's open Monday to Saturday; in July and August, it also opens on Sunday, and it's closed the last 2 weeks of February.

You'll also find tourist information kiosks at the **Portland International Jetport** (© 207/775-5809), near the baggage claim, open daily year-round, plus brochure kiosks at the **Maine Mall** in South Portland and at the **Portland Transport Center** at Thompson's Point

Portland's free weekly newspaper, the *Portland Phoenix* (www.conwaydaily sun.com/portland_phoenix), offers good listings of local events, films, night-club performances, and the like. Copies are widely available at restaurants, bars, convenience stores, and in newspaper boxes in the Old Port and around downtown.

Exploring Portland

Visitors to Portland usually begin with a quick stroll around the historic **Old Port** ★. Bounded by Commercial, Congress, Union, and Pearl streets, this area near the waterfront has some of the city's best commercial architecture, a clutch of boutiques, some of the state's best restaurants (seafood is a special strength here), and one of the densest concentrations of bars on the eastern seaboard. **Exchange Street** is the spiritual heart of the Old Port, with the most boutiques, eateries, and coffee shops.

The city's finest harborside stroll is along the **Eastern Prom Pathway** ★★, which wraps for about a mile along the waterfront beginning at the Casco Bay Lines ferry terminal at the corner of Commercial and Franklin streets. This paved pathway is suitable for walking or biking and offers expansive views of the islands and sailboats in the harbor. The pathway skirts the lower edge of the **Eastern Promenade** ★★, a 68-acre hillside park with broad, grassy slopes extending down to the water. There's also a tiny beach here, though it's often off-limits for swimming. The pathway continues on to **Back Cove Pathway,** a 3.5-mile loop around tidal Back Cove.

The peninsula's two main residential neighborhoods, **Munjoy Hill** and the **West End,** top gentle rises overlooking downtown. **Congress Street,** Portland's main artery of commerce, connects these two neighborhoods. The western reaches of Congress Street (roughly btw. Monument Square and State Street) is home to Portland's **Arts District** ★, where you can find the handsome art

If you're in town from September through May, try to squeeze a theatrical performance or a concert at one of Portland's premiere performing arts outfits.

The **Portland Stage Company** (25A Forest Ave.; www.portlandstage.org; ℓ 207/774-0465), one of the outstanding regional theaters in the Northeast, performs an eclectic schedule of classic and modern shows from Shakespeare to Noël Coward to Neil Simon; it also a track record of developing and producing new American work.

Portland Symphony Orchestra (20 Myrtle St.; www.portlandsymphony.com; ℓ 207/842-0800) knocks your socks off in a series of pops and classical concerts at the Merrill Auditorium in Portland City Hall.

museum, several theaters, the campus of the Maine College of Art (located in an old department store), and a calliope of restaurants and boutiques.

Atop Munjoy Hill, above the Eastern Promenade, are another cluster of good restaurants, grocers, and a coffee shop, not to mention the distinctive **Portland Observatory** (see below). Just north of the hill, the post-industrial, still gritty **Bayside** neighborhood crams a half-dozen of the city's best taprooms, multiple craft distilleries, a few good coffee roasters, and restaurants from barbecue joints to oyster bars all inside of 2 square miles.

Children's Museum and Theatre of Maine ★ MUSEUM   The centerpiece exhibit in Portland's kids' museum is its camera obscura, a room-size "camera" located on the top floor of this stout, columned downtown building next to the art museum. Children gather around a white table in a dark room, where they see magically projected images that include cars driving on city streets, boats plying the harbor, and seagulls flapping by. This never fails to enthrall, providing a memorable lesson in the workings of lenses. That's just one attraction; there are plenty more, from a simulated supermarket checkout counter to a firehouse pole to a mock space shuttle that kids pilot from a high cockpit.

142 Free St. www.kitetails.org. ℓ **207/828-1234.** $11.50, or $2 from 5–8pm 1st Fri of month. Daily 10am–5pm (open until 8pm 1st Fri of month).

Maine Narrow Gauge Railroad Co. & Museum ★ MUSEUM   In the late 19th century, Maine was home to several narrow-gauge railways, operating on rails 2 feet apart. Most of these trains have disappeared, but this nonprofit organization is dedicated to preserving the examples that remain. There's a small fee for admission to the museum only, while a more expensive ticket also includes a short ride on the little train that putters along Casco Bay at the foot of the Eastern Promenade. Views of the islands are attractive; the ride itself is slow, but your kids will undoubtedly enjoy it.

58 Fore St. www.mainenarrowgauge.org. ℓ **207/828-0814.** Museum admission $3 adults, $2 seniors and kids 3–12; train fare (includes museum admission) $10 adults, $9 seniors, $6 kids 3–12, free for ages 2 and under. May–Oct daily 9:30am–4pm (trains run on the hour); closed Nov–Apr.

Portland Head Light & Museum ★★ LIGHTHOUSE   A short drive south from downtown Portland, this 1794 lighthouse is one of the most picturesque in the nation. You'll probably recognize it from advertisements, calendars, or posters. The light marks the entrance to Portland Harbor and was occupied continuously from its construction until 1989, when it was automated and the graceful keeper's house (built in 1891) was converted to a small, town-owned museum focusing on the history of navigation. The lighthouse itself is still active, and therefore is closed to the public, but visitors can stop by the museum or browse for lighthouse-themed items in a gift shop. The surrounding grounds of Fort Williams Park are great for picnics; if you're traveling with kids, plan extra time for them to enjoy its two playgrounds and a brand new children's garden full of winding paths, hopscotch stones, and tunnels.

1000 Shore Rd. (in Ft. Williams Park), Cape Elizabeth. www.portlandheadlight.com. ℭ **207/799-2661.** Free admission for grounds; museum $2 adults, $1 kids 6–18. Park grounds open daily year-round sunrise–sunset (until 8:30pm in summer); museum daily Memorial Day–Oct 10am–4pm, weekends only mid-Apr to mid-May and Nov to early Dec.

Portland Museum of Art ★★★ MUSEUM   The modern main building of Portland's art museum, designed by I. M. Pei & Partners and opened in 1983, is an arresting red-brick presence on Congress Square, and it's top-rate by every standard. The museum features selections from its own fine collections along with a parade of touring exhibits. (Summer exhibits are usually targeted at a broad audience.) The museum, which began as the Portland Art Society in 1882, has over the years amassed particularly strong holdings of American artists with Maine connections, including Winslow Homer, Andrew Wyeth, and Edward Hopper, and it has fine displays of Early American furniture and crafts. The museum shares with Colby College the Joan Whitney Payson Collection, which includes wonderful European works by Renoir, Degas, and Picasso, among other titans. Recent special exhibitions have brought the art books of Henri Matisse, photographs from Maine's pioneering Rose Marasco, a retrospective of photorealist painter Richard Estes, and a juxtaposition of Warhol's *Mao* with the *Mona Lisa*. The museum's film series, shown on an auditorium big-screen, is a worthy substitute for the arthouse cinema Portland lacks. If you're into American masters, check out the tour of the **Winslow Homer Studio at Prout's Neck** in Cape Elizabeth, offered on Mondays and Fridays in the summer ($55, van trip from museum, call to reserve well ahead). Homer spent the last 26 years of his life there, staring at the rockbound coast and creating some of his most famous works.

7 Congress Square. (corner of Congress and High sts.). www.portlandmuseum.org. ℭ **207/775-6148.** $15 adults, $13 seniors, $10 students, kids 14 and under free; free admission Fri 4–8pm. Sat–Wed 11am–6pm, Thurs–Fri 11am–8pm; closed Mon–Tues from Columbus Day to Memorial Day.

Portland Observatory ★ MUSEUM/LANDMARK   Atop Munjoy Hill, above the Eastern Promenade, this quirky shingled tower dating from 1807 was originally built to signal the arrival of ships into port. Exhibits inside provide a quick glimpse of Portland's past, but the real draw is the expansive view from the top of the city and the harbor.

138 Congress St. www.portlandlandmarks.org. © **207/774-5561.** $10 adults, $8 seniors and students, $5 kids 6–16. Daily Memorial Day–Columbus Day, 10am–5pm; last tour at 4:30pm.

Wadsworth-Longfellow House ★★ HISTORIC HOME   This red-brick 18th-century home is one of three structures encompassing the famous Portland writer Henry Wadsworth Longfellow's boyhood home; it also has one of the state's best historical archives: a history campus, if you will. This home was built by Gen. Peleg Wadsworth, grandfather of the poet, and is still furnished in early-19th-century style with some original furniture. Adjacent is the Maine History Gallery, a decent museum inside a former bank.

487-489 Congress St. www.mainehistory.org. © **207/774-1822.** $15 adults, $13 seniors and students, $3 kids 6–17. May daily noon–5pm; June–Oct Mon–Sat 10am–5pm, Sun noon–5pm (tours on the hour); Nov–Apr closed.

Where to Stay in Portland

Portland's lodging market is subject to extreme seasonal shifts. In the off-season, there's a genuine glut of empty rooms around town, and deals can be had. In the summer, there's a dearth, and rates are surprisingly high for a small city. Budget chains cluster near the airport. Airbnb rentals abound and are a popular alternative.

If you're looking for something central, the **Hilton Garden Inn** at 65 Commercial St. (www.hilton.com; © **207/780-0780**) is a decent chain choice right across from the city's ferry dock. It's convenient to all the Old Port's restaurants, bakeries, and pubs—not to mention the islands of Casco Bay. You'll pay for the privilege of being in the heart of the waterfront, though: Double rooms mostly run from about $189 up to $449 per night. The **Holiday Inn by the Bay,** 88 Spring St. (www.innbythebay.com; © **800/345-5050** or 207/775-2311), offers great views of the harbor from about half the rooms, along with the usual chain-hotel creature comforts. Peak-season rates are approximately $210 for a double. Budget travelers seeking chain hotels typically head toward the area around the Maine Mall in South Portland, about 8 miles south of the attractions of downtown.

Take Me Out to the Sea Dogs

The **Portland Sea Dogs** are a minor league Double-A team affiliated with the Boston Red Sox (a perfect marriage in baseball-crazy northern New England). They play through summer at Hadlock Field (271 Park Ave.; www. seadogs.com; © **800/936-3647** or 207/879-9500), a small stadium near downtown that still retains an old-time feel despite aluminum benches and other updating. Activities are geared toward families, with lots of entertainment between innings and a selection of food that's a couple of notches above basic hot dogs and hamburgers. You might even catch future pro stars. The season runs from April to Labor Day.

Inn at Park Spring ★ This small, tasteful B&B is located on a busy downtown street in a historic brick home that dates back to 1835. It's well located for exploring the city on foot, and the friendly owners keep the place in good shape. Guests can linger or watch TV in a front parlor, or chat at the communal dining table in the adjacent room (communal breakfasts are a highlight—unless you're shy). The rooms are all corner rooms, and most are bright and sunny. Especially nice is Room 1, with its sleigh bed, hardwood flooring, and wonderful views of the historic row houses along Park Street, and periwinkle-hued Room 4, on the third (top) floor, which gets abundant afternoon light and is furnished with a king bed, big sitting room, and nice bathroom. The Portland Museum of Art (p. 631) and the city's children's museum (p. 630) are only 2 blocks away, the Old Port a 10-minute walk.

135 Spring St. www.innatparkspring.com. © **800/437-8511** or 207/774-1059. 5 units. Jun–Oct $230–$295 double; off-season $115–$195 double. 2-night minimum weekends. Rates include full breakfast. Free parking. No children 9 and under. **Amenities:** Free Wi-Fi.

Pomegranate Inn ★★ Located inside a 19th-century Italianate home in Portland's lovely West End, this is arguably the city's top B&B. Eight rooms feature individually distinct design touches, painted floors, faux-marble woodwork, and gas fireplaces. The carriage house room includes a private terrace whose sliding doors open onto a small garden, and breakfasts are a highlight. Also don't miss the flowery second-floor balcony and third-floor conservatory.

49 Neal St. www.pomegranateinn.com. © **800/356-0408** or 207/772-1006. 8 units. $159–$409 double. Rates include full breakfast. Children 16 and older only. **Amenities:** Afternoon refreshments; free Wi-Fi.

Portland Regency Hotel ★★★ Centrally located on a cobblestone courtyard in the middle of the Old Port, the Regency boasts one of the city's premier hotel locations. But it's got more than location—this is also one of the most architecturally interesting hotels in southern Maine. Housed in an 1895 brick armory, the hotel is thoroughly modern inside and offers attractive rooms, appointed and furnished with all the expected amenities. There are several types of rooms and suites, each fitted to the place's unique architecture; for a splurge, ask for a luxurious corner room with a handsome (nonworking) fireplace, sitting area, city views out big windows, and a Jacuzzi. The small health club is one of the best in town (it includes a sauna and hot tub), and the downstairs level conceals a restaurant and a lounge.

20 Milk St. www.theregency.com. © **800/727-3436** or 207/774-4200. 95 units. Early July–late Oct $250–$440 double, $329–$522 suite; off season $115–$240 double, $189–$309 suite. Valet parking $20 per day. Some rooms allow pets $75 per day. **Amenities:** Restaurant; bar; free airport transfers; babysitting (with prior notice); conference rooms; fitness club w/aerobics classes; Jacuzzi; room service; sauna; spa; free Wi-Fi.

The Press Hotel ★★★ If it's not the best urban lodging in Portland, it's certainly the most fun. The Press Hotel was constructed over the bones of the former headquarters of the *Portland Press Herald* newspaper, and there's a

let's get hopping: THE BEERS OF PORTLAND

Portland is the beer capital of New England—and it holds its own against most of the rest of the country, too, with more craft breweries per capita than any American city. In general, Maine's craft brew scene is characterized by liberal pour laws that make tap rooms as popular as bars, plus a penchant for embracing (and reviving) Old World styles.

For starters, there's the granddaddy of Belgian-style beer in the U.S. Head west out Forest Avenue (off Congress Street) a few miles, then turn right on Riverside Street and take the next right into an industrial park to find **Allagash Brewing ★★** at 50 Industrial Way (www.allagash.com; ✆ **800/330-5385** or 207/878-5385), a legend of a craft brewer that's gained nationwide recognition for its Belgian-style white, double, and triple beers. Allagash offers daily tours from 11am to 4:30pm. While the company's flagship brew, Allagash White, holds a special place in many beer lover's palates, the brewery is still crazy experimental—taps pouring at the spacious and rustic tap room include hard-to-find seasonal and limited release brews: wild-fermented beers, beers brewed with coffee or fruit or ginger, dry-hopped and barrel-aged beers, you name it.

While you're at this far-flung corner of town, don't miss the other breweries in the neighborhood, including several at 1 Industrial Way, across the street from Allagash. Try the milk stout or the slightly sour, easy-drinking Lawn Mower saison from **Austin Street Brewery** (www.austinstreetbrewery.com; ✆ **207/200-1994**), then duck next door into **Foundation Brewing Company** (www.foundationbrew.com; ✆ **207/370-8187**), which brews (among other things) IPAs in the crisp, fruity, none-too-bitter New England style.

Head down to the East Bayside District to find several of Portland's buzziest brewers, including **Oxbow Blending and Bottling ★** (www.oxbowbeer.com; ✆ **207/350-0025**). This Portland outpost of a farmhouse brewery headquartered up the coast, in Newcastle (p. 642) pours Old World farmhouse ales in a huge former warehouse decorated with an oh-so-Portland mix of b-boy graffiti and reclaimed barn wood. A bit hard to find (49 Washington Ave., head into the alley next to the coffee shop), this place is a party on a Saturday night. **Rising Tide Brewing Company** (www.risingtidebrewing.com; ✆ **207/370-2337**) at 103 Fox St. has a great patio with lawn games and food trucks and excels at lower-alcohol brews.

Off the peninsula, beer lovers literally line up around the block at Thompson's Point (p. 629) when **Bissell Brothers ★** (www.bissellbrothers.com) releases cases of its newest batches. The 2,500-square-foot tap room (complete pinball, wall murals, and lofted hangout space) is often packed by noon with devotees of Bissell's bright, strong, often opaque ales.

Incredibly, this list only scratches the surface of the 30ish craft brewers operating in Greater Portland. You can taste a bunch at the Old Port's superb **Novare Res Bier Café** (4 Canal Plaza; www.novareresbiercafe.com, ✆ **207/761-2437**), a modern-day rathskeller with a bottle list 500 strong and an emphasis on obscure Euro imports. The **Maine Brew Bus** (www.themainebrewbus.com; ✆ **207/245-1940**) will shuttle you around from tap room to tap room (tour options vary widely, $40–$70 per person). For an exhaustive list of brewers and a map of the Maine Beer Trail, visit **www.mainebrewersguild.org**.

"golden days of journalism" theme throughout the building that's more fun than it sounds, from the art installation of vintage typewriters in the lobby to the wallpaper made of old headlines to the mod Inkwell bar. Rooms are clean and contemporary, done up in muted blues and grays, with vintage furniture, local art, and a really generous number of outlets and USB ports. The restaurant, **Union,** is one of Portland's best.

119 Exchange St. www.presshotel.com. ☏ **207/808-8800.** 110 units. July–Aug $400–$600 double, $719–$799 suite; May–June and Sept–Oct $180–$350 double, $549–$619 suite; Nov–Apr $159–$199 double, $449–$539 suite. **Amenities:** Free bicycles; art gallery; restaurant; bar; fitness room; room service; spa; free Wi-Fi.

Where to Eat in Portland
EXPENSIVE

Central Provisions ★★ NEW AMERICAN   Small plates done right. Central Provisions made various national Best New Restaurant lists when it opened in 2014, and it's only upped its game since. The ever-changing menu skews way local and divvies up simply: hot, cold, raw, and sweet. Maine tuna crudos are a mainstay on the raw menu, and they're typical of the restaurant's style: simple, fresh, flavorful, and elegantly plated. On a Friday night, this place is date-night central. Grab a seat at the long bar with the scenesters (on a bar stool made from Maine-forged iron and recycled burlap) or head to the basement for more of a rathskeller feel. There's a limited menu available late and between lunch and dinner.

414 Fore St. www.central-provisions.com. ☏ **207/805-1085.** Small plates $8–$26. Lunch Tues–Sat 11am–2pm; dinner Sun–Thurs 5–10pm, Fri–Sat 5–10:30pm. Reservations not accepted.

Drifters Wife ★★ WINE BAR   This lauded wine bar opened as a handful of tables in a larger retail wine shop back in 2016—at the time, *Bon Appétit* called it one of the country's 50 best new restaurants. It's since expanded, so that the restaurant envelops the smart wine shop; while chef Ben Jackson is no longer working with two induction burners and a half-size oven, the plucky character of the place hasn't changed. Jackson turns out exquisitely plated (really, they're works of art) shareable portions of fresh local veggies and just-caught fish: maybe a head-and-all Atlantic mackerel with pistachio butter and fresh veggies, or chicken livers on toast with pickled egg and cucumbers. The wine list (like the picks at the on-site Maine & Loire wine store) skews organic and biodynamic and additive-free.

59 Washington Ave. www.drifterswife.com. ☏ **207/805-1336.** Main courses $18–$30. Tues–Sat 4–10pm. Reservations encouraged (online only).

Five Fifty-Five ★ NEW AMERICAN   When husband-and-wife Steve and Michelle Corry opened Five Fifty-Five in 2003, neither "small plates" nor "farm-to-table" were entrenched in the American foodie lexicon. The Corrys were instrumental in introducing both ideas to Northeast diners. Still, Five Fifty-Five's regulars love it for its large-plate signature dishes like truffled lobster macaroni-and-cheese, striploins and hanger steaks, hand-rolled pastas, and other maximalist stalwarts. Wine aficionados, take note: The wine list here is tops, one of the best in the entire state.

555 Congress St. www.fivefifty-five.com. ✆ **207/761-0555.** Small plates $9–$15, main courses $20–$38. Daily 5–9:30pm; Sun brunch 9:30am–2pm. Reservations recommended.

Fore Street ★★ CONTEMPORARY GRILL   Fore Street has emerged as one of northern New England's most celebrated restaurants. Chef Sam Hayward routinely pops up in magazines like *Saveur* and *Food & Wine,* his restaurant was often in *Gourmet*'s 100 Best, and so forth. Hayward's secret is simplicity: local and organic ingredients are used where possible, and the kitchen avoids fussy presentations. The dining space centers around a busy open kitchen where a team of chefs constantly stoke the wood-fired brick oven and grill, which feature prominently in the culinary philosophy here. The menu changes nightly, but entrees might run to spit-roasted pork loin, grilled duckling, grilled marinated hanger steak, or a piece of pan-seared bluefish; the wood-roasted mussels are also a big hit. Finish with a dessert such as chocolate soufflé, hand-dipped chocolates, or gelati—these are often accented in summer by seasonal Maine berries or fruits. Though it can be difficult to snag a reservation here on summer weekends, management always sets aside a few tables each night for walk-ins. Get there early and grab one.

288 Fore St. www.forestreet.biz. ✆ **207/775-2717.** Main courses $26–$40. Sun–Thurs 5:30–10pm; Fri–Sat 5:30–10:30pm. Reservations recommended.

Piccolo ★★ ITALIAN   The cuisine of central and southern Italy takes center stage at this postage stamp of a restaurant (only about 20 seats) at the edge of the Old Port, where the ever-changing menu skews fresh and rustic: chef Damian Sansonetti plates up cavatelli with lamb neck ragout, grilled swordfish with beans and salsa verde, and other dishes his mom and grandma once made. Pastry chef Ilma Lopez is one of Portland's hottest culinary talents, and her airy Italian donut holes, called *zeppole,* are a highlight. The tasting menu on Sunday nights is as fun and daring as the tiny room is social—there's one 6:30 seating, and reservations are a must. At once cozy and sumptuous, Piccolo is my pick for the best date night in Portland.

111 Middle St. www.piccolomaine.com. ✆ **207/747-5307.** Main courses $19–$27. Wed–Sun 5–10pm; Sun brunch 10:30am–2pm. Reservations recommended.

MODERATE

BaoBao Dumpling House ★ ASIAN FUSION   Buzzy chef Cara Stadler opened this casual-hip dumpling depot as a more relaxed alternative to her much-praised and more formal Tao Yuan restaurant in nearby Brunswick. It's fun ordering a la carte off the inventive dumpling menu—options like shrimp and bacon, Kung Pao chicken and peanut, and lamb and black bean chili play around with classic formulas for the small, steamed bundles beloved in China and beyond. As befits the hangout vibe of the narrow, sparsely adorned dining room, BaoBao has a great bar, with a really well curated selection of Maine craft beers, a nice sake list, and some bracing house cocktails. Kids welcome.

133 Spring St. www.baobaodumplinghouse.com. © **207/772-8400.** Small plates $6–$14. Wed–Thurs 11:30am–10pm; Fri–Sat 11:30am–11pm; Sun 11:30am–9pm.

Benkay ★ SUSHI Among Portland's sushi restaurants, Benkay is the longtime fave, usually teeming with a lively local crowd lured by the affordable menus. Chef Seiji Ando trained in Osaka and Kyoto; his sushi, sashimi, and maki rolls deliver a lot for the price, and there's a wide range of choices and combinations. Standard Japanese bar-food items such as tempura (deep-fried vegetables), *gyoza* (dumplings), teriyaki, *katsu* (fried chicken or pork cutlets), and udon (thick noodles) are also served. For dessert, consider the green tea ice cream: deliciously bitter . . . and good for you. Sort of.

16 Middle St. www.sushiman.com. © **207/773-5555.** Main courses $12–$24. Mon–Fri 11:30am–2pm and 5–9:30pm; Sat–Sun 11:30am–11pm. Reservations not accepted.

Duckfat ★★★ CAFE James Beard-award-winning chef Rob Evans left the fine dining world years ago to open this beloved bistro serving hand-cut Belgian-style fries with curried mayo, truffled ketchup, and other gourmet sauces, plus amazing *poutine* (Canadian-style fries with cheese curds and gravy), esoteric panini sandwiches (house-smoked brisket or duck confit, anyone?), beignets, and to-die-for milkshakes (with crème anglaise). The beer list is impeccable, and there is always a wait. Don't let it deter you—no one in Portland doesn't like this place.

43 Middle St. www.duckfat.com. © **207/774-8080.** Main courses $9–$14. Daily 11am–10pm. Reservations not accepted.

East Ender ★★ NEW AMERICAN The best brunch in town (in my opinion) nails a delicate balance of sweet, savory, and experimental in a room that's laid-back and welcoming. The plate of chicken and yeast-raised waffles will feed you for days, particularly if you are wise enough to also indulge in the house-made daily doughnut beforehand. Dinner is equally fun and exciting; the East Ender's schtick is serving comforty faves that are inventive on the margins, like grilled duck with sauerkraut and gruyere, or a patty melt with lobster (and bacon jam) instead of beef, or chili-lime Brussels sprouts. It's the kind of joint where you can wear a sport coat or a flannel shirt and not feel out of place either way. There's a lunch menu of comfort food and sandwiches, too; note the kitchen closes for 2 hours at 3:30 to flip from lunch to dinner service (though the bar remains open).

47 Middle St. www.eastenderportland.com © **207/879-7669.** Lunch and brunch main courses $9–$15; dinner main courses $14–$24. Mon–Thurs 11:30am–9:00pm; Fri–Sat 11:30am–10pm; Sun 11am–2pm.

Eventide Oyster Co. ★★★ OYSTER BAR/SEAFOOD Maybe no restaurant is as emblematic of contemporary Portland dining as Eventide. The offerings are of the old-school Maine seafaring variety: a rotating selection of oysters (overwhelmingly local in season, many from the oyster mecca of the Damariscotta River), a brown-butter lobster roll that's a rich and inventive twist on the state's favorite proletarian treat, or a full-on clambake option, complete with a hardboiled egg nestled in a bed of rockweed. But the room is stylish and modern, with the raw bar occupying a huge hunk of gorgeous Maine granite, the accouterments are adventurous (think ginger and kimchi toppings on your half-shell), and the clientele (especially late) tends towards the young and urbane. Eventide's a little on the dear side compared to no-frills oyster pubs on up the coast; it's also one of Portland's most fun dining experiences.

86 Middle St. www.eventideoysterco.com. ℂ **207/774-8538.** Dozen oysters $29; sandwiches and small plates $7–$15. Daily 11am–midnight.

INEXPENSIVE

Becky's ★ DINER   This Portland institution resides in a squat concrete building at the not-so-quaint end of the waterfront. It's been written up in *Gourmet* magazine, but that's where the comparison to "fine dining" ends; this is a diner, Maine-style, complete with drop ceilings, fluorescent lights, and scruffy counters, booths, and tables. It opens early (4am) for the local fishermen grabbing a cup of joe and some eggs before heading out onto (or in from) the water; later in the day, it attracts high school kids, businessmen, and just about everyone else. The menu is extensive, offering what you'd expect: sandwiches, fried haddock, corn dogs, tuna melts, and milky bowls of chowder with just-caught fish. It's notable for its breakfasts, including more than a dozen omelets, eggs any way you want 'em, pancakes, French toast, and five types of home fries.

390 Commercial St. www.beckysdiner.com. ℂ **207/773-7070.** Breakfast items $4–$11; lunch and dinner items $4–$17. Daily 4am–9pm (weekends until 10pm in summer).

Blue Rooster Food Company ★ SANDWICHES/GLOBAL   Great sandwiches, although most locals stop in for the piled-high tater tots or the creative hot dogs, natural-casing franks served with pineapple and bacon, pickled ginger and wasabi mayo, cheese curds and gravy, BBQ and jalapenos, you name it. Not much seating in this counter-service joint, so best to park it on a bench somewhere in the surrounding blocks of the Old Port.

5 Dana St. www.blueroosterfoodcompany.com. ℂ **207/747-4157.** Sandwiches and hot dogs $5–$12. Mon–Wed 11am–6pm; Thurs–Sat 11am–2am; Sun noon–6pm.

Gilbert's Chowder House ★ CHOWDER/SEAFOOD   Gilbert's is a very popular waterfront spot with tourists, and is nautical without taking the theme too far. The reasonable prices keep locals coming, too. The chowders are okay, if unspectacular; other choices include fried clams, haddock sandwiches, and various seafood you can order either broiled or fried. There's also a basic lobster dinner with corn on the cob and a cup of clam chowder. Limited microbrews are on tap, and they serve decent cheesecake for dessert, among other choices.

92 Commercial St. www.gilbertschowderhouse.com. ℂ **207/871-5636.** Chowders $5–$14; sandwiches $5–$16; main courses $12–$22. Daily 11am–9pm.

MIDCOAST MAINE

Bath: 33 miles NE of Portland. Boothbay Harbor: 23 miles E of Bath, 41 miles SW of Rockland.

Longtime Maine travelers might be heard to utter how the rocky, central stretch of the coast, known as the "Midcoast," is both its loveliest section *and* its most overdeveloped. And these grousers have a point, especially along Route 1, where both the seasonal and year-round population has boomed in recent decades. But turn off the main roads and you'll easily find another Maine, full of some of the most pastoral and picturesque meadows, mountains, peninsulas, and harbors in the entire state.

Traveling north, highlights of this coastal route include the shipbuilding town of Bath, pretty little Wiscasset, and the Boothbay region on the southern end of the Midcoast; the lovely **Pemaquid peninsula;** lost-in-time Monhegan Island; and finally, the power trio of Camden, Rockland, and Rockport (which, though they're solidly part of what Mainers call the Midcoast, are covered in the next section, "Penobscot Bay," see p. 646).

Essentials

ARRIVING

The coast is best accessed via Route 1, which you catch in Brunswick by taking exit 28 off I-295. Freeport is on Route 1, about 16 miles north of Portland. The downtown is reached by taking I-295 north to either exit 20 or 22, then following signs. From Route 1 in Damariscotta, turn south down Route 129/130 to the Pemaquid Peninsula. (Coming from the north or northeast, take Route 1 through Waldoboro, then turn south down Route 32.)

VISITOR INFORMATION

The **Maine State Information Center** (℗ 207/846-0833), just off exit 17 of I-295 in Yarmouth (which isn't yet in the Midcoast, but you'll almost certainly pass through here to get there), is crammed with glossy brochures, and its helpful staff is particularly well informed about the middle reaches of coast. It's open daily, year-round; and even when it's closed, the attached restroom facilities are open. At the **Freeport Information Center,** at 23 Depot St. (www.freeportusa.com; ℗ 207/865-1212), you can pick up a map and directory of businesses, restaurants, and overnight accommodations. The **Damariscotta Region Chamber of Commerce** (www.damariscottaregion.com; ℗ 207/563-8340) operates a walk-in information center in the middle of town at the corner of Main Street and Vine Street.

Exploring Freeport ★

If Freeport were a mall, L.L.Bean would be the anchor store. It's the business that launched this town to prominence, elevating its status from just another Maine fishing village near the interstate to one of the state's major tourist draws for the outlet centers that sprang up here in Bean's wake.

Freeport still has the look of a classic Maine village, but it's a village that's been largely taken over by those outlet shops; most of the old historic homes and stores have been converted into upscale stores purveying name-brand clothing and housewares at cut-rate prices. Banana Republic occupies an exceedingly handsome brick Federal-style home; a Carnegie library became an Abercrombie & Fitch, pumping club music (oh, the inhumanity); and even the McDonald's is housed in a tasteful, understated Victorian farmhouse, for crying out loud—you really have to look to find the arches.

Still, strict planning guidelines have managed to preserve most of the town's local charm, at least in the downtown section. (Huge parking lots are hidden from view off the main drag.) As a result, Freeport is one of the more aesthetically pleasing places to shop in New England—even though crowds and traffic can be intense during the peak season.

Seeking out the real Maine? Ask directions off the main road to **South Freeport,** which consists of a boat dock, a general store, and a good lobster shack (see p. 645) on a point of land.

Seeking a bargain? You've come to the right place.

FREEPORT SHOPPING

Freeport has more than 140 retail shops spaced out between exit 20 of I-295 (at the far lower end of Main Street) and Mallet Road, which connects to exit 22. Some shops have even begun to spread south of exit 20 toward Yarmouth. The bulk of them are "factory" or "outlet" stores. If you don't want to miss a single one, get off at exit 17 and head north on Route 1. The bargains can vary from extraordinary to "huh?" Plan on wearing out some shoe leather and taking at *least* a half-day if you're really intent on finding the best deals.

The sometimes-changing rotation of national chains here has recently included Abercrombie & Fitch, Banana Republic, Gap, Calvin Klein, Patagonia, North Face, Nike, Orvis, Tommy Hilfiger, and Cole Haan, among many others. You'll also find a number of high-end Maine brands represented, including Georgetown Pottery, chi-chi blankets from Brahms Mount, and beloved import emporium Mexicali Blues.

Stores in Freeport are typically open daily 9am to 9pm during the busy summer and close much earlier (5 or 6pm) in other seasons; between Thanksgiving and Christmas, they remain open late once more.

Casco Bay Cutlery & Kitchenware ★   Long known as Freeport Knife for its signature product, this store still sports a wide selection of knives for kitchen and camp alike, including blades from Germany, Switzerland, and Japan. Also find esoteric pots, pans, and gadgets from the likes of Le Creuset, Peugeot, and Maine's Fletchers' Mill. 5 Depot St. www.freeportknife.com. © **800/646-8430.**

Cuddledown ★   Cuddledown started producing down comforters in 1973, and now makes a whole line of products much appreciated in northern climes and beyond. Some of the down pillows are made right in the outlet shop, which also carries a variety of European goose-down comforters in all

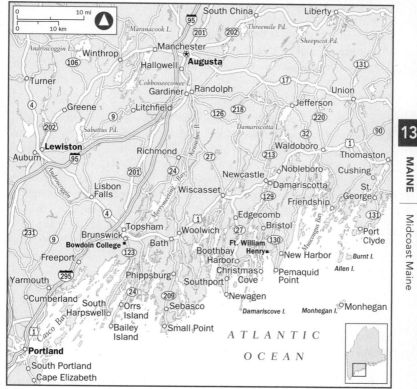

sizes and weights. Look for linens, blankets, moccasins, and home furnishings, too. 554 Route 1. www.cuddledown.com. ✆ **207/865-1713.**

L.L.Bean ★★★ Monster outdoor retailer L.L.Bean traces its roots from the day Leon Leonwood Bean decided that what the world really needed was a good weatherproof hunting shoe. He joined a watertight gum shoe to a laced leather upper; hunters liked it; the store grew; an empire was born. Today, L.L.Bean sells millions of dollars' worth of clothing and outdoor goods nationwide through its well-respected catalogs, and it continues to draw hundreds of thousands of customers through its doors to a headquarters building and several offshoots around town. The modern, multilevel main store is about the size of a regional mall, but it's very tastefully done with its own indoor trout pond, a fish tank that gobsmacks kiddos, a (famous) huge Bean boot outside, and taxidermy displays around every corner. Selections include Bean's own trademark clothing, books, shoes, and plenty of outdoor gear for camping, fishing, and hunting (and separate stores across the plaza house home goods and bike and ski gear). The staff at each store is incredibly knowledgeable—probably because Bean's policy is to encourage staff to take the gear home and try it out themselves so they can better advise their customers. 95 Main St. (at Bow St.). www.llbean.com. © **877/755-2326.**

The Mangy Moose ★   A souvenir shop with a twist: Virtually everything in this place is moose-related. Really. There are moose wineglasses, moose trivets, moose cookie cutters, and (of course) moose T-shirts. And yet somehow, hokey as this notion sounds, this merchandise is a notch above what you'll find in most other souvenir shops around the state. 112 Main St. www. themangymoose.com. © **207/865-6414.**

Thos. Moser Cabinetmakers ★★   Classic furniture reinterpreted in lustrous wood and leather is the focus at this shop, which—thanks to a steady parade of ads in the *New Yorker* and a Madison Avenue branch—has become nearly as representative of Maine as L.L.Bean has. Shaker, Mission, and modern styles are wonderfully reinvented by Tom Moser and his designers and woodworkers, who produce heirloom-quality signed pieces. Nationwide delivery is easy to arrange. There's a good selection of knotted rugs made by an independent artisan, and a worthy gallery of rotating Maine-made art on site. Finally, don't miss the outlet annex and its samples, prototypes, and refurbished pieces; you can save big bucks here. 149 Main St. www.thosmoser. com. © **800/862-1973** or 207/865-4519.

Exploring the Pemaquid Peninsula ★★★

An irregular, rocky wedge driven deep into the Gulf of Maine, the Pemaquid Peninsula is far less commercial than Boothbay Peninsula across the Damariscotta River; it's much more suited to relaxed exploration and nature appreciation than its cousin. Rugged and rocky Pemaquid Point, at the extreme southern tip of the peninsula, is one of the most dramatic destinations in Maine when the ocean surf pounds the shore.

At the head of the harbor, **Damariscotta** and **Newcastle** are twin towns with a couple of good pubs, an artisan butcher, a food co-op, and a great bookstore in **Sherman's Maine Coast Book Shop** (158 Main St.; www.shermans.com; © **207/563-3207**). There's even a fine organic distillery in **Split Rock Distilling** (16 Osprey Point Rd.; www.splitrockdistilling.com; © **207/563-2669**), and one of the coolest places you'll ever drink beer in the middle of the woods: **Oxbow Brewing Company** (274 Jones Woods Rd.; www.oxbowbeer. com; © **207/315-5962**).

The Damariscotta River that runs through the middle of town is one of the country's richest oystering grounds; paddlers can rent a boat from **Midcoast Kayak** at 47 Maine St. (www.midcoastkayak.com; © **207/563-5732**) to explore the estuary. Two-hour to full-day rentals $28 to $50.

Head south on Route 129 (Bristol Road) and you'll first hit sleepy **Walpole,** where the road splits. Keep following Route 129 (the right-hand road) and you'll pass the austerely handsome Walpole Meeting House, dating from 1772. Though it's usually not open to the public, services are held here during the summer and the public is welcome. Keep going another 10 miles; at the end of the road you'll find picturesque **Christmas Cove,** so named because Captain John Smith (of Pocahontas fame) anchored here on Christmas Day in 1614.

If instead you take the left-hand road at the Walpole split—Route 130—in 10 miles or so you'll reach the village of **New Harbor.** Look for signs west to **Colonial Pemaquid State Historic Site** (☏ **207/677-2423**). Open daily from Memorial Day to Labor Day, this state historic site has exhibits on the original 1625 settlement here; archaeological digs take place in the summertime. The $4 admission charge ($1 for kids 5–11) includes a visit to stout **Fort William Henry,** a 1907 replica of a supposedly impregnable fortress. Nearby **Pemaquid Beach** ($4 admission for ages 12 and older) is good for a (chilly) ocean dip or a picnic with the family.

On Route 32 at the eastern end of New Harbor, look for signs pointing to the **Rachel Carson Salt Pond Preserve** ★, a Nature Conservancy property, where noted naturalist Rachel Carson studied tide pools extensively while researching her 1956 bestseller *The Edge of the Sea.* Another couple miles up Route 32, you'll also find the **La Verna Preserve** ★, with 3 miles of trail and some great rocky beaches. Both preserves are wonderful spots for budding naturalists and experts alike. At low tide, you can see horseshoe crabs, periwinkles, barnacles, and maybe the occasional starfish in the tidal pools and among the rocks.

But **Pemaquid Point** ★★, owned by the town of Bristol (www.bristol maine.org; ☏ **207/563-1800**), should be your final destination; it's the place to while away an afternoon. The lighthouse is one of Maine's most photographed, the cluttered museum in the keeper's is a trip, and the gnarly rock ledges stretching out in front of the lighthouse are good for an hour of climbing. Bring a picnic and a book, and find a spot on the dark, fractured rocks to settle in. The ocean views are superb, and the only distractions are the tenacious seagulls that might take a profound interest in your lunch. Admission to the park is $3 for ages 12 and older.

Where to Stay in Midcoast Maine
FREEPORT

Reservations are strongly recommended in Freeport during peak summer season. Several new midrange chain hotels and motels south of town on Route 1 have helped accommodate the summer crush. In a pinch you might try the **Quality Suites,** 500 Route 1 (www.choicehotels.com; ☏ **207/556-5568**), or the adjacent **Super 8** (www.wyndhamhotels.com; ☏ **207/865-1408**). Both are simple, clean, and good enough for a night's rest.

Harraseeket Inn ★★   A short walk north of L.L.Bean on Freeport's main street, the Harraseeket is a large modern hotel, but despite its size, a traveler could drive right past and not even notice it—which a good thing. A 19th-century home is the soul of the hotel, though most rooms are in annexes added in 1989 and 1997. Guests can relax in the dining room, read the paper in a common room while the baby-grand player piano plays, or sip a cocktail in the homey **Broad Arrow Tavern** (with its wood-fired oven and grill, it serves lunch and dinner). Guest rooms are large and tastefully furnished, with quarter-canopy beds and a mix of contemporary and antique furnishings; some have gas or wood-burning fireplaces, more than half now have whirlpools, and some are even done up with wet bars and refrigerators. The big second-floor Thomas Moser Suite is a nod to the local furniture craftsman, with a pencil-post bed, writing desk, dresser, and flatscreen TV in the bedroom, plus a sitting room with a modern sofa, lounge chair, coffee table, Bose stereo, and stone fireplace. And a soaking tub. This inn is especially pet-friendly, with doggy beds and treats for four-footed guests.

162 Main St. www.harraseeketinn.com. © **800/342-6423** or 207/865-9377. 93 units. $150–$320 doubles; $265–$370 suites. Rates include full breakfast and afternoon tea. MAP rates available. Pets welcome ($25/night per pet). **Amenities:** 2 restaurants; bar; concierge; indoor pool; room service; free Wi-Fi.

Maine Idyll Motor Court ★

Talk about a throwback: This 1930s "motor court" is a Maine classic, a cluster of 20 cottages scattered around a grove of oak and beech trees. It could have faded into oblivion, yet it hasn't: The place is still good enough for a simple night's sleep. Most cottages come with a tiny porch, wood-burning fireplace (birch logs are provided), television, modest kitchen facilities (no ovens), and dated furniture. The cabins aren't especially large, but they're comfortable enough and kept clean; some have showers, while others have bathtubs, and a good number of the cottages have two bedrooms (one even has three bedrooms). Ask for a cottage with air-conditioning if that's important—a few units have it. Kids like the play area, while dog-walkers head for nature trails accessible from the property and picnickers fire up grill sets. The only downers are the spotty Wi-Fi service (it's best at the Maine office) and the sometimes drone of traffic: I-295 is just through the trees on one side, Route 1 is on the other side. Get past that traffic sandwich, though, and this place is a decent lowbrow value.

1411 Rte. 1. www.maineidyll.com. © **207/865-4201.** 20 units. May–Oct $71–$112 double. Rates include continental breakfast. Closed Nov–Apr. Pets on leashes allowed ($4/night per pet). **Amenities:** Playground; free Wi-Fi.

PEMAQUID PENINSULA

Seasonal homes and cottage rentals are the dominant summer lodging around the peninsula—try **Newcastle Vacation Rentals** (www.mainecoastcottages.com; © **207/563-6500**) or the usual online rental platforms (Airbnb, HomeAway, etc.). For shorter stays, you're looking at B&Bs and small, often time-worn inns.

Bradley Inn ★

The Bradley Inn is within easy hiking or biking distance to the point, but there are plenty of reasons to lag behind at the inn, too. Wander the nicely landscaped grounds or settle in for a game of cards at the pub. The rooms are tastefully appointed with four-poster cherry beds (though no televisions). The third-floor rooms are the best despite the hike up to them, thanks to distant glimpses of John's Bay, and a high-ceilinged second-floor suite occupying the entire floor is equipped with a full kitchen and dining room. The inn is popular for summer weekend weddings, so ask in advance if you're seeking solitude and quiet. A seaside spa offers a menu of wellness services, and new owners in 2017 have put a farm-to-table spin on the dining room offerings.

3063 Bristol Rd. (Route 130), New Harbor. www.bradleyinn.com. © **800/942-5560** or 207/677-2105. 16 units. $190–$275 double; $300–$475 suite and cottage. Rates include full breakfast and afternoon tea. Closed Jan–Mar. **Amenities:** Dining room; pub; free bikes; room service; spa; free Wi-Fi.

Hotel Pemaquid ★ This 1889 coastal classic isn't directly on the water—it's about a 2-minute walk from Pemaquid Point—but the main inn has the flavor of an old-time boardinghouse. Outbuildings are a bit more modern. Though most rooms now have private bathrooms and flatscreen TVs, the inn is still old-fashioned at its core, with a no-credit-cards policy, narrow hallways, and antiques, including a great collection of old radios and phonographs. It could be better, but it is what it is, and some guests love that. The two- and three-bedroom suites—one with a sun porch and one with a kitchen—are good for families, and there are cottages and a carriage house rented by the week.

3098 Bristol Rd. (Rte. 130), Pemaquid Point. www.hotelpemaquid.com. © **207/677-2312.** 33 units (4 w/shared bath). $115–$142 double w/private bath; $99 double w/shared bath; $174–$255 suite; $985–$1775 cottage weekly. 2-night minimum stay weekends. No credit cards. Closed Nov–Apr. **Amenities:** Free Wi-Fi in main lobby.

Where to Eat in Midcoast Maine

FREEPORT

Gritty McDuff's ★ BREWPUB Spacious, informal, and air-conditioned in summer, Gritty's is an offshoot of Portland's original brewpub. A short drive south of Freeport's village center, it's known for a varied selection of house-brewed beers, like the unfiltered Black Fly Stout. The pub offers a wide-ranging bar menu of reliable salads, burgers, steaks, stone-oven pizzas, cheesesteak sandwiches, quesadillas, and pub classics such as shepherd's pie and fish and chips. There's a kids' menu as well.

187 Rte. 1 (Lower Main St.). www.grittys.com. © **207/865-4321.** Reservations not accepted. Main courses $10–$17. Daily 11:30am–11pm.

Harraseeket Lunch & Lobster ★ LOBSTER Next to a boatyard on the Harraseeket River, about a 10-minute drive from Freeport's busy shopping district, this lobster pound's picnic tables get crowded on sunny days—although, with its little heated dining room, it's a worthy destination anytime. Point and pick out a lobster, then take in river views from the dock as you wait for your number to be called. Advice? Come in late afternoon to avoid the lunch and dinner hordes—and don't wear your nicest clothes. This is roll-up-your-sleeves eating. You can also order fried fish, burgers, chowder, or ice cream from the window. From Freeport, take Bow Street to South Street; continue on South Street to the South Freeport four-way intersection. Turn left at the stop sign and continue downhill to the water.

36 Main St., South Freeport. www.harraseeketlunchandlobster.com. © **207/865-4888.** Lobsters market price (typically $10–$20). No credit cards. May to mid-Oct daily 11am–8:30pm. Closed Columbus Day–Apr.

Jameson Tavern ★ AMERICAN   In a farmhouse right in the shadow of L.L.Bean (on the north side), Jameson Tavern touts itself as the birthplace of Maine. And it really is: In 1820, papers were signed here legally separating Maine from Massachusetts. Mainers still appreciate that pen stroke today. The historic Tap Room is to the left, a compact spot of beer and pub grub. The rest of the house contains the main dining room, decorated in a more formal, country-Colonial style. Meals here are either pubby or clubby: sandwiches, burgers, and fried seafood on the lighter side, prime rib and stuffed lobster on the heavier. What's new in this old place? A nice porch, open about half of the year (not in winter, obviously) for dining semi alfresco.

115 Main St. www.jamesontavern.com. ⓒ **207/865-4196.** Reservations recommended. Main courses $10–$25. Tap room daily 11am–11pm; dining room daily 11am–9pm.

PEMAQUID PENINSULA

Coveside Bar and Restaurant ★★ PUB   It's not much more than a small marina with a pennant-bedecked lounge and basic knotty-pine-paneled dining room, but this is a locals' favorite hangout in Christmas Cove. The food's pubby, the beer list is solid, and the views are outstanding. You might even catch a glimpse of the celebrity yachtsmen who tend to stop off here. Reservations are a good idea on summer weekends.

105 Coveside Rd., Christmas Cove (South Bristol). ⓒ **207/644-8282.** Main courses $11–$26. Daily 11am–9pm. Closed Nov–Apr.

Shaw's Fish and Lobster Wharf ★ LOBSTER   Shaw's attracts hordes of tourists, but it's no trick to figure out why: It's one of the best-situated lobster pounds, with postcard-perfect views of the working harbor. You can stake out a seat on either the open deck or the indoor dining room (go for the deck), or order some appetizers from the raw bar. This is one of the few lobster joints in Maine with a full liquor license, and the lobster rolls are considered by experts (okay, eaters like me) to be some of Maine's best.

129 Rte. 32, New Harbor. ⓒ **207/677-2200.** Lobster priced to market (typically $10/lb.). Main courses $12–$25. Mid-May to mid-Oct daily 11am–8pm. Closed mid-Oct to mid-May.

PENOBSCOT BAY

Camden: 230 miles NE of Boston; 8 miles N of Rockland; 18 miles S of Belfast

Somewhere around Rockland, you'll notice the northeasterly Maine coast takes a turn toward Canada, heading almost due north for a few dozen miles. The culprit behind this geographic quirk is Penobscot Bay, a sizable bite out of the coast that forces drivers to take a lengthy northerly detour in order to cross the head of the bay, where the Penobscot River flows into it at Bucksport.

You'll find some of Maine's most distinctive coastal scenery in this little region, which is dotted with offshore islands and hills rising above the shore. Although the mouth of Penobscot Bay is occupied by two large islands, its waters still churn when the winds and tides are right.

Thanks to both its natural beauty and architectural cuteness, the bay's western shore sees a steady stream of tourist traffic in summer, especially along the stretch of Route 1 passing through artsy **Rockland** and affluent **Camden.** You'll need a small miracle to find a weekend bed without a reservation in summer or early fall. Nevertheless, this is a great area if you want to get a taste of the real Maine coast. Other picturesque harbor towns to mosey through are **Rockport** (wedged between Rockland and Camden—yes, it can get confusing), **Port Clyde** (at the tip of the peninsula south of Rockland, from which the ferry leaves for remote **Monhegan,** see p. 639), or **Stonington** (on the Blue Hill peninsula, p. 662).

Essentials
ARRIVING

BY CAR Route 1 passes directly through the center of Rockland. It's about a 3½-hour drive here from Boston via I-95 and Route 1, nearly a 7-hour drive from New York City. Coming from the south, it's easier to get to Camden by turning left onto Route 90 about 6 miles north of **Waldoboro,** thus bypassing the busy downtown streets of Rockland.

BY BUS **Concord Coach** (www.concordcoachlines.com; ℂ **800/639-3317**) runs one or two daily buses to Rockland from Portland (2 hr. and 15 min., $23 one-way) and Boston's South Station (4 hr. and 15 min., $35 one-way). They also stop another 15 minutes up the road at the Maritime Farms grocery store on Route 1 in Rockport, a little more than a mile's walk from either downtown Camden or Rockport harbor.

BY AIR Surprisingly, Rockland's tiny local airport (**Knox County Regional Airport**) is served by daily direct flights from Boston on **Cape Air** (www.capeair.com; ℂ **866/227-3247** or 508/771-6944) that are often remarkably affordable. There's a local taxi on call, and rental car kiosks at the terminal. The airport itself is actually in Owls Head, off Route 73.

VISITOR INFORMATION

The **Penobscot Bay Regional Chamber of Commerce** (www.camdenrockland.com; ℂ **800/562-2529** or 207/596-0376), staffs an information desk in **Rockland** on Park Drive by Harbor Park, open daily from Memorial Day through Labor Day, on weekdays the rest of the year. The chamber also dispenses helpful information daily year-round from its center at the Public Landing (waterfront) in **Camden** (ℂ **207/236-4404**), where there's also free parking—though spaces are pretty scarce in summer.

Exploring Rockland ★ & Environs

Located on the southwestern edge of Penobscot Bay, Rockland has long been proud of its blue-collar waterfront roots. Built around the fishing industry, the city historically dabbled in tourism but never really waded. With the recent decline of local fisheries and the rise of Maine's tourist economy, though, that balance has shifted. Rockland is swiftly being colonized by restaurateurs, innkeepers, artisans, and other folks who are transforming the place from fish-processing center to arts-and-crafts mecca.

The waterfront has a small park from which windjammers come and go (see box p. 650), but even more appealing is Rockland's downtown—basically, one long street lined with historic brick architecture. Rockland is best as a sensible local base for exploring a beautiful coastal region, especially if you like your towns to be a bit rough and salty around the edges.

Lobsters in the Limelight

The **Maine Lobster Festival** (www.mainelobsterfestival.com; ℂ **800/562-2529**) takes place at Rockland's Harbor Park the first weekend in August (plus the preceding Thurs–Fri). Entertainers and vendors of all sorts of Maine products—especially, of course, the famous Maine crustaceans—fill the waterfront parking lot for thousands of festivalgoers who enjoy the pleasantly buttery atmosphere. The event includes the Maine Sea Goddess Coronation Pageant. Admission is $5 to $10 per day for adults, $2 for kids; food, of course, costs extra. Four-day passes are also available.

Center for Maine Contemporary Art ★★★ MUSEUM   The sleek new headquarters of the CMCA opened in 2016 to much fanfare, and the architecturally striking building on the old waterfront (its spiky roofline is meant to recall the waves) has been drawing crowds ever since to its three galleries filled with cutting-edge (often sculptural or multimedia) contemporary art. In the courtyard outside, a piece from Maine artist Jonathan Barofsky's 24-foot *Human Structures* series (he has similar sculptures permanently installed in San Francisco and Beijing) gives you a pretty good idea what you're in for: work that's modern, a little abstract, and a little whimsical.

21 Winter St. www.cmcanow.org. *C* **207/701-5005.** $6 adults, kids 12 and under free. June–Oct Mon–Sat 10am–5pm, Sun noon–5pm; Nov–May Wed–Sat 10am–5pm, Sun 1–5pm; 1st Fri of month 5–8pm with free admission.

Farnsworth Museum ★★ MUSEUM   Rockland, for all its rough edges, has long and historic ties to the arts. Noted sculptor Louise Nevelson grew up in Rockland, and in 1935 philanthropist Lucy Farnsworth bequeathed a fortune to establish the Farnsworth Museum, which has since become one of the most respected little art museums in New England. Located right downtown, the Farnsworth has a superb collection of paintings and sculptures by renowned American artists with connections to Maine—not only Nevelson, but also three generations of Wyeths (N. C., Andrew, and Jamie), plus Rockwell Kent, Childe Hassam, and Maurice Prendergast. The exhibit halls are modern, spacious, and well designed, and shows are professionally prepared. Equally interesting is the museum-owned **Olson House** ★, a 25-minute drive southwest from Rockland, in the village of Cushing; it's perhaps Maine's most well-known home, immortalized in Andrew Wyeth's famous painting *Christina's World.*

356 Main St. www.farnsworthmuseum.org. *C* **207/596-6457.** Museum $15 adults, $13 seniors, $10 students 17 and older, free for kids under 17; add $5 for admission to Olson House. June–Oct daily 10am–5pm; Nov–Dec Tues–Sun 10am–5pm; Jan–Mar Wed–Sun 10am–4pm; Apr–May Tues–Sun 10am–5pm.

Owls Head Transportation Museum ★ MUSEUM   You don't need to be a car or plane buff to enjoy this museum, located 3 miles south of Rockland on Route 73. Founded in 1974, the museum has an extraordinary collection of cars, motorcycles, bicycles, and planes, nicely displayed in a tidy, hangar-like building at the edge of the Knox County Airport. Look for an early Harley Davidson motorcycle and a sleek Rolls-Royce Phantom dating from the roaring '20s.

117 Museum St., Owls Head. www.ohtm.org. *C* **207/594-4418.** $14 adults, $10 seniors, under 18 free. Daily 10am–5pm.

Exploring Camden ★★ & Rockport

A quintessential coastal Maine town at the foot of the wooded Camden Hills, the affluent village of Camden sits on a picturesque harbor that no Hollywood movie set could improve on. It has been attracting the gentry of the eastern seaboard for more than a century. The mansions of the moneyed set still

During the transition from sail to steam, captains of fancy new steamships belittled old-fashioned sailing ships as "windjammers." The term stuck; through a curious metamorphosis, the name evolved into one of adventure and romance.

Maine is the windjammer cruising capital of the U.S., and the two most active Maine harbors are **Rockland** and **Camden.** Cruises last from 3 days to a week, during which these handsome, creaky vessels poke around tidal inlets and small coves that ring beautiful Penobscot Bay. It's a superb way to explore the coast the way it's historically always been explored—from out on the water, looking in. Rates run between about $110 and $180 per day per person (which is $300–$1,200 per person for an entire trip); the best rates are offered early and late in the season. Ships range in size from 50 to 130 feet, and accommodations range from cramped and rustic to reasonably spacious and well appointed. Most are berthed in the region between Boothbay Harbor and Belfast—they cruise the Penobscot Bay region during summer, and some migrate south to the Caribbean for the winter.

Cruise schedules and amenities vary widely from ship to ship, even from week to week, depending on the captains' inclinations and the vagaries of Maine weather. An array of excursions is available, from simple overnights to week-long expeditions gunkholing among Maine's thousands of scenic islands and coves. A "standard" cruise often features a stop at one or more of the myriad spruce-studded Maine islands (perhaps with a lobster bake on shore). Ideally, look at a couple of ships to find one that suits you before signing up.

Several **windjammer festivals** and **races** are held along the Maine coast throughout the summer; these are perfect events to shop for a ship on which to spend a few days. Among the more notable events are **Windjammer Days** in Boothbay Harbor (late June) and the **Camden Windjammer Weekend** in early September. If you can't do that, contact the **Maine Windjammer Association** (www.sailmainecoast.com; © **800/807-9463**) for a packet of brochures or simply check its good website of member ships and comparison-shop. If you're trying to book a *last-minute* windjammer cruise on a whim, stop by the chamber of commerce office on the Rockland waterfront (see p. 648) and inquire about open berths.

dominate the town's shady side streets (many have been converted into bed-and-breakfasts), giving Camden a grace and sophistication that eludes many other coastal towns.

The best way to enjoy this town is to park your car—and that might require driving a block or two off of busy Route 1, which runs right through the center of town. Camden is of a perfect scale to explore on foot, with plenty of boutiques and galleries. Don't miss the scenic, bowl-shaped **town park ★★** on the hill behind the town library: It was designed by the firm of Frederick Law Olmsted, the famed landscape architect who designed New York City's Central Park.

Some longtime visitors say that all this attention (and Camden's growing appeal to bus tours) is having a deleterious impact on the atmosphere; yes, there are T-shirt shops here. And there are occasional cries raised about the

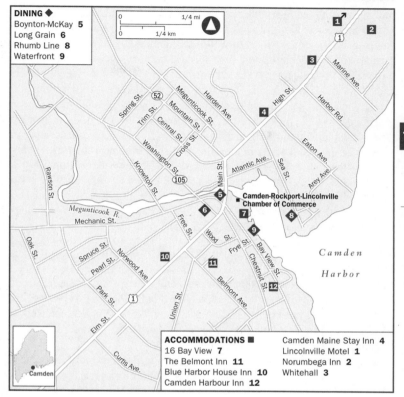

DINING ◆
Boynton-McKay **5**
Long Grain **6**
Rhumb Line **8**
Waterfront **9**

0   1/4 mi
0   1/4 km

13

MAINE | Penobscot Bay

Camden Harbor

ACCOMMODATIONS ■
16 Bay View **7**
The Belmont Inn **11**
Blue Harbor House Inn **10**
Camden Harbour Inn **12**

Camden Maine Stay Inn **4**
Lincolnville Motel **1**
Norumbega Inn **2**
Whitehall **3**

increasing snootiness of the place. As long as you don't expect a pristine, undiscovered fishing village, you'll be in good shape to enjoy it.

The Camden area is great to explore by bike. One nice loop several miles long takes you from Camden into the cute little village of **Rockport ★**, which has an equally scenic harbor and fewer tourists than Camden. There's a boat landing, a park with a small beach and usually a food truck, and a few art galleries and restaurants. Bike rentals ($26–$50 per day), repairs, maps, and local riding advice are available at **Maine Sport** (www.mainesport.com; ✆ **207/236-7120**), located at 115 Commercial St. in Rockport. High end mountain bikes and road bikes are available, along with cheaper hybrids, motor-assist e-bikes, and kiddie trailers.

The Camden-Rockport Historical Society has prepared a 9-mile bike or car tour with brief descriptions of some of the historic properties around the two adjacent towns. The brochure describing the tour is free; check for it at the Penobscot Bay Chamber visitor center (see p. 648). The brochure also includes a 2-mile walking tour of downtown Camden.

The 6,500-acre **Camden Hills State Park** ★★ (© **207/236-3109**), about a mile north of the village center on Route 1, ranges from a seaside lower section to an upper section with fine bay views. There's an oceanside picnic area, camping at 107 sites, a variety of well-marked hiking trails, and a winding toll road up 800-foot Mount Battie with spectacular views from the summit. The day-use fee is $6 for non-Maine resident adults, $2 for nonresident seniors, and $1 for kids ages 5 to 11. (The fee's only charged mid-May to mid-Oct.) If hikes and mild heights don't bother you, I definitely recommend an ascent to the ledges of the park's **Mount Megunticook** ★★. The best time for this 30-to-45-minute hike is early in the morning, before the crowds have amassed (and while mists still linger in the valleys). Leave from near the park's campground—the trail head is clearly marked—and follow the well-maintained path to open ledges. Spectacular views of the harbor await, plus glimpses of smaller hills and valleys. Depending on your stamina level, you can keep walking on the park's trail network to Mount Battie, or into lesser-traveled woodlands on the east side of the Camden Hills.

Where to Stay Around Penobscot Bay

CAMDEN

Camden vies with Kennebunkport, Maine, and Manchester, Vermont, for the title of "bed-and-breakfast capital of New England." They're everywhere. The stretch of Route 1 just north of the village center—called High Street here—is a virtual bed-and-breakfast alley, with many handsome homes converted to lodgings. Others are tucked away on side streets.

Despite the preponderance of B&Bs, though, the total number of guest rooms in town is still too small to accommodate the crush of peak-season visitors, and during summer or fall, the lodging is tight. It's best to reserve well in advance. You might also try **Camden Accommodations and Reservations** (www.camdenac.com; © **800/344-4830** or 207/236-6090) for help in finding anything from overnight rooms to seasonal rentals. In the name of keeping these folks in business, Camden has recently cracked down a bit on townsfolk offering private rentals through Airbnb and VRBO, prohibiting standalone properties (as compared to spare rooms) from renting for any duration shorter than a week. Further permitting and inspection regulations may be forthcoming, but for now, there are still tons of properties available in summer via these online rental platforms.

There's good camping at **Camden Hills State Park** (see above), which is open from mid-May until mid-October. Sites cost $35 to $45 per night for non-Maine residents in summer ($10 discount for residents), depending on whether you snag one of the new water-and-electrical hookup sites or not. There's a discount from mid-September until the park closes in mid-October.

16 Bay View ★★   Until this boutique hotel opened in late 2015, Camden strangely lacked any true waterfront hotel lodging. A former movie-house and restaurant, 16 Bay View is just steps from the harbor, with views of the waves and the tall-masted ships from the top-floor accommodations and the rooftop terrace. You'll pay for it, of course—the hotel pitches to a luxury crowd, and the fireplaces, free-standing pedestal tubs, and Cuddledown bedding give the rooms a pretty genteel feel. Continental breakfast (good pastries and quiches) is delivered in-room each morning. The clubby bistro/bar/lounge feels like a world away from the busy Camden street scene in midsummer (and the tapas plates are pretty yum).

16 Bay View St. www.16bayview.com. © **844/213-7990.** 21 units. July–Oct $269–$379 double, $415–$649 suite; May–June and Nov–Dec $188–$299 double, $349–$499 suite; Jan–April $149–$239 double, $259–$399 suite. Rates include full breakfast. Some rooms accommodate pets ($35 per night). **Amenities:** Restaurant; lounge; rooftop bar; free Wi-Fi.

The Belmont Inn ★ A handsome, shingle-style 1890s home with a wrap-around porch, the Belmont is set in a quiet residential neighborhood of unpretentious homes away from Route 1. The inn has an understated, Victorian sort of theme throughout, featuring for instance numerous floral prints by Maine artist Jo Spiller (there's also a guest room with great morning light named after Spiller). All units have polished wood floors and are furnished simply with eclectic antiques and country touches such as cast-iron stoves, sleigh beds, writing desks, and wingback chairs. Downstairs, there's an elegant common room with a fireplace alcove and built-in benches. One room, the Allen Room, magically becomes a suite (and costs more) when the owners open a little door connecting it to a sitting room.

6 Belmont Ave. www.thebelmontinn.com. © **207/236-8053.** 6 units. $169–$279 double; $269–$329 suite. Rates include full breakfast. No children 11 and under. **Amenities:** Free Wi-Fi.

Blue Harbor House Inn ★ On busy Route 1 just south of town, this pale-blue 1810 farmhouse has been an inn since 1978. It's decorated throughout with a floral country look. Rooms and suites vary in size; some are smallish, with slanting angles and low ceilings, but you can expect touches such as four-poster beds, clawfoot tubs, wicker furniture, Jacuzzis, triptych mirrors, writing desks, and slipper chairs in various configurations. And the exposed wood floors are absolutely lovely. The best rooms are the carriage-house suites, with their private entrances and extra amenities—two, Captains Quarters and Compass Rose, share a private outdoor patio. The early evening hours feature a nice cocktail service, with cocktails made to order and lovely hors d'oeuvre for a small extra charge. (Fun fact: One of the owners used to work as a cocktail bartender on the real *Love Boat* cruise ship; Gopher, Isaac, and Julie would be proud.)

67 Elm St. www.blueharborhouse.com. © **800/248-3196** or 207/236-3196. 11 units. $125–$189 double; $159–$199 suite. Rates include full breakfast. **Amenities:** Dining room; shared refrigerator; library; free Wi-Fi.

Camden Harbour Inn ★★★ This 1871 mansion sits in a quiet neighborhood on a rise with a view of the sea and mountains beyond, on the way to Rockport—think of it as Camden's "quiet side." This had been just another fusty, Victorian-era hotel until 2007, when it got a complete makeover from the two Dutchmen who bought it. No longer a creaky place of floral wallpaper and simple antiques, it's now one of the region's more renowned luxury inns, a member of the Relais & Châteaux collection, with a spa, gourmet restaurant, even a wine refrigerator in every room. The place is all about modern design. All rooms have private bathrooms and flatscreen TVs, of course, but most also feature water views, fireplaces, and/or terraces. The New Amsterdam Suite is one of the poshest in town, with its king-size featherbed and two private decks; other suites are designed in Taiwanese, Thai, and Mauritian themes. The inn is within walking distance of downtown, and there's an excellent French-influenced, farm-to-table restaurant, **Natalie's ★**, as well.

83 Bayview St. www.camdenharbourinn.com. ✆ **800/236-4266** or 866/626-1504. 20 units. Mid-June to mid-Oct $399–$475 double; $499–$1,490 suite; late Oct–early June $235–$295 double, $325–$699 suite. Rates include full breakfast. 2-night minimum weekends in peak season. **Amenities:** Restaurant; bar; spa; free Wi-Fi.

Camden Maine Stay Inn ★   The Maine Stay is one of Camden's friendliest bed-and-breakfasts. In a home dating from 1802 (later expanded in Greek Revival style in 1840), it's your classic slate-roofed New England manse in a shady yard within walking distance of both downtown and Camden Hills State Park (see p. 652). Guest rooms, spaced out over three floors, have ceiling fans (only a few have televisions). Each is distinctively furnished in antiques; expect lots of frilly and floral things, handsome exposed wooden floors, and wicker furniture. Note that top-floor rooms have foreshortened ceilings with intriguing angles. The downstairs Carriage House Room unit, away from the buzz of Route 1, is popular: Its French doors lead to a private stone patio, while a Vermont Castings stove keeps things toasty inside. Interesting tidbit: The inn's owned by two Italian innkeepers—one from the south of Italy, one from Milan (the north).

22 High St. www.mainestay.com. ✆ **207/236-9636.** 8 units. $140–$320 double and suite. Rates include full breakfast. Children 12 and older welcome. **Amenities:** Restaurant; free Wi-Fi.

Lincolnville Motel ★★★   It's far from the most opulent lodging on the Maine Coast, but it might be the most fun. Built as a motor-court motel in the 1950s, this set of six cabins and a four-room motel got a lighthearted, minimalist refresh when Alice Amory reopened the place in 2015. The outdoor pool is full of goofy inflatable animals; the comfy little housekeeping cabins are appointed with mini-fridges, fresh flowers, and record players. Each has its own little deck, and the common spaces (a big shared yard and library) have a social vibe when the place is filled up. Not the place to stay if you want seclusion; terrific if you'd like to make friends (and enjoy one of the region's best values).

4 Sea View Dr. www.lincolnvillemotel.com. ✆ **207/236-3195.** 10 units. $85–$165 double; $105–$175 two-room cabin. Closed mid-Oct to mid-May. **Amenities:** Outdoor pool; library; free Wi-Fi in common area.

Norumbega Inn ★★ You'll have no problem at all finding the Norumbega: just head north out of town and look for the castle on the right. Well, it's actually a stone mansion (built in 1886 by telegraph system inventor Joseph Stearns), but it *looks* like a castle. Wonderfully eccentric and full of curves, turrets, angles, and rich materials, this hotel's on the National Historic Registry. There's extravagant carved-oak woodwork in the lobby, a stunning oak-and-mahogany inlaid floor, and a roomy solarium. When Sue Walser and Phil Crispo took it over in 2013, the building had sat empty a couple years after some ups-and-downs with previous owners. They replaced a lot of dated furnishings and bedding, made some structural repairs, added heated bathroom floors, and rebuilt the awesome decks out back, which overlook a sprawling lawn and glittery sea. In short, the place is feeling much fresher than its 130 years. The two suites here rank among the finest in northern New England: the bright and airy Library Suite, in the original two-story library (so big it has an *interior* balcony, surrounded by books and a sliding ladder), and the sprawling Penthouse with its superlative bay views, king-size bed, and huge oval tub. Phil's Culinary Institute of America training pays off at breakfast, and multi-course tasting dinners are an option as well.

63 High St. www.norumbegainn.com. ✆ **877/363-4646** or 207/236-4646. 11 units. June–Oct $289–$389 double, $439–$539 suite. Rates include full breakfast. 2-night minimum in summer, Sat–Sun, and holidays. **Amenities:** Lounge; library; free Wi-Fi.

Whitehall ★★ Set at the edge of town on busy Route 1, Whitehall is a venerable Camden institution, thanks partly to its association with local poet Edna St. Vincent Millay, who was "discovered" here by a guest who went on to fund Edna's college education. But with new ownership and a $1.7-million, bottom-to-top renovation in 2015, the place feels a lot less like a musty historic tribute to an obscure poet. You'll still find grand columns, gables, a long roofline, and atmospherically winding staircases, but gone are the antique furnishings and Oriental carpets, which have been replaced by bright patterned upholstery, a whole lot of upcycled barnwood, iPads and Apple TVs in every room, and accents of grasscloth and highly patinaed metal. It's less of a country inn and more of splashy boutique feel now (though a few rooms still share a hallway bathroom). The patio, with its firepit, is a terrific respite on cooler evenings.

52 High St. www.whitehallmaine.com. ✆ **800/789-6565** or 207/236-3391. 40 units, some w/shared bath. July–Oct $279–$389 double; mid-May to June $139–$219 double. Rates include full breakfast. Closed Nov to mid-May. **Amenities:** Restaurant; bar; concierge; free Wi-Fi.

ROCKLAND

Rockland has enjoyed a bit of a hotel boom in recent years, and short-term rentals have proliferated on platforms like Airbnb. Not much for budget chains on this stretch of the Midcoast, but there's a **Hampton Inn** (www.hamptoninn3.hilton.com; ✆ **207/594-6644**) surrounded by big-box stores in adjacent Thomaston.

250 Main Hotel ★   This boutique hotel has a high-design, industrial-chic feel that calls to mind urban condos—which is just what the building was initially intended to be, although it eventually became a hotel for lack of demand. The developer's loss is travelers' gain. Running with Rockland's revived identity as an arts destination, the hotel hasn't found a wall that it couldn't decorate with local art, from crisp landscape photography to watercolors to reimagined 1950s tourism propaganda—there's even artist-designed wallpaper. Rooms are individually designed/decorated, and both they and the common areas are filled with midcentury modern furniture in bright colors and lots of showy reclaimed wood. If none of that is mod enough for you, each room has a complimentary concierge tablet to play around on. On a summer evening, the rooftop deck overlooking the harbor is a pretty unbeatable place to unwind (and they pour wine up there).

250 Maine St. www.250mainhotel.com. © **207/594-5994.** 26 units. Memorial Day–Columbus Day $319–$449 double; rest of year $169–$269 double. **Amenities:** Free Wi-Fi.

LimeRock Inn ★   This turreted, Queen Anne–style inn sits sleepily on a quiet side street just 2 blocks off Rockland's main drag. Attention has been paid to detail throughout, from the kingly choices of country Victorian furniture to the Egyptian cotton bed sheets. All eight guest rooms are welcoming and colorful, bordering on whimsical; among the best are the Island Cottage Room, a bright and airy south-of-France-like chamber wonderfully converted from an old shed (it has a private deck and a Jacuzzi); the Turret Room, with a canopy bed, cherry daybed, and French doors leading into a bathroom with a clawfoot tub and shower; and the elegant Grand Manan Room, with a big four-poster mahogany king bed, fireplace, and double Jacuzzi that puts one in mind of a southern plantation home.

96 Limerock St. www.limerockinn.com. © **800/546-3762.** 8 units. $129–$249 double. Rates include full breakfast. **Amenities:** Free Wi-Fi.

Samoset Resort ★★   Established in 1889 on a scenic hill just outside Rockland (technically it's in Rockport), the Samoset was meant as a grown-up summer camp for the wealthy. Even the cathedral-ceilinged lobby, constructed of massive timbers salvaged from an old grain silo in Portland, is worth photographing. This is not the original building—the original was shuttered, auctioned off, and destroyed by fire decades ago. But the place has bounced back big-time as a noted golf resort and luxury property, thanks to a number of exciting recent upgrades. A few years back, a new heated pool and hot tub were added on the hill's highest point, with sweeping views of the bay, plus a tiki bar serving frozen drinks and light meals. Rooms vary in position and view, but many have balconies or porches with grand Penobscot Bay views; all have rich wood-and-leather headboards, flatscreen TVs, and marble vanities. Bathrooms are extra-big, some with whirlpool tubs. The golf course remains one of the most scenic in New England, while the quiet local roads are perfect for strolling, and there's even a mini-lighthouse adjacent to the property. Check out the good health club, then head to dinner—your options include seasonal

Marcel's, serving excellent resort fare, and the **Breakwater Grill,** serving lighter fare year-round. All in all, a great luxury comeback.

220 Warrenton St., Rockport. www.samosetresort.com. © **800/341-1650** or 207/594-2511. 178 units. Early July–late Aug $309–$369 double, $439–629 suite; late Apr–early July and late Aug–Nov $199–$339 double, $279–$589 suite; Nov to mid-Apr (weekends only) $139 double, $279–$429 suite; $619–$1,849 cottages year-round. MAP rates available. **Amenities:** 3 restaurants; babysitting; children's programs; concierge; fitness center; golf course; golf school; health club; Jacuzzi; indoor pool; outdoor pool; room service; sauna; 4 tennis courts; free Wi-Fi.

Where to Eat Around Penobscot Bay
CAMDEN

In addition to its fine-dining options, many of which are in the lodgings listed above, downtown Camden has a wealth of places to nosh, snack, lunch, and brunch. Some unbeatable breakfast skillets, for instance, are served up at busy **Boynton-McKay,** 30 Main St. (www.boynton-mckay.com; © 207/236-2465), a former pharmacy that's now a locals' favorite breakfast stop (and a great place for picking up picnic supplies, should you be so inclined.) Note that it's closed on Mondays. Just up the street, pick up a bag of gourmet groceries at **French & Brawn** (www.frenchandbrawn.com; © **207/236-3361**) on Main Street at the corner of Elm.

Long Grain ★★★ THAI   If you'd have told me WASPy little Camden had some of the county's best Thai food, I wouldn't have believed you, but here's Long Grain. The glossy food mags have all sung its praises (the restaurant's Chicken Khao Soi soup was even a *Bon Appétit* cover girl in 2013), and even after an expansion to new digs (with an onsite Asian market) in 2018, the impossibility of a walk-in table most summer nights is a pretty good vote of confidence. Chefs Paula Palakawong and Ravin Nakjaroen turn out fragrant and flavorful dishes of ramen, pad seaw, and pad kemao (all with house-made noodles), along with terrific curries, pork dumplings, lemongrass mussels, and more. Call way ahead for takeout.

20 Washington St. www.longgraincamden.com. © **207/236-9001.** Main courses $13–$18. Tues–Sat 11:30am–2:45pm, 4:30–9pm. Reservations highly recommended.

Rhumb Line ★★ SEAFOOD   Way-fresh seafood served at picnic tables, right on the dock, in a building shared with a boatbuilder and overlooking the harbor. No place filled with so many yachties should feel this welcoming and unpretentious, and yet Rhumb Line does. There's some indoor seating too, but it has to be blowing pretty hard outside for that to be more appealing. Go fancy with gorgeously plated oysters or chilled lobster off the raw bar, or else make like the dockworkers and dig into a basket of perfectly fried whole belly clams, a terrific lobster roll, blackened haddock tacos, and other coastal proletarian faves.

59 Sea St. www.rhumblinecamden.com. © **207/230-8495.** Raw bar $12–$19; baskets and main courses $12–$26. Mid-May to mid-Oct Wed–Mon 11:30am–9:30pm. Closed rest of year.

Waterfront ★ ECLECTIC It's not the most glamorous place to dine in greater Camden, but that might be why locals like to lunch here so much. That and the view. The wide deck out back is maybe the best alfresco dining on the Midcoast, with the waves lapping at pilings right beneath you and the green hump of Mount Battie looming behind. Find a little bit of everything on the menu, from steaks to a chicken enchilada to really nicely executed Maine seafood classics. I highly recommend the mussels in white wine appetizer, and all the salads are substantial enough to be meals. Service is unfussy, and there's certainly no dress code.

48 Bayview St. www.waterfrontcamden.com. ℰ **207/236-3747.** Lunch main courses $11–$20; dinner main courses $16–$30. Daily 11:30am–9pm.

ROCKLAND

Cafe Miranda ★★ ECLECTIC A Midcoast institution, Cafe Miranda has one of the longest, craziest menus in New England. Hidden on a side street, it's a tiny, contemporary restaurant with a huge ever-morphing menu of big flavors and hip attitude. "We do not serve the food of cowards," owner-chef Kerry Altiero is quoted right on top of the menu, and he's right. I could write a whole book on the regularly changing menu here, but Altiero already did in 2014—*Adventures in Comfort Food,* which pretty well sums it up. Small plates and entrees could include things like grilled lamb patties with parsley and garlic; "50 MPH tomatoes" deep-fried and served with spicy ranch dressing; a "squash-o'-rama" (roasted squash with cheese); fire-roasted feta with sweet peppers, tomatoes, "really good" olives, and herbs; a Portuguese seafood combo of mussels, shrimp, clams, fish, and sausage steamed in wine and pummeled with parsley; "Aunt Fluffy's Pasta" (penne with veggies, caramelized onions, and Romano); the "Polish hippie" (grilled sausage with horseradish, arugula, and beets!); "Old Bleu" (handmade pasta tossed in blue cheese and basil cream); chicken paprikash; steaks; or, of course, the immortal "Pitch a Tent": sausage, gravy, onions, garlic, and mushrooms beneath a "tent" of pasta. Share everything with your fellow diners, because you'll never eat at a place this original again. Altiero again: "It's comfort food for whatever planet you're from." Amen.

15 Oak St. www.cafemiranda.com. ℰ **207/594-2034.** Lunch $11–$20, small plates $12–$19, main courses $15–$27. Mon–Thurs 11:30am–2pm and 5–8:30pm, Fri–Sat 11:30am–2pm and 5–9pm, Sun 10:30am–2pm and 5–8:30pm. Reservations strongly recommended.

Drift Inn Canteen ★ SEAFOOD Discovering a great meal at an unassuming seafood shack on a quiet coastal road is why you came to Maine, right? Drift Inn's "dining room" is a set of picnic tables under an awning in what is actually someone's backyard (with little buckets full of citronella and bug spray because, duh, Maine summer). It has a limited barbecue menu, but what it really excels at is fried fish. Magic batter and a perfect fry makes for light and golden fish and chips, fried clams, and more, served in a basket lined with faux newspaper. There's a big yard for the kiddos to play in. To get here, head west out of Rockland on Route 1 to Thomaston (3 miles), then go south on Route 131 another 14 miles.

686 Port Clyde Rd., Tenants Harbor. www.facebook.com/driftinncanteen. © **207/372-1068.** Sandwiches $6–$14, seafood baskets $10–$23. Memorial Day–Labor Day Tues–Sat 11:30am–7pm, Sun 12–5pm.

Home Kitchen Café ★ DINER Sizeable portions of classic breakfasts (omelets, benedicts, French toast) and a handful of standout Latin-influenced dishes (terrific migas, huevos rancheros, and chorizo frittatas). Expect short lines on the weekend, but throwback diner Home Kitchen has a lot of seats, including an old-school breakfast counter and a nice upstairs patio. Don't leave without grabbing one of the locally legendary (and huge) cinnamon rolls ("sinnies") or sticky buns ("stickies"). Lunch is burgers, sandwiches, and big sandwiches on homemade bread with house-smoked meats. Home Kitchen also has a trio of quick-service takeout options on the next block: **Close to Home** (subs and burritos), **home sweet home** (a bakery), and **Cone Home** (ice cream).

650 Main St. www.homekitchencafe.com. © **207/596-2449.** Breakfast and lunch items $8–$12. Mon–Sat 7am–3pm, Sun 8am–3pm.

Primo ★★★ MEDITERRANEAN/NEW AMERICAN Primo opened in 2000 and quickly developed a buzz as one of northern New England's top eats; it still is. The restaurant occupies two nicely decorated floors of a century-old home, a short drive south of Rockland's downtown. Owner/chef Melissa Kelly graduated first in her class at the Culinary Institute of America and won a James Beard Foundation award for "best chef in the Northeast" in the 1990s and again in 2013. Her Italian-inflected menu reflects the seasons and draws from local products wherever available (much of the meat and produce the kitchen's working with comes off the restaurant's expansive farm). Start with an appetizer such as wood-fired pizza with artisanal mushrooms, planked octopus with chickpea salad, seared foie gras over poached strawberries, antipasti, or fried and roasted local oysters paired with rémoulade sauce and house-cured Tasso ham. Entrees might run to seared diver scallops with fettuccine, local halibut over a white bean puree, monkfish medallions with peekytoe crab–risotto cakes, grilled steak or duck, tuna au poivre, or chicken with lavender-and-honey roasted figs and a sweet ricotta gnocchi. Finish with one of co-owner/pastry chef Price Kushner's inventive desserts: warm Belgian chocolate cake, an espresso float, a rhubarb-strawberry tartlet with vanilla gelato and strawberry sauce, homemade cannoli, a bowl of hot *zeppole* (small Italian doughnuts) tossed in cinnamon and sugar, or an apple *crostata* sided with pine-nut-and-caramel ice cream. The wine list is outstanding. It's hard to get a last-minute table here during summer; failing that, order off the menu from the cozy upstairs bar.

2 S. Main St. (Rte. 173). www.primorestaurant.com. © **207/596-0770.** Main courses $33–$48. Summer daily 5–10pm; call for dates and hours in off season; closed Jan–early May. Reservations highly recommended.

13

MAINE

Penobscot Bay

Suzuki's ★★★ JAPANESE Keiko Suzuki Steinberger started surprising diners in Rockland with her distinctive brand of sushi back in 2006. The mostly self-taught sushi chef (she did a brief stint at Tokyo's Sushi Academy) relies heavily on the local catch, so expect to find exquisitely plated and unconventional sashimi, maki, and nigiri made with halibut, herring, mackerel, tuna, whelks, or clams. Chef Keiko was a 2016 James Beard Foundation semifinalist; more than a decade in, her kitchen staff (all women) are at the top of their game.

419 Main St. www.suzukisushi.com. ✆ **207/596-7447.** Sushi $3–$11, noodle dishes $14–$25. Tues–Sat 5–9pm.

THE BLUE HILL PENINSULA ★★

Blue Hill: 136 miles NE of Portland, 248 miles NE of Boston.

Forming the eastern boundary of Penobscot Bay—though you must drive north and then *south* to get there, diverging from Route 1 by a good 15 miles or more—the **Blue Hill Peninsula** is a little piece of back-roads paradise. The roads are hilly, winding, and narrow, passing through sprucey forests, past old saltwater farms, and over bridges, touching down at the edges of inlets and boatyards from time to time. And the light is nearly always a special, misty color of yellow.

The essayist E. B. White recognized a special quality here: He bought a farm and memorialized the experience in great little books like *One Man's Meat* and *Charlotte's Web*. (White's ashes are buried in a village cemetery on the peninsula.) While they may take a little extra time to find, the island of **Deer Isle** and villages like **Brooklin** and **Blue Hill** are well worth building into any Maine-coast itinerary.

There's also a strong countercultural streak running through the area; somehow, though, the boat-builders, fishermen, artists, and ex-hippies all get along just fine. Together they've create a unique blend of quiet water views, handpainted boats, small-town churches and general stores, tiny art galleries, organic produce, and grassroots radio: a place that could only happen in Maine.

Essentials
ARRIVING
Coming from the south on Route 1/Route 3, turn south onto Route 15 about 5 miles east of Bucksport, and drive about 12 miles to reach Blue Hill, at the juncture of routes 15 and 172.

The island of Deer Isle is connected to the mainland via a high, narrow, suspension bridge built in 1938—still a bit scary to cross during high winds. You get to the bridge via one of several winding roads that split off of Route 1. Coming from the south or west (Portland or Camden), turn onto Route 175 in Orland, then connect to Route 15 and continue to Deer Isle. From the east (Mount Desert Isle or Canada), head south on Route 172 to Blue Hill, where you can pick up Route 15 to Deer Isle.

For Blue Hill information, contact the **Blue Hill Peninsula Chamber of Commerce** (www.bluehillpeninsula.org; ✆ **207/374-3242**), located at 16 South Street. The **Deer Isle–Stonington Chamber of Commerce** (www.deerisle maine.com; ✆ **207/348-6124**), staffs a seasonal information booth just beyond the bridge on Little Deer Isle. The booth is normally open daily from May through October, its opening hours dependent on volunteer availability.

Exploring Blue Hill ★★

The town of **Blue Hill ★★**, population 2,400, is easy to find—just look for the dome of Blue Hill itself, which lords over the northern end of (of course) Blue Hill Bay. Set between the mountain and the bay is the quiet and historic town, clustering along the bay's shore and a little stream. There's never much going on here, which seems to be exactly what attracts repeat summer visitors; it might also explain why two excellent bookstores are located in this dot of a town. Many old-money families maintain lovely retreats along the water or in the hills around here, but the village center offers a couple choices for lodging even if you don't have local connections (see p. 662). It's a good place for a quiet break.

One good way to start your exploration of this area is to climb to the open summit of **Blue Hill ★★**, from which you can get good views of the bay and the bald mountaintops of nearby Mount Desert Island. The trail is free. To reach the trail head from the center of the village, drive north on Route 172 about 1½ miles, then turn west (left) on Mountain Road at the Blue Hill Fairgrounds. Drive another ¾ mile and look for the well-marked trail on the right; park on either shoulder of the road. The moderate ascent is about a mile long and takes about 45 minutes; there are no tricky, death-defying stretches along the way, and you'll know you've arrived when you spy the fire tower.

Blue Hill has traditionally attracted more than its fair share of artists, especially potters. Family-run **Rackliffe Pottery** (www.rackliffepottery.com; ✆ **888/631-3321**) on Route 172 (Ellsworth Rd.), uses native clay and lead-free glazes. Visitors are welcome to watch the potters at work. It's open year-round.

The best "museum" in town is the **Jonathan Fisher House ★★** (www.jonathanfisherhouse.org; ✆ **207/374-2459**), on routes 176 and 15, a half-mile west of the village. Fisher, Blue Hill's first permanent minister, was a small-town Renaissance man: Educated at Harvard, he not only delivered sermons

---

Antiquers Alert

If you're an ardent antiques hunter (or collector of bizarre experiences), it's worth your while to detour to the **Big Chicken Barn** (www.bigchickenbarn. com; ✆ **207/667-7308**), a sprawling antiques mall and bookstore on Route 1 between Ellsworth and Bucksport (15 miles northeast of Blue Hill). The place is of nearly shopping-mall proportions—more than 21,000 square feet of stuff in an old poultry barn. It's open daily from 10am to 6pm during summer, 10am to 5pm in the spring and fall, 10am to 4pm in winter.

in six different languages (including Aramaic), but was also a writer, painter, and inventor of boundless energy. On a tour of this home, which he built himself in 1814, you can view a clock with wooden works and a camera obscura Fisher made, plus pictures he painted and books he wrote, published, and bound by hand. The house is open July to mid-October, Thursday through Saturday 1 to 4pm. Admission is by donation; $5 per person is suggested.

Exploring Deer Isle ★★

The island known as **Deer Isle** is well off the beaten path, yet worth the long detour from Route 1. Looping, winding roads cross through forest and farmland, and travelers are rewarded with sudden glimpses of hidden coves. An occasional settlement even crops up now and again. This island doesn't cater exclusively to tourists the way many coastal towns and islands do; it's still largely occupied by fifth- or sixth-generation fishermen, farmers, second-home owners, and artists who prize their seclusion here.

The main village—**Stonington,** on the island's southern tip—is still a rough-hewn sea town. Despite serious incursions over the past 10 years by galleries and enterprises partly or wholly dependent on tourism, it remains dominated in spirit by fishermen. This village does now have a handful of inns and galleries, but its primary focus is to serve locals and summer residents, not travelers. *Outside* magazine once named this one of America's 10 best towns to live in if you're an extreme/outdoorsy type—that may be true, if you don't mind living several hours removed from the nearest significant population centers and airports in Maine. Still, you could pick a worse place to avoid civilization, and the mailboat that runs visitors out to **Isle au Haut,** an island outpost of Acadia National Park (see p. 667), helps boost Stonington's outdoorsy cred.

Deer Isle, with its network of narrow roads to nowhere, is ideal for rambling. It's a pleasure to explore by car and is also inviting to travel by bike, although careening fishermen in pickups can make this unnerving at times. Especially tranquil is the narrow road between the town of **Deer Isle** and **Sunshine** to the east. Plan to stop and explore coves and inlets along the way. To get here, follow Route 15; south of Deer Isle, turn east toward **Stinson Neck,** continuing on this **scenic byway** ★ for about 10 miles over bridges and causeways.

Stonington ★★, at the southern end of Deer Isle, consists of one commercial street that wraps along the harbor's edge. While B&Bs and boutiques have made inroads here in recent years, it's still a slightly rough-and-tumble waterfront town—a good place for taking pictures and eating fish.

Where to Stay on the Blue Hill Peninsula

BLUE HILL

Blue Hill Inn ★   The Blue Hill Inn has been hosting travelers since 1840 on one of the village's main streets, within walking distance of everything. It's a Federal-style inn, decorated in a Colonial American motif; creaky wooden floors stamp it with authenticity. The innkeepers have pleasantly furnished all rooms with antiques and down comforters; a few units in the main house have wood-burning fireplaces (main house rooms are open only from mid-May through the end of October), while a large contemporary suite in an adjacent, free-standing building has a cathedral ceiling, fireplace, full kitchen, living room, and deck (and it's open year-round). Most rooms lack telephones. Breakfasts here are very good, maybe because the eggs are fresh from the innkeepers' own coops.

40 Union St. www.bluehillinn.com. © **207/374-2844.** 13 units. Late June–Sept $195–$280 double; $295–$405 suite; discounts in spring and fall. Rates include full breakfast and afternoon pastries. 2-night minimum in summer. Main inn closed Nov to mid-May, 1 cottage open year-round. Children 13 and older welcome. Cottage accommodates pets. **Amenities:** Dining room; wine and cocktail service; library; free Wi-Fi.

The Farmhouse Inn ★   Comfortably situated on 48 acres about 3 miles north of Blue Hill's village center, this circa-1870 inn has some of the most relaxing and comfortable common areas in the region. New owners in 2015 renovated the place top to bottom, so it still feels like a handsome old barn, but all the guest rooms have private bathrooms and bedding and décor with a bright country-modern feel. The in-house restaurant and bar serves nice tapas plates ($7–$11) and pub fare ($14–$18). On summer evenings, guests gather with evening cocktails around a fire pit out back.

578 Pleasant St. www.thefarmhouseinnmaine.com. © **207/374-5286.** 9 units. $150–$220 double, $200–$225 suite. **Amenities:** Dining room; wine and cocktail service; free Wi-Fi.

DEER ISLE & STONINGTON

Inn on the Harbor ★   This appealingly quirky waterfront inn has the best location in town—perched over Stonington harbor and right on the main street. The furniture's a little on the dated side, but comfy anyway—big overstuffed grandma chairs—and more than half of the guest rooms overlook the harbor. The more inexpensive rooms are a bargain, in or out of season: This is a good spot for resting up before or after a kayak expedition, or as a base for day trips out to Acadia National Park (see p. 667). All units, named for the boats of state's historic windjammer fleet, have in-room phones (cell service in Stonington can be spotty); the recently updated American Eagle Suite, the most expensive unit, has a glass-fronted woodstove, private kitchen, and private deck.

45 Main St. Stonington. www.innontheharbor.com. © **800/942-2420** or 207/367-2420. 13 units. June–early Nov $170–$275 double and suite; early Nov–May $100–$210 double and suite. High season rates include continental breakfast. Children 12 and older welcome. **Amenities:** Spa services; free Wi-Fi.

Pilgrim's Inn ★★   Set just off a town road and between an open bay and a mill pond, this handsomely renovated historic inn was built in the mid-island town of Deer Isle in 1793 by Ignatius Haskell, a prosperous sawmill owner. His granddaughter opened the home to boarders, and it has housed summer guests ever since. The interior is tastefully decorated in a style that's informed by Early Americana but not beholden to it. The guest rooms are well appointed with antiques and decorated in muted colonial colors; expect lots of white, a little bit of lace, and subdued flowery prints. Especially intriguing are rooms on the top floor, showing off some impressive diagonal beams. Other accents include private staircases, cherry beds, antique tubs, gas-burning stoves, and fireplaces; breakfasts are big and fancy, running to goat-cheese pancakes, eggs Benedict, smoked salmon, and the like. Three cottages near the main building allow pets and have kitchenettes for fixing your own meals.

20 Main St., Deer Isle. www.pilgrimsinn.com. ℂ **888/778-7505** or 207/348-6615. 17 units. $169–$259 double; $229–$299 cottage. Rates include full breakfast. Closed mid-Oct to mid-May. Pets allowed in cottages only ($25 fee). Children 10 and older welcome in inn, all children welcome in cottages. **Amenities:** Restaurant; pub; library; bikes; free Wi-Fi.

Where to Eat on the Blue Hill Peninsula

BLUE HILL

The **Fish Net** (ℂ **207/374-5240**), at the north end of Main Street (near the junction of routes 172 and 177), is where locals go for quick meals of takeout fried fish, lobster rolls, clam baskets, and ice-cream cones. It's open seasonally—figure mid-April to Columbus Day, at most. If it's a sweet fix you're after, **Black Dinah Chocolatiers** (www.blackdinahchocolatiers.com; ℂ **207/374-2228**), at 5 Main St. (which they share with a florist), makes fancy little chocolates—pear and champagne truffles, peanut butter–filled frogs, choc-covered sea salt caramels. Their tasting room (open Mon–Sat 8:30am–5pm, Sun 11am–4pm) has a vintage soda-fountain counter where you can sit and sample with an espresso—or a mug of sipping chocolate.

Arborvine ★★ SEAFOOD/FUSION   The Arborvine gives sleepy Blue Hill a top-flight eatery in a beautifully renovated Cape Cod–style house. The restaurant's interior is warm and inviting, with rough-hewn timbers, polished wooden floors, and a cozy bar area. The intriguing main courses change nightly but might feature haddock Niçoise, broiled Stonington halibut with grilled polenta, roast duckling with apple-ginger compote, galettes of Maine crab and shrimp, or a locally raised and wood-fired Cornish game hen. Yummy desserts could include a Grand Marnier–spiked chocolate mousse; chocolate cake with raspberry ganache; a lemon mousse napoleon; a gingery vanilla crème brûlée; or a Bartlett pear in puff pastry sided with macadamia nut-flavored cream, pomegranate sauce, and a bit of cinnamon ice cream. In 2011, the owners (their son, actually) opened the **DeepWater** brew pub in an adjacent barn, so you can actually park your car and have two restaurants to choose from. The brewpub's not as impressive, but if you're after a good burger, nachos, or sports, you have an option.

33 Tenney Hill. www.arborvine.com. ℂ **207/374-2119.** Main dining room main courses $28–$34; brewpub main courses $11–$18. Summer Tues–Sun 4:30–9pm; off-season Fri–Sun 5:30–8:30pm.

STONINGTON & DEER ISLE

Aragosta ★★ NEW AMERICAN/SEAFOOD   Chef Devin Finigan has worked alongside some of the best names in contemporary American cooking—Thomas Keller, Michael Leviton, and fellow Mainer Melissa Kelly, among them—so she brings a pedigree to Stonington's white-tablecloth dining mecca. Aragosta goes in big for the farm-to-table ethos: The beef and the bacon on the burger were raised locally, the oysters come out of the Bagaduce, the produce (most of it) was farmed nearby, and obviously the *aragostas* (that's "lobster" in Italian) were pulled in a few dozen yards outside the front door. Fancy as the weekly changing menu is, the cedar-shingled Aragosta maintains charmingly rustic touches, from wide-plank wood flooring to wooden menu covers. Sit outside on the small deck, and you can hear the chatter of the lobstermen as they offload what may become your dinner. Hours are reassessed with each year and each season, so call ahead.

27 Main St., Stonington. www.aragostamaine.com. © **207/367-5500.** Lunch main courses $12–$17; dinner main courses $26–$33. Memorial Day–Columbus Day lunch Wed–Sat 11:30am–3:30pm, dinner Thurs–Mon 5–9pm. Closed Columbus Day–Thanksgiving; dinner and weekends only Thanksgiving–Memorial Day. Hours/seasons prone to change. Reservations recommended peak season and weekends.

Stonecutters Kitchen ★ SEAFOOD   On a dock near the Isle au Haut ferry and attached to a general store, this laidback counter-service joint is lively and boisterous, usually as crowded as it is unpretentious. Come for fried seafood and steamed lobster, although there are sandwiches and creative pizzas, if you're ready for a break from seafood. The lobster stew brims with chunks; travelers have been known to find reasons to linger in Stonington longer just to indulge in a second bowl. There's a general store onsite too, with groceries win and beer, if you want to get your meal to go and make a picnic out of it.

5 Atlantic Ave. (on the dock), Stonington. www.stonecutterskitchenme.com. © **207/367-2530.** Lobsters market priced; lunch main courses $10–$19; dinner main courses $14–$26. Thurs–Sun 11am–8pm, takeout daily.

MOUNT DESERT ISLAND ★★★

Bar Harbor: 160 miles NE of Portland, 270 miles NE of Boston

Mount Desert Island is home to spectacular **Acadia National Park,** and for many visitors, these two places are one and the same. Yet the park's holdings are only *part* of the appeal of this wonderful island, which is connected to the mainland by a short causeway. Besides the parklands, you'll find scenic harborside fishing villages and remote backcountry roads aplenty, lovely B&Bs and fine restaurants, oversize 19th-century summer "cottages," and the historic tourist town of **Bar Harbor.**

Mount Desert Island is split almost precisely in two by a deep inlet known as Somes Sound. The eastern side is much more heavily developed. Bar Harbor is the center of commerce and entertainment, a once-charming resort now in danger of being swallowed whole by all its T-shirt and trinket shops. The island's western side has a more serene, settled air and teems with more wildlife than tourists; the villages are mostly filled with fishermen and second-homers, rather than actual businesses. Locals call it the "quiet side."

Mount Desert Island & Acadia National Park

This island isn't huge—it's only about 15 miles from the causeway to the southernmost tip at Bass Harbor Head—yet you can do an awful lot of adventuring within this compact space and see many different kinds of towns and landscapes. The best plan is to take it slowly, exploring if possible by foot, bicycle, canoe, and/or kayak, giving yourself a week to do it. You'll be glad you did.

Essentials

ARRIVING

BY CAR   Acadia National Park is near Ellsworth, reached via Route 3. Normally travelers take Route 1 to Ellsworth from southern Maine, but you can avoid coastal congestion by taking the Maine Turnpike to Bangor, then picking up I-395 to Route 1A and continuing south into Ellsworth. Though longer in terms of miles, it's a quicker route in summer. From Ellsworth, bear right onto Route 3 and continue about 15 minutes to the island causeway in Trenton. Cross the bridge and you're on the island. From here, routes 3 and 233 go to Bar Harbor, about 10 miles southeast of the causeway; Route 198 goes to Northeast Harbor, and Route 102 leads to Southwest harbor.

BY PLANE Year-round, there are several flights daily from Boston (and, seasonally, Newark NJ) on small planes to the **Hancock County-Bar Harbor airport** (www.bhbairport.com) in Trenton, just across the causeway from Mount Desert Island. Contact **Cape Air** (www.capeair.com; *©* **800/227-3247**) or **PenAir** (www.penair.com; *©* **800/448-4226**) for Boston flights, or **Elite Airways** (www.eliteairways.net; *©* **877/393-2510**) for Newark. From the airport, call a taxi, rent a car, or—best of all—ride the **free shuttle bus** (see p. 668) to downtown Bar Harbor from late June through mid-October.

VISITOR INFORMATION

Acadia staffs two visitor centers. The **Thompson Island Information Center** (*©* **207/288-3411**) on Route 3 is the first you'll pass as you enter Mount Desert Island. This center is maintained by the local chambers of commerce, but park personnel are often on hand to answer inquiries. Open daily at 8:30am mid-May through mid-October, it's a good first stop for general lodging and restaurant information. If you're interested primarily in information about the park itself, continue on Route 3 to the National Park Service's **Hulls Cove Visitor Center,** about 7½ miles beyond Thompson Island. This attractive stone-walled center has professionally prepared park-service displays, such as a large relief map of the island, natural history exhibits, and a short introductory film. You can also request free brochures about hiking trails and the carriage roads, or purchase postcards and more detailed guidebooks. The center is open daily from mid-April through the end of October. Information is also available year-round, by phone or in person, at the **park headquarters** (*©* **207/288-3338**), on Route 233 between Bar Harbor and Somesville, open daily (except closed weekends in summer). You can also make inquiries online at **www.nps.gov/acad**. The **Bar Harbor Chamber of Commerce** (www.barharborinfo.com; *©* **800/345-4617**) stockpiles a huge arsenal of information about local attractions at its offices on 2 Cottage St. (downtown, 2 blocks from the pier).

Exploring Acadia National Park ★★★

It's not hard to understand why Acadia is one of the crown jewels of the National Park system. (It's among the top ten most visited U.S. national

---

Fjord Tough?

Mount Desert Island is divided deeply right down the middle into two lobes (almost like a brain) by **Somes Sound,** a tidal inlet that's often called the Lower 48's only true fjord—that is, a valley carved out by a glacier and then subsequently filled in with rising ocean water. As many a Mainer will tell you, however, the feature is more properly classified as a fjard, a close hydrogeological cousin, which is less steep and shallower, the result of a flooded glacial lowland but not a truly scoured glacial trough. You'll find that many around MDI leave the finer distinctions to the geologists (and the Scandinavians, who take this stuff quite seriously) and simply refer to Somes Sound as a fjord. Whatever vowel you prefer, it's no less dramatic to gaze upon.

parks.) The landscape here is a rich tapestry of rugged cliffs, pounding ocean surf, fishing and leisure boats lolling in harbors, and quiet forest paths.

Acadia's terrain, like so much of the rest of northern New England, was shaped by the cutting action of the last great glaciers moving into and then out of the region about 18,000 years ago. A mile-high ice sheet rumbled slowly over the land, scouring valleys into deep U-shapes, rounding many once-jagged peaks, and depositing boulders at odd places in the landscape—including the famous 10-foot-tall Bubble Rock, which appears perched precariously on the side of South Bubble Mountain.

A **free summer shuttle-bus service** ★★, known as the Island Explorer (www.exploreacadia.com)—propane-powered, with racks for bikes—serves multiple routes covering nearly the entire island and will stop anywhere you request outside the village centers, including trail heads, ferries, small villages, and campgrounds. (Bring a book, though; there are lots of stops.)

All routes begin or end at the central **Village Green** in Bar Harbor, but you can and should pick up the bus almost anywhere else to avoid parking hassles in town. Route no. 3 runs from Bar Harbor along much of the Park Loop, offering easy, free access to some of the park's best hiking trails. The buses operate from late June through mid-October; ask for a schedule at island information centers, in shops, or at any hotel or campground.

HOW acadia national park CAME TO BE

In the 1840s, Hudson River School painter Thomas Cole brought his sketchbooks and easels to remote Mount Desert Island, which was then home to a small number of fishermen and boatbuilders. His stunning renditions of the coast were displayed in New York City museums and galleries, triggering a tourism rush as urbanites flocked to the island to "discover" nature and "rusticate" in wood-beamed lodges and Victorian inns. By 1872, national magazines were touting Eden (the town of Bar Harbor's name before 1919) as a summer getaway. It attracted the attention of wealthy industrialists and soon became the summer home of Carnegies, Rockefellers, Astors, and Vanderbilts, who built massive "cottages" (mansions, really, in the shingle style of the time) with dozens of bedrooms.

By the early 1900s, the island's popularity and growing development began to concern people. Textile heir George Dorr and Harvard president Charles

Eliot, aided by the largesse of John D. Rockefeller, Jr., began acquiring and protecting large tracts of the island for the public to enjoy. These parcels were eventually donated to the U.S. government, and in 1919, the land was designated Lafayette National Park—the first national park east of the Mississippi—named after the French general.

Renamed Acadia National Park in 1929, the park has now grown to encompass nearly half the island in piecemeal holdings. A world-class destination for those who enjoy outdoors adventure, the park seems to share more in common with Alaska than New England: You can see bald eagles soaring overhead, whales breaching below, cliffs and fir-topped mountains at nearly every turn.

In between, you'll find remote coves perfect for beach picnics; lovely offshore islands accessible only by sea kayak; clear ponds and lakes with nary a boat in them; and uncrowded mountaintops with views of it all and outstanding foliage in fall.

Regulations

The usual national park rules apply. Guns may not be used in the park; if you have a gun, it must be "cased, broken down, or otherwise packaged against use." Fires and camping are allowed only at designated areas. Pets must be on leashes at all times. Seat belts must be worn in the national park (this is a federal law). Don't remove anything from the park, either man-made or natural; this includes cobblestones from the shore. A proposed transportation plan to help alleviate park traffic would involve an online reservation system to visit some of the park's most beloved attractions, including Cadillac Mountain and Sand Beach. The earliest it might be imposed is 2020, but as of this writing, the plan was still in its public comment phase. Enjoy reservation-free travel within the park while it lasts.

ENTRY POINTS & FEES Entrance fees to the park are collected at several gates from May through October; the rest of the year, entrance is free—one of this nation's great outdoor bargains either way. You can also grab a pass online at **www.yourpassnow.com** or at several other spots around Mount Desert Island and the mainland (see **www.nps.gov/acadia** for a full list). A 1-week pass, which includes unlimited trips on the Park Loop Road (closed in winter), costs $30 per car from May through early October; there's no additional charge per passenger once you've bought the pass. Hikers, cyclists, folks riding the Island Explorer Bus, and anyone else traveling without a vehicle must pay a $15-per-person fee (motorcycles and up to two passengers are $25).

You can enter the park at several points in the interwoven network of park and town roads—a glance at a park map, available free at the visitor center, will make these access points self-evident. The main point of entry to Park Loop Road, the park's most popular scenic byway, is near the official park visitor center at **Hulls Cove** (on Route 3 just north of Bar Harbor); the entry fee is collected at a tollbooth on the loop road, a half-mile north of Sand Beach.

SEASONS While spring is forgettable in Acadia—often intensely foggy or rainy—summer is the peak tourist season. The weather in July and August is warm (in the 70s or 80s/low to mid-20s Celsius), with afternoons frequently cooler than mornings owing to the sea breezes. Light fogs occasionally roll in from the southeast on a hot day, which gives a magical quality to the landscape. Sunny days are the norm, but come prepared for rain; this is the Atlantic Coast, after all. Once or twice each summer, a heat wave somehow settles onto the island, producing temperatures in the 90s (30s Celsius), dense haze, and stifling humidity, but this rarely lasts more than a few days. August in Acadia is when both heat and traffic peaks—traffic jams on the Park Loop Road and at the top of Cadillac are, sadly, the norm, and Bar Harbor is a zoo. If you can come earlier in the summer or hold off until September, consider it.

Soon enough (sometimes even during late August), a brisk north wind will blow in from the Canadian Arctic, forcing visitors into sweaters at night. Fall here is wonderful. Between Labor Day and the foliage season in early October, days are often warm and clear, nights have a crisp tang, and you can avoid the congestion, crowds, and pesky insects of summer. It's not that the park is empty in September; bus tours proliferate at this time, and it's when the cruise ship season kicks into high gear in Bar Harbor. But both the cruise and tour bus crowds tend to stick to the pavement—hikers and bikers need only get a minute or two off the road to find relative solitude on the trails and carriage roads.

Winter is an increasingly popular time to travel to Acadia, especially among those who enjoy cross-country skiing on the carriage roads. Be aware, though, that snow along the coast is inconsistent, and services—including most restaurants and many inns—are often closed down outright in winter. Expect to stay in either a really cheap motel or an expensive resort, and to often eat what locals do: pizza, burgers, and sandwiches.

RANGER PROGRAMS   Frequent ranger programs are offered throughout the year. These include talks at campground amphitheaters and tours of island locales and attractions. Examples include an Otter Point nature hike, walks across the carriage roads' stone bridges, cruises on Frenchman Bay (rangers provide commentary on many trips), and discussions of the changes in Acadia's landscape. Ask for a schedule of events and more information at any visitor center or campground.

GUIDED TOURS   **Acadia National Park Tours** (www.acadiatours.com; ✆ **207/288-0300**) offers 2½-hour park tours from mid-May through October, departing twice daily (10am and 2pm) from downtown Bar Harbor. The bus tour includes three stops (Sieur De Monts Springs, Thunder Hole, and Cadillac Mountain) and imparts plenty of park trivia, courtesy of the driver. This is an easy way for first-time visitors to get a quick introduction to the park before setting out on their own side trips. Tickets are available at Testa's Restaurant (at 53 Main St.) in Bar Harbor; the cost is $32.50 for adults, $20 for children 12 and under.

DRIVING TOUR: DRIVING THE PARK LOOP ROAD

The 20-mile **Park Loop Road ★★** is to Acadia what Half Dome is to Yosemite—the park's premier attraction, and a magnet for the largest crowds. This remarkable roadway starts near the Hulls Cove Visitor Center and follows the high ridges above Bar Harbor before dropping down along the rocky coast. Here, spires of spruce and fir cap dark granite ledges, making a sharp contrast with the white surf and steel-blue sea. After following the picturesque coast and touching on several coves, the road loops back inland along Jordan Pond and Eagle Lake, with a detour to the summit of the island's highest peak, Cadillac Mountain.

From about 10am until 4pm in July and especially August, anticipate big crowds along the loop road, at least on days when the sun is shining. Parking lots sometimes fill up and close their gates at some of the most popular destinations, including Sand Beach, Thunder Hole, and the Cadillac Mountain summit, so try to visit these spots early or late in a day. Alternatively, make the best of cloudy or drizzly days by letting the weather work to your advantage; you'll sometimes discover that you have the place nearly to yourself.

Ideally, visitors should try to make two circuits of the loop road. The first time, get the lay of the land. On the second-time circuit (one pass gets you all-day access), plan to stop frequently and poke around on foot, setting off on trails or scrambling along the coastline and taking photos. (Scenic pull-offs are strategically placed at intervals.) The two-lane road is one-way along some of its coastal sections; in these cases, the right-hand lane is set aside for parking, so you can stop wherever you'd like, admire the vistas from the shoulder, and click away.

From the Hulls Cove Visitor Center, the Park Loop initially runs atop:

1 Paradise Hill

Our tour starts with sweeping views eastward over Frenchman Bay. You'll see the town of Bar Harbor far below, and just beyond it the Porcupines, a cluster of islands that look like, well, porcupines. Sort of.

Following the Park Loop Road clockwise, you'll dip into a wooded valley and come to:

2 Sieur de Monts Spring

Here you'll find a rather uninteresting natural spring, unnaturally encased, along with a botanical garden with some 300 species showcased in 12 habitats. The original **Abbe Museum** (© **207/288-3519**) is here, featuring a small but select collection of Native American artifacts. It's open daily from late May to September, 10am to 4pm; admission is $3 for adults, $1 for ages 6 to 15. (A larger and more modern branch of the museum in Bar Harbor features more and better-curated displays; a ticket here gets you a discount there. See p. 673 for details.)

The Tarn is the main reason to stop here; a few hundred yards south of the springs via a footpath, it's a slightly medieval-looking and forsaken pond sandwiched between steep hills. Departing from the south end of the Tarn is the 2.7-mile loop known as the **Dorr Mountain Ladder Trail** (you'll climb several granite-embedded rungs before summiting the 1,270-foot peak).

Continue the clockwise trip on the loop road; views eastward over the bay soon resume, almost uninterrupted, until you get to:

3 The Precipice Trail

The park's most dramatic hiking track, the **Precipice Trail** ★★ ascends sheer rock faces on the eastern side of **Champlain Mountain.** It's only about half a mile to the summit, but it's nevertheless a rigorous climb that involves scrambling up iron rungs and ladders in exposed places (those with a fear of heights and those under 5 feet tall should avoid this trail). The trail is often closed midsummer to protect nesting peregrine falcons;

at these times rangers are often on hand at the trail-head parking lot to suggest alternative hikes.

Between the Precipice Trail and Sand Beach is a tollbooth where visitors have to pay the park **entrance fee.**

Picturesquely set between the arms of a rocky cove is:

4 Sand Beach

Sand Beach ★★ is virtually the only sand beach on the island, although actually swimming in these cold waters (about 50°F/10°C) is best enjoyed only on extremely hot days or by those with hardy constitutions. When it's sunny out, the sandy strand is crowded midday with picnickers, tanners, tide pool explorers, and book readers.

Two good hikes begin near this beach. **The Beehive Trail** overlooks Sand Beach; it starts from a trailhead across the loop road and heads up steeply to reach a pond called The Bowl .8 miles later. From the east end of Sand Beach, look for the start of the **Great Head Trail,** a loop of about 2 miles that follows on the bluff overlooking the beach, then circles back along the shimmering bay before cutting through the woods back to Sand Beach.

About a mile south of Sand Beach is:

5 Thunder Hole

Thunder Hole ★ is a shallow ocean-side cave into which the ocean surges, compresses, and bursts out violently like a thick cannon shot of foam. (A roadside walking trail allows you to leave your car parked at the Sand Beach lot and hike to this point.)

If the sea is quiet—as it sometimes is on midsummer days—don't bother visiting this attraction; there'll be nothing to see. But on days when the seas are rough, and big swells are rolling in all the way from the Bay of Fundy, this is a must-see, three-star attraction; you can feel the ocean's power and force. The best viewing time is 3 hours before high tide; check tide tables, available at local hotels, restaurants, and info kiosks, to figure out when that is.

Just before the road curves around Otter Point, you'll be driving atop:

6 Otter Cliffs

This set of 100-foot-high precipices is capped with dense stands of spruce trees. From the top, look for spouting whales in summer. In early fall, raftlike flocks of eider ducks can sometimes be seen floating just offshore. A footpath traces the edge of the crags.

At Seal Harbor, the loop road veers north and inland back toward Bar Harbor. On the route is:

7 Jordan Pond

Jordan Pond ★★ is a small but beautiful body of water encased by gentle, forested hills. A 3-mile hiking loop follows the pond's shoreline, and a network of splendid carriage roads converges at the pond. After a hike or mountain-bike excursion, spend some time at a table on the lawn of the Jordan Pond House restaurant (see p. 685).

Shortly before the loop road ends, you'll pass the entrance to:

8 Cadillac Mountain

Reach this **mountain** ★ by car, ascending an early carriage road. At 1,528 feet, it's the highest peak touching the Atlantic Ocean between Canada and Brazil. During much of the year, it's also the first place on U.S. soil touched by the rays of sunrise. But because this is the only mountaintop in the park accessible by car (and also because it's the island's highest point), the parking lot at the summit often gets jammed.

Exploring Bar Harbor ★

Bar Harbor provides most of the meals and beds to travelers coming to Mount Desert Island, and it has done so since the grand resort era of the late 19th century, when wealthy vacationers first discovered this region. Sprawling hotels and boardinghouses once cluttered the shores and hillsides here, as a newly affluent middle class arrived by steamboat and rail car from the city in droves to find out what all the fuss was about.

The tourist trade continued to boom through the early 1900s—until it all but collapsed from the double hit of the Great Depression and the advent of car travel. The town was dealt yet another blow in 1947, when an accidental fire spread rapidly and leveled many of the opulent cottages in town (as well as a large portion of the rest of the island).

In the last few decades, however, Bar Harbor has bounced back with a vengeance, revived and rediscovered by visitors and entrepreneurs alike. Some see the place as a tacky place of T-shirt vendors, ice-cream cones, and souvenir shops, plus crowds spilling off the sidewalks into the street and appalling traffic. That is all true. Yet the town's history, distinguished architecture, and location on Frenchman Bay still make it a desirable base for exploring the island, and by far, it has the best selection of lodging, meals, supplies, and services on the isle. (If you want to shop, fine-dine, or go out at night, you've pretty much *got* to stay here.)

The best water views in town are from the foot of Main Street at grassy (and free) **Agamont Park** ★★, which overlooks the town pier and Frenchman Bay. From here, stroll past The Bar Harbor Inn on the **Shore Path** ★★, a wide, winding trail that follows the shoreline for half a mile along a public right of way. The pathway also passes in front of many elegant summer homes (some converted into inns), offering a superb vantage point from which to view the area's architecture.

The **Abbe Museum** ★, 26 Mount Desert St. (www.abbemuseum.org; © 207/ 288-3519), opened in 2001 as an in-town extension of the smaller, simpler museum at the Sieur de Monts spring in the national park (see p. 671), showcasing a top-rate collection of Native American artifacts. It's Maine's only Smithsonian affiliate and one of the best museums in the state. A new core exhibit in 2016 shows off the museum's collection of Wabanaki artifacts and

Bar Harbor

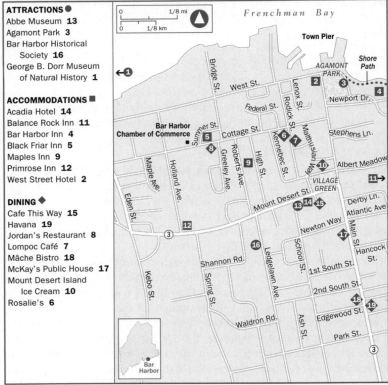

contemporary art, organized around a sculpted, two-story ash tree; it incorporates interactive elements of oral history and storytelling. Temporary exhibits might focus on anything from (impressive) Wabanaki basket-making to student art from Maine's tribes. From May through October, it opens daily from 10am to 5pm; the rest of the year, it's open Thursday to Sunday only. Admission costs $8 for adults, $4 for kids ages 6 to 15, and is free for younger children.

A short stroll around the corner from the Abbe Museum, the **Bar Harbor Historical Society,** housed in a 1918 former convent at 33 Ledgelawn Ave. (www.barharborhistorical.org; ℂ **207/288-0000** or 207/288-3807), showcases artifacts of life in the old days—dishware and photos from those grand old hotels that once dotted the town, exhibits on the noted landscape architect Beatrix Farrand, and so forth. Scrapbooks document the devastating 1947 fire, too. The museum is open from June through October Monday to Friday from 1 to 4pm; admission is free. Even during the off season, entrance can sometimes be arranged.

Just at the northern edge of the town, on Route 3 with a spectacular bay view, is the campus of the **College of the Atlantic** (www.coa.edu;

📞 207/288-5015), a school founded in 1969 with an emphasis on environmental education. The college's campus, a blend of old and new buildings, features the **George B. Dorr Museum of Natural History** (www.coamuseum. org; *📞 207/288-5395*) at 105 Eden St. Its exhibits focus on interactions among island residents, from the two-legged to the four-legged, finny, and furry. It's open Tuesday through Saturday from 10am to 5pm; admission is by donation, though I'd toss in at least $5 per adult and $2 per child (more if you're deeply appreciative of the place).

Exploring the Rest of Mount Desert Island

Down one peninsula of the eastern lobe of the island is the staid, prosperous village of **Northeast Harbor** ★★, long a favorite retreat of well-heeled folks. You can see shingled palaces poking out from the forest and shore, but the village itself (which consists of just one short main street and a marina) is also worth investigating for its art galleries, restaurants, and general store.

One of the best, least-publicized places for enjoying views of the harbor is from the understated, wonderful **Asticou Terraces** ★★ (www.gardenpreserve. org; *📞 207/276-3727*). Finding the parking lot can be tricky: Head a half-mile east (toward Seal Harbor) on Route 3 from the junction with Route 198, and look for the small gravel lot on the water side of the road with a sign reading ASTICOU TERRACES. Park here, cross the road on foot, and set off up a magnificent path of local stone that ascends the sheer hillside, with expanding views of the harbor and the town.

When leaving Northeast Harbor, think about a quick detour out to **Sargent Drive,** a one-way route running through Acadia National Park along the shore of Somes Sound, which affords superb views of the glacially carved inlet. On the far side of Somes Sound, there's good hiking. The nearby towns of **Southwest Harbor** ★★ and **Bass Harbor** are both home to fishermen and boatbuilders, and though the character of these towns is changing, they're still far more humble than Northeast and Seal harbors.

Outdoor Activities on Mount Desert Island

CARRIAGE RIDES ★★

Several types of carriage rides are offered by the park's official concessionaire, **Carriages of Acadia** (www.acadiahorses.com; *📞 877/276-3622*). Departing daily in season from stables about a half-mile south of the Jordan Pond House (just north and inland from Seal Harbor), these 1- to 4-hour tours might take in sweeping ocean views from a local mountaintop or a ramble through the Rockefeller bridges. There's a special carriage designed for passengers with disabilities, and you can even charter your own carriage for a private group. Reservations are recommended; figure to pay about $20 to $36 per adult, or about $12 to $14 per child, for a tour.

GOLF

There are several good golf courses on Mount Desert Island. The **Kebo Valley Golf Club** (www.kebovalleyclub.com; *📞 207/288-3000*) at 136 Eagle Lake Rd. in Bar Harbor (a short walk or drive from downtown) is one of the oldest in America, open in some form or another since 1888; it's a beauty. (*Golf Digest* awarded it four stars.) Greens fees run from $49 to $99 per person for 18 holes (they're highest in summer), and it can get very busy on peak summer weekends—try to reserve well ahead.

HIKING

Hiking is the quintessential Acadia experience, and it should be experienced by everyone at least once. The park has 120 miles of hiking trails in all, plus 57 miles of carriage roads, which are great for easier walking. Some traverse the sides or faces of low "mountains" (which would be called hills anywhere else), and almost all summits have superb views of the Atlantic. Many of these pathways were crafted by stonemasons or others with aesthetic intent, so the routes aren't always the most direct—but they're often incredibly scenic, taking advantage of natural fractures in the rocks, picturesque ledges, and sudden, sweeping vistas.

The **Hulls Cove Visitor Center** has a brief chart summarizing area hikes; combined with the park map, this is all you need to find one of the well-maintained, well-marked trails and start exploring. Cobble together different loop hikes to make your trips more varied, and be sure to coordinate your hiking with the weather; if it's damp or foggy, you'll stay drier and warmer strolling the carriage roads. If it's clear and dry, head for the highest peaks (Cadillac, The Bubbles) with the best views.

BIKING

The 57 miles of gravel **carriage roads ★★★** built by John D. Rockefeller, Jr., are among the park's most extraordinary, somewhat hidden treasures. They were maintained by Rockefeller until his death in 1960, after which they became somewhat shaggy and overgrown. A major restoration effort was launched in 1990, though, and today the roads are superbly restored and maintained—and wide open. Though built for horse and carriage, they are ideal for cruising by mountain or hybrid bike (the crushed-stone paths are rough for thin tires) and offer some of the most scenic, relaxing biking found anywhere in the United States. (Note that bikes are allowed onto the island's free shuttle buses.) A useful map of the carriage roads is available free at any visitor center on the island; more detailed guides can be purchased at area bookshops, but they really aren't necessary. Remember that anywhere carriage roads cross private land (mostly between **Seal Harbor** and **Northeast Harbor**), they're *closed* to bikes, which are also banned from hiking trails.

Mountain bikes can be rented along Cottage Street in Bar Harbor, with rates generally in the neighborhood of $25 for a full day or $15 for a half-day (which is 4 hours in the bike-rental universe). High-performance and tandem bikes cost a bit more than that, children's bikes a bit less. Most bike shops include locks and helmets as basic equipment, but ask what's included before you rent. Also ask about closing times, since you'll be able to get in a couple of extra hours with a late-closing shop. The **Bar Harbor Bicycle Shop,** 141 Cottage St. (www.barharborbike.com; ℂ **207/288-3886**), gets many people's vote for the most convenient and friendliest. You could also try **Acadia Bike & Canoe,** 48 Cottage St. (www.acadiabike.com; ℂ **800/526-8615**).

Where to Stay on Mount Desert Island

BAR HARBOR

Bar Harbor is the bedroom community for Mount Desert Island, with hundreds of hotel, motel, and inn rooms, plus Airbnb rentals of every stripe, with few real bargains among them. They're invariably filled during the busy days of summer, and even the most basic rooms can be quite expensive in July and August. It's essential to reserve as early in advance as possible.

Expensive

Balance Rock Inn ★★★ Tucked down a quiet side alley just off Bar Harbor's main drag, the Balance Rock (built in 1903 for a Scottish railroad magnate) reaches for and achieves a gracefully upscale Long Island beach house feel. The entrance alone is nearly worth the steep rack rates: You enter a sitting room, which looks out onto the sort of azure outdoor swimming pool you'd expect to find in a Tuscan villa, and just beyond looms the Atlantic. Rooms are as elegant as any on the island, with a variety of layouts, some with sea views; some have whirlpools and saunas, while the penthouse suite adds a full kitchen. The comfortable king-size beds are adjustable using controls and have been fitted with feather beds and quality linens. A poolside bar, piano room, gracious staff, and fragrant flowers lining the driveway complete the romance of the experience.

21 Albert Meadow. www.balancerockinn.com. ✆ **800/753-0494** or 207/288-2610. 27 units. $300–$595 double, $575–$725 suite. Rates include full breakfast. Closed mid-Oct–early May. Some rooms accommodate pets ($40 per pet per night). Children 10 years and older welcome. **Amenities:** Restaurant; poolside bar; fitness room; fire pit; heated outdoor pool; fitness center; free Wi-Fi.

The Bar Harbor Inn ★ The Bar Harbor Inn, just off Agamont Park, nicely mixes traditional style with contemporary touches. On shady grounds just a moment's stroll from Bar Harbor's downtown, this property offers both convenience and charm. The shingled main inn, which dates from the turn of the 19th century, has a settled, old-money feel with its semicircular dining room and a buttoned-down lobby. Guest rooms, located in the main building and two outbuildings, are much more contemporary. Units in the Oceanfront Lodge and main inn both offer spectacular bay views, and many have private balconies. The third wing, the Newport Building, lacks views and its furnishings are a little dated, but you can save a little on rates here. Guests have access to a spa with Vichy showers, aromatherapy, heated-stone treatments, and facial treatments, while the somewhat formal **Reading Room** dining room serves resort meals with the best dining-room views in town.

1 Newport Dr. www.barharborinn.com. ✆ **800/248-3351** or 207/288-3351. 153 units. Mid-May to mid-Oct $289–$449 double; mid-Mar to mid-May and mid-Oct to Nov $149–$389 double. Rates include continental breakfast. 2-night minimum stay mid-June to Aug weekends. Closed Dec to mid-Mar. **Amenities:** Dining room; lounge; fitness room; Jacuzzi; heated outdoor pool; room service; spa; free Wi-Fi.

West Street Hotel ★★ Opened in 2012, the West Street already feels as if it's always loomed over the water on the northern edge of town. Maybe that's because it's so conspicuous, its pale multicolored facade stretching the better part of a block. The theme is nautical luxe; the rooms are fairly snug, but well-appointed with mahogany furnishings and leather chairs. The real genius of the place is that every room has a small private balcony with a view of the harbor—it's a terrific thing to wake up to, and you'll feel well above the bustle of the Bar Harbor street. (This is even truer when you're splashing in the rooftop pool.) Guests have access to amenities just down the road at the Bar Harbor Club sister property—another pool, tennis courts, a fitness center, and spa.

50 West St. www.theweststreethotel.com. ✆ 877/905-4498 or 207/288-0825. 85 units. July–mid-Oct $339–$449 double, $559–$959 suite; mid-May–June and mid-Sept–late Oct $259–$399 double, $419–$635 suite. 2-night minimum stay July–Aug weekends. Closed Nov–early May. **Amenities:** Restaurant; bar; 2 pools; tennis courts; marina; fitness center; spa; free Wi-Fi.

Moderate

Acadia Hotel ★★   The simple, comfy Acadia Hotel is nicely situated overlooking Bar Harbor's village green, easily accessible to in-town activities and the free shuttle buses running around the island. A handsome and none-too-large home dating from the late 19th century, the hotel gave most of its rooms the remod treatment in 2014, and the place feels fresh, with patterned upholstery, flat-screens and refrigerators in every room, new paint jobs, and a stylish new suite with a picture window looking out at Cadillac Mountain. Some rooms are slightly underground, a few steps down, but they get plenty of light. A new lobby and additional guest rooms in a brand-new building next door debuted in 2017. The rates have inched up from a few years back, but all things considered this is still arguably the best value in a pricey town (particularly in winter, as it's the rare MDI hotel open year-round).

20 Mt. Desert St. www.acadiahotel.com. ✆ 888/876-2463 or 207/288-5721. 21 units. June–Labor Day $129–$299 double, $409–$499 suite; May and Columbus Day–Nov $99–$159 double, $249–$319 suite; Dec–Apr $89–$139 double, $249 suite. **Amenities:** Free bikes; outdoor hot tub; free Wi-Fi.

Black Friar Inn ★   The seasonal Black Friar, tucked on a Bar Harbor side street overlooking a parking lot, is a yellow-shingled home with quirky pediments and an eccentric air. A former owner "collected" interiors and installed them throughout the home, including a replica of a pub in London with elaborate carved-wood paneling (it's now a common room); stamped-tin walls (look in the breakfast room); and a doctor's office (now one of the guest rooms). Rooms are carpeted and furnished in a mix of antiques; most are smallish, though the big suite features nice paneling, a sofa, wingback chair, private porch, and gas fireplace. Other rooms sport such touches as rose-tinted stained-glass windows, brass beds, and a sort of mini spiral staircase. The least expensive units are the two garret rooms on the third floor. The inn, which is also home to a small restaurant and pub, generally asks a 2-night minimum stay.

10 Summer St. www.blackfriarinn.com. ✆ 207/288-5081. 6 units. July to mid-Oct $150–$210 double; May–June, mid-Oct to mid-Nov $90–$150 double. Rates include full breakfast. 2-night minimum July–Oct. Closed mid-Nov to Apr. Children 12 and older welcome. **Amenities:** Restaurant; pub; free Wi-Fi.

Maples Inn ★   A modest home tucked away on a side street in a row of Bar Harbor B&Bs, the Maples is an easy walk downtown to a movie or dinner. The current innkeepers, who took over the place in 2015, are an outdoorsy young couple, and the inn tends to attract other adventuresome types; find them swapping stories about their day's exploits on the handsome front porch or lingering over breakfast to compare notes about hiking trails. Rooms are small to medium-size, but you're not likely to feel cramped—they have private bathrooms, wicker furniture, pencil poster beds, and handsome antique wooden writing desks. The two-room White Birch has a fireplace, a lacy canopy bed with a down comforter, and a bright blue-and-white decor; Red Oak has a private deck with rocking chairs. Gourmet breakfasts are served in a sunny dining room or taken on the porch; Chef Matt is big on local ingredients, even smoking his own trout.

16 Roberts Ave. www.maplesinn.com. ⓒ **207/288-3443.** 7 units. Mid-June to mid-Oct $139–$229 double and suite; May to mid-June and mid-Oct to late Oct $119–$189 double and suite. Rates include full breakfast. 2-night minimum stay in summer, 3-night minimum on holiday weekends. Closed Nov–Apr. Not appropriate for children under 12. **Amenities:** Afternoon snacks; free Wi-Fi.

Primrose Inn ★★   This handsome Victorian stick–style inn, originally built in 1878, is one of the most notable properties on the "mansion row" along Mount Desert Street. Its distinctive architecture has been preserved, and was perhaps even enhanced during a 1987 addition of rooms, private bathrooms, and balconies. This inn is comfortable, furnished with "functional antiques" and modern reproductions; many of the spacious rooms have a floral theme, thick carpets, marble vanities, canopy beds, sitting or reading rooms, and handsome day beds, wingback chairs or other furniture. (Two newer "premium" rooms also have private entrances and are stocked with king beds, gas fireplaces, and such other amenities as a porch or whirlpool tub.) Breakfasts of eggs Florentine, Belgian waffles, blueberry pancakes, and the like are a hit (and there's a fridge full of free soft drinks whenever you're parched).

73 Mount Desert St. www.primroseinn.com. ⓒ **877/846-3424** or 207/288-4031. 15 units. Mid-June–Labor Day $212–$288 double; mid-May to early June and Sept–Oct $155–$277 double. Rates include full breakfast and afternoon tea. 2-night minimum stay summer and fall. Closed late Oct to mid-May. **Amenities:** Library; free Wi-Fi

AROUND THE ISLAND

Consider tenting at one of the many privately owned campgrounds dotting the island; you can obtain a complete listing and guide from any tourist office on Mount Desert Island. Just remember that some campgrounds fill up ahead of time or by midday; and advance booking, if possible, is always better.

Acadia Yurts ★   You're not going to find a quieter stretch of what MDIers call "the quiet side." And you won't find more idiosyncratic accommodations than the six giant round tents on this 5-acre stretch of woods. They're fitted with queen beds, full kitchens, showers, air conditioning—all the comforts of home. They're also as light and open as can be (what with the built-in sky-light), and plenty sturdy (the walls are wooden; only the ceiling is fabric). A community barn and a seasonal spa yurtlet make for gathering spaces, as do the fire pits outside each yurt. They're spaced out enough that you can maintain privacy, but as all rentals are weekly, you're likely to make friends. The proprietors are a 30-something couple with deep MDI roots. One of their sweet touches: All the artwork was made by students from Mount Desert Island High School.

200 Seal Cove Rd., Southwest Harbor. www.acadiayurts.com. ✆ **800/307-5335** or 207/244-5335. 6 units. Late June–early Sept $1500 per week. Mid-Apr to mid-June and mid-Sept to Nov $1,050–$1,200 per week. Pets welcome ($100 weekly fee). **Amenities:** Yoga and spa tent; library; grills; fire pits; free Wi-Fi.

Asticou Inn ★ The Asticou Inn, which dates from 1883, occupies a prime location at the head of Northeast Harbor. It was once one of those "must-see" hotels on the island, but then slid slowly into a state of neglect. New ownership in 2010 really turned the place around; since 2015, when the company that formerly ran the park's beloved Jordan Pond House (see p. 685) started managing the inn and its restaurant, reviews have been overwhelmingly positive. The rooms are furnished in a simple summer-home style; some have clawfoot tubs, others have fireplaces or kitchenettes, but none have phones or TVs. (Also, importantly, less than half have ocean views.) There are four outbuildings scattered about the property, containing 17 cottage-like units, and these might be my first choice: they're more secluded, a bit more luxurious. Dinner in the airy, wooden-floored main dining room focuses on seafood—and now they also have the popovers that attract park visitors to Jordan Pond House.

15 Peabody Dr., Northeast Harbor. www.asticou.com. ✆ **207/276-3344.** 48 units. Main inn July–Aug $210–$350 double; May–June and Sept–Oct $140–$260 double; cottage units July–Aug $270–$390, May–June and Sept–Oct $195–$330. Rates include continental breakfast. Closed late Oct to mid-May. Some rooms accommodate pets. **Amenities:** Dining room; outdoor pool; concierge; room service; tennis court; free Wi-Fi.

The Claremont ★★ Early prints of the venerable Claremont show an austere, four-story wooden building overlooking Somes Sound from a grassy rise; it hasn't changed much since. The place offers classic New England grace. (It's somehow appropriate that one of New England's largest croquet tournaments is held here each August.) Most guest rooms are bright and airy, outfitted in antiques, old furniture, and modern bathrooms. There's also a set of 14 cottages of varied vintages and styles in the woods and on the water, all with fireplaces and kitchenettes; they sleep from two to seven people each. The dining room, **Xanthus ★**, offers fabulous views and a menu of lobster, crab cakes, fish, scallops, pork, and steaks.

22 Claremont Rd., Southwest Harbor. (From Southwest Harbor center, follow Clark Point Rd. to Claremont Rd. and turn left.) www.theclaremonthotel.com. ✆ **800/244-5036.** 44 units. July–Aug $312–$444 double or cottage; late May–June and Sept to mid-Oct $150–$312 double or cottage. Hotel room rates include breakfast (not cot-

tages). 3-night minimum in cottages. Closed mid-Oct to late May. **Amenities:** Dining room; lounge; babysitting; free bikes; library; croquet; rowboats; tennis court; free Wi-Fi.

Inn at Southwest ★   There's a late-19th-century feel to this mansard-roofed Victorian home, which thankfully stays spare rather than frilly. All guest rooms, named for Maine lighthouses, are outfitted simply in contemporary and antique furniture; all have ceiling fans and down comforters. Among the most pleasant rooms is Blue Hill Bay on the third floor, with its yellow-and-blue color scheme, big bathroom, sturdy oak bed and bureau, and glimpses of the harbor. The snug Owls Head room has a cool headboard made from a sturdy old door. Breakfasts give you good incentive to rise early: entrees could include Belgian waffles with raspberry sauce, poached pears, or blueberry French toast.

371 Main St., Southwest Harbor. www.innatsouthwest.com. © **207/244-3835.** 7 units. $115–$235 double. Rates include full breakfast. Closed Nov to mid-May. **Amenities:** Fire pit; free Wi-Fi.

Kingsleigh Inn ★★   In a 1904 Queen Anne–style home on Southwest Harbor's bustling Main Street, the Kingsleigh has long been a reliable place to bunk down in the area. Its living room features a wood-burning fireplace and fine art, while sitting and breakfast rooms offer further refuge. All units are outfitted with thoughtful touches like sound machines (to drown out the ambient "noise"), fresh flowers, wine glasses, heated bathroom floors, and thick robes. Flowery prints and wallpapers bedeck the rooms, most of which are small to moderate size, though a few have private decks. Three-course breakfasts are genuinely artistic—expect choices like asparagus frittata, local-spinach eggs Florentine, raspberry-stuffed French toast—always preceded by a shot of an esoteric juice (watermelon? celery, anyone?) and followed by dessert, believe it or not.

373 Main St., Southwest Harbor. www.kingsleighinn.com. © **207/244-5302.** 8 units. $160–$215 double; $265–$325 suite. Rates include full breakfast. 2-night minimum stay. Closed Nov–Mar. Children over 12 welcome. **Amenities:** Wine service; library; free Wi-Fi.

CAMPING IN ACADIA NATIONAL PARK

The National Park Service maintains two campgrounds on Mount Desert Island and another campground on the **Schoodic Peninsula,** to the north.

Both of the campgrounds on MDI are extremely popular; during July and August, expect both of them to fill up by early to midmorning. The more popular of the two is **Blackwoods ★★** (© **207/288-3274**), on the island's eastern side, with about 300 sites. To get there, follow Route 3 about 5 miles south out of Bar Harbor; the Island Explorer bus (see p. 668) stops here as well. Bikers and pedestrians have easy access to the loop road from the campground via a short trail. This campground has no public showers or electrical hookups, but an enterprising business just outside the campground entrance provides clean showers for a modest fee. Camping fees at Blackwoods are $30 per night from May through October, $15 per site in April and November.

The **Seawall** ★ (☎ 207/244-3600) campground is located over on the quieter, western half of the island, near the tiny fishing village of Bass Harbor (one of the Island Explorer shuttle bus lines also stops here). Seawall has about 215 sites, and it's a good base for cyclists or those wishing to explore several short coastal hikes within easy striking distance. However, it's quite a ways from Bar Harbor and Sand Beach on the other side of the island. Also, many of the sites involve a walk of a few dozen to a few hundred yards from where your car's parked; wheelbarrows are available to tote your stuff, but for families, it might not be the best choice. The campground is open mid-May through September. Camping fees at Seawall are $22 to $30 per night, depending on whether you want to drive directly to your site, or can pack a tent in for a distance of up to 300 yards. There are also no electrical or water hookups here.

Schoodic Woods Campground ★, a pristine 94-site campground in the park's mainland section, has an amphitheater, ranger programs, and a handful of secluded walk-in sites (some with terrific views of MDI's peaks across the water). Camping fees range from $22 for the hike-in sites to $40 for full electric/water RV hookups (open late-May to early Sept, reservations necessary in midsummer).

Advance **reservations** can be made for any of these campgrounds by calling ☎ 877/444-6777 between 10am and midnight (only until 10pm in winter), or by using the reservations system online at **www.recreation.gov**. An Acadia pass is also required for campground entry.

Where to Eat on Mount Desert Island

In addition to the selections listed below, you can get good local pizza at **Rosalie's** on Cottage Street (www.rosaliespizza.com; ☎ 207/288-5666); eat upstairs or down, or take out a pie to go. There's also a solid natural foods market, **A&B Naturals** (www.aandbnaturals.com; ☎ 207/288-8480) at 101 Cottage St., which has prepared foods and a good little cafe inside.

Mt. Desert Island Ice Cream ★, 7 Firefly Lane (www.mdiic.com; ☎ 207/460-5515), right beside the tourist office, is an institution. It gives all the appearances of being just another ho-hum scoop shop of the vanilla-chocolate-strawberry ilk, but there's little conventional about a place featuring gourmet concoctions spiked with tarragon, chili, and wasabi, among other flavors. (President Barack Obama sampled a coconut cone during a surprise 2010 visit.) There's another branch at 325 Main St. (and, for your trip home, one on Exchange Street in Portland).

BAR HARBOR
Expensive

Havana ★★★ LATINO/FUSION   Havana excited foodies all over Maine when it opened in 1999 in what was then a town of fried fish and baked haddock. The spare decor in an old storefront is as classy as anything you'll find in Boston, and the menu can hold its own against the big city, too—I've had a meal at Havana that I sometimes pause and reflect on, years later. Chef/owner Michael Boland's menu is inspired by Latino fare, which he melds nicely with

New American ideas. Appetizers are deceptively simple: appetizers of crab cakes with avocado mayo and corn salsa, duck empanadas, mussels with chorizo and sofrito. Entrees could include choices as adventurous as a lobster poached in butter served with a saffrony potato empanada; paella made with local lobsters and mussels; breast of duck with a blueberry glaze; chile rellenos stuffed with amazing barbecue pork; or lamb shanks braised with chili and pineapple. Then desserts skew simple again (see the pattern?): apple empanadas, caramel and cream, churros with caraway chocolate ice cream. The Obamas dined here the last time they swung through Bar Harbor; I bet the President and First Lady stop to think about their meal from time to time, too.

318 Main St. www.havanamaine.com. *ⓒ* **207/288-2822.** Main courses $25–$42. Daily 5–10pm. Winter/spring hours generally Tues–Sat 4:30–9:30pm. Some brief seasonal closures—call ahead. Reservations recommended.

Mache Bistro ★★ NEW AMERICAN   An old Bar Harbor standby that found its way into new digs in 2014, little Mache Bistro has developed a devoted local following. The old space was ticky-tack enough that it gave the place a sort of cult appeal, masking the kitchen's sophistication; the new one is sophisticated without being any less welcoming. Like its neighbor, McKay's, a couple blocks away (see below), the new Mache is a former residential home, and the handsome bar and copper and dark wood finishes don't make the place any less approachable than when it had plywood floors. Chef Kyle Yarborough's menu changes monthly; small plates could include crispy pork belly with fig pancetta, stuffed peppers with lobster goat cheese, or a wine-poached pear with Maytag blue cheese. Main courses, which have a little Southern flair, run to smoked duck confit, slow-roasted pork with chorizo and vegetables, grilled hanger steak with a blue cheese butter, or scallops with charred onion and caper relish.

321 Main St. www.machebistro.com. *ⓒ* **207/288-0447.** Small plates $7–$12; main courses $21–$32. Tues–Sat 5:30–9pm. Closed late Oct–early May. Reservations recommended.

McKay's Public House ★★ CLASSIC AMERICAN   If there were no other reason to like McKay's, the fact that it's open year-round would speak well for it. But there are plenty of other reasons, beginning with the fact that it's true to its name—this is a genuine public gathering place, and one of those spots in Bar Harbor where the line between locals and tourists pretty well dissolves. Part of that homey feel might come from the fact that it's literally an old Victorian home, with the fireplaces and wainscoting and shady porch that some family likely enjoyed back in the day. The atmosphere is somewhere between drinks-after-work and date night, the menu full of upscale pub food like a terrific lamb burger and steak frites, along with nicely trimmed rib-eyes and chops and some standby pastas. Get there early to snag a table on the beautifully landscaped patio—good Main Street people-watching from out there.

231 Main St. www.mckayspublichouse.com. *ⓒ* **207/288-2002.** Main courses $13–$32. Daily 5–9:30pm. Closed Nov. Reservations recommended during peak season.

Moderate

Café This Way ★★ ECLECTIC   Café This Way is the kind of place where they know how to do wonderful Asian and Mediterranean things with simple ingredients. It has the feel of a hip coffeehouse, yet it's much more airy and creative than that. Bookshelves line one wall, and there's a small bar tucked into a nook; oddly, they serve breakfast and dinner but no lunch. Breakfasts are excellent though mildly sinful—it's more like brunch. Go for the burritos, corned beef hash with eggs, a build-your-own benedict, or the calorific Café Monte Cristo: a French toast sandwich stuffed with fried eggs, ham, and cheddar cheese served with fries and syrup. Yikes. Dinners are equally appetizing, with tasty starters that might run to fingerling poutine with tomato-chile jam, grilled chunks of Cyprus cheese, or lobster spring rolls. The main-course offerings of the night could include anything from lobster cooked in sherry cream or stewed in spinach and Gruyere cheese to sea scallops in vinaigrette; grilled lamb and steaks; coconut Thai mussels; or tikka masala with local veggies. There's always a tasty vegetarian option, as well. Talk about eclectic.

14½ Mount Desert St. www.cafethisway.com. ☎ **207/288-4483.** Breakfast items $8–$12, dinner main courses $19–$29. Mid-Apr to Oct, Mon–Sat 7–11:30am; Sun 8am–1pm; dinner daily 5:30–9:30pm. Dinner reservations recommended.

Lompoc Cafe ★ AMERICAN/ECLECTIC   The Lompoc Cafe has a well-worn, neighborhood-bar feel to it—waiters and other workers from around Bar Harbor congregate here after-hours. The cafe consists of three sections: the original bar, a tidy beer garden just outside (try your hand at bocce), and a small and open barnlike structure at the garden's edge to handle the overflow. Most of the beers are local (ask for a sample before ordering a full glass of blueberry ale). Bar menus are normally yawn-inducing, but this one has some surprises—terrific mussels in broth, respectable shrimp and grits, a pho-like Vietnamese noodle bowl. There's also quite a little wine list, and some house cocktails like the blueberry-mint-and-rum Acadian. The outdoor tables are fun, and live music acts often play here.

36 Rodick St. www.lompoccafe.com. ☎ **207/288-9392.** Sandwiches and main courses $11–$21. Tues–Sun 4:30–9pm. Closed late Oct to mid-May. No reservations.

Inexpensive

Jordan's Restaurant ★ DINER   This unpretentious breakfast-and-lunch joint has been dishing up filling fare since 1976, and offers a glimpse of the old Bar Harbor. It's a popular haunt of local working folks and retirees, but staff are also friendly to tourists. Diners can settle into a pine booth or at a laminated table and order off the placemat menu, choosing from basic fare such as grilled cheese sandwiches with tomato or slim burgers. The soups and chowders are all homemade, and there are some crab dishes (the only lobster's in an omelet, on a salad, or on a roll—no shore dinner here). But breakfast is the star, with a broad selection of three-egg omelets, muffins, and pancakes made with plenty of those great wild Maine blueberries (best when they're in season). With its atmosphere of "seniors at coffee klatch" and its rock-bottom prices, this is *not* a gourmet experience, but fans of big breakfasts, Americana-style cuisine, and classic diners will enjoy it.

80 Cottage St. www.jordanswildblueberry.com. © **207/288-3586.** Breakfast and lunch items $5–$13. Daily 5am–2pm. Closed late Nov–Mar.

ACADIA NATIONAL PARK

Jordan Pond House ★★ AMERICAN   The secret to the Jordan Pond House? Location, location, location. The restaurant traces its roots from 1847, when a farm was established on this picturesque property at the southern tip of Jordan Pond looking north toward **The Bubbles,** a pair of glacially sculpted mounds. In 1979, the original structure and its birch-bark dining room were destroyed by fire. A more modern, two-level dining room was built in its place—less charm, but it still has one of the island's best dining locations, on a nice lawn spread out before the pond. Afternoon tea with popovers and jam is a hallowed tradition here, though you can (and should) get them anytime. The lobster stew is expensive but very good. Dinners include classic entrees like New York strip steak, steamed lobster, pasta, and lobster stew.

Park Loop Rd. (near Seal Harbor). www.jordanpondhouse.com. © **207/276-3316.** Dinner reservations recommended. Afternoon tea $11, sandwiches $12–$20, Main courses $15–$27. Mid-May to late Oct daily 11am–9pm.

AROUND THE ISLAND

In addition to the choices listed here, you'll find ice-cream, pizza, sandwich, and takeout-seafood shops scattered about the island. Even most of the village grocery stores offer good prepared sandwiches or meals.

Beal's Lobster Pound ★★ SEAFOOD   Some says Beal's is among the best lobster shacks in Maine, and it's certainly got the right atmosphere: Creaky picnic tables sit on a plain concrete pier overlooking a working-class harbor, right next to a Coast Guard base. (Don't wear a jacket and tie.) You go inside to pick out lobster from a tank, pay by the pound, choose some side dishes (corn on the cob, slaw, steamed clams), then pop coins into a soda machine outside while you wait for your number to be called. The food will arrive on Styrofoam and paper plates, as it should. There's also a takeout window across the deck serving fries, fried clams, and fried fish (sensing a theme?), plus ice cream.

182 Clark Point Rd., Southwest Harbor. www.bealslobster.com. © **207/244-3202**. Lobsters market priced. Summer daily 11am–9pm; after Labor Day 9am–5pm. Closed Columbus Day–Memorial Day.

The Burning Tree ★★ SEAFOOD   Located on a busy straightaway of Route 3 between Bar Harbor and Otter Creek, The Burning Tree is an easy restaurant to blow right past; that would be a mistake. This low-key and surprisingly elegant place serves some of the best and freshest seafood dinners on the island, with New American twists. Some of the produce and herbs comes from the restaurant's own gardens, while the rest of the ingredients are bought locally whenever possible. Everything's prepared with imagination and skill—expect unusual preparations like a New Orleans–style lobster,

lobster fritters (great idea), sage and almond flounder, and Swiss chard leaves stuffed with scallop mousse, plus old standards like grilled salmon and halibut (served with inventive and tasty sauces). Don't miss the house cocktails, which use local fruits and berries when possible.

69 Otter Creek Dr., Otter Creek. ℂ **207/288-9331.** Main courses $19–$26. Mid-June–Columbus Day Wed–Mon 5–10pm. Closed Columbus Day to mid-May. Reservations recommended.

Coda ★★ NEW AMERICAN/TAPAS   Southwest Harbor's newest restaurant was built from the ground up in 2015 and has an idiosyncratic mission: to be the live-music mecca of this town of 1,800 people, in addition to serving farm-to-table shareable plates. So the few tables and long bar in the rustic, barnlike room are oriented towards a small stage (there's a great patio, too). The music skews rootsy and globally influenced, and so does the menu. You might share a spaetzle and cheese, braised beef cheeks with bourbon jelly, or an inspired pairing of lobster and grits. Chef Carter Light takes the DIY ethos seriously: smokes his own sausages, makes head cheese from the head of a locally reared pig, that sort of thing. Somebody behind the bar takes the whiskey list seriously. All in all, a fun and tasty hangout that wouldn't feel out of place in some western mountain town.

18 Village Green Way, Southwest Harbor. www.codasouthwestharbor.com. ℂ **207/244-8133.** Small plates $10–$17. Tues–Sat 5–9pm; Sun 6–9:30pm. Closed late Oct–Jan. Inquire about winter hours, which are subject to change. Reservations recommended weekends.

XYZ ★★ MEXICAN   This place is a true "foodie find." You'd be forgiven for doubting the authenticity of the Mexican food served in this shacklike bungalow a stone's throw from the crashing north Atlantic off Seawall Lane—yet it serves *very* authentic Mexican cuisine. Owners Janet Strong and Bob Hoyt are well-traveled in the Mexican states of Xalapa, Yucatán, and Zacatecas (thus the restaurant's acronym). No burritos here; this is campesino chow, a bit elevated. Expect lots of pork and chicken dishes and mole sauces, with a pile of local lettuce and corn tortillas on the side. The *sopa de aguacate*, chilled avocado soup with just a hint of tequila and chiles, is a must as an appetizer. Reservations are a must, too, as the place only seats a few dozen.

411 Main St., Southwest Harbor. www.xyzmaine.com. ℂ **207/244-5221.** Main courses $26. Mon–Sat 5:30–9pm. (Call first; hours can vary.) Closed Columbus Day–late June. Late season hours can be unpredictable (call ahead). Reservations recommended.

WESTERN MAINE ★

Bethel: 70 miles NW of Portland; 135 miles NE of Concord, NH; 180 miles N of Boston

Maine's western mountains make up a rugged, brawny region that stretches northeast between the White Mountains and the Carrabassett Valley. Yes, the Whites are higher, and the Maine coast is a lot more picture-postcard and convenient for travelers. But you can find natural wonders here in western Maine that those other places can't touch: huge azure lakes and sparkling little ponds; forests thick with spruce and fir; mossy, mossy woods (to borrow from Thoreau); and more mountains and foothills than you could tramp through in a lifetime.

Bethel ★★

Bethel was once a sleepy resort town with one of those family-oriented ski areas that seemed destined for mothballs. But a brash entrepreneur took over **Sunday River** ski area (7 miles north of town) in 1980 and spent the '80s and '90s transforming it into what it is today; one of New England's largest, most vibrant, and challenging ski destinations.

With the rise of Sunday River, the sturdy town of Bethel itself has become a destination, but without taking on the artificial, packaged flavor of many other ski towns (there are no outlet malls here). This village is still defined by the stoic buildings of the respected Gould Academy prep school; a broad, green village common; and the Bethel Inn, a sprawling, old-fashioned resort that's managed to stay ahead of the tide by adding condos without ever losing its pleasant, timeworn character or lovely appearance.

ESSENTIALS

ARRIVING   Downtown Bethel is a simple turnoff from the intersection of two busy roads, routes 26 and 2. Get there from Portland or Boston via the Maine Turnpike (I-95), taking exit 63 ("Gray") and heading west on Route 26 for about an hour. From New Hampshire, drive east of Gorham on Route 2 for 20 to 30 minutes.

In fall and winter, there's a helpful free shuttle called the **Mountain Explorer** ★ (www.mountainexplorer.org; *©* **800/393-9335**), which runs between downtown Bethel and the ski resorts' various lodges about once per hour. The bus operates daily from late December through mid-March, weekends only through mid-April. See the website for the detailed schedule.

VISITOR INFORMATION   The **Bethel Area Chamber of Commerce** (www.bethelmaine.com; *©* **800/442-5826** or 207/824-2282) has offices at 30 Cross Street (also referred to as Station Place), behind the movie theater. It's open Monday to Saturday from 9am to 5pm and Sunday from 9am to 3pm.

DOWNHILL SKIING

Sunday River Ski Resort ★★★   Sunday River is recognized as one of the best and most family-friendly ski mountains in New England with great, well-maintained terrain. Unlike ski areas that developed around a single tall peak, Sunday River expanded along an undulating ridge 3 miles wide that encompasses *eight* peaks—so simply traversing the resort, stitching a run together via the various chairlift rides, can take an hour or more. As a result, you're rarely bored. The descents offer something for everyone, from deviously steep and bumpy runs to wide, wonderful intermediate trails. Sunday River is also blessed with plenty of river water for snowmaking and makes tons of the fluffy stuff. The superb skiing conditions are, alas, offset by an uninspiring base area; the lodges and condos here tend to be on the dull side,

A scenic drive THROUGH GRAFTON NOTCH

The 33-mile drive from Bethel through **Grafton Notch State Park ★★**, which straddles Route 26 as it angles northwest into New Hampshire, is one of my favorites in Maine. It's both picturesque and dramatic, and unlike the Kancamagus Highway over in New Hampshire, it's never stop-and-go.

You begin by passing through fertile farmlands in a broad river valley before ascending through bristly forests to a glacial notch hemmed in by rough, gray cliffs on the hillsides above. Foreboding **Old Speck Mountain ★★** towers to the south; views of **Lake Umbagog ★★** open to the north as you continue into New Hampshire. The foliage is excellent in early October most years. Public access to the park consists of a handful of roadside parking lots near scenic areas. The best of the bunch is **Screw Auger Falls ★**, where the Bear River drops through several small cascades before tumbling dramatically into a narrow, corkscrewing gorge carved long ago by glacial runoff through granite bedrock. Picnic tables dot the forested banks upriver of the falls, and kids seem inexorably drawn to splash and swim in the smaller pools on warm days.

This is as good a state park as you'll find in northern New England, yet it's incredibly affordable. From mid-May through mid-October, access to the 3,000-acre park costs $4 per nonresident ($1 for kids and seniors); get a pass at the self-pay station in any of the parking lots.

Note that there are no services along the way; gas up and buy food in Bethel. This route attracts few crowds, but it's popular with thoroughgoing Canadian tourists *and* Canadian logging rigs loaded up with Maine timber (drive carefully and yield the road if necessary) headed for the Maine coast or I-95.

architecturally, and the nightlife doesn't measure up to, say, Aspen or even nearby Sugarloaf (see "Where to Dine," below). Anyway, you won't care, because the trails here are usually so good that they're often crowded all weekend even though there isn't a town or city of significant size for over an hour in any direction. Come on a weekday, though, and you may have the place to yourself. There's good night skiing, with good discounts to match.

Skiway Rd., Newry (Turn off rtes. 2/5/26 at brewpub onto Sunday River Rd.; after 2½ miles, bear left onto Skiway Rd.). www.sundayriver.com. ⓒ **800/543-2754.** Day lift tickets $105 adults; discounts for seniors, youths, night skiing, and advance purchase.

OTHER OUTDOOR ACTIVITIES

BIKING An easy, scenic route for touring cycles follows winding **Sunday River Road ★** several miles into the foothills of the Mahoosuc mountain range. Start at the Sunday River ski resort (see above); follow the same directions, but continue past the resort and west alongside the river through a tranquil scene marked by a little cemetery and a covered bridge. Eventually, you head into forested hills (the road turns to dirt). This dead-end road is lightly traveled beyond the resort, and views from the valley are rewarding throughout. Ask locally, or consult a local cyclists' hangout (such those listed below) for a map.

Serious mountain bikers should head for the **Sunday River Mountain Bike Park** ★★ (www.sundayriver.com; ⓒ **800/543-2754**) at the ski area, with dozens of lift-accessed trails of every skill level covering some 25 miles open during summer and fall weekends. Experienced riders will enjoy taking their bikes by chairlift to the summit, then careening back down on service roads and ski trails. Visit the South Ridge Lodge first for your rental, and then hit the slopes. An adult trail pass costs $10 per day; an adult pass including all-day chairlift rides costs $39 (about half-price for kids 12 and under). Cycle rentals ($80/day, plus $10 for a helmet) are also available. The park is open from spring through Labor Day, Thursday through Sunday, then Friday through Sunday until early October.

Families and beginning mountain bikers might hit the nine miles of gentle trail at **Bethel Village Trails** ★ (www.mahoosucpathways.org; ⓒ **207/200-8240**), a mostly wooded network that begins at **The Bethel Inn Resort** (see p. 690) and here and there crosses the resort's golf course. **Barker Mountain Bikes** (www.barkermountainbikes.com; ⓒ **207/824-0100**) rents mountain bikes ($35–$65 per day) and fat bikes ($35 per day, appropriate for road or trail) from the shop at 53 Mayville Road (Route 2). In the winter, Barker Mountain rents fat bikes right from the Bethel Inn Resort. No shop in town rents skinny-tire road bikes, but Sunday River rents motor-assisted e-bikes ($35 for a half-day) out of the South Ridge Lodge.

BOATING Canoe/kayak/SUP rentals and shuttles for exploring the Androscoggin River can be arranged by **Bethel Outdoor Adventure** ★ (www.betheloutdooradventure.com; ⓒ **207/824-4224**), on Route 2. You can also hire a guide here to take you out by canoe or kayak. If idly floating is more your speed, tube rentals are available as well.

GOLF Bethel has two excellent courses. The **Bethel Inn Resort**'s course ★ (www.bethelinn.com; ⓒ **207/824-2175**) is an unusually scenic 18-hole golf course right next to the inn; the course is somewhat flat but undeniably attractive. Greens fees for 18 holes are $50 per person; twilight rates are about half-price. Clubs and golf carts can be rented, and the club also has a driving range. Tee times are not mandatory, but they're strongly recommended in high season, which includes fall, when the setting borders on the spectacular. The course is open early May through late October, weather permitting.

The ski resort's **Sunday River Country Club** ★★ (www.sundayrivergolfclub.com; ⓒ **207/824-4653**) has its own obviously splendid views and some lovely mountainside golfing. It's expensive: Greens fees range from $70 to $120 per person (cart included and required). Twilight rates are a little less than half, though.

HIKING The **Appalachian Trail** ★★★ crosses the Mahoosuc Range northwest of Bethel. Many who have hiked the entire 2,000-mile trail say this stretch is both the most demanding and the most strangely beautiful. The trail doesn't forgive here; it gives up switchbacks in favor of sheer, rocky ascents and descents. (It's also hard to find water along this part of the trail during the high summer months.) Still, it's worth the effort for serious hikers.

One stretch of the trail crosses **Old Speck Mountain** ★★, which, at 4,170 feet, is (surprisingly) Maine's third-highest peak. Even weekend walkers can tackle this hike. Look for the well-signed parking lot where Route 26 intersects the trail to the state park; park, pay, strap on boots (some parts are muddy), and join the A.T. right from the parking lot. In just .1 mile, you'll intersect the Eyebrow Trail—this moderately difficult side trail ascends an 800-foot cliff called The Eyebrow, but don't walk it if you're afraid of heights. Otherwise, stay on the main trail and continue up past several great notch overlooks, over rushing streams and past mild cascades, and into increasing views of the valley foliage. The summit is wooded, so there are no views from the top, but you can keep walking down into a bowl containing **Old Speck Lake** and a primitive campsite. (I don't usually recommend this, though, because the total walking time might leave you out on the trail after dark; stop at the summit, unless you're camping overnight at the lake.)

You can also take a walk on the A.T. up **Baldpate Mountain** ★, the cliff whose face and top show patches of open ledge right across Route 26 from Old Speck, on the way to distant Mount Katahdin (p. 695). The trail continues across the highway. Baldpate is higher than you might think: Its summit is only about 400 feet lower than Old Speck's. Check trail books if you're trying to decide which trail to hike. The Appalachian Mountain Club's *Maine Mountain Guide* contains information about these and other area walks; pick up a copy before arriving in the Notch—shops in Bethel should carry it—if you're a serious walker.

WHERE TO STAY IN & AROUND BETHEL

Just outside Grafton State Park's boundaries, there's camping at the **Grafton Notch Campground** (www.campgrafton.com; ✆ **207/824-2292**) for $28 per night. It's not part of the park, but privately owned. Find it on the west (left) side of Route 26, a mile or two before the entrance to the park. There's also a less-wild campground on Route 2 at the headquarters of **Bethel Outdoor Adventure** (www.betheloutdooradventure.com; ✆ **800/533-3607** or 207/824-4224). RVs and tenters are both welcome; call for current site rates.

The Bethel Inn Resort A classic, old-fashioned resort set on 200 acres right in the village, Bethel's signature inn has a quiet and settled air—appropriate, as it was built to house the patients of one Dr. John Gehring, who put Bethel on the map by treating nervous disorders here through a regimen of healthy country living. (The town was once known as "the resting place of Harvard" for the legions of faculty who were treated here.) The rambling white inn's rooms are quainter than spacious—a bit dated, even. Rooms and suites added to an outbuilding in the late 1990s are more modern, with amenities like Jacuzzis and air-conditioning (which standard rooms in the main inn still lack). You might also be placed in the row of townhouse units down by the golf course. Some spa services are available; there's a fitness center on the grounds; and the cross-country skiing at **Bethel Village Trails** ★ and **golf**

course (see above) are scenic. There are sexier places to stay around Bethel, but it's hard to beat this resort's sense of history and backdoor access to outdoor rec.

21 Broad St. (on the Common), Bethel. www.bethelinn.com. © **800/654-0125** or 207/824-2175. 150 units. Summer $165–$235 double, $225–$265 suites, $285–$445 townhouses; winter $205–$454 double, $265–$305 suites, $325–$465 townhouses. Rates include breakfast, MAP rates available. 2- to 3-night minimum stay ski season and summer weekends. Dogs accepted ($20 per night). **Amenities:** 2 restaurants; bar; babysitting; golf course; health club; Jacuzzi; heated outdoor pool; sauna; tennis court; watersports equipment/rentals; Wi-Fi (free, if spotty).

Jordan Hotel ★★ At the far western edge of Sunday River's territory, in the stunning Jordan Bowl basin, this hotel feels miles away from the rest of the resort, which it is—even staff joke about its remoteness. A modern, sprawling hotel, it manages to be family-friendly, clean, and shipshape enough, and is a positively great hotel for (experienced) skiers who want to ski out the door and be first on untracked slopes every morning. Owing to the quirky terrain, parking is inconvenient; you might have to walk quite a long distance to your room (opt for the valet parking). Rooms are simply furnished in a durable condo style, many quite spacious and most with balconies and/or washers and dryers; all now have custom-made Boyne beds, too. This hotel has become a popular destination for ski-happy families—possibly because it has day care and kitchenettes—so it wouldn't be the best choice in town for a couple seeking a quiet, romantic getaway. Otherwise, it's very good. The two hotel restaurants serve food that's a notch above ski-hill pub fare.

27 Grand Cir., Newry. www.sundayriver.com. © **800/543-2754** or 207/824-5300. 187 units. Ski season $179–$239 double, $279–$489 suite; rest of year $159–$179 double, $209–$449 suite. **Amenities:** 2 restaurants; babysitting; children's center; concierge; exercise room; Jacuzzi; outdoor pool; limited room service; sauna; spa; steam room; Wi-Fi (free).

The Victoria Inn ★★ Built in 1895 and restored periodically since, the Victoria hangs on to its antique lighting fixtures, period furniture, and the original, formidable oak doors. It's a good sleeper pick when you want to get away from resortville. Guest rooms have a William Morris feel, with patterned, flowery wallpaper, canopy-like beds, and handmade duvet covers. (If you enjoy sleek, modern hotel rooms, skip this place.) Room no. 1 is a luxurious master suite with a turret window and sizable bathroom, but most intriguing are the three "loft" rooms in the attached carriage house, each with Jacuzzis and soaring ceilings revealing some of the building's rugged original beams. These suites have small second-story sleeping lofts and sleep up to eight guests each.

32 Main St., Bethel. www.thevictoria-inn.com. © **888/774-1235** or 207/824-8060. 14 units. $139–$199 double and suite. Rates include full breakfast. 2-night minimum stay Sat–Sun and holidays. Pets sometimes accepted ($30 per night). **Amenities:** Restaurant; Wi-Fi (free).

13

MAINE | Western Maine

WHERE TO EAT IN & AROUND BETHEL

The **Sunday River** ski resort offers more than a dozen different dining experiences at last count, including comfort food in a faux-rustic dining room at **Camp,** the **Foggy Goggle** (a nightspot), and the **Mountain Room** for fine dining, a spin-off of a chain of popular Portland eateries.

There's also an excellent little natural-foods store, the **Good Food Store ★** (www.goodfoodbethel.com; ℘ **207/824-3754**), on Route 2 west of downtown Bethel but before the turnoffs to Sunday River and Grafton Notch. It's very convenient for grabbing a bite pre-hike or post-ski; the local beers, baked goods, ice creams, produce, meats, and other items are excellent (more importantly, its yard plays host to **Smokin' Good BBQ**—see below).

Smokin' Good BBQ ★★ BARBECUE   The little orange food truck outside Bethel's natural food store ain't much to look at, but that smoker sitting next to the thing is magic. Pulled pork and chicken, brisket, hot links, incredible ribs—you were not expecting to find barbecue this good in a Maine ski town. Folks line the picnic tables in summer (and, to a lesser extent, in winter) for a paper takeout tray heavy with baked beans, corn bread, and other fixings. This place inspires pilgrimages among Maine foodies.

212 Mayville Rd., Bethel. www.smokingoodbarbecue.com. ℘ **207/824-4744.** Main courses $8–$19. Fri–Sun 11:30am–7:30pm, sporadically on weekdays (call ahead). Closed mid-Apr to mid-May and mid-Oct to mid-Nov.

Sunday River Brewing Company ★ BREWPUB   This cavernous brewpub, on prime real estate at the corner of Route 2 and the Sunday River access road, has pool tables and fireplaces and an outdoor fire pit, and it's a good choice if your objective is to quaff locally brewed ales in a setting that's family friendly, if a little raucous on weekend evenings. There's better beer in Maine, but the menu is vast and the food (burgers, nachos, wings, lobster rolls, pasta, hot dogs, pork sandwiches) is simple, tasty, and affordable.

29 Sunday River Rd. (at Route 2), Bethel. www.sundayriverbrewpub.com. ℘ **207/824-4253.** Main courses $10–$24. Daily 6am–11:30pm.

BAXTER STATE PARK ★★★ & ENVIRONS

Baxter State Park: 85 miles N of Bangor, 216 miles NE of Portland

Baxter State Park is one of Maine's crown jewels, even more spectacular in some ways than Acadia National Park. This 200,000-plus-acre park in the remote north-central part of the state is unlike any other state park in New England—don't look for fancy bathhouses or groomed picnic areas (or running water in winter). When you enter Baxter State Park, you're entering near-wilderness.

Former Maine governor and philanthropist Percival Baxter single-handedly created this park, using his inheritance and investment profits to buy up the land and donate it to the state in 1930. Baxter stipulated that it remain "forever wild," and caretakers have done a great job fulfilling his wishes: You won't find any paved roads or electrical hookups at the campgrounds, and strict vehicle-size restrictions keep all RVs out, too. You *will* find rugged backcountry and remote lakes. You'll also find **Mount Katahdin,** a granite monolith that rises above all the sparkling lakes and boreal forests around it.

To the east lies **Katahdin Woods and Waters National Monument ★,** established in 2016, which adds another 80,000-plus acres to the North Woods wildland recreation complex. Access to the monument is still on the hairy side—you'll want a high-clearance vehicle—but the National Park Service continues to add infrastructure and interpretive elements (signage, campsite improvements, maybe front-country boardwalks) with each passing year. In the meantime, there's excellent hiking, paddling, and mountain biking to be had on the existing trail system (and something to be said for getting there before the crowds do).

Essentials

ARRIVING

Baxter State Park is 85 miles farther north past the city of Bangor, and the local tourism office says it takes about 5½ hours to drive here from Boston, about 10 hours from New York. To find the park, take I-95 to Medway (exit 244), then head west 11 miles on Route 11/157 to the mill town of Millinocket, the last major stop for supplies. Go through town and follow signs to Baxter State Park.

Another, lesser-used entrance is in the park's northeast corner. Follow I-95 to exit 259, and then take Route 11 north through Patten and west on Route 159 to the park. On the way, you'll pass signs for the two entrances to Katahdin Woods and Waters National Monument—the southern entrance is about 12 miles west of tiny **Sherman,** the north a mile-and-half before the Baxter north entrance gate.

The speed limit throughout Baxter is 20mph, and neither motorcycles nor ATVs are allowed inside its boundaries. (No pets are allowed inside, either, though they're welcome in the monument.)

VISITOR INFORMATION

Baxter State Park provides maps and information from its park headquarters at 64 Balsam Dr. in Millinocket (www.baxterstateparkauthority.com; ✆ **207/ 723-5140**). Note that no pets are allowed into the park. Both there and at the monument, all trash you generate must be brought back out. You can also find maps and info at the **National Park Service welcome centers** in Millinocket, at 20 Penobscot Ave. (www.nps.gov/kaww; ✆ **207/456-6001**), and, in summer only, at the **Patten Lumbermen's Museum,** at 61 Shin Pond Rd. in Patten (www.lumbermensmuseum.org; ✆ **207/528-2650**).

For information on canoeing and camping *outside* of Baxter State Park or Katahdin Woods and Waters National Monument, contact **North Maine Woods, Inc.** (www.northmainewoods.org; ✆ **207/435-6213**), the consortium of paper companies, other landowners, and concerned individuals that controls and manages recreational access to private parcels of the Maine woods.

A few dozen black bears dwell in Baxter State Park, and while they're not interested in eating you, they do get ornery when disturbed (it's a mama-bear protective thing). And they get *very* hungry at night. The park has published the following tips to help you keep a safe distance from the bears:

o Put food and anything else with an odor (toothpaste, repellant, soap, deodorant, perfume) **in a sealed bag or container** and keep it in your car.

o If you're camping in the backcountry without a car, put all your food, dinner leftovers, and other "smelly" things in a bag and **hang it between two trees** (far from your tent, not close to it) so that a bear can't reach it easily.

o *Never* keep food **inside your tent.**

o **Take all trash** with you from the campsite when you check out.

o **Don't toss food** on the trail.

o Finally, do I really need to say this? **Do not feed the bears,** or any other animals in the park, for that matter; they might bite the hands that feed them.

For help in finding cottages, rentals, and tour outfitters in the region, contact the **Katahdin Area Chamber of Commerce,** 1029 Central St., Millinocket (www.katahdinmaine.com; ℭ 207/723-4443), open weekdays 9am to 1pm.

PARK FEES Baxter State Park visitors driving cars with out-of-state license plates into the park are charged a flat fee of $15 per car per day. (It's free for Maine residents, as well as to any occupants of a rental car bearing Maine plates.) This fee is charged only once per stay if you're coming to camp; otherwise, you need to pay each day you enter the park. You can cut your costs by buying a **seasonal pass** for $40 at the gate. The national monument charges no entrance fee.

Outdoor Activities
CANOEING

The state's premier canoe trip is the **Allagash River ★★**, starting west of Baxter State Park and running northward for nearly 100 miles, finishing at the village of Allagash. The **Allagash Wilderness Waterway** (www.maine.gov/dacf/parks/water_activities; ℭ 207/941-4014) was the first state-designated wild and scenic river in the country, protected from development since 1970. Most travelers spend between 7 and 10 days making the trip from Chamberlain Lake to Allagash. The trip begins on a chain of lakes involving light portaging. At Churchill Dam, a stretch of Class I to II white water runs for about 9 miles, and then it's back to lakes and a mix of flat water and mild rapids. Toward the end, there's a longish portage (about 450 ft.) around picturesque Allagash Falls before finishing up above the village of Allagash. About 80 simple campsites are scattered along the route; most have outhouses, fire rings, and picnic tables. There's a small nightly fee to use them.

Whereas you need a week to paddle the Allagash, the **East Branch of the Penobscot ★**, along the eastern edge of the Katahdin Woods and Waters National Monument, is another of Maine's classic river trips and a fine shorter alternative. It's a 3-day paddle (26 river miles) from Grand Lake Matagamon near the north entrance to where the river meets the monument's south entrance ford at Whetstone Falls. The first day involves multiple short portages over wild-tumbling rapids and falls; after that, the river smooths out for a mellow 2-day float and chance to spot moose, deer, eagles, and maybe even an elusive lynx. Great fishing for native brook trout, too. About a dozen riverside campsites (free, first-come-first-serve) allow you to break up the trip in a bunch of different ways. Nearby **Bowlin Camps Lodge** in Patten (www. bowlincamps.com; © **207/267-0884**) offers guided trips and shuttles.

HIKING

BAXTER STATE PARK   With 180 miles of maintained backcountry trails and 46 peaks (including 18 that are higher than 3,000 ft.), Baxter State Park is a serious destination for serious hikers. The most imposing peak is 5,267-foot **Mount Katahdin ★★★**, the northern terminus of the **Appalachian Trail**. Allow at least 8 hours for the round trip ascent up Mount Katahdin, and abandon your plans if the weather takes a turn for the worse while you're en route. Katahdin trails close to day hikers by early morning in peak season, once the trailhead parking lots fill—non-residents can (and must) make a $5 parking reservation up to two weeks before their hike. The two-week window does not apply to Maine residents, who can book any date in the summer as soon as reservations open in April.

Some of the most popular routes depart from **Roaring Brook Campground.** Hikers can first ascend to dramatic **Chimney Pond,** set like a jewel in a glacial cirque, then continue upward toward Katahdin's summit via one of two trails. (The **Saddle Trail** is the most forgiving, the **Cathedral Trail ★** the most dramatic.) The descent begins along the aptly named **Knife Edge,** a narrow, rocky spine between Baxter Peak and Pamola Peak. Do not take this trail if you are afraid of heights: In spots, the trail narrows to 2 or 3 feet with a drop of hundreds of feet on either side. Obviously, it's also not the spot to be if high winds move in or thunderstorms are threatening. From the Knife Edge, the trail follows a long and mostly gentle ridge back down to Roaring Brook.

Katahdin draws the biggest crowds, but the park also maintains numerous other trails where you'll find more solitude and wildlife than on the main peak. One pleasant day hike is to the summit of **South Turner Mountain,** which offers wonderful views across to Mount Katahdin and blueberries for picking (in late summer). This trail departs from Roaring Brook Campground, and requires about 3 to 4 hours for a round trip. To the north, more good hikes begin at the **South Branch Pond Campground.** My advice? Talk to rangers and buy a trail map at park headquarters first.

KATAHDIN WOODS & WATERS   Shorter day hikes are the order of the day at the national monument. Two of the best spur off of the scenic **Katahdin Loop Road** in the southwest corner of the monument. A 4-mile out-and-back hike up the little granite hump of **Barnard Mountain** shows off some pretty exposed ledges as you ascend the switchbacks. The 9-mile out-and-back hike to the 1,964-foot summit of **Deasey Mountain** begins an easy ford off the Loop Road, climbs steeply past a massive erratic boulder and through some old-growth woods, then culminates with terrific views of Katahdin's eastern face.

WHITEWATER RAFTING

One unique way to view Mount Katahdin is by rafting the west branch of the Penobscot River. Flowing along the park's southern border, this wild river has some of the most technically challenging white water in the East. At least a dozen rafting companies take trips on the Penobscot, with prices around $90 to $115 per person, including a lunch. The trade group **Raft Maine** (www. raftmaine.com; © **800/723-8633**) can connect you to one of its member outfitters. Among the better-run outfitters in the area is **New England Outdoor Center** (www.neoc.com; © **800/766-7238**), on the river southeast of Millinocket. An anchor of the region's outdoor-recreation ecosystem, NEOC offers trips and experiences of every kind in all seasons—guided fishing, moose-spotting, and photography tours, rafting trips, even its own groomed ski trails come winter—and has a good restaurant and a range of lodgings (see p. 697).

Camping

Baxter State Park has eight campgrounds accessible by car, and two more backcountry camping areas that must be walked into; most are open from mid-May until mid-October. Don't count on finding a spot if you show up without reservations in the summer; the park starts processing requests on a first-come, first-served basis the first week in January, and dozens of die-hard campers traditionally spend a cold night outside headquarters to secure the best spots. Call well in advance (as in, during the previous year) for the forms to mail in. The cost of camping inside the park ranges from $15 to $32 per site (a night in a bunkhouse is $12 per person per night), while entire cabins can be rented for from $57 to $135. Reservations can be made by mail, in person at the headquarters in Millinocket (see p. 693), or (sometimes) by phone, though phone inquiries are *only* taken less than 14 days from arrival. Don't call them about any other dates. And remember: **They don't accept credit cards inside the park,** only when reserving by mail or online ahead of time.

North Maine Woods, Inc. (see p. 693) maintains a small network of primitive campsites on its 2-million-acre holdings. While you may have to drive through massive clear-cuts to reach them, some are positioned on secluded coves or picturesque points. A map showing logging-road access and campsite locations is available for a small fee plus postage from the North Maine Woods headquarters. Daily camping fees are minimal, though you must also pay an access fee to the lands.

There are a few drive-in campsites (notice I'm not saying campgrounds) at the **Katahdin Woods and Waters National Monument,** but they are still underdeveloped and not for the faint of heart—little more than fire pits and, at one site, a pit latrine. They're free, though, first-come-first-served, and noted on the park map.

Where to Stay & Eat in the Katahdin Area

Lodging and dining are both pretty bare-bones around the Katahdin region, where a sprinkle of B&Bs, lodges, hunting camps, and (often pretty run-down) roadside motels make up the bulk of your lodging options. On the upside, more and more folks around greater Millinocket are availing themselves of Airbnb and other online rental platforms, where you can often find super-affordable rentals and cabins.

On Grand Lake Road, which leads to both parks' north entrances, **Matagamon Wilderness Campground and Cabins** (www.matagamon.com; ✆ 207/446-4635) has spacious riverside campsites, six rustic cabins, a small family restaurant, and a camp store (it's a clutch beer and/or ice cream stop when leaving the park). **Shin Pond Village** (www.shinpond.com; ✆ 207/528-2900) is a similar camp-lodge-store-restaurant complex on Route 11, between Patten and the north entrances.

The only place in the Katahdin region that can fairly be described as don't-miss dining as the **Appalachian Trail Café** ★ in Millinocket, at 210 Penobscot Ave. (✆ **207/723-6720**), which has less to do with the hearty breakfasts and lunches than the vibe—chatty locals mingling with jubilant thru-hikers just off the Appalachian Trail (their names, in Sharpie, adorn the café's walls and ceiling). This is a great place to pick up tips on the day's hiking/fishing/exploring itinerary.

Mt. Chase Lodge ★

Mike and Lindsay Downing took over this classic sporting lodge in 2015 (Lindsay's parents ran it for decades before), and they've set about turning it into the most pleasant basecamp in these parts. The main lodge and its eight rooms share a definite hunting camp vibe (indeed, hunters make up a lot of the clientele), with mounted animal heads on the wall, quilted bedspreads, plank wood walls, and furnishings made out of birch stumps. Rooms are cozy and share hallway bathrooms, except for #8, which has its own bathroom. In the Maine hunting lodge style—and because meals are included—lodge rates are per person. The five cabins (plus a yurt) sleep three to eight people and have the same rustic vibe. All have full bathrooms; some have full kitchens. The Downings' deep knowledge of the area is a huge selling point—they've been recreating at the adjacent national monument since before anybody even proposed a national monument. And they do a terrific job in the **dining room,** serving up family-style breakfasts and dinners. Dinners are open to non-guests by reservation and might include pan-seared salmon with blueberry chutney or roast pork loin with apples, onions and fennel, along with some of Mike's beautiful (and tasty) sourdough breads.

1517 Shin Pond Rd., Mount Chase. www.mtchaselodge.com. ✆ **207/528-2183.** 13 units. $98–$150 doubles; $139–$189 cabins. Rates include full breakfast and dinner. 2-night minimum stay in cabins. Cabins accommodate pets ($10/night fee). **Amenities:** Restaurant; lounge; free kayaks; free Wi-Fi in common areas.

New England Outdoor Center ★

One of the region's top outfitters (see p. 696), NEOC also offers a wide range of cabins and lodges. Some have a pioneer feel, with bunk beds and wooodstoves, original to the 1960s cabin village this place evolved out of; others multi-bedroom retreats of brand new construction, with heated floors, flatscreen TVs, modern furniture and fixtures, and comfy queen beds. Some have premium Katahdin views. The NEOC's cheery, rustic-mod **River Drivers Restaurant** ★ is open daily (you can prepay for dinners as part of your lodging rate) and serves great pub food along with big-feed dinner entrees like rib-eye steaks and crab-stuffed haddock roulade. The lounge in front of the big fieldstone fireplace is a pretty unbeatable spot to unwind with a beer or a cocktail, especially in winter.

30 Twin Pines Rd., Millinocket. (Look for signs 9 miles NW of Millinocket, on road to Baxter State Park.) www.neoc.com. ⓒ **800/634-7238** or 207/723-5438. 21 units. $245–$641 cabins/lodges (sleep 4–14). 2-night minimum peak summer and winter weekends. Some cabins accommodate pets ($20/night fee). **Amenities:** Restaurant; lounge; free kayaks and canoes; fire pits; rental snowmobiles; beach volleyball and basketball courts; free Wi-Fi.

13

MAINE | Baxter State Park & Environs

PLANNING YOUR TRIP TO NEW ENGLAND

For such a small area, New England is surprisingly diverse. You can deep-sea fish or admire autumn colors from a mountaintop, and dine on anything from pancakes slathered in local maple syrup to futuristic sushi. Yet if you wake up in Boston, you can be in any of the region's other five states in the blink of an hour or less.

As such, it's a wonderful destination for adventurous families and peripatetic travelers. In most of the region, crime is nonexistent to low. In fact, your primary worries involve choosing the right time of year to visit; determining the most scenic way to get from point A to point B (a car is almost a must in mass-transit-challenged New England); and selecting from among many natural treasures, roadside attractions, and historical tours and walks that lure visitors season after season. This chapter covers many of the critical aspects of planning your trip.

ARRIVING

By Plane

Nearly all the major airlines fly into Boston's **Logan International Airport**, your likely hub of arrival or connection if you're coming by air. For more information, contact the airport at © **800/235-6426** or check the airport's website at www.massport.com/logan-airport.

Commercial carriers also serve other important locales. Bradley International Airport is convenient to **Hartford,** Connecticut and **Springfield,** Massachusetts. You'll also find flights to **Burlington,** Vermont; **Manchester,** New Hampshire; **Portland,** Maine; **Providence,** Rhode Island; and **Worcester,** Massachusetts. Airlines most commonly fly to these airports from New York or Boston, although non-stop flights and direct connections from hub cities, such as Chicago, Dallas, and Washington, D.C., are available.

All three major New England islands—**Martha's Vineyard, Nantucket,** and **Block Island**—can be reached by plane. Even smaller towns and cities are served by feeder airlines and charter companies, including those flying into air strips in **Rutland,** Vermont; **Rockland,** Maine; and **Trenton,** Maine, near Bar Harbor.

Just remember that many flights to small airports are aboard turboprop planes; ask ahead if that makes you nervous.

While flights into smaller airports are convenient, it's almost always cheaper to fly into Logan, and then rent a car and drive (or take a bus or train) to your destination. On the other hand, Logan can become congested, security lines are long, delayed flights are endemic, and traffic can be nightmarish—so the greater expense of flying into smaller hubs might be offset by speedier check-ins, departures, and arrivals. You may also want to compare prices for flights into New York City and Albany, New York, which are only a short drive from the New England area.

Thanks largely to the arrival of **Southwest Airlines** (www.southwest.com; ✆ **800/435-9792**), low-cost airfares are available from some destinations into New England's second-tier airports. Manchester-Boston Regional Airport has grown into a bustling spot, and Southwest flights to and from Hartford, Providence, and Portland are also among the best deals you'll find. Travelers researching airfares do well to check these alternative airports.

The regional airline **Cape Air** (www.capeair.com; ✆ **800/CAPEAIR** [227-3247]) flies to 10 smaller airports around New England from its base in Boston, but also has flights to the New York City area (the Westchester County airport), to Chicago, St. Louis, Montana, and Puerto Rico, among other destinations.

Discount airline **JetBlue** has also ramped up its presence in New England. You can fly JetBlue to Portland, Boston, Worcester, Hartford, Providence, and even Hyannis on Cape Cod and the islands of Nantucket and Martha's Vineyard. Call ✆ **800/538-2583,** or check online at www.jetblue.com.

Visitors from Europe in search of a bargain should consider Norwegian Air's remarkably affordable transatlantic flights to Boston or Providence. Call ✆ **800/357-4159,** or search online at www.norwegian.com.

By Train

From Boston and New York City, commuter train lines radiate out to the suburbs (which include stations in Rhode Island and Connecticut), but train service in northern New England is limited to four **Amtrak** (www.amtrak.com; ✆ **800/872-7245**) lines: two running to Vermont, one to Maine, and another across central Massachusetts.

Amtrak's *Vermonter* departs from Washington, D.C., once a day (around 8am weekdays, a half-hour earlier on weekends), with stops including Baltimore, Philadelphia, and New York City before following the Connecticut River north. New England stops include New Haven and Hartford in Connecticut, Springfield and Northampton in Massachusetts, and in Vermont, Brattleboro, Bellows Falls, White River Junction, Montpelier, Waterbury, and Essex Junction (near Burlington), finally arriving in St. Albans some 13 hours after leaving Washington. A one-way adult fare for the full route starts at $72 (New York City to Brattleboro fares start at $48). The return train leave St. Alban's at 9:15am and arrives in D.C. around 10pm.

The *Ethan Allen Express* departs New York's Penn Station once daily (at 2:15pm Mon–Thurs, 5:48pm Fri, or 3:10pm Sat and Sun) and travels somewhat more quickly, moving north along the Hudson River through Albany, New York, before veering into western Vermont, stopping at Castleton and terminating in Rutland (near Killington) after about 5½ hours; return trains leave Rutland at 7:46am Monday through Friday, 5:10pm on Saturday and Sunday. A one-way adult fare between NYC and Rutland starts at $73.

Amtrak relaunched rail service to Maine in late 2001, restoring a line that had been idle since the 1960s. The *Downeaster* operates five times daily between North Station in Boston and Portland, with three trips per day continuing north to Brunswick, Maine. If you're coming from elsewhere on the East Coast, you will need to change train stations in Boston—a slightly frustrating exercise requiring either a taxi ride or a ride and transfer on Boston's aging subway. The *Downeaster* stops in Woburn and Haverhill, Massachusetts; Exeter, Durham, and Dover, New Hampshire; and Wells, Saco, and Old Orchard Beach, Maine, on its way to Portland. Travel time is 2 hours and 25 minutes between Boston and Portland. Trains continuing to Brunswick also stop in Freeport. Bikes are allowed to be on- or off-loaded at Boston, Woburn, Portland, and Brunswick (an $8 charge applies). One-way fares from Boston to Portland start at $29.

The *Lake Shore Limited Line* connects Boston with points west including Albany and Buffalo, New York; Cleveland and Toledo, Ohio; and Chicago, Illinois. (Massachusetts stops include Worcester, Springfield, and Pittsfield.) Departing from Chicago daily at 9:30pm, you'll be in transit for almost a full day, arriving in Boston near 6pm (sleeping cars are available on this train). The return train leaves Boston's South Station at 1:20pm and arrives in Chicago the next morning at 9:45am. One-way fares start at $91.

International visitors might want to buy a **USA Rail Pass,** good for 15 days ($459), 30 days ($689), or 45 days ($899) of multi-segment travel anywhere in the United States on **Amtrak.** The pass is available online or through many overseas travel agents. Reservations and tickets are required and should be booked as early as possible.

By Bus

Getting around by bus is a dependable option in these parts, and the national bus company **Greyhound** (www.greyhound.com; 🕐 **800/231-2222** or 214/849-8100 outside the U.S.) was the early leader in this kind of travel. Many take the bus to Boston's big depot at South Station, then switch to a regional carrier. But Greyhound now has competition busing to and from Boston (and some other New England cities). There are now nearly a dozen smaller bus companies operating along these routes (even a luxurious alternative, **LimoLiner** [www.limoliner.com; 🕐 **844/405-4637**]). Although you will probably wait for the bus to pick you up from a street corner, rather than a bus station, consider using **Megabus** (www.megabus.com; 🕐 **877/GO2-MEGA** [462-6342]) or **Boltbus** (www.boltbus.com; 🕐 877/BOLTBUS [265-8287]), which offer some of the lowest fares available. You can compare options on one easy-to-use site called **Busbud** (www.busbud.com), which searches the major discount sites, upstart bus companies, as well as Greyhound and New England–based Peter Pan.

By Car

Several interstate highways serve New England. **I-95** parallels the Connecticut shore, then turns north through Providence and Boston, after which it strikes northeast along the New Hampshire and Maine coast before heading north toward the Canadian border. **I-91** heads north from New Haven, Connecticut, through Massachusetts, and along the Vermont–New Hampshire border. The Massachusetts Turnpike **(I-90)** makes an east-west jaunt from Boston to the Berkshire Hills (for a price—although electronic tolling means you won't have to slow down or stop). Your E-ZPass transponder will work on the MassPike, saving you money and the hassle of paying tolls online or by mail.

From Boston, you head south on **I-95** to reach Rhode Island, north on **I-95** for Maine, northwest up **I-93** for New Hampshire and the White Mountains, or southwest on **I-84** into the heart of Connecticut. In Concord, New Hampshire, **I-89** splits off from I-93 and heads into Vermont. Stay on I-89 if you want to reach Montpelier and Burlington; exit northward onto **I-91** at White River Junction if you want to visit St. Johnsbury and the Northeast Kingdom.

The most picturesque way to enter New England is from the west. Drive through the scenic Adirondack Mountains to Port Kent, New York, on Lake Champlain, then catch the car ferry across the lake to Burlington, Vermont.

International visitors should note that quoted rental car rates in the U.S. typically do not include insurance and may not include taxes and fees. Read fine print or ask your rental agency about additional costs. Many rental-car agencies have non-negotiable minimum age requirements, and some impose a surcharge for young drivers (generally between the ages of 18 and 24).

GETTING AROUND

By Car

Travel can be confusing in this region at times, as there are few straight roads, but GPS takes the guesswork out of finding your way. North-and-south travel is relatively straightforward, thanks to **four major interstates** crisscrossing the region. But traveling east and west sometimes involves a zigzagged route.

On the other hand, New England is of a size that touring by car can be done comfortably—so long as you're not determined to see all six states in a week (see chapter 3 for suggested itineraries). **Maine is a lot bigger** than all the other New England states; beware that overview maps don't fully convey the state's size. (Portland is closer by car to New York City than it is to Fort Kent.)

Traffic is generally light compared to that of most urban and suburban areas along the East Coast, but there are a few big exceptions. Traffic in or around **Boston** can be sluggish anytime, and Friday afternoons and evenings in the summer are positively infuriating; the tentacles of Beantown traffic extend all the way to I-495, which you may need to use to get from the New York area to, say, coastal Maine. Be prepared for unexpected delays if you'll be driving anywhere near Boston. I-95 almost always gets snarled up around

New England Driving Distances

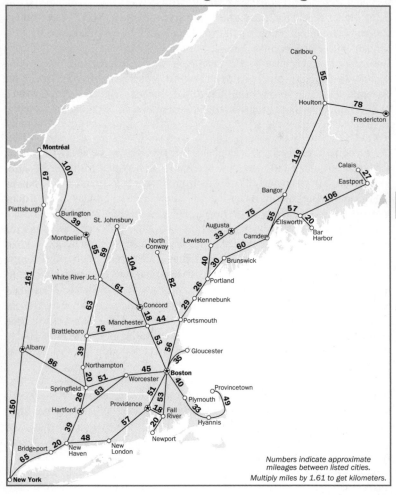

Numbers indicate approximate mileages between listed cities.
Multiply miles by 1.61 to get kilometers.

New Haven, where it intersects with I-91. Other notorious choke points that can back up for miles include Route 1 along the Maine coast on summer weekends; the roads leading to the two bridges that enter Cape Cod; or attractive New England back-road routes during the height of foliage season. Try to avoid being on the road during big summer holiday or foliage weekends; if your schedule allows it, travel on weekdays rather than on weekends, and hit the road before or after morning and evening commuter rush hours.

Note that insurance is almost never included in rental car rates in the U.S. Be sure you actually need insurance before you buy it. Many are covered by their own car insurance and/or credit cards and can avoid this significant add-on cost.

By Train

As noted above (p. 700), **Amtrak** provides limited rail travel around the region, but it's quite expensive. In coastal Connecticut, frequent **MTA Metro-North Railroad** commuter trains to and from New York City and within the state are a *much* cheaper option than Amtrak. A trip between New York City and New Haven, for instance, costs $17.75 to $30 one-way on Metro-North, versus $43 or more (and 40 min. longer, with far fewer departures) on Amtrak. Check the system's website at **www.mta.info/mnr** for schedules and fares. For information on commuter rail options around the Boston area, see p. 64 in chapter 4.

By Bus

Once you're in northern New England, **bus service can be spotty.** You'll be able to reach major cities by bus, but few of the smaller towns or villages. Tickets range from about $13 one-way from Boston to Portland, to $22 and up for Boston to Burlington. Buses can fill up on Fridays, Sundays, and around major holidays or holiday travel times; reservations are always a wise idea.

　　Greyhound (www.greyhound.com; ℂ **800/231-2222**) operates in all six states—though mostly just along the interstate highways—with frequent departures from Boston. **Concord Coach Lines** (www.concordcoachlines.com; ℂ **800/639-3317** or 603/228-3300) serves Maine and New Hampshire, including midcoast Maine and some smaller towns in the Lake Winnipesaukee, Merrimack Valley, and White Mountains areas. Buses on the Maine routes play complimentary (PG-13 rated or below) movies en route. **C&J** (www.ridecj.com; ℂ **800/258-7111**) connects Boston with Portsmouth and Dover, New Hampshire, and Newburyport, Massachusetts, on buses that promise Wi-Fi access.

By Ferry

New England has a lot of coastline and a few very popular islands, and so it's not surprising that ferry service is active here. A variety of ferries serve **Martha's Vineyard** (see p. 267) and **Nantucket** (p. 292), mostly from ports on Cape Cod. Ferries to **Block Island** (p. 466) leave from Point Judith, RI, New London, CT, and Long Island, NY. Boston Harbor Cruises also operates a fast ferry from Boston to **Provincetown,** at the tip of Cape Cod (p. 182). See chapter 4 for details on commuter and sightseeing ferries around Boston Harbor, and chapter 13 for information about local ferry services around the Maine coast.

MONEY & COSTS

Travelers are in for some sticker shock in New England during peak travel seasons. From June through August, and again in October, there's simply no such thing as a cheap motel room here. Even no-frills mom-and-pop motels can (and do) happily charge $100 a night or more for a bed that might rate just a notch above camping in a tent. Bland business hotels at highway exits or airports, miles from sights or good restaurants, charge far more. Even Airbnb coaches its hosts to raise rates when demand for rooms is high.

WHAT THINGS COST IN NEW ENGLAND	US$
Small cup of coffee at Capitol Grounds in Montpelier, VT	1.75
1 ride on the "T" subway in Boston	2.75
Admission to the Vermont State Fair in Rutland	10.00
Adult admission to the Portland (ME) Museum of Art	15.00
Adult admission to the Museum of Fine Arts, Boston	25.00
Dinner (plus alcohol, tax, and tip) at The White Barn Inn, Kennebunk, ME	125.00
3-course dinner (no alcohol) at Pine Restaurant at the Hanover Inn, NH	55.00
Haddock boat at the Lobster Shack at Two Lights, Cape Elizabeth, ME	19.99
Cheeseburger at Louis' Lunch in New Haven, CT	6.25
1 night at Hampton Inn Portland Airport (ME), plus tax	189.00
1 night at The Liberty Hotel, Boston	459.00

So if you're visiting in summer, fall, or ski season (it's likely you are), **lodging** will occupy a bigger chunk of your budget than you expected. Luckily, however, meals, gas, and day-to-day expenses are generally more affordable here than in a major city elsewhere in the country. You can find excellent entrees at upscale, creative restaurants for around $25, comparing favorably with similar dishes at big-city restaurants that would top $35.

Throughout the book, we've selected a wide range of hotel types to present you with interesting options in all price ranges. Book in advance, and online, and you'll usually pay less (see the box on p. 708 for web strategies). In the winter, especially, it's sometimes possible to get the price of a luxury hotel down to a mid-range level. And don't forget to check **Airbnb** (www.airbnb. com), **HomeAway** (www.homeaway.com), **VRBO** (www.vrbo.com), and other vacation rental entities. These websites, offering either rooms in or entire private homes or apartments, are a popular alternative in New England. Prices can sometimes be as much as $50 to $75 less than you'd pay for a hotel room.

STAYING HEALTHY

New Englanders consider themselves a healthy bunch, which they ascribe to clean living, brisk northern air, vigorous exercise (leaf raking, snow shoveling, and so on), and few stresses apart from realizing that Tom Brady can't play for the Patriots forever. You shouldn't face any serious health risks when traveling in the region.

Regional Health Concerns

Exceptions to the above statement? Well, yes—you may find yourself at higher risk when exploring New England's inviting countryside. Watch out for:

o **Poison ivy:** This sometimes shiny, three-leafed plant is common throughout the region. If you touch it, you could develop a nasty, itchy rash.

- **Giardia:** That crystal-clear stream might look pure, but it could be contaminated with animal feces. When ingested by humans, *Giardia* cysts can cause diarrhea and weight loss. Carry your own water for day trips, bring a filter to treat water, boil your water, or treat it with iodine pills.
- **Lyme disease:** Lyme disease has been a growing problem in New England since 1975, when it was first identified in Old Lyme, Connecticut. Left untreated, it can damage the heart and nervous system. The disease is transmitted by deer ticks, which are difficult to see—but check your socks and body daily anyway (ideally with a partner). If you develop a bull's-eye-shaped rash, 3 to 8 inches in diameter (the rash may feel warm but usually doesn't itch), see a doctor right away. Other symptoms may include muscle and joint pain, fever, or fatigue.
- **Rabies:** Transmitted through animal saliva and especially prevalent in skunks, raccoons, bats, and foxes, rabies **is almost always fatal if left untreated** in humans. Infected animals tend to display erratic and aggressive behavior; the best advice is to avoid wild animals. If you're bitten, wash the wound and immediately seek medical attention.
- **West Nile Virus:** Although the number of human cases reported in New England is small and this mosquito-borne illness is rarely fatal, precautions against mosquito bites are a smart move. Avoid standing water, and wear long sleeves and pants, socks, and insect repellant when outdoors, particularly between dusk and dawn.

SPECIAL-INTEREST TRIPS & TOURS

Outdoor-Oriented Trips

Want to learn a new outdoor skill or expand your knowledge? You can find plenty of options in New England. Here are three of the best:

- **Learn to fly-fish on New England's fabled rivers.** Among the most respected schools are the two offered by the region's outdoor gear and apparel powerhouses: **Orvis** (www.orvis.com; ✆ **888/235-9763** for retail, ✆ **866/531-6213** for fly-fishing classes) in Manchester, Vermont, and Dennis, Massachusetts; and **L.L.Bean** (www.llbean.com; ✆ **800/441-5713**) in Freeport, Maine, and at other locations in Connecticut, Massachusetts, New Hampshire, and Vermont. L.L.Bean also offers workshops on many *other* outdoor skills through its outstanding **Outdoor Discovery Schools;** call ✆ **888/270-2326** for details.
- **Learn about birds and coastal ecosystems in Maine.** Budding and experienced naturalists can expand their understanding of marine wildlife while residing on 333-acre Hog Island in Maine's wild and scenic Muscongus Bay through the **Hog Island Audubon Camp** for teens, families, and adults (http://hogisland.audubon.org; ✆ **843/340-8673**).

- **Sharpen your outdoor skills.** The **Appalachian Mountain Club** (www. outdoors.org; ☎ **617/523-0636**) offers outdoor adventure classes, many taught at AMC's Highland Center at Crawford Notch in New Hampshire's White Mountains (p. 593). You could learn plein air painting, wilderness first aid, or backcountry orienteering. Free activities are offered daily. Courses with fees often include accommodations.

Active Tours

New England also lends itself to adventures that combine fresh air and exercise with Mother Nature as your instructor in a vast, beautiful classroom. These experiences range from 3-day self-guided inn-to-inn biking trips to weeklong canoe and kayak expeditions. These reputable outfitters will get you started.

- **Allagash Canoe Trips** (www.allagashcanoetrips.com; ☎ **207/280-1551** or 207/280-0191), leads 5- to 7-day canoe trips down Maine's noted and wild Allagash River and other local rivers. You provide a sleeping bag and clothing; they take care of everything else.

- **Bullfrog Adventures** (www.bullfrogadventures.com; ☎ **207/234-2158**), will take you on a canoe camping adventure on a rigorous Maine river or a more placid lake or pond.

- **Country Walkers** (www.countrywalkers.com; ☎ **800/234-6900**), has a glorious color catalog (more like a wish book) outlining supported walking trips around the world. Among the offerings: walking tours in coastal Maine's Acadia National Park and northern Vermont. Trips generally run 5 nights and include all meals, beer and wine, and lodging at appealing inns.

- **Maine Island Kayak Co.** (www.maineislandkayak.com; ☎ **207/766-2373**), has a fleet of seaworthy kayaks for half- and full-day trips up and down the Maine coast. The firm has plenty of experience in training novices.

- **VBT** (www.vbt.com; ☎ **855/445-5513**), is one of the more established and well-organized touring operations, with an extensive global bike tour schedule. VBT offers trips in Massachusetts, Vermont, and Maine, including a 6-day Cape Cod and Martha's Vineyard trip with abundant scenic highlights and picnics in remarkable spots.

- **The Wayfarers** (www.thewayfarers.com; (☎ **800/249-4620** or 401/849-5087) has an extensive inventory of trips, including 4-night Maine coast walking vacations and 5-night trips in the White Mountains. Trips typically involve moderate day hiking coupled with nights at comfortable hotels.

Historic Tours

Historic New England is a nonprofit that owns and operates 37 properties around New England, ranging from 17th-century homes to a still-working 18th-century farm. Members tour all of the organization's properties for free and receive other benefits. Memberships cost $50 per year for individuals or $60 for an entire household. For more information, visit www.historicnew england.org, or call the organization's Boston headquarters at ☎ **617/227-3956**.

TURNING TO THE internet OR apps FOR A HOTEL DISCOUNT

Before going online, it's important that you know what "flavor" of discount you're seeking. Currently, there are three types of online reductions:

1. **Blind deals sites where you agree to an overnight rate without knowing which hotel you'll get.** You'll find these on such sites as **Priceline.com** and **Hotwire.com**, and they can be money-savers, particularly if you're booking within a week of travel (that's when the hotels resort to deep discounts to get beds filled). As these companies use primarily major chains, you can rest assured that you won't be put up in a dump, particularly if you choose a property with a 3-star rating or above.

2. **Discounts on chain hotel websites.** In 2016, all of the major chains announced they'd be reserving special discounts for travelers who booked directly through the hotels' websites (usually in the portion of the site reserved for loyalty members and with advance payment required). These are always the lowest rates, though discounts can range from as little as $1 to as much as $50. Our advice: search for a hotel that's in your price range and ideal location and then, if it is a chain property, book directly through the online loyalty portal.

3. **Use the right hotel search engine.** They're not all equal, as we at Frommers.com learned in 2017 after putting the top 20 sites to the test in 20 cities around the globe. We discovered **Booking.com** listed the lowest rates for hotels in the city center, and in the under $200 range, 16 out of 20 times—the best record, by far, of all the sites we tested. And Booking.com includes all taxes and fees in its results (not all do, which can make for a frustrating shopping experience). For top-end properties, both Priceline.com and HotelsCombined.com came up with the best rates, tying at 14 wins each.

4. **Last-minute discounts.** Booking last minute can be a great savings strategy, as prices sometimes drop as hoteliers scramble to fill rooms. But you won't necessarily find the best savings through companies that specialize in last-minute bookings or apps like HotelTonight. Instead, use the sites recommended above.

5. **Or skip hotels altogether.** See p. 705 for our discussion of the savings you can find with online vacation rental sites.

It's a lot of surfing, but in the hothouse world of accommodation pricing, this sort of diligence can pay off.

Escorted General-Interest Tours

The price for a structured group tour usually includes everything from airport transfers to hotels, meals, admissions, and transportation. Despite the fact that these tours require big deposits and predetermine your itinerary, many people crave the one-stop shopping they offer. And it's true—they do let you sit back and enjoy a trip without having to drive *or* worry about little details. They take you to a maximum number of sights, usually with the least amount of hassle. They're particularly convenient for people with limited mobility, and they can be a great way to make new friends.

If you're interested, dozens of companies operate bus tours of New England. **Tauck World Discovery** (www.tauck.com; ✆ **800/788-7885**), founded and still based in New England, is just one of many outfits offering fall foliage tours, for instance. Their 12-day autumn itinerary weaves together the region's iconic places and tastes and the spellbinding storytelling of filmmakers Ken Burns and Dayton Duncan.

For more information on escorted tours, see our own website at **www.frommers.com/destinations/boston/planning-a-trip/escorted-package-tours**.

[Fast FACTS] NEW ENGLAND

Disabled Travelers
Public transit in major cities is largely accessible. Most brand-name hotels are accessible, but smaller historic properties (even luxury inns) sometimes aren't. The National Park Service's **Access Pass** is available at no cost to disabled travelers; it gives pass bearers free lifetime entry to national parks, including **Acadia National Park** (p. 667) and the **Cape Cod National Seashore** (p. 247). You can get the pass at any national park. For more information, go to www.nps.gov/planyourvisit/passes.htm.

Drinking Laws The legal age for purchase and consumption of alcoholic beverages is 21 in all six New England states; proof of age is required and often requested at bars, nightclubs, and restaurants, so bring ID when you go out. Do not carry open containers of alcohol in your car or any public area that isn't zoned for alcohol consumption. The police can fine you on the spot (although in Connecticut and Rhode Island, it is legal for passengers in a vehicle, but not the driver, to consume alcohol).

Don't even think about driving while intoxicated.

Emergencies For fire, police, and ambulance, find any phone and dial ✆ **911.** If this fails, dial ✆ **0** (zero) and report an emergency.

Family Travel New England has traditionally been a destination for family summer vacations, particularly in the beach towns along the coast. There are plenty of family-oriented attractions and several sites that are a great way for kids to learn about American history. See our list of "the Best Family Activities" in chapter 1 (p. 7) for suggestions, or follow "10 Days by the Sea with Families" itinerary in chapter 3 (p. 46) for ideas. Be sure to ask about family discounts when visiting attractions. Note, however, that a fair number of small inns cater only to adults or require that children be a minimum age. We've noted such restrictions in our listings in the various state chapters.

Gasoline New England's gas prices are a bit higher than the U.S. average; at press time, the price was somewhere around $3.00 per gallon. There are very few "full-service" gas stations in New England—you'll generally have to pump your own gas—and, if you do find one, you'll often pay up to 10¢ extra per gallon. Taxes are always included in the listed per-gallon price of gas. International travelers should note that 1 U.S. gallon equals 3.8 liters or .85 imperial gallons.

Health All large and small cities in New England maintain good hospital facilities, and some smaller towns have them, too. The quality of care is very good here. If health is a serious issue for you, check ahead with your accommodations (or search for options online) to find the nearest emergency-room service or 24-hour clinic. See "Staying Healthy" (p. 705) for information on some specific health risks in the area.

Insurance Use insurance marketplaces such as InsureMyTrip.com and SquareMouth.com. Both work with only vetted companies and will quickly give you an array of possible policies, based on your age and travel plans.

Internet Access You'll have little trouble finding a

coffee shop or hotel with Wi-Fi access. A few hotels still charge a fee for this service. Some more historic buildings may not be equipped with Wi-Fi in all rooms, but there's usually a hot spot somewhere for guests to use. On some of the more remote islands and country areas, service may be spotty. Most **public libraries** in the New England states—even those in small towns—offer free Internet access.

Legal Aid If you are "pulled over" for a minor infraction (such as speeding), never attempt to pay the fine directly to a police officer; this could be construed as attempted bribery, a much more serious crime. Pay fines by mail, or directly into the hands of the clerk of the court. If accused of a more serious offense, say and do nothing before consulting a lawyer. Here, the burden is on the state to prove a person's guilt beyond a reasonable doubt, and everyone has the right to remain silent, whether he or she is suspected of a crime or actually arrested. Once arrested, a person should contact a family member, trusted friend, or attorney as soon as possible. International visitors should call their embassy or consulate.

LGBT Travelers New England has a strong LGBT community and destinations that draw LGBT travelers from all over the world including Provincetown and Northampton, MA, and Ogunquit, ME. The Vermont

Gay Tourism Association's website showcases LGBT-friendly lodgings, shops, and restaurants (**www.vermont gaytourism.com**).

Mail At press time, domestic postage rates were 35¢ for a postcard and 50¢ for a letter. For international mail, a first-class postcard or letter of up to 1 ounce costs 1.15¢. For more information, go to **www.usps.com**.

Senior Travel New England offers older travelers a wide array of activities. Mention you're a senior whenever you make travel reservations. Travelers over 65 (and sometimes younger) qualify for reduced admission to theaters, museums, ski resorts, and other attractions, as well as discounted fares on public transportation. The National Park Service's **Senior Pass** is available for $80 to travelers age 62 and over; it gives pass bearers free lifetime entry to national parks, including **Acadia National Park** (p. 667) and the **Cape Cod National Seashore** (p. 247). You can get the pass at any national park. For more information, go to www.nps.gov/planyourvisit/passes.htm.

Smoking Smoking is banned in all public places (restaurants, bars, offices, hotel lobbies) in all six New England states, with the exception of the casinos on tribal lands in Connecticut (see p. 420). Recreational use of marijuana by adults ages 21 and up is legal in Maine, Massachusetts, and Vermont.

Taxes The United States has no value-added tax (VAT) or other indirect tax at the national level. However, states, counties, and cities can add local taxes to purchases—including hotel bills, restaurant checks, and airline tickets. These taxes will *not* appear as part of the quoted prices; they'll be added when you pay. (Some items, such as food, clothing, and footwear, are exempt: Policies vary from state to state.)

Sales, dining, and lodging taxes in New England, as of 2018, are as follows: **Connecticut** charges 6.35% on sales and 15% on lodging. **Maine** charges a 5.5% sales tax in stores, 9% at hotels, 8% at restaurants, and 10% for auto rentals. **Massachusetts** charges 6.25% on sales and meals, 5.7% for hotel rooms (8.45% in Boston, Cambridge, Worcester, Chicopee, Springfield, and West Springfield). **New Hampshire** charges *no* sales tax in stores, but a 9% tax on lodging and dining. **Rhode Island** charges 7% on sales, 8% for restaurant meals, and 13% on lodging. **Vermont** charges a 6% sales tax on purchases, 9% tax on hotel rooms and restaurant meals, and 10% tax on alcohol purchased in restaurants. Vermont towns and cities can (and resort towns do) also add an additional 1% local tax to meals, lodgings, and purchases.

Time All New England states are in the **Eastern time zone** (the same zone as New York City) and 5 to 6 hours behind the time in

London. Why 5 to 6? Because **daylight saving time** is in effect from 2am on the second Sunday in March to 2am on the first Sunday in November. Daylight saving time moves the clock 1 hour ahead of standard time.

Tipping In hotels, tip **bellhops** $1 per bag ($2–$3 if you have a lot of luggage) and tip **housekeeping staff** $2 to $5 per day. Tip the **doorman** or **concierge** if he or she has provided you with some useful service. Tip a **valet-parking attendant** a few dollars any time you get your car. In restaurants, bars, and nightclubs, tip **service staff** and **bartenders** 15% to 20% of the check (assuming the service was decent), tip **coatroom attendants** $1 per garment, tip **taxi drivers** 15% to 20% of the fare. Tip **skycaps** at airports at least $1 per bag ($2–$3 if you have a lot of luggage). And tip **hair stylists, barbers,** and **spa therapists** 15% to 20%, too.

Toilets Public toilets can be found in hotel lobbies, bars, restaurants, museums, department stores, railway and bus stations, and gas stations. Large hotels and fast-food restaurants are often the best bets for clean facilities. Restaurants and bars in resorts or heavily visited areas may reserve their restrooms for patrons.

Index

See also Accommodations and Restaurant indexes, below.

General Index

Restaurants

Map List

Photo Credits

Frommer's New England 2019, 16th edition

Published by
FROMMER MEDIA LLC

ISBN 978-1-62887-396-2 (paper), 978-1-62887-397-9 (ebk)

Editorial Director: Pauline Frommer
Editor: Holly Hughes
Production Editor: Erin Geile
Cartographer: Roberta Stockwell
Photo Editor: Meghan Lamb
Cover Design: Dave Riedy

Front cover photo: Old barn surrounded by autumn trees in Vermont countryside: SNEHIT / Shutterstock.com.

For information on our other products or services, see www.frommers.com.

FrommerMedia LLC also publishes its books in a variety of electronic formats. Some content that appears in print may not be available in electronic formats.

Manufactured in the United States of America

5 4 3 2 1

ABOUT THE AUTHORS

Kim Knox Beckius is a Connecticut-based travel writer who has hugged a baby moose, tasted 38 different whoopie pies in one sitting, and sent hundreds of free fall leaves in the mail to autumn lovers around the world. She is a *Yankee Magazine* Contributing Editor, owner of EverythingNewEngland.com, New England Expert for TripSavvy.com (formerly About.com) and the author of seven books including *Backroads of New England* and *New England's Historic Homes & Gardens*. She lives in the Hartford area.

Leslie Brokaw has worked on more than a dozen Frommer's Guides to Québec and New England. She is an editor for MIT Sloan Management Review and teaches at Emerson College. She and her family live outside of Boston.

Brian Kevin is the editor in chief of Down East magazine and has written for Outside, Travel + Leisure, The New York Times, Audubon and other magazines. His work has been recognized or anthologized in Best Food Writing, Best American Essays and Best American Sports Writing and he's the author of The Footloose American: Following the Hunter S. Thompson Trail Across South America. He lives in Hope, Maine.

Herbert Bailey Livesey has written about food and travel for over 40 years, authoring or contributing to *Frommer's Montreal & Quebec City, Frommer's Europe*, and *Frommer's New England*. In addition, he wrote and revised five guidebooks in the earlier *American Express* series, which were translated into 11 languages. Scores of his articles have been published in *Travel + Leisure, Food & Wine, Playboy, New York*, and *Yankee*.

Laura Reckford has been exploring and writing about Cape Cod, Martha's Vineyard and Nantucket, as well as other parts of New England, for more than 20 years. She is the founder and CEO of Cape Cod Wave, an online magazine covering the culture and character of Cape Cod. She is also the executive director of the Falmouth Art Center. She resides in Falmouth, MA.

Barbara Radcliffe Rogers is co-author of seven guidebooks to Italy, three to Spain, and several others covering Europe, Atlantic Canada, and New England. She writes regularly for Global Traveler Magazine and other magazines, newspapers, and websites. Her taste for travel began when she moved to Verona, Italy, soon after graduating from Boston University, and she has since visited every country in Western Europe, and much of Eastern Europe and Latin America. Barbara currently lives in New Hampshire. Wherever she is, she's likely to be skiing in the winter and kayaking in the summer and discovering new flavors for her blog, Worldbite.

Award-winning travel writer **Bill Scheller** is a 30-year Vermont resident. His books include *America: A History in Art; Colonial New England on Five Shillings a Day*; and, with his wife Kay, *Best Vermont Drives*. Among his more than 300 published articles are numerous features in Yankee magazine on his adopted state. He lives in Randolph, Vermont.

Stillman Rogers is a travel writer and photographer, co-author of guidebooks to Portugal, Italy, and Spain's Canary Islands, as well as the eastern U.S. and Canada. His photographs have been published in books, magazines, and regularly on Global Traveler's family travel website, WhereverFamily. He writes about destinations and skiing and has a monthly newspaper travel column. His first foreign travel was after graduating from Harvard, when he was stationed in Italy for 3 years; Italy still remains one of his favorite subjects for photography.

Erin Trahan is an arts journalist who specializes in film, TV, and travel. She is a regular contributor to WBUR, Boston's NPR news station, and she teaches at Emerson College. She has written extensively for Frommer's Travel Guides. Erin lives in Marblehead, MA.